Mastering
Microsoft® SharePoint®
Foundation 2010

Mastering
Microsoft® SharePoint®
Foundation 2010

Callahan

WILEY

Wiley Publishing, Inc.

Acquisitions Editor: Agatha Kim
Development Editor: Jim Compton
Technical Editor: Kevin Lundy
Production Editor: Christine O'Connor
Copy Editor: Kim Wimpsett
Editorial Manager: Pete Gaughan
Production Manager: Tim Tate
Vice President and Executive Group Publisher: Richard Swadley
Vice President and Publisher: Neil Edde
Book Designers: Maureen Forys, Happenstance Type-O-Rama and Judy Fung
Compositor: Jeff Lytle, Happenstance Type-O-Rama
Proofreader: Nancy Bell
Indexer: Nancy Guenther
Project Coordinator, Cover: Katherine Crocker
Cover Designer: Ryan Sneed
Cover Image: © Pete Gardner/DigitalVision/Getty Images

Library of Congress Cataloging-in-Publication Data

Callahan, C. A., 1967- author.
 Mastering Microsoft SharePoint Foundation 2010 / C. A. Callahan. — 1st edition.
   p. cm
 ISBN 978-0-470-62638-2 (pbk.)
   978-1-118-05681-3 (ebk.)
   978-1-118-05683-7 (ebk.)
   978-1-118-05682-0 (ebk.)
 1. Intranets (Computer networks) 2. Web servers. 3. Client/server computing. 4. Microsoft Office SharePoint server. I. Title.
 TK5105.875.I6C346 2011
 006.7′8—dc22
            2010047414

Dear Reader,

Thank you for choosing *Mastering Microsoft SharePoint Foundation 2010*. This book is part of a family of premium-quality Sybex books, all of which are written by outstanding authors who combine practical experience with a gift for teaching.

Sybex was founded in 1976. More than 30 years later, we're still committed to producing consistently exceptional books. With each of our titles, we're working hard to set a new standard for the industry. From the paper we print on, to the authors we work with, our goal is to bring you the best books available.

I hope you see all that reflected in these pages. I'd be very interested to hear your comments and get your feedback on how we're doing. Feel free to let me know what you think about this or any other Sybex book by sending me an email at nedde@wiley.com. If you think you've found a technical error in this book, please visit http://sybex.custhelp.com. Customer feedback is critical to our efforts at Sybex.

Best regards,

Neil Edde
Vice President and Publisher
Sybex, an Imprint of Wiley

This book is dedicated to Charles, who once again, with patience and strength, had my back. There aren't words enough to express my gratitude for the sacrifices he made during the long process of creating this book. Except maybe, thank you. Thank you very, very much.

Acknowledgments

I'd like to take a moment to show my gratitude to the people who made this book possible. To start, Charles Firth and Trudy Hutzler. Charles revised the chapters he wrote in the *Mastering Windows SharePoint Services 3.0* book, Chapters 9 and 10. He also co-wrote Chapter 13 (with Trudy), as well as tirelessly helped me with the long process of editing the chapters of a book so long. Trudy started out as a reader-reviewer (more on them in a moment) and became not only the contributing author of Chapter 15 but the go-to person if I needed help with anything related to the book. From assisting with edits to picking up half a chapter at the 11th hour, Trudy was there, and I am very grateful.

Partway through the process of writing the book, we discovered that it was a little long on content, so Sandy Ussia was brought in and did a great job, quickly, editing down Chapters 6 and 7, with an assist on Chapter 8. Throughout the process of writing the book, reader-reviewers loyally read every chapter, often several different incarnations of the same chapters, as well as answering any question I had concerning what readers would want in the book. I owe a lot to those reviewers: Bob Moffit, Chris Smith, Jennelle Crothers, and John D'Ambrosio, with an extra special thanks to Liam Spinage and Doug Greenwood, who went far beyond your average reviewers in terms of reading content and giving feedback. Those two had a real impact on the writing of the book, they were with me every step of the way, and I am truly grateful for their help.

In addition to these fine folks, there were several editors who did the work necessary for the book to be published by Sybex. Among them I'd especially like to thank Kevin Lundy, the technical editor. He was also one of the technical editors for my last book and once again did a great job checking over technical details of each and every chapter, no matter how long or how difficult. I want to thank him for the tireless job he did to help me make sure the information on these pages is as accurate as we could make it. Finally, I'd like to give a shout-out to Jim Compton, the developmental editor, for working for so very long, on so very much information, written and revised by so many people. It takes real fortitude to edit that much material, so thank you for that. To Agatha Kim, the acquisitions editor, who made this all possible; to Kim Wimpsett, the copy editor; to Nancy Bell, the proofreader; and to Christine O'Connor, the production editor for the last book and this one—thanks.

About the Author

Callahan is the author of *Mastering Windows SharePoint Services 3.0*. A SharePoint Services MVP, she has been a Microsoft Certified Trainer for more than a decade and holds numerous Microsoft certifications. She is the founder and principal trainer for CallahanTech, providing customized training and courseware for businesses and IT professionals. Dedicated to teaching the ins and outs of Microsoft products, Callahan focuses on the practical aspects of using those products and making them work vs. talking about what they can do for you (should you be able to get them to work). She is a frequent presenter at conferences and other technical events, such as Windows Connections. A big believer in the IT community, she particularly enjoys speaking at user group meetings and SharePoint Saturdays (free, professional, one-day conferences; see www.sharepointsaturday.org), as well as volunteering at Microsoft's TechEd conferences whenever possible. She also does free webcasts and live online presentations. See her SharePoint blog at http://servergrrl.blogspot.com for links to past material and information about upcoming events.

Contents at a Glance

Contents

Introduction

This book is intended for IT administrators to get a handle on SharePoint Foundation and is an update of *Mastering Windows SharePoint Services 3.0*. It is meant to be used both as a reference for overworked network administrators who don't have a lot of time to spare slogging through articles and forums, and as a cover-to-cover guide to mastering the fundamentals of SharePoint Foundation (and then some). Most of us don't have time to waste struggling with the ins and outs of a new product. We just need it to work. We also don't have time to waste on taking classes, so having a reference to use at work (or at home) can be handy. SharePoint is a really complicated beast—poorly documented, with oddly named settings, in even odder places. It's not for the faint of heart.

SharePoint is several things at once. It is a developer's platform, leveraging components such as ASP.NET, Windows Identity Foundation, and PowerShell. It is a robust front end over the power of SQL Server on the back end. And finally, it's a web collaboration tool, a useful front end to help increase the productivity of the information worker. It's a network product, it installs on a server, and it inevitably ends up being the responsibility of the server administrator.

When I started using SharePoint, I just couldn't find any detailed, accurate documentation for the free version (at that time, WSS). There was almost nothing reliable out there that was for administrators using WSS (unlike the paid-for SharePoint Server product). A large percentage of the documentation, especially the books, that I could find about SharePoint were written for developers. There was almost nothing for the busy administrators who have an entire network to run, for whom SharePoint is essentially just another server role. And, I've found, that is still the case with SharePoint Foundation today.

With SharePoint Foundation, I feel an obligation to let the world know about the product's power, its extensive capabilities, and the fact that those capabilities are free. I fear that many organizations are being oversold the SharePoint Server product, when they would be much better off with SharePoint Foundation. SharePoint Foundation might do all they need and more, without having to spend so very much on the software and client licenses (notice the plural—there can be need for two per user). Too many businesses have found, with their SharePoint Server installations, that the capabilities they use day to day aren't actually the ones they paid for.

So when I was asked to revise *Mastering Windows SharePoint Services 3.0*, I couldn't say no (well, I considered it, but I finally agreed because the cause was good). That's why this book is here. It is the book I would have bought if it had been available when I was looking. I tried to fill it full of suggestions, tips, tricks, and concepts that would help you navigate through the maze of hype about SharePoint to reach the truth—what it really is, what it really does, and how to use it. The intent was not particularly to hold your hand but to show you, administrator to administrator, what SharePoint Foundation is all about.

Because of the time constraints, not all chapters were written by me; I had to ask for help. Several people came forward to give me a hand, and I would like to be sure that you, the reader, know who put the effort into generating that material. Charles Firth stepped up and revised the two chapters he wrote in the previous version of the book: Chapter 9, "Sites, Subsites, and Workspaces," and Chapter 10, "Site Collections and Web Applications." Chapters 6 and 7, although originally written by me, were revised to be shorter by Sandy Ussia. She also assisted in revising Chapter 8 "Introduction to Libraries," as well. James Finley wrote the majority of Chapter 14, "STSADM and PowerShell," as well as the tables in the bonus online material, "PowerShell Cmdlets and STSADM Operations at a Glance." Trudy Hutzler rose to the challenge and wrote Chapter 15, "Migrating from Windows SharePoint Services 3.0 to Microsoft SharePoint Foundation 2010." That chapter had some serious hardware requirements, crossing multiple machines (she used nine virtual machines for that chapter alone), as well as multiple versions of SharePoint, SQL, and server OSs. And finally, in the 11th hour, Charles and Trudy teamed up to write Chapter 13, "Maintenance and Monitoring," and a great job they did with it. Thanks again to those fine men and women for the work they did.

To write about SharePoint, I found myself writing about *doing* SharePoint. So, there are lots of screenshots and step-by-step instructions. The way to learn about SharePoint is by using it. It really doesn't make sense until you do. This isn't a high-level book all about the theory of SharePoint—that would be too easy. No, this is largely a real-life scenario, tutorial kind of book, chronicling what I know about SharePoint, as quickly as possible.

This book is intended to give you solid insight into how things work, how to do them, and how to understand them well enough that you can take ownership of SharePoint as an IT administrator. It was a slow, painstaking process to explore all those dark places, set all of those settings, and take all of those screenshots. But the hope is that if I do it here, however briefly, you will see how it works, and then you can apply it in your environment. Of course, despite my best efforts, there were simply some topics I could not cover in the time I had to write the book. But I wanted to give you enough information, enough confidence, that if there was something I didn't do in the book, you would be able to do it without me.

Who Should Read This Book

This book was intended for IT professionals, network administrators, or anyone with a Windows Server administrative background who needs to come up to speed on SharePoint Foundation. The contents of this book were written assuming the reader would have experience with Windows Servers, particularly IIS and Active Directory, with a basic understanding of SQL. This book is primarily for administrators (but anyone interested in what makes SharePoint Foundation tick might find it worth reading), so although we do some work with PowerShell and SharePoint's command-line tool, STSADM, we do no developing here. If you are an administrator who has been informed that you must install SharePoint Foundation, if you've inherited SharePoint Foundation, or if you plan on administering it the future—this book is for you.

What Is Covered in This Book

This book was meant for the intrepid IT professional, administrator, or student of all things server related. It takes you through what an administrator should know, part by part, chapter by chapter:

Part 1: Preparing for Microsoft SharePoint Foundation 2010

Chapter 1, "SharePoint Foundation 2010 Under the Hood": The concepts you need to be prepared for before installing SharePoint, from what installations to expect to performance and capacity planning, to features that may take extra effort or resources to use.

Chapter 2, "Standalone Installation": A detailed look at how to install SharePoint Foundation in a single-server implementation, with a glance at how it looks all set up, and post configuration tasks.

Chapter 3, "Complete Installation": A detailed look at how to install SharePoint Foundation on the first server in a server farm. It also provides detailed information concerning the initial configuration of services and accounts to get up and running.

Part 2: Using Microsoft SharePoint Foundation 2010

Chapter 4, "Introduction to the SharePoint Interface": The landmarks and terminology of the interface itself.

Chapter 5, "Introduction to Web Parts": What web parts are, what they are for, where you can put them, what the built-in ones do, and how to configure them. All without leaving the browser. No development here.

Chapter 6, "Introduction to Lists": What lists are, really—how they work, what they do, how to customize them and reuse preexisting lists and templates. This chapter also explores the preexisting lists of a team site.

Chapter 7, "Creating Lists": How to create your own lists from list templates or from scratch. This chapter covers how to create list templates and connect related lists; it also takes a glance at workflows, by using the three-state workflow that comes with SharePoint Foundation.

Chapter 8, "Introduction to Libraries": What libraries are, how they work, how to customize them, and how to make your own. There are several types of libraries; not all of them work as you expect them to.

Chapter 9, "Sites, Subsites, and Workspaces": What subsites and workspaces are, how to create them, and how to use them. It also covers what site templates are and what templates are available out of the box.

Chapter 10, "Site Collections and Web Applications": What site collections and web applications are. Moving up to the big stuff, you'll learn how and why to create new site collections or even new web applications, extend existing web applications, configure anonymous access, how alternate access mapping works, and more.

Part 3: Administering Microsoft SharePoint Foundation 2010

Chapter 11, "Central Administration": This reference chapter focuses on how to use the Central Administration pages and how its settings are used to administer SharePoint. It explains what Central Administration is and how to use it. You'll learn what settings are available and what each one does, when to use them, and what they're for. There are extensive references to where those settings are covered in depth under specific administrative topics elsewhere in the book.

Chapter 12, "Users and Permissions": An in-depth look at individual permissions and their levels, user and group management, and configuration of authorization options. Coverage includes using Policy for Web Applications to secure web applications, restricting site collections using permissions and groups, breaking inheritance, as well as securing lists and list items, with a look at managing administrators at the farm level and the new Delegated Administrators group.

Chapter 13, "Maintenance and Monitoring": How to monitor, back up, and restore SharePoint. You'll learn how to recover from disaster, from using the Recycle Bin to recover a lost list item to rebuilding the server farm.

Part 4: Special Topics in Microsoft SharePoint Foundation 2010

Chapter 14, "STSADM and PowerShell": An introduction to PowerShell for SharePoint, covering the fundamentals of the new tool in SharePoint's arsenal. This chapter provides insights in how to manage SharePoint using PowerShell and the command-line administrative tool, STSADM. You'll see how to do more than the Central Administration website will allow—there's always more power at the command line.

Chapter 15, "Migrating from Windows SharePoint Services 3.0 to Microsoft SharePoint Foundation 2010": The ins and outs of the two methods of migration: database attach and in-place, with tips and tricks concerning preparation and planning, and details of how to migrate from start to finish, standalone and server farm.

Chapter 16, "Advanced Installation and Configuration": Covering some of the more advanced configuration tasks and strategies, from network load balancing to creating external content types for Business Data Connectivity to configuring multi-tenancy. Do the fancy administrative tasks that others hesitate to do.

I have some extra material that, although not crucial to the book, I enjoyed writing and want to make available to you. The material is organized as two "bonus" chapters: "Web Parts, Lists, and Libraries; Extras, Tips, and Tricks" (otherwise known as Bonus Chapter 1), and Bonus Chapter 2, " PowerShell Cmdlets and STSADM Operations at a Glance," which is filled with convenient tables listing many PowerShell Cmdlets and their corresponding STSADM commands. These are yours, free of charge, so feel free to download them from www.sybex.com/go/masteringsharepointfoundation2010 at any time.

Behind the Scenes: The Making of *Mastering Microsoft SharePoint Foundation 2010*

The writing of this book was done entirely on a 13" MacBook Pro, most of it on Server 2008 R2 (boot from VHD, dual boot with Windows 7). I used VMware vSphere client (all day, every day for about a year) to access the virtual machines I used to do steps and take all the screenshots in this book. I wrote the book using the portable apps version of Open Office Writer. I needed something portable since I was going to be moving between operating systems on my laptop, not to mention that it's free, which is always good. For music, I used XMPlay and VLC media player. Although in the VMs themselves, all screenshots were taken with Snagit from TechSmith, I used Lightscreen for any screenshots I had to take from my desktop. For managing and viewing those screenshots, I used FastStone Image Viewer, an excellent product.

For those who like the nitty-gritty details, here is a rundown of the background of the book as far as network and resources go. The SharePoint network I used throughout the book was run in a set of VMs on a large Dell server running VMware ESXi that I happen to have in my home. My coauthors, technical editors, and some reviewers accessed virtual machines configured like my own using my ESXi server remotely. For the contributors, it was in order to have screenshots and step-by-step exercises that matched the domain, server, and user naming structure that I was using for the book. For the technical editor, it was to ensure he had all the resources he needed to edit every step in the book for technical accuracy. At times there were more than 30 VMs running simultaneously for the creation of this book, for one reason or another.

The network configuration for the book:

Internal Active Directory Domain: dem0tek.lcl

Email domain: dem0tek.lcl (with a brief foray into dem0tek.com for incoming email and alternate access mapping)

Servers:

RR1.dem0tek.lcl: This was the SQL 2008 server for SharePoint. For convenience sake, it was also the Routing and Remote Access Server for the virtual network.

DC1.dem0tek.lcl: This was the domain controller and the MailEnable email server. It also contained the shares used for backup and restores in Chapters 13 and 15.

SPF1.dem0tek.lcl: This was the first SharePoint server on the network. It was the Standalone installation server used in Chapter 2. I also reused it for the Office Web Apps installation in Chapter 16.

SPF2.dem0tek.lcl: This was the second SharePoint server on the network. This server is the one installed using the Server Farm, Complete installation and used RR1 for its SharePoint databases. Used for most of the book, it should become familiar to readers.

SPF3.dem0tek.lcl: This was the SharePoint server installed specifically to play second fiddle to SPF2. SPF3 was the server added to the SharePoint server farm in Chapter 16 to demonstrate load balancing and SharePoint services management.

In addition to the servers, for the chapters that required Office or SharePoint Designer, I used a VM running Windows 7 Ultimate, with Office 2010 Professional Plus, 32-bit, and SharePoint Designer 2010, 32-bit, installed.

There are a number of user accounts that show up throughout the book, but in fact there are numerous users for the dem0tek network that didn't really get any recognition. Doing my best to create fictitious names that were truly fictitious, I created names in a few broad categories, most notably herbs and semiprecious stones (believe it or not). The herbs were, by and large, the information workers (although several of them, particularly Saffron, are power users). The semiprecious stones were staff and IT technicians. Because most of my work was done at the administrative level, I tended to log in as my SharePoint administration utility account, but there were other accounts available to log in with if necessary. You might recognize Saffron, Jasper, and Citrine when you see them.

So, now you know what was going on in the background during the writing of this book.

There's SharePoint and There's SharePoint

I tend to refer to SharePoint Foundation 2010 (or SPF) as "SharePoint" in this book for readability and convenience (because I am not fond of using the same long name or acronym over and over for more than a few hundred pages). However, it is important to point out that there are two kinds of SharePoint: SharePoint Foundation 2010 and SharePoint Server 2010. And because of that, you will see that I do use the full name, SharePoint Foundation, when I need to make it clear which kind of SharePoint I am referring to. It should stand to reason that I will otherwise default to SharePoint meaning SharePoint Foundation, since that is the topic of the book.

SharePoint Foundation is the newest version of a product previously called Windows SharePoint Services (that was confusingly referred to as Windows SharePoint Services, no matter what version it was). That version of SharePoint was called Windows SharePoint Services (WSS) because it was considered a Windows Server service or component. (The 2.0 version of Windows SharePoint Services was even available as a component under Add/Remove Programs for Server 2003 R2.) But between the release of WSS 3.0 and the start of the SharePoint Foundation beta, the product was moved from being a Windows Server service to a full-fledged member of the SharePoint Product family. And along with the move came a change in name— from Windows SharePoint Services to SharePoint Foundation.

As a Windows service, the single-server install of WSS 3.0 could use the free, robust Windows Internal Database (WID or SSEE, SQL Server Embedded Edition), which has no database size limits. But because SharePoint Foundation is no longer a Windows service, the stand-alone installation now has to rely on SQL Express 2008, with its 4GB database limit instead. This change seems counterintuitive; why is this an upgrade if the databases have a limit for the standalone installation that the previous version didn't? But now you know why.

Along with the new name, SharePoint Foundation also got an overhaul of its infrastructure, adding service application capabilities (such as Business Data Connectivity) and other features, truly making it the foundation of the paid-for SharePoint Server 2010 product.

Let me step back and reiterate: There are two kinds of SharePoint. One is the free version, which contains all the fundamental functionality of SharePoint, known as SharePoint Foundation. And there is the paid-for version, SharePoint Server 2010. The paid-for version is essentially an add-on to the foundational version, adding numerous enterprise capabilities. Often those who use the paid-for version of SharePoint never realize that the features they use daily are not the parts they spent their money on.

DIFFERENT VERSIONS, DIFFERENT FEATURES

A number of good websites list exactly what capabilities are available with SharePoint Foundation vs. the SharePoint Server 2010 versions, Standard and Enterprise. You can find the list Microsoft offers (slightly slanted toward the Server product but still good) by doing a search for *SharePoint 2010 edition comparison*.

Just to be clear, using SharePoint Foundation and SharePoint Server 2010 is not entirely an either/or situation. They are basically two different products, but there is a relationship there.

SharePoint Foundation is free and is a complete product by itself. After it is installed, it will work perfectly fine on its own. However, if you buy and install SharePoint Server 2010, SharePoint Foundation is installed first and then SharePoint Server 2010 is installed *on top of* it (or as part of it; this is an automated part of the SharePoint Server 2010 installation). Microsoft SharePoint Server 2010 requires SharePoint Foundation to be installed before it will even run.

So, SharePoint Foundation does not need SharePoint Server, but SharePoint Server does need SharePoint Foundation, because its functions are the foundation of all things SharePoint Server. When you pay for SharePoint Server 2010, you pay for the extras it offers in addition to the usefulness of SharePoint Foundation.

In addition to the two types of SharePoint, it bears mentioning that there is a 2010 version of SharePoint Designer as well. SharePoint Designer is a free-for-download, no-coding product meant to be used by administrators and designers to customize SharePoint (both Foundation and Server 2010). It is a single-purpose tool, meant only to work with the 2010 types of SharePoint, and it lets you enhance your SharePoint sites with additional custom workflows, web parts, and pages (or edit the ones you have), customize your sites, and create connections to external content using Business Data Connectivity service.

ANXIETY, TREPIDATION, AND LICENSING

SharePoint Server 2010 requires a Standard Client Access License (CAL) for standard features, and to unlock the Enterprise features, it also requires an Enterprise CAL for each user. That's two CALs for each user, plus the cost of SharePoint Server 2010.

SharePoint Foundation, however, is still considered to be a quasi-server component, because it uses Internet Information Services (IIS) to host its web applications, and IIS uses the server's license model. No additional licensing is required (beyond the server CALs and the licensing for SQL).

There is one possible caveat. It's something called an External Connector license and is required when external users are going to be authenticating to the domain and using SharePoint Foundation. In that case, the external user is using an account that is not a licensed account for that server or using a machine that is not licensed for server access, depending on the server's licensing model. Since those users are not covered under the Server's license, they must be covered elsewhere; thus, the External Connector license comes into play. (For SharePoint Server 2010, you purchase a license for SharePoint Server 2010 for Internet Sites, in either the Standard or Enterprise version.)

The External Connector license is a per-server license for Windows Server 2008 or 2008 R2. It is purchased per server, not per client. This means a server with this license can legally allow an unlimited number of external clients to authenticate and access its resources.

Keep in mind that a license is required for external users who are authenticating and using (that includes contributing or editing material) the resources on the SharePoint server. Because the SharePoint server is an IIS web server, there is no license required for users if they are accessing the server anonymously, such as someone who is only looking and doesn't need to contribute to the site.

The scenario in which the External Connector license (or any other license) is required varies, so definitely contact Microsoft Licensing to see whether the External Connector license is a requirement for you.

That about covers it for where SharePoint comes from and what it's capable of doing today. This book will cover the ins and outs of SharePoint Foundation to give you the best bang for your buck and the most information about what you can get out of the free version before you buy the expensive add-on.

The Mastering Series

The Mastering series from Sybex provides outstanding instruction for readers with intermediate and advanced skills, in the form of top-notch training and development for those already working in their field and clear, serious education for those aspiring to become pros. Every Mastering book features the following:

- The Sybex "by professionals for professionals" commitment. Mastering authors are themselves practitioners, with plenty of credentials in their areas of specialty.

- A practical perspective for a reader who already knows the basics—someone who needs solutions, not a primer.

- Real World Scenarios, ranging from case studies to in-depth tips and tricks, that show how the tool, technique, or knowledge presented is applied in actual practice.

- Skill-based instruction, with chapters organized around real tasks rather than abstract concepts or subjects.

- Self-review test "Master It" problems and questions, so you can be certain you're equipped to do the job right.

How to Contact the Author

For more information, questions, or suggestions, please feel free to email me at callahan@ callahantech.com. I can be followed on Twitter by using cacallahan. I've also got a blog, if you'd like to stop by at http://servergrrl.blogspot.com that I created specifically to support this book (and the previous version). It is there that I will write all the stuff that I didn't get a chance to here (including late-breaking information, such as changes caused by Service Packs, updates, and new server operating systems); add more concepts; fix any errata that may turn up (hey, we're all human here); and more. And if this book ends up with another edition, you can hear about it there and even offer me suggestions as to what should be in it the next time around.

Sybex strives to keep you supplied with the latest tools and information you need for your work. Please check their website at www.sybex.com, where they'll post additional content and updates that supplement this book if the need arises. Enter **SharePoint Foundation** in the Search box (or type the book's ISBN—**9780470626382**), and click Go to get to the book's update page.

Part 1

Preparing for Microsoft SharePoint Foundation 2010

Chapter 1

SharePoint Foundation 2010 Under the Hood

SharePoint Foundation (SPF) is a nifty web-based collaboration, data management, communication, idea-creating, problem-solving tool that costs you nothing (assuming you already have a licensed server). SharePoint Foundation 2010 needs to run on Windows Server 2008 (Standard Service Pack 2 or higher).

SharePoint Foundation has its needs, its shortcomings, and its weaknesses, but overall, it is a surprisingly useful, flexible, and powerful web-based tool for any administrator. The best part is that using it doesn't require any web development skills at all. As a matter of fact, this book is being written for IT admins specifically because they seem to be the people who are ultimately responsible for managing SharePoint, without really being trained for it. This book should help fill in some of those holes in training.

So, what is SharePoint? SharePoint comes in two flavors for the 2010 version: SharePoint Foundation 2010 (SharePoint Foundation) and Microsoft SharePoint Server 2010 (SharePoint 2010). SharePoint Foundation is a free download and falls under the server's license model. However, SharePoint 2010, which during installation installs SharePoint Foundation and then installs its added components, costs thousands of dollars (depending on volume license) and requires at least one Client Access License (CAL) for each user.

The free version doesn't require separate CALs for each user (assuming each user already has a standard CAL for server access) and is the foundation for SharePoint. The paid-for version just adds more functionality to the foundation. So yes, SharePoint Foundation 2010 is free and (as the name implies) is the foundation for the more expensive SharePoint components.

What does SharePoint do? It presents a web interface for people to collaborate, communicate, and share data in an environment that is consistent, easy for administrators to control, designed to store data and documents, and very scalable. SharePoint can be installed on a single server, or it can be installed on numerous web front-end servers sharing the client load in what is called a SharePoint *server farm*.

Fundamentally, SharePoint is a collection of web pages containing web parts and lists on top of a database. However, SharePoint takes advantage of that simple framework and uses it to offer lists, libraries, workspaces, team sites, blogs, wikis, site collections, workflows, and web parts. With these tools, you can offer shared calendars, discussions, file libraries, surveys, and more. For process management, you can require document checkout, co-authoring, content approval, and versioning. You can even establish workflows to trigger alerts and other changes based on where documents or list items are in a process. Some lists and libraries can be set up with their own email accounts, so people can email entries without going to the SharePoint site. Existing external data can used to populate certain lists. And when integrating with Office 2010, users can seamlessly work on files and documents using Outlook, PowerPoint, Word, Excel, and the rest.

This chapter will give you an idea of what you need to know to prepare for installing SharePoint Foundation. This kind of product does require planning. This isn't an "install it and then think about what you want to do with it later" kind of product. To make sure the initial installation and configuration of your SharePoint implementation goes smoothly, it is a good idea to know what you are going to need for success before you start.

In this chapter, you'll learn to

◆ Determine the software and hardware requirements you need for installing SharePoint Foundation.

◆ Identify the three ways of installing SharePoint Foundation.

◆ Set up the necessary accounts that SharePoint needs to run.

◆ Recognize the new features and requirements of SharePoint.

Hardware Requirements

Trying to pin down the exact hardware requirements for a product like SharePoint is tough (And when I say SharePoint, I generally mean SharePoint Foundation in this book unless I specify otherwise.). There are many different ways to use it; therefore, there are many ways to configure the resources.

Microsoft has some suggested hardware requirements. This time around, Microsoft seems to be hedging its bets and beefing up the requirements. Your mileage may vary, but chances are good that these suggestions will easily handle an average server load. There is no suggested minimum anymore, only "recommended" requirements.

Processor   64-bit, multi-core (4 preferably), 2.5 GHz per core minimum.

RAM   4 GB for developer or evaluation installations (usually meaning single-server, testing situations, not production loads), 8 GB or more for production use. Microsoft is serious about the 8 GB recommendation. SharePoint uses IIS Web Sites and application pools, which, for each one, use a considerable amount of RAM. So, the more IIS Web Sites (which correspond with a SharePoint "web application") you need, the more RAM you'll need.

Disk   80 GB, NTFS. More disk space is recommended, depending on your storage needs, such as SQL databases (if you are going to do a single-server install) or anything else running on the server.

DISK SPACE: BIGGER IS BETTER

I have noticed that, for the virtual machines I am running for this book, about 28 GB are used just for Server 2008 R2 and SharePoint Foundation. Generally, plan for about 28 GB just for OS and SharePoint, if nothing else. Also keep in mind that log files and indexes can grow to be unexpectedly large very quickly, so 80 GB is a good suggested minimum.

Planning for storage is particularly important if you are running SQL and SharePoint on the same server (as is the case in a single-server environment). You will need to plan for the storage space of SharePoint pages in IIS, SMTP mail store (if you enable incoming email), indexing files used for search, all storage space the databases would use for site lists and libraries, and all other databases SharePoint uses for additional services, such as Logging and Business Data Connectivity. As you can see, the space that SharePoint might need for its files is not the only space you'll need. In this case, everything is stored in one place. Size it well, and guard it carefully.

DVD Drive   This is not really required for SharePoint but is useful.

Display   Microsoft avoids mentioning a recommended resolution. I've found 1024×768 on the client is a functional minimum. Pages don't display well at lower resolutions. To avoid any scroll bars, many pages in SharePoint are now better viewed at resolutions closer to 1152×864 or higher.

Network   Microsoft, again, doesn't mention a real requirement here. But I find that 1 Gbps is a good recommendation.

These recommendations are just starting points; however, they are more than adequate for most simple SharePoint server farm installations. Most single-server or simple server farm installations can probably handle 1,000 people creating an average load on the SharePoint server, without seeing a lag in operations per second. Commonly, each gigahertz of processing power in a SharePoint server can handle about nine operations per second.

Software Requirements

To make all that SharePoint goodness possible, the following roles and technologies must be installed and running on the SharePoint server. These are the underlying technologies that make SharePoint function. Without them, SharePoint won't even install.

For this version of SharePoint, these prerequisites are pretty lengthy. So to make installing SharePoint Foundation easier, most of the software prerequisites (after you install the operating system, of course) can be installed automatically on the server during setup by selecting to install prerequisites on the preinstallation screen. Keep in mind that this version of SharePoint is all about 64-bit; it cannot be installed on a 32-bit operating system, nor can its databases be stored in 32-bit SQL.

Operating System   SharePoint requires a 64-bit operating system. In production, the server needs to be at least Server 2008 SP2 (during installation, if the server is not up to Service Pack 2, it will be installed—you have been warned). It is suggested to use Server 2008 R2 or higher.

The prerequisites installer will also install some hotfixes to support claims-based authentication (a security token–based authentication method now supported by this version of SharePoint). For Server 2008, it is KB976394. For Server 2008 R2, it is KB976462.

Windows Server 2008 and 2008 R2 come in different versions, and SharePoint Foundation will install on Standard, Enterprise, and Datacenter. It will not install on Core, Web Server, or Foundation. Installing SharePoint on a domain controller is not supported.

WINDOWS 7

For the sake of developers, Microsoft has finally made it possible to install SharePoint on a Windows 7 workstation. It takes additional modifications, but it can be done. This is for development and testing purposes only, but there are numerous blogs and articles detailing the tweaking necessary to make it work.

Web Server and Application Server Roles   For Server 2008, IIS 7.0, or 2008 R2, IIS 7.5, with IIS 6.0 compatibility must be installed. This makes sense. SharePoint is web-based because IIS allows Windows Server (2008 or higher) to host websites and service HTTP requests from clients. Many SharePoint capabilities are dependent upon and colored by the functions and needs of IIS. For example, IIS contains Web Sites, which hold web pages. In SharePoint, IIS Web Sites are considered to be web applications and contain web pages organized into sites and subsites, called *site collections*. SharePoint web applications are considered containers and security boundaries for those site collections, largely because of the built-in properties of IIS Web Sites and their management (for example, specifying application pools and whether anonymous access is allowed). Those settings may be configured in SharePoint but are applied to the IIS Web Site (aka web application). This explains why anonymous access is enabled at the web application level and then trickles down to each site collection contained within. The IIS server role must be installed before SharePoint can be installed. An additional SharePoint feature that depends on IIS is incoming email, which requires that the SMTP service be enabled in IIS.

Database   SharePoint obviously requires a database on the back end in order to store data. Currently, SharePoint only supports SQL Server for its content and configuration databases (although external data can be accessed from other types of data sources in other ways).

SQL Server   SharePoint Foundation requires the 64-bit version of either SQL Server 2005 SP3 with Cumulative Update (CU) 3, SQL Server 2008 SP1, CU2, or SQL Server 2008 R2. This pricey SQL package is a database powerhouse. Network-aware, it can be made to support clustering and more. It is ideal for handling the huge amounts of data a large server farm might generate. It can also be clustered for failover scenarios (which SharePoint can support). SQL Server is possibly overkill for small offices that are considering SharePoint. However, if you already have SQL Server 2005 SP3 CU3, 2008 SP1, CU2, or SQL 2008 R2 on your network, then by all means use it.

SQL Server 2008 Express   If you don't have SQL handy (and don't want to shell out the cash to install and use it), you can do the poor man's single SharePoint server install, as discussed in Chapter 2, "Installation Standalone." This will install SQL Server 2008 Express during SharePoint's initial setup. SQL Express is a free, local-only database (meaning that it cannot be remotely accessed). With SQL Express, SharePoint can create and manage its databases just fine. The catch is that the Express version of SQL cannot support any other SharePoint servers accessing it and has a hard database size limit of 4 GB (you can upgrade it SQL Express 2008 R2, which can support 10 GB after install). It is not as robust as its big brother SQL 2008, and it has no graphical tools built in with which to manage and update it. The previous version of SharePoint used a different kind of single-server database engine, which had no database size limitations.

MIGRATING?

If you are considering upgrading to SPF from WSS 3.0 and you have a basic or single server installation, you will need to do a few extra things to prepare for the upgrade because of this database version change. See Chapter 15, "Migrating from WSS 3.0 to Windows SharePoint Foundation 2010," for details.

It's important to realize how pivotal SQL is to SharePoint. In addition to hosting nifty-looking websites, SharePoint's real primary purpose is to store and access data from its databases. SharePoint is really an extensive database front end. It's all about lists (and a special kind of list called a *library*, discussed in Chapter 8, "Introduction to Libraries"). Lists contain data in records and fields (or, visually, rows and columns). Therefore, SharePoint logically requires databases on the back end to hold all that data.

As you know, SharePoint does not necessarily need to be installed on the same server as the databases themselves, although it can be if you need it. That is the beauty of SQL Server: it can be accessed remotely. This means that a SharePoint server just needs to be pointed at a nearby SQL server to create and use a database there. This is convenient for several reasons, such as separating resources and storage, helping eliminate the SharePoint server as a single point of failure, and scalability. If a SQL database can be accessed by one SharePoint server, then it stands to reason that other SharePoint servers can access the same database. Being able to share the SQL databases is what makes server farms possible. Using this approach, multiple installations of SharePoint can be pointed to the same configuration and content databases, so they can do load balancing and share the same consistent configuration and administration settings.

This is obviously why SharePoint requires SQL. It is also where you see a functional split between installing SharePoint to be hosted by a single server and installing SharePoint to be managed across a server farm. Single-server installations only need local access to a database, and they can easily use SQL Express to accomplish that. A server farm requires a remote SQL server that all SharePoint front-end servers can share.

You also may notice that there are a lot of references to service packs, cumulative updates, and hotfixes. At this point, Microsoft has so many products out in the middle of its release cycles, and those products have numerous fixes and improvements, that some of the features SharePoint requires must have underlying technologies with specific modifications applied. So, keep that in mind if you have other technologies that share the same resources (such as SQL) but require those modifications *not* be made. There may be incompatibility issues to contend with.

This version of SharePoint has greatly improved integration features with SQL, as well as more functionality in terms of claims-based authentication, communicating with external data sources, command-line scripting, and more. To facilitate that, this version of SharePoint has a number of additional features and components it needs in order to function properly.

The following components can be installed (if you have Internet access) during the installation process, by clicking Install Prerequisites on the SharePoint Foundation installation screen (Figure 1.1).

Windows PowerShell 2.0   This feature is extremely important for SharePoint Foundation, because SharePoint uses PowerShell to run a number of things in the background, and PowerShell is swiftly replacing STSADM as SharePoint's fundamental command-line interface. A number of SharePoint commands and capabilities depend on PowerShell 2.0.

SQL Server 2008 Native Client   Even if you're not running that version of the server for your databases, you need it anyway. This is used to create new applications or enhance existing applications that need to take advantage of new SQL Server 2008 features. It's needed to support some new, under-the-covers database capabilities in SharePoint.

Microsoft Windows Identity Foundation   Sometimes also known as Windows Identity Framework, it extends .NET's Cardspace support and makes it possible for SharePoint to support claims-based, security token system authentication. It particularly supports claims-based authentication for ASP.NET applications and Windows Communication Foundation services.

FIGURE 1.1
The SharePoint
Foundation instal-
lation screen

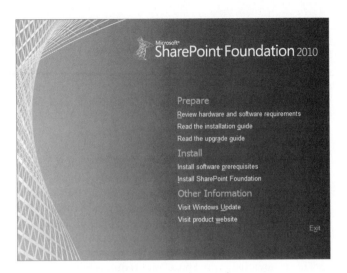

Microsoft Sync Framework Runtime v1.0 (x64): This improves SharePoint's ability to synchronize data with ADO.NET-enabled data sources or FeedSync feeds (such as RSS or Atom).

Microsoft Chart Controls for the Microsoft .NET Framework 3.5 Installs new assemblies for ASP.NET and Windows Form Chart Controls. It's particularly useful for visualization with Visual Studio.

Microsoft Filter Pack 2.0 This installs and registers ifilters with the Windows Indexing Service, which integrates with search services to index the contents of Microsoft-supported files, such as `.docx`, `.zip`, `.pptx`, `.xlsm`, `.zip`, and so on.

Microsoft .NET Framework 3.5 SP1 .NET (and subsequently ASP.NET) are required by SharePoint. This service also contains the Windows Workflow Foundation, Communication Foundation, Presentation Foundation, and Cardspace. It also supports ASP.NET Ajax, Language Integrated Query (LINQ), and web protocol support for WCF services (including Ajax, JSON, REST, POX, RSS, ATOM, and so on), as well as new classes in .NET Framework's base library. This is required for Server 2008 but already built into Server 2008 R2.

Microsoft SQL Server 2008 Analysis Services ADOMD.NET This improves data analysis, business intelligence capabilities, and data warehousing capabilities of SharePoint using SQL (it is backward compatible with earlier versions of SQL).

ADO.NET Data Services Update for .NET Framework v3.5 SP1 This supports Windows Communication Framework (WCF) in accessing data and exposing that data via web services over HTTP. This capability, along with the fully fledged WCF, enables SharePoint Foundation to perform Business Connectivity Services, discussed in Chapters 3 and 16. This is installed with Analysis Services.

Microsoft Speech Platform Runtime (x64) and Language – TELE (en-US) An optional service but installed automatically by the prerequisite installer, it assists SharePoint accessibility with speech recognition and speech synthesis. It also requires an appropriate language pack. There is a little more configuration needed (especially if you are going to use additional language packs) concerning a registry key change. Search TechNet for more details.

SQL 2008 R2 Reporting Services SharePoint 2010 add-in Also an optional service, this add-on is convenient if you are using SQL 2008 R2 with Reporting Services installed, have

SharePoint installed on the same server, and want to use Report Builder (or another tool) to make reports that can be stored in (and read from) a SharePoint library.

Of course, from the client side, users will need a browser to access the SharePoint sites.

Browser support comes in two levels. Level 1 describes browsers that are fully supported, and SharePoint is considered optimized for their access. Not surprisingly, the only browser that supports all of SharePoint's advanced features is Internet Explorer 7 or higher, 32-bit (yes, 64-bit IE is not entirely compatible with all SharePoint features). This is largely because of SharePoint's use of proprietary ActiveX controls. Mozilla's Firefox 3.5 or higher is a quasi level 1 browser, but some ActiveX features, such as Datasheet view, do not function.

Level 2 browsers are mostly supported, but they are intended to be used to do rudimentary things with SharePoint, such as reading and writing in the SharePoint sites, and to do basic SharePoint administration. Anything that truly requires ActiveX will not work for level 2 browsers.

So, what browsers are considered level 2? Any browser that isn't IE 7, 8, or higher, or isn't Firefox 3.6. That means any IE version older than 7 (or IE for Mac), Safari 4.04, Opera, and so on. IE version 6 and lower are definitely not supported.

The bottom line is that Microsoft wants you to use the most recent versions of Microsoft IE to use SharePoint—that and Office 2010, of course.

Office 2010 is really integrated with SharePoint; half the things you can do with SharePoint you can do *better* with Office 2010. Don't get me wrong, though; Office 2007 can integrate too, but not as completely as Office 2010. Keep in mind that SharePoint prefers you use the 32-bit version of Office 2010 to integrate; not all features are supported with 64-bit Office at this point (sadly enough).

There you have it. That's SharePoint Foundation under the hood—a Windows Server operating system, IIS 7.0 or higher with 6.0 support, PowerShell, .NET Framework 3.5, a handful of additional components that extend .NET 3.5, filtering, and SharePoint's use of SQL, specifically 64-bit SQL Server 2005 SP3 CU3 or higher (or you can let SharePoint install SQL Server 2008 Express). These roles and technologies, working in tandem, power SharePoint. The strengths and weaknesses of this underlying infrastructure lend their particular traits to SharePoint. Knowing about them teaches you both how SharePoint works and how to manage it, especially when it comes to troubleshooting.

INSTALLING SHAREPOINT: SINGLE SERVER OR SERVER FARM

Now that you know what you need to have on the server before you even consider installing SharePoint, let's take a look at what you need to know *about* the installation process itself, which I'll take you through in Chapters 2 and 3.

There are essentially two ways to install SharePoint. Either you don't have a copy of SQL running on your network (or even on the same server) that you can use to host SharePoint's databases or you do.

SharePoint may come in two sizes (Standalone and Server Farm; see Figure 1.2), but it can actually be installed three different ways: Standalone, Standalone Server, and Complete. The last two options are under the heading Server Farm (see Figure 1.3) and indicate that the SQL Server 2008 Express database won't be installed locally; instead, the installation process will prompt for SQL server and database information.

Standalone The Standalone install assumes that you are going to use only one server *ever* to run SharePoint and that you don't have a copy of SQL handy to use for its databases. What it does in that case is install SharePoint assuming all necessary services are going to run locally and that you need it to install the free SQL Server 2008 Express version of SQL on the same server.

FIGURE 1.2
SharePoint Foundation installation types

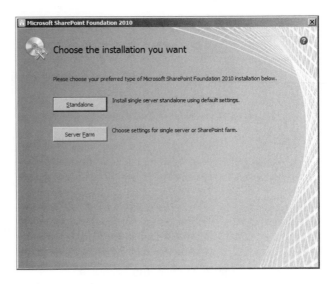

Server Farm, Stand-alone This installation is essentially the same as the Standalone install you get by just clicking the Standalone button. Use this installation method if you intend to install SharePoint on one server only (you cannot use it as a server farm server), and you want SharePoint to install and use the SQL Server 2008 Express database engine on the same server. The only difference between this install type and Standalone is that it gives you the option to specify the location of your search index files.

FIGURE 1.3
The two Server Farm options for installation

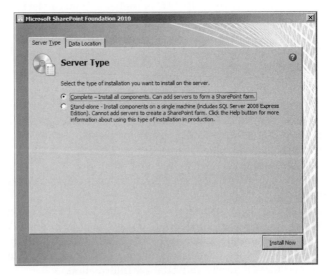

Server Farm, Complete This installation method is intended to, at its very simplest, let you specify to SharePoint, during installation, the SQL Server deployment you want it to use instead of installing SQL Server 2008 Express locally. Even if a full version of SQL Server is installed on the same machine as you are installing SharePoint, SharePoint will not notice if you don't specify that you want a Complete installation.

That's because Standalone and Server Farm Stand-alone install SQL Server 2008 Express without your involvement; they don't give you a chance to specify anything. This means that if you have SQL Server *anywhere* on your Windows network (2005 SP3 CU3 or 2008 SP1 CU2) and you want to use it to house your SharePoint databases, then the Server Farm Complete install is the only type that lets you specify where your databases will go.

The other reason to use a Server Farm installation method would be if you want a server farm topology. A SharePoint server farm uses more than one server to support SharePoint. This can be simply one SharePoint server and one SQL server, or it can be scaled up to a more complex topology, such as numerous SharePoint servers (generally called web front-end servers) and a SQL database cluster. The simplest server farm consists of a database server and a server with SharePoint installed on it, so the two functions are separated between two servers. Together they are a server farm. Of course, there is more to it than that. Usually, people create bigger server farms, comprising more SharePoint servers all using the same SQL databases. This is appropriate if they have a lot of SharePoint sites and they want to spread HTTP requests between servers to improve performance; typically this means having multiple SharePoint servers and even multiple, clustered database servers. You can also separate roles such as incoming email, central administration, or services such as Search, Business Data Connectivity, Sandboxed Code, or the Subscription Settings Service.

If you choose to do a Server Farm installation, you can specify whether the SharePoint server you are installing is the first on the farm or you are adding it to an existing server farm. The first SharePoint server on a server farm is kind of like the first domain controller in a domain. Because it's the first, it tends to hold all the services and is the one used to set up the databases. Choosing to add a server to an existing server farm means that the installation will install only the files needed to make that new server a web front-end server to help support the first server with client requests.

Server farms work because the databases that hold all the information about SharePoint and its server farm configuration settings (including which other databases on the server contain what data for what sites) already exist in a configuration database on the SQL server. All you have to do at that point is specify which configuration database the new server will share with the first server, and presto change-o, you've got a new SharePoint server with the same configuration and content.

THE GORILLA IN THE ROOM

Something that isn't mentioned much is that server farms, in addition to having front-end servers that all access the same databases, are usually configured to do load balancing, using Windows Network Load Balancing software, DNS round-robin, or a hardware load-balancing device. Real server farm, load-balancing functionality requires additional setup using something other than SharePoint. Installing additional SharePoint front-end servers is only one part of it.

To make matters worse, there has been little documentation about how to do load balancing. So, check out Chapter 16, "Advanced Installation and Configuration," for a brief demonstration of how to do simple network load balancing with SharePoint.

The differences between the kinds of SharePoint installations are not the stuff of rocket science. However, if you intend to do more than run everything on one server or if you don't want to end up with the SQL Express database engine, you really need to understand those differences before you install SharePoint.

SharePoint Sites and Databases

This section briefly outlines the IIS Web Sites and the databases that SharePoint will create during installation.

SharePoint IIS Web Sites

SharePoint needs at least two different IIS Web Sites (otherwise known as SharePoint web applications) to function. Most of the web applications contain the web pages that you will access to either administer SharePoint or actually use SharePoint's lists, subsites, and libraries. In addition, SharePoint Foundation adds another IIS Web Site during installation to support web services, such as Business Data Connectivity, Security Token Service, and Topology.

At the minimum, say for a simple Standalone installation, you will have these three IIS Web Sites available on the SharePoint server:

The Central Administration V4   This web application is used to control the configuration and administration of all servers on the server farm, as well as all web applications. This site is set up on a unique port, completely different from the standard one for HTTP. If you do a Server Farm installation, you can specify the port or use the one suggested. If you do a Standalone installation, the port will be chosen at random for you during installation and configuration (or you can specify your own). The range is somewhere between 1023 and 32767. The unique port helps obscure this site from anyone surfing the standard ports on the server.

The SharePoint Site   The default name for the first SharePoint web application (that isn't dedicated to Central Administration) is usually SharePoint-80. SharePoint tends to want to name its web applications with SharePoint, a dash, and the web application's port number (or host header and port number). It will contain the first top-level site for SharePoint, just to get you started (or in a Server Farm installation, you can create it yourself—or have the configuration wizard do it). Web applications were meant to contain site collections, which are collections of sites. Each one starts with a top-level site, but they can also include additional subsites. Web applications can contain as few as one site collection with one top-level site, or many site collections, each with multiple subsites. Because a web application is essentially a container for your SharePoint sites, when you configure settings at the web application level, they can affect *all* sites contained therein.

SharePoint Web Services   This web application, on a random port for both HTTP and HTTPS, is the one that does not contain any web pages to be used for any standard reason. This web application is used exclusively by SharePoint web services to use all of the nifty features and components available for SharePoint. It allows them to make external connections to data not stored in SharePoint's databases, handle security token for claims-based authentication, or manage the farm's topology.

Keep in mind that these are the web applications that are created during simple Standalone SharePoint installation. You can create more if you'd like. If you inherit a SharePoint server and find that more than three web applications are being used by SharePoint, that's fine. Someone probably added more for a good reason (see Chapter 10 for more information about how and why to create additional web applications) or enabled additional services, and now you are responsible for them. Congratulations.

THE SHAREPOINT DATABASES

SharePoint, of course, creates databases during the course of its installation. Each SharePoint web application needs at least one content database to contain its data. The Central Administration web application also accesses the server farm's configuration database (which stands to reason, because that is where all the configuration settings are for SharePoint). Because SharePoint is capable of performing full-text, site-collection-wide searches, Search also has its own database. In addition, there will be a logging database, as well as a database for Business Data Connectivity.

This means that six databases will be created when SharePoint is installed as a Standalone server (meaning most services will be enabled and configured automatically). The following list describes them using the default names. When you do a Complete installation, you can choose to specify the database names if you need a different naming convention. However, even for the Complete installation, SharePoint will suggest the default names below.

SharePoint_Config_(*GUID*)　This is the configuration database for SharePoint. It holds all the configuration data and settings for the entire server farm. What makes separate SharePoint servers all members of the same server farm is that all of them use the same configuration database. This makes it possible for all those servers to have the same configuration settings. When you do a standalone server installation, the database will be called SharePoint_Config_(a string of random alphanumerics to generate a unique global ID or GUID). If you do a server farm installation, the suggested default (which you can easily change) is simply SharePoint_Config.

WSS_Search_*Servername*　This is the database that contains all the search data acquired when the index (or content access) service crawled through the SharePoint site collection. Search is an interesting beast in SharePoint, both overly simple and potentially complex.

WSS_Content　This is usually the content database for the first web application made in SharePoint for SharePoint sites (it's the default, unless you are doing a Complete installation and choose to name it something else). It will contain information about the site collections that the web application contains, and it will contain all the list, library, and web part metadata, documents, and attachments. Keep in mind that you can have more than one content database for a web application, and it easy to grow out of the first one pretty quickly.

SharePoint_AdminContent_(*GUID*)　This is the content database for the Central Administration web application. Because the Central Administration website is just like any other SharePoint website, it is prone to the same strengths and weaknesses. Site settings can be changed, including those for the master page. Novices should not do this. As a matter of fact, no one should. They could potentially delete the document library folder containing the help files and more.

EXTRA DATABASES

This version of SharePoint does come with some additional services that, when enabled and configured, require their own databases. Their default names are as follows:

WSS_Logging This database is used by SharePoint's diagnostic logging and usage to store logging and usage data.

Bdc_Service_DB_(*GUID*) This is the database used by SharePoint to store Business Data Connectivity data. If you use external data sources to have external lists and list fields in SharePoint, this database is critical for storing the information SharePoint needs to make those connections happen.

Subscription Settings Service Database This database doesn't necessarily have a default name like the others do, because it has to be configured by hand in PowerShell (so you explicitly have to name it). It is not enabled in a Standalone server installation by default. However, if it is enabled in your environment, chances are good the person who did so will give the database a name related to the service. The Subscription Settings service can be enabled to offer multi-tenant, subscription-based hosting on the SharePoint server to separate customers, departments, whatever group or organization that requires isolated administration, authentication (if configured), and feature management. For more information about it, see Chapter 16.

Although each web application gets its own content database initially, you can add more content databases to a web application if necessary. Web applications can contain more than one site collection, and each site collection can contain multiple sites that can contain lists and libraries that *can* get really big (I'm not guaranteeing anything; I'm just saying that they *can*). Frankly, using a single database to contain large sites full of data can be an invitation for that database to become really slow and unwieldy. There is always a reasonable limit to how much any one database can hold, and it's surprising how quickly that limit can be reached. Don't think of it as a bad thing; it just means that people are using the sites.

To help you cope, SharePoint allows you to add extra content databases to web applications to keep up with the ever-increasing data load. This is why it is possible to have several content databases for one web application. In addition, you can configure database capacity settings (by limiting the number of site collections per database) so that you can be warned when a database is getting too big and be prepared to add a new database. Site collections themselves can have quotas that limit their size in megabytes to give you further control. This is particularly important should you be using a Standalone installation.

Overall, this means that SharePoint uses IIS Web Sites to drive the web applications that hold site collections. Those site collections can each contain a lot of data. Additionally, a SharePoint server farm can have a number of web applications, each with several content databases. This means your SharePoint implementation can contain numerous content databases. However, there can only be *one* configuration database for each server farm. The configuration database specifies the configuration for the whole farm and, therefore, must be the only one. It is shared by each of the SharePoint servers in a farm configuration. That's why, during installation, if you choose to do a Complete installation and you specify you'd like to add the server to an existing farm, you just indicate the SQL server and the configuration database, and you're basically done.

SharePoint Service Accounts and Services

After it installs, SharePoint creates and enables a number of services and application pools in order to work properly. To be able to do their jobs, these services need to run with some sort of account context. Some of those services do work only on the local machine and therefore can get away with using local accounts. But some will need to access the SQL server or other servers on the network and therefore should not use local accounts. There is also a service or two that, because of the work it does (or from a troubleshooting standpoint) should be a unique account, not shared by any other service.

Depending on how you install SharePoint, you may have to create domain accounts to apply to those services. As a matter of fact, SharePoint has a health analyzer in which there are rules that certain services must have unique domain accounts. To understand SharePoint and keep it in good working order, it helps to know what those services are, what they do, and what access their accounts need while remaining secure.

Service Accounts

Depending on how SharePoint is installed, you may have the following service accounts:

Setup Account (Standalone Install)   To install SharePoint, you must be logged in on the server with an administrative account. If your server is not in a domain, this account needs to be the local Administrator (or the equivalent). On a domain, the account can be a domain admin. The account must be able to install software locally and should also be allowed to add and start services on the server.

With a Standalone installation, all other service accounts used by SharePoint are set up automatically (using local system or network service accounts). It really is the easiest installation, in addition to being the cheapest. Although it is not really scalable, it is convenient. It is also a great way to get an understanding of what SharePoint and its services look like when running, and it gives you a chance to simply get started using SharePoint. Once you've explored its functions, it makes it easier to then do a Complete installation and configure the services manually, because you will know how they work.

THE CHEESE STANDS ALONE

You don't have to install SharePoint in a domain environment. You also can install SharePoint on a stand-alone server in a workgroup with no domain controller.

Just install SharePoint using the Standalone option on the server (or, if you don't want to use SQL Server 2008 Express, install SQL on the server, and then install SharePoint using the Complete option).

If you choose a Standalone install, the databases and services setup will be done for you by SharePoint using the administrative account you used to log in. It will specify that all services will run using local system or network service server accounts.

Having both SharePoint and SQL on the same server means that all the database and service management can be done without needing to access anything on a different server and therefore only need to use local accounts.

Local users and groups will be used to give users access to SharePoint in that scenario, rather than going through a domain controller. You can still support incoming email in that scenario by enabling SMTP in IIS and then setting it up in Central Administration.

It just goes to show that SharePoint is scalable down as well as up.

Setup Account (Complete Install)   In a domain server farm install, the setup account should be a domain admin (you can use local administrator accounts to install SharePoint on each individual server, but it is easier simply to use one setup account that is a domain admin). This account should be allowed to install SharePoint on any server in the domain, and it must be able to access the SQL server that SharePoint will be using to build databases.

On the SQL server, the setup account must have these SQL server security roles on the target SQL server: Login, SecurityAdmin, and DBCreator.

Farm Account   Also known as the *configuration database account*, this account is powerful and critical to SharePoint. It does not need to have administrative privileges, but it should be a domain account. All other rights for this account will be configured automatically by the setup account during installation. The setup account adds the farm account to the SQL server's Logins, DBCreator, and SecurityAdmin roles. This is why the farm account ends up being the owner (DBO) of most of the SharePoint databases.

This account is the Central Administration application pool identity. This means that it is *the* account that accesses and changes the configuration database for the server farm. It is also the account used to power the SharePoint Timer service, which is in charge of any jobs that need to be started and stopped at different times (such as getting incoming mail, managing quotas, and managing alerts). This account should be guarded and not used for anything else (except for the one rare occasion of setting up a super-admin account in PowerShell).

THE DBO EXCEPTION

Oddly enough, the farm account does not become the DBO of the configuration database for the server farm, because the setup account creates that database during installation and then assigns ownership of it to the database access account. This means that, by default, the setup account is the DBO, but the farm account holds an owner role. This also means that, in a pinch, the setup account can be used to do farm administration in PowerShell, if necessary.

Content Database Access Account   Also known as the *content database account, web application account*, or web application *application pool account*, this is the account that uses the content database(s) of a web application. There should be one of these per web application—although under some circumstances (as is the case in businesses with security policies that limit service accounts), web applications can share an account. This account should be a domain user and otherwise is given (and requires) database ownership of all content databases associated with the web application it is working for.

If you are going to have more than one web application, you may want to consider creating a content database access account for each of them. This helps give the account least privilege (if it is compromised, it can only affect that web application; if it fails, it causes only one web application to fail), and it is easier to troubleshoot if each web application has its own content database access account. However, each application pool does use server resources to function, so some organizations actually require there be a limited number of application pools for a SharePoint implementation. It can be a balancing act, but it's something to keep in mind when planning accounts for SharePoint.

Search Account   This account should be a domain user. It directly accesses the Search database. Because it takes the questions entered into the search field in SharePoint and queries the Search database records with them, it is considered the query account.

Content Access Account   Also known as the *index, gatherer,* or *crawler account,* this account analyzes all the content in SharePoint site collections. It must be a domain user, and it will automatically be given full read rights to all web applications. It also has access to the search database to write in the information it has gathered. Often administrators just use the search account for both search and content access services.

ADDITIONAL SERVICES MIGHT NEED LOVE TOO

If you enable the new Business Data Connectivity service, Sandboxed Code, or Subscription Settings service, they will need their own service accounts as well. Keep in mind that content database and service accounts like Search (but not Index, strangely enough), will require that their account be registered in SharePoint as a managed account before being applied. So, it is a good idea to plan for the accounts, create them in Active Directory, and then register them as managed accounts soon after SharePoint installation.

Optional SharePoint Admin or SharePoint utility Account   I also suggest you consider a general-purpose SharePoint administrator account. This account should be a domain admin (or at least a local admin for each SharePoint server) so it can install tools locally on all SharePoint servers on the farm, run the SharePoint command-line tools, and be used as an administrator for Central Administration and new site collections you may create. It comes in handy for me when I need to troubleshoot a site or a setting in Central Administration. I always know that account's name and password, and it is usually the first administrator of most site collections I create (of course, this may not be allowed to remain after handing the collection over to its rightful owner, but it's convenient during setup).

PREPARING FOR POWERSHELL

New with this version of SharePoint are SharePoint-specific shell cmdlets (pronounced "command-lets"). Microsoft is going all out with PowerShell, hoping that customers will prefer to use it rather than the old favorite, the STSADM command-line tool.

With STSADM, the permissions required to run a command depend on what you want to do. It has to be run on the SharePoint server locally (or at least on a server in the farm), so the account needs to have local administrative rights on the server. If you are doing farm-related commands, such as creating a web application or starting a service, the account also needs to be a farm administrator. If the commands are only for a site collection, the account needs local admin rights on the server and needs to be a site collection admin for the site collection being worked on.

With PowerShell, things are different. Maybe because the tool is so new or maybe because it has been more the focus of developers than administrators, PowerShell requires the accounts that use it to be very powerful, possibly insecurely powerful. For an account to use PowerShell, it must be a local administrator of the SharePoint server. Then it must have ownership rights to the farm's configuration database, as well as be a farm administrator (meaning that the account will be added to the WSS_Admin_WPG group on the SharePoint server). If that account also has to do *any* work in a specific web application (site collection, and so on), it must also be an *owner* of the content database in SQL related to the web application (or site collection). So, for a farm administrator to be able to work on anything the farm needs, the account needs to own (have the owner permission in SQL of) all content databases and the configuration database of the farm.

There is a PowerShell cmdlet (otherwise known simply as a *command*) that is used to give accounts PowerShell admin rights, add-spshelladmin. This command has to be run by an account with the rights to do so in order to apply the correct permissions to the added account so it too can use PowerShell.

This causes a chicken-and-egg scenario: you need to give shell admin rights to accounts to work in PowerShell, but there is no account available to run the command to give the rights to other accounts...except for the farm account.

The farm account should never, ever, ever be logged in and used as a normal account. This account, if made (very temporarily) a local administrator of a SharePoint server, could open the SharePoint Management shell (Start menu ➤ All Programs ➤ Microsoft SharePoint 2010 Products ➤ SharePoint 2010 Management Shell) and be used to give shell admin rights to the accounts or AD security group that need it. Then, when you are done using it, log the account out, log back in as a normal administrator, and remove the farm account from the local administrators group (SharePoint hates it when the farm account is a local admin, and there may be an error saying so, if it notices what you've done).

When an account is added as a shell admin account, it is added to the configuration database in SQL with the owner role and a SharePoint-specific role called SharePoint_Shell_Access. If you want to have an account also be able to manage a content database of a web application via PowerShell, they need to be added as a shell admin specifically to that database (or databases). In doing so, the comdlet adds the SharePoint_Shell_Access role to the database and then gives the account rights to it. Conceivably, you can have different shell admins with rights only to make changes to the configuration database (by owning it) and to only a certain content database that you have specified. Usually I use an account that is added as a shell admin to all databases for the farm. I consider it my PowerShell super-admin account.

Keep in mind that site collection administrators should not be given PowerShell capabilities if you only want them to be capable of managing their own site collection. PowerShell admins are able to manage everything in a web application they are given rights to (which contains site collections, so they'd manage all of them) or nothing. Site collection administrators will still have to use STSADM for their command-line work.

There is an entire chapter dedicated to getting you up to speed with PowerShell (Chapter 14, "STSADM and PowerShell"), but I wanted to give you some advanced warning when planning for SharePoint, that there may be the need to give a few accounts a lot of power to do damage, not just to every database related to SharePoint but potentially to SQL as well (since every account will need a login role).

In my case, I plan to give my SharePoint admin account the right to be a shell admin for the whole farm in order to be able to use it, at will, to do work—making it my super-admin account (see Chapter 14 for more about how that's done). Initially, we will be doing a lot of work either in Central Administration or with STSADM. Later in the book, as you get the hang of using SharePoint, we will begin to do more and more with PowerShell.

SharePoint Services

The following services are created by SharePoint and are generally required for proper functioning. It might be handy to know what they are before you conduct your first installation.

SPAdminV4 (SharePoint Foundation 2010 Administration)   This is the administrative service for SharePoint. It runs on every SharePoint server locally and is in charge of checking the configuration database for changes. It keeps track of what server on a server farm is running what service and is used by SharePoint to access local resources per server. This service runs as the WSSADMIN process in Task Manager.

SPTimerV4 (SharePoint 2010 Timer)   This is the service in charge of actually triggering and running jobs for SharePoint. Because it uses the farm account identity, it usually doesn't have administrative permissions on the local server; however, it does have ownership permissions to do what it needs to do on both the configuration and content databases. If it needs to do something administrative on the local machine, it calls on the SPAdminV4 account to do it. This service runs as the OWSTIMER process in Task Manager.

SPSearch4 (SharePoint Foundation Search V4)   This is the Search service for SharePoint. It runs on the SharePoint servers that are running the Search service. This service runs the mssearch and mssdmn processes in Task Manager.

SPTraceV4 (SharePoint 2010 Tracing)   This service also installs on each SharePoint server locally. It is used for error tracking and analysis and controls the trace logs. This service runs as the wsstracing process in Task Manager.

SPWriterV4 (SharePoint 2010 VSS Writer)   This service integrates with SQL's VSS writer service, inherited from SPS 2003, and works with SharePoint's backup and recovery capabilities. It makes it possible to use Windows Volume Shadow Copy when doing backups. This service runs as the SPWRITER process in Task Manager and starts only when necessary. So, it's not always running.

SPUserCodeV4 (SharePoint 2010 User Code Host)   This service is specifically for something called *sandboxed solutions*. Basically for developers, SharePoint now allows certain controls and limits for running solutions. This service executes code in a "sandbox." In the past, solutions could unintentionally take up a lot of server resources because of unhandled exceptions, abnormal process termination, and the like. So, now solutions that are installed on the server farm, if they are scoped to be sandboxed solutions, can be managed (limited or stopped) by this service. This service runs as the SPUCHostService process in Task Manager. It is not always enabled by default.

BAD SOLUTION, NO DINNER FOR YOU...

Solutions can be pointed to the User Code service and, using something called *solution affinity*, be made to run only on the servers that have this service started. Any sandboxed solution (which now includes site templates) is allowed only so many "resource points" within which to run. If a solution exceeds its allowed points, it's turned off. The user using the solution may not know what's going on or be able do anything about it, but now you can sleep safely, knowing that at least it isn't crashing the server.

A few services that SharePoint uses straddle the line between a SharePoint capability, service application (which uses an application pool identity to function), and a simple service. They include the following:

Business Data Connectivity Service (BDC)   This Business Data Connectivity Service application enables external connection types, such as non-SharePoint SQL databases, which allows SharePoint to surface that non-SharePoint data in external lists. It uses the Web Services web application in IIS and has its own application pool identity to function. Although it isn't a separate service running in the Services console or Task Manager, it has its own database and an identity, which you can specify. This service is also known as Business Connectivity Service (or BCS) in some documentation.

KEEPIN' IT BRIEF

Most of these services, if you were to look at them in Central Administration, would start with the words *Microsoft SharePoint Foundation* and then the actual unique task the service does, such as User Code Service. I've taken the liberty of shortening these titles to avoid too much repetition.

Application Discovery and Load Balancer Service Application   This service simply supports load balancing and discovery of farm-scoped applications. It doesn't really have its own service account and has no configuration settings to speak of.

Subscription Settings Service   This service, for the most part, is not surfaced for configuration in Central Administration. A number of service applications normally used by SharePoint Server 2010 have been moved to SharePoint Foundation, and this is one of them. The Subscription Settings service applies to something called *multi-tenancy*. This kind of SharePoint setup requires configuration via PowerShell; it cannot be done in Central Administration. It basically uses a GUID to put site collections together in a "subscription." Very much the way SharePoint online works, it allows for a SharePoint implementation to be configured in such a way that each department or client has their own SharePoint "deployment" with limited administrative surface. This service also allows the farm administrator to create "feature packs" or group together features and then apply them to certain subscriptions, giving those site collections only the features available in the pack. For more about multi-tenancy, see Chapter 16.

Workflow Timer Service   A subservice of the SharePoint Timer service that runs the farm, this service simply sets the number of workflow events that are processed every timer interval for the server.

Central Administration and Web Application   Both are services you'll see in every SharePoint farm. The Central Administration service runs only on SharePoint servers that are hosting the Central Administration site. On most server farms, only one server needs to host that site. Web Application is the service that lets SharePoint have web applications, serve pages, and so on. It is fundamental to SharePoint, and every SharePoint server runs it. If you enable Central Administration on a SharePoint server that did not originally have it running, it will generate a web application on the server locally to support Central Administration's site collection. If you disable the Web Application service, the server will stop answering user requests for web pages. This is useful if you want to run services, such as Search or BDC, but not waste that server's resources offering pages to users.

 Real World Scenario

USER ACCOUNT MODES

When you install SharePoint, it automatically defaults to using Active Directory (AD) to supply the user accounts to be used as users for the SharePoint sites. This means that you need to have the user account in AD (or on the local server in a non-domain, standalone environment) before it can be added as a user in SharePoint. This user account mode is called Active Directory Domain Account mode.

However, there is another user account mode available, called Active Directory Account Creation mode (ADAC). This lets you create the account in SharePoint *first* and then adds it to an organizational unit (OU) that you set up specifically for SharePoint in AD. This mode has limitations; the account has to be added as an email address, the same email account cannot be added as a user to more than one site collection, and it disables several settings in Central Administration, particularly those that have to do with configuring or managing site collections so that they can only be run in the command interface (with STSADM or PowerShell).This mode focuses quite a bit on applying and isolating accounts per site collection.

Enabling ADAC is an advanced setting and can be done only during the installation of SharePoint. It is a one-shot thing; it defines the way user accounts are applied to SharePoint, period. There is no easy way to undo the choice, because it is locked in as the user account mode in the configuration database for the whole SharePoint farm by the time installation is complete.

You get the chance to select the ADAC account mode by clicking the Advanced Settings button during configuration. If you miss that button and complete the installation, the default Domain Account mode will be applied.

Although SharePoint Foundation still supports ADAC (SharePoint Server 2010 does not), it has been overshadowed by the capabilities of the Subscription Settings service, which uses multi-tenancy to isolate site collections more effectively and can either isolate users in their own OU in AD or use forms-based authentication (FBA), which lets you use a SQL database to store user accounts for web applications (and the site collections within them) instead of AD.

Because of this, I will point out the Advanced Settings button during Chapter 3, "Complete Installation," but I will be focusing more on multi-tenancy in this book instead (Chapter 16). FBA is rather fiddly and outside the scope of the book, but it can be applied per web application (or extended web application) and, like multi-tenancy, is better than the "all-or-nothing" approach of ADAC.

Authentication Types

In conjunction with IIS, SharePoint supports several ways to allow users to authenticate. They are not exclusive; you can apply multiple types of authentication to a web application. IIS will apply the most restrictive method first. If that fails, it will try the second most-restrictive method, and so on, until it finally refuses the client or lets them log in.

ASP.NET Impersonation Authentication This authentication type allows an ASP.NET application to use a specified account to act as its identity or run as a user authenticated by IIS (such as IUSR if Anonymous Access were enabled).

Windows Integrated Authentication This authentication type requires the user to have a domain account or a local account on the SharePoint server. This, of course, is the method that Microsoft prefers and is the one used throughout this book.

Digest This also works with Active Directory, but it sends the username and password as hashed values. It can be used if Windows Integrated Authentication is blocked by a firewall or not being passed by a proxy server. It is also available on WebDAV servers.

Basic This type will send authentication information across a network as clear text, which is obviously not a great idea. It is sometimes required by mobile devices.

Anonymous Access This type allows users to establish an anonymous connection with IIS by using an anonymous or guest account.

Usually ASP.NET Impersonation and Windows Integrated Authentication are enabled by default for SharePoint web applications.

Authentication Methods

In addition to those authentication types, SharePoint offers two Windows authentication methods during installation. These protocols don't just govern how authentication data is passed on the network for users trying to access SharePoint; they govern how SharePoint service accounts themselves access resources.

NTLM This secure protocol encrypts usernames and passwords over the network. It simply sends data to the authenticating authority and back. This protocol does not require additional configuration, and is the simplest to use.

Kerberos This secure protocol encrypts data but handles authentication differently than NTLM. Kerberos is based on *ticketing.* A username and password are passed to an authentication server, which sends back a ticket to allow the authenticated user to access network resources. The user *and* the authentication server (or Key Distribution Center) must trust each other. This means that service principal names must be set for the SharePoint servers and database access accounts so resources on the network can be accessed by SharePoint on behalf of the user. The account and the servers must be trusted for delegation in some circumstances.

Although Kerberos can be the best option for authentication, NTLM is still suggested in many cases, because using Kerberos requires the database access account to have a service principal name, which could be a greater danger to the network if that account is compromised. And even though outside the network, authentication is tighter with the mutual authentication process of Kerberos, using it to authenticate can be a problem due to time synchronization. Another consideration is that, in some situations, the Index service used by the Search service (discussed next) cannot authenticate using Kerberos (on custom ports in particular) and therefore cannot index sites that require it. That said, Kerberos can be a little faster and is more secure than NTLM. Further, it can also be used for those service applications that do pass-through authentication. For more information about Kerberos and how to configure it, see Chapter 16.

Claims-based authentication   Not technically an authentication method, SharePoint now also supports claims-based authentication. This allows SharePoint to support standard Security Assertion Markup Language (SAML) tokens, giving it the option to support non-Windows accounts in a Kerberos ticket kind of way. It also makes it possible to use security tokens to better protect authentication using forms-based authentication. If you enable claims-based authentication for a web application, you can still use NTLM or Kerberos, but claims-based is the option that supports forms-based authentication as well.

SharePoint Search

The Search service for SharePoint Foundation is basically the same one used for the previous version (WSS 3.0). The interface has changed a little and is now called SharePoint Foundation Search. Search basically does two things:

◆ It responds to search queries.

◆ It crawls through site collections and indexes data.

This is why Search has two services, the Search service and the Index service (or content access service), and their corresponding service accounts. Both services use the search database; the Index service merges its collected data with it, and the Search service queries it. Only one Index service can exist on a server farm, but there can be more than one server running the Search service on a farm. (Each server would share the Index service.) The Index service requires read access to all content databases of all the web applications that will be searched. When a web application is being created, you can assign a search server to service its content database. This is useful if you have more than one server running Search.

The Index service will scan the content databases of the web applications per the schedule you set up when you enable Search. The changes that it finds are temporarily stored in index files on the SharePoint server that is running the Index service and then merged with the search database after a set period of time. Meanwhile, the Search service, when responding to a user query, will check the index files and the database to be sure that all results are accurate. This is why there can be only one server running the Index service on a farm, because those files have to be in one place. When installing SharePoint using either the Complete or Server Farm Stand-alone installation, you can use the option to save the index files to a different location. Consider setting aside a different drive or partition on the server to handle the possible large amount of files. (If you do specify where the index goes and if you decide to move it later to a different server, be sure the same path is available for the index files on the new server to avoid issues.)

Search has some strengths and weaknesses that you should know about before you install SharePoint:

◆ Search doesn't have much of an administrative surface. The GUI settings are limited to what service accounts are used, the search database name, and how often the site collections will be indexed. Indexing is primarily incremental, but even that can strain resources if you do it too often. What little management you can do with Search is through the SharePoint command-line tool STSADM or PowerShell. See Chapter 14, "STSADM and PowerShell," for more details.

◆ Search can search only site collections (or more precisely content databases). It cannot search file shares, email servers, or other locations. If you want to search content outside site collections, consider shelling out the money for SharePoint Server 2010 (which, for the added cost, can search multiple external sources or even multiple SharePoint server farms), Microsoft Search Server 2010, or installing Search Server 2010 Express.

◆ Search uses a top-down approach. When you conduct a search query on a site, it will search that site and all subsites under it. If you conduct a search query on a site at the top of a site collection (the first site created in a site collection), it will search the data contained in its search database and index files for that site and then systematically check all other subsites below it. However, if you are already on a subsite and start to search, it will search from there and work its way down the subsites below it, ignoring the sites above it in the collection. In other words, Search always searches down and never up. Unless you absolutely know which subsite has the data you are looking for, you should always perform searches from the top level of a site collection.

◆ Search is security filtered and searches along a path. Therefore, it generally only returns search queries per site collection. That means if you are looking for a document and you have several site collections, you need to know what site collection it's in or search each site collection until you find it. Site collections are considered a hard-search boundary because of two things. Site collections are usually at the top of a path, like `http://server/sites/sitecollection1`. Everything within and under the sitecollection1's top-level site would be included in a search. Then those results are further filtered by the querying user's permissions. Normally a user is a member of one site collection but not the other. This usually works fine for most users, but if you are, say, the owner of more than one site collection in a path, check the URL of your search results to be sure they are from the correct collection.

◆ Search does whole-word, exact-match queries. If there are multiple words in a query, AND is implied between the words (orange juice is considered orange AND juice and would return only results that contain both values). Punctuation is ignored, as is the word *and*. However, strangely, the word *or* is neither ignored nor recognized as part of the query logic and is treated like part of the query text itself.

◆ Unfortunately, Search for SharePoint Foundation doesn't accept wildcards or Boolean logic, but it does allow for keyword exclusions or additions by using the plus (+) or minus (–) signs. Search will also support property filtering. Property filtering means that search can recognize some field names and properties, such as file type, content type (used for libraries particularly), author, title, or subject. To filter in the search field by property, the syntax is `property:query`; for example, `filetype:txt` will result in all text files in the site collection. Searches are scoped in a way (but not as well as the previous version). Search will be scoped depending on where you initiate the search. If you are on a list or library, even though the search field will say "Search this site…," it will actually only return results for that list or library. However, on the search result page, you can then change the scope to "This site" (which strangely also places you one step from the site's home page, regardless of the list you were originally on when you first initiated the search), and it will search the whole site for your query.

◆ The search results are displayed on a page organized by relevance. Results are displayed with the link to it and some summarizing information (see Figure 1.4).

FIGURE 1.4
The Search
Results page

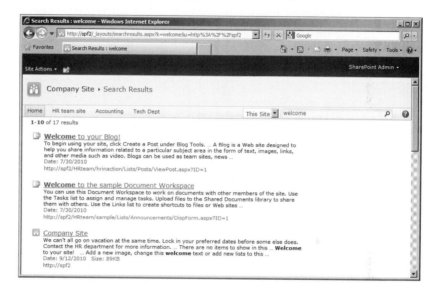

◆ In a server farm, there is usually only one Search service and one Index (content access) service running. However, if you have a large and busy server farm, it might be good to have a server dedicated to searching and indexing, or you could run more than one server with the Search service enabled. Search prefers Windows Authentication and may cause errors in an anonymous environment (make sure the site is set to always search .aspx pages). In addition, the Index service prefers NTLM authentication, so it can have problems accessing a web application that requires Kerberos if it is using a nonstandard port (ports 80 and 443 are considered standard). Search generally uses the default zone address for the web applications it indexes, so it might be best to keep that zone's authentication method to NTLM (and to consider using extended web applications to host Kerberos or anonymous access).

◆ Search does perform security trimming, which means it includes security information when it is indexing site collections and excludes items from a query based on the permissions of the person asking.

◆ Sites and lists can be excluded from indexing if you'd like them to be unsearchable. This can be useful for lists with item-level security (which can confuse security trimming), and may cause some items to be displayed in the search results for those who can't open them.

INDEXING AND GATHERING

The Search service's Index service is an old hand-me-down from SPS 2003 and MOSS. The Index service is a powerful feature that you don't need to monitor. It takes care of itself and does its own thing. (SharePoint Server 2010 has extensive added configuration features for indexing.) Its only content sources are the content databases that SharePoint uses. It uses ifilters and protocol handlers to parse documents, filter out formatting, and find words in documents. It can distinguish between relevant words and irrelevant words or "noise." It can handle only 64 MB of indexed words per document. If it maxes out, it doesn't really notify you; it just doesn't index any more of the document, which is another reason to keep uploads and document files from becoming bloated.

The ifilters that come with SharePoint can handle Office 2007/2010 file types, text files, HTML, and TIFF files (the file type usually created by scanning faxes and documents). If you'd like to be able to index other types of files, a number of additional ifilters are available from their manufacturers.

SharePoint and Email

SharePoint integrates easily with email. However, it does take some consideration concerning how you'll configure email when you're planning to install SharePoint.

In addition to being capable of sending alerts and notifications (which requires properly configured outgoing email), SharePoint can be set up to receive incoming email. This is because several lists and libraries can be enabled to receive email. The primary benefit is that you can send a new item to the list (or library) without going to the SharePoint site if you know that list's email address. And you can do all of this from the comfort of your email program. There's no need to open a browser.

To manage incoming email, the SharePoint server should have the SMTP service set up locally (make sure it has started). It is best to have SMTP enabled before you install SharePoint. When SharePoint receives email, it pulls it from the default drop directory that SMTP uses or from the directory you specify. It gives it to the correct list or library, which parses the email for the subject line, message body, and other pertinent header information. It then applies the information to the appropriate fields in the list record.

Incoming email has another interesting feature called SharePoint Directory Management Service (DMS). This service integrates SharePoint with Active Directory and Exchange. To use it, you need to create a unique OU, give the server farm account extensive access to it, and assign the content database accounts local administrative rights to the SharePoint server. SharePoint can allow users to create distribution lists that show up in the OU and add the list and library incoming email aliases to the Exchange global address list (GAL). Of course, this obviously requires Exchange, and more specifically it works best with Exchange 2003, because it integrates so deeply with AD. Later versions of Exchange can support DMS but may require considerable additional configuration.

DON'T LET THEM SCARE YOU

Despite occasional documents stating otherwise, SharePoint Directory Management Service does not have to be running for SharePoint to handle incoming email. In its simple, straightforward way, incoming email works fine without it. If you don't want to increase the complexity of your SharePoint install, don't use SharePoint Directory Management Service. It is an option, not a requirement.

Alternate Access Mapping

When you initially install and start using SharePoint, accessing it by using the NetBIOS name of the server works fine, but what if you want your users to be able to access it the same way they do other Web sites or be able to access it from the Internet? You can't resolve that server name among all the other machine names on the Internet, so you need it to resolve to a DNS name. Alternate Access Mapping (AAM) is about mapping a SharePoint web application to an alternate address other than the default. This way, you can have an internal, default name of http://spf2 and an Internet URL of http://SharePoint.dem0tek.com, both pointing to the same server (and more importantly, to the same content).

AAM specifies alternate access to a web application by internal URLs, public URLs, and zones. An internal URL is what the web application responds to. A public URL is what the web application returns to the user in the address bar and in the links for all search results. Web applications can have five public URLs associated with it (at which point they are called *zones*). So, you can have a Default zone (that's the default URL for the web application, which is the root path for all the site collections it might contain), an Intranet zone, Internet zone, Extranet zone, and a Custom zone.

There is also another use for AAM—extending web applications. An extended web application is just an IIS Web Site that points to the same content database as an existing web application. This is done if you want to use some other URL, security settings, or authentication type to access the same data (essentially if you want to use different IIS Web Site settings to access the same content, like anonymous or Kerberos). That way, users can have more than one way to access the same data, especially if you want to have different types of authentication for the content, depending on what URL the user uses.

Because an extended web application is just sharing the same content database as an existing web application, it is considered just another URL used to access the first web application's content. This is why an extended web application is not given its own name in the web application list but is considered a *zone* of the existing web application. In that case, one of the public URL zones is taken up with the URL of the extended web application. You might want to note that there are a limited number of AAM zones available to extend (Intranet, Internet, Custom, Extranet) per web application. The Default zone is the original web application's URL, so obviously that is not available to be used for extending.

So, when planning your URL structure and how users are going to access SharePoint, keep AAM in mind.

Managed Paths

When planning for SharePoint, it's a good idea to keep in mind how you would like to structure your site collections. Site collections are composed of a top-level site and all the sites that stem from it (called *subsites*). The top-level site is usually accessed by using the web application's URL and then the path to the top-level site's home page. When creating a site collection, you must decide what its URL path will be. When you create your first site collection in a web application, you can give it the *root* address for that web application, or you can specify a path. What this means is if you create the first web application on server SPF2, then its URL can be http://SPF2, using port 80, which is the root address for the URL. But if you create a second site collection in that web application, it needs to have a different path, because it can't use the same URL. This is where managed paths comes in. By default SharePoint has a sites wildcard managed path for additional site collections. The URL for that path would be, on the same server, `http://spf2/sites/`. What this means is if you create that additional site collection, it can be something on that path, such as `http://spf2/sites/something`.

You can, of course, create your own managed paths, depending on your required topology. This is useful if you are planning to have one web application, say, per region, and then site collections for each office. Then you might consider creating a managed path for the London office, Beijing office, Helsinki, and so on.

A site collection makes a good user account or permissions boundary because you can add users once to the top-level site, apply permissions to them either individually or in groups, and if the subsites inherit permissions (which they do by default), those users will be able to access subsite resources with those permissions as well—but for that site collection only. The other site collections are unaffected by the comings and goings of users in any other site collection.

Another thing to consider with managed paths is that if you have additional non-SharePoint websites or web software you want to run in the same IIS Web Site virtual directory, SharePoint automatically ignores anything that is on a path not specified as a managed path.

User Accounts and Permissions

For anyone to use SharePoint, there must be users. SharePoint leans toward organizing users and permissions based on the users' roles. So, a site owner would need to have full control of the site, but a member would only need to be able to contribute.

SharePoint controls the user permissions that can be applied at the web application level. So if necessary, you could block certain permissions entirely from ever being applied to users in the site collections that the web application contained. At the site and site collection levels, individual permissions can be combined to create permission levels, which are then applied to users or groups.

Individual Active Directory (AD) users can be added to SharePoint, but you can also simply add domain security groups as well. Doing so lets you add numerous users to SharePoint that might require the same permission levels at one time. It is also easier for SharePoint to handle because it has limitations on how many separate security principals it can manage at one time. It's actually considered a SharePoint best practice to use AD security groups to add users rather than individual domain users for that reason (the same applies if SharePoint is on a non-domain server, only they'll be local server users and security groups).

SharePoint uses SharePoint groups to organize users. There are three SharePoint groups built in, Members, Visitors, and Owners, but you can also make your own. When you create a SharePoint group, you assign permission levels to the group (permission levels are combinations of individual permissions). Then, when you add a user, you choose the SharePoint group they should belong to, and that group's permission levels automatically apply to that user. Default permission levels include Full Control (all permissions), Read (permissions that only allow a user to view the site and its contents, but not add, edit, or delete), and Contribute (permissions that allow users to read, add, edit, or delete site content). So when planning your user management strategy, keep permissions, permission levels, and SharePoint groups in mind.

Another thing to consider is that you can apply user policies to a web application that affect all the site collections contained in them. A user policy is when you add a user to the web application and explicitly allow or deny them permissions to access the web application (and therefore all site collections contained therein). A user policy at the web application level overrides permissions at the site collection level. This means a user account, given the correct permissions in a user policy, can log into any site collection in the web application, even if that account is not a member of the site collections in any way. This also works from the standpoint of denying a certain user or security group permission; so even if they are added to a site collection within a web application, they will not be able to make use of the denied permissions. Keep this in mind as you plan for user accounts and permissions while designing for your web applications and site collections. For more on users and permissions, see Chapter 12.

Performance Planning

By now you may have made some plans concerning what OS you'd like to have on your SharePoint Foundation server; what installation option you'll use; and what accounts, services, user account mode, and authentication you'll implement. You may have decided how you'll handle Search (such as putting the index files on a separate drive), set up email, manage paths, and alternate access mapping, and you've mapped out the user accounts, permission levels, and groups you'll need.

Now you need to determine whether your server is big enough for the job—today and into the future.

KEEPING UP-TO-DATE

Planning for performance and storage is more an art than a science. And as time passes (and more people use the most current version of SharePoint), the ideas about the current best method for performance or storage planning change to suit. So, be sure to check online to see what the most recent best practice is for planning for SharePoint.

How do you plan for that? There are really two points of concern, performance and storage. In terms of performance, it's good for you to determine how many operations per second (OPS) your server will need to do under normal (or even extreme) loads. (Storage is measured in input/ouput operations per second, or IOPS, which is a a little different.)

There are probably as many different ways to plan for performance as there are people using SharePoint, but for a ballpark, general estimate, there is a tried-and-true formula from WSS 3.0 to help you with your plans. This formula is very simple, but it can give you a good idea of how to avoid being underpowered in terms of simple user activity.

Essentially, you need to answer the following questions:

1. How many people are supposed to use SharePoint? (Users)

2. What percentage are *really* going to use it? (Percent active users)

3. How many operations per day do they do on average (how many documents edited, list entries added, searches done, and so on)? (Operations)

4. How many hours do the users work in SharePoint on an average day? (Work hours)

5. Does an average work day have particular peaks in performance? (Peak factor)

To calculate the operations per second, multiply items 1, 2, 3, and 5 together and then divide that number by the number of hours those people are going to be working a day by 360,000 (which is 100 percent conversion × 60 minutes per hour × 60 seconds per minute). Altogether, that will show you how many operations per second your server needs to efficiently handle.

To show you what I mean and illustrate that the suggested hardware requirements are probably adequate for your needs, assume your office has 1,000 people who are going to use SharePoint, and 60 percent of them will be actively using SharePoint daily. You estimate that each user probably performs about 50 operations a day. (Most of them will spend more time editing a document than retrieving it from the document library or uploading it.) Let's say your office has, at maximum, 9 hours of work time a day and a peak factor of 4. *Peak factor* is a scale between 1 and 5 that refers to how often or how likely there are to be peaks in normal daily usage. One indicates that there is practically no particular time of peak usage during a business day, and 5 indicates that practically the entire day is a peak use time. I never go less than 4, just in case.

MEMBERSHIP IN CLUB SHAREPOINT IS NOT ALWAYS ALL-INCLUSIVE

Many businesses don't always allow every employee access to SharePoint. Therefore, when you determine who will use the SharePoint sites, don't just include everyone in the company by default. To help ensure that your calculations are as accurate as possible, consider exactly who will do what.

Let's summarize the data we have:

Users: 1,000

Percent active usage: 60

Operations: 50 (per person, per day)

Work hours: 9

Peak factor: 4

And the formula that uses that information is as follows:

$$\text{Users} \times \text{Usage} \times \text{Operations} \times \text{Peak} \times (360{,}000 \times \text{Work hours})$$

Or in our case:

$$1{,}000 \times 60 \times 50 \times 4 \times (360{,}000 \times 9)$$

That will bring you to the operations per second that your server needs to deliver for your users. In this case, that number is 3.7 operations per second (OPS).

Given the standard formula shown previously, using a quad-core, 2.5 GHz per core processor and 8 GB of RAM should be enough to handle at least 10 user operations per second. All *you* need is 3.7 operations per second for 1,000 people doing 50 operations a day. You can see why I think the starting hardware requirements are sufficient for most small to medium businesses.

Remember, just like the processor, RAM is important, if only so the server can render pages efficiently. Keep in mind that each web application a server hosts does increase the amount of RAM the server uses. Having more web applications means more RAM. Indexing is also RAM-intensive. Keep in mind that SharePoint often rapidly increases in use and increases in the percentage of people using it. As SharePoint catches on, you might find yourself at peak usage more often than not. That's why you need to monitor how your SharePoint server handles the stress of use, just in case. If you can afford it, consider calculating your OPS requirements and then doubling them to prepare for the inevitable, large increase in use.

Additional Performance Considerations

You'll want to keep an eye on these items that will increase your processor's load:

Alerts   Users can set alerts on changes in a list or library. Alerts are scheduled and, therefore, keep the SharePoint Timer services busy. Limit the number of alerts your users can have running at any given time. It will save your processor. Alerts can be configured with a user limit or disabled altogether.

Indexing   The server that will be indexing site collection content will have to support the increased load on the processor. If you can, try not to index every five minutes or less. Instead, it's better to index every hour or at certain times of the day. This can be difficult if you expect SharePoint to index and search new items almost instantaneously; just keep it in mind if you are trying to squeeze as many operations per second as you can from your server. Indexing can be RAM-intensive. If your server is taking a long time to index documents and indexing is peaking your RAM usage, consider increasing the RAM on the server doing indexing.

Usage and Health logging   SharePoint can analyze site usage and deliver detailed reports. However, analyzing the usage logs takes a considerable amount of processor power. Try to schedule the analysis to occur during a long downtime, usually sometime around 3 a.m.

Web Parts   Your developers may go crazy with the power of web parts. Be careful; some web parts (depending on what they do and how they were coded) can be resource hogs. Stay well below 50 web parts per page—and that includes the hidden ones. Home pages, where web parts are usually found, can be overwhelmingly busy.

Web Applications   Although web applications may not, by themselves, increase processor load, they do take up about 50 MB or more apiece in RAM on the SharePoint server (especially if they are using different application pool accounts). This is one of the reasons that you might want to consider consolidating site collections into as few web applications as possible.

Features and Solutions   Custom features and solutions can be added to SharePoint and scoped at the farm, web application, or site collection level. Be sure to test those added components to know how many resources they use when active. Realize that although now there can be sandboxed solutions, or solutions that are deeply throttled in terms of the resources they're allowed to use, and scoped to be added and activated at the site collection level, no matter how frugal they are, if you have many solutions or features they can impact the server's CPU and RAM over time.

Storage Planning

When you're considering performance issues, don't forget to plan for adequate storage. If you plan to have SharePoint and the SQL Server 2008 Express database on the same server, you'll need extra RAM because SQL uses quite a bit. But more specifically, it will require much more storage space than SharePoint alone. Even if your SharePoint databases—particularly the content databases, which holds all SharePoint's precious content—are stored on a different SQL server, planning for storage is still important.

Consider that the maximum default size allowed for document uploads is 50 MB. A large multimedia Word document can often about 5 MB, so a maximum of 50 MB is usually more than sufficient. Of course, you can adjust the size; this is just a good default. And of course, if you upload more than just Word files, you may need to change that limit.

It goes without saying that storage needs will depend on how your users will use the lists and libraries on your SharePoint sites. For example, assume they are creating marketing materials to send out every quarter, and they are storing and collaborating on the materials in a document library. If they create five major documents each quarter, that would be 20 large documents per year, possibly up to 10 MB per document. That could be 200 MB of space for those documents alone. If other people manage the images for the document in a picture library and the material had 10 large, full-color pictures per document, that could be 2,000MB (2 GB) per year for that picture library in addition to its related document library. You could need gigs and gigs of hard drive space—and that doesn't include versioning.

If you have versioning enabled in your document libraries, there will be multiple copies (as many copies as you allow when you set up versioning) of each document. Therefore, if versioning (say four major versions and three minor versions per document) were enabled in the previous scenario, then at least 1.4 GB per year would be needed for versioning in the marketing document library alone. Keep in mind that versioning can be allowed for most lists as well.

Most list entries, when stored in the content database, are tiny—just a few kilobytes, if that. However, if you enable attachments for the lists or libraries, those files (by default less than 50 MB) will be saved with those list items, increasing the size of your content database in ways you may not have intended. And don't forget about incoming email. If you configure an incoming email–enabled list or library to save original emails, those emails (including attachments) need to be stored in the content database too.

You also need to consider that, depending on what you allow, users can easily create their own document workspace subsites from a document if they need additional team work to collaborate. When a document workspace is spun off of a document, it takes a copy of the original document with it. An additional site will need to be stored in the content database, and a copy of that document with its own versions will be stored on that site. That document will very likely be returned to the original library, and the workspace will probably be deleted when the project is done. Until then, however, that document (and its workspace) is yet another thing requiring storage. You can also allow users to create their own site collections (with Self-Service Site Creation); this adds yet more storage overhead to the SharePoint content databases.

Finally, remember that the more stuff you have in SharePoint, the more stuff you will have in the search database. It holds the indexed search data for documents, list entries, and page content (it *does not* index attached files); that data is stored on the SharePoint server itself and merged regularly into the search database. To make sure that it returns only the entries that the user making the query is allowed to see, Search also records the Access Control List information for every indexed entry.

Generally, Search is only allowed to store indexed word entries that equal about 40 percent of the original document's size, with a maximum of 64 MB of stored words for a single document. That means if you have 20 documents in a library, the search database can have (maximum) 1.3 GB of entries for that library alone. Of course, if the documents themselves never exceed 50 MB (which should have less than 64 MB of unique words to store) and Search sticks to its 40 percent limit for each document, then that would be no more than 20 MB of indexed entries per document and therefore (going with our scenario) about 400 MB stored in the search database for that one document library.

When you're deciding how much storage space your SharePoint server should use in SQL, consider this:

♦ You need to have an idea of what your users are going to do. Estimate how many documents they are going to be collaborating on and storing. Think about what lists they will be using and how they will be used.

♦ Plan how you are going to manage attachments and versioning.

♦ Plan how you are going to manage user websites—especially ones generated for document and meeting workspaces.

♦ Plan on using site collection quota templates to keep site collection storage in check (in addition to limiting site collections per content database). Remember the Recycle Bins as well. The end-user Recycle Bin contents at the site level are part of the site collection's quota, so keep an eye on it. But the second-stage, site-collection-level Recycle Bin can have a quota that is a certain percentage of its site collection's quota, but keep in mind that is in addition to the site collection's quota. That can cause an unexpected increase in storage requirements if you aren't prepared. Remember to empty your Recycle Bins to save space.

♦ Also, on the SharePoint server, always leave some room for the paging file; try to go for at least the same amount as the server has in RAM.

Once you can estimate what you need, double that space. At least, always have 25 percent more space than you expect to need. Always leave room to bloat. You will never go wrong.

It's great if SharePoint works, but if you have no more room to store SharePoint's data, the users will be upset. There is a standard formula going around that might help in estimating for user storage:

Database size = $((D \times V) \times S) + (10\ KB \times (L + (V \times D)))$

D = documents

S = average size of documents

L = list items (harder to average, but smaller; suggested three per document)

V = estimated number of versions

10 KB= constant (the estimated amount of metadata used by SharePoint)

So, in this case:

D = 200 yearly (that's 20 documents and 10 pictures per document)

S = 10240 KB (that's 10 MB per document/picture, in kilobytes)

L = 600 (rounding to three times the documents, a rule of thumb considering that there is likely to be a couple discussion items and a calendar entry per document)

V = 7 (estimating the number of versions for the documents)

So the formula would be as follows:

$((200 \times 7) \times 10240KB) + (10KB \times (600 + (7 \times 200))$

or 14, 336,000 + 20,000 = 14,365,000KB

14,356,000KB is about 13.6909 GB (rounded up to 14)

This averages to a storage size of about 14 GB (estimating high of course) per year. Then you need to factor in the storage space that Search will need (about 40 percent of the size of stored files, or in the case of 14 GB, factor in an additional 5.6 GB).

Keep in mind that your environment may be different; after you install your SharePoint server, make sure you monitor the activity. Create a test group that represents a small but measurable sample of your expected users. See how many of them use the server, when they use it, how they use it, and how much they store on the server. Then multiply the increase in resources based on their activities by an estimate of how many more users will be doing the same sorts of things when the server goes live. If you don't think the suggested hardware will be up to the task, improve it. Plan for at least 20 percent more growth than you expect— just in case. It's better to find out that your system is not adequate now than to find out when everyone is using it.

Storage is well worth the price you pay for it (and is often inexpensive). Use RAID to make your storage fault tolerant; mirror the web servers, and cluster your SQL servers if you can (especially now that SharePoint is failover aware). If there is drive failure, you'll be grateful you did.

Software Limitations

In addition to its hardware limitations, SharePoint has some software limitations. Microsoft beat the heck out of some servers to see how they performed; and they found that when certain objects reached a maximum number, performance degraded significantly. Previously, the list of limitations for SharePoint was considered a guideline of acceptable performance. Now it is considered software boundaries and limitations.

These boundaries and limitations come in three types:

Boundaries Hard limits that cannot be exceeded by design.

Thresholds Limits that have a default value for best performance, but that value can be changed.

Supported Limits Recommended limits, based on testing. Surpassing these limits could result in performance issues and possible "deleterious" effects.

Tables 1.1–1.3 list the object limitations you need to know. At this point, you may not really realize the importance of some of these objects, but you will. It's always good to know up front what limitations there might be for something in case you might end up being responsible for it. These are not the full and comprehensive tables (which are available on TechNet; just search for *SharePoint 2010 software boundaries and limitations*); they simply list the most relevant to SharePoint Foundation in a standard installation. (Note that much of what is available online is related to the SharePoint Server product more than SharePoint Foundation.)

Table 1.1 contains the software boundaries for this version of SharePoint.

TABLE 1.1: Software boundaries for SharePoint Foundation 2010

OBJECT	MAXIMUM VALUE	TYPE OF OBJECT	DETAILS
Zone	5 per web application	Web application limit	This limit is hard-coded per web application as Default, Intranet, Internet, Extranet, and Custom.
List Row Size	8,000 bytes per row	List and library limits	Each list or library item can take only up to 8,000 bytes (actually 7,744) in the underlying database.
File Size	2 GB	List and library limits	The default maximum file size that can be uploaded is 50 MB, but that can be changed. The absolute maximum is 2 GB.
Bulk Operations	100 ops per bulk operation	List and library limits	The user interface only allows for a maximum of 100 items to be selected at once for bulk operations (such as copying to a library from Explorer view).
ECT (External Content Type) in Memory	5,000 per web server	BDC service limit	Only 5,000 different ECTs can be in memory per server at any given time.
External System Connections	500 per web server	BDC service limit	The default maximum is 200, but the boundary is 500.

Table 1.2 describes a number of the software thresholds for SharePoint Foundation. Remember that thresholds are default settings, many of which can be changed. These thresholds are suggested for best performance.

TABLE 1.2: Software thresholds for SharePoint Foundation 2010

OBJECT	MAXIMUM VALUE	TYPE OF OBJECT LIMIT	DETAILS
List View Lookup	8 join operations per query	Lists and libraries limit	Any list view can only have eight lookup fields (and that includes People And Groups and Workflow progress fields). More than that will be blocked. Can be changed in Resource Throttling per web application.

TABLE 1.2: Software thresholds for SharePoint Foundation 2010 *(CONTINUED)*

OBJECT	MAXIMUM VALUE	TYPE OF OBJECT LIMIT	DETAILS
List View	5,000 items	Lists and libraries limit	The default maximum number of items that a query can process at one time. Can be changed in Resource Throttling per web application.
List View for Auditors and Administrators	2,0000 items	Lists and libraries limit	The default maximum of items that an object model database can query at one time. Works with the Allow Object Model Override setting. Also a Resource Throttling setting.
Subsites	2,000 per site view	Site limit	Enumerating the number of subsites for a site collection starts to degrade performance above 2,000; it also degrades the performance of the All Site Content page and Tree View.
Co-Authoring	10 concurrent editors per document	Lists and libraries limit	The recommended limit is 10, but the boundary is 99. More than 10 coeditors on a document can cause conflicts and degradation in performance.
Security Scope	1,000 per list	Lists and libraries limit	This is the maximum number of unique security settings per list or library. A security scope can contain the ACL (access control list) for an object and the security principals related to that ACL as well.
Single Line of Text	276 per list	Column limit	There should be no more than 276 single-line-of-text-columns per list.
Multiple Lines of Text	192 per list	Column limit	
Choice	276 per list	Column limit	
Number	72 per list	Column limit	
Currency	72 per list	Column limit	

TABLE 1.2:   Software thresholds for SharePoint Foundation 2010 *(CONTINUED)*

OBJECT	MAXIMUM VALUE	TYPE OF OBJECT LIMIT	DETAILS
Date and Time	48 per list	Column limit	
Lookup	96 per list	Column limit	
Yes/No	96 per list	Column limit	
Person or Group	96 per list	Column limit	
Hyperlink or Picture	138	Column limit	
Calculated	48	Column limit	
Web Parts	25 per wiki or web part page	Page limit	This is an estimate based on simple web parts. Above this threshold, and performance suffers. If the web parts are more complex, expect performance degradation sooner.
Workflow Postpone	15	Workflow limits	15 workflows are allowed to be executed against a database at any given time. After that, additional workflows will be postponed. Those new requests count against this threshold.
Workflow Timer Batch Size	100	Workflow limits	This is the standard limit that the workflow timer job can pick up at any one time. Configurable. Additional workflow timer job instances can be started to handle more batches if necessary.
Database Items Returned per Request	2,000 per database connector	BDC service limits	The default maximum of 2,000 is used by the database connector to restrict the number of results that can be returned per page. The boundary is 1,000,000.

Table 1.3 describes a number of the supported limitations for SharePoint Foundation. Remember that supported limitations are ones that, although they are not hard boundaries or thresholds that can be changed, are suggested limits because tested performance has been found to degrade after these limits are reached.

TABLE 1.3: Software limitations for SharePoint Foundation 2010

OBJECT	MAXIMUM VALUE	TYPE OF OBJECT LIMIT	DETAILS
Content Database	300 per web application	Web application limit	With 300 content databases per web application, end users may not see a change in performance, but administrative operations such as creating a new site collection will experience a decrease in performance. Using PowerShell for administration might help.
Managed Paths	20 per web application	Web application limit	Managed paths are cached on the web server, and beyond 20, there is a degradation in performance.
Application Pools	10 per web server	Web server, application server limit	It does depend on the server's RAM and the workload the farm is servicing. However, this is a good rule of thumb. If you need more, test thoroughly for performance issues.
Content Database Size	200 GB per database	Content database limit	There is no hard limit, but it is strongly suggested to limit individual content databases to 200 GB apiece. Larger databases are acceptable for a single site repository, such as a records center, but it is not suggested.
Site collections per Content Database	2,000 recommended; 5,000 maximum	Content database limit	This limit is based on how long it takes to upgrade. Also, the more site collections there are in a content database, the smaller they should be.
WebSite	250,000 per site collection	Site collection limits	Note that creating many subsites simultaneously may fail at this limit. Sites have a way of increasing quietly; it is easy to have more than you think.
Site Collection Size	100 GB per site collection	Site collection limits	Site collection size should never exceed 100 GB unless it is the only site collection in a content database.
Documents	30,000,000 per library	List and library limit	This value depends on how well you organize the data in the library, using folders, nested folders, and using views.

TABLE 1.3:   Software limitations for SharePoint Foundation 2010   *(CONTINUED)*

OBJECT	MAXIMUM VALUE	TYPE OF OBJECT LIMIT	DETAILS
Major Versions	400,000	List and library limit	Passing this limit can have surprising performance effects, causing issues with file open, save, delete, and view history.
Items	30,000,000 per list	List and library limit	You can create very large lists using standard views that filter by metadata and by using folders. This value can also vary depending on number of columns and how the list is used.
Number of SharePoint Groups a User Can Belong To	5,000	Security limit	This is consistent with Active Directory guidelines. Can be affected by size of tokens, the number of groups SharePoint is caching, and how long it takes to do security checks.
Users in a Site Collection	2 million per site collection	Security limit	You can add millions of people to a website using security groups (instead of individual users). The limit particularly affects the manageability and ease of navigation in the user interface.
Active Directory principals/ Users in a SharePoint Group	5,000 per SharePoint group	Security limit	Activities affected by this limit (or exceeding it) are fetching users to validate permissions and rendering the membership of a view.
SharePoint Groups	10,000 per site collection	Security limit	When greater than 10,000, the time it takes to execute operations increases significantly
Security Principal: Size of the Security Scope	5,000 per ACL	Security limit	The number of security prinicipals per access control list for an object. The size of the scope affects the data used for security check calculations. There is no hard limit, but the bigger the scope, the longer the calculation takes.

TABLE 1.3: Software limitations for SharePoint Foundation 2010 *(CONTINUED)*

OBJECT	MAXIMUM VALUE	TYPE OF OBJECT LIMIT	DETAILS
SharePoint Search Service Applications	20 per farm	Search limit	Multiple servers can run Search. More than 20 (particularly if there are other service applications running on the farm) degrades performance.
Indexed Items (and Crawl Log Entries)	Recommneded 10 million, 100 maximum per Search service application	Search limit	Although search can index 100 million items, it is suggested to keep the limit to 10 million for best performance.
Alerts (that can be searched)	1 million per search application	Search limit	This is the tested limit.
Blog Posts	5,000 per site	Blog limit	Tested limit for maximum number of blog posts per site
Blog Comments	1,000 per post	Blog limit	Tested limit for blog comments per post, per site

These hardware and software factors should help you avoid the slow decay of your SharePoint server's performance. Remember to monitor, monitor, monitor. It does no good to have logs if you don't read them. Be prepared for the need to scale out or upgrade before someone else has to tell you to do so. If you ever overestimate the performance requirements, it's good to know that too.

So, that's it. You've seen behind the curtain of SharePoint and learned about its requirements, capabilities, limitations, and services. Now you are ready to get started installing it. Chapter 2 covers preinstallation steps, Standalone installation, and post-installation steps; Chapter 3 covers Server Farm Complete installation and runs through the post-installation steps as well.

The Bottom Line

Determine the software and hardware requirements you need for installing SharePoint Foundation SharePoint has some stringent software and hardware requirements. Be sure you know what you need before you become the proud owner of your own SharePoint server or servers. SharePoint depends on Windows Server components and services in order to function.

Master It What software architecture is required for both the server OS and SQL to successfully install and run SharePoint?

Identify the three ways of installing SharePoint Foundation   Choose the best three ways of installing SharePoint Foundation for you. With SharePoint, how you choose to install it defines how it works. Making the wrong choice can come back to haunt you. Know what you're in for, and choose the correct installation type for your business.

Master It   If you were going to install SharePoint on one server (no existing SQL server) for a small business of about 50 people, what installation type would you choose?

Set up the necessary accounts that SharePoint needs to run   When SharePoint is installed on a domain, it needs user accounts to assign to its services. Knowing what permissions and roles those accounts require will help you avoid problems when installing and running SharePoint.

Master It   What is a Database Access Account? Is it known by any other names?

Recognize the new features and requirements of SharePoint   SharePoint has features that require additional planning and setup to function properly. Make sure you know what they are and what they require.

Master It   What new feature of SharePoint Foundation allows SharePoint to access data from external data sources?

Plan for hardware requirements   Don't let SharePoint outgrow its hardware before it really gets started. Prepare for growth. Establish your company's baseline operations per second and storage needs before installing SharePoint.

Master It   What is the formula to calculate the storage requirements that a SharePoint server would need in a given environment?

Chapter 2

Standalone Installation

Generally, installing a new software product is not the most important part of working with it, and you might be wondering why a whole chapter (much less two) might be devoted to it.

This is why: SharePoint can function differently depending on how it's installed. Also, to install SharePoint at all, the server must be prepared properly. Without preparation, there will be no SharePoint. SharePoint has to be prepared for, installed properly, and finally, some settings must be configured simply to use the product. Therefore, devoting some pages to preparation, installation, and post-installation configuration makes plenty of sense.

In this chapter, you will learn to

- Prepare for the installation of SharePoint

- Install SharePoint using the Standalone installation option

- Determine what gets created when SharePoint installs

- Perform the initial configuration tasks after a SharePoint install (and understand why you perform them)

Preparing for SharePoint Foundation 2010 Installation

To install SharePoint, you'll need to do some preparation. This section will discuss the little things that SharePoint requires before it can install and do its thing. Luckily, with this version of SharePoint, it is not necessary to hunt down and individually install all the prerequisites before the SharePoint installation. Instead, SharePoint's installer has a splash page that allows you to prepare for the installation and select to have the prerequisites checked and installed for you.

Chapter 1, "SharePoint Foundation 2010 Under the Hood," outlined the hardware and software technologies a SharePoint installation requires. Here's a quick recap:

- SharePoint Foundation (SPF for short) is a free Microsoft download, but obviously this means you can't skip downloading the installation file in order to have SharePoint Foundation on your server (a previous version of the product was built in as a server role at one point). The current installation file will be conveniently named `SharePointFoundation.exe`. Since it can install only on 64-bit systems, there isn't a 32-bit version.

- Windows Server 2008 (Service Pack 1 or higher) or Server 2008 R2 or newer is required. The OS architecture *must* be 64-bit. Therefore, the hardware, obviously, must support 64-bit operations. There are no 32-bit options here, not even for evaluation. SharePoint installation is supported on the Standard, Enterprise, and Web editions of Windows Server. It cannot be installed on a Server Core, and installing it on a domain controller is not supported. (Although there are hacks to get it to work, doing so is not suggested.) Also, SharePoint needs PowerShell 2.0 to install. (In the registry, search for *powershell* or *powershellversion*, and you'll see what version you have.) If you have version 1.0 installed (the default for Server 2008), PowerShell 2.0 is backward compatible and will install to the same folder. Note that if you are running Server 2008 with Service Pack 1 (SP1), the SharePoint installer will upgrade you to Service Pack 2, so be warned if anything else on the server needs SP1 only.

◆ Web Server/Application Server role, meaning Internet Information Services (IIS) 7.0, with 6.0 compatibility and ASP.NET enabled. The prerequisite installer will enable this role for you if you don't have it, as well as enable the settings and features that SharePoint Foundation requires.

◆ Microsoft SQL Server 2008 Native Client.

◆ The hotfix for Microsoft Windows (KB976462 for Server 2008 R2 or KB976394 2008 SP2).

◆ Windows Identity Foundation (WIF), which is considered a hotfix (KB974405).

REBOOT WARNING

If you don't have the Windows or WIF hotfixes already on your server, be prepared for the server to abruptly reboot after the prerequisites have installed. If you have anything else to do on the server that's not related to the installation, do it before you click Finish at the end of the prerequisite installation.

◆ Microsoft Sync Framework Runtime v1.0 (x64).Microsoft Chart Controls for Microsoft .NET Framework 3.5

◆ Microsoft Filter Pack 2.0 (really called Microsoft Office 2010 Filter Pack)

◆ Microsoft SQL Server 2008 Analysis Services ADOMD.NET

◆ Microsoft Server Speech Platform Runtime (x64)

◆ Microsoft Server Speech Recognition Language—TELE(en-US)

◆ SQL 2008 R2 Reporting Services SharePoint 2010 Add-in

All of these fiddly bits will be installed for you if you choose to have the SharePoint installer handle the prerequisites, as we'll do later in this section. The only thing you really need to set up on your own is SMTP if you want to enable incoming email for SharePoint.

SOMETIMES THE EASIER PATH IS NOT THE WRONG PATH

Because the prerequisite installation process works so well (and saves so much time and effort), I am simply going to use it and not run you through the step-by-step process of downloading and installing all the moving pieces manually. Using the prerequisite installer also ensures that all the Web Server role settings are exactly as SharePoint needs them, because its own installation tool will configure them.

The caveat for the easy path is that Internet access is required for the prerequisite installer to grab the bits to install (unfortunately, they're not all simply available with the installer). If the server you are going to be installing SharePoint on is not connected to the Internet, you will need to have all the prerequisites on hand to install manually.

◆ Along with installing SharePoint, you must always remember that SharePoint depends on SQL databases of some sort on the back end. If you are doing the Standalone installation detailed in this chapter, SharePoint will be installing SQL Server 2008 Express. Otherwise, you will need to have a 64-bit version of SQL Server (2005 SP3 or higher) somewhere on the network.

ABOUT THAT STANDALONE INSTALLATION...

If you're considering the Standalone installation type and therefore will be using the built-in SQL Server 2008 Express database engine, you might want to consider enabling Remote BLOB Storage (RBS) to help it handle large files. There are a few steps to it, and you need to download the management tools, but it is doable. Check out Chapter 15, "Migrating from WSS 3.0 to Windows SharePoint Foundation 2010," or go online to TechNet and look up the "How to: Enable Filestream" article and then use the article "Install and Configure Remote BLOB storage (SharePoint Foundation 2010)" for more information.

Using Remote BLOB Storage is particularly important if you are upgrading from Windows SharePoint Services 3.0 to SharePoint Foundation, because WSS 3.0 used a built-in database (WID) that did not have a 4 GB limit for each database. Thus, it is critical that Remote BLOB Storage be enabled if your WSS 3.0 databases are over 4 GB, because SharePoint is going to need help handling databases that are technically too big to migrate. For more, see Chapter 15.

In addition, consider upgrading the SQL Express 2008 that SharePoint installs to SQL Express 2008 R2, which increases the database size limit from 4 GB to 10 GB. That is also covered in Chapter 15.

◆ Something else to consider before starting the installation is the account you are going to install it with, commonly called the *setup* account or installation account. This chapter and the next demonstrate the two different installations, Standalone and Complete. For the Standalone installation, all the services will be running on the same server, so all you need in order to do the installation is an account that is allowed to install software on the machine and start services. This is usually an account that is part of the Administrator's group on the local server. Because this chapter covers the Standalone option, I won't go into creating additional, specific accounts right now, but I will describe it in detail in Chapter 3, "Complete Installation."

Initiating the SharePoint Foundation 2010 Installer

After you have made sure your server meets the hardware prerequisites listed in Chapter 1 and that you are prepared for the software prerequisites, services, features, and roles that will be installed on the server, then it's time to prepare for SharePoint.

Make sure you are logged in to the server you are going to install SharePoint Foundation on with an administrative account for the server, and double-click the SharePointFoundation.exe installation file (Figure 2.1).

FIGURE 2.1
The SharePoint Foundation installation file

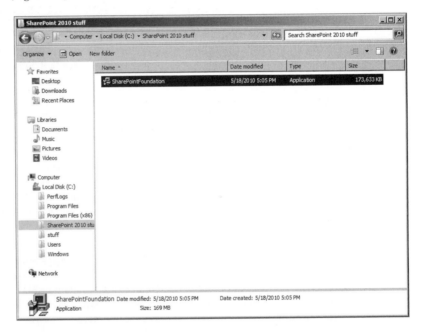

You may get a warning (depending on your security settings), checking to see whether you really want to open the file. And if you do, click Run to proceed. (If you right-click SharePointFoundation.exe and choose Run As Administrator, you will not get the warning dialog box.)

The installer will then extract some files, busy itself for a bit, and then briefly display the splash screen for SharePoint Foundation 2010. Finally, you'll see the installation screen.

On the installation screen (Figure 2.2), you can see that there are quite a few options to prepare you for installation before you begin, very much like the SQL Server installation process. You have the opportunity to review the requirements for installing hardware, installing software, or upgrading SharePoint (under the Prepare heading), and there are links to visit Microsoft pages (under the Other Information heading). The options you are most interested in for this chapter's sample Standalone installation are Install Software Prerequisites and Install SharePoint Foundation.

FIGURE 2.2
The SharePoint
installation screen

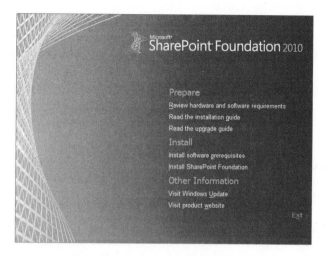

Installing Software Prerequisites

Once you are ready to install, you have two options: install the prerequisites required for SharePoint's installation or install SharePoint. In this example, let's assume you don't have any of the prerequisites installed on the server, so you might as well let SharePoint install them for you.

1. Given that, click Install Software Prerequisites.

   That will open a wizard page titled Welcome To The Microsoft SharePoint 2010 Products Preparation Tool (Figure 2.3). This is the wizard that will install and configure all the prerequisites for SharePoint for you. It lists, for your convenience, all the items that will be installed and/or enabled in preparation for a SharePoint install. These are the items listed earlier in this chapter and detailed in Chapter 1.

2. After checking out the prerequisites to be sure you want them on your server, you can click the link to learn more (if you have Internet access). When you are ready, click Next to begin.

FIGURE 2.3
The Microsoft
SharePoint 2010
Products Prepara-
tion Tool

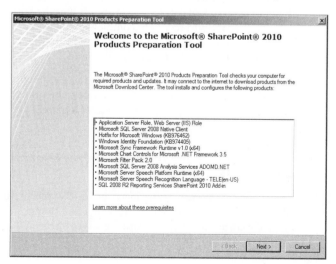

3. You'll then see the end-user license agreement (EULA) page. You must, of course, accept the license agreement in order to move on with the prerequisites. When you're finished reading it, click the check box to agree to the terms of the license agreement, and then click Next.

At that point, the preparation tool will begin installing prerequisites. You can watch as each of the expected items gets installed and configured (Figure 2.4). The really nice thing about this part of the tool is that it reports when it started the prerequisite installation process and how long each part is taking. It will also display, in real time, exactly what items it is installing.

FIGURE 2.4
Installing
prerequisites

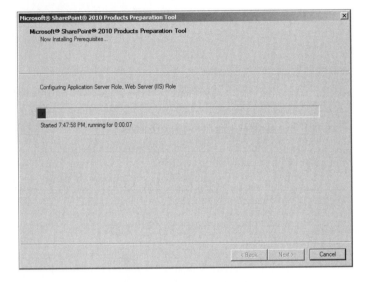

When the prerequisite installation is finished, the tool will display a Your System Needs A Restart... page, displaying what was installed. If there were any problems, this page will list what failed so you can fix it, but more often than not, the prerequisites install without a hitch. You can see in Figure 2.5 that the hotfixes and several other prerequisites require the server to reboot to complete installation. Your prerequisite installation might not require a reboot, and in that case, it will simply indicate that the process is complete and everything installed successfully.

4. Closing out of the preparation tool will trigger an abrupt reboot (if required). If you are ready for the server to reboot and complete the prerequisite installation, click Finish. (You can also review the prerequisite installer log file if you need to do so, by clicking the link on that page before finishing.)

JUST TO BE SURE

It may not be a bad idea to run Windows Update after reboot, to see whether any of the new items installed require any patches or updates before continuing. Also, be sure to check the event logs to be sure there are no hidden issues with the server you need to resolve before continuing.

When the server reboots and you log back in with the same administrative account you used for the prerequisite installation, the preparation tool will start running again. It may look like a restart, complete with a progress bar, but all it's doing behind the scenes is dealing with the effects of the hotfixes.

FIGURE 2.5

Installation almost complete; requires a restart

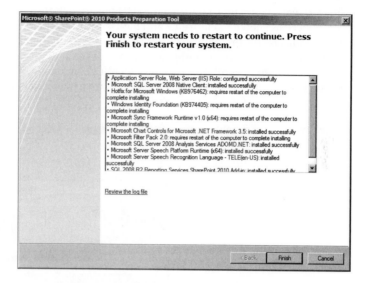

5. When it's ready, the installer will display an Installation Complete page, as shown in Figure 2.6. You can see that the Application server role has been configured successfully, and all other prerequisites appear as "(no action taken)." This means that those prerequisites were installed successfully before the reboot and then, after reboot, were not reinstalled. You can safely click Finish to complete the prerequisite installation process; the server will not reboot this time.

FIGURE 2.6

Installation complete this time

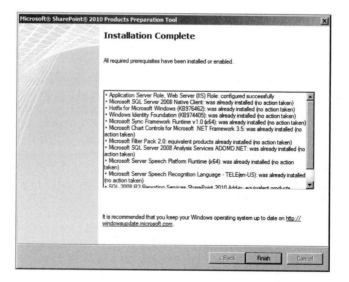

Before you install SharePoint, let's see what was changed with the prerequisites and set up SMTP for incoming email.

Confirming Prerequisites Installed

To start, you should find a bunch of new folders in both the Program Files and Program Files x86 folders, as shown in Figure 2.7 and Figure 2.8. The folders selected in these figures are those added by the prerequisite installation and tell you that it worked. In the Program Files folder, there are folders for the SQL 2008 native client, Microsoft Sync Framework, .NET 3.5 (the Reference Assemblies folder), Windows Identity Foundation, MSBuild (which has to do with Windows Workflow Foundation, another requirement of SharePoint), and ADOMD.NET (the Microsoft.NET folder).

FIGURE 2.7
The Program Files folder after the prerequisite installation

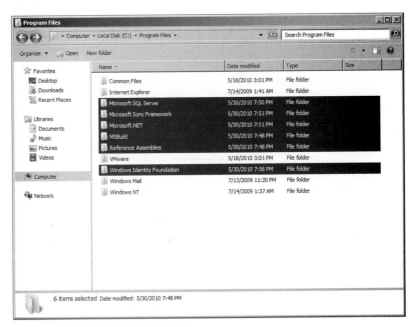

Like Program Files, the Program Files x86 folder also contains folders for SQL Server (for the SQL native client and Reporting Services add-on), Microsoft .NET, Windows Identity Foundation, MSBuild, and Reference Assemblies. In addition, unique to Program Files x86 are the Microsoft Chart Controls and MSECache folders. Interestingly, the chart controls and the cached information about the SharePoint installation are both x86 material.

If you've been counting, that still leaves the Microsoft Filter Pack 2.0 and speech recognition missing. Those files are located under Program Files ➤ Common Files ➤ Microsoft Shared, in the Filters and Speech folders, respectively. You can see in Figure 2.9 that the creation date of those folders is much later than the other folders (in fact, it matches the date of the prerequisite installation).

FIGURE 2.8
The Program Files
x86 folder after
the prerequisite
installation

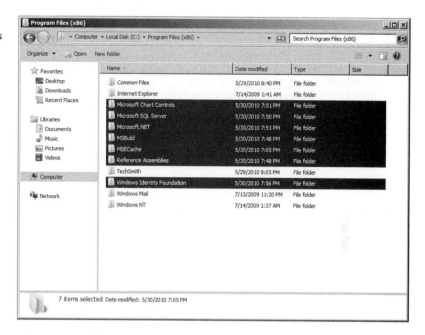

And of course, after you've checked the file system for the prerequisites, you can also do a final check on the Programs And Features list (Figure 2.10) just to be sure.

FIGURE 2.9
The Filters
and Speech
folders found

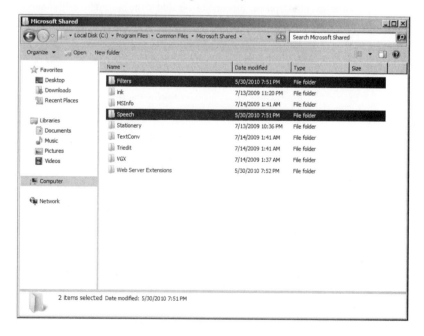

FIGURE 2.10
The Programs
And Features list
displays installed
prerequisites.

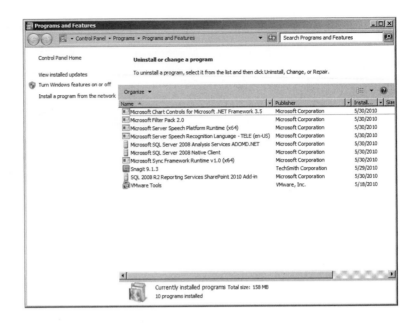

WHAT ABOUT THOSE HOTFIXES?

To check the two prerequisite hotfixes, you will need to go to Programs And Features and click the
View Installed Updates link on the left side of the page. This will show you the hotfixes (and whatever
other updates you might have installed).

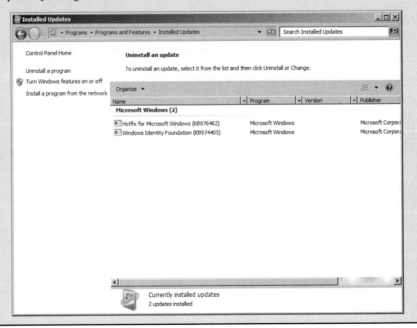

Now that you know the prerequisites have been installed, it's time to take a look at the server role that was added, IIS.

Checking the Web Server Role

There are a few ways to see whether IIS is installed and to discover how it's configured; this examination will also let you understand more clearly what changes SharePoint makes to IIS after it installs. You will first check the Server Manager console to see what it says under Roles And Features and then check the IIS management console and see what it looks like at this point.

WHEN IS AN APPLICATION NOT AN APPLICATION?

Keep in mind that Server 2008 and 2008 R2 split some of the services out from IIS and consider them Application server roles. Essentially, Microsoft makes this distinction because you can offer applications from the server that have nothing to do with web services. However, web services generally require application server capabilities. So, there is some overlap, and a requirement is for the Application server role to be enabled when web server is also enabled.

---

1. To that end, open the **Server Manager** console (it's usually a button on the taskbar showing a gray server and toolbox, or you can get to it from the Administrative Tools off the Start menu).

2. Once the console opens, you'll be able to see the server summary in the content pane on the right of the window. If you click the plus sign next to **Roles** in the navigation pane on the left and click **Web Server (IIS)**, you will see information pertaining to the IIS role in the content pane (Figure 2.11).This area is useful for managing the IIS server role. It will not only prove that the role is enabled but also show you the system services running for that role (so you can be sure each service is running as it should), as well as the events related to that role (again checking that all is well). It will also let you check the Best Practice Analyzer for the role, which is always handy.

   Forty-one role services have been enabled as part of the prerequisite installation; that's practically everything but some custom logging, FTP services, WebDAV publishing (interestingly enough), and IIS hostable web core. Of particular interest is the IIS 6.0 compatibility (Figure 2.12). Not only does SharePoint need this, but when you enable SMTP services (as we will in a moment), it'll use the IIS 6.0 console as well.

   So, we've confirmed that IIS has been enabled and that many associated services are also running as a result of the prerequisites install. To make certain all is well, let's take a look at the IIS management console.

You could access the IIS manager console right inside the Server Manager console, but I'd like to prove something. So, let's access IIS by going the long way.

1. Close out of the Server Manager.

2. Click the Start button on the taskbar, and go to **Administrative Tools**.

FIGURE 2.11

The Web Server
role enabled in the
Server Manager
console

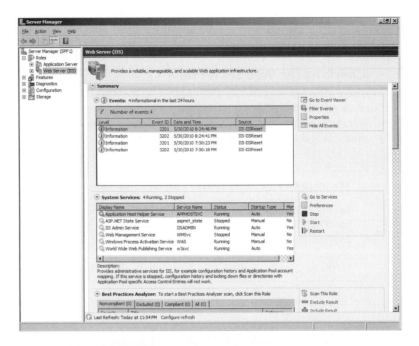

FIGURE 2.12

Web Server role
services, IIS 6.0
compatibility

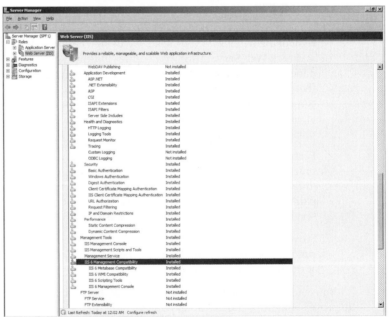

On the Administrative Tools menu, you can now see that there are two versions of the
IIS management console available (Figure 2.13; I've outlined the console listings for easy
viewing).

FIGURE 2.13

Administrative Tools menu after prerequisite install

3. Let's take a look at both of them, because you need to know what they're both for. To start, let's check out the latest and greatest IIS console for the operating system (either 7 or 7.5). To do so, select **Internet Information Services (IIS) Manager** from the menu (they don't bother to indicate the version, since it's the one that is native to the OS).

This will open the IIS manager console. In the navigation pane on the left side of the console, you'll notice that Start Page is selected, and beneath it is an icon for the local server (in my case, SPF1). If you click the plus sign next to the local server icon, it will drop down a short list containing Application Pools and Sites items. And if you click the plus sign next to Sites, you'll see that there is only one default site (Figure 2.14).

FIGURE 2.14

The IIS manager console

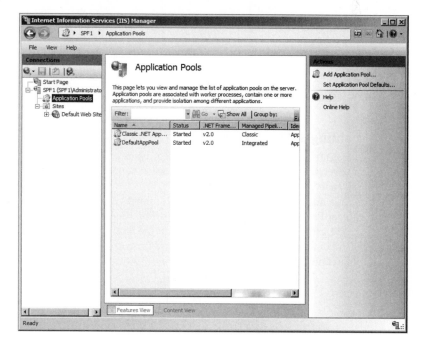

If you were to check further, the application pools available on installation are just a classic .NET pool and a default pool. There's nothing yet SharePoint related. And under Default Site there is only a folder containing necessary bits for ASP.NET, nothing more.

Because there will be quite a few changes made when SharePoint installs, it's always good to know what state IIS was in before installation. You can't really be in control of something if you don't really know anything about it.

Now on to the other IIS 6.0 manager console. Close out of the currently open IIS manager console.

1. Go to Start on the taskbar, choose **Administrative Tools**, and click **Internet Information Services (IIS) 6.0 Manager**. It'll open a completely empty console. There isn't even a local server listed. It is primarily used behind the scenes for IIS 6.0 compatibility at this point. There is simply nothing in there yet (Figure 2.15).

FIGURE 2.15
IIS 6.0 Manager

2. Close out of the console.

Enabling SMTP Server

It's reassuring to know that all the prerequisites are installed, configured, and enabled. However, there is one prerequisite that wasn't enabled, because it's an optional feature: SMTP service.

For a number of SharePoint lists and libraries to support incoming email, Simple Mail Transfer Protocol (SMTP) must be enabled on the SharePoint server. This will allow those lists and libraries to have an email address on the SharePoint server and have items emailed to them, instead of requiring the user to log in and browse to the list or library to create a new item or upload one.

WHAT IS SMTP?

For those who need it, here is a quick SMTP primer as it relates to SharePoint. Simple Mail Transfer Protocol is an industry standard and is used to send mail from server to server. SMTP uses port 25 to do its work, so that port has to be available for its use. This means you can't enable SMTP (and therefore SharePoint's incoming email) if you've installed SharePoint on the same server as Exchange (unlikely, but it could happen). That is because Exchange is already using that port and doesn't share.

When you enable SMTP for IIS, it will create a number of folders under the IIS's folder `LocalDrive:\` `Inetpub` in a folder called Mailroot. This folder will contain a Drop folder, in which mail sent to the server will be stored. It is this folder that SharePoint checks for email sent to the local lists or libraries. If email is found addressed to one of the lists or libraries, SharePoint will read the email header and contents; parse the information for title, content, and attachment information; and deposit the mail as an item for that list or library.

Interestingly, despite that SMTP is generally used to focus on *sending* mail rather than receiving it, using SMTP for receiving mail for its SharePoint services is rather clever.

Think about it; SharePoint Foundation is free (and the very first version of SharePoint, the impetus for all this, was free as well). So, it needs to use what is already available on the server at no extra cost to do what it needs to do, as well as using only Microsoft products to get jobs done. So, it uses IIS and SQL. IIS is particularly the focus of SharePoint because the front-end servers must handle web pages and use ASP.NET. So, if someone wanted the capability of sending items to lists and libraries in SharePoint rather than logging in, how would they do it, for free, with nothing more than what is already available?

SMTP, of course. It has its shortcomings, but it allows the pickup and drop-off email messages on the IIS server. SharePoint only uses the drop-off capability, the ability to get the messages meant for its server address, but that still works. This also explains why the default for the server address for incoming email is the SharePoint server's name in DNS. It's already set, so just use what works.

SMTP also has Pickup, Queue, and Badmail folders. These are relevant if you are using SMTP to send mail from the IIS Web Sites to other servers (and other addresses outside the domain). However, the folders aren't really used for receiving email. (Although Badmail can be, if a message isn't address correctly.)

Only one SharePoint server in the farm needs to have SMTP enabled, because SharePoint really supports only one SMTP drop location per farm. However, this installation may be the only server on the farm, and it will certainly be the first one, so it is a good idea to at least learn how to enable SMTP and set up incoming email and to have the first server be the one that supports incoming email at least until other servers are online.

Back in the day, to enable SMTP, you'd go to Add/Remove Programs, click Add/Remove Windows Components, and scroll down to SMTP. Now, with Server 2008 and 2008 R2, SMTP is a server *feature*. There are a couple of ways to go to enable server features, but we're going to use the Server Manager console.

1. Open the **Server Manager** console, and either scroll to the server features summary on the summary page or click **Features** in the navigation pane (Figure 2.16). That will bring up the list of server features already enabled in the summary area. To the right of that list is an **Add Features** link. Click that to add our new feature, SMTP.

FIGURE 2.16

Features Summary
in Server Manager

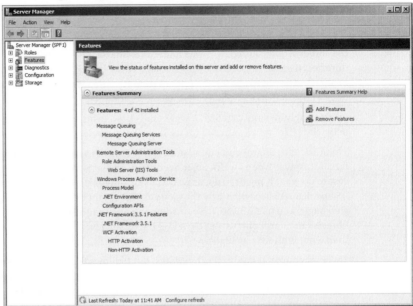

When you click the Add Features link, the Add Features Wizard opens, displaying the Select Features page, which lists the available features for the server. Features already enabled have a check mark in the box next to them; those with a subset of features enabled are filled in.

2. Scroll down in the Features list until you can see **SMTP Server** listed (Figure 2.17). Select its check box.

3. When you select SMTP Server, a dialog box will open, displaying the additional subfeatures that must be enabled in order to enable SMTP (Figure 2.18). You can't avoid installing them if you want SMTP, so click the **Add Required Role Services** button.

This will take you back to the Add Features Wizard, but now there is a check mark in the box next to SMTP Server.

4. To continue with enabling SMTP, just click **Next** in the wizard window.

This will bring you to the Web Server (IIS) page. Here you can read about what the Web Server role does. You'll also find information about the Windows Resource Manager and what the default installation of IIS does, as well as links for additional information. This is very useful if you've never seen or used IIS before.

As you can also see on this page of the wizard (Figure 2.19), there are a few steps to cover before SMTP is enabled. They are entirely automated, but it is nice to have a road map of what's going to happen.

FIGURE 2.17
The Add Features
Wizard, SMTP
Server listed

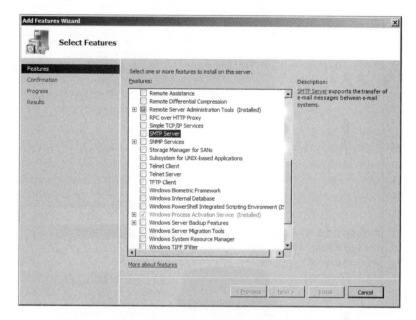

FIGURE 2.18
The dialog box for
additional role ser-
vices and features

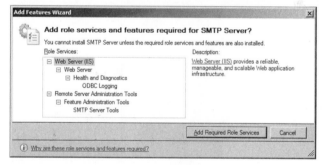

5. Click **Next** to continue with enabling SMTP.

This will take you to an IIS role services page (Figure 2.20). This just shows you what IIS role services are available for the IIS role, along with which ones are enabled and which ones aren't. Basically everything that is checked but grayed out is already enabled, any that are black but checked are required for enabling SMTP (ODBC Logging; all the other requirements were already enabled), and the only things not enabled at this point are FTP Services, Custom Logging, WebDAV publishing, and IIS Hostable Web Core.

FIGURE 2.19

The Web Server (IIS) page of the Add Features Wizard

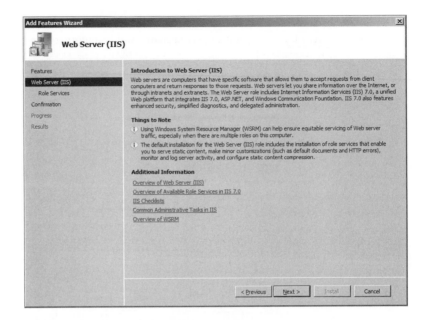

FIGURE 2.20

The Select Role Services page of the Add Features Wizard

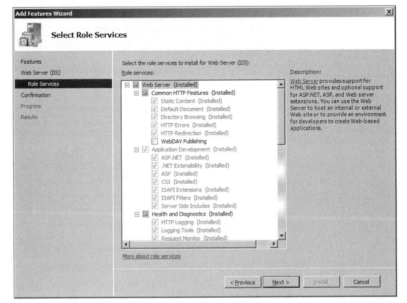

6. Click **Next** to continue.

The next page of the wizard simply confirms the selections you made (or were made for you) in the previous pages of the wizard. It is a good habit to stop and look at this page before proceeding. It's all too easy to click past it and then realize afterward that you've done something wrong that could have been avoided if you'd read the confirmation page.

This particular confirmation page (Figure 2.21) indicates that ODBC Logging has been enabled (under Health And Diagnostics in the role services list) and that the administration tools for SMTP services, as well as SMTP Server itself, will be installed.

FIGURE 2.21

The confirmation page for the Add Features Wizard

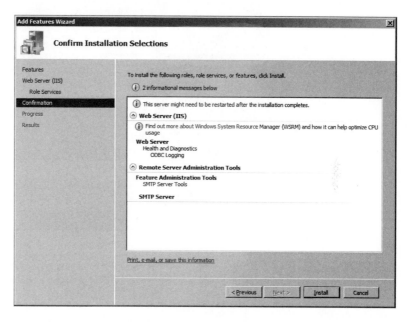

7. If everything looks good on the confirmation page, click **Install** to install the SMTP feature.

    The next page will simply display the progress of the installation, indicating what is being installed, until the installation is complete. The final page will display the installation results (Figure 2.22), indicating the success of each install.

    It will also indicate whether there are any problems, even if enabling the feature and installing role services is successful. In our case, because this is a new server, we haven't enabled Windows Update yet. So if you see any warning icons, don't panic until you read what they're about. Some are more informational than others.

8. To exit the wizard, just click **Close**.

    This will put you back on the Server Manager console. The SMTP Server feature will be listed in the feature summary area. But to really see where SMTP was put, open the IIS manager console by selecting Start ➤ Administrative Tools ➤ Internet Information Services (IIS) 6.0 Manager.

    Now there is something in the IIS 6.0 Manager console. As you can see in Figure 2.23, the local server is listed, and beneath that (if you look) is SMTP—actually [SMTP Virtual Server #1]. This is where you will manage SMTP outside of SharePoint (and there are a few things you can do here that you can't do in SharePoint).

FIGURE 2.22
Installation
Results page

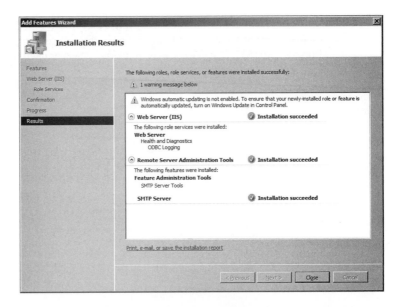

FIGURE 2.23
The IIS 6.0 man-
ager console with
SMTP enabled

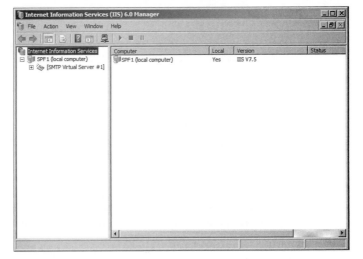

"ISN'T THERE AN SMTP EMAIL SETTING IN THE IIS 7 CONSOLE?"

Yes, there is a SMTP setting in the IIS manager console for the more recent version, but that only uses an existing SMTP set up somewhere else; it isn't where you configure SMTP even if it's enabled locally. The IIS 6.0 console is for that.

In addition, if you'd like to check to see what folders were created for SMTP, open `%intepub%\mailroot`. As expected, the folders stored there are Badmail, Drop, Pickup, and Queue (Figure 2.24). It never hurts to know where those are, should you need to troubleshoot incoming email someday.

FIGURE 2.24
The SMTP service
email folders

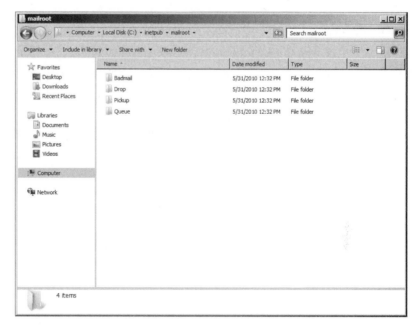

Now that you've enabled SMTP, proven that all the bits that needed to install have installed, and proven that IIS is up, running, and compatible with 6.0, let's move on to the Standalone installation of SharePoint Foundation.

Feel free to close out of the IIS console, any extraneous windows, and Server Manager for that matter (if you haven't already); you won't need them after this point.

Standalone Installation of SharePoint Foundation

This section of the chapter shows how to do a Standalone installation and what happens when you do. (After the installation is complete, we will finish up with some extra configuration tasks in the "Post-Installation Configuration Tasks" section of the chapter. These are tasks you'll have to do regardless of which type of installation you've done.) Now that the hotfixes and other prerequisites have successfully installed, the actual SharePoint installation process can begin. Keep in mind that the account you are logged in with when you start the installation must have local administrative rights (in order to install software, make changes to services, and so on). It will be considered the installation or setup account.

1. To start, double-click the **SharePointFoundation.exe** executable (as you did before in order to install prerequisites).

2. Once the SharePoint Foundation 2010 installation screen comes up, you can click the **Install SharePoint Foundation** link.

   Once you've started the installation, a gray screen will come up very quickly, saying "Please wait while SharePoint prepares the necessary files." There might also be a quick command prompt window as well.

3. Next up is the EULA page; feel free to read the license agreement. Click the check box to accept the terms of the agreement. The **Continue** button will remain grayed until you accept. Click it to continue with the installation.

This will bring you to the part of the installation where your choice of installation type defines your SharePoint infrastructure. These innocuous buttons, as shown in Figure 2.25, are pretty important.

FIGURE 2.25

Choosing between Standalone and Server Farm

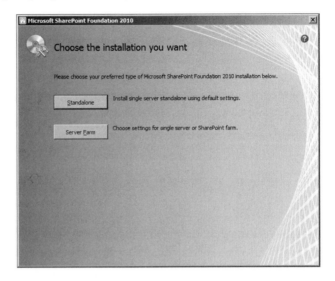

This Choose The Installation You Want page has two buttons on it, and little else. Once you click one button or the other, you can cancel the install, but there will be no back button.

"MAY I HELP YOU?"

You may be tempted to look for some help before proceeding. Clicking the help icon is the only way to get help during the installation process.

The help available during installation is often more useful than you might've come to expect from SharePoint (with only a few technical errors). When in doubt, it doesn't hurt to ask for help.

The Standalone button is the one you click if you want to have the simplest, fully automatic, single-server installation, complete with the installation of SQL Server 2008 Express edition on the server to manage databases. This type of installation is intended for implementations that will have *only one* server in the server farm, *this* server. No other server can share the configuration database to spread the load of users accessing the SharePoint web pages. When considering a Standalone installation, keep in mind the SQL Server 2008 Express CPU and RAM limitations. Express can support only one CPU, has a 1 GB memory limit for its buffer pool, and, of course, has that infamous 4 GB database size limit.

In addition, during a Standalone installation, all server configuration will be done automatically for you, using standard settings and local service accounts. The implementation of a Standalone server is good for demonstration, for evaluation, or if you are in an environment that does not require more than one server or full-blown SQL server software and if you don't mind the 4GB database limitation of SQL Server 2008 Express (although you can upgrade it to the 2008 R2 version, which supports up to 10 GB, which may help). Immediately after you click the Standalone button, the installation will just begin with little interference from you.

The Server Farm button, in contrast, takes you to a page that offers you two options: to, once again, do a Stand-alone or a Complete installation (OK, maybe not quite so much contrast if it's offering Standalone twice). It is the Complete button that you will click if you truly want to have more control over the settings of your SharePoint configuration, use an existing SQL installation for the databases, and do not install SQL 2008 Express on the local server. Use the Complete installation type if you intend to build a SharePoint server farm to spread the web-accessing load between more than one server—all pointing to the same configuration database in SQL for their server farm configuration settings.

Strangely, the Stand-alone server button available after you choose Server Farm is exactly the same as the first Standalone button, except in this setting you get to choose where the index files to be used by Search will go. Otherwise, there is no difference. Why SharePoint offers Standalone more than once, I don't know.

Now that you are reminded of the perils of selecting the wrong installation type, let's move on.

4. To continue with the Standalone installation, simply click the **Standalone** button.

The Installation Progress page will come up, with a progress bar and the statement "Installing SharePoint Foundation 2010..." below it (Figure 2.26).

It is during the installation part of this process that the prerequisites are verified, necessary files are installed, and the SharePoint services will be created but not yet started (Figure 2.27).

FIGURE 2.26
Installation
Progress page

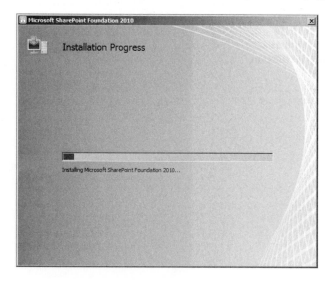

FIGURE 2.27
SharePoint
services in Task
Manager

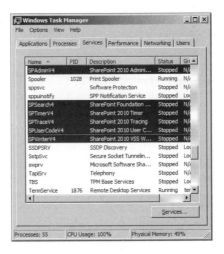

It might take a while for the installation progress bar to complete. Then the installer will begin applying updates (Figure 2.28), which may take even longer.

FIGURE 2.28
Applying updates
during installation

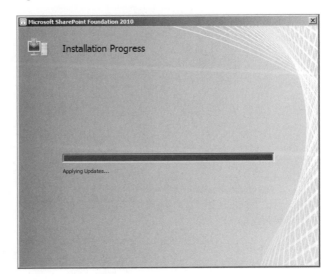

It is, strangely enough, during *this* part of the installation process where the installer installs SQL Server 2008 Express, creating the necessary essential storage location and structure (Figure 2.29) and starting the SQL services (Figure 2.30).

FIGURE 2.29

SQL Server 2008 Express storage location

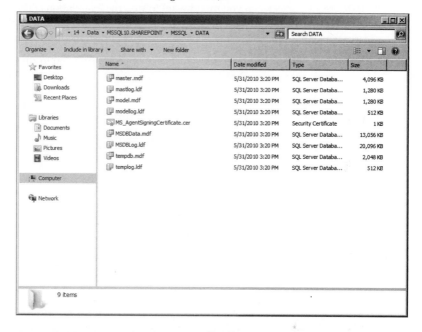

"WHERE IS THE SQL EXPRESS LOCATION?"

The location of the SQL Server 2008 Express files is `%Program Files%\Common Files\Microsoft Shared\Web Server Extensions\14\Data\MSSQL10.SHAREPOINT\MSSQL\DATA`, if you are eager to check it yourself. We'll be revisiting it later when we check to see what databases are added after the SharePoint installation.

FIGURE 2.30

SQL services in Task Manager

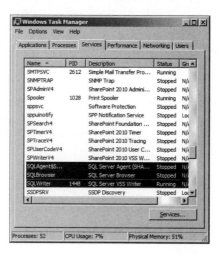

When SharePoint is done adding updates, it will promptly move to configuration. As I mentioned earlier, the installation of SharePoint comes in two parts: first installing the necessary files and services and then configuring SharePoint to operate.

There are times when you might want to stop the installation at this point and configure later, but for this installation, we don't need to do so. Since configuration doesn't require any assistance from you, it doesn't hurt to just get to it so you can finish the installation and see what happens.

1. On the installation screen, which is now prompting you to run the configuration wizard, make certain the Run The SharePoint Products **Configuration Wizard Now** box is selected (Figure 2.31), and click the **Close** button. This will trigger the configuration wizard to begin.

FIGURE 2.31
The prompt to start the configuration wizard

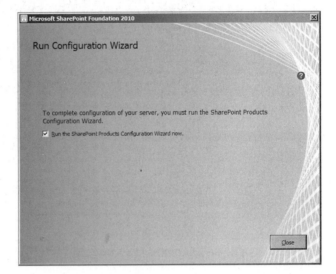

2. After a moment the SharePoint Products Configuration Wizard will open. Click **Next** to continue.

3. At this point, a dialog box will open with a warning that certain SharePoint services may have to be restarted during configuration. Since the services aren't actually doing anything right now (because SharePoint isn't configured), click **Yes** to continue (Figure 2.32).

The configuration wizard will then start in earnest (Figure 2.33), performing various configuration tasks (10 in all).

Some tasks will zip by, and others will take a while (such as creating the configuration database, securing resources, configuring and registering search, provisioning the Central Administration site, creating sample data, and so on). All configuration tasks will occur without prompting you for any assistance. This part may take a while, depending on your system's hardware.

FIGURE 2.32
The Reset Services
warning

FIGURE 2.33
The configuration
wizard at work

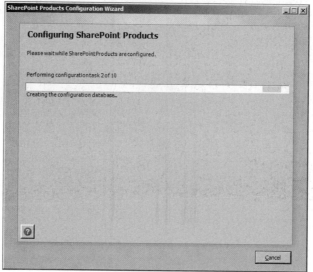

Because of the preparations made by the SharePoint installer and prerequisites, the configuration wizard is able to set up SharePoint for you. Under the hood, this means that the wizard creates SharePoint's configuration database, which is the database that holds all the configuration settings for SharePoint (thanks to SQL Server 2008 Express). It also creates an IIS Web Site (thanks to IIS) for configuring SharePoint Central Administration as well as a default web application and site collection you can start using right away. In addition, SharePoint creates the content databases for both Central Administration and the default first web application for you, which is, again, only possible thanks to the SQL Express instance on the local server. Because SharePoint already knows what local service accounts to use, Search and other services are started and configured automatically and are ready and working as soon as you finish the configuration wizard. As a matter of fact, as soon as you complete configuration, a browser window will open and access your freshly built SharePoint site.

When the wizard is finished, you will see a Configuration Successful page, as shown in Figure 2.34. At the bottom of the page will be instructions describing what will happen when you close the page and how to log in to the browser (as well as a reminder to add the site to the browser's trusted zone).

FIGURE 2.34
Configuration
Successful page

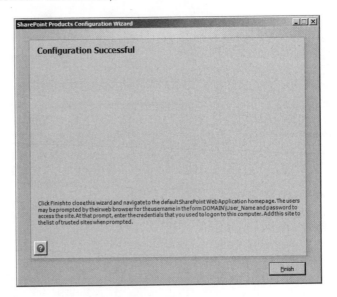

4. To finish configuration and just start using SharePoint, click **Finish**.

Immediately after the wizard closes, the default browser will open. In most cases, on Server 2008 or 2008 R2, that will be Internet Explorer 7 or 8.

FREQUENT PROMPTING GETTING YOU DOWN?

For the purposed of full disclosure, the browser I'm using is Internet Explorer 8 (unless I state otherwise), and, outside of this exercise, I generally have Enhanced Security Configuration (ESC) disabled for administrators, which means I'll be prompted less often for authentication and warned less about untrusted sites (useful when you're writing a book or working within your office network, but not so good when you're browsing the dangerous byways of the Internet).

I disabled ESC by going to Server Manager and in the server's Summary pane clicking the Configure IE ESC link in the Security Information section.

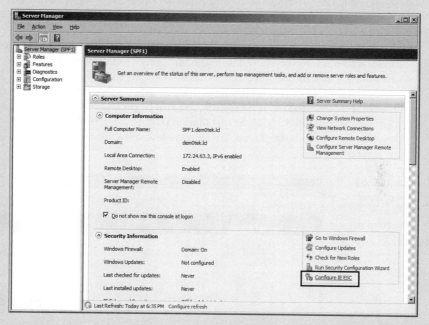

A dialog box comes up with two sections, one for disabling ESC for administrators and one for disabling ESC for users. I just clicked Off in the Administrators section and clicked OK.

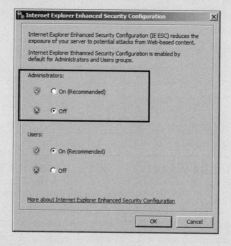

I don't advocate disabling security features in production (or even in every testing situation), but the setting is there if you think you need it

You may be prompted for a username and password. If so, use the username and password of the account you were logged in as during installation and configuration. If you are not prompted to log in, it is because the browser simply passed through the login credentials of the account you are currently using on the server. Since you just finished installing SharePoint, that should be the correct account to use (SharePoint doesn't know any other user accounts at this point).

If you're following my example, you've installed SharePoint using the server's local administrator's account, so you should be logged in using spf1\administrator, because our server name is spf1 and the local account we used to install SharePoint is administrator.

After you log in (if you need to), you may be asked to add the site to Trusted Sites for the browser. Feel free to do so if necessary. You will be presented with the default home page of your new SharePoint Standalone installation (Figure 2.35). Notice on the top right of the page that your username is displayed. This always lets you know the current account with which you are logged in.

FIGURE 2.35

First glimpse of the new SharePoint site

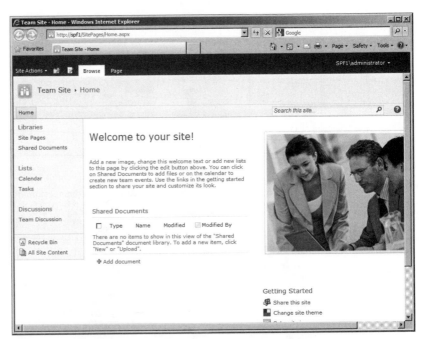

The new top-level site uses the Team Site template, which is a standard, default template for many SharePoint sites that offers some sample lists, libraries, and so on. You can see in the address bar of the browser that the address of the site is the address of the server itself (http://SPF1 in our case). SharePoint sets up the first SharePoint website (or as it's called, *web application*) simply to listen for and respond to traffic on port 80. So, any requests that are addressed to that server's address on port 80 (the default port for HTTP traffic, and the default port for anything typed into a browser) will be directed to the SharePoint website and therefore will be served the home page you saw in Figure 2.35. You can have SharePoint respond to other kinds of addresses, such as a fully qualified domain name (FQDN), but for right now, the machine name is the default.

SharePoint can seem a little anticlimactic when you first get a glimpse of it. The interface consists of some tabs (Browse and Page, reminiscent of the Office 2010 ribbon bar tabs) and icons on the top left of the screen; beneath the tabs are the title of the site (Team Site by default) and the name of the page you are on (Home in this case). Under the title is a Home tab, which is on the left above a navigation bar, called a Quick Launch bar, that goes down the left side of the page containing links to lists, libraries, and other objects in the site. In the center of the page is the web part area, now formatted as a wiki page (for those of you familiar with wikis), containing a web part and some rich text and a picture as examples. At the top right are the Account menu (which always indicates the account you are logged in with), with the search field and the help icon below.

SharePoint is not supposed to be busy and intimidating but easy on the eyes, uncluttered, and easy to use. If you are not intimidated, then SharePoint has achieved its objective. For details about using the new SharePoint Foundation interface, see Chapter 4, "Introduction to the SharePoint Interface."

That's it. That's all it takes to install SharePoint using the Standalone option. You are on the home page of your first SharePoint site, ready to add users, explore the existing lists and libraries, and do all the things you need to make it your own. You can immediately begin to use and manage it without much, if any, additional effort. All databases and services were created and configured automatically for you.

However, I don't know about you, but helplessly watching a wizard do mysterious things to my server, regardless of the immediate outcome, makes me nervous. One of the first things I do, after a product is installed and running, is check to see what actually changed on the server in order for the product to function properly. It's also helpful to get to know what a good installation looks like, under the hood, so you'll recognize what's missing should an install go bad. So, now that SharePoint is up and running, let's see what actually happened during the SharePoint Standalone installation.

We won't be going back to the site for a while, so feel free to close out of the browser (until we come back later). In addition, you're done with the installation, so feel free to exit the SharePoint Foundation 2010 installation screen, because you've obviously finished using it.

Confirming Changes in the File System

During the installation process, SharePoint had to create a file structure to store the files it requires on the server. This structure was called the *12 hive* in the previous version because the topmost folder had a 12 as its name, and all folders organized beneath it were used by SharePoint, rather like the way settings are organized in the registry. Now the folder has gone up to 14 (obviously Microsoft skipped version number 13) and is supposed to be called the *SharePoint root* (although many will still call it the *14 hive*). This folder structure starts with a 14 folder, and all other folders and files organized beneath it are solely required by SharePoint. This is the root file structure for all things SharePoint. Any file SharePoint needs that isn't in a database, particularly those web or design based, is located here (although, with a Standalone installation, the database files are stored in the SharePoint root as well). This file structure needs to be the same for each SharePoint server in the farm (with the exception of indexing files).

The physical path to the SharePoint root is `%Program Files%\Common Files\Microsoft Shared\Web Server Extensions\14`. As you can see in Figure 2.36, there are a number of folders located within the root, each with a particular use. This is where many of the virtual directories listed in IIS for SharePoint are physically located. You'll see proof of this in a moment. This structure is important enough to make a point of backing up regularly—particularly since most customizations, such as new templates, solutions, and so on, are stored here and nowhere else.

FIGURE 2.36
The SharePoint root

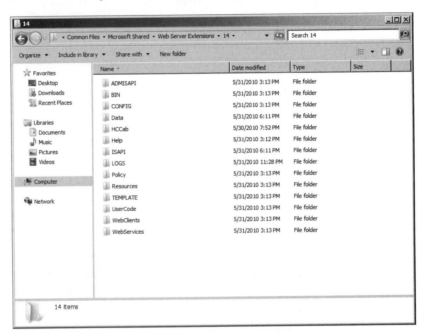

Confirming Sharepoint Security Groups

To access those SharePoint root folders, SharePoint creates some user groups on the local server to manage security (it adds the necessary accounts to the correct group and then adds the group to the access control list with the correct permissions to the folders). To see what groups were created, open the Computer Management console (Start ➤ Administrative Tools ➤ Computer Management), click Local Users And Groups, and open the Groups node, or you can open the Server Manager, open the Configuration node, and click Local Users And Groups to access Groups.

As you can see in Figure 2.37, SharePoint created three groups.

FIGURE 2.37
SharePoint Security Groups

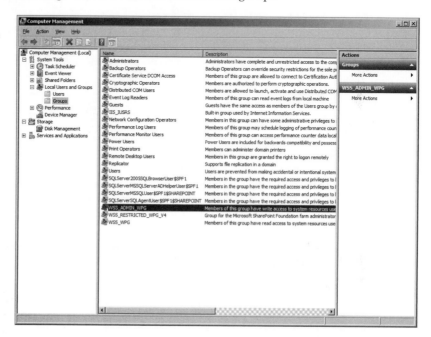

WSS_WPG   Used by accounts that need read access to resources, usually web application pools.

WSS_ADMIN_WPG   Used by accounts that also need write access and is usually the farm account, farm administrators and setup account.

WSS_RESTRICTED_WPG_V4   Usually populated only by the farm account and used by the SharePoint administration service. This service is the one that runs interference between SharePoint and the local computer should SharePoint need to make service changes locally— such as making changes to IIS, doing IIS resets, starting and stopping services, and so on.

And now that you know the groups exist, you can check the permissions of the SharePoint root folders, check the groups, and understand why they are there, as you can see in Figure 2.38. It shows the Security tab (which I displayed by right-clicking the Config folder in the SharePoint root and choosing from its menu), and you can see that two SharePoint groups are assigned permissions and that WSS_WPG does have only read, list, and execute rights to that folder.

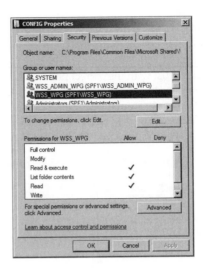

FIGURE 2.38
The WSS_WPG in
the Config folder
permissions

These security groups and their members are not really important for a Standalone installation, because all of the accounts used by SharePoint are local to the computer. However, these groups and where their permissions are applied can be useful should you want to make changes to the accounts used by SharePoint or you need to troubleshoot permissions. They are also very important to know during the Complete installation, because most accounts, in that context, will be domain users and not local.

> **SQL HAS GROUPS, TOO**
>
> You might have noticed in Figure 2.37 that there are also a number of groups on the server for the SQL services to manage the local installation of SQL Express. These groups will not be available for SharePoint installations that don't also have some version of SQL installed locally.

Confirming the Installation of Databases

Now that you know that SharePoint's root folders are there, let's see about the databases. During the prerequisite installation phase, you got a glimpse of the folder SQL Server 2008 Express used. If you go back there now (conveniently buried deeply in the SharePoint root at %Program Files%\ Common Files\Microsoft Shared\Web Server Extensions\14\Data\MSSQL10.SHAREPOINT\ MSSQL\DATA), you can see in Figure 2.39 that there are more than just the requisite SQL databases (such as Model and Master). Now there are a number of new databases (and their logs) in existence, and each is used by SharePoint:

Bdc_Service_DB_(*GUID*)   This is automatically generated for use by the new Business Data Connectivity capabilities available to SharePoint Foundation.

SharePoint_AdminContent_(*GUID*)   Since Central Administration has its own website on a separate (custom, randomly generated) port from the default website, it requires its own web application. Each web application gets its own database. Thus, this is Central

Administration's content database. If you were to customize the Central Administration website by adding a list or two or filling the existing ones (they're not easy to find, but they are there) with data, those customizations would be stored in this database.

FIGURE 2.39

SharePoint databases for a Standalone installation

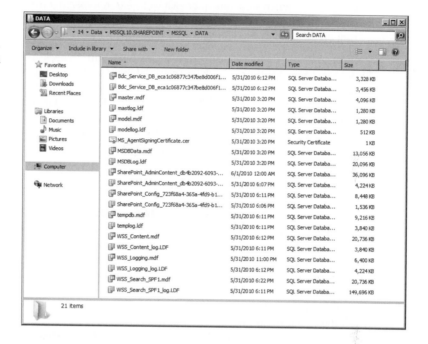

SharePoint_Config_(*GUID*)   This is the all-important configuration database containing all the configuration information about this server implementation. Any settings made in Central Administration that relate to SharePoint overall go here.

WSS_Content   This is the content database for the default first site that you logged into in the browser. Any data you add to the lists or libraries on that site, as well as changes made to the site, are stored in this database (except for customizations such as added solutions, which are stored in the SharePoint root).

"I THOUGHT THIS WAS SHAREPOINT FOUNDATION, NOT WSS"

You may have noticed that the security groups for SharePoint, and the content database, still have "WSS" in the name. That's not surprising, since the name change to SharePoint Foundation occurred only during the beta of this product. It had been Windows SharePoint Services for years prior to that (and SharePoint Team Services before that, which is why the command-line tool, now being deprecated, is still called STSADM).

WSS_Logging   This database is used by Usage and Health analysis to store log data.

WSS_Search_(*servername*) This is the database created by SharePoint to be used by the Search service. The data collected by Search's indexing service is first stored locally on the server that runs the service, but for the long run, that information gets shipped to the Search database. So when someone queries a site, Search looks first in the database for the results, in the change logs for the content databases, and then in the index files stored in the SharePoint root on the server for recent changes.

Although SQL Express doesn't have any robust, built-in backup features, you can use the file system backup utility to back up these databases in case of emergency. This makes it even more important that you know where the database files (and their logs) are located and which ones relate to what part of SharePoint. See Chapter 13, "Maintenance and Monitoring," for more information about disaster recovery. In addition, you can install the SQL Management Studio Express to manually back up and restore the SQL Server Express databases. Chapter 15 also details how to install the SQL Management Studio for SQL Server Express.

Now that we're done looking at the SharePoint root and the SharePoint databases, feel free to close the Explorer windows.

Confirming the Services and Their Accounts

SharePoint requires many of its services to interact directly with services and resources running on the server. This means that these services must have an account identity to make requests. (It also means that those accounts must be able to log in as a service; keep that in mind if your environment uses group policies to disallow such login, because exceptions might have to be made.)

When SharePoint is installed using the Standalone method, all services are configured automatically using local system accounts. This is why everything is up and running as soon as you finish the configuration wizard.

But to make sure of what services were installed, which ones are running, and which accounts they're using, you'll need to take a look at the Services console.

TIPS AND TRICKS FOR THE SERVICES CONSOLE

There are several ways to open the Services console. You can select it in the Server Manager console, under Configuration in the navigation pane; you can click the Services button on the Services tab in the Task Manager (my usual method, because I always have the Task Manager open to track CPU and RAM usage in real time); and, of course, you can go to Start ➤ Administrative Tools ➤ Services or use the search field in the Start menu to find it.

To do that, open the Services console (Start menu ➤ Administrative Tools ➤ Services). The services we are looking for start with either *SQL* or *SharePoint*.

As you scroll down the console (if it is sorted by service name), the first services related to the SharePoint installation that you'll come across should be the six SharePoint services: SharePoint 2010 Administration, Timer, Tracing, User Code Host, VSS Writer services, as well as the SharePoint Foundation Search V4 service. Not all of these services need to be running; some, like the VSS Writer service, stop and start when needed (the Timer service is an exception; it must be Started, meaning running, in order for SharePoint to work). Each one of the services has a short description in the Description field if you'd like to know more about them. Most importantly, the console indicates which services are running and which account they are using as their identity.

As you can see in Figure 2.40, the administration service, which is critical for a server farm, isn't even enabled by default on a single-server install (which can cause issues later when you are trying to do backups to an off-server location). Also note that all of the services are using local service, local system, or network system accounts for their logon identities.

FIGURE 2.40

Windows Share-Point Services in the console

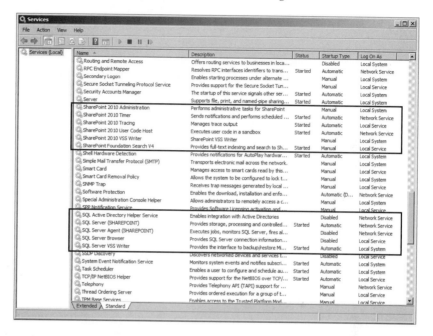

Just below the SharePoint services (you may need to scroll a little), you'll also find the five SQL services listed: SQL Server , SQL Server Agent, SQL Server Browser, and SQL Server VSS Writer. There might also be a SQL Active Directory Helper if your server is member of a Windows domain.

The most significant SQL service is, of course, the SQL Server service, which is started (which means it's running) and is using the local server's Network Services account. As you can see, the other services (variously set to disabled or automatic depending on whether they're needed) also use local service, local system, or network service accounts. There are no nonlocal accounts in sight.

After confirming that the SharePoint and SQL server services are listed, let's move on to the rest of the SharePoint components.

Knowing what services are running that relate to SharePoint, knowing that it's OK if some are not always on, knowing which ones must be running, and knowing what their service accounts are all help you really understand the underpinnings of the product.

Feel free to close out of the Services console.

Confirming IIS Web Sites and Application Pools

When the prerequisites were installed, IIS was enabled, and you checked the console to see what was available by default.

Now that SharePoint has installed, that has changed. If you open the IIS console (not the one for IIS 6.0), open the icon for the server (double-click or click the plus sign), and then open the

Sites icon in connections pane on the left, you'll see that, in addition to Default Web Site (which has been stopped), there are three new Web Sites available (Figure 2.41). Also note that you can tell at a glance what ports each website uses in the workspace (the central area of the console) under Bindings. It's very convenient.

FIGURE 2.41

SharePoint Web Sites in IIS

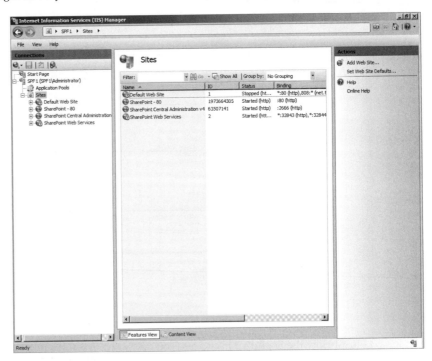

"What Are Those Things Called, Anyway?"

The IIS 7.0 (or 7.5) console has three areas where a lot of obscure things can happen. Gone are the days that that middle area remained static, the contents there always the same depending on what location or object you're looking at. Most of the areas are still called *panes*. The skinny one on the left, which could be called the navigation pane, or navigation tree, is called the *connections* pane now, although the icons you can click there that might have subobjects beneath them are still often referred to as *nodes*. The skinny pane on the far right of the console is called the *actions* pane. The options it displays can vary greatly, depending not just on what is selected in the connections pane but what view you are using in the pane we have not discussed, the one in the middle.

The middle pane seems to be a bit of a conundrum. It displays things based on what was selected in the connections pane. It used to be considered the content pane because it showed you the contents of whatever you had selected. But with IIS 7 and 7.5, it does significant, and somewhat schizophrenic, double duty.

There are two buttons at the bottom of the middle pane: the Features View button and the Contents button. This means that the middle pane's contents, *and* what appears in the actions pane, change significantly depending on which view button you select.

It makes giving instructions a little more complicated because options in the actions pane may not even be available for something unless you are in the correct view in that middle pane. My apologies on that—I didn't invent the new layout; I just have to use it.

Some people just opt for using the names of the other two panes when referring to them, but always calling the middle area the "middle pane." Others refer to it as either the Features pane or the Contents pane, depending on which view is selected. I think giving the same area two different names is confusing. I've considered calling it the "views" pane, since it's defined by the two view buttons, but since we're going to be working with SharePoint, which uses views extensively, I chose not to do that. After extensive searching, I did find a document on TechNet (titled "About the IIS Manager UI (IIS 7)") that formally names that middle pane the workspace of the console. This is why I am called it *workspace* in this chapter, even though few others appear to be doing so. Now you know why.

CHECKING SHAREPOINT-80

The SharePoint-80 site was created by the SharePoint configuration wizard for the Standalone installation. The wizard stopped the default IIS Web Site, created a new IIS Web Site named SharePoint-80, and assigned it port 80 (since the default site was stopped, it wasn't needed anymore). A folder was added to the default website's virtual directory at %inetpub%\wwwroot, called wss, with a folder in it called VirtualDirectories. A folder called 80 was then created within VirtualDirectories, containing files new sites will need. The SharePoint-80 IIS Web Site is set to use NTLM and Windows authentication (not anonymous) and points a bunch of virtual directories toward folders in the SharePoint root. Its home page is the one you've seen already.

To confirm that the address the IIS Web Site uses is 80, make certain the workspace is set to Features View (the button is at the bottom of the pane), and click the SharePoint-80 Web Site icon. In the actions pane on the far right of the console, you can confirm the address under Browse Web Site (Figure 2.42).

To see where the site's virtual directory is located, click Explore in the actions pane (first item), and it will open an Explorer window showing you the files in the 80 folder (Figure 2.43).

FIGURE 2.42
Confirming the
SharePoint-80 port

FIGURE 2.43
Exploring the
SharePoint-80
virtual directory

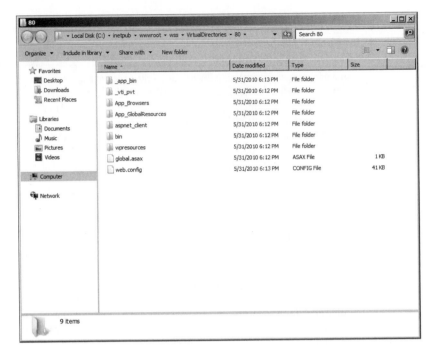

If you click the Content View button in the workspace, it will show you the files and subfolders you know are in the IIS Web Site's virtual directory, but in addition, folders listed there with little redirect arrows (Figure 2.44) are actually virtual directories pointing to corresponding folders in the SharePoint hive.

FIGURE 2.44
The Content view
of SharePoint-80

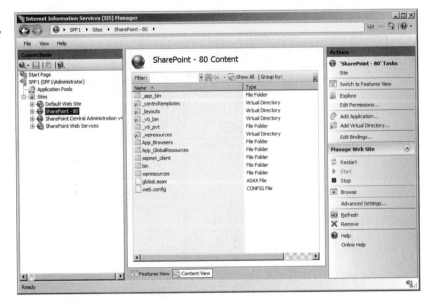

To see what I mean, select the layouts icon in the workspace, and click Explore in the actions pane. It will open a window to show you the files in the layouts folder, under the templates folder in the SharePoint root (as you can see in the window's address bar in Figure 2.45).

FIGURE 2.45
Exploring the layouts virtual directory

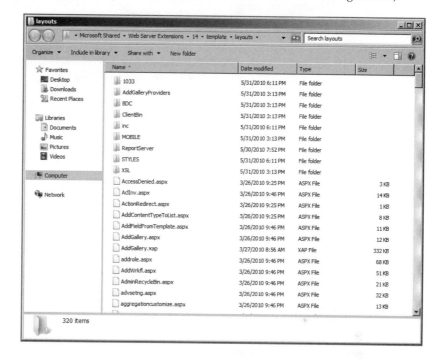

This gives you an idea of why all those folders are there, what they mean, how they relate to the files and file structure SharePoint created on the machine, and why they might be important to protect in case of catastrophe.

"WHY DO SOME OF THE IIS WEB SITE ICONS HAVE QUESTION MARKS?"

It's not because IIS has questions about them or that they are not functioning properly. IIS Web Sites with the question mark on their icon have multiple bindings, meaning they have a number of different protocols, which can be bound to different ports. This is usually the case if the site is used by applications that need to listen and respond to more than just HTTP traffic.

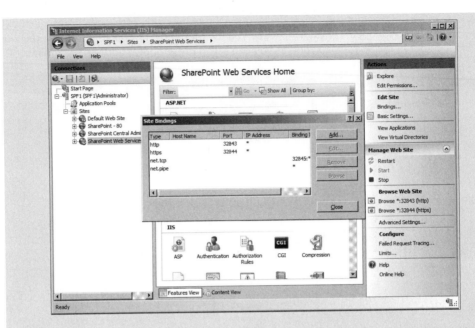

You can also see it listed in the content pane of the IIS console when you select the Sites folder in the navigation pane. The Bindings column shows what ports are bound and listening for each IIS Web Site (you can see it in Figure 2.41 earlier).

CHECKING CENTRAL ADMINISTRATION V4

The Central Administration v4 site uses a separate IIS Web Site than SharePoint-80. Because Central Administration is so important to SharePoint and all of its contents, the configuration wizard set it up to use a completely different port, one generated randomly so that users are unlikely to mistakenly attempt to access it. It shares some of the same virtual directories with other SharePoint IIS Web Sites, but it uses a folder named after whatever its port address is in the wss folder (in my example, it's "2666") and unique files in the virtual directory admin from the ADMIN folder in the SharePoint root, `%Program Files%\Common Files\Microsoft Shared\Web Server Extensions\14\TEMPLATE\ADMIN`. This is one of the reasons why the pages in Central Administration don't conform to the design of normal SharePoint sites.

If you click the Web Site icon for Central Administration v4 and make sure you're in Feature view in the workspace, you can easily see that the port for Central Administration in the actions pane is unique and different from Sharepoint-80 (Figure 2.46). Keep in mind that your port number will be different.

Something else to remember is the link that shows you that the port can literally be used to browse to the site—so if you're in the console and you need to open Central Administration quickly, you can.

FIGURE 2.46
Confirming the
Central Adminis-
tration port

LOOKING JUST A LITTLE FURTHER: IIS WEB SITE AUTHENTICATION

Something we didn't check with SharePoint-80 that bears knowing is the authentication type used for the IIS Web Site. Both SharePoint-80 and Central Administration use the same method, Windows authentication. To confirm, you can click Features View at the bottom of the content pane and then double-click the Authentication icon. It will open a dialog box showing that, out of all the authentication options IIS can support, the types enabled are ASP.NET impersonation (so SharePoint can use the authenticated user's credentials when accessing pages, views, and objects) and Windows authentication.

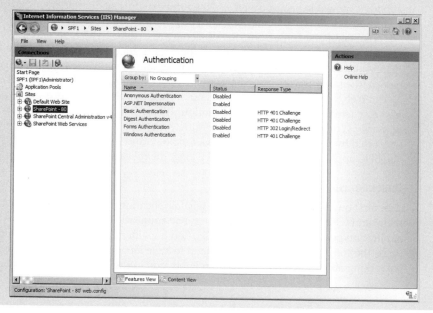

While you are looking at authentication, select Windows Authentication in the content pane, and then click Providers in the action pane. It will show you that, for Windows authentication, IIS can support either NTLM or negotiating Kerberos.

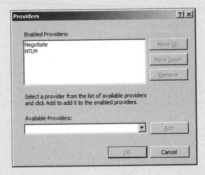

You might be tempted, now that you know this is here, to make changes to the settings that affect SharePoint in IIS. Don't. SharePoint doesn't like it, or more specifically, the configuration database that is shared by the farm and is used by SharePoint to keep track of all its settings won't know you made the change unless you do it through SharePoint's GUI or command-line tools. However, if you made changes to authentication on SharePoint-80 in SharePoint, it would change the settings here.

CHECKING WEB SERVICES

The third IIS Web Site is a new feature of this version of SharePoint, Web Services. It was decided that some of the features used in the paid version of SharePoint (SharePoint Server 2010) should be moved to be more a part of the infrastructure of SharePoint and less a complete (and complicated) add-on. That way, it would be built into SharePoint Foundation, too.

Thus, SharePoint Foundation, the version we're working with here, gets a Web Services IIS Web Site, along with the chance to actually use Business Data Connectivity (BDC) and have a number of features listed in Central Administration that we cannot really use—unless we upgrade to the paid version (then they'll work great, because the underpinnings have been there all along).

The Web Services IIS Web Site does not have any web pages to browse to, per se, and listens on only custom ports, set up by the configuration wizard, to accomplish particular, obscure, primarily Windows Communication Framework tasks. The web services applications that are supported by this IIS Web Site are BDC, topology, and security token management (Figure 2.47). The BDC application is the one with the long, inexplicable GUID as its name.

CHECKING THE APPLICATION POOLS

As a final quick check, we need to see what application pools have been created, who is using them, and what identities they are using. The applications each have to run with their own application pool and therefore an application pool identity. Unfortunately, because they are set up by the configuration wizard, they tend to have long, obscure, GUID-like names. To see what I'm talking about, click the Application Pools icon in the connections pane (Figure 2.48).

As you can see in the workspace, application pools were created for the SharePoint-80 and Central Administration v4 IIS Web Sites (and conveniently named after them). Any application pool with a white circle/black square icon is stopped. In our example, that includes the Web Services site; the applications within it actively need application pools, but the IIS Web Site itself is just a container.

To see what the account identity is for an application pool (I'm going to use SharePoint-80 for this example), just select the application pool in the workspace, and click Advanced Settings in the actions pane.

FIGURE 2.47
Web Services
IIS Web Site and
applications

FIGURE 2.48
SharePoint appli-
cation pools

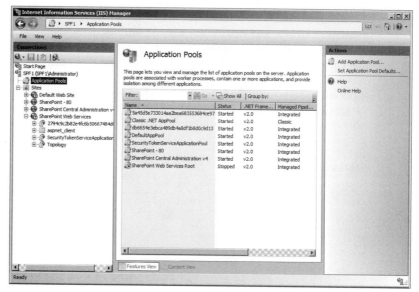

This will open a dialog box listing the advanced settings for the selected application pool (Figure 2.49). In the Process Model section, the Identity field lists the user account the application pool is using for its identity. In this case, because you did a Standalone installation, the SharePoint-80 Web Site is using the Network Services account. So if SharePoint-80 needs to access its content database or do any other function, it does so using the Network Services account.

FIGURE 2.49
Advanced Settings
for application pool
identity

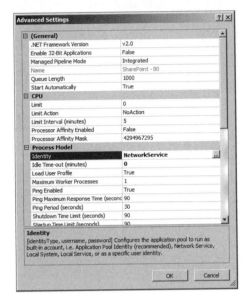

There are several application pools with long GUIDs. Unsurprisingly, they belong to the applications under Web Services. There is an easy way to figure out which application pool goes with which application.

Back in the connections pane, select the application under the Web Services IIS Web Site that you'd like to check, and then click Advanced Settings in the action pane. This will open a dialog box with the application pool listed in the first field. If the name is such a long string of characters that you can't see all of it (and if the first 12 or so don't help), you might need to click the ellipsis button (...) to bring up a small dialog box that more clearly shows the full name. My example is the application that is using the long GUID as a name (which I know is for the BDC), and I did pull up the small dialog box just so you could see the full name of the application pool (Figure 2.50). In the Advanced Settings dialog box, the virtual path matches the GUID name for the BDC application.

How Do You Know That Application Is for the BDC?

You can get an idea as to which web services application is which by viewing its contents in the workspace. In the case of the BDC application, its WCF-related SVC file give it away.

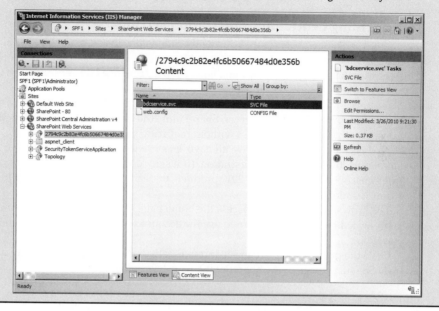

FIGURE 2.50
The application's application pool

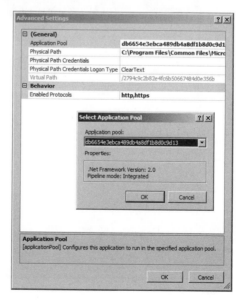

Now that you know what changes have been made in IIS by SharePoint and are able to check all the pertinent information concerning your SharePoint responsibilities there, it's time to finish up confirming the install—by going to the Central Administration website and seeing what settings SharePoint made during the Standalone installation.

Confirming Central Administration Settings

When SharePoint was configured during the Standalone installation, the Central Administration Web Site was created to use a unique port. Having checked it out in IIS, you know what that port is, so you can just open a browser and enter `http://thelocalserversname:uniqueportnumber` (mine would be `http://spf1:2666`).

However, there is an easier way. For your convenience, SharePoint places a shortcut in the Start menu of the SharePoint server, SharePoint 2010 Central Administration, that will open the browser with the correct address without requiring you to memorize it.

And because it's something we all have, let's use that. Go to the Start menu and click SharePoint 2010 Central Administration. (If it's not directly on the Start menu, click All Programs, open the SharePoint 2010 products folder, and click SharePoint 2010 Central Administration there.)

The browser will open and access the home page of the Central Administration site. You may be prompted to log in, so be sure to use the account you were logged in as when you installed SharePoint.

Once the page loads, you can see immediately that the layout is definitely different from the Team Site home page of the SharePoint-80 top-level site (Figure 2.51).

FIGURE 2.51
The Central Administration home page

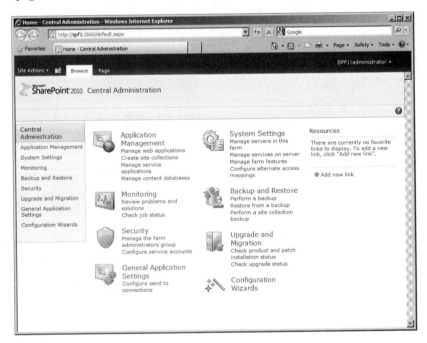

Although some elements are the same—the dark blue/black bar along the top with the ribbon bar buttons, the Site Actions tab, and the Account menu—much of the rest of the page is different from the standard SharePoint site home page. There is the title of the site, of course. Along the left is a navigation bar (essentially a Quick Launch bar for getting to settings) that echoes the same links that are displayed, essentially, in the middle of the page, where the web parts would be. That middle area is taken up with links to settings organized under seven headings (and a link for configuration wizards, of which there are none for the Standalone installation). On the right of that area is a lone web part, Resources, for adding links to useful resources for administrators who use the site.

SHORT-LISTED

The eight headings give you the direct links to the settings page of the configuration tasks most often done. There are more options under those headings than are displayed on the home page. That's probably one reason why the headings are repeated in the navigation bar on the left.

Because there is an entire chapter dedicated to Central Administration later in the book (Chapter 11, "Central Administration"), I'm not going to go through all of the settings available at this point. To confirm what happened during the Standalone installation, you just need to check the services running on this server and see what was enabled and what wasn't. Keep in mind that there are two additional post-installation tasks to complete as well, configuring email and creating user accounts. Those tasks are the same regardless of installation type, so I am going to cover them in detail later in this chapter.

You know that in IIS SharePoint created two IIS Web Sites: SharePoint-80 and Central Administration v4. To confirm that their corresponding web applications are listed in SharePoint, select the heading, Application Management. Then on the Application Management page, click Manage Web Applications.

CONFIRMING WEB APPLICATIONS

As you can see in Figure 2.52, the two web applications that you expected are available. Remember that the Web Services IIS Web Site simply provides services and is not meant to be used by SharePoint to host any pages, so it is not considered a web application.

To get back to the Central Administration home page, just click Central Administration in the navigation bar (usually referred to as the Quick Launch bar) on the left.

CONFIRMING SERVICES

To see what services are running on this server and to check their settings to see how they were set up (should you want to change it), click Manage Services On Server, located under the System Settings heading on the Central Administration home page.

FIGURE 2.52

SharePoint Web
Sites in Central
Administration

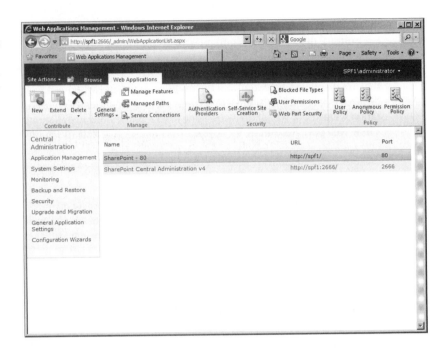

In the Services On Server page, you get the opportunity to see all the services available for configuration on the server. Because SharePoint set them all up for you during the configuration wizard, most of them should be running.

As you can see in Figure 2.53, the services listed are those mentioned in Chapter 1: Business Data Connectivity, Central Administration, Claims to Windows Token Service, Incoming Email,

Subscription Setting Service, Sandboxed Code Service, Web Application, Workflow Timer, and SharePoint Foundation Search. Most of them have been started automatically, configured with a local system account.

FIGURE 2.53
Services On
Server page

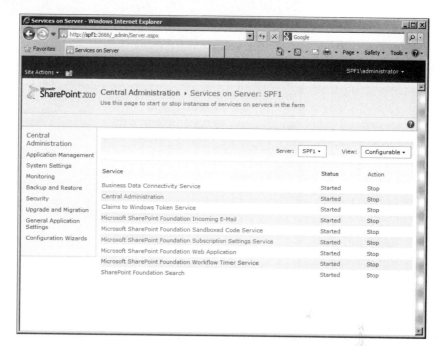

IT SAYS STARTED BUT REALLY IT'S STOPPED...

You might notice on the Services On Server screen that the Incoming Email service appears to have been started, but that is actually a bug introduced in this version of SharePoint—the Incoming Email service has to be configured by an administrator in order to start, and we haven't done that yet. As part of this bug, SharePoint is also unable to know whether the Outgoing Email service is configured. Regardless of this oversight in the interface, both services do work after you configure them to work. See the "Post-installation Configuration Tasks" section of this chapter to see how to set up incoming email to actually work.

Ideally, sometime after this book publishes, Microsoft will make a hotfix or service pack available to fix these issues. Until then, don't be caught off guard by the misinformation in the Services On Server page.

What you may not be able to see in black and white is that all the services except Incoming Email and Workflow Timer display in dark gray. The two exceptions are blue, showing that they are links that can be clicked. This is because those two services have additional settings that can be configured.

If you click Workflow Timer Service in the Services list, it will take you to the Workflow Timer Settings page (Figure 2.54).

FIGURE 2.54
The Workflow
Timer Settings page

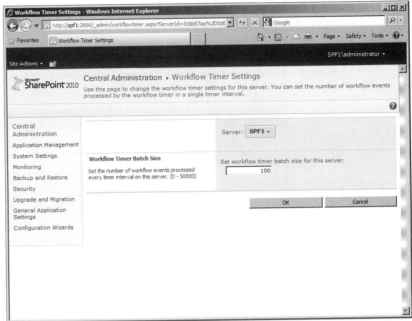

As you can see, the Workflow Timer service manages how many workflows will run per timer job interval. On this page, you can change how many occur per interval. The default is 100, and because you have to assume that SharePoint would know what a good default setting is, you can leave it as is (especially since this example installation won't crush the server with workflow activities any time soon).

TIMER JOB?

The SharePoint server Timer job service (as opposed to the one for workflows) is the most important service on the server because it runs all the jobs that SharePoint needs, from diagnostics, search, and alerts to backups, workflows, usage data, and password management. It is the little service that actually carries most of the load of SharePoint by itself. Its identity is the same as the one used to access SharePoint's configuration database. It is the big reason why that account is considered *the* farm account.

The other service that was configurable in the Services list was SharePoint Foundation Search. To configure it, navigate back to the Services On Server page using the new Navigate Up button as described in the "The Navigate Up Button" sidebar below.

THE NAVIGATE UP BUTTON

Going back to the Services on Server page introduces an interesting part of the new SharePoint page design (which we will explore further in Chapter 4): the Navigate Up button. Gone are the standard breadcrumbs that let you simply click a link and go back to the page you were previously on.

We could use the page title/breadcrumb, but it only goes back to the Central Administration home page, which is one page too far. So, there are just two options: click the back button in the browser itself (which is bad page design), or click the Navigate Up button to the right of the Site Actions tab in the dark band at the top of the page (generally referred to as the *top ribbon bar*). As you can see below, the button drops a navigation tree that will show you every single page you clicked to get to where you are, letting you navigate with precision. Use the Navigate Up button to go back to the Services On Server page.

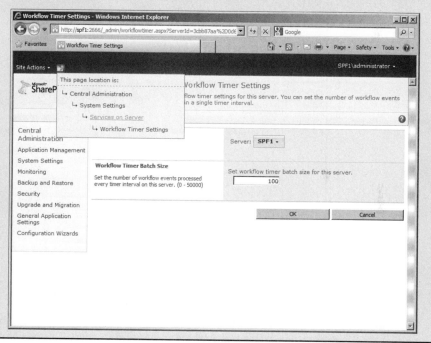

The other service that is running but can be configured from the Services On Server page is SharePoint Foundation Search. To just see what configuration settings are available for the service (and how SharePoint set it up) without affecting its running state, click the title of the service in the Services list.

THE DIFFERENT VIEWS OF THE SERVICES ON SERVER PAGE

While we're here, I want to show you something. On the right side of the Services On Server page is a View menu box. Currently it is showing the Configurable services (which is a misnomer, since a lot of them aren't configurable, at least not here). To see *all* the services, click in the View menu and select All. It will show you additional SharePoint services. Most of which are not configurable.

On the configuration page for SharePoint Foundation Search, there are enough settings that you need to scroll down quite a ways to set them all. You'll be configuring Search in Chapter 3, but I did want to show you how the account identity that Search is using is the one we expected—Local Service. Search does actually use two services to work: Search and Index (otherwise known as Content Access or the crawler). Right now they are the same account, and SharePoint considers that perfectly acceptable (Figure 2.55).

FIGURE 2.55
Search configuration settings, service accounts

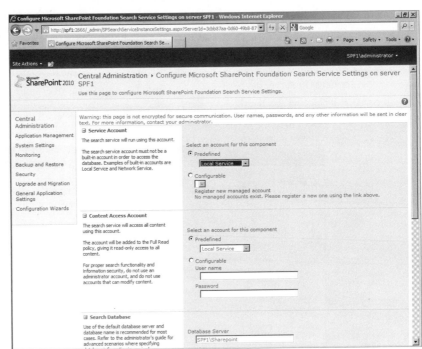

No Managed What?

In Figure 2.55, you can see that SharePoint is using a local service account for Search, but you may have also noticed the warning that there are no managed accounts. This version of SharePoint supports managing its service account passwords (unexpectedly changed or expired passwords were the bane of the previous versions of SharePoint) and encourages—in fact, *requires*—most of its services to use accounts that have been added as managed accounts in SharePoint so it recognizes them. However, if you're using local system, service, or network service accounts, that doesn't apply. So, worry not.

Speaking of warnings, the warning that the data on the page is not encrypted appears because we are not using SSL for the site. In this scenario, we are accessing the site from the *same server* the pages are on, so this is not a problem. If you are worried about security within your private network, you might want to consider getting an SSL certificate for the Central Administration site. For more information about using SSL with SharePoint, see Chapter 16, "Advanced Installation and Configuration."

That's it for simply confirming that everything is OK with the Standalone installation. We've proven that we can access the first SharePoint site at port 80 for the server, the file system is set up, and the databases are in place and accounted for. We checked IIS for the SharePoint applications' corresponding IIS Web Sites, complete with virtual directories (which tie back to the SharePoint root file system) and application pools. Last but not least, we checked out Central Administration itself and saw that it was up and working on the correct port, and we took a peek at the services that are running on the server.

Now it's time to move on to the post-installation configuration tasks.

Post-installation Configuration Tasks

This is the point in the process where a few more things need to be done in order to have their implementations truly up and running. There are many settings that can be configured in SharePoint to suit your environment, but there are a few that commonly need to be set up before you are really ready to go.

When you install SharePoint using the Standalone option, most settings are configured for you, using local accounts. This lets you see what a running and correctly configured SharePoint Foundation server looks like. When you install SharePoint using the Complete option, you will need to configure most of the services yourself (as well as create your first web application and site collection). The Complete installation gives you much more control over how services are configured, but it is more complicated to implement initially.

With either type of installation, there are still several tasks you must perform before your implementation is complete, the primary task being configuring email settings. Even the Standalone installation cannot predict what your email server name might be in your environment, so you will need to set that up yourself.

Once outgoing and incoming email are configured, our final post-installation task will be to set up some user accounts. Right now the only farm administrator for this installation is the one you used to install SharePoint. We need to add more administrators, both at the farm level and at the site collection level, as well as at least one average user to log in with for testing purposes. Then the implementation will be ready for work.

Configuring Outgoing Email

To configure SharePoint to be able to do outgoing email, you need to specify the email server, such as your ISP or Exchange server. SharePoint can't know that on its own—thus it waits, unconfigured, until you get around to it. SharePoint requires outgoing email to be configured so it can send out notifications and alerts.

To configure outgoing email, in Central Administration go to System Settings. On the System Settings page (Figure 2.56), click Configure Outgoing E-mail Settings under E-mail And Text Messages (SMS).

FIGURE 2.56

The System Settings page

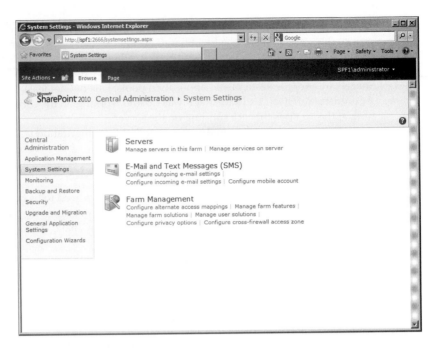

On the Outgoing E-mail Settings page, you'll see that there is, finally, only one section of settings, which contains only a few fields.

1. The first setting is to specify the outgoing SMTP server. This is usually your office email server, configured to already handle outbound and inbound email. Mine is running on my domain controller, DC1, so I am going to enter **dc1.dem0tek.1c1** into that field. You can also just use the server name, instead of the FQDN.

2. The second field, the From address, specifies the address that recipients will see in the From field of the email. It doesn't need to be a real address, just something appropriate. I'm going to keep it simple, though, and use a real address on my email server: **sharepoint@dem0tek.1c1**.

3. The third field, Reply-To Address, needs to contain a real email address that the recipients will be able to send return email to. I am going to use the same real address, **sharepoint@dem0tek.1c1**.

See Figure 2.57 for an example of my settings.

4. The fourth field on this page has to do with the character set used for outgoing email. My server uses the default character set listed, so I did not change it. If you need to, to comply with your environment, do so here.

5. When all your outgoing email settings are correct, click **OK** to finish.

That will take you back to the System Settings page in Central Administration.

FIGURE 2.57
The Outgoing
E-mail Settings
page filled in for
the sample instal-
lation

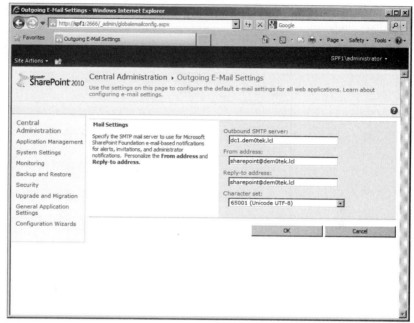

DON'T FORGET TO REANALYZE

The Health Analyzer may consider not having outgoing email configured a problem. So if you wait
a week or longer after installing SharePoint to configure outgoing email, it will generate an error
warning you about it. After you've finished setting up outgoing email, be sure to clear the entry
on the Problems And Solutions page (click Monitoring in the Quick Launch bar, and click Review
Problems And Solutions under Health Analyzer) by opening its details and clicking Reanalyze Now
in the ribbon.

Configuring Incoming Email

SharePoint can receive incoming email for lists enabled to accept it and redirect messages to
those lists so they can add them as list items. This requires the SharePoint server and, more particularly, the SharePoint Timer service to know where to get the incoming email addressed to its
lists, what the email alias for the server is going to be, and whether the SMTP service is allowed
to accept email from any servers or only servers considered safe, to avoid spam.

1. To configure those settings, since we're on the System Settings page in Central
   Administration already, just click the **Configure Incoming E-Mail Settings** link under
   E-Mail And Text Messages (SMS).

   Once on the incoming email's configuration page (Figure 2.58), you'll notice there are
   only four sections: Enabling Incoming E-Mail, Directory Management Service, Incoming
   E-Mail Server Display Address, and Safe E-Mail Servers.

FIGURE 2.58
Incoming E-Mail
Settings page

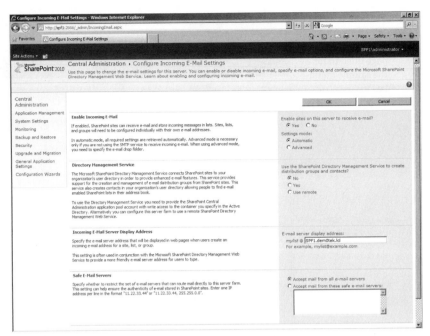

THE DIRECTORY MANAGEMENT SERVICE

Something to mention before we begin is Directory Management Service (DMS). This service allows SharePoint to integrate with Exchange (primarily 2003, but 2007/2010 works with addition configuration) through Active Directory in order to be able to add SharePoint's incoming email enabled objects to the Exchange global address list (GAL). An organizational unit (OU) must be dedicated to the service, and permissions must be applied correctly. It is a pretty complex setup to add some addresses to the GAL. You are not going to be configuring DMS at this time, because it isn't necessarily a required feature for most networks.

2. To configure incoming email, you first need to enable it. In the Enable Incoming E-Mail section, click **Yes** for **Enable Sites On This Server To Receive E-mail**.

   In the same section, you can choose either to allow the locally installed SMTP service to handle incoming email or, if you haven't installed SMTP, to specify a drop folder used by some other SMTP server to leave mail.

3. You already have SMTP installed on the server, specifically so that you could use its services, so leave **Automatic** selected.

4. For **Directory Management Services**, leave the default selection of **No**. You will not be configuring that setting at this time, but you can always go back and change it later if everything else on the network is configured correctly for its use.

The Incoming E-mail Server Display Address setting is a clever use of SMTP and DNS. Because the domain's DNS server already has a record for this server's FQDN, any internal email server is going to query local DNS. Since the SharePoint server is listed in DNS by its FQDN, the internal email server will check the email addressed for the server, recognize its address in DNS, and give it to SMTP on the server (make sure the internal email server is set up to be allowed to relay to the SharePoint server; SMTP already defaults to accepting all email), which will put it in a folder that the SharePoint timer job knows to check for email. This address won't work for users outside the internal network, but internally it works very conveniently, with no additional setup.

You can set up a more friendly email address later if you'd like, by configuring a new zone in DNS, adding an MX record that points to the SharePoint server, and then configuring the local SMTP service to recognize the domain.

5. But for now, let's leave the default display address.

The last section, Safe E-mail Servers, is where you specify the servers allowed to send email directly to the SharePoint server or to accept mail from all E-mail servers. If you choose Accept Mail From These Safe Email Servers, you then specify safe server IP addresses. Any email the SMTP server gets from an IP address that doesn't match the safe list is discarded.

6. In my environment, there is only one email server, and no one from outside the internal network can send email to the server, so I'm going to keep this section blank for now. You can check Figure 2.58 for the settings I used.

To recap:

◆ We enabled incoming email.

◆ For Settings mode, we left the default Automatic.

◆ We did not enable DMS.

◆ We left the display address as the FQDN for the server for now.

◆ We left the Safe E-Mail Server field blank for now.

7. If all the settings are correct, click **OK**.

"IS THIS THING ON?"

Sometimes the SMTP service in the IIS 6.0 console might not be running by default. Make certain you check. In the IIS 6.0 console, open the local server node, and right-click the [SMTP Server #1] icon. If it is not running, click Start in the pop-up menu or in the console toolbar. You can also check in the Services console to confirm that startup type is set to Automatic for the Simple Mail Transfer Protocol service. If it is Manual, then every time the server reboots, you'll have to manually start the SMTP service.

Very quickly (since there were no additional services or resources to set up), you'll be brought back to the System Settings page. This setting is what makes it possible, while configuring different lists and libraries, to give them email aliases to receive email. As a matter of fact, if you're ever in the settings of a list or library that should be able to receive incoming email but it can't, chances are good someone forgot to enable it in Central Administration.

 Real World Scenario

SPECIFYING A DIFFERENT DOMAIN ALIAS FOR INCOMING EMAIL

If you want your incoming email address default to be something that external clients might be able to use, then using the FQDN of the SharePoint server for the email alias is probably a bad idea.

There are four parts to specifying a different domain alias for incoming email: the SMTP service on the SharePoint server, the DNS on your network, your office email server, and the incoming email address on the SharePoint server to the new domain alias. (This does not include the steps for enabling external mail to get to your internal mail server, just how to get that email to the SharePoint server once it's on the network.)

To start, you need to decide what you want the address to be; for my example, I am going to use dem0tek.com.

Then follow these steps:

1. Go to the IIS 6.0 management console by choosing Start ➢ Administrator Tools ➢ Internet Information Services (IIS) 6.0 Manager. Remember that it is the 6.0 version of the IIS console that contains the SMTP settings.

2. Verify that you can see the nodes under your local computer in the navigation pane of the console; if you can't, click the plus sign next to the local computer icon.

3. Click the plus sign next to Default SMTP Virtual Server node (it should be started, if not, start it). Select Domains. The local server will be listed as a default domain.

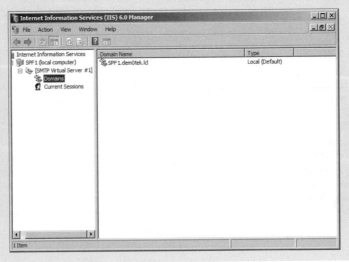

4. If you want the SMTP service to recognize and accept email from a different domain besides the default local server name, right-click Domains in the navigation pane or details pane. In the pop-up menu, select New. From that menu, select Domain. That will trigger the New SMTP Domain Wizard.

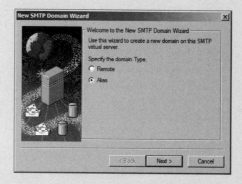

5. Because you are creating a new alias for the SMTP server to accept, make sure Alias is selected, and click Next.

6. On the next screen, enter the domain alias you want the SMTP service to accept. My example uses dem0tek.com.

7. When you are done entering your domain alias, click Finish. You should now see your new domain alias in the IIS console

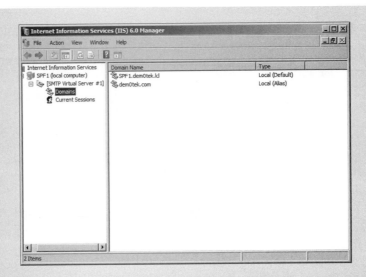

Next, you need to let DNS know what the new domain alias is by creating a new Forward Lookup zone if one doesn't already exist. Then you need to create records there to point at the SharePoint server. Assuming you don't have them yet, follow these steps:

1. On the server hosting DNS (usually the first domain controller on the network), open the DNS Management console by choosing Start ➤ Administrative Tools ➤ DNS.

2. Right-click the Forward Lookup Zones node in the navigation pane, and select New Zone.

3. In the New Zone Wizard Welcome screen, click Next. Choose Primary Zone for the zone type, and click Next.

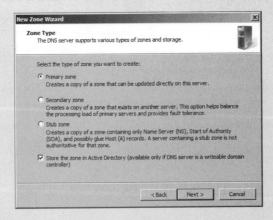

4. On the next screen in the wizard, you can choose how the new zone information will replicate to other servers in the domain. My example uses the default. Click Next.

5. In the Zone Name field, enter your domain alias. My example uses dem0tek.com. Click Next.

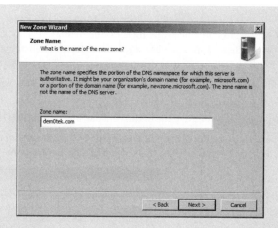

6. In the Dynamic Update screen, choose the update process that best suits your network. My example uses the default. Click Next.

7. The Completing The New Zone Wizard screen will display the new zone name, the lookup type (forward), and the fact that it's an Active Directory–Integrated Primary zone. Click Finish to complete the process.

You should now have a new zone listed under Forward Lookup Zones in the DNS console. My example is dem0tek.com.

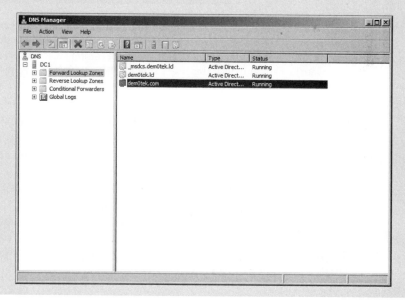

In the zone, you should to create a host record to let DNS know that there is a machine with the name of your SharePoint server using the domain alias. It is not strictly necessary; you can simply add the MX without it, but it is considered bad form. Then using that A record, you can create an MX record to let DNS know that the new host is a mail server. To do that, follow these steps:

1. To add a host record for the SharePoint server to the new zone, double-click the new zone to open it.

2. Right-click in the detail pane of the console, and select New Host (A) from the pop-up menu.

3. In the dialog box, enter the machine name of the SharePoint server in the Name field. In the IP Address field, type the IP address of your SharePoint server.

What about the two check boxes at the bottom of the dialog box? I do have a reverse lookup zone, and email servers often use reverse lookup to confirm legitimate server addresses, so I am going to put a check mark in the Create Associate Pointer record. However, in this example, I don't want just any authenticated user to update the record, so I am going to leave that option deselected. To add the host record to your new zone, click Add Host.

(If your environment requires it, you can add a cname or alias record to map the new domain name to the SharePoint server instead of a host record. That means the MX record will have to refer to the server in its native, internal domain.)

4. A pop-up will tell you the host was added successfully. Close that pop-up, and click Done to close the New Host dialog box.

5. You now need to create an MX record for the SharePoint server. Right-click in the details pane, and select New Mail Exchanger (MX) from the pop-up menu.

6. In the FQDN field, enter the name of the host record you just created. My example is spf1. dem0tek.com. You can set the mail priority if you'd like. My example uses the default of 10. When you're done, click OK. Your DNS server now knows what to do with requests for email addressed to your new domain alias.

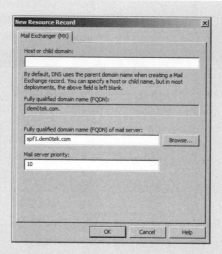

Now you need to make sure that your email server can forward email to your SharePoint server. For Exchange, you need to create an SMTP connector that points to the new MX record in your new DNS zone. For most email server products (the one I am using included), you need to enable relay on the SMTP service for that server. Generally, that means you would go to the email product's console and specify your relay settings.

Usually you can either specify the address of the SharePoint server and select Only The List Below or leave the list blank and select All Except The List Below. With this second option, it will exclude whatever you specify in the list (if it's blank, that means it excludes no addresses). In my example, I specified that only the IP addresses listed were acceptable relays (I included the server itself, because the product had itself in there, and the IP range of only servers inside the office).

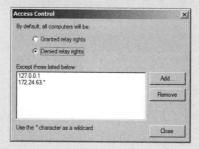

Finally, you need to go back to the SharePoint server and make the incoming email address for the server match your new domain alias. Follow these steps:

1. In SharePoint Central Administration, go to the Operations page, and click the Configure Incoming E-Mail Settings link.

2. On the Configure Incoming E-Mail Settings page, scroll down to the Incoming E-Mail Server Display Address section, and change the address in the field to your new domain alias. My example uses dem0tek.com.

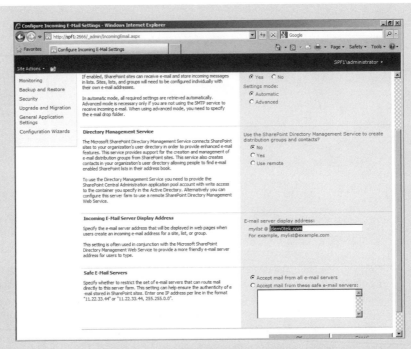

3. After you change the incoming email alias and click OK, it will take you to the Operations page of Central Administration.

The new domain name for the incoming email address will now show up when configuring incoming email for a list (for this example I am enabling the Announcements list with an alias to email to).

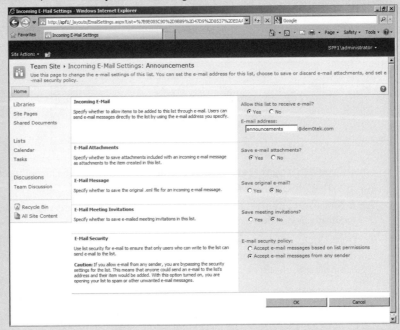

Later, when you enable incoming email on libraries or lists (something we do in Chapter 6, "Introduction to Lists") and a user in the office sends email to that list, the email will go to the drop folder on the SharePoint server.

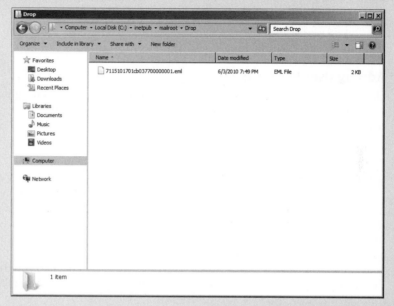

Then it will be picked up by the SharePoint Timer service (which usually checks about every 30 seconds), parsed, and placed in the correct list (I emailed an off-site party notice to the list).

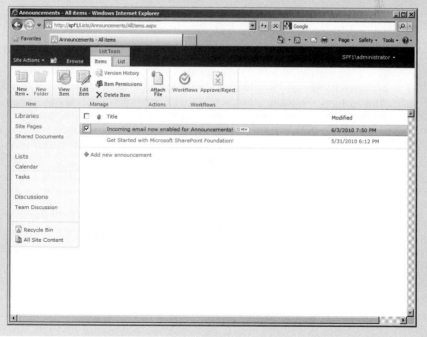

Now you can configure your libraries and certain lists to receive incoming email for an address other than the server's internal network FQDN. Not all lists can do email; they don't have fields that map to a simple email header. However, a developer could create some custom email event handlers if you wanted.

Adding User Accounts

SharePoint is almost ready to go, except that no one else but you can log in. It's time to add some users. Specifically, we need to create accounts for farm administrators, site collection administrators, and end users.

Farm Administrators

Right now, we have only one account we log into Central Administration with, and that's the account we used to install SharePoint, otherwise known as the setup or installation account. In a server farm situation, that account generally should be used only to install SharePoint and, as such, should be retired as our Central Administration account of choice. In a single-server implementation, that account is often simply a server administrator account. Regardless, it probably shouldn't be the only account available for administering SharePoint.

For an account to be able to access Central Administration and do all the administrative tasks there, it must be a member of the Farm Administrators group (even in a Standalone installation) for that implementation.

1. There are several ways to add more user accounts to the Farm Administrators group, but the easiest is to go to the Central Administration home page, and under the Security heading click **Manage The Farm Administrator's Group**.

ADDING SECURITY GROUPS INSTEAD OF USER ACCOUNTS

If you are adding more than a few users, you might want to consider adding an Active Directory security group instead of a single user account to the Farm Administrators group. It not only can be done, it's encouraged because SharePoint can only handle so many security principals, and a single user account and a single security group are considered a single principal, even if the group can contain many user accounts. Then you can add and remove user accounts to the security group in AD and it automatically changes their access to SharePoint without additional effort.

It will immediately take you to the People And Groups – Farm Administrators group page.

As you can see in Figure 2.59, there are two items listed: the `Builtin\Administrators` group and the setup account (in my case, that's the local server's Administrator account, `spf1\administrator`).

FIGURE 2.59

The People And Groups – Farm Administrators page

As I mentioned earlier, the local Administrators group is a member by default, just in case. However, that isn't always a good idea, and often people remove such a general group (since it includes all domain admins, and it is possible that you might not want all of them to be able to have full control of SharePoint).

The setup account should not be used to log in regularly. So, here's how to add more.

Keep in mind that the account should have administrative rights to the server (generally as a domain admin so the person can go from server to server in the farm if need be). That way, they can log in locally if necessary, run the SharePoint configuration wizard, `psconfig` (the command-line tool for configuring SharePoint, instead of using the wizard), STSADM, and PowerShell (although PowerShell requires a little more configuring).

2. On the Peoples And Groups – Farm Administrators page, there are three options above the list of user accounts: New, Actions, and Settings. To begin the process of adding a new user, click **New**.

That will bring up a Grant Permissions box, where you will enter the name or names of users or AD security groups that you'd like to grant permission to become members of the Farm Administrators group.

3. In the Users/Groups field, enter the name of the account you want to add to the Farm Administrators group (Figure 2.60). In my case, I'm going to use my SharePoint utility account, `dem0tek\shareadmin`.

To resolve the name to the display name in Active Directory (to be sure you used the correct account name), you can click the Check Names button (looks like a torso with a check mark next to it) below the box you entered the account name into. This is what I did in Figure 2.60. You can also use the address book icon (called the People Picker) next to Check Names to browse through users in Active Directory to find a group or username. By the way, I always click the Check Names button to make sure SharePoint can resolve the username with AD.

FIGURE 2.60

The Grant Permissions box

4. If you've entered a user account, click **OK** to add the user to the Farm Administrators group.

The account is now a member of this Farm Administrators group list.

If you'd like, you can log out as the setup account and log in as the account you just added, by clicking the Account menu in the top-right corner of the page (it lists the account name that you're logged in with currently) and selecting Sign In As Different User.

Log in with the newly added account. It should put you back on the People And Groups page you were on before; only the Account menu will now show the new account name rather than the account you used to install SharePoint (Figure 2.61).

FIGURE 2.61

Logged into Central Administration with the new Farm Administrators account

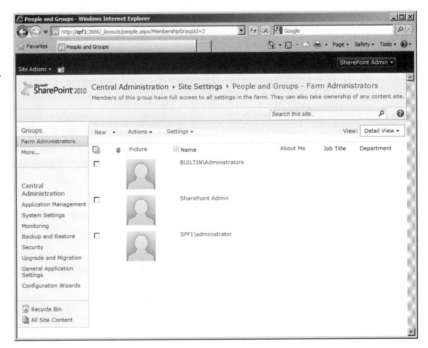

Now you know how to add a user (or security group if you desire) to Central Administration's Farm Administrators group.

POWERSHELL AND STANDALONE INSTALLATIONS

PowerShell is a new command environment for managing SharePoint. In order to use PowerShell, you must be logged in with an account that can use PowerShell. Once logged in with a PowerShell admin account, you can run the Add-SPShellAdmin command and use it to create more PowerShell admins.

Now often this causes a bit of a conundrum, because to give an account PowerShell admin rights, you have to be logged in with an account that already has PowerShell admin rights.

However, for Standalone installations it's easy. Because the databases are on the same server as SharePoint, and because the account you used to install SharePoint owns those databases, it's easy to use that account to either do your PowerShell tasks, or at least use it, once SharePoint is completely configured, to create other PowerShell admins.

If you are interested in practicing with PowerShell, a Standalone installation is the easiest to get started in terms of permissions. For more about PowerShell, see Chapter 14, "STSADM and Powershell."

SITE COLLECTION ADMINISTRATORS

Now that you know how to add farm administrators to manage Central Administration, it's time to go one level down and see how to add administrators to site collections.

In both of the SharePoint installation types, among the elements created, whether manually in a Complete installation or by the configuration wizard in a Standalone installation, were a web application (remember SharePoint-80 in IIS?) and within it a site collection for you to get started with. The first site created in a site collection is, by default, the top-level site. There can be other sites that stem off that one, but there always has to be one top site. The top-level site contains all the settings for the site collection.

To administer that site collection, create lists, add users, and change settings, there must be site collection administrators. A site collection administrator will have power over not only the top-level site of a site collection but all subsites contained therein. Permissions and settings trickle down by default from the top-level site to all subsites (although subsites can be configured to break inheritance), and that means site collection administrator control trickles too.

As with Central Administration, in the Standalone install, SharePoint, by default, used the only account it knew—the account that installed it, to be the site collection administrator. Either way, our site collection has one administrator. In case of emergency, there should be at least two.

To add a site collection administrator to a site collection after the collection has been created, open the browser (preferably Internet Explorer of course), use the server address (mine is http:// spf1), and log into the site as a site collection administrator (my account is spf1\administrator).

1. Once logged in and on the home page of the top-level site, click the Site Actions tab (top left), and select Site Settings from the bottom of the drop-down menu (Figure 2.62).(You

could also go to Site Permissions on the menu, then select Site Collection Administrators in the ribbon bar; it is another way to get to the same Site Collection Administrators box.)

FIGURE 2.62
Site Actions menu, site collection home page

FROM CENTRAL ADMINISTRATION

For you diehard administrators out there, you can also edit the site collection administrators from Central Administration, under Application Management ➢ Site Collections ➢ Change Site Collection Administrators.

The Site Settings page is a pretty powerful place to be for a site administrator. You can configure the look and feel of the site, users and permissions, and site administration as well as site collection administration overall (Figure 2.63).

2. To add an administrator to the site collection, under the Users And Permissions heading, select **Site Collection Administrators**.

It will open a simple Site Collection Administrators page, with only one setting, a field in which to add more accounts.

FIGURE 2.63
The Site
Settings page

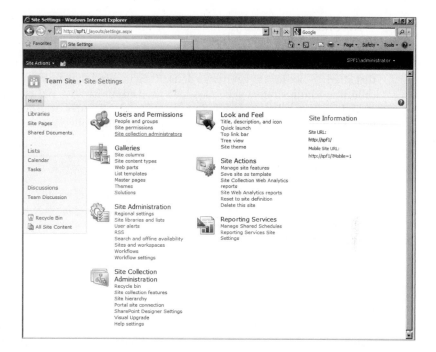

3. The syntax is standard, consisting of account names separated by semicolons. The account that was added during the installation is there (and works because we're logged in with it). To add another account, just click in the name field after the semicolon and add one. In my example, I will add my SharePoint utility account and click the Check Names button, at the bottom right of the field, to make sure the name resolves (Figure 2.64).

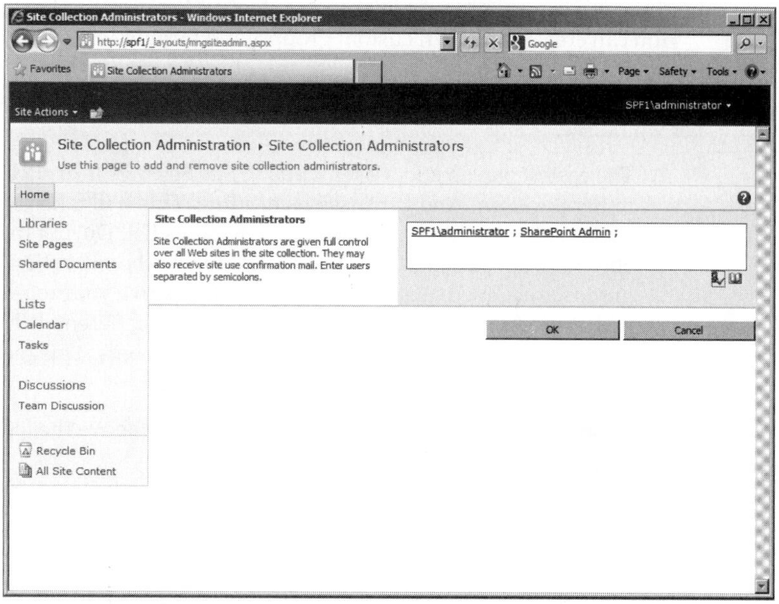

FIGURE 2.64
The Site
Collection Admin-
istrators page

4. Once you've added your accounts (site administrators can be added only one by one; no AD groups for them), click **OK** to finish.

That will bring you back to the Site Settings page. Now if you needed, you could log in as that alternate account to get things done. Keep in mind that, unlike a farm administrator, site collection administrators generally don't need administrative rights to the server.

To learn more about managing sites, see Chapter 9, "Sites, Subsites, and Workspaces." To learn more about site collections, see Chapter 10, "Site Collections and Web Applications."

ONE FOR ALL AND ALL FOR ONE

Keep in mind that SharePoint can handle only so many discrete objects, so adding a few large security groups containing many users is better than each user added individually. This especially works for site collection users (but not site collection administrators). However, it's not uncommon to see administrators added individually because their tasks are usually specific, high priority, and high skill.

ADDING USERS

And finally, a quick look at adding users. Chapter 12, "Users and Permissions," is dedicated to users and permissions. But just to get you started, here are the basic steps.

There are three premade user groups for a SharePoint site: Owners, Members, and Visitors. Owners have full control, members have contribute permissions, and visitors have read permissions. SharePoint has many individual permissions (such as read, write, view, edit), which are usually combined into *permission levels*, generally based on the tasks a group of users might need to perform. Full control permission level gives the members all the permissions available, the contribute level gives them the permissions a contributor would have, and finally, visitors have only the permissions for reading content and navigating the site, but no contributions.

You can create your own custom groups (and permission levels), but for now, these will do.

Currently the site has only two accounts able to access it, and only at an administrative level. What you need is at least one user account you can log in with to see what the average site member would see.

1. The easiest way to add a user while in Site Settings is to click People And Groups, under the Users And Permissions heading. This will take you to the People And Groups page, set by default to open into the Members list. During the Standalone installation, SharePoint used the name "Team Site" during the site collection creation process, so my groups are named Team Site *something*. If you give your top-level site a different title while creating the site collection, yours will be different. What really matters, though, is not the site name but the fact that they are members. This means they are site contributors, which are average users.

2. To add a user to the Members group, click New above the (currently empty) list area (Figure 2.65).

FIGURE 2.65
People And Groups, Members page

This will open the Grant Permissions box (Figure 2.66). It is here that you specify the user account (or accounts) or AD security group you'd like to add to the Members group for this site collection. I am going to add a user named Saffron. She is something of a power user, and she needs at least Members permissions on this site.

FIGURE 2.66
The Grant Permissions box for user accounts

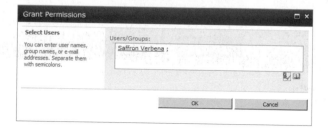

3. Type the username you want to add in the box (feel free to verify it with the Check Names button or browse the People Picker address book for a name if necessary).

4. Click **OK** to finish adding the new user.

Your user will be added to the Peoples And Groups list, in the Members group (Figure 2.67).

FIGURE 2.67
The new user
added to the
Members group

And, to see what a user sees when they are on the home page (see Figure 2.68), go to the home page, and log in as that user. (On the Account menu, where your account name is at the top right, select Sign In As Different User.)

FIGURE 2.68
Home page, logged
in with new user
account

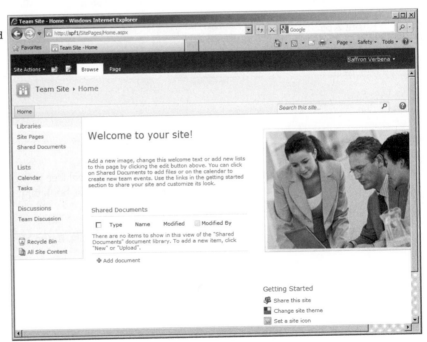

> ### GETTING TO THE HOME PAGE
>
> You can use the Navigate Up button to get back to the home page, or you can click the name of the site in the title area of the page to get back to the home page. The title can work like a breadcrumb, and you can use it (if it's being displayed) to get back to the home page from practically anywhere on the site. You could also click the link to Home just below the Site Actions tab. This user's home page looks the same, but the Site Actions drop-down menu has only about five thing on it.

Congratulations. You did the Standalone installation, and you have a full-featured SharePoint installation. You understand what it took to get here, from the file system changes to IIS to SQL Express. You know what services are running, and even what account identities they are using, and you know where to check to make sure everything is OK. You've used Central Administration, accessed the default SharePoint site, configured outgoing and incoming email, and added user accounts where you need them. Now you are ready to begin the task of mastering SharePoint (or learning about doing a Complete installation). Well done.

The Bottom Line

Prepare for the installation of SharePoint.   SharePoint has certain software and hardware requirements before it can be installed. In addition, some of those requirements vary depending on the type of installation you choose. It is good to know what to install, how to install them, and in what order to be prepared for installing SharePoint.

> **Master It**   SharePoint has a number of prerequisites that must be installed before it is installed. Do they each need to be downloaded and installed separately?

Install SharePoint using the Standalone installation option.   Several types of SharePoint installations are available: Standalone, which is a single-server installation that installs without intervention with all default settings and uses a SQL Server Express database; Server Farm Standalone, which is essentially the Standalone installation but with an additional configuration option before installation begins; and Server Farm Complete installation, which allows you to manage all configuration options and specify the SQL server that will manage the databases. Each installation type has its strengths and weaknesses, and it's good to know about them before you begin.

> **Master It**   Can you install and use SharePoint if you don't have a SQL server on your network?

Determine what gets created when SharePoint installs.   From Standalone to Complete, it is good to know every step of the way the repercussions of each installation, configuration, and service that SharePoint adds and/or enables.

> **Master It**   What is one way to confirm that the SharePoint services are running properly on the server?

Perform the initial configuration tasks after a SharePoint install (and understand why you perform them).   After installation, SharePoint can require additional configuration before you can call it your own. It is good to know what the necessary settings are to quickly get SharePoint up and running to the point where an administrator can start working on it.

Master It   Does incoming email require Directory Management Service to function?

Chapter 3

Complete Installation

This is the second of two chapters concerning the installation of SharePoint Foundation. The previous chapter covered the Standalone installation of SharePoint, from the prerequisites to post-installation tasks. That type of installation, sometimes considered "one-click," configures most of the services required by SharePoint to use local system, service, or network service accounts, and it installs SQL 2008 Express to manage its databases. The Standalone installation was meant to be truly a one-server product, with everything on that server.

In this chapter, you are going to do another SharePoint installation, but this time you'll configure SharePoint to put its databases in an existing installation of SQL (either on a different server or on the same server). SQL Server, unlike SQL Express, can be remotely accessed, and therefore its databases can be accessed from other servers. This will allow SharePoint to share its configuration settings with other SharePoint front-end servers in a server farm topology. Because of that, there will be a few additional steps to prepare for before installation should begin.

Because SharePoint will have services that require access to other servers on the network, authentication and permissions become an issue. This is why using Active Directory with SharePoint is so useful, with all the servers on the same domain (or in a trusted domain), allowing them to share domain user accounts.

In this chapter, you will learn to

- ◆ Prepare for a Complete installation
- ◆ Install SharePoint using the Complete installation option
- ◆ Determine what service accounts SharePoint requires and how to set them up
- ◆ Manually configure necessary SharePoint services

Preparing for a SharePoint Complete Installation

SharePoint, as much as it might try, cannot be installed without some prerequisites already on the server and configured first. In addition, the Complete installation requires a little more preparation before installation than the Standalone version.

The previous chapter went into considerable detail concerning installing the prerequisites. I will cover them here as well, in case you need it, but for more step-by-step detail, feel free to check out the beginning of the previous chapter. (I am assuming, because a Complete installation is more advanced than a Standalone, that those of you doing it might need less explanation. If that is not the case, in Chapter 2, "Standalone Installation," you'll find detailed coverage of behind-the-scenes confirmation of every change during the prerequisite installation and, for the most part, configuration process, complete with information about the IIS consoles, sidebars about customizing incoming email, and more.)

Preparing User Accounts for a Complete, Server Farm Installation

SharePoint needs a few accounts to use as the identity of several of its services, as well as a specially configured installation (or setup) account. In addition, I tend to create a SharePoint administrative utility account, one I use to do general administrative work in SharePoint. It helps to have these accounts prepared before SharePoint is installed.

The Setup Account

The setup account that is used to run the SharePoint installation and configuration is critically important, particularly for a Complete installation. This is because it will need to create SharePoint's configuration database, assign the farm account the right to own that configuration database, and give the farm account the right to create more databases and give other accounts access to them.

The setup account also will be used to run the SharePoint preparation tool and the installation and configuration wizard, as well as to create the SharePoint root file structure. This will give the farm account the necessary permissions to folders and the subsequent right to assign access to other accounts as needed.

The setup account must have the right to log on locally to the server where SharePoint will be installed and have permission to install software and start/stop services locally (particularly when working with IIS). In a domain setting, this account is usually at least a domain admin (or a member of the Administrators group on each server where the installation will be run). The setup account must have SQL login, securityadmin, and dbcreator fixed roles on the SQL server in order to be able to create the necessary databases in SQL, assign roles to other accounts in SQL, and give them ownership to the correct databases.

Real World Scenario

Setup Account, Meet Server Farm

As you know, the account you use to install SharePoint in a server farm configuration must be able to install software and start services on each of the servers in the farm. You could use an account that has been added as a local administrator to each server, or you can make the setup account a member of the Domain Admins group for the Active Directory domain. In addition, in a server farm configuration, the setup account must also be assigned special roles on the SQL server. If you are not responsible for these tasks, you can simply ask the appropriate Active Directory administrator to create an account that is in the Domain Admins group and then ask the SQL DBA to add that account to the Logins, DBCreator, and SecurityAdmin roles.

However, if you need to do it, here's how.

To add a user to Active Directory and add them to the Domain Admins group, follow these steps:

1. Open the Active Directory Users And Computers console by choosing Start ➢ Administrative Tools ➢ Active Directory Users And Computers.

2. Click the Users node, and then click the Add Users button (it looks like a head with a sparkle on the back of it).

3. In the New Object – User dialog box, enter something appropriate into the User Logon Name field, and fill in either or all of the First, Last, Initial, or Full Name fields. Keep in mind that what appears in the Full Name field is what will be displayed in the Active Directory Users And Computers console. If you only add a logon name, the Next button will remain grayed out. I entered **setup** for First Name, **account** for Last Name, and **setupacct** for User Logon Name. This means that the account, setupacct, will often display as the setup account.

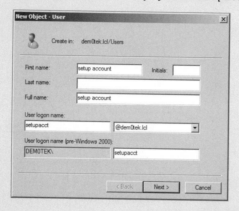

4. Click Next, and enter a password. I suggest you uncheck User Must Change Password At Next Logon. Depending on your environment's password policy, you might want to select the Password Never Expires and User Cannot Change Password check boxes. That way, if the account is compromised, it makes it harder for the attacker to change the password to one you don't know.

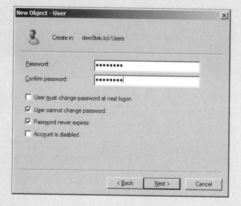

5. Click Next when you have finished setting up the password. Confirm that the name, logon name, and password settings are correct, and click Finish. The account you created will be highlighted in the console.

6. To add the new setup account to the Domain Admins group, right-click the username, and select Add To A Group from the pop-up menu.

7. In the Select Group dialog box, verify you are selecting from the correct location (it should be your domain).

8. In the Enter The Object Names To Select field, enter **domain admins**, and click the Check Names button. If the name resolves, its formal display name should appear. In this case, **domain admins** should become title-capitalized and underlined, which means that Check Names found it. Click OK.

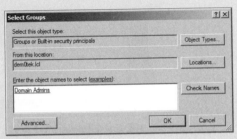

9. A dialog box should notify you that the Add To Group operation was successful. Click OK.

To add the setup account to the correct roles in Microsoft SQL Server, follow these steps. (In my case, the version is SQL Server 2008 SP1 CU2, but the same applies to 2008 R2, as well as SQL 2005 SP3, CU2, although the interface is a bit different.)

1. On the server running SQL, open the SQL Server Management Studio console by choosing Start ➢ All Programs ➢ Microsoft SQL Server 2008 (or whatever your version is) ➢ SQL Server Management Studio.

2. Make sure you are connecting to the correct server (and server instance if necessary) and server type (in this case, database engine), with the correct authentication, username, and password. Click Connect (my example server is RR1, and I am using the default account for Windows authentication). See the following graphic for more information.

Keep in mind that you need to add the setup account to the SQL Server Logins role, so it can be added to the SecurityAdmins and DBCreator roles.

3. To do this, open the Security node in the Object Explorer pane.

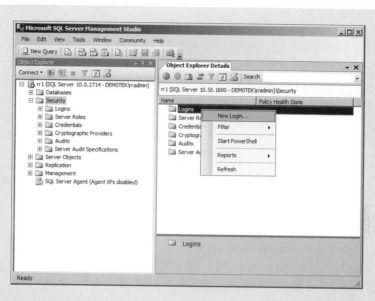

4. Right-click the Logins node or right-click Logins on the Summary page in the detail pane. In the pop-up menu, select New Login.

5. In the New Login window that appears, enter the name of your setup account in the *domain* *username* format in Login Name field (my domain is demotek, and my setup account is setupacct).

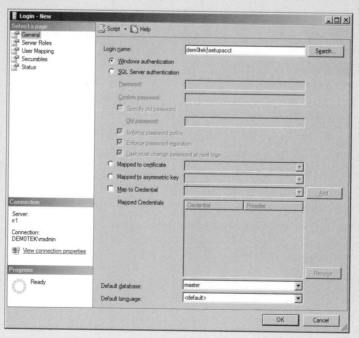

6. While you're creating the setup account as a login role, you can add it to the necessary server roles. To do this, select Server Roles on the Select A Page pane on the left side of the New Logins window.

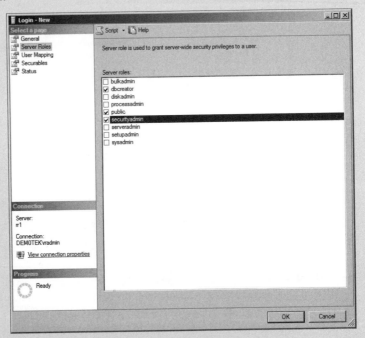

7. Check DBCreator and SecurityAdmin in the Server Roles list (Public is selected by default for a login role for SQL 2008), and click OK. That should take you back to the SQL Server Management Studio console. Your setup account should be a Logins account, and the setup account should be added to the SQL Logins, DBCreator, and SecurityAdmin roles.

Although the remote connections setting is usually enabled by default with SQL 2008 and higher, to verify that your SQL server is prepared for remote access from the SharePoint server, right-click the server instance in the Object Explorer pane, and go to Properties in the pop-up menu.

In the dialog box, select Connections from the Select A Page column. On the right, make certain the Allow Remote Connections To This Server box is checked. Click Cancel to close the dialog box if it is already checked; if not, select it, and click OK.

You can also confirm if TCP/IP is enabled for remote access specifically by opening the Configuration Manager (Start ➤ All Programs ➤ Microsoft SQL Server 2008 ➤ Configuration Tools ➤ SQL Server Configuration Manager).

In the console, select SQL Server Network Configuration ➤ Protocols for *InstanceName* (mine is the default MSSQLSERVER). It will display the available protocols. Make certain TCP/IP is enabled.

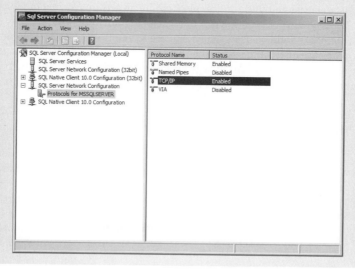

If you are using SQL 2005, you will need to enable remote access manually (it is not automatically enabled, as it is for SQL 2008). So if a server farm install keeps failing no matter how perfect your settings, you will need to do the following:

1. Use the SQL Server Surface Area Configuration Tool. You can select it by choosing Start ➤ All Programs ➤ Microsoft SQL Server 2005 ➤ Configuration Tool ➤ SQL Server Surface Area Configuration.

2. In the SQL Server 2005 Surface Area Configuration window, in the Configure Surface Area For Localhost section, select Surface Area Configuration For Services And Connections.

3. In the window that opens, in the list of services and connections on the left, make certain you are using the correct server instance (mine is the default MSSQLSERVER instance), and then select Remote Connections. In the configuration area on the right of this selection, you'll specify whether SQL Server 2005 will allow remote connections, which SharePoint needs. Choose Local and Remote connections, and then select Using TCP/IP and Named Pipes (because locally that is what SQL uses). This will make SQL available to SharePoint.

4. When you've made your selections, click OK. Close the SQL Server 2005 Surface Area Configuration window.

SERVICE ACCOUNTS

As you know, additional accounts should be specified during the configuration of SharePoint in a server farm scenario. In a single-server environment, the local service and network service accounts will work fine as the account identities for all SharePoint's services. Domain accounts come into play only when the SharePoint services may need to access resources (such as databases on a remote SQL server) that are not on the local server.

For a server farm installation, in addition to the setup account, the server farm (or just "farm account)," Search, Index (content access), and Content Database (web application, database access, or just database account) services also require an account context in which to run.

The following is a rundown of the service accounts we need, plus my example of the domain user accounts I will be using. None of these accounts is more than simple domain users (so if you are using the instructions from the "Setup Account, Meet Server Farm" sidebar, do not add these accounts to the Domain Admins group). They do not need administrative rights to anything. Any permissions to SharePoint folders or databases will be assigned by the farm account as needed.

SICK OF EXPIRING PASSWORDS?

One of the problems with having numerous domain accounts used as identities for all of these services is managing password changes for the accounts. This is one of the reasons some businesses limit the number of service accounts used with SharePoint. Previously, if an account was used by an application pool or service and that account's password changed, there was no automatic way for SharePoint to know, and because it didn't know, it would use the wrong password when prompted (behind the scenes). This means the password for the service accounts had to be manually updated for any service account used by SharePoint. This has changed with SharePoint Foundation.

SharePoint Foundation now supports managing accounts. Not only can it sense and adapt to any change in the passwords of its managed accounts, but it can be configured to generate a random, strong password for its accounts itself—either on a schedule you set or a certain number of days before the domain's password expiration policy deadline. It can also just send you an email warning of an impending change, as well as a warning if it does not succeed with a password change.

Keep this in mind when creating your service accounts. It is usually standard procedure to create the domain user accounts with the password policy set to never expire, and the user can't change their password. Now, depending on the domain's password policies, that is a less important issue. In the case of accounts you plan to have SharePoint manage, it is a good idea to set passwords so that the user isn't obligated to change them upon login, but that the password *does* expire and the user *can* change them. Most of the accounts that SharePoint will use to manage services or access databases will be required to be registered as managed accounts before they can be used.

Farm Account   This account is the one used by all SharePoint servers in the farm to access the farm's configuration database and run SharePoint-specific services; it is added as an owner of the configuration database during installation. It will create all the other databases used by SharePoint, add the necessary accounts to SQL and give them the correct database access, as well as add accounts to the appropriate SharePoint related groups on the SharePoint servers. It also is the SharePoint Timer service account (as well as the Workflow Timer) and the application pool identity for Central Administration. The simple domain user account I created for this purpose is *spffarm*. This account is added during installation as a managed account, but by default, SharePoint does not do anything with its password. This account is also the only one that, by default, is able to use PowerShell to manage everything when SharePoint is installed in a farm configuration. For more about PowerShell, see Chapter 14, "STSADM and PowerShell."

Search Account   This account is one of the owners of the Search database, and it answers Search queries. My account for this one is *spfsearch*. This account is required to be registered as a managed account.

Index Account   This account is one of the owners of the Search database and is otherwise known as a content access account, crawler, gatherer, or indexer. It crawls and indexes SharePoint content. It must have read access to all Search-enabled content databases. I'll be using *spfindex* for this account. Interestingly, it doesn't need to be set up as a managed account before it is used.

Content Database Account   This account owns and accesses the content database of a web application, such as the first SharePoint site. For this account, I'll be using *spfcontent*. This account is required to be a managed account. In some environments, you might want to consider using a different content database account for each of your web applications, especially since accounts can be managed by SharePoint. In this book, additional web applications will be created, and will be using their own content database accounts. For more about that, see Chapter 10, "Site Collections and Web Applications."

"I WANNA HOLD YOUR HAND..."

Please take note of the account names I am using for these services, because you will see them throughout the entire book. The Complete installation built in this chapter will be used in hands-on examples for the rest of this book. If you substitute your own account names here, be sure to use those same account names when you see my corresponding names in later chapters.

BDC Account   This account is the one used by SharePoint to pass data back and forth between a user (accessing an external list or external lookup field), SharePoint, and an external data source (often a non-SharePoint SQL database) using the Business Data Connectivity service. BDC supports claims-based authentication, and it can use its own credentials or pass through the user's credentials to access external data (however, that requires the user to have the right to directly access the external database). Often the BDC uses the farm account as its identity, but it is not a bad idea to create a unique account for this service. Keep in mind that this service is optional, if you don't plan to use it, you don't need to configure it. For this account, I am using *spfbdc*. This is another account that must be managed.

Sandboxed Code Service Account   This service is used by SharePoint to manage solutions that are deployed in a "sandboxed" fashion, not to the whole farm but to a single site collection with restrictions on the resources it can use. These sandboxed solutions (sometimes known as *user solutions*) don't require farm administration permissions but can be uploaded to a site collection and activated by a site collection administrator (or site owner). However, activation won't work unless the Sandboxed Code service is started. When it starts, it will use the farm account by default, despite the fact that it will trigger errors and is not recommended. It is suggested you use a different domain account for the service instead. This service is optional and doesn't need to be enabled if you are not going to deploy sandboxed solutions. For this account, I am using *spfusrcode*. This is another account that must be managed.

Remember that defining these accounts is necessary only if SQL and SharePoint are going to run on different servers. However, it is considered good practice to use separate accounts if you are going to have other servers running SharePoint on the farm to support user requests.

IF YOU'RE CONSIDERING POWERSHELL

If you are going to use an account to do work in PowerShell, it will need to be a shell admin, which means they will have the dbowner fixed role in SQL for each database on the farm you will use the account to manage, and be a member of the WSS_Admin_WPG group on the SharePoint servers. Consider creating a domain security group for this process, to avoid having to configure individual accounts. See Chapter 14 for details.

When SharePoint initially installs, someone needs to configure it. Therefore, when Central Administration (the first SharePoint site made so that you can further configure and manage SharePoint) is created, the setup account and (just in case) the built-in Administrators group are added as farm administrators by default. Farm administrators are users added to the Central Administration site for the purpose of administering SharePoint. (They are called farm administrators even if SharePoint is installed on only one server.) You can add additional users to Central Administration to be authorized as farm administrators (or remove them) as needed.

When you create other site collections, they do not have these accounts available for login by default, so you must specify the primary and secondary administrators for the site before the site is created. At that point, to get into the site, you must log in with one of those accounts (the primary is obviously required, and the secondary generally isn't).

Real World Scenario

A SHAREPOINT ADMINISTRATION UTILITY ACCOUNT

Many administrators may use their own accounts to manage SharePoint, but I prefer to keep my SharePoint administrative account separate from my personal domain account. Because of this, I have a Domain Admins account called *shareadmin* (its display name is SharePoint Admin, as you'll see throughout the book) that I use specifically to manage and administer the server the SharePoint run on, as well as SharePoint itself.

The account doesn't need to be a Domain Admin, as long as it is a local administrator for each of the SharePoint servers. Essentially, the account must have the right to install software, run tools, and manage server roles (such as IIS) and services locally on all SharePoint servers on the domain.

In addition, to administer SharePoint, I add the account to Central Administration as a farm administrator. This makes it possible for the account to be authorized to manage SharePoint, create and configure new web applications and site collections, do backups, and more. This account, with those rights and permissions, can use the SharePoint command-line tool, STSADM, to manage SharePoint from the command line. It also can install and administer SharePoint-specific features and solutions, web parts, and other utilities.

To be capable of using PowerShell to administer the entire farm, I also add it as a shell admin, specifying that it have rights to all databases. This makes it possible to do all the cmdlets to administer the farm. See Chapter 14 for details about configuring accounts to be PowerShell shell admins.

Finally, there are times, when creating new site collections, testing new templates, or taking over a site collection, that I might use that utility account as a primary or secondary site collection administrator. This makes it possible for me to log into the site collection, configure it, and test it before replacing the account with the rightful owner's account when all work is complete.

Overall, my SharePoint admin account is used for all of my SharePoint needs. It allows me to go from the desktop of the server running SharePoint to the command line to use STSADM (or PowerShell) to configure and manage SharePoint to the SharePoint administrative interface, all without having to change logins.

This account may not fit all network security models, but I have found it useful enough to mention.

Complete Installation of SharePoint Foundation 2010

The installation of the Complete installation's prerequisites and SharePoint itself is the same as it is for the Standalone type. For details concerning the exact steps of the SharePoint prerequisite process, see Chapter 2. However, here's a quick recap:

◆ To have every SharePoint prerequisite on hand, be sure to have Internet access. The prerequisite installation process of the SharePoint Foundation installation does access the Internet for most of its bits.

◆ Download the SharePoint Foundation installer, `SharePointFoundation.exe`, from the Microsoft Download Center.

◆ Log into the server where you install SharePoint, as the setup account (in my case dem0tek\setupacct).

◆ Double-click SharePointFoundation.exe, and on its installation screen (Figure 3.1), select Install Software Prerequisites to run the preparation tool. Use that preparation tool to install, enable, and configure the SharePoint prerequisites (take notice of what prerequisites were installed from there as well).

FIGURE 3.1
The SharePoint
Foundation 2010
installation screen

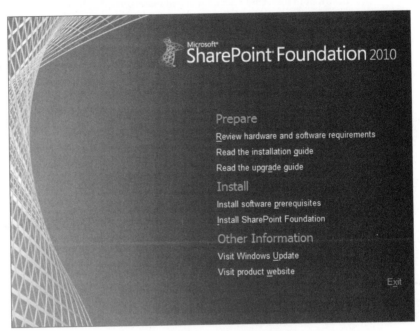

◆ Because the preparation tool installs some hotfixes, the server may reboot when installation finishes. Be prepared for that.

◆ Log back in as the setup account. Prerequisite installation will complete.

SOMETHING ELSE TO CONSIDER

For the sake of convenience, on the SharePoint server, I have also disabled User Access Control (UAC) and Enhanced Security Configuration (ESC) for administrators on Internet Explorer. UAC can block even domain admins from being able to do standard administrative tasks in SharePoint (such as create new web applications). However, if your environment requires these features to be enabled, you may be prompted more often to log in locally to SharePoint sites, and you may occasionally see options in Central Administration grayed out or missing when they otherwise wouldn't be.

◆ Check to be sure the preparation tool worked as it should, enabling IIS and installing software, updates, add-ins, and so on (check in Programs And Features in the Control Panel).

◆ Add the SMTP server feature (open the Server Manager Console, choose Add Feature, select SMTP Server, let it add the required role services, and go through the wizard). Make sure that the Internet Information Services (IIS) manager console and IIS Manager 6.0 console are available and that the 6.0 console has SMTP running (if it doesn't, start it; you can set SMTP in the Services console from manual start to automatic so if the server reboots, you don't have to manually restart it).

◆ Consider checking for updates in case any of the prerequisites are due. Also check the Event Viewer for any hidden or unexpected issues.

The following prerequisites are installed for SharePoint:

◆ Application Server role, Web Server (IIS) role

◆ Microsoft SQL Server 2008 Native Client

◆ Hotfix for Microsoft Windows (KB976462 for Server 2008 R2 or KB976394 for Server 2008)

◆ Windows Identity Foundation (KB974405)

◆ Microsoft Sync Framework Runtime v1.0 (x64)

◆ Microsoft Chart Controls for Microsoft .NET Framework 3.5

◆ Microsoft Filter Pack 2.0

◆ Microsoft SQL Server 2008 Analysis Services ADOMD.NET

◆ Microsoft Server Speech Platform Runtime (x64)

◆ Microsoft Server Speech Recognition Language – TELE(en-US)

◆ SQL 2008 R2 Reporting Services SharePoint 2010 Add-in

WHILE YOU'RE AT IT, SQL NEEDS LOVE, TOO

While you're preparing for the SharePoint installation, you might want to consider any prerequisites that the SQL database may need to complete before you use it for your SharePoint database.

The TechNet article "Hardware and Software Requirements (SharePoint Foundation 2010)" is the link to the Service Packs and cumulative update (CU) packages needed by SQL to support the 2010 versions of SharePoint. (Go to TechNet, http://technet.microsoft.com, and search for the article title.)

◆ SQL Server 2005 Service Pack 3 needs CU 3, KB967909.

◆ SQL Server 2008 with Service Pack 1 needs CU 2, KB970315.

◆ As of the writing of this book, SQL Server 2008 R2 doesn't not require any updates, but that could change, so check the TechNet article for more information.

> Many CUs require that you actually *request* them (and the CUs we need are no exception). The request will require an active email account, where you will receive an email with a link to the CU download and a time-limited password to use to extract the CU so you can use it (yes, it's just a password-protected zip). The CU password lasts only seven days, so don't request it until you know you'll use it within that time.
>
> Keep in mind also, when you are extracting the files, that depending on your server's security, it may not let you put the files on the root of the drive, even though that may be the default location for the file when it extracts. Since it's a one-time-use file, put it where your account can reach it, such as the desktop, download folder, or a share.

Because this installation type will be using an existing installation of SQL, be sure that your SQL server is up-to-date with its service packs, cumulative updates, and other assorted patches. You, of course, need to know what the SQL server name is (and the instance that SharePoint will be using, if your server has more than the default). You don't need to precreate the configuration database, although the configuration wizard might give you that impression. It will create a configuration database for you, using the information you provide during the configuration process.

Finally, keep in mind what the farm account's username and password are, because they are required to configure SharePoint.

> **NAME THAT DATABASE...**
>
> If your DBA requires you to let them build the databases and has created the configuration database for you, then you need to know the name of that database before you can install SharePoint. Remember that the setup account must have the correct permissions in SQL for this to work, because it will be need to be able to assign the farm account to the configuration database and get things rolling. For more information about using precreated databases for SharePoint, see the TechNet article "Deploy by using DBA-created databases (SharePoint Foundation 2010)." It implies that everything must be done using PowerShell, but that is not always the case.

Running the Installation Wizard

Once these preparations are complete, it's time to actually do a SharePoint Complete installation.

1. Run the SharePoint installer (double-click the `SharePointFoundation.exe` file that you downloaded and originally used to run the preparation tool). That will bring you to the SharePoint Foundation 2010 installation screen.

2. On the installation screen, click the Install SharePoint Foundation link.

3. There might be a pause while the installer prepares files, and then the EULA page will come up. To install, you must accept the terms of the agreement, of course; then click Continue.

   That will bring up the critical page that defines the installation type (Figure 3.2). On this page are two buttons, Standalone and Server Farm. Choose the installation you want.

4. For our Complete installation, you first have to click the Server Farm button.

WARNING

When you have a choice of two buttons, one is always the default. For this reason, do not hit Enter on the keyboard at this point, unless you want to simply start the Standalone installation, because its button is the default.

FIGURE 3.2

The Choose the Installation You Want page

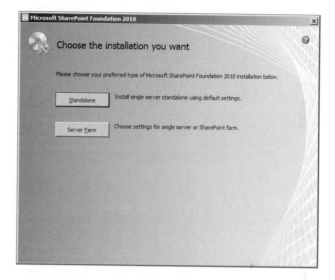

Once you've selected Server Farm, a new page will come up with some tabs and two radio buttons (Figure 3.3), one for Stand-alone and one for Complete. Toward the top of the page are two tabs, Server Type and Data Location. The radio buttons are on the Server Type tab.

FIGURE 3.3

Server Farm installation options

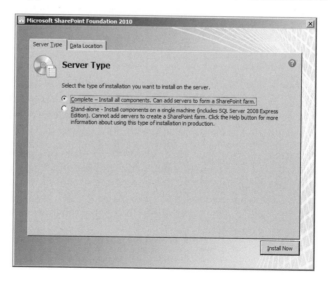

DEJA VU? STANDALONE VS. STAND-ALONE

You might be wondering why there is a Stand-alone option here as well as Complete. Installing SharePoint here with the Stand-alone option is no different from doing a Standalone installation, *except* for the Data Location tab. That tab lets you choose where the index files will be stored (they can take up a lot of space, so it's not a bad idea to put them on a different drive than the OS and SharePoint itself). That's the only difference between the Standalone installation type and the Stand-alone installation option under the Server Farm button.

So if you want to install SharePoint as a standalone server but want the option to put the index files somewhere other than the SharePoint root, here is where you do that installation.

The Data Location tab is only for specifying the location of the index files for either type of install, Complete or Stand-alone. To change their location (such as a different drive on the server), click the Data Location tab (Figure 3.4).

FIGURE 3.4
The Data
Location tab

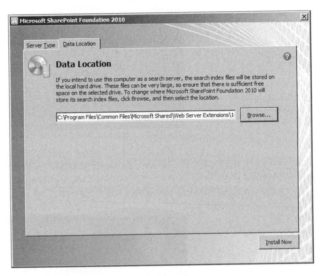

You can see that there is one field and one option available to specify the data location of the index files. You could choose not to enable Search for this server (although I can't imagine why), making this option moot. But since that's unlikely, it's nice to have this option.

In this case, I am going to keep the default data location, but I am going to take a moment to find out where that default location is, which just so happens to be the SharePoint root at %Program Files%\Common Files\Microsoft Shared\Web Server Extensions\14\ Data. That makes sense, since the root will have all the correct permissions and be easy to back up. The downside to this is that the index files will be on the same drive as the operating system, so if it fills up, there will be problems running the server at all. Keep that in mind if you are expecting a lot of data to index, putting the index files on a different drive may be a life-saver.

Now that you've taken a glance at the Data Location tab and confirmed where the index files will go, let's move on with the installation. Go back to the Server Type tab and make absolutely certain that you've selected the Complete option. Keep in mind that, for some reason, Stand-alone is selected by default.

5. While you're on the Server tab and you've confirmed that Complete is selected, click Install Now.

The Installation In Progress page will open with a progress bar. It might take a while, but when it finishes installing files, the Run Configuration Wizard page will open (Figure 3.5). Make certain the Run The SharePoint Products And Technologies Wizard Now box is selected.

FIGURE 3.5

The Run Configuration Wizard page

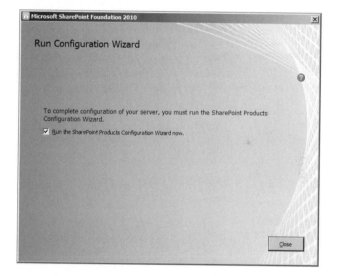

A Quick Check of Installation Changes

During the Standalone installation, we checked to see what happened during the install. So, as a quick recap, before moving on to configuring SharePoint, here's a reminder of what happened.

The SharePoint services were created but not started (partially because you haven't assigned any service accounts for them), as you can see in Task Manager in Figure 3.6. (In the figure below, notice that the accounts of these services are not listed in the Group column. In the Services console, they're temporarily assigned Local System, but we have to change that before they are started.)

In IIS nothing has changed yet (which is standard; IIS doesn't get populated until the configuration phase), and no security groups have been created, but the SharePoint root has been created and at least partially populated (Figure 3.7).

FIGURE 3.6

The newly installed services viewed in Task Manager

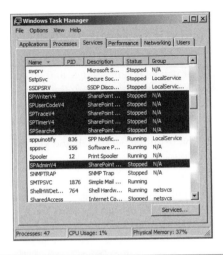

FIGURE 3.7

The SharePoint root file structure during installation

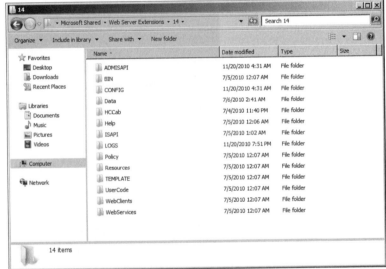

SERVICE CONNECTION POINT ERROR

You might notice, after you finish the installation and configuration, that there is a SharePoint error in the application log of Event Viewer about a service connection point. This is caused by a new (and, in my opinion, not quite ready for prime time) feature of SharePoint that allows Active Directory to keep track of SharePoint installations. It requires that you configure Active Directory, using ADSI Edit (available under Administrative Tools on the Domain Controller), to create a container called Microsoft SharePoint Products, give authenticated users Create serviceConnectionPoint Object permissions to it, and ensure, generally using Group Policy, that the servers have a registry key for HKEY_LOCAL_MACHINE\SOFTWARE\Policies\Microsoft\SharePoint, with a string value for ContainerDistinguishedName that exactly matches the distinguished name of the Microsoft SharePoint Products container.

Once you do that and that group policy applies to all servers on the domain, whenever SharePoint (2010 or higher) is installed on one of those servers, it generates a connection point object in the container in Active Directory. It also helps if you do not configure SharePoint using PowerShell but, instead, the standard GUI interface or `psconfig` command. For more details on how to set it up, look for the TechNet article "Track or Block SharePoint Foundation 2010 Installations."

If you don't need to use Active Directory to track your SharePoint installations, you can safely ignore the error.

Running the Configuration Wizard

Now that you have an idea where you are in terms of changes, let's start configuration.

1. Back on the Run The Configuration Wizard page in the installation wizard, click Close to get started (I know it seems odd to click Close to start a wizard, but that's how it's done).

   If you accidentally or intentionally remove the check from the Run The Configuration Wizard page (so that the installation wizard closes and doesn't continue with configuration), you can just go to Start ➢ All Programs ➢ Microsoft SharePoint 2010 Products and click SharePoint 2010 Products Configuration Wizard.

   The first page of the configuration wizard, the Welcome To SharePoint Products page (Figure 3.8), indicates that in order to configure SharePoint, you must know the SQL server's name, the name of the configuration database (if it has been premade for you), and the account name and password of the farm account.

2. If you have the SQL server and farm account information handy (and if you don't, go get it), click Next.

3. A dialog box warns you that SharePoint services will be stopped or reset during the configuration process. That should be fine, since those services aren't being used by anything yet, so click Yes.

FIGURE 3.8
The Welcome To SharePoint Products page

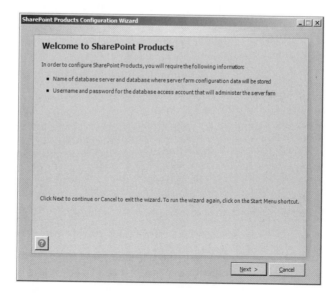

The next page that opens is Connect To A Server Farm (Figure 3.9). This page is one to keep in mind if in the future you will be adding another server to the farm. It offers you two options; you can choose Connect To An Existing Server Farm if this installation is not the first and you want to add this server to an existing SharePoint implementation's configuration database. Otherwise, you can select Create A New Server Farm if this is the first installation of SharePoint and a new configuration database has to be created.

FIGURE 3.9

The Connect To A Server Farm page

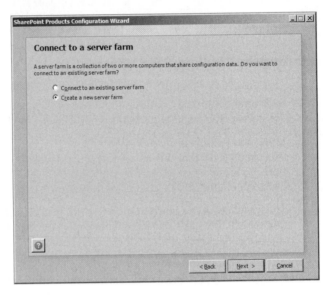

4. In our case, this is the first Complete installation, so we have to create the new configuration database. Therefore, select Create A New Server Farm, and click Next.

5. You'll see the Specify Configuration Database Settings page. Because you chose to create a new farm, this page is where you specify the farm's configuration database information. As you can see in Figure 3.10, you need to enter the SQL Server's name (it prefers the NETBIOS name for the server, actually) and configuration database. The server name for the SQL 2008 server on my network is RR1, so that's what I am using.

6. There will be a suggested default name for the configuration database (unsurprisingly, SharePoint_Config). You can change it if you'd like, but for this example, I'm going to keep it for clarity's sake.

   In addition to specifying the SQL server name and database, this page is also where you specify the farm account that will ultimately own that database and run SharePoint. For my example, I am going to use the farm account I created earlier. The syntax for the username is *domain\username*. So, in my case, that would be dem0tek\spffarm (since dem0tek is the domain name I'm using for this book).

7. Enter the farm account's username and password before continuing.

8. Be sure to check all the information on this page carefully; then click Next to continue.

   The next step in the configuration wizard is new to this version of SharePoint, the Specify Farm Security Settings page (Figure 3.11). The passphrase you enter here (you can change it later if necessary) is used during the configuration wizard when you add new servers to the farm. SharePoint wants you to use a phrase instead of a single password because it should be more secure. However, it just really needs to be complex and at least eight characters.

9. Enter a passphrase at this time. I'm going to use *MasteringSPF2010* as mine. Then click Next to continue.

FIGURE 3.10
Specifying configuration database settings

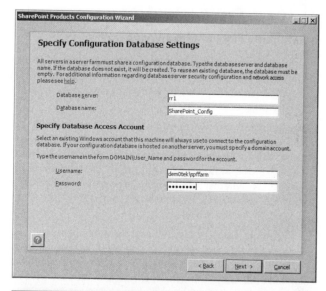

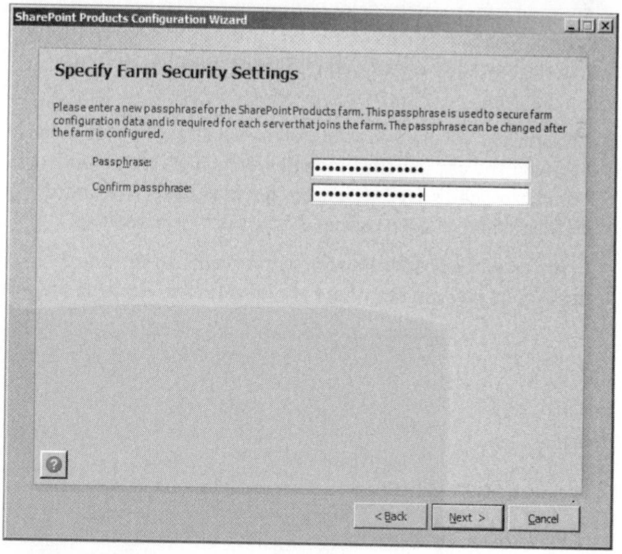

FIGURE 3.11
Specifying a passphrase in farm security settings

The Configure SharePoint Central Administration Web Application page of the configuration wizard is where you can configure both the port and the authentication type that will be used to access Central Administration. You can either allow SharePoint to assign a random port number for Central Administration's web application or specify your own (the Standalone installation just assigned a port for you). SharePoint generates the port number from a range between 1024 and 65535. Often ports below 1023 are being used by the server (or you can't be sure which are available), so the higher the port number, the more likely it's not being used.

 Real World Scenario

VERIFYING PORT NUMBER USAGE

Let's say you have an appropriate port number that might be easier to remember than the random one SharePoint chooses for you. Before you assign an alternate port number for your new Central Administration site, you may want to be absolutely certain that your server is not using that port for anything.

The quick and easy way to confirm that is to use an old but still useful tool—PortQuery. An older version, portqry.exe, used to be available on the Windows Server CD in the Support folder's support.cab file. However, if you have Internet access, just download the newer version, portqryv2.exe, which is available from Microsoft. This command-line tool is used to query the ports of a server to see whether a port is being filtered (by a firewall usually), has a service listening to it (and therefore not available for assignment to anything else), or has nothing listening to it (and therefore is available for you to use).

PortQueryv2 is a tool primarily meant to troubleshoot services such as Active Directory and Exchange. However, in this case we can use it to see if the port we want to use for Central Administration is being used by some other service. To do this, go to the folder in Windows Explorer where you've installed portqryv2 (it usually extracts to the local drive's portqryv2 folder), Shift+right-click in an empty space in the folder window, and select Open Command Window Here from the pop-up menu. This will open a command prompt already in that directory—no navigating needed. Then run the portqry command with the following switches:

```
portqry -n IPaddressofserver -p both -e yourport
```

This means we are running the portqryv2 executable, with the -n, or name, switch (this is not optional and can use the machine name, FQDN, or IP address; otherwise, it defaults to 127.0.0.1), -p, or protocol, switch (I like to check for both TCP and UDP just in case), and the -e, or endpoint, switch, which is used to specify the port I'm checking.

In my case, the IP address of my SharePoint server is 172.24.63.4, and the port I am going to check is 9876. As you can see, there are no services listening on port 9876 using TCP or UDP.

```
Administrator: C:\Windows\system32\cmd.exe

C:\PortQryV2>portqry -n 172.24.63.4 -p both -e 9876
Querying target system called:

 172.24.63.4

Attempting to resolve IP address to a name...

IP address resolved to spf2.dem@tek.lcl
querying...
TCP port 9876 (unknown service): NOT LISTENING
UDP port 9876 (unknown service): NOT LISTENING
C:\PortQryV2>
```

Port Queryv2 is an invaluable troubleshooting tool and definitely should be a standard in your server toolkit.

If you use PortQueryv2 frequently or you have to teach junior administrators how to use it a little too often, you might want to consider the graphical user interface add-on called the PortQueryUI tool. It is simple to install. Download the `PortQryUI.exe` installer, and double-click it. It will install the necessary files to a folder called PortQryUI on the local drive. Then simply navigate to the PortQryUI folder using Windows Explorer or the command prompt, and run the `PortQueryUI.exe` executable. The interface is easy to use, and it has convenient predefined queries for common services and a means to specify your ports manually. For easy access, you can create a shortcut to it on the Desktop, which is what I do.

To use PortQueryUI to check whether any services are listening to port 9876, just specify the port you want to check, make certain you are checking both TCP and UDP, and click Query. It will generate the same report that the command-line PortQuery tool did but in an easy-to-use interface. Check out the predefined queries for hours of fun.

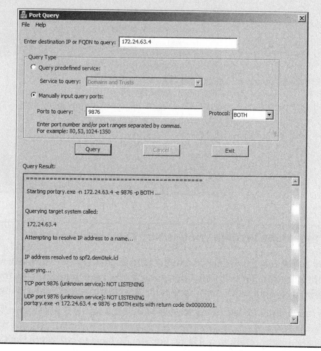

10. To make it easier to remember, I am going to specify a custom port for Central Administration that I made certain was not being used by the server already, *9876* (to do that, you need to check Specify Port Number in order to activate the field). At this point, you can keep the default (just make note of it), or you can enter your own custom port number (after verifying that it's not being used by the server for anything else).

In the Configure Security Settings portion of the page are the options for what IIS will use as the authentication provider for Windows Integrated Authentication, either NTLM or Kerberos. Although Kerberos is more secure, it takes more configuration to get to work correctly, and there are network time and realm considerations. Further, search tools (particularly the index account) sometimes have issues trying to access sites with Kerberos authentication (especially those with custom ports).

11. So for this example, since NTLM works perfectly fine for most intranet situations, especially when just using Central Administration, my choice at this point is NTLM. See Figure 3.12 to see my settings.

FIGURE 3.12
The Configure
Security
Settings page

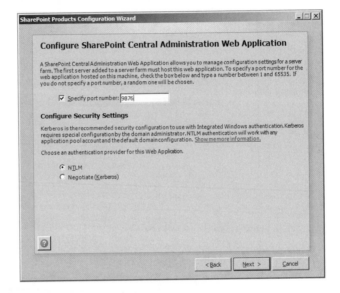

> **WHEN MORE INFORMATION IS NOT THAT INFORMATIVE**
>
> You might be curious about using Kerberos and try the Show Me More Information link in the Configuration Security Settings area. It will take you to a page for general information about Kerberos overall, with nothing specifically helpful about configuring Kerberos for SharePoint.
>
> To learn more about using Kerberos as your authentication method with SharePoint, go to KnowledgeBase article 832769. With this version of SharePoint, you no longer have to run the script the document refers to initially, but you do have to complete the Configure A Service Principal Name For The Domain User Account and Configure Trust For Delegation For Web Parts To Access Remote Resources sections. Enabling Kerberos is also covered in Chapter 16, "Advanced Installation and Configuration."

By the way, if you want to change your Central Administration site port number after this process is complete, you will have to rerun the SharePoint configuration wizard, disable the Central Administration site, and then reenable the site to specify a new port. Just changing it in IIS will not let the configuration database for the farm know it has been changed.

12. If you are certain your settings are correct, note your port number, and click Next to continue with the configuration.

This will take you to the Completing The SharePoint Products Configuration Wizard page. Here you'll see a summary of the settings that will be applied to your SharePoint installation.

It is here that you can confirm your settings (and go back to change them if there was a typo). The settings in my example (Figure 3.13) indicate my SQL server name, the configuration database name, the fact that this server will host the Central Administration web application (as the first server on the farm, this is obligatory), the URL for Central Administration (this is the address that will be used to access the site), and the authentication provider.

FIGURE 3.13

The Completing The SharePoint Products Configuration Wizard summary of settings that will be applied page

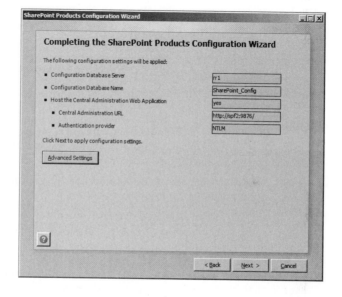

You might have also noticed an Advanced Settings button. Chapter 1, "SharePoint Foundation 2010 Under the Hood," mentioned the two user account modes available in SharePoint: Active Directory Domain Account mode and Active Directory Account Creation mode. The Advanced Settings button takes you to a page to configure Active Directory Account Creation Mode.

SharePoint requires an authentication provider to authenticate user accounts. It queries the provider about that user; then, if the provider approves it, the user is allowed to use SharePoint. Once the user logs in, SharePoint can apply its permissions to secure that user's access to its resources.

Central Administration in particular must use Windows integrated authentication (although you can use other kinds for your web applications if you want). But if SharePoint is running on a domain and using Windows Authentication, it can use Active Directory (AD) to store the user accounts that can be added to SharePoint. That's called Domain Account mode and is the standard user account mode for SharePoint. This mode requires that the user account already exist in Active Directory before it can be added to SharePoint.

In contrast, Active Directory Account Creation (ADAC) mode, which also uses Active Directory, will add an account to Active Directory *after* the account has been added to SharePoint. This method requires that SharePoint have access and control over an OU in AD to put the user accounts in. As you can imagine, ADAC does have its shortcomings and is more complex to configure, but it offers an alternative for those who want to be able to add users to AD from SharePoint, rather than vice versa. This can be useful to those who want to allow SharePoint access to users who don't originally have an account in AD.

Sadly, this setting is likely to be deprecated (meaning removed) in future releases because using forms-based authentication is easier and does not impact the entire farm, only the web application you configure to use it.

We are not going to be using ADAC for this implementation, so do not configure it.

13. Instead, take a good look at the summary, make sure there are no errors, and then click Next to continue.

SERIOUSLY CONSIDERING ACTIVE DIRECTORY ACCOUNT CREATION MODE?

If you are considering using Active Directory Account Creation Mode (ADAC), there are a few more things to consider.

Keep in mind that with Domain User Account mode, you need to have the user in AD before you can add them as a user in SharePoint. With ADAC, you add the user to SharePoint, and then they are added as users in the OU you made for SharePoint in Active Directory.

So, to use ADAC, you must set it under Advanced Settings during installation; otherwise, you won't be able to use it. There is no going back.

To use ADAC, you must have an organizational unit in Active Directory ready to contain the users. The OU must be set to have the correct permissions to manage it; namely, the farm account and content database accounts for the farm must be delegated the right to create/delete/manage user accounts and read all user account information in that OU. If you are using ADAC, only users created in the OU are available as users in SharePoint; you cannot add a user from elsewhere in AD that isn't in that OU. Nor are those users available to be added to groups or other resources in AD. Further, because users are intended to be added on a per-site-collection basis, if you want to apply a user you've already added to one site collection, you can't. You'd have to add them again with a slightly different username. As (I have to assume) a convenience, users are added in ADAC using their email address, which is used to generate their username. This can be challenging if they are added to ADAC over and over again because they need access to multiple site collections.

If you are going to enable ADAC for your user accounts, keep in mind a few things:

◆ You cannot upgrade a SharePoint Foundation server to SharePoint Server 2010 if it is running in ADAC mode. SharePoint Server doesn't support it.

◆ You cannot change your mind. If you decide the setup is too hard and you would rather go back to the default Domain Account mode, you are out of luck. During a SharePoint installation, you choose one user account mode or the other, and that is it for the whole farm forever. The setting is unchangeably burned into the configuration database. You cannot change it without reinstalling. This is why the Standalone install just goes for the default Domain Account mode automatically.

♦ You have to set the minimum password age to zero (which means never). If you set it to something else, users cannot change their own passwords. When a user is added to SharePoint with this user account mode, the user is sent their username and password (so outgoing email must be configured properly before users are added to the farm). Because passwords are assigned, it is best practice to allow users to change them to something more personally private and relevant. They can't do that if Active Directory is using a minimum password age of anything other than zero.

♦ If you use ADAC mode, you must learn how to manage a lot of SharePoint administration using the command-line tool STSADM or PowerShell. (See Chapter 14 for more.) You cannot do a lot of administration from the GUI with ADAC, because the HTML interface has features that depend on Domain Account mode. It won't let you create site collections in the GUI or allow users to create their own site collections (called *Self-Service Site Creation*). The potential inconvenience of this is enough to make administrators think twice about using ADAC mode.

♦ As you know, running any IIS Web Sites on a domain controller, let alone SharePoint, is not recommended. But specifically, ADAC mode is not supported on a domain controller.

At this point, configuration begins in earnest. The Configuring SharePoint Products page comes up, and a progress bar indicates activity, while the text around it describes what is happening. There are 10 configuration tasks for the wizard to complete, from creating the configuration database (the one that may take the longest) to provisioning the Central Administration web application to registering services to creating sample data.

When the configuration is complete, a last page of the wizard will come up, indicating the configuration was successful (and if it wasn't, it will tell you what went wrong so you can fix it). It also details the configuration settings it applied (these details should be identical to the summary of settings you saw before the configuration—but always check, just in case), as you can see in Figure 3.14.

FIGURE 3.14
The Configuration Successful screen, with a summary of settings applied

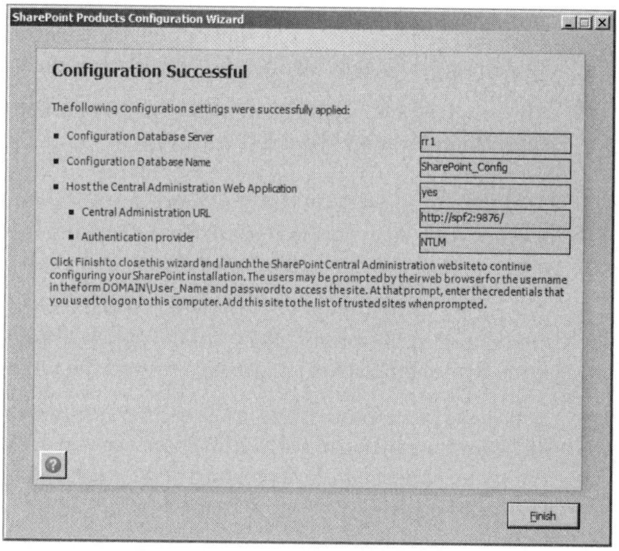

Below the settings on the page is a paragraph detailing what will happen after the wizard is finished. To continue configuring SharePoint, you have to go to Central Administration. To access Central Administration at this point, you will need to log in using the setup account, with the domain\username format. Central Administration should automatically come up in the browser (preferably IE, of course) as soon as the wizard is finished.

14. If the settings are correct, click Finish to close out of the configuration wizard and prepare to do more configuration tasks.

The browser may take a moment to display the page, but it will open immediately to offer you the option to participate in the Customer Experience Program, as shown in Figure 3.15. Feel free to select the option that most suits you. In my case, I will choose not to participate.

FIGURE 3.15
The Help
Make SharePoint
Better box

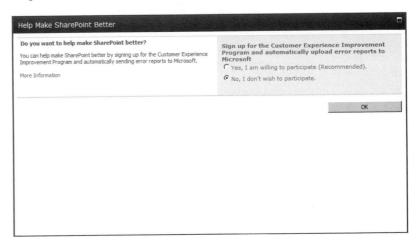

If you later decide to change that option, the Customer Experience Program setting is located under System Settings ➤ Farm Management ➤ Privacy Options.

15. After clicking OK on the Help Make SharePoint Better box, you will be taken to the Initial Farm Configuration Wizard (Figure 3.16).

At this point, SharePoint has only this Central Administration site; there are no other sites to work with. Also note that Search, outgoing and incoming email, diagnostic logging, and other services are not configured, because they need (or at least, should have) your input.

The Farm Configuration Wizard (which is the wizard available only for SharePoint Foundation at this point) offers you the option of being walked through setting up the farm, while being able to select services and the type of site.

This looks like a good option for first-time administrators, but I have found it doesn't actually give you much control over how services are set up, and you can end up with a default site set up almost exactly as if you'd done a Standalone install.

FIGURE 3.16
The Farm Configuration Wizard

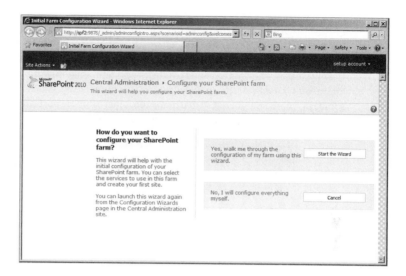

IDENTITY CRISIS

When SharePoint adds a new web application, it assigns the application a virtual directory in the wss folder under the default site for IIS. This virtual directory generally, if the ISS Web Site is unique by its port, names the folder after that site's port number. This means that Central Administration's folder should be 9768 (at least in my case; you might've used a different number)—but it isn't. SharePoint randomly gave it a different number. Something I think you should know.

To see what number SharePoint used to name the virtual directory for the Central Administration website, open the IIS Manager console (Start ➤ Administrative Tools ➤ Internet Information Services (IIS) Manager), double-click the local server node, and double-click Sites in the Connections pane until you can see the icon for Central Administration v4. Click the plus sign next to Central Administration in the Connections pane.

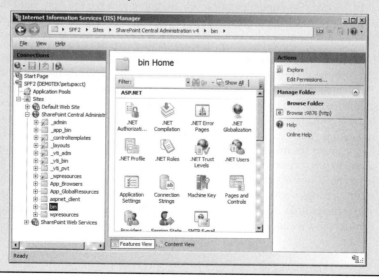

Click a virtual directory icon in the Connections pane *without* an arrow on it (in my example I selected the **bin** folder). While the folder is selected, click Explore in the Actions pane. This will open an Explorer window to the folder and show you the exact contents of that virtual folder and incidentally the physical location of that folder in the file system. That means it will show you the folder name SharePoint is using for the virtual directory. (In my example, SharePoint named my folder 7973 for some reason—remember, it *should* name the folder after the port used by the IIS Web Site, but there is a glitch in this process for Central Administration.)

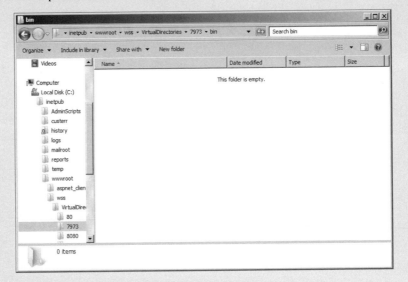

Now you know what that folder is for and why *not* to delete it.

16. So for this implementation, we are going to forgo the easy walk-through and do this ourselves. Select the No, I Will Configure Everything Myself option, which is actually the Cancel button.

This will bring you back to the Central Administration home page (Figure 3.17) and finish the installation process (you can also close the installation screen if it's still open for any reason).

Chapter 2 introduced the Central Administration home page in detail. Briefly, it has the dark blue bar at the top (considered a top ribbon bar), containing the Site Actions tab, the navigation button, and a few ribbon bar tabs on the left. On the right side of the bar is the account menu, indicating your login account. Also on the right, just below the title area of the page, is a tiny help icon. In the middle of the page are the seven headings with commonly used tasks beneath them, for your convenience. On the left is the Quick Launch bar, which basically repeats the seven headings. If you click a heading, it will take you to the page containing *all* the configuration settings (loosely organized by task), which far outnumber what is on the home page. The settings links available per heading on the home page are a fraction of the tasks available throughout the site; they're just available here as a convenience.

FIGURE 3.17

The Central Administration home page

Some settings pages for Central Administration have a limited menu of options to choose from, along the lines of a single link to use or the menus from the previous version of SharePoint (containing drop-downs for New, Actions, and Settings). Others will comply with the current version of SharePoint's ribbon bar design (like Office 2007 or 2010). Don't be alarmed if they vary.

PSCONFIG, THE WIZARD BEHIND THE CURTAIN

Now that you've seen how the installation and configuration wizard works, I'll let you in on a secret: all it is doing is using a command called PSCONFIG at the command line. Behind that nice, appealing interface, PSCONFIG is hard at work doing the installation.

What does that mean to you? It means you can use that command, too. And because it is a command, you can script it to automate installations.

You may have noticed that the installation had two parts: the installation of the necessary files, or *binaries* as they are called, for SharePoint (using your standard setup.exe), and then the configuration of SharePoint (which is done with psconfig.exe).

If you plan to install SharePoint with the PSCONFIG command-line tool, then don't complete the configuration of SharePoint after the file installation. Clear the Run The SharePoint Products And Technologies Configuration Wizard box when that screen comes up, and click Close. The files you need to configure SharePoint and truly install it are in place, and now all you have to do is complete the process.

SharePoint puts its command-line tools in the %Program Files%/Common Files/Microsoft Shared/web server extensions/14/bin folder on the local server. To use the PSCONFIG command, open a command prompt (Start ➢ Run, type **cmd**, and click OK), and navigate to that bin folder.

To see what PSCONFIG can do, type **psconfig /?** at the command prompt. It will offer you three command options:

```
-cmd [parameter]
```

This command indicates that PSCONFIG should run as a command based on the specified parameter. Parameters can be further modified by additional options.

```
-help [parameter]
```

This lets you get help information about a particular parameter and how to use it.

```
-?
```

This is the equivalent of using /? after the command and simply displays the syntax and parameters used with the command.

The following parameters can be used with PSCONFIG:

◆ Setup: This parameter just runs the SharePoint setup. You can use the LCID option (to specify language) with this parameter.

Keep in mind that Setup.exe is an executable in its own right and can run on its own with its own options. For example, to repair an installation, you would run Setup/repair at the command line first and then PSCONFIG's setup. Setup.exe is what is used to install the SharePoint binaries.

◆ Standaloneconfig: This installs SharePoint as a standalone server, with the Windows Internal Database. This also uses the LCID option.

◆ Configdb: This is used to specify the configuration database for the installation, with additional parameters to specify whether it should create a database, connect to an existing database, or disconnect. With this parameter, you can specify the domain for the farm, its organizational unit (if it will be using Directory Management Service), and even the database for the Central Administration site. This parameter is used if you are doing a command-line installation of a SharePoint server that will be part of an existing server farm.

◆ Helpcollections: This installs the SharePoint help file collections.

◆ Secureresources: This enforces security on SharePoint resources such as files, folders, and registry keys.

◆ Services: This parameter is used to register SharePoint services and has two additional modifiers: install, which registers the SharePoint services on the local server, and provision, which installs and registers the SharePoint services for a Stand-alone server, setting them as online.

◆ Installfeatures: Although the command-line tool STSADM can also work with SharePoint features, this parameter is used to register the SharePoint features for the server farms that are on the local server.

◆ Adminvs: This parameter is used to create a new Central Administration web application and has additional options to specify the port and type of authentication. This parameter also has the option to unprovision, or remove, a Central Administration web application.

◆ Evalprovision: This does a Basic SharePoint installation. Intended to install SharePoint conveniently for evaluation, it has three options: provision, which simply installs SharePoint; port, which allows you to specify the port used by the default SharePoint web application (if not specified, 80 will be used); and overwrite, which will overwrite an existing IIS Web Site with the new web application. Normally, if you specify a port that is already in use by SharePoint, it will be shut down, and SharePoint will create its own website without disturbing the first one. With overwrite enabled, it will replace the existing web application.

◆ Applicationcontent: This parameter copies the web application binaries, files, and other shared application data for SharePoint to the web applications. This is good if you think those files may have been removed or corrupted.

◆ Quiet: A standard installation parameter, this will run the configuration wizard steps without output. The data is written to a psconfig.exe[date].log file.

◆ Upgrade: This parameter is what SharePoint uses to upgrade (or migrate) existing WSS 3.0 installations. This parameter has the option to do side-by-side or in-place upgrades. It has an option, reghostonupgrade, which reverts customized pages to the WSS defaults. Other options include inplace, preserveolduserexperience, and passphrase. Other parameters, such as force, wait, and finalize, are used to control the upgrade process. For more on upgrading SharePoint, see Chapter 15, "Migrating from Windows SharePoint Services 3.0 to SharePoint Foundation 2010."

The syntax for using PSCONFIG is as follows:

```
psconfig.exe -cmd [parameter] -parameteroption
```

An example of this is as follows:

```
psconfig.exe -cmd setup -lcid <1033>.
```

If you are going to use PSCONFIG to automate the installation of servers in your server farm, make certain that the installation of binaries (the initial installation step before configuration) has been run on each server to install the necessary files PSCONFIG requires locally. You can string parameters together to have one long command, but keep in mind that they execute in a certain order. The order shown here is the order they run, with the upgrade going last.

So if you don't like the graphic user interface or were wondering how to automate your SharePoint installation, PSCONFIG might be what you've been looking for.

Initial Farm Configuration

At this point, you need to manually do some configuration tasks that were done automatically in the Standalone installation. They are as follows (roughly in the order they'll be done in this chapter):

◆ Configure managed accounts. New with this version of SharePoint, you have to register the accounts used by web applications and services if you want to use something other than the farm account for their application pool identities. Managed accounts allow SharePoint to manage the passwords for those accounts, avoiding password expiration or issues that might be caused by changing the account passwords outside SharePoint. It helps to configure all the managed accounts you are going to use for the farm, before you start configuring services and web applications.

> ### THERE'S CONVENIENCE, AND THERE'S CONVENIENCE
>
> You could start to create a web application (or configure a service) and register a managed account to use for their application pools on the fly, but to do that, you need to interrupt the configuration of the long list of settings to go to the page to register the account, and when you get back, all of the settings you entered before registering the new managed account may have to be reentered. It's much easier to simply know what accounts you want to manage first, register them, and then enable the services and create web applications that need to use those accounts.

- ◆ Configure the Search service. You might think it odd to configure Search first, before even creating the first SharePoint web application, but during the configuration of a web application, you select the Search server you want to index its content from a drop-down list. It helps to have Search configured *before* the web applications.

- ◆ Configure the Health and Usage data collection. Enabling the Health and Usage data collection enables SharePoint to run the Health Analyzer tool and to generate usage reports. Although this is not required, it is good to have data being collected from the start.

- ◆ Configure the Business Data Connectivity (BDC) service. You only need to enable Business Data Connectivity if you have any external databases you'd like to be able to access as an external list or lookup field in SharePoint. I am going to demonstrate this feature later, so I have to enable it.

- ◆ Configure the Sandboxed Code service. First you start this service, and then you need to specify its service account. It does not require its own database. This service, like Business Data Connectivity, is optional. It's used to run sandboxed solutions uploaded to site collections. The solutions will not be able to be activated if this service is not running. If you aren't going to use sandboxed solutions, this service does not need to be started.

> ### WHAT'S THE SERVICE APPLICATION GOT TO DO WITH IT?
>
> Both Health and Usage as well as BDC are considered service applications and can be applied per web application, meaning they show up as options on the web application configuration page when creating a web application. If these services are not configured before the web application, their settings won't be available to be selected while creating web applications.

- ◆ Create at least one web application to contain SharePoint sites (in addition to Central Administration, without which you couldn't administer SharePoint).

- ◆ Create a site collection to go into that web application. Remember that a web application is just an empty container, defined by its address and security settings. Without a site collection, even if it's no more than a single top-level site, there would be no pages for users to open in a browser at that web application's URL.

Before we move on to enabling services or creating a web application, let's register some necessary service accounts.

Registering Managed Accounts

Unfortunately, you can't just click a link to register accounts from the Central Administration home page. This is one of those tasks you have to go a page or two down to find the settings you're looking for.

In this case, you need to click Security in the Quick Launch bar. That will bring you to the Security page, listing the SharePoint tasks considered related to security (Figure 3.18).

FIGURE 3.18

The Security page

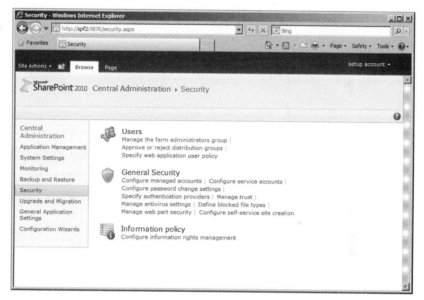

1. Click Configure Managed Accounts under General Security, which will bring you to a page that is already populated with the farm account that you entered during the configuration wizard (see Figure 3.19).

2. Click the Register Managed Accounts link above the list. That will, finally, open a page where you can enter the data required to register an account. As shown in Figure 3.20, I've filled in the fields to register my search service account.

"WARNING: THIS PAGE IS NOT ENCRYPTED…"

You may have noticed the warning at the top of the Register Managed Account page. It is saying that the server is not using an SSL certificate or otherwise encrypting traffic between your browser and the server on your network. Generally this is not a problem, since you are accessing the data internally, but if it is, consider using SSL to secure traffic to the Central Administration site. In my case, I am working in the server itself, so there is no browser traffic from a client to the server to intercept.

FIGURE 3.19
The Managed
Accounts page

FIGURE 3.19
The Managed
Accounts page

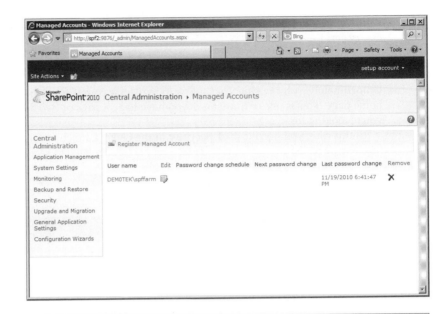

FIGURE 3.20
The Register
Managed
Account page

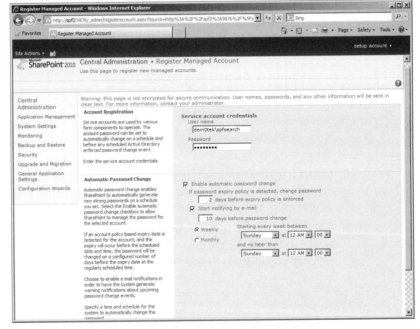

The Register Managed Account page contains two sections: Account Registration and Automatic Password Change.

The Account Registration section is where you enter the account's username and password. Remember to use the correct syntax, `domain\username` (or for a nondomain, workgroup environment, `servername\username`).

3. In this case, we are going to first register the search service account (for some reason the index, or "content access," account doesn't need to be registered). So, enter the account you intend to use for the Search service, which for me is dem0tek\spfsearch.

The second section, Automatic Password Change, is where you can configure SharePoint to manage password changes itself. This feature is not enabled by default, but you can enable it here, causing additional settings to propagate in this section (so be prepared to scroll a bit more to get to the OK button).

Once it is enabled, you have one main option, to allow SharePoint to automatically change the account's password. When that is selected, the other options in this section become available. These specify when, before expiring, the password will be changed by SharePoint (the default is two days) and whether SharePoint should start sending a notification email before the password change will occur. It's odd that the notification can be sent out only weekly or monthly, but the notification window before expiration can be considerably shorter. It's also odd that you can't just ask for the notification here without also enabling SharePoint to change it to a password only SharePoint knows (notification without password change can be set in the Password Settings page, as you'll see later in this chapter).

4. At this point, I am just going to go for broke and enable automatic password change to change the password two days before the password expires and start warning at 10 days out, with a weekly notification schedule, Sunday at midnight (the default time for the weekly schedule), as shown in Figure 3.20. Keep in mind that SharePoint can't send out any notifications without having outgoing email configured, something we'll set up later in the chapter.

YOU ARE UNDER NO OBLIGATION...

Keep in mind that you are not obligated to use the automatic password change setting. If you created these accounts with passwords that don't change and can't be changed by the user, then don't enable Automatic Password Change. Just enter the account username and password to register the account so SharePoint can use it for its services or web applications.

---

5. Click OK to finish registering the account.

On the Managed Accounts page, your new account will be listed, with its password change schedule (which indicates, correctly, that you didn't schedule anything for the other account).

In addition to Search, web applications require managed accounts for their application pool identities, and the BDC and Sandboxed Code service require managed accounts. To register the web application's content database account and the other service accounts, just go back through the steps you used to register the Search account and create one for the content database access account.

As a quick recap, you go to Security ➤ Configure Managed Accounts ➤ Register Managed Accounts. In the Register Managed Account page, enter the account to manage (in my case dem0tek/spfcontent for the content database account, dem0tek\spfusrcode for the Sandboxed Code service, and dem0tek\spfbdc for the BDC service; remember that you can register only one account at a time). Choose to enable Automatic Password Change if you'd like, and configure it as you see fit. Click OK to register one account, and then return to the Managed Accounts page to click the Register Managed Account link and register the next account until you're done.

FIGURE 3.21
Settings config-
ured for the regis-
tered account

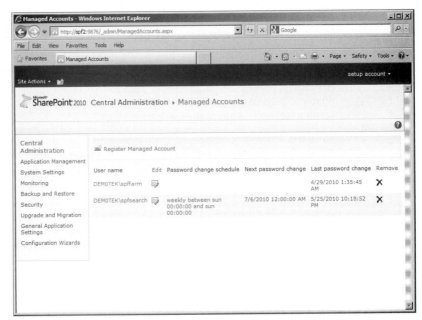

In the end, you should have at least five managed accounts, one for the server farm, one for Search, at least one web application content database access account, one for the Sandboxed Code service, and one for the BDC service (Figure 3.22). You might notice that the farm account doesn't have any password schedule. That is because when it was configured during the installation of SharePoint, there was no option to set up its password schedule. To edit that, you can click the Edit icon for the account if you'd like. I am going to leave it for now.

PASSWORD EXPIRATION POLICY?

It helps to know what the domain policy is for password expiration if you are going to use managed accounts, because this feature might require some planning. The default domain policy for Server 2008 is a maximum password age of 42 days.

Something else to consider is the lockout policy. If SharePoint should make a mistake too many times while trying to change the password, lockout could be enforced.

You can use the Group Policy Management console (installed by default on Server 2008 R2) at Start ➢ Administrative Tools ➢ Group Policy Management to check your policy (if you have the right to access the domain controller; if you don't, ask your AD admin to do it). Once in the console, open the domain node, and then select the Default Domain Policy (keep in mind that, in your environment, there might be other policies in force). In the Details pane, select the Settings tab, and then display the details for Security Settings ➢ Account Policies/Password Policies.

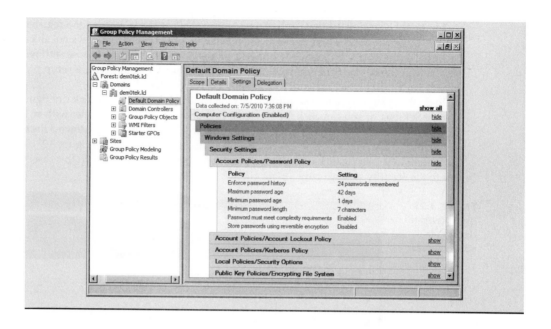

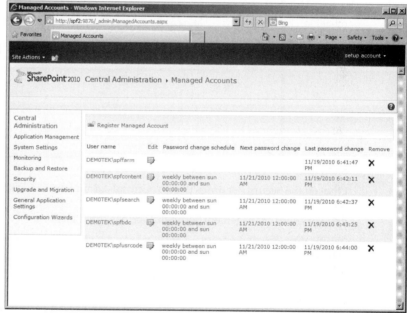

FIGURE 3.22
The Managed Accounts page with new managed accounts available

You might have noticed that configuring Automatic Password Change for a registered account is missing details about where its notification email is actually sent or that it's not able to just send out email notifications without also changing passwords. That's because those settings are, as you may have guessed, on a different page. So to complete the Managed Account setup process, we have to pay a visit to the Password Management Settings page.

To do that, you could click Security in the Quick Launch bar and then click Configure Password Change Settings, or you can click the Navigate Up button (it looks like a folder with an arrow, in the top ribbon bar, left side, next to the Site Actions tab). That button drops down a breadcrumb of sorts, which shows you the path you've taken to get to the page you're on (Figure 3.23). It is a very convenient way to navigate back up to the pages just above where you are. In this case, we'll navigate to the Security settings page.

FIGURE 3.23
Using Navigate Up to get to a previous page

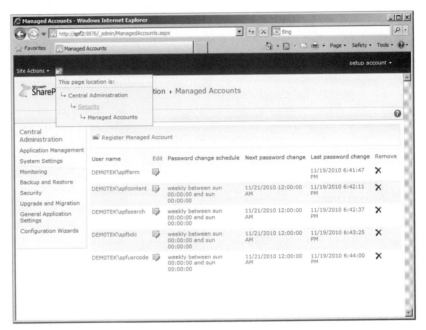

Once on the Security settings page in Central Administration, click the Configure Password Change Settings link.

The Password Management Settings page has three sections:

Notification Email Address   This is where you enter the email address the password notifications get sent to. Unfortunately, it allows only one.

Account Monitoring Process Settings   Here you can still get notifications on upcoming password expiration without giving SharePoint the right to change the password itself. It is set to 10 days before password change by default.

Automatic Password Change Settings   This doesn't do what it says it does. This section is used to indicate the number of seconds SharePoint waits after notifying services that it is going to change a password *before* it does change it. Of course, that happens only if you enabled automatic password change on any of your managed accounts to begin with. There is also a setting for the number of tries it makes to change a password before failing. The default, in seconds, for the wait before changing a password is 45, and the number of tries is 5. Both these defaults are fine.

In our case, we only need to enter an email address for the password change notification emails to send to. In my case, that would be `sharepoint@dem0tek.lcl` Figure 3.24). Then click OK to keep the change and leave the page. Keep in mind that, although managing passwords is great, there may be times when services are unavailable while passwords are changing.

FIGURE 3.24

The Password Management Settings page

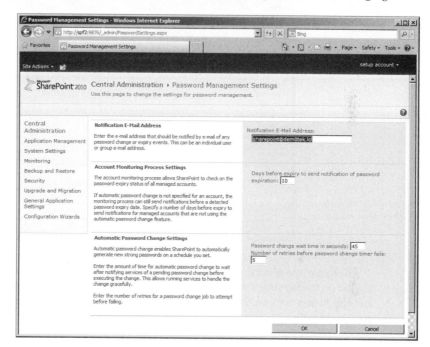

Configuring Search

Now that we've registered some managed accounts, let's configure Search and, in the process, see what services are available on the server.

To do that, you can click Manage Services On Server, under System Settings on the Central Administration home page. Or click System Settings in the Quick Launch bar, and on the System Settings page select Manage Services On Server.

That will open the Services On Server page (Figure 3.25).

As you can see, a number of services are available for the server farm. Even though the View menu identifies these as the "Configurable" services (to see all services, change the view to All), for most items, the only configuration possible is to start or stop the service; there are no configurable settings for most services here (despite the menu on the right indicating the list is configurable). Only the last two services, shown in blue on the screen, are truly configurable: the Workflow Timer service and Search. The Workflow Timer service just schedules how many workflow events can run during each SharePoint Timer job service interval (since the timer job obviously schedules all tasks SharePoint requires in timed intervals). And Search is what answers queries by accessing the search database; it works along with the indexer, which does a lot the heavy lifting in terms of indexing all searchable data.

FIGURE 3.25

The Services On Server page

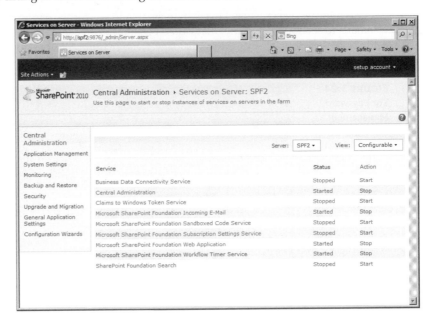

Of course, the service you need to enable early on is Search. There is a bit of a trick to it. In the list on the Services On Server page, you can see the title of the service, the Status column, and the Action column. To change the configuration of a service without changing its status, you can just click the service's title. But to both configure and start a service, click Start in the Action column for the service.

1. Since that's what you need to do to configure and start the Search service (because it's obviously set to Stopped at the moment), click its Start link in the Action column. That will open the Configure Microsoft Foundation Search Service Settings On This Server page (you have to love those wordy titles).

   This configuration page has several sections to work with, so it's useful to break this into two parts, configuring the accounts for Search then configuring the database information and index schedule.

   The first two sections (Figure 3.26) are used to configure the service accounts Search requires. The Service Account section is where you enter the username and password of the user account you'd like SharePoint to use as the Search service's identity.

2. To specify an account, enter a username in the domain\username syntax. In my case, I'm using the managed account, dem0tek\spfsearch, that I set up earlier. Don't forget to enter the password.

FIGURE 3.26

The Service Account and Content Access Account sections of the Search service settings

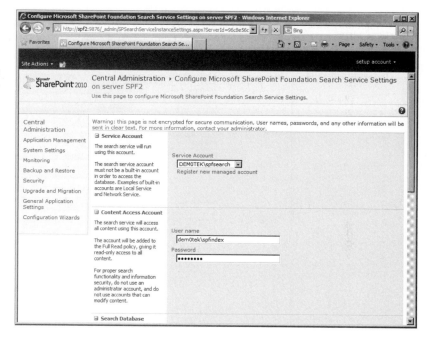

The Content Access account section is for specifying the index account that will be used to access all the sites and their content in any web application configured to use Search. SharePoint initially sets the default as a local service account. This isn't a good idea, since this service will need to be assigned roles to the Search database on a different server.

3. So, enter the index account you created for this purpose in Active Directory (don't forget the password). In my case, I'm using dem0tek\spfindex. Don't be surprised that the index account doesn't need to be managed. I don't know why Microsoft chose to do that, but that's just the way it is. And for that reason, you should make sure that the account has a password that doesn't expire and can't be changed by the user (should it be compromised).

The next three sections, shown in Figure 3.27, are used to configure the search database, that database's failover server (if your SQL server is configured to have one), and the index schedule.

In the Search Database section, you indicate the SQL server where the Search database will go, the database name, and what kind of authentication is required (because some SQL servers use their own SQL authentication for database access rather than the Windows integrated authentication).

4. As you can see in Figure 3.27, SharePoint knows what its default SQL server name is (since it's using it for the configuration database), and it has a suggestion for a database name. For convenience's sake, I am going to keep the default settings (in my case, *rr1* for the server, and *WSS_Search_SPF2* for the database name).

FIGURE 3.27
Configuring
Search's database,
failover server, and
indexing schedule

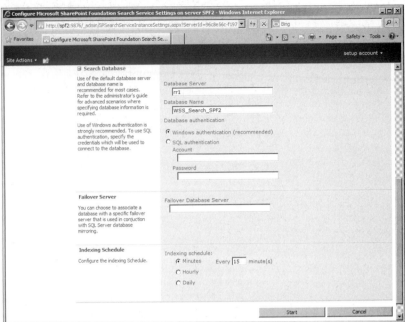

5. For authorization, I am going to keep the default Windows authentication; use the correct authentication method for your server.

6. In the Failover Server section, I am going to leave that field blank, because I don't have my SQL server set up in a failover cluster, so I don't have a failover server to specify here. If you do have a failover server, enter the server name here.

In the Indexing Schedule section, you can see that there are several options. You can specify the intervals in which SharePoint indexes changed data: hourly, between a time range within an hour (so if you have other things timed to run at the top of the hour on the network or the server, the index service can be set to run at a different point in the hour every hour), or daily between a range of time. The default is hourly around 49 minutes after the hour, every hour.

7. You can, of course, change this setting, and you can reconfigure it again whenever needed. For my purposes, I need to have the index work more frequently, so I am going to change it to every 15 minutes. Mind you, this is not a good setting for production because the indexing service can use a lot of resources on the local server. But when you're learning SharePoint for the first time and you are experimenting with Search, it's best if you don't have to wait an hour after you make a change for the change to show up in the search results.

NO GOING BACK

If you do want to reconfigure the index schedule for Search, I suggest you simply edit the settings by clicking the title of the service on the Services On Server page to do so.

If you stop the service and then start it again (which is what happens if you click Stop and then reconfigure the settings in the Action column to change settings), Search will require a whole new database. It cannot reuse the existing Search database on restart if it had been stopped. Building the Search database and reindexing everything can take time and resources, so stopping and restarting Search during production (especially during busy times) is not recommended.

8. Make certain the settings for Search are correct, and then, to start the service, click the Start button at the bottom of the page.

This will start the service. A Processing page will come up, and then, if all goes well, you'll be back on the Services On Server page with the Search service indicating that its Status is Started (Figure 3.28).

FIGURE 3.28
The Search service now appears as Started on the Services On Server page.

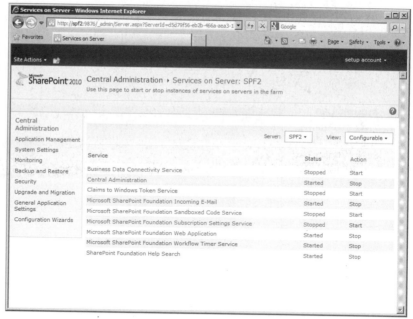

In addition, if you go to the Services console, you can see that the SharePoint Foundation Search v4 service is now using the service account you assigned it (Figure 3.29).

FIGURE 3.29
The Search service
account in the Ser-
vices console

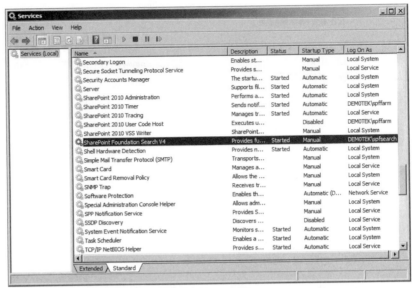

Finally, if you check in the Event Viewer (under Administrative Tools off the Start menu)
under Windows Logs ➤ Application, there will be events indicating that the Search service has
started (Figure 3.30) and a master merge has begun, although this is primarily of help information because no web applications have been created yet.

FIGURE 3.30
The Event Viewer
reports that the
Search service has
started.

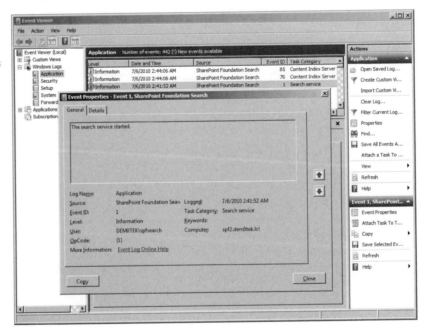

So, we've successfully started the Search service, which means it will be available to be applied to the web application when we create it.

IS YOUR VSS SERVICE NOT PLAYING WELL WITH SHAREPOINT?

After enabling Search, you might see the occasional Volume Shadow Copy service error in the Application log in Event Viewer, which basically says there was an unexpected error and access was denied (event ID 8193).

If you do a little digging, you'll find that the search account (which drives the `mssearch.exe` service referred to in the details of the error) requires full control of the registry key listed in the error:

`Hkey_Local_Machine\System\CurrentControlSet\Services\VSS\Diag`

Once that account has access to that key, the error goes away. Beware; online there are articles saying the content access account (which usually means the indexer) requires permissions, but in fact it's the account that runs the Search service itself, which in my case is `dem0tek\spfsearch`.

Registering managed accounts and enabling Search before creating the first web application (so you can put your first SharePoint site collection it in) are good ideas, since both settings are needed before proceeding. However, there are a few additional quick configurations we should get done before we get to web applications.

I'm talking about Business Data Connectivity (BDC), a new service available with this version of SharePoint, as well as data collection for usage and health information and sandboxed solutions.

Starting and Configuring the Business Data Connectivity Service

The BDC service is enabled in two stages: starting the service and configuring a new service application for it. You can start the service first and then configure the application, or vice versa.

STARTING THE BDC SERVICE

For this example, we are going to start the service first and then configure it.

1. To start the BDC service, go to the Services On Server page (System Settings in the Quick Launch bar and then Manage Services On Server). You may already be there, since this is where you ended up after starting the Search service.

    On the Services On Server page, the Business Data Connectivity service itself does not have any settings to configure from there, but by default it is not started, as you can see in Figure 3.31.

FIGURE 3.31
The Services On
Server page shows
that Business
Data Connectivity
is inactive.

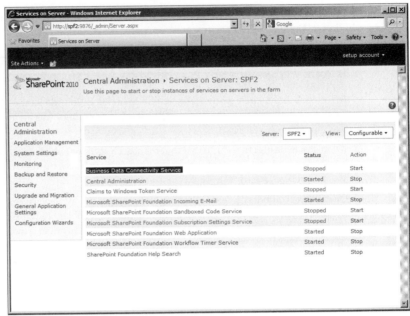

The BDC service, when completely configured, creates an application under the Web Services Web Site in IIS, has its own application pool identity, and has to create a BDC database in SQL. Given that it does use those resources, you can see why SharePoint allows you to opt not to start the BDC. However, it is a great resource to have, the Standalone installation has it enabled by default, and we are going to enable it now.

2. To start the Business Data Connectivity service, just click Start in the Action column.

A processing page will come up for a moment, and then the Services On Server page will reappear, only with the BDC service started.

This doesn't mean the service is ready to be used, however. You still need to configure its database and service account. To do this, you need to get to the Manage Service Applications page, by clicking Application Management on the Quick Launch bar, then clicking Manage Service Applications under the Service Applications heading on the Application Management page.

CONFIGURING A SERVICE APPLICATION

Once on the Manage Service Applications page (Figure 3.32), you'll see two services running, but neither is Business Data Connectivity. To rectify this, click New on the ribbon bar, then select Business Data Connectivity (the only option available under New).

The background of the page may darken, and a Create New Business Data Connectivity Service Application box may pop up with the configuration settings for a new web application. This is a new UI feature of this version of SharePoint. If you find the box a little restrictive because of all the fields and text you have to scroll through, you can maximize the box (as I've done in my screenshots).

The settings here are very much like those used by web applications, because the BDC service needs a lot of the same resources: a service account, application pool, and database of its very own.

Again, it's useful to divide the settings into two groups, roughly by screenful. The first group consists of the Name and Database sections, shown in Figure 3.33 with the settings completed.

FIGURE 3.32
The Manage Service Applications page

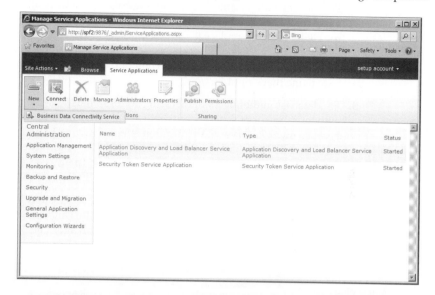

FIGURE 3.33
Name and Database sections, creating a new BDC

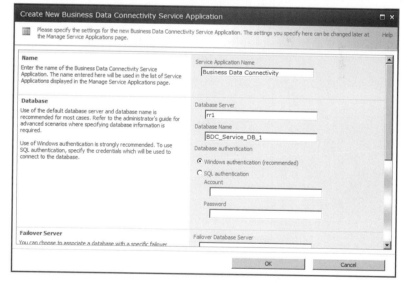

1. To create the new service application, you first need to enter a name for the service. I'm going to use the practical and descriptive *Business Data Connectivity* for the name.

2. In the Database section, you need to specify the database location, name, and type of authentication used to access it. The database server used during installation and

configuration is usually listed in this section by default for the Database Server name. In my case, it is correct. Make sure it is correct for you, or enter the correct server name. Beneath the server name field is the Database Name field, already filled with a default name for a BDC database. I like most of the database name, but I am going to get rid of the GUID part and replace it with the number 1. This means my BDC database name will be *BDC_Service_DB_1*. This database keeps track of all the BDC-related configuration data, such as external systems and content types. You can follow my lead, or use a database name that's right for you.

3. For database authentication, there are two options: the default setting of Windows authentication or SQL server authentication. Windows Authentication is correct for me, because my SQL server authentication is Windows integrated. However, if your SQL server used SQL authentication, this is where you would enter the username and password this service would use to access the server. In my case, I'm keeping the default selected for database authentication, as you saw in Figure 3.33.

The next two sections of settings to create a new service application are Failover Server and Application Pool, as shown in Figure 3.34. The Failover Server section is used if database mirroring is enabled in SQL and you have an alternate SQL server for this service to point to.

FIGURE 3.34
Application Pool section, creating a new BDC

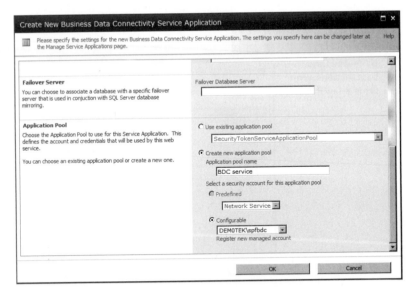

4. In my case, I have only one SQL server installed, so I am going to leave the Failover Server section blank.

In the Application Pool section, you can either assign the service an existing application pool or create a new one. I'm going to create a new one in this case. The BDC might be doing a lot of the work in the future, and I'd rather not have it share an application pool with any other service.

5. To create a new application pool in this UI, you first need to name it and then apply a service account to it, as you can see in Figure 3.34. In this case, I am going to name the pool *BDC service* (which will be its name in IIS), and in the Select A Security Account For This Application Pool area, I am going to select the managed account I created earlier for this server, *dem0tek\spfbdc*, in the Configurable Account field (using a local built-in account is a bad idea and is grayed out for that reason). Feel free to name the application pool whatever you'd like, and use the account you created and registered earlier for the BDC service.

6. That's it. If all the settings you want for configuring the BDC service are complete, click OK to create its service application.

The Processing page will come up for a little while, during which an application pool, database, and web service application will be created.

When processing is complete, a really redundant success notice will come up if it was successful (depending on what you named your service), a failure notice with information as to what went wrong if it didn't. As you can see in Figure 3.35, mine created the new Business Data Connectivity service application successfully.

FIGURE 3.35
New Business Data Connectivity Service Application created successfully

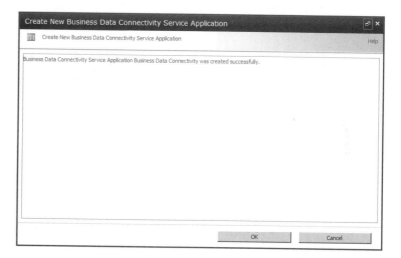

If you click OK in the notice box, you'll be brought back to the list of service applications. Notice that Business Data Connectivity is now listed (with a supporting proxy) on the page (Figure 3.36). It will also be listed on the Services On Server page.

WHAT ARE THOSE OTHER SERVICES?

The other two service applications listed relate to the web services that were displayed in IIS earlier: the Topology application handles load balancing and discovery (and is referred to in SharePoint as the Application Discovery and Load Balancer service for that reason), and the SecurityTokenServiceApplication handles the, well, Security Token service, the service used by SharePoint for claims-based authentication.

FIGURE 3.36

Manage Service Applications page with Business Data Connectivity available

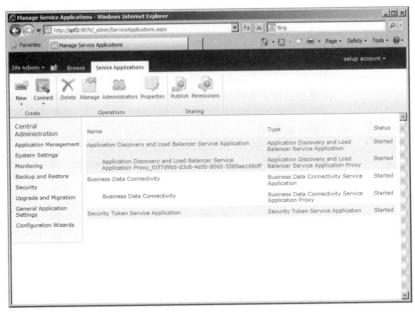

Business Data Connectivity is now ready for external data types to be configured. You'll need SharePoint Designer 2010 (the 2007 version won't work), Visual Studio 2010, or some coding experience to do that. Since SharePoint Designer (or SPD as it's called) is free and works great for setting up at least your basic external content types, I will be using it to demonstrate using external content types with the BDC to make external lists in Chapter 16.

Now that we have Business Data Connectivity configured and running, it's time to enable Health and Usage data collection before finally creating our web application and site collection.

These services are not absolutely required, but they are important enough to make it a habit to configure them at the installation of any self-respecting SharePoint farm.

Enabling Usage and Health Data Collection

SharePoint has essentially two options to gather data: diagnostic logging and the Usage and Health data collection. Diagnostic logging works entirely on the server; the logs are stored there, and the events are presented there. The Usage and Health data collection is different. When you enable that set of features, it requires a database to be created in SQL (along with all the others for SharePoint). The analysis of the data itself can be resource-consuming, so be sure to schedule it for nonpeak hours.

To enable and configure data collection settings for usage and health, click Monitoring in the Quick Launch bar, and then click Configure Usage And Health Data Collection in the Reporting section.

This will open the configuration page for usage and health (named Configure Web Analytics And Health Data Collection, just to confuse you). This is one of those pages with a lot of settings, but for our purposes there are only two settings you want to change—currently the Usage and Health data collection is not enabled; you just have to enable it. Most of the other settings are correct as the defaults and can be altered later.

This page has sections for enabling usage collection and the events it reports, data collection settings in terms of a path for the local usage logs (as well as their size limit), enabling health data collection, scheduling health data snapshots, and logging, as well as specifics about the logging database.

The first three sections of this configuration page are Usage Data Collection, Event Selection, and Usage Data Collection Settings (Figure 3.37).

FIGURE 3.37
Configuring Usage Data Collection and Event Selection settings

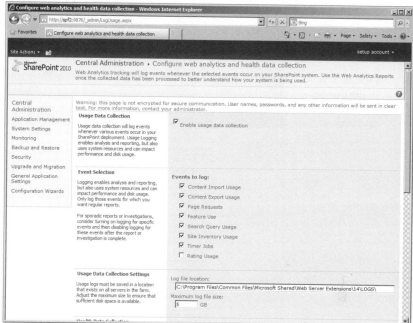

Usage data collection gathers all the events for a given set of events (that you can configure) so that data can be analyzed and reported on to better understand SharePoint's usage. Keep in mind that usage analysis takes up a lot of resources, which is why, later in the page, it's important to have a schedule for it to use.

1. Click the Enable Usage Data Collection box in order to enable this service (that will put a check in the box).

2. In the Event section, there are a number of events that usage data collection can use to generate reports. It is generally a good thing to enable as much data gathering as possible during the early days of a deployment (especially if you are in testing) to set a baseline and find any issues early. For that reason, I am leaving practically all of the events enabled in this section. After you have gotten your baseline information and developed a feel for what events you *don't* need to gather information on, then you can come back and disable them. One event that can safely be disabled from the start is Rating Usage, which is not used for SharePoint Foundation.

3. In the Usage Data Collection Settings section, there is the obligatory path to the local usage log files. You can change that if you'd like (these logs can grow pretty large), but make sure that the location where you put them will be the same for all SharePoint servers in the farm and that WSS_ADMIN_WPG group has Full Control, WSS_WPG has at least Read and Write, and the SPTrace service account has at least Modify permissions for the location. Also in this section is the setting to throttle the amount of space these logs take up. The default is 5 GB, which is fine for our purposes. So, leave the settings in this section as they are.

The last three sections for this page are Health Data Collection, Logging Data Schedule, and Logging Database Server (Figure 3.38).

FIGURE 3.38
Health data collection and log database settings

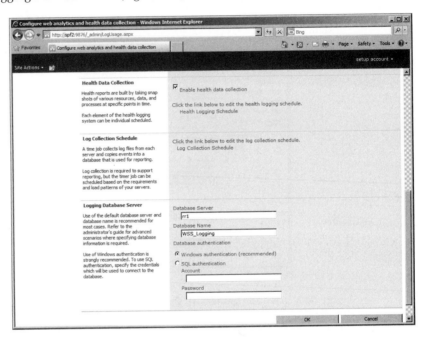

The Health Data Collection section contains settings for enabling health data collection and a link that will take you to the timer job page for all of the health data collection jobs so you can change their scheduling if you'd like.

4. In our case, we want to enable health data collection, so be sure that setting has a check in the check box next to it.

Also in this section is a link to edit the health logging schedule. We are not going to edit the schedule (which already has all jobs configured with default schedules), because it leaves this page (and any changes you made may be wiped). Always save your changes first, then come back to this page to work with the schedule. The default schedule works fine without editing in most cases. Below the Health Data Collection section is Log Collection Schedule. It will take you to a timer job page as well, displaying the timer jobs used to generate usage logs so you can reschedule them. They are already configured with a default schedule, which works for me.

5. Finally, the last section is for configuring the SQL database information concerning the logging database. This is where the database server name for the server to hold the database must be specified (mine has the default RR1 server already in the field), as well as the database name (again, the default *WSS_Logging* is fine for me) and how SQL requires authentication—either Windows authentication, which is what my server uses, or SQL authentication, which will require username and password credentials. If your server requires SQL authentication, enter the correct credentials. The default, Windows authentication, is fine for me.

So for the last three sections, you changed only one setting, and that was to enable health data collection.

6. Check all settings on this page to make sure they are correct, and then click OK.

The Processing page will come up, as a database is created, and then you will be dumped unceremoniously back onto the Monitoring page. If you wait a day, though, there will be usage data available for the health reports.

Also, to confirm that the data collection has been enabled, you can check the Manage Service Applications page, as you can see in Figure 3.39 (to get to the page, click Service Applications ➤ Manage Service Applications on the Application Management page).

FIGURE 3.39

The Manage Service Applications page with the Usage and Health Data collection started

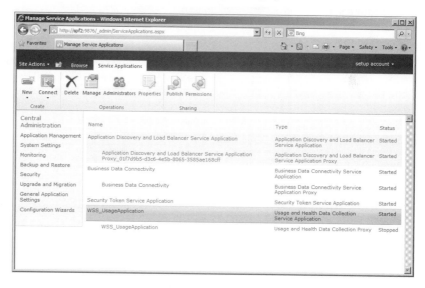

Service applications are available farm-wide, but they are applied per web application (that's why they are listed under Application Management and not System Settings). It's actually the service application's proxy that is associated with a web application. Proxies are organized by two groups, default and custom. Default is the first one and the one with all services available by, well, default. Custom simply displays all the services, but you can select which ones you do or do not want available for the web application. You can customize what a web application will get in terms of service applications during the web application's configuration (or, after a web application is created by using the Service Connections button on the Web Applications Management page).

Starting Sandboxed Code Service

The Sandboxed Code service is one of those services that is either on or off. That's it. To start the Sandboxed Code service, simply go back to the Services On Server page and click Start for the service. It will take a moment and then start.

However, there is a trick to running the Sandboxed Code service, and it is this: there is no configuration surface for it from the Services On Server page, but it does require an account identity to run with. Because of that, it starts using the farm account. That is not a good idea because it should have its own account identity to run with, and the Health Analyzer service will quickly generate an error saying that the farm account shouldn't be running so many services.

So, how do you fix it?

Go to the Service Accounts page (click Security on the Quick Launch bar, and then click the Configure Service Accounts link under General Security). This page, shown in Figure 3.40, is used to check services that are running on the server that require service accounts. It lets you see what account they are using and change them if necessary. This is the only place you can change the account for the Sandboxed Code service in Central Administration.

FIGURE 3.40

The Service Accounts page

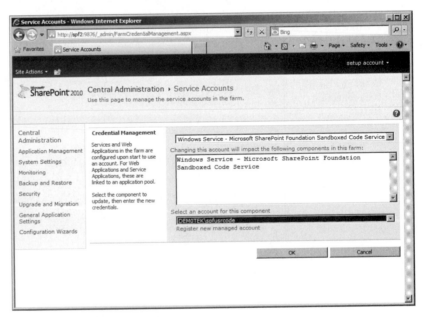

On that page are two fields and a box that will display any services the selected service impacts. In the first field (that doesn't seem to have a name), select the component you want to change (in this case, Windows Service – Microsoft SharePoint Foundation Sandboxed Code service). That will populate the description box with only the name of that service (because no other service is affected in this case). Finally, the second field, at the bottom of the section, is where you select the managed account you want to use for the service. By default, it will display the farm account. That is what you need to change. In my case, the account I'll change it to would be the account I registered earlier for this service, dem0tek\spfusrcode. Use the account you registered for this service earlier.

Once you've selected the correct account, click OK to keep the change. It will take a moment as SharePoint adds that data to the configuration database and makes the change elsewhere on the server. Then the service will have a new account. If you have more than one SharePoint server in the farm, you might want to run an IISRESET on those other servers so they pick up the change quickly. Now that you've configured and started the Search, BDC, Sandboxed Code, and Usage and Health Data Collection services, as well as registered managed accounts, we're ready to create our first web application.

Creating the First SharePoint Web Application

SharePoint web applications are just containers that define the address, security, and authentication for the site collections they contain. When you want to have a SharePoint site, first you create a web application. That creates a corresponding IIS Web Site, which defines access to its pages with a URL address (machine name and port number or host header), as well as specifying authentication, and can be configured with an SSL certificate to secure communications.

Web applications need to keep the content that makes up the sites they contain in a database. Each web application, therefore, has at least one content database. Also, logically, those web applications need to be able to *access* their databases, even if they are on a different server in the domain. Because of this, they use their corresponding IIS Web Site application pool identity to access resources. Further, those account identities must be assigned the correct permissions in order to do their jobs. So when configuring web applications, assigning the address, authentication, security, and content database account are the focus of configuration.

To start the process of creating a web application, you can simply click Application Management in the Quick Launch bar on the left. Once on the Application Management page (Figure 3.41), you can see that there are a number of additional tasks and headings than were listed under the Application Management heading on the Central Administration home page. On this page, click Manage Web Applications to get started.

FIGURE 3.41
The Application Management page

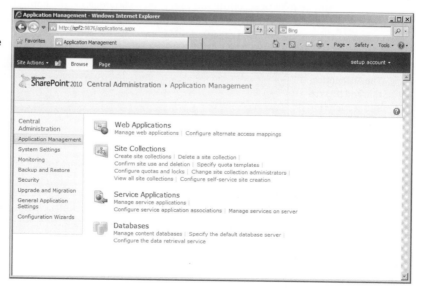

The Web Application Management page uses an Office-like ribbon bar for most of the tasks concerning web applications (this also means the page can be deceptively complicated in terms of the settings it can contain under one innocent-looking ribbon bar).

As you can see in Figure 3.42, the center of the page is the list area that displays the existing web applications. Currently there is only one, Central Administration v4, but we are going to add another.

1. To create a new web application, click the New button on the ribbon bar.

FIGURE 3.42
The Web Application Management page

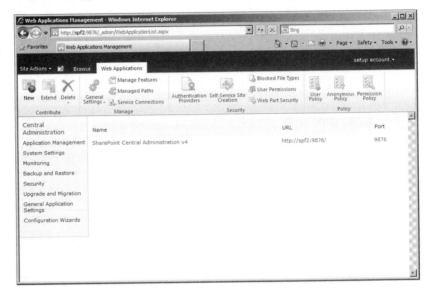

The New button will open a Create New Web Application form box. It has many settings, so you may want to maximize it. Regardless, unless you have a huge monitor, there will still be a lot of scrolling. Be prepared. And because the configuration of a web application has a lot of settings, I'll do this in pieces, starting with the Authentication and IIS Web Site sections (Figure 3.43).

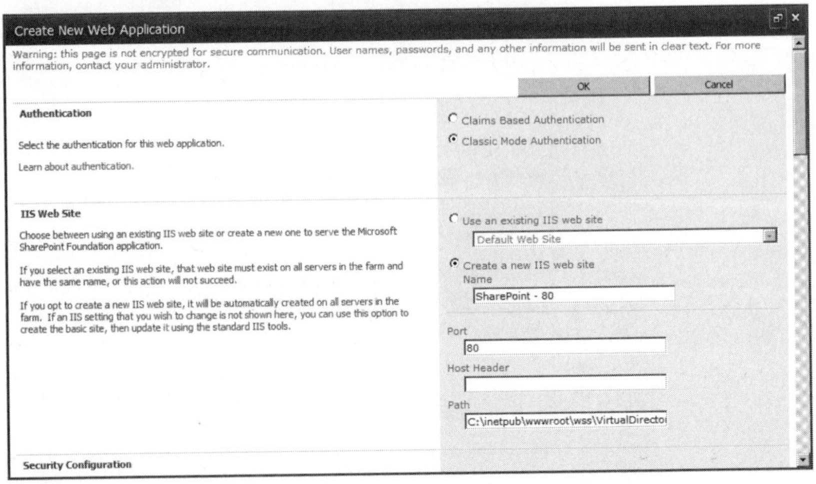

FIGURE 3.43
The Authentication and IIS Web Site sections for creating a new web application

The settings in the Authentication section are new to this version of SharePoint. Microsoft is trying to be more flexible with SharePoint's authentication capabilities, offering either the old-fashioned Windows authentication classic mode or claims-based authentication. Classic mode authentication doesn't take advantage of any of the new claims-based, token-passing features of Microsoft's Windows Identity Foundation (WIF) technologies. It works exactly like the perfectly functional mode used by the previous versions of SharePoint, with the exception of forms-based authentication. With this version of SharePoint, if you want to do FBA, the web application has to be set to claims-based authentication.

Claims-based authentication uses the new Windows Identity Foundation technologies and supports more than one authentication type per zone; it also handles alternate forms of authentication, such as forms-based, better.

2. For our uses, the classic authentication mode (the default) is fine, so keep it selected.

The next section, IIS Web Site, contains the settings particular to IIS and critically important to how users will access the site. The settings here are directly passed to IIS when the web application is created.

3. You have the option in the IIS Web Site section to either use an existing IIS Web Site or create a new one. In this case we are going to create a new one. That option is selected by default, so keep it.

SOMETIMES RECYCLING ISN'T SUGGESTED

If you had created an empty IIS Web Site and wanted to use it for your new SharePoint web application, you could specify it here. However, because the mechanism that causes SharePoint to propagate changes to the rest of the servers in the farm is triggered by creating a *new* website, you would have to go to each SharePoint server on the farm before creating the web application and manually add it there before you create the new web application. The new website you create here will be added to all the SharePoint servers on the farm as a matter of course.

---

4. Beneath the Create A New IIS Web Site radio button is the field where you can name the Web Site object. This will be displayed both in IIS and in SharePoint. Currently, the default *SharePoint-80* is listed. That name is actually fine, so we'll keep it for simplicity's sake. However, you can name it anything you like, in case, for example, you need to comply with company policy.

The next two settings, Port and Host Header, have to do with Web Site addressing. You basically get two options; either use the server's name and a unique port number to access the sites in the web application or apply a host header.

5. As this is the first web application to really host SharePoint sites on the server, it might as well use the default port 80 to respond to HTTP requests, as well as the server name for the address. So keep the default. In the future, you can always use alternate access mapping or extend the web application if you want to use a different address to access the web application's content. But this does mean that all other web applications on this server will need to use either a different port or a host header for its address. This means that the address for this web application will be just the server name; the default port doesn't need to be specified for the address in most browsers. They automatically use port 80.

6. The last setting in this section, Path, is more informational than anything; most people just keep the default. The Path field contains the actual physical path on the hard drive to the folder that will be the home directory (otherwise known as the virtual directory) for the web application. If you click in the field and scroll to the right, you'll eventually see that the name for the directory will be the port number for the site, as it should be.

The next sections, shown in Figure 3.44, cover the Security Configuration, Public URL, and Application Pool settings for this web application.

FIGURE 3.44

The Security Configuration, Public URL, and Application Pool settings for creating a new web application

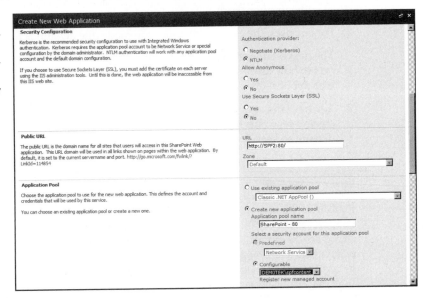

The Security Configuration settings available are the choice of an authentication provider, whether to allow anonymous access, and whether to use an SSL certificate to secure the site.

Every web application gets five zones to use for alternate addressing and security. The first zone for a site is, by default, the considerately named default zone. This is the first zone that the indexer uses when trying to access and index (or crawl) content. The indexer prefers NTLM authentication, so it's considered best practice (and simply prudent) to have the first zone for a web application use NTLM. Kerberos is supported, but it does require additional configuration, and the indexer cannot handle Kerberos on custom ports (should you be using one).

For our purposes, choosing the prudent course works. So, keep NTLM as the authentication provider. Along those lines, you won't enable anonymous access or an SSL certificate at this time. For more information about using a SSL certificate with SharePoint, see Chapter 16.

7. So, for the Security Configuration settings, keep the defaults, making sure that NTLM is the authentication provider, that Allow Anonymous is not enabled, and that Use Secure Sockets Layer (SSL) is set to No.

AMBIDEXTROUS

When you enable claims-based authentication for a web application, it is able to support several authentication types simultaneously: forms-based authentication, which can simply use a SQL database to contain usernames instead of Active Directory; trusted provider authentication, which takes advantage of Active Directory Federated Services (ADFS) if you're using it in your environment; and Windows authentication, which uses NTLM, Kerberos, or Basic. This means for one claims-based web application, you can use all of the authentication types. Not only that, but with Windows authentication alone you can enable NTLM, Kerberos, *and* Basic authentication access for one zone (try *that* with classic mode). Being able to support NTLM alongside the other authentication types should assist Search in accessing the web application's content and indexing it.

The Public URL section is interesting. Like many settings in SharePoint, this one has a particular use if some other technology is configured elsewhere. The Public URL is the address that users are supposed to use to access the site, is the address returned to the browser of the users if they successfully access the site, and is the address that will be at the beginning of all links contained in the web application. This setting is also used for load balancing; it actually used to be called the *Load Balanced URL* in previous versions of SharePoint. Microsoft didn't change that capability of this setting, just its name. In other words, when you have more than one SharePoint front-end server in the server farm, it is assumed that some load-balancing technology will be employed to balance the load of requests to the servers. The load balancer (be it hardware or software) will intercept the traffic to the public URL and route it to the appropriate SharePoint server in the load-balanced cluster. Therefore, there must be one URL that each SharePoint server knows is the primary one for that web application.

8. Needless to say, this setting is pretty useful to know about. By default it will use the address specified above it (whether server name or host header) and then the port—in our case, that's the server name and port 80. This is fine to accept for right now, since we are not load balancing just yet. If you are going to enable SSL, it's the public URL that must match the certificate address (depending on the certificate type). Watch out for that appended port in that case. Again, that's not our issue here, so leave the default.

The last section in this set is Application Pool. It's here that you indicate whether you want to use an existing pool (not really recommended) or create one specifically for this web application's use. In addition, you need to specify the account identity used by the application pool.

9. We are, of course, going to create a unique application pool for this web application. The default name is always the name you gave the Web Site, which works for me because it's not only convenient, but it's logical and makes it easier to figure out which application pool goes with which IIS Web Site. So, keep the default.

The application identity, or security account, is another thing altogether. The options are to either use a local built-in account (bad idea, and it's grayed out anyway) or use a "configurable" account.

At this point, it might be good to point out that this field only allows registered managed accounts (Figure 3.44). As such, it's a good thing we've already registered the account for this web application; otherwise, we'd have to either stop and do that or use an existing account. (That's not a good option for us at this point, since all other accounts will be used by other, often busy, services.)

10. In this case, the account I recently registered to be used for a web application was *dem0tek\spfcontent*. In my case, I needed to click the down arrow and select it from the registered accounts list. If the account you plan to use wasn't the default for you, select it in the configurable field before continuing.

The last sections to configure to create a web application are Database Name and Authentication, Failover Server, Search Server, Service Application Connections, and Customer Experience Improvement Program, shown in Figure 3.45.

FIGURE 3.45

The final settings in the Create New Web Application window

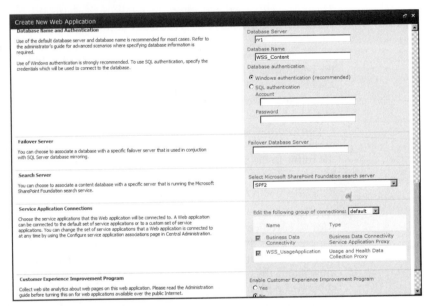

For the Database Name and Authentication sections, a lot of the defaults are fine. This section requires a SQL database name, a name for the content database of this web application, and how SharePoint is supposed to authenticate to access the content on the SQL server.

11. Be sure to specify the SQL server name (SharePoint already knows mine, *rr1*). You can also name the content database for the web application (the default of *WSS_Content* works for me, so I'm not going to change it).

12. Finally, if your SQL server uses SQL authentication, select it and enter the correct credentials in the username and password fields below the SQL authentication option. My SQL database server supports Windows authentication, so I am keeping that option selected.

13. For the Failover Server section, I plan to leave it blank, since I don't have SQL configured for failover. If you did, this is where you would specify the failover SQL server that SharePoint could use if SQL were set up to support SQL Server database mirroring.

14. In the Search Server section, select the Search server that you want to index this database. We enabled Search on this server, so select its name in the drop-down field (mine is *SPF2*, as you saw in Figure 3.45).

The next section, Service Application Connections, bears a closer look. Because we configured the Usage and Health data collection service application (going by WSS_UsageApplication) and Business Data Connectivity service already, they are available to be selected. They are enabled by default for this web application because the default is selected in the field. If you wanted to be able to select one or neither of them, you could click in the Edit The Following Group Of Connections field and select [custom].

15. However, for our purposes, keeping the default group selected for the Service Applications Connections is fine.

16. Finally, the Customer Experience Improvement Program section has two options, Yes or No. Since I chose No (I don't want to participate) during installation, there is a warning in this section that if I choose Yes, I want to participate in the program for this web application, and I have to enable it farm-wide. I am going to select No here. Feel free to make your own choice.

So to recap, my settings are as follows:

1. In the Authentication section:

   A. Classic Mode Authentication

2. In the IIS Web Site section:

   A. Create a new IIS Web Site.

   B. Name: SharePoint-80

   C. Leave the port at 80.

   D. Leave the host header blank.

   E. Keep the default path.

3. In the Security Configuration section:

   A. Leave the Authentication Provider as NTLM.

   B. Do not allow Anonymous.

   C. Do not use Secure Sockets Layer (SSL).

4. In the Public URL section, leave the default URL as is.

5. In the Application Pool section:

   A. Make sure that Create New Application Pool is selected.

   B. Keep the default name, SharePoint-80.

   C. Select Configurable for the security account.

   D. Select the managed account we created for content databases; mine is dem0tek\ spfcontent.

6. In the Database name and Authentication section:

   A. Make sure the database server name is correct. Enter the correct one and the instance if necessary.

   B. Leave the default database name as it is or change it if you want.

   C. Leave Windows Authentication, unless your SQL server requires SQL authentication. In that case, enter the correct username and password in the appropriate fields.

7. In the Failover Server section, leave the field blank, unless you have a failover server available. If you do, enter its name in the Failover Database Server field.

8. In the Search Server section, select the local server's name, since that's where you enabled Search. It should be the only option in the field.

9. In the Service Application Connections section, leave the default selected.

10. In the Customer Experience Improvement Program section, select the option No.

If all your settings are correct, click OK (either at the bottom of the page or at the top).

A progress box will come up. After that finishes, you'll get an Application Created notice in the same box, indicating that, if this is the first time the application pool has been used with SharePoint, it may take a while for the IIS Web Site associated with this web application to be propagated to the other SharePoint servers on the farm. In addition, this web application still needs a site collection before it is finished (Figure 3.46). Remember that without a site collection, navigating to the web application's URL will bring up nothing.

FIGURE 3.46
The Application
Created notice

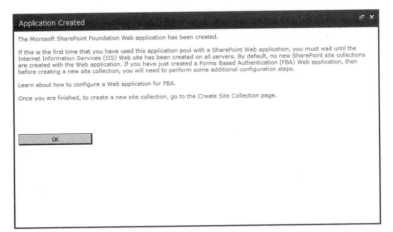

Although it is not required, I find it is always a good idea, if I can afford to do so, to open the command prompt (you may need to use elevated privileges) and run an IISRESET command, just to make sure IIS is clear about the new web application and all of its settings.

Although the web application has been created, it's just an empty container waiting to be filled with SharePoint site collections. So, let's get started.

Creating the First Site Collection

Now that there is a web application to put it in, it's time to create a site collection. In the Application Created box, there is a link to Create Site Collection; click it to begin. (If you closed the box, go back to the Application Management page in Central Administration, and click the Create Site Collection link.)

Immediately, the notification box turns into a Create Site Collection settings box, which unfortunately wastes some screen real estate. (If you created your site collection using the Create Site Collections link under Application Management in Central Administration, the settings will be offered on a normal browser page and not in a box.)

In the Create Site Collection box, there are, again, enough settings that it's useful to group the sections together roughly by screenshot.

Remember that a web application is completely empty without a site. Sites are organized into site collections in SharePoint, even though they all start with just one top-level site. In the case of our web application, this is going to be the first one in this SharePoint implementation, so it can have the coveted HTTP://servername URL. This address is very easy for users to understand and use (second only to www.servername.com). This site collection we are getting ready to create can have its top-level home page at that root address of the web application's URL. Only one site collection can use that address per web application; all others must use a different path.

Often the first site in the first web application, because of the simple address, is used as a portal site—a nice, general, all-purpose site that might have links in it to other sites or site collections. For that reason it usually has the most generic of all templates applied to it: the Team Site template. Although a number of site templates are available out of the box with SharePoint Foundation, the Team Site template is a good top-level site template. A standard, welcome-to-the-site-collection site, with announcements, discussions, and tasks lists and a document library, it is a good all-around starter site—useful from the start, with good bones to add things to later.

There are six sections on this settings page. The first three sections of the Create Site Collection page, shown in Figure 3.47, are Title And Description, Web Site Address, and Template Selection.

1. In the Title And Description section, you can, unsurprisingly, enter the title and description for the site collection's top-level site. The title of the site will appear on most of the pages of the site (if the title breadcrumb area is showing), but the description will appear only on the home page. (Unless you create a wiki library, which, inexplicably, uses the site's description in its title area instead of its own.) Feel free to enter something appropriate. In my example, I am going to use *Company Site* for my title and *Corporate Collaboration* for the description.

   In the Web Site Address section, the only web application available, the one you just made, is already prepopulated as the root of this site collection's address. The drop-down list at the end of the URL gives you the option of just starting the site collection from the root URL (which displays as just a forward slash in the field) or having the site collection's top-level site start at http://servername/sites/.

2. We are just going to place the site collection at the root of the URL, so keep the default selection for the Web Site address.

FIGURE 3.47
The Title and
Description, Web
Site Address, and
Template Selection
settings for creat-
ing a site collection

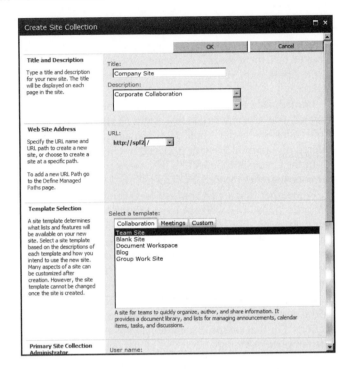

WHAT'S SITES GOT TO DO WITH IT?

In this case, http://servername/sites is considered a managed path and allows you to configure a logical address structure for site collections within a web application that are not going to be at the root of the URL. As you can imagine, you can configure additional managed paths. Because this is the first site collection, you don't need to worry about having a unique address. But if there were another site collection added to this web application (and there can be many if you'd like), it would need to use a different URL path, because the root would be taken. It's at that time that creating managed paths becomes more relevant. Managed paths will be covered more deeply in Chapter 10.

The next section is Template Selection. It is here that you can choose to apply one of the pre-made site templates that SharePoint has available for you. There are three tabs orga-nizing the available options. The templates offer standard samples of lists, libraries, and web parts that you might want to have on a site, based on what the site is for. The tabs are arranged by the purpose of the templates. Under Collaboration are the standard Team Site template, as well as Blog, Document Workspace, and Group Work (a new addition to the templates explored in Chapter 9, "Sites, Subsites, and Workspaces"); under Meeting are templates that use a different site definition than the collaboration templates and relate to types of meetings, and under Custom is the option to simply not apply a template (assuming you want to upload one, in the form of a solution file, to the farm and then apply it). If you click either the Collaboration or Meeting tab, you can select a template and see a brief description of its purpose beneath the list.

3. For our needs, the Team Site template is ideal, so that is what I am going to choose for this example. Feel free to select the template of your choice.

The last three sections of the page are Primary Site Administrator, Secondary Site Administrator, and Quota Template (Figure 3.48).

FIGURE 3.48

The Primary Site Administrator, Secondary Site Administrator, and Quota Template settings for creating a site collection

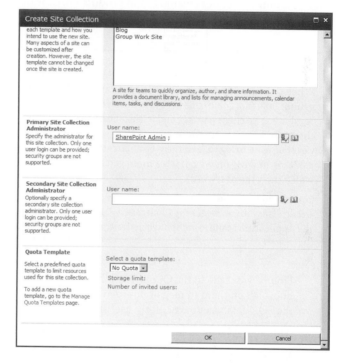

Each site collection must have at least one site administrator. This account not only has administrative rights to each of the sites in the collection (the first, top-level one, and any other subsites that are added to it) but also has rights to specific settings that affect the whole site collection, such as content types, template galleries, and administrative recycle bin.

4. In the Primary Site Administrator field, I am going to add my SharePoint admin utility account, *shareadmin*. Having an account specified in this field is mandatory.

User Name fields have a check name and address book icon next to them. These icons allow you to check the account name you entered against Active Directory to be sure it is correct (if it resolves the account name, the name will change in the field to the display name for the account in AD), or, in the case of the address book button (also referred to as the People Picker), it opens a dialog box where you can search for a username by first, last, full, or account name. It queries the authentication provider you are using for this web application. In our case, the People Picker is integrated with Active Directory, so you don't need to specify the domain name. In my case, after using the Check Name button, my account name, *shareadmin*, changed to the account's display name of *SharePoint Admin*, as you can see in Figure 3.48.

A secondary site administrator is always a good idea (actually, having several isn't a bad thing), just in case the primary administrator goes on vacation or is out sick while site collection administration needs to be done.

5. However, just for this example, you can afford to leave the Secondary Site Collection Administrator field blank. But in production, consider always having two accounts to administer site collections.

ONLY TWO MAY ENTER

When creating a new site collection, you can configure only two accounts for access. Those fields cannot take more than one account (despite the semicolon that is added to a username after you resolve it with check names), and it must be a user account, not a security group. Keep in mind that these two accounts are the only ones allowed to log in (aside from the farm account, which should never be used to log in, and the web application's content database account, which you eventually can't log in with anyway, if it's a managed account with password change enabled, because you won't know the password).

You can add more accounts to the site collection's administrator's group once you get to the site. Otherwise, you can select the Change Site Collection Administrators link under Site Collections on the Application Management page in Central Administration to change the accounts if necessary.

Finally, we come to the Quota Template section. All site collections can have a size limit quota set on them in megabytes to avoid having one site collection take too much space in the SQL database (particularly useful if you are using the Standalone installation).

6. Although it's a great idea, we have not configured a quota yet, so leave it blank.

Keep in mind that you can create a quota and go back and apply it to the site collection later (for more on that, see Chapter 10).

NUMBER OF INVITED USERS?

You may have noticed a Number Of Invited Users field in the Quota Template section. If you were to create a quota template to be applied to site collections, there would be no setting for number of invited users. So, what is that setting for?

It applies to site collection only if your farm is using Active Directory Account Creation mode. Because ADAC is really focused on site collections, especially in terms of user accounts, you can set a limit on how many users are invited per site collection. That's just one more SharePoint mystery solved.

7. So, if you've entered a title and description, specified the URL path for the site collection (remember, mine's at the root), selected a template, and entered a primary site collection administrator, click OK to create your site collection.

A Processing page will open for a moment, and then a Top-Level Site Successfully Created box will come up. I know that what you were creating was a site collection (it said so on the top of the configuration page), but all site collections start with just one, top-level site. This just proves it (Figure 3.49).

FIGURE 3.49
Top-Level Site
Successfully
Created box

At this point, you could just click OK and end up back in Central Administration, or you could click the link to the new site collection to open a new browser window to the new site collection's URL. If you do that, be aware that the setup account was not given explicit permission to access the collection, so you will have to log in with a site collection administrator's account.

8. I'm opting to check out the new site collection in a different browser window, so click its URL link in the box.

It will, as expected, open the new site collection in a different browser window. You will be greeted by an Access Denied page (Figure 3.50). See, I told you that the site administrator accounts were the only ones allowed access.

FIGURE 3.50
Access
Denied page

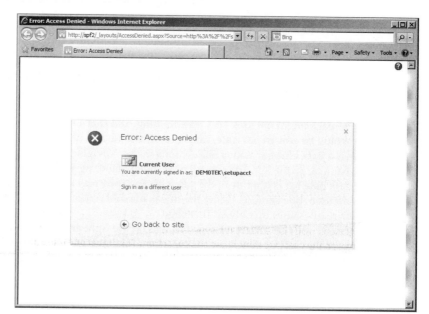

When, for any reason, you are denied access to a page in SharePoint, this Access Denied page comes up, indicating what account you're logged in with and giving you a link to try logging in again as a different user (or go back a page to one where you were allowed access). In this case, all you need to do is log in as the site collection administrator. For me, that would be *shareadmin* (make sure the prompt displays the correct domain for the account; if it doesn't, use the domain\username syntax).

9. So, just click Sign In As A Different User to get a login prompt (Figure 3.51).

FIGURE 3.51

Signing in as a different user

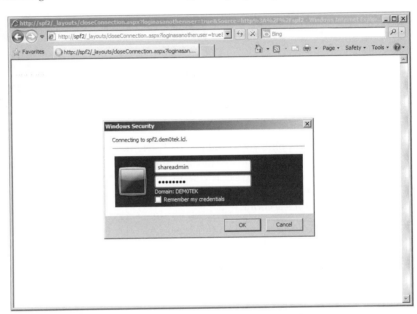

10. Type in the site collection administrator's username and password (the prompt can also offer to remember the credentials so as to not prompt you so often). Click OK.

And voila! The Company Site home page fills the browser.

Congratulations, you've reached the first page of the top-level site in the first site collection in your first web application.

The page might not look very intimidating, and that's rather the point (Figure 3.52). The site should be easy to navigate, easy to understand, and not overly cluttered. At the top of the page is a dark blue bar with a Site Actions menu, Navigate Up and Edit Page buttons, some ribbon bar tabs on the left, and the Account menu (showing your login name) on the right. Below the dark blue bar is the title of the site with an arrow and the name of the page itself (a sort of breadcrumb/title combo). Below the title is the description of the site (Corporate Collaboration), which really shows up only on this page.

Beneath the title area is a Home tab, and on the right are the Search field and help icon. Below them are the Quick Launch bar on the left and the web part or *rich content* area (the main content area for most pages in SharePoint) in the center. We will be covering SharePoint's interface in much more detail in the next chapter, but this at least gives you an idea what to expect from the Team Site home page.

FIGURE 3.52
The new site collection's home page

And we've done it. This SharePoint Complete installation is configured as completely as the Standalone installation, only using domain accounts and databases on a full-blown SQL server rather than SQL Express.

At this point, it's a good idea to go through and quickly confirm what was changed by your configuration settings. You've created databases for Search, BDC, and usage and health, as well as the web application, so now let's confirm they are there. You should also check IIS for the application pools and Web Site changes.

So, let's go see what SharePoint has wrought.

Confirming Configuration Changes

During the prerequisites and installation, we checked to see what changes occurred on the server, and now it's time to see what the final configuration changes did. Again, I'll go through this a little faster than in the Standalone installation, because it's already been done in the previous chapter.

You know the SharePoint root, at `%Program Files%\Common Files\Microsoft Shared\Web Server Extensions\14`, was created; we saw that earlier.

The SharePoint services running on the server are the same, but Search uses the search account you configured, and the SharePoint timer job uses the farm account (Figure 3.53), and the User Code Host service uses the account you specified earlier for the Sandboxed Code service. The other SharePoint services are using local accounts because they interact with the local server. The service applications we configured don't run within the context of SharePoint and don't have their on services on the server per se.

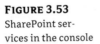

FIGURE 3.53
SharePoint services in the console

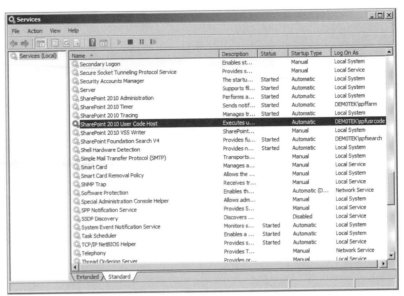

Now we should check IIS. There will be much more in the IIS console, because during the initial configuration we created the SharePoint-80 web application and assigned it an application pool identity. We also set up the Business Data Connectivity service application, which should show up under Web Services. SharePoint also, during configuration, created the Central Administration website and a site dedicated to web services, like the Topology service and Security Token service.

But before we get to IIS, on the SQL server, there should be six new databases, and on the SharePoint server, new service accounts should have been added as members to the new SharePoint local security groups.

Confirming SQL Databases

You know that SharePoint created a number of databases during installation and configuration, and you know that those databases need to have certain accounts accessing them.

If you are able, go to the SQL server and check out the databases. I'll show you how to check the permissions on a database or two, with the idea that once you know how to do it, you can check the others on your own.

1. Log into the SQL server (mine is RR1), and open the SQL Management Studio (for SQL 2008, go to Start ➤ All Programs ➤ Microsoft SQL Server 2008 folder ➤ SQL Management Studio). Log in using the correct account.

2. In the SQL Management Studio window, open the Databases node in the Object Explorer pane. Underneath you should see (Figure 3.54), in addition to whatever SQL-related or non-SharePoint databases you might have, the six databases that SharePoint made (you might have configured different database names): configuration (SharePoint_Config), search (WSS_Search_SPF2), logging (WSS_Logging), BDC (BDC_Services_DB_1), SharePoint-80's content database (WSS_Content), and Central Administration site's content database (Admin_Content_(*GUID*)). The names of most of these databases should be familiar to you, since you specified them as you configured their services.

FIGURE 3.54

SharePoint's databases on the SQL server

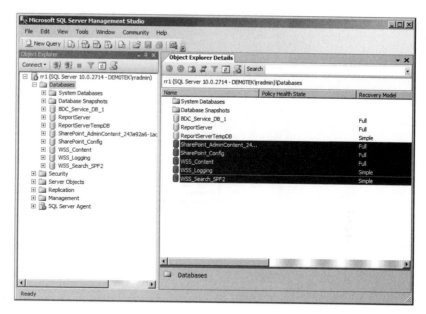

It helps to know what accounts have been assigned access to the databases. If you remember, originally only the setup account had roles set up on the SQL server. But when configuration began, the setup account added the farm account to the SQL server's login roles, as well as the DBCreator and SecurityAdmin roles. This let the setup account step away from managing SQL for SharePoint any longer and let the farm account do it.

To this end, the configuration database for SharePoint was created by the setup account, but the farm account was given ownership of it after. From that point on, the farm account is the dbo (static database owner role) for all SharePoint databases, but it may assign other SharePoint accounts access to those databases depending on what they require.

To check to see what the users are for the configuration database, take the following steps (you can use the same method on all databases):

1. Select the database (in my case, SharePoint_Config, which you might remember was the default name for it during configuration, which I kept) in the Object Explorer pane.

2. In the details pane, open the Security folder, and then open Users.

   As you can see in Figure 3.55, all accounts that might need to be able to read (or change) the configuration database have been added. Of specific note is that the farm account is there (in my case, dem0tek\spffarm), and the setup account isn't.

   That's because the setup account is *the* static dbo for the database. It created the configuration database during installation and then handed off ownership of it to the farm account later.

3. To prove that (and find the setup account), double-click dbo in the details pane.

FIGURE 3.55
Configuration
database users

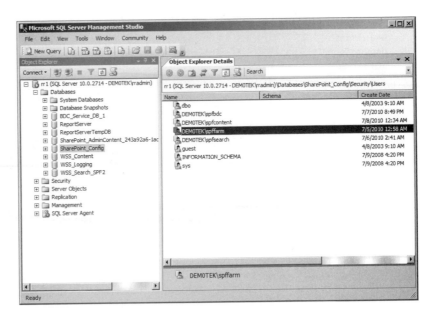

As you can see in Figure 3.56, in the dbo's properties dialog box, the login name is actually the setup account (mine is dem0tek\setupacct). This is the only database that the setup account owns. After the farm account is specified, it takes over the creation of SharePoint databases and assigning rights to them.

FIGURE 3.56
The configuration database dbo account

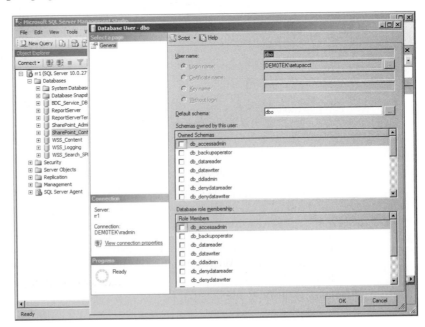

If you close out of that dialog box and double-click the farm account in the details pane, you'll see a dialog box for this account (Figure 3.57). If you scroll down in the Role Members list, you'll see that the account is set as a database owner.

WHAT ARE THOSE OTHER ROLES?

SharePoint_Shell_Access is the role added to SharePoint databases for the use of PowerShell, and WSS_Content_Application_Pool is a role added for any account that is an application pool account (which the farm account is, for Central Administration).

FIGURE 3.57

The farm account's role on the configuration database

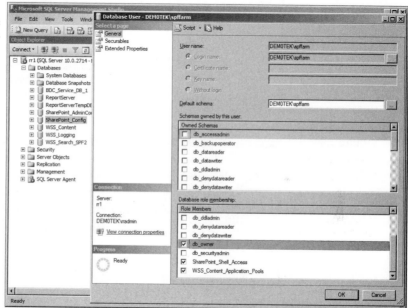

If you close out of the dialog box and double-click one of the other accounts, such as the search account, you'll see in its dialog box (if you scroll down the Role Members list) that it might have access to the configuration database, but only with the WSS_Content_Application_Pool role (Figure 3.58), meaning that it basically has the same rights to the configuration database as a content database account.

To see what account has the right to access the content database for the web application you created (WSS_Content in my case), just click it in the Object Explorer, open the Security folder in details pane, and then open Users.

You'll see, as in Figure 3.59, that the content database account (my example is dem0tek\ spfcontent) is the only one listed.

FIGURE 3.58
The Search
account's role on
the configuration
database

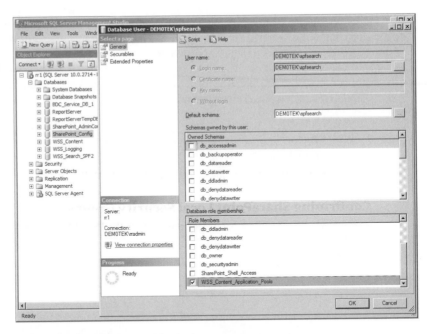

FIGURE 3.59
Content database
account

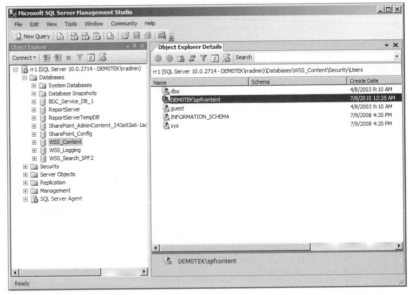

If you were to double-click that account, it would show that it held a db_owner role in the Role Members list, which is fitting, since that is its database.

And if you go back to the Users list and double-click the dbo for that database, the login for that role will be, unsurprisingly, the farm account. That's because the farm account created the database and then handed off the owner role to the content database account. So, it's the true dbo, but the content database account has ownership rights, too.

If you check each of the other databases, you'll see that the correct accounts have access and that the farm account actually made their databases for them, too.

This indicates that even though the configuration was done on a page on the SharePoint server, there wasn't any smoke and mirrors. The databases you named (except for the one used by Central Administration's site collection, which has that ugly long GUID) yourself, and the accounts you assigned are assigned to them, as expected. The setup account did its job, and the farm account continued it.

You did it. These are your SharePoint databases (there may be more or fewer databases on your SQL server, depending on how it's configured and what products are using it in your environment).

Now let's go back to the SharePoint server to check the security groups and IIS.

Confirming SharePoint Local Security Groups

To confirm the local security group changes on the local SharePoint server, open the Computer Management console (Start ➤ Administrative Tools ➤ Computer Management), open the Local User And Groups node in the navigation pane, and click the Groups folder in the content pane. (I'm assuming you've used the Computer Management console before.)

If you scroll down the list of groups on the server, you should see WSS_WPG, WSS_ADMIN_WPG, and WSS_RESTRICTED_WPG.

For WSS_WPG, the accounts in this group generally only need read access to resources on the server. If you double-click, it should contain a lot of the service accounts you assigned: farm account, search account, content database account, and, oddly enough, the BDC account (Figure 3.60).

For the WSS_ADMIN_WPG group, whose members generally need both read and write access, only the setup account and server farm account are members (Figure 3.61).

FIGURE 3.60
WSS_WPG
members in
the SharePoint
security group

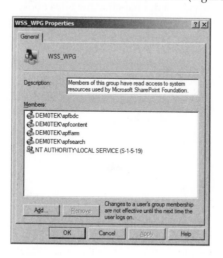

And for the WSS_RESTRICTED_WPG group, the lone member is the farm account. That stands to reason because that is the account, on behalf of the whole SharePoint farm, that speaks to the SharePoint Administration service, which has a local system identity.

So now, if you should have to troubleshoot permissions or set up a folder that will need them, you know what groups are available on the SharePoint servers and what their members are.

FIGURE 3.61
WSS_ADMIN_
WPG group
members

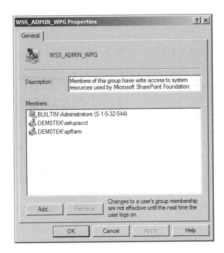

Confirming IIS Web Sites and Application Pools

When you created the SharePoint-80 web application, it created a corresponding IIS Web Site. Also, whenever you created an application pool account, SharePoint added it to IIS.

So, let's take a glance and see what changed:

1. Open the IIS Manager console (Start ➢ Administrative Tools ➢ Internet Information Services (IIS) Manager).

2. Once in the console, in the connections pane, open the local server node (if it isn't already), and double-click the Sites node icon (Figure 3.62). There will be, in addition to the Central Administration and Web Services Web Sites, a SharePoint-80 (or whatever you named your web application) Web Site as well.

FIGURE 3.62
New SharePoint
Web Site in IIS

3. If you select the new Web Site (mine is SharePoint-80) and then click Advanced Settings in the Actions pane on the right, the dialog box (Figure 3.63) will indicate its application pool (conveniently named after the Web Site instead of a random GUID).

FIGURE 3.63
Confirming the application pool in Advanced Settings

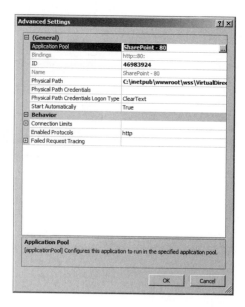

4. Click the plus sign next to the icon for Web Services; you'll see three service applications: Topology, the Security Token service, and an application unappealingly named with a long, random GUID. That's the Business Data Connectivity service (Figure 3.64) we configured earlier.

FIGURE 3.64
BDC Service application GUID under Web Services

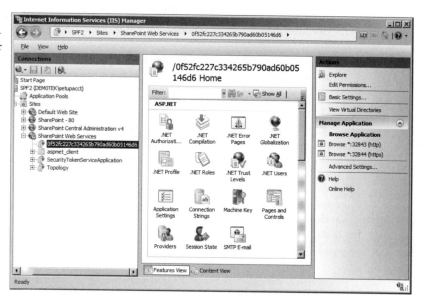

5. If you select the BDC service's GUID in the connections pane and check its advanced settings, you'll see yet another long random GUID for its application pool name. Keep it in mind (you can see mine in Figure 3.65).

FIGURE 3.65

The BDC Service application's advanced settings

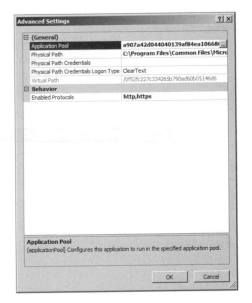

6. To check the application pools, double-click the Application Pools node in the connections pane. In the workspace, you'll see a pretty long list. Two of the application pool names are just random GUIDs (compliments of Web Services service applications); one is named after the web application you created, one is the SecurityTokenServiceApplicationpool, and, of course, there is Central Administration.

7. To confirm the account identity for the application pools, you can scroll over in the workspace (that middle pane) to see it listed per application pool, or you can select a particular application pool in the connections pane and then click Advanced Settings in the Actions pane.

For example, in Figure 3.66, in the IIS console you can see that SharePoint-80 is using the account I assigned to it when making the web application, dem0tek\spfcontent.

Using the Advanced Settings dialog box gives you the added bonus of additional information about the application pool. Select an application pool in the workspace, such as the one for the BDC service (that long random GUID you saw earlier), and then click Advanced Settings in the Actions pane. In the dialog box, the account identity that we assigned for the application pool will be displayed (Figure 3.67), as well as additional information.

So, you've confirmed that your initial configuration of SharePoint is complete, and you are now at the same point of configuration that we were with the Standalone installation, only you've done most of it yourself.

To really use SharePoint, though, you have a few more things to attend to. To be able to send out alerts and those password change notifications, outgoing email needs to be configured. For the lists and libraries able to receive email to do so, incoming email needs to be configured. And finally, you should at least add some additional users to Central Administration and your SharePoint top-level site.

So, let's move on to the post-installation tasks.

FIGURE 3.66
Application Pools available in IIS

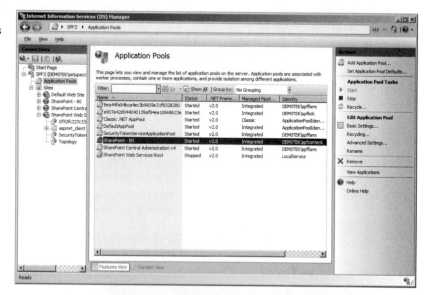

FIGURE 3.67
The BDC application pool identity in Advanced Settings

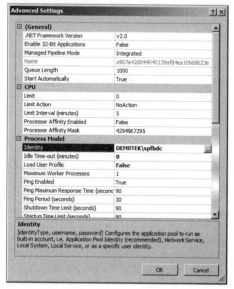

 **Real World Scenario**

USER PROFILE AND DCOM ERRORS GETTING YOU DOWN?

There is a good chance that, after you install and configure SharePoint, there will be a few known errors in the event logs. Troubleshooting these errors is covered in detail in Chapter 13, "Maintenance and Monitoring," but I just wanted to let you know that there are known fixes for them. Here are some brief suggestions.

For the DCOM event ID 10016 Distributed COM error in the System log; there will likely be two DCOM objects that need to be dealt with. One is the IIS WAMREG admin service; its CLSID starts with 61738644. This is caused because SharePoint doesn't properly give content database access accounts the permission to launch or activate the DCOM object locally. You will need to give that account local activation permission to the DCOM object to clear that error (or better yet, give the WSS_WPG group permission; that way, you won't need to do this every time a new content database account is used). For server 2008 R2, you will first need to go the object's corresponding key in the registry and give the account you are logged in with ownership of the key and full control of it. Then you can go to the Component Services console, select the DCOM component you need, go to its properties, and then add the necessary account (or group) to the Launch and Activation permissions.

If you get the same event ID error, but for CLSID that starts with 000C101, then that is because the farm account wasn't given the correct permissions to the MSIServer DCOM object. To fix this error, use the steps used for the other CLSID , but add the farm account to the launch and activation permissions for the 000C101 object (it won't be listed by its name) so it can do local activation.

In the application event log, you may also get event ID 1511 errors because the server cannot find a local user profile for the content database account (the account causing the problem will be listed in the error). SharePoint uses a user profile for content database accounts but just can't seem to get it right. So if you do have this problem, do an IISRESET on the server to unlock the profile (in case IIS was using it). Then log in locally on the SharePoint server with the offending account. Change some things on the desktop (if it indicates that it was using a temporary profile, make changes, and log out and log back in again, until your changes stick and it doesn't say it's using a temporary profile), then log out and log back in as your SharePoint administrator. You might want to do another IISRESET just in case and then check the user profile properties to make sure the account now lists as having a local profile. It might take a few tries, but that usually works.

Post-installation Configuration Tasks

At this point, you've finished the Complete installation for your server farm, but there are still a few more things you need to do to have your implementation truly up and running. Specifically, although SharePoint now has Central Administration, a SharePoint-80 web application, Search, BDC, sandboxed code, and usage and health enabled, it is missing email.

This is because email configuration requires information that the installation process cannot predict, and it requires custom configuration far outside of SharePoint's control. However, considering some of the configuration tasks you've done, configuring incoming and outgoing email is pretty easy. Once that is done, you'll need to create accounts for farm administrators, site collection administrators, and at least one user.

These procedures are the same for either a Complete or Standalone install, so I am just going to review them quickly here. For more details, see "Post-installation Configuration Tasks" in Chapter 2.

Outgoing Email

Outgoing email must be configured in order to send out notifications and for alerts to be enabled at the site level. If you have not enabled outgoing email, lists and libraries will not display an Alert Me button on the ribbon bars.

You can configure outgoing email for each individual web application you create or set up outgoing email as the default for the farm. At the least, the farm-wide outgoing email settings should be configured.

Briefly, to configure outgoing email for the farm, in Central Administration, on the System Settings page, click Configure Outgoing E-Mail Settings, under the E-Mail And Text Messages (SMS) heading.

On the Outgoing E-Mail Settings page (Figure 3.68), configure the following:

1. Specify your outgoing SMTP server. This is usually your office email server, configured to handle outbound and incoming email. In my example, that would be my domain controller, `dc1.dem0tek.lcl` (you can just use the server's NetBIOS name if you want; in my case that would be DC1).

2. In the second field, specify the address the recipients will see in the From field of the email. It doesn't need to be a real address, just something appropriate. To keep things simple, I am going to use a real address I set up for outgoing email, `sharepoint@dem0tek.lcl`.

FIGURE 3.68
The Outgoing
E-Mail
Settings page

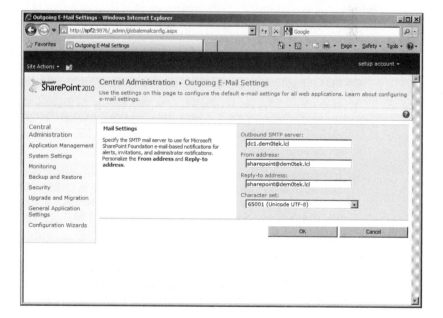

3. The Reply-to address has to be a real email address that the recipients can reply to if necessary. In my case, I am using `sharepoint@dem0tek.lcl` again.

4. The fourth field has to do with the character set used for outgoing email. The default character set listed (UTF-8) is used by my server and is a good standard, variable-length, character-encoding system for Unicode. It can represent every character in the Unicode character set and is backward compatible with ASCII. If your environment requires a different character set, feel free to select it from the drop-down list. I am keeping the default.

Don't Forget to Reanalyze

The Health Analyzer may consider not having outgoing email configured a problem. So if you wait a week or longer after installing SharePoint to configure outgoing email, it will generate an error warning you about it. After you've finished setting up outgoing email, be sure to clear the entry on the Problems And Solutions page (click Monitoring in the Quick Launch bar; then, under Health Analyzer, click Review Problems And Solutions) by viewing the error item and clicking Reanalyze Now in the toolbar.

Incoming Email

SharePoint has a feature that allows users the convenience of emailing items to several of its lists and libraries, rather than having to log in, navigate to the list or library, and then add the item. To make this capability possible at the list level, it must be configured here in Central Administration. Incoming email does require SMTP, which should have been added during the prerequisite portion of the installation process (see the "Installation and Configuration" section of this chapter for more).

To configure incoming email in Central Administration, go to the System Settings page, and click the Configure Incoming E-Mail Settings link.

On the Configure Incoming E-Mail Settings page (Figure 3.69), do the following:

1. Select Yes under the Enable Sites On This Server To Receive E-Mail? question in the Enable Incoming E-Mail section. Since SMTP is already set up on the local server, I have chosen Automatic for the Settings Mode; it will automatically use the SMTP drop folder for incoming email.

2. Incoming email does not require Directory Management Service. That service requires Exchange to be integrated with Active Directory in order to add the incoming email–enabled lists and groups to Exchange's global address list. We are just enabling incoming email right now, so we should keep the Directory Management Service setting at No.

3. Incoming email requires a display address for each incoming email–enabled list or library. By default it will append the alias for the list or library to the display address (usually the server's fully qualified domain name) for incoming email addresses. I am going to keep that default, because Active Directory and DNS already know about this server, so emails can be routed to the SMTP drop folder easily. For more information on changing that display address, see the Chapter 2 sidebar "Specifying a Different Domain Alias for Incoming Email."

4. To avoid having any rogue email servers spam the incoming email–enabled lists or libraries, you can specify exactly what servers are considered safe to accept email from. I am not worried about rogue servers, so I am keeping the setting Accept Mail From All E-Mail Servers. If rogue servers are a worry in your environment, feel free to specify the safe server IP addresses here. Once all of the settings are correct, click OK. That will take you back to the System Settings page.

FIGURE 3.69
The Incoming E-mail Settings page

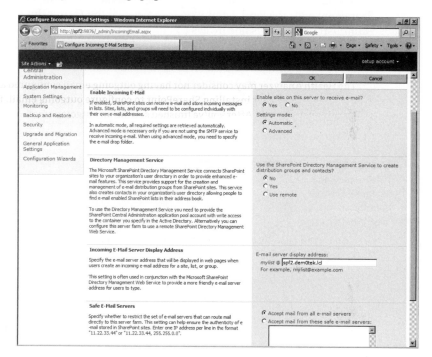

INCOMING EMAIL IS STARTED?

There is a bit of a bug in this version of SharePoint that incorrectly displays both incoming and outgoing email. For incoming email, it incorrectly shows it as started on this Services On Server page, even when it hasn't been configured yet. For outgoing email, it will display in Servers In Farm as "NOT CONFIGURED" when it is in fact configured and working fine. Keep that in mind if you know what you've configured and what you haven't.

User Accounts

Obviously SharePoint is useless without users, and it can't be administered without administrators. Therefore, no installation is complete until you know how to add more accounts to SharePoint. Here is a very brief look at adding accounts.

FARM ADMINISTRATORS

When the farm was created during installation, the setup account became the farm administrator by default. It is not a good idea to continue to use it as a working farm administrator account, since you shouldn't log in with it unless you are going to install SharePoint (or some other SharePoint-related product that requires a setup account configured as ours is). Therefore, it is a good idea to add at least one more account. Further, just as a backup, SharePoint adds the local Administrators group to the Farm Administrators in Central Administration. This is not always a good idea; therefore, it is good to add your own farm administrators and remove the local Administrators group from the list.

1. To add a farm administrator, in Central Administration, on the Security page, click Manage The Farm Administrators Group.

2. On the People And Groups – Farm Administrators page (Figure 3.70), click the New button in the Action bar (what we call the bar with the New, Actions, and Settings drop-down buttons).

FIGURE 3.70
The People And Groups – Farm Administrators page

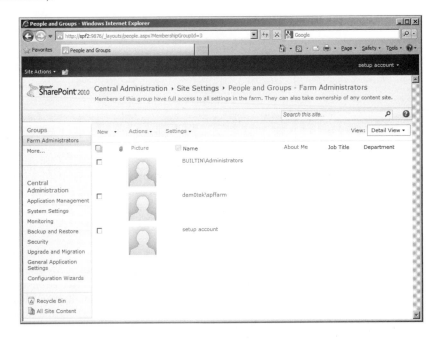

3. In the Grant Permissions box (Figure 3.71), enter the name of the users you want to add as farm administrators (or you can add an Active Directory security group if you prefer). I'm going to add my SharePoint Admin account, *shareadmin*.

4. You can have a welcome email sent to the new administrator or choose not to have it sent. In my case, I am going to disable it, because I don't need it. Then click OK to finish adding the new farm administrator.

FIGURE 3.71

The Grant Permissions form box

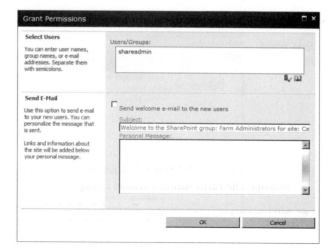

BUILT-IN ADMINISTRATORS

As you saw in Figure 3.71, the BUILTIN\Administrators group for the local server is a member of the Farm Administrators group by default. Often, after SharePoint is installed and you've added your own farm administrators, it is a good idea to remove the BUILTIN\Administrators group from the Farm Administrators membership so as to keep server administrators who may not be qualified to administer a SharePoint farm from doing so.

To remove the group, click the check box next to it in the page, and choose Actions in the Action bar. In the drop-down menu, select Remove Users From Group. This will remove the selected item (in our case BUILTIN\Administrators) from the Farm Administrators group. Now only the farm account (don't ever remove the farm account), the setup account, and the accounts you add will have access to the farm at the administrator level. For more about managing the farm administrators group or users and permissions in general, see Chapter 12, "Users and Permissions."

SITE COLLECTION ADMINISTRATORS

When creating a site collection, you can add two site collection administrators (a primary administrator and a backup). But often you need more site collection administrators to take care of day-to-day management of a busy site collection. In this case, we added only one site collection administrator during installation. Therefore, it's a good idea to add at least one more.

If you have only one site collection administrator, you can add the secondary one via Central Administration, choosing Application Management ➤ Change Site Collection Administrators to display the page shown in Figure 3.72.

But to add more accounts to site collection administrators than just those two, you can go to the site collection itself.

1. While on the site collection, click Site Actions, and select Site Permissions from the menu, as shown in Figure 3.73.

FIGURE 3.72
The Site
Collection Admin-
istrators page

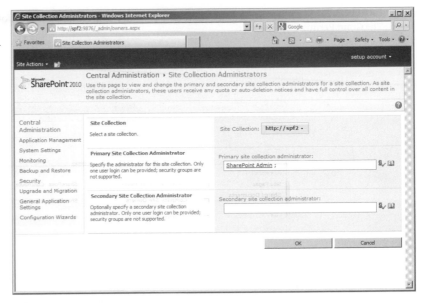

FIGURE 3.73
Choosing Site Per-
missions from the
Site Actions menu

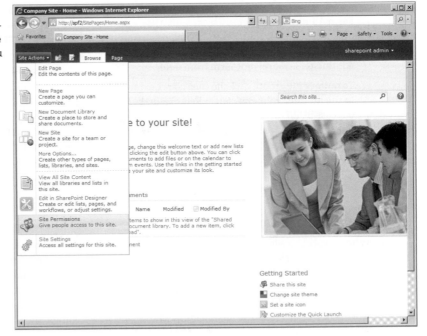

2. On the Site Permission page (Figure 3.74), click the Site Collection Administrators button in the Edit Ribbon.

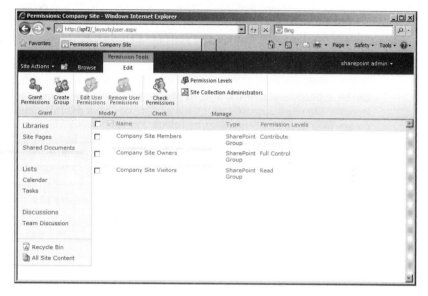

3. In the Site Collection Administrators form box (Figure 3.75), enter the accounts (no groups accepted here) separated by semicolons. When done, click OK. That will add those accounts as site collection administrators.

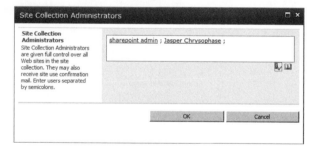

ONE FOR ALL AND ALL FOR ONE

Keep in mind that SharePoint can handle only so many discrete objects, so adding many individual users as a part of a few large security groups is better than each added individually. This especially works for site collection users, but administrators (specifically site collection administrators) tend to be added individually because their tasks are usually specific, high priority, and high skill.

SITE USERS

Of course, the point of SharePoint is to have users use its resources. So, it stands to reason that you need to add user accounts as soon as possible. It is always a good idea, when setting up SharePoint, to have at least one account set up as a site member, so you can check and see what things look like to a user with only member permissions (as opposed to the administrative permissions most of us have most of the time).

User permissions are managed in sets (such as read, edit, delete, and manage personal views) called *permission levels*. Those permissions levels are generally applied to groups (although they can be applied to individual users if necessary). There are a few groups pre-made for site collections: Members, Owners, and Visitors. Owners have the full control permission level, which means they have all permissions available. The Members group uses the Contribute permission level, which basically gives the user the right to see lists, libraries, and pages; create personal views and page versions; add, edit, and delete list/library items; and recover items from their Recycle Bin. They are not allowed to configure site, list, or library settings. The Visitor group has only read permissions to the site; they can't contribute or configure settings. (For more about user groups, permissions, and permission levels, see Chapter 12.)

1. To add a user to a site or site collection (obviously you need to have administrative permissions or be an Owner to do this), on the site click Site Actions in the top ribbon bar and select Site Permissions from the menu (just as we did to add site collection administrators).

2. On the Site Permissions page, click the Grant Permissions button.

3. In the Grant Permissions box (Figure 3.76), enter a username, AD security group, or email address of a user into the Users/Groups box in the Select Users section. Separate the entries by semicolon.

FIGURE 3.76
The Grant Permissions form box

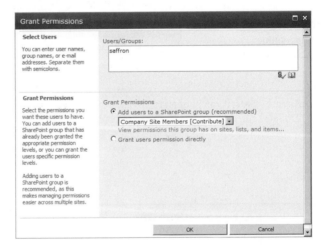

4. Select the SharePoint group to which the user(s) will be added in the Grant Permission section (or you can apply a permission level directly to the selected users instead).

5. Choose to send, or not send, the new users a welcome email.

6. Once you have configured all sections, click OK to add the user (or users) to the site.

You have now completed the final configuration tasks for a Complete installation of SharePoint. You server is up and running and ready to be used. You now know how to install and configure SharePoint manually, from managed accounts to enabling and configuring services to creating your first web application and site collection. You've confirmed the changes made by SharePoint to the file system, IIS, and SQL. You now know every account being used and every service running. You are truly ready to master administering SharePoint. Congratulations!

DO YOU SPEAK MY LANGUAGE?

SharePoint Foundation can support sites that use a different language for its menus, settings, object names, and descriptions. All you have to do is download and install language packs for SharePoint Foundation, one pack per language. Once a language pack is installed, when you create a site, the option to use a different language than the default becomes available. An existing site cannot have a new language applied to it, unfortunately. So, before you create any sites, you might want to install your language packs first.

To get language packs for SharePoint, go to the Microsoft download center, and search for "Language Packs for SharePoint Foundation 2010".

On the download page, be sure to choose the language you want, click Change to commit it (otherwise, even with the correct word in the field, it will download the default English pack), and then click the Download button.

Once the file is downloaded to the SharePoint server, just run it (if you have other SharePoint servers in the farm, install it on the others as well). The language pack will be added so that all sites created after this point will have the option to choose either the default language or the language from the pack you installed.

A few caveats: if you happen to be migrating SharePoint from one version to another (or to a different server) and you are using language packs, install them before you run the configuration wizard on the new server. Also, if you happen to install Office Web Apps on your server (more about that in Chapter 16) and want to install language packs after that point, you must use the language packs for SharePoint *Server* 2010, not SharePoint Foundation.

Keep in mind that each language pack uses the same file name, unfortunately. So if you need to use several, download them to different locations.

The Bottom Line

Prepare for a Complete installation. SharePoint has certain software and hardware requirements before it can be installed. In addition, some of those requirements vary depending on the type of installation you choose. To be prepared for installing SharePoint, it is good to know what to install, how to install it, and in what order.

Master It During the installation process, in what way does the Complete installation vary from the Standalone installation?

Install SharePoint using the Complete installation option. Several types of SharePoint installation are available: Standalone, which is a single-server installation that installs without intervention with all default settings and uses a SQL Server Express database; Server Farm, Stand-alone, which is essentially the Standalone Installation but with an additional configuration option before installation begins; and Server Farm, Complete installation, which allows you to manage all configuration options and specify the SQL server that will manage the databases. Each installation type has its strengths and weaknesses, and it's good to know about them before you begin.

Master It Does SQL have to be on a different server when you install SharePoint using the Complete installation option?

Determine what service accounts SharePoint requires and how to set them up. The SharePoint Complete installation requires you to have accounts available to be used by its services. It is best if the accounts are created ahead of time. They should use the least possible privileges on the domain. In addition, most services require you to register and manage their service accounts.

Master It List three service accounts that SharePoint uses and what they are used for.

Manually configure necessary SharePoint services. Because the Complete installation does not make assumptions about if and how you want to configure services, it leaves you to configure them yourself. This lets you specify details, such as indexing schedules, service accounts, database names, and more.

Master It Is there a service account that you have to configure in a Complete installation that does not require a managed account?

Part 2

Using Microsoft SharePoint Foundation 2010

Chapter 4

Introduction to the SharePoint Interface

When you look at a SharePoint site for the first time, you might think it looks like a normal web-site—and it does. The beauty of SharePoint is its simple usefulness as well as its versatility. At first glance, you can see many of SharePoint's standard features. Most of the attributes of a SharePoint web page are focused on ease of navigation and consistency of design. It may not be a blinking, glittering extravaganza of art and animation, but it gets the job done.

Remember that the point of SharePoint is to be easy for users to navigate and understand, while being really flexible for administrators. Consider it a framework—filled with potential but not truly complete until you make it your own.

Microsoft has particular terminology for most of SharePoint's web page features and attri-butes, which I will point out as we go. This will give us a common language to work with for the rest of the book when referring to web page features and attributes. For the few objects or features that have no official term, I'll establish one for the remainder of the book.

From the start, let's look at the interface of the SharePoint top-level site we created when install-ing SharePoint (either Standalone or Complete). I chose to use the Team Site template for my top-level site because it is a good, standard starting point for most site collections. It has the most commonly used lists, libraries, and web parts, as well as standard navigation tools that are a good introduction point for all things SharePoint. In Chapter 9, "Sites, Subsites, and Workspaces," you will look at the other templates available for sites straight out of SharePoint's box.

In this chapter, you'll learn how to

- ◆ Identify SharePoint's navigation tools and understand how to use them
- ◆ Find a list or library
- ◆ Use the Quick Launch bar
- ◆ Use the ribbon bar
- ◆ Understand a content page

The Team Site Home Page

The home page of any site is like the foyer of a building. It is intended to be the entrance every-one uses to get into the site. It has navigational elements, much like a building directory, that allow you to see at a glance where else you can go in the site and how to get there. In addition, like a bulletin board in a foyer, the home page has an area to display announcements and other information that the administration might think visitors would find important.

> **BONUS MATERIAL**
>
> This chapter goes over the interface of the home page, lists, libraries, and administrative pages rather quickly. I am assuming that you've browsed the Web before, so a lot of the navigational functionality will be somewhat familiar, and you may have used Microsoft Office 2007 or 2010 at some point, so the ribbon bars may not be that new to you. The only thing you really need to brush up on are some of the features unique to SharePoint and the terminology.
>
> However, if you desire more details and explanation, I have an extended version of this chapter available online.
>
> To get a copy of the extended version of this chapter, go to:
>
> www.sybex.com/go/masteringsharepointfoundation2010.

To see what I mean, let's open the team site home page:

1. In the installation chapters, we created a site collection at the root address of the server. So, open a browser that SharePoint supports, and enter the name of the server you installed SharePoint on in the address bar (in my case, that would be `http://spf2`). If you chose a different address for your site collection, enter that instead.

> **PREFERRED BROWSERS**
>
> Keep in mind that SharePoint works best with Internet Explorer 7.0 or higher. It will open in Firefox 3.6 and higher, or Safari 4.04 and higher, but they don't entirely support every SharePoint function.

2. To see all the options available, you should log in with an account that has administrative permissions to the site. In my case, that would be the site collection administrator account I set up in Chapter 3, "Complete Installation" (`dem0tek\shareadmin`). If you are not logged in with that account locally, you may see either a prompt to log in (depending on how your browser is configured) or an Access Denied page with the option to log in as a different user.

   Either way, make sure you are logged in with an account that can access the site with administrative privileges.

> **ACCESS DENIED, BUT YOU CAN REQUEST ACCESS...**
>
> You may have noticed on the site's Access Denied page that there are two links to choose from: Log In As A Different User and Request Access. Request Access is on by default but can be disabled. It allows a user who has been denied access to something to send a "request for access" email to the outgoing email address specified for the site (it uses the reply-to address you set up for outgoing email in Central Administration if you don't specify one).

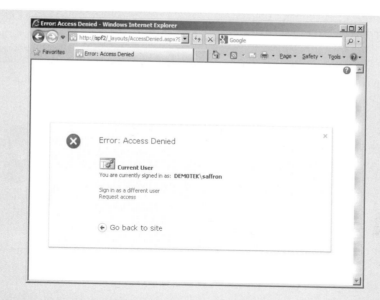

If you typically log into your workstation with one account and log into SharePoint with another, consider configuring your browser to simply prompt for a password by default in order to avoid the hassle of having to wait to be denied so you can log in as a different account.

In Internet Explorer, go to Tools ➤ Internet Options while on the site. In the Internet Options dialog box, click the Security tab make sure the zone that the site should be in is selected, and click the Custom Level button. In the Custom Level dialog box, scroll down to the last settings under User Authentication ➤ Logon, and select Prompt For Username And Password.

3. Once you are logged in, it might take a moment while ASP.NET compiles the page, and then the home page for your first SharePoint site will appear (Figure 4.1).

Team Site Landmarks

For us to have a common vocabulary for these features, I'll briefly go over the highlights of what's on the page, what each item is called, and what each item does. Remember, this is the interface for a home page created with the Team Site template. You may have chosen a different template for your top-level site, so don't worry if your home page looks different on your server. Every site template in SharePoint has the same underlying capabilities, but they are laid out differently based on each one's core task, such as blogging, meeting management, or document management. Don't be alarmed if your site doesn't look exactly like mine. Many of the navigation features are the same. Figure 4.2 shows all the page landmarks.

FIGURE 4.1
A typical
SharePoint site
home page

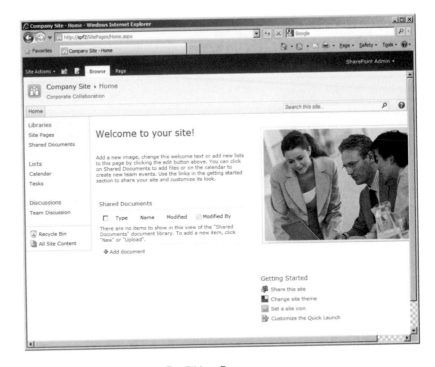

FIGURE 4.2
The home page
with landmarks
indicated

Each of the components on the page has a purpose. Here's a quick rundown of where everything is and what it does, starting on the home page (from the top left):

Top Ribbon Bar   That dark bar across top of the page is a consistent element for all pages on the site. When you scroll down a page, it doesn't move. When you access a ribbon bar for a page, it essentially hangs off the top ribbon bar, with the ribbon tool tabs appearing on the top ribbon bar. It contains a menu for working on the page and the site; buttons for editing, viewing, and managing the page; and a menu for user tasks, such as logging out and viewing user information.

Title Area   The area below the top ribbon bar contains the title and description for the site (the description appears only on the home page, however) and an icon for the site that can be customized. The title also acts as a breadcrumb, indicating the page you are on and the pages to take you back to the home page, with little arrows between each page link. If you are on a list or library, the title breadcrumb appends its view to the end of the path.

Top Link Bar   This area is used primarily as a navigation tool and is meant to contain links to subsites in the collection. It currently contains a link for the home page. In this version of SharePoint it does double duty, containing the search field and help icon on the right side of the page as well.

RIBBON BAR SHENANIGANS

Unfortunately, when a ribbon is enabled and hangs off the top ribbon bar, it covers both the title area and the top link bar. When those areas are covered, you lose the title breadcrumb, a convenient means to navigate back to the home page, and you also lose access to the search field and the help icon (big oops on that one). That's why Microsoft has a Browse tab on the top ribbon bar—so you can click it to get rid of the ribbon bar and uncover the title area and top link bar. But what if your users are new and need to use Help to figure out how to get rid of that ribbon? I guess they'll just have to call you.

Quick Launch Bar   Below the top link bar on the left of the page is the Quick Launch bar. This navigational device contains links to lists and libraries on the site, as well as to a page containing links to All Site Content (in case something you want to access isn't on the Quick Launch bar) and to the Recycle Bin for the logged-in user (in case they accidentally delete something and want to restore it). The types of items listed, such as libraries, lists, discussions, are organized under headings.

QUICK LAUNCH TIPS

The Quick Launch bar has a few hidden gems of its own.

During the process of creating a list or library, you are given the choice whether or not to add it to the Quick Launch bar. There can be lists or libraries that are useful to contain files used by the site itself (such as pictures or pages), and it's a good idea to obscure them from unnecessary exploration by users.

To see all the lists, libraries, and subsites of a site, simply click All Site Content at the bottom of the Quick Launch bar.

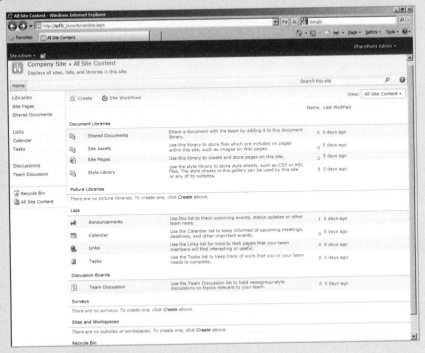

You can filter the page using the View menu located above the content of the page on the right (you'll also notice the page has the standard Quick Launch bar, top link, title area, and top ribbon bar). The page organizes lists and libraries by type as much as possible, such as document libraries, picture libraries, discussions, and so on, as well as listing subsites and a link to the Recycle Bin. For each type of object, the page displays how many items it contains and when last it was modified (very useful). The page even gives you access to the site's workflows (click the Site Workflows link at the top of the page). You can even get to the Create page to create new lists, libraries, or subsites from the All Site Content page.

You can also use the headings on the Quick Launch bar to access the All Site Content page. For example, if you wanted to see all the lists for the site, you could click the Lists heading in the Quick Launch bar, and it would take you to All Site Content, filtered to show just lists.

There are some types of site content, such as discussion lists or picture libraries, that don't get a heading on the Quick Launch bar until a list or library of that type is created. Once the heading is there, even if the list or library itself is deleted, the heading stays, even if it doesn't have anything under it.

At the end of the Quick Launch bar is the link to the Recycle Bin, a tool that should be familiar to anyone who has used a Windows computer. If a user deletes an object, it will go to the Recycle Bin for about 30 days (by default). Each user has a Recycle Bin and can get to it from the Quick Launch bar or All Site Content page to restore an object.

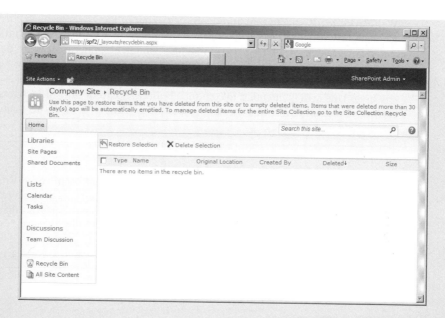

If a user deletes an item from the Recycle Bin, it actually goes to a "second-stage" site collection Recycle Bin. In either case, the bins are permanently emptied of items once they reach the 30-day deadline. The Recycle Bins are not a good alternative to regular backups. Recycle Bins are not entirely private; although users cannot see each other's garbage, site administrators can see everything in the Recycle Bins in case there is an issue. Also, keep in mind that they add to the storage size of a site collection. So if the site collection is getting too full, emptying Recycle Bins (don't forget the second-stage ones) is a good thing.

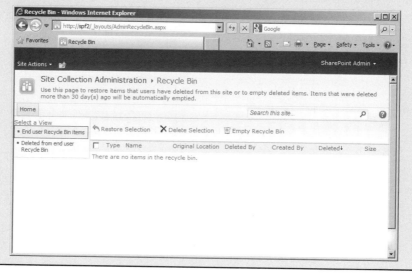

Web Part Area/Rich Content   In the center right of the page is the web part area. For the team site, because it uses new wiki page capabilities, that area is able to contain web parts as well as rich text, inserted images, and tables—whatever a Microsoft Word document could contain. (It's essentially a Word document configured with a text layout of two columns by default.) And because of that, on a team site home page, the web part area is called a *rich content* area. This area is intended to contain a bulletin board of things, such as announcements, calendars, and other information that would be worthwhile to users accessing the site.

WEB PARTS?

Web parts are little ASP.NET controls designed to display the content of a page, list, folder, library, or whatever. Unassumingly powerful, web parts can actually pull data to display almost anything displayable from the Internet and more. Out of the box, there are web parts that display a summary view for each list and library created in SharePoint (and more). They give you an "at-a-glance" view of new entries for the list they contain and an opportunity to check out the entry or list with a single click. We'll be doing more with web parts in Chapter 5, "Introduction to Web Parts."

Top Ribbon Bar Details

On the top link bar, a few features need explaining:

The Site Actions Menu   The Site Actions menu is security-filtered, meaning that what it displays depends on the permissions of the logged-in account—all possible options or only those allowed for that user. It is also the only straightforward place where you can access the administrative settings for the site; if there is no Site Actions menu, there is no easy way to get to the site settings.

For a site administrator, the Site Actions menu contains the following (shown in Figure 4.3):

FIGURE 4.3
The Site Actions
menu

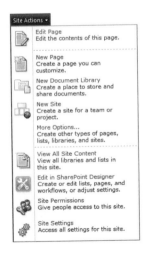

Edit Page   This menu item does the same thing that the Edit Page button in the top ribbon bar does. It simply puts the page you are on into edit mode. The ribbon bar changes to reflect the tools used in edit mode of the page (you'll learn much more about editing the page in Chapter 5).

MENU SECTIONS

You might have noticed the dotted line breaking up the Site Actions menu into three groupings. The first group contains only the Edit Page option. Next is the group whose options create new things, and finally is a group with more advanced settings, usually seen only by administrators, such as Site Settings or Edit In SharePoint Designer. If the logged-in account does not have the right to manage the site, the user will see only a subset of the items being described: Edit Page, New Page, and View All Site Content. Someone with only read rights to the site (such as an auditor), will have just View All Site Content available.

New Page   The home page of a team site is now a wiki page stored in the Site Pages library. This menu item starts the process of creating a new wiki page as if you'd clicked the New button in the Site Pages library. It's a quick way to create a new wiki page right from the home page of the site.

As an administrator, you can create a new wiki page and make it the home page instead. This is useful if users have gotten overly creative with the original home page and need to have it replaced for a while. (Unfortunately, site members can also create a new wiki page from here, as well as edit or delete the home page.)

New Document Library   This menu item takes you immediately to the New Document Library configuration page. It saves you a step compared to going to another page (such as Create) to choose to create the document library and *then* creating it. Instead, you start from here.

New Site   Like the previous item, this menu item immediately takes you to a New Site configuration page, allowing you to start creating a subsite beneath the top-level site without delay.

More Options   This menu item is the catchall for any other site object you'd like to create, such as a list or different kind of library, that doesn't have its own menu item under Site Actions. It takes you to the Create page, where you can choose from all the options to create things on the site.

View All Site Content   This menu item takes you to the All Site Content page. Not all site content needs to be listed on the Quick Launch bar. Otherwise known as the "I know I put that list around here somewhere" page, All Site Content is the one place where everything that is associated with the site is listed.

Edit In SharePoint Designer   This is a new menu item, indicating the close relationship that this version of SharePoint has with its free, desktop SharePoint editing product SharePoint Designer (sometimes referred to as SPD). Only SharePoint Designer 2010 works with SharePoint Foundation 2010. It can be installed on the SharePoint server or on a different server or workstation (as long as that machine has network access to the SharePoint server).

SharePoint Designer integrates with SharePoint and allows you to do additional editing of pages, lists, web parts, and more, without having to learn how to write code.

When you select the Edit In SharePoint Designer menu item, it will open the local copy of SPD (or prompt you to download it if there isn't one), load the page, and allow you to extensively edit the page.

BUT I WANT TO HEAR MORE ABOUT SPD

SharePoint Designer is an entirely different product than SharePoint Foundation and is beyond the scope of this book. There are also many, many books and articles dedicated to SharePoint Designer. Chapter 16, "Advanced Installation and Configuration," covers a few necessary functions using SharePoint Designer concerning Business Data Connectivity, but for the most part, it is outside the focus of this text.

Site Permissions   This menu item takes you directly to the permissions page for the site. Previously, People And Groups was a permanent listing on the Quick Launch bar that allowed everyone easy access to the Members page of People And Groups so you could see who was a member and add new ones quickly.

For this version of SharePoint, People And Groups has been removed from the Quick Launch bar, and the easiest way to add users or otherwise see the permissions and security settings is to go to Site Permissions first.

Site Settings   To administer a site (and the whole site collection, if it is the top-level site), there must be access to the site settings. This is the only direct way to get to the underlying settings for the site/site collection from the home page. This menu item takes you to the Site Settings page, filled with important configuration options. This item is obviously not listed if the logged-in account does not have the right to manage the site.

Navigate Up   This button is one of the most consistent navigational aids on the site. When selected, it will display a tree view of the entire true path back to the page where you started (with rare exceptions). This means that even if you took a shortcut to get to a settings page, which is usually available only off the main Site Settings page, you could get to Site Settings by using the Navigate Up button (since hitting the browser's Back button or the title breadcrumb won't do it). Further, there are pages and situations in which the title area breadcrumb and Quick Launch bar are not available for navigation, making the Navigate Up button a requirement.

Edit Page   This button shows up in the top ribbon bar only if the home page is set to be a wiki page from the Site Pages library and the person logged in has the right to edit documents in that library. In that case, clicking the Edit Page button puts the page in edit mode, changing the top ribbon bar to include Editing Tools toolset tabs (Format Text and Insert) used to edit the page and activating the Format Text ribbon. This allows the user to edit and save the page that will be viewed by everyone who visits the site. This surprisingly powerful feature is available to anyone with the permissions given to default members of the site—if the home page is set to be a wiki page.

The Browse Tab   The page can be in either of two modes: to be browsed like any other web page or to be edited. When it is in browse mode, this tab displays the title area and top link bar (complete with the search field and help icon). This tab is handy when you need to navigate, use the search field, or get help while the ribbon bar is active.

The Page Tab   This tab triggers a ribbon bar for doing tasks specifically on that page (it does include a tab for editing the page, which acts like the Edit Page button). Tasks such as editing the page, emailing a link to the page, setting an alert (so you'll be notified if the page changes), and making the page a home page (redundant in this case) are standard.

WHEN ONE THING DOESN'T LOOK LIKE THE OTHER

For a team site, the home page is actually a wiki page, and the tools in the Page ribbon reflect that, with buttons for managing page permissions, page history, the wiki library the page is stored in, and incoming links (which is very much a wiki thing).

If the home page were just a normal web part page, it would have a slightly different ribbon. In such a page, the web part area can contain web parts only, so there are no extra ribbon bar tabs for formatting text or inserting tables. The Page ribbon is all a web part page gets in edit mode and is mostly concerned with managing that specific page (or that page's more limited, mobile equivalent using the Edit Mobile Page button).

However, some buttons will always be grayed out for a web part home page, such as Version History, Workflows, or Approve/Reject. Those buttons appear on the Page ribbon of a web part home page because web part pages, such as wiki pages, are stored in a library, where those features can be enabled, but a web part home page stands alone and is not in a library, so they'll never work there.

So if your users ever ask why the Page ribbons are different between the two types of home pages or why some home page buttons are never available, now you know.

The Account Menu   The Account menu, always located on the right side of the top ribbon bar, isn't just a display of the account currently logged in, as you can see in Figure 4.4. It's also a menu of user-related tasks, such as looking at and editing user information, signing in as a different user, requesting access (so you can send an email requesting access or more privileges), or signing out.

FIGURE 4.4

The Account menu

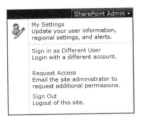

USER INFORMATION

On the Account menu, the logged-in user can access their user information page from the My Settings option.

On this page users can enter their user information into the fields; configure their own regional settings, such as time zone, time format, and locale (which uses the site's settings by default); or manage alerts.

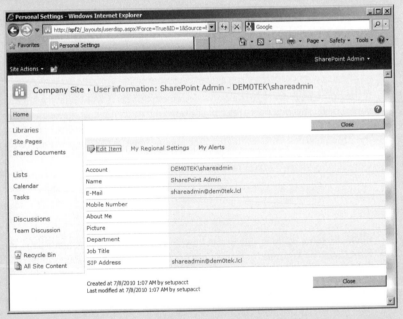

Alerts are email notifications users can set to let them know if there have been changes to a page, list, or library item. They are resource-intensive to run, because the SharePoint Timer job, while it's busy running SharePoint, must also schedule and execute alerts for all users. So, it is good both to limit the number of alerts users can set (which you configure in Central Administration) and to encourage them to delete the alerts they no longer need themselves.

Top Link Bar Details

In the top link bar are a few items that deserve a closer look:

Home Tab   In most cases (unless you specifically remove it), there is a tab in the top link bar for the home page (even if you're on the home page). If the site collection has subsites, their links can be located here for easy navigation.

Search   Also located in the top link bar is the search field, used to search for content anywhere in the site collection. Search is security-filtered, meaning that if there is a site, document, or list item that your account is not allowed to see, it won't show up in the search results. This field directly relates to the Search service that we enabled in the installation chapters. To use it, just enter the word (or words) for which you are looking, exact matches only. Search doesn't perform partial-word matching or Boolean logic, but it can do additions or exceptions. You can include or exclude words using the plus (+) or minus (−) sign (for example, orange -juice +zest).

A Few More Details About Search

Search will index list item contents (the contents of all fields of all lists and libraries), as well as the contents of files stored in libraries, as long as those file types can be indexed. Indexing uses ifilters (index *filters*) specific for the file type they will be indexing. SharePoint can index Office files, as well as HTML and TIFF files, automatically. To index other kinds of files, you'll need to get ifilters for them.

Search works in a top-down fashion. This means that if you search for something from the home page of the top-level site (where we are, for example) and there are documents that also contain that word in subsites below this top-level site, they will show up in the search results. However, if you search from a subsite for something in the top-level site, you won't find it, because search goes down only, not up. So when in doubt, search from the top-level site.

The built-in search capability of SharePoint Foundation only searches for things inside the content databases of the web applications that are configured to use Search; it doesn't search outside SharePoint. When you search from the home page, it searches the whole site. If you search from a list page, it searches for the query in that list only (even though the field says Search This Site); then, if the query fails in the search results page, you can specify to search the whole site (and subsites).

So if you don't know exactly where in a site collection a list item or document is, search for it from the home page of the top-level site. If you know what you want is in a particular list, go to that list and search for it there. And remember that if you still can't find an item, you might not have permission for it, and therefore it might be getting filtered out of your search results.

Help Icon   The question-mark icon to the right of the search field is the only place to get help in SharePoint. It will open a small help window, with a short list of general help topics and a search field of its own in the top right. Like many Microsoft products, SharePoint has a pretty hit-or-miss help function. As of this writing, occasional help documents actually suggest checking online for better, more up-to-date information.

Home Page Ribbons

Although you've now seen all the standard landmarks on the home page, we've mentioned only in passing the ribbon bars that can hang off the top ribbon bar and how they're triggered—either by the Edit Page button or the Page tab.

It's time now for a quick rundown of what happens when you click one of those two buttons—covering just enough to give you a feel for what the ribbon bars look like, what they're meant for, and how they differ.

THE PAGE RIBBON

The Page tab activates a relatively simple, single-purpose ribbon (practically the simplest ribbon for the site), on which most of the buttons just relate to the page itself. In this case, I will describe the Page ribbon of a home page that displays its web parts in a rich content area, but even if you just have a standard web part page for your home page, you'll get the idea.

To activate the Page ribbon, just click the Page tab in the top ribbon bar. You'll notice that when the ribbon is activated, the title area and top link bar are both covered (Figure 4.5).

Ribbon bars are divided into section, as you can see in Figure 4.5. The Page ribbon has five sections: Edit, Manage, Share & Track, Page Actions, and Page Library.

FIGURE 4.5
A home page with
the Page ribbon
activated

THE DIFFERENCE BETWEEN A RICH CONTENT AND A WEB PART PAGE

The rich content area of the home page is based on a wiki page in the Site Pages library (earlier in the chapter you saw what that kind of page looks like). However, if the home page were set to be a normal web part page, it would not have that Word-document, multimedia look to it—just web parts, as shown here.

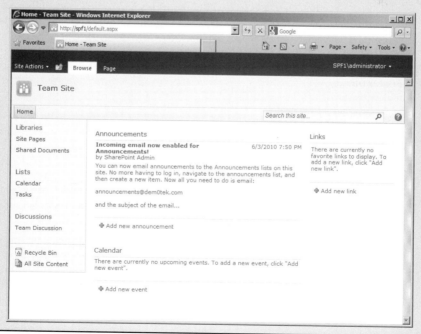

Edit

In the first section, Edit, are two buttons, Edit and Check Out.

Edit   Figure 4.6 shows the Edit button's drop-down menu. Like several ribbon bar buttons, this one changes state depending on what you are doing. If you are currently editing a page, it turns into a Save drop-down button. If you are not yet editing the page, it's an Edit drop-down button. When you click this button while it says Edit, it will put the page in edit mode *exactly* as the Edit Page button in the top ribbon bar does. So if you happen to be managing the wiki area of the home page with the Page tab and want to edit it, then using the Edit drop-down button would be convenient.

FIGURE 4.6
The Edit button's
drop-down menu

The Edit drop-down button has several options available: Save, Save & Close, Save And Keep Editing, Stop Editing, and Edit In SharePoint Designer.

Check Out   As is standard in most libraries in SharePoint, the management of document editing is available in the form of versioning and document checkout. Because the home page is also a document in the Site Pages library, Check Out and Check In options are available. Clicking the Check Out drop-down button on this page will place the document in its corresponding library into a checked-out state, meaning that the user who checked it out is now the only one who can edit it until they check it back in (or an administrator forces the checkout to be disregarded). The drop-down button changes to Check In for the user who checked it out. For users with administrative privilege to the site, list, or item, the button's drop-down options will also include Discard Check Out and Override Check Out (Figure 4.7).

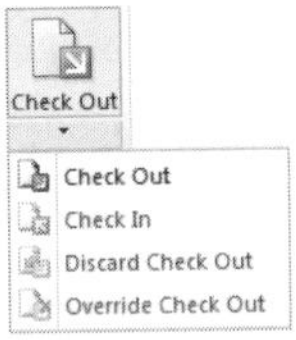

FIGURE 4.7
The Check Out
drop-down menu

Manage

In the next section, Manage, there are five buttons, several of which are grayed out because they're not applicable. (In typical ribbon bar behavior, it doesn't hide the buttons that can't be used; it just leaches the color out of them):

Edit Properties   The Edit Properties drop-down button is disabled on this particular ribbon but can be accessed from the item in the Site Pages library. Interestingly, this button is not available on any of the tabs while you are editing the page using the Edit Page button. That is because Edit Properties (like the Format Text and Insert ribbons) is all about actually editing the page's contents. The Page tab is about managing the page, including its properties, name, and so on.

Rename Page   This button opens a field in which to change the filename. It's grayed out now because we are using the page as our home page (the filename is literally Home), so it is not a good idea to rename it.

Page History   This button takes you to the page displaying the history of edits of the wiki page, if version history is enabled for the library that contains it.

Page Permissions   The Page Permissions button, located below Page History, takes you to the Page Permissions page so you can change the file's permissions. This option is grayed out if your account doesn't have the right to change permissions.

Delete Page   This button, when available, pops up a box asking whether you are sure you want to delete the page. If you confirm that you are sure, it moves the page to your Recycle Bin (for later restoration when you realize deleting it was a mistake). Since the page is being used as the home page, this button should be grayed out.

Share & Track

In the Share & Track section there are only two options, Email A Link and Alert Me. The Alert Me button occurs only if you've configured outgoing email for the farm or at least the web application containing the site.

Email A Link   This button will trigger your local computer's email client to send the page's address in an email.

Alert Me   Because the rich content area of the team site home page is a wiki page that is actually contained in the Site Pages library (there's a link to it on the Quick Launch bar), you can configure an alert to let you know if this page (or any other in the library if you want) changes. Also, in this button's drop-down menu (Figure 4.8), you can go to the page to manage alerts overall for the logged-in user.

FIGURE 4.8
The Alert Me drop-
down menu

ALERT DETAILS

The user must have an email address listed in their user information to get the alerts. In addition, new with this version of SharePoint is the option to get Short Message Service (SMS) messages for the alerts—if it is configured on the server. Keep in mind that doing SMS requires that SharePoint have a paid-for account from an SMS provider.

Page Actions

In the Page Actions section there are two buttons, Make Home Page and Incoming Link.

Make Homepage   This button is not particularly useful for the home page of the site (since it already *is* the home page), but if you were on a different wiki page in the Site Pages library and wanted to make *it* the home page (and you had the permissions to do so), you could replace the current home page with the page you are on. This button is missing entirely from the Page Actions section if you don't have permission to use it. Users who have only member permissions or lower don't even see this button (a rare occurrence of security trimming in a ribbon bar).

Incoming Links

Incoming Links   Because wiki pages can have links to (and from) other wiki pages, the Incoming Links button will take you to a page where you can check if there are any other pages in the Site Pages library that use wiki-formatted links to point to the page. Because this is the home page and we just created the site recently, there aren't any.

Page Library

The last section of the ribbon bar is Page Library, which has buttons to manage the library that contains the home page. There are three buttons in this section: Library Settings, Library Permissions, and View All Pages. Users with member permissions or lower can use only the View All Pages button; the other two (Library Settings and Library Permissions) will be grayed out.

Library Settings

Library Settings   This button will take you to the Settings page for the library where the page is located (Site Pages in this case). Not really useful for the home page, it's useful when there is no other way to get to the library settings while you are on the library page itself.

Library Permissions

Library Permissions   This button takes you to the permissions page of the library (where the page you're looking at is located). This is useful if you realize you'd like to block users from being able to edit Site Pages from here. These permissions affect the entire library (and all its contents, not just the home page).

View All Pages

View All Pages   This button simply takes you to the library where the wiki page is located— in our case, the Site Pages library. The view for the library (because all lists and libraries can have different views to display and organize their items) will be set to All Pages, so as to better view all pages there. Learn more about views in Chapter 6, "Introduction to Lists."

THE EDIT PAGE TOOLS

The Edit Page button appears only on a wiki page and therefore only on a home page that uses a rich content area based on a wiki page (which is a good way to tell at a glance what type of page you're looking at). It is essentially a shortcut for putting the page into edit mode. You can do the same thing from the Page ribbon by clicking the Edit button.

The Edit Page button triggers more than one ribbon. Ribbon bars tend to be context-sensitive, meaning that if you are on a page that needs to have content edited, such as a Word document, and needs to be able to insert web parts, then tabs for both functions will appear in the top ribbon bar—or as many as needed to do all the work necessary for that context. In this case, when the Edit Page button is clicked, it triggers an Editing Tools toolset of ribbon tabs in the top ribbon bar, containing Format Text and Insert tabs. Clicking these tabs will activate their corresponding ribbons to do their corresponding tasks.

The Format Text Ribbon

To see the first Editing Tools ribbon in action, click the Edit Page button on the home page. This causes the page to go into edit mode and activates the toolset, opening the Format Text ribbon, shown in Figure 4.9.

FIGURE 4.9
The Format
Text ribbon

As you can see, the ribbon contains seven sections: Edit, Clipboard, Font, Paragraph, Styles, Layout, and Markup.

EDIT

The Edit section of the Format Text ribbon is just like the corresponding section of the Page ribbon. It contains two buttons:

Save & Close   When you're not in edit mode, this appears as the Edit button, but since you're already editing, it toggles to a save state. Its drop-down menu (Figure 4.10) allows you to toggle between states.

FIGURE 4.10
The Save & Close
drop-down menu

Check Out   This button is provided because the home page is actually a page in the Site Pages library, and documents in a library can be checked out. This button has a drop-down menu (Figure 4.11) containing the options Check Out, Check In, Discard Check Out, and, if you are logged in as an administrator, Override Check Out. If the page is not checked out, then Check Out is the only option available. If this were just a web part page, this button wouldn't be available.

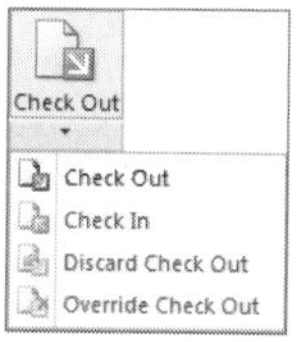

FIGURE 4.11
The Check Out
drop-down menu

The Clipboard section of the ribbon contains the standard Cut, Copy, Paste, and Undo functions that use the Clipboard in Windows and should be familiar to anyone who has ever used a text editor.

The Font section of the ribbon also contains the standard buttons and drop-down menus available for text editing in Windows. Standard-issue Font and Font Size menus are available, as are the usual Bold, Italic, Strikethough, Subscript, Superscript, Highlight, and Font Color buttons. There is also a Clear Format button at the end of the section, in case your formatting gets out of hand and you need a fresh start.

In the Paragraph section are the paragraph-related buttons: Bullet, Numbering, Outdent, Indent, Paragraph Reading Order (left or right), and Paragraph Alignment buttons. These are all standard for a text editor.

STYLES

The next couple of sections are less standard and more interesting, starting with Styles.

Styles   This drop-down menu (Figure 4.12) contains some styles to quickly format selected text in the rich content area. The styles it lists help create a standard format for captions, references, tag lines, bylines, comments, and even a normal style. This helps avoid manually formatting those common styles and helps keep them consistent from wiki page to wiki page.

FIGURE 4.12
The Styles
drop-down menu

LAYOUT

The Layout section also contains only one button, Text Layout.

Text Layout   This drop-down button has nothing to do with text styles of any sort but instead controls the background layout of the rich content area. By default, the area has two columns in which text, pictures, tables, and web parts can be inserted. But you have a number of other options to choose from in terms of column and header/footer layout (Figure 4.13).

MARKUP

The last section, Markup, contains some interesting and convenient settings, with at least one that is likely to generate some support calls from unwary users.

Markup Styles   The Markup Styles drop-down button applies some standard markup styles to selected text. This has a wide selection of different styles that are easily applied to great effect (Figure 4.14). It also employs the live preview feature, where you select text and hover your mouse over the style to see it applied. The styles available are Headings (1 through 4), Colored Headings (1 through 4), Horizontal Rule, Paragraph (or basically a reset to default text style), and Callout styles 1 through 4.

FIGURE 4.13
The Text Layout
menu

FIGURE 4.14
The Markup
Styles menu

LIVE PREVIEW

The neat thing about the styles in the drop-down menu (for both the Styles and Markup Styles buttons) is that they apply a *live preview* to the selected text when you hover over them. This is very convenient for seeing what the style will do before committing to it. So if you had your cursor in a paragraph on the page and then hovered your mouse over, say, Callout 2 in the Markup Styles drop-down, it would display what the style looks like before committing to it.

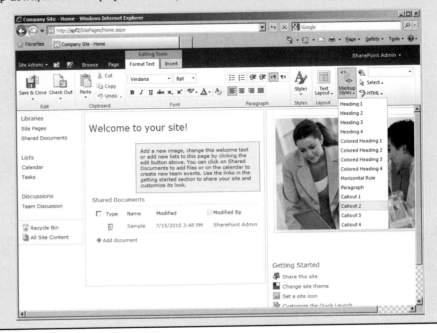

Languages The icon shown here, for an untitled list box called Languages, is used to simply mark selected text as being in a different language. It does not change the text into a different language (that would be too cool); it just marks it in the HTML code as being in a different language than the default on the page.

Select Below Languages in the Markup section is a white arrow pointing up to the left with an associated drop-down list. Select is actually a cool feature, allowing you to select an entire text division (what it calls one of the columns or zones of the page), paragraph, or other HTML element. (It seems to ignore web parts.) It indicates the selection with a red dotted line around the area (Figure 4.15). The Select list options change depending on where the insertion point is in the wiki page, obviously.

FIGURE 4.15
The Select drop-down menu, hovering over the Text Division option

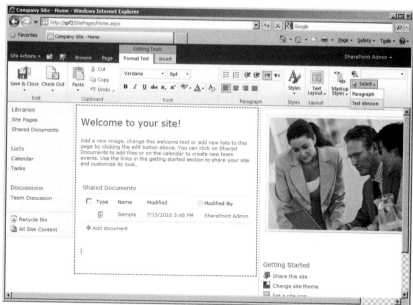

HTML The HTML drop-down button is probably one that inexperienced users should not mess with. Its options (Figure 4.16) allow you to edit the source HTML of the selected zone or convert the underlying entire page to XHTML compliance (from which there is no return). If you have code or web parts that rely on the page not being XHTML, that change may cause some issues.

FIGURE 4.16
The HTML drop-down menu

The Insert Ribbon

Now that we've taken a glance at the Format Text ribbon, it's time to check the Insert ribbon.

To activate the Insert ribbon, make sure the home page is edit mode, and then click the Insert tab in the Editing Tools toolset on the top ribbon bar.

The Insert ribbon (Figure 4.17) has four sections and contains buttons related to inserting tables, pictures, links, files, and web parts.

Insert assumes that wherever the insertion point, or cursor, is in the rich content zones on the home page is where you are going to insert something. Keep that in mind when you use any of the buttons, lest you put something where you didn't intend.

FIGURE 4.17
The Insert ribbon

TABLES

In the Tables section is one drop-down button, Table.

Table   This drop-down button displays the grid shown in Figure 4.18, allowing the user to drag-select exactly how many cells the table they want to insert will have. Also, at the top of the drop box is the Insert Table option, which pops up a box to enter the size, rows, and columns that you want the table to have. It is a little odd that there are two listings of Insert Table in the drop-down, one that brings up a box where you can type your parameters and one that obviously is a header for the drag-select area, but that's what we've got.

FIGURE 4.18
The Table drop-down box

MEDIA

The Media section has only one button in it, Picture.

Picture   The Picture drop-down button allows you to insert a picture from either the local computer (or file share) or an existing URL address, as shown in Figure 4.19.

FIGURE 4.19
The Picture drop-down menu

The From Computer option requires that you browse to a picture file available locally or from a file share. This will actually upload the picture to a convenient Site Assets document library and then use the link to it from there—all library items that can be opened in the browser get their own URL.

The From Address option lets you specify the URL for a picture that already has one; it will pull the image from the address. You can also specify alternate text that will be displayed if the users are blocked from accessing that address for any reason, such as a firewall or permissions issue. Be sure to test the URL by logging in with member and visitor accounts to be sure those users can see the picture, too. (I have test accounts of each group just for that reason.)

LINKS

The Links section has two buttons, Link and Upload File. The options in this section are intended to insert either a link or a file at the insertion point somewhere in a rich content zone.

Link   Clicking the Link button opens an Insert Hyperlink box where you can enter the text that will appear as the link on the page, as well as the address the link will go to.

Upload File   Clicking this button will open a box that will let you specify (or browse to) a file to upload. The file itself will be put in the Site Assets document library, and then SharePoint, using its address in the library, will display its contents on the page. Be sure to test this thoroughly, because not all file types may appear as you expect.

WEB PARTS

The last section for the Insert ribbon bar is Web Parts, which contains buttons for inserting existing web parts, web part templates, and list view web parts. It also provides a button for actually creating a list on the fly specifically to be displayed in a web part for the page.

Web Part   This button causes a web part workspace to open below the ribbon bar (pushing the rest of the page further down), as shown in Figure 4.20. Existing web parts are generally organized into categories. The workspace has a column for these categories on the left and then a column to display the web parts in a selected category to the right of that. On the far right is a large About The Web Part area to display the text description of the web part you selected in the web part column. At the bottom of the About The Web Part area is the Add button to insert the web part into the zone where you have your insertion point. The insertion point usually appears at the top of the left zone; then you can move the web part around from there. You can't select and add more than one web part in the workspace or drag and drop them, unfortunately.

FIGURE 4.20
The Web Parts
workspace

Existing List   The Existing List button opens the web part workspace again, filtered to show just web parts related to lists or libraries; thus, it has only one column and the wide About The Web Part description area. It is in the Web Parts column that you can see every web part that is generated automatically when its underlying list is created; you might need to use the scroll buttons if there are a lot of them. Remember, every single list and library gets its own web part, so this is an easy way to add a web part to the home page for a quick glance at its contents and get to it quickly, rather than going through the Quick Launch bar. The About The Web Part section has an Add button that lets you put the web part in the zone you selected.

New List   This button is an interesting addition to the Web Parts section. Instead of choosing from web parts or lists already available, New List brings up a box where you can choose from a selection of the different kinds of list or library templates available on the site

(Figure 4.21), to create a quick, empty list or library web part. It will then insert that web part into the selected zone.

FIGURE 4.21
The Create List box

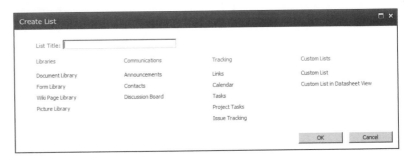

ESCAPING EDIT MODE

To get out of edit mode on the page, you first have to decide whether you want to save or close. If you want to save changes, just click the Save & Close button that the Edit Page button in the top ribbon bar has turned into, or click Save &Close on the Format Text ribbon bar. To close without saving, click the down arrow on the Save & Close button on the Format Text ribbon and select Stop Editing to exit edit mode.

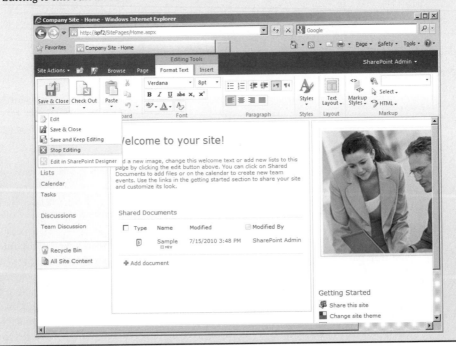

That's it for the ribbons associated with editing the home page. Now that you have taken a look at these ribbons, you will recognize their buttons should you come across the Editing Tools set again.

Site Pages

A SharePoint site has a number of different kinds of pages. There are pages intended to be seen when a person first logs into the site (the home page, usually), pages to hold settings (such as Site Permissions), pages that hold lists of links to settings pages (such as Site Settings), pages to display the contents of something administrative (such as the Recycle Bin or the Themes Gallery), and pages for list and library content.

List and library content is displayed on content, or *view*, pages. A list or library can have more than one view page, because there may be more than one way the data needs to be displayed. These pages are designed specifically for viewing and managing lists. Lists and libraries are often differentiated from each other in common SharePoint parlance, but frankly they are fundamentally the same thing. A *list* is essentially a table of data stored in the content database. This table has rows and columns. Each row is a record, and each column is a field. Because lists are made up of columns and rows, it's easy for Microsoft to integrate them with Excel (as well as Access), making it easy to create a list from a spreadsheet or export an existing list to a spreadsheet. Of course, you need to have Microsoft Excel for this; no other spreadsheet program is compatible to my knowledge.

Every list has fields for keeping track of who created a record, whether that record was modified, when it was modified, and by whom. Because of this, you can track changes in a record, making it possible to trigger alerts when changes are made. You can trigger an alert based on whether anything changes in a list or whether an item you created or modified was changed. Further, because SharePoint knows when a new record was created or modified in a list, it's pretty easy to do RSS feeds from there. As a result, lists are capable of doing alert and RSS feed actions.

In addition to being able to do alerts and RSS feed actions, lists and libraries have additional functions that can be enabled to further extend their usefulness. These capabilities are configured in the Settings page for a list or library and include things such as folders, content approval, versioning, or allowing attachments.

Lists are made unique by their intent. When you create an Announcements list, for example, it's for specific announcement-related things, such as meetings or events. As a result, its records (generically referred to as *list items*) generally contain fields useful to recording announcements, such as the announcement title, a description, and an expiration field to stop displaying when the event has passed.

Libraries, on the other hand, are lists that are intended to focus on the management of particular kinds of files (for example, document libraries manage document files, specifically Microsoft Word documents by default). This means that their records include a field meant to contain a file. That file's file type and name are considered the focus of the record, and those fields are the first two generally displayed. Activities in a library are specific to what you might do to add, edit, or manage a document that might be stored in a record there. In other words, even libraries are lists. Lists can vary because they are intended to be used for different reasons. Generally, they share the same content page layout, most of the tools, and other features of the interface. But they do have their differences, depending on what they were meant to be used for. This becomes somewhat important because the actions (and ribbon bars) available per list vary depending on that list's intent.

For example, an Announcements list and a document library should be used for different reasons and in different ways. Therefore, the interface for these two kinds of lists should differ to some degree, despite the standard content page interface. To see what I mean, let's open an Announcements list and then open the Shared Documents library to see what differences there are. This will familiarize you with both the content page interfaces and how they may vary.

A Quick Look at a List: Announcements

The Announcements list is a list like any other, and as such, its ribbon bars and tabs are pretty much the same as in any other list. This comes in handy because, if you become familiar with them here, you will recognize those elements in other lists, too.

When the Team Site template was applied to the top-level site, several lists and libraries were generated from the site's list of list and library templates. One of those is Announcements, a list based on the Announcements template. However, you can't access this list from the Quick Launch bar, because it was meant to be displayed on the home page in an Announcements web part. But with the wiki page turned on for the home page, the list doesn't appear (though you can add it if you want).

This means that the only way to get to the Announcements list from the home page is to use the All Site Content page. You can get to this page in several ways: by using the Site Actions menu and clicking View All Site Content, by clicking All Site Content in the Quick Launch bar, or, since Announcements is a list, by clicking the List heading in the Quick Launch bar. The last option takes you to the All Site Content page, filtered to display only lists, and it's what we'll do here. Why scroll if we don't have to?

Once on the All Site Content page, click Announcements in the Lists section. Assuming you got there by clicking the Lists heading in Quick Launch, notice that the View menu on the right of the content area is set to Lists (Figure 4.22).

FIGURE 4.22
The All Site
Content page,
filtered to Lists

On the Announcements page (Figure 4.23) there are some familiar landmarks: the Quick Launch bar on the left, the Top Link bar with its search field and help icon, the Top Ribbon bar with a List Tools toolset containing Items and List tabs, and the Title area.

To the right of the Quick Launch bar is the content area, along the top of which are the column headings indicating fields that list items can contain. (The list may not be limited to those fields, since the current list view could be customized not to show every field. You'll learn more about views in Chapter 6.) This list is already preconfigured with fields and even comes propagated with a list entry for our use (entitled Get Started with Microsoft Foundation!). At the bottom of the content area of the list is also a convenient Add New Announcement link.

In the title area, you can see that the title is essentially a breadcrumb, leading from the home page to the Announcements page, as you can tell by the arrows between the page titles.

However, on each list or library page, there is a new function for the title area breadcrumb. Now the breadcrumb is appended conveniently after the name of the page, with the title of the view being used to display the list's data.

As you can see, for this view there are two fields displayed in the list. Just as in Excel, column headings can be clicked to sort or filter the column. This list also has an Expires field, but it is not displayed because the purpose of this view is to display the date the announcement was posted (or modified) and the title of the announcement in a web part on the home page.

FIGURE 4.23

The Announcements list page

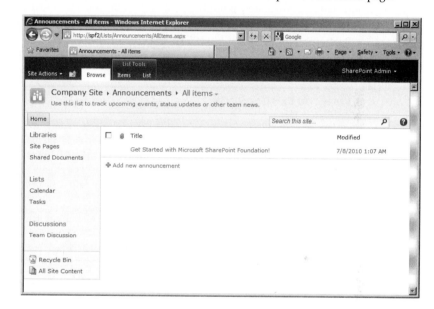

Lists are used to enter data, but they are also used to display it as well. You can create different views to organize and display data to better effect than just showing all fields organized alphabetically.

This means that knowing what view you are in when looking at a list can be helpful. It's also useful to know that you can click the view name displayed in the breadcrumb for a drop-down list of any other views for the page. (You can see in Figure 4.24 that I've made no other views for the list; only All Items is available to use.) That drop-down also can contain options to modify the existing view (which takes you to a page to modify the view) or create a new view (which takes you to a page where you can choose from some nice view templates or make a copy of an existing view).

FIGURE 4.24

The drop-down list of views in the title breadcrumb of the Announcements list

This also allows you, before you open any ribbon bars, to be able to tell at a glance what the views of that page are. Of course, the ribbon also has a view field available in it (as you will see). It needs to have this because when it's active, it covers the title area, and you can't see the breadcrumb anymore.

So, without touching the ribbon bar tabs, you can do two things by default in the list: take note of, change, modify, or create a view, and add a new item to the list.

Often, when someone goes to a list, it's to either see what's already there or add something new. So, it's nice to know, if you are in a hurry, that you can easily do those tasks without having to click a ribbon tab and wait for it to draw the buttons.

Having said that, if you want to see what else you can do with the page, you'll need to take a look at the page's top ribbon bar and the ribbon tools it offers. In addition to the standard Site Actions tab and Navigate Up button, you'll find a Browse tab (like the one on the home page, this will immediately uncover the top link and title area of the page and essentially turn off the ribbon bar) and the List Tools toolset, containing Items and List tabs.

On the whole, it makes sense to have ribbon bars that manage either the items in the list or the list itself.

A VIEW YOU CAN COUNT ON

If you land on a completely default, unmodified list or library, its default view is always the `AllItems.aspx` page (or in the case of wiki libraries, `AllPages.aspx`). If you look back at Figure 4.23, you'll note that the title of the view in the breadcrumb for the list is All Items, but the name of a view can be easily changed. However, the underlying filename can't be changed. That's why sometimes, as in the case of the Team Discussions list, the view can be called Subjects but it is still an All Items page; you can see `AllItems.aspx` at the end of the URL in the browser address bar.

Each view for a list or library is actually its own page, and All Items is usually the default one made for the list before you make your own. This is a useful thing to know when you need a good idea of what a list might contain when you're new to it. When in doubt about a view, check its address in the browser.

THE LIST TOOLS ITEMS TAB

If you click the Items tab under List Tools, it will activate the Items ribbon bar, which has four sections: New, Manage, Actions, and Workflow. These are standard for most lists. For convenience, this ribbon bar is also triggered by simply selecting an item in a list. Many of the buttons in Figure 4.25 would be grayed out if no items have been selected to which button actions can be applied.

A SELECTION TIP

If you want to select a list item to work with its ribbon, either click the item's check box or, when it's highlighted, click in the highlighted area. The name of the item is the active link for the list item (in most cases, the field name would be Title), so it will open the item's View Item box for you to see its contents. Nice, but not what you wanted, so don't click the name of the item if you don't want the View Item box.

Also, keep in mind that every item has its own drop-down menu. If you hover your mouse over a list or library item until the item is highlighted, a drop-down arrow will appear at the right end of the Title column (or whatever the linked field is called). If you click the arrow, a menu will appear with an abbreviated list of actions available for the item. The actions in the menu coincide with buttons on the ribbon bar that require you to select an item before applying. This way, you are already on the item, and you can just apply the action from the drop-down. It's very convenient and is covered in depth in Chapter 6.

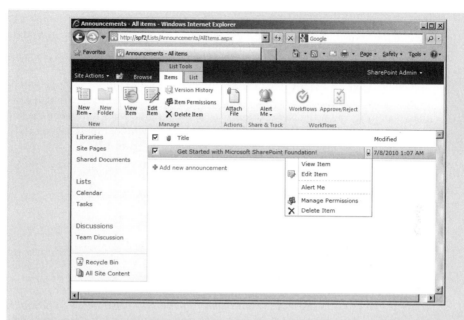

Finally, in this version of SharePoint there are check boxes next to each item so that more than one item can be selected. This allows you to apply a ribbon bar action to more than one item at once.

FIGURE 4.25
Selecting an item in the Announcements list triggers the Items ribbon bar.

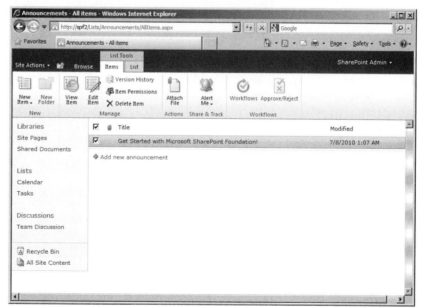

New

Up first in the Items ribbon bar is the New section, with two buttons, New Item and New Folder.

New Item   A list or library can actually contain items of different types (such as quotes and service orders). Items (or *records* if you are old-school) can be defined by what are called *content types*, which specify what kind of attributes a list or library record can have. A list can be configured to support more than one content type. And because of that, it can have more than one thing under the New button. One of them will always have to be the default, but it never hurts to peek under that New drop-down to see whether there is something else there. In the case of this list, there is only a New Item listed (Figure 4.26).

FIGURE 4.26
The New Item
drop-down menu

THE NEW ITEM FORM BOX

The New Item button displays a box containing the fields available for data entry for this list. This is considered a *form*. It comes up in a box rather than opening a separate page (unless you configure the list not to launch forms in a dialog box). Forms open for editing, viewing, or creating new list or library items. They contain the fields for the list or library item and also display a very abbreviated ribbon appropriate for the form so you can do some common tasks right there.

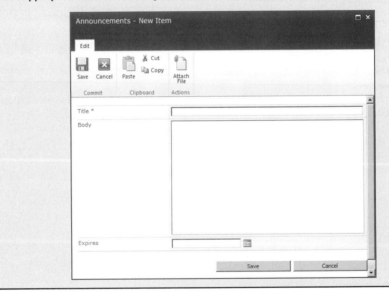

New Folder   Lists and libraries can contain folders to organize their items. This option is generally not enabled by default on lists (and will be grayed out if that's the case), but it is on libraries. Folders help emulate that old file share feeling for users who are more accustomed to that kind of organizational structure, as well as help organize items in very large lists for easier viewing.

Manage

Next in the Items ribbon bar is the Manage section, which contains buttons for managing list items. They include View Item, Edit Item, Version History, Item Permissions, and Delete Item.

View Item   This button opens a form box with the same fields displayed by New Item but allows you to only view the selected item's fields and properties, because you are supposed to be viewing the data that has been already entered for the item. This box also has an abbreviated ribbon bar, with Manage and Action sections.

Edit Item   This button opens a form box so you can actually edit or do additional data entry for the selected item in the list, complete with its own abbreviated ribbon containing buttons for saving or canceling changes, clipboard actions, and deleting or attaching files.

Version History   Version History is a list (or library) capability that, if enabled in the list settings, saves a copy of the list item every time there is a change made, so you can restore an item to a previous version if a recent change was wrong, and you can see the history of changes for that item. If the button is grayed out and you have an item selected, then version history is not enabled for the list.

Item Permissions   This button allows you to manage permissions for the selected item. It displays a permissions page where you can check and change the item's permissions.

✕ Delete Item

Delete Item   This button is used to delete the selected item. A deleted item goes to the Recycle Bin of the user who deleted it.

Actions

The next section, Actions, contains only one button, Attach File.

Attach File   Lists can allow you to attach files to a list item (like a resume, directions, or a picture). If Attach File is enabled in the list's settings and you click it, it will open a box where you can upload the file. Unlike inserting a file on the home page or adding one to a library, this will add the file to the list item itself, so it will not have its own URL address to access from elsewhere.

SITE RESOURCES

Files added to libraries are contained in the site and therefore have their own address in the site. Because of that, they can be used as a resource elsewhere on the site; for example, a picture can be stored in a picture library and then used to display on the home page.

Share & Track

The next section, Share & Track, appears *only* if you have outgoing email configured in Central Administration for the farm. (I learned that the hard way; don't let it happen to you.) It contains only one button, Alert Me.

Alert Me   The Alert Me button displays essentially the same drop-down menu as the one on the Page ribbon, allowing you either to create an alert (a list item must be selected first) or to go to the Manage My Alerts page. Alerts for a list item can be configured to trigger a notification if a change is made to anything on the list, such as someone else changes any item or if someone changes an item created or last modified by me. Also, if the list has any special fields or functions (such as the Announcements list's expiration field), an alert can be set to notice if those fields are changed or an item is created with those fields filled with data.

Workflows

The last section of this ribbon bar, Workflows, contains two buttons, Workflows and Approve/Reject.

Workflows   The Workflows button is grayed out back in Figure 4.25, because there are no workflows associated with the list in my example. If there were, clicking the button would display the Workflows page for the item, where you could view the state of the workflows associated with the list item and add them too.

WHAT IS A WORKFLOW?

A workflow is basically a series of automated tasks that streamline a process, such as sending an email to the person assigned to a list item when someone changes a field from Started to Completed. SharePoint Foundation has one workflow available to be configured out of the box (the Three-State workflow), but you can create more by using SharePoint Designer 2010 or Visual Studio 2010. For more about the Three-State workflow and workflows in general, see Chapter 7, "Creating Lists."

Approve/Reject   This button is a bit oddly placed in the Workflows section because it has nothing to do with workflows. Lists and libraries can allow content approval to be enabled. This means that any added or edited items have to be approved by a user with the permission to do so (like an administrator) in order to appear on the list for anyone but the approver and the editor/author. This button displays a box to either approve or reject the selected object. If approved, it can be viewed by everyone on the list; if not approved or rejected, the item can remain invisible to all but the author/editor and approver.

THE LIST TOOLS LIST TAB

The ribbon bar buttons for this tab relate specifically to the list, not to selected items in the list. This ribbon bar has seven sections, containing many buttons (Figure 4.27), some of which are pretty tiny.

View Format

The first section of the List ribbon is View Format. Lists or libraries are usually viewed using the views created for the list. But if you have an Office product installed locally, you also have the option of viewing the list as if it were a spreadsheet. This is useful for doing large amounts of data entry. The buttons in this section let you toggle between two ways to view the list, Standard view or Datasheet view.

Standard View   This button lets you view the list using the views offered in the Views drop-down menu in the Manage Views section of the ribbon. These can include Gannt chart views, calendar views, or standard report-type views, whatever you might have created. Otherwise, the standard view is usually the All Items view, which the list makes upon creation. That is initially the default view all users see when accessing a list, you can customize it or make other views to set as the default instead, if you'd like.

Datasheet View   This button enables the list to be displayed as a datasheet (spreadsheet), with a number of cool spreadsheet features such as totaling columns and adding a row. This will not work if you don't have an Office product installed (preferably 2007 or higher), because Office products (even just Word) install Office capabilities that include allowing SharePoint lists to be viewed as a datasheet.

Datasheet

The four buttons in the Datasheet section are enabled only if Datasheet view is active. These buttons are New Row, Show Task Pane, Show Totals, Refresh Data.

New Row   The New Row button lets you insert a row into the datasheet. This is a quick way to add new records (items) to the list.

Show Task Pane   Datasheet view can include a pop-out task pane of actions and commands that can be applied to items in the view. This pane can be hidden, and this button is a convenient way to open the pane. If you click this button while the pane is showing, it will hide the task pane as well.

Show Totals   This button adds totals to bottom of the columns in Datasheet view. It's very useful for a quick, temporary view of a column's totals, because clicking the button a second time will turn totals off.

Refresh Data   This button refreshes the data in the list to include any changes other users might have made while the page has been open.

Manage Views

The Manage Views section contains four buttons, a scroll bar, and a Views drop-down list. This section is all about views. And that is good, since the title area breadcrumb is inaccessible while this ribbon is active, meaning, without this section, users would not be able to change, modify, or add a view while the ribbon is active.

Create View The Create View button opens a Create View page (as shown in Figure 4.28, it's not merely a dialog box), where you can choose to create a view based on some view templates (or use SharePoint Designer if you have it installed), or you can base a new view on the settings of an existing view listed below the templates. See Chapter 5 for more about views.

Modify View This button displays a drop-down list (Figure 4.29) with two options to modify the current view. The simple Modify View option takes you to a page with the settings of the current view so you can modify them. The second option, Modify View In SharePoint Designer (Advanced), opens SharePoint Designer, which requires it to be installed locally. The Modify View button is useful if you see something in the view you need to change.

FIGURE 4.28
The Create View page

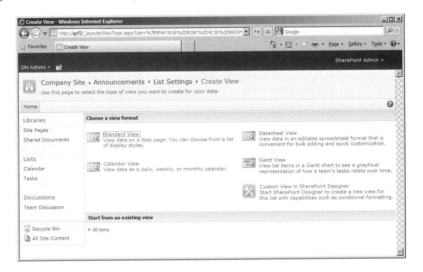

FIGURE 4.29
The Modify View drop-down menu

Create Column You can use this button to add a field (or column if you're thinking in terms of Datasheet view) to the list. When clicked, it opens a box where you can enter the settings to create a new column.

Navigate Up The Navigate Up button actually has nothing to do with views. Lists and libraries can have folders enabled. If a list has folders and you are in a folder looking at items, you can click the Navigate Up button to go up one level to the folder's parent. Although it looks like the Navigate Up button in the top ribbon bar, this button takes you up only one level in the library; it does not drop down a path tree to navigate to the home page.

Current View The Current View menu initially displays the current view but, when clicked, displays a drop-down list of all views available for this list; in my example, there's only one at this point.

The Current View menu provides the only access to the other views for the list from within the ribbon bar (which you can deactivate by clicking the Browse tab in the top ribbon bar).

Because Add and Modify are already buttons in the ribbon, those options aren't available in the Current View drop-down like they are in the title area breadcrumb drop-down.

Current Page   Views can be set to display only a certain number of items per page. This is good management of resources; if the list has many items, it's easier for SharePoint to display fewer items at a time than to send all the data about the whole list to your computer at once. If that option is enabled, Current Page will let you scroll forward and backward, paging through list items.

Share & Track

The next section is Share & Track, which includes buttons for emailing a link of the selected item, setting up an Alert Me notification, and going to the RSS feed page for the list.

E-mail A Link   This E-mail A Link button requires the local computer you are accessing the site from to have an email client available. If it does, the button will open a window to send an email. The link to the list will have been pasted into the body of the message, ready for sending.

Alert Me   Like the Alert Me button for other ribbons, this displays a window (Figure 4.30) where you can create an email alert for changes on the list or you can choose to manage alerts for the user. Remember that the alert won't work if SharePoint doesn't know the user's email address. Alerts set at the list level, as opposed to the item level, have slightly different, additional general options for alert triggers: All Changes, New Items Are Added, Existing Items Are Changed, and Items Are Deleted, as well as the list item alert triggers.

RSS Feed   The RSS Feed button takes you to the list's RSS feed page so you can subscribe to it (Figure 4.31).

FIGURE 4.30
Creating a new alert for the Announcements list

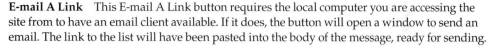
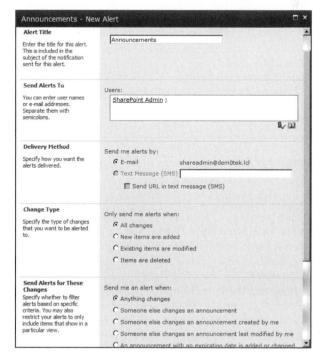

FIGURE 4.31
The RSS feed page
for the Announce-
ments list

FIGURE 4.31
The RSS feed page
for the Announce-
ments list

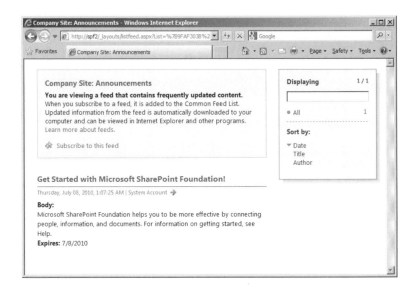

DOES YOUR LIST RIBBON BAR LOOK SOMEWHAT DIFFERENT?

SharePoint expects its pages to be viewed full-screen at a resolution of at least 1024×768. If you don't have the browser window maximized (and I often don't in order to save space in the book), some ribbons might compress sections, causing them, and their buttons, to look a little different from what I am describing.

So if you can't see all the buttons in each section (or if a section is missing), try maximizing the browser window. And for those sections compressed to one icon, click the down arrow beneath them. The menu will display all the buttons in that section (bigger than the ones on the original ribbon in some cases).

Connect and Export

The next section is Connect And Export. It contains six small buttons, only three of which actually have labels and most of which relate to integrating SharePoint with a corresponding Microsoft product. If you don't have the appropriate software installed locally, the buttons will be grayed out.

Sync To A SharePoint Workspace   SharePoint Foundation 2010 strongly supports clients using SharePoint Workspace (formerly known as Groove, in case you've worked with the product). The Workspace software is installed on the clients locally and lets users have SharePoint sites (meaning their lists and libraries) stored locally so they can work while offline and then use the button shown in Figure 4.32 to synchronize with SharePoint when they go back online. The Workspace client interface allows users to drag and drop files on the local computer into a library or list, before synchronizing with the site. Microsoft considers Workspace to be a SharePoint client in the same way that Outlook is an Exchange client.

FIGURE 4.32
The Sync To
SharePoint Work-
space button

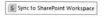

SHAREPOINT WORKSPACE

SharePoint Workspace is a client product and won't be deeply covered in this book. However, there are many articles online and other books available that allow you to explore the product in depth.

 Connect To Outlook   Many lists in SharePoint have fields that make them perfect for working on and integrating with Outlook (such as the contact list or calendar). Therefore, it makes sense to have a button on the ribbon bar for the list to connect Outlook to it. This button is grayed out if you don't have Outlook installed.

 Export To Excel   Because a list is really a table of columns and rows, it easily lends itself to being exported to Excel. People often like to manipulate the data in a list far more than just changing the view. So, the Export To Excel button gives the user the option to export the data to Excel for additional work (or even as an emergency backup—lists can be created from Excel spreadsheets as well).

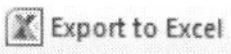

 Create Visio Diagram   If the list contents support it and you have Visio installed, you can create a Visio report based on the list's content.

 Open With Access   If you have Access installed, you can open the list in Access if you'd like. I've used this feature to generate quick mailing labels from a list—very convenient.

 Open Schedule   This button integrates the list with Microsoft Project, opening it in Project if you have it installed locally. As the button name implies, this option works best with lists that contain date fields, preferably date ranges.

Customize List

The Customize List section contains buttons that are possibly more powerful than your average user should have knowledge of. Luckily, for your average site member, these buttons are grayed out. (Although the users can still see the buttons and be tempted by them, they can't use them.) Buttons in this section include Modify Form Web Part, Edit List In SharePoint Designer, and New Quick Step.

 Modify Form Web Parts   The drop-down shown in Figure 4.33 is an interesting new option for this version of SharePoint. All list and library view pages in a site are also essentially web part pages. That means every view page of a list or library can be treated like a web part page if you want, web parts can be added to make the page more useful or interesting, and users can have their own personal view of the pages, while leaving Shared view alone. (Yes, being able to do that can create some confusion in some users.)

FIGURE 4.33
The Modify Form
Web Parts drop-
down menu

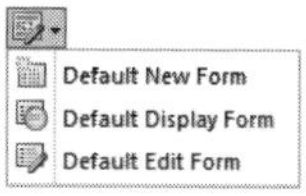

A CAVEAT

If you do add web parts to a list or library page, it changes the page from a list view page, with a drop-down View menu in the title breadcrumb and default toolset in the top ribbon bar, to a generic web part page. You can still get to a different view using the Current View menu, but the title breadcrumb view menu won't be available until the added web parts are removed from the page.

But now the form boxes that users use to create, view, or edit a list or library item can be modified as well, meaning that web parts can be added to those pages if needed for some reason. Generally, only those with administrative privileges can make these changes.

When you click the Modify Form Web Parts button, you can choose which type of forms used by the list you want to edit. In the case of Announcements (which is a simple list), you can modify the New, Edit, or Display forms.

IF YOU DO CHOOSE TO MODIFY A FORM

If you select one of the Modify Form Web Parts button options (such as Default New Form), it will take you to a different page, in which the form page is in edit mode and you can add web parts to the top area of the form. Notice that it has a Web Part Tools ➤ Options tab in the top ribbon bar, which opens a ribbon that lets you work with any web parts you might add.

Notice that the form page has even more ribbon bar tabs relating to managing the page, inserting things into it, and working with the web parts themselves.

Edit List In SharePoint Designer   This button simply opens the list for editing in SharePoint Designer. If you do not have SPD installed locally, however, this button will pop up a box suggesting that you download the program, with assistance for choosing the language and architecture and a Download button to get you started (Figure 4.34).

FIGURE 4.34
The box prompting to download Share-Point Designer

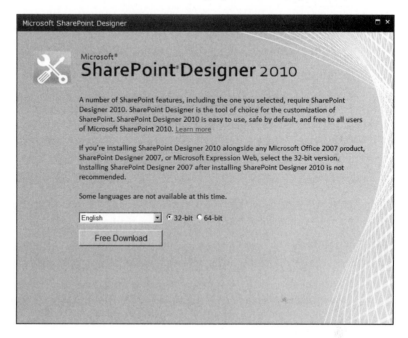

New Quick Step   This button requires SharePoint Designer to be installed locally; otherwise, it will prompt you to download the program. It lets you create a custom ribbon button to apply to items in the list, by essentially creating a macro with the limited options available for workflows and then assigning it a button. When you create one of these buttons, a new section appears, Quick Step, where these custom buttons are stored. Keep in mind that those added buttons might require some scrolling if your users (or you) don't have a high-resolution screen.

Settings

The final section of this ribbon, Settings, contains buttons used to modify settings directly related to the list. Two of its buttons, Workflow Settings and List Permissions, are somewhat redundant because their settings are also displayed on the List Settings page.

List Settings   The first and largest button in the Settings section, List Settings will take you to the List Settings page (Figure 4.35). This page contains the links to specific settings pages, such as Versioning, Validation, Permissions, and Workflow, as well as settings for the list such as columns and views. It also contains information concerning the exact URL, description, and email address of the list if the list is incoming email enabled.

FIGURE 4.35
The List
Settings page

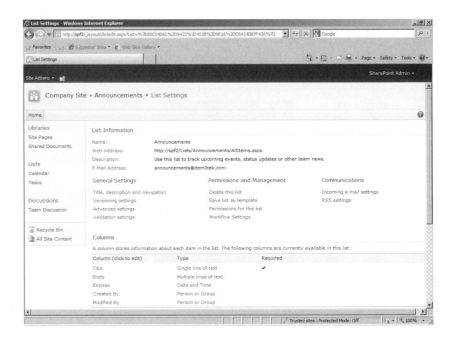

FIGURE 4.35
The List
Settings page

List Permissions   The List Permissions button takes you to the Permissions page for the list. Most objects on the site inherit the site's permissions, but you can break inheritance and set specific permissions on just about any object. For more information about permissions and inheritance, see Chapter 12, "Users and Permissions."

PERMISSION, PERMISSIONS EVERYWHERE

You may have noticed that not only does the site have a Permissions page, the home page has permissions, as do lists and list items. (And as you might expect, document items and libraries will have them, too.) The reason the Permissions option keeps showing up is because practically everything on the site (except maybe web parts) can be individually secured if necessary.

Workflow Settings   This little button produces a big drop-down menu (Figure 4.36), with options to open the Workflow Settings page, add a workflow (there is a Three-State workflow available for the site), or create a unique workflow just for the list or a reusable one to apply anywhere on the site (both requiring SharePoint Designer to create, of course).

FIGURE 4.36
The Workflow
Settings drop-
down menu

So, that's it for the Announcements list. We've explored the title area and seen that the list's view is appended to the end of the title bar breadcrumb. We've learned that, even before opening a ribbon, we can see the list's view (and modify it or create a new one from the title drop-down) and add a new item to a list. We've covered the two ribbons generally available to all lists, Items and List, combined under List Tools in the top ribbon bar.

Now it's time to see the similarities and differences between lists and libraries, by taking a quick look at the Shared Documents library.

A Quick Look at a Library: Shared Documents

As I mentioned earlier in the chapter, a library is just a list whose sole purpose is to manage files. The Team Site template creates a nice sample document library called Shared Documents for you to get to know.

Because a library is just another kind of list, a number of the buttons on the ribbon bars for a library are the same as they are for lists, but there are some significant sections, particularly for documents, that are different and deserve to be explored.

1. First, just to take a look at a library, let's go to Shared Documents on the Quick Launch bar.

2. After you've clicked Shared Documents, it will open to a standard document library page.

A document library page has the usual top ribbon bar at the top, the title area and top link bar below that, and the Quick Launch bar on the left. In the center (to the right of the Quick Launch bar) is the area where the library items will be listed, complete with column headers along the top of that area and an Add Document link at the bottom. In this view, the title breadcrumb is appended to the view of the page (it's the default view All Documents; if you look at the address bar, the page name is `AllItems.aspx` as expected). It looks pretty much like the Announcements list page we saw previously.

But if you look closer at the top ribbon bar, its toolset has changed. It was List Tools for the Announcements list, with tabs for Items and List. For a document library, it's Library Tools, and the tabs are Documents and Library (Figure 4.37).

FIGURE 4.37
The Shared Documents document library's content page

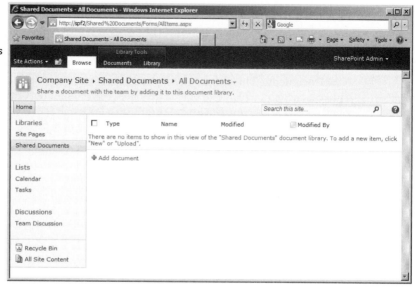

THE LIBRARY TOOLS DOCUMENTS TAB

To get an idea of what tools might be located in the Documents ribbon bar, click the Documents tab in the Library Tools toolset on the top ribbon bar (Figure 4.38). Keep in mind that libraries focus on files, or specifically (because they are so popular) Word documents, especially the Shared Documents library. Because of this, document libraries in particular really integrate with—or more accurately, *rely* on—you having some version (2007 or newer) of Office, or at least an Office product or two, installed locally.

FIGURE 4.38
A document library with the Documents ribbon active

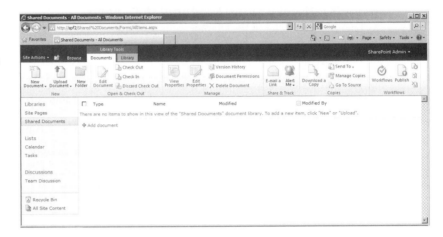

The Documents ribbon may look similar to the Items ribbon we looked at earlier, but there are some subtle differences. There are six sections: New, Open & Check Out, Manage, Share & Track, Copies, and Workflow.

New

In the New section there are three buttons: New Document, Upload Document, and New Folder. You might notice that the New Folder button is not grayed out (as it was with the Announcements list), because having the option of creating new folders is enabled for libraries by default. Let's take a brief look at the buttons:

New Document This drop-down button has only one option, New Document (Figure 4.39). Unlike a list item, which will open a new item box to enter data into the list item's fields, when you click the New Document drop-down button, it will check the library's associated template and try to open it locally so you can create a new file.

FIGURE 4.39
The New Document drop-down menu

"DENIED..."

The default New Document template for a document library is usually Microsoft Word. If you don't have Word installed locally, you will be unable to create a new document. You can still upload documents, though.

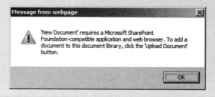

Upload Document   If you cannot create a new document, you can still upload an existing document to the library. Using the Upload Document drop-down menu (Figure 4.40), you can upload one document at a time, or, if you have an Office product installed locally, multiple documents at once (if you don't have an Office product installed locally that option is grayed out, as it is in my case). If you click the button, its default is to upload just one document, which you can browse for. It will store the file in the library.

FIGURE 4.40
The Upload
Document drop-
down menu

A QUICK UPLOAD, AND A NOTE

Just so we can see what some of the buttons do (this is the Documents ribbon, so it really doesn't work without something selected), I am going to upload a sample file. However, you'll find a much more thorough library demonstration in Chapter 8, "Introduction to Libraries."

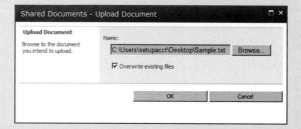

You may be wondering why the option to upload multiple documents isn't available. When an Office product of any kind is installed, it installs a bunch of Office components (many of which have nothing directly to do with the product you installed). One of them is essentially an upload manager, making it possible for you to upload more than one document at a time. No Office products installed? You can still upload documents one at a time (or drag and drop them using Open with Explorer window, which is mentioned later in the chapter and also covered in Chapter 8.)

New Folder

New Folder   This button allows you to create a new folder in the library, letting you then organize files (and even more folders if necessary) in the folder. This option lets the library maintain the same document structure as the file shares users might be familiar with. Also, if a library gets too large, it is easy to display document items per folder than the whole flat list of thousands.

Open & Check Out

The Open & Check Out section is unique to libraries. It contains the Edit Document, Check Out, Check In, and Discard Check Out buttons. Remember that buttons can be grayed out and unavailable, as you can see in Figure 4.38, if a document item is not selected in the library for them to apply to or the library doesn't have that feature enabled.

Edit Document

Edit Document   Just like the New button, the Edit Document button needs Office to work, because it is used to open a selected file to edit it. To be specific, Edit Document needs the Office product associated with the selected file's file type to work. But if you were to select a Word file and click Edit Document, it would open the file in Word for you to edit. When you save it in Word, it should save the changes to the document library.

Check Out   Check Out, a button we originally saw on the Page ribbon, is used to mark a file to be checked out for editing. When a file is checked out, it is set as read-only for all accounts but the one that checked out the file. This lets that one user edit the file, helping avoid simultaneous editing and change loss. Checkout can be configured in the library's settings to be *required* (a file cannot be edited without being checked out first). For more about checking documents in and out, see Chapter 8.

Check In   For any document that can be checked out, there has to be a way to check it back in. The Check In button takes a document that you are done editing and changes its state to checked in so it is no longer set to read-only and is available for others to edit.

Discard Check Out   This button forces a document to be checked back in (discarding the changes of the person who has it checked out). This function is useful if you need to abandon changes you've made to a document while you had it checked out.

OVERRIDE?

Note that unlike the Page ribbon, this Documents ribbon for some reason doesn't also offer the Override Check Out option, which allows those with the correct permissions to discard the checkout of other users.

Now with this version of SharePoint, Discard Check Out acts like Override Check Out does. Even though the Discard Check Out button's tooltip implies that the feature works only with items you have checked out personally, that is true only if you don't have the Override Check Out permission enabled for your account (site administrators do by default; site members don't). So if you are looking for Override Check Out in a document library, it's Discard Check Out now.

Manage

The Manage section contains the View Properties, Edit Properties, Version History, Document Permissions, and Delete Document buttons. Most of these buttons are the same as those in the Items ribbon bar's Manage section, but some do have a subtly different use.

View Properties   In a library, the fields for a list item to which a document (or other kind of file) is attached are considered *property fields* for the document. Because a library is a list, you can customize the fields so as to capture better metadata about the document. To see the fields for the document, you click View Properties. This button allows you to view the item.

Edit Properties   This button, like View Properties, has to do with the fields associated with a document item. It lets you go in and change or add data to the fields for a document item by bringing up a form box containing the fields to edit.

WHY BOTHER WITH LIBRARY ITEM PROPERTIES?

Keep in mind that you can add fields such as topic tags, author name, editors, and so on, to library items to make the properties more useful, especially for searching and views (which can be looked at like reports). Chapter 8 covers this topic in more detail.

 Version History   This button opens a box displaying the version history of a document—if versioning is enabled for the library.

Document Permissions   This button takes you to the selected document item's permissions page.

Delete Document   This button, like its equivalent in the Items ribbon for a list, deletes the selected document (after prompting to be sure) and puts it in the user's Recycle Bin.

Share & Track

The two buttons in the Share & Track section, E-mail A Link and Alert Me, are both pretty self-explanatory and were described in detail earlier in the chapter.

Copies

The Copies section (along with parts of the Workflows section) is unique to libraries.

It has four buttons: Download A Copy, Send To, Manage Copies, and Go To Source. This section is focused on a feature specific to libraries—sending documents to other libraries as part of the document management process.

Download A Copy   If you have an Upload button, why not have a Download button too? If you don't want to edit a file from the library and then save it locally, you can just click this button and be prompted to simply download a copy. There will be no synchronizing going on between the copy in the library and the downloaded one. It's just an independent copy, downloaded to a location you specify.

Send To This button sends the selected document somewhere else. As shown in Figure 4.41, its options include a different library or document workspace. If you have a particular send-to destination specified in the library settings, it will list the library name as an option as well.

FIGURE 4.41

The Send To drop-down menu

WHAT DO YOU MEAN, SEND TO?

Often the editorial process of a document requires that it start in one library, with one group of people working on it, and then move to a different library for a different team to work on it (or possibly to be archived after the project is done).

To support this, you can send (essentially copy) a document to another location, meaning a different library. You can also configure a library's settings to specify a default library location (one default send-to location per library). The copy of the document is linked to the original, and it can be synchronized with that version if that original, or *source* document, is updated. Keep in mind synchronization is one way, from the source to the copy. Changes to the copy cannot be used to update the original.

A standard SharePoint feature for managing documents is to allow a document to calve off its own subsite, solely focused on working on that document, so the other option in the Send To drop-down is Create Document Workspace. Although this option is really about creating the workspace subsite for the document, the document stored in that workspace is actually still linked to the originating document and can be synchronized from that original, so creating the workspace is like an elaborate Send To.

Manage Copies The Manage Copies button is used to open a box listing the selected source document's copies. If a copy of a document is sent to another library, there will be two copies of the same document. When you do a Send To, the documents are linked in one way—from the source to the sent copy. This means that changes made to the first document can be forced onto the sent one from here, keeping them synchronized.

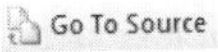

Go To Source The Go To Source button is used on a document in a library that is the destination of the Send To, to go to the library of the original source document. Sometimes it's hard to remember where an original document is stored. In that case, you can select the document that is a copy and then click Go To Source. It will immediately take you to the library containing the original document.

Workflows

The final section, Workflows, contains one button about workflows and four buttons about version control and content approval (Publish, UnPublish, Approve/Reject, and Cancel Approval). Why the section is called Workflows since only one button in five relate to it, I do not know. All the buttons in the section can be grayed out if they are not applicable, in other words, if their function is not enabled or available.

Workflows

Workflows   This button is the same as the one for the Items ribbon for a list. It can be used only if there is a workflow associated with the document item; otherwise, it's grayed out. If the button was active, you could click it and go to a page to see the status of the workflow, manage it, or start a new one on the selected document.

Publish

Publish   This button does not actually publish the selected document anywhere. Instead, it promotes a minor version of a document to a major version—which, according to SharePoint, is *publishing* the document. To explain further, you can set a library to allow versioning, with two options. You can have flat versions, meaning that every time a document is saved to the library a copy is saved in Version History, and a whole number assigned to that version (so you can roll back to a previous version if your current saved changes were a terrible mistake). Or you can have major and minor versions, with the option, when saving, to give the version a whole number (making it major) or a decimal number following the last major version's number, such as 1.3, making it a minor or draft version.

If a document is a draft version, you can *publish* it up to a major version, changing that version of a document to the next *whole* number, rather than its decimal version number. If the button is grayed out, then versioning is not enabled.

Unpublish   This button is what you click if you want to demote a document's current version *down* to a minor version from a whole number (so instead of being version number 2, it's 1.1). Equally as important as the Publish function, this button is also grayed out in my example because versioning is not available for this library.

Approve/Reject   This button, has, like its predecessor, nothing to do with workflows and is the same as the Approve/Reject button in the Items ribbon for lists. Approve/Reject requires Content Approval to be enabled for the library (and if it isn't, the button is grayed out). When it's enabled, a document edited or saved to the library must be approved before anyone but the author/editor and the approver can see it.

HIDDEN DRAFT

One of the big reasons content approval works the way it does is Draft Item Security. When you enable Content Approval, the Draft Item Security setting becomes available, which gives you the ability to display minor, or draft, versions only to those who are authors of the document or to someone with the Approve Items permission (such as a site administrator). You can change that Draft Item Security setting and allow anyone with read or edit rights to see drafts if you want, but that rather defeats the purpose of Content Approval.

Cancel Approval   When you click this button and Content Approval is enabled, the selected document item will be demoted from a whole number to a decimal number, or draft version (rather like unpublishing, but approval has been explicitly revoked). And in that case, if draft item security for content approval is enabled, then the item will become invisible to everyone but the author/editor and approver until it is approved again.

THE LIBRARY TOOLS LIBRARY TAB

The Library tab in the Library Tools activates a ribbon bar in which the sections and buttons are specifically for managing and maintaining the library.

To open the Library ribbon bar, click the Library tab in the top ribbon bar. This ribbon is almost exactly identical to the List ribbon bar we saw earlier for the Announcements list. That makes sense, since a library really is just a list. I'll mention each section briefly, in case you need a reminder. There are a few buttons missing and one important one added, so I'll cover them as we go (Figure 4.42).

FIGURE 4.42
The Library Tools
Library ribbon

To start, the ribbon has seven sections: View Format, Datasheet, Manage Views, Share & Track, Connect & Export, Customize Library (as opposed to List), and Settings.

View Format   This section contains the buttons to toggle the view format of the library from Standard view to Datasheet view, which allows you to view and work with the library as a datasheet. This works only if you have an Office product (2007 or higher preferred) installed on the computer you are using to browse the site. If you are using Office 2010, it must be the 32-bit version to use Datasheet view; the 64-bit version does not support it.

Datasheet   This section has buttons for doing things specific to working in Datasheet view: New Row, Show Task Pane, Show Totals, and Refresh Data.

Manage Views   This section is exactly the same as the one on the List ribbon bar, containing the buttons Create View, Modify View, Create a Column, Navigate Up, and Current View, as well as a Current Page scroll bar for scrolling through pages of items in a view.

Share & Track   The Share & Track section, exactly like the one for the List ribbon, contains three buttons: E-mail A Link, Alert Me, and RSS Feed.

Connect & Export   This section contains fewer buttons than a List ribbon's does, because a library can integrate with only a few Office products well. Thus, there is a button called Sync To SharePoint Workspace and then small buttons called Connect To Outlook and Export To Excel. The last button in this section, Open With Explorer, really has nothing to do with connecting or exporting and is more about how the library is viewed. Opening the page in an Explorer window is unique to libraries and cannot be done with lists.

Open With Explorer   If your computer supports it, you can open the library into an Explorer window. (If you are browsing from Server 2008 R2, it doesn't support this capability natively.) The documents will show up as icons for files. The users can drag and drop files from their desktop to the library in this view (which can wreak havoc if there are required fields or content approval). This view is especially comforting for users more familiar with file shares than libraries (you can see why in Figure 4.43, complete with the sample file I uploaded earlier). It can also be useful for bulk uploading.

FIGURE 4.43
A library open
in an Explorer
window

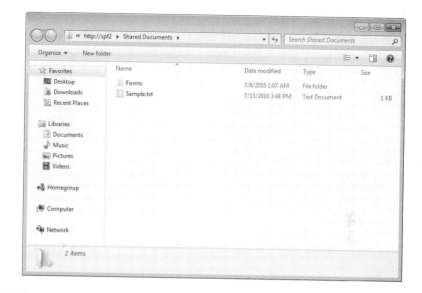

THE FORMS FOLDER

An interesting thing about viewing a document library using Windows Explorer is that it contains, by default, a folder called Forms (although you see it only if your local computer is set to see hidden folders and you have administrative permission on the site). This folder contains the forms that are used for the library, such as those for different ways to view the content of the page or the form used to upload files. Within the folder, the Webfldr file is actually the Explorer view listed in the View menu. The Repair Form, a troubleshooting tool, can be found here as well, and it's worth keeping in mind. This page will allow you to reconnect a document if it somehow becomes disconnected from its content type's template.

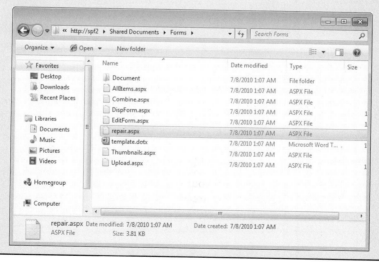

Customize Library   The Customize Library section contains the same buttons as its equivalent on the List ribbon bar, which will be grayed out for most nonadmin users: Form Web Parts drop-down, Edit Library In SharePoint Designer, and New Quick Step.

Settings   The last section on the Library ribbon, Settings, contains three buttons: Library Settings, Library Permissions, and Workflow Settings.

So, that's it for the library ribbon bars. You've now learned about the different content pages and seen that they have a lot of similarities, such as the ability to select items (even multiple items at once) in a list. You've seen that items can have a drop-down menu containing actions specific to the item, that the content pages (for either a list or a library) can be different views of the same data, that common page elements (such as the top link bar, Quick Launch bar, and top ribbon bars) remain, and that the lists have reliable, similar ribbon bars.

You've also learned that practically every object that can be edited, managed, or added has its own ribbon bar (or two) to contain the actions that can be applied to them. Because you've seen so many in this chapter, when you come across a new one later in the book, you should be able to recognize its layout and quickly understand its buttons.

Now that we've explored the home page and the two main kinds of content pages, let's briefly look at administrative pages.

A Quick Look at Administrative Pages

Administrative pages in SharePoint are all over the place in terms of their page formatting.

For example, the Create page is a kind of administrative page that is really nothing but a page of links, with no need for a toolbar of any kind (Figure 4.44). This page actually is quite dynamic; if you move your mouse over an object title, a description will appear in the top half of the page (note the advertisement for Silverlight, which I am not installing since I am currently browsing on the server). Also note that this page has no Quick Launch bar or search field.

FIGURE 4.44
The Create page

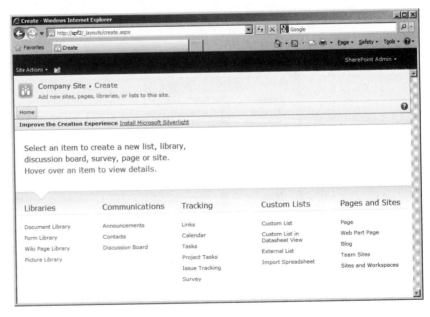

SILVERLIGHT AND THE CREATE PAGE

If you have Silverlight installed, the Create page changes its look. It doesn't necessarily make it more useful, just different looking. So if your Create page doesn't look like Figure 4.44, then you probably have Silverlight installed.

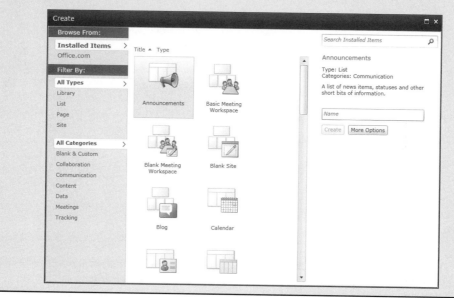

The Site Settings page is another administrative page that contains nothing but links; however, this one does comply with standard site page design, containing a Quick Launch bar and title area (Figure 4.45). It's on the Site Settings page that you administer everything about a site, from permissions to look and feel to managing features. For the top-level site, you also have settings related to the site collection as a whole. And for this reason, the page doesn't need more than headings to organize the links, and it links to configuration pages, very much like the category pages in a Central Administration site for the farm (see Chapter 11, "Central Administration," for more information).

Then there is the Recycle Bin. As you saw in the sidebar "Quick Launch Tips" earlier in this chapter, this page follows the formatting of the previous versions of SharePoint, with links above the list of items enabling you to take action on a selected item—Restore Selection and Delete Selection (if there were anything deleted to select). In addition, it has all the normal navigation aids, as well as the search field and help icon.

And there is also the Site Permissions page (Figure 4.46). This page is formatted to be more current, with a Permission Tools ribbon bar.

As you can see, there are buttons in the Site Permissions ribbon relevant to working with site permissions—which brings up a good point. Generally, with administrative pages, if what is going to be done on that page is particularly complicated, with a number of different settings and configurations, it is likely to have a ribbon bar. Although the page might have an action bar of links from the previous version of SharePoint, if you don't see a ribbon bar, it is usually because the particular page doesn't need it. For example, a new document library page has no ribbon bar or links, because it is needed only to accept configuration settings to create a new site (Figure 4.47). Many pages in Central Administration are designed this way.

FIGURE 4.45
The Site Settings page

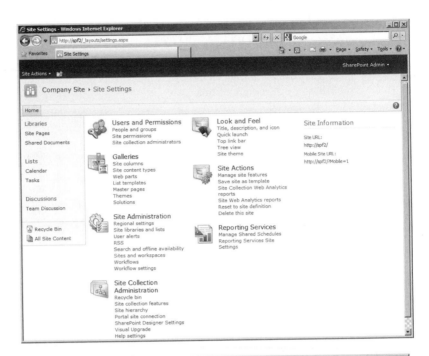

FIGURE 4.46
The Site Permissions page

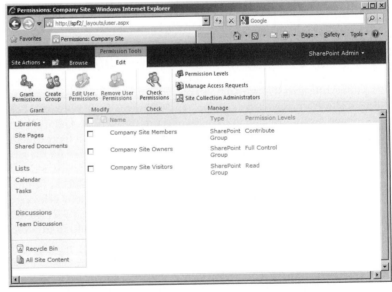

This brings up another good point. For those of you who will be working in Central Administration, the pages there are also administrative pages, basically by definition, and as such their format is dictated by their function and varies accordingly. There isn't as much simple standardization as a site with its content pages and home page.

Fundamentally, administrative pages are laid out the way they need to be to get the job done and should be approached on a case-by-case basis.

FIGURE 4.47
A new document
library page

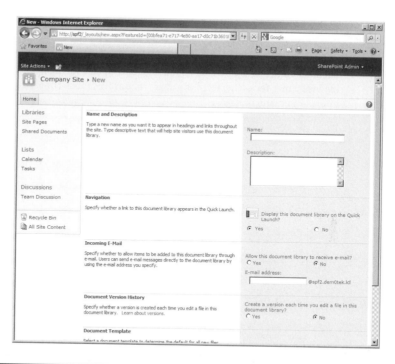

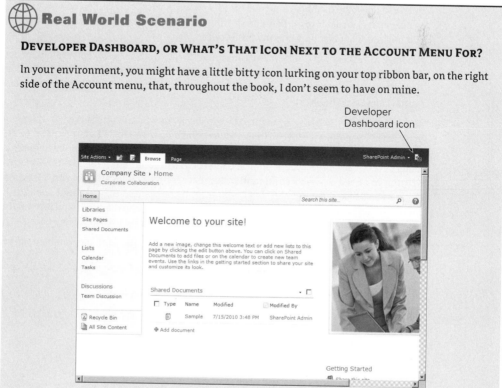

Real World Scenario

DEVELOPER DASHBOARD, OR WHAT'S THAT ICON NEXT TO THE ACCOUNT MENU FOR?

In your environment, you might have a little bitty icon lurking on your top ribbon bar, on the right side of the Account menu, that, throughout the book, I don't seem to have on mine.

Developer
Dashboard icon

That icon is a toggle button to display, or not display, the *developer dashboard*. The developer dashboard is a little extra capability added to this version of SharePoint that appends a section to the bottom of site pages that allows you to see troubleshooting information about the page, including load times for each part of the page, request response times, database query times, exception information, and more.

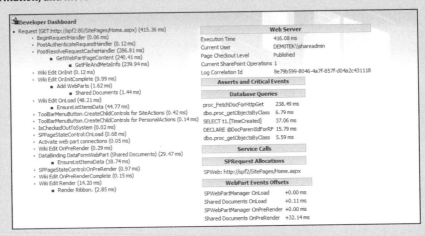

Keep in mind that it can add a lot of content to the bottom of the page. For that reason, you can choose to leave the dashboard turned off (the default), turn it on (which will take up a lot of space on every page), or set it to on-demand (letting you turn it on or off for each page at will, generating that button). That last option is my preferred setting.

You have to set this capability at the command line, using STSADM, PowerShell, or code of some sort. These tools are discussed in Chapter 14, "STSADM and PowerShell," but briefly, I find it much easier to use the single-line STSADM command than several lines of PowerShell script to manage the developer dashboard.

Remember that STSADM was meant to be run locally on a SharePoint server (or at least one of them in the farm), you must be logged in to a SharePoint server as a local administrator to use STSADM (it helps to be a farm administrator as well) and STSADM.exe is located in the SharePoint root BIN folder (%ProgramFiles%\Common Files\Microsoft Shared\Web Server Extensions\14\ BIN), so you need to have a command prompt accessing that location to run STSADM. For more about STSADM and PowerShell, see Chapter 14. If you wanted to, you could open the PowerShell console instead, because it can do STSADM commands just like the command prompt, but without having to navigate to the BIN folder, if you have the correct permissions configured.

Keep in mind that the developer dashboard is a farm-wide function; once enabled, it is enabled for all pages of all sites in all web applications.

Here's how it's done:

◆ To simply have the dashboard display at the bottom of all pages at all times (good if you're a developer and are developing preproduction), enter the following:

```
stsadm -o setproperty -pn developer-dashboard -pv on
```

◆ To turn off the dashboard, enter the following:

```
stsadm -o setproperty -pn developer-dashboard -pv off
```

◆ To enable the dashboard as an on-demand capability (with the nifty button in top ribbon bar), enter this:

```
stsadm -o setproperty -pn developer-dashboard -pv ondemand
```

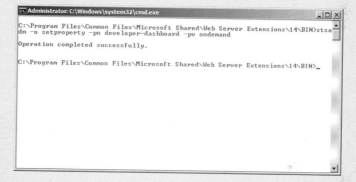

Now you know what that icon is, what it does, and how to enable it for your farm (or disable it, if you want).

The Bottom Line

Identify SharePoint's navigation tools and understand how to use them. SharePoint makes a point of ensuring that a user always has a way to get where they need to go without using the Back button in the browser. Recognizing these features makes navigation easier and increases productivity.

Master It List three ways to get back to the home page should you be in a list or library.

Find a list or library. SharePoint uses the Quick Launch bar as a quick, convenient, and consistent way for users to find the SharePoint lists and libraries they need to access.

Master It How do you find a list or library if it is not on the Quick Launch bar?

Use the Quick Launch bar. The Quick Launch bar is more than a list of lists. It also contains an easy way to navigate through all contents of a site, access people and groups, check the Recycle Bin, and create new site contents.

Master It By default, when SharePoint is initially installed, the Quick Launch bar does not have Surveys as a heading. Why?

Use the Top Ribbon bar.   The interfaces containing the settings and actions to apply to objects in this version of SharePoint are ribbon bars. These ribbons contain buttons and drop-down lists to apply changes, access settings, or to configure whatever is selected in the environment.

Master It   Is there a limit to how many ribbon bars there can be for a selected item or page?

Master It   There is a button that appears on both the top ribbon bar and in the Documents ribbon for a library. Is seems to be the same button, does it do the same thing when used from the top ribbon bar as it does from the Documents ribbon?

Understand a content page.   All lists and libraries contain content. To display that content in a consistent and easy to use manner, SharePoint uses content pages. This simply refers to list or library pages that contain content. Otherwise known as view pages, they can be configured to display the list or library data in different ways, depending on your needs.

Master It   Every page on the site has at least one feature that is consistent throughout the site. What is that new consistent feature? What unique attribute does it have that allows it to remain always in view?

Chapter 5

Introduction to Web Parts

Web parts are an interesting addition to SharePoint. They were meant to be a convenient way to display things on the home page of SharePoint sites. They were so handy that now they can be added to most pages of the site. Somewhat like sidebar gadgets, web parts are independent little applications that pull and display information from anywhere data might be available, such as the content database, file shares, or web pages. They are resizable, movable, and self-contained. Numerous companies have been built on customizing SharePoint web parts into all kinds of useful things, probably well beyond the expectations of the original SharePoint developers.

Most web parts have a number of features in common. They have a title bar, a central area to display content, borders, and, in the case of some web parts such as those used for list views, toolbars. They can be configured to hide some features, such as the title bar or borders, or they themselves can be hidden from user view. They can also be added to pages that can hold web parts, be rearranged, be minimized, be exported, be imported, and even be deleted.

There are numerous books about how to develop web parts, so this chapter covers only the basics concerning what SharePoint offers out of the box in terms of List View web parts, web part templates, and some user-specific, aggregating web parts. With that knowledge, you can more easily understand what is available for you to work with and customize before paying someone to do it for you.

For this version of SharePoint, there are two kinds of pages that can contain web parts: wiki pages and web part pages (the latter of which can include the home page, list or library content pages, and even the forms used to manage list or library data). For this reason, working with web parts is a little more complicated now, not because the web parts have changed necessarily but because the pages that can contain them have.

In this chapter, you'll learn how to

- Identify web parts
- Use edit mode
- Distinguish between Personal and Shared versions
- Work with web parts
- Export and import web parts

Using the Home Page as a Wiki Page

Because one of the most popular site templates that SharePoint offers is the Team Site template, it's a good idea to take a look at its home page. For this version of SharePoint, Microsoft wanted to show off its new and improved wiki pages by using one as the home page for the site. This gives us an opportunity to both explore a wiki home page and its web parts and get a head start on mastering wiki pages in general.

Exploring a Web Part

If you are following my example, you should be on the home page of the SharePoint site, in my case `http://SPF2`, for this chapter. You may need to log in (be sure to use an administrative account, such as the site collection administrator). I logged in using my SharePoint Admin (*shareadmin*) account that I created in the installation chapters.

On the home page, you should see the top ribbon bar, title area, Quick Launch bar, and web part/rich content area. In the rich content area, there is, sadly, only one web part available—Shared Documents (Figure 5.1). This is a List View web part displaying the contents of the Shared Documents library (which is also listed on the Quick Launch bar on the left side of the page, for your convenience).

FIGURE 5.1

The Shared Documents web part on the home page

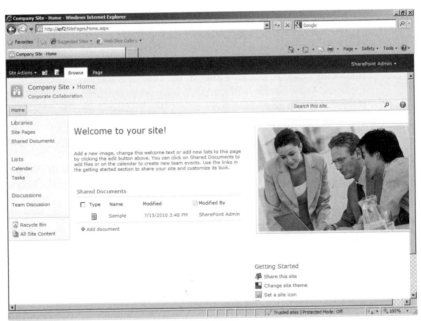

The rest of that central area is considered a rich content area (or wiki page), so you can edit it like a Word document, adding images, formatting text, and so on. This means the text above the Shared Documents web part, the picture across from it, and even the list of links below the picture are all just stuff on the wiki page itself, not web parts.

Web parts are usually dynamic. They show the contents of something, such as a list, library, or folder (all of which can change as their contents change). Web parts aren't usually just for looking pretty, although they can be if that's what you want.

A List View web part has a title that corresponds with the title of the list or library it's displaying, an area below the title where (as you can see with the Shared Documents web part in

Figure 5.1) the items in the list would be displayed, and an Add A New Item link that will take you to the new item page for that list.

> ### IT'S ALL JUST A LIST TO ME
>
> Only one kind of web part displays the contents of libraries and lists, and that's the List View web part. There is no library view web part, probably because a library is just a list with a focus on the documents attached to record.

If you move your mouse over the Shared Documents web part (especially in the title bar area), you'll see that the title bar sort of activates, showing you a check box on the right side and a down arrow.

The down arrow will give you a menu offering you options to manage the web part on the page (Figure 5.2). The options will vary depending on whether you are allowed to edit the web part or change its state. For example, the Minimize option rolls up the web part content to the title bar like a window shade, and when the web part is minimized, the Restore option returns it to full size. This menu can have more options depending on whether you are editing the web part or just looking at, as we are now.

FIGURE 5.2

The Shared Documents web part drop-down menu

Next to that drop-down menu is a check box. It indicates whether the web part is selected. If you select the check box—in fact, if you click the web part at all—it selects the web part and triggers the top ribbon bar to offer the Library Tools toolset of ribbons, assuming you actually want to work in the library from the home page (Figure 5.3). If the web part were based on a list, the List Tools toolset would appear instead.

FIGURE 5.3
Selecting a web part triggers ribbon bars related to the web part's contents.

FIGURE 5.3
Selecting a web part triggers ribbon bars related to the web part's contents.

To unselect the web part, you can clear the check box, or if that doesn't work, just click in an empty space on the home page somewhere other than the web part itself.

The web part title is usually a link (you can configure it). In this case, it links to the content page of the Shared Documents library if you click it (Figure 5.4).

FIGURE 5.4
The Shared Documents library content page

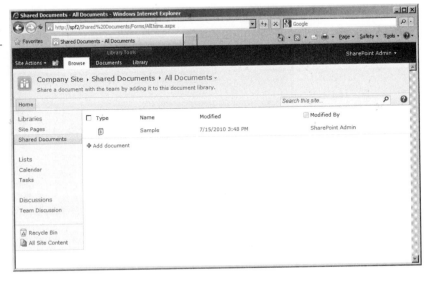

There are several ways to get back to the home page. You can click any of these:

♦ The Home tab in the top link bar, below the title area. (In our case, the Home tab is the only one there because there are no other sites in this site collection.)

♦ The name of the site itself in the title breadcrumb.

♦ The Navigate Up button in the top ribbon bar. (Then click the name of the site there.)

Note that, with the breadcrumb and the Navigate Up button, the name of the site is synonymous with the home page.

Click whichever navigation option you'd like to get back to the home page to continue to explore the only web part there: Shared Documents.

On the Shared Documents web part, below the title, is a set of columns from the document library's list (essentially a summary view). You can filter the contents by these columns just like you could in the list (or library) by clicking the column heading titles (which will trigger a drop down menu with filter options). At the bottom of the web part can be an Add Document icon and link, which works like the Upload Document button in the ribbon for the library. For most lists, that link is an Add Item link and triggers the New Item form box so you can enter a new list item right there.

As you can see, a List View web part allows you to quickly view what's in the library or list, add a new item or document immediately, or go to the list or library itself in case you need to do more than what is offered on the home page. To add to that, this version of SharePoint allows you to activate the list or library's ribbon bars right from the home page by just selecting the web part.

So, we've checked out the one web part available on the Team Site home page. Now it's time to get into the nitty-gritty of adding, removing, moving, and modifying web parts. Once you've learned the basics on the home page, wiki or not, you can apply that knowledge to any other page that can accept web parts.

WORD DOCUMENTS AND WIKI PAGES...THE SIMILARITIES ARE STRIKING

Just as a reminder, the rich content area of a Team Site template home page is meant to contain text, inserted tables, pictures, and even files (convenient if someone wrote something in a document and you just want to add it to the home page), as well as web parts.

When inserting anything into a rich content area, you need to put your insertion point where you want the content you are inserting to go. Even web parts will be added to wherever the insertion point is. It's a sort of point of landing for whatever you are inserting, text or not. Also, when you are dragging selected objects around the rich content area, remember that nothing can be dropped where there isn't already a paragraph mark or insertion point. I realize, in that case, that being able to view nonprinting characters would be nice, but sadly the Format Text ribbon doesn't have that option available.

Adding text, formatting it, inserting tables, pictures, and so on, into a wiki-rich content page is just like working in a Word document (or Publisher for that matter). And because of that, I am going to assume you already know how to do it. That said, there are some great things you can do with the "wikiness" of the home page to make it more visually interesting. And if that is the case, you might want to explore the Format Text ribbon to familiarize yourself with what it can do for you.

To edit the home page, you need to go into edit mode. Edit mode is a little different on a wiki page than it is on a regular web part page, so I will explore both types, starting with the wiki page (since that's what the site is using as the default at the moment).

Using Edit Mode on a Wiki Page

To put the home page into edit mode on a Team Site, you can either click the Edit page button on the top ribbon bar or click the Page tab and then click the Edit button on the ribbon. Clicking the Edit page button is easiest, so that's what I am going to do.

That will put the page into edit mode (Figure 5.5). You'll notice that the Edit page button has now turned into a Save & Close button, which matches the state of the Edit button (now a Save & Close button) on the ribbon bar. The top ribbon bar will now have an Editing Tools toolset, with two tabs: Format Text and Insert.

FIGURE 5.5

The Home page in edit mode

The rich content area of the page now has two zones with blue borders around them. There should also be a blinking cursor at the top of the left zone, waiting for you to start typing and letting you know where it thinks the current insertion point is.

Assuming you know how to work with the rich text–type stuff on the page (the picture, the text, and so on), I am going to show you simply how to work around those objects to insert, delete, and modify web parts.

WANT MORE COLUMNS FOR WEB PARTS?

By default, the rich content area of a wiki page has only two columns, but if you use the Text Layout button in the Format Text ribbon, you can actually change the underlying layout of the rich content area, allowing for header and footer areas and more than two columns if you'd like. Two columns work for me at this point, but you can get far more creative if you feel the need.

Inserting a Web Part

So, we have the Shared Documents web part in the column on the left, below the sample welcome text (you may want to delete or edit that at some point, but I am going to work around it for now).

Often home pages have web parts on them that helpfully display the tasks or documents a user is working on at the moment. Their contents are filtered by the logged-in user's account, so the web parts display only the items related to that user. It helps make the home page more user specific and user friendly.

I'd like to add a user-related web part to the home page. And while we're at it, we'll see about moving, deleting, and modifying a web part, as well as explore a few other interesting types of web parts.

Keep in mind that I am not going to use every single available web part, but I am going to cover enough that you will be able to master them on your own, depending on what you need to do with them.

One of the consistent things in a SharePoint site is that if a page can go into edit mode, chances are good that web parts can be inserted or added to them. And that insertion interface is pretty consistent, no matter where you are as well.

So, we'll start with inserting a web part on the home page. And to do that, we'll need to take a look at the Insert ribbon, so click the Insert tab on the top ribbon bar.

To be able to insert a web part on the home page, the page needs to be in edit mode, you need to put your insertion point in the column where you want to eventually insert the web part, and the Insert ribbon needs to be displayed.

The Insert ribbon has buttons organized in sections (formally considered *groups* by Microsoft, but since SharePoint already uses groups elsewhere, I'm going to call them *sections*). The Insert ribbon has only a few sections: Tables, Media, Links, Web Parts.

I intend to add a web part to the left column of the rich content area (and then move it later). When you first go into edit mode, the insertion point does end up at the top of the left column by default. If you were to insert a web part, it would land right where that cursor is blinking. I want to insert the web part right above the Shared Documents web part, so I am going to put my insertion point there. Feel free to put your web part wherever you want; just be sure to click there first, or else you'll have to drag the web part around by its title bar until it's positioned correctly.

In the Web Parts section of the ribbon bar are buttons related to web parts (mostly List View web parts). The first is, intuitively enough, the Web Parts button. To select a web part (or built-in web part template) to insert, click the Web Part button. It will drop down a web part workspace (that will push the rest of the page farther down) beneath the ribbon bar, as you can see in Figure 5.6.

FIGURE 5.6
The web part
workspace

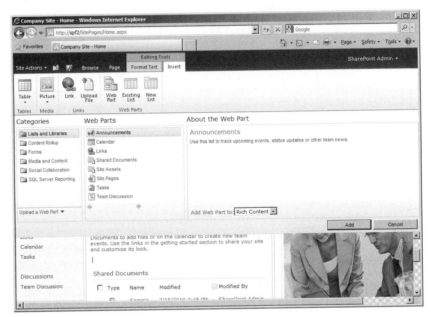

EXPLORING THE WEB PART WORKSPACE

The workspace has three columns: Categories, Web Parts, and About The Web Part. Existing web parts (that means web parts that are built in, web parts that occur whenever a list or library is created, or web parts you import to the page or site collection web part gallery) are organized under categories (some of which don't really make sense to me). If you select a category, such as Lists And Libraries, it will display the web parts available for that category in the Web Parts column. And if a web part is selected (usually the top one is by default), it will display a little blurb about it in the About The Web Part column.

Also in the About The Web Part column is the Add button and the currently useless Add The Web Part To selection field. The only option in the field is Rich Content because that's all there is to a wiki page. That control becomes more useful when you are working on a true web part page because the zones are more clearly defined. With a wiki page, the zones are just columns defined as the layout in the wiki page itself and therefore can't really be "seen" by the workspace (that's why clicking where you want the web part to go first is so important—otherwise, you'll be doing a lot of dragging and dropping).

OTHER WEB PARTS BUTTONS

Because this chapter is about exploring web parts, I am primarily going to focus on the Web Parts button on the Insert ribbon. However, the two other buttons in the Web Parts section are Existing Lists and New List.

Existing Lists will open a web part workspace, just like the Web Parts button will—but there will be no category. It will display only existing list or library web parts.

New List is an interesting button. Rather than creating a new list for the sake of use (well, primary use) on its own content pages, you can create a list or library on the fly here in edit mode on the home page purely to put its List View web part on the home page. The New List button will open a little Create List pop-up box so you can enter a new title for your list and choose from the list templates there to apply to the new list.

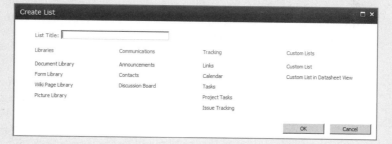

The next chapter is dedicated to all things list (as the one after it is about libraries), so it would be redundant, and unnecessary, to get distracted by making new lists here. And that's why we're focusing on just doing web parts for now.

EXPLORING WHAT WEB PARTS ARE AVAILABLE OUT OF THE BOX

Before we drop any web parts on the page, let's take a moment to briefly explore what web parts there are available by default in SharePoint Foundation on a Team Site. Keep in mind that if you didn't use the Team Site template for your site, you might have different lists or libraries available by default.

Lists and Libraries

The first category of web parts available in the web part workspace is Lists And Libraries. For each list or library created, there is a List View web part, which is a web part specifically designed to display the contents of a list or library. In fact, a content page for a list or library is really nothing more than a web part page containing one web part—the web part for that particular list or library. Thus, every list or library needs its own web part. But that requirement also makes it possible to have a list or library's contents displayed practically anywhere on a site, making it especially easy to add relevant lists or libraries to the home page, for the users' convenience.

Under the Lists And Libraries category, by default, are the following web parts (indicating that they are existing lists or libraries on the site): Announcements, Calendar, Links, Shared Documents, Site Assets, Site Pages, Tasks, Team Discussion. These are the lists and libraries generated by the Team Site template when the site was built. If you aren't using that template for your site, you might not have exactly the same items listed (and you won't have the wiki page as your home page either).

Content Rollup

Under the Content Rollup category are the Relevant Documents and XML Viewer web parts.

Relevant Documents The Relevant Documents web part makes sense as a roll-up web part—not only is it filtered to show just the documents relevant to the account that you are using to log into the site, but it actually aggregates or "rolls up" all the documents from all the site's libraries that might be relevant to your account. This means that any document you are working on in any library will be listed, unlike the Shared Documents web part, which displays all documents for that library only. And since documents can be considered content, well, I guess that makes it a good thing to have in this category. This web part is one of two that I consider "user-specific" web parts; both personalize any page they're on by filtering its contents by the account logged in.

XML Viewer The XML Viewer web part, however, doesn't seem to be a natural fit for the title of this category. What it is supposed to do is take XML, translate it to XSL (using XSL translation, XSLT), and then show the data. I guess, if you work with the right code, you could have it do some content roll-up. I've used the XML Viewer web part to display the result of a little HTML or XML script I might need (like a Google gadget or something). It's not necessarily what it's meant for, but as an admin, I sometimes have to go with what works.

Forms

The Forms category contains only one web part, HTML Form.

HTML Form This web part is very simple and powerful. What it does is flatly demonstrate a web part capability that a lot of people still don't use—web part connections. When two web parts (or more) are on the same page and they have content displayed that they both have in common, you can connect them by that content. When web parts are connected, one web part can be used to filter the data of another web part.

As is often the case with lists, one list will have a unique record for something, such as a customer, and another list will have a bunch of records, such as sales, related to each customer. If you use a lookup field in the sales list for the customer field so that the data-entry person only needs to select a customer name in that field rather than type it in, then those two lists are connected (or related, if you will). In that case, if you put web parts for both lists on a page, you could connect them using their common fields. Then you could select a customer from the customer list, and it would filter the display of records from the sales list to show only the sales that relate to that customer.

What an HTML Form web part does is even easier. It gives you only a field to type in and a Go button. When you add it to a page, you have to configure it to connect with some other List View web part on the page, specifying one of its fields to filter. Then, to use the form, you just type in a word (exact match only), and it will look at the connected list and return only the records that have a matching value in their field.

It's a lovely, simple way to demonstrate web part connections, which is why I suspect Microsoft even has the web part available for use.

Media and Content

In the Media And Content category, there are a number of web parts, such as Content Editor, Image Viewer, Page Viewer, Picture Library Slideshow, and Silverlight.

Content Editor   The Content Editor web part (CEWP) has been somewhat diminished in its capabilities for this version of SharePoint (I suspect in order to increase partner opportunities). This web part is primarily intended to simply contain content, like a Word document, to be displayed in a web part. It also can display the contents of a file if it can be accessed by a URL address. It no longer has a rich-text editor or source editor built into it.

Instead, it allows you to basically format its content as any other rich content on a wiki page. However, the web part can be minimized, moved around on the page as a chunk more easily, and exported and imported to other pages or site collections.

WHAT, CEWP HAS NO SOURCE EDITOR?!

Previously, the CEWP was a jack-of-all-trades, able to contain rich content or, using the source editor, HTML code, Java, and JScripts. However, for this version of SharePoint, there is no source editor for the CEWP. You can edit the web part's HTML source by clicking in its content area and then using the Format Text ribbon's HTML Source button. However, SharePoint now modifies any script you enter into that source box, possibly rendering it inoperable. Instead, you can try putting the scripts you do want in a text file and refer to that using the content link field for the CEWP. The web part still supports displaying the contents of a file without modification, so your code will work as expected. It's an awkward workaround, but a workaround nonetheless.

Image Viewer   The Image Viewer web part is meant simply to display an image. You just configure the web part with the URL address of the image to display (the easiest way to do this is upload the file to a library on the site that all users can read and then use its address—each file in a library has a URL). This web part is used to add simple pictures to the web part page. It is particularly useful for inserting a graphic element on a page that isn't a wiki.

Page Viewer   The Page Viewer web part is still just as powerful as it always has been, because there's no deprecation here. The Page Viewer web part uses an iframe (which can be exploited for cross-site scripting, so be aware) to display the contents of a file, a web page, or even a shared folder. Unlike the CEWP, the Page Viewer web part can handle HTML FORM elements. So if you need to use FORM in your HTML script, put it in a file, and run it through the Page Viewer, rather than the Content Editor web part.

Picture Library Slideshow   This web part is a bit of eye candy, using up resources (*serious* CPU resources on the client machine) flipping through the pictures in a picture library. But, it can be useful, possibly showing the progression of a building project or displaying a montage from a successful event. You can configure the web part to show all the pictures in a picture library or just selected ones (you can't specify how many times it cycles through them, though) and whether it shows the title and description of each, as well as how long you look at each one before moving on.

Silverlight   The Silverlight web part is meant to contain Silverlight code to display something made in Silverlight. Because Microsoft is hoping that Silverlight will be as ubiquitous as Flash, this could be a useful little web part. However, this web part is not for people who don't know how to code for Silverlight.

Social Collaboration

The Social Collaboration category contains two web parts, Site Users and User Tasks. I'm not sure why User Tasks is there (I think it would be much better placed in the Content Rollup category), but there you go.

Site Users   I have a feeling the Site Users web part is finally going to come into its own with this version of SharePoint. This web part is meant to display the users on the site and indicate (if you have online presence or smart tagging enabled and set up properly) their online status. Back when People And Groups was available in the Quick Launch bar, this web part was redundant. If the users wanted to know the account names of other site members, they could just use People And Groups. It would also show their online status.

Now, however, People And Groups is not that easily available, since it has been removed from the Quick Launch bar. But this means that having an easy way to click a member of the site (and see their user information) or see whether they're online on the home page could be kind of useful. This web part is on the home page of a Document Workspace by default.

If the web part is added to the top-level site or to a site set to not inherit permissions from its parent site, it will have an Add New User link. This link will take the user to an Add New User page, even if they do not have the right to add users (and therefore will fail to be able to do so, no matter what they type in, even though it lets them fill in all the fields as if they were going to succeed). I'm not crazy about that, but at least you know what you're getting into.

User Tasks   The User Tasks web part, like Relevant Documents, filters its display by the logged-in account, showing only the tasks for that user (essentially personalizing it), as well as aggregating all relevant tasks for the user on the site, regardless of which task list (if there is more than one) the task was actually created in. It is because of this aggregating or "rollup" behavior that I think it should have been put in the Content Rollup category.

SQL SERVER REPORTING

You might have noticed an additional category, SQL Server Reporting, for web parts. This category contains the web part template to create a Reporting Services Report Viewer web part (and can be used to display reports). Reporting services has considerable configuration requirements, and is pretty non-standard at this point.

Although we might not explore every single one of the types of web parts individually, we are going to do enough that you can get the hang of them and work with them on your own.

To that end, let's insert a few web parts and see what happens. To start, we'll work with the Relevant Documents web part. This web part, as was listed earlier, lets the users see all the documents they are working on in the site, regardless of what library they might have them in. Of course, once this web part is set up, we won't be needing the Shared Documents library anymore.

 **Real World Scenario**

NOT THE ONLY BUILT-IN WEB PARTS

Keep in mind that the Team Site template generated the built-in web parts when it was applied. Other site templates can have a few other web parts specific to their applicable tasks, such as blog web parts for the Blog template or meeting-related web parts for the Meeting Workspace templates.

As a matter of fact, if you grow particularly fond of a web part from a different site template, you can go to the web part gallery (select Site Actions ➤ Site Settings, and click Web Parts in the Galleries category), activate the Documents ribbon, and click New Document (yes, all galleries are really document libraries). It will trigger a form box in which you can select any, or all, of the web parts available by default for the out-of-the-box templates for SharePoint Foundation. It is there that you will likely find your favorite web part. Select it, and click Populate Gallery.

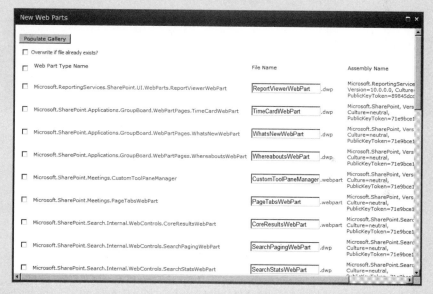

That will make your selected web parts available in the site collection's web part gallery and therefore available in the web part workspace.

ADDING A WEB PART

Keep in mind that there is no way to insert more than one web part at a time (there used to be, with the previous versions of SharePoint, but not this time), so if you do want to add more than one, you'll have to add them singularly. In this case, we're adding a user-specific web part, but you can use this process to add any web part available in the workspace to a page.

1. To keep from having to drag the web part to relocate it later, be sure to click in the rich content area where you want the web part to go. Then click the **Insert tab** in the Editing Tools toolset.

2. On the Insert ribbon, click the **Web Parts** button to open the web parts workspace.

3. In the workspace, to insert the Relevant Documents web part, select the Content Rollup category in the Categories column, select Relevant Documents from the Web Parts column, and click **Add** in the About The Web Part column.

After a moment while SharePoint thinks about it, the Relevant Documents web part should be inserted right where you indicated it should (Figure 5.7).

FIGURE 5.7
Inserted the Relevant Documents web part

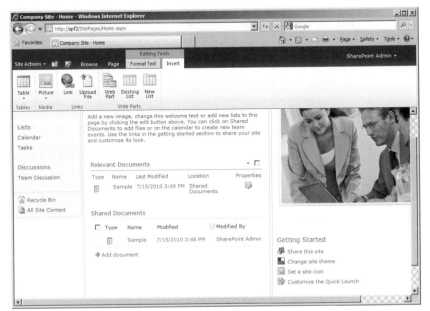

MOVING A WEB PART

If the web part isn't where you want it (now that you can see where it landed), feel free to move it around by clicking and dragging the title bar until it suits you.

In my case, I'd like to move it into the right column, beneath the stock photo. To do so, while in edit mode, make sure there is an insertion point in the area you want to put your web part. If not, click above it (it might be beside a picture or web part) and press Enter, just like you would to insert something into the text in Word.

Once you have a point to move the web part to, click the web part's title bar (make sure you are in edit mode), and drag it to the new position where you want it on the page (you should get a four-headed arrow as you drag to the new position). As you can see in Figure 5.8, I've moved Relevant Documents to the right column below the photo.

The Relevant Documents web part will display all documents relevant to the logged-in user, so it may seem redundant right next to the Shared Documents web part. Because it's more useful, because it shows documents from all libraries on the site and not just that one, it now makes the Shared Documents web part obsolete and makes a good argument for removing it from the page.

Another nice thing about the Relevant Documents web part is that it has a column to display the name of the library the listed item is located in. It's very convenient to see at a glance not just relevant documents but their location as well (and of course, you can check the document properties of any item by clicking the convenient Properties icon for each one). Keep in mind that the Relevant Documents web part may indicate it has no data to display for you right now (although mine does have a sample file added in the previous chapter). This will change when more documents are added to libraries on the site.

FIGURE 5.8
Moved the Relevant Documents web part

CHANGING WEB PART SETTINGS

Now that we've gotten comfortable with inserting a web part into a wiki page, let's take a little closer look at the web part.

All web parts have configuration settings. Most settings have to do with the way the web part will be displayed on the page, but some settings are web part–specific and have to do with the web part's contents as well.

In the case of the Relevant Documents web part, you can set whether the web part should show documents last modified by, created, or checked out by the logged-in user account. These differences can be useful and almost justify having more than one of these web parts on the same page— one to show all documents created by you on the site (regardless of who has modified it or checked it out or what library it's in) and one to show all documents you have currently checked out.

In our case, I'd like to display all documents checked out by the user in the Relevant Documents web part.

1. To edit a web part, you click the **down arrow** in the web part's title bar (if the web part isn't selected, the down arrow may not appear until you move your mouse over the web part). Once you click the down arrow, it will drop down a menu of options affecting the web part (Figure 5.9).

FIGURE 5.9
Edit Web Part
option in Relevant
Documents drop-
down menu

THE INCREDIBLE MISSING OPTIONS

When you click the down arrow in the title bar of a web part when the wiki page is *not* in edit mode, you will have the option to minimize (which collapses the web part into its title bar, making larger web parts much easier to drag and drop), export (if the web part can be exported; web parts unique to the site, like lists, cannot), or edit the web part.

But if the page is in edit mode, the drop-down menu will also display the options to delete the web part (this is a permanent deletion of the web part, it does not go to the Recycle Bin) and create a web part connection (if there is a web part on the page with common fields to connect the two; otherwise, that option will be grayed out). If the page is a web part page, the down arrow menu for the web part will also include Close. This closes the web part from the page but parks it in a closed web part category for the page (and only for that page) in the web part workspace in case you want to return it later. Closing is gentler than deleting and still removes the web part from the page without deleting it altogether. Later in the chapter you'll see how to close and restore a web part.

---

2. To edit the settings of the web part, you select **Edit Web Part** from the menu. If you click that option in the web part title bar's drop-down menu, it'll open a web part tool pane (Figure 5.10). (It may take a moment to open.) The tool pane takes up a few inches of the right side of the window, so it will shove everything to the left.

The tool pane contains setting sections that vary depending on what the web part is for. Generally, though, most web parts have the following sections because they contain settings relevant to the appearance, layout, or allowed actions on (or by) the web part while on the page.

In the case of Relevant Documents, there is also a Data section. This section is used to manage what data is displayed in the web part, such as limiting how many items can be displayed at once or what kind of data will be included.

FIGURE 5.10

The Relevant Documents web part tool pane

Appearance

As you can see in the tool pane, Appearance is the first section and is automatically expanded when the tool pane opens. It contains the following options:

Title   This is the field for the title of the web part (currently Relevant Documents).

Height and Width Settings   You can manually set the fixed height or width of a web part (in various units of measure, from inches to picas). Or you can choose to have the web part automatically fit the zone (or column) to better accommodate all resolutions.

Chrome State   This is the chrome state of the web part, whether it displays as normal (all content showing) or minimized (where the web part has collapsed or rolled up into the title bar like a window shade)

Chrome Type   This refers to whether the web part will have borders, a title, both, or neither (essentially considered its *chrome*).

3.   In this case, I am going to leave the defaults as they are; the title will be Relevant Documents, the height and width of the web part will automatically adjust to fit the zone or column the web part is in, the web part will not appear minimized by default, and it will have borders and a title bar.

Layout

Below the Appearance section (you might need to scroll down) is the Layout section. To see the settings under Layout, click the plus sign in that section's heading. It will drop down and display settings related to where the web part goes on the page and whether it displays (Figure 5.11).

FIGURE 5.11
The Layout
section of the web
part tool pane

In the Layout section are the following settings:

Hidden   This setting is used to hide the web part from view but still have it on the page. This is useful if the web part does something programmatically to the page or other web parts but doesn't display anything useful to the users. This setting is grayed out and cannot be enabled because no web parts can be hidden on a wiki page.

Direction   This setting allows you to specify the alignment of the text in the web part. If you choose None, the default layout (generally based on the regional settings and language pack for the site) for the web part will be used.

Zone   This setting, like Hidden, is grayed out in this example. On a normal web part page, this field not only would indicate what zone (essentially the column) the web part is in but would let you specifically change it from here. However, in a wiki page, web parts can be dragged around only among the rich content to be moved.

Zone Index   This setting is also currently grayed out. It lets you specify the order of the current web part, among the other web parts in the zone. So if you had two web parts, the first would probably be in zone index 1, the second in 2, and so forth. If you put a web part above the web part indexed as 1, it would likely be zero (0). Both the Zone and Zone Index settings are useful for moving a web part to a different location on the web part page without having to drag it around.

4. Again, I am going to leave the defaults in place, because the current look of the web part is fine for me, and otherwise most of the settings are grayed out.

Advanced

Beneath the Layout section is the Advanced section. This section has a larger array of settings than the other sections, from settings that allow user actions on the web part to what error message is displayed if the web part cannot be imported.

At the top of the Advanced section are settings with check boxes so you can allow (checked) or deny (unchecked) their use.

Allow Minimize   When this setting is enabled, the user can click the down arrow in the web part title bar and collapse the web part so only the title bar is showing. This can be useful for the user who needs to be able to see other web parts with this one out of the way. If this setting is disabled, the Minimize option will not be available.

Allow Close   This setting is currently grayed out because web parts on a wiki page cannot be closed. On a web part page, however, a web part can be closed, which removes it from the page but places it in a Closed web part category in the web part workspace to be returned to the page later if necessary.

Allow Hide   This setting would allow the user to hide a web part on a page if they didn't want to see it. Disabling this allows you to prevent the user from hiding a web part (a good thing if it is important). However, web parts can't be hidden on a wiki page anyway, so this is currently grayed out.

Allow Zone Change   As we'd discovered with the Layout settings, wiki pages don't allow web parts to specify their zone or zone index, so this setting is grayed out too. But, on a web part page, this setting, if enabled, would allow the user to change the web part's location on the page if the user were allowed to put the page in edit mode.

Allow Connections   This setting is available on a wiki page as well as web part pages. With this setting, you can allow users to connect this web part to another that has at least one common field. If it is disabled, the Connections option on the drop-down menu will not display for the users.

Allow Editing In Personal View   This setting allows this web part to be edited by the user when they are personalizing the page (opening the tool pane and changing settings as we are now). If it is disabled, the option to edit the web part's settings (and therefore open the tool pane) is disabled. Sadly, the wiki page doesn't *have* a Personal view, but this option is still available for configuration (Figure 5.12; note that not all of the following settings for this section are shown).

FIGURE 5.12
The Advanced section of web part tool pane

Export Mode   With this setting, if you were to export this web part (not all can be exported), you can specify whether all data it contains will be exported or only nonsensitive data.

Title URL   This setting allows you to make the title of the web part a link to somewhere else by specifying a URL. It is a good idea to make sure that all users able to see the web part also have the permissions necessary to go to the URL specified.

Description   The contents of this field display with the name of the web part in the tooltip that pops up when you move your cursor over the web part's title.

Help URL   This setting lets you offer a separate page or location to provide the user with help for the web part. Usually this is blank.

Help Mode   This setting specifies how the help URL would be opened:

>   **Modeless**   Opens a separate window but lets you work around it

>   **Modal**   Opens a separate window but doesn't let you go back to work on the web part without closing the window

>   **Navigate**   Navigates away from the page the web part is on to the help URL

Catalog Icon Image URL   This field lets you specify the URL to a tiny, 16×16-pixel icon for the web part to display in the catalog of web parts in the web part workspace.

Title Icon Image   This field lets you specify a little image, preferably 16×16 pixels, to put in the title bar of the web part.

Import Error Message   This field, which you can edit, contains the text that appears if you fail to import the web part. Many web parts can be exported from a page to import elsewhere.

5. For this example, I will leave the settings in the Advanced section as they are, but it's nice to know they're there.

Data

Finally, the last section for this web part is Data. This section is not available to all web parts, but it is for Relevant Documents. It also varies greatly, depending on the web part. Because of that, I am not including it in the list of standard web part settings.

Be aware that there can be other web part settings that crop up depending on what the web part does, such as Ajax Options or, my favorite, Miscellaneous. But you can generally depend on the previous three sections to be consistent (although some settings may be grayed out), throughout most web parts.

The Data section in the tool pane for the Relevant Documents web part has five settings, three for why documents would be displayed (Include Documents Last Modified By Me, Include Documents Created By Me, and Include Documents Checked Out To Me; they are check boxes, so you can select more than one), one for whether the Location column would display a link back to the originating library, and one for the maximum number of items allowed to be displayed.

MAXIMUM IS THE FINAL OFFER

Be careful about the maximum number of items shown. If the maximum is 15 and the user has 20 documents that qualify for the web part, well, only 15 will show, and there will be no indication that any are missing.

So, be sure to estimate high on the maximum number of items displayed if you are worried about users calling you when they forgot about a document because it wasn't in their web part. The highest number allowed for the maximum items settings is 10,000. I know that would be ridiculous for a home page, but if a user is working on 10,000 documents at one time, they have bigger issues.

6. In this case, I'd like to include only currently checked-out documents in this web part, so I am going to clear Include Documents Last Modified By Me and check **Include Documents Checked Out To Me** because in most cases, if I am currently modifying a document, then I have also checked it out of the library to do so. I'm going to keep **Display A Link To A Containing Folder Or List** enabled, and I am going to increase the Maximum Number Of Documents displayed to **25**. For your environment, that maximum number really depends on what your users do with documents versus a reasonable number of documents displayed on your home page. Figure 5.13 shows the settings I chose.

FIGURE 5.13

The Data settings for the Relevant Documents web part

7. Check to make sure the data settings are complete, and then click **OK** to leave the tool pane. This will apply your settings and close the pane (regaining that window real estate for the page).

As you can see in Figure 5.14, my Relevant Documents web part is now displaying no documents (even though I'd added a document to the Shared Documents library in the previous chapter). Why? Well, the account I am logged in with doesn't have any documents checked out. That will change in Chapter 8, "Introduction to Libraries," where we will fill that web part in no time.

FIGURE 5.14

The Relevant Documents web part is now empty after the data settings update.

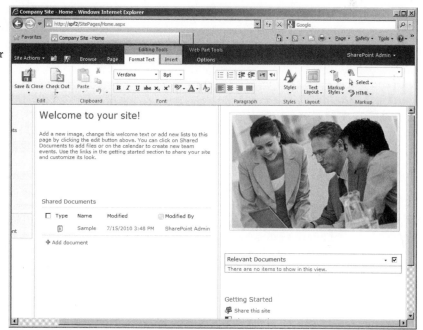

Now that we have a Relevant Documents web part that shows the user all of the documents relevant to them (in terms of what they are currently working on) across all libraries on the site, we don't really need the Shared Documents web part anymore. It displays the web parts for only one library.

So, let's delete it from the page. It's easy, and we can always add it back from the Lists And Libraries category later if we change our minds (although this incarnation of the web part, had we changed any settings to customize it, would be truly deleted).

Deleting a Web Part

1. To delete a web part from a wiki page, make sure you are in edit mode (and have the right to delete web parts), and then click **Delete** in the down arrow menu on its title bar (Figure 5.15). Remember that the down arrow doesn't show up until you move your cursor over the web part to activate it.

FIGURE 5.15
The drop-down menu for Shared Documents web part, Delete option

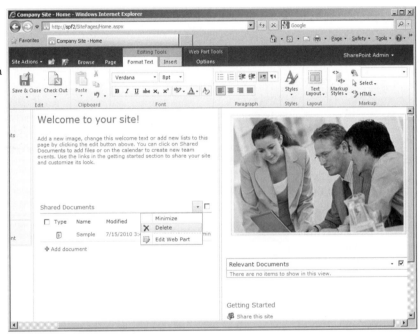

Once you click Delete, you'll be warned that this will permanently delete the web part, which means it won't be in the Recycle Bin for the site or in a closed web part category—this copy of the Shared Documents List View web part will be gone. This doesn't delete the Shared Documents library as a whole or delete it from the Lists And Libraries category in the web part workspace, should you want to drop another copy on the page again, but the one you had there with its configurations will be gone. This is something to keep in mind about deleting web parts, particularly those you have extensively configured (you might want to export a copy before you delete, just in case you change your mind later).

2. Click **OK** to delete the web part.

Once the Shared Documents web part is gone, its column will react to the change and rearrange. This is likely because nothing particularly large is in that column right now. All web parts so far are set to automatically fit their zones. The left column will get a bit smaller, and the right one will get a little larger (Figure 5.16).

FIGURE 5.16
The Shared Documents web part deleted

And that's it for deleting a web part. It's that's easy.

Built-in Web Part Templates

So, we've learned about web part settings and even set some. Most List View web parts, although they have the Appearance, Layouts, and Advanced sections, don't necessarily need much configuring. However, there are web parts that *require* configuration in order to even display any content.

Those are the built-in web part templates, such as the Content Editor web part, Forms, or Page Viewer.

It turns out that the people who make web parts tend to use the same framework over and over to build a number of different web parts. Rather than requiring us to rebuild that framework from scratch each time, Microsoft made built-in web parts for SharePoint that are basically templates of the basic framework for a lot of the types of web parts that might be used. These include Page Viewer, Image Viewer, XML Viewer, Silverlight, Picture Library Slideshow, Content Editor, and even the Form web part. These web parts are empty when you add them to the page; you must configure them in order for them to work. All built-in web parts require you to specify the source of the content, be it a file, folder, or URL (depending on the type of web part). The Content Editor and XML Viewer web parts additionally allow you to create the content right there. (Content Editor uses a rich content environment like the wiki page, and XML Viewer uses a text editor accessible from the tool pane.)

For our purposes, we have a home page populated with a useful web part, a photo, and some welcome text. That is a good start. But for this scenario, there is a vacation request notice that requires the user's attention as soon as they reach the site. It's a good candidate for being added to the home page.

This will give us an idea of how a built-in web part works, and it will demonstrate when it is good to just add text and pictures to the home page and when it's good to add text and pictures to a Content Editor web part on the home page that can be exported and applied elsewhere (as well as showing you *how* to apply it elsewhere).

INSERTING A BUILT-IN WEB PART TEMPLATE

Take the following steps to insert a built-in web part template:

1. To insert the Content Editor web part, make sure the home page is in edit mode, and then pick a place to put the web part on the page, making sure there is an insertion point there for the web part. In my case, I'd like it to go right above the "Welcome to your site!" title at the top of the left zone. (You may need to click in front of the title and hit Enter so you can put your insertion point above it, if you are following my example.)

2. Once you have an insertion point on the page, click the **Insert tab** on the top ribbon bar, and then click the **Web Parts** button on the Insert ribbon.

3. Once the web part workspace is displayed, click the **Media And Content** category. This will display the Content Editor web part in the Web Parts column so you can select it.

4. After selecting the Content Editor web part, click the **Add** button at the bottom of the About The Web Part area.

There may be a pause while the web part loads, and then it should show up at the insertion point. Figure 5.17 shows my new web part at the top of the right column.

You'll notice that the web part has only a title bar and contains the sentence "Edit this Web Part to add content to your page." That is a good suggestion, so let's start configuring this web part and then add content.

FIGURE 5.17
Inserted the
Content Editor
web part

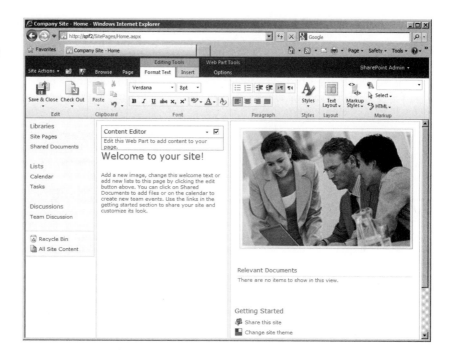

CONFIGURING A BUILT-IN WEB PART TEMPLATE

CONFIGURING A BUILT-IN WEB PART TEMPLATE

This web part needs both content and configuration. To start, let's change the title of the web part and disallow it to be minimized or edited (even on a web part page) by the users so they can't ignore it that easily. Then we'll add some content.

1. To configure the web part, click the down arrow on its title bar, and select **Edit Web Part**.

   The tool pane for the Content Editor web part will come up on the right side of the page (Figure 5.18). Notice that, in addition to the standard Appearance, Layout, and Advanced sections, there is a setting at the top of the pane that relates specifically to this web part. If you wanted to, you could point this web part to an existing file to display its contents. This is not what we are here for, but it's good to know.

FIGURE 5.18
The Content Editor
web part tool pane

2. The title for this web part, at this point, is just Content Editor, which is not too unique. A good rule of thumb is that each web part must have a unique title. So, to rename the web part to something more relevant, click the **Appearance** section header to expand it.

3. In the Title field, replace Content Editor with something more appropriate for a vacation request announcement (I'm going to use **Vacation Request** for mine, as shown in Figure 5.19).

FIGURE 5.19

Changing the web part Title and Chrome Type in the Appearance section of tool pane

In this case, this Content Editor web part is going to be focused on displaying its contents and doesn't really need to display a title bar. Further, you can have the web part simply look like it's part of the rich content of the zone, by removing its borders too.

4. To set the web part to not display a title bar or borders, you click the Chrome Type drop-down menu and select **None**.

When the web part is out of edit mode, the boundaries that make it look like a web part will disappear. This will leave it without a title bar (and its drop-down menu). But since we don't want users editing the web part, a little inconvenience is a good thing.

5. Once those settings have been changed, expand the Advanced section. In that section, **disable** the **Allow Minimize** and **Allow Editing** In Personal View settings by removing their check marks (if they have them, Figure 5.20).

6. Once those settings are complete, click **OK** to close out of the tool pane.

Back on the home page, which is still in edit mode, you'll see that the title for the web part (now selected because we've been working on it) displays the new title. As you can see in Figure 5.21, mine is Vacation Request. Notice that there is a title bar even though we set the chrome type to show none. In edit mode, all web parts must have a title bar. It's out of edit mode that the chrome type setting applies.

Now that we've configured the web part, let's create the Vacation Requests content. This is going to be done like a flyer, with some text and a nice vacation picture to encourage users to send in their vacation requests for the summer before all the best days are taken.

FIGURE 5.20
Advanced settings,
Content Editor
web part

FIGURE 5.21
The newly con-
figured Vacation
Request web part
on home page

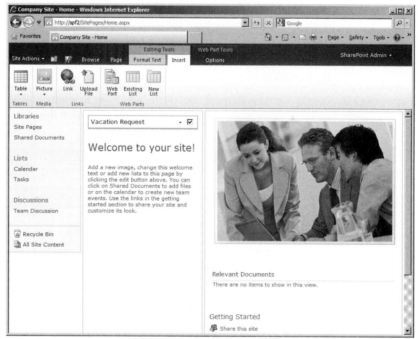

Because most of us have access to Windows servers and workstations, the picture I am going to use for this exercise is `Azul.jpg`, a background picture on most Windows machines (except Server 2008 R2, ironically) located under `%Windir%\Web\Wallpaper`. I copied the file to my SharePoint server for this scenario. You can use any appropriate picture you'd like, although sadly, you won't find them natively on the 2008 R2 server without installing the desktop experience feature (which I don't intend to do).

For this exercise, I am going to upload the picture file to the site when adding it to the web part. This is a convenient new feature that lets you store resources, such as pictures, used in web parts or wiki pages in a library on the site called Site Assets. You can use this library to manage those resources all in one place. That way, no matter what happens to the original file (if it is moved, deleted, or renamed), it won't matter, because the copy being used on the site is stored on the site. Also, because sites can be saved as templates, keeping all resources that web parts or pages might be pointing to *in* the site makes the template more portable.

Editing a Content Editor Web Part's Contents

Configuring complete, it's time to edit the web part's contents:

1. To do that, you need to click the down arrow in the title bar of the web part and edit the web part again.

   This will open the tool pane, which we don't need, but it will allow you to click the holder text in the web part's contents and start editing (Figure 5.22).

2. To edit the web part, click **Click Here To Add New Content** in the web part.

   Once you've clicked that text, the web part will be ready to edit. Don't worry about it being so small; once we've finished editing and closed the tool pane, there will be more room.

   As soon as you click the text, the content area of the web part will actually get smaller, but there will be an insertion point blinking in there, so take heart.

3. For my Vacation Request web part, I am going to enter content appropriate for a reminder concerning vacation requests, starting with Vacation Request Reminder. Feel free to enter your own content.

FIGURE 5.22
The Content Editor web part in edit mode

4. Once I've entered my catchy first sentence, I am going to hit Enter twice, enter some more text concerning the vacation requests, and put the insertion point back beneath the first line of text, to be ready to insert that vacation image of a beach I mentioned earlier (see Figure 5.23 to see my full example). Be sure that you make room in your content area for your image, and position your insertion point where you want the picture to be.

FIGURE 5.23

Added text and preparing to insert a picture into the Vacation Request web part

5. To insert an image into the Content Editor web part, click the **Insert tab** in the top ribbon bar. You will see a Picture button with a down arrow.

There are two options for inserting a picture into the web part: either you upload a picture currently accessible from your computer to a library on the site (such as Site Assets) or you specify an address for the file's location.

Uploading to the site works in this case because I don't intend for this web part to be used anywhere but this site, and it makes it easy to manage where the picture is and who can access it while it is in a site library. All files stored in libraries have their own URL, so it is easy to display a library file in a web part.

FROM ADDRESS

You might not want to store the image for a web part in a local site library if you plan to import the web part to a different site collection (where the users won't have access to this site's libraries) or even a different web application. In that case, you should choose From Address in the Picture drop-down menu. The pop-up box will require an address and alternative text. The address field will accept addresses using `http://`, `ftp://`, `file://`, or the UNC `\\` protocol. Make certain that the location of the image file is available to all users who will be accessing the site.

6. To upload a picture, in the **Picture** button's drop-down menu, select **From Computer**. It will open a dialog box letting you browse to the file you want to use. You can also choose to store the file in any library on the site by selecting it in the Upload To field (Figure 5.24). Site Assets is selected by default and works for me. Browse to the image file you want to use in your web part (I am using Azul.jpg).

7. Once you've selected your image file, make sure the library to upload to is correct, and click **OK**.

FIGURE 5.24
The dialog box for inserting a picture with the From Computer option

8. This will bring you to a form box triggered by the library, confirming the filename and asking for a title for the image (Figure 5.25). I don't need a title for the file and the file-name is fine, so I am just going to keep the defaults and click **Save**.

FIGURE 5.25
Saving the file to the Site Assets library

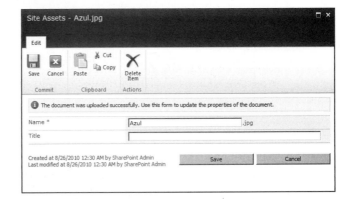

That should put you back on the web part with the picture inserted. In my case, the picture is huge (because it was meant to be a desktop background), so I have to resize it by grabbing the handle squares at the corners of the picture and dragging it inward until it's as small as I want it. Feel free to resize your picture. When it's sized appropriately, you might want to format the text around the picture as well.

When you're done formatting text and resizing the image, you should have something that catches the eye, is easy to read, and encourages the users to follow through with the reminder.

9. Click **OK** in the tool pane to close it and see what the web part looks like before saving changes on the page (for a look at my example, see Figure 5.26).

FIGURE 5.26
The Vacation
Request web part,
configured and
formatted

10. To save your changes and see what it looks like when the users see it (not in edit mode), click the Save & Close button on the top ribbon bar (or you can use the Save & Close button on the Page or Format Text ribbon). The new web part will lose its title bar and borders (Figure 5.27), and the blue boxes around the two columns will disappear.

FIGURE 5.27
The Vacation
Request web part
out of edit mode on
the home page

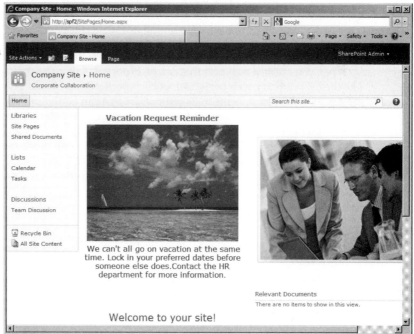

Congratulations, you have configured a built-in Content Editor web part. Now that we've created something that looks practically seamless on the wiki page, let's see what it looks like on other pages.

It's time to export this reminder so it will be available elsewhere.

Exporting a Web Part

Now that you've gotten a feel for what it takes to customize a web part, you can understand why you might want to export a copy. Doing so backs up the web part and makes it possible to use it elsewhere. To avoid creating it again from scratch, you can export it and then import it to the page where you want to display it. Thus, the Export field under Advanced in the tool pane carries a little more weight.

When you use a built-in template to create a web part, it is unique to the page upon which it was created. To reuse that web part, you would have to package it as a web part definition file (.dwp), which happens when you export it and then import it to the page where you want to put it or, if you want to make it more widely available, to the whole site collection.

AN EXTENSION BY ANY OTHER NAME...

In the old days, .dwp used to also stand for "Dashboard web part." So if you see it called that, don't be surprised. Like many things from Microsoft, over the years, the name of this extension has shifted from its original meaning to something else.

I am going to show you how to export a web part and how to import it to a different page. The first step is to access the web part you're going to export (and make sure it exports the correct data) and then export it. After the export, we can then import it anywhere.

When you create a web part that can be exported (web parts that are specific to the site itself, like the list or library web parts, cannot be exported), you should give it a unique name. If there are any external components to its contents, such as an address to a file or folder, that location must be accessible to all users who see the web part, particularly those using the site where the web part will be imported.

To export a web part, you usually don't have to be in edit mode (although you can be). If the web part has a title bar and you are allowed to export it, Export will be an option on the title bar drop-down menu. See Figure 5.28 for an example of the Relevant Documents web part's drop-down menu.

FIGURE 5.28
The Relevant Documents web part drop-down menu displaying the Export options

However, for this example, the chrome type for the Vacation Requests web part was set to show no title bar. That means it has no drop-down arrow to do anything to it while simply browsing the page. This is a good deterrent to users who might not mess with a web part without a title bar, but don't let it stop you from exporting it.

To export a web part that doesn't have a title bar, you have to go into edit mode on the page first. That will cause the title of the web part to be displayed, at which time you can minimize, export, or edit the web part as you want.

BEFORE YOU EXPORT, CHECK YOUR DATA

Some web parts can have personal data in them for users on the site. In that case, you might want to change the Export mode. Vacation Requests doesn't, so I want all data to be exported. But to check the Export mode of the web part, click Edit Web Part in the title bar's drop-down menu.

In the tool pane, expand the Advanced section, and scroll down to the Export Mode field. It will say either Export All Data or Non-Sensitive Data Only. In my case, I want to make sure it exports all data, so I'll be sure to specify that (if it isn't already selected).

Since this Export mode option is here, you might as well use it if there are web parts you are exporting with sensitive data.

To get out of the tool pane, click OK (or Cancel if you made no changes).

---

1. To export the Vacation Requests web part, click the **Edit page** button in the top ribbon bar of the home page.

2. When the home page is in edit mode, go to the title bar of the web part you want to export, and click the **down arrow**.

3. In the drop-down menu, click **Export**.

   Once you've selected Export, you might be prompted to save the page before focus leaves it (because a dialog box will come up to set up the export). Although we haven't made any changes yet, feel free to click OK to continue (you may have to do this twice).

4. A file download dialog box will open. Click **Save** to save the exported file to a location that you can access easily again to import the file later (Figure 5.29).

FIGURE 5.29
Saving the
exported web part

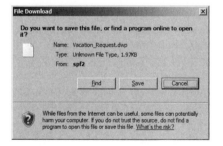

After you've saved the file, you might be prompted to open the file or file location as if you were going to run it right now. That's not really necessary at this point.

That's it. You've explored web parts on a wiki home page. You added, deleted, moved, exported, and edited the settings of web parts.

MORE PORTABLE THAN RICH CONTENT

Since we've made the Content Editor web part, you can see how easy it is to edit, add, or remove from a page, and you know you can easily move it around. Also, by just changing the chrome type, the content can look as if it were on a wiki page. It also can give a wiki look to an average web part page. Overall, despite it seeming redundant on a wiki page, the Content Editor web part does still have its uses.

That should give a good start, not only on how to work with a wiki page but on how to work with web parts in general.

As a matter of fact, I mentioned at the beginning of the chapter that the home page of other site templates, as well as list and library content pages, are web part pages, not wiki pages. We've worked on a wiki page so far, but that kind of page is outnumbered by web part pages, so let's turn our attentions toward working with web parts on a web part page for a moment so you can see the similarities and differences firsthand.

Using the Home Page as a Web Part Page

The home page has the option to roll back and be a standard web part home page. Currently, there is a site feature enabled by default that makes the home page a wiki page. This feature is called Wiki Page Home Page (creatively enough). All you have to do is deactivate that feature, and the home page will display the web part page that was hidden all along.

LOW-TECH SOLUTIONS

Because the wiki home page of a site using the Team Site template is actually a file named Home in the Site Pages library, users who don't have the permissions necessary to deactivate features on the site *can* accidentally disable the "wikiness" of the home page by deleting the home page in the Site Pages library. If they do that, all they need to do is restore it from their Recycle Bin to return it to its rightful place.

If losing the wiki home page due to user error is a concern for you, I suggest checking out Chapter 12, "Users and Permissions," to learn how to lock down the Home file in the Site Pages library so users cannot edit its contents or delete it.

To do that, you first need to finish working on the home page as it is (we'll reactivate it after we're done). So to keep your changes, click Save & Close in the Format Text ribbon (if you're still in edit mode), or you can simply click Stop Editing the page if you don't want to save your changes.

Then, once the page is out of edit mode, we need to go to the Site Features page of the site and deactivate the wiki page feature.

Keep in mind that the web part home page and the wiki home page are truly separate pages, so what you do on one does not happen on the other. This means if there is a web part on the wiki home page that you want on the web part home page, you are going to add it again from the web part workspace and configure it, or have to import it to the page and insert it.

Disabling the Wiki Home Page Feature

1. To get to the Feature gallery, click the **Site Actions** menu, scroll to the bottom, and click Site Settings.

No Site Settings in Your Menu?

If you can't see the Site Settings option in the Site Actions menu, the account you are logged in with doesn't have permission to change site settings. Log in with an administrative account.

---

2. This will bring you to the Site Settings page, which we will be exploring in detail in Chapter 9, "Sites, Subsites, and Workspaces." For now, we just need to go to the Site Actions heading (redundant, I know) and click the **Manage Site Features** link (Figure 5.30).

FIGURE 5.30
The Site
Settings page

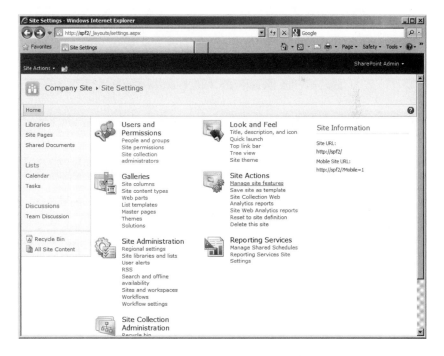

In the Site Features page is a list of the features available by default for a site that is using the Team Site template. You can see in Figure 5.31 that the last feature, Wiki Page Home Page, is Active.

FIGURE 5.31
The Site
Features page

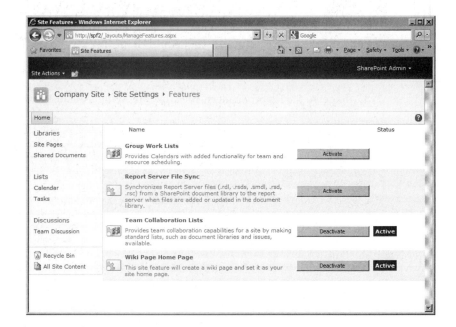

3. To deactivate the Wiki Page Home Page feature, click its **Deactivate** button. It will warn you that you are getting ready to deactivate a feature, that anything depending on the feature might not function, and that data might be lost. In this case, there is nothing to lose, so click **Deactivate This Feature** (Figure 5.32).

FIGURE 5.32
The Deactivate
Feature Warning
page

This will take you back to the Site Features page, where the feature's button will now be labeled Activate.

OTHER FEATURES

You may have noticed the other features listed for the site, and although they will be explained a little more in Chapter 9; the only other feature active by default on a Team Site is Team Collaboration Lists. This feature is what makes the list and library templates, such as Issue Tracking, Tasks, or Picture library, available for use in creating new lists and libraries on the site.

Once the feature has been deactivated, go back to the home page.

Once there, you will see that it has reverted to being a web part home page (the page is now just a standard `default.aspx`, as you can see in the address bar in Figure 5.33), and now it contains the Announcements List View web part. Announcements is a list created specifically to have its contents displayed on the home page and comes prepropagated with a "Get Started with Microsoft SharePoint Foundation!" item, for your convenience. The page also contains Calendar and Links List View web parts based on the site's existing Calendar and Links lists.

Notice that the Vacation Request web part we made isn't there, nor is the Relevant Documents web part—both of those are on the wiki home page, not the underlying web part page. This proves that the web part home page is an entirely different page from the wiki home page. This can be useful to know in case you'd like to swap between the two for any reason (such as a mistake on the wiki page that needs to be removed from view quickly).

In our case, since the home page now does not contain the Vacation Request web part, we can import it to the page so it will be visible once again. Relevant Documents, on the other hand, can easily be added from the web part workspace because it is a built-in web part for the site.

FIGURE 5.33
A web part home page

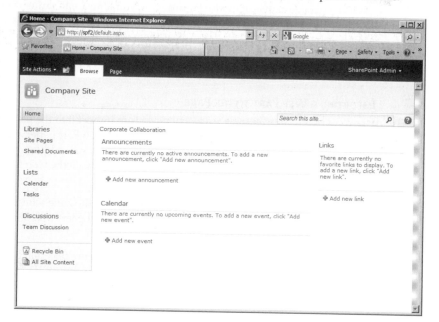

Using Edit Mode on a Web Part Page

One of the interesting and useful features of a web part page is the fact that it can have two different ways of viewing it. Considered "versions," web part pages can have a *shared* version, one that an administrator sets up and all users see, and a *personal* version, which is a personalized version of the page that users with the correct permissions can modify to suit themselves.

Personal versions of a web part page can be seen only by the user personalizing it. A personal version of the page always starts by being based on the shared version, and at any time, the user can reset the page contents back to the shared version if they change their mind. There can be (as you know) web parts configured to not allow users to close, move, edit, or modify them on the page. And those web parts continue to be unmodifiable, even in a user's personal version of the page.

Most of the time, administrators work on the shared version of a home page, adding, configuring, and organizing the web parts so everyone can see them. So, we'll work on the shared version of the page first, importing the Vacation Request web part to the web part page.

To work with web parts on a shared version of a web part page, you first need to go into edit mode.

Going into edit mode on a web part page is different from a wiki page to a certain degree. Because there are two different versions of a web part page, there are two different edit modes, one that makes changes to the shared version and one that makes changes to the personal version. In addition, the web part area contains only web parts, so there is nowhere to put rich content in the zones (except in Content Editor web parts), and because of that, no Format Text ribbon bar will be available in either edit mode.

To edit a page's shared version, you can click the Page tab in the top ribbon bar and select Edit Page, or you can go to Site Actions and click Edit Page in the menu. If you use the Site Actions menu to edit the page, it will not trigger the Page ribbon. I am going to click the Page tab and click the Edit Page button.

Once the page is in edit mode (Figure 5.34), you'll notice that there is only one ribbon bar, Page, to access the page-editing tools. This is because most of what is done on a web part page is adding web parts. To that end, notice that there is an Add A Web Part box at the top of each zone (conveniently labeled Left and Right). This is how you open the web part workspace and select web parts to add to the page.

IMPORTING A WEB PART TO THE PAGE

There are two ways to import a web part; one is to import it to the page where you want to add it, and the other is to import it to the site collection's Web Part gallery. This will make it available for all pages in the site collection. In our case, we are simply adding it to the page.

To import a web part to a page, you first need to activate the web part workspace. It is there that you can upload a web part.

1. To do that, click the **Add A Web Part** box above the zone where you want the web part to, eventually, go. I want to add the web part to the left web part zone, so I will click that Add A Web Part box.

   The web part workspace will open. Notice in Figure 5.35 that the Add Web Part To drop-down menu in the About The Web Part column indicates that it expects to add a web part to the left zone. Now that you are editing a web part page, you can specify the zone you want to add the web part to.

FIGURE 5.34
A web part page in edit mode

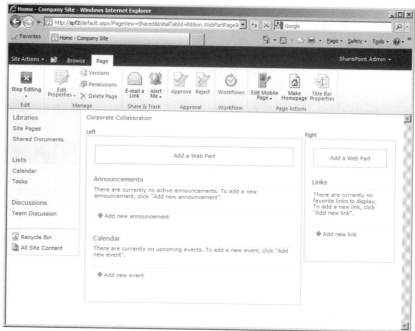

FIGURE 5.35
Uploading a web part in the Web Part workspace

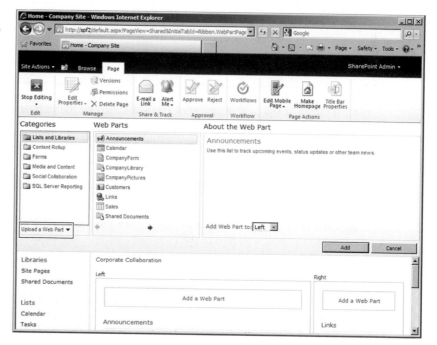

Below the Categories column is an unassuming down arrow next to the label, Upload A Web Part. It is here that you import a web part to this page.

2. Click the down arrow next to **Upload A Web Part**. That area of the workspace will change to display a field and a Browse button.

3. Click the **Browse** button, navigate to where you saved your exported web part, select and Open it. That will bring you back to the workspace, with the path to the web part you want to upload listed in the Upload A Web Part field (Figure 5.36).

FIGURE 5.36

The file displayed to upload in the web part workspace

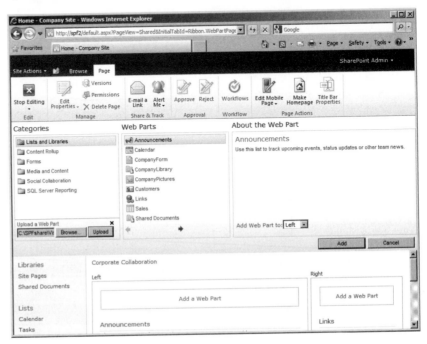

4. If the file is the correct one, click **Upload** to upload the web part to the workspace.

   This will take you back to the home page as if nothing happened. It is a little shocking. But what *did* happen is that a new category in the web part workspace was added called Imported Web Parts, and the uploaded web part is now listed in that category.

5. To actually add the imported web part to the page, click **Add A Web Part** at the top of the zone you want to use.

6. Once the web part workspace is open, click the **Imported Web Parts** category, and select your imported web part in the Web Parts column. See Figure 5.37.

7. Click the **Add** button on the bottom right of the workspace to add the web part to top of the web part zone.

That will close the web part workspace and drop the web part in the zone you'd selected. The My Vacation Request web part will now appear at the top of the left web part zone.

To get out of edit mode, click **Stop Editing**. That will display the page as users will see it when they access the site (Figure 5.38). Notice that the web part has no title or border and looks like rich text added to the web part page.

And that's it. That's how you import a web part to a page. This works for either web part or wiki pages. The Upload A Web Part option is available in the web part workspace either way.

FIGURE 5.37
The web part workspace with imported web part available

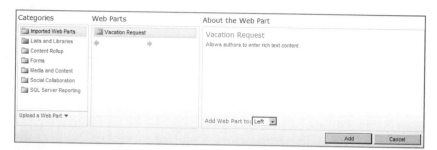

FIGURE 5.38
Imported web part added to the web part page

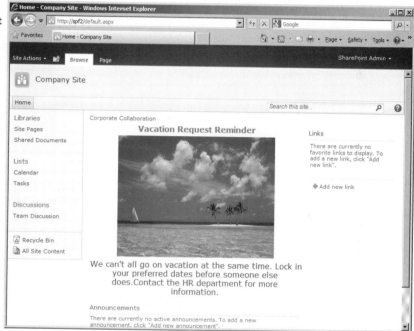

IMPORTING TO A SITE COLLECTION

There are times when you have a web part that you'd like to make available to all sites in a site collection. (Remember, a site collection is a collection of subsites that start with a top-level site—the subsites inherit templates, permissions, navigation, and so on, from the top-level site.)

To add a web part to an entire site collection so that it shows up in the web part workspace in every site, you simply add it to the site collection's web part gallery.

1. To access the web part gallery, go to Site Actions, and click Site Settings at the bottom of the menu.

2. On the Site Settings page, in the Galleries category, click Web Parts.

3. This will bring you to a library filled with the web parts available for this site collection.

4. To add a web part, just click the Upload Document button on the Documents ribbon.

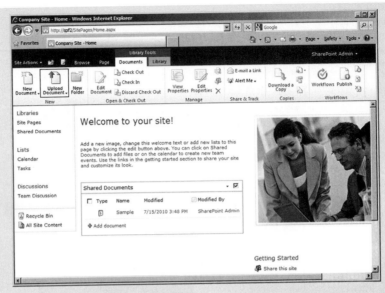

This will open a standard Upload File dialog box. Browse to the web part file you want to upload, and then click OK.

That will open a form box (slightly different from a dialog box; it has fields to fill out) containing the information to confirm about the web part file before it is added to the library. You can change the title, filename, and description. If you want to organize your web parts in the gallery, you can specify the group it should go in. Site templates have an ID that starts with #. You can recommend that a particular web part be suggested for a particular site template by using its ID. Most web parts for the site don't use this setting.

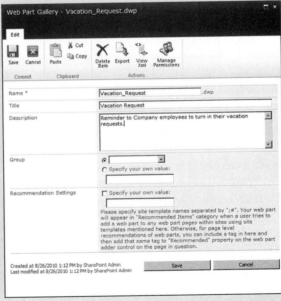

Once the information on this page is correct (I am going to change the description because it defaults to the one for Content Editor web parts), click Save.

That will add the web part to the gallery.

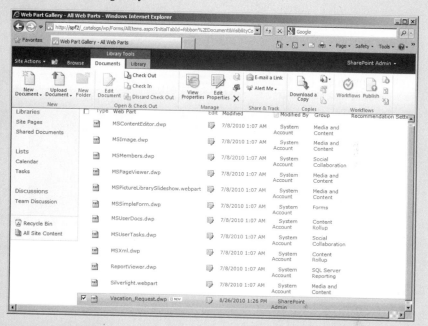

And now, any site in the site collection can add the web part to any page that can be edited via the web part workspace (remember that list and library content pages are also web part pages). The web part workspace creates a miscellaneous category for web parts added to the site via the gallery.

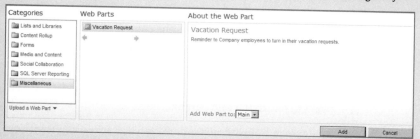

For this example, I am using the Vacation Request web part. But generally, if you are going to create a web part to be imported to other site collections, the resources that web part uses should be located, not in a single site's library but on a network share, accessible by all users. So in the case of Vacation Request, if you are going to be importing it to other site collections or servers, you should use the Picture button's From Address option and specify the network location of the file instead of uploading it to a site library.

CLOSING A WEB PART

There are times when a web part is on a page that you'd like to remove temporarily, just to get it out of the way. There is a way to do this on web part pages. You can close the web part, instead of minimizing or deleting it.

When you close a web part, it puts it in a Closed web part gallery to be returned to the page at your leisure.

To close a web part, simply click its title bar, and select Close in the menu (Figure 5.39).

FIGURE 5.39
Closing the Calendar web part

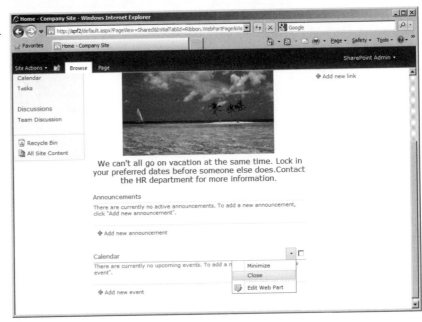

The web part will disappear from the page.

RETURNING A CLOSED WEB PART

1. To get it back, put the page in edit mode, and click Add A Web Part above the zone you want to return the web part to.

   In the web part workspace, there will be a new category, Closed Web Parts (Figure 5.40).

FIGURE 5.40
The web part workspace, Closed Web Parts category, Calendar web part

2. Select that category, select the web part you closed, and click Add at the bottom right of the workspace.

This will return the web part to the page again (Figure 5.41). However, it will be put at the top of the zone, so you may have to move it back to where it was originally located (I'm leaving the web part where it is for the moment).

FIGURE 5.41

The returned web part on the home page

What if the page isn't in a library, like a web part home page? The you append ?contents=1 to the URL for the page (in my current example, that would be `http://spf2/default.aspx?contents=1`).

That will trigger a repair page so you can get rid of the bad inserted web part.

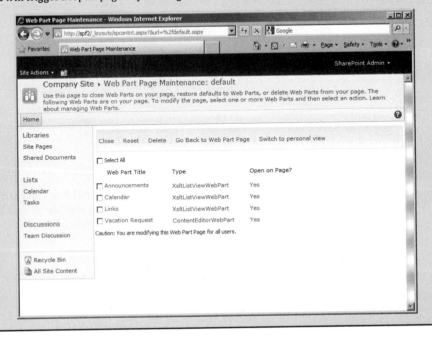

EDITING THE PERSONAL VERSION OF A WEB PART PAGE

Just to be thorough, let's take a quick look at how to personalize a web part page. As I mentioned earlier, web part pages can have a personal version. The shared version is used as a base, and then the user (if they have the permission to; site members do by default) can make changes to the page to suit themselves. This version of the page does not change the shared version everyone else uses. No one else can see this person's personalized page (which can cause some help-desk issues). If the user makes a mistake and wants to reset their page to the shared version, they can.

To personalize a page, click the **Account** menu (the menu with your account name on it on the top right of the top ribbon bar).

Web part pages have extra options. At the bottom of the menu, select **Personalize This Page** (Figure 5.42).

FIGURE 5.42

The Personalize This Page option in the Account menu

That will put the page into edit mode, personal version (see Figure 5.43). You can then move, close, and minimize the web parts you are allowed to modify (notice that the Vacation Request doesn't have a title bar in this edit mode because we configured it to be unable to be edited in personal view).

Just to demonstrate, feel free to add some web parts (now that you know how), close web parts, and so on. In my case, I am going to add a User Tasks web part, close the Calendar and Link web parts, and then click Stop Editing to finish. See Figure 5.44 for the example of my changes to my personal version of the page (I selected the Browse tab to get rid of the Page ribbon).

To see the page in the shared view, click the **Account** menu, and select **Show Shared View**, now available in the menu (Figure 5.45).

It will display the shared version of the page (Figure 5.46). The Show Shared View option in the Account menu will offer either Show Shared View or Show Personal View, depending on which one you are in at the time.

FIGURE 5.43
Editing the personal version of a web part page

FIGURE 5.44
Personal view of the edited web part page

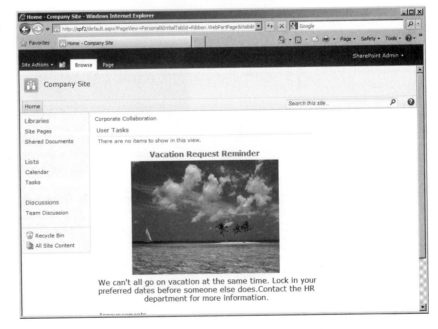

FIGURE 5.45
The Account menu with the Show Shared View option

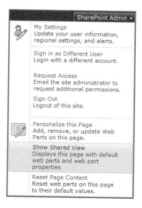

FIGURE 5.46
The Shared View of the web part page

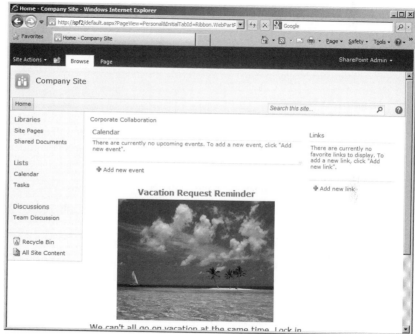

"*I* DIDN'T PUT THAT WEB PART ON MY PAGE…"

If a new web part is added to a shared version of a web part page, it will show up in the personal version of the page, until that user removes it from their version (if they can). Consider letting users know that a new web part is being added if you know your users are personalizing web part pages—it will cut down on support calls. Also, keep in mind that list and library content pages are web part pages, so users can be maintaining their own, personal view of those pages as well. Adding web parts to a list or library content page will disable the title breadcrumb and default ribbons, but it can be done. And if you do add web parts to a content page, it might disrupt the users, unless you let them know.

RESETTING PAGE CONTENT

To simply do away with the personalized changes you've made, reset the page content. Resetting page content simply clears the personalized version of the page and resets it to match the current shared version of the page.

1. To reset personalized content, make sure you are in the personal view of the page, click the **Account** menu, and select **Reset Page Content** (Figure 5.47).

FIGURE 5.47
The Account menu, Reset Page Content option

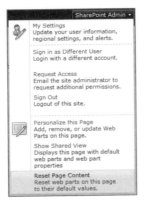

A dialog box will open warning you that all personalized web parts will be reset to their shared values and any private web parts (web parts you added to you view manually) will be deleted. That's fine.

2. Click **OK** to reset the page contents.

The page will return the personal view to the current shared version's state.

Enabling the Wiki Home Page Feature

Now that we have explored the web part page lurking under the wiki home page of the Team Site, it's time to reenable the wiki home page feature. To do that, you simply activate the Wiki Page Home Page feature again.

1. To enable the wiki home page, go to **Site Actions**, and click **Site Settings** in the menu.

2. On the Site Settings page, select **Manage Site Features** in the Site Actions category.

3. In the Site Features page, click the **Activate** button for the **Wiki Page Home Page** feature (Figure 5.48).

Once the feature is activated, go back to the home page. You will see that it is back to its original settings before the feature was deactivated (Figure 5.49). No harm done.

That's it. We've covered two kinds of pages that can hold web parts: a web part page (list and library pages are web part pages) and a wiki page. You've learned what web parts are available out of the box with SharePoint Foundation (the Server version has more, since you paid for them), as well as why there are List View web parts and what they do. You've edited web parts and configured their settings. You've added web parts to different pages, deleted one, closed one, and returned one from a closed state. You've also exported a web part and imported a web part to a single page, and know how to import one to a whole site collection.

FIGURE 5.48
The Site Features page, to activate Wiki Page Home Page feature

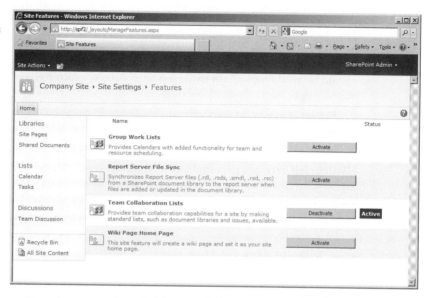

FIGURE 5.49
Wiki home page returned

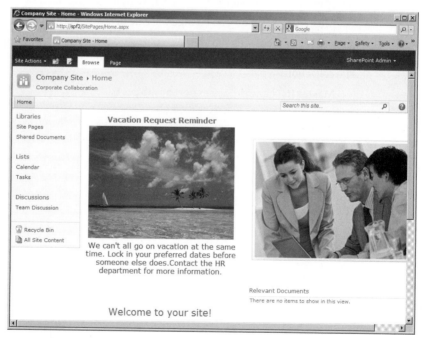

This is only the beginning for web parts, but at least we've covered enough of the basics that you can get the hang of the rest from here.

The Bottom Line

Identify web parts. Web parts are small, independent applications intended to quickly and conveniently display the contents of lists, libraries, folders, or pages.

Master It What are List View web parts?

Use edit mode. To work on web parts in SharePoint, the page containing the web parts should be in edit mode. Edit mode is a page state in which web parts can be moved, removed, added, imported, and edited. No data entry occurs in edit mode.

Master It How do you enter edit mode to edit a shared version of a page? How do you know for certain that you are editing the shared version?

Master It How do you edit a wiki page home page?

Distinguish between personal and shared versions. SharePoint offers the luxury of allowing users to have their own personal version of any web part page in which they can rearrange, remove, or add web parts to their pages for their convenience.

Master It How can a user tell whether they are viewing the personal or shared version of a page?

Work with web parts. Adding, moving, removing, and customizing web parts while in the browser are all possible with SharePoint. There are built-in List View web parts to quickly populate the home page with web parts relevant to users. There are also built-in web part templates to easily customize web parts with no coding necessary.

Master It How do you change the title of a web part?

Export and import web parts. Web parts aren't just static little applications. You can customize them, export them to a web part definition file, and import them to a different page or site collection.

Master It How do you export a web part?

Chapter 6

Introduction to Lists

Lists are what power SharePoint. Lists are everywhere in SharePoint, from discussions to document management, site galleries, and calendars. All of the data, communications, and collaboration are handled in lists. Every library is actually a kind of list—heck, every time there is a repository of something in the site or site collection settings (such as themes or web parts), that is actually a list.

Lists are important to SharePoint, so if you understand lists, you go a long way toward really understanding one of the main reasons SharePoint exists—to make, use, support, display, and manage lists.

I could write a whole book about lists, but because this is a book about SharePoint in general, this chapter and the next are meant to give you, the administrator, an overview of what lists can do and how to use them (and how your users will be working with them) so you have an idea of what to expect when asked about lists and how to use, create, manage, and customize them in the course of your workday.

In this chapter, you'll learn how to

◆ Use and modify a list

◆ Modify a view and create a view

◆ Customize a list

What Is a List? (Fundamental Concepts)

To begin with, lists are located in SharePoint sites. Sites are stored in web applications, and every web application has at least one *content database* to store its data contents. Every time you create a list, the data goes into the content database for the site. Lists are meant to offer a consistent interface for users to view and enter data. Lists have a very spreadsheet-like, tabular feel to them; their fields are typically referred to as *columns*, and the rows, or records, are referred to as *list items*.

Each list is displayed on a content page. A *content page* is simply a way to display the contents of a given list. Usually, when you generate a display of a database's contents, the display is called a *report*. In SharePoint, it's called a *view*. You can create surprisingly useful views using SharePoint's built-in view customization tools, which give you all kinds of control over how to display and manipulate the data that you put into a list. The trick is that a content page is defined by a view, and a list can have several ways to view it, which means (unbeknownst to the users) that a list can have several different content pages, each providing a different way to view the data. This is also why the terms *view page* and *content page* for lists can be synonymous.

So, you know that lists are contained in tables in the content database. You also know that you can manipulate the data in a list by creating different views and that each view of a list is in fact its own page. But, the fact that they are simply tables in the content database implies something else that is important about lists: how they can be connected by common data.

SharePoint allows you to format a field as a *lookup field* to display the data that was entered into a common field in a different list. For an administrator, or someone who is designing these lists, the concept of common field data is important to keep in mind. It is possible to have an Inventory list, a Customer list, and a Vendor list and then create a Sales list that has lookup fields for the customer name, vendor name, salesperson name, and inventory name. The Sales list becomes a kind of middle list, linking the other lists for ease of data entry as well as to avoid data duplication issues.

In addition to the ability to use lookup fields to access field information from one list within another list, you can also *connect* lists by their common fields using List View web parts (which you learned about in Chapter 5, "Introduction to Web Parts").

SharePoint has a number of different lists that are ready to use by default. You can also make a list based on a template and customize the heck out of it, or you can simply make a completely new list if you want. You can even make a list template out of your favorite lists, to be used elsewhere. For convenience, list fields can be created based on field templates available for the site collection called *site columns*, so when you're adding fields to your lists, you don't always have to make common fields from scratch. You can even create entire list items and save them as a template, known as a *content type*, to be applied to other lists when you create them. You can add extra features such as workflows or templates to the content types for additional usefulness. All in all, even the simplest list can have an array of settings, features, and capabilities in SharePoint. We'll explore all of these features over the course of this chapter and the next.

BONUS MATERIAL

This chapter gives you a good overview of working with the basic features of SharePoint lists. However, if you desire more details, explanation, and demos, I have an extended version of this chapter available online.

To get a copy of the extended material for this chapter, go to www.sybex.com/go/masteringsharepointfoundation2010.

Exploring a List: Announcements

To start, let's take a look at a representative list. One of the simplest lists created in the Team Site template is the Announcements list. To access the Announcements list, you can click the Lists link either in the Quick Launch bar or on the ubiquitous All Site Content page, which shows all the objects on the site. Clicking Announcements will take you to the Announcements list's content page (Figure 6.1).

FIGURE 6.1

The Announcements list

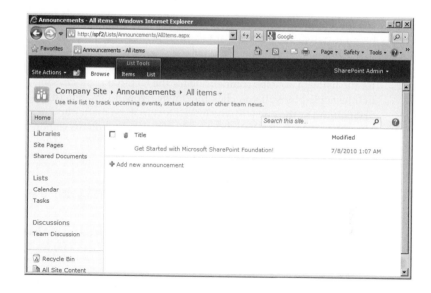

On the content page of the Announcements list, you can see the sample Get Started with Microsoft SharePoint Foundation! list item. This is automatically generated when the Team Site template is applied. Notice that, in the content area of the page, the field headings are Title and Modified (with a selection box and a column to indicate whether there is a file attached to a list item). Above the content area is the title area, within which is a title breadcrumb indicating a path back to the site's home page from this list. Appended to the end of the breadcrumb is the current view, which is usually a little lighter in color than the rest of the breadcrumb and which has a down arrow next to it. (The default view for this list is All Items. This means all record items available for the list, not necessarily all the fields available for each item.) Below the title area is the top link bar, with a tab to get to the Home page if you'd like, and the search field and help icon on the right. Above the title area is the top ribbon bar, containing Site Actions on the left, with the Navigate Up button to its right, as well as a Browse tab (to activate the title area should a ribbon bar be covering it) and the List Tools toolset (the Items and List ribbon tabs). To the far right in the top ribbon bar is the Account menu, indicating the account you are currently logged in with (always useful). On the left below Site Actions, of course, is the ever-present Quick Launch bar.

In the content area itself below the list items, as a convenience, is also an Add New Announcement link, which will allow you to add a new list item really quickly, without having to activate the Items ribbon bar.

If there are any list items, they'll be displayed beneath the headings in the content area. To sort any list items you might have, you can click a column heading. To open a list item and view its contents, simply click its title, or whatever field in the item appears to be a link. You might also notice that when you move your mouse pointer over a list item, it highlights, and a selection box appears to the left of the item. That box will allow you to select the item, although simply clicking in the highlighted area will also select it. When you select an item, the Items ribbon becomes active in case you want to do something to that particular item. However, you don't necessarily have to use the ribbon to work on an individual item.

You may have also noticed that a down arrow appears on the right side of the title column for the list item; it helps compensate for the fact that right-clicking isn't available for list items in Internet Explorer. If you click the down arrow for an item (it is always at the end of either the first column or the one with the linked text in it, no matter how wide it is), a menu pops down, offering you approximately the same actions that the Items ribbon bar offers plus actions specific to that individual item.

Creating a New List Item

To create a new list item, you can either activate the Items ribbon and click New Item or just click the Add New Announcement link.

1. I'm going to choose the easiest option and click the Add New Announcement link in the list's content area. (It's also the fastest option; there's no waiting for the screen to draw the ribbon bar.)

   In the Announcements – New Item form box (see Figure 6.2), you'll notice that although the list showed an attachment column, a title column, and a modified column, when you create a new item, there are other fields in that record: Body and Expires. Because the Modified date field is a default field that you cannot change, it's not available for data entry. Keep in mind that the default view of the list generally doesn't have all the fields available for the record. It shows what Microsoft thought would be relevant for the Announcements list.

FIGURE 6.2
The Announce-
ments – New
Item page

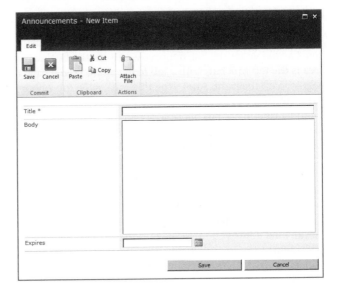

MORE RIBBON BARS

You might've noticed that the Announcements – New Item form has its own abbreviated ribbons.

The Edit ribbon, for editing the item, contains the following:

◆ A Commit section, with Save and Cancel buttons.

◆ A Clipboard section, with Paste, Cut, and Copy buttons.

◆ An Actions section, with only one button, Attach File. This makes sense (not as the only action button) because the list showed a paper clip attachment heading on the content page.

If you click in the Body field of the Announcements – New Item form, you'll see an Editing Tools toolset come up (not to be confused with Edit), with tabs for typing in the Body field. This is because Body is an enhanced content field, and like the Content Editor web part, the text can be formatted, tables and images can be inserted, and so on. You've seen those ribbons before, so I am not going to list their buttons here. Most forms have their own abbreviated ribbon bar, letting you do several of the tasks you can do with the ribbons out on the list itself.

2. I am going to use **Welcome to the site!** for the title of my new announcement. The body of the text is going to welcome new members, which you can write yourself.

   Below the Body field is the Expires field, which controls the length of time this announcement is visible in the web part. If you leave its Expires field blank, the announcement will always be displayed in the Announcements web part on the home page.

3. Because this is a welcome announcement, I don't want it to expire, so leave the Expires field blank, and click Save (either the Save button at the bottom of the box or the Save button in the Edit ribbon) to go back to the Announcements list.

   In the Announcements list, a new item is displayed (see Figure 6.3) for my new announcement. Notice that the Body field of the list item is not displayed in this view. There is also no Expires field listed.

FIGURE 6.3
A new
announcement

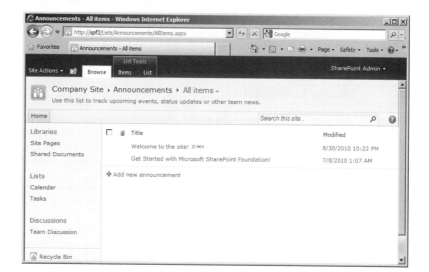

THE NEW ICON

A green exclamation mark (!) is assigned to all new list items in SharePoint, and a little green "NEW" appears next to them for the first 24 hours of their existence. It should disappear after a day. If the !NEW icon bothers you, check out KB article 825510. Even though the article is for a previous version of SharePoint, the operation and parameters still apply.

As you read in Chapter 4, the top ribbon bar tabs are context sensitive, activate depending on where you click, and have ribbons that drop down under them. There is also always one field in every list item that is linked to the view list item form. This means that if you click that linked item, the item's view form opens. (That form has its own ribbon bar that makes options such as Edit Item available to the user.)

SECRETS OF A LINKED FIELD

The linked field for an item is usually the "name" or "title" field. Keep this in mind when you are messing with the way a list is viewed, because if the name or title fields are not displayed, the user may not be able to access that list item to edit or view item contents easily. There is a way around it—by using an Edit icon for each list item (add the Edit icon column to the view). However, it is still good to know that there are limitations to what fields are automatically (and inflexibly) assigned as the link for an item.

Of the List Tools tabs, the List ribbon is largely focused on things you can do in the list, such as editing or deleting; however, for each item, there is the Items ribbon to work on it specifically. In addition, each list item has a drop-down menu, as I mentioned earlier in the chapter.

The options in the drop-down list will, of course, depend on your permissions for the list, the permissions for that particular item, and, even in some cases, what kind of list it is. Keep in mind that if you cannot access the drop-down menu of an item (if it is an ActiveX control, your browser may not support it), you can also access the item-specific commands by going to the Items ribbon as well as into that item's view form box (which will have item-specific buttons available).

LIMITED PERMISSIONS?

I am logged in as *shareadmin* on my server. That account is the primary site owner, so I have all possible rights to all items at this point. This is why I have all the options possible to work on any list, list item, site, web part, and so on. If you are working on a list in SharePoint and don't have all of those options, the chances are good that you are logged in and working with an account that has limited permissions.

To trigger the Item drop-down menu in the Announcements list, move your mouse pointer over the Title field of the new Announcement item (in other lists, be sure to move your mouse pointer over the field that is linked). It will highlight the Title field. While the field is highlighted, you'll notice a drop-down arrow at the end of the Title field (or column, if you will). You can click this arrow to get the drop-down menu for the item to appear (as shown in Figure 6.4). The drop-down arrow will always be at the end of the column of the linked field.

FIGURE 6.4

A list item's drop-down menu

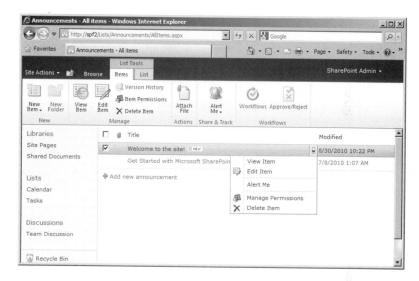

This menu will have the following items:

View Item   This menu option is the same as what you see when you click the title for an item. It brings up the box displaying the contents of that item.

Edit Item   This menu option opens the Edit box for that item so you can change or add data to the editable fields (fields such as Created Date or Last Modified are automated and cannot be accessed or changed by a user; nor can calculated fields).

Alert Me   This menu option gives you an easy way to create an *alert* (an email sent to you alerting you to changes) on a list.

Manage Permissions   This menu option allows you to specify permissions and security at the item level. That's how granular security is.

Delete Item   This does exactly what you'd expect. Click it, and you get a warning that this item will be deleted. If you OK it, the item goes to the user's Recycle Bin for the site.

If one or more workflows, content approval, or versioning are enabled on the list, options for them may also appear in the list item's drop-down menu.

Viewing a List Item

With your item created, the first thing you should do is verify what it looks like:

1. To view the contents of the Welcome To The Site! item, do one of the following: click View Item on the item's drop-down menu; select the item so the Items ribbon bar becomes active, and then click the View Item button; or click the item's title link while on the content page for the list.

In the View Item form box for that item's contents, you'll see the data you entered for this new item earlier, in the fields Title, Body, and Expires (which in my case is blank). Notice at the bottom of the form, in Figure 6.5, that there is also other item information not contained in an editable field—the name of the person who created or modified the item, as well as the item's create and modify dates.

FIGURE 6.5

The View Item form

On this View Item form, there is an abbreviated ribbon containing buttons for editing the item, managing its permissions, deleting it, or creating an alert. Because version history is not enabled for this list, the Version History button is grayed out.

2. To close the item and go back to the list, click Close. This will take you back to the Announcements list.

Editing a List Item

As an example of how to edit a list item, you'll now edit the new Announcement list item you've created:

1. To begin, you can select the item and click Edit Item in the Items ribbon bar, or you can click the down arrow in the Title column for the item and select Edit Item from the drop-down menu.

2. This page illustrates that there can be more fields of data for an item than may be displayed in a list view. In the Edit Item box, enter yesterday's date in the Expires field. (Feel free to enter your birth date instead of yesterday's date—but I'm not volunteering mine.) Notice the Edit ribbon bar for the box just as there was for viewing or creating a new item, and if you click in the Body field, as expected, ribbon tabs for editing come up (Figure 6.6). Click OK.

FIGURE 6.6
Edit announce-
ment to expire

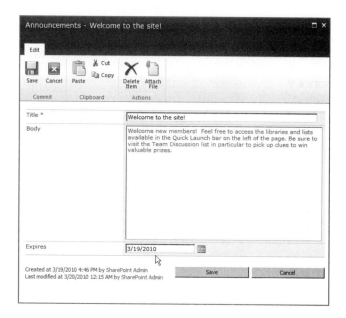

Back on the content page, nothing has changed, because the edit occurred within a field for the item that isn't displayed in this view.

The default view of the list is currently displayed, letting you know the titles of the announcement items and when they were most recently modified. But what's missing is when they are scheduled to expire. That would be a useful thing to see at a glance. To provide that ability, you need to add the Expires field to the current view (the most convenient view since it is the default).

To add a field to the current view, you have to modify that view.

Modifying a List View

To modify an existing view, do either of the following:

◆   Click the down arrow at the end of the title breadcrumb (it follows the name of the view, which in this case is All Items), and select Modify This View (Figure 6.7). If you can't see the title area because there's a ribbon bar in the way, click the Browse tab in the top ribbon bar; that will get rid of the ribbon and reveal the title area.

◆   Or, you can use a button in the ribbon to modify the view by clicking the List tab in the List Tools toolset in the top ribbon bar and then clicking the Modify View button in the Manage Views section.

This may be the first time you've seen a settings page for a view. So, let's stop here for a second and examine some of the sections. Knowing what the sections are will let you recognize this information when you make changes later to lists and views.

In Figure 6.8, you can see the Name section, which contains the name of the view and the name of the page for that view. The name of the view will be part of the URL for that page. The RSS Feed link next to the Web Address field will take you to the RSS Feed page for the list.

FIGURE 6.7
The View drop-down menu to modify the view

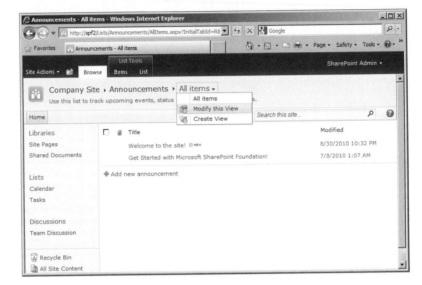

FIGURE 6.8
The first section of the Edit View page

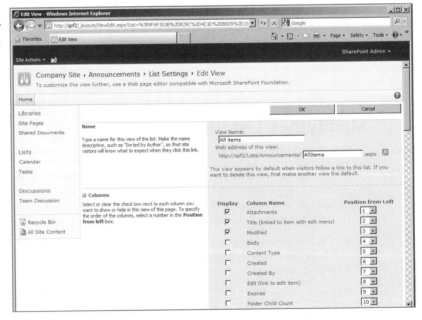

Columns are in the second section of this Edit View page (Figure 6.9). These are the fields for the list item (this helps prove that a list is just a table, because behind the scenes a field is called a *column*). The check marks under the Display heading show that the fields that actually display in this view are Attachments, Title, and Modified. That should seem reasonable because you've seen the list using this view, and you know those fields are displayed.

FIGURE 6.9

The Columns section of the Edit View page

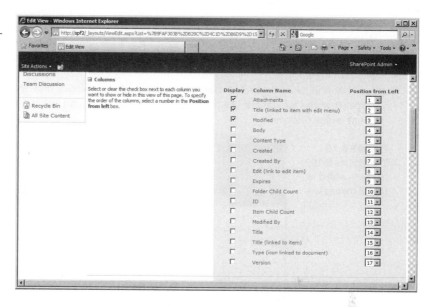

What may not be so familiar is that the list items have many more possible fields than even the ones you used when you did the data entry for the new item. Title, Body, and Expires are the only fields for this list into which you can enter data. All the other fields for this list are automated and will be filled because something happened in the software (triggers include when the record was created, who created it, what was modified, when it was modified, and who modified it).

Other automated fields can be those used by email. If a list has incoming email enabled, then incoming list items will be received via email, and information about that needs to be recorded in the list item. This means that there can be fields such as Email From, Sender, Subject, To, and Cc. If those fields aren't in the list of columns for your Announcements list, then you haven't enabled incoming mail for that list yet. (Once created, the fields remain even if you disable incoming email for a list.) We will be enabling email on a list a little later in the chapter, by the way, so if you don't have the email fields in your list yet, you'll see how to get them later. In addition, there are automated fields for the ID (automatically gives the list items unique, consecutive numbers), the type (if this list has multiple types of new items that can be created), and the version (if versioning is enabled).

The next several sections of the Edit View page are not shown here but have to do with fancying up the view itself. Remember, a view is a sort of report of the data. As with most reports, you can organize what data is displayed and how it is displayed by using Sort, Filter, Total, and Style. You can organize data in folders in a view, and you can also specify whether this view will be available as a view on a mobile phone or PDA. (SharePoint is mobile-compatible, as long as the mobile device can access the local network.)

This brief tour was simply to show you what was available on this page; we are not going to get that fancy with the view just yet. For now, let's keep it simple and just add the Expires field to the existing view.

Adding an Existing List Field to a View

To add the Expires field, while on the Edit View page, simply put a check mark next to the field (Expires in our example) in the Columns section, and click OK at either the bottom or the top of the Edit area.

That will take you back to the Announcements list. Notice now that a new column, Expires, appears at the far right of the list (Figure 6.10). Now you can see at a glance when an announcement is due to expire.

FIGURE 6.10
The Expires field has been added to the All Items view.

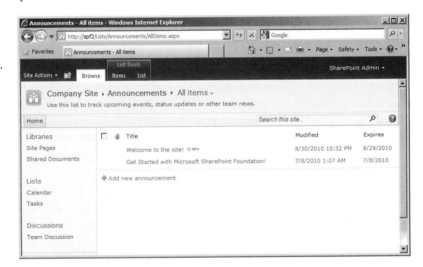

Removing a Field from a View

To further modify this view, let's remove the Modified date field and replace it with the Created By field. I find it easier to search for an announcement based on its author than when it might've been modified.

1. To change the view, go back once more to the View menu at the end of the title breadcrumb, and select Modify This View.

2. In the Columns section on the Edit View page for this list, remove the check mark next to the Modified field name to remove it, and put a check mark next to the Created By field to add it (Figure 6.11).

   If you clicked OK, the Modified column would be removed from the current view, and Created By would be added. However, because Created By is being added at this point, it will be positioned at the far right or last place in the field order. I would rather it were

located where the Modified column was. So, before we click OK, let's change the order of
our fields to specify the location of the Created By field.

FIGURE 6.11
Adding and remov-
ing fields from the
default view

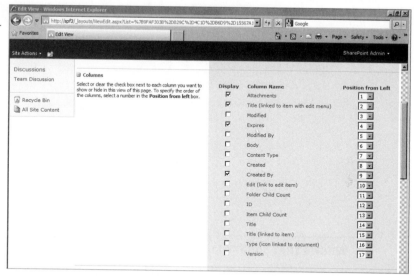

Changing the Order of Fields in a View

While we are modifying the fields we are displaying, let's change their order. Field order is
important. Highest-priority data should be the leftmost column in a record (unless the user is
reading a language that does not go from left to right; if that is the case, adapt accordingly).
Generally, the more important or unique a field is for an item, the closest to the left it should
be. But when fields are created, they are added to the list of fields alphabetically, and when you
choose to display a new field, it is added to the far right of the view, so there is a good chance
fields will need to be rearranged to be optimally located.

In this example, let's place the Created By field third from the left and have the Expired field
be last, or the one farthest to the right.

To do this, notice the Position From column in the Columns section of the Edit View page,
with its drop-down boxes that contain numbers. Currently, the Attachments field is first from
the left, then Title, and then Modified.

1. To change that order, just make sure the Position From field numbers are in the order
   you'd like. In this case, the Created By field should be third and the Expires field fourth.
   To do this, make certain that the number of the position for the Created By field is 3 and
   the position of the Expires field is 4.

2. Once your positions are complete, click OK to finish editing the view, and go back to see
   the fruits of your labor.

Back on the Announcements list, in the All Items view, notice that the Created By field is
displayed, the Modified field is not (it still exists; it's just not being used in this view), and the
Expires field is now in the fourth position (see Figure 6.12).

FIGURE 6.12
The fields are rearranged in the All Items view.

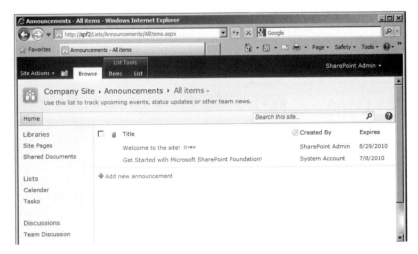

WHAT'S THAT SQUARE THING?

Did you notice the little rounded square next to the heading of the Created By column? That's the Online Presence icon. If Online Presence is enabled on the web application, this site is in, and if your company uses Office Communications server (or Lync) and client-side Communicator 2007 R2 or later, the names of the people in the column will have a little Online Presence icon next to them. The icon will be green if the person is online. Of course, it helps if that person is using Communicator too.

Modifying a List

List views are good for manipulating the view of the data in a list, but they are only as useful as the data they display. To make the Announcements list more useful, let's categorize announcements so we can see at a glance what would be Informational, Emergency, or Celebratory. We could even filter announcements by their category, letting us know quickly how many are important to read.

To do this, we need to modify the list itself (rather than modifying a view of the list's data) by adding a column. There is a convenient button to do this.

On the Announcements list, click the **Lists** tab in the top ribbon bar, and select Create Column in the Manage Views section (I know, it's not actually adding the column to the view but to the underlying list; welcome to Microsoft). This will bring you to the Create Column box. Let's take a few minutes to get familiar with the layout of this box before continuing.

NO HELP

One thing you'll notice about these new form boxes is that they don't bother to offer help.

In addition, the only help button available for SharePoint is in the top link bar—and the top link bar is obscured by the ribbon bar most of the time. So even if you could click the darkened background, there'd be no help to click. There is, by the way, no help button on the ribbons anywhere.

It's a good thing you have a big book about SharePoint to help you, because there's not much help available in the interface.

Create Column has two sections of settings, Name And Type and Additional Column Settings, with an optional section called Column Validation (we'll get to that shortly). The Name And Type section is important because the column type you choose here defines what settings will be available in the Additional Column Settings section below. Additional column settings vary depending on the type of field you choose.

The Name And Type section contains the Column Name field and radio buttons to choose the type or format the field will be. As I describe each field type here, you might want to click each radio button to see the additional column settings that appear.

Single Line Of Text   This type of field accepts text only and will display it on a single line. It can be configured for a maximum number of characters and have a default value. The maximum number of characters is 255, even though it is unlikely that you will be able to see all those characters on a single line.

Multiple Lines Of Text   This type of text field doesn't have a character limit but instead can enforce a line limit. It is also able to support rich text or even enhanced rich text (including tables, images, and hyperlinks). If the field has modifications, it also has the option of whether to replace the original text with the changes or append it.

BEFORE YOU CONSIDER APPENDING

Choosing to allow text to be appended in a Multiple Lines Of Text field requires that versioning be enabled on the list. Versioning is used in this case to keep track of who modified the text in the multiple-line text box and whose text is whose.

Thus, to allow appending text in this field, you must enable versioning first. This is one of the many instances in SharePoint where you may need to interrupt your current configuration process to go configure something else first.

Choice (Menu To Choose From)   This type of field is for offering the user a choice among a set list of options that you supply. It can be set to offer those choices by radio button, drop-down list, or check box (which means the user can choose several of the options rather than just one). There is also a setting to allow the user to fill in the field with a value rather than pick one of the choices.

Number (1, 1.0, 100)   This field type will accept numbers only. You can specify the decimal places, minimum/maximum, default value, and whether the value is represented as a percentage.

Currency ($, ¥, Euro)   This is a numbers-only field that also formats the content to display as currency. It allows you to choose from a list of currency formats. As with a Number field, a Currency field also can be configured for decimal places and minimum/maximum value.

Date And Time   This field formats the content to a date and time value. You can specify whether it displays only a date or displays a date and time. You can have the field default to today's date and time or specify a default.

Lookup (Information Already On This Site)   The lookup field allows SharePoint to do something that has been done in Access for years: pull data from a column in one table and use it in another. For example, if you have a Vendor list on your site that contains data in a column such as Vendor Name, you can create a lookup field in a different list (say, Inventory) that refers to the Vendor Name field from the Vendor list. The field in the Inventory list will display the existing vendor names from the Vendor list in a drop-down list for the user to pick from. To configure this field, you first choose the list from which to get information and then choose the column in that list from which to get the information. You can also configure this field to allow multiple selections for the field. This will lay out the field as two list boxes, rather than a drop-down, where you can choose data from the box on the left (which pulls from the list you are looking up) and click the Add button to put your choice(s) in the box on the right, which adds the data to the field.

A lookup field is commonly used to keep someone from having to type the same data over again if it is already available in a different table. This will help prevent typing errors during data entry and will ensure that changes in the underlying list field propagate through to all related lookup fields (such as when a vendor's name changes). In addition, using List View web parts, you can display related data from the two lists you've connected via the lookup field. We'll take a look at how to do this in the next chapter.

Yes/No (Check Box)   This field is a single check box. If it is checked, the value is Yes; if it is not checked, the value is No. It's that simple. You can also specify a default value of either Yes or No.

Person Or Group   This field pulls directly from the People And Groups list for the site, like a lookup list for site user accounts. You can configure whether to allow multiple selections for this field; allow the selection of People Only or People And Groups (it defaults to People Only); limit the field to All Users or a particular group of users (also really useful); and which of the user fields to show, such as Account, Email, Job Title, and even Name With Presence, Picture, or Picture with Details.

Hyperlink Or Picture   This field is formatted to display only a URL (such as HTTP, FTP, or FILE); it is going to be accessed from the browser, and therefore the location of the file the field is referencing must be user-accessible.

If you choose to use this field as a hyperlink, it will simply display a link. If you choose to use it to contain a picture, you enter the path to access the picture file via the network or the URL of the file in a library, and then that picture will be displayed in the field.

Calculated (Calculation Based On Other Columns)   This really powerful field enables you to use complex formulas to perform calculations. As a matter of fact, it is formatted to only do calculations, so you can't actually type in a calculation field when doing data entry. SharePoint just does the math in the background and uses the field to display the results.

You can use field names (from this list only, unfortunately), known variables like [Today] or [Me], common math, and even complex formulas and functions ranging from text and logical functions to trigonometry.

The Calculated field has a Formula box with a convenient Insert Column box next to it listing all the list fields created so far. This means if you want to calculate using another field in the list, you need to create that other field before you create the calculated field. Enter the formula you want to be calculated in the Formula box, and double-click the field name you want to add to the formula (which puts itself in the formula for you). You can also specify the data type that the formula is going to return, such as currency, number, or single line of text. Yes/No is also an option.

External Data   For this field to be available, the Business Data Connectivity service must be enabled on the server, and a configured external data source (such as a non-SharePoint database) must be available. Then this field works like a lookup field, pointing to a field in the external source.

External data fields and external lists are both covered in Chapter 16, "Advanced Installation and Configuration," along with more details about managing the Business Data Connectivity service. This new feature of SharePoint Foundation deserves to be the focus of an entire section of a chapter.

All fields in a list can be configured to require data. When a user is adding a new item record to the list, they won't be able to finish it until there is a value in each required field.

Most data fields can also have a default value and/or a calculated default value. The calculated value in that case must be a simple calculation (no field references, just variables, functions, formulas, or simple math). Using a calculation value for a field is nice because the field can have a simple calculation in it (like a default expires date for example), or you can override that value by typing something into the field manually. Calculated fields don't have that option. They only do calculations based on the content of other fields or the value of a variable at the time the item record was created and are not available for the users to change.

In addition, all fields have a setting that adds them to the default view. If you don't want a field to be added to the current default view of the list, remove the check from the Add To Default View box when you are creating the field. This is simply a convenience. As you've already learned, you can add or remove fields from a view at any time.

Adding a Field to a List

Now that you are familiar with all the settings in the Create Column page (via the Create Column button in the List ribbon), let's add a Category field to the Announcements list. This field should require the person entering the data for a new announcement to choose a category for it.

1. In the Name And Type section (Figure 6.13), enter the name of the field. My example uses **Category**.

FIGURE 6.13
The Name And
Type section

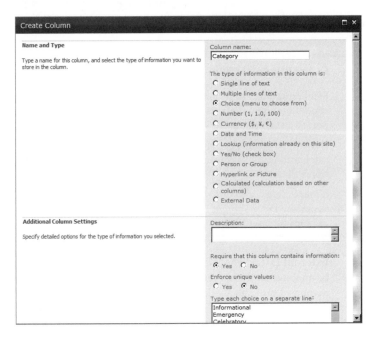

2. From the data types listed, select the type of field Category will be. Because this field will allow users to apply one of a limited number of categories to an announcement, we will use the **Choice** type.

3. The Additional Column Settings section has now changed to display settings that relate to a Choice field. First is the ubiquitous Description field. When we add a description to a field, it ends up on the data entry form for the item right below the field. It can be considered help text, used to assist users in understanding what they are supposed to enter in the field. However, in some cases, if the field's contents are self-explanatory, the description can be distracting and take up space. For this example, I am not going to enter a description. I can always edit the field's properties and change it later if I need to do so.

4. There is an option to require information in this field. My example requires the users to choose a category when they create an announcement, so this option is going to be **Yes**. Additionally, the field cannot enforce a unique value among all items in the list, since there are going to be only three options to choose from, so be sure to set Enforce Unique Values as **No**.

5. Next is the text box in which you actually type the choices. It seems a bit low tech, but you can replace the placeholder text with your choices. For my example, I am going to use **Informational**, **Emergency**, **Celebratory** (see Figure 6.14). Each choice should be entered on a separate line, and you can easily have more than three choices if you want.

   Note that if you find yourself entering a great number of choices (or editing the field to increase the choices over time), you may want to consider creating a separate list with a field to contain the choices and then using a Lookup field against that list.

FIGURE 6.14
Adding choices to the Category field

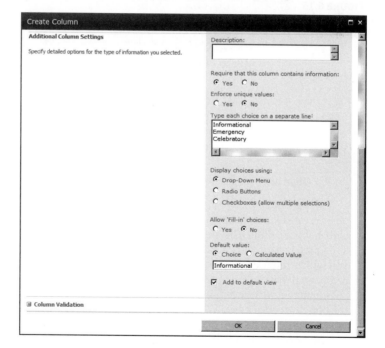

6. Below the choices are the options that determine how the choices will be displayed: in a group with radio buttons, in a drop-down menu, or with check boxes so users can choose more than one (the data is stored in a comma-delimited field). My example uses the drop-down menu.

7. You can also decide whether to let users fill in the field with their own value. In this example, the users shouldn't do that because the announcement items will be filtered by a category. So, set the Allow Fill-In Choices to No.

You can choose to have a default value among the choices or a calculated value. You may notice that the default value became Informational as soon as you finished typing your choices in. If you leave it that way, as soon as you click OK, the default value will be that first choice in the list. If you want the default value to be different, simply type it in the default value field yourself. My example uses the first choice because Informational is likely to be a good default.

8. Also at the bottom of the page is the option to add the field to the default view. Leave it checked so that this field is listed in the All Items view for the list. It will be added, by default, as the field farthest to the right in the view.

You may have noticed a Column Validation section heading at the bottom of the box (Figure 6.15); this is new in SharePoint Foundation. It allows you to indicate a calculation that the data in the field must meet to pass (basically, the calculation must be true or an error occurs). In our case, there is no validation necessary, since the users can select only one of three options in a drop-down menu.

FIGURE 6.15
The Column Validation section

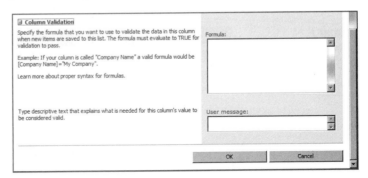

9. When all settings are finished, click OK to complete the column-creation process.

There should now be a Category field in the list view of the Announcements list. For the previously created items, there will be no data in the category field, but you can use what you learned earlier about editing a list item to add categories if you like. Note that because we made Category a required field, if you go into the Edit Item form, you will see a red asterisk next to Category, and you will be required to enter a category before you will be permitted to save any edit. All new records will have at least the default value of Informational (or whatever you chose for the default).

You may have noticed, if you were editing the new item, that the category field was added to the bottom of the item's list of fields on the Edit Item form. However, since it is required, I would like to put it near the top of the data entry page for the item record, for visibility and convenience. To accomplish that, we will need to rearrange the fields in the list.

Changing the Order of Fields in a List

You may remember that we rearranged fields earlier in the All Items list view, but we didn't actually change the order of the underlying fields of the list. We only changed the order in which the fields were displayed. But now that we are considering data entry, the order of the fields in the underlying list becomes important.

To change the order of a list's fields, you must modify the list itself by using list settings. The List Settings page is a significant configuration page. Right now we are just going to mess with the order of list fields. We will be getting to the other settings later in the chapter.

1. To go to the List Settings page, we need to be in the List ribbon (which we should be already to create a column). In the List ribbon, click the **List Settings** button in the Settings section at the end of the ribbon.

The List Settings page has several sections. Topmost is the List information, and below that is General Settings, which has links to all the important settings pages for this list. Beneath General Settings is the Columns section, which is devoted to all column-related activities, such as adding, removing, editing, ordering, and indexing columns. The last section relates to the list's views, focusing on the views that exist (in case you want to edit them), creating new views, or making new views with an existing view as a base, which is convenient.

EXTRA DATA

If you are on a list with content types (covered in Chapter 8, "Introduction to Libraries") enabled, there may be a Content Types section displayed on the List Settings page as well. The Columns section will then be below that. With content types enabled on a list, the list can contain more than one kind of list item; this is useful for lists that might contain both sales quotes and sales orders, for example. The two different kinds of list items might contain different fields, have fields in a different order, or have different settings enabled.

We are going to focus on the Column section. All the current fields in this list are in this section. They are displayed in the order that you see when you are creating or editing an item. You can see their data type and whether they are required. Also in this section are the following options:

Create Column This field links to the same Create Column page as the Create Column menu item from the Action bar's Settings button. You use it to create a new field for the list.

Add From Existing Columns This option lets you choose from the site's existing shared columns. Shared columns are premade fields, essentially field templates, that can be added to lists anywhere in the site collection. Fields that you create for lists cannot just be added later to this list of site columns; you need to create them from the Site Columns gallery page. Many columns are already set up to be shared across the site by default. These columns are pulled from the prebuilt lists and list templates of a team site (or whatever site template you are using).

Column Ordering All the fields for this list (there are more than you'd think) and their order are displayed on the page for this option.

Indexed Columns   *List indexing* is a pretty big concept. If you have a list that may grow to thousands of items, you might consider indexing. When you have such a huge list, SharePoint can take forever to show all the items in an All Items list view. Microsoft suggests either limiting the views by a hard limit (such as 100 records at a time) or filtering the view by a particular field so the user sees only a subset of all items. However, if a list is so large that even filtering is difficult because sorting through all of those records takes a long time, then you should index a field.

For example, if you are certain that the Announcements list is going to quickly become huge, with thousands of item records, you could index the Category field. Then you could create a view of the list that filters by category. This would allow SharePoint to pull up and organize the item records more efficiently because it has already analyzed that column's data. The catch is that it would take up RAM and processor resources to always keep that column analyzed (and it would stress the database engine itself a little). The more indexed columns there are, the more resources it takes to index that list. Therefore, you should index only one or two fields per huge list, because the resources required to index more than one or two fields would actually slow the list down.

Along those lines, you should index only those lists that you really need to index. Indexing takes up server resources. If you aren't having any speed issues working with a list, chances are it isn't too big, so don't index it. Microsoft suggests that a view have no more than 1,000 to 2,000 items in it per list (of course, you would want to limit each page of the view to far fewer items). Keep that in mind, and filter views to return fewer items than that limit to avoid having a list drag to a halt when someone tries to go to its content page.

TIPS FOR MANAGING HUGE LISTS

If you are going to have humungous lists of data, you might want some advice. Some of this information may be beyond what we have done so far, but just keep it in mind as you progress through the book.

♦ Limiting the number of items that can be displayed in a view (for example, to 100 at a time) does not really help the performance of a list as much as indexing does. Nor does limiting the number of fields in a view (though it helps). It's the number of item records being pulled from the content database that matters. Limiting items in a view does help in terms of waiting for all items to render in the browser, though, so by all means use it. Every little bit helps.

♦ Views have some sorting, filtering, and grouping options that can be a little complex. Filtering a list with an OR parameter negates the usefulness of an indexed column because SharePoint must deeply analyze and do comparisons with some other field in the list as well as the indexed one.

♦ Like a library, a list can be organized by folders, with list items stored in those folders. This organization can help break up the view of items, and it can help manage large lists. Then you can create views for each folder, further filtering the data (remember to index the field on which the filter is based). Folders with 2,000 or more item records will negate any performance improvements, though, so be careful. Basically, 2,000 is the magic number, give or take (although at 1,000, performance is better). Try to stay under that limit if you can.

♦ When filtering a view, make sure the primary, first column being filtered is the indexed one. You can filter, sort, and group by a lot of columns in a view, but make sure that the main focus of the filter is the indexed column and that the filter significantly reduces the items viewed.

♦ A list can have more than one indexed field, but it is not recommended. For example, if you had two different, popular ways to view a list, each filtered by a different field, then you could index those focus fields for the sake of the two different views, as long as they both reduce the number of items to around 2,000 or less (preferably far less).

In addition, this version of SharePoint includes *list throttling*. Set at the Web Application level in Central Administration, list throttling essentially limits the number of items returned from the underlying content database for a list view (trying to exceed that limit will cause failure). The default is 5,000 items, but that can be changed. For more on throttling list views, see Chapter 10, "Site Collections and Web Applications."

Now that you know a little about managing list columns, let's change our column order. Take the following steps to change the order of the List's fields:

1. Click the Column Ordering link in the Columns section. The Change Field Order page that appears has only one section. It simply displays the fields for the list. The Category field we created is at the end of the list, logically, because it was the last one made.

2. In my example, we want Category to appear between the Title field of the announcement and the Body field. To place it there, click the down arrow in the Position from the Top drop-down box for the Category field and change the number to **2**. This will instantly change the order of the fields, placing Category in the second position (see Figure 6.16).

FIGURE 6.16
Changing the field order of Category

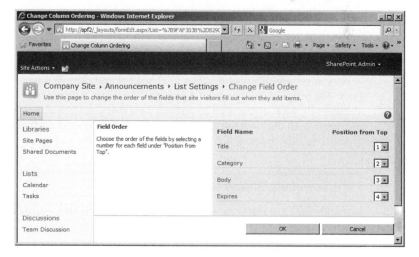

3. To finish, click OK.

This will take you back to the List Settings page. In Figure 6.17, you can see that the Category field is the second field in the list. However, the point is to see how it changes the order of data entry for the item, so in the breadcrumb in the title area of the page, click Announcements to get back to the Announcements List content page.

FIGURE 6.17
The List Settings
page with newly
positioned fields

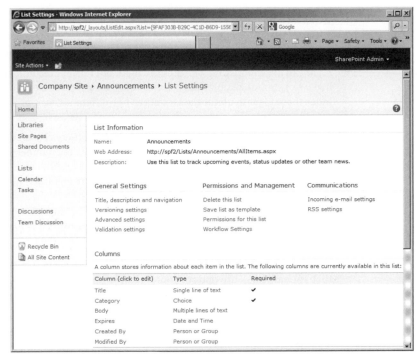

The fields are not in a different order on the Announcements list page. This is because we didn't move Category in the view; we moved it in the list itself. To see this for yourself, create a new item as you've done previously, and add some data. Note that the Category field is now the second field on the page and that the category has defaulted to Informational as its value. Feel free to choose a different category for your new item.

As you can see, it's easy to add a field to a list and change the order of the fields for data entry. The order of fields in a list is meant to facilitate data entry.

However, what if you need to do bulk data entry, such as entering several announcements at one time? With the New button method, you'd have to enter each item individually. If you want to populate a list quickly, you need to use *Datasheet view*.

BIG WINDOWS, BIGGER BUTTONS

It is possible that the buttons in the ribbon bar shown in these figures don't quite match those on your screen.

SharePoint will rearrange buttons to conserve space on the ribbon based on the size of windows. Most of the figures show windows that are not maximized (to save space); but that doesn't mean you shouldn't maximize your windows. The buttons will always be available in the correct section, regardless of window size; they just might be smaller or under a large button for the section with a drop down to show you the items in the section. Don't worry if your buttons are not *exactly* arranged like the ones in these figures.

Entering Data via Datasheet View

The Datasheet view of a list uses an Office feature to make a small spreadsheet out of the list view so you can enter data more quickly. This means you'll need to have at least one 32-bit Office Professional product (Word, PowerPoint, Excel, and so on, preferably Office 2007 or 2010) installed on the computer you are using to access SharePoint before you can work with a list in Datasheet view. If you try to edit a list in Datasheet view without having an Office product installed, a dialog box will warn you that the list cannot be displayed (Figure 6.18).

FIGURE 6.18
The datasheet
warning dialog box

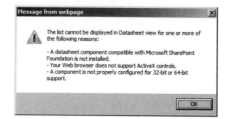

> ### WEB "ACCESS"IBLE DATASHEET
>
> If you have any Office 2007 (or higher) product installed, the list view will turn into an Access Web datasheet. (This makes sense in a way, because Access is a database product; it should work with SharePoint to manage data.) If you don't, but you do have an Office 2003 product installed, you'll get a simple, Excel-like datasheet.

To enable bulk data entry for a list in a datasheet on a machine that has an Office product installed, click the Datasheet View button in the List ribbon.

As you can see in Figure 6.19, Datasheet view takes the current view you are using on the content page and makes it into a spreadsheet of data. Note that the only fields available for data entry are the ones in the view you were using when you clicked Datasheet View. In my example, the All Items view doesn't display the Body field, so I can't fill in the Body field in the Datasheet view. On the other hand, you can create a standard view that shows only the relevant fields that you want to fill with data when you enable the Datasheet view.

For demonstration purposes, let's populate several fields of announcement titles and categories with the intention to fill in the Body field later. This will create a few list items and give us enough data in the list to explore more complex views later in the chapter.

The datasheet itself has standard rows and columns, a border across the top containing the field headings, a border along the left side for selecting rows and indicating a new row, and the top-left corner of the border for selecting the entire sheet.

CUSTOM FILTERING

All the field headings have a down arrow next to them. This is a standard spreadsheet table feature that allows you to filter and sort a field from that drop-down. You can also use it to perform custom filtering. Just click the down arrow of the column you'd like to filter, and select Custom Filter. That will open the Custom Filter dialog box in which you can do three levels of complex filtering of that field's data in the list.

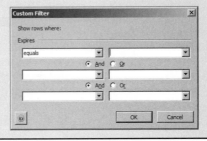

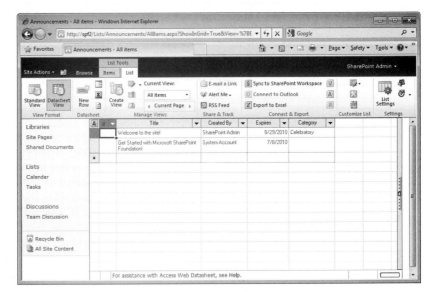

FIGURE 6.19
The Datasheet view

When a list is in Datasheet view, it acts like any spreadsheet. You can add and delete rows and columns, fill columns, cut and paste, and so on. In addition, fields that contain multiple-choice data simply drop down for you to choose from the list just as you did in the New Item window. As a matter of fact, because the Choice field has a default value, Informational, it will autofill with that value if you skip over it to go to the next row.

1. To add a new item record, simply go to the last row of the datasheet and start typing in the fields. You'll find that you can type in the Title field but not in the Created By field. Why not? Well, Created By is a field that gets filled based on your login information. It wasn't meant to be editable. System fields populated by data SharePoint generates (Created By, Modified By, and Creation Date, to name a few) will show up as read-only in the datasheet when you try to enter data into them (see the bottom-right corner of Figure 6.20).

Caution: You might think that calculated columns would also be read-only, but that's not the case; if you type a value in that datasheet cell, calculated values for that field will be overwritten in every item. This can be easily fixed by reentering your calculation formula.

FIGURE 6.20
A field set to
read-only in the
datasheet

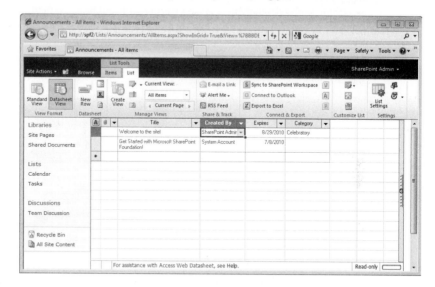

2. After you've filled the Title, Expires, and Category fields (see Figure 6.21 for an example), simply move to the next row to fill in a new list item record. It's that simple. Adding items in bulk is pretty easy. Remember, you can cut and paste data from Excel or Access to the datasheet as well. Of course, because the datasheet is based on the All Items view, we cannot access the Body field from here, but you get the point. Data entry using the Datasheet view is definitely more convenient than clicking the New button when you need to enter a lot of data.

FIGURE 6.21
Bulk data entry in
a datasheet

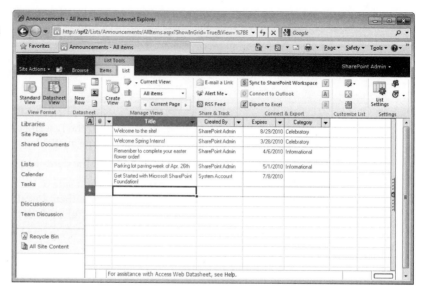

THE MULTIPLE LINE FIELD AND DATASHEET VIEW

Assume, for example, that you want to do all your data entry in Datasheet view. Sooner or later you are going to add the Body field (or some other multiple-line text field) to the Datasheet view. That might be a problem. When you add the Body field to a view so you can see it in Datasheet view, it may be read-only.

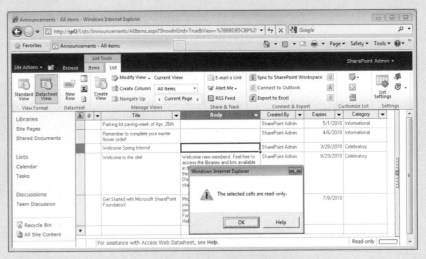

The interesting thing about multiple-line text fields and Datasheet view is that a datasheet creates completely blank records when you start on a row. When a multiple-line text field is not set to allow Append (which allows the field to be edited and added to once it has been saved), the field in Datasheet view is locked as read-only.

To make it possible to append a Body field in Datasheet view, you must allow Append Changes To Existing Text in the multiple-line text field's settings (see "Modifying a List" earlier in this chapter). To make matters more complicated, you must enable versioning on the list (see "Versioning Settings" in Chapter 8, "Introduction to Libraries.").

Versioning is list-wide and causes the list to keep a copy of every change to every list item, which increases the complexity and size of the list. Consider the ramifications of this just to be able to do bulk data entry for a multiple-line text field—do the costs outweigh the benefits? However, if this is your preferred method of data entry or the list is going to have versioning set on it anyway, go ahead.

When Datasheet view is enabled, the buttons in the List ribbon's Datasheet section are no longer grayed out. The following buttons become available:

New Row   Inserts a new row at the bottom of the datasheet.

Show Task Pane   Opens a task pane on the right side of the datasheet for integration tasks with Excel or Access (even if you don't have them installed). You can also open the task pane by clicking the grip bar on the far right side of the Datasheet view. See Figure 6.22 for an example.

Show Totals   Adds a Total row to the bottom of the datasheet, making it possible to go to the bottom of a column and perform a calculation on the data there. The types of total calculations possible for each column depend on that column's contents and data type.

Refresh Data   If anyone working on the list has cut and pasted a lot of data, has calculated fields that are not quickly updating, or has this data linked with data in Excel or Access, refreshing the data will reload the list data and pick up those changes.

FIGURE 6.22
The Datasheet task pane

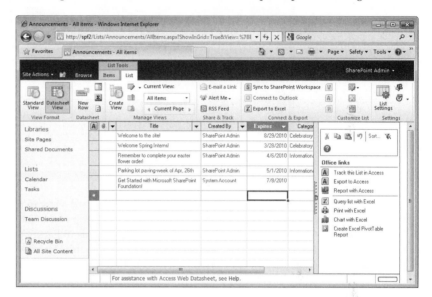

The Total row in Datasheet view is really convenient should you need to sum, average, or count items in a list by column. Here's how to add one:

1. First, add the Total row by selecting Show Total in the Datasheet section of the List ribbon (it's a small button with a sum symbol on it).

2. Then click in the field in that row that corresponds with the column you'd like to total. A drop-down arrow will appear in the selected field, allowing you to choose from the calculations available there. For example, if you want to see the latest expiration date for the Announcements list, enable the Total row, then click in the field for the Expires column, and select Maximum.

3. This may generate a set of number symbols (????), but that only means the column is not large enough to display the total with the down arrow in the field, so click away from the field, and the total will display. Or if necessary, you can increase the width of the column (move your mouse pointer over the right edge of the column header until the pointer turns into a double-headed arrow and then drag the column until it is a few characters wider than it was), and the correct maximum date will appear (Figure 6.23).

FIGURE 6.23
The maximum
date in the
Total row

FIGURE 6.23
The maximum
date in the
Total row

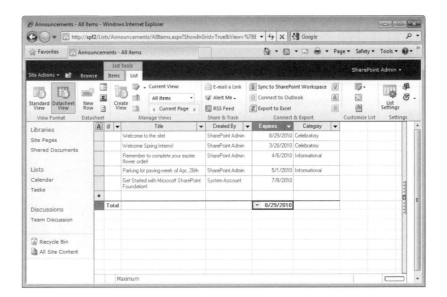

If you were to go back to Standard view (click Standard View in the List ribbon) with that Total field enabled, the total would be displayed at the top of the list.

If you find a list with a total that is hugging the top, as in Figure 6.24, and don't want it there, simply change the view to Datasheet (click the List ribbon's Datasheet View button). Then go to the Datasheet section of the ribbon, and select Show Totals to remove the Total row, which will remove the field calculation as well. When you go back to Standard view, the total won't be at the top of your list. Getting a quick summary of a column of data in a list using Datasheet view is one of those conveniences that not everyone knows about.

FIGURE 6.24
The Total
displayed in
Standard view

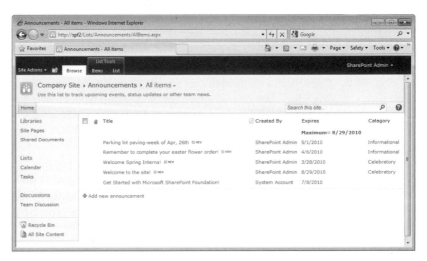

That should give you an idea of the possibilities of bulk data entry using Datasheet view. Let's return to Standard view and customize some views to filter the new data we've entered.

SUPER BULK DATA ENTRY

If you already have a lot of data in an Excel spreadsheet and no existing list to put it in, then consider the ultimate in bulk data entry—creating a new list by importing a spreadsheet. As long as you have Excel installed, it's easy. Just go to More Options on the Site Actions menu. On the Create page, select Import Spreadsheet under Custom Lists. Fill in the list name and description, browse to the spreadsheet, and click Import.

What that does is start a wizard that opens Excel and tries to figure out what fields in the spreadsheet will be in the list. Confirm the field selection, or specify the field range and click Import. You might be asked to reenter your credentials to confirm, and then SharePoint will create the list. The catch to creating a new list by importing a spreadsheet is that sometimes the field formats are not perfect and need to be reconfigured (then data will have to be copied and pasted back in for that column because resetting the data type wipes the data in the field).

Formatting fields in SharePoint is pretty simplistic. Phone numbers, for example, can't be set to display with parentheses and dashes, but otherwise importing an entire spreadsheet can save a lot of time by skipping the process of creating a new list, creating all the correct fields, and cutting and pasting the data in Datasheet view. It simply gives you a whole new list filled with the data you need to get started.

For more about creating a new list, check out the "Create a Custom List" section of Chapter 7.

Back in Standard view, we now have considerably more data with which to work. When a list begins to fill up with data, it is natural to want to filter the data so you can more easily focus on the items you want to work with. For example, you may want to see whether there is a pattern of emergency announcements in the last year or see how many celebrations there have been. Because the list items can be categorized, it's natural to want to filter or organize the list by these categories. To do this, we'll simply create a few new views.

Creating a New List View to Group by Category

When you create a new list view, you have some options. You can create a view based on an existing view, or you can create a new view based on a particular view format, which is essentially a view template, such as a calendar or datasheet.

In this case, we are simply going to create a standard view (which is what the All Items view is), add the fields in the order we want, and then group (and even total) the information by category for easy viewing. Remember that Standard view is laid out like a standard report, and because of that, it has many of the data organizational features that a report would.

To create a new list view, follow these steps:

1. While in Standard view, click the Create View button on the List ribbon (alternatively, you can click the Browse tab in the top ribbon bar, click the view's down arrow in the title breadcrumb, and select Create View). That will take you to a Create View page (it's actually a View Type page, as you can see in the address bar). As you can see in Figure 6.25, you can choose a format to base your new view on, or you can start from an existing view.

FIGURE 6.25
The Create
View page

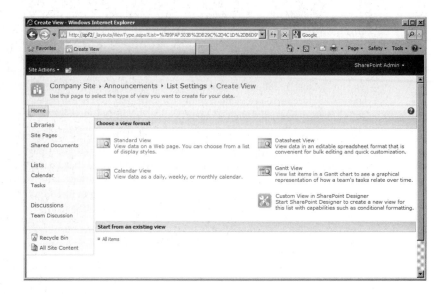

The view formats are as follows:

Standard View   This is your standard report format, with the option to organize the data by groups, total, filter, and so on.

Datasheet View   If you find yourself in Datasheet view more often than not, you might want to consider creating a Datasheet view in which to work. This view is also good if you are going to be doing regular bulk data entry, because you can create the view with all the fields you plan to use.

Calendar View   This view uses any date field a list item might have to display that item on a particular date, such as a deadline. (This works great for birthdays and anniversaries as well.) The Calendar view can be displayed in week, month, or day format. Calendar view also has a new capability with this version of SharePoint, Calendar Overlay (like Outlook, Google, or Yahoo, you can have one Calendar view show a number of different schedules as separately colored items).

Custom View In SharePoint Designer   This obviously requires SharePoint Designer to be installed locally (if it isn't and you choose this option, it will offer to download it for you so you can install it). If selected, it will open SharePoint Designer so you can create a list view from scratch and employ some of the additional formatting SharePoint Designer offers. SharePoint Designer is outside the scope of this book, but there are a number of great books that extensively cover the product's interface and capabilities.

Gantt View   This view is similar to a Calendar view but turned on its side. Like a calendar, this view focuses on dates. This view requires that there be two date fields to create a range of time, such as a start date and an end date, or the period of time a project or event is scheduled to last.

2. We are going to use a Standard view to group our data, so select Standard View from the group of view formats. The Create View page is very similar to the Edit View page for a standard view but is actually a ViewNew page in the address bar. The View configuration sections are as follows:

Name This section allows you to name the view. Keep in mind that a view name will be used in the web address for that page, so try to keep the name to a single word and as short as possible. Remember that when you create a view or site and use two words or more in its name, the spaces are represented by %20 in the web address. This means that, for example, "The Technical Resource Filter View" will end up with a page address of `The%20Technical%20Resource%20Filter%20View`. Given that SharePoint allows only 260 characters in a web address, you will need to keep your names descriptive but short, minimizing spaces. Once you've saved a view, you can edit its name and web page address if necessary within the Edit View page, but it's best to simply name the view correctly the first time; as always, planning ahead is important.

BREVITY VS. READABILITY

I've said that you should avoid spaces in your view names and make them as short as possible. The same advice applies to column names and list names so that they can be more easily referenced later in URLs and possible code references. But your users are used to seeing real words separated by spaces. What to do? You can create each of these short names as recommended, but then you can go back and edit the view, column, or list, and change the name only. You will see that the underlying reference in SharePoint remains the same, but the name displayed is much more user-friendly.

The Name section also contains a setting for making the view the default view. The default view is the one that will open when a user opens the list from a List View web part or from the Quick Launch bar.

Audience This section lets you decide whether the current view is going to be Public or Personal. As with a web parts page, users with the correct permissions can create a view of a list that only they can see (Personal) or that everyone can see (Public).

Personal views are good for creating complex or obscure views that relate only to what you personally are doing with a list or library, and they help avoid having a huge list of views from which other users must choose. Keep in mind that if users are allowed to create their own Personal views, troubleshooting them can be challenging, since only the user can see that view. Note that one of the Public views must be a default so that when a user drops by, they see the default until they choose another view.

Columns In this section, you choose the existing list fields that will appear in the view, and you determine the order in which they are placed. A computer screen can display only so many fields across, so determining which fields to display and which to not display is an art in itself, dependent upon the business and user requirements for that view. Usually, the more important a field is, the farther to the left side it is displayed.

Sort This section lets you specify the sort order of the items in the view. Unfortunately, in SharePoint you can sort only by two fields. (This has been a disappointment for me a time or two.)

Filter Filtering lets you display only the list items whose data matches particular criteria. The set of criteria available for filtering is standard but useful, including Greater Than, Less Than, Equal To, Not Equal To, Contains, and Begins With. Another nice thing about filtering is that you can filter by more than two columns of criteria. You can simply keep adding more columns to filter by, combining them with And or Or logic.

CREATE DEFAULT PUBLIC VIEWS

Keep in mind that if you have a list that contains thousands or even tens of thousands of items, it's best to create default Public views that limit the number of items displayed automatically. Doing so will help the list come up more quickly for users navigating to that list. Alternatively, you can create a Personal view as each user and teach them how to filter with it to better manage and manipulate the data in the lists for themselves.

Inline Editing   When enabled, Inline Editing adds an Edit button to each item record. If you click it, any field that is editable becomes available to edit (for example, text fields become text boxes). A little red X (cancel) button and a little floppy disk (save) button become available to save or cancel the changes and get out of edit mode for that item. Note that it works only for views that use the default style.

INLINE EDITING DOES CHANGE THINGS

Once inline editing is enabled, it becomes the default way to add new items to a list, changing the Add New item (Announcement, for example) to just a plus sign, as shown here.

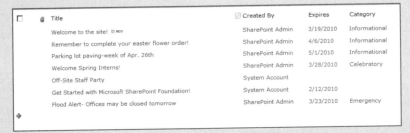

When the plus sign is clicked, a new item is started in the list view, with Save and Cancel buttons and the fields active to accept data. If you don't want that as the default data entry behavior, don't apply this setting to any views intended for data entry.

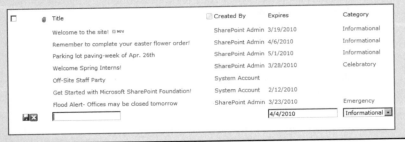

Tabular View   This option is on by default and enables the selection check box at the beginning of each item record so you can select one or more than one item at a time.

Group By   Organizes the items displayed in the view by groups. Like Sort, Group By has a two-column limit. The criteria by which to group are standard. Choose the first column to group by and determine the sort order, and then choose the second column and its sort order. A nice thing about grouping is you can choose whether the groups are collapsed or expanded by default. (If a group is collapsed, a plus sign will appear next to the heading for the group. When you click it, the items in that group will be exposed.) For those huge lists, the number of groups to be displayed per page can be limited. The default is 100.

Totals   This is very much like the Total row in Datasheet view. You select the fields from which to calculate totals from those selected to display in the view. The data type for those columns will define what calculations can be done for the field. As we've seen, totals for those columns will be displayed at the top of the list, not the bottom.

Style   This section presents some limited formats available for the view. You can choose Basic, Boxed, Newsletter, Shaded, Preview Pane, or Default.

PREVIEW PANE IS UNIQUE

Preview Pane style is different from most of the others: it lists the title of the items on the left and leaves the majority of the content area in the middle of the page available to display the contents of a list item. Hover your mouse pointer over a list item title to display the contents of that item. The display will include only the fields that are set to be visible in the view, but it is pretty dramatic. It's an interesting way to display items in a contacts list, a glossary-type application, or any time you want to display more fields than can fit horizontally on the screen.

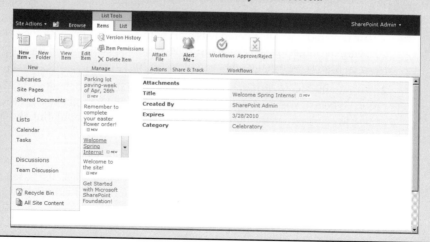

Folders If folders are used to organize items in a list, you can choose to make the view folder-aware and display only the items in the open folder. (Then, if you want to see items in a different folder, you will have to go to it to apply this view to them.) Otherwise, you can set the view to be *flat* or folder-unaware so that when the view is applied, it will display all items in the list that comply with its criteria, regardless of what folder they might be in. If list items are organized by folder in order to manage a large list, consider ensuring that the view is set to be folder aware, or show items inside folders, in order to continue to limit the number of items displayed in the view at one time.

Item Limit This section allows you to specify how many items can be displayed per page for the view, or even a cut-off limit for all items to be displayed in this view, period. The default is 100 items per page, with no cut-off limit.

Mobile If you'd like the view to be available for mobile devices, you can leave it enabled in this section (the default). Notice that it can be enabled only for Public views but can be made a default view for mobile access for the list, allowing you to create a view just for mobile users. You can also specify how many items will display per page (the default is three) and what field is displayed for each item as well.

SPEAKING OF MOBILE

If your mobile device uses DNS and can access the network the SharePoint server is on, it can easily access a pared-down version of the SharePoint web pages.

Now that we've seen our options, let's group our view by category and list the latest expiration date:

1. Name the list view. My example uses **GbCategory**. Remember to keep the name short but easy to remember; my example uses a view naming scheme. All of my Grouped By views are prefaced with *Gb*, filtered lists start with *Fb*, and so on, with the field that is the focus being the largest part of the name. The most important part of the naming process is to keep it short, so use the scheme that works for you.

2. Also in the Name section is the option to make this the default view for the list (instead of All Items). We won't do that in this example, but it might be a great idea if you are trying to cut down on the number of items automatically populating the content page of a list every time a user goes to that list.

3. For the audience, we are going to keep this a Public view.

4. For the columns, we are going to keep the ones already selected based on the All Items view (see Figure 6.26). They work for us at the moment. Remember, you can always modify a view later if you want to change it.

FIGURE 6.26

The Name, Audience, and Columns sections of the Create View page

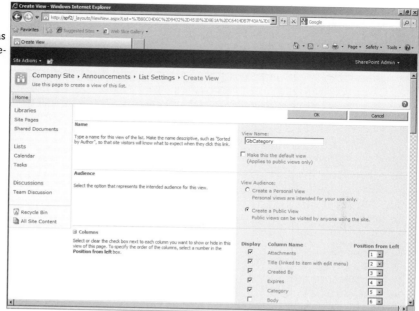

5. We are not going to sort or filter our view data, and we don't need to inline edit, but we are going to use Group By. Click the plus sign in the Group By section to expand it.

6. In the Group By section, in the First Group By the Column drop-down list, select Category. By default, groups are sorted in ascending order. That's fine in this example, so leave the default. At the end of the section are options to have the groups expanded or collapsed by default and the number of groups displayed per page. Let's keep the defaults of collapsed by default and the per page display of **30**.

7. Click the plus sign in the Totals section to expand it, and click the down arrow in the Total field next to Expires. Select Maximum from the calculations there (Figure 6.27). Notice that Average is supported only if the view is Datasheet. That's nice to know, but we're not using it for this view.

8. Expand the Style section, and choose Shaded. This will shade the background of every other row to help them stand out a little.

   There is no need to enforce an item limit on the list, because it's simply not that big. The list itself isn't organized by folder, and my example does not use any mobile devices to access the list. That means that after choosing the style for this view, we're done.

9. Click OK to create the new list view.

FIGURE 6.27
The Group By and
Totals sections

In Figure 6.28, you can see that the GbCategory view displays the categories collapsed, with the calculation (which is the maximum expires date) at the top right of the list, in the Expires column. Also notice, in the address bar, that the filename for the view is GbCategory.aspx.

FIGURE 6.28
The new
GbCategory view

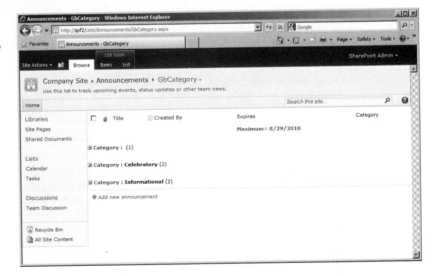

IT DOESN'T LOOK LIKE A DIFFERENT PAGE

Because the page header area and Quick Launch bar never change, you may think you are on the same page and that you have changed only the view of the data.

But look in the address bar as you switch views on a list. You'll see that you are going to a different page for each view. It's just that SharePoint has the header and Quick Launch bar as a common design theme for all content pages, which can be misleading. What is different between the pages is the view of the contents. That's why they're called *content pages*.

This becomes particularly important if you are adding web parts to a particular view of a list. When you change the view, the web parts disappear because they were on the other view's content page.

As for the categories, you might have noticed that there is a blank category (in which there is one item). To see what list item might be grouped by that category, click the plus sign next to the category heading to expand it.

In my example, the Get Started with Microsoft SharePoint Foundation! Announcement was generated as soon as the site was built before the Category field was added. Because of this, that list item has no category assigned (see Figure 6.29). This example is a good one if you ever need to search through a list of items to see whether there is any data missing in a field. Group by that field (sorting ascending), and the blanks will come out on top. Then you can edit them, adding the necessary data, until there are no more blanks.

FIGURE 6.29
The expanded empty Category group

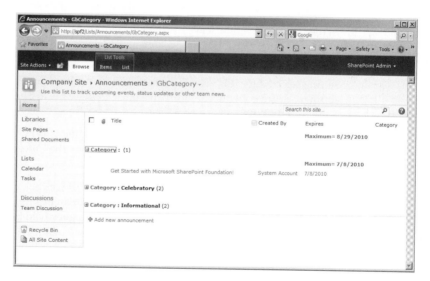

Another useful feature of this view, as you can see in Figure 6.29, is that a calculation is listed for each grouping as well. In my example, only the latest expiration dates for each category appear, but this can be useful for doing total profit or averages; in this case, we can scroll to the Emergency announcements, expand that group, and see the most recent expiration dates and the announcements that are still active.

Now that you've seen how easy it is to create a new Standard view and exploit some of the reporting power of that format, let's create another Standard view. Only this time, it will filter out all list items that don't match our criteria.

Creating a New View to Filter by Category

When you're in a list, you can search for a particular item. You can click the header of a column and try to sort items. However, the fastest way to isolate several items that have data in common is to use filtering. Remember, you can filter by as many columns as you'd like until you get your desired results. What's even better is that you can create a view to be used to filter a list's content display and simply modify it over and over as needed. It becomes less of a static view and more of an ad hoc one. Not only that, but filtering is one of the best-practice methods for opening and using very large lists.

Let's create a new Standard view to use as our filtering tool for the list:

1. Click the view name at the end of the title breadcrumb, and select Create View.

2. Then select Standard View on the Create View ➢ View Type page.

3. On the Create View ➢ View New page, name your view something short but memorable. My example uses MainFilter, and it is not the default view. Because we plan for it to be reconfigured as needed, it doesn't follow the Fb naming scheme mentioned earlier.

4. We could make this view private, but select the Public View option so other users can take advantage of it, if they know it's there, and have the permission to modify public views.

5. In the Columns section, leave the default columns selected. We can change this at any time by just modifying this view later.

6. Scroll down to the Filter section, where we are going to do our work. You can see that the setting selected for this view is currently Show All Items In This View. To apply the filter settings we are going to configure, we must change this to **Show Items Only When The Following Is True**.

7. Beneath that in the Filter section are the Show the Items When Column, Criteria, and Data fields. In this example, we are going to filter by the Category column, so select that in the first field.

8. The second field in the section is the Criteria field. If we click it, a list of possible criteria to filter the field by drops down (see Figure 6.30 for an example). In this case, we will choose Contains because we want to filter the Category field by its contents. For the Data or Argument field that the criteria are going to work against, type **info**. Informational is one of the Announcement categories, and using part of the word demonstrates that SharePoint doesn't require an exact match for this criterion.

   We could continue with other criteria and arguments by clicking the And or Or radio button and fill out the When Column information, which would indicate that you want to combine the filtering criteria of more than one set, and you could always add more. However, filtering by one argument in the Category field works in this case.

FIGURE 6.30
The Filter criteria
for a new view

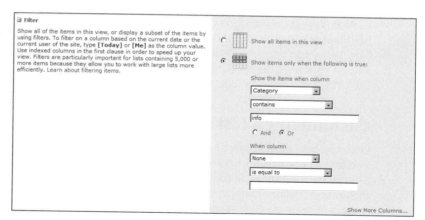

9. Click OK to create and apply the new view.

The view in my example isolates the two Informational items that were created earlier in the chapter and displays them exclusively, as shown in Figure 6.31.

FIGURE 6.31
The new
MainFilter
view

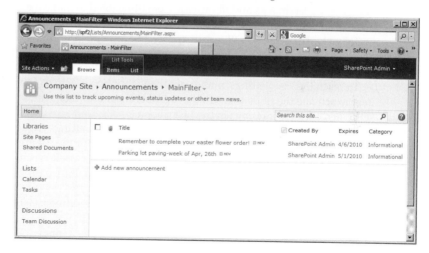

10. To turn off the view and see all items in the list, simply click the View menu at the end of the title breadcrumb (or click in the Current View menu in the List ribbon), and select the All Items view.

Keep your filter view in mind, and when you need to filter the list in any way, just go to the view and modify it to match your criteria. If you find yourself often using a particular set of filter criteria, just create a new filter view specifically for that. You should consider setting its audience to Personal, so no one else can see it or change it.

At this point, you've worked with announcements. You now have the list views the way you like them, you've rearranged the fields for better data entry, and you've added a category field. Now, more than ever, your announcements are useful. People will read them with renewed interest (or at least they will in this scenario; your mileage may vary). It's time to customize the list further, increasing both its usefulness and the control you can have over it.

Customizing a List

Once you have a list's columns the way you like them and you've created your views (both Public and Personal), it's time to expose the real backbone of your list: its settings.

Lists are more than just columns, data, and views. You can secure them independently of the site that contains them; you can even secure individual items differently from those around them. You can set versioning of the list items, in case someone edits data incorrectly (you won't lose the original data if you need to return to it). You can configure item management rights, set content approval, and allow incoming mail. Lists, particularly in this version of SharePoint, can be more complicated than you think.

One setting that greatly enhances the convenience of a list is Incoming Email. When this setting is enabled, users can simply email any announcement they need to make. In this version of SharePoint, certain lists and libraries are email-enabled to make it easier for users to add items to a list without having to open a browser or leave their email client.

To enable incoming email for a list, as well as other configuration settings, you must go to the list's List Settings page. Sure, you've been to the List Settings page before, but only to mess with columns and views—now it's time to look into the links at the top of the settings page.

To reach the List Settings, make sure the List ribbon is active (you may have to select a list item to activate the ribbon tabs in the top ribbon bar and then choose List in the List Tools toolset). Then click List Settings in the List ribbon.

In the List Information section at the top of the List Settings page for the Announcements list, you'll see that the name, web address, and description for the list are displayed. In Figure 6.32, note the address. The list is part of the path, but the page itself is actually the `AllItems.aspx` page. This is because that is the default view for this list. If incoming email has been configured, the email address will be listed as well.

Beneath the list information are the categories of list settings: General Settings, Permissions And Management, and Communications.

Under the General Settings category are the following items:

Title, Description And Navigation   This configuration page contains three fields: one for the name of the list so you can change it (it will not, however, change the name in the path of the web address), the description (to be edited as well), and the option to change whether this list is displayed in the Quick Launch bar.

Versioning Settings   This page has three sections: Content Approval, Item Version History, and Draft Item Security. With Content Approval, you can require approval for new and changed items before they are published as content. With Item Version History, you can keep a copy of a list item every time it is modified. With Draft Item Security, if you allow major and minor (draft) versions, you can limit who can see the draft versions until they are published as a major version. Versioning, especially the way it works with content approval, will be covered in much more detail in Chapter 8.

Advanced Settings   This is sort of a catchall page. There are sections for the following:

- Enabling content types for this list (more on those in Chapter 8)

- Setting item-level permissions

- Allowing attachments for list items (which is useful if you want to add a resume or other file to a list entry)

- Whether to enable folder organization for the list

- Whether to allow Search to return results for this list

New in SharePoint Foundation are the following advanced settings:

- Allowing list items to be downloaded for Offline Client. For Office integration and SharePoint Workspace, users can cache copies of selected lists or libraries for work offline.

- Allowing or denying Datasheet view for bulk data entry. Datasheet view can be disabled if you don't want bulk data entry to be allowed.

- Disable Dialogs. This causes the forms used for item view, new item, or edit item to be opened on a page instead of in a dialog box (which is the default behavior).

FIGURE 6.32
The List
Settings page
for the Announcements list

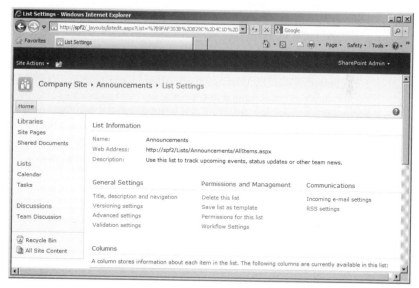

In the Permissions And Management category are links that either do something to the list or configure explicit accounts and permissions for it:

Delete This List   Click this link to go to a page that gives you the option to delete this list. Remember, lists are SharePoint objects; therefore, if you delete them, they will go to the SharePoint Recycle Bin for a while before actually being removed. If you want a list permanently deleted so it does not take up space on the site or the server's hard drive, you have to remove it from the SharePoint Recycle Bin as well.

Save List As Template   Basically, any list can be made into a template for later use. Making the perfect list can be time-consuming, and when you're done, you might want to back it up to use on a different site. By making a template of a list, you can ensure that the design (and optionally the list content) is not only saved but also easily available to be used anywhere else in the site collection. List templates are saved to the List Template Gallery on the top-level site. Templates are saved as `.stp` files and can be used to back up lists against catastrophe. (See Chapter 13, "Maintenance and Monitoring," for more about backing up and restoring.)

Permissions For This List   This link goes to a page listing the users and groups that have access to the site. Most lists inherit their permissions from their parent site. It's under this option that you can actually break inheritance and set up unique permissions for a list. Permissions are complex and are covered in detail in Chapter 12, "Users and Permissions," but suffice it to say you can specify what groups, and even what permission levels, are specifically allowed for this list from those available for the site collection. It's also here that, if you choose to work with unique permissions, you can decide whether a user can make an access request if they were refused access to something on the list.

Workflow Settings   This is an interesting configuration page. Out of the box, SharePoint Foundation has only one sample workflow (but you can make many more using SharePoint Designer or Visual Studio). The sample Three-State workflow that comes with SharePoint Foundation was actually designed to work with a type of list called Issue Tracking. It was meant to generate a Tasks list item when a new issue is created and a second task to review the first one.

Workflows are first added to a site like task-oriented templates that lay out a process in which a change of state in a list or a library item can trigger an email, alert, or new list item. A workflow is a flow of actions that continue the human process of working with documents, tasks, or data. A workflow template can be made available to lists on a site and then applied as an instance with a unique name and settings to a particular list (or library).

Workflows for lists are managed by the SharePoint Workflow Timer service and, therefore, do consume server resources to run. Keep that in mind when you are deciding to apply a workflow to a list.

BAD FIT, BUT STILL POSSIBLE

Ironically, the sample Three-State workflow does work for our Announcements list to a degree, because the workflow requires only a trigger field, which in this case needs to be a Choice field with three choices in it. Therefore, this list qualifies for the sample workflow.

However, the Three-State workflow was meant to create a Tasks list item (in a specified Tasks list on the site) when triggered by the selection of an item in a Choice field (such as New, Started, Completed). Then it will email the person to whom the task is assigned to let them know they have a new task and then create another task if the Choice field state changes again. We have no reason to add a list item to a Tasks list for an announcement, but the option is there if we need it. In the next chapter, we will create a list that's better suited to demonstrating the sample workflow.

Finally, in the Communications category are the following items:

Incoming E-mail Settings   Available only if incoming email is enabled in Central Administration first, this link takes you to the page where you can enable incoming email for the list. Not all list templates can support this feature. Incoming email means that you can send email to the list and have it parse the email's fields and apply them to existing fields in the list itself. The Announcements list has fields that easily map to email fields: Body, Subject, Created By, and Attachments. With incoming email enabled, users just need to know the email address of the list. Then they can email an announcement to the list, and it will be correctly managed and made into a list item.

Incoming email settings include enabling the incoming email, specifying the email address (actually, the incoming email domain portion of the address is configured in Central Administration for the entire farm, so only the specific alias for the list is set here), and whether to allow attachments, save the original email, or save email invitations to the list (should the list be invited to something, usually only done intentionally for discussion lists or announcements). You can also set whether the list applies its permissions to the received email items; the list can accept all email as a new item from anyone or accept it only from those allowed to contribute to the list. This helps avoid spam.

RSS Settings   All lists have an option to subscribe to an RSS feed by selecting View RSS Feed in the Actions drop-down menu. RSS feeds can be enabled or disabled at the Central Administration level for each web application. Then RSS can be further controlled at the site-collection level, at the site level, and even by list. RSS tends to be enabled by default and, at the list level, displays all the contents of an entry unless you set it to truncate the multiline text field (in this case that would be the Body field) to 256 characters. No more, no less. You can modify the title and description for the RSS feed for the list, or you can leave the default list name and description there. You can even change the image that shows by default if you'd like. If you do change the image, make it easy on yourself and put the image in the folder on the SharePoint server where all the images for the site reside:

```
%program files%\common files\microsoft shared\web server extensions\14\
template\images
```

Other settings specify what fields will display for the feed, as well as the item limits of maximum items to show in the feed (the default is 25) and maximum days to include an entry (the default is 7).

So, that's it for the List Settings page; you have the General Settings, Columns, and Views sections (and Content Types if they are enabled).

Now that you've had a quick overview of each link for the List Settings pages, let's configure the Announcements list.

Enabling Incoming Email

In Chapter 2 (or Chapter 3, if you did the complete installation), you learned how to configure the capability to offer incoming email at the list or library level for the farm in Central Administration. SharePoint's incoming email feature lets users simply email an item to a list or library, instead of having to open a browser, log in, browse to the list or library they want to work in, and then add an item or document. Being able to email something to a list or library is a real convenience. For details, see "Specifying a Different Domain Alias for Incoming Email" in Chapter 2, which provides behind-the-scenes additional information about configuring incoming email for the farm.

Only a few lists and libraries are set up with the correct event handlers so they can be configured to accept incoming email out of the box. Announcements, Calendar, Discussions, Document Library, Form Library, and Picture Library all can accept incoming email and turn them into list or library items. So, let's enable incoming email for the Announcements list and see how it's done.

Make certain that you are on the List Settings page for the Announcements list, and take the following steps:

1. In the Communications category, select Incoming Email Settings.

2. The Incoming E-mail Settings page that appears (see Figure 6.33) has five sections. In the first section, Incoming E-mail, select Yes to enable this feature. That enables you to type in the E-mail Address field.

FIGURE 6.33
The incoming email settings

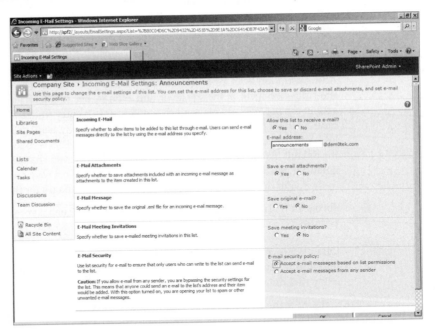

3. An email alias is required for the list to receive email. We'll use **announcements**; note that the domain will already be displayed.

4. In the second section, we will choose Yes to save attachments with the list item, in case someone has a photo, directions, or document they need to keep with the announcement item.

5. If you don't want to keep a copy of the email that has been sent to this list, set Save Original E-mail to No in the E-Mail Message section. If email is successfully converted into a list item, then you have a copy of its contents in the list already, and you are adding

to the size of the list in the content database by having each list item also keep a copy of its originating email as an attachment.

6. We'll leave E-Mail Meeting Invitations set to No.

7. The final setting is for the list's email security policy. The list can accept all email from anyone who gets the address right (bypassing the list's own security), or it can use the list's permission settings to block emails from people who don't have the right to contribute to the list. To help the list avoid being spammed, select Accept E-mail Messages Based On List Permissions.

8. Once you've completed configuring your settings for incoming email, click OK at the bottom of the page.

SOME INCOMING EMAIL CAVEATS

With Server 2008 R2, SMTP might need to be started manually (especially after a reboot), so before enabling incoming email, you might want to go to the IIS 6.0 console and make sure SMTP is running (even if you've configured it to automatically start in the Services console, it can be stopped).

Another possible issue is that the list can't know what SharePoint member's user account an email is coming from if that user doesn't have their email listed in their user information.

If you can't be sure all your users have their email listed in their user information and you still need to use incoming email for lists, you might want to consider accepting email *not* based on list permissions but instead just accepting email from any sender.

---

9. If you have an email client handy (and you are logged in as someone with permission to contribute to the list), you can send an email to the list using the new email alias you specified (see Figure 6.34). This will add a new item to the list via email.

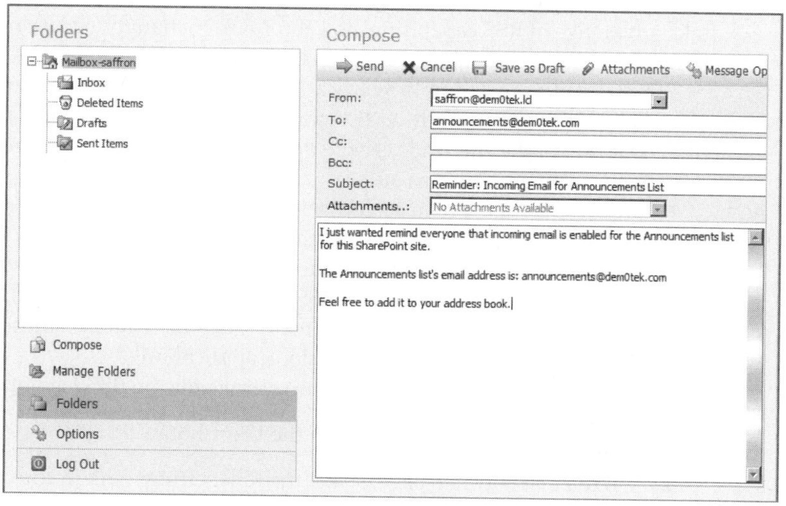

FIGURE 6.34
Email reminder being sent to the Announcements email alias

The SharePoint Timer job is in charge of checking the SMTP Drop folder every few minutes to gather email for SharePoint and then distributing it to the correct lists. Therefore, in a few minutes the email will appear in the Announcements list (Figure 6.35).

FIGURE 6.35
A new list item is created via incoming email.

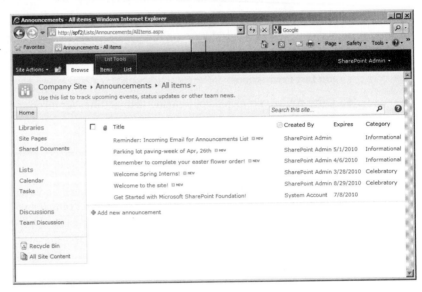

Now you know two ways to add items to a list: within the list itself or via email. It would also be good to know how a user can be alerted when something is added to the list. They could just check the web part on the home page every day, but to make it easier, lists and libraries come equipped with two ways for users to keep track of changes, *RSS feeds* and *alerts*.

Checking the RSS Feed Settings

Because SharePoint is accessed through the browser, it makes sense that a user would want to take advantage of RSS capabilities to keep track of changes occurring on their favorite lists or libraries.

RSS stands for Real Simple Syndication (or Rich Site Summary to some people). In SharePoint, RSS is essentially XML made up of channel tags that contain elements such as the title, URL link of the site, and website description, as well as elements for each item and their optional subelements such as author, category, and comments.

RSS readers are used to keep contact with RSS feeds to which the user has subscribed (Internet Explorer has an RSS reader feature). They regularly check for changes by doing regular updates, although some browsers don't perform updates effectively and force the user to update manually. Subscribing to an RSS feed for a list allows one to be alerted when there is a change to the list without having to directly visit the list to see those changes. Updates can also be received directly into the user's Outlook application.

Take the following steps to check the settings for the RSS feed of the Announcements list:

1. Click the List Settings button in the List ribbon.

2. On the List Settings page, select the RSS settings link in the Communications category.

On the Modify RSS Settings page, as you'll see in Figure 6.36, RSS is already allowed for the list by default (because it is on by default in the site collection).

FIGURE 6.36

The RSS settings

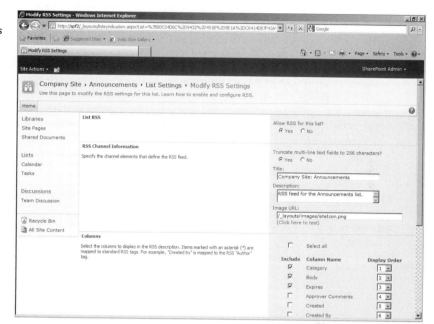

In the RSS Channel Information section of the page, you can see the title, the description, and even an image you can specify for the feed. You can truncate longer multiple-line fields to 256 characters, and the person reading the feed can click the link for the item to read its full contents.

3. To follow my example, leave the defaults for the RSS channel as they are, except for one: enable truncation for the longer fields (such as the Body field of an announcement). That makes it easier to skim down an RSS feed while looking for relevant items.

4. All the columns available to be displayed from the Announcements list are in the Columns section. My example leaves the defaults fields as they are.

5. In the Item Limits section, let's leave the defaults. The maximum number of entries displayed on the feed page is **25**, and it displays those items that have changed in the past seven days.

6. At the bottom of the page, you could click the Default button to reset the default values for the RSS settings. However, because we made a change (truncating multiline fields) that we want to keep, click OK to commit the settings and go back to the List Settings page.

To actually subscribe to an RSS feed for a list, you first need to go back to the List content page (click Announcements in the title breadcrumb at the top of the List Settings page). Then, while on the list, click the RSS Feed button in the List ribbon.

That will take you to the RSS Feed page for the list. The RSS Feed page lists the items in the list. An area at the top of the page describes the page and gives you a link to subscribe to the feed. On the right is the area that gives you a search field to search within the feed page, as well as a way to sort the items by author, date, or title.

To subscribe to the feed, click the Subscribe to this feed link in the yellow area at the top of the RSS Feed page (see Figure 6.37).

When you subscribe to a feed in Internet Explorer 7.0 or higher, the browser picks up on the subscription and gives you an opportunity to check your feeds by going to the Favorites Center (click the yellow star on the top left of the browser window or use the menu). Also, when you add a feed, you can be prompted to add it to your favorites bar at the top of the page for easy use (you can refresh the feed by just right-clicking and choosing Refresh). Each kind of browser handles RSS feeds differently, so your performance may vary. Remember that the feed needs to be checked occasionally; therefore, if your computer is offline for a while, your feeds will likely be out of sync—remember to refresh in that case.

FIGURE 6.37
The RSS feed for the Announcements list

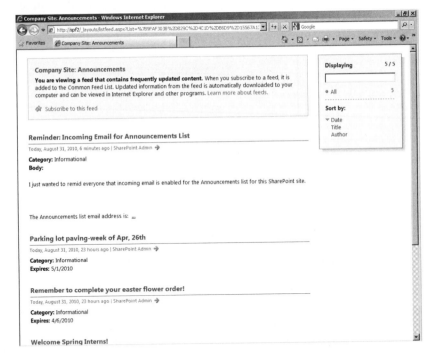

Setting Alerts

Another way to keep up with changes made to a list is to set email alerts. User alerts initially are set and managed at the web application level and are limited web-application-wide, not by site or site collection. They can also be completely disabled at that level. (Although alerts will most often be implemented directly by your users, as an administrator, you may be responsible for providing basic instructions for this and similar customization features; this section will help you do that.)

Unlike RSS feeds, alerts actively notify the user by email when there is a change made to a list item. The user can decide what kind of change can trigger the alert, to a certain degree, and control when the alerts are sent, from immediately to once a week. SharePoint actively sends the user an email when the notification is triggered, which means more resources are used than the more passive RSS feeds. However, setting alerts does mean that the user will be more likely to notice any changes than with RSS, which requires opening the browser or feed reader to see the update. Another plus is that a user can set an alert for someone else so that person can be informed when a new item or changes to an item might involve them.

LIMIT YOUR ALERTS

Alerts are managed by the SharePoint Timer service and do take some processor effort to generate and track. For this reason, it is common practice to limit the number of alerts that a user can have going at any one time. This setting is configured at the web application level (Central Administration ➤ Application Management ➤ Manage Web Applications ➤ General Settings, in the Alerts section). The default maximum is 500. But commonly that number is changed to something far lower, particularly if you are using multiple web applications for your sites.

Regardless, keep that limit in mind before teaching your users to go alert-crazy. It may be better for them to subscribe to an RSS feed on a list to track changes instead.

For the Announcements list, it would be good to have an alert set up for the list overall. There are three ways to set up an alert: in the drop-down list for an item, in the ribbon for the list (or library, if that's where you are), or in the Items ribbon for a selected item. In our case, I am going to focus on changes to the list overall (also, creating an alert from the List ribbon gives you a few more, redundant, options). Keep in mind that because the Alert Me button on either an Items or List ribbon looks the same and is in a similar place, it's easy to set an alert on the wrong ribbon.

1. To enable an alert on a list, make sure you're on the List ribbon, click the Alert Me button, and then select Set Alert On This List.

2. On the New Alert page that appears, the first section gives you a chance to give a more descriptive name for the alert. The default title for the alert is the list name (or list item) from which it stems. For now, let's keep that title.

3. In the Send Alerts To section (at the top of Figure 6.38), the default email address is fine, since I'm setting it for myself. You can see that you are allowed to enter not only someone else's email address but also as many other people's email addresses as you like. Use semicolons to separate them.

   Be careful. Alerts can keep the SharePoint Timer service very busy. Teach users to limit alerts to only those lists that are the most important to them. The desire to alert *other people* might overcome their caution, however, particularly if they know that everyone is limited in the number of alerts they are allowed. Encourage them to keep the number of alerts they set for *anyone* to a minimum.

   Also note that, if SMS is set up in Central Administration and the user account has a mobile phone number listed, alerts can be sent as SMS text messages instead of email.

There are basically two change triggers (or a combination of both) that can cause an alert to be sent:

FIGURE 6.38
The New Alert page

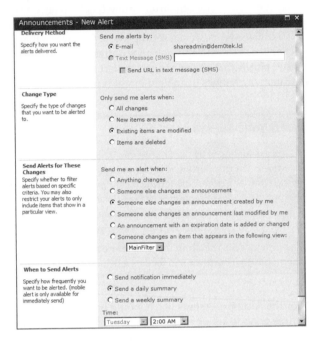

Change Type   This section is available if the alert is set for the list; list items don't have this section. If an item in the list changes in a certain way, a notification will be sent. These notifications can be triggered by any changes in the list, when a new item is added, when existing items are modified, or when an item or items are deleted. (That last one is good for administrators.)

Send Alerts For These Changes   This trigger uses more specific criteria to launch a notification; if anything changes on the list, someone else changes an announcement, someone else changes an announcement created by you, someone else changes an announcement last modified by you, an announcement with an expiration date is added or changed (unique to the Announcements list because it refers to expiration), or changes are made to an item when in a particular view (this option is available only if you have views that do filtering).

All Changes and Anything Changes are the default trigger settings for an alert. In other words, if you keep the default Change Type and Send Alerts For These Changes, then any change that is made to any item will cause an email to be sent.

4. In my example, I am going to set the Change Type to **Existing Items Are Modified**. Set Send Alerts For These Changes to filter those modifications down to **When Someone Else Changes An Announcement Created By Me**.

The settings for scheduling when email notifications based on the criteria will be sent are in the When To Send Alerts section of the alert settings. The options are as follows:

◆ Immediately

◆ Send In A Daily Summary

◆ Send In A Weekly Summary

You can set up an exact day and time of the week for the weekly option and an exact time of day for the daily option. Immediate alert emails send a separate email for every single alert. Daily and weekly alerts summarize all changes (based on the alert criteria) for that length of time.

5. Set the schedule for this alert to a daily summary. When you select Send A Daily Summary, the Time field below the setting will become available to choose the time the summary will be sent. For this example, choose **2 a.m.** (it's always a good idea to schedule alerts for slow periods of activity on the server).

If the alert you are setting up is simply informational, a weekly summary might work for you. I tend to go for a daily summary for most of my alerts, under the assumption that I need to know quickly what's going on but am going to be so busy, day to day, that I'll have only a short time to get to alerts once a day. Use your best judgment when it comes to scheduling alerts. Try to balance the need to know about changes immediately with the need not to unnecessarily tie up the SharePoint Timer service with sending out too many alerts.

6. When you've finished with your settings, click OK to finish configuring the new alert.

See Figure 6.39 for an example of a daily summary email that a user would receive.

FIGURE 6.39
Daily summary email alert

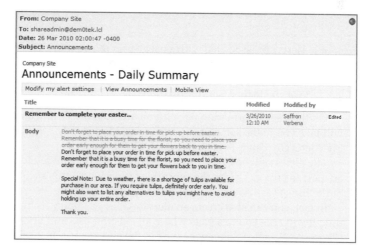

As the weeks pass, you may forget exactly how you set up your alert for this list. What if you want to make a change? What if you want to delete the alert because you don't need it anymore? How do you bring up the alerts you've created?

It's easy. There are several ways to access a user's alerts. The two most convenient ways are as follows:

◆ From the Alert Me button drop-down menu. Originally we chose to set an alert on the list, but the other option in that menu was Manage My Alerts (Figure 6.40).

FIGURE 6.40
Alert Me menu,
Manage My Alerts

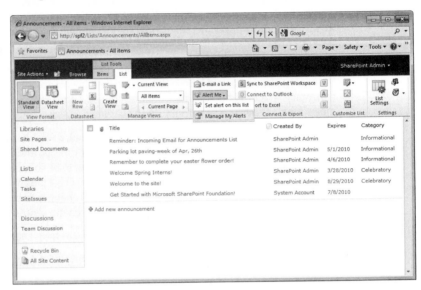

◆ Alerts are associated with a user's user information. Once logged in to an account, you can go to your account's user information directly by clicking the Account menu at the top of any page of the site in the site collection. In the drop-down, select My Settings. This will take you to the User Information page (Figure 6.41).

On the User Information page for an account, the Action bar contains a link to My Alerts; it will take you to the same page as choosing Manage My Alerts under the Alert Me button on the My Alerts On This Site page (Figure 6.42).

The alerts will be organized by frequency. You can delete a selected alert here or just click an alert to edit it. This is the central location for all this account's alerts for the site, regardless of the list.

In fact, you can also create an alert for a list or library from here. Simply click the Add Alert link. It will take you to a page where all existing lists and libraries for the site are displayed (Figure 6.43), called `Subchoos.aspx` in the address bar. Just select the radio button next to the list or library for which you'd like to create an alert, and click Next at the bottom of the page. You will be taken to a New Alert page for that list or library (called `Subnew.aspx` in the address bar), where you can configure an alert.

FIGURE 6.41
The User Information page, My Alerts

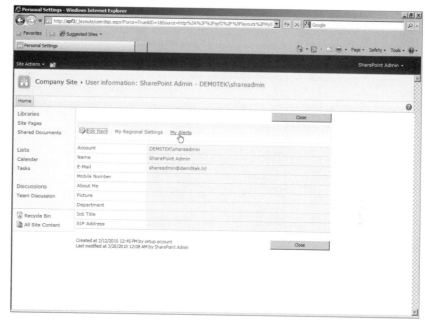

FIGURE 6.42
The My Alerts On This Site page

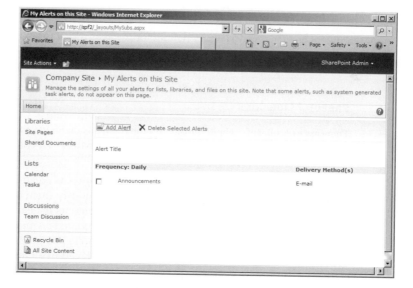

In addition, as an administrator, you can delete users' alerts if necessary by going to Site Actions, then going to Site Settings, and choosing User Alerts in the Site Administration section.

So, you now know how to work with lists in SharePoint. You've seen how to add a list item individually and in bulk using Datasheet view. You've added fields to a list, created new views, enabled incoming email for a list, configured RSS, and created an alert. Now that you have the fundamentals of lists down, it's time to explore the other lists that are available on the Team Site.

FIGURE 6.43
The New Alert page
for the whole site

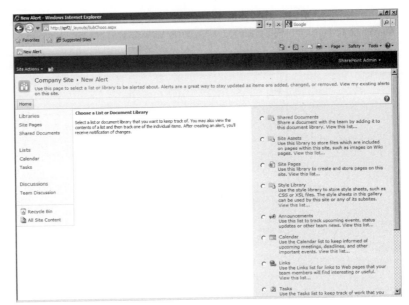

Exploring Prebuilt Lists

SharePoint creates several lists by default for the Team Site template. These lists are each useful in their own right and also demonstrate the flexibility of lists. The lists are basically there to
teach you how to exploit these capabilities and encourage you to use them on their own.

PREBUILT LIBRARIES

There are a number of prebuilt libraries for the Team Site in this version of SharePoint as well. Those
libraries, and the reasons SharePoint provides them, will be covered in Chapter 8.

Each list that is prebuilt for the Team Site template was created from a list template. You
can use that template to create your own lists and modify them to suit yourself. You can also
modify prebuilt lists as you did with the Announcements list earlier in the chapter.

One of the preexisting lists for the Team Site template is Announcements. You're familiar
with the simple items for this list. The Announcements list, practically more than any other
(except maybe the Links list), was meant to be displayed in a List View web part. The special
field, or trait, for this list is the Expires field. Even though it is nothing more than a date field,
the web part for this list uses a view that filters the items to display so that only items that
have not expired will be shown in the List View web part.

To get the most out of those prebuilt lists, we should explore them to see what they are
about: Calendar, Links, Task, and Team Discussion.

Calendar

The Calendar list is an Events list where the default Public view is a Calendar view that organizes events not by title but by date in a calendar layout. Also, this list has a few calendar-

specific fields, such as All Day Event and Recurrence. This list also specifically integrates with Outlook (preferably 2007 or higher). Because this list has to do with dates and meetings are often scheduled this way, list items for this list can be used to create new meeting workspace subsites beneath this site. Users cannot use this feature unless they have the right to create subsites (note that SharePoint doesn't stop them from trying to use the option, but it will fail to do anything).

Often businesses can require (or end up with) more than one calendar on their SharePoint sites. This can cause confusion, because users must remember in which calendar they put an event. To combat this (and to at least appear to have the capability that most calendaring products have), this version of SharePoint introduces *calendar overlays*. With this feature, a single calendar can now host the schedule of other calendars on the site. You can actually pull data from calendars in other site collections. However, if the users don't have access to those other calendars or site collections, they will see the overlay listed but not the events they contain.

In addition, calendars can also be created to support *group calendaring*, which adds two views to a calendar so you can do comparisons between the schedules of two users who have events on the calendar. This option is meant to be a quick check, and therefore the user accounts you added to the view to compare don't persist after you leave the page.

To access the Calendar list, click the Calendar link on the Quick Launch bar (usually on the left side of whatever page you're using), or select Calendar from the lists on the All Site content page for the site.

By default, the content page is in Calendar view (Figure 6.44). Notice that on the top left of the window, above the Quick Launch bar, is a mini calendar in Year view, with a link below so you can get back to today's date in the view easily. The area below that displays what calendars are in the view; in this example, we haven't added any, so it shows only one. In the top link bar is the Calendar Tools toolset, with Events and Calendar tabs (essentially Items and List tabs for a calendar).

FIGURE 6.44

The Calendar list in Calendar view

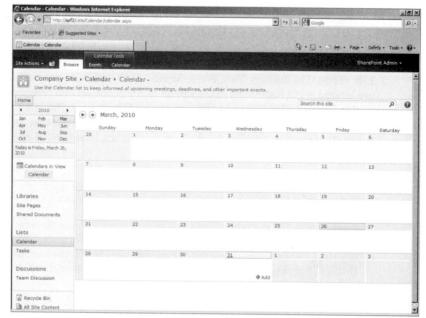

REALLY JUST AN EVENTS LIST

If you click View menu in the title breadcrumb, you'll see that there are views for All Events and Current Events. Because this is really an Events list, these views are not a surprise. If you select the Event view, you'll find that it is the Standard view for the list.

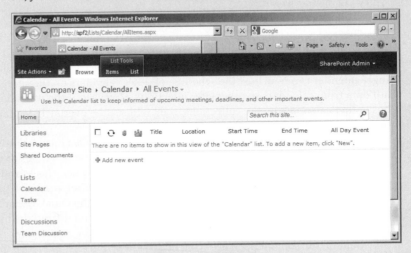

Notice that the toolset in the top ribbon bar changes back to List Tools and that the column headers are Title, Location, Start Time, End Time, and All Day Events (for those items that are flagged as All Day). There are also columns for Recurrence, whether the item has an attachment (such as directions or itinerary), or whether it is associated with a meeting workspace.

You may have noticed that there is no means to change the Calendar view to display dates by day, week, or month. This is because the option to do so has been moved to the Calendar ribbon (rather than being a static part of the display). If you click the Calendar tab in the Calendar Tools toolset in the top ribbon bar, you can see that, aside from the first few sections, it is basically a List ribbon. The buttons (Day, Week, Month) to change how the dates in the calendar are viewed are located at the beginning of the ribbon in the Scope section (Figure 6.45).

Because calendar items can stack up in the date squares, the calendar might show three or four and then have an indicator that there are more events but they are collapsed. To expand to see all of them or collapse events so only a few are listed on a date, use the buttons in the Expand section of the Calendar ribbon.

THE CONVENIENCE OF ADDING AN EVENT IN CALENDAR VIEW

If you want to add an event while in Calendar view, you can use the New Event button in the Events ribbon. But more easily, you can simply double-click the date for the event, opening a New Event box, or you can move your mouse pointer over the date box and click the Add link that will show up. Another trick is to first drag across and select several date boxes and then click Add to get a date range.

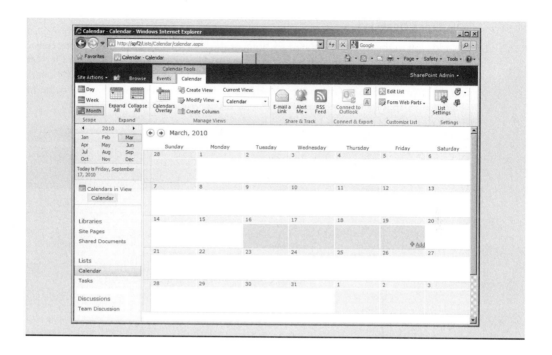

FIGURE 6.45
The Calendar
ribbon

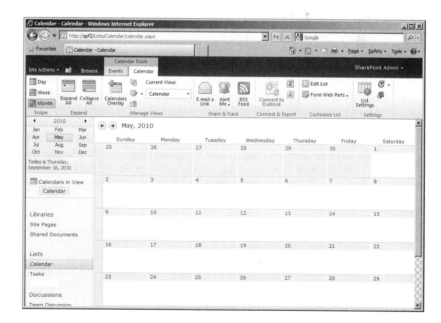

CALENDAR OVERLAYS

In addition to the calendar-related sections of the Calendar ribbon, there is one new button in the Manage Views section that adds functionality to the calendar—Calendar Overlay.

Clicking this button takes you to a page to see the list of additional calendar overlays you might have added to the calendar already, as well as the option to add a new calendar. Note, in Figure 6.46, that there is a limit of ten calendars per view.

FIGURE 6.46

Calendar Overlay Settings page

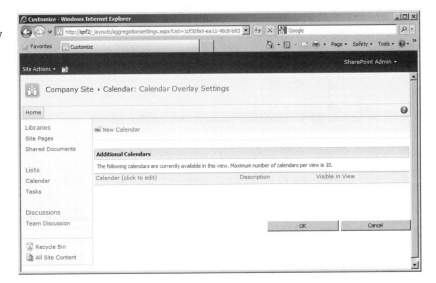

Right now, there are no additional calendars. We won't walk through creating a new calendar right now, although calendar overlay does require another calendar to already exist on the site. But because this is a new feature in SharePoint Foundation, I will walk you through the calendar overlay settings page and show you an example calendar I've created.

If you had a calendar to add, you can click the New Calendar link at the top of the content area. Interestingly, it will take you to a Customize Calendar page, rather than a pop-up box. This page has two sections: Name And Type and Calendar Overlay Settings.

In Name And Type are fields for the name of the calendar overlay (of course) and what type of data the calendar overlay is going to pull from. Right now the only options are SharePoint or Exchange calendars.

EXCHANGE CALENDAR OVERLAY

To use a calendar overlay from Exchange, the calendar requires the Outlook Web Access (OWA) URL and then the actual URL for the Exchange calendar rather than a simple URL of a SharePoint site (such as http://spf2).

The settings for the Calendar Overlay Settings section are more numerous and complex (Figure 6.47). Here's a quick rundown:

Description   This allows you to add a description to the overlay, so when you move your mouse pointer over an event related to this overlay in the calendar, this description will display, indicating which calendar the event stems from.

Color   You have a limited number of color options to choose from (oddly, fewer colors than the number of calendars allowed). Using the default site theme, the options are Light Yellow, Light Green, Orange, Light Turquoise, Pink, Light Blue, two different shades of Ice Blue, and White. The colors available depend upon the theme applied to the site.

Web URL   This field is used to indicate the URL of the site where the calendar you want to overlay is located. When you click the Resolve button, this field will try to resolve to a site and then populate the next two fields with data.

List   This actually doesn't display the lists, but rather the *calendars* at the site to which the above URL resolved. Use this field to select the calendar you want to use for the overlay. You could use calendars from any other site in the collection, or even other site collections, just make sure that the users have permission to see those other calendars.

List View   Use this field to select the view to use for the calendar overlay, if the calendar selected for the List has alternate views. This is very useful if there are filtered views.

Always Show   A site member viewing the calendar in a Public view (such as the default Calendar view) can't edit the overlay settings directly. But on the Calendar Overlay page, they can choose via check box to show or not show an overlay. However, you can set an overlay to always show, blocking members from being able to stop showing an overlay in the view.

See Figure 6.48 for the example overlay I created (my overlay events are yellow, with a green event for the primary calendar for comparison). The overlay itself is listed in the Calendars In View list on the left side of the page.

Another consideration is that a calendar overlay actually adds a calendar's events to the view of a different calendar, aggregating events from several different calendars into one. Since calendars are just event lists with a calendar type view, you can create additional views for them. And when you do, the new view (if you make it as a calendar type) can have other overlays than the default view that everyone uses.

This also means that if you add a calendar web part to a page somewhere, the overlays you set on the calendar when on its content page (usually in the default view content page itself) will not show up in the web part, only the calendar's own events. This lets you choose different overlays and overlay colors for the calendar when viewed on different pages (this works for different views on the calendar itself as well).

If you want to have more than ten calendar overlays for a calendar, don't despair. Since the limit is per view, create several Calendar views for a calendar, and add the extra overlays there.

Further, because overlays are applied not just from other calendars but from *views* of those other calendars, you can create some filtered views by category (for example) on a calendar and then create overlays, not just of that calendar's data but of that calendar's *filtered* data, so you can see events specifically organized by a category, location, or whatever.

FIGURE 6.47
The Customize
Calendar page's
overlay settings

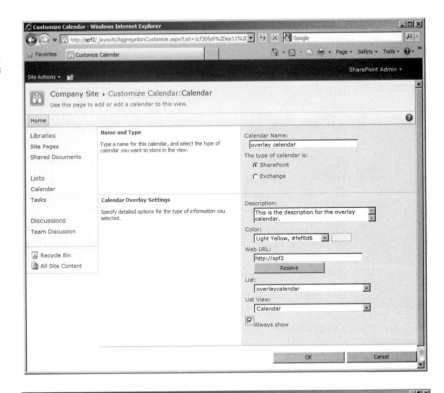

FIGURE 6.47
The Customize
Calendar page's
overlay settings

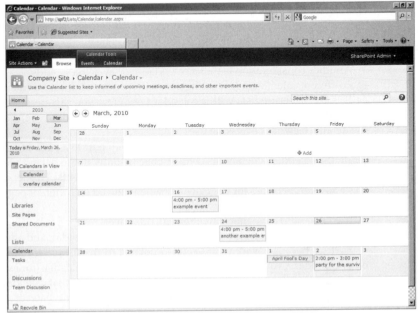

FIGURE 6.48
Calendar view
with new overlay

Real World Scenario

COMPARING THE WEEK

There is another calendar feature that you can use only if you enable it during the calendar's creation, and that's Group Calendar Option.

If you enable that option, it will add two new buttons to the calendar's Calendar ribbon, Day Group and Week Group.

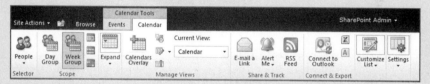

The buttons allow you to view the calendar in a strange, quasi-Gantt view. It shows your personal schedule (if you've added it here), one week at a time, and it has a field to add another user.

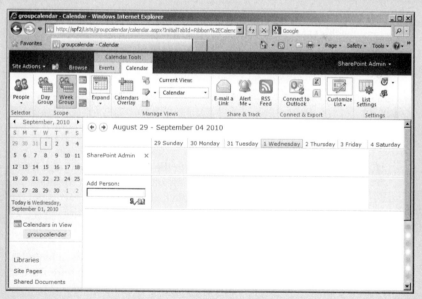

When you are looking at the schedule for several people, it is easy to create an event with them invited already. With the Group Calendar option enabled, a Free/Busy field appears, showing you the invited users' schedules in that calendar.

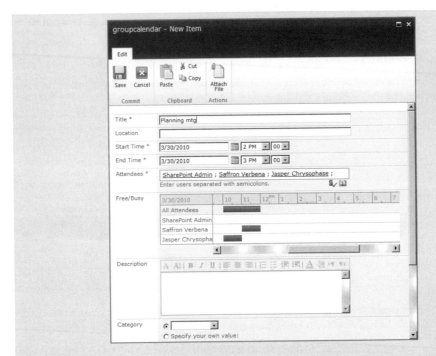

I assume this view exists to allow users to add someone to a calendar quickly, to see whether they have anything scheduled for that week, and to be able to add an event to the calendar with both of you attending.

Links

Like Announcements, this simple list was specifically created to be displayed in a web part. It demonstrates the use of a hyperlink field.

1. To get to the Links list, you can go to the All Site Content page from the Quick Launch bar (Links List View web part was meant to be used on the home page, but when it's a wiki page, as in the Team Site template, the Links web part is not there).

2. Once you are on the content page for Links, click New Item in the Items ribbon, or click Add New Link in the content area to create a new item.

   You can see in Figure 6.49 that there are only a few fields: a hyperlink field (with a link to click to test the URL to make sure it works), a description for the URL, and a multiple-line field for notes about the link.

3. You can enter a hyperlink, description of the URL, and notes (see Figure 6.50 for my example). If you click OK, the item will appear in the list's content page.

   This list doesn't have fancy views or a lot of fields. It was meant to be a utility to add more interaction on the home page (although the Items ribbon does have a Change Order button, since the order in which links are displayed in a web part can be important). The items in this list were meant to be displayed in a web part so the users don't have to go to the list directly.

Now, if there were a Links web part on the home page (or wherever you put it), it would display the new link for use.

FIGURE 6.49

A New Links page

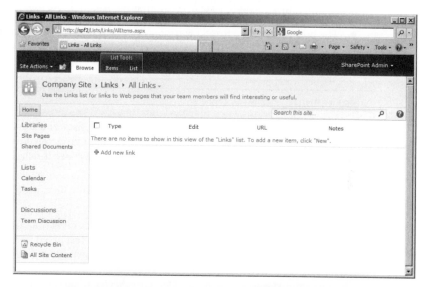

FIGURE 6.50

Links – New Item form

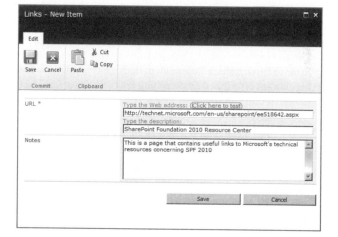

LINKS AREN'T JUST FOR WEB PAGES

A hyperlink field is actually just a *path field,* a field that will hold a path or address that, when selected in the web part, will open whatever is at the end of that path. That's why the field is often called Hyperlink or Picture field.

This means that the hyperlink field for a Links item does not have to be a web address. It can be a path to a document or image in a public share, or even a folder if all users have access to it. Hyperlink fields are not something to be ignored. Get creative. Imagine what you could offer your users with a link on the home page.

Team Discussion

All collaborative sites should have at least one discussion forum. The Discussion list demonstrates SharePoint's *content type* feature, in that the list contains two different types of list items:

- The post that starts a thread, variously referred to as a *post, thread, topic, subject,* or *discussion*
- Replies

SHAREPOINT, THE NEW GREEN

SharePoint is all about recycling. It has templates of sites, lists, and libraries so you can reuse them. If you create or customize a list to perfection, SharePoint gives you the option to make a template of it for the site collection, so you can reuse it too. No effort needs to be duplicated there.

In fact, if you create a field for a list that is ideal and you know that you will want to format a field just like it for a different list, you can make it a site column first, which is sort of a template for a field, so you can apply its formatting to other lists.

Given SharePoint's proven interest in recycling, it stands to reason that SharePoint also goes one step further and has content types. Content types are a sort of list item template and can be created from list items that you really like: create a list, which will have a list item (which you know is a record in that list's underlying table) with all the fields, or metadata, that you want. If it really works for you and you can see the need for it in other lists, you can then go to the Site Content Types page to create that list item as a content type and use that content type in other lists. You can create a new list, enable content types, choose the list item you want to use for that list, and never have to re-create any of those fields.

Content types are usually based on an existing base content type (like the Item content type for all lists, which contains a Title field, period). So to create your favorite content type, just pick the existing content type that suits what you are trying to create, add some of those premade site columns to flesh it out, and you have your own custom list item.

Hence, you can create a list that contains the list items from several other lists in it, such as a sales quote, sales order, and bill of sale all in one list. You can create custom content type list items, document library items, or folders for your new lists if you desire.

I will be covering content types as they relate to document libraries in Chapter 8.

So, SharePoint recycles lists, libraries, and sites with templates. It has a Recycle Bin (or two) to protect the accidental deletion of items. It even allows the recycling of well-made list items with content types and useful fields with site columns. That's SharePoint, very effort-conscious.

I suggest you experiment with content types to see how they might improve your lists for your organization.

Most lists and libraries have one kind of content. In a list's case, this means that an Announcements list has one kind of item, an announcement. Link lists have one kind of item, a link, and so on.

Beginning with the previous version of SharePoint, when you create a list or library, you can use more than one content type. This gives you considerable flexibility when making complex lists. Each content type has its own fields and can even have its own workflows associated with it. There is even a unique content type for folders, so their contents can automatically inherit certain fields and traits.

EXPLORING THE DISCUSSION CONTENT TYPES

If you go to the list settings of the Team Discussion list (via the List Settings button on the List ribbon), you would see on the List Settings page that content types are enabled, because there is a Content Type section, and that there are two content types shown, Discussion and Message.

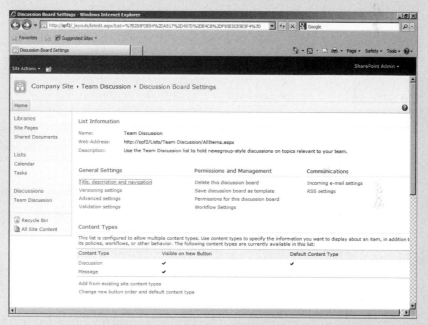

You can also tell that the Discussion content type is the default; it appears at the top of the New Item drop-down and is the one triggered if a user simply clicks the New Item button.

The base content type for the Discussion list is a folder. You can see this by clicking Discussion in the Content Types list and following its parentage up (it can be a child of a child of a parent content type) to the original folder.

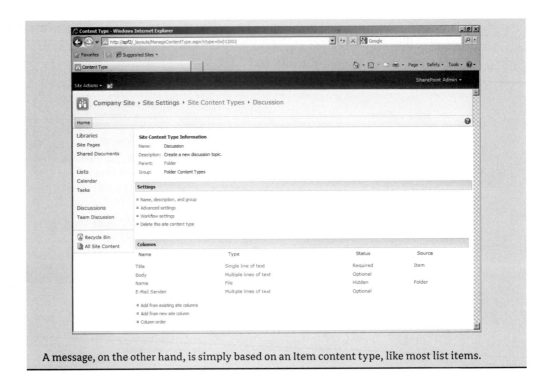

A message, on the other hand, is simply based on an Item content type, like most list items.

To use the Team site's Discussion list, just click the Team Discussion list in the Quick Launch bar.

1. To add a new discussion item, click Add New Discussion, or click the New Item button on the Items tab of the List Tools ribbon.

2. The first discussion item in this example is going to be a welcome message (see Figure 6.51). Notice that the body field is an enhanced content field; you can format the text and insert tables, images, and so. After adding text to the Subject and Body fields, just click Save to create your new discussion item.

Back at the Team Discussion list, you will notice that the discussion item looks pretty standard for a list item: Subject, Created By, and Last Updated fields, as well as a Reply field showing the number of replies the discussion has had.

1. To reply to a discussion, you first need to view it by clicking the item's Title field or by selecting View Item in the drop-down menu at the end of the title column. Strangely, Reply is not an option on the drop-down menu.

2. Once you are viewing that item's contents, click the Reply button on the far right of the bar at the top of the topic (Figure 6.52).

3. To reply, simply enter some text in the Body field. Note that there is no Subject field because it is simply a reply to the subject of the discussion topic. When you are done adding text to your reply, click Save to finish.

FIGURE 6.51
A new discussion item

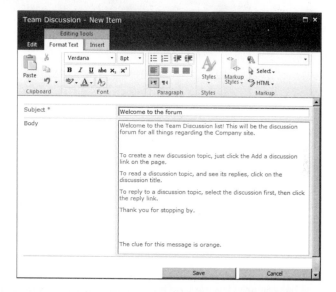

FIGURE 6.52
View a discussion item to make a reply.

Once you are done, you'll be back on the discussion page. Notice that there is now a reply beneath the original topic (Figure 6.53).

FIGURE 6.53
Discussion with
Reply

What you are viewing here is different from most View Item pages, because the discussion item is really a folder content type, which contains the reply items. Therefore, when you click View Item from the drop-down menu for a discussion item, it shows you the discussion's metadata or *properties*. But if you actually click the discussion's subject (which is usually a link to view an item), it opens the discussion folder and shows you the items it contains. In this case, the discussion folder will show some of the fields of its properties (these were added to the default view of the folder to give context to the replies) and the discussion's replies. As you can see in Figure 6.53, both the discussion topic and the reply are displayed, but you can still view the properties of either item by clicking their View Properties link.

While you are viewing the discussion and can see the reply, notice that the view is Flat in the View menu. There is also a Threaded view, which indents the replies so you can see whether someone is replying to a reply or to the original discussion.

Tasks

A Tasks list actually has several nifty traits. Task items demonstrate Choice fields, the People And Groups field, a multiple-selection lookup field, two date fields (to create a start and end range), and a folder-based content type (like the Discussion list), in addition to the standard Task item.

To get to the prebuilt Tasks list on a Team Site, click the Tasks link under the Lists heading in the Quick Launch bar. This list can create two kinds of tasks for this version of SharePoint: a Task item and now a Summary Task item.

Generally, whenever a list has more than one type of type of list item, or *content type*, the New button in the ribbon has a down arrow showing the types, so you can select which one you want to create. The top item in that drop-down is usually the default item for the list (although that can be changed). In our case, the standard Task item is the default.

A Task item is simply a list item, with useful fields relating to a task. A Summary Task item is actually a folder, with the same fields as a normal task item, designed so that tasks for a large project can be organized in some way, for example by milestones.

1. To create a new task, you can click Add A New Item. The New Item box displays all kinds of interesting fields:

Title   This is the only required field. A Title field is standard for most lists. The first field created by default is the Title field, and because it's required, it cannot be deleted.

Predecessors   New to this version of SharePoint, this is a simple lookup field set to allow multiple selections. It allows you to choose which items, among the tasks in the list, should be done before this one. This field doesn't just let you select one value; it lets you select multiple tasks in this list to precede this one.

This field seems cool, but bear in mind that this predecessor thing is primitive—there is no mechanism to enforce the fact that the tasks you choose should be predecessors. However, predecessors will be indicated within a Gantt chart view of a Tasks list.

Priority   This is a Choice field with three options: High, Normal, and Low.

Status   This is a Choice field with five options, ranging from Not Started to Waiting On Someone Else.

% Complete   This field is a number field formatted to be displayed in percentage value.

Assigned To   This setting uses the People And Groups field and is essentially a lookup field to the People And Groups list for the site (as well as anyone in Active Directory in most cases). It is considered a People Picker field (yes, that's its name) that you use to type in the name of the person or group the task is assigned to. You can enter a username (the user's Active Directory account, not their full name) and check it with the Check Names button, or you can use the Browse button and actually browse the Active Directory users for the domain. This means that you can assign a task to someone who isn't a member of the site. In addition, you can assign tasks to SharePoint groups or even security groups in Active Directory rather than a single person. You cannot assign a task to two or more users in this field, however. Only one user or group is allowed to be used with this type of People Picker field.

ASSIGNING TASKS TO NON-SHAREPOINT USERS

If you don't want users to be able to assign tasks to someone who doesn't have an account in SharePoint, check out Chapter 14, "STSADM and PowerShell," to learn more about using the `setproperty` operation and the property name of `peoplepicker-onlysearchwithinsitecollections`.

Description   This field is a rich-text multiple-line field.

Start Date   This is a standard date field.

Due Date   This is also a standard date field. However, if you fill in both the start and due dates of a task, you can then create a Gantt view to track the task's progress (or you can create a Calendar view to do the same thing if you prefer).

Figure 6.54 illustrates a sample Tasks item. Notice that the task will automatically email the accounts in the Assigned to field if they have an email address in their user information.

2. Feel free to fill the fields with a start date and due date within the next several days. There are no preceding tasks, since this is the first, so you cannot select one yet. I am going to assign the task to the account I am logged in with (*shareadmin*) by just typing the username in the field and clicking Check Names to resolve the account name to its full username in Active Directory (you don't need to Check Name if you are sure the account you typed in is correct, but it helps avoid errors). I am going to keep the defaults of a normal priority, not started yet, and therefore no percentage complete. Once you have filled in all fields as you wish, please click Save to save the new task.

FIGURE 6.54

Tasks – New Item

Back in the Tasks list (Figure 6.55), let's create a summary task and put a task in it (while making that first task its predecessor).

1. To create a summary task, make sure the Items ribbon is active, and click the down arrow below the New Item button. Select Summary Task from the drop-down menu (Figure 6.56).

FIGURE 6.55
Tasks list with
new task

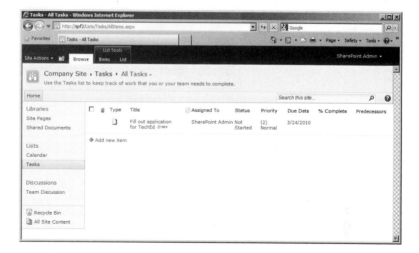

FIGURE 6.56
Summary Task
option in New
Item menu

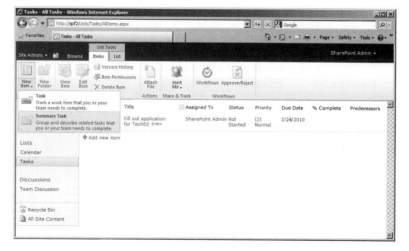

2. This will open a New Item box identical to the previous one, despite that this list item is a type of folder. This summary task is going to contain a task that will be only the first of several, so I am going to call this **Preparations for Conference**. Notice that the original task that I created is now listed as a possible predecessor for this summary task (Figure 6.57). Go ahead and make the first task a predecessor of the summary task (assuming, in this scenario, that the first task should be completed before this summary task and its subtasks can start). To do that, click the first item that was created in the possible values box, and click the Add button to put it in the selected values box.

3. The rest of the fields can be filled as you wish, except make the date range of the container several days long starting with today. I'm going to assign it to my account. When you are done entering data, click Save.

Back in the list, you can now see that there is a task and a summary task in the list (and the summary task has a predecessor listed), as shown in Figure 6.58.

FIGURE 6.57
Creating
Summary task

FIGURE 6.58
Task and
Summary Task
items in Tasks list

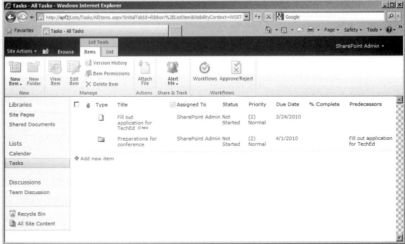

To put tasks in the summary task container, just click the summary task's title. That will put you on a page that looks no different, except the browser tab for the page shows the name of the folder—I mean summary task—rather than the list itself (Figure 6.59).

1. In the Summary task, let's add a new task that will require the first task we made to precede it. Click Add New Item in the page or New Item in the Items ribbon.

2. In the New Item box, there are now two items listed in the Predecessor field's possible values (Figure 6.60). Give the item a title (the only required field for a Task item), and select the original task as a predecessor to this task (you can double-click the item to put

it in the selected value box instead of clicking the Add button if you want). It isn't strictly necessary to do, because the container for this task has done the same thing, but it demonstrates that a task in a folder can still access and use tasks in a lookup from outside the folder (and vice versa).

FIGURE 6.59
View of Tasks list within Summary task

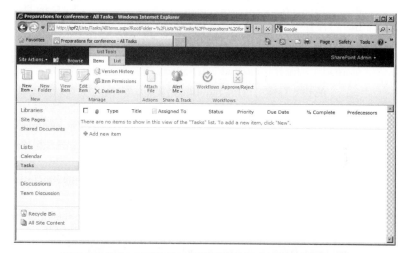

FIGURE 6.60
Create task item within Summary task

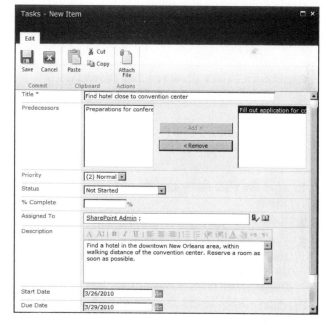

3. Fill out the other fields as you see fit. I am going to again assign the task to my account in the People Picker field and schedule it within the next few days. Click **Save** when you're done.

There will be a new subtask listed in the summary task container. You've now learned to create a task, a summary task, a task in the summary task container, and how to connect a task to a predecessor task.

To get back up to the original Tasks content page, click either the Navigate Up button in the top ribbon bar or the Navigate Up button in the List ribbon. The button in the ribbon navigates only up the tree of the list; the one on the top ribbon bar navigates around the whole site.

Back on the Tasks list, the All Items view is not impressive by default. However, because of the useful fields that are contained in a task (Assigned To, Start Dates, End Dates, and Priority), there are several really useful views for this list.

Click the View menu in the title breadcrumb (you might need to click the Browse tab in the top ribbon bar to see it), or you can click Current View menu in the List ribbon. You'll see several more views for this list that you haven't already seen:

Active Tasks   This Standard view is filtered by the Status field, if its value is not equal to Completed.

By Assigned To   This Standard view is sorted by Assigned To and then Status.

By My Groups   This view filters by Group assignments if any were made.

Due Today   This view will display all tasks due today; that is, it filters by Due Date being equal to the variable [Today]. Within the items due today, the view sorts by the date the tasks were entered into the list.

My Tasks   This view filters the Tasks list where the value of the Assigned To field equals the variable [Me]. It is also sorted by Status and Priority.

The Tasks list is a good example of why you should conscientiously enter data in all the necessary fields of a list item. Those fields can only be sorted, filtered, grouped, and so on, if they have data in them. Views can be powerful, but they are not really relevant if the data is not there.

CREATING A GANTT VIEW FOR THE TASKS LIST

One of the reasons someone would create a Gantt view for a list would be to track a series of tasks—say, making preparations to attend a conference. As long as those tasks have start and end (due) dates, they can have a Gantt view. In addition, the predecessor field is specifically meant to be surfaced in a Gantt view.

To create a Gantt view of the Tasks list, follow these steps:

1. Click the View menu and select Create View, or click the Create View button in the List ribbon.

2. In the View Type page that appears, select the Gantt View format.

3. In the View New page for a Gantt view, the only settings that are different from the Standard view are in the Gantt Columns section. Otherwise, you name the view (keep it short), decide on whether it will be public (my example is public), and decide which fields will be displayed. (Pay attention to which columns you want to use in this view.)

The Gantt Column section of the settings has five fields available to configure:

Title   This field is what is going to be displayed next to the activity bar representing the start and end dates. Usually, it is the title of the list item.

Start Date   This is the Start Date field for the activity bar. This field's date must always precede the date that you will use for the end date.

Due Date This is the end date for the task. This field must have a date that, for every list item, occurs after the Start Date.

Percent Complete This optional field lets the Gantt view indicate by color how far along a task is toward completion.

Predecessors This optional field allows the Gantt view to draw an arrow from a task's predecessor to this task.

4. For the example Gantt Column values, use the traditional Title field for the title, Start Date for the start date, and so on. As you can see, Gantt view was meant to work with a Tasks list.

5. Once the settings for the view are complete to your satisfaction, click OK to create your view.

The Gantt view for this version is a little different (and a bit more awkward) than the previous version. Now the view area is split, with a divider you can drag to move, between the fields of the list items on the left and a horizontal calendar with a bar for each date range. The date ranges have bracket indicators at each end of the start and end date range of a task. Summary tasks are indicated by a gray bar, with triangles indicating the start and end dates.

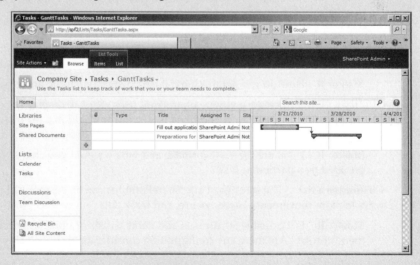

Note, however, that there is no indication of the subtask in the summary task container, nor its relationship with the original task. However, the summary task is a link in the Gantt view, so you can click it to see a Gantt view of the tasks within it.

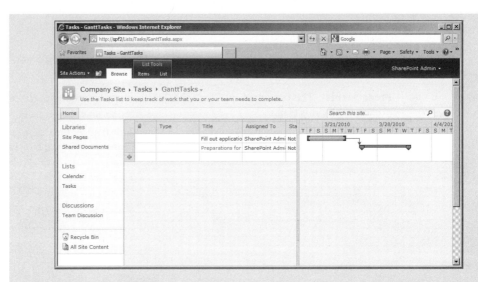

Note, however, that there is no indication of the subtask in the summary task container, nor its relationship with the original task. However, the summary task is a link in the Gantt view, so you can click it to see a Gantt view of the tasks within it.

In the next chapter, we'll create some lists—several from templates and at least one from scratch.

The Bottom Line

Use and modify a list.   Lists are the collaboration core of SharePoint. With the content stored in a database, lists can be used to track data, hold discussions, manage issues, and more.

Master It   How do you get to a list if it isn't displayed on the home page?

Modify a view and create a view.   SharePoint uses views to display the content of lists. Much like reports, views can be modified to display any field in a list in any order. Custom views can be created, with four different view formats to choose from.

Master It   What are the view formats, and which would you choose to display data grouped by a particular field?

Customize a list.   The settings of any SharePoint list can be customized in a number of ways to more conveniently store, secure, and track data.

Master It   Is it possible for users to add items to lists or libraries without having to use their browser? Are there any configuration considerations, or is it simply built in?

Chapter 7

Creating Lists

In Chapter 6, "Introduction to Lists," you learned how to effectively use existing SharePoint lists, from entering and editing data to manipulating views to customizing list settings. In this chapter, you'll go beyond that. Now that you have the basics on what a list is and how to use it, it's time to explore creating lists, first in terms of creating lists from the convenient list templates available on a Team Site and then onward to creating an entirely custom list.

SharePoint contains several kinds of list templates. The preexisting lists we explored in the previous chapter were among the types of lists that can be generated from these templates. Most of these lists were designed to do a particular task, demonstrate the use of new data types, or integrate with Office.

In this chapter, you will learn to

◆ Create a list from a template

◆ Create a custom list

◆ Display related lists through connected web parts

Creating New Lists with Existing Templates

SharePoint contains several kinds of list templates. The preexisting lists you explored in the previous chapter were among the types of lists that can be generated from these templates. Most of these lists were designed to do a particular task, demonstrate the use of new data types, or integrate with Office (2003 or higher, although 32-bit 2010 is preferred).

In this chapter, using the site's Create page, you'll create entirely new lists based on the list templates not covered yet: Issue Tracking, Surveys, and Contacts. I will give you an overview of Issue Tracking and Surveys, saving Contacts for last, because that list type lends itself easily to the bread and butter of using a template, customizing it to suit your needs.

IMPROVE THE CREATION EXPERIENCE

When you go to create a new list, the Create page is slightly different from any other in this version of SharePoint. It also has a banner suggesting you install Silverlight.

In most production environments, installing unnecessary software that requires a lot of updates is not suggested. Therefore, the banner suggestion is for those who are accessing SharePoint from workstations.

For that reason, in my examples, I do not have Silverlight installed. If your system does, the Create page may look a little different.

For the most part, it functions in the same way, but instead of opening a page to enter settings for the new thing you create, the Silverlight version shows those settings in the Create box.

Issue Tracking

The Issue Tracking list is meant to capture data about troubleshooting issues, which are not uncommon in any collaborative solution. It is very much like a Tasks list (discussed in the preceding chapter) but includes a Related Issues lookup field for indicating what other issues in the list might be related to the one you are entering. In addition, the Issue Tracking list was meant to demonstrate the one workflow that SharePoint Foundation has to offer: the Three-State workflow, which was designed to take an issue and trigger a task item to be created in the Tasks list based on assignment. This list integrates with Outlook, Access, and Excel. Issue Tracking also has versioning enabled to allow its comment field to append new data to the field.

Perform the following steps to create an Issue Tracking list from an existing template:

1. Go to the Create page by clicking the Site Actions menu and selecting More Options from the drop-down menu. (You can also click the List heading in the Quick Launch bar and then click the Create link at the top of the content area of the page; or you can just go to All Site Content and click Create there.)

   Once on the Create page (Figure 7.1), you can move the mouse pointer over the link for Issue Tracking (in the Tracking category) and see that its description is displayed in the area above the template categories.

FIGURE 7.1

The Create page

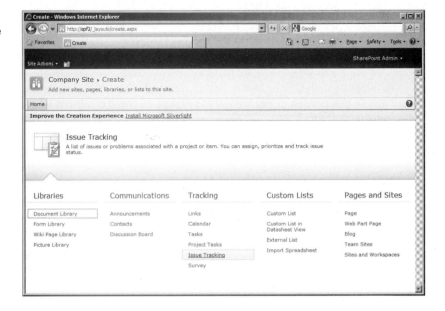

THE CREATE PAGE: ADDITIONAL CATEGORIES

The Create page is used as the primary location to create any object that is not a web part or in a list or library. The first three categories—Libraries, Communications, and Tracking—are pretty obviously just displaying the list templates available on the site. The Custom category contains links to create custom lists. Use Custom List to create a list from scratch in the browser, or use Custom List In Datasheet View to create a list that is already in Datasheet view by default. External List uses an external source to create a list, which requires the Business Data Connectivity service to be configured and an external data source to be set up. Using external data is a new feature of SharePoint Foundation; the previous versions of Windows SharePoint Services could not use external sources for lists or lookup fields. For more on external data sources, see Chapter 16, "Advanced Installation and Configuration." The last selection, Import Spreadsheet, allows you to import a list from an Excel spreadsheet.

The final column on the Create page is primarily used for creating new web and web part pages, as well as subsites (either specifically using the Blog or Team Site template or opting to apply one of the other site templates through Sites And Workspaces).

2. To create an Issue Tracking list from a template, just click its link on the Create page. That will take you to the New page (see Figure 7.2).

3. Fill in the Name and Description fields with something appropriate (my example is SiteIssues). Remember that the name of the list will be part of the URL for the list, so keep it short and avoid spaces. Recall from Chapter 6 that you can go back later and add spaces, yet the URL will keep the original name.

4. For the Navigation setting, you can choose to have the list show up on the Quick Launch bar or not. My example has it on the Quick Launch bar, so keep the default, Yes.

FIGURE 7.2

The New page to create an Issue Tracking liste

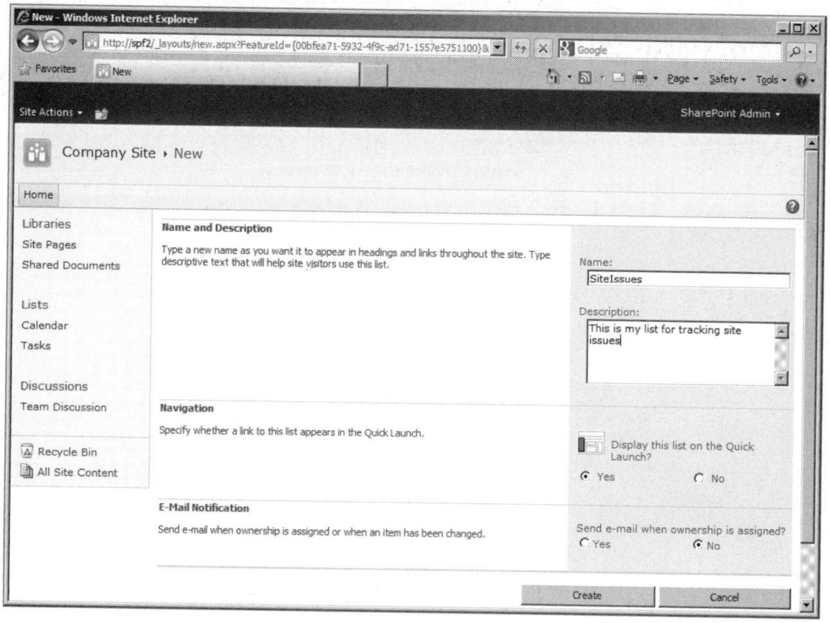

5. For E-mail Notification, you could have the list send an email message should ownership of the list item be assigned to someone other than the person who is creating it now. This setting may be useful, but for now let's leave the default setting of No. Keep in mind also that SharePoint has to use processor and RAM resources for email notifications because those functions are performed by the Timer job.

6. Once your settings are complete, click **Create** to create the Issue Tracking list.

ISSUE TRACKING LISTS ARE MEANT TO BE REVISITED

Some lists are *static*, meaning that they contain data that can be stored permanently and never changes.

Lists such as Issue Tracking are meant to be revisited, and the items can be edited to reflect changes in the status of an issue through to its completion. This is an important point. If you've ever tried to keep an issues list and it failed, with nothing ever seeming to be started or finished, it might be because a user, while actually working on the issue, had to also remember to go in and update the list item but failed to do so. The only way an issues list will work is if everyone actually participates in keeping it *dynamic*.

The new Issue Tracking list should appear with the list's name and description (see Figure 7.3). This list comes with three views: All Issues, Active Issues (which filters out the closed Issues), and My Issues (which filters the Assigned to field by the [Me] variable).

FIGURE 7.3
The new Issue
Tracking list

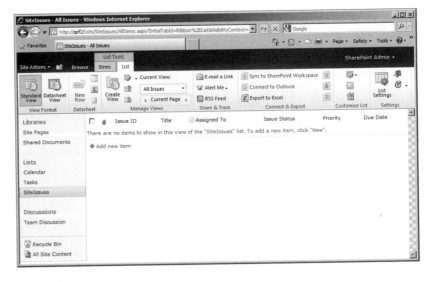

KEEPING IT SHORT

You might have noticed in Figure 7.3 that the list's name is part of the URL in the browser's address bar, demonstrating the usefulness of a short list name. Try to avoid spaces. Giving your lists or libraries short names is important in terms of the URL length (about 260 characters before a query string—query strings usually start with question marks). Folder names, no matter how nested, are usually added to the URL in a query string, which are limited only by the browser (most can have URLs with a query string of more than 2,000 characters).

Just as a bit of trivia, when you are creating subsites, consider that, in order to be able to make a list or library there, the new list page adds /_layouts/new.aspx (18 characters) to the path to get to the New page. So, it will be hard to create a new page if you exceed 242 characters.

To really see what the Issue Tracking list is all about, create a new item, as follows:

1. Start by clicking the Add New Item link at the bottom of the content area (or click the New Item button in the **Items** ribbon). This will take you to the New Item form box (Figure 7.4).

FIGURE 7.4
Creating a new issue item

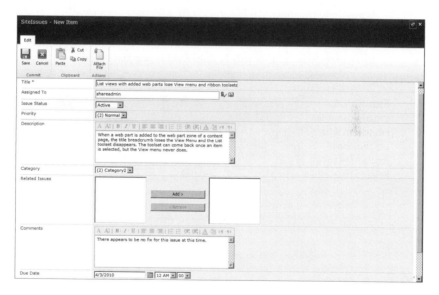

2. Enter a Title (which is required). The Assigned To field is a People And Groups data field. Assign the issue to the user account under which you are logged in by clicking in the field and entering your username. The Issue Status field, which is simply a Choice field, can be Active, Resolved, or Closed. Leave it Active for now. The Priority field (also a Choice data field) can be left at Normal.

3. Feel free to enter a description in the Description field. Under normal circumstances, this field would be very important for resolving the issue and for use as historical data later.

4. The Category field is unfinished in comparison to the other fields, as if to encourage you to customize it. It does contain three generally nondescriptive categories. Leave it at the default of Category2.

Related Issues is a lookup field with the option to allow you to choose more than one item from the lookup. An interesting thing about this particular lookup field, just like its equivalent in the Tasks list, is that it accesses not the value of a field in a different list but the value of the Title field of items in this list. This allows you to track multiple issue items that might relate to one another in some way. This is pretty clever, and it illustrates an essential way to demonstrate lookup fields. Right now there is no value to select because this is the first item in this list.

The Comments field is simply another multiple-line rich-text field. Again, this field would be a good place to add documentation about the issue.

5. Finally, at the bottom of the page is Due Date. Feel free to give the item a due date of the end of the week (or sometime in the future), and then click **OK** to finish creating your new issue item.

If you were to create another issue item, the first item's title would appear in the Related Issues field (as shown in Figure 7.5). To add the item in the box on the left to the box on the right (to select it), either double-click your selection or click it and then click Add. If there had been more items in the list, you could choose any number of items to relate to your new issue. Remember, the point of this lookup field is not just to look up the value of a field but to allow you to choose more than one.

FIGURE 7.5
Creating another issue item with the previous item added in the Related Issues field

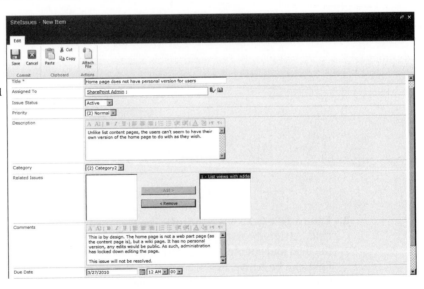

You have created, used, and viewed the Issue Tracking list, but you aren't done with it yet. The interesting thing about the Issue Tracking list is that Microsoft chose it to demonstrate workflows.

The Three-State Workflow

Workflows are a pretty simple and nifty concept. You know that you have lists. You know that you have libraries. What if you wanted to automatically create a task in a Tasks list when a document is marked Ready For Review (this would be a custom field you'd create in the library) and you want the user to see that they have a new task when they log in and view their User Tasks web part on the home page?

You could do it with a *workflow*, which is simply a programmatic process that is triggered by an event or change in its associated list. The trigger can send an alert, create a new list or list item, or change the state of a field (or more, with SharePoint Designer/Visual Studio). Workflows make SharePoint's lists, as well as document management and collaboration, more useful by automating and standardizing the organization's processes.

Workflows can be added to SharePoint as reusable workflows (workflows that are made to be usable on any site), as site workflows, as templates (as solution or .wsp files), or they can be assigned to a particular list, library, or content type.

On a list where you want to apply a workflow template, select the template in Workflow Settings (under List Settings), then name it, configure it specifically for that list, and what you want it to do. At that point, a workflow instance is associated with that list to be triggered by a change in that list, which can then effect changes in other lists—send notifications, and so on—depending on how the workflow is designed.

My example uses the out-of-the-box sample workflow called Three-State, which is available for any list or library in the site collection (but really was originally designed for the Issue Tracking list). This workflow utilizes a field with three choices and a Tasks list. When an item is created in a list with which this workflow is associated, the workflow will check the state of a choice field you specify to see whether a particular option (in this case, Active) is selected. If so, the workflow will check the Assigned To field and create a new item in a specified Tasks list for the site, that is assigned to that person for the issue (and email them). When that task item is set as completed, the Issue Status field of the issue item that spawned it is changed to the second option (Resolved).

If the Issue Status setting of an issue item is changed to Resolved, an email is sent to either someone you specify or the person to whom the issue was assigned, telling them to review this issue and change it to Closed if necessary (which is the third stage of the workflow).

Want More Workflow Functionality?

To really use more than the one sample SharePoint Foundation workflow available out of the box, you must create workflows using SharePoint Designer or Visual Studio. Yes, you must download or buy (and install) another product to be able to use all the features of a free product. However, for workflows, it might be worth the effort (or, if you can use Visual Studio, the price).

Setting Up a Three-State Workflow

To demonstrate how it works, let's set up a Three-State workflow for the new Issue Tracking list:

1. While on the Issue Tracking list, make sure the List ribbon is active, click the Workflow button's drop-down arrow in the last section of the ribbon, and select Add A Workflow (Figure 7.6).

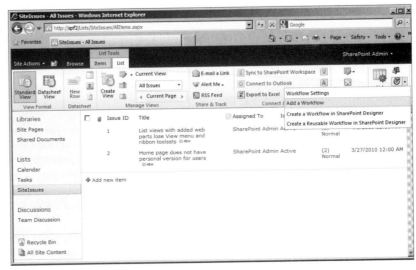

FIGURE 7.6
Adding a workflow

2. The Add A Workflow page has five settings. (Note that the button at the bottom of the page is Next, not OK, which means there are more pages to this process.) The first section, Workflow, will list the different workflow templates that are available for that list. Right now there is only one, so select Three-State.

3. In the Name section, you should enter a meaningful name for the workflow that will be applied to this list. In this example, it will be named CreateTask (Figure 7.7).

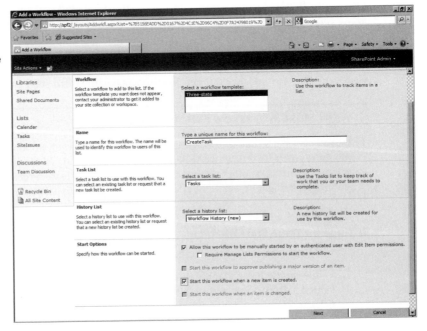

FIGURE 7.7
The first page
of configuring a
workflow instance

4. In the Task List section, you specify the list in which to create a task item. You could select **New Task List** from the Select A Task List drop-down menu to create a new Tasks list specifically for this workflow. However, for our example, keep the existing Tasks list as the one in which this workflow will generate items.

5. Like most things in SharePoint, a workflow can have a history, essentially a log, to record what it has been doing. Since this is the first time you've used workflows, there is no existing workflow history to choose from the drop-down. You'll have to create a new one, so keep the default.

Workflows can be called to action by several triggers, such as manually being started (and you can decide who can do that), creating an item, changing an item, or approving a document.

6. Because this Issue Tracking list already has some items, you will need to allow a workflow to be started for them manually. You can either allow anyone who can edit an item to start a workflow for an item or limit that option to only those who have permission to manage a list. My example allows anyone with edit rights to start a workflow on an item if they want. However, I'd also like to start the workflow when a new task item is created from this point on as well, to avoid any human error. Make sure that Allow This Workflow To Be Manually Started and Start This Workflow When A New Item Is Created are selected.

7. Click **Next** to continue creating your workflow instance.

8. On the next page, you customize the workflow. This workflow requires a Choice field with at least three options available, such as the Issue Status field, which has three states (Active, Resolved, and Closed). Keep that field choice and its three options (see Figure 7.8).

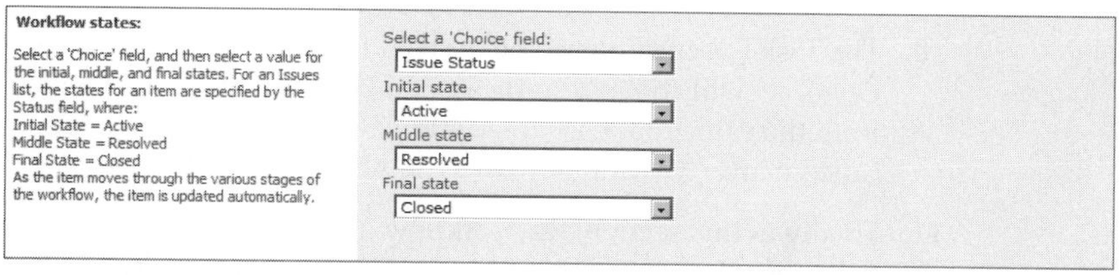

FIGURE 7.8
The Workflow States section of customizing the workflow

Workflow states:

Select a 'Choice' field, and then select a value for the initial, middle, and final states. For an Issues list, the states for an item are specified by the Status field, where:
Initial State = Active
Middle State = Resolved
Final State = Closed
As the item moves through the various stages of the workflow, the item is updated automatically.

Select a 'Choice' field:
Issue Status
Initial state
Active
Middle state
Resolved
Final state
Closed

ONE WORKFLOW CAN GO A LONG WAY

The Three-State workflow can work with any list that has at least one Choice field with three options available and either an Assigned To field or one person to whom all tasks are sent. If you are creative, this versatility will allow you to use the Three-State workflow in a host of other situations—as long as you want a task item to be created in a Tasks list.

When an item is created in this Issue Tracking list, the default value in the Issue Status field is Active. This is considered the initial state for this workflow.

The settings to specify what happens when the workflow is initiated are in the second section of this page (Figure 7.9). This section lets you specify what data is used for the new task item's fields as well as the email details that will be sent to the task assignee.

FIGURE 7.9

Specifying what you want to happen when a workflow is initiated

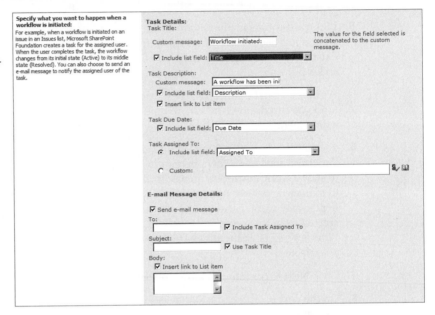

9. The default value for the Title field of the task item generated from an issue is that issue's ID number. Change that value to Title, because the issue title is much more descriptive than its ID field.

10. The Task Description can be derived from the Description field of the issue, and the Due Date will come from the issue's Due Date field. The new task assignment can be set from the value in the issue's Assign To field, or you can specify someone explicitly in the Custom area. My example uses the Assign To field value.

11. Finally in this section, the workflow gives you the option to send an email to the assignee to let them know they have a new task. You can specify to whom the email is sent or allow it to default to the assignee, and you can enter an email subject or use the task title in the email (rather than the default of the item ID, which isn't very descriptive). You can even customize the body of the message if you'd like, but make certain a link to the task is included for the recipient's convenience. For this example, we'll use all of the defaults but set the title to be included instead of ID.

In the third section of the Customize Workflow page, you decide what to do when the issue is Resolved (which is considered the middle state of the workflow). This step creates a new task for the assignee to review the task they were originally assigned, to be sure it can be closed. When that task is completed, the original Issue Status field value is changed to Closed.

Therefore, this section looks essentially the same as the previous section, but with some different defaults (see Figure 7.10).

12. The default settings are all correct for this example, so keep the defaults.

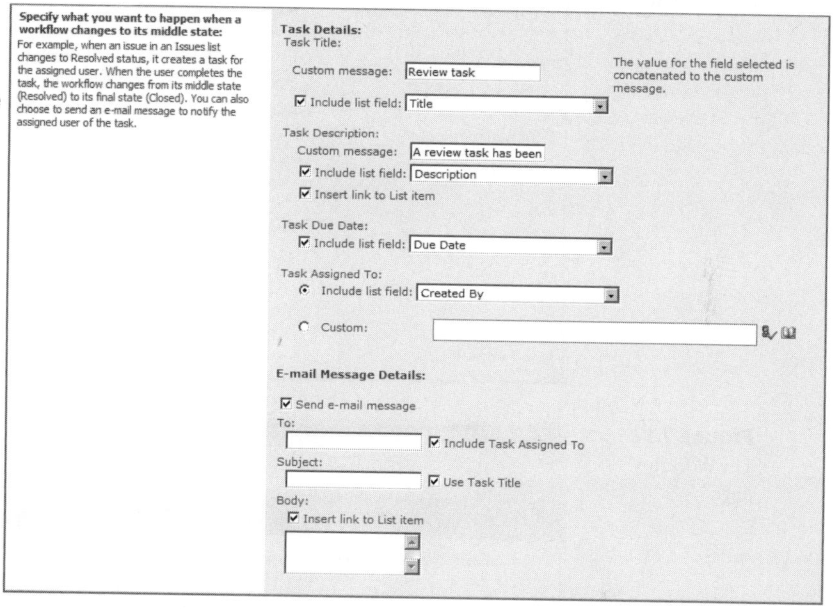

FIGURE 7.10

Specifying what happens at the middle stage of the workflow

13. When all your settings are the way you'd like them (you can edit them later if necessary), click OK to finish creating your workflow instance for this list. That should put you back on the Issue Tracking list, ready to use the Three-State workflow.

Starting a Workflow on an Existing Item

This workflow was set to be started either manually or when a new item is created. Take the following steps to start the workflow on one of your existing items:

1. Select an existing list item to trigger the item menu, and then select Workflows, which now appears in the item drop-down menu (see Figure 7.11).

2. On the Workflows page (Figure 7.12), you can select from the workflow instances that might be available to be started for this list item. Currently running and completed workflows are also shown. To start the workflow for the item, just click the button for the workflow, in this case CreateTask.

The Operation In Progress page may appear for a few moments while the workflow starts for that item.

3. Back on the Issue Tracking list, there is now a new column indicating that the CreateTask workflow is in progress. To see whether a task item was created in the Tasks list, click that list's link in the Quick Launch bar. As you can see in Figure 7.13, a new workflow-initiated task has been created.

FIGURE 7.11
The Workflows option on the drop-down for the list item

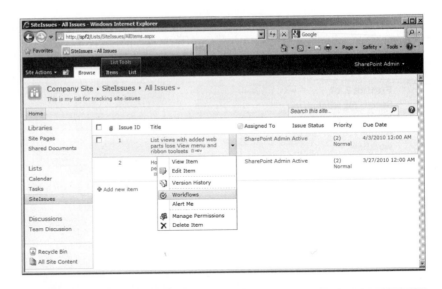

FIGURE 7.12
The Workflows page

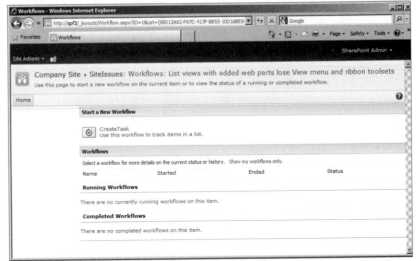

If you view the task item (see Figure 7.14), you'll see that the description of the task includes a link to the originating issue. This item also has a notice saying that it will email the assignee the contents of the item, in case this is a security issue.

4. To cause the second stage of the workflow to trigger, you need to set the status of this task item to Completed, so click Edit Item in the Items ribbon bar of the item's **View** page (since we're already here). On the Edit page, change the Status field value to Completed, and click Save.

Back on the Issue Tracking list, the originating issue item's status will change to Resolved instead of Active (see Figure 7.15).

FIGURE 7.13
A new workflow-
initiated task

FIGURE 7.14
The contents of the
workflow task item

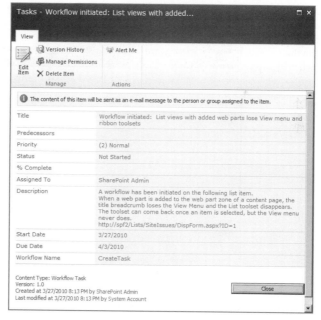

5. As you may remember from our workflow customization, when the first task is complete and the issue item changes to Resolved, a second task is created to review the first task's resolution before closing the issue. To confirm this and finish the workflow, go back to the Tasks list.

You will see the second task initiated by the workflow (Figure 7.16).

FIGURE 7.15
The Issue item is
now resolved.

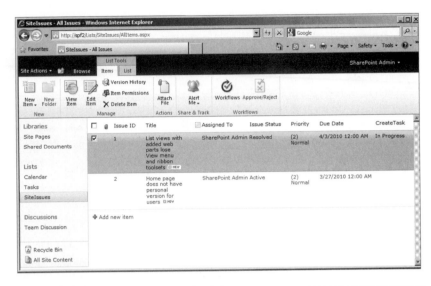

FIGURE 7.16
The second
workflow-created
task in the
Tasks list

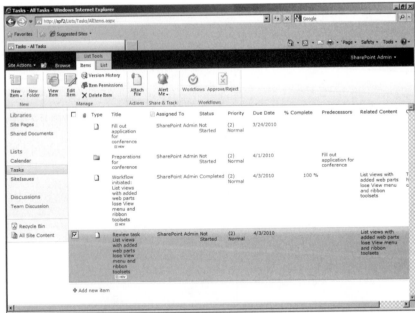

If you edit the item and change its status to **Completed**, the status of the originating
Issue item will be set to **Closed**, and its CreateTask workflow will be marked Completed
(Figure 7.17). Alternatively, if someone manually sets the issue's status to Closed, without
completing the review task, it will still complete the workflow.

FIGURE 7.17
The originating Issue item is closed, and the workflow is completed.

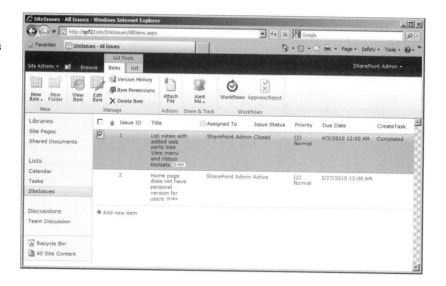

STATUS CHECK

If it appears that your workflow for a list item is not working or you want to know why a workflow hasn't completed, you can check the workflow's status by selecting Workflows from the item's drop-down menu and then selecting the running workflow on the Workflows page. That workflow's status page will open, allowing you to see a report of its activities and history. If the workflow seems to be malfunctioning, it is here that you can deactivate it (Terminate This Workflow Now), which removes it from the item and causes it to delete the tasks it has made.

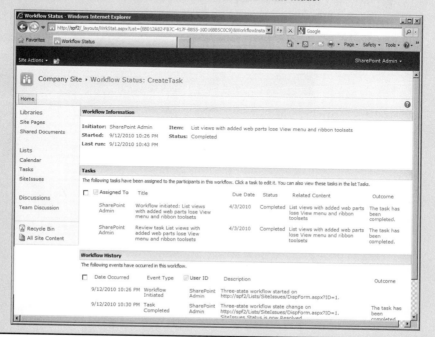

Surveys

Another SharePoint list template that you might be called upon to implement is Surveys. *Surveys* have no default fields, so when you create the survey, all questions you create for the user to answer (that is, the fields) must be custom created. Surveys have a unique graphic view of the results available, and certain fields (Choice and Yes/No) can use a very rudimentary kind of branching logic that can be implemented after the questions are created.

In terms of design, if you have a string of questions, SharePoint will try to keep them on a page. If you don't want to group questions on a page or you want to separate them so that users will have to click Next between questions, you can use the page separator option in the section while you're creating a question. When you are doing branching logic, any question branching forces a page break, so you'll have to click Next to get to the rest of the questions. You might want to consider where your branching questions are in the survey so you can group your questions accordingly.

CREATING A SURVEY

Creating a survey is like creating any other list. You need to go to the **Create** page, either by clicking Site Actions ➤ More Options or by clicking the List heading in the Quick Launch bar and then clicking **Create** at the top of the All Site Content page.

Keep in mind that once you create a survey and choose to display it on the Quick Launch bar, a Survey heading will appear there so the new survey can be listed beneath it. Once that heading is created, even if you delete the survey, the heading will remain (unless you manually delete it).

1. On the Create page, click the link for Survey in the Tracking category.

   The **New** page that opens (Figure 7.18) will have the same settings as any other new list—Name And Description and **Navigation**. In addition, it will have Survey Options settings: **Show User Names In Survey Results** and Allow Multiple Responses. Here you can decide whether the survey will be anonymous to other users and whether you will allow users to retake the survey.

FIGURE 7.18
The New page for the Survey list

2. For this example, name the survey SimpleSurvey (or whatever you'd like), and put a link for it on the Quick Launch bar. Don't show usernames, and don't allow multiple responses (see Figure 7.18); then click Next.

You will immediately start to create the first field for the survey, which is actually a question (see Figure 7.19).

FIGURE 7.19

The New Question page for a survey

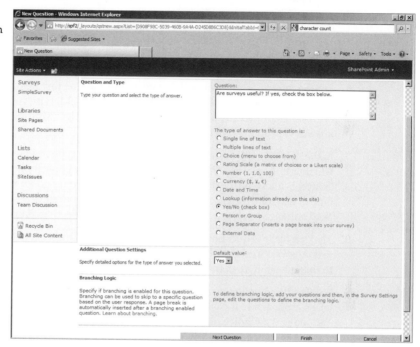

AN EXTRA QUESTION

Survey questions may seem familiar, because most of them are the standard field types of any list, but there is an additional field, Rating Scale. This type of question will allow for several subquestions to be rated on a number scale you specify. We aren't using it in this example, but it is pretty self-explanatory.

---

3. My example uses a simple Yes/No question. Type some text (such as **Are surveys useful? If yes, check the box below**), and select **Yes/No** for the type of answer.

4. In the Additional Question Settings section, you have to choose a default value. Yes is the default. Keep it for this example.

The last section on the New Question page actually has no settings; it's the Branching Logic section that simply reminds you that you can use it after all the questions have been created.

> **YOU HAVE TO TELL THEM EVERYTHING**
>
> The default settings for surveys are pretty basic. For example, the Yes/No option for a question merely displays the question and a blind check box. That's it. No explanation is offered in the interface as to what the check box is about; therefore, you'll need to define what the box value actually is in the question, such as "Check the box below if you are over 18 years of age."

5. At the bottom of the page, click Next Question to finish this question and start on the next one.

6. For the next question, you will create a multiple-line text field where you ask the user to explain why they answered No. In the Question field, type your request for an explanation (my example is **If no please explain**). Then select Multiple Lines Of Text for the answer type to give them room to tell you.

7. In the Additional Question Settings section for this type of answer, you can determine whether this answer is required (it is in my example), specify how many lines of text this answer is allowed (the default of six is fine, or you could go for more), and determine the type of text for this field (plain text, rich text, or enhanced rich text). This survey doesn't need enhanced rich text for images and tables, so selecting Plain Text (the default) will work.

8. That's it for this question's settings, so click Next Question to create the next one. If the user answers Yes, they'll go directly to this third question. If they answer No, they'll go to this question after they explain why not.

9. For this third question, as the meeting point after the branching logic for this example, let's simply ask **Is it easier to do a survey if you know your answers are anonymous?** and make it a **Choice** question.

10. In the Additional Question Settings section, do require a response. Do not require unique values, because there are going to be only three values, so by the fourth person, you've run out of unique answers.

11. For my example, the choices will be **Yes**, **No**, and **It makes no difference**. You can display the choices in a drop-down list, with radio buttons, or with check boxes (to choose more than one). Let's go with the Radio Button default. Don't allow a fill-in value, because there are always jokers out there, and it will skew the average. Keep the default value as Choice, because that means that Yes will be the default because it is the first choice.

    The Choice field has the option of Column Validation, but because there are only three options to choose from, you will not do validation here.

12. That's enough questions to demonstrate the point, so finish creating the survey by clicking Finish at the bottom of the page. That will take you not to that list's content page but to its **List Settings** page (see Figure 7.20) so that you can rearrange the questions or set up branching logic.

FIGURE 7.20

The new survey's list settings page

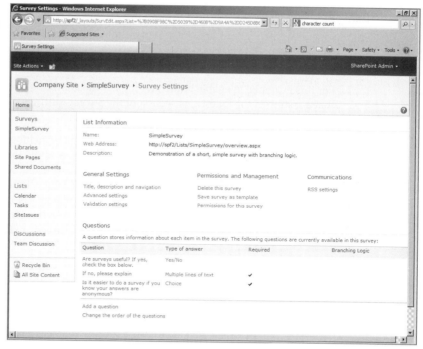

NO GIVEBACKS

By default the survey is set so users cannot edit each other's entries, but they can edit (and delete in order to redo) their own. But you can set the item permissions under Advanced Settings in the list settings not to allow users to edit or delete their own entries. This means that if they are halfway through and click Save, they won't be able to go back. Right now, they can.

However, there is one caveat to changing this setting. For some reason, branching logic requires the Edit Item permission. So if the survey branches, the user gets an Access Denied error, and their response is saved as only half-finished. Half-finished survey responses are considered drafts (versioning is on by default and cannot be changed), but not even a site administrator can access the unfinished/draft versions of responses. So, no one but the user can see their half-finished response, and they're not allowed to edit or delete it. And, if the list is set to not allow multiple responses, the user will be given an error if they try to do the survey again.

Bottom line: resign yourself to either allowing users to edit or delete their responses in a survey or creating the survey to do absolutely no branching logic.

BRANCHING LOGIC

Survey questions are laid out in a linear pattern. Question 2 follows question 1, and so on. But with branching logic, you can cause questions to stop going in order temporarily, skipping to a different question in the list based on the answer given.

1. For this example, to enable branching logic if the answer is No to the first question, select that question in the Questions section of the Survey Settings page. My example uses "Are surveys useful? If yes, check the box below."

   On the Edit Question page, scroll to the bottom, to the Branching Logic section (see Figure 7.21). There are two possible choices for which to apply the branching logic: Yes and No. For each choice in this case there are several options listed: No Branching, which jumps to any of the subsequent questions in the survey, or Content Type (see the "An Extra Option" sidebar). In this scenario, if the answer to the first question is No, then the user should be directed to the next question (the explanation). However, if the answer to the first question is Yes, the user should skip the second question and go directly to the last one.

FIGURE 7.21

The Branching Logic section

2. To do this, branch the Yes answer by selecting the last question in the Jump To field so you can skip over the "If no, please explain" question. For the No answer, you can either not branch, which would cause it to simply go to the next question, or specify that it go to the explanation question directly.

3. Once you've set your branching logic, click OK to finish editing the question. Back on the list settings page for the survey, there should be a check mark in the Branching Logic column next to the first question.

AN EXTRA OPTION

You'll see that there is an option for a content type in the Possible Choices drop-down list, and you'll see later that it shows up at the bottom of the Graphical Summary view of the survey results as well. But because content types cannot even be on this list, there is no reason for that option to appear in the possible choices for branching or in the graphical summary.

USING A SURVEY

To see how surveys and branching logic work, let's create a Survey list item; that is, you'll respond to the survey.

1. Go to the Survey list (SimpleSurvey in my example) by either clicking its link in the breadcrumb above the page title or clicking the survey's link in the Quick Launch bar. Notice that there is a new Surveys heading in the Quick Launch bar now that a survey has been built.

The Survey list's default view is a little nonstandard (Figure 7.22). There is no toolset in the top ribbon bar, just the old Action bar from the previous version of SharePoint, complete with a Respond To This Survey button, as well as an Actions menu and a Settings menu (you can export the list to Excel or create an alert or RSS feed under Actions, and Settings lets you either add questions or go to Survey Settings). There's even the old View menu to the right of the Action bar. That's really all you need for a survey; this is just a list that is presented a little differently (I guess they forgot to update it before they released the latest version).

2. To create a new Survey list item, click Respond To This Survey.

FIGURE 7.22

A new Survey list

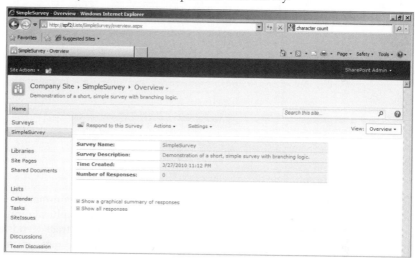

Unlike most new item pages, surveys display their fields in a group until a branch in logic occurs. This means that the first question is displayed by itself, waiting for you to choose Yes or No so it can decide what to display next (see Figure 7.23 to see the first question).

Notice that there is a question and a check box (selected by default, of course). That's it. There is no explanation of what the box is for unless you provide it in the text of your question. Keep that in mind.

3. If you answer Yes to this question, it will jump to the last question of the survey; if you answer No (clear the check box) and click Next, it will go to the next question, the one that follows in a normal linear manner. There is no jumping. To demonstrate that, clear the check box so the answer is No, and then click Next.

FIGURE 7.23

The first question
in a new survey

SimpleSurvey - New Item			□ ×
	Next	Save and Close	Cancel

Are surveys useful? If yes, check the box below.

☐

| | Next | Save and Close | Cancel |

As you can see in Figure 7.24, the rest of the questions in the list are displayed on the same page because there is no branching logic to interrupt the flow. Also notice, at the bottom of the page, that the name of the person creating and modifying the survey item is obscured by asterisks because you chose not to show names.

FIGURE 7.24
The rest of the survey questions

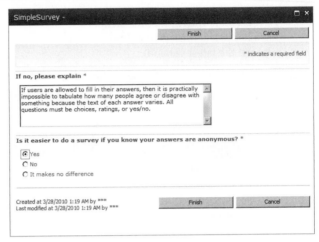

4. To complete the survey, click Finish.

Back on the **Survey List** content page, the Overview (summary) view of the list merely shows that there has been one response. You can also view a graphical representation of the responses in the Graphical Summary view (Figure 7.25) so you can track trends and opinions. (Of course, if you had more than one response to the survey, it would mean more.)

FIGURE 7.25
A graphical summary of the survey

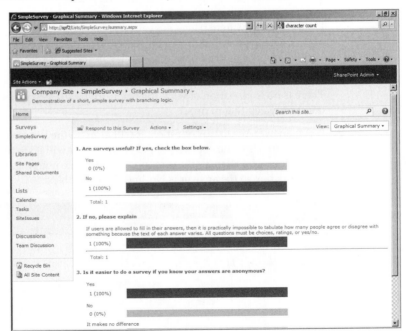

I hope this quick overview of the logic of surveys has given you an idea as to what you can and cannot do with this simple list and its interesting views.

Contacts

The Contacts list doesn't have a workflow associated with it, doesn't do branching logic, and doesn't have a fancy graphical summary. Its fields correspond closely to the contact records in Outlook for easy integration and synchronization with Outlook (preferably 2010). And because it is so easy to modify, this section is going to focus on not just the list but some of the things you can do with it.

Do the following to create a Contacts list:

1. Click Site Actions near the top left of any content page or the home page and then select More Options from the drop-down menu, or go to the All Site Contents page (most easily by clicking the Lists heading on the Quick Launch bar) and click Create.

2. On the Create page, select Contacts from the Communications category. This list is going to be used for customer contacts for this example, so on the **New** list page, let's name it Customers. Feel free to give it a description, and add it to the Quick Launch bar.

3. When you've completed these settings, click OK. This will take you to a standard Contacts list content page (Figure 7.26).

FIGURE 7.26
New list based on Contacts list template

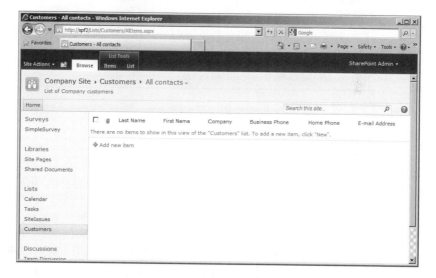

To see what fields a Contacts list has, feel free to click Add New Item to open the New Item form (and Cancel when you're done). Notice that the Last Name field is the only required field for this list. There are a lot of fields available to fill out for a contact item. Take special notice of the Full Name field. Even if you fill in the First Name and Last Name fields, you'll need to type the full name of the contact manually. You can edit that field so the full name is pulled from the values of the First Name and Last Name fields. This will save time when entering data into the list, and if it is pulled into Access or Excel to generate mailing lists, the Full Name field can be used for addressing.

To accomplish this, you need to **delete** the original Full Name field and add a new Full Name calculated field. On the Customers content page, click the Settings button in the Action bar, and select List Setting.

DEFAULT CALCULATED VALUE

You might wonder, "Why not keep the original Full Name field and just add the suggested calculation as the default value? That way, we could get the combined (concatenated) values of the first and last name fields in this field, but we could also edit it as we want."

Well, that is a good point. A calculated field isn't really editable; it runs under the covers. But here's the thing about text fields, or any field that can also have a little calculation as its default value: fields like that (and this also goes for column validation) cannot refer to any field outside of themselves for their calculation.

So if you want a field that contains values based on other field values, you need to use a calculated field. That's why if you want a full name field that automatically pulls the first and last name values and concatenates them, you need to delete the original single-line-of-text field and replace it with a calculated field instead.

However, something to keep in mind concerning calculated default values is that, like a view filter, they support what is considered *volatile* variables like [Today] and [Me]. True calculated type fields cannot naturally support variables like [Today].

So if you need to do a calculation that refers to other fields in the list, the calculated field type is your friend. If you need to have a default calculated value but want to give users the option to override that value and enter something else or if you need to use a volatile variable in your calculation, consider the default calculated value.

DELETING A FIELD

Take the following steps to delete a field:

1. On the List Settings page for the list (on the Lists ribbon, click List Settings to get to the page), select the field you want to delete (Full Name in our case) from the list of fields in the Columns section.

2. When the page opens to edit that field, go to the bottom of the page. In addition to the OK and Cancel button is the Delete button. Just click Delete; it's that simple.

3. A dialog box will warn you that the column and all of its data will be deleted. You don't have any data to lose yet, so click **OK**. But note that this is a good reminder that you should customize a list *before* you enter data.

Once the Full Name field is deleted, it's time to create a new and improved Full Name field. I'll use this field to demonstrate calculation. Because calculated fields aren't available for editing, it won't show up on the **New Item** form box when users are doing data entry.

IF YOU DELETE SOMETHING BY MISTAKE

When you delete a field from a list, it's permanently gone; it doesn't go to the Recycle Bin. When SharePoint says that something you are about to delete is going to be deleted permanently, it means it.

However, there are many things that can be deleted in a SharePoint site that are not permanently deleted but go to the Recycle Bin. Objects such as list items, lists, and library items, including items from galleries, such as templates, all go to the Recycle Bin when deleted. And there they stay, taking up space in the content database for the site, for 30 days (that can be changed administratively). If a user deletes an object on the site, such as a document or list item or even a list, they have 30 days to restore it. And if they delete an item from the Recycle Bin by mistake, there is an administrative, site-collection-level Recycle Bin to recover it from. But if the item is 30 days old, it's deleted from that level as well.

In my example, several list items and some site templates have been deleted. To recover one of these items, I just put a check mark in the box next to it and click Restore Selection in the Action bar. This will put the item back where it was originally.

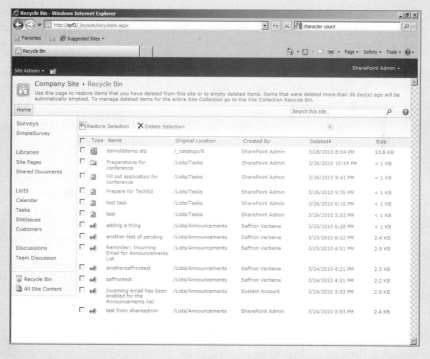

Things that are permanently deleted are list columns, sites, workflows, user accounts, web parts, and site columns.

CREATING A CALCULATED FIELD

To create a column, do the following:

1. As you've done before, go to the **Column** section of the List Settings page for the list, and click Create Column (I am assuming you've been following along from the previous chapter. For more details about creating columns, see Chapter 6.).

2. Because the original Full Name field has been deleted, that name is available for use in this list, so you can name the new field Full Name.

3. For the data type, choose Calculated, which is at the bottom of the list. Once **Calculated** is selected, the Additional Column Settings section will change to reflect the needs of a calculated data type.

4. For the description, you can use the Combined First Name and Last Name fields. Always describe any calculated fields so that you will be reminded later what the field was intended to do.

   Because calculated formulas in lists often refer to values in other fields of a list, there is a convenient Insert Column field populated by the field names of the list right next to the roomy Formula box. We are going to use a formula to *concatenate* (string together two or more text values) the data in the First Name and Last Name fields to create the value of the Full Name field. This is a common text calculation. You can explore the help files for more formulas, because this calculated field can do all kinds of functions, even trigonometry if necessary.

5. To do the concatenation (see Figure 7.27), click in the Formula box. The formula for concatenating fields is as follows:
   `[First Name]&" "&[Last Name]`

   Normally, like Excel, SharePoint formulas start with an equal sign. However, because you are going to use a box specifically for formulas to create the field, the equal sign is understood; you don't need to type it, but SharePoint will add it later. Field names are always in brackets, the ampersands (&) indicate the concatenation, and you are inserting a space (which has to be in quotes) between the two words. If you don't insert the space, the first and last names will run together into one word.

6. You can choose the data type that will be returned by the formula. A single line of text is good for our purposes, but, depending on the situation, you could also choose something like date and time or even Yes/No.

7. Be sure the Add To Default View box is selected, and click **OK**.

   Back on the List Settings page, in the Columns section, your new column will be listed. You can change the order of the column so it is closer to the First Name and Last Name fields if you'd like (using the Column Ordering link below the list of columns); however, because users will not be entering data in that field, it really only needs to be in the right place in whatever views you create.

8. To see the new field in action, go back to the list's content page (you'll see a new column for Full Name at the end of the list in the content area, just waiting for data), and click Add New Item. Enter whatever data you'd like for the new contact item (see Figure 7.28

for my example). Notice that there is no Full Name field in the New Item form box to enter data into, because, as I said earlier, a calculated column is not editable.

FIGURE 7.27
Calculated field settings

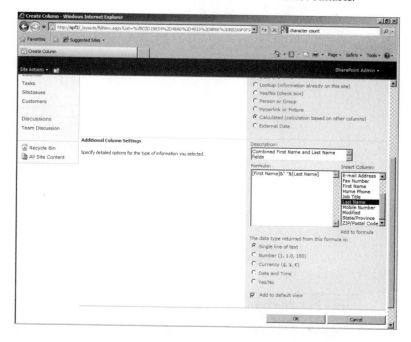

9. Click Save to finish.

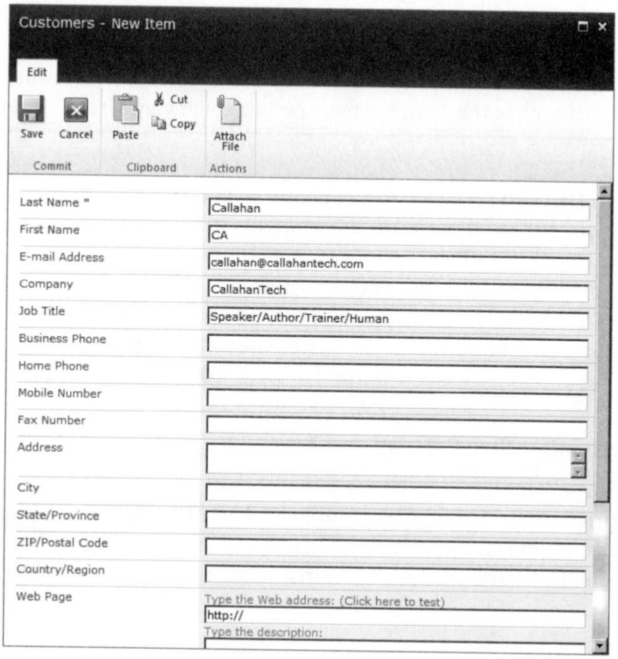

FIGURE 7.28
New contact item data

On the list's content page, you can see that the First Name and Last Name fields are combined in the **Full Name** field (Figure 7.29) on the far right of the view.

FIGURE 7.29

The Full Name field
in the List view

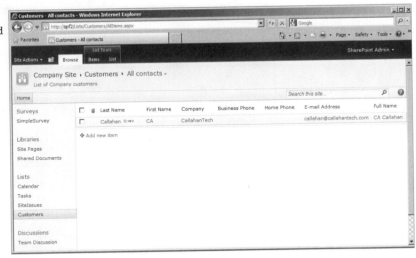

USE ONE FIELD TO VIEW TWO NAMES

You will likely want to consider modifying this view by removing the First Name and Last Name fields from the view and replacing them with just the Full Name field. The data can still be entered normally when you create a new item, but your *view* will be of the full name in one field to save horizontal space.

However, be aware that if you do remove Last Name from the view, there will be no field in the view that will trigger a drop-down menu or be linked to the edit form (because the Last Name field has that honor). But with the ribbon bar available, that's not a big issue. You could also add an Edit link column to the view. For more details about views, see Chapter 6.

This contact list is full of useful fields, but there is another field I would like to add. In appreciation of our customers, we try to find out their birthdays for a more personal touch. The marketing staff sends out automated cards to clients to celebrate their birthdays, so we have collected dates for many of our customers.

A Birthday field is one that can be useful in several different kinds of lists. This brings us to the concept of *site columns*. Site columns are templates of common fields. If you create a field you like and expect to use it in other lists, make it a site column. Then you can use it elsewhere.

ADDING A SITE COLUMN TO A LIST

SharePoint has a pretty large number of site columns already available based on its numerous preexisting lists and list templates. It's convenient to know that those fields are already there before you end up making something similar yourself. Many standard fields such as Company, Due Date, and Address are already available as site columns. Unfortunately, you can't just select a column you've created in a list and make it a site collection; you have to set it up specifically from the Site Column Gallery page to make it available to more than one list. To use its convenience, you have to plan for it. In other words, if there are fields you plan to use over and over, create those fields as site columns specifically, and then use them in your lists.

In our case, the Birthday site column already exists; you just need to add it to your list. Take the following steps to create a new field for a list from a site column:

1. Go to the List ribbon, and select List Settings.

2. On the List Settings page, scroll to the bottom of the Columns section, and click the Add From Existing Site Columns link. Site columns are organized in groups, such as Base Columns, Core Contact And Calendar Columns, Core Task And Issue Columns, and the like. You can also make your own groups to organize your site columns in a way that will be intuitive to you.

   The columns available under All Groups are pretty numerous—and at this point, probably pretty familiar. Most fields in most existing SharePoint lists have been made site columns as well, which is really convenient. Just remember, you can't have two fields in a list with the same name, so don't try to add a field with a name you already have in a list.

3. In the list of available site columns, you'll see the Birthday field (Figure 7.30). Just double-click it, or click the **Add** button to move it from **Available Columns** to the **Columns To Add** box. (When you do that, the field will no longer be shown in the Available Columns box. This helps enforce the fact that a field cannot be added twice to a list.)

FIGURE 7.30
The Add Columns
From Site
Columns page

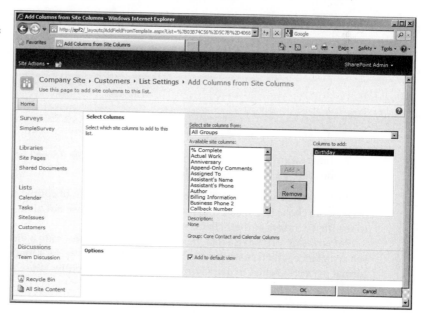

4. This column does not need to be added to the default view of the list, so remove the check from the Add To Default View option, and click OK.

5. Back on the List Settings page, you should see the Birthday field (formatted for Date and Time) in the Column section. Go back to the list's content page, and edit the item you created earlier (move your mouse over the item, click the down arrow on the right side of the Last Name column, and select Edit Item in the drop-down menu, or select the item and click Edit Item in the Items menu).

6. In the Edit Item box, you'll have to scroll down (because when a field is added to a list, it is appended to the bottom of the existing set of fields), but the Birthday field is right there (Figure 7.31).

FIGURE 7.31
New Birthday field
from site column

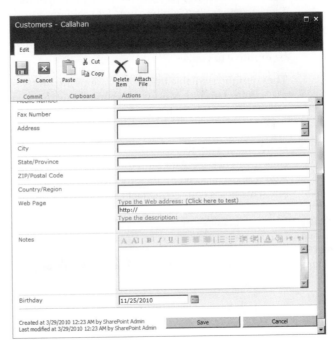

7. Enter your birth date in the field (well, my example doesn't have the correct year for me, but you get the point), and click **OK**.

You'll be back at the Customers content page. There is, of course, no Birthday field listed because we chose not to add it to the default view, because not all users who view the list need to see the birthdays of their clients so easily.

But now that you have a date field on this list, you can create a view by birthday so you can see at a glance which customer birthdays are approaching. As a matter of fact, there is a view format perfectly suited to displaying birthdays conveniently—the Calendar view.

CREATING A CUSTOM SITE COLUMN

Site columns are pretty useful, and they become even more useful when you create your own. Site columns are the property of an entire site, so once created, they can be added to any list on the site. In my case, I'd like to create an Expiration site column with a default value of 10 days after the date the list item is created.

To create a site column, follow these steps:

1. Go to the Site Actions menu, and select Site Settings.

2. In the Galleries category, select Site Columns. The Site Columns Gallery page displays all the site columns in groups.

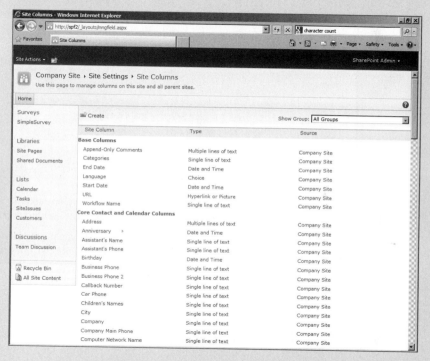

3. To create your own site column, just click Create. This will take you to a page filled with the standard sections for creating a new field, except this page also has a Group section to specify to which site column group you want to add this field. You can create your own group, or you can use the default Custom Columns group, as I'm doing here.

4. The Expiration field I'm creating is a date field, with a default calculated value of today's date plus 10 days ([Today]+10). Because the field has a calculated value, be sure to include a description.

5. Once you've set up the field the way you like it, click OK. The new site column will show up in the Custom Columns group and is ready for use anywhere that a list in this site collection needs it.

Note that if you want to further customize a custom site column, you must do it at the gallery level. And when you do that, those customizations will then affect the site column's settings site-wide.

CREATING A CALENDAR VIEW

A Calendar view of a list is just another way to display the list items. You may recall that in Chapter 6 you created some new views of lists, but they were standard views; that is, they were still in a list format. Also in Chapter 6, you looked at the site's built-in calendar, which I said is just a Calendar view of an Events list. But you can create a Calendar view of any list that contains a date field.

Take these steps to create a Calendar view:

1. On the Customer list, go to the Create View page by clicking Create View on the List ribbon. (Or use the breadcrumb drop-down or List Settings page.)

2. In the Create View page that opens, choose the Calendar View format.

3. For the **View** name, my example uses Birthdays, in this case you want to make this a Personal view so it won't be available to other users.

4. Because you are tracking a single date, use the Birthday field for both the Begin and End fields for the Time Interval section (see Figure 7.32).

FIGURE 7.32

Settings for the new Calendar view

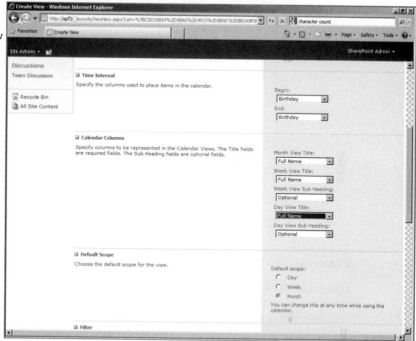

5. In the Calendar Columns section, you can choose what kind of information is listed (within the limited amount of space you have in the calendar format) for each kind of display: Month, Week, and Day. For the Week and Day views (because those displays give you room for a second line), you can have two lines of information about the list item displayed for the date on which it will appear. My example doesn't need subheadings, so we'll use Full Name as the Title field for Month, Week, and Day views.

6. The default scope for the calendar is going to be Month (which is the default selection for that section).

7. This view can also be filtered if the list is large; however, you don't need to do that here, so you can leave that setting alone.

8. Once you've completed all your settings, click OK to finish.

The Birthdays view is done and is now available on the Customers List content page (that is, your view of it, since you made this a Personal view), you can see it in Figure 7.33.

Note that in a Calendar view, if you click the link for the item listed on a date, it will simply go to that list item's View page to see its content; unlike a Standard view, it won't generate a down arrow when you hover over it.

FIGURE 7.33
The Birthdays
Calendar view

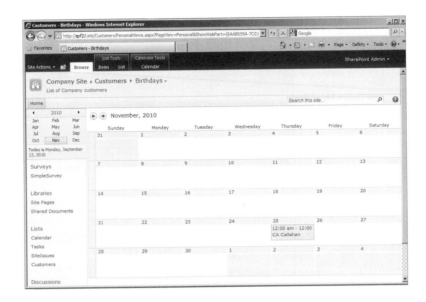

PERSONAL AND MOBILE VIEWS

Most views, *if* they are public, have a mobile page enabled automatically. Unfortunately, even though this view was set to be personal, the Mobile section still displays on the Create View page (though not when editing the view later). Personal views don't have mobile views.

ADVANCED SETTINGS

Now that the list is available for data entry, you might want to consider some permission management. To keep users from intentionally or accidentally messing up other users' client data, you might want to limit what list items can be edited by whom. This way, the only data users can mess up is their own.

IDENTITY SWAPPING

To log in as a different user, go to the Account menu, and select Sign In As A Different User. This will trigger a Log In prompt so you can enter that other user's credentials. Remember, though, that if there are web parts or Explorer views displaying folder content, the permissions of the user you are actually logged in as will take precedence over the SharePoint login. This means you might be able to view content that the other user cannot. Keep this in mind if you are testing their access.

There are two ways to manage the edit permissions of list items:

◆ Go to Advanced Settings in the List Settings, and select to do Item-Level Permission, such as allowing only Edit access to users for the list items they created.

◆ Choose to manage the permissions of an item from the Item drop-down menu (which has some caveats).

This chapter explains the Advanced Settings, namely, Item-Level Permissions for a list. However, if you want to explore managing the permissions for lists and individual items in more detail, visit Chapter 12, "Users and Permissions."

To manage the edit or view permission of list items as a whole, follow these steps:

1. Go to the List ribbon, and click List Settings (make sure you are logged in with an account that has permission to change list settings).

2. On the List Settings page that opens, click the Advanced Settings link in the General Settings category. The advanced settings are pretty much standard for all lists, so what you learn here can be applied to other lists as well. This page has five sections:

    Content Types   Enabling Content Types lets a list have more than one kind of item in it.

    Item-Level Permissions   This is the section you need to work with now. As you can see in Figure 7.34, this section lets you set the Read permission for each item to let users read all items or only items they created, as well as set the Edit permissions to allow users to create and edit all items on the list, create items but edit only their own, or create none. None truly means they can create and edit no items on the list, overriding their actual user permission levels for the list.

A LOST FEATURE

You might be looking for the setting that allowed someone to create an item but not to edit it subsequently. This capability was particularly useful with surveys, where you would like a candid response, because you can prevent the user from deleting or editing their first response.

It made sense—users could be allowed to create items and edit all items, create items and edit only the ones made by the individual user, or create items but not be able to edit.

But alas, this version of SharePoint no longer has that option. Apparently being able to create an item is inexplicably, and tightly, tied to being able to edit at least that item itself in lists. Keep that in mind if you are used to the item-level permissions of the previous version of SharePoint.

You can edit the list's permissions manually to remove the Edit Item permission from the users, but that is not the easiest option.

Attachments   This section lets you enable or disable file attachments for list items. Attachments (such as directions or pictures) can be especially useful for customer contact items, for example in a scenario where a sales rep leaves and their replacement needs to know what the customer looks like or how to get to their office.

Folders   For my example, we don't need to organize the Customers list in folders. Most lists are flat for easy viewing. However, in some cases, using a second level to organize list items is a good idea, so this option is available.

Search   This option is set to Yes by default. If you don't want this list's contents to show up in search results, set it to No.

Offline Client Availability   This setting is meant to integrate with SharePoint Workspace so users can download content from the list to work on offline. There can be security and other issues with this, so the option is here to allow or deny downloading for offline clients.

SHAREPOINT WORKSPACE

SharePoint Workspace comes with Office 2010 Pro Plus and is a client-side product (basically the old Groove client, minus some features) that lets users work with SharePoint locally. The users connect SharePoint Workspace to the site and select which lists or libraries to work with.

The product lets users easily drag and drop files from their desktops to libraries, allows the user to work with a list's or library's content while offline, and then lets them (ideally) synchronize with those resources when they are back online.

Obviously, there will be lists (such as those containing confidential client information) that you might not want stored offline on someone's laptop. In this case, you would want to be sure to change the Offline Client Availability setting to No.

Datasheet   This option can be set to No if, for some reason, you do not want users to be able to do bulk data entry or editing on the list in datasheet view. It is enabled by default.

Dialogs   This option is set to Yes by default and is why all forms open in a sort of Flash/Silverlight dialog box. If you want the forms to open to their own page instead of a box, set it to No.

FIGURE 7.34
Item-level permissions for the Customers list

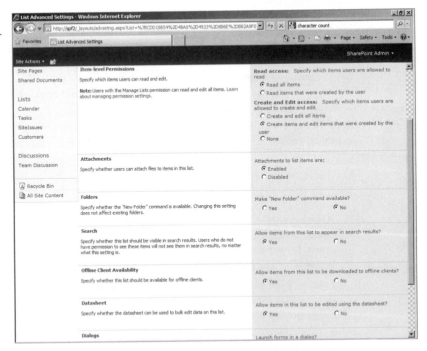

3. For our purposes, everyone should be able to see all the Customer contacts but only be able to edit the ones they entered themselves, so change the Create and Edit Access setting in Item-Level Permissions to Create And Edit Items that were created by the user.

4. For all other settings, leave the defaults as they are.

5. If your settings for this page are complete, click **OK** to finish.

Now when users add items to this list, they will be able to edit their own items but not any-one else's. (Note, however, that if they do attempt to edit someone else's item, the edit form will open and let them fill in the fields, but they will get an error message only when they attempt to save—not an optimal user experience.) Remember, you can always go back and change these settings if circumstances change.

So, we've explored the existing lists and list templates of a SharePoint site, as well as custom-ized them, but we've never created a custom list. And now, it's time.

Creating a Custom List

To create your own list from scratch, you can either import a spreadsheet from Excel or create a standard list and set up the fields yourself before adding data. My example will show you the more difficult one of the two: how to create a custom standard list. Creating a list has at least two essential steps. First you create the list; then you create the fields for the list. You will need to create the fields from scratch, unless you use site columns. It's at this point you begin to see the true value of site columns.

When you create a custom list, there will always be a Title field created for you; this is the field that has the link to view the item, and the drop-down menu will be triggered from its column. Because of this, the Title field shouldn't be deleted but instead repurposed, if you can, as the primary field for the list. Calling it Title often works, but sometimes it would be better as Company Name, Project, or Product Name.

You have done a lot with lists so far, as you've explored preexisting lists and list templates, but there are a few things you need to experience before you are done. For that reason, you are going to create a simplified Sales list with fields that demonstrate the processes of creating a lookup field, using validation, using the custom site column you created earlier, and inserting related lists (otherwise known as connecting web parts).

First you'll edit an existing field (might as well not waste it) and create a Salesperson field so you can assign sales orders to people. You should also have fields for item sold and quantity, as well as currency-formatted cost and price fields. And, while you're at it, you'll use the custom site column created in the "Creating A Custom Site Column" sidebar earlier in the chapter for an expiration date on the sales order items.

1. To start creating the custom list, go to More Options on the Site Actions menu.

2. On the Create page that appears, select Custom List in the Custom Lists category.

3. The New list page has only two sections (Figure 7.35), both of which should look famil-iar to you if you've created a list from a template before: Name And Description and Navigation. In the Name And Description field, enter the data pertinent to this list. Remember to keep the name for the list short because it will be part of the web address for the list and its views.

4. In this case, let's call this list Sales and leave the description blank (you can always change it later by going into the list's settings and selecting Title, Description, And Navigation).

FIGURE 7.35
Creating a new
custom list

FIGURE 7.35
Creating a new
custom list

5. For Navigation, leave the default, and ensure that this list will have a link to it in the Quick Launch bar.

6. To complete the custom list creation, click Create.

That's it; you are at your new list's content page (notice that it comes up with the **List** ribbon already active, for your convenience). As you can see in Figure 7.36, there are already two fields in this list: Attachment and Title. The Attachment field is indicated by the little paper clip icon. Fields for ID, Created By, and Modified By are also created, but they are not displayed in the default view.

FIGURE 7.36
A new custom list

Editing an Existing Field

There were a few fields already created for this custom list by default. One of them is required automatically and can't be deleted: the **Title** field. Although Title is as good a name as any for a default single-line text field, it would better suit our purpose if it were renamed. Take the following steps to do so:

1. Click the List Settings button in the List ribbon.

HEY, WHERE'S INCOMING E-MAIL?

There is no link for incoming email in the Communications category on the List Settings page for this list because custom lists don't have the built-in email handlers that many of the prebuilt lists do. Do not despair, though. You can choose a prebuilt list that does do email and customize it.

---

2. Since the Title field already exists, you are going to change it a little to fit the list better. Remember that it is a built-in field, and it generally is the field used to open a list item, so it's best to try to keep the field and just rename it as a Sales Order field. To edit the Title field, click its link in the Column section. That will open the Change Column page. Go to the first section, and change the name to Sales Order.

3. To prevent problems later, you don't want any duplicate sales order names, so in the Additional Column Settings section, set Enforce Unique Values to Yes (see Figure 7.37). Unique value fields must be indexed, which does take some resources to filter and sort huge lists and therefore should be used sparingly.

FIGURE 7.37
Changing the Title column to Sales Order

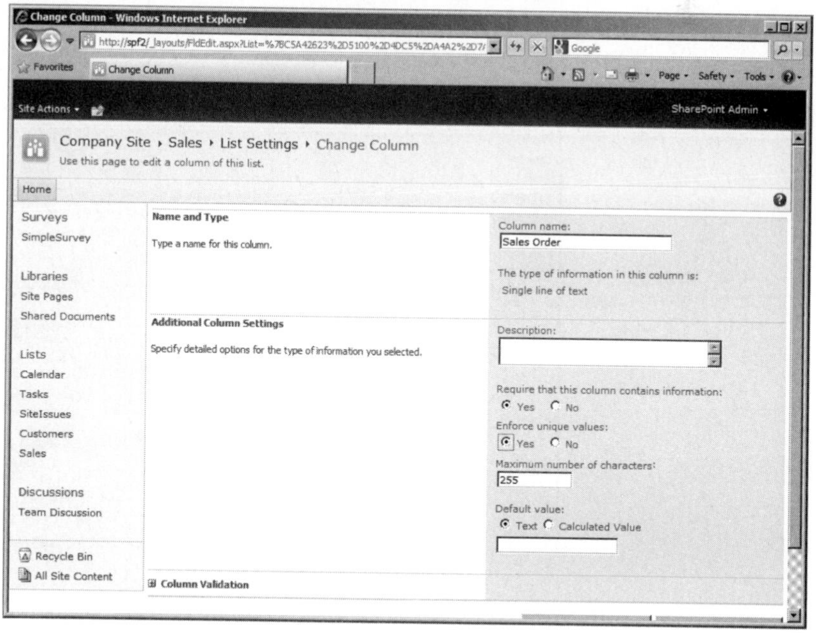

4. The rest of the defaults are fine (no description, require the field, maximum number of characters, no need for column validation), so leave those settings as they are.

   Notice that you can't change the data type for the Title field; it has to be a single line of text.

5. Once your changes are done, click OK. A dialog box will come up warning you that enabling Enforce Unique Value requires that field to be indexed. To accept that and finish editing the field, click OK in the dialog box. That will take you back to the List Settings page.

That should change the name of the Title field to Sales Order, making it a little more relevant, and cause the field to have to be unique from now on.

And now you are ready to create the other fields for this list.

Adding a Person or Group Field

On to creating the Salesperson field. You *could* make this a simple text field and have the users just type in the name of the salesperson for the sales orders. But why introduce possible typing errors when users could use simply look up the name via the Person Or Group field? Since my salespeople are members of this site, this is a perfect fit.

1. To start, click Create Column in the Columns section of the List Settings page.

2. On the Create Column page (Figure 7.38), use Salesperson (obviously) as the column name of the Salesperson field.

FIGURE 7.38
The new Salesperson field in the Create Column page

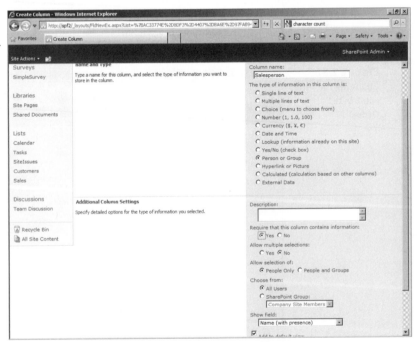

3. For the data type, choose Person Or Group.

4. In Additional Column Settings, require that this field contain information. Do not allow multiple selections (only one salesperson gets commission per sale), and allow this field to have only a person's name (People Only), as opposed to allowing groups as well.

5. You can allow the field to choose from a particular site group or allow it to access all groups (SharePoint or Active Directory) to resolve the username that is entered. For this example, I'll leave it set to **All Users**, but you might choose to only display users in a Sales group, for example.

Because the Person Or Group field is essentially a lookup field for the People And Groups list, you can decide what data from the user information of the person you are selecting will appear in the field. If you type a username in the field, the value returned could be their name with the Presence button next to it (if you have that enabled) or may be the picture or description from their user information or their email address.

6. Leave Show Field set to Name (With Presence) (in case your organization wants to make use of the **Presence** feature), check the Add To Default View box, and click OK.

Back on the List Settings page for this list, you can see that the new Salesperson field has been created. There are several more fields to create before this list is done.

Adding Single-Line Text, Number, and Currency Fields

For this example, the Sales list is also going to need some simple fields to display the name of the item being sold, as well as the item's cost, price, and quantity being sold. To add them, you'll continue working with the Create Column page (shown earlier, in Figure 7.37; this page's settings will change depending on the column type you choose). While you're at it, you'll finally do a little field validation on the quantity field to see how it works.

1. To create the Item Sold field, while in List Settings, click Create Column, and enter the following values:

Column Name: Item Sold

Type: Single line of text

2. In Additional Column Settings, require that this column contain information and otherwise keep all defaults (don't enforce unique value, 255 character maximum, no default value, no column validation, and add to default view), and click **OK**.

3. To create the Cost field, click Create Column, and enter the following values:

Column Name: Cost

Type: Currency

4. Set this field's other settings as follows: require that this column contain information, and specify a minimum value for this column at 5.00. This means that it will not be possible to save the item unless the value of this field is greater than or equal to 5.00. Leave the decimal and default values as they are. Leave the Currency format at the U.S. default. Do not configure Column Validation. When you are done, click OK.

5. To create the Price field, do the same: click **Create Column** on the List Settings page, and set Column Name to Price And Type to Currency. Require the field, and set the minimum value of 5.00. Otherwise, keep the defaults (including no column validation). Click OK.

At this point, you can see that it's not hard to add field after field to a list (having to configure the settings can get tiresome, but that's what site columns are for). However, the next three fields for this custom list are a little fancier. The first one is a field with validation; then you'll do a Customer lookup field. The lookup field will connect to the Customers contact list so that the data entry person won't need to type in a customer's name if it already exists in the Customers list. Finally, you'll add the custom site column.

Adding a Field with Column Validation

Column validation lets you configure a simple formula on the field; the value that is entered during data entry must meet the formula's criteria, or the list item will fail to be created. At that point, a configurable error message will appear beneath the offending field in the new item form, indicating what kind of value is acceptable and requiring that the error be corrected. In this example, you've chosen to allow no more than 10 of each item per order because of shipping issues. So if any value over 10 is entered into the Quantity field, it should be red-flagged before the item is saved to the list so that the user can correct it.

1. To create the Quantity field that you are going to validate, click Create Column, and enter the following values:

    Column Name: Quantity

    Type: Number

2. Require the field, and set a minimum value of 1 (so there can be no zero quantities). Otherwise, keep the rest of the defaults; don't enforce unique value, keep automatic decimal places, no default value, don't display as a percentage, and add the field to the default view.

3. To expand the Column Validation section, click the section title or the plus sign next to it.

    In the Column Validation section are two settings, Formula and User Message (Figure 7.39).

    The syntax for entering a formula can be a little picky (there is a link to open Help so you can look for more information on formulas). Even though you are obviously referring to this field, you must enter the field name in brackets anyway (SharePoint will strip the brackets off and add an equal sign after you save; although I added it in the figure below, you're not obligated to start the formula with equals). Finally, the actual calculation or argument itself has its own syntax. In this case, you need to be sure that the value of this field is less than or equal to 10. Remember, for validation, you are entering the value that defines the parameters that the data in the field has to fall within, so this calculation must be *true* to pass, not be the criteria by which the data fails.

4. So in this case, the formula in the Formula field should be entered as follows:

    `[Quantity]<=10`

FIGURE 7.39

Configuring column validation

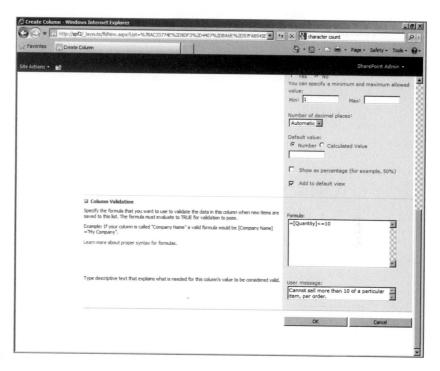

5. The User Message field should contain text that explains why the failure occurred and what should be done to fix it. Enter appropriate descriptive text. In our case, as you saw in Figure 7.39, I entered **Cannot sell more than 10 of a particular item per order**. It's also good practice to state within the field description what values are valid; this will help prevent errors to begin with.

6. When you've finished configuring column validation and the rest of the settings, click OK.

TROUBLESHOOTING COLUMN VALIDATION

Often, if the column validation formula, or more specifically the syntax used in the formula, is wrong, SharePoint won't let you create the field (yeah, just for the formula, you won't be able to create the whole field). The error will, unhelpfully, offer some links to help or troubleshoot SharePoint, but it often won't really tell you what went wrong. Thankfully, if you just click the Back button on your browser, it will go back to the Add Column page, which will still have your settings. (Remember when good UI design made sure you never left the page to navigate?)

Something to keep in mind is that if you use any text in your formula other than a field name, you must put it in quotes. Otherwise, the formula will think you're referring to some other field, which is a no-no.

Adding a Lookup Field

The Customer field for this list would be perfect as a lookup field. The user can only select from existing customers in the Customer contact list, so they can't mistype or make one up. It also creates a nice connection between the Sales and Customer lists.

One shortcoming of lookup fields has been that often when someone needs to look up one field from a list, they actually need information from more than one field in the same list. For example, pulling the customer's company name is useful in the Sales list, but it would be even more useful to also have the contact and their phone number as well. And have them linked, so if you choose a certain company, then the company contact and phone number would propagate with the correct data corresponding to the company name.

And this version of SharePoint can do just that.

In addition, because there will now be a relationship between the two lists, you can indicate what should happen in the *target* list (the list you are adding the lookup field to) if the record is deleted from the *parent* list (the list that is being looked up): should it also delete the related items in the target list, or should it throw up a warning not to delete that record because it has associated records in other lists? This capability was decidedly lacking in the previous version of SharePoint. And although it is rudimentary, it can be very useful.

TO HELP THE LOOKUP WORK BETTER

Just to give SharePoint an assist, consider, in the Customer list, setting whatever field you use for the lookup to Enforce Unique Values so there won't be any confusion if there are more than one record with the same value.

---

1. To create the Customer field, click Create Column.

2. For the Column name, use Customer. Choose Lookup for the data type.

3. In the Additional Column Settings section, require that this column contain information. Do not enforce unique values.

4. Also in that section, select Customers in the Get Information From field. This selects the list that the lookup field will be accessing (Figure 7.40).

5. Choose Company as the column to which the lookup field will connect.

6. Do not check the box to allow multiple values, because there should be only one customer per sales order. Allowing multiple selections would make it possible to choose more than one company from the Customers list for each item in this list. Keep it in mind for other lists you might make, but it's not appropriate here.

Under Add A Column To Show These Additional Fields are the other fields available in the Customers list (note that choice, calculated, or lookup fields don't show up here) to display in the list along with the lookup field. They are considered *projected* fields, meaning the extra data is pulled for your viewing pleasure in this list, but the data they contain is not saved in this list. These additional fields will be displayed with their field name appended to the lookup field name by a colon (you'll see in a moment). They also will come immediately after their associated lookup field in the view, by default.

7. In this example, I am going to select to show **Full Name** and E-mail Address as additional fields (Figure 7.40).

FIGURE 7.40
Adding a
lookup field to
a custom list

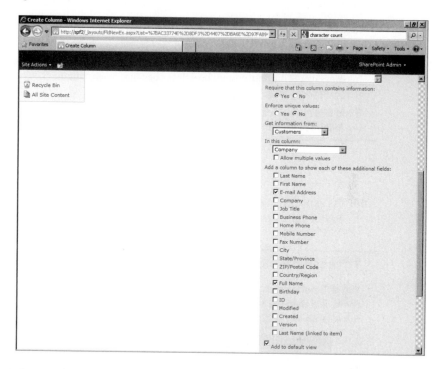

Beneath the additional fields section is the **Relationship** section, which contains the settings concerning what happens if an item is deleted from the lookup field's source list. Should it not enforce the relationship and do nothing to the items in this list that relate to the items in the source list that are being deleted? Or, if enforced, should the source list be *restricted* from deleting an item that is used by this list, or should the item (or items) on this list that relate to the original list be *cascade-deleted* when the original customer record is deleted (if we decide we won't need to keep the sales order if the customer is gone, for example).

In this example, you want to keep sales order data history to track sales, regardless of any loss of clients, so let's enforce relationship behavior and not allow customer records to be deleted from the Customers list when there are related items in the Sales list (you can add a Yes/No field to indicate active versus inactive customers in the future if you must).

8. To enforce relationship, check the Enforce Relationship Behavior box, and make sure Restrict Delete is enabled (Figure 7.41). Keep in mind that because you are enforcing, SharePoint will need to index the column. The overhead unnecessary indexing entails is a good reason to think carefully before enforcing relationship behavior.

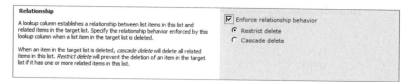

ENFORCE RELATIONSHIPS

By enforcing a relationship between the Sales and Customers lists, this means that if there is a customer record in the Customers list that an item in the Sales list is using in its lookup field, then you shouldn't be able to delete it.

If you try it, the Delete button or menu item will not be grayed out, but it will fail with the following message: "This item cannot be deleted because an item in the [Lookup] list is related to an item in the [Source] list."

If you had enabled cascading delete, then if you deleted a list item in the source list, the records in the lookup or related list (like this one) would simply be deleted.

9. Keep all other defaults, and click **OK**.

10. As expected, you will be prompted to accept that enforcing that relationship behavior will require the field to be index. Click OK to accept.

TITLE LENGTH TOO LONG?

You will notice that the generated field titles are a little lengthy, with the lookup field name, a colon, and then the additional field name. If the field titles take up too much space, you can select the column on the List Settings page and edit its title to make it more to your liking.

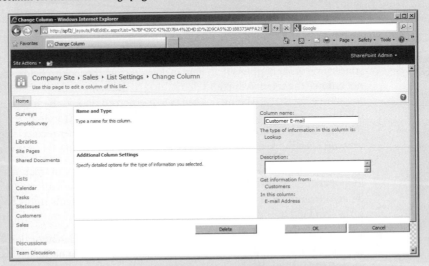

You can also see on the Change Column page that it indicates what list and what field in that list the column pulls from.

That should add Customer as a field, as well as its additional display fields (see Figure 7.42). Although the additional fields appear just after the lookup field, they are for show only and have nothing to do with data entry, so their order in the underlying list doesn't matter. If you decide to add additional display fields for this lookup, edit the lookup field here (in this case, Customer). If you want them to display in the view in a different order, you can easily modify the view to suit your needs.

FIGURE 7.42
The new lookup and additional fields

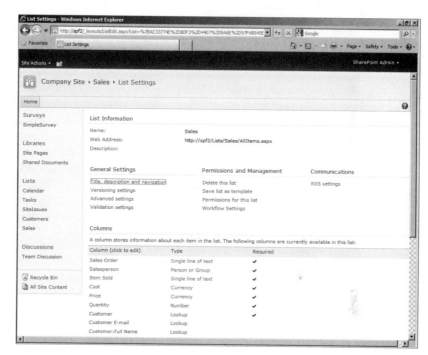

The final field to create for this list is Expiration, which was a site column that you created earlier in the chapter.

Adding a Custom Site Column

One of the beautiful things about site columns is their ease of use. Yes, it's a little inconvenient to have to go directly to the Site Column Gallery to create your own site columns (rather than just clicking a setting on a field you've already created and tested in a list to add it to the gallery). Regardless, site columns can't be beat for their convenience when creating or modifying lists.

1. To add the custom site column we created earlier to the Sales list, simply click Add From Existing Site Columns in the Columns section of the List Settings page. This is the same sequence you followed to add the existing Birthday site column to the Customers list earlier.

2. You'll be taken to the Add Columns from Site Columns page, where you can select Custom Columns from the Site Columns Groups drop-down menu. This is the group that contains the site column you added earlier in the chapter.

3. Select **Expiration** for this example from the Available Site Columns list, and click the Add button. Allow the column to be added to the default view.

4. Click OK to finish.

INDEXING COLUMNS

You didn't explicitly set any column indexing in the exercise, because that is primarily done only in the case of extremely large lists (around 10,000 items) or, as you saw, in the case of enforcing relationships or unique value (there's a moral there somewhere). However, if you are planning to have huge lists, consider indexing columns. Indexing a column in a large list helps the server organize and filter those list items more quickly. Indexing is resource intensive, and you should index as few columns per list as possible, because the amount of RAM it takes to index a column begins to take its toll.

To maximize how quickly a list can propagate a view when a user accesses it, it is a best practice to create views that limit the number of items seen at one time. To make those views work better, they should filter by a field that is indexed. Try to use the same indexed field as the main focus in as many views as possible. Index additional fields only if they are going to be the focus of views that cannot contain the original indexed column.

To set a column to be indexed, go to the list's List Settings page, and in the Columns section select Indexed Columns. That will take you to an Indexed Columns page, displaying any already indexed columns. Click the Create New Index link to open the Edit Index page, where you can select the field you want to index as well as an optional secondary field to index. To delete an index from a field, select it on the Indexed Columns page, and click Delete at the bottom of the Edit Index page for that index.

Keep in mind that SharePoint sometimes creates indexes that shouldn't be deleted. In addition, there is a limit of 20 indexed fields per list, in case that affects your list design.

---

5. That's it. The custom list is complete. To give it a test run, go to the list's content page (click the list name in the title breadcrumb at the top of the List Settings page), and then click Add New Item.

On the new Sales – New Item form (Figure 7.43), note that the required fields are indicated with a red asterisk. The Salesperson field is a People Picker. The Customer field is a drop-down list, indicating that it is a lookup field; it defaults to the first list item in the Customers list. Finally, you can see that the Expiration field is there, with a default date of 10 days from today.

Let's enter some data and see what happens. Remember that you have a validation formula active for the Quantity field.

1. In the **New Item** form, enter a sales order name in the Sales Order field (see Figure 7.44 for sample data).

2. For the Salesperson field, enter the account name of one of your users, and then click Check Name to resolve it.

3. Enter a fictitious name for the Item Sold field.

4. For the Cost field, enter any number, but for Price, try entering a number that is less than Cost, to see whether that mistake will be allowed.

5. For Quantity, enter a number that is larger than 10; that should kick off an error message when you save, if your column validation is working.

6. For the Customer field, keep the company that defaults there, because it's the only item in the Customers list right now.

7. And for the sales order expiration date, the default 10 days from now is fine. If I can't turn this sales order into a sales invoice by then, then it will probably be canceled.

8. If all the field contents are satisfactory, click Save to try to finish adding the new item.

FIGURE 7.43
A new item for the new custom list

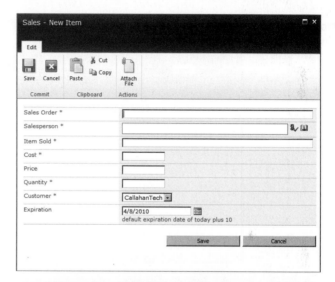

FIGURE 7.44
Sample sales order item

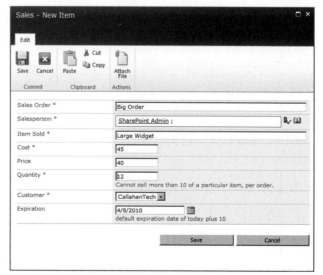

As you can see in Figure 7.44, my Quantity was just over 10, which is not allowed according to the column validation set earlier. And therefore, my save failed. My error message for the Quantity field validation is now displayed, and the cursor is in the Quantity field, ready for the mistake to be fixed.

9. Change the value in the Quantity field to 10 or less, and click **Save** again.

That should work. Your item should save, and you should end up on the Sales list content page. Notice, in Figure 7.45, that my new item is listed, complete with the additional fields and their content.

FIGURE 7.45
Custom list with new sales order item

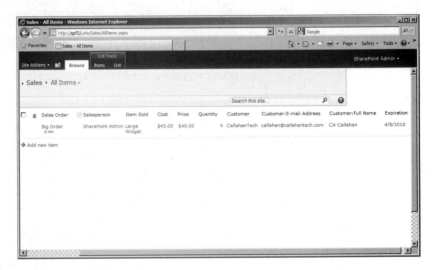

As you can see, field (or column) validation is working. But there was an unfortunate data entry error concerning the price being lower than the inventory cost of the item. That isn't a good thing. Wouldn't it be nice if you could have some sort of validation that could compare two fields and, if one were higher than the other, alert the user and not allow those values to be saved? Column validation can't see other fields in the list, so it can't be used. But there is list validation.

List validation is just like column validation, but it can do calculations that refer to any of the fields in the list.

Configuring List Validation

To configure list validation on this list, go to the List Settings page.

1. On the List Settings page, click the Validation Settings link under General Settings.

On the Validation Settings page, there are two sections: Formula and User Message. The Formula section has a field selection box, allowing you to calculate based on other field values (letting you select the field names rather than type them in).

2. In this case, you need to ensure that the value in the Cost field is less than the value in the Price field, so enter the formula [Cost]<[Price]. (To select the fields to put in the Formula box, just double-click them or select them and click the Add To Formula link.)

3. In the User Message box, enter an appropriate warning (see Figure 7.46 for my example). Once you've entered your formula and user message, click Save.

FIGURE 7.46

The List Validation settings

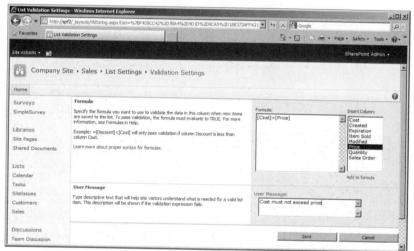

4. That should take you back to the List Settings page. Go to the list by clicking its name in the title breadcrumb, and let's test the List Validation setting to see whether it works.

5. Back on the Sales content page, click Add A New Item.

6. Fill all the fields as you want except Cost and Price; there, enter amounts such that Cost is higher than Price. You already know the column validation for the Quantity works, so enter a value of 10 or less.

7. Once you've entered your data, click Save. The save should fail, with your list validation user message displayed *at the top* of the form (Figure 7.47). This is because there may be more than one field involved in this issue. The list validation error goes on top (and there can only be one), and each field's error message goes beneath its field.

8. So there you have it. Edit the Price field so that its value is greater than Cost, and click Save.

Back on the list, you'll see the fields that were added to the default view, complete with their data. That's it. You now have your very own custom list including lookup, site column, and a People And Groups field. Both list and column validations are in force, so data entry is more likely to be accurate.

FIGURE 7.47
A list validation
error message

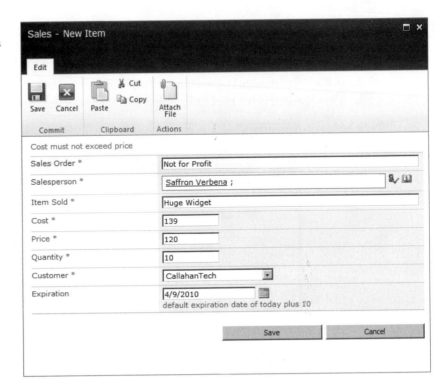

 Real World Scenario

WISH YOU COULD REUSE YOUR LIST ELSEWHERE? MAKE IT A TEMPLATE

Let's say that you customized the heck out of a list. You added a lot of cool calculated fields, did a lot of field validation, and so on. You know that that list would be useful elsewhere, and you aren't looking forward to re-creating it later, when you create subsites.

Well, you don't necessarily have to do so. You can make a list template (as Contacts and Tasks are) out of a list. It will become available on the Create page just like all the other templates and will be stored in the List Templates gallery for the site collection. There are some caveats; for example, templates can't hold on to security settings. Also, any lookup fields that reference another list won't work if that list doesn't exist where the template is going to be applied.

Lists can be made into templates with or without content. That is, you can save only the design or save the design with the data as well. Templates usually have a 50MB size limit (although that can be increased to 500MB at the command line), so it is often better to simply save a list template without data. That is also the case if any of the data was confidential or was protected with specific permissions.

To create a list template, just do the following:

1. Go to the list's List Settings page, and click Save List As Template. That will open a **Save As Template** page, with fields for **F**ile Name, Template Name (this is how it will be listed in the gallery and on the Create page), and Description, as well as whether the template will include content.

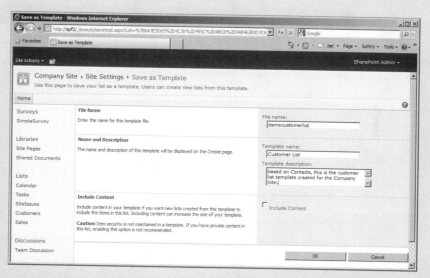

2. Just fill in the fields as you want, and click **OK**. You'll get an Operation Completed Successfully page with a link to the List Template Gallery so you can take a look at it. In the List Template Gallery, the template will be listed by its filename first.

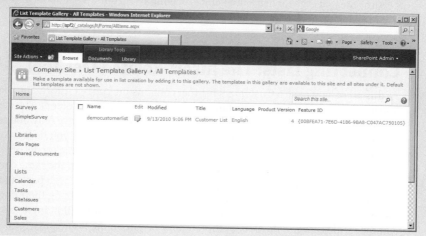

3. Then, to apply the template, just go to the Create page. It will be listed there (mine is under Communications, since it's based on the Contacts list). If you hover your mouse pointer over the template's name, your description will be displayed.

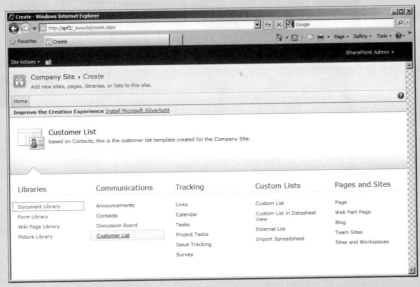

Lists can also be downloaded from the List Template Gallery (which is just a library) and then uploaded to List Template Galleries of other site collections as well. The list template files make decent backups. Just remember that anything that was linked via lookup won't work, and permission settings will be wiped.

Also note that even though SharePoint is moving away from .STP (SharePoint Template Package), list templates are still saved in that format.

Connecting Lists: The Insert Related List Tool

At this point, you have a Customers list that contains the contact information for your customers. You also have a Sales list that contains sales orders for those customers. The customers can (and ideally do) place more than one sales order, but each order can have only one customer. And each single list item in the Customers list is a record of a customer. So, you have a common customer field (Company) between the two lists, linking them. One list is the *parent*, or has one record per value, and the other is the *child*, or can have multiple records with the same common value.

As long as they have a field in common, you can connect the web parts of two lists to filter the view of one with the selected record of the other; synchronizing their data makes them both more useful. This helps list view web parts be more dynamic, allowing users to capitalize on the commonalities among the data of the site's lists right on the home page (or any other web part page for that matter). See Chapter 5, "Introduction to Web Parts," if you need a refresher on list view web parts.

This means you can put the web parts of the Customers list and the Sales list on the same page. You can then create a connection between them so that if you click an item in the Customers web part, the corresponding Sales web part will change to show only records that match the common field data from the selected Customers list item.

In this version of SharePoint, Microsoft has gone out of its way to encourage users to connect web parts by adding a button to the Web Tools ➢ Options ribbon called Insert Related List. It basically adds the related list view web part to the page (it drops down a menu displaying the lists that have lookup fields pointing at the web parts on the page you're editing, so you can select one). Then it configures the connection between the two for you.

The Insert Related List button has its limits, as you'll see, and isn't quite as flexible as doing the web part connections yourself, but at least it gets you started.

To see what I'm talking about, let's first enter some more records into the Customers and Sales lists and then use the Insert Related List button to add the Sales list web part to the Customers list content page.

1. Go to the Customers list in the Quick Launch bar. On the Customers page, choose Add New Item, and create some new customers. You can also change the view to enable inline editing if you'd like to edit inline on the page, or better yet, you can enable Datasheet view—remembering that with both of those options, you can only enter data on fields in the view.

2. Once you have at least three customers (see my example in Figure 7.48), go to the Sales list's content page.

FIGURE 7.48
The Customers list with additional items

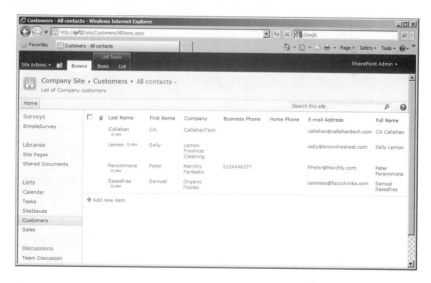

3. For this example, you want to have at least two sales orders that look up the same customer from the Customers list and at least one that uses a different customer (see Figure 7.49 for my example; be careful about the validations).

FIGURE 7.49

The Sales list with additional items

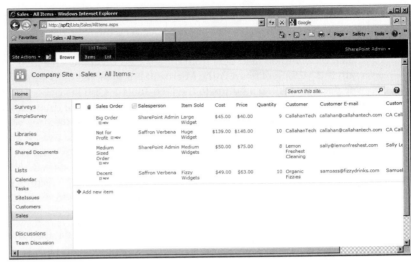

Once both lists have these additional entries, it's time to connect the lists so you can see how related lists work.

To use Insert Related List, you must go either to any view of the content page of the list that is the *source* (or parent) of the relationship between the lists or to a wiki or web part page with that source list web part on it. The page must be in edit mode, so you can insert the web part of the list that has a lookup to that source.

If you were just adding that inserted web part to the page, it would be placed by default at the top of the zone. However, since it's being filtered by the source list, an inserted related web part is placed below the source list.

To see this in action, let's go to the Customers list. It doesn't have to be the source list's content page, but that's convenient, since the Customers list view web part is already there. (If you want to do this on the home page, add the Customers web part to the page first), but you need to put the page into edit mode. You can personalize the page (Account menu, Personalize This Page) if you want to insert a related list web part to just the logged-in person's version of the page, or you can edit the default view (or a new view) of the list (Site Actions, Edit page).

1. For this example, you will just personalize the page by going to the Account menu on the Customers list and clicking Personalize This Page.

2. Once the page is in edit mode, click the Web Part Tools Options tab.

   In the **Options** ribbon, there is an Insert Related List button.

3. Click the down arrow below the Insert Related List button to access the drop-down menu. If there are any lists using the lists on the page (there can be more than one list view web part here) as a source, they will be available to be selected in the Insert Related List drop-down menu.

   In this case, the only list using Customers as a lookup source is **Sales** (Figure 7.50).

4. To insert a Sales list view web part below the existing Customers web part on the page and connect the two, click Sales in that Insert Related List drop-down menu.

Immediately, the related web part is dropped on the page *below* the original web part, and the original web part on the page displays a Select column containing diagonal two-headed arrows for use in filtering the related web part (Figure 7.51). It's that simple.

FIGURE 7.50
Selecting a list with the Insert Related List button drop-down menu

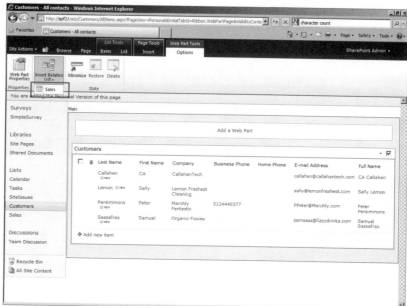

FIGURE 7.51
The related list web part inserted

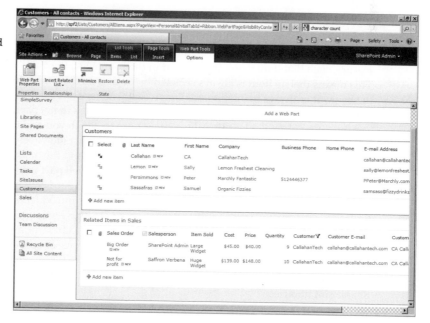

5. Click the Page tab, and then click Stop Editing to get out of edit mode.

Once out of edit mode, you can see the page as a user would. Note that you can create views on the underlying lists specifically to be used for web parts with only the fields you want to display, and then you can edit the web part to display that view.

6. To see how this related list stuff works, click the double-headed selection arrow next to the customer item that has several sales orders related to it.

When you do, the Sales web part will be filtered to just show the sales orders for that customer (Figure 7.52).

FIGURE 7.52
The Sales web part filtered

One thing to note with connected lists is that the web parts don't have a "clear selection" feature, such that if no items are selected in the source list, then all items of the related list show. This means that an item is always selected by default on the source list, and therefore the related list below it is always being filtered. But at least you have a related list web part on the page. Now, at a click of a mouse, you can see all the sales orders that a particular customer has made.

Something else to note is that the content page to which you add the related list web part is now considered a web part page (since there are two list view web parts on it), so the title breadcrumb no longer has a view menu at the end of it, and the default tabs for the list will not display. To get the tabs, you have to select the list view web part you want them to affect. If you remove the additional web part, the page reverts to a standard content page.

Congratulations! That should just about do it for your introduction to lists. I've covered built-in lists, list templates, custom lists, list modification, views, overlays, branching logic, calculations, validation, enforced relationships, related list web parts, and more. Lists have many options and can become complex; however, you should have enough information to experiment and make your own lists. If you're curious about versioning and using your own content types, continue to Chapter 8, "Introduction to Libraries," for more on those features as I discuss SharePoint libraries.

LIST VIEW WEB PARTS AND THE COMMON FIELD CONNECTION

So, you've seen the training wheels version of connecting web parts, using related lists. Now it's time to look under the hood and see how easy connecting web parts really is.

If you were to put two web parts on the same page that had a lookup field in common, such as Sales and Customers, you could connect them, like Related Lists, but with more control.

1. First put the page into edit mode; then click the down arrow in the title bar of the web part you'd like to use to filter the other web part, and select Connections.

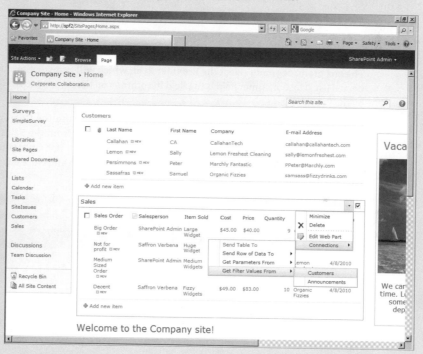

2. It will pop out a menu of options for the kind of connection you want to make:

Send Row of Data To: If this option is selected, this web part will be the one that filters the other by what item is chosen from its contents.

Get Parameters From: Generally not applicable for list view web parts, this option is used to send parameters from one web part, such as a data view web part, to another.

Get Filter Values From: If this option is selected, the contents of the web part will be filtered to match the common field data from the item selected in the other web part.

3. In this case, Sales is going to get filter values from the other list view web part on the page (in our example that will be Customers) and be filtered by it (essentially choosing to make the connection from the list being filtered, instead of the one forcing the filter). When the option is selected, it pops out the list of possible web parts to connect with. When you select the list you want to connect with, a Configure Connection dialog box will open.

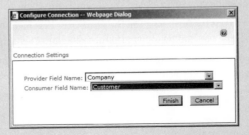

The box prompts you to select the Provider field, which will provide the data to filter the connected list. The Consumer field is the field in common on the connected list that will be filtered by the Provider data.

4. In my example, the Provider field is the Company field from the Customers list, and the Consumer field is, conveniently enough, the Company field from the Sales table (they're not always going to have the same field name; it's the data that counts). Once you've finished specifying the connection settings and are back on the page, finish and close out of edit mode. Your lists will be connected.

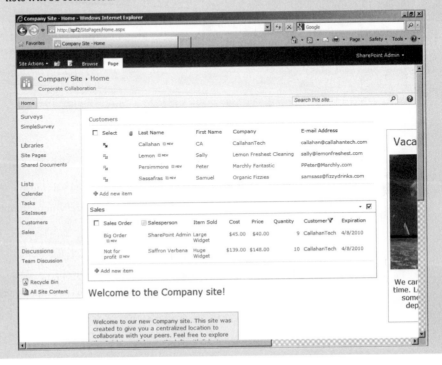

5. If you change the view of the content in either list and the common field is not displayed in both of them anymore, it will break the connection. To remove the connection on purpose, bring the Configure Connection box back up (in edit mode, click the down arrow in the title bar, click Connections, and select the existing connection between the web parts).

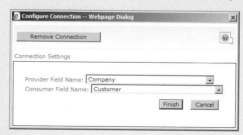

6. In the dialog box, a Remove Connection button will be available. Use it to remove the connection between the two lists.

If you wanted to get fancy, you could have a web part be the row provider and filter several other list view web parts on the page. So, when one record in the row provider is chosen, it filters all the connected web parts. Or have one web part filter another, and that web part filter another, and so on.

The Bottom Line

Create a list from a template.   SharePoint has, in addition to a few convenient prebuilt lists, ready-to-go templates of common lists. This makes it very easy to simply create a new list based on an existing template and then customize it, rather than having to create one like it from scratch.

> **Master It**   What list template creates a list that is meant to work with the Three-State workflow? How would you go about creating that list?

Create a custom list.   In addition to the prebuilt lists and the templates, SharePoint has the option to create custom lists from scratch. Lists can be custom made in two ways: by importing from an Excel spreadsheet or by manually building one. All lists require at least one field (by default the Title field) and include system-generated columns for ID, Created By, and Modified By.

> **Master It**   You're creating a custom list to track inventory. You need to make sure that, during the data entry process, the item number field is never left blank and is unique for each item and that purchase levels never exceed storage levels.

Display related lists.   This version of SharePoint has expanded its capabilities regarding related lists, from enforcing relationships and allowing additional related fields to more easily displaying related data in list view web parts.

> **Master It**   How would you go about filtering the contents of one list based upon the value in another, related list? What is the essential element that allows you to do this?

Chapter 8

Introduction to Libraries

SharePoint libraries are lists intended to be used for managing documents. Their list items are focused on the files attached to them, with features specific to handling the creation and editing of those files, such as requiring check-in/checkout, versioning, and content approval. Libraries make it easier for users to work together on documents in a consistent and secure manner. Libraries are often the most compelling reason people even consider using SharePoint. They are generally the foundation of the collaborative work users might need to accomplish, whether that involves sharing documents, spreadsheets, slide shows, or forms.

In this chapter, you'll learn how to

- ◆ Create a library
- ◆ Use the different kinds of libraries
- ◆ Set check out, content approval, and versioning
- ◆ Manage content types

What Are Libraries?

Libraries are lists that are known by, and focused on, the kinds of files they will contain. There are four types of libraries:

Document Library   The name *document library* rather obscures what this type of library really is. A document library is a list that creates a new file of some type whenever you create a new list item. The file type depends on what template you associate with the list itself (and doesn't have to be a document template). If you enable content types, the file type depends on what type of library list items (and their associated template) you want to have available for the list. This list also has features such as content approval, versioning, RSS, and incoming email. In addition, libraries can also mark their list items as checked in or checked out, locking the list item and its attached file as read-only on checkout and unlocking the item upon check-in to the library. This feature is unique to libraries. Document libraries also have an option to open the library with Explorer that lets you see the contents of the library as file system icons instead of list items. SharePoint document libraries are supposed to replace file shares; opening the library in Explorer helps make users comfortable with the transition. This view makes it easy to drag and drop files that need to be stored in a library from a file share. In addition, document libraries can make good use of content types and folders that may not be clearly useful for other types of lists. A document library can also spawn a document workspace subsite. This kind of list is meant to integrate with Office, because the templates associated with library list items are mostly Office templates such as Word, Excel, PowerPoint, or even InfoPath. In addition, like any list, a document library can also be opened in Access, exported to Excel (well, the metadata anyway), and connected to Outlook.

Form Library This type of library requires Microsoft Office InfoPath, preferably InfoPath 2007 or newer. InfoPath is a program that creates forms for users to fill out. More specifically, it lets you design your own form templates; when a user opens the template, it creates a *form instance*, which allows the user to fill the form with data. InfoPath 2010 comes in two flavors, InfoPath Designer and InfoPath Filler. You design and publish InfoPath forms to a forms library using InfoPath Designer, and the users can fill out the form using InfoPath Filler. InfoPath files are XML files, and they require InfoPath to be installed locally on the machine from which you will be using the library. This type of library is useful for companies that process vacation requests, purchase orders, and other kinds of InfoPath forms that need to be filled out by the users. Because InfoPath forms are based on templates, if you move a file from one form library to another, you'll need to relink it to its template.

Picture Library This type of library is intended to store images that you can access elsewhere on the site; each image file is given a direct URL that can be referred to in an image web part or hyperlink field of a list item (such as an item in a Contacts list). You may have noticed that images aren't inserted into fields of web parts (such as the Content Editor) or RSS pages; instead, these features all refer to an image's location and display the image from there. No embedding is necessary. Image files in a picture library are stored in the content database, so they are convenient to the entire site and are backed up when the content databases are backed up. A picture library uses the Picture Manager that is installed with Office (preferably 2010, but 2007 and 2003 have one, too) to edit images and add multiple images to the library. A user who does not have an Office product installed will only be able to upload one picture at a time to the library. The picture library also has several unique views, and this version of SharePoint even has a picture library slide show web part, if you would like to add a slide show from one of your picture libraries to a page (the web part takes a lot of processor power for the client viewing it, though).

Wiki Library This type of library is basically a document library of HTML files that support the wiki syntax when linking to other files in the same library. This library is unique insofar as it displays the contents of the wiki file called Home instead of displaying its contents in a list on its content page. To access the actual content page for the library, you can click the library's link in the content breadcrumb. A wiki library has versioning enabled by default, and it does not allow content types. Unlike the other library types, it does not support Open with Explore, so you cannot drag and drop multiple files into the library. Wiki libraries have no means to upload existing pages.

Creating a library is easy, but before you create one, you need to do some planning first. You should ask yourself these questions:

◆ Is there a maximum file size you want to allow on SharePoint sites? The default is 50 MB.

◆ Are there any types of files you do not want to be uploaded to a library? Some file types are helpfully blocked by default in Central Administration. You may want to block different files or unblock the defaults. This setting applies per web application, so you need to keep it in mind when planning for document libraries.

- Does the library or certain files require special permissions?

- Does the library require checkout/check-in, versioning, or content approval?

- Should the library have a single kind of file template associated with it, or should it have content types enabled so you can have several kinds of templates available to be created from the same library?

- Is the list going to contain thousands of documents? If so, should this library be organized as a list or as folders? (When creating a view for a list containing folders, remember to decide whether the view should display content from those folders in the library's default view.)

- Like any list item, a library item has fields such as Name, Title, Created By, and so on. What additional fields do you want to create for your library items? They will become the metadata or properties associated with the file attached to the library item.

LIBRARY PLANNING FOR WORKFLOWS

Like any list, a library can have new fields for categorizing, organizing, and creating workflows. For example, to enforce a review process, you can create a choice field called Status with three choices, and an Assigned To field; then you can apply the Three-State workflow to the library and create tasks in a Tasks list (with email notifications) for each document. If your organization has custom document management workflows, consider their needs when creating your libraries.

To get a feel for libraries in general, let's use the document library called Shared Documents that is created by default for the team site. To get to the Shared Documents library, simply click its link in the Quick Launch bar.

The Shared Documents content page looks very much like any list. It has a content area to display the library items, and the fields for the All Documents view are Type, Name, Modified, and Modified By. The Type field will display an icon relating the type of file or template used for the library item. This is useful if you are uploading or creating different files of different types in this library. People can accidentally give two kinds of files the same name, such as the ProjectPlans Word document and an accompanying ProjectPlans PowerPoint presentation. You can tell them apart by their file type icon.

The ribbon bars are a little different because they include the capacity to upload a file (rather than just create a new item), to check in or check out a document, and to view the page in an Explorer window. Otherwise, the Documents and Library ribbons contain the buttons you would expect in any standard list. When you first get to a library, you can see the title area. To see the ribbon bars, you can click on their tabs in the top ribbon bar or simply click on an existing item in the library, which will also activate the Documents ribbon. (see Figure 8.1)

Libraries can be used to create new documents—depending on how the templates those new documents will be based on are managed—or you can upload existing files to the library. Keep in mind that templates apply to only what is newly created in a library. Any templates associated with the library are not a limitation on the types of files (text files, image files, audio files, and so on) that can be *uploaded* there. You can upload any kind of existing file (unless it is explicitly blocked administratively) to a document library.

FIGURE 8.1
The Shared
Documents
content page

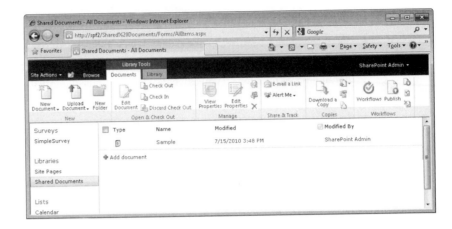

Uploading a Document to a Library

To upload one or more files to a library, just click the Add Document link at the bottom of the library's content area, which opens the Upload Document box (see Figure 8.2). It has a check box that allows you to save over an existing file and add the changes you've made to that file's version history (if versioning is enabled).

FIGURE 8.2
The Upload Docu-
ment box

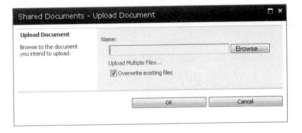

Notice also that, if you have an Office (2003, 2007, 2010) product installed, you could choose to upload multiple files, which would open a page where you can browse to a location and select more than one file to upload. (You can also choose to upload multiple files by clicking the down arrow under the Upload Document button in the Documents ribbon and choosing it from the drop-down menu.)

My example keeps things simple and uploads only one file (named `uploaded` in this case). Simply browse to the file you'd like to upload, select it, and click Open in the Choose File dialog box. Once the path for the file is listed on the Upload Document page, click OK to add the file to the document library. (Keep in mind that you can only browse to a file; you cannot type in the path manually.)

When you add a file to a document library, it actually creates a library list item and adds the file to it. In Figure 8.3, you can see by the icon in the Type column that the file type for my example's new library item is a Word document. SharePoint will try to figure out what the file type is and indicate it; otherwise, it will display a default file icon. The name of the file is the linked field for the library item.

FIGURE 8.3
FIGURE 8.3
An uploaded file in
the Shared Docu-
ments library

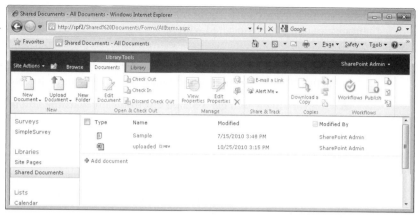

WHAT'S THAT SAMPLE FILE?

You may have noticed there was already a file in the library that we didn't upload. Actually, I uploaded that file, named `sample.txt`, in Chapter 4, "Introduction to the SharePoint Interface," to demonstrate how the interface works.

In a standard list, if you click the linked field of an item, it will open the item's View page and display that list's field contents. But because a library is so focused on the files associated with the library item, the linked field is linked to the *file*, not the library item itself. So in this case, if you click that library item's linked field, it will trigger the appropriate application to open the file and allow you to work on it. To see the fields of the actual library item, you must specifically select View Properties from the item's drop-down menu.

In addition to the Name field, there are the Modified Date and Modified By fields, which are automatically filled in upon creation of the library item and when any edits are made to the item or its attached file. There are other fields that can be used for an item in this library as well, such as for the item ID, file size, or version, but they are not available in the default All Items view for document libraries (I mention them in case you'd like to use them in a custom view of your own).

By default, the Shared Documents document library uses a Word 2007/2010 document template. This is why, while working in the Shared Documents library, I will be working with documents. But keep in mind that you can have a document library focused on PowerPoint presentations just as easily as you can Word documents. Then you would be creating and working on presentations instead of documents. Don't be limited by the name of the type of library or my simple example; document libraries can use other kinds of templates and therefore focus on other kinds of files.

Creating a New Document

When you create a new document in a library rather than uploading an existing one, it creates a new file based on the template associated with the library, opening the file in the correct application (you must have that application installed locally). When you save the file to the library for the first time, it also creates the library item for the file and populates the item's fields with the properties of the file associated with it.

To create a new document based on the library's template, follow these steps:

1. Click on the Documents tab in the top ribbon bar if the Documents ribbon is not already active. Then click the New Item button in the Documents ribbon.

2. You very likely will get a dialog box ironically warning you that some files can harm your computer and that you are opening a `template.docx` file from the SharePoint server. Click OK if that Warning dialog box appears.

3. A new Word document will open. Simply type some text into the document, and save it.

   You'll be prompted to name the file; my example uses `newdoc` (Figure 8.4). In the Save As dialog box, the file is being saved to the Shared Documents library on the SharePoint server, which is `http://sp2` in my example.

FIGURE 8.4

Saving a new document to the Shared Documents library

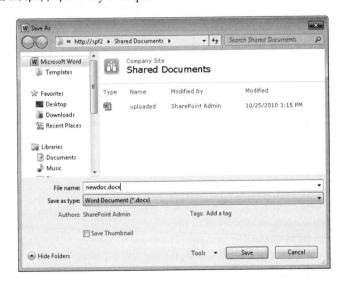

4. Name the file, and click Save.

5. Close the Word document.

TEMPLATE VERSIONS

The Shared Documents library is set to use a Word 2007/2010-compatible `.dotx` template. However, you can create a document library that uses a `.dot` template if you need the backward compatibility.

Two Word documents are now in the Shared Documents library.

If you select a document in the list, it will activate the Documents ribbon and enable most of the buttons. The document name field is capable of triggering a drop-down menu at the end of its column, the same as any item in any list, to edit, view properties, and do other individual item tasks. You will see some familiar list item options and some new ones (these options can change depending on the configuration of the library and even the item itself):

View Properties   This option is used to see the metadata, or field data, for the library item. It corresponds to the View Item option in a standard list; however, in this environment, you should think of the item fields as document properties.

Edit Properties   This option lets you edit the metadata of the library item.

Edit In Microsoft Office Word   As the option says, it allows you to open the library item's attached file for editing in Microsoft Word. For this to work, of course, you must have Word installed locally on the machine with which you are browsing the site. This menu item is also triggered when you simply click the name of the library item. The menu item will reflect the type of the attached file (if SharePoint can identify it).

Check Out   This option locks a document from being checked out and makes it read-only for everyone but the person checking it out. This helps limit the amount of overlapping work that might be done on a document simultaneously. When a user is done with a document, they can check it back in, making it available to be edited by someone else. Check Out is not required by default. If it is required, then no document can be edited unless it is checked out. Thus, to edit a document, a user must check it out; otherwise, it will be read-only. Check Out can be overridden by someone with the permission to do so, usually an administrator or list manager.

Alert Me   This setting is the same as for standard lists; it means you can configure email notification if there are changes made to library items, based on a limited set of criteria, such as changes made only to documents you created or to all documents.

Send To   This menu option has several functions. Items in a library can be sent to other libraries and locations. As SharePoint and its document libraries have evolved, libraries have become more connected to other libraries and site resources; a document workspace can be generated from a document in a library, or finished documents from a library can be sent to a final archive library.

By default, Send To offers the options to email a link, create a document workspace for the document, download a copy, or send a copy of the document to another location (such as a different library). There is also an option in the overall library settings to define a custom library or location to use as a default place to send a copy of the document. Documents sent to a different library can be updated with changes from the original library. The secondary location is generally meant to be an archive. What that means is the secondary location cannot update changes made to the document copy there *back* to the original library. The updates are only one-way.

Manage Permission   This option lets you apply unique permissions to the library item. Because all objects on the site inherit that site's permissions, you first would break inherited permissions and then alter the permissions for the item to fit.

Delete   This is the option that removes the document and its library item from the library and puts it in the user's SharePoint Recycle Bin. Remember that when things are deleted from lists or libraries, they are not completely gone until either they are also removed from the Recycle Bin or the Recycle Bin times out and all items of a certain age are deleted (30 days by default).

Most people focus on the documents in a library, but they are just attachments for the library list items. You can create fields for any library item just as you could any list. You can require that those fields be filled out before the item and its document are saved. This makes it possible to require users to enter data that can be used to track documents, search for them, or trigger workflows.

DROP-DOWN MENU OR RIBBON BUTTON?

There are two ways to access the tasks available for a document item. One is to use the buttons on the Documents ribbon, and the other is to use the drop-down menu associated with each item. Because a number of the buttons in the ribbon are without labels and are organized in sections that might initially seem unintuitive, I've opted to do most of the exercises here using the item drop-down menu, rather than the ribbon buttons. The menu is organized simply, and all options are labeled for easy identification. There is no need to scan through the ribbon to see which buttons are grayed out and which aren't. However, feel free to select an item and then use the ribbon bar buttons instead of using the drop-down menu.

Right now there are very few editable fields for this library. To see what those fields are, in the item's drop-down menu, select Edit Properties. In Figure 8.5, you can see that the Name and Title fields are available for data entry. Name is the only required field, and it is automatically populated with the filename of the document you upload or create from a template in the library. The Title field is not required; therefore, you generally don't get prompted to fill in the Title field when you create a document, which is why it is empty.

FIGURE 8.5
Edit properties of library item

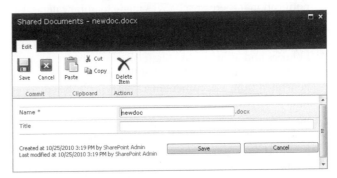

DETERMINING THE WORD VERSION

As you probably know, Word changed its file format between the 2003 (.doc) and 2007 (.docx) releases. In a SharePoint document library, you can see which Word documents are formatted for 2003 and earlier and which are Word 2007 or later in the Type column. Documents that are formatted as .docx have a square blue outline with the top-left corner folded down behind the stylized *W* of the icons; .doc documents have a completely square blue outline behind the *W* on their icons.

If you are further looking to confirm the file extension of a document in the library, don't try to view it, because that form doesn't display the extension; instead, choose Edit Item. That form shows the file extension.

Adding a Required Field to a Library

One of the nice things about having a library item associated with a document is that its fields can be used as the document's properties. So if you want additional fields that better identify a document, you can add them to the library item. Better yet, by setting a field to be Required, you can force the property to be filled in when a user creates, uploads, or edits a document in the library. My example creates a Project metadata field that requires the user to enter a value so anyone can see at a glance which projects are associated with which documents.

Adding fields to a library is exactly like adding fields to a list, although how the library handles fields is different, as you'll see in a moment.

1. Simply click the Library Settings button in the last section of the Library ribbon (click the Library tab in the Library Tools toolset in the top ribbon bar if you need to activate the ribbon).

2. Then, on the Document Library Settings page, in the Columns section, click Create Column. (There seem to be only four columns by default for this library, but that is not the case; the columns displayed are the only ones that are editable by the user.)

THE CREATE COLUMN BUTTON

You might have noticed that you can also use the Create Column button in the Manage section of the Library ribbon to create a column. This will pop up the settings in a dialog box instead of a page, but I prefer pages because more settings can be seen without scrolling. Feel free to use the button if you prefer.

---

3. On the Create Column page, as you can see in Figure 8.6, name the column (for my example, the column is named Project). Keep the data type set to Single Line Of Text, give it a description, and require that the field contain information, which is the whole point of this required field. For the other settings, do not enforce a unique value, do keep the default maximum characters, make sure to leave the default value blank, and add the field to the default view to ensure that the field shows up in the default view of the library. The field doesn't require validation.

4. Once the settings are complete, click OK to finish creating the new Project field.

FAST ENOUGH FOR YOU?

I am assuming that you've at least glanced through the preceding chapters about lists, so I am going rather quickly through creating a new, required field. To get a detailed look at columns, data types, settings, and more, check out Chapters 6 and 7.

---

5. On the Document Library Settings page for the library (where you should be able to see that the new field is in the Columns list and is required), click the library's link in the Quick Launch bar, or the Shared Documents link in the title breadcrumb, to get back to the library's content page. Project should be a new column heading on the right of the content area.

FIGURE 8.6

Setting properties
for the new column

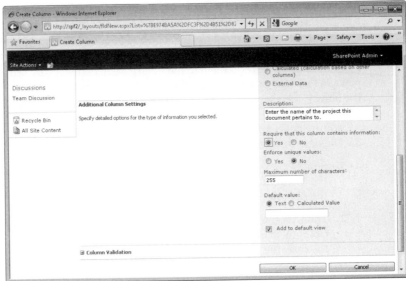

Of course, the required field will be blank for the documents already in the library because they were created before the field was. However, because the field is required, if these documents are edited, the field will have to contain data before their changes can be saved—and of course, this field will need to be filled in for new documents as well.

Editing a Document with a Required Field

To prove that we can't save a document that doesn't have required fields filled in, let's edit the document we created.

1. To edit a document in a document library, there are a few options (from this point, I'll probably always suggest only one). You can simply click its filename or click the down arrow at the end of the Name field to trigger the item's drop-down menu and select Edit In Microsoft Office Word. You can also select the item and click Edit Document in the ribbon.

2. A Warning dialog box will come up reminding you that you will be opening a file. Make sure it displays the filename you want, and click OK.

   Word might prompt you for your SharePoint login. Your login does two things. It confirms that you can access the location of the file. And if you want to use the shared workspace pane (available only to versions prior to 2010) to work with the document, your login tells Word who you are so it can propagate the pane with the correct data.

3. If you open the document in Word 2010, you will likely get a warning like the one in Figure 8.7, because the document now has required properties. If you get the warning, click the Edit Properties button. It will open the Document information panel and display the editable fields for the document library.

WHAT, NO LOGIN PROMPT?

If you are feeling left out because you didn't get prompted to log in, fear not. If you are logged into the client computer with the same account used to access the library and the site's address is a local intranet zone in that computer's Internet Explorer, then you may not get the prompt to log in because it will pass the local user's credentials transparently.

FIGURE 8.7
The properties warning in Word 2010

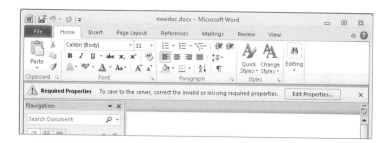

SERVER PROPERTY FIELDS

The fields for the library are considered server property fields, because most Word documents come with properties of their own, such as summary, author, tags, and so on. If you use the document properties, rather than the server document properties, they will not show up in SharePoint. Make sure you are looking at the server properties to access the document library fields for the document.

In Figure 8.8, the Project field is marked with a red asterisk. This means it must contain data if you want to save the changes you will be making to this document. Also displayed in the information panel is a Location field, showing you the URL of the location where Word thinks the document came from and where it will be shared to.

FIGURE 8.8
Document Properties – Server fields for a library document

4. As a test, edit the document but don't fill in the required field, and then click Save to save your changes. You will immediately get an Error dialog box warning you that this file cannot be saved because some properties are missing or invalid. This means, in this case, that you did not fill in the Project field. To fix the issue, click the Go To Document Information Panel button in the dialog box (Figure 8.9). It will take you back to the Document information panel so you can enter the required data. (If you are using a version of Word prior to 2007, a pop-up box will appear when you save changes instead of an information panel. You can enter your data changes in the pop-up box.)

FIGURE 8.9
Required field
warning dialog box

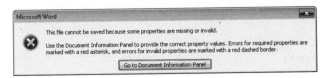

5. In the Document information panel, enter data into the Project field. In my example, I used the word *Example* as the data in the Project field. Then click the convenient Retry Save button, which will be located just below the Document information panel in a Required Properties banner. Now that the field has data in it, the Save function will work fine. Close Word, and go back to the Shared Documents library in SharePoint.

   Back in SharePoint, as you can see in Figure 8.10, the newdoc item (or whatever you named your document) now has data in its Project field. If your users are using Word 2010, encourage them to use the Document information panel. This provides a convenient way to see the library item fields for the document and easily manage data.

FIGURE 8.10
The new document
with Project field
data in the library

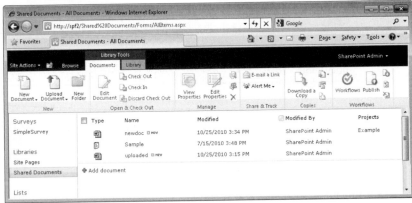

6. The Document information panel generally doesn't open automatically unless there is an empty field that requires data. To open it manually within Word 2010, select the File tab.

   On the right side of the document's information page, the properties for the document will be displayed. There users can edit or fill in fields (Figure 8.11) without the information panel. Remember that there are two kinds of properties: Word and Server (SharePoint). Be sure the users are on the Document Properties – Server information.

7. Now that there is a required field, if you upload a file to the Shared Documents library, you will be prompted to fill in the required field before the upload can finish. To demonstrate this, click the Upload Document button in the Documents ribbon, and upload a file

(my example is called Sample2003 and was created in Word 2003). After you choose a file to upload and click OK, the Properties dialog box for the document item will prompt you to enter data in the required field (as you can see in Figure 8.12). Notice that Word 2003 automatically uses the first line of the document for the Title field; Word 2007 and 2010 don't do that.

FIGURE 8.11
Document information page properties

FIGURE 8.12
The Library item properties page during file upload

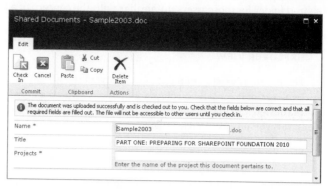

When you upload a file that requires its fields to contain data, the file will be in a checked-out state (unavailable to everyone but you) until you fill in the required fields. Basically, the document can be uploaded, but it's not considered "done" and ready to be seen by anyone else until all the necessary fields are filled out.

> ### REQUIRED FIELDS AND WORD 2003
>
> Required fields work differently in Word 2003 than they do in Word 2007 or 2010, and maybe better, for two reasons. The first is that when a field is required, it doesn't show up as an error and is, therefore, less likely to cause any user anxiety. If a field is required, a box pops up when the document is being saved, or the application is closed, prompting users to enter data in the required fields.
>
> The second reason required fields work better in Word 2003 is that when a field is required for a document in a library, every time the file is edited, the prompt to enter data in the fields pops up during the Save process. This regularly reminds the user that those fields are there and can be edited, for example changing the status of a document from Editing to Completed. The user isn't obligated to change the data; they can just save it as is. Neither Word 2007 nor 2010 reminds the users of the required fields (at least not consistently) if the field is not empty. That means once a field has data, the user must remember to edit the field manually if the required field contains information that needs to be updated.

Opening the Library with Windows Explorer

Libraries have an additional way of being viewed as well. Because SharePoint was originally used mainly for document management, Microsoft knew that companies would need a quick, familiar, and easy way to dump documents from a file share into a document library. Because of this, libraries (except the wiki library) can be opened with Windows Explorer.

Opening the library with Windows Explorer opens a Windows Explorer window and displays the library like a web folder so you can simply drag and drop files into the library from a location on the local machine or a network share. You may think that's no big deal, but remember, a library is actually located in the content database. This feature allows you to see the library as if it were a shared folder for those users unfamiliar with the concept of a list holding their files.

> ### EXPLORER VIEW
>
> The previous version of SharePoint allowed the library to be opened in a separate window in Explorer, or it actually displayed Explorer view in the browser itself. This was compatible with the design idea of keeping the users in the familiar interface of the browser. That is not the case in this version, as it only supports opening the library in a separate Explorer window.

Unfortunately, there is one (maybe inconsequential) thing to worry about when viewing any library with Explorer: the library stores its template, forms, and standard view pages (like `allitems.aspx` or `upload.aspx`) in the library in a folder called Forms. Most users will not be able to see the Forms folder, but administrators/owners will (particularly if they have their folder options set to show hidden files on the machine they are using to access the library). So, teach them to be careful not to accidentally drag and drop files into that folder. Keep in mind that the Forms folder is a system folder, and adding another folder to the library with the same name can cause intermittent issues with the original folder. You can use the Forms folder to access and easily edit the template for the library, as well as access the standard ASPX pages for the library such as AllItems.aspx (which is the All Documents default view for the library).

SERVER SAYS NO

The Server OS does not have the WebClient service installed by default, which is required in order to use the Open With Explorer capability. To be able to open libraries in Explorer while on the server, you have to install the Desktop Experience feature on the server, which will install the WebClient service (along with a bunch of stuff you probably don't want). Then you need to start the service.

To open Explorer to display the library's contents in a separate window (Figure 8.13), activate the Library ribbon, and then select the tiny Open With Explorer button in the Connect & Export section. You may be prompted for your SharePoint login credentials again to make certain you have the right to access the library as a web folder.

FIGURE 8.13
The Open With
Windows Explorer
window

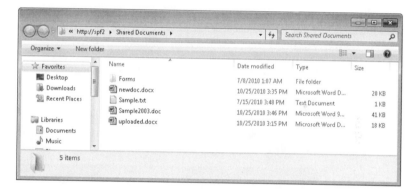

PERMISSIONS AND OPEN WITH EXPLORER

Your login permissions on the local computer will impact which user account SharePoint will use when accessing a resource. Because Explorer is part of the operating system, it will use the locally logged-in account as the context allowed to access that library, regardless of the credentials you use to log in to SharePoint in the browser.

This is generally not a problem for most users. If their workstations are part of the domain, they are logged into that machine with the same login they would use in SharePoint. However, if you are testing what Open With Explorer might look like for a user with lesser permissions than you have, from your machine it might look like they have access to more than they actually do. You need to log on locally as that user and then access SharePoint to see the full effect of their permissions. This also affects the way Page View web parts work if they are accessing shares where permissions might be an issue.

To easily move files from a file share to the library, simply drag and drop them into the Explorer window. For example, a document named `Security Management.docx` was dragged and dropped from a folder on my hard drive to the library in Figure 8.14. Transferring files this way is essentially the same as uploading them; the files will be considered checked out and unavailable to other users until data is entered into the required fields and the files are checked in.

FIGURE 8.14
A document added to the library using Open with Explorer

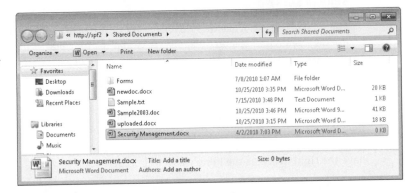

BULK LOADING

It's easy to add multiple documents to a library, either using an Explorer window or doing an upload of multiple files using the Upload button on the Action bar. If you upload multiple files at once, remember that if they have required fields, they are checked out until you fill in those fields, and then you can check them in. Keep in mind that an uploaded file is not visible to any other user until it is checked in.

If you choose to upload multiple files on a machine without Silverlight, the interface will look like this (personally I prefer it this way):

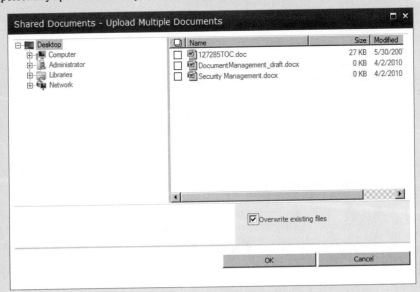

With Silverlight, it will look like this:

You can then use Datasheet view to more easily fill in the required fields of those items in bulk, rather than entering each item individually. Chapter 6, "Introduction to Lists," covers Datasheet view and manipulating views in general.

Of course, as an administrator, not only are you going to need to know how to use Open With Explorer, you are going to need to be able to troubleshoot it as well. Because of this, there are some details that you might need to know about how Open With Explorer works with SharePoint in order to support it.

SharePoint's Windows Explorer capability uses Web Distributed Authoring and Versioning (WebDAV) to make Open With Explorer possible. Occasionally, there are issues using Explorer with SharePoint. Here are two of the most common problems and their solutions:

Common Tasks Bar Shows Up on Left Side of Explorer Window   Explorer is controlled by the user's Folder Option settings on the computer they are using to access SharePoint. To get rid of that bar, open Windows Explorer on that computer, go to the Tools menu, and select Folder Options. Set the folder to use Windows classic folder view.

Open with Windows Explorer Won't Work   This particularly occurs on servers, which don't have WebDAV enabled by default. Make certain that the WebClient service is running on the computer being used to access the library. For Server 2008 or 2008 R2, you will need to install the Desktop Experience feature on the server itself (using Server Manager) to make WebClient available. It will then need to be enabled (the role just makes the services available).

STUPID FOLDER TRICKS

As you know, if folders are enabled, you can add them to lists and libraries. This feature is enabled by default on most libraries, and the button is usually the third one in the Documents ribbon.

Folders are essentially containers. They can contain library items or other folders. Adding a folder and double-clicking it essentially "opens" it so you can add documents to it. This lets you organize your documents and lets users who prefer file shares be more comfortable. However, there is one interesting thing about folders and SharePoint. Have you noticed that there is no Move button or menu item?

So, what do you do if you have a document in the library, you have made a folder, and now you want to put that document in that folder?

Well, you could edit the document and then Save As specifically to that folder in the library (but that would leave you with two copies, one in the folder and one not—until you deleted the first one). You could download the file and then upload it to the folder (by opening the folder first and then clicking the Upload button). Or you could drag and drop it.

That's right—Explorer to the rescue. The easiest way to move files around in a library is to open the library in Explorer. Then just drag and drop the file into the folder (or back out again). Keep in mind that, if the library requires check out, moving files might mark them as checked out

Requiring Checkout

As I've mentioned before, a document that is marked Checked Out (in a standard view, a checked-out document is indicated by a green arrow on the bottom-right corner of the Document Type icon) is set to be read-only for everyone but the person who checked the item out. When you check out a document, only you are allowed to edit it until it's checked back in.

Requiring Check Out is a good thing. If it is set, then users cannot open a document without explicitly choosing to check it out for editing (which locks it for everyone else) or to open it only for reading. If you don't check out a document when Check Out is required, then all you can do is read it, and changes made to it cannot be saved back to the library.

YOU CAN USE FORCE

Don't panic. As an administrator, you can force a document to be checked in if someone leaves the company with a document checked out or simply forgets to check a document back in for too long. Their changes will be discarded, but at least the document will be available for others to work on it. I'll cover this a little later in this section.

Keep in mind that there is an issue with allowing Check Out to be voluntary. A user can choose to check out a document they are editing by clicking Check Out on the document's selection box drop-down menu before opening it or by choosing to check the document out when prompted by Word when it is being opened. However, this can be a hit-or-miss thing, because they can still edit the document even if it is not checked out, and, meanwhile, so can anyone else. This means that if Require Check Out is not enabled and the user forgets to check out the document, while they are editing it, someone else can also open the document and edit a copy of it as well. This can cause essentially two versions of the document to exist, one with the edits of one person and another one with the edits of the other. The last person to save the document will have their edits displayed as the most recent document, making the other person's edits seem as if they have been "lost" because they were saved as an "older" version of the document.

To require that a document automatically prompts to be checked out when someone edits it and cannot be checked in by anyone but that person, you must enable the requirement under the library settings.

A setting at the bottom of the Versioning Settings page allows you to require Check Out. The Versioning Settings page actually has all kinds of useful settings that we will revisit later in the "Versioning" section of this chapter.

Take these steps to access the Require Check Out setting:

1. Click Library Settings in the Library ribbon.

2. On the Document Library Settings page that appears, select Versioning Settings under the General Settings category.

3. On the Versioning Settings page, scroll to the bottom to the Require Check Out section (see Figure 8.15), and select Yes to require documents be checked out before they can be edited.

FIGURE 8.15
The Require Check Out setting

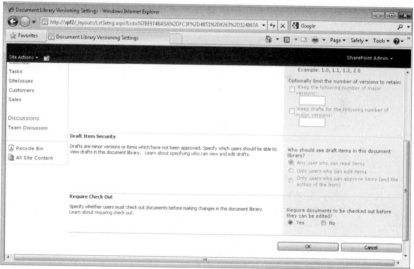

4. Then click OK to finish. That should take you back to the Document Library Settings page for the library.

To return to the content page, click the name of the Shared Documents library in the title breadcrumb.

Checking Out a Document

Back on the Library content page, let's see what happens if we try to edit one of the documents that now require check out. There are two ways to check out a document:

◆ Manually do so by selecting Check Out in a document's drop-down menu or selecting the item and clicking the Check Out button in the Documents ribbon.

◆ When check out is required, simply open the document. It will prompt you to either check the document out or open it read-only.

1. For an example of the second method, click the new document you created earlier (my example is Newdoc) to edit it in Word.

As you can see in Figure 8.16, with Require Check Out enabled, when you prepare to open a library document, the prompt won't just ask you whether you want to read or edit the document; it will ask whether you want to read or check out *and* edit the document.

FIGURE 8.16
The dialog box for choosing Read Only or Check Out And Edit a library document

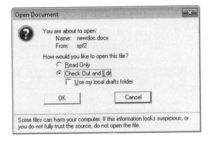

SAVING A DOCUMENT LOCALLY

SharePoint also can let you save a copy of the document locally in case you need to work offline. I would rather not have two copies of the document at any one time, so I do not save a draft copy to a local folder. However, if that is allowed in your environment, it lets the users work on a document they have checked out while disconnected from the network. After working on the document locally, when they reconnect to the network and are able to access the SharePoint server, they can save their changes to the library. When they do, they will be prompted to check the document back in if they are done working on it.

To edit the document, you must check it out.

2. Select Check Out And Edit from the two options, and click OK. This will open the file in Word to be edited. You may be prompted for your login credentials.

3. Make some changes, and then save and close the document.

4. When you try to close the program, you will be prompted (see Figure 8.17) to check in the document so others can see the changes. If you save but don't check in the document, it will still be set to Read Only for everyone else, allowing you to continue to edit the document without anyone else accessing it until you check it in. Also, your saved changes will not be visible to anyone else until the document is checked in.

FIGURE 8.17
The Check In prompt after editing a document

If another user clicks the Check Out button, a dialog box informs them that the document is checked out by someone else (Figure 8.18). They could save a copy of the file locally and work on it there; however, that is not a good idea because it doesn't show the changes of the version currently being edited by the person who has it checked out.

FIGURE 8.18
Read Only or Notify dialog box options

OLD SCHOOL

In Word 2003, if you open a document that is checked out, you don't really get any warnings. It only lets you know that the document is set to Read Only after you try to save the changes you made after opening it.

That leaves us with the need to check that document back in.

Checking In a Document

There are two ways to check in a document: within the Library content page by selecting Check In on the drop-down menu for the item (or selecting the item and clicking the Check In button in the Documents ribbon) or after you save changes and are closing out of Word. For example, our newdoc file is checked out and open in Word. Go ahead and save the document back to the library. You will be prompted to check it back in (Figure 8.19).

FIGURE 8.19
Check In dialog box for version comments

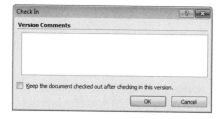

You should type a comment in the box. Do not select Keep The Document Checked Out After Checking In This Version, because versioning isn't enabled yet (we will be doing that later in the chapter), and click OK to finish.

> **CHECKING IN WHILE STAYING OUT**
>
> You might think this is a contradiction of terms, keeping the document checked out after checking it in, but you can save a copy of your changes as a version of the document in the library and then keep it checked out to work on it some more. This lets you make a backup version of the document in the library, just in case.

In the Shared Documents library, newdoc no longer has the green arrow indicating it is checked out. It is free to be checked out by other contributors. If another user accesses the document now, it will show all changes, including those withheld from everyone else while the document was checked out. This really indicates why no one should be using the document until the user who checked it out is finished editing it.

Discarding Checkout

What happens if someone checks out a document for too long? What would happen if documents are left checked out because of a user emergency or because the user left the company? To recover a document that is checked out by someone else, you can log in as that user and check in the document for them, or you can go into the Document Library settings and discard their checkout.

As you know, you can have items that may be checked out with no saved changes and no versions in the library (for example, if a file is dropped into a library in Explorer). However, if a document has been changed at least once in a library, then it can be "rolled back" to its state before it was checked out most recently. This is useful in those situations when the document must be returned to the library to be checked out by others. In that case, the administrator or someone with the permission Override Check Out can click Discard Check Out in the item's drop-down menu (Figure 8.20). You could also select the item and click the tiny Discard Check Out button (it has the same icon) in the Documents ribbon.

FIGURE 8.20
Discard Check Out
in the item drop-
down menu

Either way, this will check in the document and discard the changes made to the document and its property fields while it was checked out (basically reverting it to its most recent version before checkout).

Managing Checked-Out Files

If the document has never been checked in, if it was uploaded by someone, or if it was left checked out and otherwise has no versions to roll back to, then it needs to be managed in a different way. Changing that file from checked out to checked in requires that someone take ownership of it:

1. Click the Library Settings button in the Library ribbon.

> ### A BIT OF SLEIGHT OF HAND
>
> To do this exercise, I logged in as a user (saffron) other than our usual SharePoint admin (shareadmin) and dragged a document into the library without entering data in the Project field. That left the document checked out without any changes. Then I logged back in as shareadmin to continue this process. This created a document that the administrator could take ownership of for this demonstration.

2. In the Document Library Settings page, click Manage Files Which Have No Checked In Version under the Permissions And Management category.

On the Checked Out Files page (Figure 8.21), you'll note that although there may be many checked-out files in the library, only those with no checked-in version are listed (see the subheading below the breadcrumb). Earlier in the chapter, a document was dragged into the library using Explorer. It should still be waiting for you to enter data into its required field so you can check it in. However, you already own that library item, so you don't need to take ownership of it (it's in the Files Checked Out To Me section). Note that the file is a link and has no check box next to it to select it. That's because to check that document in, all you need do is simply check it in yourself back on the library's content page. If there are documents that are checked out but don't belong to you, they will be listed under Files Checked Out To Others.

FIGURE 8.21
The Checked Out Files page

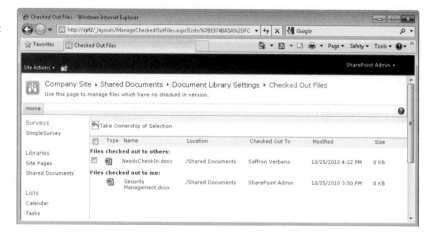

3. In my example, the document checked out by someone else is `NeedsCheckIn`. To check in that document, you need to take ownership of it and then check it in yourself. To take ownership of a document, put a check in the check box next to it, and then click Take Ownership Of Selection.

4. You'll be prompted with an Are You Sure dialog box; click OK if you're sure.

5. Then go back to the Shared Documents content page (click Shared Documents in the title breadcrumb). The document item will show up in the content area of the library (for your view only, since it's still checked out, but now you own it).

6. To check in the document in this case, you still need to fill in the required field. So, add data to the Project field by selecting Edit Properties from the drop-down menu.

7. In the Edit Properties page, enter some data into the Project field, and click OK.

8. To check the document in, simply select Check In from the drop-down menu (Figure 8.22). You might have noticed the option to discard checkout is listed, but you cannot discard checkout because there is no previous version to go back to.

FIGURE 8.22
A document being checked in after a change in ownership

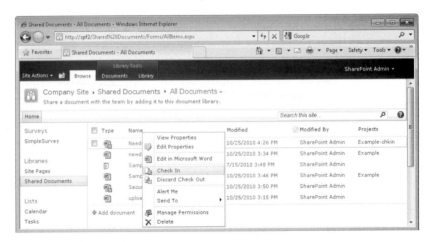

9. Selecting Check In will trigger a Check In box where you can enter a comment and decide whether to keep the document checked out after checking in this version. Make certain that the setting is No, because the whole point of this exercise is to check in the document.

10. Once you've entered a comment, click OK to finish checking in this document item. The document will no longer be checked out and can now be worked on by other people allowed to contribute to the library.

So, you know how to create, upload, and edit a document. You've learned how to add a required field to the library and know what effect that has on saving documents. You've learned about using the Open With Windows Explorer feature of a library and how to manage Check In and Check Out. Now it's time to move on with configuring a library. A library can be configured, to support versioning, as well as content approval, content types, and even incoming email and RSS. Versioning is one of the important features of document management. Keep in mind that each version of a document is a copy of that document and can take up quite a bit of space. If storage is an issue, consider limiting the number of versions.

CO-AUTHORING

A new feature of Office 2010 is co-authoring, which allows two users to work on a Word, PowerPoint, or OneNote 2010 file simultaneously. Instead of locking an entire file for check out, co-authoring locks the document *by paragraph*, allowing multiple people to work in one document at one time but on different paragraphs.

This method does have its drawbacks:

- It requires that all users working on the document to be using the 2010 version of their software. If someone on the team opens the document in, say, Word 2007, it will lock the document as read-only for everyone else.

- The file must be saved as a 2010 version file for Word and PowerPoint. OneNote can support co-authoring with either 2010 or 2007 files.

- You cannot co-author Excel files using the Office 2010 client (but, oddly, you can if you are using Office Web Apps). So if you are doing full-featured work with Excel spreadsheets, even if they are 2010, you will not be able to do co-authoring.

- Word 2010 need to be set to allow store random numbers to improve Combine accuracy (a Trust Center, Privacy Option, document-specific setting).

- The file cannot be co-authored if it contains ActiveX controls, OLE objects, SmartArt, Chart, or Ink objects; contains HTML framesets; is to be published as a blog entry; or, in the case of a Word document, has subdocuments (as most master documents do).

- It is not compatible with check out. Checking out a document sets it as read-only for everyone else, which defeats the purpose of co-authoring. This is something to consider if you have a library of Office 2010 documents that are only going to be worked on by people using Office 2010. You can safely not worry about editing conflicts, because Office 2010 manages that inside the document.

Co-authoring does support versioning. Every time one of the authors saves their changes, it updates that change in the document for all other authors to see as soon as they save their changes (as soon they click Save), and it saves a version of that document in the library.

Co-authoring simply works. If a user opens a Word 2010 document, for example, from a library, and then another user also opens that document in Word 2010, it will indicate that two people are using the file in the status bar of the window (and generate a little pop-up for a moment to let you know when they opened the document).

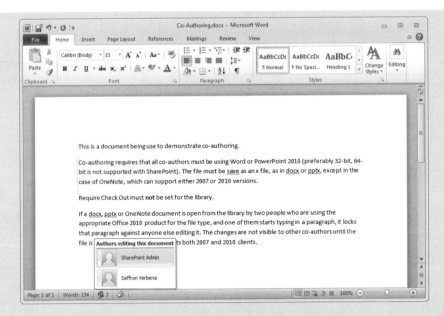

If one user types in a paragraph, it is indicated to all other users with the document open in Word 2010. This will lock the paragraph that user is editing (and indicate which user is editing it), but the rest of the document will be available to edit for everyone else.

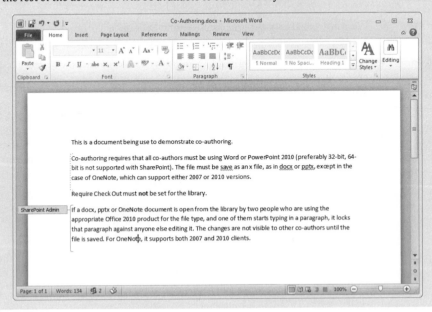

The changes a user makes in their paragraph aren't readily visible to everyone else until that user clicks the Save button. Then it will automatically update in the document for everyone currently editing it as soon as they click Save as well, which causes the document to refresh and show everyone's saved changes).

This process is new with Office 2010. It does have its limitations, but it is a great step toward simultaneous, real-time collaboration.

Versioning

All lists, including libraries, can do versioning (which means that the principles you learn here can be applied to other lists as well). SharePoint keeps a copy of a list item whenever a change is made so the user can "roll back" to the previous version of the item if necessary.

Thus, every time a document that is attached to a library item is edited and the changes saved to the library, it is considered a new version of the document and its library item. Versions are saved (you can enforce how many) to the version history of that library item, and versions can be restored or deleted there. When a version of a document is restored, it becomes the most recent version and is the one that will be opened when you click the link for that document in the library. The version that is being replaced as the most recent is pushed down one place in the list—it is not deleted. SharePoint also supports major and minor (or draft) versions of an item. Major version numbers are whole numbers, like 1.0 or 2.0. Minor versions are indicated with decimal numbers like 1.1, 1.2, and so on.

When a document is edited, saved, and checked into a library, it is considered a minor version until you choose to publish the version as a major version. That elevates the version number from a minor version, such as version number 1.2, to a whole number, such as version 2.0. If you enable content approval on a library that also has versions enabled, documents will remain as minor versions until they are approved (more on that in a few pages).

Do the following to enable versioning:

1. Click Library Settings in the Library ribbon.

2. On the Document Library Settings page, click the Versioning Settings link in the General Settings category.

3. The Versioning Settings page has a content approval section. In a library, you can choose to have a document remain in a draft state until approved. This can be useful with document management. However, we are not going to do content approval just yet, so leave this unchecked.

   Other sections for this page are Document Version History, Draft Item Security, and one you've already seen, Required Check Out.

   Document Version History is where you set how versioning will be handled by this library. It's here that you actually enable versioning, configure it to use only major versions or major and minor versions, and set limits on the number of those versions.

Enabling major and minor (draft) versions unlocks the Draft Item Security section. That is where you can also limit the ability to see a minor version of a document to anyone who can read items in the lists, only people who can edit items, or only those allowed to approve items if you enable content approval.

4. In this library, let's allow the creation of both major and minor versions. See Figure 8.23 for the settings to limit the number of versions allowed per document in this library to six major versions and allow only five of those to have drafts. For draft item security, let's allow anyone who can read items in the library to be able to see minor versions of documents. This will change when you enable content approval.

FIGURE 8.23
Versioning settings

5. Once the settings are complete, click OK at the bottom of the page to finish enabling versioning.

6. Now that versioning is enabled in the library, let's go to the library's content page and start creating document versions. To do this, click the Shared Documents link in the breadcrumb above the title of the page.

NO MINORS ALLOWED

If versioning is enabled but major and minor versioning is not selected, then all versions are major versions using a whole-number versioning scheme.

7. When you're on the Shared Documents content page, click the down arrow for one of the library items to access the drop-down menu. In addition to the standard menu items, there is now a Version History option (Figure 8.24).

FIGURE 8.24
The version options for library items

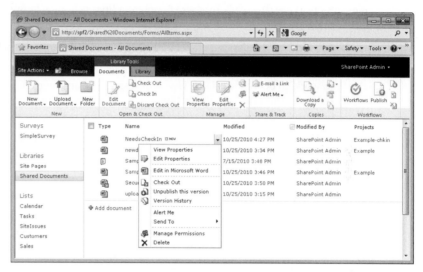

In addition, now when you select an item, the tiny Version History button in the Manage section of the Documents ribbon will be available.

On library items that are not checked out, there is also a publishing option. Publishing takes a draft or minor version and makes it a major version. If the document has only a major version available or the most recent version of the document is a major version, the menu will display Unpublish This Version. If the most recent version of a document is a minor version, Publish A Major Version will appear so you can elevate it to major.

8. My example is going to use the uploaded file from earlier in the chapter (my example is literally *uploaded*). Like all other documents in this library, it currently has only one version; this is why the publishing option in the item's drop-down menu is Unpublish This Version. Select Version History from the item's drop-down menu.

In the Version History box, you can see that there is only one version of this document in my example (Figure 8.25). Because it is the only version, it is a major version by default. Published major versions are indicated by the highlighted color of the background surrounding the entry (it varies depending on the theme you use).

FIGURE 8.25
The Version History page for uploaded.docx

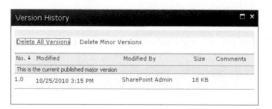

Creating a New Minor Version of a Document

Now that you've verified that there is only one version of this document in the library, it's time to make more. Versions are created when you edit a file in a library (or its library item). The most practical way to create another version of a library item is to open the item's file and edit, just as any user would.

1. Close out of the Version History box to go back to the content page.

2. From there, click the filename for `uploaded`, or the name of the file with which you want to work, to open it in Word. This will trigger a Warning dialog box for you to confirm the filename and offer you the option to read or check the file out and edit it. Select the Check Out And Edit option, and click OK.

3. In Word, edit the document and add whatever text you'd like. The file `uploaded` in my example also requires that the Project field contain data, so make certain it's filled in too.

4. When you are done, save the changes and close Word.

5. When you are prompted, choose to check in the document (Figure 8.26).

PROMPTING MAY BE OPTIONAL

Remember that you will be prompted to choose minor or major when using Word 2007. With 2003, it will save the document as a minor version by default.

FIGURE 8.26
Check In with versions enabled

6. When you check in the edited document in a library that has major and minor versions enabled, SharePoint asks you which version you'd like this document version to be. For my example, I would like to make this a minor version. So, make sure that 1.1 Minor Version is selected and add a comment. Do not keep the document checked out, and click OK.

7. On the Shared Documents library content page, the file is there and is not checked out. If you take a look at the item's drop-down menu, you'll see that where it previously said Unpublish This Version, it now says Publish A Major Version. If you click Version History

in the item's drop-down menu, you can see that there are now two versions of the document, 1.0 and 1.1 (Figure 8.27). The most recent and minor version is at the top of the list (and will be the version associated with the Name field if you click it).

FIGURE 8.27
The version history for recently edited item

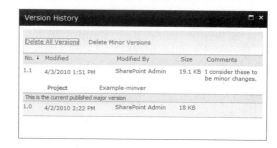

Creating a New Major Version of a Document

If you edit the document again, you will see that the most recent version, despite its minor status, will be the one that opens. This means you can edit it until you think it is ready to be considered a major version of the document. You can promote a minor version of a file to a major version by publishing it. You might do this if you change your mind about the appropriateness of the version type you chose when you checked a document in. Usually, though, a minor version of a document simply needs to be edited, and then the final changes are checked in as a new, major version. Take the following steps to create a new major version of a document:

1. Make sure you're in the document library (Shared Documents in this example), and click the filename for the library item you are working on (mine is `uploaded`). When prompted, check out and edit the item.

2. Once the item is open, you'll see that the changes made in the recent version are there. Add additional text, save the file, and then close out of Word.

3. You will be prompted to select the version type for the changes you just made to the document. Notice in Figure 8.28 that there are now three version options for this document: 1.2 Minor Version (Draft), 2.0 Major Version (Publish), and Overwrite The Current Minor Version. Select 2.0 Major Version (Publish), and add a comment. If you choose to publish the version, the Keep The Document Checked Out option is grayed out.

FIGURE 8.28
The Check In prompt

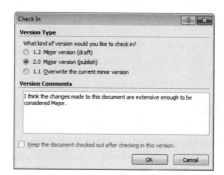

4. When you are done with the Check In settings, click OK.

5. In the Shared Documents library, the document is not checked out, but otherwise it looks unchanged. To see how the version history looks, select it from the item's drop-down menu.

On the Version History page (Figure 8.29), the topmost 2.0 version is now the published major version and is highlighted with a background color appropriate for the site theme to indicate at a glance that it is not a minor version.

FIGURE 8.29

The Version History page with a new major version

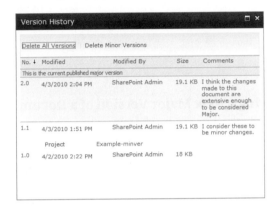

On the Version History page you can do several things with the saved versions of the document. You can restore any one of the previous versions to the top of the list (which means that version is edited when you click the linked field for a document in the library).

You can delete a previous version (or even delete all minor versions), but not the current version. A current version of a document will need to be replaced at the top of the list before it can be deleted. This is usually done by creating a different new version or by restoring a previous version of the document to the top of the list. On the Version History page, you can also view the properties of the document for each version if you'd like (View on the drop-down menu). This is where having users fill in Status or Progress fields would come in handy to track the progress of a document via its fields.

To either unpublish or delete, restore, or view the properties of a version on the Version History page, just move your cursor over the version's date and time (which is the linked field for this list), and click the down arrow in the selection box that appears around it. In the drop-down menu are Restore, View, and Delete for the previous versions. If you select the most recent, major version of the document (Figure 8.30), it will not have a Delete option and will have an Unpublish This Version option instead—just as it would on the library's content page for the document.

Unpublishing a Major Version

If you unpublish a major version of a document, it is demoted to a minor version. To see how this works, in the selection menu of the current, published version of the document, select Unpublish This Version. (Note that you could also do this from the item's drop-down menu on the content page.) The document version will not be removed from the top of the list; it will still be the most current version and the one that will be edited from the content page; however, its version number will go from a major whole number to a minor (draft) decimal number, 2.0 to 1.2 in my example (Figure 8.31).

FIGURE 8.30
The drop-down menu for the current version of the document

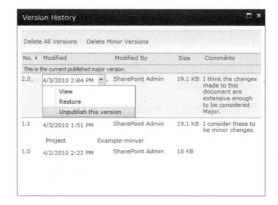

FIGURE 8.31
Unpublishing a published version of a document

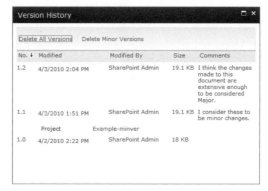

Remember that draft numbered documents can be hidden from users who can only read documents in the library. If content approval is enabled, those allowed to approve items can see a minor version of a document. Similarly, if you publish a minor version of a document to a major version, it will become viewable by those who otherwise couldn't see it in draft form. Keep these things in mind as you manage who sees what in a library.

Back on the Shared Documents content page, if you access the item's drop-down menu, you will see that the Publish A Major Version option is now listed, because we unpublished the current version to a minor version. If we publish the current version of the document, it would be brought back up to version 2.0 once again. However, at this time, let's leave the most recent version of the document in a minor state.

Restoring a Previous Version of a Document

Let's say that the edits for the most recent version of this document are going in the wrong direction and you need the document to be restored to previous edits. To restore a previous version of the document to the top of the version list, you first need to check it out.

Why do you need to check out a document before you restore a previous version of it? It's because you previously set Require Check Out on all document items in the library. So if you are going to roll back all changes to a document and its properties, you need to check out the document.

1. In this two-step process, select Check Out from the drop-down menu for the library item you've been working with (my example is `uploaded`). A dialog box will ask you to confirm that you want to check out the file (don't store a copy in a local drafts folder); click OK. That will simply add a green arrow to the bottom-right side of the content type icon for the document.

2. The next step is to select Version History from the item's drop-down menu. In the Version History box for the document, notice that simply checking out a document causes it to generate a minor version without even opening the file yet (Figure 8.32).

FIGURE 8.32
The checkout created another version before edits.

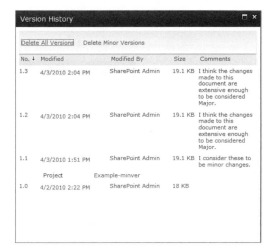

3. To restore a previous version (my example uses 1.1), simply select Restore from the version's drop-down menu. You will be warned that you are going to replace the current version with the selected version. That's fine, so click OK.

4. You'll see that the most current version of the document is a copy of the old version 1.1 (it will be the same size), but it will have been renumbered to assume the most current version number available. To verify that it is the correct version (the less current one, the one that does not have the major-version, final changes), click the Time And Date link for it.

   That will open the document (with the requisite warning that you are opening a document), and because you checked it out, it will otherwise open without prompting you because it is not set to Read Only. Take a look; the last edits you made in the document should be missing. So if those edits weren't what you wanted, you could continue the document from this point.

5. You are just looking and won't be making any changes at this time, so close the document, leave it checked out, and go back to the Version History box.

VERSION WARNING

If you open a version of a document in Word 2007 that isn't the most recent, it will warn you that there are newer versions and try to encourage you to make a copy. Although I appreciate the warning about the version being less than new, I can't understand Microsoft's intentions with the option to make a local copy of the older version of a document. Luckily, this doesn't seem to be default behavior with Word 2010.

Now that you've had some fun, you can return version 1.2 to its rightful place at the top of the Versions list and delete the version you just created. To do that, just select Restore from the drop-down menu for version 1.2. You might be prompted with a warning; click OK if you get one.

That will leave the truly most recent version as the correct one. When you make a previous version of a document the official, most recent version by restoring it, that version sits in limbo, uncertain as to its version number until you assign it. Depending on how you check it in, the version can overwrite the version it replaced, have its own minor version number (leaving its predecessor alone), or be made a major version (again, not overwriting anything).

6. To finish off committing to the restored version, check in the document you've been working on by going back to the Library content page and selecting Check In from the item's drop-down menu.

7. This will trigger a Check In box with the three options concerning how to handle the current version number for this version (Figure 8.33). In this example, let's publish it as a major version (committing 2.0 as the version number), make a comment, and then click OK to check in the document.

FIGURE 8.33
The Check In page with version options

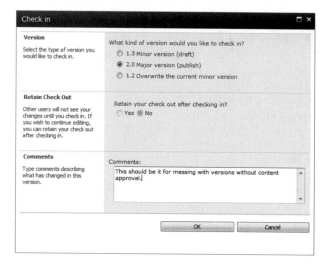

If you were to go to back to the version history of the document you've been working with, you should be familiar with each version, including the most current major version you just checked in and the original version of the document with which you started. Versions are useful; just remember that you can restore an older version to the current version position, but that doing so doesn't delete the version that was replaced. That version won't be deleted unless you manually do it.

To delete a version, simply go to the version history of the document, and select Delete from the version's drop-down menu. You'll then be prompted with a warning that the version will be sent to the SharePoint end-user Recycle Bin. Click OK, and the version will be deleted. In fact, using the links at the top of the Version History page, you can even delete all minor versions or all versions altogether (except the most current, which can't be deleted from this page).

VERSION LIMITS

Just a word about those limits you set for the maximum number of major and minor versions kept for items in a library. They are not as exact as you might hope. Version history focuses on the major versions and will generally keep only the limit you imposed, plus one (the most recent major version). If you reach beyond that one-over limit, the oldest minor and major versions will be deleted.

As for minor versions, you might think that the second setting for limiting versions directly limits draft versions. It doesn't. Major versions can have up to 511 draft versions apiece. What the draft limitation does is limit the number of major versions that will be allowed to have drafts. Go over that number, and the oldest major version will lose its drafts.

At this point, you've gotten an idea of how versions work, what major (publish) and minor (draft) versions are, and how to manage them. However, the real usefulness of minor versions can be seen when content approval is enabled. Let's take a look at how content approval works and why minor versions are referred to as drafts.

Using Content Approval

Content approval means that new items or new versions of items in a list or library require approval before they can be seen by everyone able to view a list (depending on how it's set up). With a normal list, after content approval is enabled, new items start out with the status of pending. Then a person with the right to approve list or library items can decide to either approve or reject an item and add comments to explain their decision. If an item is approved, it can be viewed by everyone who can read list or library items. If an item is rejected, it remains pending and can be seen only by the administrator, someone who can approve items, and the creator of the item. This means that new items go through the simple process of pending approval and then being either approved and therefore visible to all or rejected and therefore continuing not to be visible to all.

If you use content approval in conjunction with versions in a library, then drafts can come into play (if you enable them). No longer does content approval have just the approval levels of Pending, Rejected, and Approved; in a library with versioning, it has Draft, Pending, Rejected, and Approved.

Enabling Content Approval

When you enable content approval, major and minor versions work differently than they do without it. When a document is checked in as a minor version, its approval status is Draft. If that document is published as a major version, its status becomes Pending. Only Pending versions can be approved; you cannot approve a minor version. When that Pending document is approved, that's it. It's approved, and everyone can finally see it.

If a major version is rejected, it is indicated as such and treated as if it is still pending, meaning that others can't see that version of the document, and it is still not editable by anyone but the owner or people allowed to view draft documents.

Seeking Approval

The approval process may sound a little complicated, but it works like this in practice: when you are jotting down ideas for a document and creating a really rough draft of what you have in mind, you might want to save a copy to the library for safekeeping. If you don't want everyone to read it, you can save it as a minor version. That makes it a draft in the library that is not ready for approval yet and not visible to average contributors of the list—if you set draft item security correctly.

You keep working on it, fleshing it out. You then save your changes to the library again, but this time you save the changes as a major version. Now they are pending approval, so the people on your staff who can approve items in the library are aware that they need to look at the document now.

Then one of them reads the pending document and either approves it for everyone to work on or rejects it from general consumption with a comment so you can see what you need to fix in order for the document to be ready to be contributed to.

Every time a user opens the document and edits it, a new version is saved, in which they can decide whether their changes are minor or major, and the approval process starts again.

To enable content approval on a library, follow these steps:

1. Go to that library's content page; click Library Settings in the Library ribbon.

2. On the Document Library Settings page, click the Versioning Settings link in the General Settings category.

   The Versioning Settings page will appear (Figure 8.34). The first section, Content Approval, is where you choose Yes or No to require content approval for submitted items. The Draft Item Security section is where you can configure who can see a draft or unapproved document item.

3. To configure your Content Approval settings on this page, click Yes in the Content Approval section.

4. In the Draft Item Security section, select Only Users Who Can Approve Items (And The Author Of The Item) for this example.

5. All other settings on this page have already been configured, so click OK. Go back to the Shared Document library's content page.

FIGURE 8.34
Setting the Content Approval and Draft Item Security settings

The Shared Documents library should now be set to require content approval. There is a new column in the All Documents view indicating the approval status of the items, and two new views (Approve/Reject Items and My Submissions) to help you keep track of approved items. Any item that was a major version in the library prior to enabling content approval is automatically approved—because everyone has been looking at it anyway. Minor items are considered drafts.

Let's create a new document item and see how content approval works. In this demonstration, you are going to create the document as a SharePoint site collection administrator, so make sure that is how you are logged in now. Later you can log in to a workstation as a normal user with edit permissions on the library to see what that user would see, but you will be working in the library with administrative privileges.

1. Click the New Document button in the Documents ribbon to create a new document.

2. You might get a Warning dialog box reminding you which document template you are opening. You can safely ignore the warning about the template, and click OK.

   You might be prompted for your SharePoint username and password because Word needs to know who you are in case you want to use the Shared Workspace task pane. This occurs particularly if you are logged into SharePoint with an account that doesn't match the one with which you logged into the computer.

3. When the document opens, enter a relevant value in the Project field in the Document information panel.

4. In the document, enter some sample text.

5. When you finish the document, click Save, name the document (my example uses `approvaltest`), and then close Word.

6. Check in the document as a minor version, enter a comment (my comment is "keeping it minor"), do not keep the document checked out, and click OK.

As you can see in Figure 8.35, the new document is in the Shared Documents library with its approval status listed as Draft. All other documents are shown as approved because their most current versions were major versions (and they were already visible) when content approval was enabled.

FIGURE 8.35
The new draft document in the Shared Documents library with content approval enabled

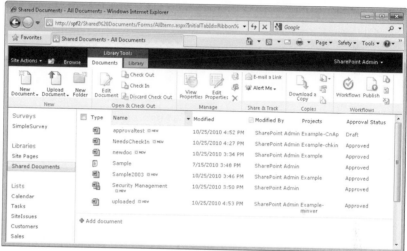

You are able to see that the new document is a draft version because you own the document and you have approval rights. However, if you happen to log on to a different workstation using a standard user account with edit permissions and look at the Shared Documents library, you will be unable to see the new document. It will not show up in the user's view of the library because it is a draft (minor) version and not approved.

Let's see what can be done with the new document as far as content approval and versioning. (Of course, you need to be logged in as someone allowed to do content approval.)

In the drop-down menu for the new document, you have the standard options—nothing that indicates content approval is enabled. As you can see in Figure 8.36, Approve/Reject is not listed for this draft document because only major versions are allowed to be approved or rejected.

ELEVATING A MINOR VERSION TO A MAJOR VERSION

If you elevate this draft version of a document to a major version, the approval status will change from Draft to Pending, which will allow you to approve or reject a document.

1. In the drop-down menu for the new document, select Publish A Major Version. A Publish Major Version page will appear. As you can see in Figure 8.37, the Comment box contains the comments you made when you created the version, so you can add to them if

you'd like before making this minor version a major version. You don't get a new blank Comment box, because you are not creating a new version of the document; there were no changes made to it or its properties. You are just changing the version number.

FIGURE 8.36
The options available for a draft version of a document

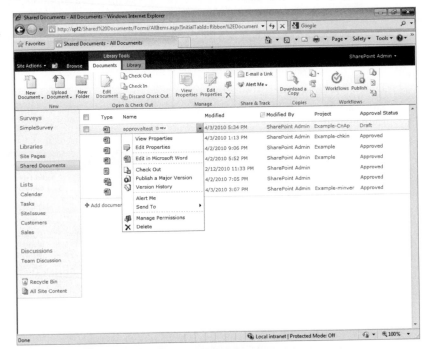

FIGURE 8.37
The Publish Major Version dialog box

2. Add to the comment about the change in version if you'd like, and click OK. On the library's content page, you can see that the new document now has Pending approval status (Figure 8.38).

3. Check out the item's drop-down menu; it will have two new options. Now that the current version of the document item is a major one, you can approve/reject the item or cancel approval (Figure 8.39).

4. Before you change the approval status of this version of the document, verify that there is only one version of the document. In the item's drop-down menu, select Version History (Figure 8.40).

FIGURE 8.38
The approval status change for the new document

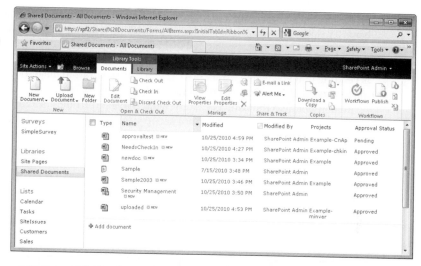

FIGURE 8.39
Approve/Reject is now available for the document item.

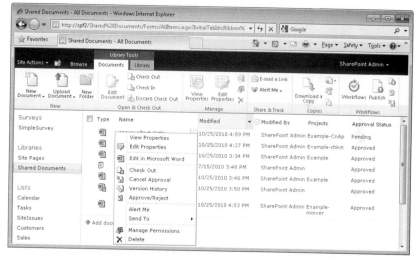

FIGURE 8.40
Version of pending document

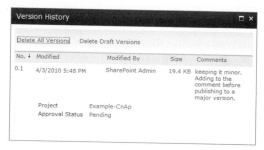

As you can see in Figure 8.40, there is only one version for this document, and the version number is 0.1. Although you might think that publishing a document to a major version may change the version, with content approval enabled it doesn't. Publishing a document only moves the document from a Draft state to a Pending approval state (you can see that its Approval Status setting is Pending in the Version History box). If you go from draft to major or even save a document as a major version, the version will not actually change to a whole number until it is approved.

Remember also that this is exactly what drives draft item security. People who are not allowed to see draft versions cannot see a version of a document if it is not approved. Pending, Rejected, or Draft items are not viewable by anyone who can't approve items and isn't the creator of the items with our current draft item security setting. If the version is not a whole number and draft item security is set to allow only authors and approvers to see a draft version, then users will not be able to access or even know about a draft version of a document until it is made a major version and then approved. This process is designed to help prevent a document from exposing data that might still be speculation or poorly worded and revealing it to less-informed, less-qualified, and possibly less-secure library users.

WHAT DO YOU MEAN IT'S ALREADY CHECKED OUT?!

There is an interesting glitch in the way the library displays versions when content approval is enabled and Draft Item Security is set to allow only those who can approve items to view drafts. If a document was approved in the past, even if its current version is in a draft stage, that past version will be displayed to all users as Approved. Users may be tempted to click the document so they can edit it.

When they do, the document might fail to open (depending on the version of Word you are using) with a clear error.

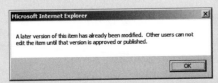

In other cases (say, with Word 2010), the user might be able to open it, but it will unexpectedly be read-only (even if they checked it out before opening it), and they will not see the latest version of the document but the previous, approved one. Further, there will be a warning saying the document is checked out to someone else, even if they just checked it out themselves.

In other words, with Draft Security set to allow only the author or approvers to see draft items, a new document that is in a draft state and has never been approved will be completely invisible to users who don't have the right to approve items (or are not the item creator) until the item is approved and suddenly appears in the library. However, if a previous version of the document was *ever* approved, the document will not be invisible. In fact, it will not correctly display its status (Pending, Rejected, or Draft) to nonapproving users because they are not supposed to see the status. All they will see, mistakenly, is the approved version of the document listed.

This is unfortunate. It can make trying to figure out what can be edited and what can't be edited very frustrating. One way around this problem is to let users who can edit items see draft versions of documents, so they at least know when a document's current version is a draft. Just remember, that means they can access it too.

Now you know that a minor version of a document is considered a draft and cannot be approved. Only versions waiting to be major can be approved—or rejected for that matter. Most people edit a document several times, save the changes as minor versions, and then when they are comfortable, either check in their final changes as a major version or take their most current minor version and publish it to a major version. What can confuse people is the fact that if they indicate a version should be major, all that does in a content approval–enabled library is change its status to Pending, meaning the document is going to major as soon as it is approved.

To approve a document item that is pending, follow these steps:

1. In the document item's drop-down menu, select Approve/Reject.

ANOTHER WAY TO APPROVE/REJECT

You can also approve/reject a version by viewing a document item's properties and clicking the Approve/Reject button in the ribbon bar. You can do basically anything in the item drop-down menu that you can do in the ribbon bar for the properties view.

---

2. The Approve/Reject box (Figure 8.41) has three options: Approved, Rejected, and Pending (the current state). To approve this version, select Approved, and enter some text in the comment box. Click OK.

FIGURE 8.41
The Approve/
Reject box

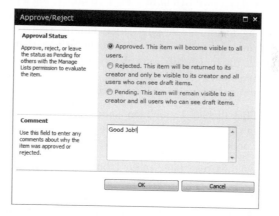

On the content page for the Shared Documents library, the document (approvaltest in my example) now shows Approved in the Approval Status field. If you were to log in to a workstation as an ordinary site member and go to the Shared Documents library, it would finally be visible to that user.

WHAT IF YOU WANT TO CHANGE YOUR MIND?

What do you do if you changed a document version from minor to major by mistake? If you checked in a document as a major version, but you meant it to be minor, can you correct the error? You can kick it back down to Draft status by clicking Cancel Approval. That basically unpublishes the version of the document and returns it to a minor version number and draft status.

You know what versions are, you know what content approval is, and, more importantly, you know how they work together. You should have some idea as to how to use these features in your business or whether they should be used at all. Eventually though, you are going to outgrow the existing Shared Documents library. To prepare for that eventuality, let's create our own document library so we can customize the library's template and explore content types.

Creating a Document Library

Because document libraries are so useful and so versatile, chances are good that you are going to need to create more than one. Keep in mind that although you can upload any allowed file type to a library, libraries can be created to focus on a particular type of file, custom template, or group of content types. Libraries have also evolved to be used to focus on a particular part of the document management process. Because copies of files can be sent from one library to another, a document can start in a library focused on writing and editing, and a copy can then be sent to a library focused on content approval by the legal department and then on to the library used for preparing documents for publication. Finally, a copy can be sent to an archive for backup, while the originals are all removed from the libraries earlier in the process. Regardless of how libraries fit into the scheme of your collaborative needs, it's likely you'll need to know how to create more than one.

Creating a library is just like creating any other list:

1. Click the Site Action menu, and select More Options... from the drop-down menu (or you can click one of the headings in the Quick Launch bar and then click Create in the All Site Content page).

2. On the Create page, in the Library category, select Document Library.

SO MUCH FOR IMPROVING THE CREATION EXPERIENCE

For creating lists and libraries, I am using a machine with Silverlight not installed.

The problem is that if you have Silverlight installed and you want to create a new library, it will not display the option to enable incoming email in the New Library interface. That setting is simply missing. If you want to enable that feature easily while creating the library (or list), do it from the server or a non-Silverlight workstation.

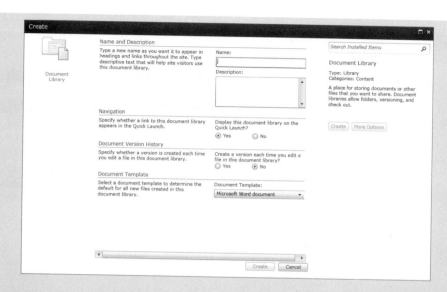

If you have Silverlight installed, the New page is a box rather than a page (and the Create page is different as well, as discussed in Chapter 6). After selecting Document Library from the Library category in the Create box, you must click the More Options button below the library name field in order to get the necessary settings displayed here (otherwise you won't have the option to set anything but the name, not even a description):

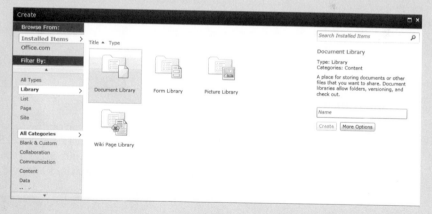

I am not really a fan of the Silverlight version of the New page for that reason. Be prepared for identifying Silverlight-influenced interfaces, because what might be considered an "improved experience" by Microsoft may actually be less useful.

3. On the New page, in the Name And Description section, give the new library a name and description. I've entered **CompanyLibrary** as the name and **Official company documents and materials** as the description for my example (Figure 8.42).

FIGURE 8.42

The new document library settings

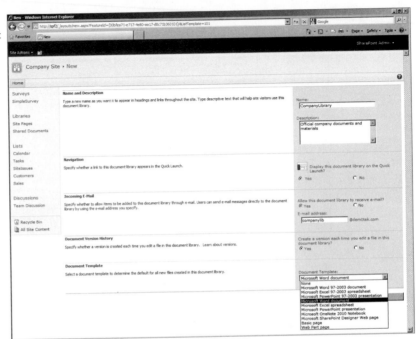

4. In the Navigation section, you will be offered the choice of whether to display a link for this library on the Quick Launch bar; keep the default setting of Yes.

5. In the Incoming E-mail section, you have the option to enable incoming email for this library. Most libraries can receive files attached to email and translate them into document library items. (Note that incoming email cannot be enabled for any list or library on a site if it is not first configured at Central Administration.)

This library should be email-enabled, so select Yes to allow this document library to receive email. This setting is useful for those busy employees who may have their email up but may not want to browse, log in, and navigate to the library to upload a file. They can simply email to the library with the document attached, and it will be added to the library automatically.

6. My example uses the email alias `companylib` for the library.

You can also conveniently enable Document Versioning while creating a document library so it is ready to start versioning before the first document is added.

7. In the Document Version History section, select Yes to create a new version each time a document is edited in the library.

The Document Template section contains powerful and sometimes overlooked settings for a document library. For one thing, it is unfortunately named. It isn't just for documents. In Figure 8.43, you can see that there are more templates to base a document library on than one that just makes documents. Yes, you can choose a Word document (either 97/2003 compatible or 2007/2010 compatible), but you can also choose a PowerPoint presentation, an Excel spreadsheet, OneNote sections, and even SharePoint Designer web pages. You can also use libraries for basic web pages and web part pages. (The library's ability to have a template for web pages helps make wiki libraries possible.)

8. Choose Microsoft Word Document in the Document Templates drop-down list. This will apply a Word 2007/2010 `.dotx` template to the library.

9. Click Create to finish. You should end up on the content page of your new document library. In the Quick Launch bar in Figure 8.43, you can see that CompanyLibrary is listed. The address bar indicates that you are on the `CompanyLibrary/Forms/AllItems .aspx` page (there may be some extra URL query string characters after it, but the page is `AllItems.aspx`). This is the default view for the library.

FIGURE 8.43
The new
CompanyLibrary
content page

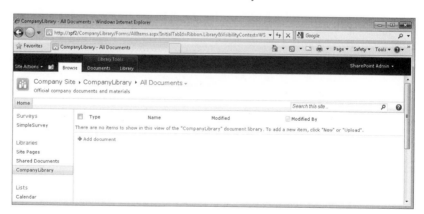

Replacing a Library's Template with an Existing Template

Before you create any documents in this library, let's replace that blank Word template with one of your own. In this example, you are going to replace it with an existing company letterhead template that was made elsewhere. Two easy phases are involved in using your own template for a library. The first phase adds the template to the Forms folder in the library. The second phase configures the template setting for the library to point to the new template.

1. Make sure you have the template file you want to use. Then go to the Library ribbon in the content page of the library, and click the Open With Windows Explorer button to use Windows Explorer to display your library's contents.

2. Because you are an administrator, you are able to see the Forms folder in the library. Open this folder, which is the default location for the library's template.

3. Drag and drop (or copy and paste) your existing template into the Forms folder. If you can't see the Forms folder, try setting your Windows Explorer folder options to show hidden folders. The new template should appear in the Forms folder (see Figure 8.44). My example uses a template called dem0tek_red.

FIGURE 8.44
A new template in the Forms folder

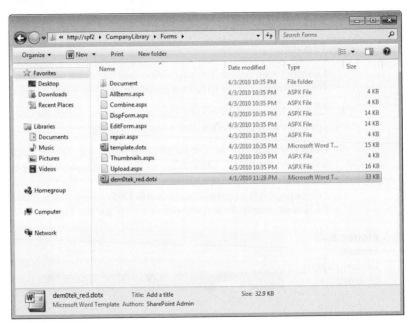

4. Now that the template is in the library's Forms folder, you can configure the library to use it. Click the Library Settings button in the Library ribbon.

5. On the Document Library Settings page, select Advanced Settings in the General Settings category.

Although we are only going to change the document template at this time, take a quick look at the advanced settings for a document library:

Content Types By default, content types are not enabled on document libraries. This means the library by default is associated with one kind of library item and one particular template file, such as PowerPoint presentations, Excel workbooks, or Word documents. When you click the New button in a library associated with one template, it tries to open a file based on its associated template.

If you want a library to be able to create, edit, and store different kinds of library items and/or files, enable content types. When you do this, you can choose to have several kinds of library items, each associated with its own template and using its own fields. This means the library stops being associated with one template (and the Document Template settings gray out) and leaves the template association to the content types instead.

OFFICE FILES ARE A MUST

Unless you've configured SharePoint to support Office Web Apps, if you don't have the necessary Office program installed on your computer, SharePoint will fail to open that file (or if it can open it, say in WordPad, it will have problems editing and saving it as a version of the original file). You cannot edit a file from a library without the appropriate program running locally. You can save the file, open it in a program that will work (but is not recognized by SharePoint as a Microsoft Office product) to edit it, save the file, and then upload it to the library again. However, SharePoint, being a Microsoft product, is specifically designed to work with other Microsoft products.

Document Template This is the section with which you are going to be working. Here you can specify the path to the template you would like to use for this library. Make sure the path is accessible to all users (and in our case it is, because we put the template in the Forms folder of the library).

Opening Documents In The Browser Because some files can be displayed in either the browser or the client application, this setting lets you specify whether you want the item to always display in the browser or open its appropriate application when applicable. For this version of SharePoint, there is an added reason to open documents in the browser—Office Web Apps. This feature can open documents in the browser with a subset of the Office ribbon bar buttons for limited use. It is available only at the server level and requires Office 2010 client licenses (depending on the version). The default is to open documents in the browser. But if Office Web Apps is not installed on the server, it will default to opening documents in the client application.

Custom Send To Destination Because you can send a copy of a file from one library to another, you can specify a default library to send to; users will be able to select this easily in the item selection menu. If the library they are working in has an archive library or a legal department library that the document needs to be passed to when it's done, it will be displayed on the document's Send To menu. Send To keeps tabs on copied documents and gives you the option to update the copy in a new library when the document is checked in with changes in the original library. The destination name is what will appear in the drop-down, and the URL is actually the web address of the other library.

Folders Some users feel more comfortable if they can find their files in folders. Some companies need to have more structure than a mere flat list or library to store their data. When you have huge libraries and lists (around 10,000 items), it helps to break up the view of the data by storing some of it in folders within the list or library. Libraries have folders enabled by default. They can be created (if you have the permissions to) by clicking the down arrow of the New button and selecting New Folder from the drop-down menu. You can disable this feature if you'd like and enable it later if necessary.

Search   This option is set to Yes by default. It lets you specify whether the library should be searchable or whether it should be exempt from being indexed by Search and available for searching. Keep in mind that if someone does not have the right to view the library, they cannot search that library's contents. Search is aware of access control, and it will not display results to a user that they are not allowed to see.

Offline Client Availability   This option specifies whether this library allows users to download items for offline use. This particularly relates to the new SharePoint Workspace available with certain versions of Office 2010. The default is Yes.

Site Assets Library   One of the interesting offshoots of this version of SharePoint's use of wiki pages is that it comes with the option to specifically distinguish libraries on the site as site asset libraries, to be used to store things uploaded to wiki pages such as the home page. There is already a Site Assets library for the site, so it stands to reason that the default for this is No.

Datasheet   This option is used to disable Datasheet view if you don't want users doing bulk data entry in the library. It is enabled by default.

Dialogs   Most forms used by libraries and lists can open either in dialog boxes or as classic SharePoint form pages. This option is enabled by default, and when it is, forms such as View, Edit, and New open in those boxes that black out the page behind them. If you would rather the forms did not open in those boxes, disable this setting.

Now that you have a good idea of the settings available on this page, let's finish setting up the new template for this library.

6. To do that, go to the Document Template section of the Advanced Settings page. In the Document Template field, change the filename for the template from `Template.dotx` to the filename of the template you put in the Forms folder. My example is `dem0tek_red .dotx` (Figure 8.45) so the field should have the path `CompanyLibrary/Forms/dem0tek_ red.dotx`. Keep all other default settings as they are, and click OK. That will take you back to the Document Library Settings page.

7. To test your new template for the library, click the library's name in the title breadcrumb for this page to get back to the content page.

8. On the library's content page, click the New Document button in the Documents ribbon to create a new document based on your template. If it prompts you about opening a file, it is referring to your template file. Click OK.

9. My example uses Dem0tek letterhead as the template (Figure 8.46). Enter some text into your new document. Save the document, naming it as you want (my example is `Congratulations`). Close Word. Remember that you enabled versioning when you created the library. Also keep in mind that you didn't specify major or minor versions, require checkout, or require content approval.

On the library's content page, you'll see your new document based on the custom template you assigned to the library.

Now you have a library dedicated to creating Word documents using a custom template. It is useful to have a library that a user can simply go to, click the New Document button, and create a document using a particular template.

FIGURE 8.45
Assigning a custom document template

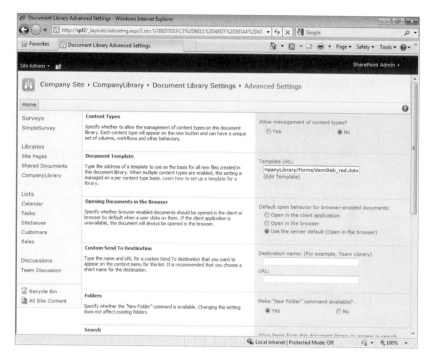

FIGURE 8.46
Creating a new document using a custom library template

However, what if you needed a document library that supported more than one kind of document template? Sure, you can upload multiple different types of documents, but I am talking about having multiple types of New Document options under the button so users will have the option to choose between a set of templates you control for that library. What I'm talking about here is content types, and libraries can easily have more than one.

CUSTOMIZE THE DEFAULT TEMPLATE

What do you do if you don't have an existing template but would like to customize the blank template for the library? Click the Edit Template link under the Document Template field in the Advanced Settings page of a library. This will open the template in its corresponding Office product, where you can customize it to your heart's content. When you are done, save it. The changes will be saved to the template file for the library in the library's Forms folder. This means when you next use the New button in the library, it will create a document from your new and improved template.

Using Content Types

Content types are basically templates for standard list or library items. The item properties you can specify in a content type include the fields of the item, the template that might be associated with it, and even what kind of workflow works with that item.

Content types are stored in a gallery for the entire site collection. So if you create a content type to be used for a particular library, it's actually available to be used in a different list or library elsewhere in the collection.

Because content types are general item templates available to the whole site collection, the fields they use must be available to the whole site collection as well. Therefore, if you want to add a field to a content type, it must be available, or created, as a site column (which you worked with in Chapter 7, "Creating Lists"). Site columns are available from their own gallery and can be used anywhere in the site collection.

Earlier, I mentioned that you can define a library by its template. This means that when you click the New button, a library will always create new documents that use its associated template. However, content types allow a library (or list) to have more than one template or list item type available under the New button.

A good example of this would be a library that contained documents for a project and also presentations for that project. Because the library would be focused on the materials necessary for the project overall, it would need to contain templates for both the written project documentation (Word 2010) and the project slides (PowerPoint 2010).

To create this scenario, you enable content types in the library's properties, which will disable the single template association. Then add the content types appropriate for your library. Many of the content types for existing default list and library items are already in the content types gallery. So, it is easy to use an existing content type as a base and customize it a little to work in your new list or library.

First, you should create a new document library that will hold your project work. Next, you will enable content types on that library and then choose among the existing content types to make available two kinds of templates for the library.

1. To create a new document library, go to Site Actions at the top left of the page, and select New Document Library from the drop-down menu.

2. On the New page, fill in the fields necessary to create the new library. My example uses the library name Projects. Add a description, enable incoming email (the alias in my case will be *projects*), and enable versioning. It doesn't matter which template you select during the library setup, because it will be disabled when you enable content types. Click Create when configuration is done.

Enabling Content Types

To have more than one item type for a library and therefore have the opportunity to associate more than one template with the library, you must enable content types. To do so, follow these steps:

1. Go to the Library ribbon, and click Library Settings.

2. On the Document Library Settings page, click Advanced Settings. On the Advanced Settings page, select Yes in the Content Types section. Click OK to finish.

3. On the Document Library Settings page, you can see that the Content Types section already has one item: Document. This is the default library item, which in this case is a library item with a Word 2007/2010 template associated with it. We will be, conveniently, keeping this library item.

Also notice in Figure 8.47 that there is a brief description of content types under the section title. Basically, the library can now contain different list item types complete with their own associated file templates, fields, workflows, and more. This example is a simple way to introduce you to the concept in case it is something you might need. All lists and libraries have items (or more precisely, records), but with content types, they can have more than one kind of item if necessary.

FOLDERS AS CONTENT TYPES

To make things more complicated, folders are considered items in a list or library, which means their properties can be modified and they can be used as content types. This is how they work in discussion and task lists. There are online articles and books dedicated to working with lists and libraries and integrating them with Office. They go into more detail about content types and folders than we can here.

Although you already have a nice, default, blank template for your documentation files, you need to add a template for project-specific slides. You should use a customized template for the project's PowerPoint presentations so users can get started with the correct slide layout when they are working with this project library.

FIGURE 8.47

The Content Types section

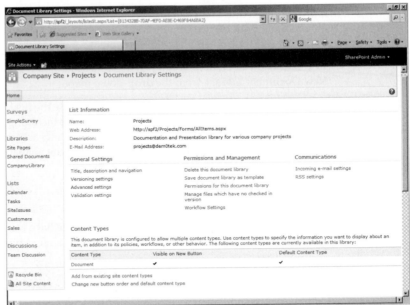

Creating a New Content Type

When you create a new content type, it needs to have a parent content type to be based upon. So when you create a new content type, say for a document library, you can use the default document item content type as the base. Then you can configure it, for example by specifying particular fields or the template that will be associated with it to make it unique. Once a content type is created, it can become a base for other new content types if necessary.

Parent content types available by default in SharePoint fall under certain headings:

Custom Content Types This is the content type group where content types that you create are listed, unless you specify otherwise.

Document Content Types These content types are what are likely to be stored in a document library, such as a document (the default content type for a library, which contains default fields and is associated with the template assigned to the library), web page, picture, and even master page. There is also the Link to a Document content type, which is used to link to a file in a different location, a la Send To linking.

Folder Content Types This list of content types is short. There is the content type associated with discussions, the default for simply creating a new folder, and now also a Summary Task folder type.

Group Work Content Types The Group Work site template, new in this version of SharePoint, has its own unique lists, calendars, libraries, and, correspondingly, its own content types. They are not necessarily meant to be used outside of that site.

List Content Types The content types in this group are the standard items applied to most default lists, such as Contacts, Announcement, Issues, and Tasks. Included is the option Item, which is used in custom lists as the default for list items and enforces the Title field requirement.

Special Content Types   There is only one content type listed in this group by default, Unknown. This content type allows libraries to accept any file that is uploaded to the library regardless of file type (unless it is blocked administratively). If you can't upload files to the library, but you were able to before, make certain that this content type was not removed from the library's settings.

In this case, you are going to need to create a content type, based on the standard document library item, but associate it with a custom PowerPoint template. To do this, you'll need to go to the site collection's content type gallery.

To create a new content type, follow these steps:

1. Go to the top of any site page, click Site Actions, and then select Site Settings.

2. On the Site Settings page, select Site Content Types from the Galleries category (Figure 8.48). As with the Site Columns page, you can see that the site content types are organized in groups.

FIGURE 8.48
The Site Content Types Gallery

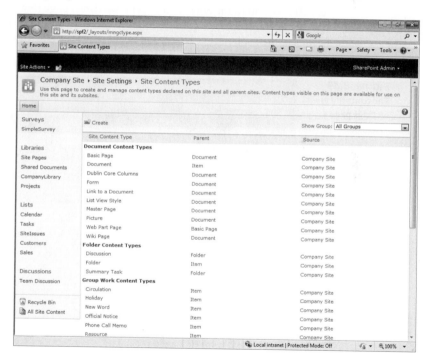

3. You can look through this list and see that there doesn't seem to be a content type available for creating PowerPoint presentations. Therefore, you are going to have to create one yourself. To create the new content type, click Create at the top of the content area of the page.

   When you create a content type, you generally base it on a parent or an existing content type to save time. In this case, you just need a standard document library item but with a different template.

4. To that end, on the New Site Content Type page (which opened when you clicked Create), in the Name and Description section, name the new content type (ProjectSlides in my example) and enter a description, such as **Document content type to be associated with a PowerPoint template**.

5. Under Parent Content Type, you can see that, in the Select Parent Content Type From field, there are several groups of base content types listed. Because you are working with a document library, you should choose Document Content Types. Because you chose that group, in the Parent Content Type field below you can choose Document. This creates an association with the preferred template, with the same fields as the content type that is the default for the library.

6. You can decide whether you want to list your new content type under the general Group heading Custom Content Types or create one yourself. My example uses the default. If all the settings are good, click OK to create your new content type.

This will take you to the new content type's settings page (Figure 8.49). There you can change the name and description, set up workflows you want to use with this content type, delete the content type, or configure its advanced settings, which is what you are going to modify.

FIGURE 8.49

The content type's settings page

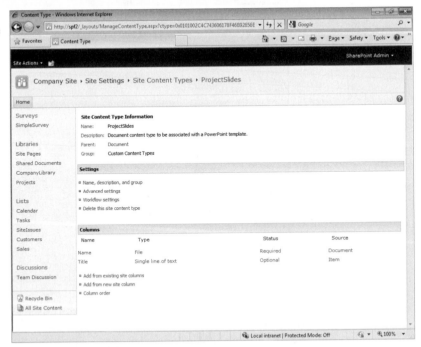

7. Click Advanced Settings. The content type's Advanced Settings page has three sections: Document Template, Read Only, and Update Sites And Lists (see Figure 8.50 for my example).

Document Template This section is where you specify the template that will be associated with this content type. This is a convenient place for you to upload the template to SharePoint that will be used for this content type. Alternatively, if the document template already exists in another library, you can specify its URL in this section.

FIGURE 8.50

The content type's Advanced Settings page

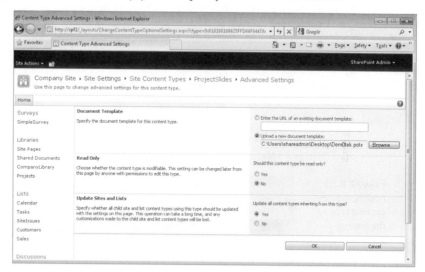

Read Only This section allows you to restrict the editing of the content type's settings. If you do want the content type to be read-only and unmodifiable, keep in mind that this setting can be changed by someone with the right to edit content types.

SOME TIPS ABOUT THAT READ ONLY SETTING

If a content type is set to Read Only, on the content type's settings page all configuration settings you might have wanted to use disappear except for the Advanced Settings page (the page you need to be able to access to disable Read Only). In addition, if you do set a content type to Read Only and change your mind, disabling Read Only might disconnect any workflows that might be associated with that content type. Be sure to specify the workflow association again after disabling Read Only.

Update Sites And Lists Settings in this section can be particularly useful. As you know, you create new content types by basing them on existing content types. What you might not have considered is that SharePoint remembers the connection. And if you change a parent content type, those changes can trickle down to all content types based on that parent. It is in this section that you can choose to allow changes made to this content type to be inherited by all content types based on it (the default), or not.

8. For the Document Template section, I am going to upload a PowerPoint template, dem0tek.potx, from my local drive. Keep the defaults for the Read Only and Update Sites And Lists sections, and click OK to finish the advanced settings for this content type.

The advanced settings are the only thing changing at this time for this content type; however, keep in mind that you can make changes at any time, including adding more fields if you'd like from either existing site columns or site columns that you create yourself.

Now that you have created a new content type, you can apply it to your library:

1. Go to the new library you created and enabled content types for (my example is Projects) by clicking the library name in the Quick Launch bar.

2. In the library, click Library Settings in the Library ribbon.

3. On the Document Library Settings page, in the Content Types section, click Add From Existing Content Types.

4. In the Add Content Types page, in the Select Content Types From field, choose the Custom Content Types group—because that's where we put the new content type. If yours is in a different group, choose that one.

5. In the Available Site Content Types box, select the new content type (my example is ProjectSlides, as you can see in Figure 8.51), and add it to the Content Types To Add box. Then click OK.

FIGURE 8.51
Adding the new content type to the library

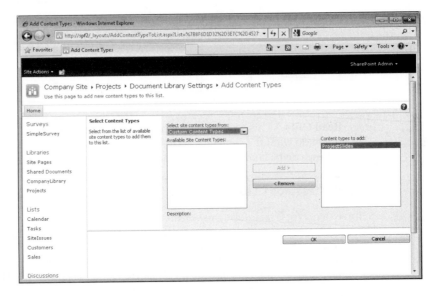

You should now be back on the Customize page for the library. In Figure 8.52, you can see two content types for the library. The default is the document type, and they are both visible under the New button. You could change the order of the content types under the button, making the new one the default. However, I am fine with the document being the default, because that will probably be the template users will use most often.

Now that the library has its two different templates associated with it, you can use your content types for the library:

1. Go to the library's content page by clicking its name in the title breadcrumb or in the Quick Launch bar.

2. Back on the content page of the library, click the down arrow next to the New Document button in the Documents ribbon. In Figure 8.53, you can see that two

items are now listed. The first item, Document, will be the default if you click New without going to the down arrow.

FIGURE 8.52
Two content types
for the new library

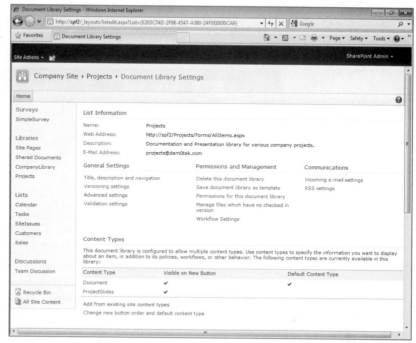

FIGURE 8.53
Two template
options under
the New
Document
button

3. To see this for yourself, click away from the drop-down menu, and then click the New Document button. SharePoint will use the default blank document template for Word.

4. Add some text, save, and close. Name the document (my example is Firstproject). That should put your new document in the library.

5. To use the PowerPoint template, click the down arrow next to the New Document button, and select the new content type (my example is called ProjectSlides) in the drop-down menu. This will open a presentation in PowerPoint using the template you uploaded.

6. Create some slides, and enter whatever text you'd like. Then save the file (my example is Firstpresentation), and close PowerPoint.

On the content page of the library, you can see that two documents are stored there (Figure 8.54). In the Type column, notice that the two file types are different. `Firstproject` is a Word document, and `firstpresentation` is a PowerPoint file.

FIGURE 8.54
Two different content type items in the library

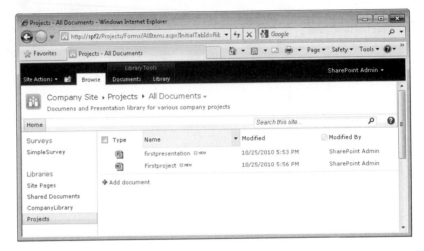

Because these content types are based on the same parent (Document), they have the same fields. If you want to add fields to the library, they can be added to both content types as if they were one kind of library item. While you are creating the field, simply select Add To All Content Types at the bottom of the Create Column page, as you can see in my example of a new field for Projects in Figure 8.55. Keep in mind that this will affect only the content types applied to this library. The change will not propagate up to the content types stored in the content types gallery.

FIGURE 8.55
Adding a new field to all content types on the Create Column page

WHEN IN DOUBT, RELINK

If you change the template used by a content type in a library, you may have to relink documents that were using the template to reflect the change. Otherwise, they may not open properly when users try to read or edit the document. If you have changed a template and are now having problems opening files in a library, there is a repair page available to relink the file to its template.

You can see the page, in the Forms folder, in Explorer view. To open it, just append the filename to the end of the URL for the library. In other words, instead of AllItems.aspx, the path should end in repair.aspx. In my case, that would be http://spf2/Projects/Forms/repair.aspx.

This will open the Repair page for that library, in which you can select the file that needs to be relinked to its template. The library will check the file for its content type and then check that content type's template. If the URL pointer for that file's template doesn't match the updated one for the content type, the file's pointer will be changed to match. That should fix the problem. Remember, repair.aspx is your friend.

Now you have a library dedicated to creating Word documents using a custom template, as well as a library used to store custom documents and presentations. After you've worked on the documents in these libraries, you might want to send a copy to another library to be archived or viewed by a larger group of people. So, let's take a look at what Send To can offer to make managing files between libraries easier.

REPORT BUILDER CONTENT TYPES

Those of you who have Reporting Services configured for SharePoint in your environment may have heard that you can create a Reporting Services library to generate and store reports that pull data from databases on the SQL 2008 R2 server.

You might have looked for a Reporting Services library template. Sadly, there isn't one. That is because, when Reporting Services is configured, all it does is add three content types to the site collection (if the Reporting Services feature is activated).

To create a library that will generate reports, you first create a document library. Then you enable content types for that library. Then, select Add From Existing Content Types on the library's settings page, and select the Report Builder Report content type, as well as the additional Report Data Source and Report Builder Model content types (they allow you to create new data sources and report builder models in the library, as well as just reports).

Remember that Report Builder 3.0 is the product needed to create Reporting Services reports. This product is to Report Server what SharePoint Designer is to SharePoint. Report Builder 3.0 is free and creates reports very much like Crystal Reports does. When the user clicks to create a new Report Builder report (data source or model, or to edit an existing one), Report Builder 3.0 should be the tool that opens. If the user doesn't have Report Builder 3.0 installed locally, when they use the New Document button to create a new Report Builder report, data source, or model, it will trigger a prompt to install the software. This is because it is part of SQL Server 2008 R2's Report Server implementation as a ClickOnce application, so it will install automatically if the product isn't already available. This is convenient, because you don't need to worry about preinstalling the software so users can use the library. If they have Report Builder 3.0 already on their computer, when they choose to create a new report, data source, or model, it will open Report Builder 3.0.

Using Send To

Earlier in this chapter, you saw that SharePoint has a Send To feature that makes it convenient to copy a file from one library to another. When you're working with a great many documents, using one library to store everything might not be a good idea. The number of finished documents can far exceed the number of documents in progress. Because of this, people often have *archive libraries*, where finished projects can be moved to simplify the organization of the primary library. From that idea also spring things such as a legal library, where documents can be copied to after editing to be checked by the legal department. Sending documents from one library to another in some environments is a natural part of the process. Send To was designed to address this process.

SEND TO CAPABILITIES

Send To can send documents to other libraries on a site, to a different library somewhere in the site collection, or to a library in a different web application if you are using Office 2007 or newer (other Office products aren't web application–aware).

In a document item's drop-down menu, Send To has options that correspond to the buttons in the Copies section of the Documents ribbon:

Other Location   This option allows you to send a copy of a document from one library to another. You can specify a default location for this option to encourage users to send finished copies to a particular library as part of a document management process.

Email A Link   You can email a link to the document to someone if you'd like them to read or edit the document.

Create Document Workspace   Like its predecessors, SharePoint Foundation offers the option to create a workspace subsite to work on a particular document. Creating a document workspace will be covered in Chapter 9, "Sites, Subsites, and Workspaces."

Download A Copy   This option simply lets you quickly download a copy of a document to your machine in case you may be going offline.

The most useful and most frequently used option when you're using Send To is sending a copy of a document to another library (Other Location).

You can send a copy of a document from one library to another using two different methods: linked or unlinked. A *linked* copy can be updated with whatever changes were checked in from the originating document. That way, the archived copy does not become obsolete or out of sync with the original. An *unlinked* copy is completely independent from the original and will not be changed when the original changes.

SharePoint lets you specify whether a copy should be linked or unlinked by choosing, oddly enough, whether you can prompt for updates. This option is unfortunately worded. SharePoint doesn't actually prompt you to update copies of a document after you check it in. This inconsistency makes the feature seem unfinished somehow. For now, if you want a document to send its changes to a copy that might be stored in a different library, you need to remember to force it yourself.

Microsoft intends this option to be used to send a finished copy of a document to a different library to be archived. That means the destination library should not be actively editing the document. To this end, the destination or target library for the document copy must *not* require check out, or updating from the original document will not work.

As an example, let's send a copy of a document from the Shared Documents library to the CompanyLibrary as a reference for future documents and keep it linked. That way, when you change the document in the originating library (Shared Documents), you can update the copy in the destination library (CompanyLibrary).

ELUSIVE "UPDATE COPIES"

SharePoint will offer to let you update copies if major and minor versioning are enabled and you are publishing a document to a major version. At that point, it will display a section in the dialog box offering to update copies.

You will not be prompted to update copies when you save and check in a document, but it will offer to update copies if you manually check the document in after the document changes have been saved to the library.

But that's the closest it gets to a prompt for updates. If the library does not have major and minor versioning enabled and you aren't working with a minor version, even this option isn't available. There is no way, just looking at the library or checking in a document, to tell whether it needs to update its copies, until you go to the Manage Copies page.

Sending a Copy of a Document to a Library

To send a copy of a document in the Shared Documents library to the CompanyLibrary (or whatever you named your library), follow these steps:

1. Go to the Shared Documents library. Find the document you'd like to send to the other library. My example uses the newdoc we created earlier in the chapter.

2. Select Send To in the item's drop-down menu. The Send To options will pop out.

3. In the Send To pop-out menu, select Other Location (Figure 8.56).

FIGURE 8.56
Preparing to send a copy of a document to a different library

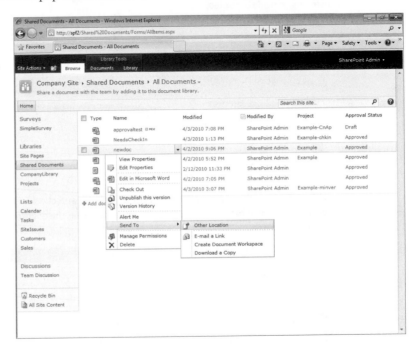

The Copy box will open. It has two sections: Destination and Update (see Figure 8.57).

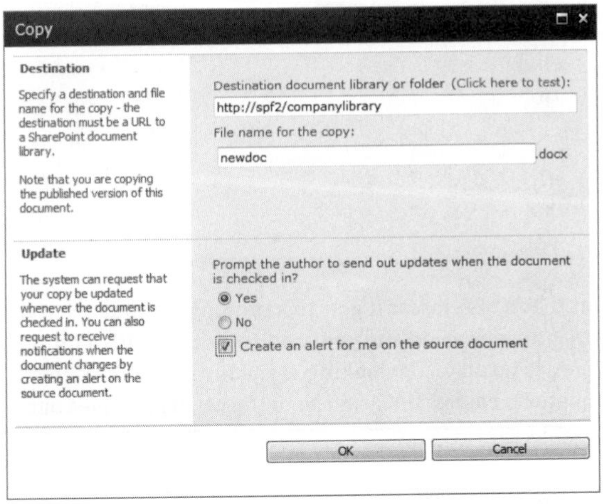

FIGURE 8.57
Sending a copy of the document to a different library

The Destination section is where you specify the location of the library where you'd like to put the document copy. My example is sending a copy from the Shared Documents library to the CompanyLibrary you made earlier. Because you can send documents to libraries outside this site (such as a different subsite, site collection, or even a different web application), you need to specify the correct URL for the destination library's location.

4. In the Destination section, enter the URL for the destination library. My example specifies `http://sp2/companylibrary`, because that is the URL of the site where the library is located and the library name. You don't need to copy and paste the library's URL here; you can use the library's real name, even if it has spaces in it. Just keep in mind that SharePoint specifies sites by their URL, not their title. So, it's best to get in the habit of using a URL.

CONFIRMING THE URL

If you're not sure of the URL or library name, click the Click Here To Test link to open a window to the location. If an incorrect library comes up, correct the address and try again.

---

5. The Update section is where you decide whether the copy should keep a link with its original. To make this a linked copy, choose Prompt The Author To Send Out Updates When The Document Is Checked In. That option implies that a prompt will pop up when you are updating an original, but it won't. It is really just meant to link the copy. The only sort of prompt you will get appears when you are publishing a minor version to a major version; there is a radio button to select to update copies. Otherwise, you'll need to remember to update copies yourself.

IF YOU DON'T NEED A LINK

If you don't want a copy to be linked, choose No for The Author To Send Out Updates When The Document Is Checked In. Also keep in mind you can unlink a copy from its original at any time.

The Update section also has the option to create an alert for the original document's library, so you can get an email to let you know that the document has been changed. This will let you make sure that, if you need to keep the copy updated, you know when to force the update.

6. Choose Yes to prompt the author to send out updates. You can always unlink the copy later. You can also enable an alert on the original so you will be aware when changes are made (although this doesn't always work I've found, so check your user alerts to see whether it really sets; then set it yourself if it doesn't).

7. Once you've entered the correct location for the document copy and other settings, click OK to continue the copy process.

8. A Copy Progress dialog box will appear to confirm your selection. Check the path, and make sure it is the correct document (it may look like a Copy box and have a status of

waiting for user confirmation; it's the same thing). If you are sure the path is correct, click OK to complete the copy. The dialog box will process for a few moments, add a copy of the original document to the other library, and then announce its success.

9. To confirm that the Send To worked, open the library where the copy was sent (CompanyLibrary in my example). The copied document should be there. You may notice that, looking at the document, it doesn't indicate it is a copy. One easy way to tell whether a document is a copy is if the Go To Source Item option appears in the item drop-down menu (Figure 8.58).

FIGURE 8.58
The copied document is in the new library.

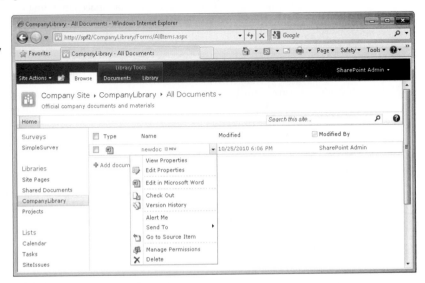

10. Click Go To Source Item. It will take you to a View Properties page for the original document. In this page, the ribbon bar has the option Manage Copies (pay attention to that "hand holding paper" icon, because the button for Manage Copies in the ribbon bar looks like that but doesn't have a label). This is one place you can check to see what copies of a document you have made, and you can manually update copies from here. When you update a copy of a document, you are *overwriting* the copy with the changes from the original. If versioning is enabled in the copy's library, the changes will be saved as the most current version.

DON'T CHECK OUT COPIES

Never enable Require Check Out on a destination library for copies. If you do, the updates will not work.

Now that you're on the original document in the originating library, let's check it out, make changes, and then check the document back in.

1. You can open a document for editing from within a document's View Properties page by clicking the document's filename. The link is the same as if you clicked the filename in the library's content page. However, it may not prompt you to check out the document to edit it. It may open the file as a read-only copy until you click the Check Out button in the information panel or link in the task pane.

2. Open and edit the document by clicking its name (make certain it is checked out first)—perhaps add a sentence to the end of the text, as I do in my example—save, close, and check the document back in. It does not matter if the change is a major or minor version.

3. After you close Word, you should be taken back the original View Properties page. If you click Manage Copies on the ribbon bar, it will take you to a Manage Copies page (Figure 8.59). You will see the copies of this document either that prompt for updates (those that are linked) or that do not prompt for updates (those that are unlinked). You should have a document listed in the linked documents section.

UNLINKING AND RELINKING DOCUMENTS

If you are in the Manage Copies box and need to unlink a document copy or relink it by prompting for updates, you can edit its properties using its Edit button. Notice that it suggests you set an alert yourself on the source document if you want to be notified of changes, instead of offering to do it for you.

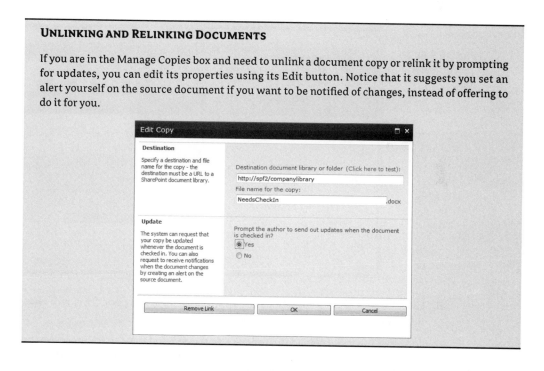

---

4. To force an update to the copy of the changes made to the original document, click Update Copies at the top of the box. This will take you to the Update Copies page, where you can select to update particular linked copies or update all at once (Figure 8.60). Simply select the copy you want to update, and then click OK. The Copy Progress dialog box will appear again, proving that it will overwrite a newer copy of the original over the first copy. Click OK in the Copy Progress dialog box to continue the process.

FIGURE 8.59
The Manage
Copies page

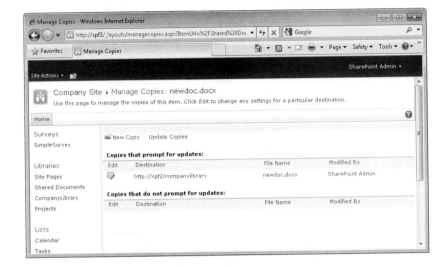

FIGURE 8.60
Update Copies
page

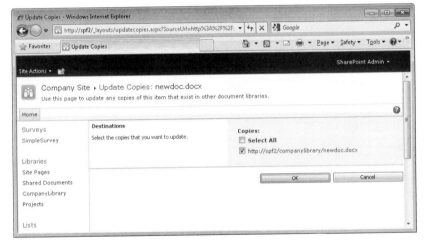

5. Click Done when the copy is successful to close the dialog box. This will take you back to the original document's View Properties page.

6. To see whether the copied document was indeed updated, go to the destination library (CompanyLibrary), and open the copied document. You can open the document as read-only because that's all you need to do with it. The most recent changes you made to the original document should be there.

TEMPLATE? WHAT TEMPLATE?

Because the copied document was not created using the New button, it doesn't use the nifty custom template that documents use in the CompanyLibrary. This demonstrates that new documents in the library use the template, and those created elsewhere do not.

There is an additional, and easier, way to update copies from an original in the content page of a library. Just follow these steps:

1. Go back to the original library (Shared Documents).

2. In the drop-down menu for the document you copied (my example is newdoc), select Send To.

3. In the Send To pop out menu, you'll see the Existing Copies option (Figure 8.61). If you click that, it will take you to the same Update Copies page that you used earlier from the Manage Copies page. Feel free to update any copies you'd like. In our case, it's not really necessary, but it's nice to know the option is here.

FIGURE 8.61
Existing Copies option on original document

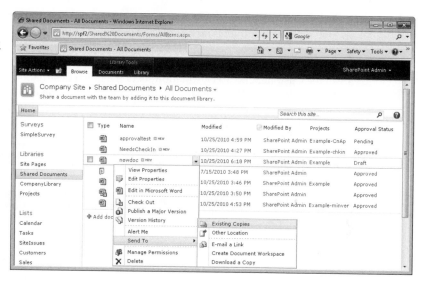

A FEW MORE SEND TO DETAILS

If you only want to make a copy of a document in another library without being able to update that copy, simply send that copy to the other location, but choose No to the prompt for updates.

Then, if you check the item selection menu, there will be no Send To ➤ Existing Copies option because you chose No for the prompt for updates action. If you go to the Manage Copies box for that document, you will see that the document is listed under Copies that do not prompt for updates.

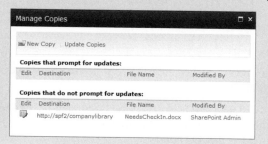

This means that the copy is not set to be updated. To link the original with the copy, just click the edit icon for the copy and change the Update setting to Yes on the Edit Copy page.

Keep in mind that if you are going to change the update options of a copy, you must change them at the original document's properties, not the copy's properties.

Configuring a Library with a Default Send To Location

Now that you know how Send To works, you can see how useful it can be. But, wouldn't it be nice if you could specify a particular default library that the users could just select to Send To instead of having to specify the URL themselves?

1. To configure the Send To destination for the Shared Documents library, go to the Library ribbon, and click the Library Settings button.

2. On the Document Library Settings page, click the Advanced Settings link.

3. In the Custom Send To Destination section, enter a destination name (keep it short because it will be listed in small pop-out menus) and the URL to the library (notice that there is no link to test the URL). In my example, I am going to use companyLib as the name and the Company Library URL (Figure 8.62).

FIGURE 8.62
Advanced Settings page, with custom Send To destination

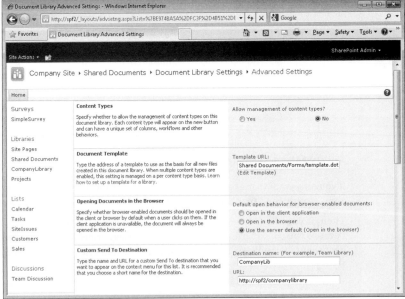

4. Once you've finished entering your destination name and URL, scroll to the bottom of the page, and click OK.

5. This will take you back out to the Document Library Settings page. Click the name of the library in the title breadcrumb (or the link in the Quick Launch bar) to return to the Shared Documents library.

6. To see whether it works, select a document that doesn't already have a copy sent to a library (in my case, I am using `NeedsCheckIn`), let's try sending a copy to the new Send To destination.

7. In the drop-down menu on your selected document item, choose Send To, and in the pop-out menu you'll see your new destination listed (Figure 8.63).

FIGURE 8.63
Library's custom Send To destination in menu

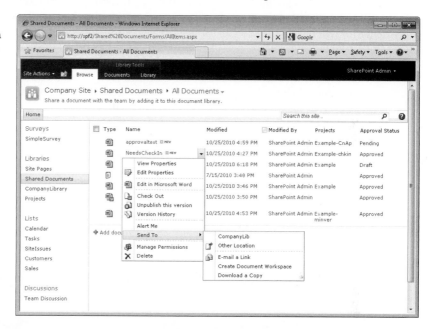

8. If you click it, you'll see the familiar Copy page for the document (but with the destination already filled in). Just decide whether you want the copy linked, and click OK.

9. This will bring up a confirmation page; just click OK. Then, when the copy operation is done, click Done at the top of the content area. Feel free to check the Manage Copies page for the document to see whether the process worked, or go to the destination library.

That's about it for using Send To to send linked copies of documents to other libraries in SharePoint.

DOES IT WORK IN THE RIBBON?

Up until this point you've done a lot of Send To work in the item menu, but if you were to click the Send To button in the Library ribbon, its drop-down menu would also display the destination configured for the library. It's all the same to SharePoint.

So far, you've added documents and fields to libraries and configured versioning, required checkout, content approval, and Send To. You've created content types, configured library templates, and even created other document libraries. That's about all there is to document libraries.

However, a few other kinds of libraries are available in SharePoint. They are very similar to document libraries; they simply were meant to store and manage different file types.

Picture Library

Picture libraries are intended to store all the pictures a site or site collection might require (with thumbnail views, download options, and slide shows). Each image file stored in a picture library will have a URL so you can use it elsewhere. This comes in handy if you have, for example, a contact list of employees. You can then enter the URL of the employee's photograph into a field (that uses the hyperlink or picture column type) in the contact list.

Picture libraries are not listed under Libraries on the Quick Launch bar; instead, the heading is generated when the first picture library is created and set to appear on the Quick Launch bar. Then, even if the library is deleted, the heading will remain.

To see how a picture library works, let's create one:

1. Click Site Actions, and then click More Options from the drop-down menu. On the Create page, click Picture Library in the Libraries category.

2. As you can see in Figure 8.64, the settings for a new picture library are similar to those of any other library. You can enable incoming email and versioning, and you can determine whether the link for the library will be on the Quick Launch bar. Name the library (mine will be CompanyPictures for this example), give it a description, and enable incoming email (my example's alias is *pictures*). Keep the defaults for navigation and versioning. When the settings are complete, click Create.

FIGURE 8.64
Creating new picture library settings

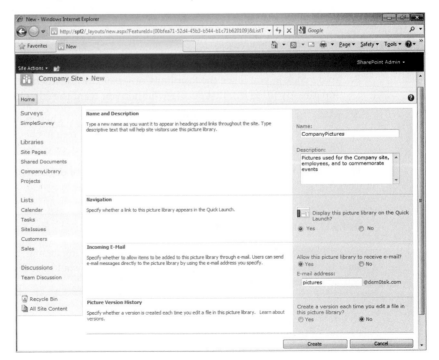

This will take you to the new picture library. You might notice, right off, a bit of a difference in the interface for this library. It doesn't use ribbon bars. That's right. Everywhere else, ribbons are all over the place, but not for the picture library. It uses old-style Action bar buttons (all of which have menus beneath them). You might notice in the address bar of the browser that the URL doesn't have the ribbon query string appended to it, just a nice, clean, and simple URL. Also, there is the classic View menu on the right of the Action bar, in addition to the View menu in the title breadcrumb. Here's a quick summary of the Action bar buttons:

- The New button can only create a new folder because the library is intended for uploading pictures. You can't create pictures here.

- The Upload button will offer to upload only single files if no Office product is installed, and will add the option to upload multiple files if an Office product is installed.

- The Settings button drops down to display options to create a column, create a view, or go to the library settings.

- And finally, the Actions button is where practically all the, well, *action* is. It offers some tasks specific to picture libraries.

   Edit   This will open your operating system's default application to edit image files. SharePoint prefers the Microsoft Office Picture Manager.

   Delete   This will delete a selected picture.

   Download   This is the opposite of upload, of course. It will copy the selected picture to your local computer.

   Send To   This is not the Send To you were expecting. It inserts a selected picture in an email or document you select.

   View Slideshow   This uses the Slideshow view to cycle through the pictures in the library.

   Connect To Client   This option may also be called Connect To Outlook. It, obviously, integrates with Microsoft Outlook. When selected, it opens Outlook and displays the library's contents in the Outlook window.

   Sync To Computer   This requires SharePoint Workspace to be installed on the local computer you are using to access the site. It will make a synchronized copy of the library in the workspace so the user can access it locally while offline.

Of course, View RSS Feed and Alert Me, standard in all lists and libraries, are on the menu as well.

Once images are added to the library, you can view them in All Pictures view, which shows each picture as a thumbnail with a check box so you can select it. You can also select particular images to view together. If you click the View menu and select All Pictures view, an alternate menu will appear. In it, you can choose Details, Thumbnails, or Filmstrip (see Figure 8.65 for an example).

When you upload pictures one by one, you are afforded the chance to fill in the fields for each picture, such as the title, date the picture was taken, description, and tags to search for the picture by. If you choose to upload multiple files, that should trigger the Office Picture Manager (this works best with Office 2010). However, that type of upload doesn't let you edit each picture's fields (its properties or metadata).

To access a picture's fields (to edit them after upload for example), use the All Pictures page's Details view. That's the standard "all items" view of the picture files, letting you access the item's drop-down menu (Figure 8.66).

FIGURE 8.65
The Filmstrip view and the All Pictures View menu

FIGURE 8.66
All Pictures page's Details view

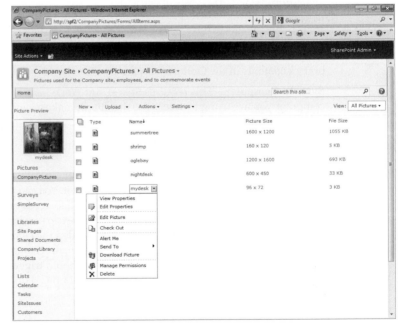

The Wiki Page Library

The wiki page library is just a library of web pages. You actually have considerable experience with the new wiki pages for this version of SharePoint if you've done any work with the home page (as you did exploring the SharePoint interface in Chapter 4). For the Team Site template, Microsoft has chosen to use a wiki page as the home page.

Wiki pages support rich content and can have pictures, tables, and even web parts inserted into them. Text can also be significantly formatted. Also, like any web part page, any wiki page can be made into the home page with a click of a button in the ribbon bar.

There is already a modified wiki page library on the team site called Site Pages. It contains the home page for the site. However, you'll create a new wiki library here so you can really see how it works:

1. To create a wiki library, go to More Options in the Site Action menu, and then select Wiki Page Library from the Libraries category on the Create page.

2. On the New page for your new library, simply specify the name and description of the library and allow it to display the library on the Quick Launch bar. Wiki libraries don't support incoming email and, like the picture library, can't be assigned a template because all wiki pages are going to be HTML pages. For wiki libraries, versioning is enabled by default, so the option isn't available during creation. Wiki libraries are very simple libraries meant to do one thing: contain web pages that link to one another. Then click Create.

As you can see in Figure 8.67, the wiki library in my example is called CompanyWiki. In the Quick Launch bar, it is listed under Libraries.

FIGURE 8.67
The new wiki library

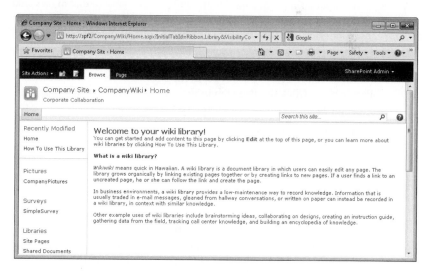

One of the more unusual things about a wiki library is its default view. A wiki library opens with a view that displays a default file in the library named Home. The title of the text in the page might be "Welcome to your wiki library!" but the filename is Home. As a matter of fact, there are only two pages in this library so far, by default—Home (the page you're looking at now) and How To Use This Library.

Site Pages Doesn't Seem like a Wiki Library

The Home page for the Site Pages library has been modified to be the actual home page for the site (if the wiki home page feature is enabled). Because of that, its default view is the All Pages view, not the Home page for the library.

You might notice that there is no ribbon toolset in the top ribbon bar for this library, unlike Shared Documents or any lists. This may be because the Page tab on the top ribbon bar was *meant* for the wiki page. The menu there is very much like the Documents and Library ribbons rolled into one for wiki pages. There is a standard Library Tools toolset for this library, but you can't get to it from here.

When you reach the wiki library for the first time, there is the ever-present top ribbon bar, as well as the title area, top link bar (with the search field and help icon), and the Quick Launch bar on the left of the page. A new section has been added above the Quick Launch bar just for the wiki library displaying the most recently modified pages.

Where's the Description?

Because of the shenanigans needed to make a wiki the site's home page, this library's description does not actually show up in the title area as it does for all other lists and libraries. Instead, the *site's* description is displayed. This is the only place, other than the home page, to do so.

Mind you, you might consider disabling the site feature that makes wiki home pages possible and therefore maybe getting your description back for the wiki library. And that may work, but the description you gave the site will also stop displaying on the home page.

To get to the library's actual content page (and the Library Tools), you need to activate the Page ribbon. Click the Page tab in the top ribbon bar (Figure 8.68).

In the Page ribbon are some buttons you've seen before and some that are unique to wiki pages:

◆ Edit and Check Out (it is a library after all) in the Edit section.

◆ Edit Properties, Page History, Page Permission, and Delete Page, as well as a Rename Page button in the Manage section.

◆ E-mail A Link and Alert Me! in the Share & Track section.

◆ The Page Actions section contains Make Homepage and an Incoming Links button. The Make Homepage button, available on the Page ribbon for content pages also, will make the page you are on *the* home page, replacing the home page you currently have. This has no "undo" feature, so be careful about using it. To undo, you can either reapply the original wiki page or delete the page (if you are using a web part home page). The Incoming Links button helps manage the links in the library by showing what pages have links to the page you are on.

◆ The Page Library section of the ribbon is unique to the wiki library. It contains the buttons to manage the library while on a wiki page. The Library Settings button gives you access to the library's settings, and Library Permissions has an equivalent function. The last button, View All Pages, takes you *under* the wiki page you are on to see the content page for the library itself. At that point, you'll see the list of pages in the library in a standard view, with the normal Library Tools toolset to work with.

To get to the Content page for the wiki library, click the View All Pages button on the Page ribbon. Here you can see that there are two wiki documents by default, Home and How To Use This Library (Figure 8.69).

FIGURE 8.68
Page ribbon in wiki library

FIGURE 8.69
The All Pages view of the wiki library

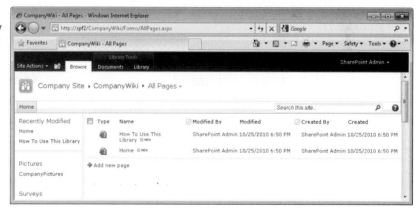

The library items have the standard drop-down menus. In addition, the Library Tools tabs are available in the top ribbon bar, with the standard Documents and Library ribbon buttons.

Adding a Wiki Page

To add a wiki page to the library, take the following simple steps:

1. Click New Document in the Documents ribbon of the wiki library or by using the Site Actions menu. This will pop up a simple New Page box (Figure 8.70).

FIGURE 8.70
Adding a new
wiki page

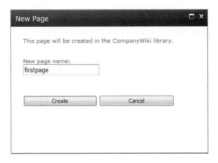

2. All it needs is a name. I am going to use firstpage for my example. Then click **Create**.

A new wiki page will appear, with a blank area (a lot like an empty web part zone) to start working in. Because wiki pages are rich content pages, just like the home page, you can edit the heck out of them; change their layout; and insert pictures, links, web parts, tables, and even entire files if you'd like. In addition, you can use the wiki syntax to easily make a link to another page in the library.

3. To follow my example, just enter some text and a link to the other library pages for more info. The syntax for wiki links is two square brackets around the page name (for example, [[home]]). When you start typing the link, the page will try to help suggest the page name for other pages in the library. This is useful both for avoiding typos and in case the names are long (Figure 8.71).

FIGURE 8.71
Editing a new
wiki page

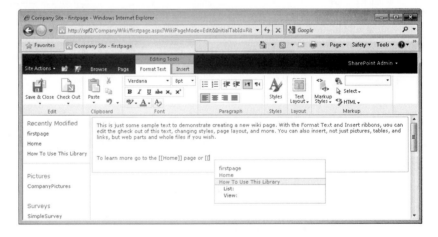

Begin the syntax with two open brackets, and a drop-down listing the other pages in the library will appear. Just highlight the page name you want and hit Enter, and the link will complete itself.

4. Once you are done working on the page, click the Save & Close button in the Documents ribbon.

The finished page will show the links as the page names in a different color than the rest of the text, indicating to the reader that they should click them.

If you create a wiki link to a page that doesn't exist, the library will indicate the link is empty by putting a dotted line under it. When you click it, it will try to get you to create the page and its content.

Editing a Wiki Page

Editing an existing wiki page isn't as intuitive. No matter how you select a page in the View All Items page, the Edit Documents button on the Documents ribbon will remain grayed out.

To edit a wiki document, you first have to open it (you are already on the page you just created); then click the Edit button (the paper and pencil to the left of the Browse tab), or click the Page tab in the top ribbon bar and *then* click the Edit button on the ribbon.

That will put the page back into edit mode so you can do more work there.

Wiki pages can also be edited in SharePoint Designer if you want by clicking the down arrow on the Edit button in the Documents ribbon and selecting Edit In SharePoint Designer from the menu.

For this version of SharePoint, there is no explicit wiki site template, but you can use the Team Site template and just replace the home page with a Welcome To The Wiki Library Home page. That will focus the users' attention on that library and its documents.

The Form Library

This library doesn't get a lot of press because it requires Microsoft, more specifically InfoPath Filler, to be installed locally on the user's computer (unless you have an InfoPath Forms Server on your network). However, if you are using InfoPath extensively at your company, you might want to take a look at it.

This library is created like any other:

1. Get to the Create page (go Site Actions, go More Options, or go to the All Site Content page and click Create).

2. From the Create page, click the Form Library link.

The New page has your standard fields for library creation (including incoming email, oddly enough). It even has a Document Template field, but the only option is to use an InfoPath form template. That is because the template is just a holder, and you will need to use InfoPath to publish a form template up to the library. Forms are usually considered *templates*, and when people fill out a form, it is considered a *form instance*.

After you create your library (my example is CompanyForm), it will look like any other. All the settings are generally the same, but there is also a Relink Documents To This Library setting on the library's Settings page, because it is not uncommon for forms to become unlinked from their parent template.

To use the library, you must first publish a form template to the library. If you are using InfoPath 2010, it comes in two flavors: Designer and Filler. Designer is used to create InfoPath forms, and Filler is used to, well, fill them out. Users would only need InfoPath Filler to use the library.

Publishing an InfoPath Template to a Form Library

To create a form, save it, and publish it to a SharePoint InfoPath library, you have to use InfoPath Designer.

In my example, I opened InfoPath and used a sample template (see the Travel Request form in Figure 8.72). It was saved as `companytravel.xsn` locally.

FIGURE 8.72
The Travel Report template in Info-Path Designer

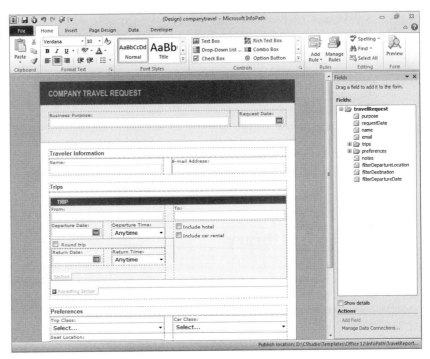

Once the form template is designed the way you like it and you've saved it locally, the form is ready to be published to the library:

1. In InfoPath, click the File tab, select Publish, and then click the SharePoint Server button (Figure 8.73). (Alternatively, if you haven't used this template elsewhere, you can click Quick Publish in the Quick Access toolbar and then specify in the wizard that you want to publish to SharePoint.)

2. This opens a Publishing Wizard dialog box for you to choose where you want the template to be published. Specify a URL for the site containing the form library (Figure 8.74). My example uses `http://spf2`. Enter the URL, and click Next.

   The next screen (Figure 8.75) wants to know whether the form will be associated with a form library or a content type. It also warns that, because there is no enterprise-level InfoPath services on the SharePoint server or an InfoPath server on the network, the InfoPath forms will not be browser-enabled. The user must use InfoPath Filler to fill out forms in a form library.

FIGURE 8.73
InfoPath
Designer back-
stage, Publish page

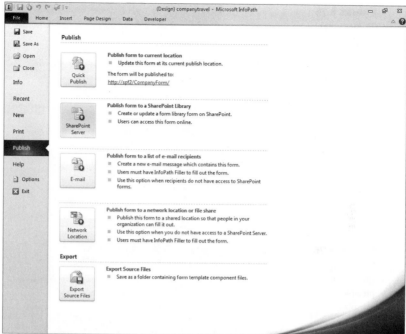

FIGURE 8.74
Enter the path for
the site.

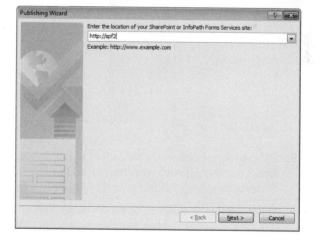

3. Make sure Form Library is selected, and click Next.

4. On the next screen of the Publishing Wizard, you can see that InfoPath has found all the possible libraries that might need a form template (Figure 8.76). Choose Update The Form Template In An Existing Document Library, and select your form library (my example is CompanyForm). Then click Next.

FIGURE 8.75
Choose what should be associated with the template.

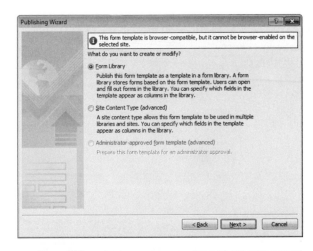

FIGURE 8.76
Choose the form library to which to publish the form template.

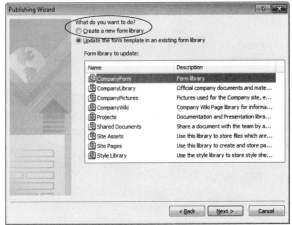

5. The next screen shows the fields that will be available for the library list item itself (the form's metadata if you will). You can add or remove fields here. Doing so does not affect the form template's fields. For this example, let's leave them as is, and click Next.

6. The last screen is to verify whether the settings are correct. If they are correct (Figure 8.77), click Publish to publish the form to the form library.

7. After the form template publishes to the library, you will get a screen that says "Your form template was successfully published." You can open the form library from there if you'd like, or you can click Close to finish. Check the box to Open This Form Library, and click Close to return to the form library.

Back on the form library, it will look no different. The template in the library's Advanced Settings page will appear as simply Template.xsn, and you can't view this kind of library in Explorer to see whether the template is in the Forms folder. The easiest way to tell whether the template published correctly is to try to create a new instance of the form.

FIGURE 8.77
Verify the publishing settings.

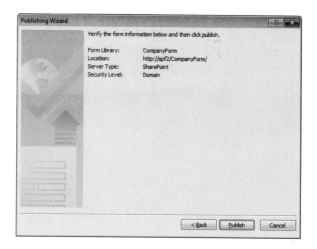

Filling Out a New Form in the Form Library

So, from a workstation that has InfoPath Filler installed, click New Document from the Documents ribbon. That will create a form instance of the template (Figure 8.78). Feel free to fill some of the fields with data, save it (my example is called *myrequest*), and close out of InfoPath Filler.

FIGURE 8.78
InfoPath form instance being filled out

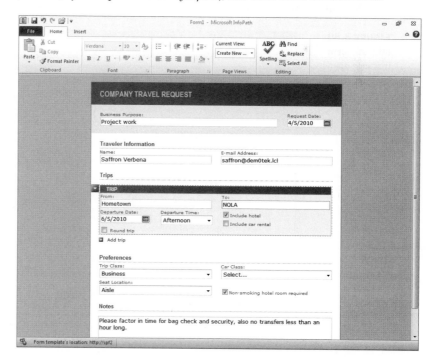

Back on the library, you can now see a saved instance of the form (Figure 8.79).

FIGURE 8.79

The Travel Request
form made from
the form template

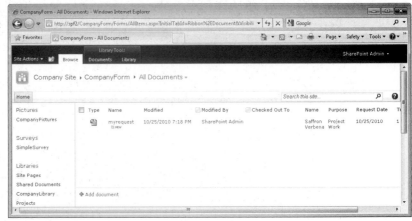

If you open it on a computer with InfoPath Filler installed, you can edit the form. If you open it on a machine that *doesn't* have InfoPath installed, it will still open but as an XML file in the browser. In that fashion, you can at least see all the data in the fields, but you can't edit it. It's a little crunchy but, in a pinch, useful (Figure 8.80).

FIGURE 8.80

InfoPath form
instance open in
browser

That's it for libraries in general. I hope this chapter has given you a basic understanding about how to use libraries, what they are, what they are meant to do, and what they *actually* do.

The Bottom Line

Create a library.   A library is a kind of list that focuses primarily on the files that are attached to the list items. There are several different types of libraries, depending on the type of file they are intended to store. Creating a library is as easy as opening the Create page, selecting the type of library, and configuring it. There are several different types of libraries.

Master It   If you do not have any Microsoft Office products installed on your machine, what two main features of document libraries are not available?

Use the different kinds of libraries.   Document libraries can be created for any type of file, but SharePoint has four main kinds of libraries with different features and views. These four libraries are the document library, form library, wiki page library, and picture library.

Master It   You're restructuring the content of some of your libraries and are planning on moving content from one library to another. What key facts do you need to keep in mind regarding wiki libraries when it comes to moving or uploading files?

Set checkout, content approval, and versioning.   Require Check Out forces users of a document library to check out a document if they intend to edit it. This helps enforce version management by allowing only one person to edit a document at a time. When a document is checked out, it can be only be read by other users, but they cannot edit the document until the person with it checked out checks it back in.

Content approval can allow items to remain invisible to most list or library viewers until someone with approval rights approves the item. In a library with content approval and major and minor versions enabled, only major versions of a document can be approved.

Versioning means that whenever a list or library item (or its attached document) is changed, that change is saved as a different version. That means that if an edit was a mistake, you can restore a previous version of the item.

Master It   Brian has left the company, but some of the documents in your Shared Documents library are still checked out by him. Several of the documents have multiple versions stored, but one was a new document that Brian uploaded to the server recently. What three methods are available to check these documents back in?

Manage content types.   By default each library (like most lists) has one content type. The content type of a library item is one that can have a single template associated with it such as Word documents, PowerPoint presentations, or Excel spreadsheets. However, it is possible to have a document library with multiple content types, allowing the library to create a mix of documents and multiple templates.

Master It   You have a general document library for the public relations department. They want to use the library to manage a large number of different file types—from Word to pictures to movie clips to more obscure things. Many of them were created in products other than Office. More importantly, the type of files they're going to use is likely to change over time. How should you configure the content types for this library?

Chapter 9

Sites, Subsites, and Workspaces

You've seen all the amazing things you can configure with lists and libraries. Now it's time to look at what you can do to the site overall and how to leverage SharePoint to provide multiple sites for multiple purposes and users. Adding new sites to a site collection is easy, and you can customize these sites to do almost anything. From adding additional Team Sites to providing blogging and wiki services, SharePoint offers numerous site types and configuration offerings.

In this chapter, you'll learn how to

- ◆ Create and customize a new site

- ◆ Adjust a site's settings for administrative purposes

- ◆ Understand the different types of SharePoint site templates available

Definitions and Concepts

To better understand the different types of SharePoint sites, let's first review some core definitions and concepts:

Site   A site is simply a shorter way of saying a SharePoint website. A site (as opposed to a site collection) is a collection of web page documents, connected by links, usually under a single URL, such as `http://spf2/default.aspx` and `http://spf2/lists/tasks/allitems.aspx`. A site in SharePoint is either a top-level site or a subsite in a site collection.

Site Definition   Each SharePoint site is based on a site definition. This determines what all sites based on the definition can do, what web parts are available, whether any custom features are loaded, and how libraries and lists are configured. The site definition is the underlying framework for SharePoint sites.

Site Template   A site template is similar to the site definition in that it determines how a site is displayed; what premade lists, libraries, and web parts are created; and what settings and configuration are available. It essentially refines the potential of a site definition into discrete sites for different purposes. A site template is used to generate the site and is applied when a site is created; once the site is created, the template is done, and the site can be customized further. All templates have, as their base, a site definition. Site templates require a site definition to work from. Thus, regardless of which template you use for a site, they all have the same capabilities set by the site definition; they differ only in which capabilities have been applied, what is prebuilt, how it is laid out, and how it looks.

SITES CAN BE BASED ON TEMPLATES OR SITE DEFINITIONS

The sites we will be looking at are those created by the default templates available with SharePoint Foundation. However, it is possible, if you are a developer, to create a great site definition and simply use it to create a site, avoiding the need for a template. Site definitions can even contain information for separate basic sites based on their settings and features (which is what meeting workspaces use). The details are beyond the scope of this book, but it does need to be said, should you come across a fancy site definition and are told it can be applied to a site without a template. Most often, though, for the convenience, people create templates based on an existing site definition and use those instead.

Site Collection   A site collection is just that, a collection of sites under one starting address. Often they are created to be a grouping of related sites. The first site in the collection is called the *top-level site*, and all subsequent sites below that are called *subsites*. All sites in a site collection can share users and permissions and many galleries and can reside in the same basic path. Each site is created based on a template, including a blank one if you simply want to customize it from the ground up in SharePoint Designer. Site collections are contained in web applications. There can be more than one site collection per web application. For web applications with one content database, 2,000 site collections is the supported limit. For more about site collections and related topics, see Chapter 10, "Site Collections and Web Applications."

Top-Level Site   This is the first and "top" site in a collection. All site collections require at least one site: the top-level site. This is the site that holds the settings for administering the entire site collection. Although the top-level site is created based on a template just like all others, its security settings and galleries can affect all other sites in the collection. See Chapter 10 for more about top-level sites and their settings.

Subsite   This is a site that resides under another site. Often the upper site is called the *parent site*, and the subsite is called a *child site*. All top-level sites and their subsites reside in a site collection. A site considered "under" another site is one that has its address further down the path from the site "above" it, such as `http://spf2/subsite1/`. Subsite1 is a child of the top-level site located at `http://spf2`.

Self-service Site   This is a site collection (not a site) that is user-created and user-controlled. The ability to create self-service sites is administratively enabled per web application and is not on by default.

When creating SharePoint sites (whether top-level sites or subsites), you can use site templates based on site definitions to configure the new site to do exactly what you need. By default, SharePoint has several existing site templates:

- Team Site
- Blank Site
- Document Workspace
- Blog

◆ Group Work Site

◆ Meeting Workspaces (there are several different types of meeting workspace templates to choose from, all using the same site definition)

◆ Custom

Before we dig deeper into what these sites can do and how they differ from each other, let's first take a closer look at how to create a new subsite and apply different settings from custom themes to site administration. Once you've seen how you can modify any site, we'll examine each of the default templates and even create one.

Creating a New Subsite

Before creating a new subsite, you need to keep the overall structure of your site collection in mind. At first, creating a new subsite below your main site is straightforward; however, as your SharePoint deployment grows, you'll need to keep track of where a subsite is located relative to other sites. In a similar fashion to designing organizational units (OUs) in Active Directory, it pays to plan ahead before creating a new subsite. Consider the purpose of the new site, user access desired, and how long you intend the site to exist. Subsites can be created with the intention of being temporary, such as a workspace for a project, or permanent, such as a team site for a particular department or organization.

For this example, we'll build a new team site for the human resources (HR) department to give them a place to work and share documents without cluttering the main site. It will need to be just like the main Company Site but designed specifically for human resources.

To create a new site, follow these steps:

1. Go to the New SharePoint Site page by clicking **Site Actions** and choosing **New Site**, as shown in Figure 9.1. For this example, the site will be created off the top-level site.

FIGURE 9.1
The Site
Actions menu

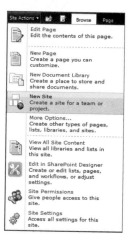

The New SharePoint Site page will appear, as shown in Figure 9.2. This is where you enter the initial settings for the new site.

FIGURE 9.2
The New
SharePoint Site
page: (top) the first
three sections;
(bottom) the last
three sections

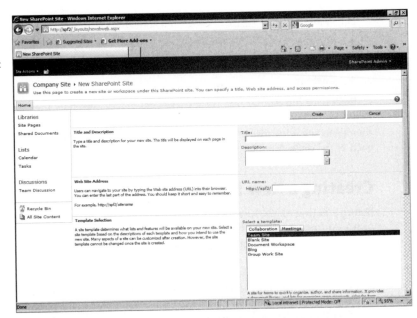

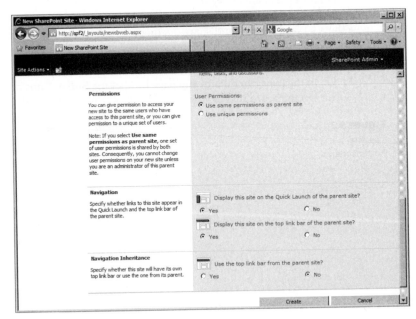

2. The Title And Description section is pretty clear. Enter a name for the site (my example is **HR team site**). For the description, enter something useful to describe the purpose of the site; my example will contain forms, data, and documents pertaining to the human resources department. This site is intended to be a resource for all employees and staff.

3. For Web Site Address, you can set the URL for the site. SharePoint has a limit of 260 characters in a single URL, so keep this short—you could end up placing more sites, libraries, and workspaces below the new site. It's a good idea to use one word without spaces. Enter an appropriate web page name; my example uses **HRteam**.

URL LIMIT DETAILS

Microsoft's documentation says that SharePoint has a limit of 260 characters in URL paths, which includes the protocol, server name, and file path, ending with the filename and extension (such as `http://spf2/subsite1/documents/Shared%Documents/allitems.aspx`).

However, SharePoint has a maximum character limit of 255 characters for a single line of text field, so you might want to consider that your URL limit instead. It might not seem to have much to do with the URL in the address bar, but if you are going to use the Send To capability of libraries or use links to access SharePoint resources (such as adding links to the Quick Launch bar, top link bar, or Links list), then you can't enter URLs longer than 255 characters into their fields.

This is why many people will say that SharePoint doesn't support more than 255 characters in a URL. It's not technically accurate, but it could be considered practically so.

Something you might have noticed is that SharePoint adds extra parameters to URLs, appending things such as view names to the path (the parameter usually starts with a question mark at the end of a URL path). The URL path character limit affects the URL path only; parameters have no impact on the limit. With added parameters, the URL can easily exceed 260 characters. You may have seen this and wondered why the page still opens. Now you know why.

---

4. Under Template Selection, there are a number of templates you can use to speed up the design and layout of your new site. Each template pulls data from a site definition. Under Collaboration, you'll see the Team Site, Blank Site, Document Workspace, Blog, and Group Work Site templates. The Blank Site option creates a completely blank site so that you can customize it using SharePoint Designer or Visual Studio. Under Meetings are the choices for each Meeting Workspace definition. For this example, choose **Team Site** to create a main site for the HR team. This template has, as you know, a lot of useful lists and web parts already premade and is perfect for HR's uses.

5. For Permissions, you have two basic choices: Inherit or Custom. You can choose Inherit to have this site use permissions from the parent site. Choosing Custom will force you to create the permissions manually. If you choose to inherit permissions, you can later edit the site, break inheritance, and move to a custom permission set if you need. For more details on permissions, see Chapter 12, "Users and Permissions." For now, leave the default in place, and use the same permissions as the parent.

WHAT IF YOU CHANGE YOUR MIND?

Don't worry. All of these settings, even the site name and URL, can be changed after the new site is created.

The only option you can't change is the template used. After a site is created, you can't apply a different template. That being said, anything on the Create page is available anywhere in the site collection. This means that if you want a list for your subsite, but it doesn't seem to be available by default, you can easily create it from resources available for all sites in the collection.

6. For Navigation, you have the option to have this new site appear as a link on the parent site's Quick Launch bar and top link bar. Adding the links lets people who go to the main site easily move to the HR team site. Selecting No for both will not place the link on the Quick Launch bar or top link bar, but people can still get to the new site by using View All Site Content on the main page or by entering the URL directly in their web browser (`http://sp2/HRteam/`). Set both of these options to **Yes** so users can easily visit the HR team site from the top-level site.

7. The Navigation Inheritance option sets the new site's top link bar to be the same as the parent site's. This is not always a good idea; it really depends on the new site's intended use. Consider your new site's role and whether the top-level site's top link bar is appropriate. Choosing No will give the new site a new top link bar, with a default Home link that goes to the top page of the new subsite (and not the parent site). This means there won't be an easy way to get back to the parent site from the subsite's home page, but that makes users focus on this site. Choosing Yes will mean this site won't have its own bar; it will use the bar from the parent site (in which case the Home link goes to the parent site). Leave this option set to the default **No**. When you have finished with your settings, click **Create**.

That's it! You now have a new site for human resources, as shown in Figure 9.3. It looks just like the main site. Remember to keep your current path in mind (using the breadcrumbs and Up One Level button) so you keep track of these sites and the page you're using. Another thing to consider is changing the theme of the subsite to make it easy to distinguish whether you are on the top-level team site or the human resources team subsite.

FIGURE 9.3

The HR team site

Site Settings

Your new site is obviously a lot like the old site because it's based on the same template. Fortunately, SharePoint is very customizable, and a lot can be done to the sites to make them unique without any web development.

To edit the site's settings, go to the Site Actions menu, and choose Site Settings. You'll see the page shown in Figure 9.4.

FIGURE 9.4

The Site Settings page for a subsite

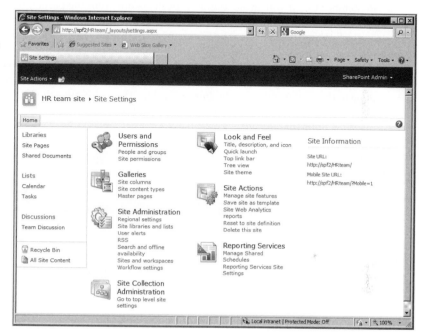

Users and Permissions

Users and permissions are covered in more detail in Chapter 12, so for now let's just see how they relate to the new HR team site compared to the main Company Site.

PEOPLE AND GROUPS

This page indicates who has what permissions to the site and what groups they belong to. Remember that if you chose to inherit permissions from the parent, this page reflects the people and groups created at the top-level site. And any changes made here will actually be made on the Site Settings page for the Company Site (the top-level and parent site in this example), not just to this HR team subsite. In Figure 9.5, notice the single line referring to the Members group of the site: "Use this group to give people Contribute permissions to the SharePoint site: Company Site." Anything you do on this page—adding groups, users, and so on—is actually done to the permissions for the Company Site. This is because the HR team subsite doesn't have its own permissions, so if you want to see what permissions are affecting it, those are the permissions of the parent site.

FIGURE 9.5
People And
Groups page

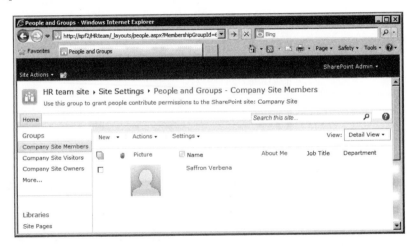

If you want to break inheritance (and have this site use its own, custom permissions), you need to click Site Permissions on the Site Settings page (you can go back to the Site Settings page by clicking its link in the title breadcrumb). For more about users, groups, permissions, and breaking inheritance see Chapter 12.

SITE PERMISSIONS

The Site Permissions page displays the permission levels applied to the groups of the parent site and therefore to the subsite. This page is where you can drill down to see what permissions and permission levels are being applied to the subsite. There are also buttons to manage those settings on the parent and to break that permission inheritance between the two. To break inheritance, simply click the Stop Inheriting Permissions button, as shown in Figure 9.6. (We're just looking at this point, so leave everything alone for now and don't break inheritance.) There are also buttons to add users (Grant Permissions) and create a new user group (Create Group), both of which add users or groups to the whole site collection. The Check Permissions button conveniently lets you check the permissions on the site being applied to a user.

FIGURE 9.6
Editing the site permissions

MOVING FROM CUSTOM TO INHERITED PERMISSIONS

If you break inheritance and use custom permissions (or start with custom permissions from initial creation) and later decide you want to inherit permissions from the parent site, enabling inheritance will erase any custom permissions you might have set.

Look and Feel

The Look And Feel category on the Site Settings page focuses on what the end users care about: the user interface. Everything in this category is designed to modify the site for ease of use and layout.

TITLE, DESCRIPTION, AND ICON

This section allows you to edit the site's title and description. Those fields are identical to the fields on the New SharePoint Site page.

The page also lets you change the website address (the site's URL). Changing the URL will cause searches to fail until the next time the index service runs (because all the paths will change). For details on setting the index frequency, see Chapter 3, "Complete Installation."

Finally, this section has Logo URL And Description. This feature wasn't present during creation, and it is a great way to customize a new site. The new icon replaces the SharePoint "playtoy people" icon in the top-left corner of the page. You can enter a URL for a new image hosted elsewhere, but you probably have a company logo or team photograph you'd like to place on the web server directly (files in the SharePoint root are replicated between SharePoint servers, so each accesses files from there locally, making for quick load times). In that case, the full path to the suggested location is `C:\Program Files\Common Files\Microsoft Shared\Web Server Extensions\14\TEMPLATE\IMAGES\`. You can also easily navigate to this location in the IIS Manager (see Figure 9.7) should you not remember the exact path.

1. For this example, place your new logo in the images directory (or directory of your choice). It can be any image file you like, but consider its size. Because it's going to be placed at the top left of every page in the site, you'll probably want to use something small. (60×60 is recommended.) Once the logo is in place, you can use a relative path in the Logo URL field.

2. Change the logo for the site. My example uses a small GIF; you can use whatever you like.

3. For the logo URL, enter **/_layouts/images/imagefilename**, and click **OK**. See Figure 9.8 for my example.

The site icon will change immediately, and you'll have a custom icon for the site.

FIGURE 9.7
The IIS images location

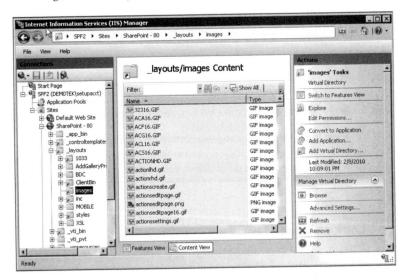

QUICK LAUNCH

The Quick Launch link on the Site Settings page lets you add, edit, and delete links from the Quick Launch bar (not disable or enable the Quick Launch bar, which is done in tree view settings for some reason). On the Quick Launch page (Figure 9.9) are links to add new links or new headings or to change the order of the existing links and headings.

FIGURE 9.8
Editing the logo

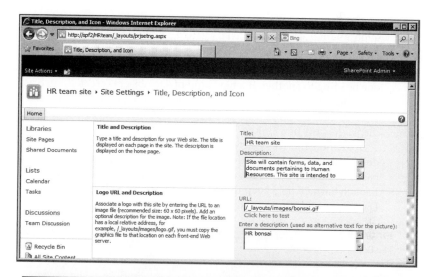

FIGURE 9.9
The Quick Launch
settings

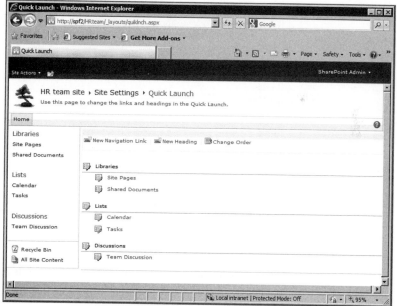

The existing links (Site Pages, Shared Documents, Calendar, Tasks, and Team Discussion) were autocreated. Autocreated links cannot be deleted or changed, only renamed; they are *managed.* If the list or library they refer to is deleted, the link is also deleted.

Links that you create yourself are manual links. A manual link can be any browser-readable link. It can be part of the SharePoint site, an external link, or anything else your browser can read. Quick Launch doesn't manage these links. If you manually create a link to a page that later disappears, the link will stay. This includes manual links to pages within this site or site collection.

Links are sorted in groups under a heading (Libraries, Lists, or Discussions in my example). These heading can also be added, removed, and edited. You can also edit a link to move it from one heading to another. If a new kind of site object is created, such as Survey or Picture Library, the heading for that type of object is added, along with the managed link. Something to keep in mind is that the Quick Launch can only support about 50 links by default, before it simply stops displaying any new links.

To demonstrate how easy it is to remove links or headings from the Quick Launch bar, let's delete the Discussions heading. Maybe it's company policy to remove it from the Quick Launch bar to avoid distracting the users with the discussion list. Getting that heading off the Quick Launch bar will help keep things neat. To delete the heading, click the Edit button next to the Discussions heading, and then choose Delete. See Figure 9.10.

FIGURE 9.10
The Edit
Heading page

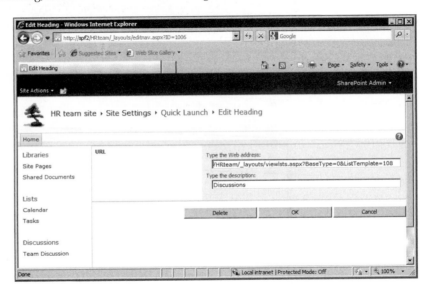

Deleting a heading will also delete any links underneath it. If you ever want to delete a heading and retain the links, you'll need to edit each link and move it to a new heading.

Once you confirm the deletion, you can see that the Discussions heading is no longer on the Quick Launch bar. See Figure 9.11.

FIGURE 9.11
The modified
Quick Launch
bar with no
Discussions

THE TOP LINK BAR

If a site inherits the top link bar from its parent site, the only choice you have if you want to customize it is to stop inheriting links (if you do stop inheriting links, you can change your mind and go back to the top link bar settings and use Links From Parent again). However, if this is a top-level site or the subsite is not inheriting the top link bar, then you can add, edit, and delete links from the bar without that additional step. The HR team site is not inheriting the bar, so it's easy to edit the top link bar directly. See Figure 9.12.

FIGURE 9.12
The Top Link Bar settings

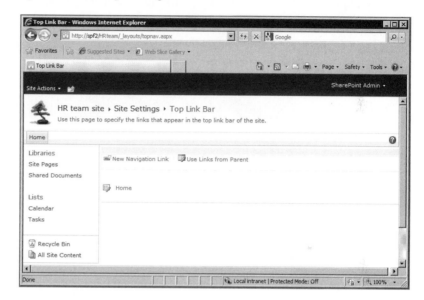

To add a link, use the New Navigation Link button. To edit or delete a link, click its Edit button. To change the order in which the links appear on the bar, click Change Order (Change Order is visible only if there is more than one link on the top link bar).

GOING YOUR OWN WAY WITH THE TOP LINK BAR

When a subsite doesn't inherit its top link bar from its parent, it cuts its top link bar off from all sites above it and effectively considers itself to be a "top" site. This means there will be only one link in its top link bar, and that will be the "home" tab that points to itself. All subsites of that site, if they inherit the top link bar, will consider that parent subsite to be the top, home tab of their top link bar. This can be used to create a kind of mini site collection, where you can have a collection of subsites that don't use the top link bar to conveniently point back up the collection to the more top-level sites.

However, keep in mind that the Navigate Up button at the top of all SharePoint pages will always have a link to the top-level site, regardless of whatever you do with the Quick Launch and top link bars. This is a good example of why SharePoint has built-in navigational redundancy.

Just like the links on the Quick Launch bar, the autocreated links on the top link bar are managed. They'll disappear if the referenced site is deleted. However, manually created links (even links to pages on the SharePoint site) are unmanaged and will remain if the referenced page is deleted.

Let's create a new link to an external website (for example, your company's site, webmail interface, local news, weather, or whatever). My example creates a link to Google, as shown in Figure 9.13. Put the URL for the link in the web address field, and then type a description. The description is what will be in the top link tab, so keep it short. When you are done, click OK to create the new link.

FIGURE 9.13
The new link

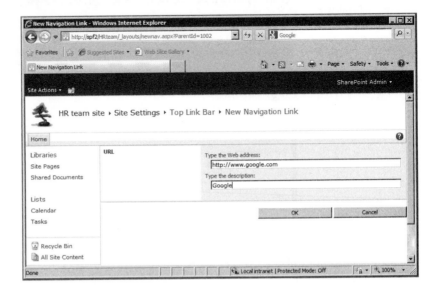

A Google link appears on the top link bar, as shown in Figure 9.14. Clicking this link will take you to www.google.com. Obviously, this will cause your browser to leave your SharePoint site. The only way to return to SharePoint is to use your browser's Back button.

FIGURE 9.14
The modified top link bar

TREE VIEW

By default all SharePoint sites have the Quick Launch bar for navigation on the left side of most pages. However, there is an alternative: tree view. This view can be used instead of or in addition to the Quick Launch bar. The Quick Launch bar contains site links grouped logically, whereas the tree view shows the full site hierarchy in a physical sense. It behaves the same way as the tree pane in Windows Explorer or most MMC consoles. You can enable just the Quick Launch bar (the default), just the tree view, both, or neither. See Figure 9.15.

FIGURE 9.15
The Tree View page

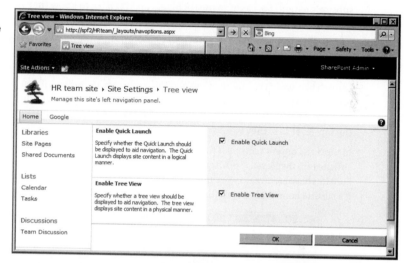

When you enable both settings, a new Site Contents section will be added to the Quick Launch bar showing the site's contents using the tree view. Enabling neither doesn't reclaim that space (meaning disabling Quick Launch too); it just leaves the All Site Content link and the Recycle Bin in place (moving them up the page), and removes all the other headings and links. This flexibility in controlling what links are on the Quick Launch bar, what order they go in, whether there should be a display of site hierarchy, or even whether there should be much of anything there at *all* allows you more control over what the users see conveniently and therefore what they *use* conveniently. And keep in mind that the navigation design decision affects *all* pages on the site except settings pages. So, give it some serious thought when planning your subsites.

For this example, let's go ahead and enable both, then click OK.

TREE VIEW IS A POWERFUL THING

We've created a subsite beneath the top-level site. And because location has its privilege, the child sites directly beneath top-level sites are added to the parent site's Quick Launch and top link bars.

However, if the child site spawned a child site of its own, such as the HR team site having an HR blog subsite (called HR in Action!, for example), that subsite would not be on the top link bar of the main Company Site. It's too far away from the top-level site for it to even realize the sub-subsite was created.

This is because the HR blog is inheriting the top links from its parent site, the HR team site, which has its own, unique top link bar. This means that the HR blog has the same top link bar as the HR team site, which is different from the top link bar on the main company site because the HR team site is not inheriting the main company site's top link bar.

The bottom line is that sub-subsites are not naturally listed in the Quick Launch bar or top link bar on the top-level site or any level above the subsite's parent (depending on the inheritance of these navigation features). The only site that will always have a link to it (if you don't disable it) is the sub-subsite's parent. So, to get to the HR blog, you first have to know that you need to go to the HR team site and then click the HR Blog link in the Quick Launch bar or top link bar to get to the HR blog.

If you want users to be able to find and access all subsites in the site collection more conveniently from the top-level site, consider enabling tree view for the top-level site. This will add the Site Content section to the Quick Launch bar area. (It can take up a lot of space and clutter the Quick Launch bar, which is why so many people leave it off.) However, if you have Site Content on (which is what the tree view is called when enabled), you can use it to see what sites are where at any level throughout the site collection. And if you had your subsites inheriting the Quick Launch bar from the top-level site, they would automatically have the Site Content section available as well.

In the Site Content section of the Quick Launch bar (on the far left of the page), the lists, libraries, and subsites are displayed. Subsites are indicated first, with the rest of the local content displayed below. Subsites have arrows, so you can expand them in the hierarchy to see what content they have available. If a subsite has sites beneath it, they will be displayed with arrows so you can expand them as well.

So if you have a lot of subsites that contain subsites and you don't want to have to add them manually to the top link bar or to the Links List View web part of the top-level site, consider tree view.

SITE THEME

Site themes are a convenient and dramatic way to change the appearance of a SharePoint site. Because SharePoint pages are rendered on the fly, changing the appearance using themes is easy. The theme changes the colors and fonts for the site. It does not change the actual content in any way. There are 20 built-in themes, but you can also design themes in PowerPoint 2010 and import the resulting .thmx file to the Theme Gallery on the top-level site and use it for the site throughout the site collection.

When you access the Site Theme page (Figure 9.16), you see the colors and fonts for that theme displayed in a palette. On the palette, the top row shows the main colors used. The first four colors are the big ones; these will have the greatest impact on the site. The remaining six are for minor things (borders, text color for menu items, group title colors, and so on). So, focus on the first four colors for the big stuff. The rest of the palettes are the accent colors, used for tinting or shadowing (such as with the top link bar).

FIGURE 9.16
The Site
Theme page

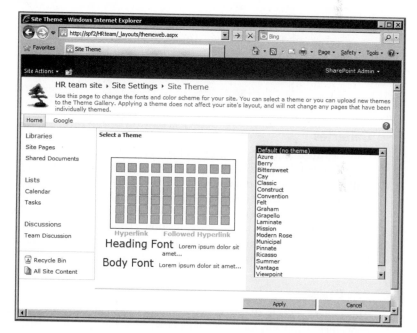

Browse through the themes, pick one you like, and change your site. My example uses Graham. After you apply your theme, go back to the HR team site (or whatever you named your subsite) to check it out, as in Figure 9.17. The site now has a custom logo and a new theme, and the Site Content section should appear on the Quick Launch bar.

FIGURE 9.17

The newly themed
HR team site

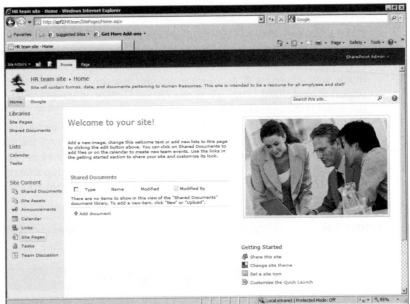

Galleries

Galleries are for storing customized lists, sites, web parts, and more (usually in the form of template files, but there are exceptions). There are even galleries for site columns and content types. Galleries are generally document libraries, used to organize and make available those files for download, upload, and so on. There are seven galleries; three are available at all site levels, and four site collection galleries are accessible only from the top-level site, although their contents are applicable throughout the site collection. (These will be covered in Chapter 10.) Items added to the site-level galleries are for that site specifically. The galleries that are available at all site levels are for site columns, site content types, and master pages.

SITE COLUMNS

This gallery collects all the premade columns available to the lists and libraries in the site (think convenient templates for list fields). Once again, this gallery displays inherited columns, and everything here is available to all subsites. You can create new site columns that apply just to this subsite (and not the parent site) or edit any of the inherited columns. You can find more details about site columns in Chapter 7, "Creating Lists."

SITE CONTENT TYPES

This gallery contains all the content types for this site. Content types are a kind of list item template. Or more precisely, they are the definition files for site list or library item types, which can include the templates for documents and pages that can be generated in document libraries, such as Word files or basic web pages. The gallery is available to the site and all subsites and shows the content types inherited from the parent site. Chapter 8, "Introduction to Libraries," explains content types in more detail.

Master Pages

Master pages are HTML files (actually, they support XHTML) that reference the ASP.NET-based code that controls general features for the site's pages. General features in this case are things that appear on every page of the site, such as navigation, header, footer, and content areas. The master page has the code for the top ribbon bar, top link bar, Account menu, the help icon, and the Quick Launch bar. Site definitions have a master page, and templates create an initial master page when a new site is first created. Every site has, by default, a `default.master` file, which is backward-compatible with WSS 3.0 (for visual upgrades when migrating), as well as master pages for the current version of SharePoint: `v4.master` and `minimal.master` (a basic, starter master page). You can add custom master pages (or create and edit them in SharePoint Designer or Visual Studio) and add them to the site using the Master Page Gallery, as shown in Figure 9.18. You can also download them and import them into other sites or even other servers. When you change a master page for a site, either a top-level site or a subsite, it changes only that master page for that site. Even though there may be other sites in the site collection using the same template and their own copy of the same master page, they are not going to be affected. If you change a site's master page, it affects only that site. If you change a site definition, the change will be reflected in all sites that are based on that site definition.

FIGURE 9.18
The Master Page
Gallery

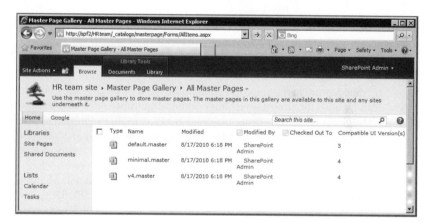

Site Actions

This section is focused on making changes to the site as a whole, rather than certain portions or particular settings. Designed for the site administrator, it handles site-wide settings, from available features to deleting the site altogether.

Manage Site Features

This option shows all the features deployed to the site. All you can do on this page is activate or deactivate the features available. See Figure 9.19.

FIGURE 9.19

The Manage Site
Features page

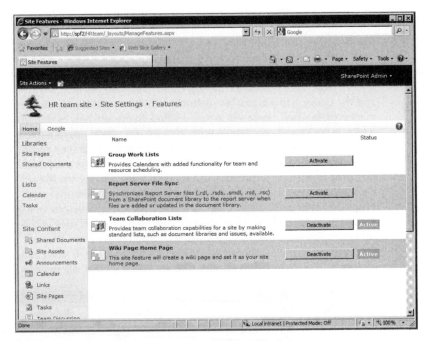

Site features are customizations that extend or modify the existing SharePoint site. Features can be used for almost anything—something minor such as a change to one of the existing menu options or something major such as a complete overhaul of SharePoint to provide ecommerce solutions. Features are typically written by third-party companies to integrate their software solutions into SharePoint or by helpful developers, many of whom give them away free over the Web.

At the core of a site feature is a `feature.xml` file, which tells SharePoint what to do. Each feature can also contain supporting files (additional XML, ASPX, DLL, or other files) if needed, but they aren't required. Many features do everything they need to do in the single `feature.xml` file. Everything involved with a feature is tucked away in a named folder that is stored at this path:

```
C:\Program Files\Common Files\Microsoft Shared\web server extensions\14\TEMPLATE\
FEATURES\
```

Features are usually provided by installation packages called *solutions*. Solutions can appear as custom SharePoint installation files (`*.wsp`). You can find step-by-step instructions for installing solutions (like additional features) in Chapter 15, "Migrating from WSS 3.0 to Windows SharePoint Foundation 2010."

A feature can be scoped to apply at a certain level of a SharePoint farm, be that the entire farm, per web application, or even per site collection (and therefore can be uploaded to the site collection's solutions gallery to be activated there). If a feature has be deployed (at whatever level it is scoped), that often just makes it available to be activated or deactivated at the site level.

The available site features vary from site template to site template (particularly as to which have been activated). For the Team Site template, the features available out of the box are as follows:

Group Work Lists   The new site template, Group Work Site, offers resource and team scheduling for the site calendars. This is a feature that is actually available to most site templates; it's just not turned on, or *activated*, for non–group work sites. You can activate it to use the group work calendar capabilities if you like. For more on the Group Work Site template and what it can do, see the "Group Work Site" section later in this chapter. By default this feature is not activated for a team site.

Report Server File Sync   This feature generally requires that you have Reporting Services enabled on the SQL Server and in Central Administration, as well as configured for the site, so you can synchronize reports made with SQL Server Reporting Services' Report Builder in a document library, with the data the reports reference in SQL Server. As you can see, this feature has quite a number of requirements and is usually off by default.

Team Collaboration Lists   This feature allows the site to offer most of the list and library templates available for use on a team site. If it is off (and the Wiki Page Home Page feature is off), you can create subsites, workspaces, and web part pages, and that's it. All other list and library templates are gone. Even making a custom list is not an option. This feature should always be activated by default.

Wiki Page Home Page   This feature forces a file named Home in the wiki library Site Pages on a team site to be the site's home page. The rich content area of a wiki page replaces the web part area of a standard home page. Interestingly, if this feature is activated and Team Collaboration Lists is deactivated, it will cause wiki library templates and the creation of new wiki pages to still be available when all other list and library templates go away. This feature tends to be activated for a team site by default. To revert the home page of the site to a web part page, deactivate this feature (something we do in Chapter 5, "Introduction to Web Parts").

SAVE SITE AS TEMPLATE

After you've done a lot of work on a site—adding your custom logo, adjusting a theme, creating new lists or document libraries, customizing the top link bar or Quick Launch bar—you may want to make a copy of that site to make a new one just like it later. This is where saving it as a template can come in handy. You can use the saved template to create new sites.

The site template can also include the actual data content of the site, including all the items in the lists, document libraries, and workflows. Include the content only if you really want all this data to be part of the template. For example, it might be nice to have a custom list as part of the template, but you probably don't want to include all your private human resource documents.

In general, "content" consists of the items inside lists and libraries but not those lists and libraries themselves. So, the template "without content" will still include a Shared Documents library, but it will be empty. Web parts are not considered content and will be included in the template either way, but if the web part references any particular item in a list or library (such as a picture in a picture library), it will not be included unless you include content. Naturally there are exceptions—for example, the wiki home page (contained within the Site Pages library) is included with the template, even if you chose to not include content.

One item that is not included in the template (regardless of whether you choose to include content) is your custom icon. No matter what, you'll have to relink the icon on the new site.

Real World Scenario

THE SITE TEMPLATE SIZE LIMIT

By default, there is a 50 MB limit to the size of a site template. Anything larger will fail to be created. You can change this size limit using the STSADM command-line tool, up to a maximum of 524,288,000 (500 MB). To change the size limit, open a command prompt on your SharePoint server, navigate to the SharePoint root BIN folder (or just open the PowerShell console), and run the following:

```
stsadm -o setproperty -pn max-template-document-size -pv <size-in-bytes> -url
<site_url>
```

Replace *<size-in-bytes>* with the desired size—for example, 100000000 would be approximately 100 MB. Replace *<site_url>* with the site collection's URL, for example http://spf1. STSADM is discussed in greater detail in Chapter 14, "STSADM and Powershell."

1. To create a template out of the HR team site and save what you've done so far as a template, click the **Save Site As Template** link.

2. On the Save Site As Template page, enter a title and description for the template, as shown in Figure 9.20. In this example, you don't need to include the content. Then click **OK** at the bottom of the page to complete the process. When it's saved, it will let you know; click **Continue** to return to the main page.

We'll come back to this template later and see how to use it.

FIGURE 9.20
Saving the site as a template

![Screenshot of the Save Site as Template page in Windows Internet Explorer. The browser address bar shows http://spf2/HRteam/_layouts/savetmpl.aspx. The page shows "HR team site ‣ Site Settings ‣ Save as Template" with sections for File Name (File name: hrtemplate), Name and Description (Template name: HRteam, Template description: A template built from the HRteam site), and Include Content with an unchecked checkbox. OK and Cancel buttons appear at the bottom. A left navigation pane lists Libraries, Site Pages, Shared Documents, Lists, Calendar, Tasks, and Site Content items including Shared Documents, Site Assets, Announcements, Calendar, Links, Site Pages, Tasks, and Team Discussion.]

PRIVATE CONTENT IN SITE TEMPLATES

Keep in mind that saving the contents of a site in a template means that data might be available to anyone allowed to create a site elsewhere in the collection; a site's security settings are not saved with the template for the site. Beware of the temptation of saving secure content with a site template unless you intend to download it from the gallery and remove it from the list before anyone gets to use it for nefarious purposes.

SITE WEB ANALYTICS REPORTS

It's always a good idea to keep track of how much a site is being used. Perhaps you need to monitor some sites for inactivity to help you decide whether to delete them, or maybe you need to know which users are frequently accessing the site. When usage analysis is enabled in Central Administration (discussed in Chapter 3), the web analytics reports become available for all sites in the server farm.

HEY, WHAT HAPPENED TO MY SITE WEB ANALYTICS REPORT?

To use the Site Usage Report and the Site Collection Usage Summary, you need to enable Usage Analysis Processing. This is done in SharePoint Foundation Central Administration. Follow these steps:

1. Connect to Central Administration.

2. Once you've logged into Central Administration, navigate to Monitoring ➢ Reporting, and click Configure Usage And Health Data Collection. This will take you to the page shown here.

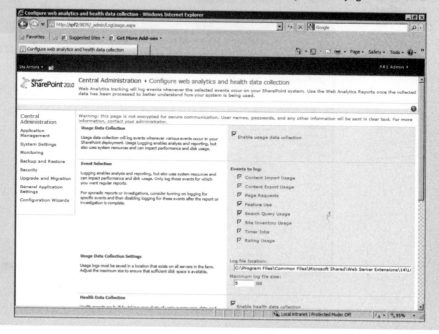

3. Check the additional events you want to track, but keep in mind that the more you log, the larger the log files will be (and the more space they'll consume in the database).

4. For the Usage Data Collection settings, you can change the Log File Location setting or leave the default in place:

```
C:\Program Files\Common Files\Microsoft Shared\web server extensions\14\Logs
```

My example leaves the default in place. You can also change the maximum log size (the default is 5 GB). You can change the maximum log size here if you want; I'm keeping the default.

5. You can edit the schedule for the health data collection; this takes you to the Job Definitions page.

6. Log Collection Schedule lets you schedule how frequently the server pulls the logs from the file structure (above) and places them into the logging database.

7. Logging Database Server is where you choose what database to store the log files—typically they're stored in a separate database (you don't want to fill your content database with log file information).

8. Click OK. You've enabled usage reports; now all you need to do is wait a day or two before you can check them out.

Let's take a look at web analytics reports for the HR team site. See Figure 9.21.

FIGURE 9.21
Web Analytics
Reports page

Seven reports are available on the Quick Launch bar for this page:

Number Of Page Views   Shows the number of page views the site has received each day. A page view is simply every time the page is rendered (viewed).

Number Of Unique Visitors   Displays the number of logins (users) that accessed the site each day.

Number Of Referrers   Shows how many referrers were logged each day. A *referrer* is the URL that directed people to the site. This is probably the least-used report, because most SharePoint pages are accessed directly or referred from another page in the same site.

Top Pages   Lists the most frequently accessed pages.

Top Visitors   Displays the users who have accessed the site, listed by frequency of visit.

Top Referrers   Displays the referrer URLs that directed people to the site.

Top Browsers   Displays the browser identified, sorted by the beloved count. At the time of this writing, this report was identifying IE8 as IE7, so you should treat IE7 as "IE7 or later."

When viewing a report, you'll also notice an Analyze tab appears at the top of the page next to Browse. Clicking this tab will open a ribbon containing two buttons: Previous Day and Previous Month. Both of these buttons are grayed out and do nothing. They appear to be designed for use with SharePoint Server 2010 (and not SharePoint Foundation).

WHAT EXACTLY DO THE "TOP" REPORTS CALCULATE?

You may be wondering where the reports get the numbers listed under Count in the Top Pages, Top Visitors, Top Referrers, and Top Browsers reports. For example, does Top Visitors calculate the count based on the number of times users logged in or based on the total page views? And how far back does the metric go in time? Is this a list of top visitors today, this week, this month, or since the site was created?

In WSS 3.0, it was possible to view reports on the top pages, visitors, and browsers as well. These were calculated by counting page views, and you had the option to see it broken down by each day or with a monthly summery.

Now, with SharePoint Foundation, it's not so clear—it appears the count is still calculated by page views, but there is no date range specified. Since the first three reports (Number Of Page Views, Number Of Unique Visitors, and Number of Referrers) display data going back one month only, it's likely the metrics for the "Top" reports is similarly truncated, covering data for one month. But at the time of this writing, this is not explicitly stated anywhere in SharePoint or Microsoft's TechNet documentation.

RESET TO SITE DEFINITION

Resetting a site to the default definition completely removes any extensive customization of either a single page or the entire site. As you can see in Figure 9.22, there is no Undo button.

That's the bad news. The good news is that *customization* doesn't mean exactly what you might think it does. Nothing you've done so far—the custom logo, the theme, the top link bar, or the Quick Launch bar—has edited the site's definition. From a site definition perspective, you've done *nothing* to customize this site; you've only changed some settings and maybe augmented it. It's still a team site. Resetting its definition won't change anything. However, if the site had been customized using SharePoint Designer, clicking the Reset button can reset it to the default. This is sometimes handy if someone completely corrupts a site using SharePoint Designer.

FIGURE 9.22
Resetting to the site definition

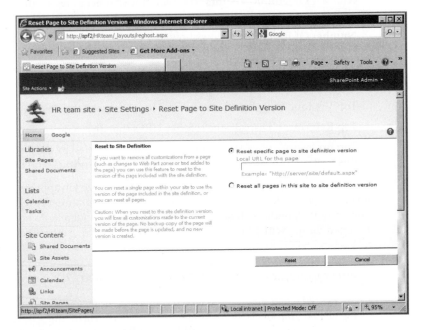

SITE DEFINITIONS VS. SITE TEMPLATES

Site templates are used to speed up new site creation. You've looked at them briefly and even created a custom template from the HR team site. So, what's a *site definition*?

Templates are used when you're creating a site—and that's it. Once a site is created, the template no longer matters. You can customize the site well beyond the template.

Site definitions are more important. The site definition defines what can and cannot be available in a template based on it. The site definition controls what *type* of site the site is—a meeting, a blog, a wiki, a team site, or even Central Administration. Site definitions are the underlying XML and ASPX files used to generate the page regardless of what kind of theme, logo, or change you apply to the site. Under the hood, every site still adheres to its site definition. The core files are located in C:\Program Files\Common Files\Microsoft Shared\web server extensions\14\ TEMPLATE\SiteTemplates in their own folders.

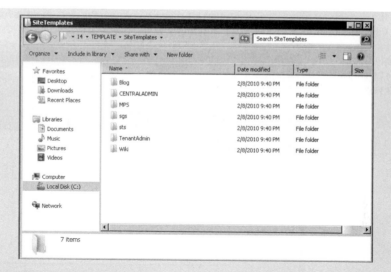

There are seven existing site definitions:

◆ Blog (for blog sites)

◆ CENTRALADMIN (for the Central Administration site)

◆ MPS (for meeting sites)

◆ sgs (for SharePoint group work sites)

◆ sts (for SharePoint team sites)

◆ TenantAdmin (for tenant admin pages, used with multi-tenant hosting)

Wiki (in case there are older WSS 3.0 wiki sites; deprecated)Site definitions have their own `v4.master` file, which is a master page that determines the layout of their web pages.

A site template takes all the potential of its site definition and narrows that down to its own application of the layout, theme, prebuilt lists, web parts, and so on, of that definition. For example, you can have a Meeting Workspace site definition and from that make a template for a social, basic, or decision meeting workspace. Each one is based on the same definition but laid out differently based on the presumed use. All have the same potential; they just apply it differently for your convenience. This explains why everything in SharePoint looks so similar and has the same interface. Many of the sites are using the same site definition under their particular theme and template. It also explains why meetings, wikis, and blogs look different from normal team sites.

DELETE THIS SITE

The last option under Site Actions is to simply delete the site, as shown in Figure 9.23.

Deleting a site is not something you do lightly, because it deletes the entire site—all web parts, lists, discussions, document libraries, documents in the libraries, customizations, unique permissions, you name it. Sites don't go to the Recycle Bin; if you delete a site, it will be deleted permanently. There is no Undo, no Recycle Bin, and no chance to correct a mistaken deletion. Make sure you've salvaged anything you need from the site before you destroy it. For example, if you're about to delete a document workspace because the document is finished, make sure you copy the final version of the document to the parent site first.

FIGURE 9.23
The Delete This
Site page

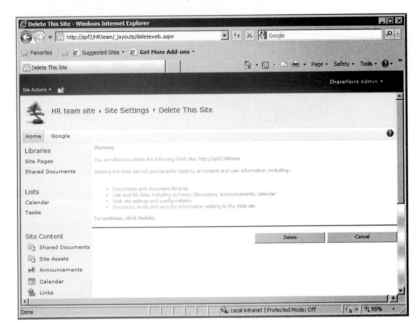

Site Administration

This section provides administrative links to change site behavior and appearance beyond the general look and feel. Most site administration settings are applied or configured right after site creation and then left alone.

REGIONAL SETTINGS

The Regional Settings page deals with location-specific settings, such as Time Zone, Date, Calendar, and so on. By default, a new site is given the same settings as its parent site. So, it's a good idea to examine these settings (shown in Figure 9.24), especially settings such as Define Your Work Week, which can really impact the way the calendar works for all site participants unless they explicitly override it with their own regional settings. Letting the site know your organization's daily start and end times will assist in tracking appointments (or overtime) and ensure that the calendars are created with the correct settings.

The settings you can adjust here include the following:

Locale This setting determines the world region, such as English (US) or English (UK). This will determine such things as the way dates are displayed (3/28/2010 or 28/3/2010), decimal points or decimal commas, and other regional-specific modifiers.

Sort Order This setting changes the sort order for lists and libraries. The sort order determines the way alphabetically sorted lists are handled. Certain languages have different sort orders for characters. Although American English speakers are used to seeing X-Y-Z at the end of the alphabet, users in other regions may not be.

FIGURE 9.24

The Regional
Settings page

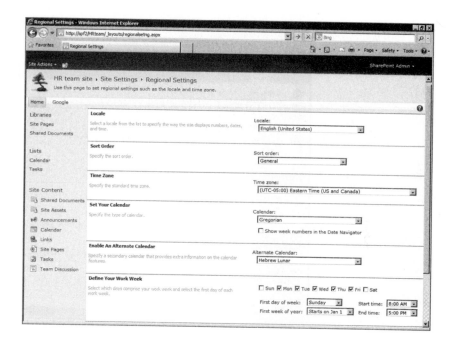

PERSONAL REGIONAL SETTINGS

By clicking the Account menu and choosing My Settings, an individual user can adjust their regional settings to differ from the site's regional settings. For example, a user can set their time zone to PST even though the site is in the EST zone. The only exception is Sort Order, which cannot be adjusted by individual users.

Time Zone   The setting ensures that all posted announcements, modification dates, and other time listings are adjusted for your local time zone.

Set Your Calendar   This setting determines the calendar you use in your daily life. Most people will use Gregorian, but you can adjust this for custom calendars, such as Buddhist.

Enable An Alternate Calendar   If you need to track dates in two calendar forms, this setting allows you to have one calendar that easily shows both forms—for example, if you need Gregorian and also need the Hebrew Lunar calendar, enable the alternate calendar for Hebrew Lunar and easily see both, as in Figure 9.25.

Define Your Work Week   With this setting, you can choose which days are considered "work" days (such as Monday through Friday) and when work starts and stops (such as 8 a.m. through 5 p.m.). You can start the week on Sunday or Monday—or even Thursday if you like.

Time Format   With this setting, you can choose whether you want 12-hour or 24-hour time displayed. This setting can change automatically if you change the Locale setting, so make sure you double-check it if you make any changes to this page.

FIGURE 9.25
The alternate calendar

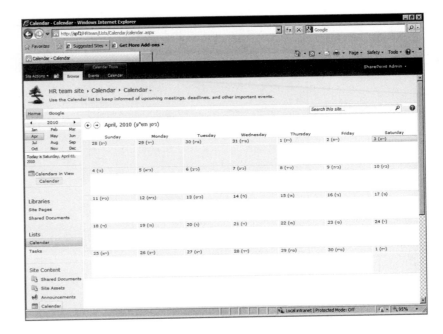

SITE LIBRARIES AND LISTS

This settings page, shown in Figure 9.26, provides you with a list of all the site's lists and libraries, with easy links to the Settings page for each one as well. These links take you to the same places that the specific list or library's settings will take you. For more details about customizing lists and libraries, see Chapters 6 through 8.

USER ALERTS

This setting gives you an easy way to see user alerts on lists or libraries. You can't see a complete list of all alerts for the site, but you can display alerts for individual users (see Figure 9.27). The only thing you can do to an alert from here is delete it; no editing or creation is possible. You can find more information about alerts in Chapter 6, "Introduction to Lists."

RSS

This setting is available under the category of Site Administration at every site, from the top level to the lowest subsite. However, at the subsite level, it allows you to enable or disable RSS feeds for the site and to specify channel elements for the RSS feeds on the site (see Figure 9.28). On the top-level site, the settings are the same, but there is an extra option to allow or disallow RSS feeds for the *entire* site collection from there, not just the top-level site. So, make certain that option is not disallowed if you want RSS to work at all for any site in the site collection. If RSS is disabled at the site collection level, the RSS option will not appear on Site Settings for any of the subsites in the collection.

Really Simple Syndication (RSS) is the protocol for what are commonly called *web feeds*, which frequently update web content you can subscribe to so your computer will automatically download any updates. RSS feeds are frequently used for the Announcements list. With RSS enabled, you can have your web browser subscribe to this list so any new announcements will appear in the feed.

FIGURE 9.26
The Site Libraries
And Lists page

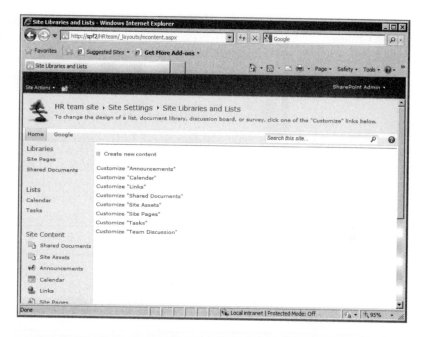

FIGURE 9.27
The User
Alerts page

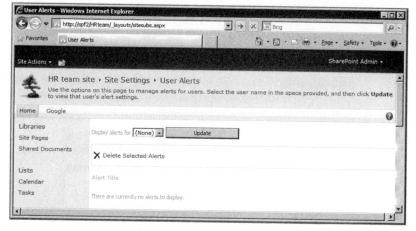

You can apply additional channel elements to the feed, tagging it with a copyright, editor name, and webmaster name. These tags are seen by some RSS readers and are a good idea to have. The elements entered in this location will be applied to all RSS feeds throughout the site.

The Time To Live setting determines the minimum *refresh time* permitted for the site. The refresh rate is the shortest amount of time an RSS reader has to wait between update checks. Although it sounds like a good idea to keep this rate low so updates are frequent, remember that every RSS reader out there could be constantly hitting the site for updates if you make this setting too low.

FIGURE 9.28
RSS settings

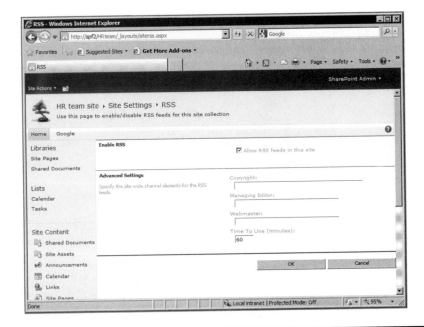

How Do I View RSS Feeds?

You can view an RSS feed in Internet Explorer by clicking the RSS Feed button. This button is active only when you're looking at a page that has a corresponding feed. When you click the button, the page changes to the RSS view.

Click Subscribe To This Feed to add the feed to your browser list of feeds and place the feed in a folder. Doing so works similarly to making a favorite (or bookmark).

When you've subscribed, you can see the RSS feed on your Feed tab under Favorites.

Note that Internet Explorer by default uses NTLM/Kerberos credential pass-through. This means that the feed will be able to autoupdate only if you are logged in to the local machine with the same account that you use for SharePoint. You can change the username/password used (if it's different from your Windows account) by editing the feed's properties.

A lot of third-party RSS viewers, including other web browsers and custom applications, are available as well, if you would rather use something other than IE.

SEARCH AND OFFLINE AVAILABILITY

As shown in Figure 9.29, you can disable search indexing if you don't want this site or any of its contents to show up in search results. Note that Search is already permissions-aware, and users will not see results they do not have permission to see. In general, it's OK to leave indexing turned on (even on sites with private information) because unauthorized users can't search the site anyway. However, sites using fine-grained permissions or connected web parts with different permissions *can* allow unauthorized users to see restricted items in their search results.

FIGURE 9.29
Search and offline availability

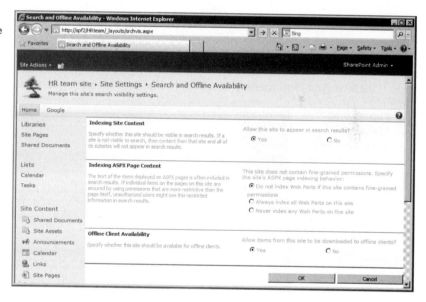

Fine-grained permissions restrict parts of a site above and beyond the main site permissions. For example, suppose you have a document library (with certain inherited permissions) and you decide to change the permissions on one document item in the library to make it more restrictive than the rest of the library. In that case, users with permission to the document library could see this restricted document in their search results. They won't be able to open it (the link will fail), but even seeing the name of the document could be a security concern.

Another security concern occurs when web parts link to another web part containing different permissions. For example, a Contacts list (with relatively open permissions) connected to a list of performance evaluations (with more restrictive permissions) could cause the more restricted information to be listed in the search results when it shouldn't.

It is unfortunate, but in the case that you need to use such fine-grained permissions or web part connections, Microsoft recommends that you disable the indexing for the site. Fortunately, the Indexing ASPX Page Content section will tell you whether you're using fine-grained permissions, and SharePoint has the default behavior of disabling indexing if such permissions exist. This also explains why Search suddenly does not work for a site's new information when it did before you enabled unique permissions on a list item.

Most of the time, you'll want to leave the default in place and allow indexing for most sites and disallow indexing on those sites with fine-grained permissions or linked web parts. However, if being able to search is more important than letting users see the search results for list items and files they can't open anyway, then you can enable search to always index ASPX pages regardless.

New in SharePoint Foundation is the ability to restrict caching of the website for offline client access. By default, clients can cache the site locally, allowing for access when offline. Setting this to No will prevent the client from using offline file caching on the site and will require an active connection at all times.

SITES AND WORKSPACES

The Sites And Workspaces page (shown in Figure 9.30) displays a list of subsites below the current site. Because the HR team site has no subsites, let's look at this section under the main Company Site. So, navigate up to the Company Site, go to its Site Settings page, and then click the Sites And Workspaces link under the Site Administration section.

FIGURE 9.30
The Company Site's "Sites And Workspaces" page

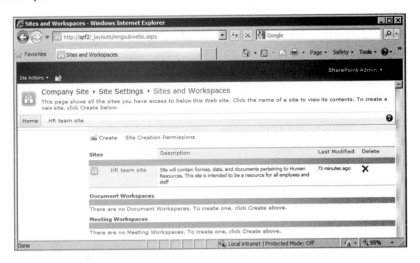

The HR team site you created is displayed here in the Site Content tree view. Clicking the site's name takes you to that site.

Clicking the Create button takes you to the New SharePoint Site page.

THE SITE CREATION PERMISSIONS BUTTON

On the top-level site, the Sites And Workspaces page also has a handy Site Creation Permissions link. (Subsites don't have this feature, even if they themselves have subsites beneath them, if they all inherit permissions from the top-level site.) Clicking the Site Creation Permissions button will display a partial list of permission levels for the site.

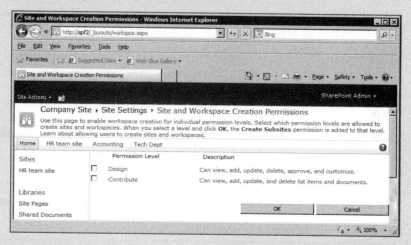

By selecting the box beside a permission level and clicking OK, you're assigning the Create Subsites permission for that permission level (and therefore giving the power to create new subsites to any groups or users with that permission level). The Site Owners group already has the right to create subsites, and by default the Visitors group cannot have the right to create subsites, because they have only read rights to the site. That leaves the Contribute and Design permission levels, both of which could be granted with the Create Sites permission.

By clicking the permission level's name, you can manually edit the permission levels to give each level the specific permissions you want. See Chapter 12 for more about permissions and permission levels.

Let's create another site below the main site, so we can use the site template we made earlier:

1. Click **Create**.

2. Here you'll find yourself at the familiar New SharePoint Site page (Figure 9.31). I'm going to name the site **Accounting** and leave the description blank.

3. For Web Site Address, the path is already displayed, so enter the last part of the path indicating the site. For my example, that is **Accounting**.

4. For the template selection, let's apply the template we saved from the HR team site earlier. If you click the Custom tab, you'll see our custom template! Let's pick that, leave all the other settings at the default, and hit **Create**.

FIGURE 9.31
Creating a site
from a custom
template

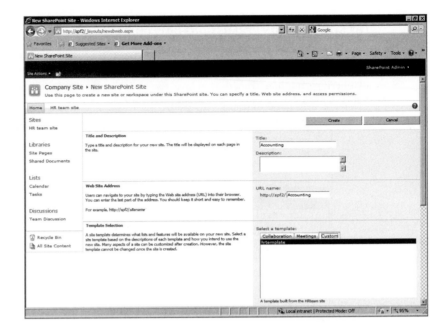

As you can see in Figure 9.32, the new site is exactly like the one from which the template was created, except that the custom icon is gone and the content is missing (unless you selected the Include Content box when you created the template). All your custom links in the top link bar and Quick Launch bar are there, the theme is applied, and any edits or additions you made to the home page are all there.

WORKFLOW SETTINGS

This section is merely a rendered list of all the currently in-use workflows on the site. You cannot make any changes from here. There's no way to add, edit, or delete workflows from this gallery. SharePoint Foundation comes with one workflow by default: the Three-State workflow, but even this will not show up unless it's actually in use. You can obtain other workflows from third-party software developers or build them using SharePoint Designer or Visual Studio 2010. For more information on workflows, see Chapter 7.

Reporting Services

New in SharePoint Foundation is built-in integration with SQL Server 2008 R2's Reporting Services. This allows SharePoint to integrate with the SQL Server reporting server to provide easier access to reports generated by SQL Server Reporting Services. In other words, this integration does not enable additional report features for SharePoint; it simply allows you to store, edit, and view SQL Server reports (created initially using Report Builder, a separate product meant to generate reports from data in databases in SQL) via the SharePoint library.

FIGURE 9.32
A new subsite made from a custom template

If you have a SQL Server instance running Reporting Services for SharePoint, you can configure Reporting Services for SharePoint. This builds a new database that can run in SharePoint Integrated mode. Fundamentally, this allows you to use SQL Server Reporting Services to store reports in a SharePoint library, allowing direct access to the reports via the SharePoint interface. Once the reports (and related content types) are in the library, they can be accessed by any users with permission in SharePoint and can even be viewed directly using a Report Viewer web part (also new to this version of SharePoint).

Reporting Services first needs to be set up on SQL Server 2008 R2 where a copy of SharePoint has been installed and added to the SharePoint farm; then you need to configure the correct URL, integration, and authentication settings in Central Administration, which will attach the SharePoint farm to the reporting service (it will work only with SQL Server 2008 R2, not SQL Server 2008). Once it's connected, you can activate Reporting Services on any site in the farm.

Should you be interested in setting up SQL Server 2008 R2 with Reporting Services and you want a handy way to store and access the reports generated, consider using this SQL Server integration capability.

Managing Shared Schedules

Shared schedules are used to run reports unattended. They're typically first created on a report directly (via the library where the report is stored). When a schedule is set as shared, it can then be used by other reports (when configured to run unattended). Here you can see the currently configured shared schedules and pause, edit, expire, or even delete them. (Expire causes the schedule to stop running at a certain date but does not delete the schedule.)

This link does not go anywhere productive unless you have Reporting Services configured and attached to a SQL Server report server.

REPORTING SERVICES SITE SETTINGS

This link takes you to the Reporting Services Site Settings page, shown in Figure 9.33.

FIGURE 9.33

Reporting Services Site Settings page

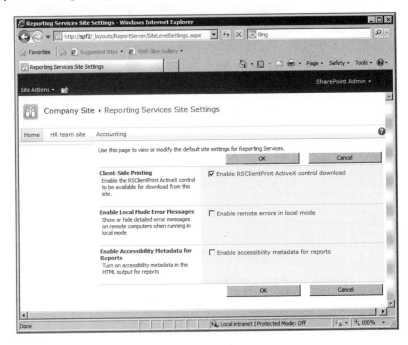

Here you can enable three options:

Client-Side Printing   This enables the RSClientPrint ActiveX control for the SharePoint site. This ActiveX control allows the users to print the reports to their local printer directly (Internet Explorer required, obviously).

Enable Local Mode Error Messages   New with SharePoint Foundation 2010 is the ability to run the SharePoint Reporting Services in *local mode*, which lets you store and view reports in the library without an active connection to a SQL Server Reporting Services server (but connected to another data, such as Access 2010). This option allows you to display any errors that pop up on the remote computer when running reports.

Enable Accessibility Metadata For Reports   When generating reports in HTML format, you can have the server also write the accessibility metadata into the HTML code. This is applicable only for simple table or matrix structured reports, and it simply identifies rows and columns, header cells, and frame titles. This is designed for rendering the HTML report accurately on multiple disparate platforms (for example, seeing the report on a mobile phone browser).

Site Collection Administration

On a subsite, this category contains only a single link: Go To The Top-Level Site Settings. This takes you to the Site Settings page for the top-level site, which is where all Site Collection settings and administration is done. Site Collections (and their settings) are covered in Chapter 10.

Additional Default Site Templates

Now that you've seen all the ways to customize and control sites, let's take a closer look at the different types of sites available in SharePoint and how they differ from each other. Choosing a template during site creation will prebuild the site with lists, libraries, and custom features designed for that type of site. This speeds up the customization process, since you're starting from a prebuilt default that will (ideally) contain what you need. There are several existing site templates, and each contains key differences in layout and intent. The following templates are available choices during site creation, starting with the most common, the Team Site template.

Team Site

The Team Site template is the SharePoint workhorse. So far, everything you've done has been in a team site. Team sites are the most general and the most common sites. They're typically what administrators choose for the main site from which all other sites branch. Containing lists, libraries, some web parts, and a nice custom theme, they're perfect for your all-purpose SharePoint site. If you just need a site, you're looking for a team site.

Blank Site

Would you prefer to start with a site that is not cluttered with the trappings of someone else's idea of a site? This is the site for you. Nothing prebuilt, and no assumptions or existing libraries or lists. If you'd rather build the site from scratch with your own libraries, lists, web parts, and layout, you can start with a Blank site.

Document Workspace

A Document Workspace site is all about managing one document. There are two ways to create a document workspace: either through the Sites and Workspaces page in Site Settings, the usual New SharePoint Site page (under Site Actions ➤ New Site), or directly from a document. I've added a sample document to the HR team's Shared Documents library; from there you can create the document workspace by selecting Send To ➤ Create A Document Workspace from the document's drop-down menu, as shown in Figure 9.34. You can also select the document, go to the Documents ribbon, and in the Copies section click the drop-down menu for the Send To button.

Why would you want to have a separate site for one document? Say you have a large number of people working on one file—a legal brief, screenplay, or other complex document. That sort of collaboration will require discussion, versioning, additional documents, and other collaboration, all of which can be done in a library on the main team site. But why have all those document-specific items clutter the main site? It's better to give the document its own space so you can add supporting documents, discussions boards, and assign tasks separately from the rest of the site. Go ahead and create the workspace, and then click OK when prompted to confirm.

When the document workspace (Figure 9.35) is first created, a copy of the document is placed in the workspace's Shared Documents library. The creating user (in my case SharePoint Admin) is added to the workspace Members list. All other users who need to work on the document need to be added to the Members list; it does not inherit the permissions of the parent site. Fortunately, there is a link on the main page of the document workspace to do this. Users without permission to access the workspace will not even see it in the site hierarchy.

FIGURE 9.34
Creating a workspace

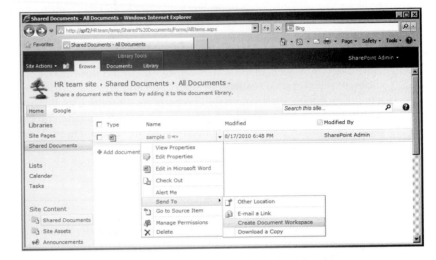

FIGURE 9.35
The document workspace

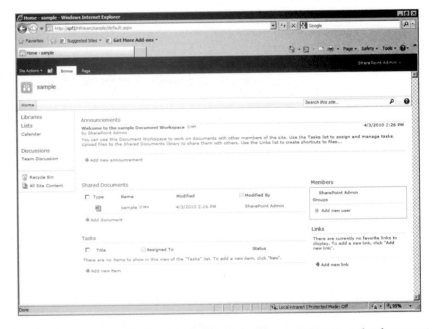

A document workspace comes prebuilt with the document library containing the document, a Tasks list to assign tasks to members, a calendar to track deadlines and milestones, and a discussion board to discuss the document's development. If you created the document workspace via the New SharePoint Site page, then the Shared Documents library will be empty (since you hadn't specified for which document the workspace was created).

WORKING ON THE WRONG COPY

When you're creating a document workspace, remember that a copy of the document is still sitting in the original document library. It's important to keep track of which copy is the primary one and keep that in the document workspace. Why else have it? The last thing you want is to have someone working on the original document while someone else is also working on a copy in the workspace. You may want to remove or check out the copy from the original Shared Documents document library to prevent confusion.

Once the document is finished and the purpose of the workspace is completed, you may want to remove the workspace to keep the server clean. Before you do so, make sure you copy everything you want to keep (in particular, the actual final document) to the parent site. Once the workspace is deleted, it's gone. Sites don't go to the Recycle Bin.

Blog

Blogs, probably the most notorious form of website, are basically public diaries and journals with frequent postings listed in reverse chronological order. SharePoint blogs support comments so users can comment on posts, with categories to organize the posts, and *permalinks*, which are fixed links to posts. From the HR team site, I've created a blog called HR In Action! using the now-familiar New SharePoint Site page. I have it set to inherit permissions and appear on both the Quick Launch and top link bars. I also set the blog to inherit the top link from the parent site (the HR team site). When the blog is created, it automatically takes you to its home page (Figure 9.36).

FIGURE 9.36
A SharePoint blog

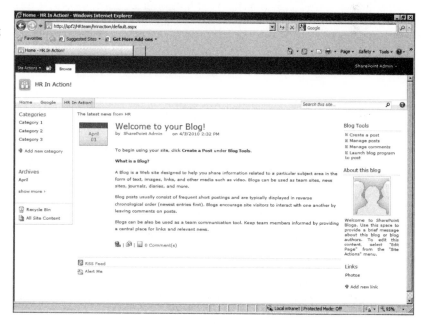

On the left side of the page is a modified Quick Launch bar, unique to the Blog template's home page. On the right side are the Blog Tools links to create and manage the posts and comments on the site. They appear only when you are logged in as the blog's creator or another user with rights to create posts. Clicking Create A Post will take you to the new post page, shown in Figure 9.37. To create a post, you can enter a title and text in the body of the post. You can assign a category and specify a published date for the post. You can save the post as a draft, or you can publish it. When published, the post appears on the home page of the blog. Blogs are based on a Posts list with Content Approval enabled, as well as lists for Comments and Categories.

FIGURE 9.37
A new post

Once the post is created, it will appear on the main page. Figure 9.38 shows an example. To edit the categories and add more, click the Categories heading in the Quick Launch bar.

Each blog post has buttons at the bottom—for providing a permanent link to the posting (which will take you to the post's permanent page), for sending a link to the posting via email, and for comments. Comments are feedback posts that are linked to the main post and are typically created by other users. When looking at the main page, you can see the Comments link below each post, with a number showing the current comment count. Clicking this link will take you to the comments (see Figure 9.39) and let you add a new comment.

Comments are actually stored in the Comments list and referenced to the main post with a lookup field to the Posts list column called Post Title. The Posts list also contains a linked field called Number Of Comments, which looks up the Comments list and does a count of comments that are related to the post's title.

SharePoint blog posts can be written and edited right there in the browser itself, or with any SharePoint-compatible blog-editing software, such as Word 2010 or Windows Live Writer.

FIGURE 9.38
A blog with a post

FIGURE 9.39
Comments

Group Work Site

The Group Work Site template is designed to manage and organize groups of people. This site will be invaluable for managers, administrators, secretaries, or anyone who needs to keep track of people, schedules, and resources, as well as anyone who needs to keep everyone in sync. If you have a busy department and need to keep track of everyone, this is the site for you (assuming you don't find its flaws too distracting, that is).

The Group Work Site template has some prebuilt lists that work best when the site's permissions are explicitly set a certain way, and for this reason, it's recommended to break inheritance when creating a group site (For more information on breaking inheritance, see Chapter 12).

Let's create one for the tech department:

1. From the Company Site, go to Site Settings ➢ **New Site**. This will again take you to the New SharePoint Site page, as shown in Figure 9.40.

FIGURE 9.40
Creating the tech department group site

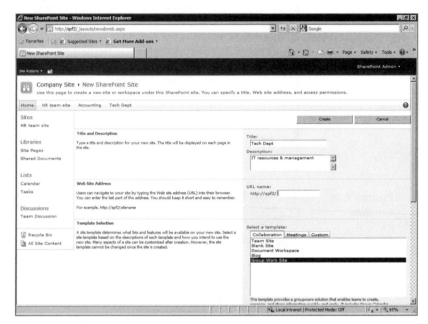

2. In this example, let's call the new site **Tech Dept**. Give it a description "techdept." Select the **Group Work Site** template. For Permissions, make sure it's set to **Use Unique Permissions**. You can leave the rest at the default settings. Click **Create**.

3. Because you selected the option to use unique permissions, you now need to set up groups for the site. See Figure 9.41. Here we build new groups for the site (or use existing groups). These are then applied to the site and can of course be changed later.

   By default SharePoint wants to set up three groups, basically the same groups we had on the company site: Visitors, Members, and Owners. You should already be familiar with these groups and their corresponding permission levels, but you can find more information in Chapter 12. Visitors have read-only access, Members can read-write, and Owners can do everything (including changing permissions).

4. With a group site, these groups really matter for the custom lists, and your assumptions based on team sites may not be accurate. With a group site, it's best to place most users in the Visitors group and reserve the Members group for people who need access to everyone's items and schedule. This will become clear as we delve into the site. For now, I'm creating a new group for both Visitors and Members, placing all the

"technicians" in the tech department in the Visitors group and placing their manager and administrative staff in Members. And of course I'm making sure I'm the Owner of the site. When you're done, hit **OK**.

Welcome to the new tech department group site, as shown in Figure 9.42.

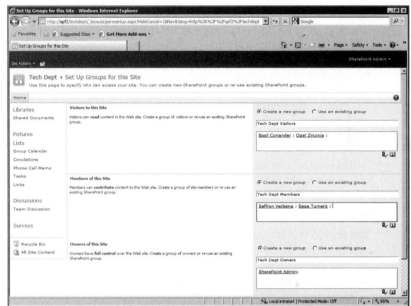

FIGURE 9.41
Setting up groups for the tech department site

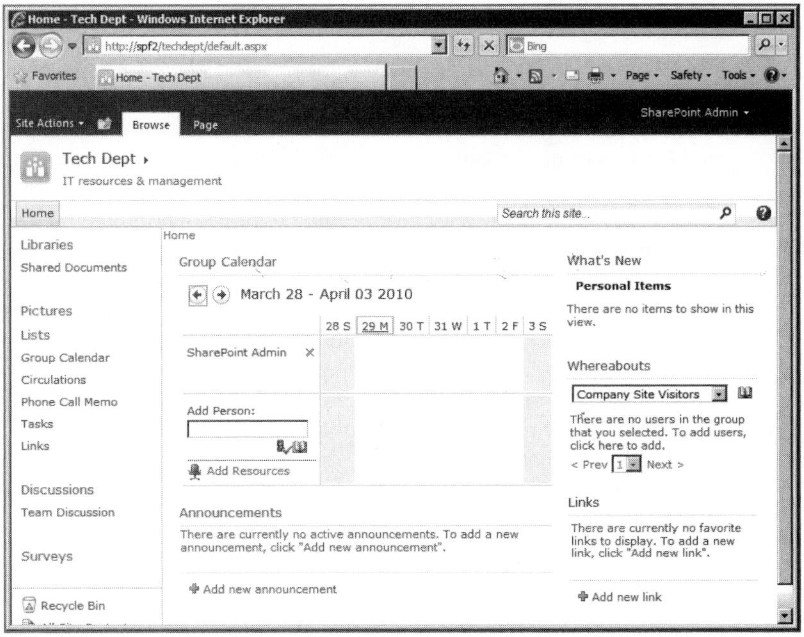

FIGURE 9.42
The tech department group site

The group site comes prebuilt with the usual Shared Documents library, a Team Discussion list, a custom group calendar, and some extremely handy lists. Let's populate these lists and take a closer look at what the group site can do.

FAMILIAR LIBRARIES AND LISTS

There is a standard document library, which will be used by the tech department to store documentation and guides. You could also create a wiki-page library for tips and tricks. There is also a Team Discussion list available for debates and discussions about technical topics. You'll also notice the Quick Launch bar has a header for Pictures, but no picture libraries, and a header for Surveys but no survey list. So, you can either create these lists and libraries or edit the Quick Launch bar to remove these unnecessary headers.

On the right side of the home page you'll see a What's New web part—this will populate with new items on the Circulation, Phone List Memo, and Group Calendar lists as they get used, all filtered by the current user (so when you log in, you can see what's new for you at a glance). At the bottom is the normal Links list web part.

There's also a Whereabouts web part, which ties directly into the Whereabouts list. This is one of two background lists.

BACKGROUND LISTS

You should look at and set up two background lists before you go much further. They don't appear on the Quick Launch bar, because they're designed to be set up first, and their primary focus is to support and enhance the other lists and the home page. These need to be populated before you can use all the features of the group site.

These two lists are Resources and Whereabouts, and you can see them if you click the Lists header in the Quick Launch bar (or if you go to the All Site Content page).

Resources

The Resources list (see Figure 9.43) is for physical items—rooms, projectors, vehicles, or any other resources that are shared within the group. These are then added to events in the group calendar, so (for example) you can list Conference Room A as a resource. Then, if an event is created for a meeting in Conference Room A, you can add the resource to the event, which marks it as booked for the duration of the meeting (even if the meeting event is later rescheduled, that resource is rescheduled with it). I'm going to quickly populate the list with some resources available to the tech department.

The Resources list also supports resource groups—a different content type for the list, used to group resources. We'll use resource groups later when it comes time to reserve resources. Think of a resource group as a filter for the type of resource. For example, you can place all the conference rooms into a resource group called Rooms. To add a new resource group, hit the arrow at the base of the New Item button and choose Resource Group. When creating the group, you can select the resources that belong in the group. See Figure 9.44.

You'll notice that you can select only existing resources, so you'll need to add all the resources first, before creating the groups. Otherwise, you'll need to edit the resource group after you've added the missing resources.

Go ahead and create a resource group called Rooms and place conference rooms into it. Now you have some resources and resource groups to work with later.

FIGURE 9.43
Resources list

FIGURE 9.44
Adding a
resource group

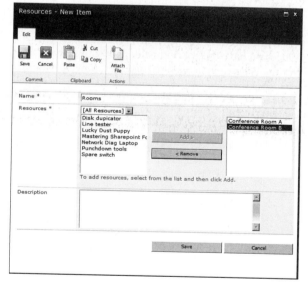

Whereabouts

The Whereabouts list is designed to track the location of people, tracking whether they're in the office, home, on vacation, or any other location you want to use. The list first needs to be populated with people. Clicking the Add New Item Link opens a People Picker, and you can quickly add some users to the list. When you're done, you'll have a list item for each user (see Figure 9.45).

FIGURE 9.45
Populating the
Whereabouts list

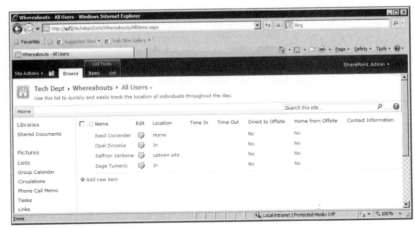

Once the users are added, you can edit the rest of the columns for each item. Pick a user, and click the Edit button to open the list item's settings. Here you can set the person's location (where they are currently), what time they came in, what time they left for the day, and if they go directly offsite in the morning or head directly home after work (and didn't actually come into the office). For the My Location field, the values In, OOF (Out of Facility), and Home are hard-coded. You can also have up to five custom locations, two of which are preset with BizTrip and Vacation (both of these can be edited or deleted). You can also have up to five values for the Contact Information field; none is populated by default. These custom values (for Location and Contact Information) are stored per user, so each user can have five custom locations.

Once you have the list populated, you can go back to the home page of the site, and you'll notice the Whereabouts web part is now showing where everyone is (Figure 9.46).

FIGURE 9.46
The home page
with the Where-
abouts web part
populated

From this web part, you can quickly update the person's location, see their work hours under Period, and even see whether any phone call memos are waiting for that person (more on phone call memos shortly).

GROUP CALENDAR

The group calendar has been modified from a normal calendar and has some interesting tricks. You'll notice it's displayed in a web part on the home page of the site, and a link to the actual calendar is also available on the Quick Launch bar. The group calendar is designed for two uses. For the techs, it'll be the way they see what events have been scheduled for them and potentially where everyone else is. Administrators can create events, assign them to techs, and also assign resources (from conference rooms to particular vehicles or tools the techs need to share).

The modifications to the regular calendar are provided by a site feature called Group Work Lists (which you can deactivate in Site Settings ➤ Manage Features). Adding features to sites is covered in Chapter 11.

The first significant change is the ability to add multiple users to the calendar so you can see everyone's events at a glance. Just enter each user's account in the Add Person field to add their name and see any events they have scheduled. See Figure 9.47.

FIGURE 9.47

Multiple people on the group calendar

Now, before you get too excited about this, there is one inexplicable flaw: this view change is not saved. So, you can view all the people you added as long as you don't leave the page and go anywhere else. For example, if you go into the Shared Documents list and come back, the additional users will be gone, reverting the view to just your account. Microsoft has confirmed that (at the time of this writing) this is the intended behavior. Baffling.

The second interesting thing is the resources picker. Clicking the Add Resources link will open a list of existing resources to add to the calendar (see Figure 9.48). This is a People Picker for list items, so although you can use it to select an existing resource, you can't add new resources this way. For that you need to go to the Resources list. When you add a resource to the calendar, it's treated like another user and shows where that resource is booked over the course of the week.

FIGURE 9.48

Adding a resource to the calendar

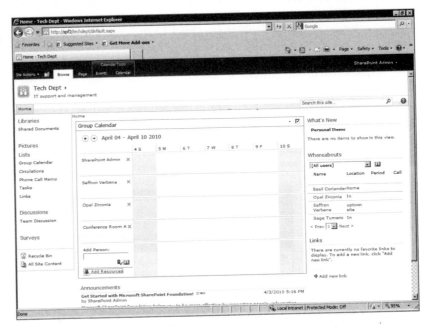

Obviously, the main purpose of the calendar is to schedule events—and with the group calendar you can assign both people and resources to the event. Let's add a new event to the calendar by simply double-clicking the date we want to have the event. (You can also go to the calendar directly and choose New Event, just like you would with any other calendar.) It will open the Group Calendar – New Item window (see Figure 9.49).

Here you can enter the title of the event, a location (not required), and the start and end times. Other settings are as follows:

Attendees Unlike a normal calendar, the group calendar allows you to specify the people who need to attend the event.

Resources The resource list is visible, and you can select what resources you want to book for the event. If the resources are in categories, you can also filter the visible list by resource group. Selecting the resource and clicking Add will assign them to the event (as will simply double-clicking the resource).

Free/Busy As you add attendees and resources to the event, they'll appear here, with bars showing the times they're already booked. This lets you see, at a glance, whether there are any known conflicts with your proposed event times.

Check Double Booking Hitting the Check button will examine the resources in the list to make sure they're not already booked. This information is already visible under Free/Busy, but you can hit the Check button to make sure. Note that this does *not* check the availability of people, only resources.

FIGURE 9.49
The Group
Calendar – New
Item window

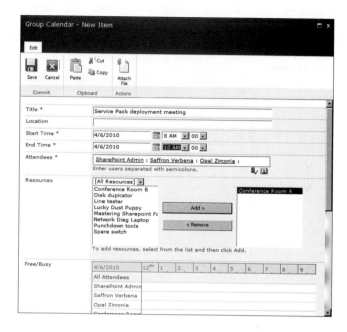

Description   This is a brief description of the event.

Category   This is the type of event, from meeting to project to party. You can use one of the prebuilt categories or add your own.

All Day Event   This defines the event as all-day and removes the start and end times.

Recurrence   Check to create an event that repeats on a set schedule.

Workspace   Checking this box will create a new meeting workspace for the event as a sub-site of the group site. Once this box is selected, choosing Save for the event will immediately take you to the New Meeting Workspace page, where you can enter the settings desired for the new subsite, including the type of meeting workspace the site will be. The newly created meeting workspace does not autopopulate with the attendees from the Calendar event, so you'll need to treat it like any other new meeting workspace and add the attendees again.

You'll find more information about this topic in "Meeting Workspaces" later in this chapter.

CREATING A WORKSPACE REQUIRES THE CREATE SUBSITE PERMISSION

To create a meeting workspace from the group calendar, you need the Create Subsite permission. By default, this is available only to Site Owners (Contribute, the permission level that Site Members use, does not have this permission). If you don't have the permission, the Workspace box will be available, and when you save the event, you'll still get to the New Meeting Workspace page, but you will be unable to choose the Inherit Permissions option, and the actual creation of the workspace with fail, giving you an Access Denied error.

I'm going to create a meeting for some of the tech staff, book Conference Room A, and not bother to make a workspace. When it's done, the event will appear on the calendar and be shown for every attendee when they log in. See Figure 9.50.

FIGURE 9.50
The new event on the group calendar

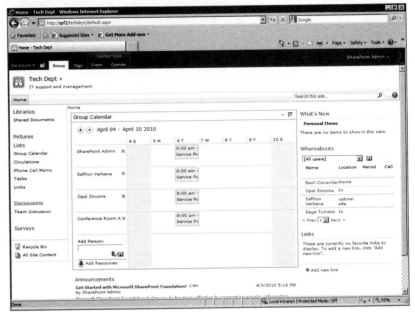

CIRCULATION

The Circulation list is probably the most confusing one on the group site, and it may not be appropriate for your site. It is designed for handouts—basically a way to replace those "CC everyone" emails you end up dealing with in the course of a day. It's intended to be sent to multiple people either for their input or for simple confirmation they've read the contents.

The list supports two content types: Circulation and Official Notice. The way these items behave depends on the permissions at the site level, which is why it's recommended you break inheritance when you first created the group site. This is where placing your general users (the techs, for example) into the site Visitors group becomes critical.

The list has several custom views:

My Unconfirmed Circulation   This view shows any circulations where you're a recipient and have not yet confirmed you've read (and, if expected, edited) the circulation. This is the default view.

My Circulation   This view shows any circulations where you are a recipient, both unconfirmed and confirmed.

Circulation From Me   This view shows any circulations you have created and sent to other recipients.

All Circulations   This shows all circulations.

Let's take a closer look at the list by creating a new circulation. Hit the New Item box to open the Circulations – New Item window (see Figure 9.51).

FIGURE 9.51
Creating a new circulation

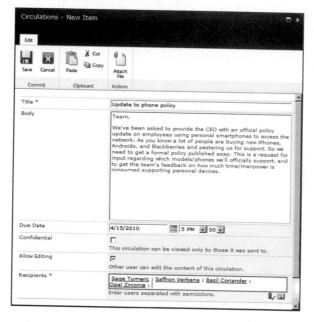

A circulation has the following fields:

Title   This is the title of the circulation.

Body   This is the text for the circulation.

Due Date   If the circulation is time sensitive (responses, confirmation, or actions need to be done by a particular date or time), you can set the due date here.

Confidential   Selecting this box allows the recipients to view and edit the circulation, regardless of their normal access to the site. It also prevents anyone other than the creator and recipients from even seeing the circulation, regardless of their normal access to the site.

Allow Editing   This box does nothing. It has no impact on who can or cannot edit the circulation. Permission to edit the file is determined by normal site permissions or the Confidential check box.

Recipients   This is a required field; it specifies the people for whom the circulation is intended.

Once you've set up the circulation, click Save. At this point, you'll be taken back to the main list, and if you're on the default view (My Unconfirmed Circulation), you won't see your new circulation (since you're not a recipient). Change the view to All Circulations to see the new circulation. If you now edit the circulation, you'll see it has a new field, Comments (see Figure 9.52). This lets recipients (if they have permission) post comments without having to touch the body of the circulation.

FIGURE 9.52

Editing a circulation

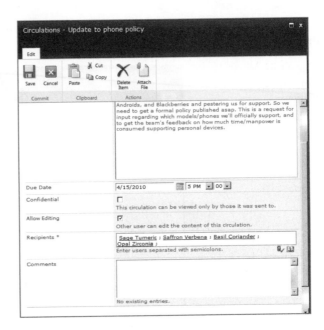

Keep in mind that if you want recipients to be able to edit the circulation, either they must be Site Members (and thus have the Contribute permission level) or you need to set Confidential (to allow them to edit). Otherwise, they will not even be able to confirm the circulation.

THE CONFIDENTIAL OPTION

The Circulation list works by playing with permissions. Whenever you create a new circulation in the list, people have permission to do whatever they normally have permission to do on the site. People who can read-write on the site (the site members) can read-write the circulations. People who can only read on the site (site visitors) can only read the circulation, so they can't edit or even confirm the circulations.

The exception to this is when you click Confidential. At that point, the following happens:

◆ The action breaks inheritance on the new circulation, removing all permissions from the item.

◆ It then adds the creator of the item (whoever you're logged in as) to the item explicitly with Full Control. And it adds the recipient(s) of the circulation (or official notice) with the permission level Contributor.

◆ It adds the recipient(s) to the site's permissions with the level Limited Access (even if they're already listed in an existing group).

This means that if something is marked Confidential, then all recipients can edit the item, regardless of what their normal permissions on the site permit. And people who were not previously able to access the site at all now have Limited Access to the site (and, if the site its self is inheriting permissions, they have access to its parent, potentially going all the way to the top-level site).

For more information on permissions, see Chapter 12.

The other content type for a circulation is the Official Notice type. This is almost identical to Circulation except for two minor things:

◆ The Allow Editing button is not available. But since it doesn't do anything, this is minor.

◆ There is no Comments field on the resulting list item. So although people can edit the notice (if they have permission, it's same rules as for Circulation), they can't place comments in the comment field (it's simply not there).

PHONE CALL MEMO

The Phone Call Memo list is designed to replace the "while you were out" paper pad or email—a way to let co-workers know that they missed a call. Like the Circulation list, the Phone Call Memo list has four views, with options to sort the list by My Unresolved Memos, My Memos, Memos from Me, and All Unresolved Memos.

1. Click **Add New Item** to create a new Phone Call Memo list. See Figure 9.53.

FIGURE 9.53
A new Phone Call Memo item

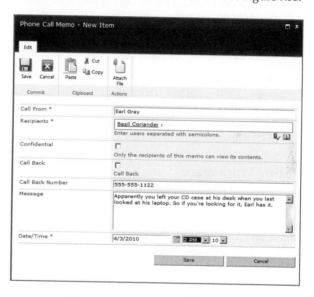

2. You'll notice this list also has a Confidential check box; it behaves the same way as it does on the Circulation list. Selecting this box allows the recipients to edit and resolve the memo, regardless of their normal access to the site. It also prevents anyone other than the creator and recipients from even seeing the memo, regardless of their normal access to the site. Once you've filled out the memo, click **Save**.

Back on the main home page for the group site, you'll now notice that the memo's recipients have an alert icon by their names in the Whereabouts web part, as shown in Figure 9.54. This icon shows up whenever someone has a new memo waiting; it's a quick way to see whether you or someone else has a memo waiting. Note that if the memo was tagged Confidential, you won't see the icon unless you're either the memo author or the recipient. Clicking this icon will take you back to the Phone Call Memo list, but it will be filtered by that person's name in the recipient field.

FIGURE 9.54
The Whereabouts
web part showing a
missed call

3. When you open the memo, you can quickly see who called, along with their number to call back (if entered) and the message. When you're done resolving the memo, you can click the **Resolve** button. (Note that you need permission to edit the item to use the Resolve button; read-only access will not be sufficient, even if you're the recipient.)

Hitting the Resolve button causes a couple of things to happen:

♦ The Resolved field is updated to Yes, and your name and the current date/time are automatically entered into the Resolved By and Resolved Date columns. These columns are hidden from the default views, but they're visible when you edit the list or create a custom list view.

♦ If this was the only unresolved memo, the icon on the Whereabouts web part goes away.

♦ The memo will no longer appear in any of the default views (which show only unresolved memos). It has not been deleted; it's just visible with a custom view. You can find more information about List views in Chapter 6. (Because it's hidden and not deleted, over time the list can fill with old, unwanted phone memos. You may want to periodically clear out old list items or write a workflow to do it for you.)

Meeting Workspace

No one likes to be told they have to attend a meeting without knowing what it's about or who else is going to be there. No one likes to leave a meeting unsure of what was accomplished and who's supposed to do what to move the project forward. Typically, meeting agendas are emailed, and people look at the email's CC field to see who is attending. SharePoint has meeting workspace templates that were designed with the needs of the meeting organizer in mind.

With a meeting workspace, you can organize the meeting attendees, agenda, and objectives; post any required documents; resolve task assignments; and record any decisions made. There are several types of meeting workspaces and different templates that adjust the site for particular needs. All meeting workspaces are based on the same site definition. This is what gives meeting workspaces their unique layout—meeting workspaces usually appear to have only one page. There are several standard lists that are made available to users as List View web parts on the workspace's home page. The meeting workspace's home page is actually a content page that can contain multiple sets of web part pages displayed in the content area. Each page is indicated (and accessed) by its tab in the content area. To start, regardless of the type of meeting workspace template you choose, each will have at least one page, considered the home page.

You can create a meeting workspace in several ways. The first is through the now familiar New SharePoint Site page (using a template on the Meetings tab). The other way is more common, and that's creating the meeting workspace based on an event in a calendar on the SharePoint site. Create one from the calendar on the HR team subsite under the company site, as shown in Figure 9.55. When creating a new event in a calendar, there is an option for creating a new meeting workspace as well.

Checking the box in the Workspace section when creating a Calendar event will take you to the New Meeting Workspace page shown in Figure 9.56; there you can create the new meeting workspace. We're going to create one for a project kickoff meeting for the HR team from their main site's calendar.

FIGURE 9.55

The new calendar event

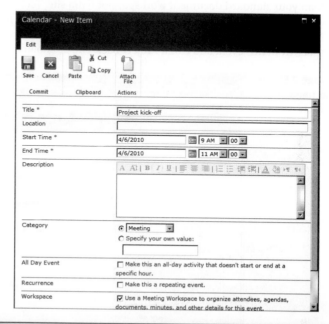

FIGURE 9.56

Create a new meeting workspace

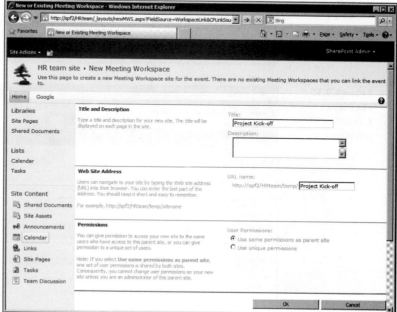

Once you've entered the meeting information and clicked OK, you will be prompted to choose the desired template (see Figure 9.57); these templates are the same templates as those listed on the Meetings tab on the New SharePoint Site page. All meeting workspaces are based on the Meeting Workspace (MPS) site definition. This is why they have a different look and feel than your standard document workspace or team site. Technically, meeting workspaces refer directly to the site definition and don't even have templates, but Microsoft tends to take liberties in referring to the different workspaces as templates. I'm going to create a Basic meeting workspace from this event and call it Project Kick-Off, as shown in Figure 9.58.

FIGURE 9.57
Selecting a
template

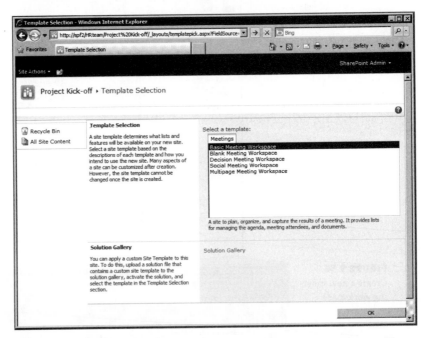

FIGURE 9.58
The Project
Kick-Off meeting
workspace

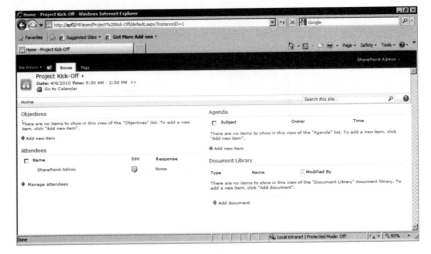

SharePoint supports linking the events in a calendar with meeting workspaces. We just created a new meeting workspace from an event, and these two items are now linked—each provides a link to the other—and are tied together. But there's a lot more you can do with these links, and there's some unique behavior in the relationships between meeting workspaces and calendar events.

If you create a repeating calendar event and then create a meeting workspace for it, the workspace will be aware of the recurrence, although it has an interesting way of showing it. It creates separate instances of the workspace (so the pages look the same but they aren't) for each meeting.

On the left side of the workspace (regardless of the template you choose) will be a Meeting Series pane showing a list of the dates of the recurring event (see Figure 9.59). You select the correct date, and the workspace will bring up the instance for that date.

FIGURE 9.59

The meeting workspace for a recurring event

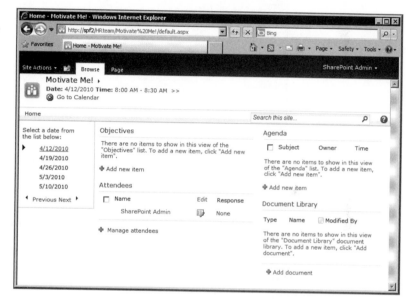

This gives you a single meeting workspace for the event, even though it occurs repeatedly. Each of the workspace's libraries and lists tracks the instances (dates) for the workspace, keeping them separate despite being in the same library, so you can have different attendees, tasks, and decisions for each event.

Sometimes you create the meeting workspace before an event has been scheduled. (You know there's going to be a big meeting, but you don't know when.) So, you create a meeting workspace from the New SharePoint Site page. When the time comes to place the meeting event on the calendar, you want to link this new event to your existing meeting workspace.

In this case, when you create the event and check the box to create a workspace, it takes you to a modified creation page called New or Existing Meeting Workspace (Figure 9.60). It's exactly like the New Meeting Workspace page shown in Figure 9.56, except for the option to either link an event to an existing meeting workspace or create a whole new workspace for it.

If you choose to link the event to an existing meeting, then you will have to choose the meeting from the drop-down menu. The catch is that the meetings available as choices must be directly off the site you are creating the calendar event on.

FIGURE 9.60
The New or Existing Meeting Workspace page

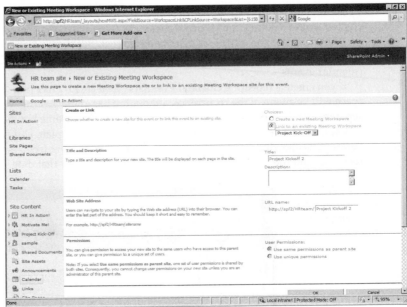

I CAN'T LINK TO MY EXISTING RECURRING EVENT WORKSPACE

You may notice the drop-down menu doesn't include your existing workspaces that were created directly from a recurring event.

Although it's possible to link events to a meeting workspace that already has one or more events linked to it, for some reason you cannot link a new event to an existing workspace if that workspace was created from a recurring event.

You also can't create a new recurring event and link it to an existing meeting workspace.

Recurring events cannot share workspaces with any other events.

When you choose the meeting to link the event to, that meeting workspace's home page spawns a new instance (with the same results as a workspace created from a reoccurring event).

Meeting workspaces maintain partial contact with the calendar event in the originating calendar; as long as they're linked, the workspace will reflect any changes made to the event. How they behave depends on the number and type of events to which the workspace is linked.

If you have a single event attached to a workspace and you make changes to the date or times of the event (for example, a meeting scheduled for 3 p.m. on Tuesday gets moved to 10 a.m. on Friday), the moment you change the event on the calendar, the meeting workspace will update to reflect the change. If you delete the event from the calendar altogether, it does not delete the workspace, but the home page of the workspace will show an alert telling you the event has been either unlinked or deleted. See Figure 9.61.

If you have a workspace linked to a recurring event, the linking gets a lot more confusing. Because there are multiple events linked, when you move/edit an event, the workspace reacts by marking the old event as unlinked/deleted and adding the updated date/time as a new event. So if you move a recurring event from every Thursday at 3 p.m. to every Friday at 1 p.m., the workspace will show both dates/times, some no longer linked to an event. You'll need to edit these instances manually. The bottom line is, it's best not to move a recurring event.

With a workspace linked to multiple nonrecurring events (several separately created events), the behavior is much better; moving one of the events to a new date/time will update the workspace correctly. And if you delete one of the linked events, going to the workspace will prompt you with an alert to do one of three things with the affected instance in the Meeting Series pane (Figure 9.62):

Move   Merge all the data from the defunct instance into one of the other (still linked) instances. So, all the attendees, objects, agenda items, and so on, are moved to the other instance, potentially making that meeting pretty crowded.

Keep   Leave the instance untouched—so you have an instance, with the old date/time and no corresponding calendar event.

Delete   Delete the instance and all the data it contains.

FIGURE 9.61
The workspace has lost its event.

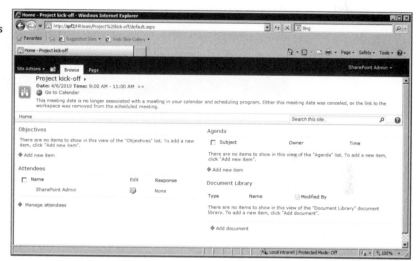

FIGURE 9.62
The Meeting Series pane has a canceled meeting.

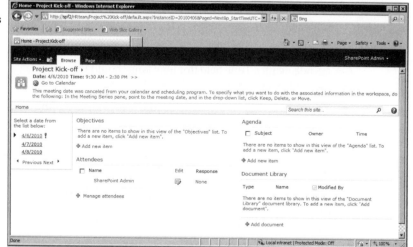

If you re-create the deleted event, it will show up as a new instance, so you could move the data from the old (deleted event) instance to the new instance and then delete the old one.

No matter how you create the new meeting workspace or if it's linked to a calendar event, you have a choice of five separate templates designed for different types of meetings. Let's take a look at how these templates differ from one another and see what you can do with them.

BASIC

The Basic meeting workspace is the general template based on the Meeting Workspace site definition. An example of a Basic meeting workspace is the Project Kick-Off meeting we created earlier, shown in Figure 9.63. This is why the home page for the site is so fundamentally different from the team site. It still has most of the features of a team site except for the Quick Launch bar. Most scheduled meetings will be fine with Basic. The Basic workspace includes some prebuilt lists, such as Agenda, Objectives, and Attendees. It also includes a document library for storing related documents for the meeting.

FIGURE 9.63
The Basic meeting page

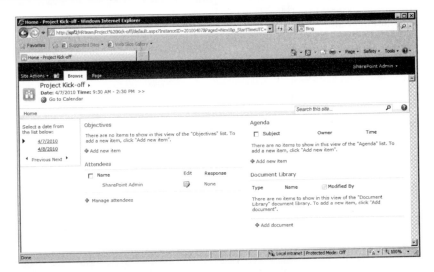

◆ The Objectives list is a simple list for notes used to list objectives for the meeting.

◆ The Agenda list item has a required Subject field, an Owner field (for whoever posted the agenda item), a Time field (for how long should this Agenda item should take to discuss during the meeting), and a Notes field.

◆ The Attendees list is a place to list the users who are going to attend the meeting. When you add a new user, two additional fields, Response and Attendance, are required. They appear in Figure 9.64.

ATTENDEES REQUIRE EMAIL ADDRESSES

When adding attendees, you may get an error stating that the user does not have an email address, which is required. To add an email address to the user object, you will need to go to Site Settings ➤ People And Groups and edit the user object to provide the email address.

◆ The Response field, which the list creator will probably leave set to None, is simply the user's response to the meeting request: None, Accepted, Tentative, or Declined.

FIGURE 9.64

The new Attendees item

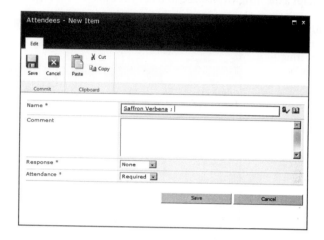

These meeting workspaces are simple sites. There is no automated way for a user to email a response and have their Response field change by default. The meeting organizer (or the attendee themselves if they have the permission to) will have to change that field manually. Also note that the attendees need to have permission to access the site in order to see it. Make certain the attendees can actually log in at least as visitors of the site.

Attendance also has three options, Required, Optional, and Organizer, which is a polite way of saying "really required because you're calling the meeting."

A quick glance at the Attendees list will show you who's supposed to attend, whether they can make it, and who's running the show (see Figure 9.65).

FIGURE 9.65

The Attendees list

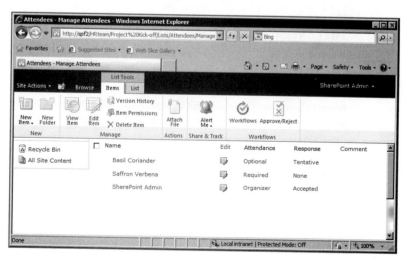

In addition, you can add other lists and therefore List View web parts to a meeting to add Tasks, Issue Tracking, and pretty much whatever else you need. Just as with team sites, you can adapt a meeting workspace to meet your needs. See Figure 9.66.

FIGURE 9.66
Adding to the meeting workspace

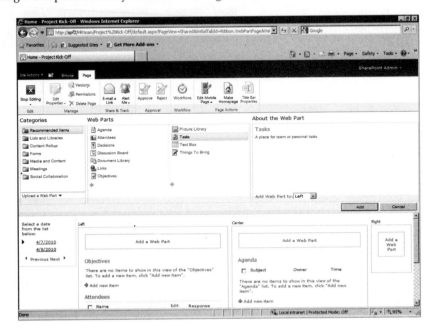

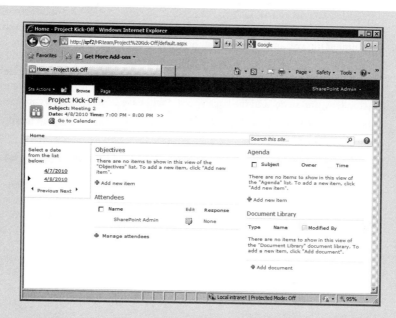

But you aren't limited to one page; you can add another page by going to Site Actions ➢ Add Page. This lets you add a page for each meeting. Note that the Site Actions menu allows you to go to the Site Settings and edit the page you're on, as well as add or manage pages.

When you add a page to a meeting workspace, it will ask you to name the page and decide whether it should appear for just this one meeting instance or all meetings (if you have more than one calendar event assigned to the meeting workspace).

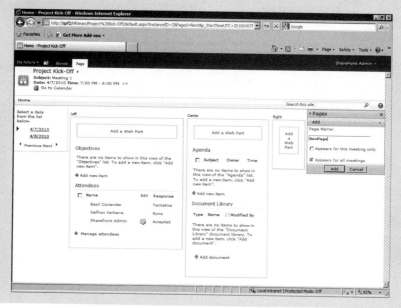

After you create a page, it starts in edit mode so you can add web parts to the new page, such as a document library, an Attendees list, or links, and then populate them with data pertinent to that meeting. (By default the new page contains no web parts.) Or, later you can click Site Actions ➤ Edit Page (just like any other web part page) and add web parts to the web part zones. For each page, the List View web parts for the meeting are incremented. So, the home page has Objectives, Agenda, Attendees, and so on, and the page you add will have Objectives1, Agenda1, and so on.

Back on the Home page, you can see the new page is now showing up under the Pages section in the Quick Launch bar.

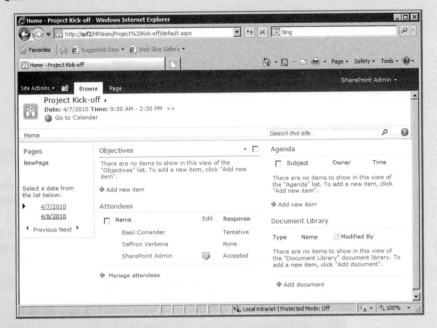

This can give you one central workspace to go to for data that's historical or shared between the different meetings, with separate pages for the collected details about the individual meetings themselves.

This is just something to think about when creating workspaces for those endlessly spawning meetings. Instead of creating a meeting workspace and then creating a subworkspace for the next one and the next, consider creating one workspace for meetings and simply adding each meeting as a separate page in that workspace's content area. It might save time, save space, and give the attendees one simple place to go for each meeting, rather than a different workspace every time.

BLANK

A blank workspace is like a blank site—no prebuilt lists, libraries, or web parts. So, you're starting from scratch with this template. It still adheres to the Meeting Workspace site definition, so it will register as a meeting workspace and can link to calendar events.

Decision

The Decision template is focused on resolving questions or issues. See Figure 9.67. It contains the base web parts of the Basic template, but it adds additional Tasks and Decisions lists.

The Tasks list allows tasks to be assigned, progress to be tracked, and a deadline set for the task, as shown in Figure 9.68.

FIGURE 9.67

A decision meeting

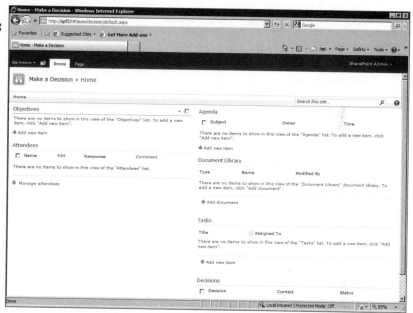

FIGURE 9.68

A new task item

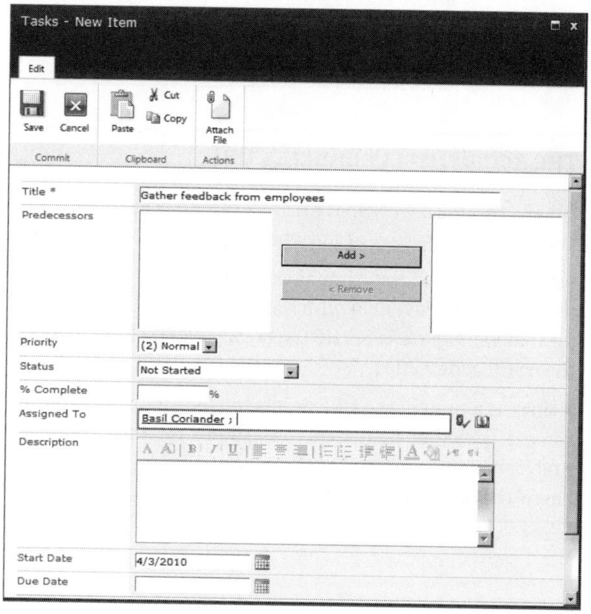

The Decisions list is used when decisions are actually being made. Each decision has a Contact field and a Status field that can contain Proposed, Pending Approval, or Final.

SOCIAL

Sometimes a meeting is less serious, and your primary goal is making sure everyone attends and has a good time. Rather than create a meeting with the objective "Have a party," why not create a social meeting workspace? The Social template is geared toward both the before-party planning (attendees, who needs to bring what, location, and timing) and after-party reminiscence, with a discussion board and photo gallery, as shown in Figure 9.69. Social meetings are considered one-shots, so the interface uses separate tabs for each list, rather than each occurrence of a meeting.

FIGURE 9.69

The social meeting workspace

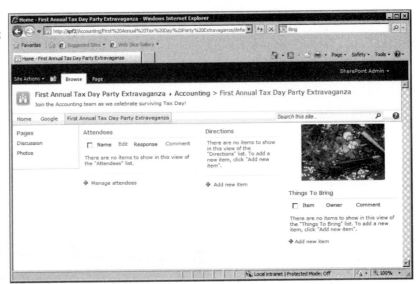

THE ACCIDENTALLY ENDLESS URL

When creating a workspace from a calendar event or document, the document or event name can automatically be part of the workspace's web address.

For example, the First Annual Tax Day Party Extravaganza social meeting workspace was generated from a calendar event in which all the defaults were kept. As you can see in Figure 9.69, the address for that workspace is particularly long and includes a lot of spaces (which URLs must render using the ASCII code %20).

If there is a typo in the URL or it is too long (such as First Annual Tax Day Party Extravaganza), you can easily change it. Just go to the site's settings under Site Actions, and click Title, Description, And Icon in the Look And Feel category. This will give you the chance to change the URL. All subsites below that workspace will also reflect the change.

MULTIPAGE

A Multipage template (see Figure 9.70) is simply a Basic template with two additional blank pages provided to do with as you see fit (just like taking a Basic meeting workspace and manually adding two new pages). The home page of the multipage site is a basic site, minus the document library.

FIGURE 9.70
A multipage meeting

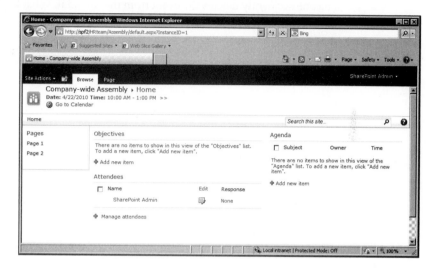

The two blank pages are really, really blank. You'll want to customize these pages by adding web parts to them before opening the workspace to users.

The Bottom Line

Create and customize a new site. Using the New SharePoint Site page, you can create a new subsite or workspace from one of several templates, or you can create a new workspace from an existing document or calendar event. The site can be customized using themes, custom logos, lists, and libraries.

Master It After you create a new site, you discover you left a space in the URL, making it hard for users to type (since it contains that darn %20 ASCII code). What steps do you need to take to safely change the URL without breaking links to the site and its subsequent subsites? Will anything fail the moment you change the URL?

Adjust a site's settings for administrative purposes. You can configure sites to inherit or set unique permissions on a site. You can also configure subsites to use tree view, manage user alerts, place the site on the top link bar, adjust regional settings, enable features such as RSS, and view usage reports.

Master It If you create a new subsite and choose to not place a link to this subsite on the parent site's top link bar and then set the subsite to inherit the top link bar from the parent, what happens when you click the Home link on the subsite?

Understand the different types of SharePoint site templates available. By default, SharePoint can create team sites, document workspaces, blogs, group sites, and meeting workspaces (from the Basic, Decision, Social, and Multipage templates).

Master It You create a new event on a calendar and select the option to create a new meeting workspace. Once it's created and you've entered attendees and objectives, someone accidently deletes the event from the calendar. What happens to the linked workspace?

Chapter 10

Site Collections and Web Applications

Until this point, you've done all your work in the first site collection that you created when you installed SharePoint. You've explored web parts, lists, and libraries, and you've even built some subsites. You've done all that in a single site collection within its web application. Now it's time to branch out and learn how and why to create additional site collections and additional web applications.

In this chapter, you'll learn how to

◆ Create and customize a new site collection

◆ Create a new web application

◆ Use managed paths

◆ Configure anonymous access

◆ Set specific zones for different access methods

Creating a Site Collection

We've mentioned site collections before; a separate top-level site and corresponding subsites from the SharePoint site collection are used throughout this book. A separate site collection is obviously very different from a subsite. But from a user perspective, it looks the same. A site is a site; it's all just different URLs. Otherwise, a top-level site looks like a subsite. It is possible to create all-new site collections, each with its own top-level site and subsites, but why would you want to do such a thing?

Unlike a new site or subsite, a new site collection does not inherit anything from the previous sites—although they all share global settings and web application settings, which will be discussed later. This lack of inheritance can be very useful when you want to separate a batch of SharePoint sites from your main site collection.

Having multiple site collections allows you to apply different settings than those of your main site collection. A separate site collection lets you do the following:

◆ Allow an entirely different group of people to be administrators for the site collection

◆ Use separate, unique users, groups, and permissions

◆ Back up just that site collection

◆ Have unique workflows, site templates, list templates, activated features, site collection solutions, content types, and site columns

◆ Specify different storage quotas

For example, say you have a branch office—a different location with its own group of people, unique needs, and documents. At first, you might be tempted to give that location its own subsite off your main top-level site. However, there will be times when this arrangement is less than optimal. For example, you'd have to give those subsite users permissions in the site collection and handle the increased administration required to restrict their account groups to their subsite.

With a new site collection, you have a whole new top-level site, with new users and groups. You could then give the branch office's IT department administrative rights to that site collection. The branch office administrator could then manage that office's own sites, permissions, and subsites— without having access to your main SharePoint site. They could have their own templates, navigation, permissions, logo, and whatever they like, and you wouldn't have to worry about them.

New site collections can be created using PowerShell or STSADM or using Central Administration. For this example, we'll be using Central Administration's interface so you can get an idea of what settings are required (because the GUI will have descriptions that the command line and shell tools won't). To create a site collection, follow these steps:

1. Open Central Administration. You can do so using the SharePoint 2010 Central Administration link in the Start menu, or you can enter the URL for the server and the port for Central Administration. In my example, that would be **http://spf2:9876**.

2. The Create Site Collections link is under the Application Management category in Central Administration. Click this link to go to the Create Site Collection page, as shown in Figure 10.1.

Here you'll configure your new site collection and the required top-level site that will start this collection.

FIGURE 10.1
The Create Site Collection page

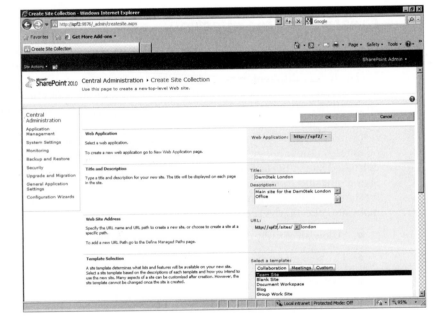

3. The first step is to choose the web application in which you want the site collection to be created. We'll discuss web applications later in the chapter, so for now leave the web application set to the default web application, which for my example is SharePoint-80, that was created during installation.

4. The Title and Description fields are treated the same way as when you create a site. They apply to the top-level site in the new site collection. Enter a title for your new top-level site (and a description if you require). My example creates a new site collection for the London office, so it uses **Dem0tek London**, with the description **Main site for the Dem0tek London Office**.

5. The Web Site Address field is where you enter the URL for the new top-level site. Unlike the URL for a subsite (which is placed in the path of the parent site), this URL starts at the top of the web application and uses a *managed path* as the location for the new site. The default managed path is /sites/; we'll discuss how and why you might want to create and use other paths later. For our purposes, this path is fine; just enter your desired URL. My example uses **london**.

6. The templates in the Template Selection section are identical to those available when you create a new subsite, but this time we are choosing the template for the site collection's top-level site. Any custom site templates you installed in the first site collection will not be available here, because this is a new site collection and not part of the first one.

   So, in the Template Selection section, for a top-level site you'd typically want to choose the **Team Site** template, which is what I am going to use in my example.

WAITING TO APPLY A SITE TEMPLATE

You'll notice the Custom tab has a Select Template Later option. This lets you create the site collection without actually creating the top-level site (or applying a template to it). You won't be able to visit the site until you pick a template, but it will create the background galleries and site collection settings. So, what's the point?

Once the site collection is created, it has a working Solution Gallery. This gallery contains solutions, which can include custom site templates (remember from the previous chapter that whenever you save a site as a template, it becomes a solution and during site creation shows up as an option on the Custom tab for templates). So when you create a new site collection, you can then add a custom template to the Solution Gallery before creating the top-level site. Then, you apply that template to the top-level site. So, during the Site Collection creation, you choose Select Template Later.

Template Selection

A site template determines what lists and features will be available on your new site. Select a site template based on the descriptions of each template and how you intend to use the new site. Many aspects of a site can be customized after creation. However, the site template cannot be changed once the site is created.

Select a template:

| Collaboration | Meetings | Custom |

< Select template later... >

Create an empty site and pick a template for the site at a later time.

Then, the first time you visit the site, it prompts you to select a template. At the bottom, you'll notice an option to instead visit the new site collection's Solution Gallery.

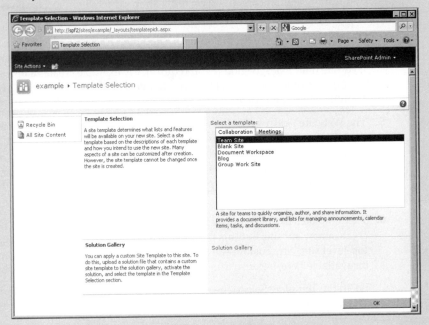

In the gallery you can upload a new solution—for example, the site template you created in the previous chapter from the HR team site. Once it's uploaded, you need to activate it in order for it to be usable.

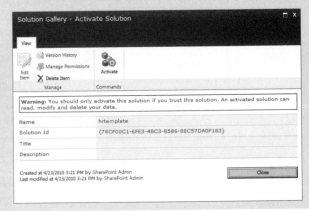

Then, back at the new top-level site's URL where you are asked to choose a site template, the HRteam template shows up as an option. Choosing it will create the new top-level site using your custom template.

It will then prompt you to choose people and groups for the new site; leave the defaults (since it's a fresh top-level site), and click OK. You now have a customized top-level site.

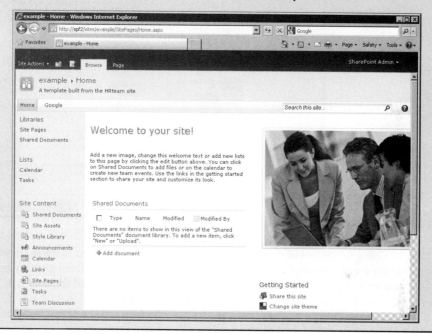

7. The Primary Site Collection administrator is the owner of this new site collection. New site collections do not inherit any permissions from any other collections; therefore, unless you enter someone's username in this box, no one will be able to log on to the new top-level site or administer it. For my example, *shareadmin* is the primary administrator (Figure 10.2). The Secondary Site Collection administrator is a second administrative account, and it's a good idea to have a second account in case something happens to the primary account or administrator. My example adds Amber, the London office's network administrator.

   The Quota Template field lets you choose which quota template to apply to the site collection. This quota will determine how large the site collection can get (in megabytes) and is needed for storage reports on the individual sites within the collection. My example uses **No Quota** because we haven't created one yet. You can always apply a quota later.

8. Once you're done, click OK. The new site will be created in the managed path (for my example, `http://spf2/sites/`).

FIGURE 10.2
The Create Site
Collection page

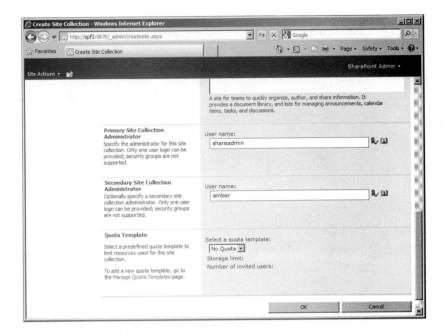

Going to the root of the server (http://spf2/) will take you to the main site collection, where there is no hint that the new site collection even exists. Even under View All Site Content, you won't see the new London site. It's completely separate, and the only way to get there is to use the new URL (http://spf2/sites/london). See Figure 10.3.

You should have a fresh, new top-level site ready to configure and build on.

FIGURE 10.3
The new
top-level site

WHAT IF THE SITE COLLECTION ADMINISTRATOR HAS BEGUN TO RUN AMOK?

If the fact that only site collection administrators can access a site collection makes you uneasy, take heart. There are things you can do, of course, to gain access to any site collection in case of emergency. Truly, the only user accounts that will be listed and available to log into the site collection just after creation will be the site collection administrators, but there are always ways around that if necessary. The hope is that you'll never need them, but here are some alternate ways to access site collections even if you aren't the site collection administrator:

◆ Any farm administrator can take over ownership of a site collection by using the Change Site Collection Administrators link on the Application Management page of Central Administration. On that page, the Farm Administrator can select the site collection and then see (and change) who the primary and secondary administrators are.

◆ The User Policy ribbon button on the Web Application Management page allows you to add an account to the web application with administrative control over all site collections therein. This page is used to apply user policies to web applications, affecting everything they contain. On the Web Application page, you can select the web application that contains the site collection(s) you want to be able to access (regardless of who the assigned administrators are) and then add the account you are going to use, assigning it Full Control (the permission level administrators have). That will give it administrative rights over all site collections in the selected web application. (For more about Policy For Web Application, see Chapter 12 "Users and Permissions".)

◆ As a last resort (otherwise you should never, ever log in with these), you can use the following:

   ◆ The web application's application pool account (accesses the web application's content database)

   ◆ The farm account (the account that accesses the configuration database, owns all the databases in the farm, and runs the SharePoint timer jobs)

   ◆ Search-related accounts: search service and the indexing for search (called the Content Access account)

All of these service accounts, by default, must have access to all sites, although the search-related accounts only have read access. They are not listed in People And Groups anywhere (as a matter of fact, the web application pool and farm accounts are considered *system accounts*), but you can still use them to access a site collection. Do not use any of them to log into SharePoint except in an extreme emergency.

Site Settings for Site Collections

Before we go to town on the new site collection—customizing the theme, adding subsites, and installing new templates—let's take a look at the settings that distinguish site collections. These are settings that will apply to the entire site collection, from the top-level site down. You'll recognize a lot of the options from previous chapters, so let's focus on those settings that apply to site collections rather than simply sites. To view the site settings, click the Site Actions menu and choose Site Settings. You'll notice a lot of the links on this page are familiar—they are site settings that simply apply to the site, and not the site collection. These are covered in the previous chapter. For site collections, we're going to focus on those settings that appear only on the top-level site's Site Settings page; these are settings in each category that affect the entire site collection.

Users and Permissions

First and foremost, you need to add users to the new site. Right now only two people have access to the site: the two site collection administrators. Just as you configured your first site, you'll need to go through the initial setup of this new site collection, and that includes adding users and giving them the appropriate permission levels. You do this in the same relative location as on any site: Site Settings ➤ Users And Permissions ➤ People And Groups. At a minimum, you should make sure anyone who needs to view or contribute to the site has access. At a maximum, you might want to consider what users you want for the entire site collection. This is where inheriting permissions comes into its own. You can add users to the top-level site, and they will be able to access any other site in the collection if that site inherits permissions. In addition, you can create your own permission levels and modify the defaults that can affect all inheriting subsites but no other site collection. This is why a site collection can be considered a permissions boundary.

You can find more information about permissions in Chapter 12.

SITE COLLECTION ADMINISTRATORS

The final link in this section is Site Collection Administrators. This lets you add, edit, or delete people from the site collection administrators group for the current site collection. See Figure 10.4.

FIGURE 10.4

The Site Collection Administrators page

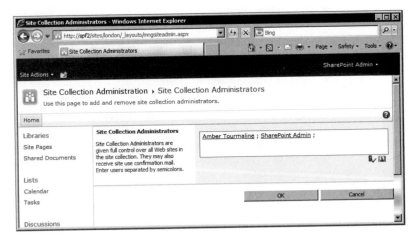

Look and Feel

This entire section is for customizing the current site (or subsite) and is not applicable to the entire site collection. All of these links are the same as for any other site or subsite and are covered in Chapter 9, "Sites, Subsites, and Workspaces." They include changing the title, description and icon for the site, Quick Launch and top link bar settings, Tree view, and site theme.

Galleries

The previous chapter explained the difference between site galleries and top-level site (or site collection) galleries. The galleries that appear only on the top-level site apply to all sites in a site collection.

While individual sites can have unique master pages, content types, and columns, the top-level galleries apply to every site in the collection and contain the same items regardless of the site they are accessed from.

The galleries that are available only at the site collection's top-level site are discussed next. The rest are for the site and are covered in Chapter 9.

WEB PARTS

The Web Part Gallery (see Figure 10.5) holds all the web parts available to the site collection (except for the List View web parts, of course; those are unique to the lists for the site and not available in the gallery). You can add, edit, and delete the web parts from it. Anything in this gallery is available for use in the entire site collection, which means this top-level site and all subsites. You can find more information about web parts in Chapter 5, "Introduction to Web Parts."

FIGURE 10.5
The Web Part Gallery

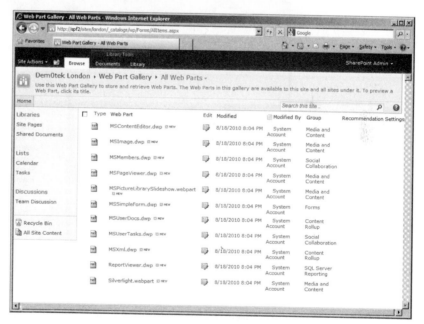

LIST TEMPLATES

You can save customized lists as templates. They are stored in the List Templates Gallery for use when creating a new list. The gallery will show you the name, date, title, language, and version of the list template. Any list that is saved as a template is saved to the list gallery. Like any library content, list templates can be uploaded to the gallery, and you can edit their title and description properties (but you cannot actually edit the list template from the gallery). You can also download list templates from the gallery. This is good for backing up the template in case of emergency. If you create a new list template, it will appear on the Create page, just like the original template it was based on (and in the correct category as well). However, unlike the prebuilt lists, the list templates you create may need to be deleted or renamed so they have their own gallery. Chapter 7, "Creating Lists," shows how to create lists and list templates.

THEME

This gallery (Figure 10.6) holds all the available site themes for use in the site collection. Themes are a quick and easy way to change the look and feel of a site. A theme consists of Office Open XML files packed in a `*.thmx` file (which is actually a compressed folder; if you change the extension to `*.zip`, you can unzip it). If this sounds familiar, it's because this is the same way themes are built and deployed in PowerPoint.

FIGURE 10.6
The Theme Gallery

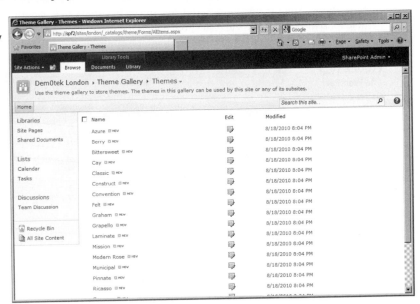

A theme changes two things: color and font. If you recall, you applied one to a new subsite in the previous chapter. The color changes are based on a palette that showcases exactly what colors are going to be used. You can see the colors and fonts used in each theme under the Look And Feel section of Sites Settings. A theme does not change the fundamental layout of the site or affect the contents (web parts, libraries, lists, and so on) in any way—it just changes color and font.

The theme's files are stored in the gallery (which is simply a document library), but copies of the default themes are also available in the file structure of the server in the following directory: `C:\Program Files\Common Files\Microsoft Shared\Web Server Extensions\14\TEMPLATE\GLOBAL\Lists\themes`.

When a new site collection is created, the server copies the default themes from this location in the file system to the newly created Theme Gallery. All sites within the collection share this gallery (which is why it's visible only in the top site's Site Settings).

Custom themes can be created in SharePoint Designer or PowerPoint and uploaded to the gallery, at which point you can apply them to any site in the site collection.

When a theme is selected for a site, SharePoint reads the `*.thmx` file's enclosed XML files for the desired colors and fonts. It then creates a new batch of Cascading Style Sheets (CSS) files that apply these colors and fonts to the layout and design of the site. These CSS files are created on the fly and stored in the site's _themes folder. (In my example, that would be `http://spf2/sites/london/_themes/`.) The first time you apply a theme to a site, it places the generated CSS files in a numerical subfolder, such as `http://spf2/sites/london/_themes/1/`. The number used the first time you set a theme is 1, then the second time it is 2, and so on. When you change themes, SharePoint does not retain the old theme's folder, so if you change the theme ten times, you'll see a _themes/10/ folder, but the previous (1–9) folders will be destroyed.

THEMES: WSS VS. SPF

Back in WSS 3.0, site themes were the actual CSS files. These files were stored on the SharePoint server in the file system, and whenever they were applied to a site, SharePoint read the CSS files and applied the settings to the web page on creation. This meant that creating new themes was a matter of editing CSS files and the corresponding XML reference file (`spthemes.xml`). Now, in SharePoint Foundation (SPF), themes are Office themes (typically made in PowerPoint) that are then used to create the CSS files by the server. This makes it easier to create new themes but harder to edit the CSS files to provide more customizations beyond color and font.

The old WSS 3.0 themes are still here, just not selectable. You can see the old themes on the SharePoint server, located in `C:\Program Files\Common Files\Microsoft Shared\Web Server Extensions\14\TEMPLATE\THEMES`.

They're hiding here in case you have migrated an existing WSS 3.0 site to SPF and have chosen not to upgrade the visuals. (For more information on migration, see Chapter 15, "Migrating from WSS 3.0 to Windows SharePoint Foundation 2010.") You can't select these themes for native SPF sites. The structure of the CSS files are different from the ones SharePoint generates from the new XML themes, and although it's possible to crack them open in SharePoint Designer and rewrite them for SPF, that's beyond the scope of this book.

SOLUTIONS

Solutions are custom modifications for your SharePoint site. A solution could be a custom site template, a site feature, a group of features, a web part, or pretty much anything that modifies SharePoint. These are placed in the Solution Gallery and activated, so they will be available for any site in the site collection and for the new subsites you are creating. When you create a site template from an existing site as discussed in Chapter 9, this is where that template is stored.

Recall that while working in the original site collection (the company site), we created a template for the HR team site in Chapter 9 (Figure 10.7) and used it to create a new subsite. If you want to use that template on this new site collection, you can access the original site collection's Solution Gallery and download the template.

FIGURE 10.7
The company site's Solution Gallery

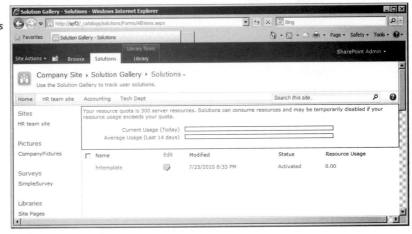

Then you can upload the .wsp file to the new site collection's Solution Gallery by opening the Solutions tab and, in the ribbon, clicking Upload Solution. The solution has to be activated before you can use it. You can activate the file during upload (using that option in the form box confirming the upload) or, once it's in the gallery, click the Activate button. This template will then be available whenever you create a new site within the Dem0tek London site collection (see Figure 10.8).

FIGURE 10.8
The Demotek London site's Solution Gallery

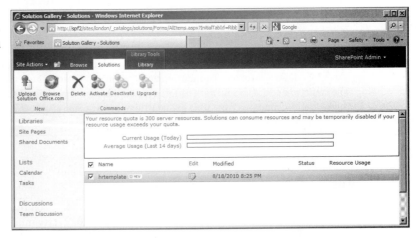

The Site Template solution actually installs a site collection feature, which it then activates. This feature, when activated, makes the template a selectable option when creating a new site.

SANDBOXED SOLUTIONS

You might have noticed that box referring to a resource quota in the Solution Gallery window. Some solutions can be uploaded to a site collection Solution Gallery (it's not just for site templates) by a site collection administrator or user with the correct permissions. Those solutions are scoped to affect only that one site collection; they can't access remote resources, connect to databases, write to disk, or access or affect the rest of the farm. Solutions designed to be uploaded and used per site collection this way, with these limitations, are called *sandboxed solutions*.

SharePoint administrators were worried about letting site collection administrators upload and use their own solutions without real farm management, which could result in these nearly unmanaged solutions sucking up resources and bringing servers down.

That's why sandboxed solutions can have a quota applied to them per site collection. That is, each site collection is allowed a certain number of resources to be used by its activated solutions. If a solution exceeds those numbers, it is disabled. That's why the box appears in the Solution Gallery, showing how much of the quota the gallery's solutions are using currently or have used in the last 14 days.

Site Actions

The majority of the links in this section apply to the individual site and are covered in Chapter 9. There is one action that applies to the entire site collection, however.

SITE COLLECTION WEB ANALYTICS REPORTS

The Summary page for web analytics reports, shown in Figure 10.9, provides you with a brief overview of the entire site collection's storage, users, and activity.

Storage   Shows you how much space (in megabytes) the entire site collection is consuming and what percentage of that space is being consumed by web discussions. If there is a storage quota on the site collection, that is also shown.

WHAT THE HECK IS A WEB DISCUSSION?

Web discussions are a legacy feature from the Office 2003 and WSS 2.0 days. They permitted you to use the SharePoint server to have discussions and comments on any browser-readable document, and they stored those discussions on the SharePoint site. Office 2003 had a handy Web Discussions toolbar you could use to start a discussion on any document you had open. This feature was removed in Office 2007 (and Office 2010). There was also a Discuss button in Internet Explorer 4.0 through 6.0, which let you have discussions on any web page at all. This was removed in IE7. But the legacy code for web discussions is still residing inside SharePoint Foundation.

Users   Shows the total number of users on the site collection and whether there is a restriction on the total permitted users for the site collection. It also provides a link to the site's Web Analytics Reports page (for the site, not the site collection).

Activity   Gives you the total number of page hits for the entire site collection and how much bandwidth has been used (on average) per day. It also provides a link to the Web Analytics Reports page for the individual site.

FIGURE 10.9
The site
collection web
analytics reports
Summary page

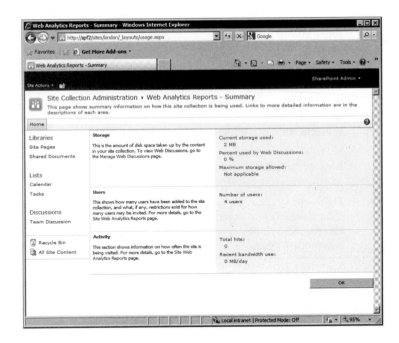

ALAS, POOR STORAGE SPACE ALLOCATION, WE KNEW YOU WELL

Back in WSS 3.0 there was an additional report you could run at the site collection level called Storage Space Allocation. This single report would show you the storage consumed by each individual site, library, or list so you could see which portion of the site collection was consuming your storage.

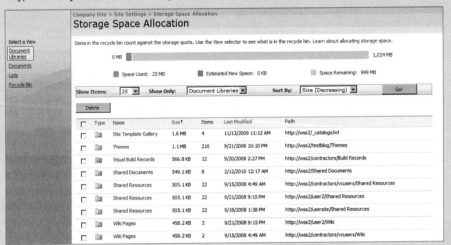

Unfortunately, this report is no longer available in SharePoint Foundation. According to Microsoft, the report was known to cause issues with SQL Server. So, rather than fix it, Microsoft simply removed the feature. So, to see the space usage of individual items in the site collection, you'll need to manually check each one.

Site Administration

This entire section is devoted to the administration of the individual site, and not the site collection, which is covered in Chapter 9. There is one small difference for the RSS page, however.

RSS

At the top-level site, the RSS page contains one additional check box not available on a subsite: Enable RSS. This option, shown in Figure 10.10, lets you enable or disable RSS for the entire site collection. When RSS is disabled at the site collection level, the RSS settings are no longer available as a link on any subsite's Site Settings page.

FIGURE 10.10

The site collection RSS page

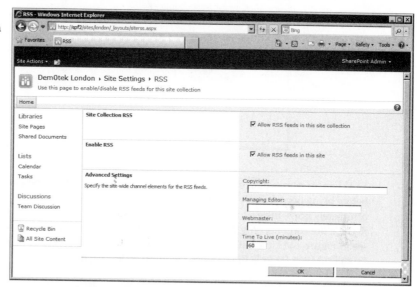

Site Collection Administration

Site collections can be administered only from the top-level site in the site collection. Any subsite has a category called Site Collection Administration that provides one link, Go To Top Level Site Settings. Clicking this link takes you to the Site Settings page for the top-level site. Here, this section contains administrative features and options explicitly for the site collection.

Recycle Bin

The Site Collection Recycle Bin shows everything deleted from the site collection—except sites. When your users delete a document or list item and then suddenly realize they made a mistake, you can easily recover the document or list item from the Recycle Bin rather than having to restore from a backup.

Each user has a personal Recycle Bin per site, which is why it is often called the end-user Recycle Bin. The personal bin shows the user only the contents of the site Recycle Bin that they deleted. There are only a few things that can be deleted that don't go to the Recycle Bin, such as sites, web parts, workflows, columns, content types, and users.

Site administrators have their own end-user Recycle Bin if they delete something on the site, but they can also access the overall Recycle Bin at the site collection level, which shows everything deleted by all users in the site collection. See Figure 10.11. The site collection–level Recycle Bin is particularly useful if a user deleted something from somewhere in the site collection but they can't remember which site. They can ask the site collection administrator to check the site collection Recycle Bin, which lists all things deleted in the site collection, regardless of which site it originally came from.

FIGURE 10.11

The site collection Recycle Bin

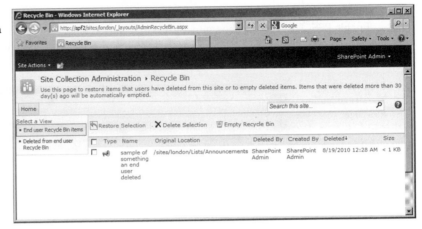

When an item is deleted, it goes to the end-user Recycle Bin, where it will sit happily for 30 days before being permanently destroyed. If a user goes to their Recycle Bin and deletes an item, it is not completely gone; instead, it is moved to the real second-stage, site collection–level Recycle Bin. This Recycle Bin contains only items deleted from the end-user Recycle Bins at the site level. As you can see in Figure 10.12, the elusive second-stage, site collection–level Recycle Bin is under the Deleted From End User Recycle Bin view, tucked in the Quick Launch area for the Recycle Bin.

FIGURE 10.12

Second-stage Recycle Bin

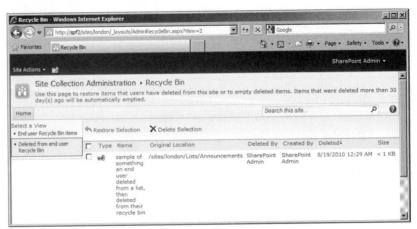

If an item is deleted from this second Recycle Bin, it's gone for good. Basically, you can restore practically anything that was deleted less than 30 days ago (or whatever the Recycle Bin default is, it can be changed per web application in Central Administration), even if the user also emptied their individual Recycle Bin.

SITE COLLECTION FEATURES

Site collection features are just like site features, except they're designed to be available for the entire site collection (see Figure 10.13). Some common features include the Three-State workflow and of course the site template we uploaded (considered an "exported" template).

FIGURE 10.13

The site collection Features page

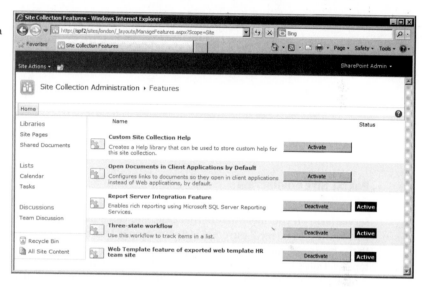

Any feature that's active is available throughout the site collection. If you click the Deactivate button, that feature turns off—it's still there, just not running. So, deactivating the Web Template feature of the exported web template HR team site will remove that template from the Custom tab during site creation. To remove the feature completely, you need to deactivate the solution that created the feature (in our example, the HR team site template solution). Features are often deployed at the farm level, as part of a solution (although features can be deployed individually at the farm level as well; it just doesn't happen that often). If a feature was made available to a site collection from that level, to completely remove a site collection feature, rather than deactivating the solution available at the site collection level, it would have to be retracted (and can be removed) at the farm level. It's a little extreme, but it can happen. At that point, the feature made available by that solution would be unavailable at the site collection level.

SITE HIERARCHY

The Site Hierarchy page provides a list of all the subsites that have been created in the site collection. From this page, you can go to a subsite's home page (by clicking its URL) or to the subsite's Site Settings page (by clicking its Manage link). Because the London site is still new, Figure 10.14 shows this page from the original Company Site site collection we've worked on in previous chapters. You'll notice all the subsites listed, but not the London site (since this is a separate site collection).

FIGURE 10.14

The company site's
Site Hierarchy page

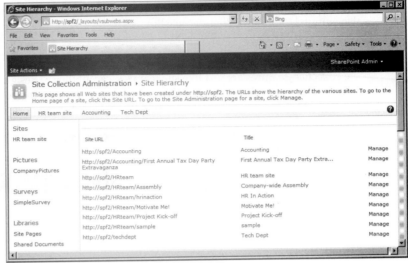

PORTAL SITE CONNECTION

Technically, connecting to a portal site is applicable only if you have a SharePoint Server 2010 server farm on your network. In that case, you can attach this SharePoint Foundation site collection to the portal (see Figure 10.15). Interestingly, this setting can be used to add a link, any link, to the beginning of a site collection's Navigate Up button. It will precede the site collection's own top-level site's home page as the first link there. Any link can be used, but usually it should be a central site that needs to be accessed from anywhere in the site collection (and that site should have a link back to the site collection that refers to it).

FIGURE 10.15

The Portal Site
Connection page

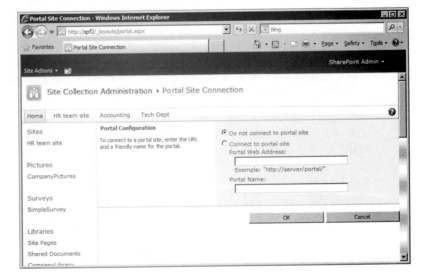

SharePoint Designer Settings

As you've probably noticed, Microsoft has decided to really push SharePoint Designer as a fun and exciting way to extend the powers of your SharePoint sites. One of the new features is letting site owners and designers (rather than just site administrators) use Designer to modify, edit, and change the sites. On the SharePoint Designer Settings page, you can control how much power and control SharePoint Designer users will have over the sites within this site collection. See Figure 10.16.

FIGURE 10.16
The SharePoint Designer Settings page

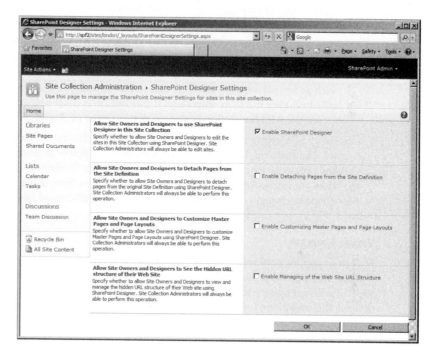

Allow Owners and Designers to use SharePoint Designer in this site collection   Unless you want to encourage your more advanced users to use SharePoint Designer, you'll want to deselect the first box (which is enabled by default). This prevents site owners and designers from editing the sites via SharePoint Designer at all.

If you do want to let them customize the sites, you can go further by also granting them the following permissions:

Allow Owners and Designers to Detach Pages from the Site Definition   Allowing owners and designers to detach pages from the site definition does two important things. In SharePoint Designer, it enables the Edit In Advanced Mode option for any pages. This lets owners and designers completely edit the page, and not be restricted to just editing the Web Parts sections. It also detaches that page from the underlying site definition, so if the definition is ever updated, upgraded, or changed, none of that will apply to this now-custom page. So, unlike other pages in the site collection, this page will have no site definition at all.

Allow Owners and Designers to Customize Master Pages and Page Layouts   This grants owners and designers the ability to change the master page for a site, making sweeping changes to the look and layout of pages in the site. This runs the risk of causing the site's appearance to break from organizational standards for sites (particularly if this is done differently for numerous sites in a site collection). Pages can also be broken if content regions or other important page structures are deleted. This setting, if disabled, causes master page and page layout to not display in the navigation pane in SharePoint Designer.

Allow Owners and Designers to See Hidden URL Structure of Their Web Site
Allowing users to view and edit all the files in the URL structure is also really powerful. This lets them see and edit *all* the files in the site, including the critical "background" files (such as templates, support files, and so on)—these can then be edited or deleted, potentially breaking the site completely. If this option is disabled, owners and designers will not see the All Files option in the navigation pane of SharePoint Designer.

Obviously, just letting designers and site owners edit the site in SharePoint Designer is a powerful tool. The additional three check boxes extend that power to profound levels and should be checked only with extreme caution. By default, site administrators have these powers, even if the boxes are unchecked. To prevent site administrators from using SharePoint Designer, you need to make changes at the web application level, as discussed later in this chapter.

Visual Upgrade

This page applies only when you're working on a server that was upgraded from WSS 3.0. During the upgrade process, if you choose an "in-place" upgrade, you have the option to either apply the visual update to WSS 3.0 sites (change their appearance to the new SPF user interface) or leave the sites alone (and still running the WSS 3.0 interface). For a database-attach upgrade, leaving the sites alone with the option to visually upgrade is the default.

When you leave the interface alone, any site still running a WSS 3.0 interface will have an option to run the visual-upgrade process on that site, from its Site Settings. In addition, when the visual upgrade has not permanently been applied, you can choose to view a site with the visual upgrade on but not apply it. This is good to test templates, web parts, and features to be sure they work with the upgraded interface. So, you can go between working in the old interface, then take a look at the new one, and back again, before committing to applying the new interface. The Visual Upgrade page (Figure 10.17) allows you to do two things to all the sites in the site collection that have not received the Visual Upgrade yet:

Hide Visual Upgrade Option   This will turn off the option in Site Settings to upgrade to the new SharePoint Foundation user interface. So, individual sites will not be able to see the site with the upgraded changes.

Apply the New User Interface to All Sites   This will run the visual upgrade on all sites in the site collection, giving them all the new SharePoint Foundation look and feel.

You can find more information about visual upgrades and migration from WSS 3.0 in Chapter 15.

FIGURE 10.17
The Visual
Upgrade page

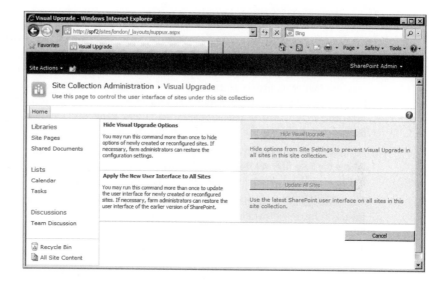

HELP SETTINGS

Ever felt that the help files for a product just weren't up to snuff? Well, with this version of SharePoint, you can write and provide your own help files. Or you can install help files from third-party providers. Help files are stored in help collections, and you can enable and disable them on the Help Settings page. See Figure 10.18.

FIGURE 10.18
The Help
Settings page

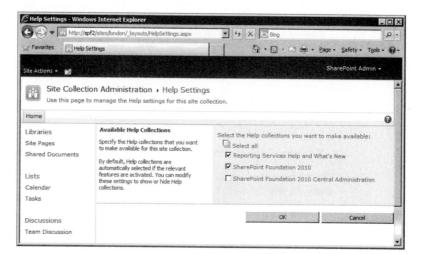

Real World Scenario

MAKE YOUR OWN CUSTOM HELP COLLECTION

This version of SharePoint makes it possible to create your own custom help collection from within the site collection (although the help pages are just simple HTML). For example, in Chapter 8, we created a custom Travel Request form and library in our original http://spf2 site collection. This was intended to be an easy and effective way for users to submit travel requests to HR for approval, but let's assume that some users are having a hard time figuring out how to fill out and submit the form correctly. Creating a help topic called "Travel Requests" would allow them to click the Help button and easily find the step-by-step information they need.

So, how do you go about creating help files? First, you need to make sure you're in the site collection where the help files are needed, which in our case would be the original Company Site, located at http://spf2/. Custom help is set at the site collection level, so be sure to be on the top-level site.

Then, once you're in the right site collection, you need to enable the Custom Site Collection Help feature. This feature is installed by default but not activated. To activate it, simply go to Site Settings ➢ Site Collection Administration ➢ Features.

1. Click Activate to turn the Custom Site Collection Help feature on.

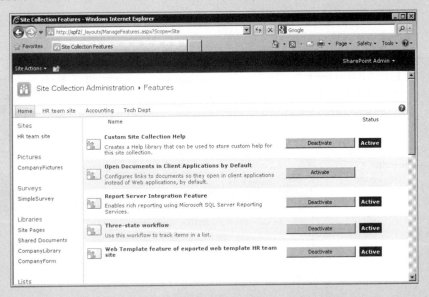

The moment you turn on the feature, it creates a new library called Site Collection Help, found under All Site Content. This custom library holds four content types:

Help Topic   Essentially a help page, or a single question in a FAQ. It is usually an HTML file and is uploaded to the library.

Help Media File   Any supportive media files for a help topic to be uploaded.

Help Category   A category used to organize help files within a collection.

Help Collection   The overarching name for the entire custom collection. It is what will show up in the Help Settings page and is what you enable or disable for the site collection.

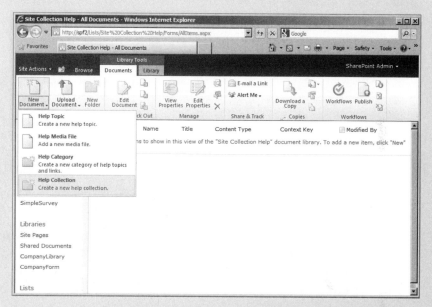

2. When creating your own help collection, the first piece is the collection itself. So go to the site collection help library, click the New Document button's down arrow, and choose Help Collection from the drop-down menu. In the form, you need to fill out the following:

   Name   This must be unique, and it's basically the name of the folder all the parts of the collection will be placed inside. In the example, I'm using `companysite`.

   Title   This is what the users will see in the Help menu, in this case **Company Site Help**.

   Locale ID   This is the ID for the language the collection will be written in. For English, it's 1033.

   Product   This is the identifier for the entire help collection, regardless of language (so you can have multiple help files, each written in a different language but all "assigned" to the same product). In the example, I'm sticking with `companysite`.

   Resources   If your help files need custom JavaScript for CSS files to work, you should enter them here. The example won't use anything that fancy.

   Display Position   This controls where the item is displayed in its enclosing category; for our example, just leave it at 0.

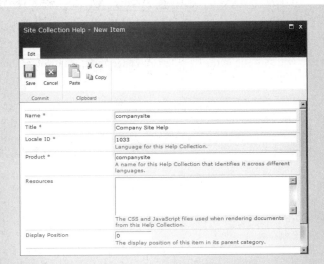

3. Once you click Save, the new help collection will be in the library; you'll see it as a folder.

4. Click the folder to go into the new help collection.

5. In the help collection, you can create help categories and help topics. Let's start with a category. Go to New Document ➢ Help Category.

A help collection is another folder, with the following fields to enter:

Name   The name of the folder, for example travelrequests.

Title   The title of the category that users will actually see in help, for example **Travel Requests**.

Context Key   An optional mapping value to connect to the category or topic from a particular page on the site. I'll use **travel**.

Display Position   Controls where the item is displayed within the collection.

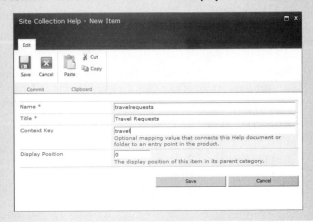

You can also upload individual help topics. These need to be HTML files, encoded in UTF-8. If they need to contain any kind of media, for example a picture, you need to upload that file separately and make sure the link in the HTML file references the correct URL for that file. Otherwise, help files are like any other HTML file. When you upload a help file, you'll notice that it's checked out to you automatically, and there are required fields you'll need to fill in before you can complete the upload process. I've uploaded a simple HTML file for testing purposes.

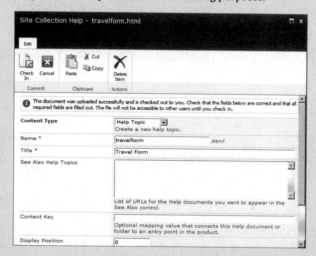

Anything placed in the help collection in this library is immediately available to the entire site collection as part of the normal Help menu. It starts out approved back on the Site Settings ➤ Site Collection Administration ➤ Help Settings page. If you go there, you'll now see that the new company site help collection is enabled for the site collection.

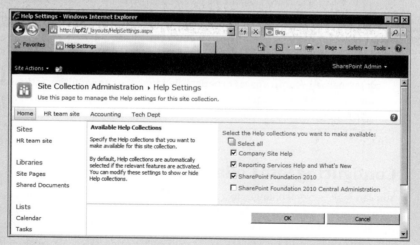

Also, when you click the help icon (the blue question mark), you will now see the new help collection listed, and you can browse by the help categories and view any of the help topics you uploaded.

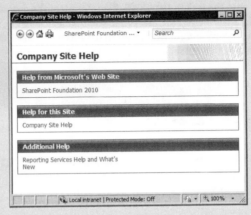

While we're on the subject, ever wonder why when you click the help icon on a particular page in SharePoint, it always takes you to the help table of contents, and not to that page's relevant help category? It's not that hard to create contextual help. Using SharePoint Designer, in advanced mode, you open the ASPX page itself that you want to have open the relevant help topic when the help icon is hit and edit a single variable, navBarHelpOverrideKey. This variable uses a key, WSSEndUser, which points to the generic SharePoint Foundation help collection. You can replace it with your custom category by using your category as the key. The syntax is simply *helpcollection_category*, for example companysite_travel. Once you save the page, the help icon on that page will go to the category you want rather than the general help page (if you have that collection available for the site collection).

At this point, you're probably wondering why SharePoint doesn't use this feature by default. If it's that easy, how come all the default pages don't use it?

The answer is simple: making this change to the code on the page *detaches* the page from the site definition. As with other advanced editing done by SharePoint Designer (see the section "SharePoint Designer Settings"), this means the page is now unique and is no longer using the site definition. It would therefore be untouched if you made any upgrades, updates, or overall site changes. Because contextual help requires pages to be detached from the site definitions, it's usually not a good idea unless you're already planning on doing major customization (despite being really tempting). And that is why even Microsoft doesn't use contextual help on SharePoint's pages.

Configuring Site Collections

You can make several changes to a site collection to customize how it behaves and what is permitted. These configuration changes can all be done through Central Administration, under Application Management. Just as with the site collection settings, these changes affect the entire site collection and can vary between site collections. As is the case with most of what you do in Central Administration, you can use PowerShell or STSADM to do them instead. However, for a convenient idea of how something is done and what settings are required, Central Administration is a great place to start. For more about PowerShell and STSADM, see Chapter 14.

> ### WHO LOGS IN WHERE?
>
> Keep in mind that if you create a site collection and log into it with the site collection administrator's account, then you have the power to administer the site collection. However, to administer site collections (and more) in Central Administration, you will need to log in with a farm administrator's account.

Configuring a site collection (such as creating storage quotas or managing paths) is a server-level administrative task, and it is not something you'd expect the site collection administrator to handle. Site collection administrators do not necessarily have access to Central Administration. In the example, Amber (the London office network administrator) does not have access to these settings, because she is just a site collection administrator. These settings should be configured during or immediately after the initial creation of a new site collection by a qualified farm administrator. The site collection administrator's responsibilities should occur in the site collection interface itself and focus on managing users, permissions, settings, and content of the sites and subsites in her care. A farm administrator should configure Central Administration–based settings. Central Administration can be accessed from SharePoint Server by going to Administrative Tools ➢ SharePoint 2010 Central Administration. Then navigate to the Application Management page.

Site Use Confirmation and Deletion

For each web application on the server, you can enable Site Use Confirmation notification and Automatic Deletion. These settings are found in Central Administration, under Application Management. In the Site Collections category, click the Confirm Site Use And Deletion link. This will take you to the page shown in Figure 10.19.

FIGURE 10.19
The Site Use Confirmation And Deletion page

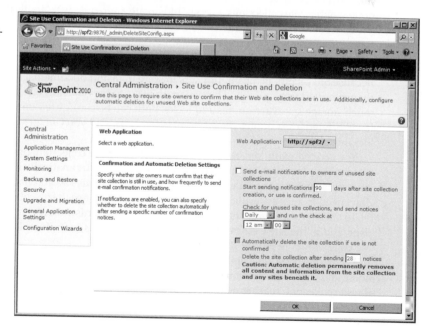

Site Use Confirmation And Deletion is focused on enabling usage confirmation first and sending a notification email to the site collection administrators for confirmation about the site. Once confirmation is enabled, however, you can also enable automatic deletion of site collections that don't get confirmation of activity over a certain number of notifications. Turning on email notifications will send the emails on a set schedule, prompting the site collection administrator either to confirm that the site collection is in use or to delete the site collection.

This page is a bit misleading because it implies that it will send notifications to only those site collections that it senses, somehow, are not active. This is not the case. When email notifications are enabled, every single site collection, regardless of popularity, will be subjected to notification emails.

The emails are sent after the number of days you specify have passed since the site collection was created—or since the last time the administrator confirmed use. This specified time can be anywhere between 30 and 365 days. The server can scan for, and send email to, site collections that are due for an email notification on a daily, weekly, or monthly basis.

If the server sends email notifications on a daily basis and a site administrator does not respond to the first email notification, the server will send another one the next day. The server won't wait another 30+ days; the site is considered "stale" until it's confirmed in use or deleted.

You can also turn on automatic deletion (deletion isn't required, but to delete, notification is required first). After a set number of email notifications have been sent with no response, the server will automatically delete the site collection. This set number of notifications can be between 28 and 168 email notifications.

Enabling automatic deletion is a wise decision if you're going to enable self-service site creation (which we'll discuss later). However, there is a risk to turning on automatic deletion: it affects all the site collections in a web application, including your main site (Company Site in my example). Because of this, it is strongly recommended you do *not* enable automatic deletion on the web application that hosts your main site collection or any other mission-critical permanent site collections. Instead, if you need it for self-service sites or other reasons, such as hosting temporary public site collections, you should create a separate web application, put those temporary site collections there, and then enable automatic deletion for them.

Quota Templates

Because SharePoint is meant for users to store data and documents, it can take up more space than expected very quickly. The two main ways to prevent site collections from consuming too much storage space are quotas and locks. Both can be configured on site collections, so you can have different disk quotas for different collections, and you can lock specific collections without locking others.

You can manually set site quotas on a particular site collection, or you can create quota templates to use for quick assignment (or to have a quota automatically assigned during self-service site creation). It's a good idea to create site quota templates so you have some consistency and don't need to keep entering quota settings manually for each site collection.

To create a new quota template, go to Central Administration's Application Management page, and in the Site Collections category, click Specify Quota Templates. This will take you to the page shown in Figure 10.20.

Using this page, you can create a new template or edit an existing one. Each template needs a name and a storage size limit. You can also set the server to email the site administrators when the site collection reaches a certain size to warn them that they are approaching that limit.

FIGURE 10.20

Creating a quota template

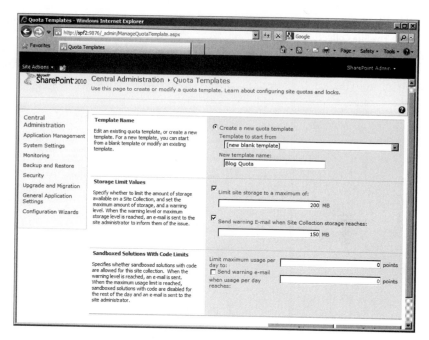

For my example, I am going to create a quota for site collections meant to contain blogs. Later in the chapter, I will provide a web application for blogging site collections, and it would be nice to have a storage quota for them.

Name the quota by entering it in the New Template Name field; mine uses **Blog Quota**. For the quota limits, set the limit to **200** MB, with a warning at **150** MB.

The third section on this page lets you set a quota for any sandboxed solutions that might be installed in the site collection. Sandboxed solutions are custom code solutions that can be installed into a site collection directly, without farm access, and are restricted from making any changes or accessing the rest of the farm. Typically, these are provided by third-party developers, and what kind of quota (if any) they need varies dramatically (the default is 300 points, and points are a combination of server resources like CPU cycles, or memory consumed). For this example, we're not dealing with any sandboxed solutions.

You can edit existing quota templates on this page, delete a template, and create a new template based on an existing one (keep in mind that those edit and delete options won't be available if you don't have an existing template in the farm yet). Although quota templates are meant to be applied to site collections, they are actually available farm-wide.

Site Quotas and Locks

To assign a quota to an existing site collection, to check the current storage used, or to lock the site collection, click Configure Quotas And Locks in the Site Collections section of the Application Management page. This will take you to the page shown in Figure 10.21. In my example, I am setting an individual quota on the London office site collection of 1024 MBs with a notification email to be sent out when the site collection reaches 800 MBs, with a quota on the sandboxed solutions of 300 points with a notification at 100.

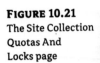

FIGURE 10.21
The Site Collection
Quotas And
Locks page

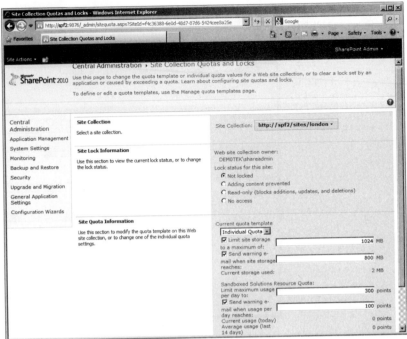

Check the Site Collection section to make sure you're editing the correct site collection before you apply a quota or lock (and change it if necessary by clicking the Site Collection drop-down menu, selecting Change Site Collection, and in the Select A Site Collection dialog box, selecting your site collection and click OK).

To apply a quota or quota template to the selected site collection, go to the Site Quota Information section at the bottom of the page. You can either select a quota template that you've previously created on the Quota Template page or choose the Individual Quota option. This option lets you set the storage quota limits on the current individual site collection (as I have for `http://spf2/sites/london`). This is useful if the site collection requires quota settings that don't fit with current quota templates.

On this page, you can also set a *site lock* on the site collection or check its lock status. (Tip: When troubleshooting why a particular site collection cannot be accessed when others can, always check here to eliminate the chance that the site collection has gone over quota or has been manually locked.)

Site locks are a quick way to prevent access to a site collection without having to go into the Site Settings page for that site collection and edit everyone's permission level. By default, site collections are unlocked. Access to the site collection, in that case, is determined by the permission level the user has on the Site Settings page for that site. Other Site Lock settings are as follows:

Adding Content Prevented   No new content (even a new field for a list item) can be added to the site collection. The site collection can still be viewed, and existing content can be updated or deleted. This is the lock setting that is automatically triggered when a Site Quota limit is reached.

Read-Only   The site collection can be viewed, but no additions, edits, or deletions are permitted.

No Access   The site is completely locked and cannot even be viewed.

When you change a site lock to any of these three options (anything but Unlocked), the Additional Lock Information text box will appear on the page, shown in Figure 10.22. This box is required for any lock to be placed on a site collection. The text in this box is shown to users when they try to access the locked site (or perform a locked action). Always enter some information explaining to your users why you've locked the site, as I have in my example.

FIGURE 10.22

The Additional Lock Information box

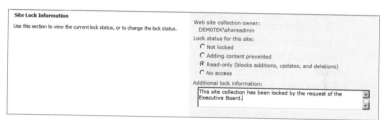

SITE QUOTA TIPS

Let's say you create a quota template for a particular type of site collection (for example, personal blogging sites for users) and set it to 300 MB. Then you create a bunch of site collections using that quota. Later you decide to upgrade everyone's disk space to 500 MB, so you edit the template to reflect the change. Any new site collections created with this template will be set to 500 MB. This will not, however, change the settings for any existing site collection that has already had the template applied. Those collections will stay at a 300 MB limit until you manually reapply the quota to the site collections on the Site Quotas and Locks page. It is possible to update quotas on a large number of existing site collections by using the PowerShell command `Set-SPSite -Identity "<Site>" -QuotaTemplate "<Template>"` and writing a script that runs this command on all the desired sites.

A site collection's quota is for everything in that site collection, including the end-user Recycle Bin. Therefore, having people delete stuff won't free up any space unless the deleted items are also emptied from the Recycle Bin. The second-stage site collection Recycle Bin, which only administrators can see, does not count toward the quota; instead, it's limited to a configurable percentage of the quota (above and beyond the collection's quota). The exact percentage is configured at the web application level, as discussed later in the chapter.

If you add a quota limit to a site collection that is already bigger than the quota limit allows, the site collection will immediately be locked. Therefore, if you're not sure, check the size of an existing site collection before applying a quota.

The next three settings for site collections are pretty self-explanatory, although very useful (and are also covered in Chapters 11 and 12). Change Site Collection Administrators lets you change who the primary and secondary administrators are for a selected site collection, and

View All Site Collections lets you see a list of all the site collections contained in a selected web application. You'll learn more about self-service site creation later in this chapter.

Creating a New Web Application

Let's move another layer up the chain and look at web applications. Suppose you want to have more user-controlled sites with automatic deletion enabled but don't want automatic deletion enabled on all your other site collections or to be forced to respond to usage notifications on your main site collections. In this case, you'll need a new web application because site use confirmation and deletion is applied per web application.

Web applications are what SharePoint uses to hold site collections. Every site collection has to reside in a web application, although a web application can contain many site collections. When SharePoint was installed earlier in the book, two web applications were created: the first site (in my example that's `http://spf2/`) and Central Administration (in this case, `http://spf2:9876/`). A web application essentially consists of two items that reside in IIS: an IIS Web Site and an Application Pool. The default `http://spf2` web application uses the IIS Web Site SharePoint-80, while Central Administration (`http://spf2:9876`) uses the IIS Web Site SharePoint Central Administration v4.

Any settings you configure in IIS on these websites affect every site collection in the corresponding web application. IIS Web Sites host security settings such as SSL, authentication, and anonymous access, making web applications security boundaries in the sense that their security settings affect all the site collections they contain, while not affecting the security of other web applications. In addition to IIS settings, SharePoint offers a lot of additional configuration that can be done at the web application level.

DID YOU REMEMBER YOUR MANAGED ACCOUNT?

Web applications make use of their IIS Web Site application pool identity to access resources such as their database in SQL. So if you want to give your web application its own, unique application pool identity (good for troubleshooting because you know exactly what account is being used by the web application but bad because each application pool does use some RAM to do its work), set it up in SharePoint as a managed account before you create the web application. You can register an account directly from the web page used to create the web application, but moving away from the settings page will wipe all the changes you made, and you'll have to start over. To set up a managed account, just go to Configure Managed Accounts under the Security heading, and then register a managed account. For more details, see Chapter 3.

Almost all web application administration and customization is done in Central Administration under Application Management. Click the Manage Web Applications link, which will take you to the Web Applications Management page, as shown in Figure 10.23.

Let's create a new web application for user blogs—one with a main site collection for the administration blogs and other information.

1. To create a new web application, make sure you are on the Web Applications Management page, and click the **New** button.

This will open the Create New Web Application form. See Figure 10.24.

FIGURE 10.23
The Web
Applications Man-
agement page

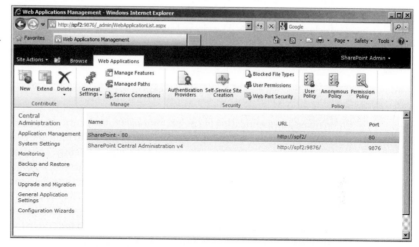

FIGURE 10.24
The Create
New Web
Application form

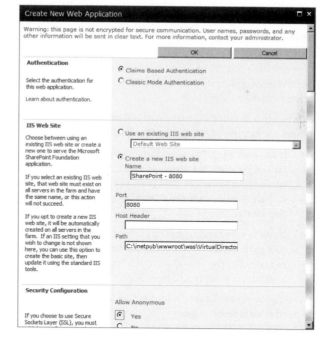

You need to work with a lot of settings to create a new web application, so let's go
through them all with the new blogging web application in mind.

Authentication   This enables access to a new feature of SharePoint Foundation 2010,
claim-based authentication. Choosing Classic Mode Authentication provides you with the
same authentication methods that were available with WSS 3.0 (the standard IIS-supported

authentication methods). Choosing Claims Based Authentication allows these as well as forms-based authentication (FBA) and SAML token-based authentication. FBA is typically used by SQL databases and LDAP, while SAML tokens are used by Active Directory Federation Services, Windows Live, and other claims-based authentication providers.

2. Because it rarely hurts to have options, let's choose **Claims Based Authentication**.

A BRIEF LOOK AT CLAIMS-BASED AUTHENTICATION

Claims-based authentication is a newer approach to authentication that is actually pretty dramatic. Instead of having an application (such as SharePoint) build multiple connections for user authentication, claims-based authentication handles things differently. The user authenticates to an issuer, who verifies their identity and provides them with a signed security token that contains their claims (credentials). Then, when connecting to the application, the user hands it the signed token. This saves having to log in again or having the application reverify the user's account with the issuer. It's been compared to an airport boarding pass. The issuer (front desk) handles the validation, confirms that the user has permission to get on the plane, and then hands them the token (boarding pass)—all SharePoint needs to do is make sure everyone has a boarding pass, without having to worry about how it was issued (NTLM, FBA, Kerberos, LDAP, Basic with a username and password login page, or the like). This is done via Security Assertion Markup Language (SAML)—basically, using XML and SSL to wrap up a nice boarding pass for use with websites.

Microsoft has been deploying claims-based authentication with its Active Directory Federation Services (the chunk of AD that issues the token to the user after they log in via normal means to AD) and Windows Identity Foundation (for writing ASP.NET code to support claims-based authentication in custom code).

Although a detailed discussion of claims-based authentication is beyond the scope of this book, there are a couple of things you should know:

◆ If you ever intend to use claims-based authentication, you need to apply it to the web application on creation. You can't create a classic mode web application and then later extend the web application to use claims-based authentication on a different zone (for more about extended web applications see the "Creating a New Public URL (by Extending a Web Application)" section later in the chapter).

◆ If you're using claims-based authentication, make sure the Default zone uses Windows NTLM authentication to ensure that the search indexer (also known as a *gatherer* or *crawler*) can log in and index the site. Otherwise, Search may not function. This is especially true if the web application is using a custom port.

And if your network ever deploys Active Directory Federated Services, rest assured that SharePoint Foundation is ready to go.

IIS Web Site   We need to specify which IIS Web Site the new web application will use. On the off chance you already created a Web Site in IIS for this web application, you could choose it from the list. In this case, we have not, so we need to create a new one.

To create a new web application, you need to enter the following information:

Description   A descriptive name for the IIS Web Site, usually something such as SharePoint-portnumber.

3. The Description field will change to reflect your port or host header selections later in the settings. You can choose to manually enter a description as well. My example uses SharePoint-8080 for this web application. (I didn't type that in; if you change the port or host header, it changes for you.)

Port   The port on which the new web application will listen. IIS Web Sites must be unique in some way in order to receive traffic. Websites can be unique either by port number or by host header (you can't mess with unique IPs in this interface). Using a port number to make a Web Site is adequate for demonstration purposes but does require that users type a port number next to the server name in their browser to access the top-level site.

4. The port suggested by default is certain not to be already in use by the server. However, you can specify a port if you know it is available. Because port 80 is taken by the first web application, SharePoint-80, my example is specifying port **8080**.

Host Header   A host header is a way to change the expected URL of the web application. Normally, because port 80 is already taken by the SharePoint-80 Web Site (which is our first web application for this SharePoint server), you would not be able to have any more websites on that port. But host headers allow you to specify a unique URL for the website that listens on port 80. As long as the host header is unique in IIS, IIS can capture user requests on port 80 for it and redirect the correct traffic to that site. This will be covered later in the chapter.

5. For this web application, my example leaves the host header blank because we are using a unique port instead.

Path   This is where the SharePoint configuration files are to be kept. My example uses the default settings. By default, IIS places the files in a folder that is named, by default, whatever the port or host header is for the web application. Here's an example: `C:\Inetub\wwwroot\wss\Virtual Directories\8080`.

6. Although you can specify a different path for your web application's data, for this example, keep the default.

Security Configuration   There are several ways you can configure security on the new web application, as shown in Figure 10.25.

Allow Anonymous   This setting turns anonymous access on or off in the IIS Web Site for the web application. Enabling anonymous access adjusts IIS settings to allow the web application to offer anonymous access as an option to the site collections, the subsites, or even individual lists and libraries. If there is a site collection or subsite (that doesn't inherit permissions) in the web application that wants to take advantage of this, the administrator has to choose to enable anonymous access at that level. Lists and libraries can be explicitly given anonymous access, but that option (to give particular lists or libraries unique anonymous access) must be enabled at the site collection or subsite where the list or library is located as well as at the web application level.

FIGURE 10.25
The Security Configuration settings

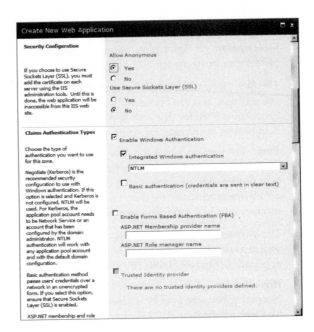

7. In this example, allow anonymous access by selecting **Yes** (the default is No) so the user blogs will have the option to be read by everyone on the network without logging in.

   Use Secure Sockets Layer (SSL)   If you want to use SSL to encrypt all the sites in the web application, you can turn on SSL (changing the path from `http://spf2:8080` to `https://spf2:8080`). We discuss more details about SSL in Chapter 16, "Advanced Installation and Configuration."

8. For this example, SSL is unnecessary, so keep **No** selected for this setting.

   Claims Authentication Types   This section changed when we selected Claims Based Authentication earlier. Now it allows us to configure Windows authentication, forms-based authentication, and SAML-based trusted identity partners (this option is grayed out because our network does not have any configured). Under Windows Authentication, you have the normal choices: Integrated (NTLM or Kerberos) and Basic (clear-text passwords). In this case, we'll be using Windows authentication and keeping the default, NTLM.

9. Keep the authentication types set to the default of **NTLM**.

   Sign In Page URL   Also with claims-based authentication is the need for a login page—either default or custom. This is triggered only if the user doesn't already have a claims token.

10. Leave the default sign-in page.

SharePoint Doesn't Authenticate

Remember that SharePoint does not do authentication, only authorization. SharePoint uses outside processes, such as Active Directory, to store user accounts and authenticate those accounts. Then SharePoint authorizes those authenticated users to access its resources.

Public URL   This shows the URL for the site—by default, this is set to the URL of the web application (either the port or a host header, if one is used).

11. Using the default URL is fine for this example, so leave this setting at its default.

Application Pool   You need to establish which application pool in IIS is going to be used by the IIS Web Site. Application pools in IIS access resources on behalf of the Web Site using an account identity that you specify. This application pool will be used by the web application to access its content database. Generally, you'll want to create a new one to keep it separate from the existing application pools. If you do create a new application pool, you will also have to provide the security account it will use to access its content database. On a single-server install, this can be the Network Service account. However, on a server farm, you'll probably want to create a new domain user just for this web application, or you could use the account you created for the original web application after installing SharePoint. Remember that the configurable application pool account must be a managed account to be available to be selected.

12. For this demonstration, I am going to keep the suggested application pool name (it usually matches the description of the web application) and use the domain account I registered earlier, dem0tek\spf8080content; feel free to use a managed account you have registered. See Figure 10.26.

Figure 10.26
The Application Pool section

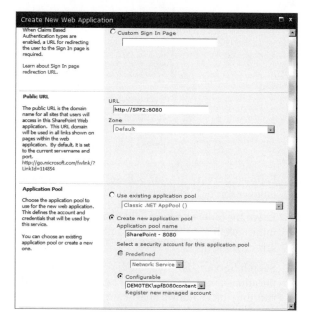

Database Name and Authentication   The web application needs a content database to store everything in—just as the SharePoint-80 web application did during the initial installation of SharePoint (as discussed in Chapter 3). You need to choose which SQL Server instance you want the database to be stored on; of course, with a Standalone server install, you'll need to use the default provided as it points to the SQL Server Express Database on the server. You can leave the database name as the default or rename it something more intuitive if you want (the default creates a unique GUID for the database, which is hard to remember). You'll also need to decide how the web application will authenticate to the database. Again, you'll most likely want to use the default Windows authentication, but if your SQL Server instance does not use Windows authentication, you'll need to supply a username and password.

13. Make certain that the correct database server is specified, the database name is acceptable, and your web application can authenticate to access the database. My example uses **WSSBlog_Content** for the database name; otherwise, the default database server and authentication method are fine, as shown in Figure 10.27.

FIGURE 10.27

The Database Name And Authentication section

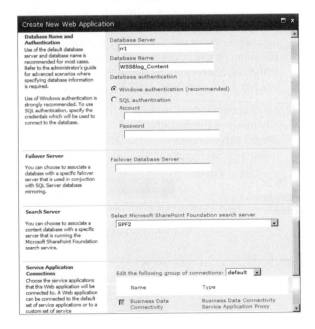

Failover Server   If your SQL server is running database mirroring, you can specify the failover server here.

14. Leave the failover server field blank if your SQL Server instance is not mirroring, which mine isn't. If your SQL Server instance is doing database mirroring, feel free to enter that server name here.

Search Server   For the search service to index the content database for this new web application, a search server must be assigned. The drop-down list shows only those servers running the Windows SharePoint Services search service.

15. Select a search server for the content database. For this example, there is only one choice (SPF2), but it is possible to move search to another server (or have search on more than one server for that matter), as discussed in Chapter 16.

> **Service Application Connections** If your SharePoint server has some application connectors installed, you can set up which ones the new web application enables. By default, the server comes with two (Business Data Connectivity Service and Usage and Health data collection), although they both do need configuration.

16. Leave the default connections in place (both checked).

> **Customer Experience Improvement Program** And you thought CEIP was just for Office! Enabling this will have the SharePoint Server instance collect data on usage, access, and behavior. The theory is that this information will assist Microsoft in making the product even better in the future, similar to the way it has updated the GUI between WSS and SPF.

17. Let's leave CEIP turned off.

18. Once you've set everything to your satisfaction, click **OK**, and wait while the new web application is built. Once the operation completes, you'll need to take some more steps to finish the creation.

19. To complete the web application creation process, you may need to manually restart IIS on the server so it finishes building the new IIS Web Site (it's not required, but can speed up the process). Open a command prompt, and enter `iisreset /noforce`. (The `/noforce` switch lets services gracefully reset but doesn't force them, which is good if you have other IIS applications running.)

If you chose to restart IIS manually, if there are other SharePoint servers in the farm, you may need to run the `iisreset` command for each of them as well. If you didn't, their IIS may not realize that they should also have a copy of the new web application.

When IIS restarts, go ahead and open Internet Information Services (IIS) Manager, which is found in Administrative Tools on the Start menu. You'll see your new IIS website and application pool, as shown in Figure 10.28.

Your new web application is up and running in IIS and available to SharePoint. Of course, it's completely empty. Going to the URL won't show anything—after all, you have no actual site there. The next step is to create a new site collection for the web application and fill it with the top-level site.

1. To create the first site collection for the new web application, go back to Central Administration ➤ Application Management, and under the Site Collections category, click Create Site Collections. Otherwise, if you still have open the Application Created box, you can click **Create Site Collection**.

2. On the Create Site Collection page, you may need to change the web application to your new one (SharePoint-8080), so the new site collection will go in this new web application. So, in the first section of the page, click the web application's name, and choose **Change Web Application.** This will take you to the Select Web Application page shown in Figure 10.29.

FIGURE 10.28
IIS shows the new website.

FIGURE 10.29
The Select Web Application page

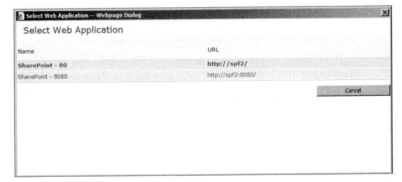

3. Choose your new web application, and click **OK**. You will be taken back to the familiar Create Site Collection page, but now the page shows the new web application. See Figure 10.30.

4. For the title, my example uses **Personal Blogs** and gives a brief description. You'll notice the Web Site Address field is showing the new URL for the web application. We're going to make this site collection the root of the web application, so the complete URL is `http://spf2:8080/`.

5. Create a new top-level site using the **Team Site** template (it makes a good portal for the user blog site collections that will be created from there), use your account (mine is *shareadmin*) as the primary administrator, and apply a quota template. (My example uses the **Blog Quota** we created earlier.) Then click **OK**. When you're done, browse to your new site collection, as shown in Figure 10.31.

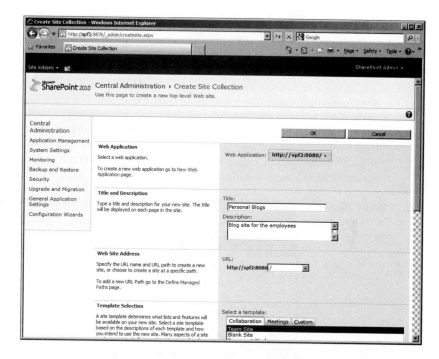

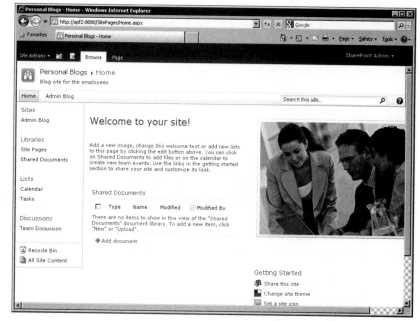

Now let's fill up the site collection. (After all, is it really a collection if there is only a top-level site?) Let's create a subsite of the top-level site. This subsite will actually be a blog for the administrators of the site collection for this example. It is intended to teach users what a blog is and how to use one before they create their own.

Use the **Site Actions** menu to choose **New Site**. On the New SharePoint Site page, name the site (I'm using A**dmin Blog**), and use the Blog template. For the URL, you can add `adminblog` to the path. In my example, that would look like `http://spf2:8080/adminblog`. Be sure to place it on the Quick Launch and top link bars of the parent site. Set it to inherit the top link bar from the parent site. When you are finished, click **OK**. When it's done, you should have a nice blog site to display to users in addition to the main Personal Blogs top-level site, as shown in Figure 10.32. For more details on creating a subsite, see Chapter 9.

FIGURE 10.32
The Admin
Blog site

Web Application Management

Now you have a new web application holding a new site collection with a basic top-level site and one subsite. As we did with site collections, let's take a look at the unique things you can do with a web application. For all of these settings, in Central Administration go to Application Management and click the Manage Web Applications link.

New and Extend

You've already created a new web application, but you may also notice an Extend button in the Contribute section of the ribbon. Extending a web application allows you to create a new IIS Web Site (with its own custom authentication, port, host header, and so on) for an existing web application—essentially providing multiple access methods to the web application. This will be covered in much more detail in the section "Alternate Access Mapping."

Delete Web Application

If you need to delete a web application, select it in the list, and click the Delete button. This will take you to the page shown in Figure 10.33.

FIGURE 10.33
The Delete Web
Application page

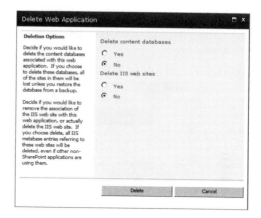

Make sure you're set to delete the right web application. If not, click Cancel. If you do accidentally delete the wrong application, check Chapter 13, "Maintenance and Monitoring," to see how to restore from backup (that is assuming you *made* a backup).

When deleting the web application, you can choose to delete the associated Web Site in IIS and/or delete the content database. Deleting the IIS Web Site will remove both the IIS Web Site and the corresponding application pool from IIS—even if they are being used by another IIS Web Site. Deleting the content database will truly delete the database in SQL. If you choose to not delete the database, it will be detached from the web application, but not deleted in SQL, so you can create a new web application and reattach it later. Content databases will be covered in more detail later in this chapter.

If you click the Delete button's drop-down menu, you'll also see an option to simply remove SharePoint from the IIS Web Site. This is used to "delete" any extensions you made for the web application (also discussed in "Alternate Access Mapping").

Let's not delete anything here.

Web Application General Settings

The Web Application General Settings button has a drop-down menu that covers a lot of options—just clicking the button will take you to the page shown in Figure 10.34. Other settings pages available via this drop-down are Resource Throttling, Workflow, Outgoing E-Mail, Mobile Account, and SharePoint Designer. This section will explore each of these pages and their settings. These settings pages often have many options listed, more than can reasonably fit in one window without scrolling. The figures for these long pages may not display every setting available because of this; however, all settings will be described regardless.

GENERAL SETTINGS

This page contains a large number of sections for configuration. Everything you see here will apply to all the site collections and sites within the web application. Some of these settings are defaults for the sites, which means they apply to site creation but can be changed on individual site collections post creation. Most of these settings, however, are applied to the web application and cannot be changed later for individual site collections. Let's adjust the general settings for our SharePoint-8080 web application.

Default Time Zone Set the default time zone for newly created sites. This is only a default setting; individual sites can be edited to change the time zone from the default to reflect local time.

1. Select the default time zone for all sites in the web application. My example uses the main office's time zone: EST.

FIGURE 10.34

The Web Application General Settings page

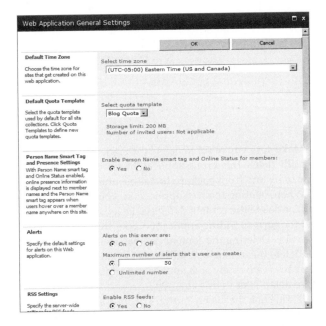

Default Quota Template Set the default quota template for newly created site collections. This setting is also a default. You can still change the quota template assigned to a site collection manually, as discussed in the "Site Collections" section of this chapter.

2. My example uses the **Blog** quota template that we created earlier in this chapter, so any site collections that are created on this web application automatically get this quota.

Person Name Smart Tag and Presence Settings This option requires MSN Messenger or Windows Messenger (or Windows Communications server and Office Communicator). Person name smart tags are small pop-ups that appear when a user hovers their cursor over a name in the SharePoint site. The tags indicate whether the person is online currently and, if so, whether they're available for chat. This feature is covered in Chapter 11.

3. This option is on by default, which is fine in this case.

Alerts User alerts are discussed in Chapter 6, "Introduction to Lists." They can be very useful, but you really don't want to let a user set thousands of alerts (your email server might complain). Here is where you can limit the number of alerts a user can set, or you can disable user alerts altogether.

4. My example changes the default of 500 to a mere **50**, so users can't go crazy with alerts. Feel free to set the limit to fit your environment.

RSS Settings Disabling RSS feeds means that there will be no RSS for any of the site collections on that web application. In fact, when RSS is disabled at the web application level, the RSS link on the Site Settings page for enclosed site collections won't even appear.

5. For this example, leave RSS turned **on**.

Blog API Settings With the rise of blogging, a large number of third-party blog-writing applications have been developed. In an effort to allow this software to connect seamlessly with actual blog servers, an RFC has been written for two application programming interfaces (APIs): Blogger API and MetaWeblog API. Blogger API, an older standard, dealt only with accessing the text on a blog. The newer standard, MetaWeblog API, also handles extra data such as common RSS-built metadata like Author, Title, Comment, and so on.

SharePoint supports the MetaWeblog API; when it's enabled on the web application, users can update, edit, or create blog posts via third-party software. If you accept usernames and passwords via the MetaWeblog API, these programs can also log in to perform the updates. Otherwise, the default authentication for the site is used.

If you do enable the API and allow the username and password to be accepted, note that these credentials are sent in clear text. Enabling SSL on the web application can reduce this security risk, as will be discussed later in the chapter.

6. Leave the Blog API enabled, and turn on username and password acceptance.

 Real World Scenario

USING WINDOWS LIVE WRITER WITH SHAREPOINT BLOGS

Windows Live Writer from Microsoft is an excellent example of a MetaWeblog API–compatible program. You can download it from Microsoft's `http://get.live.com` website.

To set up Live Writer for use with a SharePoint blog, you'll need to configure a new blogging profile as follows:

1. When you open Live Writer for the first time, it will prompt you to create a Windows Live Spaces blog. If you click Next (because you already have a blog, thank you), it will ask you for the blog type you are writing to. If the account you use to log into the local machine is the one you use to access your SharePoint blog, choose SharePoint Blog. At that point, Live Writer will ask for your blog address, will access your blog, and then will be ready to begin.

2. Name the profile, and click Finish.

You can now create a blog post in Live Writer easily.

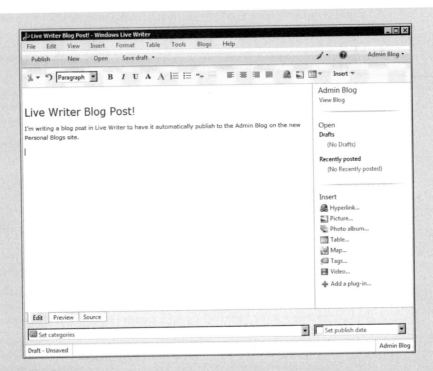

From that point on, it is easy to create blog entries in SharePoint using this (or many other) MetaWeblog API–compatible program; the configuration should be the hardest part.

Remember that MetaWeblog API is a web application setting; therefore, enabling it will provide this kind of integration for all blogs on all sites in all site collections residing in that web application.

Here are some other notes on using LiveWriter:

◆ If you log into SharePoint using a different account, you may want to choose Other Blog Service instead of SharePoint Blog. It will take you to a screen to enter the URL for your blog (for example, **http://spf2:8080/adminblog**) where you provide your username and password (assuming authentication via the API is enabled on the SharePoint server, it will be sent as clear text). When you're finished, click Next. Live Writer will check to see whether there is a web page at that address; when you are prompted for a service provider, choose MetaWeblog API.

◆ For the remote posting URL, you'll need to tack **/_layouts/metaweblog.aspx** onto the end of your blog's URL (for example, `http://server/myblog/_layouts/metaweblog.aspx`).

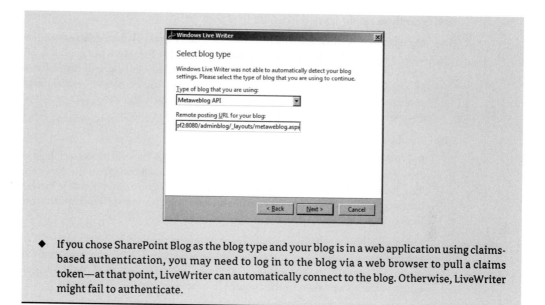

- ◆ If you chose SharePoint Blog as the blog type and your blog is in a web application using claims-based authentication, you may need to log in to the blog via a web browser to pull a claims token—at that point, LiveWriter can automatically connect to the blog. Otherwise, LiveWriter might fail to authenticate.

Browser File Handling This setting has two options. Permissive doesn't make any noticeable changes to the user's browser experience (the browser will behave the way it does on any other site). Strict attaches headers to particular file types—overriding the browser's normal behavior and instead requiring the browser to download the file (rather than attempt to render it). If you are using a page viewer web part to display a file and whenever the page opens it prompts you to download that file instead, consider changing this setting to permissive.

7. Leave the default of **Strict** in place.

Web Page Security Validation This setting determines how long a user can remain idle before having to log in again. If you have a lot of users who tend to sit idle with a form half-filled out on their screen and you're not concerned with desktop security, you may want to extend the timeout period or disable it.

8. For this example, leave the default setting.

Send User Name And Password In E-mail This setting is relevant only if Active Directory Account Creation mode (ADAC) is enabled.

When this setting is enabled, and when an account is created for a user, they will receive a notification email detailing their username and password. Without this setting enabled, the user will require an administrator to reset the password in Active Directory.

9. For my example, leave the default in place.

Master Page Setting for Application _Layouts Pages When enabled (the default), the _ Layouts page reference queries the master pages for the site. This applies to every site and site collection in the web application, so disabling this setting will radically change the appearance of these sites (assuming they had customized master pages). But if you have a problem with corrupt or badly modified master pages, this is a quick way to disable them all, preventing site administrators from using master pages.

10. For the example, leave the default in place.

Recycle Bin You can customize the Recycle Bin for the entire web application. These changes apply to every site collection and site in the web application. You can adjust how long items sit in the end-user Recycle Bin and the second-stage Recycle Bin before deletion, set the Recycle Bins to never delete anything automatically, or disable the Recycle Bins completely.

11. My example leaves the defaults in place. Items can be left in the Recycle Bin for 30 days before they are deleted, and the second-stage Recycle Bin is set at 50 percent of the site quota. This means the second-stage Recycle Bin adds 50 percent of the site collection's quota to the space taken in the content database.

Maximum Upload Size This is the maximum amount that can be uploaded in a single process to the web application. This limit applies to any single file upload or any group of files being uploaded together. For example, if you're using the Explorer view to copy and paste 50 documents to a document library in one go, you'll need to make sure the combined size of the files is less than this limit. If you're planning to transfer a large amount of data to a SharePoint site, you should first increase this limit and then decrease it when you're done.

12. My example leaves the default of **50** MB in place. Apply the maximum upload size that is appropriate for your environment.

Customer Experience Improvement Program If you decide you want SharePoint to collect analytical data for the CEIP program, here is where you turn it on. It is the same setting that you see during the creation of a new web application.

13. I'm going to leave it turned off.

When you're done configuring the general settings, click **OK**. You will be taken back to the Web Applications Management page.

RESOURCE THROTTLING

This version of SharePoint has some nice features for controlling performance, one of which is *resource throttling*. With SharePoint, one of the biggest bottlenecks is with large lists—both lists with a large number of items and those with a large number of fields. Whenever a large list is queried, it slows the entire content database down for everyone else. And that content database could be hosting every site collection in the web application. Resource throttling ensures that such large queries don't get out of hand. Resource Throttling is an option in the drop-down menu for the General Settings, and clicking it opens the page shown in Figure 10.35.

FIGURE 10.35
The Resource
Throttling page

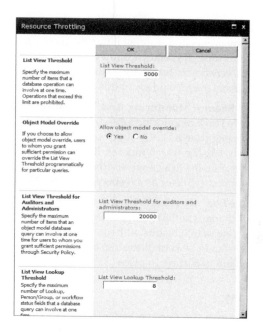

List View Threshold This limits how many items in a list can be accessed in a single database operation. For example, this limits how many items can be shown in a list view web part. The default is 5000. (The minimum threshold is 2000.) When a database query to a large list is made that exceeds the threshold, an "Expensive Query" exception error is displayed, explaining that the query has hit the threshold.

Object Model Override When enabled, this allows the previous threshold to be overridden (ignored) by custom-built queries. So if you need to run custom, large-count queries on the SQL database, you can do so. Running a command to use the override requires the command be run as an administrator (or another account with explicit permission on the web application).

List View Threshold For Auditors And Administrators This is the same threshold, but for administrators and auditors (people who have been granted either Full Control or Full Read permission via a permission policy at the web application level). The default is 20,000. This threshold is applied only when one of those accounts queries the list via an object model (so Object Model Override must also be enabled). When viewing lists normally, the standard List View Threshold setting still applies.

List View Lookup Threshold This limits how many lookup fields (fields that need to pull data from other lists) a list can contain.

Daily Time Windows For Large Queries This allows you to set a time period when the thresholds are not observed, so large list queries can be run (by anyone) without triggering an exception.

List Unique Permissions Threshold This threshold sets how many unique permission changes a list can have, including custom permissions on list items or on the list itself.

Backward-Compatible Event Handlers   *Event handlers* are custom code written and triggered by events in document libraries. They can be applied to components, such as lists, files, and even sites. This feature allows you to use older event handlers while you rewrite them for this version of SharePoint. My example leaves the default in place, because we don't have any custom event handlers at this point.

HTTP Request Monitoring And Throttling   Turning this on causes the web front-end server to run a monitoring job—and when HTTP traffic becomes overburdened (requests are slowing from a DDOS attack or just a really busy day), the server rejects low-priority requests, like the search indexer. It's recommended you keep this off, and if your web front-end servers slow to a crawl, address the cause/issue rather than throttling. This is meant to be a temporary fix (or as a response to a DDOS attack). By default it is enabled.

Change Log   The *change log* is part of the search feature set. The server keeps a log of any recent changes to the site in the change log. This allows search services to quickly provide up-to-date search results without having to reindex the entire site. You can specify how long entries should be kept in the log, or you can disable the log completely. My example leaves the default of 60 days in place.

Workflow

Workflows is the next option under the General Settings button. The Workflow Settings page (see Figure 10.36) controls whether your users can build their own workflows on the sites within this web application. When user-defined workflows are enabled, they can build custom workflows from the existing (administrator-installed) workflows.

FIGURE 10.36
The Workflow
Settings page

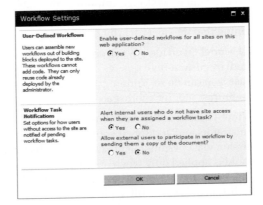

In addition, you can enable Workflow Task Notifications. There are two settings:

◆   Alert internal users who do not have site access when they are assigned a workflow task. This applies to users who are known to the authentication server (for example, they're members of Active Directory) who don't have explicit permission to the site. They receive an email prompting them to go to the Request Permissions page.

◆   Allow external users to participate in the workflow by sending them a copy of the document. For people with no permission to the document, this will email the notification and a copy of the document. If the workflow task is not a document but a list, the list item properties are displayed in a table within the email Although this workflow setting is not suggested for working with confidential or otherwise secure information, it is useful for those web applications intended for work with external users (such as company clients or customers).

Outgoing E-mail Settings

Next under the General Settings drop-down menu is Outgoing E-mail Settings. By default, a web application uses the same email settings you created during installation for the whole farm, but it is possible to give a web application unique email settings. See Figure 10.37. You'll probably want to keep the same mail server, but you might find it useful to change the sender address to be unique for this web application. My example uses blogserver@dem0tek.com. (Make certain, of course, that the email address exists on your email server.) Should your region or system require it, you can also change the character set. I'm leaving it set to UTF-8.

FIGURE 10.37
The web application email settings

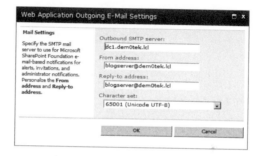

Mobile Account

This version of SharePoint supports SMS notifications (sending alerts and messages directly to cell phones). For the server to do this, you need to enter the URL of an SMS service with which you have an account for the server, along with your username and password for the account. See Figure 10.38.

SMS service can be provided by many third-party companies that integrate text messaging with SharePoint (and Outlook). Microsoft provides a link here to its Office Online website, which lists available third-party companies, based on your region and cell phone provider.

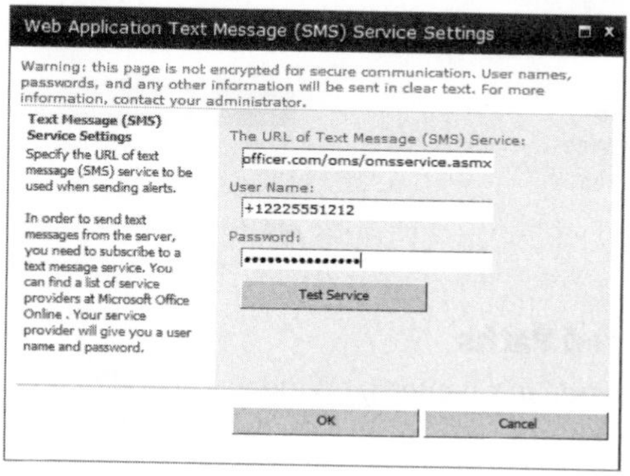

FIGURE 10.38
The mobile account settings

SHAREPOINT DESIGNER

This page (see Figure 10.39) provides the same settings as on the SharePoint Designer page for site collections (as shown in Figure 10.16)—except they apply to the entire web application and override whatever settings were configured on individual site collections within that web application.

FIGURE 10.39

The SharePoint Designer Settings page

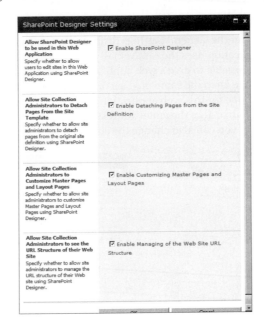

Managing Web Application Features

Like sites and site collections, web applications have features that apply to the entire web application (and the site collections therein). These can be provided by third-party companies to integrate their products into SharePoint or as part of an overall solution to customize SharePoint functionality. To view web application features, go to the Manage Web Application page and click the Manage Features button, which will take you to the page shown in Figure 10.40. If there are features installed that were scoped to apply to a web application, they would be manageable here. Currently, we have no web application features.

FIGURE 10.40

The Manage Web Application Features page

Managed Paths

As discussed in Chapter 1, "Windows SharePoint Foundation 2010 Under the Hood," uses Internet Information Server (IIS) to host and publish all of its websites. This means that everything you see through the web browser is being hosted on or accessed by IIS and is, therefore, bound by the rules of IIS.

IIS usually stores all websites in the file system. If you have a normal web page with the URL `http://www.mycompany.com/sales/default.html`, a sales folder containing the file `default.html` will reside somewhere on the IIS server (by default in the WWWroot folder). All your website content—images, pages, scripts, and so on—will reside somewhere in the file system, nested within the root path assigned in the IIS Web Site settings.

SharePoint, on the other hand, compiles its web pages on the fly based on the content in the content database. This means there is no need for separate files to be stored in the local file system for each and every page. If you create new content, such as a list named Order, or upload a document to a library, everything will be stored in the database, not in the file system. In other words, the Order list's `Allitems.aspx` page is compiled from the master page and other components that exist in the file system by default (depending on the site template or definition), but the unique data and settings for that list are all stored in the content database for the site. SharePoint web applications do have a virtual directory that contains necessary components to display web content, but most of it is information for compiling pages on the fly.

The new London site collection (in our original `http://spf2` web application) is located at `http://spf2/sites/london` because the path for the URL defaulted to `/sites/` when the site collection was created.

No matter where you look in the local file system, you'll never find a London folder with HTML (or ASPX) files in it. Instead, all that data will be in the content database, and all other pages for the site will be compiled when requested from shared components in the file system.

IIS and SharePoint distinguish between paths that are normal IIS websites (and exist in the file system) and paths that are SharePoint sites (and exist in the database) by using managed paths. A *managed path* is a path for which SharePoint tells IIS, "I'll handle this request."

With this version of SharePoint, all unspecified paths are by default *excluded*—they are not managed. For a path to be used by SharePoint (and available as a path for new site collections within the web application), it needs to be set as a managed path. SharePoint creates two managed paths for new web applications, such as the SharePoint-80 web application created earlier in the book. They can be viewed in Central Administration, under Application Management ➢ Manage Web Applications.

To see what managed paths are available for our new web application (SharePoint-8080), make sure it is selected, and click the Managed Paths button in the ribbon. See Figure 10.41. As you can see, there are two managed paths by default, the *root* and *sites*.

FIGURE 10.41

The Define Managed Paths page

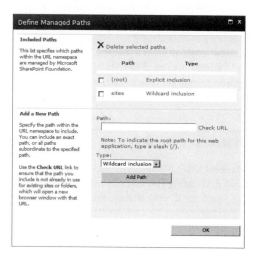

There are two types of managed paths, explicit and wildcard.

Explicit Managed Path An *explicit* managed path is a path that is itself a SharePoint site. Root is an explicit path because if you enter the root of the server into a browser (for example, `http://spf2:8080/` or `http://spf2`), you'd get to the top-level site of a SharePoint site collection. It's the end of the path; it goes no further.

Wildcard Managed Path A *wildcard* managed path is a URL that can contain multiple site collections. `Sites`, in our case, is a wildcard managed path because the path can have any number of site collections starting from there, such as `http://spf2/sites/london`, `http://spf2/sites/toronto`, and `http://spf2/sites/cleveland`.

When you create a new managed path and you want that path to host a single SharePoint site collection, it needs to be *explicit* (think of it as an explicit address, "Your top-level site address is `http://spf2/`"). If you want to host multiple site collections within the managed path, you need to make it a *wildcard* managed path. Making it a more general address, as in "Your site is somewhere under /sites/."

To create a new managed path, simply specify the path (such as `blogs`) in the Add New Path section of the page. Specify whether the path is explicit or wildcard, and then click **Add Path** (Figure 10.42). When you create a managed path, it doesn't close the page, assuming that you are going to create more. The page closes only if you click **OK**.

You can also test the URL to make certain it works and isn't already in use somewhere by clicking the Check URL button. If a page comes up for that path, it's obviously already being used, so having the URL fail to display a page when you check it is good.

TO SLASH OR NOT TO SLASH

The Define Managed Paths page says you have to precede paths that start at the root address of the web application with a forward slash. In my experience, this isn't necessary.

To specify a managed path, you have to type in each path from the web application address forward. For example, it is possible that you might want to provision some longer managed paths for members of a presales presentation team for when they use self-service site creation to create their blogs. (Self-service site creation lets users make their own site collections; we'll be covering it later in this chapter.)

In that case, instead of just adding **blogs** to the managed paths list as a wildcard path, you'd need to add **blogs/sales**. Then the presales team users could use their names to specify their sales blog addresses, such as `http://spf2:8080/blogs/sales/BasilMullien`. This also lets you organize the paths, so other teams can have blogs, such as `blogs/HR`, `blogs/mgmt`, and so on.

DON'T NEGLECT THE ROOT

Keep in mind when planning your URL namespace that SharePoint requires a site collection at the root path first before you add site collections to any other managed path. If you decide to use the /sites/ path for all your site collections for some reason, Search may not work. Weird but true.

There is no short way to specify a long managed path, which should be useful discouragement in and of itself. Remember the 260-character limit for URLs when creating paths (255 characters if you are going to do Send To for libraries or otherwise link to the path in the site).

FIGURE 10.42
Creating a new managed path

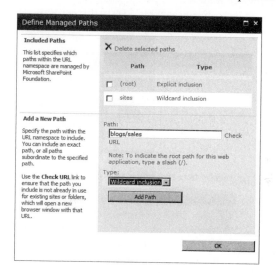

DON'T GO MANAGED PATH CRAZY

Keep in mind that these paths are for site collections in this web application, and are available for anyone creating a site collection, in Central Administration or via self-service. Subsite addresses within site collections are *appended* to site collection addresses. This means that if you had a site collection at http://spf2/london/sales and you wanted to create a subsite for presales projects, you wouldn't need to create a managed path for sales/presales to put that subsite at that address. If you add a presales subsite to the site collection at http://spf2/london/sales, its address will be http://spf2/london/sales/presales without additional effort.

A managed path is more than just the URL you use for site collections; it's a critical piece of the relationship between SharePoint and IIS; it lets IIS know what addresses to expect SharePoint to take care of.

USING EXCLUDED PATHS

If you'd like to place a traditional website in an excluded path on the IIS server while keeping the default port 80, you need to do a couple of things to make IIS display the site outside of SharePoint.

For example (and I am intentionally keeping this simple), say you want the URL http://spf2/sales/ to go to a standard website, rather than to a SharePoint site. First make certain that the site's path is not a managed path. The next thing to do is place the website files in the correct location—the root of whatever IIS Web Site is hosting port 80. As you may remember from Chapter 2, the default site was disabled, and port 80 is used by the Web Site SharePoint-80 instead.

Launch Internet Information Services (IIS) Manager, and expand the Web Sites folder. You'll see the SharePoint-80 Web Site. Click the Basic Settings action (on the right pane) to see the directory for the site. Mine is as follows:

```
C:\Inetpub\wwwroot\wss\VirtualDirectories\80\
```

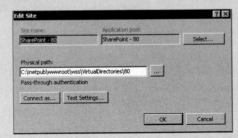

Copy your website to this location. Keep it in its own folder (my example uses Sales for the folder).

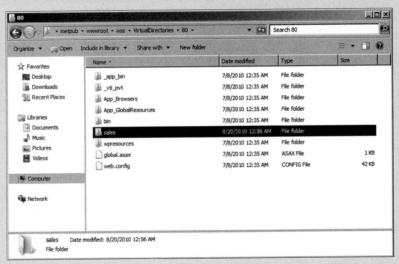

In this case, you'll have a Sales folder containing your website files (HTML, images, and so on). This example has only one file, `default.htm`.

For IIS to know that the new path is there, you may need to restart it. From the command prompt, enter the following:

```
iisreset /noforce
```

This will restart IIS, and `http://spf2/sales/` will lead to the static `default.htm` file. It will not go to SharePoint.

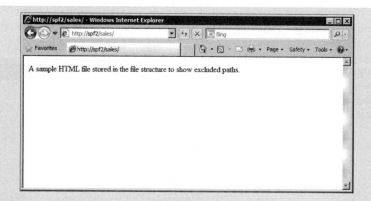

A sample HTML file stored in the file structure to show excluded paths.

Keep in mind that everything that is hosted this way uses the same IIS Web Site, which is called SharePoint-80 in this case and is used by SharePoint. Therefore, any IIS settings you have for the web application, such as Authentication (allowing or disallowing anonymous access) will also apply to this excluded path. If you want to change these settings just for the excluded path, you'll need to create a new IIS website for the path and not use one of SharePoint's.

Service Connections

This button takes you to a simple page (see Figure 10.43) that gives you the option to enable or disable access to any available service application. These are the same settings you saw during the creation process. You can find more information on service applications in Chapter 11.

Authentication Providers

Authentication providers are set by zone—which will be covered in the "Alternate Access Mapping" section. For each zone, you can quickly see what kind of authentication mode you have configured (see Figure 10.44).

This is also a good way to double-check what mode of authentication you selected for a new web application if you have forgotten—if you chose claims-based, it will say so here. If you chose classic mode, it will be shown here as "Windows."

FIGURE 10.43
Service
connections

FIGURE 10.44
Authentication
providers by zone

Then, for each zone, if you click its name, you can edit the settings (the same ones you saw during creation—enabling anonymous, setting up Windows authentication to use NTLM, and so on. See Figure 10.45.

FIGURE 10.45
Authentication settings for the default zone

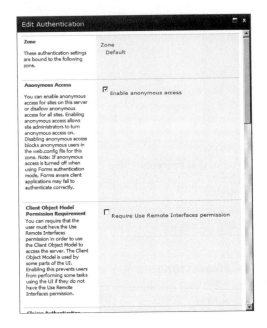

Self-Service Site Creation

With all these different sites and all the possible templates and site definitions, you could easily find yourself doing nothing all day but creating the following new subsites: new meetings, new blogs, new document workspaces, and so on. You might be tempted to give more users Create Subsites permissions so they can create their own subsites. Of course, then you'll have the nightmare of all these subsites popping up with no organization, and you'll need to deal with them (keep in mind that each subsite eats into the site collection's storage quota, if there is one).

As an alternative to letting your users create subsites on your main site collection, you can enable self-service site creation. Self-service site creation allows users (and not just farm administrators) to create their own site collections. Then you can more easily apply a storage quota to each of their site collections (they'll probably only ever use the top-level site) and apply the automated deletion feature (under Site Use Confirmation And Deletion) that can be used to delete unused site collections.

DOES ALLOWING USERS TO CREATE SITE COLLECTIONS GIVE YOU CHILLS?

Of course, giving users the right to create their own site collections (instead of creating subsites) presents its own problems. Site collections are easier to manage from Central Administration, but they are fully functional site collections, with a top-level site, the capacity to have many subsites of all kinds, and their own users and permissions. So, there is a trade-off: ease of management versus giving users carte blanche over their own collection of sites.

Enabling Self-Service Site Creation

The web application in this case was created so that users could have their own blogs, complete with a root site collection (this site collection becomes important when self-service site creation is enabled). There are basically two ways of going about allowing users to create their own blog site: allow them to create subsites in one site collection or enable self-service site creation. They both have their pros and cons.

If you allow users to create subsites in a site collection, they can create as many as they want there. That's because when you enable the permission, there is no inherent limit to how many they can create. But they at least can only overload one site collection.

On the plus side, that one site collection with all the subsites is pretty easy to back up and restore. Also, users don't need to know how to manage their own security if they simply inherit the settings from the parent site. They also can use any custom templates you may have added to the site collection. On the other hand, if you have users abusing the permission to create subsites, you will have to track down the subsites they create and delete them manually. Also, the site collection quota will affect all the subsites in the collection, meaning that one person's overloaded subsite can lock the site collection for everyone.

If you enable self-service site creation, yes, the users can create their own site collections (with their own users and security). In fact, they can create as many as they want (once enabled, there is no way to limit how many site collections the users can create), and that's pretty powerful. But you can also set up usage notification and automatic deletion, which will automate the deletion process, freeing you from having to hunt down and delete unused site collections yourself. Also, each site collection will have its own storage quota, so no one will be locking anyone else's sites with their data overload (they will be limited by the quota as well). And keep in mind that they will have to set up their own users and security for this site collection as well (which gets tiresome after a while).

Because users are permitted to have considerable independence in what they add to their blogs in this scenario, we are going to enable self-service site creation for this web application. But in addition, we will make the users responsible for regularly indicating that their site is being used. If they don't respond quickly enough, the site collection triggering the confirmation notice will be deleted.

Self-service site creation is a web application-wide setting configured in Central Administration under Application Management ➤ Site Collections. Once there, click the Configure Self-Service Site Creation link to go to the page shown in Figure 10.46. Here you can enable self-service site creation for a particular web application. (It is also possible to see these settings under Application Management ➤ Manage Web Applications. Simply click the web application and click the Self Service Site Creation button in the ribbon.) When it is enabled, all permission levels with the Self-Service Site Creation permission set (by default, everyone but Site Visitor members) allow users to create their own site collections. There is also an option to require a secondary contact for the site collections created in this fashion. Generally, this is a good idea if you're planning on enabling site use notifications, in case the primary administrator is unavailable to receive notifications for some reason.

Go ahead and enable self-service site creation, making sure to check the box for a secondary contact. Click OK.

Creating a self-service site creation site collection is a little different from creating a site collection from Central Administration. With self-service site creation enabled, users without access to Central Administration can create site collections. In addition, during the creation process, the users will not get to choose their path or their storage quota. The default managed path and storage quota set at the Central Administration level will be applied for them.

FIGURE 10.46
Self-Service Site
Collection Man-
agement page

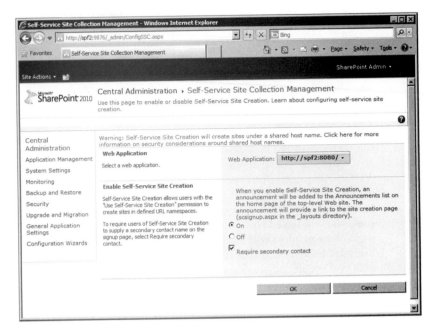

Whoever creates a self-service site collection is by default the owner of the site collection, and they can add, edit, and remove other people, groups, permissions, permission levels, subsites, and all site content. However, they still do not have any administrative rights to the original, main parent site or access to Central Administration. They're only a big fish in their own small pond. But they are still big enough to impact storage as they add to their site collections and then build up activity as the people they add join them there. It is important to regularly monitor usage to see where growth is happening. Keep in mind that self-service site creation gives users the opportunity to create a site collection of their very own, but it doesn't limit them to just one.

When enabling self-service site creation, you will want to consider setting some limits in order to manage the possible storage load that all of those user site collections could pose on whatever server is hosting the web application's data. The first thing is to place a default storage quota on your web application for all newly created site collections. We just created a new web application (http://spf2:8080) and set the storage quota on creation, so that's done. If you need to add a default storage quota to an existing site, the setting is found under General Settings.

The other key settings to consider are for automatic deletion and usage notifications under Site Use Confirmation And Deletion. These settings are shown in Figure 10.47. A lot of users will create new site collections, use them once, and leave them to linger forever. You can prevent this by enabling automatic deletion, as covered earlier in the chapter.

If you enable autodeletion, you are strongly encouraged to require a secondary administrative contact for site collection creation. The last thing you want is to have a site collection deleted because the one person getting the email notifications is on vacation. In my example, I'm going to force notification but not enable auto-delete at this point. If it looks like the self-service site creation is being abused, I will come back and enable it.

FIGURE 10.47
Enabling site
use confirmation
and deletion

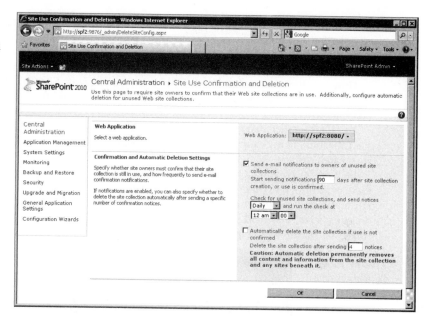

CREATING A SELF-SERVICE SITE COLLECTION

When self-service site creation is enabled, a new announcement will appear in the Announcements list on the top-level site of your root site collection. This announcement contains a link to create a new site collection (see Figure 10.48), starting with the top-level site. This is the *only* way users can use self-service site creation, so don't delete this announcement! In fact, it's recommended you add the Announcements List Web part to the home page of the top-level site. (You can find details on adding a List View web part in Chapter 5.)

If needed, you can also add the link provided in the announcement to the Links web part, top link bar, or Quick Launch bar (detailed in Chapter 9).

FIGURE 10.48
The self-service
announcement

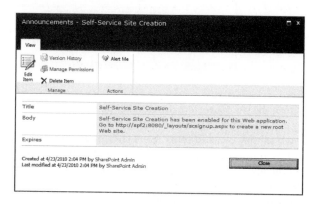

Clicking this link takes the user to a modified New SharePoint Site page. Ironically, it does not take the user to the Create Site Collection page. If you notice, in the address bar, the page is `scsignup.aspx`, which means it is in fact the site collection sign-up page and not going to just create a new subsite.

However, the page is almost exactly like any other Create Site Collection page, except there is no option to choose a site quota or specify the owner (because the person creating it is by definition the owner).

You'll also notice that you have the option to pick in which managed path to place the new site collection. In my example, Basil is going to create his blog in the blogs/sales managed path we created earlier.

Because it's creating a new site collection (not just a SharePoint site as the page title suggests), there is no option to inherit permissions or navigation; instead, there is a new section to assign any additional site administrators. If you configured self-service site creation to require a secondary contact, this field must have at least one person listed in order to be able to create the site collection (as shown in Figure 10.49).

FIGURE 10.49
Second administrative contact

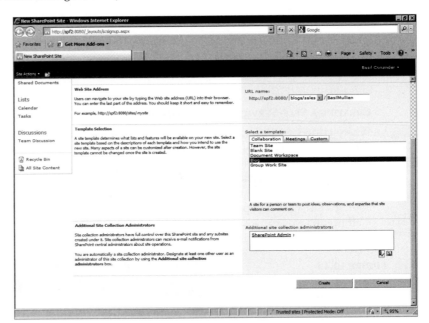

Once the site is created, it will take the user to the Set Up Groups For This Site page, where they can quickly add users to the default SharePoint groups for their site (Figure 10.50). Keep in mind that they can add other users later under Site Permissions or People And Groups in Site Settings, if they don't do so here. Once that's done, the site is fully created and can be accessed from the main URL. No link to it is created on the first site collection site; if you want a link there, you'll need to add one manually.

As a matter of fact, remember that site collections are islands; they don't have convenient links to other sites or site collections outside of themselves. You may want to consider configuring the Portal Connection setting in the top-level site of any new site collection to link to the Personal Blogs site collection so the users can get back to the site collection they started from.

Once you've finished setting up the groups, click **OK** to go to the top-level site of the new site collection (Figure 10.51).

FIGURE 10.50
Set Up Groups For
This Site page

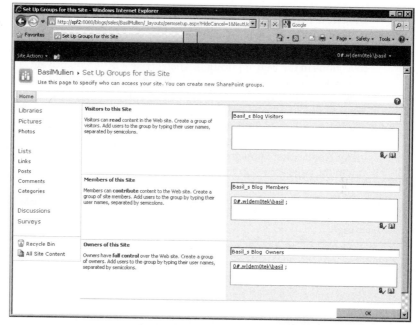

FIGURE 10.51
The new
self-service
site collection

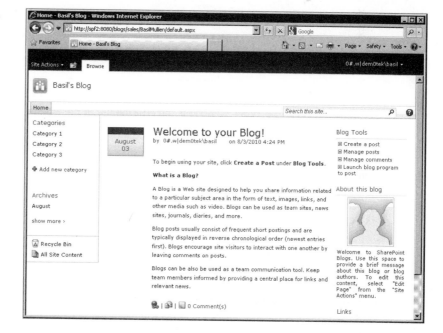

Keep in mind that the user will be the owner of the site collection, where there are a lot of configuration settings available. Some training might be in order.

Blocked File Types

By default, SharePoint blocks the upload of several file types based on the file extension. The list of blocked file types is set at the web application level. You can block all *.exe files for all site collections in the web application. Then create a different, private "IT tech team" web application, where having a library of common executable tools would be handy, so you permit .exe files. You can also restrict a web application so that it doesn't permit media files (such as .mpg, .mov, or.wmv files) to be uploaded. The sky is the limit as far as restricting file types. This is another reason web applications are security boundaries.

Blocked file types are set in Central Administration on the Manage Web Applications page under Application Management. Clicking the Blocked File Types button on the ribbon will take you to the page shown in Figure 10.52.

FIGURE 10.52
The Blocked File Types page

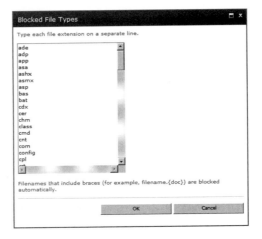

On the Blocked File Types page, you can edit the list of file extensions to block. First make sure you're editing the correct web application. If you need to make changes to all the web applications, you'll need to edit the list for each one. You can permit previously blocked file extensions by simply removing them from the list, and you can block new file extensions by adding them to the list (note that you add only the characters for the extension, not the period).

SharePoint doesn't check a file beyond the extension; therefore, if a user changes a blocked extension to a permitted extension, they'll be able to upload the file. For example, someone could take **evilhack.exe**, rename it evilhack.doc, and successfully upload it to a document library.

User Permissions

As you know, permissions in SharePoint are applied to a site or site collection using permission levels—typically Read, Contribute, Design, and Full Control. Then individual users or groups are assigned these permission levels.

A permission level is actually a collection of separate permissions, discussed in detail in Chapter 12. There are times when you don't want a particular permission to be available to *any* permission level for the web application. (For example, you may want to remove the permission

Add and Customize Pages from the web application so that even site owners, designers, or other contributors can't get this permission—it's just not available for any permission level in any site collection within the web application.)

When you do need to disable individual user permissions for the web application, select the web application on the Manage Web Applications page, and click the User Permissions button. You'll see the page shown in Figure 10.53.

FIGURE 10.53

The User Permissions page

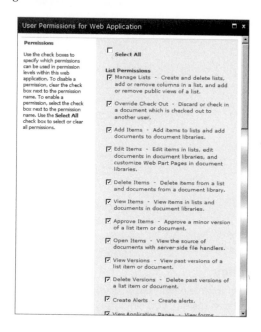

When you uncheck a permission, it is removed from the web application and no longer shows up as part of any permission level, not even Full Control.

Web Part Security

Another way you can lock down individual web applications is by using the Web Application Web Part Security button on the ribbon. It displays the Security For Web Part Pages page, shown in Figure 10.54.

This has three settings, each with two options: Allow or Prevent.

Web Part Connection   Controls the ability to have web parts connect to other web parts. As discussed in Chapter 5, this is a powerful and useful ability. It is enabled (Allow) by default. Web part connections can cause security filtering issues with search (when you connect a secure list to one that isn't so secure, secure items can show up in search results where they shouldn't), so in some situations it might be important not to allow them.

Online Web Part Gallery   Backward-compatible with custom online galleries. It once permitted users to access Microsoft's online web part gallery when they have a web part page in edit mode, so they can download and add web parts to their pages. That Microsoft online web gallery no longer exists, but there are some companies that require this setting. This is enabled (Allow) by default.

Scriptable Web Parts   Can be added or edited by contributors (users with contribute permissions) when this is enabled, so web parts with scripts can be applied and modified on web part pages. This is disabled (Prevent) by default. If you want your contributors to be able to work with content editor web parts, this setting must be enabled.

FIGURE 10.54
The Security
For Web Part
Pages page

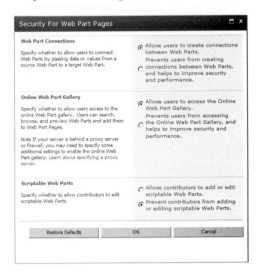

User Policy

If you want to give particular user(s) explicit rights to the entire web application (and all the site collections inside), you can apply them here. No matter what the permissions are on an individual site collection, site, or even list item, this user would have certain rights applied at the web application level. Typically this is used for service accounts (such as the search indexer), but it can be used for any other account (for example, to allow the user to bypass the List View Threshold discussed earlier).

1. To give a user access to the entire web application, in the Manage Web Applications page, select the web application (for example, `http://spf2:8080`), and click the **User Policy button** in the ribbon. This takes you to the page shown in Figure 10.55.

FIGURE 10.55
The Policy For Web
Application page

Here you can see the current user policies configured for the web application. Let's create a new policy giving saffron the policy Full Control to the web application, so no matter what happens to the site collections (such as users with self-service site collections refusing to add that account to any of their groups), the saffron user can always log in and make changes anyway.

2. First click **Add Users** to add a new user. This opens the first of the Add Users pages. You can apply the policy to an individual zone (more on zones to come) or to all zones (which is the most common use). Once you've picked the zone(s), click **Next**. To follow my example, leave it applied to all zones.

This takes you to the second Add Users page (Figure 10.56), where you can choose the user(s) you want to add (**saffron** in my example) and assign one or more of the following permission policy levels to the user:

Full Control   Access to all permissions

Full Read   Can read everything but cannot edit/delete/add anything

Deny Write   Cannot write anything

Deny All   No access at all

WHAT'S WITH THE I:0#.W|?

You may notice that some of your usernames are displayed as i:0#.W|domainname\username. This weird string appears to be appended by SharePoint whenever claims-based authentication is used, presumably to identify that authentication method. So if you see "i:0#.W|" as a prefix to your domain name, you can assume claims-based authentication is in use. I hope Microsoft will remove or hide this code in a future update to SharePoint Foundation.

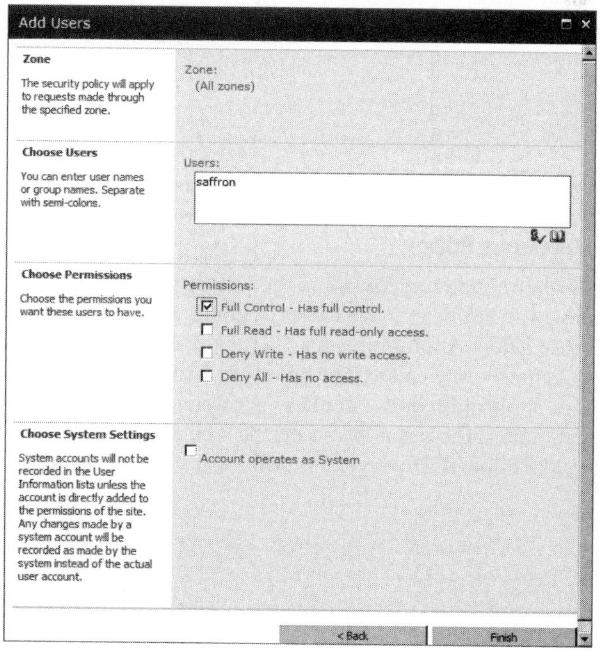

FIGURE 10.56
The Add
Users page

3. You can apply more than one permission policy level to the same user—Full Control will overwrite Full Read (if both are selected), but the Deny options will overwrite both Full Control and Full Read. So, giving someone Full Control and Deny Write will give them all the permissions except anything blocked by Deny Write. Typically you'll pick only one of these permission policy levels. I'm giving Saffron the **Full Control** policy.

4. The final option is to set this account to operate as System—this places the user in "stealth" mode—they won't show up as themselves if they post anything, and any changes or modifications are recorded as coming from a system account. Typically reserved for the service accounts, this can also be applied to actual user accounts, but in this case I'm going to leave it unchecked.

Now, with a user policy for the entire web application in place, Saffron can access any site collections in that web application, like the self-service site creation one used by Basil, even if he chose not to add her account to one of his site groups. As you can see in Figure 10.57, Saffron is logged into Basil's blog site and on the site permissions page, without being added to the site.

FIGURE 10.57
User policy user account accessing a site collection

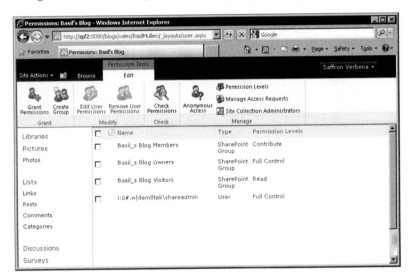

Anonymous Policy

One feature you can control at the web application level is anonymous access. When creating a new web application (or extending one, as detailed in "Alternate Access Mapping"), you can choose Allow Anonymous for the new web application. This selection does not turn anonymous access for the site collections on or off; it merely permits that option for each site collection. If a web application does not allow anonymous access, no enclosed site collection can have it. If anonymous access is allowed on the web application, then the enclosed site collections have the *option* to allow it. However, it's still turned off by default.

ADDING ANONYMOUS ACCESS TO AN EXISTING WEB APPLICATION

If you don't select the Allow Anonymous Access option while creating a web application, you can enable it later. Go to Central Administration ➢ Application Management ➢ Manage Web Applications. Choose the web application, and click the Authentication Providers button.

Then click the zone (based on the URL the users use to get to the web application's contents) on which you want to allow anonymous access. (Zones are discussed in the "Alternate Access Mapping" section. For now, we have only the Default zone.) When you click the zone, you will be taken to the Edit Authentication page.

Select the Enable Anonymous Access box and click Save to permit anonymous access for this web application.

ANONYMOUS ACCESS RESTRICTIONS

When you are in the Manage Web Applications page, if you select a web application, you can click the Anonymous Policy button to display the Anonymous Access Restrictions page (Figure 10.58) and apply restrictions to anonymous access.

FIGURE 10.58
The Anonymous Access Restrictions page

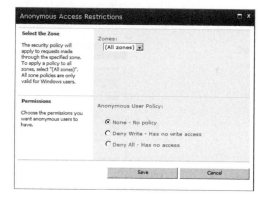

These settings override any settings for anonymous access applied at the site collection (or lower) level. So, you can force any anonymous access for the entire web application to Deny Write or Deny All, regardless of what the site administrator of the enclosed site collection does (none means no restrictions are set from this level). Deny All is the equivalent of disabling anonymous access completely on the Authentication Providers page, except that it leaves anonymous access as a configurable option in the site collections—so the individual site collections can have anonymous access permissions configured, but they're all disabled when this restriction is in place.

This approach is handy if you need to disable all anonymous access on a web application temporarily (without having to redo all the permissions on each site collection).

ENABLING ANONYMOUS ACCESS ON A SITE COLLECTION

As you may recall, you allowed anonymous access when you created the blogging web application. Now it's time to turn it on at the site collection level. Browse to your new web application, and log in as the site administrator (my example uses `http://spf2:8080`, and the login is `dem0tek\shareadmin`) to reach the top-level site. If you go to Site Permissions (under the Site Actions menu), you will be taken back to the familiar Permissions page. On the ribbon you will see a new option, Anonymous Access (Figure 10.59, top). Compare this to the Settings menu for a site collection in a web application that does not permit anonymous access, such as the main, Company Site on `http://spf2` (Figure 10.59, bottom).

FIGURE 10.59
Site Permissions on (top) a web application that allows anonymous access; (bottom) a web application that does not allow anonymous access

Go ahead and look at the Anonymous Access settings for the site collection. Click the button in the ribbon to go to the Anonymous Access page (shown in Figure 10.60).

FIGURE 10.60
The Anonymous Access page

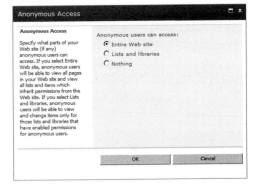

You have three options for how you want this site collection (remember, this is at the site collection level) to treat anonymous users. You can grant anonymous users access to the following:

Entire Web Site   Anonymous users have access to the entire site collection (because this is being applied at the top-level site). They can browse and read all pages, lists, and libraries.

My example grants this anonymous access level for the Personal Blogs top-level site. So, in this demonstration, anyone can view the entire site collection without having to first provide a username and password.

Lists and Libraries   With this setting, anonymous access is available to be enabled per list or library but is not set to allow access to any pages. You must manually edit the permissions on whatever list or library you want to grant anonymous access. And even then anonymous users will have to browse directly to the list or library to see it because they will not be allowed elsewhere in the site.

Nothing   No anonymous access is permitted. This is the default.

When anonymous access is granted by using the Entire Web Site setting, the anonymous user is given the Limited Access permission level by default (meaning they can only read and not write). Therefore, choosing Entire Web Site will not give them full control but will merely allow anonymous users to have limited access to view the entire site collection. You can find more information about permission levels in Chapter 12.

If you set anonymous access to allow access to the entire site, a visiting user does not need to log in to see the site (Figure 10.61). The Account menu (that usually indicates the logged-in user's name) is replaced with a Sign In link. This allows users to opt to log in if they want to contribute to the site. Of course, people who do not have a valid user account to the site will not be able to log in. Notice that for the Team Site template, a Publish ribbon tab appears for anonymous users. This is triggered because of the wiki home page but is not useful for the anonymous user because all settings are grayed out. The Site Actions menu is available, but the only option available is to see All Site Content.

FIGURE 10.61
A site with anonymous access enabled

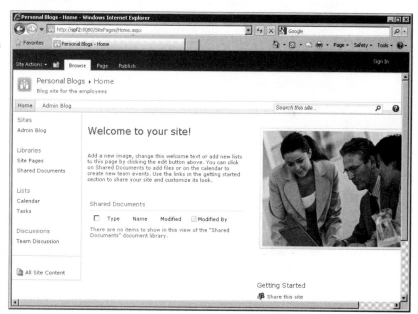

EDITING ANONYMOUS USER PERMISSIONS ON A LIST OR LIBRARY

To enable anonymous access on a site collection, you have two options: List And Libraries or Entire Site. As soon as you select Entire Site, anonymous users can view (and only view) the entire site. But if you choose the Lists And Libraries option, they are not given limited access to the entire site; their access is to the entire site by default still *None*, but you can go to the individual lists or libraries and explicitly set permissions for anonymous users there. They would have to browse directly to those lists or libraries to access them, but it would work and not violate the security of the rest of the site.

At this point, all visitors can view all content on the site, but they cannot contribute. That's basically good; we don't want visitors adding posts, but we do want them to be able to comment. So, let's give the anonymous users the right to add comments to the admin blog. All comments will be stored in the Comments list.

1. Browse to your admin blog (at `http://spf2:8080/adminblog/` in my example), and navigate to the Comments list, which can be found under All Site Content on the Quick Launch bar. (If you are not using a blog template for your site, any list will do.)

2. Once on the list, click the **List Settings** button on the ribbon (under the List Tools toolset, List tab). On the List Settings page, click **Permissions** for this list. (List settings are fully covered in Chapter 6, and permissions are covered in more detail in Chapter 12.)

3. Because the list inherits permissions from the parent site (so that everyone can read but anonymous can't contribute), you need to break that inheritance so you can set custom permissions for the list. Click the **Stop Inheriting Permissions** button in the ribbon.

4. A dialog box will remind you that this breaks inheritance. Click **OK**.

   The Permissions: Comments page will now show the unique permissions for this list. (See Figure 10.62.)

5. Click **Anonymous Access** on the ribbon bar.

FIGURE 10.62
List permissions

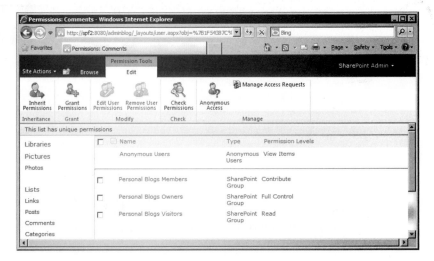

On this page (shown in Figure 10.63), you can adjust the rights of an anonymous user on the selected particular list. The following permissions are available:

Add Items   The ability to add a new item to the list or to add a new document to a library (in this example, the ability to add a new comment)

Edit Items   The ability to edit an existing item, such as an existing comment, in the list or library

Delete Items   The ability to delete an existing item

View Items   The ability to view items in the list

FIGURE 10.63
Changing anonymous access

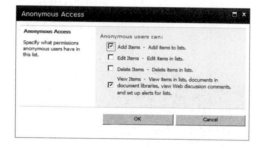

When you selected Entire Web Site for the Anonymous Access settings at the site collection level, the server gave anonymous users the View Item permission, so it will be already checked here. If you set the anonymous access for the site collection to Lists And Libraries, none of these will be checked.

6. For the comments, you'll want to give anonymous users rights Add Items and View Items (which they currently already have), but not Edit or Delete, because you don't want people to edit or delete other people's comments. Since they are all anonymous, SharePoint can't keep track of which anonymous user wrote what, so it's best they don't edit anything. Check the **Add Items** box, and click **OK**.

You should now have a personal blogs site, with an admin blogs subsite, that allows anonymous access. Open a new browser window and go to http://spf2:8080. You should be able to see the site without having to log in. As you saw earlier, the button at the top right no longer shows your name, but it provides you with the Sign In option.

For this example, let's see whether we can add a comment to the blog. Browse to the admin blog (or whatever you named your subsite) and see whether you can add a list item to the Comments list. In my case, I am going to add a comment to the default post "Welcome to your Blog." To do that, click the Admin Blog link, and click the Comments link at the bottom of the post. You'll be taken to the Comments list for that post. See Figure 10.64.

You can immediately tell whether anonymous users are permitted to create comments. The Add Comment fields will be available at the bottom of the page. That link does not appear if you don't have permission to add a comment. Go ahead and add a comment, and click Submit Comment. The new comment will be posted with no username listed (as you can see with my sample mystery comment in Figure 10.65).

FIGURE 10.64
The Comments list

FIGURE 10.65
An anonymous
comment is
posted.

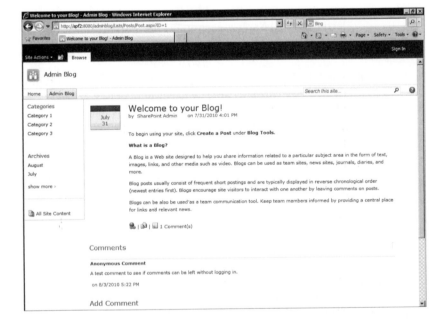

As always, think carefully before enabling anonymous access. Even though this web application isn't currently accessible from outside your network, someone could still add inappropriate comments.

Permission Policy

Web applications can also have custom permission policies. These are essentially permission levels created to be applied at the web application level and affect all site collections contained therein. We applied a permission policy in the "User Policies" section, giving Saffron the Full Control policy to access all site collections in the web application with Full Control permissions. Keep in mind that a permission policy (or permission level for site collections) is a combination of individual permissions, such as View, Delete, and Edit Items. Permission policies are different from permission levels because they have the option to explicitly allow or deny a permission, and they have two default policies premade.

Going back to Central Administration, navigate to the Manage Web Applications page again (under Application Management). Select the SharePoint-8080 web application, and click the Permission Policy button in the ribbon to display the window shown in Figure 10.66.

FIGURE 10.66

Manage Permission Policy Levels page

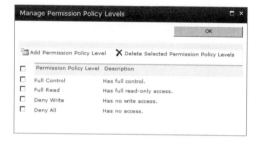

Here you can manage permission policy levels—by adding, editing, and deleting them. Let's take a closer look at the Full Control policy level. Click the name of the policy to edit it.

This opens the Edit Permission Policy Level window (see Figure 10.67), which is an actual browser window (basically using the old interface from WSS 3.0), not a form box. Editing a permission policy level gives you a couple of options.

Web Application   This section cannot be changed; it's just here to remind you of what web application is being edited (and is left over from the WSS 3.0 interface).

Name and Description   Here you can edit the name and description for the policy level.

Site Collection Permissions   You can have the permission policy level grant either Site Collection Administrator rights or Site Collection Auditor rights. As you know, site collection administrators have complete control over the site collection. Site auditors have full Read access to the entire site collection. So, these grant one or both of the settings to the permission policy level, granting that permission to every site collection in the web application.

Permissions   Figure 10.67 shows this page, where you can set the individual permissions for this policy level. Unlike customizing permission levels, when you set up a permission policy level, you also have the option to explicitly deny a permission—so even if a site collection administrator grants the user that permission explicitly, it's still blocked by the permission policy level.

For example, you can explicitly deny the Create Alerts permission for a particular user or group. So even if a site collection administrator grants them the Create Alerts permission, they will still be unable to create alerts. Make sure you document any changes made to the policies, particularly when denying a permission to aid future troubleshooting.

FIGURE 10.67
Permission policy
levels: permissions

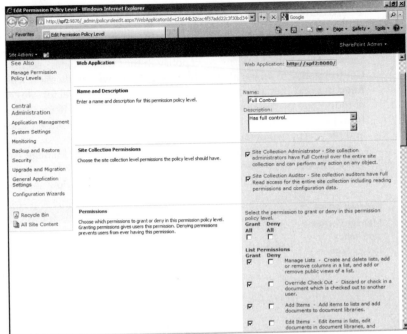

BEWARE THE DENY

Keep in mind that if you deny the Create Alert permission, nothing at the user level indicates that they have been denied until creating an alert just doesn't work. Whenever you explicitly deny any permissions, you may want to log into a site collection in the affected web application with a standard user account and see what it breaks before committing to the change.

Host Headers

Once you've started building multiple web applications on your server, you'll quickly realize that having the same URL, but different port numbers for all those web applications can be confusing. You also might be thinking about how great it would be if you could host websites with completely different URLs, especially if you want your server to be referred to by something other than its internal network server name. Host headers, an IIS feature that SharePoint is more than happy to take advantage of, can help organize the confusion.

Host headers allow you to map a web application to a custom URL. For example, rather than creating a web application with the URL http://spf2:27445/, you could set it to the URL http://tech/ or the live, external DNS name http://tech.dem0tek.com/. The really nice thing is that both of these URLs can run on port 80 rather than a custom port, which simplifies browser use. Because 80 is the default port for HTTP, the user won't need to specify a port in their browser's address bar, just the URL.

UNIQUE IS BETTER THAN GOOD; IT'S NECESSARY

Keep in mind that each IIS Web Site (and therefore each web application) must be completely unique in the way it identifies itself so IIS can pass it the correct user requests. Thus, the Web Site must have a unique URL or a custom port. Above all, the Web Site must be uniquely identifiable by IIS in order to work.

And, if you are working with host headers, the IIS server will never get the request for that URL if DNS does not have a record for it that resolves to that server's address. If the URL is used on the Internet, that domain should be registered to your company and listed on a DNS or *name* server on the Internet (in addition to having a record in the internal DNS).

Host headers should be set when a web application is created or extended. Take the following steps to try out this feature:

1. Create a new web application (Central Administration ➢ Application Management ➢ Manage Web Applications ➢ New).

2. For the New IIS Web Site, SharePoint will suggest a random port, so change the suggested port back to **80** and enter the URL to which you want the web application to respond in the Host Header field. See Figure 10.68 for my example.

3. Configure the other sections as you would any new web application: Security, Application Pool, Database, Search, and so on. Then click OK.

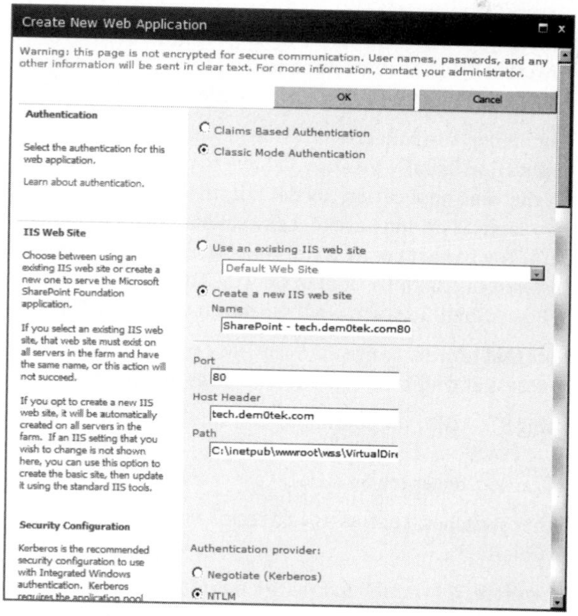

FIGURE 10.68
Setting a host header in the Create New Web Application page

After the web application is generated, you'll need to create the initial site collection (my example is *techsite* to keep with the tech theme) just as we did earlier in this chapter. Keep in mind that in order for users to successfully browse to this URL, they'll need to be able to resolve it in DNS to the IP address of your SharePoint server (so make certain that there is a record in DNS that resolves to the server's IP). Once everything is created and IIS has been reset, you'll be able to see the host header information in IIS.

Open Internet Information Services (IIS) Manager, and browse to Web Sites in the tree pane. Then in the Actions pane, click the Bindings link. The default port of 80 will be listed for the site, and it will show the host header URL, as shown in Figure 10.69.

FIGURE 10.69
The host header of the new Web Site in IIS

Of course, browsing to the new URL (in my case `http://tech.dem0tek.com`) will take you to the new site.

SITE COLLECTIONS AND HOST HEADERS

Officially, you need to create a new web application to use a host header; however, STSADM (and PowerShell) has an undocumented feature (or should we say, *underdocumented*) that lets you create a new site collection using a host header.

Remember, site collections reside in web applications, and adding a new site collection to the web application usually means you have to place the new site collection in one of the managed paths for that web application (by default, the /sites/ path). However, you can add a site collection to a web application and have that site collection use its own host header, instead of using the managed path. You cannot create a site collection that uses a host header address (which Microsoft calls a *host-named* site collection) in Central Administration; it can be done only at the command line or in PowerShell. To start, we'll see how it works in STSADM.

Note that in order to use the STSADM command, you need to be logged in as a user with permission to access and edit the content databases in SQL Server.

Using STSADM, the command to create a new site collection normally is as follows:

```
STSADM -o createsite -url http://server/sites/newsite -owneremail name@domain
.com -ownerlogin DOMAIN\username
```

Other switches, such as `-sitetemplate` to prespecify the top-level site's template, are covered in Chapter 14.

Therefore, if I wanted to create a new site called `http://spf2/sites/camper` without using a host header and using the `http://spf2` web application with *shareadmin* as the owner, I would use the following command:

```
STSADM -o createsite -url http://spf2/sites/camper -owneremail shareadmin@
dem0tek.com -ownerlogin dem0tek\shareadmin
```

If you go to that site in your browser, you'll be asked to choose the template you want to use and enter some users and groups (just as you did with self-service site creation). After you enter the users and groups, you'll be taken to the new site, where you'll see the normal, expected URL in the address bar.

You can create the same site using a host header for the site collection itself (instead of for the web application). It's still in the `http://spf2` web application and must abide by that web application's settings; however, the URL would be different, such as `http://camper.dem0tek.lcl` in my example, rather than `http://sp2/sites/camper`. Think of it as essentially *masking* the real normal web application–based address of the site collection with the host header.

The command for this would be the following:

```
STSADM -o createsite -url http://camper.dem0tek.lcl -owneremail shareadmin@
dem0tek.com -ownerlogin dem0tek\shareadmin -hhurl http://spf2
```

You'll notice two changes. The `-url` switch displays the desired host header URL (rather than the web application's managed path), and the `-hhurl` switch points to the web application in which you want to create the site collection.

Once again, if you browse to `http://camper.demotek.lcl`, you'll be prompted to choose a site template and add users and groups. Then you'll be taken to the new site, displayed with the nice host header URL in the address bar.

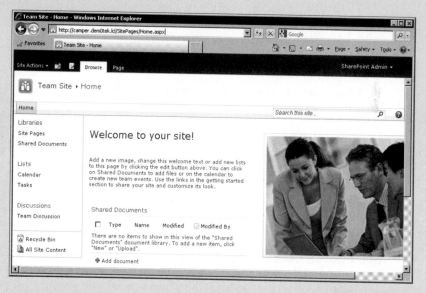

You can do the same thing in the SharePoint Management shell (or PowerShell console).

First make sure the account you are logged in with has the correct permissions to use PowerShell (you need to be a farm administrator, as well as owner of both the configuration database for the farm and the content database where the site collection is located). See Chapter 14 for details.

Then, to create the site collection, you can use the following command:

```
New-SPSite http://camper.dem0tek.lcl -OwnerAlias "dem0tek\shareadmin"
-HostHeaderWebApplication http://spf2
```

Keep in mind that this new site collection is in an existing web application, so you want to do this only if you want the site collection to be constrained by the web application settings (such as anonymous access, user permissions, custom port number, and so on). As a last caveat, also note that SSL will not work for a host header site collection unless it is using a wildcard certificate and the host header is in the same domain. Because site collection host headers are not listed in Alternate Access Mapping, searches may also return unexpected links in query results. Despite these shortcomings, the option to use site collections with their own host headers is here if you need it.

Alternate Access Mapping

With the creation of multiple web applications, multiple sites, host headers, and a complex SharePoint deployment, there will come a time when you want to start providing access to SharePoint sites from multiple places and for multiple people. At the very least, you might want to open your server to outside access, opening a port in your firewall and forwarding it to the SharePoint server. Of course, no one in the outside world is going to browse to your server using the URL http://spf2/ or http://spf2.dem0tek.1cl. They're going to use a real address, such as http://blogs.dem0tek.com. You know how to make a new web application with this URL, but what about adding the URL to an existing web application? This is done through alternate access mapping.

Alternate access mapping lets you do the following:

◆ Map a new URL to an existing web application

◆ Send a URL other than the one received back to the client browser

◆ Allow different security policies, based on the URL, for a single web application's content (with zones and extended web applications)

◆ Provide access to a web application's content on a second port

To understand how alternate access mapping works, you first need to consider how SharePoint treats URLs. Fundamentally, a URL is how a user gets to a SharePoint site. The URL is also used by SharePoint to generate links on the page. A good example of this is with search results. The links in SharePoint aren't hard-coded in an HTML file somewhere; they're generated on the fly, just as SharePoint pages are. When you perform a search request on a SharePoint site and you get back some possible results, each result shows you a clickable link to that result's location. The links need to have the correct path to work. See Figure 10.70.

Notice that the result link has the site's path (http://spf2:8080/pathtoresult) in it. This link works great if the user can resolve the URL http://spf2:8080/, but it would be pretty useless if the user were connecting to the server from outside your firewall and couldn't resolve http://spf2:8080/. In that case, all those search result links would be dead.

SharePoint resolves this issue by using alternate access mapping, allowing each web application to have up to five different public URLs. That means that the same web application, with all the enclosed site collections, can be accessed from multiple URLs, and SharePoint is smart enough to use the corresponding public URL in all its internal links and paths, making them useful again. For example, the web application http://spf2:8080 could also respond to the URL http://blogs.dem0tek.com. As such, you would have two different URLs, both pointing at the same web application content.

To work with alternate access mapping, you need to be familiar with some terms:

Public URL   This is the URL that SharePoint displays in the address bar of the browser and in all the paths and links generated on the page.

Internal URL   This the URL that is presented to SharePoint during the request for a page. This is often, but not always, the same as the public URL that SharePoint sends back.

Zone   Each public URL for a web application is associated with a *zone*. Zones are just an easy way to keep track of which public URLs go to which internal URL. When you first create a web application, the URL used becomes the public URL for the Default zone. The other four zones are named Intranet, Internet, Custom, and Extranet. The different zones don't have any intrinsic differences. The names are just for clarity, and the zones can be used for whatever you like. Zones are also used to address extended web applications (actually, they're primarily used to address extended web applications). In other words, you can take an existing web application's content databases and make a new web application (essentially a new IIS Web Site) that points to those databases; this allows two different URLs to access the same data.

FIGURE 10.70
Search results
with links

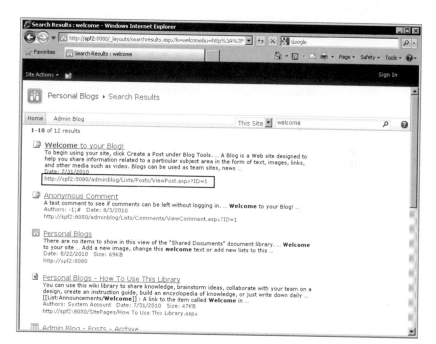

CREATING A NEW PUBLIC URL (BY EXTENDING A WEB APPLICATION)

You can create a new public URL by going to the Alternate Access Mappings page and typing one in order to associate it with an existing web application (and we will do that later). But that's not really the point. Public URLs are associated with zones because it is possible that you might want to offer a web application's contents to users who require different kinds of security, such as SSL or anonymous access. These kinds of users can be thought of as being in different zones.

The default zone users are those in the local office. Their web application doesn't need SSL, they may be allowed anonymous access (to read their co-workers' blogs), and using the server's computer name as the URL is fine. The intranet users could be the ones in adjoining buildings, maybe part of the campus, but not in the office; they should authenticate to access the site collections they are members of, and they need to use a URL that resolves outside of the office. The extranet could be the commuting users, accessing content over the Internet; they too need to use an external URL and authenticate to access their content, but they also need SSL to protect their transactions. Finally, Internet users could be customers or partners also accessing the web application's content over the Internet, while requiring anonymous access and SSL. To access the same data by a different URL but apply different security and access settings, you need to use different IIS Web Sites pointing to the same content databases. Then the users can access the same information but use different URLs, with different security applied. Zones can be used just to use different URLs to resolve to the same web application, but what they're really used for is extended web applications, whose addresses are zones and are used to access the same web application's content but use different URLs and other IIS Web Site settings (such as requiring SSL or allowing anonymous).

ANONYMOUS?

Notice that anonymous access is being offered to certain kinds of users depending on the zone they are using to access the same web application. That is why, even though anonymous access can be enabled at the web application level, it is additionally allowed or disallowed at the site collection level. Those site collections meant to contain private company data would never enable anonymous on any site, list, or library therein, despite the option being available depending on what URL accesses the site collections.

To create a new, public URL for accessing a web application using different security settings than the original, that web application needs to be extended to a different IIS Web Site. As you know from creating a new web application, the IIS Web Site determines the URL for the web application, either by setting a custom port for the main URL (such as `http://spf2:8080`) or by using a host header to give the web application a custom URL (such as `http://tech.dem0tek.com`). The IIS Web Site also determines which kind of authentication is to be used (NTLM, Kerberos, allowing anonymous access) and if SSL is going to be used.

Extending a web application creates a new IIS Web Site based on an existing web application's content. This new IIS Web Site uses the same application pool and the same content database as the existing web application. But extending a web application lets you add another URL and other IIS Web Site–based settings to access that content. This allows you to create a new public URL for the web application and adjust the security settings for that public URL without changing the existing security settings for your web application's default public URL.

For the example, we can take the blogging site collection, running in the web application `http://spf2:8080`, and extend it to the public URL of `blogs.dem0tek.com`, which, in this example, is accessible from the outside world through the firewall. While we're at it, we can set the new URL so that it doesn't permit anonymous access. This way, only people with login accounts (the company's employees) will be able to access the blogs from outside the firewall. The default, internal URL settings (for `http://spf2:8080`) will stay the same, and anonymous access will be permitted there.

DNS Is Still Critical

We're going to be doing a lot of work with new URLs, both public and internal. All of these URLs are still dependent on DNS to function. Make sure your DNS server can resolve any URL you create and it points the client to the SharePoint server. Remember that all URLs need to map to an IP address eventually, and they need DNS to do that.

To extend a web application, follow these steps:

1. To extend a web application in Central Administration, click the **Manage Web Applications** link in the Application Management category.

2. Choose the web application you want to extend (my example is `http://spf2:8080`), and click the **Extend** button in the ribbon. This will take you to the Extend Web Application To Another IIS Web Site page. See Figure 10.71.

FIGURE 10.71

The Extend Web Application To Another IIS Web Site page

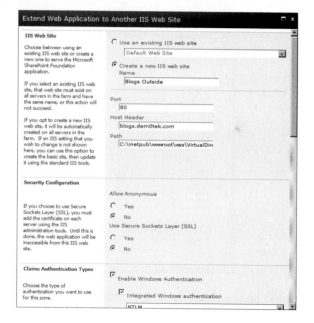

3. Under IIS Web Site, create a new IIS Web Site; mine is called **Blogs Outside** in the description. Assign it to port 80, and enter the URL you'd like it to have; my example is `blogs.dem0tek.com`, in the Host Header field.

4. Under Security Configuration, leave Allow Anonymous Access disabled, leave SSL disabled, and leave NTLM selected.

5. Leave the Sign In Page URL at the default.

6. Under Public URL, leave the new default (mine is `http://blogs.dem0tek.com:80`), and set the zone to **Internet**. You can set the zone to any of the four zones that have not

already been used. The *default* zone is being used by the main URL (`http://spf2:8080` in my example), so it's not an available choice. After you're done creating this extended web application, the *Internet* zone is no longer available should you ever choose to extend the existing web application again. Keep in mind that this means you can only have four extended web applications per web application.

7. Once you've configured the extended web application the way you like, click OK. SharePoint will extend the web application to the new IIS Web Site (no need to add any site collections). If you have DNS set up to point the URL to the server, browsing to it will show the same site, but with a new URL in the address bar and the corrected links and paths displayed on the page. So, performing the same search will provide the same results with the new URL. See Figure 10.72.

FIGURE 10.72
The same search with a new URL

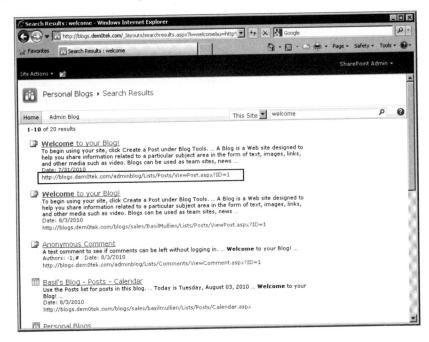

Unlike browsing to `http://spf2:8080`, using this new URL will require authentication because anonymous access was disabled for the new IIS Web Site.

CHANGES TO IIS

You can see what changes occurred in IIS from extending a website by going into Internet Information Services (IIS) Manager and checking out the newly created Blogs Outside IIS Web Site.

Select the new IIS Web Site, and click Bindings in the Actions pane to verify that it is listening on port 80. This will also show the expected host header. Click Basic Settings to see that it is using the same application pool as the original IIS Web Site (SharePoint-8080). This means all traffic bound for this new IIS Web Site will be directed to the same content database as traffic bound for the original SharePoint-8080 Web Site. Clicking application pools on the left side of the IIS console, then selecting the SharePoint-8080 Application Pool, and clicking the View

Applications link under Actions in the Actions pane will list the new Web Site's root and layout paths, as shown in Figure 10.73.

FIGURE 10.73
Application pool changes

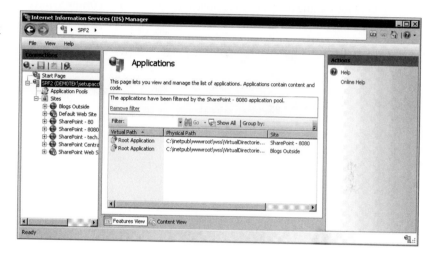

CHANGES TO ALTERNATE ACCESS MAPPINGS

Let's take a look at what SharePoint shows with this new public URL. Go to Central Administration's Application Management page, and under the Web Applications category, click Configure Alternate Access Mappings. This will take you to the page shown in Figure 10.74.

FIGURE 10.74
The Alternate Access Mappings page

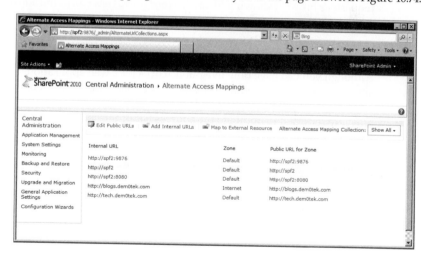

This page lists all the current internal URLs and public URLs in the SharePoint farm. Any incoming request is examined to see whether it matches one of the internal URLs. If it does, the server responds with the path shown in the corresponding public URL. If the request doesn't match an internal URL, the server responds with the public URL of the default zone on whatever port the request was received on.

If you click the Alternate Access Mapping Collection view menu (default view of this list is Show All), you can filter the view to display the mappings for a particular web application. Let's look at the original web application we extended (mine is `http://spf2:8080`), as shown in Figure 10.75.

FIGURE 10.75

The `http://spf2:8080` URLs

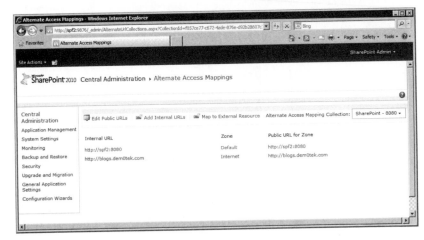

The original web application now has two internal URLs, one for the default zone and one for the Internet zone. Both mappings have an internal URL and a public URL. Therefore, any request sent to the server as `http://blogs.dem0tek.com` in my example will come back to the requester's browser showing `http://blogs.dem0tek.com` in the address bar and for all the paths and links on the page, which means they'll work fine through the firewall.

CREATING A NEW INTERNAL URL

Although you can have only five public URLs for a web application (one for each zone), it's possible to have several internal URLs for each public URL. Remember that internal URLs are the addresses that SharePoint responds to for a particular web application, and public URLs are what are returned to populate the address bar of the client's browser. To create a new internal URL for a public URL, click the Add Internal URLs link on the Action bar. This will take you to the page shown in Figure 10.76.

Make sure you've chosen the correct Alternate Access Mapping Collection option, which is the same thing as the web application, and then enter the new internal URL and choose the zone for this URL. The zone you choose needs to have a corresponding public URL (if you don't specify one, the new internal URL will be used to fill it).

My example uses a new internal URL called *blogs* for the default zone. As such, internal users who previously had to enter `http://spf2:8080` will only need to enter **blogs** (which is easier for them to remember) into their web browser to go to the Personal Blogs site collection. When they get there, it'll kick back the default zone's public URL of `http://sp2:8080`, which is fine because they can resolve that URL (if they were outside the firewall, this would be a problem). The new internal URL is displayed on the Alternate Access Mappings page (see Figure 10.77).

FIGURE 10.76
Creating a new
internal URL

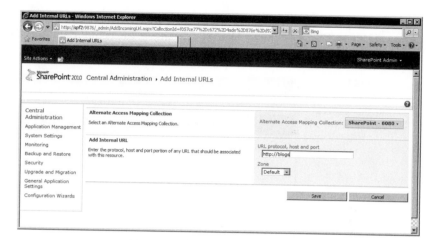

FIGURE 10.77
The new internal
URL mappings

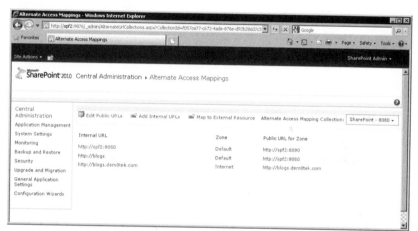

IIS BINDINGS AND AAM

In some cases, creating the new internal URL isn't sufficient; you also need to manually create the associated binding in IIS. In my example, that would mean editing the Sharepoint-8080 IIS Web Site and adding a binding for http://blogs on port 80. So if the internal URL you create doesn't work for you, that might be the fix you need.

Just as you do with all URLs, you need to make sure new internal URLs exist in DNS and point to the server.

MANUALLY ADDING A PUBLIC URL

You can also edit public URLs from the Alternate Access Mapping page. For example, you can quickly add a new public URL for an unused zone (or change the URL for an existing zone) and save the changes. The public URL will be added to the web application and automatically generate a new internal URL to match. For example, you could use the URL `http://blogserver` as the Extranet zone for the web application `http://spf2:8080`. See Figure 10.78.

FIGURE 10.78
Adding a public URL this way is a bad idea.

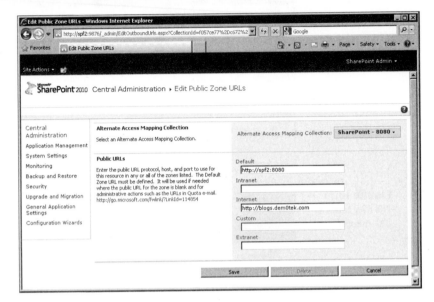

Although this method will work for browsing the web application, it has one key difference from the full Extend A Web Application process: it doesn't create a new IIS Web Site for the new public URL. This means that there are no new security settings available for the URL, and no host header exists in IIS to direct traffic to the correct web application (SharePoint does the redirect on the backend). Although editing *existing* public URLs is fine if they are extended web applications, you really shouldn't create new public URLs this way. It simply doesn't allow you the flexibility of being able to apply unique authentication or policy settings for the URL, because it doesn't have a corresponding Web Site in IIS.

REMOVING A PUBLIC URL (BY REMOVING AN EXTENDED WEB APPLICATION)

You could conceivably just delete the entry for a public URL, regardless of whether it is associated with an extended web application. But the correct way to remove an extended web application's public URL from a web application's mapping is to use the Remove SharePoint From IIS Web Site link on the Manage Web Applications page (on the Delete button's drop-down menu) This essentially removes the extended web application itself.

In the resulting Remove SharePoint From IIS Web Site window (Figure 10.79), you have the option of removing only the association of the web application with the IIS Web Site in SharePoint or removing the IIS Web Site altogether. Whether you choose to delete the IIS Web Site, this will remove the public URL from the list in Alternate Access Mapping.

Make sure you select the correct IIS Web Site and zone to remove from the extended web application.

FIGURE 10.79
The Remove Share-
Point From IIS Web
Site window

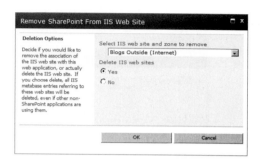

Deleting the IIS Web Site deletes, unsurprisingly, the IIS Web Site which removes any custom settings you might have—but it also keeps IIS nice and clean. If you choose not to delete the IIS Web Site, the IIS server places the Web Site into the stopped state. So, it's still there; it's just not running.

Again, it is possible to delete the public URL from within the Alternate Access Mapping page by editing the public URLs and simply clearing the field. However, doing so is not recommended because it makes no change to IIS. This leaves the Web Site running, so it accepts connections for the URL (via the host header) and points them at the web application. In this case, because the public URL has been deleted, SharePoint serves the web pages with the default URL (for example, `http://spf2:8080`), but it doesn't stop service; it just doesn't return the former public URL.

Content Databases

During the install process in Chapter 3, you worked with content databases, and you even created a new one while creating a new web application earlier in this chapter. Now let's take a closer look at what you can do with content databases and web applications. Web applications need at least one content database to put everything in, but they can support additional content databases. As mentioned in Chapter 2, content databases on a standalone install reside here:

`%SharePointRoot%\Data\MSSQL10.SHAREPOINT\MSSQL.DATA`

(As a reminder, the SharePoint root is `C:\Program Files\Common Files\Microsoft Shared\ Web Server Extensions\14`. This is sometimes referred to as the *SharePoint Root* or *14 hive*.)

With a complete install, content databases are located on the SQL Server you specified during installation.

EDITING CONTENT DATABASE SETTINGS

To manage content databases, go to Central Administration's Application Management page and click Manage Content Databases. This will take you to the Manage Content Databases page, shown in Figure 10.80.

On this page, you can see the content databases for a particular web application. As always, clicking the web application's name will let you change to a different one. Clicking a content database's name will let you edit its settings (see Figure 10.81).

FIGURE 10.80
The Manage Content Databases page

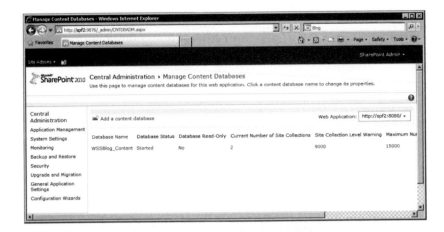

FIGURE 10.81
The Manage Content Database Settings page

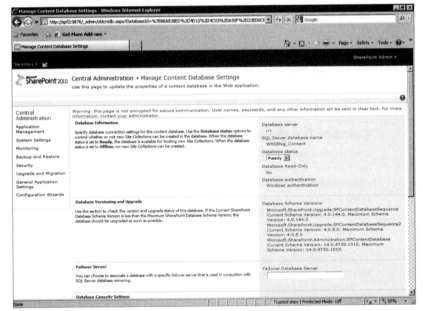

Database Information A content database can be in two states: Ready and Offline.

The default setting is Ready, which allows new sites to be created in the content database. Obviously, you'll want this if you plan to add site collections to the web application, and this is the only content database for that web application.

The other setting is Offline. This prevents any new site collections from being created in the content database. Existing site collections can still be used, and new subsites can be created within that collection, but the limit has been reached, and no more new site collections can be added.

Database Versioning And Upgrade   This provides a quick way to see the database versions in use in case the content database is running an older version and should be upgraded.

Failover Server   If you have SQL Server set up for failover services, the failover server would be listed here.

Database Capacity Settings   To prevent a database from growing too much and getting out of hand, you can limit the number of site collections that are created in a single content database. The default number is 15,000, but it can be set to whatever you like. There is also an option to send out a notification if a certain number of site collections are reached. You obviously want this to be lower than the actual limit, and the default is 9,000.

Note that on this page, the word *site* is used when describing the limit and warning level. This is a misnomer; the settings apply to site collections, not to individual sites.

When the database hits its capacity, it will go Offline—no new site collections will be permitted.

Search Server   When you created the web application, you were prompted to choose a search server for the content database. This setting is where you can change that choice if you want to transfer the search process to another search server.

Remove Content Database   Removing a content database from a web application does not delete that database; it just disassociates it from the web application. The database still exists, just as when you delete a web application and elect to not delete the content database. A removed content database can be added to a web application later or used when you create a new web application.

Preferred Server For Timer Jobs   If you have multiple timer job servers, you can have the content database use a preferred one. No Selection does not mean there is no timer job server; it just means the content database has no preference and will use whatever server is available.

ADDING A NEW CONTENT DATABASE

When the content database gets too large or hits its capacity limit, you may want to add a second content database to the web application. In this case, additional site collections can be added to the new database while still being part of the web application. A web application can have numerous databases to accommodate increases in data storage.

To add a new content database, go to Central Administration's Application Management page, and click Manage Content Databases. Make sure you're working with the web application you intend to add the database to, and click the **Add A Content Database**. This will take you to the Add Content Database page, as shown in Figure 10.82.

This page asks you to fill out the same information the content database required during the creation of a new web application; in addition, it lets you specify the capacity site limit and warning event level. Once you provide the needed information, click **OK**. You'll see the new content database listed on the Manage Content Databases page, as shown in Figure 10.83.

At this point, any new site collection created inside the web application will go to whichever database has the most available space for site collections. The available space isn't calculated by storage capacity but by subtracting the existing number of sites in the database from the database's site limit.

FIGURE 10.82
The Add Content
Database page

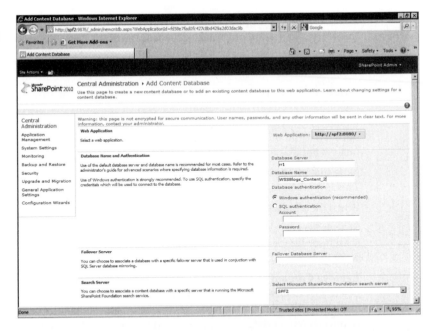

FIGURE 10.83
The Manage
Content
Databases page

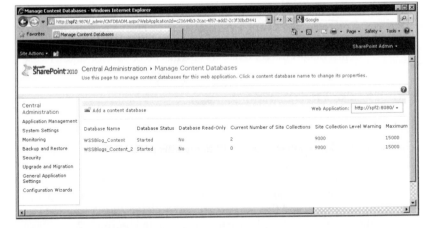

USING AN EXISTING CONTENT DATABASE

It's possible to use an existing content database. It could be one that was previously removed from a web application, or it could simply have not been deleted when its web application was deleted.

In some cases, when the web application becomes horribly corrupt and unusable, you could be forced to remove it—but, of course, that would never happen.

If you want to bring a preexisting content database back online and resurrect the sites contained in the database, you can do so by creating a new web application and entering the content database in the Database Name And Authentication section.

Of course, you'll need to know the name of the existing database and the SQL Server instance on which it's located.

When the web application is created, you do *not* want to create a new site collection to complete the install; after all, the content database already has the site collections and enclosed sites. Instead, just reset IIS by running this:

```
iisreset /noforce
```

Then go to your new web application URL, where you'll see the old sites from the content database. If, on the odd occasion it doesn't work, you can run the attach database command in STSADM or PowerShell. This will force SharePoint to realize the content database should be accessible from the web application.

The Bottom Line

Create and customize a new site collection.   A new site collection has separate permissions, its own Recycle Bins, its own storage quota, and its own site collection galleries. You can change the regional settings and grant someone site administrator rights on a new site collection without compromising your existing sites.

> **Master It**   You created a new site collection with a storage quota of 100 MB. Since then, it has hit capacity, and no one can add new documents or list items. You asked quite a few users to delete data to free up space, but it didn't appear to help. Short of increasing the quota, what can you do?

Create a new web application.   A new web application is fundamentally a new IIS Web Site with a new content database on the back end. Using a new IIS Web Site allows you to change the port for accessing the web application, use a host header, and adjust the IIS-level authentication such as anonymous access. Web applications, in addition to being a security boundary, are also a boundary for settings such as RSS, sending alerts, upload size limits, and blocked file types that affect all contained site collections. All SharePoint site collections must reside in a web application. At this level, serious changes can affect the way the site collections are accessed and controlled.

> **Master It**   You want to create a new web application but don't want to use a custom port, so you set up a host header instead. But although it appears to have been created correctly and you created a site collection, you cannot seem to access the site. What is the most likely problem?

Use managed paths.   SharePoint uses managed paths to tell IIS which paths in a URL are handled by SharePoint and are, therefore, *managed*. All other paths are considered *excluded*, and IIS is free to use them with traditional websites. You can add your own managed paths, adjusting the URL of site collections.

By default, SharePoint site collections have two managed paths: the path (root), which is explicit, and the path /sites/, which is a wildcard path.

> **Master It**   You create a new wildcard managed path at http://myserver/sales but cannot seem to place a site collection in this URL without adding another piece to the path. What is wrong?

Configure anonymous access.   One of the main features of web applications is the ability to allow anonymous access to the site collections they contain. Anonymous access can allow the site to be viewed without requiring a login while retaining all the needed permissions for authenticated users to add, edit, modify, or delete site content. Anonymous access is enabled in two core steps: first by permitting anonymous access at the web-application level and then by enabling anonymous access at the site collection level.

> **Master It**   Someone else has allowed anonymous access on the web application, and you're configuring your site collection. You want anonymous users to view only the Status list and nothing else. How do you configure the site?

Set different zones for different access methods.   Each web application can support up to five public URLs that it displays in the address bar and on the page in links and paths. Four of the public URLs can be used for manually entered alternate web addresses or used by extending the web application to a new IIS Web Site, providing a new URL (including a new port if desired), and applying different authentication policies to the same site. For example, one web application within the local network can permit anonymous access, but authentication can be required for anyone accessing the site through the Internet public URL. The five public URLs are identified by their *zone*, and additional internal URLs can be mapped to each zone.

> **Master It**   Your web application has three zones configured with extended web applications, each with their own public URL. Because of a company policy change, you need to remove the Internet zone from the web application. What is the recommended method for doing this?

Part 3

Administering Microsoft SharePoint Foundation 2010

Chapter 11

Central Administration

This chapter is intended to give you a reference point for all of those settings links on the Central Administration site. Chances are good that you will never use some of them, but it's nice to know what they are, just in case. Many of these settings are covered extensively in other chapters (and if that is the case, it will be noted throughout this chapter). However, some settings are so specific to the farm that they may not necessarily be covered while focusing on tasks in other chapters. If so, those settings will be covered in more detail here. Overall, this chapter is intended for you to find Central Administration settings all in one spot.

In this chapter, you'll learn how to

- ◆ Understand Central Administration's organization
- ◆ Configure managed accounts
- ◆ Set the server farm's default database server
- ◆ Determine where to stop and start farm services
- ◆ Manage a farm's solutions and features

The Central Administration Site Interface

As you know, SharePoint creates an administrative web application during installation. All SharePoint administration that applies to the farm as a whole, or web applications and site collections in particular, are configured in this web application's site collection pages. Those settings are stored in the farm's configuration database.

This administrative web application is called Central Administration. When this web application is created, it is assigned a unique port number for security reasons; this helps obscure the site from casual browsers. Central Administration also contains one top-level site in its primary site collection.

To access Central Administration, simply open a browser (preferably Internet Explorer 7 or higher), enter the SharePoint server address that is hosting the Central Administration site (it is often the first SharePoint server on a farm if you are not using a standalone server), and then add the port number. My example uses `http://spf2:9876`. (As you may remember, when we installed this SharePoint server in Chapter 3, "Complete Installation," that port number was selected because it was easy to remember.) This means you can access the Central Administration site from any machine with a browser on your network; you are not limited to accessing it only from the SharePoint server. However, if you want to access the Central Administration site from the server where you installed SharePoint, you can use the shortcut that SharePoint adds to the Start menu (Start ➤ All Programs ➤ Microsoft SharePoint 2010 Products ➤ SharePoint 2010 Central Administration). That shortcut just opens the browser to the site's address, such as `http://spf2:9876` (the same address my example just used). Regardless, the shortcut is useful if you have forgotten the port number for the site. Of course, you can also go into the IIS console and check the port for the Central Administration web application if you forget.

When you install SharePoint, the Central Administration site is created with your setup account as the only owner. However, unlike any other site collection, Central Administration also allows, by default, the built-in Administrators group to log in (in case of emergency, such as when the farm administrator's password is forgotten). This means if you are a domain administrator, the local server's administrator, or you are using the setup account, you can log in to Central Administration. My example uses the setup account, `setupacct`, to log in, as you'll see on the Account menu in figures throughout the chapter.

YOU USUALLY DON'T ADMINISTER SHAREPOINT WITH THE SETUP ACCOUNT, BUT...

Keep in mind that I am using the setup account to log in for simplicity's sake; this is the one account I know you can use to log in; because if it doesn't work, that means SharePoint isn't installed. Otherwise, under normal circumstances, you should never use the SharePoint setup account for anything but installing and configuring SharePoint. I've mentioned that elsewhere, but it bears repeating.

If you do not know how to add additional farm administrators, simply click the Manage The Farm Administrators Group link under Security on the Central Administration home page. It will take you to the Farm Administrators People And Groups page, where you can click New and add user accounts or security groups to the Farm Administrators group. For more information about adding farm administrators, see Chapter 12, "Users and Permissions."

In Figure 11.1, you can see that the site has a lot of the standard interface features. It has the top ribbon bar, a title area, a Quick Launch bar, and a content area. What it doesn't have is a top link bar or Search. That's right. No search for Central Administration—the one place where an administrator could really use a Search feature.

FIGURE 11.1
The Central Administration home page

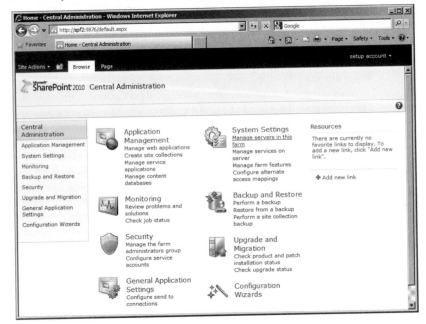

In the Quick Launch bar is the link for the Central Administration home page at the top, and below that are links to each of the settings categories for the site: Application Management, System Settings, Monitoring, Backup And Restore, Security, Upgrade And Migration, General Application Settings, and Configuration Wizards (which only contains the wizard you can use to set up the farm with the Standalone installation defaults).

In the content area of the page are the same category headings as in the Quick Launch bar, with some common settings below them. Keep in mind that not *all* the settings available for the farm (or even the most common) under those headings are displayed. The links here are what Microsoft thinks would be most useful.

Along with those category headings, and a smattering of the settings links beneath them, is a small web part zone on the right containing the Links list view web part, which has been renamed *Resources*. As you know, hyperlink fields can be used to open anything, including file shares, Word documents, and websites. This web part gives administrators the chance to add a few additional resources that might be appropriate for working on SharePoint (such as a link to the Microsoft SharePoint sites or the TechNet Windows SharePoint Foundation 2010 technical library online).

Real World Scenario

SPEAKING OF WEB PARTS

The home page of Central Administration, like most home pages, is a web part page, and although it has a section in the content area for the categories and their settings, but it also has two web part zones, one on the right (containing the *Resources* web part) and one directly below the headings. You can see and use these zones when you edit the page.

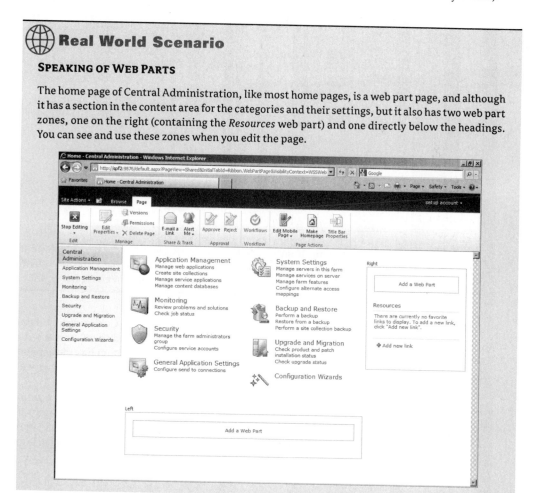

The previous version of SharePoint had a convenient Farm Topology web part for the home page. It displayed all the servers that SharePoint knows about in the network, as well as the services they provide in relation to SharePoint, such as a mail server if it's set up for outgoing email, the farm's SQL server or other SharePoint servers on the farm.

Although that web part isn't on the home page by default, it is still available to be added to the home page. Click in the Add a web part zone of your choice. Then, in the Miscellaneous category of the web part workspace, select Farm Topology Web Part, and click Add. When you finish editing the page (click Stop Editing), the web part will be available on the Central Administration home page.

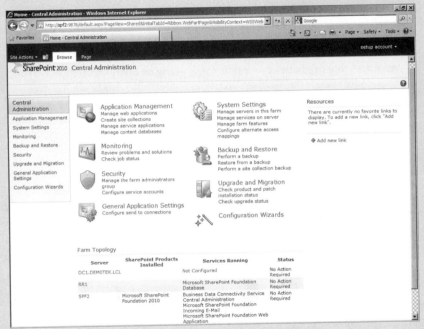

You might have noticed the unfortunate Not Configured warning for the outgoing email server. Maybe *this* is why they don't have the Farm Topology web part on the home page anymore. It is a known false negative, so if you have configured outgoing email, don't let it worry you.

Central Administration's settings—its data—are stored in the Configuration database for the farm, but the site content itself, such as web parts, lists, and so on, are stored in the AdminContent database. And thanks to that, Central Administration has the capabilities of a normal top-level site of a site collection. It's a top-level site and has a settings page of its own under Site Actions (Figure 11.2).

You may be tempted to use Central Administration as a SharePoint site for administrators, but never forget that you can't recover this site, like you can any other SharePoint site. Because it is so closely tied to the configuration database, Microsoft treats it differently. Although it can be backed up using SharePoint Backup And Restore, you can't restore it from backup. You have to reinstall it from scratch so you'll have a completely fresh configuration database on which to rebuild. This is why you should create a unique web application (or at least a different site collection) for the SharePoint administrators so you can have calendars, discussions, document libraries, wikis, and the like, to foster communication between administrators and leave Central Administration for configuration settings only. This way, you can back up and restore the administrator's content on a new server, if necessary, without issue.

FIGURE 11.2

Central Administration's site settings

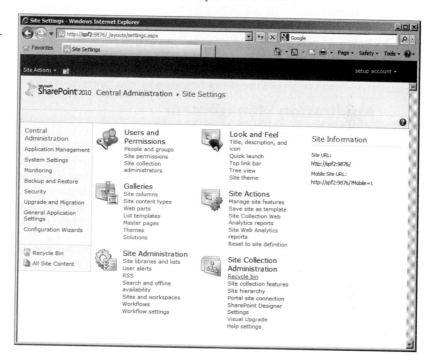

FIGURE 11.2
Central Administration's site settings

DOCUMENT THE SETTINGS

Always, always, always document the settings you make in Central Administration, as well as at the site collection, site, and even list levels of SharePoint. Documentation never hurts when it comes to restoring SharePoint. This will take effort on your part, because there is no built-in easy command to run that will generate an inventory of changes and objects you've made. However, making a point of recording your changes will come in handy later. There are some very simple spreadsheets available on the TechNet site for SharePoint Foundation; they're under Planning and Architecture, Planning Worksheets, if you'd like to try them.

Each category heading in the Quick Launch bar (or if you select the heading in the content area of the home page) opens into its own page of settings. From there you can use the Quick Launch bar, the title breadcrumb, or the Navigate Up button in the top ribbon bar to get back to the home page of the Central Administration site at any time.

Keep in mind that certain settings available in Central Administration are only there as "hooks" to connect SharePoint Foundation with SharePoint Server 2010 or other third-party products. You need to be aware of them so they don't surprise you when they appear, even though you aren't doing anything with them. Some settings require third-party products and vary so greatly that you'll need to check with your vendor to see how to integrate them with SharePoint (such as the antivirus settings).

This chapter is organized by the categories listed in the Quick Launch bar, starting with Application Management. As I go through each category and setting, most of them are covered in detail elsewhere in the book. When that is the case, I will give a brief overview of what the setting does and will otherwise direct you to what chapter to read to get more involved information.

Application Management

From the Central Administration home page, you can get to the Application Management page by clicking the heading in the content area or the link in the Quick Launch bar.

Settings organized under Application Management are those related to either web applications or site collections and their resources (such as content databases). It is from here that you can access the pages to create, delete, and manage web applications and site collections within web applications (also critical to the use of SharePoint); manage content databases; and integrate with external resources. This page is essentially the foundation of SharePoint web application and site collection administration.

The Application Management page is broken into subsets of settings (Figure 11.3): Web Applications, Site Collections, Service Applications, and Databases. These subcategories contain links to additional settings pages, which can in turn have buttons in their ribbon bars that take you to even more settings pages.

FIGURE 11.3
The Application
Management page

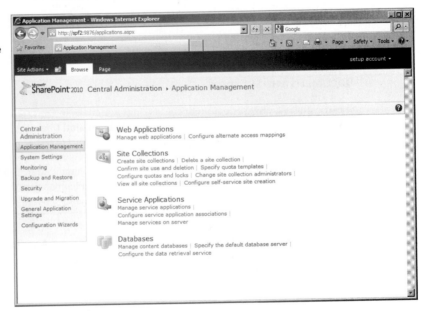

In this section, you'll work through all the settings for each subcategory of Application Management. Generally, the descriptions will be brief because most of what's here, especially anything relating to web applications and site collections, was covered in detail in Chapter 10, "Site Collections and Web Applications."

Web Applications

This subcategory is where a lot of the action is; don't let the fact there are only two links fool you. The Manage Web Applications page alone is a page full of configuration settings for web applications. In fact, this page has so many settings that some of them are also available elsewhere in Central Administration. Anything related to web applications is available from this subset. Web applications were covered in detail in Chapter 10.

MANAGE WEB APPLICATIONS

Manage Web Applications is one of the pages in Central Administration that complies with the new ribbon bar design convention. Because of that, it can be a bit of a confusing place. It contains about a dozen settings pages in which you can do just about everything you need with web applications. To access the page, simply click the Manage Web Applications link under Web Applications on the Application Management page.

WHAT'S A WEB APPLICATION?

Although web applications and site collections were extensively covered in Chapter 10, as a reminder; web applications are associated with IIS Web Sites, and they contain site collections for SharePoint. Web applications are where you apply access settings (such as authentication methods, anonymous access, or requiring SSL). Web applications are essentially address and security boundaries for the site collections they contain.

Once on the Web Applications Management page (Figure 11.4), you'll see a list of the existing web applications for the farm and a largely inactive ribbon bar. Until you select an existing web application from the list, the only button that is available is the New button.

This page contains the buttons necessary to create new web applications, extend web applications, and delete web applications, as well as manage all web application settings and requirements, from security using policies, authentication providers, and blocked file types to managing paths, features, and service connections to self-service site creation. For much more on those topics, see Chapter 10 for details.

New The New button is used to create a new web application. When you click this button, a Create New Web Application form box (Figure 11.5) comes up. This form has eight sections that allow you to specify the settings of the IIS Web Site for the web application, ranging from the authentication mode, its address and virtual directory; its security and public, load-balanced URL; the application pool name and identity; to the database server and database name, and service application associations. Creating new web applications is covered in detail in Chapter 10.

FIGURE 11.4

The Web Applications Management page

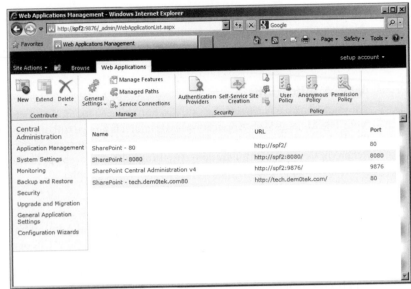

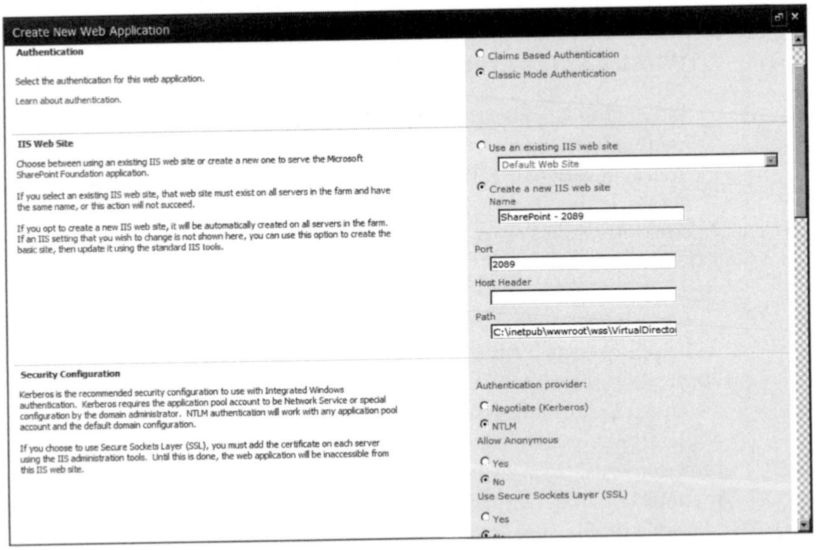

FIGURE 11.5

The first few settings of the Create New Web Application form

---

NEW BUTTON GRAYED OUT?

Depending on the OS version SharePoint is running on, there is a chance that, even logged in as a domain admin and a farm administrator, you still may not be able to see things such as the New button, Extend, or a number of the links to settings in Central Administration. If this is an issue for you, try disabling User Access Control (UAC) on the server. UAC may be blocking your account from doing administrative tasks on the local server, even though you explicitly should have permission.

If the account you are logged in with is a member of the Farm Administrators group but doesn't have administrative permissions on the local server, you may also be missing settings that require the right to start/stop services, install software, or add/remove IIS Web Sites. But that is by design. For more about farm permissions, see Chapter 12.

Extend   To use this button, you first must select a web application to extend. If you click the Extend button, it will take you to a form that is very similar to the Create New Web Application form, but with fewer choices. Remember that extending a web application simply creates a new IIS Web Site that uses the same application pool and content database as the web application it is extending (so you don't specify separate database or application pool settings). This means an extended web application is nothing but another door to the same room, so to speak. It is just another way to access the same data as the original web application, only it will use a different URL and can have different security settings. Once you've created an extended web application, it will not have its own listing in the web application list, and it cannot be managed like a standard web application because it does not have its own content database and, therefore, cannot store its own site collections and content. Extended web applications are associated with their original web application zones, of which there are four available per web application for extension. This is why extended web applications are referred to in SharePoint by their zone and URL in alternate access mappings. For more details, see Chapter 10.

Delete   This button has two options: Delete A Web Application and Remove SharePoint From An IIS Web Site. The first will strip the selected web application from the configuration database as if it had never been there. The second is particularly used to get rid of an *extended* web application (deleting is for real web applications). Web applications are covered in detail in Chapter 10, so for more information about deleting web applications, particularly demonstrating how to delete an extended web application, see that chapter.

General Settings   The General Settings button displays a catchall menu where you can easily get to the settings of a selected web application. Some of the options here are also accessible from other places in Central Administration.

To use the General Settings button, select a web application. Clicking the General Settings button will simply open the General Settings form for the web application. However, if you click the down arrow for the button, you get a number of other options: General Settings, Resource Throttling, Workflow, Outgoing E-mail, Mobile Account, and SharePoint Designer.

A more detailed description of the options for the General Settings button are as follows:

   General Settings   The General Settings form is another catchall, this time for all those settings that can be applied to a web application that can't really be classified anywhere else.

It is here the default settings for things such as time zone, quota, alerts, Recycle Bin, blog API, browser file handling, maximum upload settings, and so on, are set per web application. This page of settings was covered in detail in Chapter 10.

RECYCLE BIN FRUGALITY

Something of particular interest concerning the Recycle Bin settings in General Settings that is often overlooked is the percentage of space the second-stage Recycle Bin takes. When you create a site collection quota, the deleted items sitting in the user Recycle Bin take up space in that quota. However, if you delete items from the user Recycle Bin, they go to the second-stage, site-collection Recycle Bin. Why would we encourage you to empty the user Recycle Bins in order to free up space in the site collection quota? It's because, in the General Settings page for a web application is the second-stage Recycle Bin setting called Add A Certain Percentage Of Live Site Quota For Second Stage Deleted Items. You can enter a certain percentage (50 percent is the default) indicating how much in *addition* to the site quota the second-stage Recycle Bin can store before it maxes out and older items are automatically removed. This setting is obviously per web application and affects all site collections within it.

Resource Throttling   Resource throttling is new with this version of SharePoint. Lists in a site are all organized in one place in the content database. Previously, SharePoint had a soft display limit of about 2,000 items. When a user went to the content page of a list with 2,000 or more items, it would lag horribly and, because of its location, would likely make a lot of other lists lag for other users as well. This version of SharePoint is supposed to be so good it can support lists with millions of items, yet throttling is set to some surprisingly low numbers. I guess it is because SharePoint (or maybe the database engines on the back end) can handle a large amount of data, but it still finds it challenging to query nearly that number of things.

And, although it might be argued that this is bad design, SharePoint has tried to fix the issue by allowing you to throttle the number of things a user can do—to help avoid (but not fix) the choking and crashing that large lists or many page requests can cause. The Resource Throttling box has a number of settings that relate to how SharePoint will fail to return data if the user is trying to access a list too large or a site too busy. The settings include several list view threshold settings, object model override, and daily time window for large queries. For more details concerning these settings, see Chapter 10.

ABOUT THOSE THRESHOLDS

In Chapter 1 there were a bunch of software boundary tables that listed software limits, boundaries, and thresholds. Thresholds were performance limits that were set in SharePoint at a default level, but they could be changed administratively. These threshold settings for resource throttling are an excellent example of the defaults that limit how many items a list view will display before failing, unique permissions for a list, and HTTP request throttling (and monitoring). It is here that you can increase (or decrease) the thresholds of these settings.

Workflow   The form box for this setting has refreshingly few settings (Figure 11.6), all concerning how users will relate to workflows in all sites for the web application. The settings box contains two sections—one to allow (or disallow) users to build custom workflows from existing workflow pieces deployed to the site (but not necessarily add their own) and one to allow for workflow notification regarding users accessing workflow tasks and external users participating in document workflows.

FIGURE 11.6
The Workflow
Settings form

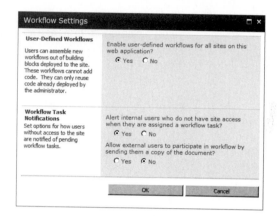

Outgoing E-mail   This settings box also has a page you can go to from the System Settings category's E-mail and Text Messages (SMS) subcategory. This setting is configured for the whole farm in Chapters 2 and 3. To be able to send out alerts and notifications, SharePoint requires a valid email address and outgoing email server. However, that page under System Settings applies to the whole farm; here, you can set the outgoing email settings per web application, overriding the farm's outgoing email settings.

The fields to configure in this settings box are Outbound SMTP Server, From Address (which can be fictitious but probably shouldn't be), Reply To Address (needs to be real so users can reply), and the default character set used for those outgoing emails.

Mobile Account   This settings box has the same settings as the Configure Mobile Account Settings page in the System Settings ➢ E-mail And Text Messages (SMS) subcategory. However, that settings page affects the whole farm; you can configure a different mobile account for individual, selected web applications here. For SharePoint to be capable of sending text messages in addition to email messages for alerts and notifications, the server must be set up with a mobile account (there will be a fee involved, much as if you'd purchased a cell phone for the server). A number of carriers support SharePoint server mobile accounts. In the forms box for this setting is a link to a page listing service providers at the Microsoft Office Online site. Once you've set up the account, you'll be provided with a URL, username, and password to use the service. You can test the account to be sure you have configured it properly, by using the Test Service button (Figure 11.7).

SharePoint Designer   Interestingly, the SharePoint Designer settings can't be set farm-wide; they are always set per web application. This setting is also available per web application under General Application Settings ➢ SharePoint Designer ➢ Configure SharePoint Designer Settings.

Because of that, the details about each option in the forms box for the setting are the same here as there. You can configure whether SharePoint Designer access is even enabled for the web application (and the sites it contains), and if it is, if site collection administrators can detach pages, customize master and layout pages, or manage the site's URL structure. For more details, see the SharePoint Designer settings in the "General Application Settings" section of this chapter.

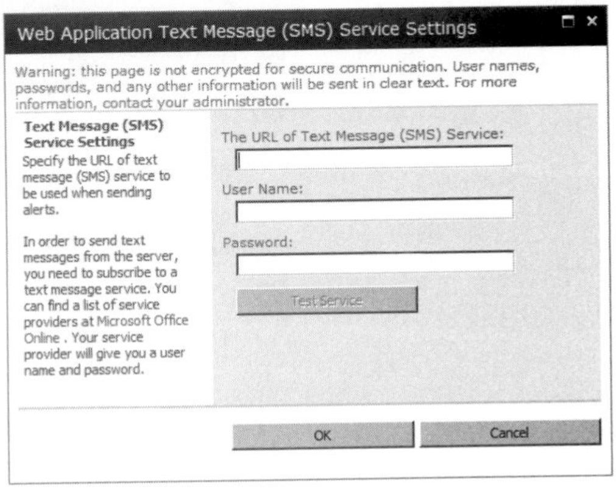

FIGURE 11.7
The Mobile
Account form box

That's it for the different settings pages available under the General Settings button. Let's move on to the rest of the buttons in the Ribbon.

Manage Features   The Manage Features form displays only existing features that have been deployed to the selected web application. SharePoint Features can be created to run in the scope of a farm, web application, site collection, or single site and can be activated or managed at that point.

Features are sort of standalone additions to SharePoint's functionality (like adding ratings, an add-on for the developer dashboard, or more control over buttons on a list's ribbon bar), which can be installed using STSADM or PowerShell and then activated at the level it is scoped for, be it farm, web application, or site collection. One of the more useful things is that after installation, a feature can be activated or deactivated at the level it is scoped; it doesn't need to be removed to turn it on and off.

When you have a feature that is meant to be used for a site collection or site, you simply see it and manage it at that level. However, to see what features are applied at the farm- or web-application level, you need to go to Central Administration—of course. Just as obviously, this is the box where you can see what features are available in SharePoint that are scoped to affect the selected web application. The box itself simply displays the installed features scoped for web applications with a column to indicate the activation status of the features. To install and uninstall features, you have to use STSADM or PowerShell.

Features can be added as part of a larger solution package. Solutions are often larger additions to SharePoint's functionality and can contain a number of features, definitions, templates, and web parts. Solutions are added to the farm and, if they are scoped for it, can be deployed at different levels in the farm, just like a feature. If a feature appears available at the site collection level but doesn't appear in the list for the web application itself, it was either scoped to apply to the whole farm, was designed to only be deployed at the site collection level (as a sandbox solution for example), or was deployed as part of a farm solution.

Manage Paths   This button opens a form that specifies what data SharePoint explicitly manages and what data it doesn't. More importantly, it specifies what managed paths are available, per web application, to make site collections. By default, in SharePoint, the first site collection made in a web application gets the coveted root path (unless you specifically configure it otherwise). That means its URL is at the root of the web application, just as in this book's example, the Company Site is at the root of SharePoint-80, at `http://spf2`. (SharePoint prefers that there is always a site collection at the root of a web application. If you decide to use the `/sites/` path for all your site collections for some reason, Search may not work.)

SharePoint offers two different kinds of managed paths, explicit and wildcard. Explicit paths mean the path you enter will be the address for a particular site collection's top-level site, such as `http://spf2/managersite`. You can then create a site collection and specifically give it that address. When you create a new web application, you are prompted to create the first site collection for that web application soon after. Usually that first site collection is put at the root of the web application, so its address would be the web application's address, such as `http://spf2`. It can be considered an explicit path in that respect. No other site collection in the web application can use that specific address. A wildcard path is a path that is general and meant to hold any number of additional site collections. That's why, when you specify a wildcard path for a site collection, it's referred to as a *site prefix*. SharePoint has a default wildcard path for web applications, `/sites/` (as in `http://spf2/sites/`), for you to put the rest of the site collections in a web application. That is only an example, though; you can create as many managed paths as you'd like. (You can see in Figure 11.8 that I am getting ready to create a `mgmt` wildcard path.) Managed paths are an important part of planning the namespace of your SharePoint sites. SharePoint managed paths are covered extensively in Chapter 10.

Keep in mind that you can make as many managed paths as you'd like, but there is a limit of about 260 characters for a web address (which will include the name of the page the user is on while there), so keep your paths as brief as you can.

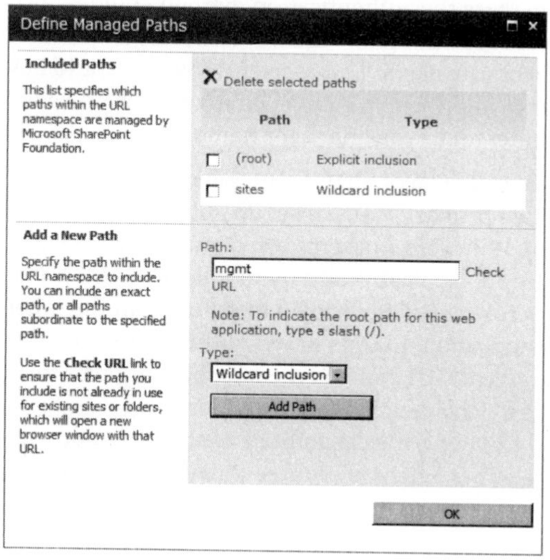

FIGURE 11.8
The Define Managed Paths form

Service Connections   Service applications available for the SharePoint farm are made available to a web application using service connection groups. The default is to have all service connections selected, but you can choose to make only certain service applications available to a web application while you're creating it by choosing [custom] (not sure why it has the brackets, but it does) in the Group Of Connections list. This will make it possible to uncheck the service applications you don't want the web application to have access to.

So, this settings form for service connections lets you change the selected service applications (Figure 11.9) associated with the web application. It thus gives you a chance to change your mind about what service applications to associate with the web application and is simply a good place to see what service applications are associated.

FIGURE 11.9

The Configure Service Application Associations page

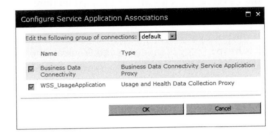

Service applications were initially enabled in Chapter 3 and covered a little more in-depth later in this chapter. The Business Data Connectivity Service in particular is covered in Chapter 16.

Authentication Providers   This setting is demonstrated in Chapter 3's SharePoint server farm installation and covered extensively in Chapter 10. In addition, it's also available in Security ➢ General Security ➢ Specify Authentication Providers.

Each web application is accessed by users using a certain authentication method (or, in some cases, several). Users must be authenticated by an outside authentication provider (SharePoint gives authorization to accounts already authenticated by an authentication provider). Usually SharePoint uses a Windows integrated provider, like Active Directory. From there the authentication method could be NTLM or Kerberos. SharePoint also supports forms-based authentication, which uses a database (other than Active Directory's LDAP) to authenticate users. This is useful if you want to have a list of users accessing content but don't want to add them to Active Directory. Forms-based authentication requires a membership provider and a role manager name.

For this version of SharePoint, which is trying to be more flexible with authentication, there are two primary ways to set up authentication—Classic, which basically assumes you are doing Windows Authentication and lets you choose from the standard IIS authentication type options; Basic (used by mobile devices), NTLM (preferred by the Search service), and Kerberos (negotiate; harder to set up than the other two but more secure). And Claims-based authentication. Claims-based authentication can require a fair amount of setup outside the SharePoint GUI, but it is the one that supports forms-based authentication (and surfaces the fields for the membership provider and role manager). Claims-based authentication can be used to extend the capabilities of standard authentication with extra requirements, by specifying either a non-AD source for authentication data or extra data in AD to further narrow down the AD users qualified for access. For example, if the user field for department were filled out in AD, you could customize the authentication to include an added filter of all people in a certain department who can authenticate, but others can't. It takes considerable customization, but it can be done. Otherwise, Claims-based authentication can simply be configured to use Windows Authentication, with the added bonus of supporting more than one authentication method, such as NTLM and Kerberos.

You cannot select Classic as the type of authentication for the web application and then try to do forms-based, either on that web application or any of its extended web applications. If you are planning on using forms-based authentication for a web application's extended web application, make sure the original web application is using claims-based (even if you are actually going to select NTLM as the authentication method for that one).

Self-Service Site Creation   Ironically, the Self-Service Site Creation setting doesn't actually give users the ability to create their own sites—it gives them the ability to create *site collections*. For this reason, this setting is a bit misnamed. The web application set to enable Self-Service Site Creation allows users to create their own site collections, with all the autonomy that implies.

The settings box for this link has only three settings in the Enable Self-Service Site Creation section: On or Off (the default) and Require Secondary Contact (which is always a good idea). See Chapter 10 for more on self-service site creation. This setting is one of those that is also listed elsewhere in Central Administration and opens in a page of its own (if you prefer pages to boxes) under Security ➢ General Security ➢ Configure Self-Service Site Creation.

THE SHARED HOST NAME WARNING

At the top of the Self-Service Site Creation page you'll see the warning "Self-Service Site Creation will create sites under a shared host name." What does that mean?

When you enable Self-Service Site Creation, it lets users create their own site collections in a web application. They will all be located in the same web application and therefore use the same base address, like http://spf2/sites. So, user 1 and user 2 will have their site collection addresses at http://spf2/sites/user1 and http://spf2/sites/user2. These addresses are basically sharing their "host name" or host web application's root URL. Because of this, if user 1 gives user 2 read permission to their site and user 2 opens a file from user 1's site in the browser that has a dangerous script in it, that script will run in user 2's account context and cause damage.

Of course, this can happen to anyone on any site. But IE is supposed to help avoid "cross-site scripting" exploits. As far as it's concerned, both user 1 and user 2's sites are just pages in the same website, so to speak. And since http://spf2 is a trusted site, then it doesn't do any cross-site script blocking of the two user site collections, apparently.

To avoid the possible yelling and screaming from administrators, Microsoft displays the warning in the Self-Service Site Creation form, with a link to an online document about the issue. It is also why Browser Handling in General Settings is set by default as Strict, so even if user 2 did click a dangerous script in user 1's site, it would prompt to download rather than running (although, wouldn't that endanger user 2 if they ran it locally anyway?).

So, now you know what that warning means, and you have a better idea whether you should allow self-service site creation in your environment. For me, the fact that users can make as many site collections in the web application as they want, all with a full site collection's quota, gives me more pause than shared host names.

Blocked File Type This setting is also available under General Security in the Security category. It allows you to set the list of file extensions that are blocked by default for the selected web application. This setting is per web application and affects all site collections within it. This setting is also covered in Chapter 10.

The box that opens when you click the Blocked File Type button contains a simple text list of file extensions that will be blocked automatically from being uploaded to any library in the selected web application's sites. To remove an extension, delete it from the list. To add one, just insert it. Keep in mind that this process is very rudimentary; SharePoint does not check beyond the file extension in terms of blocking uploads. If a user changes the extension of an otherwise blocked file to one that is acceptable, it will not be blocked from uploading.

User Permissions To do anything in a SharePoint site, users must have permission to do so. SharePoint permissions can be set to be available to be applied or not available for all sites in a selected web application from here. This box lists all the user permissions possible, organized by List Permissions, Site Permissions, and Personal Permissions. This is a useful list if only to familiarize yourself with what users can and cannot do. Also keep in mind that there are certain permissions that depend on other permissions to function, so if you enable them, those other permissions are enabled by default.

To remove a permission from being applicable within a selected web application, just clear its check box and click the Save button at the bottom of the form box (Figure 11.10). That will ensure the permission will not be available to anyone in any of the sites contained in the web application.

For considerably more details about user permissions, see Chapter 12.

FIGURE 11.10

The User Permissions form box

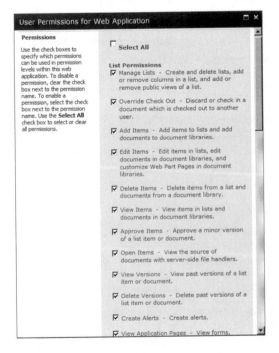

Web Part Security   This button opens a Web Part Security settings box that contains the same settings (Figure 11.11) as the Web Part Security page in the Security category, under the General Security subcategory. Applied per web application, web part security can restrict whether anyone can connect web parts (that includes administrators), use the online gallery (which isn't available for this version of SharePoint anyway), or add Content Editor or XML Viewer web parts to their pages (because those web parts can hold and execute scripts). In addition to the OK and Cancel buttons, there is also a Restore Defaults button. For more details concerning web part security, check out the information under the web part security setting in the General Security subcategory.

FIGURE 11.11

The Security For Web Part Pages form box

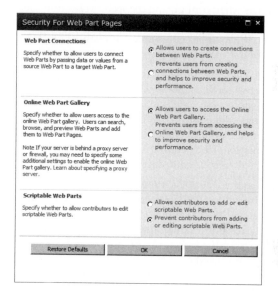

User Policy   The User Policy button opens a Policy For Web Application box that lists the user policies that are already set for the web application. Usually the farm account and, if you have it configured, Search's content access (index) account have policies here. The box lists the zone the user policy is applied to, the display name and username of the user the policy applies to, and the permission level for the user.

A *user policy* gives a user, users, or security group permissions to the web application as a whole (or just by zone). This means that those users to whom the policy applies will have those permissions to access (or be denied access to) any sites in the web application. It makes sense, for example, for search to have full read rights to all content in a web application in order to be able to index all the content in it, which is why it has a user policy with Full Read permissions by default.

To add new users or security groups (and therefore create a new user policy), you can click the Add Users link. To delete a user policy, just select it in the Policy For Web Application box, and click Delete Selected Users. You can also edit the permissions of a user if you want to give them more or fewer permissions. To use other permission levels than what are available by default, you need to create new "permission policies." Basically, anything applied to the web application overall is considered a "policy." That means configuring anonymous access, users, or their permissions for a web application are each a policy.

User policies are covered in more detail in Chapter 12.

Anonymous Policy Because this is truly a security setting, to allow nonauthenticated users to have access to content, it is reasonably applied by zone. You can apply an anonymous access policy to all the zones of a web application or to just specific zones (each can have a different policy if necessary).

Allowing anonymous access occurs in two parts—first when creating the web application such as when configuring the web application's security information (or when editing its authentication provider) and second when enabling and configuring it at the site collection level. When anonymous access is enabled for the web application, it makes it possible to configure the anonymous policy for that web application or its zones.

If you click the Anonymous Policy button, you'll get an Anonymous Access Restrictions box with two sections: Select The Zone (where you can choose all zones or a particular one if the web application has them set up) and Permissions. The Permissions section contains three settings: None (meaning there are no explicit restrictions for anonymous access), Deny Write (restricts any anonymous user accessing any site in the web application from having write permissions), and Deny All (restricts any user trying to access sites in the web application anonymously, as a fail safe).

As mentioned earlier, allowing anonymous access to a web application's contents (even if you intend to allow it for only one of the site collections in the web application) takes at least two steps. It's first applied in the settings for the web application's authentication providers (or in the settings during web application creation). That will enable the Anonymous Policy settings for the web application, in case you want to use a policy. If the Anonymous Policy button is grayed out for a web application, it's because it wasn't enabled for web application. Once Allow Anonymous is enabled for the web application, it becomes available to be allowed at the site collection level. Although anonymous access will be available to be enabled for the site collections within the web application, it must be explicitly allowed at the site collection level to be applied. So, the second step is allowing anonymous access to the site collections. At the site collection level, you can enable anonymous access to either the whole site or to selected lists or libraries. Therefore, if you just want to give anonymous access to a particular list or library, the third possible step is to enable it at the particular list or library rather than the whole site. To learn how to apply anonymous policy and how it affects access at the site collection level (or even at the list level), see Chapter 10.

Permission Policy Permission policies are basically permission levels, or combinations of permissions, that are applied at the web application level. (For more about permissions, see Chapter 12.) There are four default permission policies (or as they can also be known, *permission-level policies*): Full Control (the kind site collection administrators have), Full Read (the kind of permissions a site collection auditor would have, so they can read all pages, items, and settings), Deny Write (explicitly refuses the user write permissions to site collections in the web application, even if they are permitted them there), and Deny All (blocks the user from being able to access site collections in the web application, even if they are added as a user). This setting is also listed under General Security.

That's it for all the buttons and settings under Manage Web Applications. Now on to the only other settings link in the Web Applications subcategory, Configure Alternate Access Mappings.

CONFIGURE ALTERNATE ACCESS MAPPINGS

Alternate access mappings were covered in detail in Chapter 10. This setting is also located under the Farm Management subcategory in the System Settings category. Alternate access mappings are generally associated with web applications. Here's a basic idea of how they work.

SharePoint uses internal and public URLs for its addressing. Internal URLs are those the SharePoint server can accept, which give users access to a particular web application. Public URLs are ones that the SharePoint server returns to a user (showing up in the browser and the URLs for search results) when they access a web application using a particular Internal URL. SharePoint has five public URLs: Default (used by the web application for its real URL), Intranet, Internet, Custom, and Extranet. Each public URL is considered a zone. Remember that when you extend a web application, its address uses one of the zones available for the originating web application. This limits the number of extended web applications per original web application.

In addition to viewing and editing the zones available for a selected web application, you can also add additional internal URLs and map to external resources (Figure 11.12). When you add an internal URL, you need to specify a public URL to which it will resolve. If you can, reuse an existing public URL to conserve zones.

FIGURE 11.12
The Alternate Access Mappings page

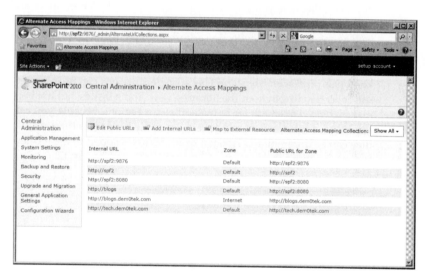

Mapping to an external resource is one of those settings that is primarily a hook for SharePoint Server 2010 or a third-party product, because it is meant to be used to mask the URL of an external resource. Setting up an external resource requires a resource name and URL. Once you create the resource, it's treated like a web application, in that it gets its own zones and can have additional internal URLs.

DELETE THE COLLECTION

If you create a new alternate access mapping collection (which is what Map To External Resource does) by accident and want to delete it, you need to view that new collection's public URLs. The Delete button on that settings page does not delete a selected public URL but instead deletes the collection. This works for deleting any alternate access mapping collection (meaning any internal URL and its associated public URLs as a set), so use it very, very carefully.

Site Collection

A web application is useless without something in it, and this subcategory is all about the site collections. The settings include creating and deleting site collections, configuring their quotas, creating self-service sites, and assigning site collection administrators. All site collection settings were covered in detail in Chapter 10, so for more information about site collections and a demonstration of what a lot of the settings do, see that chapter.

CREATE SITE COLLECTIONS

If you click the Create Site Collection link, it will open a page that looks suspiciously as though you are simply creating a site—and you are. As you learned in Chapter 10, when you create a new site collection, you are creating a new top-level address space and a site to put there. When creating a site collection, you can enter a title, a description, and the URL path for the site, as well as specify the site collection administrators, template to apply to the top-level site, and site collection quota template.

In addition, site collections can be used as user account and group boundaries (otherwise known as *permission boundaries*) because permissions can be inherited from the top-level site of a site collection throughout the libraries, lists, and subsites, but not between site collections. This makes them convenient for branch offices or regions, because you can add users at the top-level site of that site collection and have them easily propagate through all the subsites below it, but they can be different and isolated from the users added to the top-level site of a different site collection. For more about users and inheritance, see Chapter 12.

NUMBER OF INVITED USERS?

There is a field at the bottom of the Create Site Collection page that seems rather obscure. It's Number Of Invited Users in the Quota Template section. This setting can be configured only if SharePoint was set to use Active Directory Account Creation Mode during installation. In that mode, users are added to SharePoint using an email address, and the alias (part of the email address preceding the @ symbol) is used to create a user account in a specially configured organizational unit in Active Directory. In that implementation, as part of setting up a quota template, you can specify the maximum number of users allowed to be added to the site collection. That option is not available for the default, Active Directory Account Mode, which SharePoint uses during a standard installation (Standalone or Complete).

Number Of Invited Users has no relevance in this situation because this implementation of SharePoint doesn't use ADAC, and that's why the field is blank and why you can't configure it when setting up quotas.

DELETE A SITE COLLECTION

The Delete Site Collection page contains options that are pretty straightforward (Figure 11.13). To start, you must specify the site collection to delete by clicking in the Site Collection selection box and then selecting Change Site Collection.

FIGURE 11.13
The Delete Site Collection page

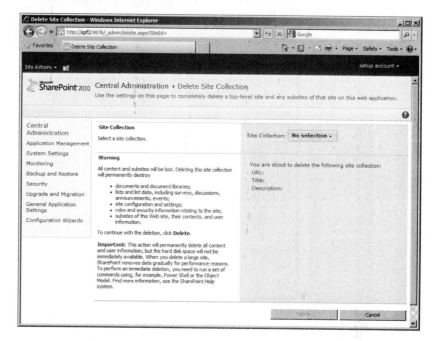

On the left side of the Select Site Collection page, select the site collection you plan to delete (make certain you are in the correct web application). More detailed information about it will appear in the right pane (Figure 11.14). If you're sure that's the site collection you want to delete, click OK.

FIGURE 11.14
The Select Site Collection page

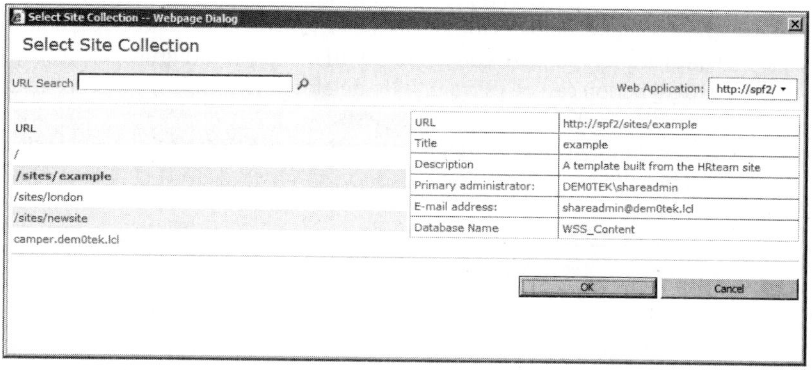

That'll take you back to the Delete Site Collection page, which will be propagated with the site collection's information. To continue with the site collection deletion, click Delete at the bottom of the page (Figure 11.15).

FIGURE 11.15
Deleting the selected site collection

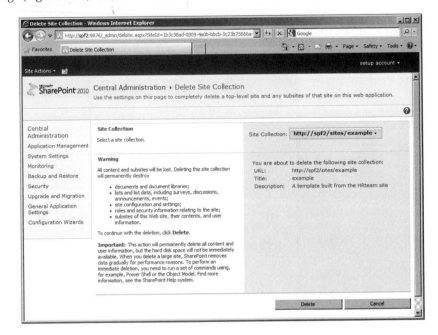

That will permanently delete the site collection and everything it contained. Before doing something so drastic, it is always a good idea to make a backup, just in case.

CONFIRM SITE USE AND DELETION

The Site Use Confirmation And Deletion page setting is useful when users create their own site collections. Although this method is not the most useful or fanciest, Site Use Confirmation And Deletion lets you determine whether and when site collection owners should be contacted to confirm that their site collection is still being used (Figure 11.16). You can even set it so that the site collection can be permanently deleted if the contact does not respond to the confirmation email in a certain number of requests.

For detailed step-by-steps instructions and descriptions about site use and confirmation, see Chapter 10.

SITE VS. SITE COLLECTION

Sometimes SharePoint says *site* when it really means *site collection*, as is the case with the Site Use Confirmation And Deletion page. This is because in prior versions of SharePoint, and in IIS, a *site* is a site collection, and a *subsite* is called a *web* or *subweb*. These old naming conventions also exist in the STSADM and PowerShell commands.

FIGURE 11.16
The Site Use Confirmation And Deletion page

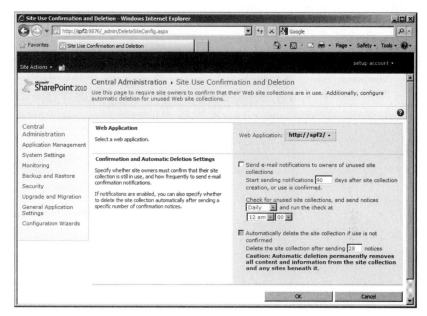

SPECIFY QUOTA TEMPLATES

This is another page that focuses on controlling the growth of site collections. Here is where you can create storage-limit templates for site collections. (Although SharePoint says sites, it means site collections.) A storage quota template can be selected as the default for site collections (useful for self-service sites), or they can also be applied to each site collection specifically. If you click the Quota Templates link, it will take you to a page with two sections: Template Name and Storage Limit Values.

As you can see in Figure 11.17, you should enter a template name in the Template Name section. In the Storage Limit Values section, specify the maximum size in megabytes that the site collection can take up in the content database. When the site collection hits that maximum, SharePoint will lock the site collection, prevent the addition of new content, and refuse all changes to that site—although it will allow you to delete things until the site collection falls beneath the maximum limit. (Do not forget to empty the end-user Recycle Bin.) You can also set a warning level; when the specified number of megabytes is reached, a warning email will be sent to the site collection owners so that they can act preemptively before the maximum is reached. When a site collection contact receives notification that it is reaching its limit, make sure they take it seriously. There is also a section for specifying a quota for sandboxed solutions per site collection. 300 points is a good general default, but you can set a different amount. Solutions that exceed that are disabled for the day and a notification can be sent. You can make as many templates as you'd like to apply to different site collection situations. See Chapter 10 for more details about quotas.

CONFIGURE QUOTAS AND LOCKS

The Site Collection Quotas And Locks page does two things:

- It lets you apply a quota template to a site collection or apply a custom quota to the site collection, instead of applying an existing quota template.

- It shows you the lock status of a given site collection and allows you to change it.

In Figure 11.18, you can see that the page contains settings for Site Lock Information And Site Quota Information—and of course, the site collection selection itself.

FIGURE 11.17
The Quota Templates page

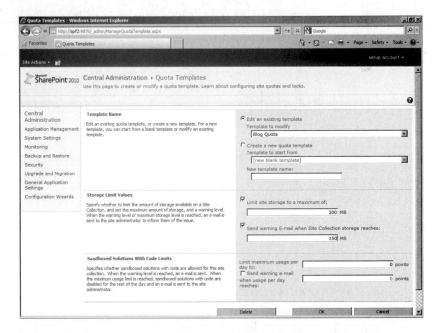

FIGURE 11.18
The Site Collection Quotas And Locks page

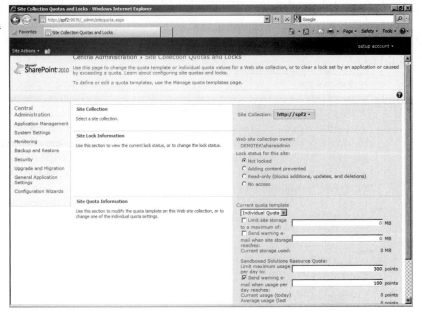

In the Site Lock Information section, there are four lock states:

◆ Not Locked

◆ Adding Content Prevented

◆ Read-Only (Blocks Additions, Updates, And Deletions)

◆ No Access

Here is where you can check the status of a site collection *and* change its lock state. This ability is very useful if, for instance, you have a rogue user doing bad things and you need to block all access to the site collection until the situation is contained.

In the Site Quota Information section, you can set the selected site collection's storage quota individually or assign an existing template to it if you'd like. This setting is useful if you want to change the quota assigned to a site collection during its creation. This section also lets you manage the resource quotas of any sandboxed solutions used by the site collection.

CHANGE SITE COLLECTION ADMINISTRATORS

As you can see in Figure 11.19, this link simply opens a page where you can see the primary and secondary administrators for the selected site collection.

FIGURE 11.19
The Site Collection Administrators page

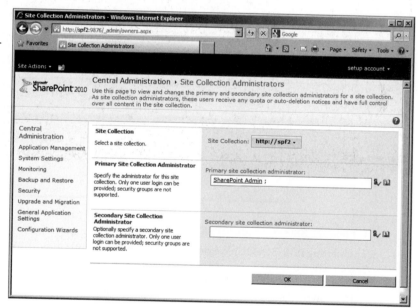

This setting is here is so a farm administrator can see who is supposed to own a particular site collection and reassign ownership if necessary—or take one over if they must. In the Primary Site Collection Administrator and Secondary Site Collection Administrator sections of the page, you can see and change the primary and secondary administrator accounts for the selected site collection. Remember that only single accounts are accepted; no security groups are allowed.

To change the site collection you want to manage, you can use the Site Collection menu to select the correct web application (if necessary) and site collection.

VIEW ALL SITE COLLECTIONS

The Site Collection List page simply lists all the site collections for a particular web application (Figure 11.20). This information is handy when you're troubleshooting why users can no longer access a site collection. If you come here and find that a site collection is gone, you'll know what the problem is. Ironically, considering it's one of the last settings in this subcategory, if you come to this setting first and select a site collection from the list, that site collection will be the default site collection selected in the Site Collection menu of most of the pages in this category. Coincidentally, this page's content is identical to the Select Site Collection box used to select a site collection to delete.

FIGURE 11.20

The Site Collection List page

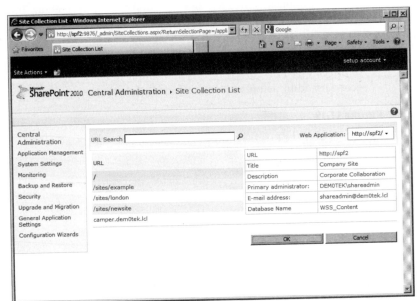

CONFIGURE SELF-SERVICE SITE CREATION

This setting is also available from the Manage Web Applications page, under the Self-Service Site Creation button.

The name is a bit of a misnomer. This option does not allow users to create their own sites, as in their own subsites in a site collection. When enabled for the selected web application, it allows users to create their own site collections. Thus, the user becomes the site collection administrator. So if you set security so that scriptable web parts won't be available for average users to use, forget about it. Users will be able to put those buggy, security-endangering, resource-hogging scripted web parts all over their site collections, for example, because they are administrators.

Also, when you enable self-service site collection, you can't limit the number of site collections a user can create (Figure 11.21). It's either enable it or not; after that, you have to hope (unrealistically) that users make only one. This is why Site Use Confirmation And Deletion is available, so at least the site collections the users have forgotten about can be deleted after a certain time. Also remember to specify a default quota in the general settings of the web application that has this setting enabled to keep user site collections from getting too large.

FIGURE 11.21
The Self-Service Site Collection Management page

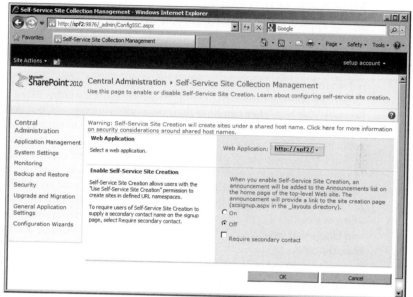

The trick to enabling self-service site creation is that you must have a site collection at the root of the web application that will contain the user-created site collections. When you enable self-service site creation, it will create an Announcements list item with a link to the Self-Service Site Creation page for the users to use to create their site collections (scsignup.aspx). Without that list at the top-level site of the site collection at the root of the web application, this option will not work. This is also why you should consider having the Announcements list view web part on the home page of the top-level site of that root site collection, because it's essentially going to be the portal through which users will go to create their site collections. You can also copy that link from the announcement into an email to send the users or make it a link in the Quick Launch or a tab in the top link bar.

The Self-Service Site Collection Management page has very few settings—Yes or No and Require a Secondary Contact. Requiring the user to designate a second person to manage a site collection is not only useful if the primary administrator goes missing, but it also helps avoid too many "practice" or "test" site collections.

Service Applications

This subcategory contains links to settings that relate to service applications. Previously, only SharePoint Server supported service applications. But as of this version, Microsoft has decided to have more of the Server infrastructure available in the Foundation product, which makes sense. Because of that, there are a few services that are surfaced but not configurable in Central Administration, and there are a few that can be enabled, disabled, and so on. One service, the

Business Connectivity Service (or Business Data Connectivity Service in some circles) is new to this version of SharePoint and very, very useful. It is manageable from this category of settings.

Manage Service Applications

Service applications themselves are new to this version of SharePoint but otherwise are familiar to those administrators who have worked with the SharePoint Server products. There are some differences. Some things have been renamed, and some have been simplified. To start, these service applications are all under the IIS Web Site named Web Services (an improvement over the old shared service providers and their limitations in the SharePoint Server product).

Service applications often have corresponding applications listed in IIS under the Web Services Web Site. They can have their own application pools, but because application pools each use quite a bit of RAM, it's considered a good idea to have as many of them use the same application pool as possible (I am not really sold on that idea, but it has merit).

The Manage Service Applications page lists the service applications that are now available in SharePoint Foundation (Figure 11.22): Application Discovery And Load Balancer Service Application, Business Data Connectivity Service (if you have an instance enabled, which I do), Security Token Service Application, and the Usage and Health data collection service (the only one without a surfaced application in IIS). The two service applications, Business Data Connectivity and Usage and Health (and their proxy connections), that can be configured in any way are in blue; the others are listed in gray text. (If you enable and configure Subscription Settings service, it can also show up on this page and in IIS. See Chapter 16 for more about that service.)

Application Discovery And Load Balancer Service Application   Assists in sharing service applications between trusts, keeps track of the service topology of the farm, and more. This is also called the Topology service because it is uses the Topology application under SharePoint Web Services in IIS.

Business Data Connectivity Service   Allows SharePoint to access external data and expose it within the web applications that associate with the service. This service must be configured in order to allow external lists and lookups. When configured, it gets its own application listed under the SharePoint Web Services Web Site in IIS. You can configure more than one instance of this service application. See Chapter 16, "Advanced Installation and Configuration," for details about using Business Data Connectivity to surface external data.

Security Token Service   The service application that makes claims-based authentication possible and allows SharePoint to support security tokens. It uses the SecurityTokenServiceApplication under SharePoint Web Services in IIS.

Usage and Health Data Collection Service   Has its own database to store data but doesn't have its own application (and therefore, application pool) in IIS. It is used to collect usage and health information for the entire farm.

Although you configured both the Usage and Health data collection service and Business Data Connectivity in Chapter 3 (see that chapter for more details), I'll quickly go over what each button does when working with service applications. There are few service applications that can be managed for SharePoint Foundation; this is an infrastructure feature more populated in the Server version of this product.

Service applications often have additional connection, or *proxy*, settings. They can have more than one connection configured. In this case, all the service applications listed have their own proxies, except for the Security Token Service application.

FIGURE 11.22
The Manage
Service Applica-
tions page

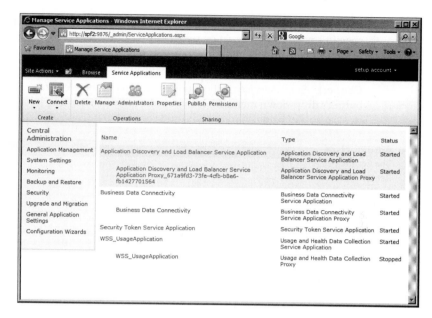

In the Manage Service Applications page, above the listed service applications, is the ribbon bar, with the following options:

New Used to create a new instance of a service application, if possible (they will be listed in the button's drop-down menu). In Figure 11.23, the only service application the New button has available is the Business Data Connectivity Service (or BDC service). This service is basically the only one, out of the box, that can have more than one instance running (and can be configured in Central Administration).

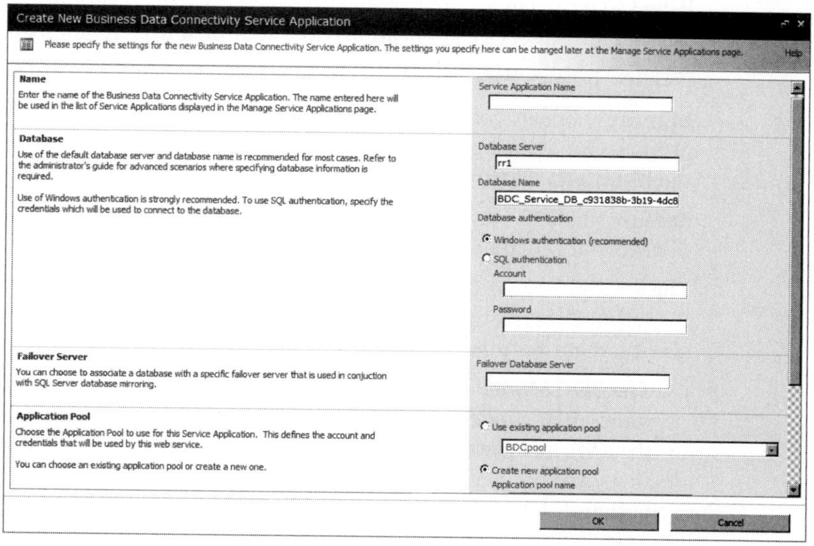

FIGURE 11.23
The Create New
Business Data Con-
nectivity Service
Application form

As you can see in Figure 11.23, a new BDC service application instance requires you to specify a name and application pool (which will be used as the BDC service application's identity). The BDC service application also requires its own database (and requisite database information such as server name, authentication, and failover).

Connect   Some service applications can be shared between farms; these will be listed in the button's drop-down menu. So if there were another farm and it had a service application that was capable of being shared, you could connect to it (Figure 11.24).

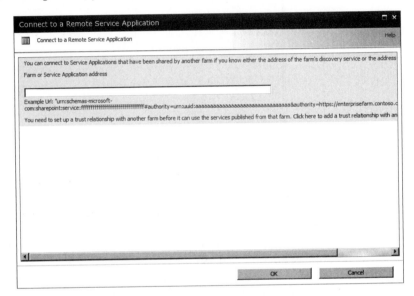

FIGURE 11.24
The Connect To A
Remote Service
Application form

To connect to a service application in a different farm, the service application must be published so it can have a published URL (that URL can be very unintuitive). Connecting to another farm's service applications does require a trust relationship with that other farm.

Delete   Deletes the selected service application or proxy.

Manage   Allows you to manage the settings of the selected service application or proxy connection. Out of the box, the BDC service and its proxy are manageable, and the settings for the Usage and Health data collection service application can be edited.

Because the BDC service application has a number of moving parts, there are a few additional bits that can be edited. We'll get to those in a moment.

The Manage page is filtered by what type of item you want to see and manage in relation to the selected service application (Figure 11.25). In the case of a Business Data Connectivity service, there are three components to manage:

The BDC Model   Basically the application definition file for the service application instance. BDC models, since they are definition files, can be exported and imported, with all the XML metadata for the BDC model, complete with localized names, properties, permissions, and proxies (if you want). When you are managing BDC models, the ribbon will have buttons for Import, Delete, and Export, as well as setting permissions. When exporting BDC models, you can choose to export all the metadata for your setup, or just the "resource" definition, containing any or all permissions, localized names, or proxies.

FIGURE 11.25

The Manage Business Data Connectivity Service page, filtered by External Content Type

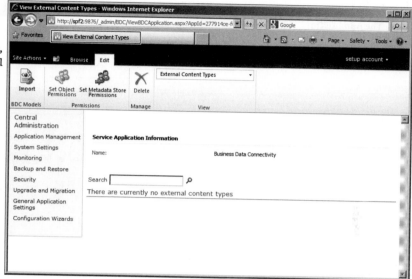

The External System   Specifies the actual external source of data and the protocol used to access it, such as a SQL server database, a web service, or an OLEDB or ODBC database using an ADO.NET connector. It can also be considered the line-of-business (LOB) system. When managing external systems, you can still import a BDC model, set permissions, and delete. In addition, there is a Settings button, but often the external systems for the BDC service application don't have any configurable settings.

The External Content Type   Specifies the actual data within the external system that is being accessed using the BDC service application instance. When you are viewing external content types, there is an Import button for BDC Models, as well as permission buttons and Delete.

Each part of a service application can be secured, and as such, each has permission settings. At the service application level, you can set up administrators allowed to invoke the selected service application. The BDC has three additional parts that can be configured, and each of those has object and metadata store permissions. Setting the Object permissions applies to that particular object, whereas modifying the permissions of the metadata store can affect all metadata used by the BDC service.

This gives you the option of securing the whole application, a BDC model, its external system connections, or the content types (which is generally what I apply permissions to for user access).

Administrators   This button takes you to a page where you can add administrators who are allowed to administer the selected service application instance (Figure 11.26). Farm administrators already have the right by default.

Properties   Click this button to see or change the settings you configured when creating the service application instance (or proxy connection). Settings such as the application pool, database, service name, and managed account are displayed (Figure 11.27).

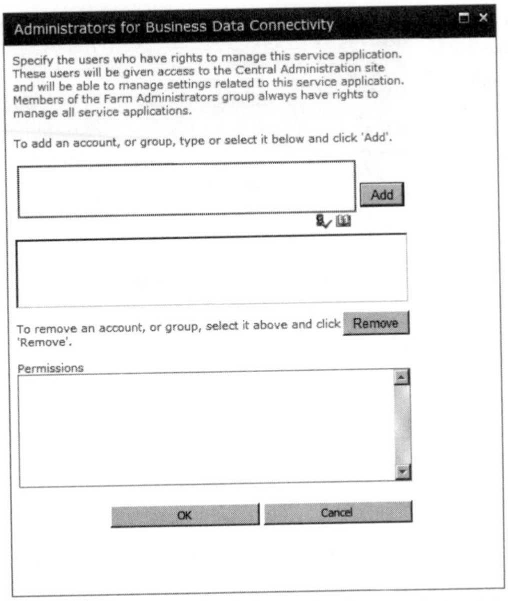

FIGURE 11.26
The Administrators form for Business Data Connectivity

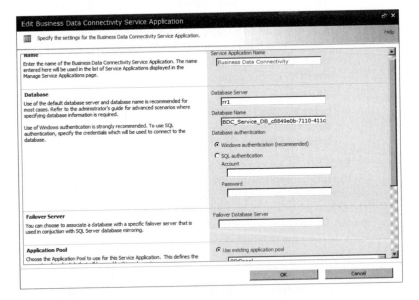

FIGURE 11.27
The Edit Service Application settings

Publish Some service applications can be shared with other SharePoint farms. To share a service application with another farm (or to consume services from another farm) there has to be an existing trust relationship. If the service application can be shared, this button will open to a box that lets you configure the connection type (HTTP or HTTPS), publish to another farm (turns the sharing feature on), and select the trusted farm (with a link to configure a trust if there isn't already one), description, and informational URL if you have a page set up for people to read about it. In addition, there is a section that displays the service application's published URL. The trusting farm that will consume the service will need that URL (Figure 11.28).

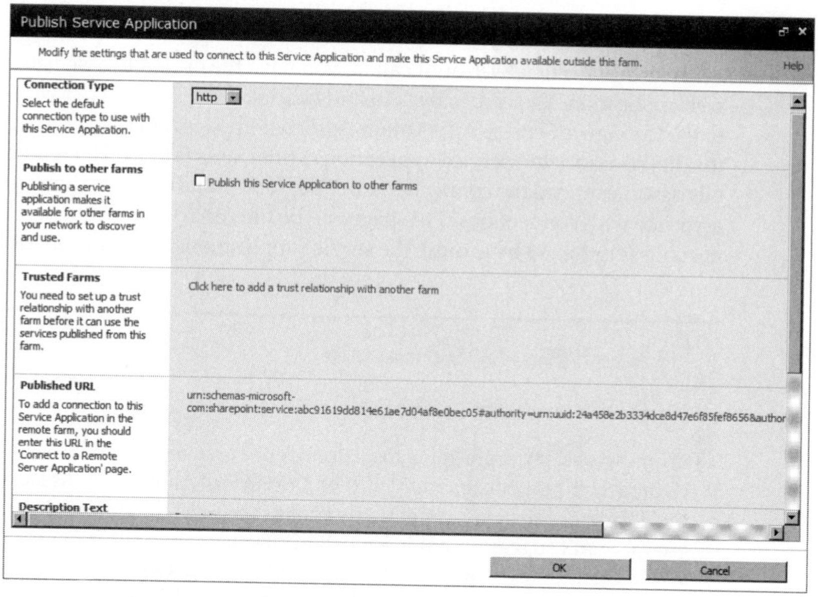

FIGURE 11.28

The Publish
Service Applica-
tion form

Permissions   This button is one of several that relates to service application permissions (Figure 11.29). These permissions have to do with allowing an account or principal (like the farm ID or system) to invoke the selected service application (or the proxy) itself. The local farm is, understandably, usually permitted by default.

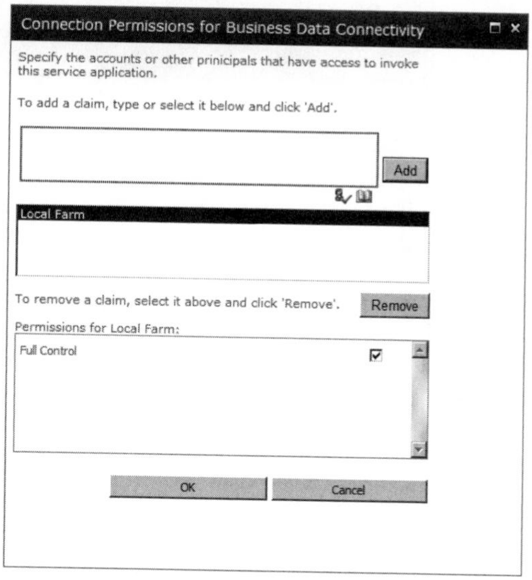

FIGURE 11.29

The Connection
Permissions form
for the selected
service application

For more about service applications, particularly the Business Data Connectivity Service, see Chapter 16.

CONFIGURE SERVICE APPLICATION ASSOCIATIONS

When creating a new web application, you have the option to associate service applications with the web application. You can go back in and change those settings per web application. Or you can go to the Configure Service Application Association page and select the web application of your choice to edit the associated service application connections (Figure 11.30). Keep in mind what you're actually associating are the connections, or "proxies," not the service application itself. Web applications associate with connections. This page can be filtered to display the web applications and their connections (organized by group), the service applications and their proxies, or both.

Real World Scenario

WHEN IS A DEFAULT CUSTOM?

In most cases, if you are going to customize the associations for web applications, you first have to change their group to [custom]. But on the Service Application Associations page, you can select the default group name and actually change the service application connections available to that group. I don't suggest it, but in a pinch, if all your web applications are using a service application and it's gone crazy, you can just whack it from the default group here and remove its association from all web applications that use that group.

FIGURE 11.30
The Service Application Associations page

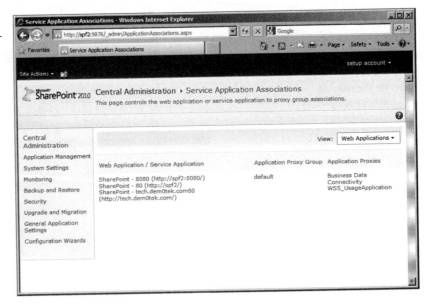

When you click the link for a web application, a Configure Service Application Associations box pops up, allowing you to keep the default group, which is all available service applications, or choose Custom from the drop-down and pick which service applications to associate.

Manage Services on Server

This setting takes you to the Manage Services on Server page, which is also, more appropriately, located under System Settings. This page lists all the surfaced services running on the server, most of which can be started or stopped from the page, and a few can configured from there.

Databases

This subcategory contains the settings links for managing content databases for web applications, setting the default database for the server farm, and, strangely, configuring data retrieval (which doesn't have much in the way of administrative control from the GUI).

Manage Content Databases

The page for this setting doesn't have a ribbon bar and simply supports one action link and a Web Application drop-down (Figure 11.31). You can either add a new content database to the selected web application (displayed in the Web Application drop-down) or click a content database listed for a web application and manage its settings.

You can have more than one database per web application, so it stands to reason that there would need to be a list of them somewhere.

On this surprisingly wide page, displayed with the database name (or names, if the selected web application has more than one database) is the database status, whether or not it's set to read-only, the Timer job server (if there is one selected) for the database, the current number of site collections in it, and the maximum number of site collections for the database as well as its notification level.

FIGURE 11.31
The Manage Content Databases page

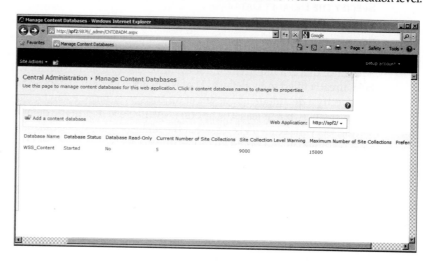

To change those settings listed, click the name of the database you want to modify. This will open the Manage Content Database Settings page (Figure 11.32) for that database. On that page, you can check the database's status (it will match what was listed on the Manage Content Databases page), its version and updates, the selected servers for SQL failover, search, and workflow timer job, as well as both the maximum number of site collections it can contain before being notified and the maximum before the database is taken offline. The database can also be removed from the web application from this Manage Content Database Settings page. For more step-by-step details concerning managing content databases, see Chapter 10.

FIGURE 11.32
The Manage Database Settings page

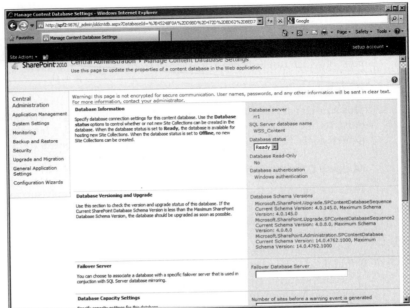

SPECIFY THE DEFAULT DATABASE

SharePoint obviously needs to use SQL databases for configuration, content, and service data. When you create new web applications, a new content database can also be created, if you aren't reusing an existing one. Either way, SharePoint needs to know where that database should be. And since that is a requirement for every database, it is convenient to have the database server field already filled in by default. That is what the Default Database Server setting is for, so you can specify a default database server for the server farm. It can be overridden during web application creation, but at least the option is available to accept the default. As an added bonus, this setting lets you see, at a glance, what the name of at least one database server is for a new network with which you might be unfamiliar.

This setting takes you to a page that simply lets you specify the default SQL server for content and service databases for the farm (Figure 11.33). It is usually propagated on a server farm with the server specified during installation, but you can change it here.

CONFIGURE THE DATA RETRIEVAL SERVICE

Data retrieval services are technologies that use Simple Object Access Protocol (SOAP) or XML to pass data from a source to the data consumer. The Data Retrieval Service page (Figure 11.34) is prepopulated by default and doesn't give you much leeway to modify it, although you can register a third-party service by using the `bindservice` operation in STSADM.

The data retrieval services supported by default are Microsoft SharePoint Foundation, OLEDB, SOAP Passthrough, and XML-URL. You can enable or disable these services entirely as a group. Initially they are all enabled for the farm (globally), but you can choose to stop inheriting the global settings so you can disable all retrieval services for the specified web application. There is no option to pick and choose among them. Under normal circumstances, you should not disable those services. Other settings on this page are basically about the size (in kilobytes) that the data source returns to the data retrieval service that requested it. The default service is OLEDB. You can enable OLEDB update queries here; they are off by default. You can also set the data source time-out period in seconds (the default is 30). This refers to how long it takes the data source to respond to a retrieval service request. You can also enable or disable the data source controls for the retrieval services to process query requests. If you disable either the data source controls or the data retrieval services, no query requests will occur. Therefore, no data will be passed from the data sources to the data retrieval services and then on to you, ultimately. You don't want that to happen.

FIGURE 11.33
The Default Database Server page

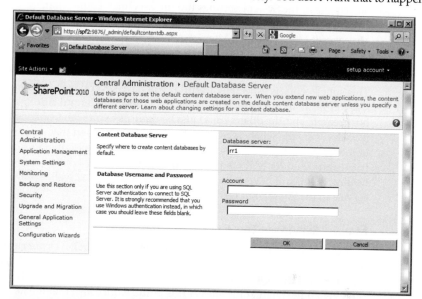

FIGURE 11.34
The Data Retrieval Service page

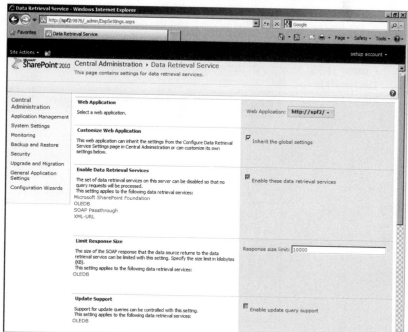

System Settings

Settings organized under the System Settings category generally apply to the server farm as a whole—including managing the server and its services, farm features and solutions, and the farm's incoming and outgoing email settings—as well as the farm's mobile account.

To get to the System Settings page, you can click the heading on the Central Administration home page or the System Settings link in the Quick Launch bar.

Once on the page you can see that there are three subcategories; Servers, E-mail And Text Messages (SMS), and Farm Management.

Servers

This subcategory is especially useful if you have several web front-end SharePoint servers in a server farm. In that case, one server could host the Central Administration page, one could host Search, and the others could just be there as extra web front end servers for load balancing (which can be the whole reason for having a farm). Given that scenario, if you had to take one of the servers offline, those services would need to be assigned to a different SharePoint server in the farm. Suddenly, it would become useful to know where your services are, what server is hosting them, and how to stop and/or move a service, as well as how to remove a server from service in the SharePoint farm.

MANAGE SERVERS IN THIS FARM

This settings page lets you see the servers SharePoint believes are running specific services it requires. In Figure 11.35, you can see that my domain controller (DC1) is the outgoing email server, RR1 is the SQL server (which is correct), and SPF2 is the only SharePoint server and is carrying all the SharePoint roles at this point. Notice also that it lists the name of the configuration database for this server farm (of which there is currently only one server), the version number for this version of SharePoint, and the database server for the configuration database (which is useful if you have more than one SQL server on your network).

FIGURE 11.35
The Servers In Farm page

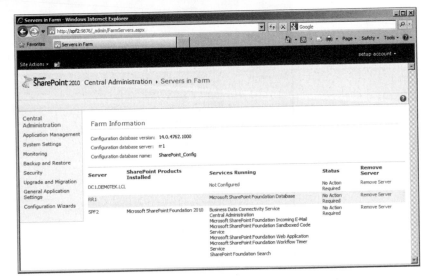

NOT CONFIGURED?

You may have noticed that the outgoing email server, in my case that's DC1, is listed as Not Configured when in fact, if you'd been through the installation chapters, you know it *has* been configured (otherwise alerts wouldn't work).

There is a known bug with this version of SharePoint that, despite being correctly configured and running fine, it can show up in Central Administration's Servers In Farm as Not Configured. This is also the service that displays as Started In Services On Server, even when it hasn't been configured yet. Obviously, this version of SharePoint has gotten confused about displaying outgoing email as a service, but don't let it worry you; it still works fine.

This page will help you figure out where the services are for the server farm. If a server has been decommissioned or has become irreparably damaged, you can remove it from the server farm here by clicking the Remove Server link. When you remove a server from the server farm, all it actually does is remove the server's entry in the configuration database for the farm, making whatever services it was responsible for available to reassign to other servers (such as Central Administration or Search). It does not uninstall SharePoint from the removed server, so if that server comes back online, it will not be recognized by the SharePoint server farm, because it is no longer listed in the configuration database. In cases where a server may be used on the network again, you should uninstall SharePoint from that server before you remove it from the server farm.

MANAGE SERVICES ON SERVER

The Services On Server page is used to manage the services running on a particular SharePoint server directly. As you can see in Figure 11.36, the services displayed by default belong to the first SharePoint server in the farm (which in my example is called SPF2). We set up the Search Incoming Email services in Chapter 3. The Central Administration service was configured during installation automatically, so the server can host the Central Administration site, and we set up the Web Application service, so it can host SharePoint web applications.

FIGURE 11.36

The Services On Server page

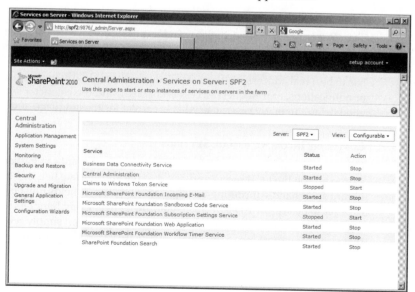

To see the services running on a different server in the farm topology, you can click the Server menu and select Change Server. This will take you to a page where you can select the server you'd prefer (Figure 11.37). This type of page is used to change the selection of Settings pages throughout Central Administration. Options, whether they are servers, web applications, or alternate access mapping collections, are laid out as links to select on a background of alternating stripes (with the selected one highlighted in yellow). Simply select your option, and it will filter the Settings page accordingly. The Services On Server page is where you start and stop services on a particular server. For an example of this, check out Chapter 16, where you'll learn how to move or add the Search service to a second server on the farm.

FIGURE 11.37

The Select Server page

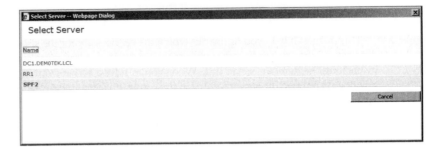

E-mail and Text Messages (SMS)

This subcategory is focused on the email settings available or required by SharePoint. New for this version is the Mobile Account setting, which allows SharePoint, when it is configured correctly, to offer alerts and message via SMS as well as email. Keep in mind that the outgoing email and mobile account settings are also available per web application (and were described) under Manage Web Applications earlier in the chapter. The options for their configuration in this section are for the farm as a whole, if nothing is set at the web application level.

CONFIGURE OUTGOING E-MAIL SETTINGS

SharePoint uses outgoing email to send notifications and alerts to users, site owners, and administrators. As you can see in Figure 11.38, you only need to let the server know the address of the outbound email server, the From address (which can be fictional), the Reply-to address (which has to be a real address, and one someone checks regularly in case users reply to their alerts or notifications, or if Request Access is enabled), and the character set for the email (UTF-8 is a good default in many cases; use what is correct for the language of your network).

CONFIGURE INCOMING E-MAIL SETTINGS

Using the defaults built into IIS's SMTP service, SharePoint can gather incoming email from a drop box on the local server and add it to the appropriate lists or libraries. Not all lists and libraries can handle incoming email, because the email fields must be mapped to the list's fields in order to be useful. You can create your own email event handlers if you want to make incoming email possible for your custom lists; however, you can simply reuse existing list templates that already support incoming email and modify them to suit your needs.

FIGURE 11.38
The Outgoing
E-mail
Settings page

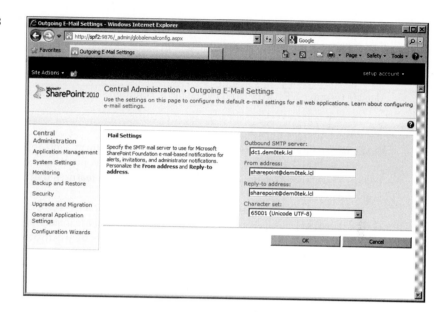

In addition to setting up incoming email, you also can enable something called Directory Management Service (DMS). This feature ties SharePoint in with Active Directory to allow SharePoint to create contact items and distribution list objects in a specific organizational unit (OU). It requires Exchange (2003 or higher, but newer versions might need additional configuration) and Active Directory, of course. Contrary to popular belief, Directory Management Service does not have to be enabled for incoming email to work. For more details concerning configuring incoming email, see Chapters 2 and 3, and for setting up incoming email on a list itself, see Chapter 6, "Introduction to Lists."

CONFIGURE MOBILE ACCOUNT

This setting is similar to the one under the General Settings button on the Manage Web Applications page. Here it is used as the default for the whole farm instead of an individual web application.

To configure a mobile account for the farm, you first have to sign up with a mobile provider, which will give you a URL of the text message service and a username and password for the account. You can test the service using the Test Service button. Be aware that mobile accounts require a fee to be paid to the mobile provider for their service. Typically the server farm is configured with this one account, as opposed to having separate ones for each web application.

Farm Management

This subcategory contains settings to manage farm-specific configuration tasks, such as farm features, solutions, and privacy options. These settings are intended to have an effect on the entire farm, from sites to web applications.

CONFIGURE ALTERNATE ACCESS MAPPINGS

This setting is also located (and explained in more detail) under Application Management, in the Web Application subcategory. The link takes you to the Alternate Access Mappings page, where you can specify the public and private URLs for web applications, as well as a link to specify an outside resource URL to be used by the farm. For more step-by-step details, see Chapter 10.

MANAGE FARM FEATURES

Features can be scoped to be applied at the level of the farm, web application, site collection, or even site. This capability is specified in the feature's contents and cannot be forced during install. The Manage Farm Features setting displays the features that are scoped to be available at the farm level.

A feature simply changes or adds to the functions that SharePoint can do. It usually consists of one `feature.xml` file and occasional supporting files that are installed in SharePoint's Features folder (where all default features are located). Features are then activated per their scope (that's why you can manage features at the farm, web application, site collection, or site level).

The only place you can install or uninstall features is at the command line using STSADM or PowerShell. However, if you have added features to your SharePoint server that are scoped for the farm level, they'll be listed here. For more about adding features to a server, see Chapter 14, "STSADM and PowerShell."

If a feature is applied, you can activate it either at the command line or on the Features page at the level for which it was scoped.

On the Manage Farm Features page (Figure 11.39), you can see whether there are any features available at that level. In my example, you can see that a feature (Office.com Entry Points from SharePoint) is available for the farm and is activated. Remember, features can be added to SharePoint as features on their own or as part of a larger solution.

FIGURE 11.39
The Manage Farm Features page

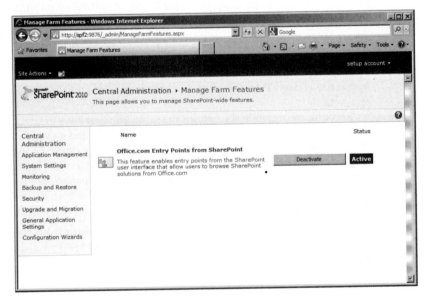

If a feature were not active, you would simply click the Activate button to activate it. The same goes for deactivation. Activating the feature will make the function available for use at the level it was scoped, which in this case is the solutions gallery at the site collection level (Figure 11.40).

FIGURE 11.40
The farm feature Office.com applied at the site collection level

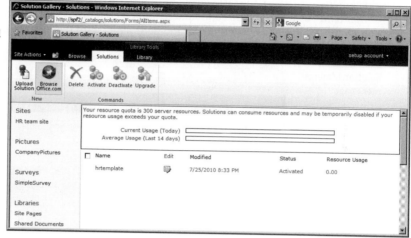

ABOUT THAT BUTTON

As of the writing of this book, the Browse Office.com button, which is the point of the farm feature shown in Figure 11.40, takes you to the Office.com website, which only contains things related to Microsoft Office products, and offers no SharePoint solutions, templates, or web parts. Maybe in the future they might offer something related to SharePoint, but at this point there seems very little reason for this button to be available in a SharePoint Solution Gallery.

To deactivate a feature scoped at the farm level, simply go back to the Manage Farm Features page and click the Deactivate button (which will then turn into an Activate button, should you want to activate the feature again). It will warn you that you are about to deactivate a feature. Click the link on the warning page to continue, and the feature will be deactivated.

INSTALLED, ADDED—WHAT'S THE DIFFERENCE?

Keep in mind that features are installed and then activated; by contrast, solutions are added, then deployed, and then components can be activated. Despite the apparent extra step, solutions are easy to create and deploy, so expect to add many more solutions for your farm than features.

MANAGING FARM SOLUTIONS

Managing solutions is very much like managing farm features in that you need to use STSADM or PowerShell to add the solution (and remove it). However, you can choose to deploy or retract a solution once it's added to SharePoint using the Solution Management page. If there are no solutions available at the farm level, the Solution Management page will suggest you use the STSADM -o addsolution command to add one (Figure 11.41). If there have been solutions added to the farm, they would be listed here, along with their deployment status.

FIGURE 11.41
Solution Management page

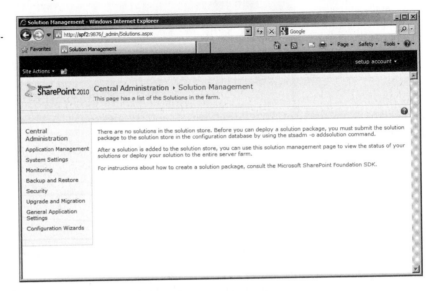

Solutions are really files packaged together in a CAB file with the .wsp extension. A solution can be as big as a site definition, containing site templates and their features and web parts, or as small as a single feature and its supporting files.

Solutions are often made of features that can be scoped to be activated at different levels of SharePoint. Thus, they can add things such as workflows to lists at the site collection level, new menu options to sites, new functionality to site settings, and more. When a solution is deployed to a web application, that only means that all of the site collections or sites in that particular web application can have access to the new features, depending on how they're written. See Chapter 15 for a demonstration of how to add and deploy solutions.

MANAGE USER SOLUTIONS

New with SharePoint Foundation, user solutions let you manage solutions uploaded and applied at the site collection level, allowing more freedom and flexibility for users other than farm administrators to deploy solutions. What makes it possible to deploy solutions that aren't regulated by the farm administrator is that they can be "sandboxed," meaning that their resources can be constrained, their reach can be limited, and some solutions can simply be blocked.

On the Manage User Solutions page (Figure 11.42), you can see that there is a section for specifying blocked solutions (complete with a customizable message). Note that although you upload the solution and specify its filename, the solution is blocked by contents, not by filename alone. Therefore, if a solution has the same name but different content, it won't be blocked. Also notice the Load Balancing section. The first option, to run all the sandboxed solutions' resources on the server that made the request, works well, but it can compromise that particular server if the solutions start to run amok or if there are too many running. The second option lets you use SharePoint's new Sandboxed Code service, which manages all the sandboxed solutions by organizing which servers run the sandboxed code (considered solution affinity). More than one server on the farm must have the sandboxed code service started for solution affinity to work.

FIGURE 11.42

The Sandboxed Solution Management page

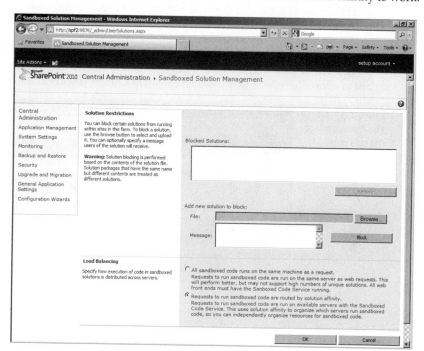

CONFIGURE PRIVACY OPTIONS

The focus of this setting is to allow you to opt in or out of Microsoft's Customer Experience Improvement Program (CEIP), Error Reporting, and Online Help.

In the case of the CEIP, you can opt in on for the farm and then select to opt in or out per web application. The Customer Experience Improvement Program collects data about your SharePoint server and how you use it, ostensibly to help improve their product. No personal or private information should be collected intentionally, and if they happen to accidentally get some, they promise not to use it to identify or contact you or your users. Very comforting, I'm sure.

Microsoft's Error Reporting settings are a little more complicated than just yes or no. Every time SharePoint throws up an error, the error report can be sent to Microsoft. Again, any personal or private information that might accidentally end up in the report shouldn't be used by Microsoft. For this option, you can opt to let SharePoint collect the error reports and send them to Microsoft, to collect error reports and send them in from any client running scripts from the server, and/or to silently send reports to Microsoft without any prompting, such as when unsuspecting users log in. The option to opt out of sending these reports willy-nilly to Microsoft is rather troubling in itself, saying that it would simply ignore errors and not collect any data—which sounds like it would simply ignore errors you need to know about in punishment for not opting to participate in the error report–sending party. You can have the server collect the error reports but not select to do anything else with them. It should then prompt you with the option, whenever an error report is generated, to send it to Microsoft or not.

Finally, the last section, External Web-Based Help, lets you choose whether to allow SharePoint to display help from external sources if they're triggered in the help pages of internal help. If you've ever used SharePoint help, you probably know that it needs all the external assistance it can get. Further, those help pages are often updated with better, more helpful, even more accurate data well after the product releases—which is why it is recommended that you opt to allow SharePoint to access external help sources (Figure 11.43).

FIGURE 11.43
The Privacy
Options page

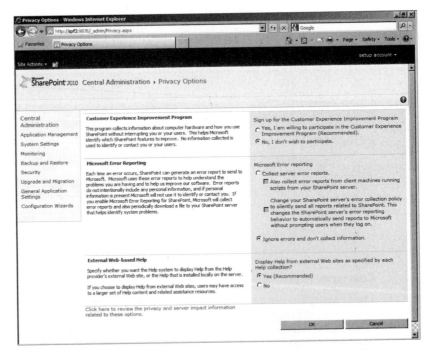

CONFIGURE CROSS-FIREWALL ACCESS ZONE

Primarily intended to be used with Microsoft's Forefront firewall products, this setting allows you to configure a zone for each web application to be used to allow cross-firewall access for mobile devices, as shown in Figure 11.44. You can simply select a zone per web application that will be used to allow for access through firewalls and then have your mobile users use that zone's URL.

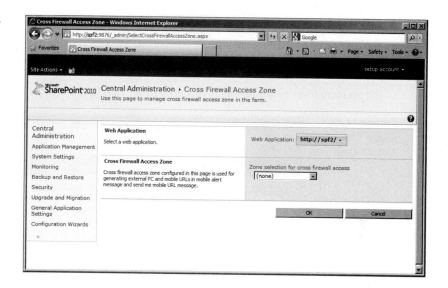

FIGURE 11.44
Configuring a
cross-firewall
access zone

Monitoring

This category contains the settings for the new Health Analyzer feature, timer jobs, as well as the reporting capabilities of diagnostic logging, usage and health data collection. Both health and the usage data collection pertain directly to monitoring SharePoint, whereas timer jobs are actually the meat and potatoes of what runs SharePoint. So, think of this section as being both about monitoring tools and about monitoring farm timer job activities. For more about these in this category, see Chapter 13, "Maintenance and Monitoring."

Health Analyzer

SharePoint has a number of moving parts and requires a certain baseline of component settings to function properly. In previous versions, there was an art to keeping in mind all the little things that help keep a SharePoint farm healthy.

New to this version of SharePoint, the Health Analyzer is a large set of preset rules that run against the server on a set schedule (that you can change). These rules, reminiscent of those found in the SPDiag product available in the SharePoint Administration toolkit V4 (and no longer found in the kit for 2010, reasonably enough), analyze certain settings or baseline functions of the SharePoint server or SQL databases to make certain they are not compromising SharePoint's performance.

Health Analyzer notifications are just that—notifications. They generally don't fix anything on their own (unless they're simple enough to fix automatically, which most aren't); they simply generate a Health Analyzer problem that indicates whether a rule has been broken. They come in three flavors: Information, Warning, and Error. If there are any Error items in the list, a red bar will be generated on the home page of Central Administration with a link to come directly to the Health Analyzer Review Problems And Solutions page. Warnings generate a yellow bar.

REVIEW PROBLEMS AND SOLUTIONS

This page lists the items generated if any Health Analyzer rules have been triggered and have found a problem (Figure 11.45). The items displayed are organized by category (such as Security, Configuration, and Availability). It will also display what server and service are associated with the problem (they're ominously considered to be "failing") and when the item was generated.

FIGURE 11.45
Review Problems
And Solutions page

Because the page is a list, items can be selected, edited, and deleted. They can also be viewed so you can see the problem's details, with information as to what exactly the problem is, a possible remedy, and a link to view the rule that triggered it. The ribbon bar while viewing an item also has a Reanalyze Now button, if the problem has been resolved and you want the list item to go away without deleting it yourself. In addition, if the problem is simple enough to fix, there may be a Repair Automatically button, which can be used to try to resolve the problem. Keep in mind that deleting an item will only remove it from the list until the rule runs again. You can also edit item severity, changing it to "success" to remove it from the list, but again, it will reappear if the issue that triggered it is not resolved before the rule runs again.

REVIEW RULE DEFINITIONS

The Health Analyzer Rule Definitions page displays all the existing rules, organized by category. This allows you to see all the rules, as well as when they are scheduled to run, whether they are scoped to apply to all servers or a particular one, whether the rule is enabled, its version, and so on (Figure 11.46). Some rules, if the fix is easy enough, can be set to try to fix the problem automatically. For this reason, rules can require considerable development, and there is no easy mechanism for administrators to create one themselves. Rules may be updated by Microsoft from time to time in order to keep SharePoint implementations in compliance with most up-to-date best practices.

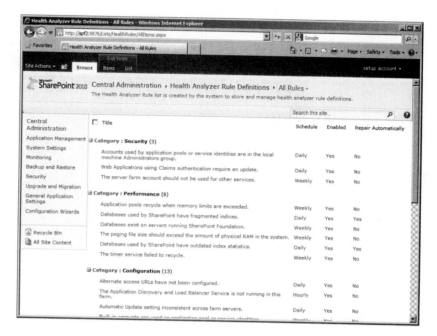

FIGURE 11.46

Health Analyzer
Rule Definitions
page

For more information about the Health Analyzer and a deeper look at the Problem and Solutions report and Health Analyzer Rules Definitions page, see Chapter 13.

Timer Jobs

SharePoint uses the Timer service to run tasks that may be scheduled, such as site deletion notification, incoming email checking, and even "one-time" jobs such as backup restore, or password change, which are all started as needed. Most of SharePoint runs on timer jobs, so although they sound innocuous, they are critical for the proper functions, big and small, of the whole server farm.

The links in the Timer Jobs subcategory both take you to the same set of list pages, discussed next.

REVIEW JOB DEFINITIONS

This opens the Timer Jobs page to Job Definitions, displaying the timer job definitions for the farm, organized by title and by the web application to which they apply. You can also see the schedule type for each job.

On the left of the page, as an addition to the Quick Launch bar, is a Timer Links section, containing links related to Timer Jobs. As you can see in Figure 11.47, Job Definitions is one of them, as are Timer Job Status, Scheduled Jobs, Running Jobs, and Job History. To see the timer jobs organized by status, scheduled jobs, running jobs, or history, you can click the links.

FIGURE 11.47
The Timer Job
Definitions page

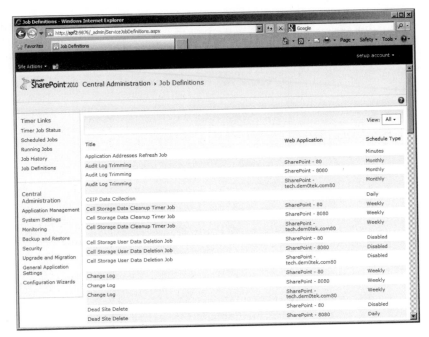

CHECK JOB STATUS

This link takes you to the Timer Jobs page, only filtered to display timer job statuses. The page will display whether jobs are initialized or running, when they are scheduled to run, and a history of previously run jobs (and whether they succeeded or failed and when). For more information about the timer job pages, see Chapter 13.

Reporting

This subcategory contains settings for reports and logs used by Central Administration. It is here that you can manage the events logged by diagnostic logging, and you can enable, disable, and configure usage and health data collection or manage trace logs. You can also do rudimentary health reports, which just show you a limited list of slowest pages and active users, either for the farm or specifically by server or web application.

CONFIGURE DIAGNOSTIC LOGGING

This settings page (Figure 11.48) lets you configure event throttling for diagnostic logging, as well as configure some trace log (otherwise known as ULS logs) settings.

Because SharePoint can overwhelm the event and trace logs with events that you might not really need, it's a good idea to be able to throttle the events that diagnostic logging records. Trace logs alone can take up a lot of space.

This settings page allows you to configure what level of events are recorded for a number of SharePoint categories (Business Data Connectivity service, Search service, SharePoint Foundation, and Reporting Services). Each category contains individual settings as well, so you can go as granular as you'd like configuring the severity listed for alerts, email, or gatherer events. You can also configure Event Log Protection, which will keep repeated events from flooding the event logs.

In addition to throttling diagnostic events, there are also settings for managing trace logs, such as the log location and maximum limit to the size of the log files.

It is often a good thing to put the logs on a different drive than the system files. If you do, just be sure that all SharePoint servers also have the same path available for their logs. Also, the WSS_ADMIN_WPG group must have full control, the WSS_WPG group needs read and execute (and read rights to the folder above it for some reason), and the account used by the Tracing service (SPTraceV4) needs read and modify rights to the location as well.

The size of the trace logs is important because they can become huge. Be aware that the default size limit setting for trace logs is 1000 GB, which is far larger than the suggested minimum drive size to install SharePoint. Consider dropping that to only a few gigabytes instead, and just keep an eye on the logs more often in case anything goes awry. Also keep in mind, to avoid going over the limit if it is getting close, SharePoint will delete the oldest logs in the folder. If keeping all the historical data in the logs is important to you, back up those logs regularly. For more details about diagnostic logging, see Chapter 13.

FIGURE 11.48
The Diagnostic
Logging page

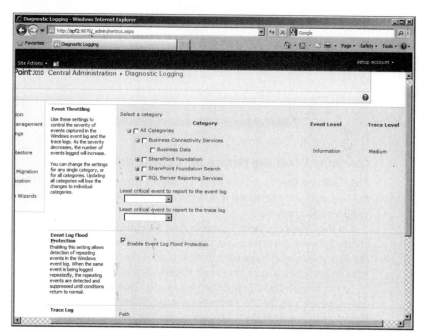

VIEW HEALTH REPORTS

This underwhelming settings page doesn't actually give you a health report. Instead, it simply shows you the slowest pages on the server, and the most active users, in a given range of time.

To use the page, choose between the two reports, specify whether you want to see results from all servers and web applications in the farm, or specify a particular server or web application. Then specify how many items to display per page and the range of time, and click Go

(Figure 11.49). The list will be populated with all of the active users or pages accessed, not just the top ones; they will be listed with information pertaining to the duration it took to load the page, database queries made by the page, and number of times a page was requested for the slowest pages, (or in the case of users) the number of requests made, when they were made, and how many were successful for Top Active Users. Also keep in mind that the page is very wide, so you may miss information if you don't scroll right. For more information about the health reports, see Chapter 13.

FIGURE 11.49
Health report,
Slowest Pages

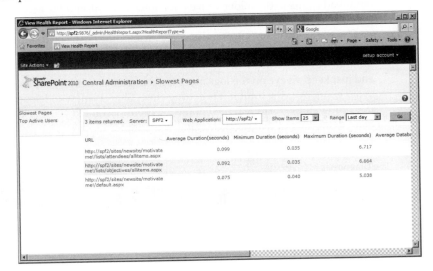

CONFIGURE USAGE AND HEALTH DATA COLLECTION

This link and the title of the settings page it displays (Figure 11.50) don't match. It's almost as if the committee that created this version of SharePoint forgot to agree on what the settings were supposed to apply to.

On the Configure Web Analytics And Health Data Collection page, you can see settings for enabling Usage data collection, complete with what events should be collected, where the log file for the data should go (make sure that location is the same for every front end server on the farm), and how large those logs can get (in gigabytes). You can also enable Health data collection here.

In the Health Data Collection section, the link to see the Health Logging schedule actually only takes you to the Job Definitions page, filtered to the SharePoint Foundation Timer service. But you can see the Health Analysis jobs list, in case you'd like to check their schedules or the last time they ran or, specifically, reschedule them to run outside of peak hours.

In the same vein, the Log Collection Schedule link also takes you to the same Job Definitions page, only filtered to the Microsoft SharePoint Foundation Usage service.

Both the Health and Usage data collection mechanisms use the same database for their data, so there is a section specifying the database server, database name, and authentication to access the database for the respective services. That database is one that can be directly queried by something other than SharePoint, such as Reporting Services.

Keep in mind that logging, whether diagnostic, usage, or health, does take up storage space on the servers and resources while the data is being logged. Schedule their timer jobs for periods of least activity if possible. Also note that during setup, the Standalone installation of SharePoint does not enable Health data collection by default, partly because it can fill the 4 GB limit of the logging database imposed by the version of SQL Express very quickly. So if you do enable Health data collection, watch the logging database for size issues. For more information about configuring the Usage and Health data collection, see Chapter 13.

FIGURE 11.50

The Configure Web Analytics And Health Data Collection page

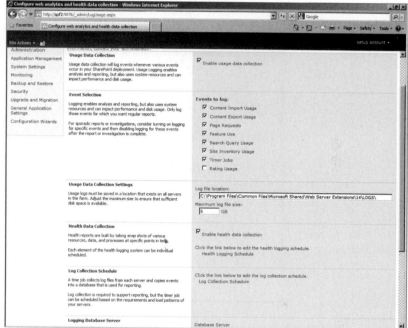

Backup and Restore

This category contains the settings for backing up and restoring the SharePoint farm, web applications, site collections, or even sites and lists if you'd like. Within the list scope, you can even recover data from detached databases if necessary.

Backing up and restoring at all levels are covered in detail in Chapter 13, "Maintenance and Monitoring"; this section goes over the highlights so you know where everything is when you need it.

Farm Backup and Restore

This subcategory contains the settings pages related to backing up and restoring big things, like the farm or web applications. Here are the links for performing backups, restores, and configuring those backup settings, as well as viewing the history of backups and restores and the job status of backups and restores.

PERFORM A BACKUP

This link takes you to the backup page, Step 1 Of 2 (Figure 11.51). It is here that you can see the parts of the farm that can be backed up. There are the web applications, configuration database, search, and the services that share the Web Services IIS Web Site, which are considered shared services, such as Business Data Connectivity (and its proxy connection settings) and Security Token

Service. There is also the sandboxed solution, SPUserCodeV4, with all of its necessary components. Essentially, anything that is particularly difficult to set up has its own application pool, service account, or database and can be backed up with the intention of restoring with the rest of the farm.

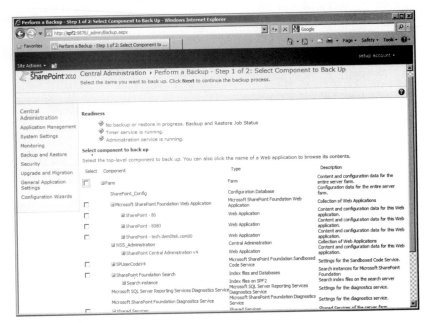

FIGURE 11.51
Performing
a backup: Step 1
Of 2 page

To create a backup of a SharePoint server farm, you need to have SharePoint installed. Ironically, to restore using a SharePoint backup, you must do so from SharePoint, meaning it has to be installed in order to run a restore.

This means that to do a full restore, you first have to install SharePoint, and then you can run the restore. It is still, obviously, worth doing, because you get all your content and settings back. But it does mean that there is already a configuration and AdminContent database running, so they don't necessarily get restored. This is why I don't encourage extensive changes to the Central Administration site itself; instead, you can make subsites or site collections in a web application to back up and restore granularly instead.

Before you perform a backup, it helps to know a few things. A backup or restore is considered a one-time, on-demand timer job. Therefore, the timer service must be running in order for the backup to happen. In addition, it helps to have the administration service (WSSADMIN in Task Manager) running when you back up, and it is critical for success when doing restores. SharePoint Backup uses the SharePoint 2010 Administration Service to access local server resources, and it uses the Volume Shadow Copy service of both the local server and possibly the SQL server that is hosting SharePoint's databases (depending on how you installed SharePoint). This is why the Administration service must be running when you do a backup. However, the Windows SharePoint Services VSS Writer service can be set to Manual and will run if SharePoint needs it. Keep in mind that the Administration service is not enabled by default on Standalone installations of SharePoint.

You must have a location to store the backups, and that location needs to be accessible from the server you are backing up (it should go without saying that you don't want to back up locally). In addition, if you are doing a backup from the SharePoint GUI, you need to give the timer service permission to read and write to the location (in our case that's dem0tek\spffarm), and if you are going to use STSADM or PowerShell to do the backup (you might want to schedule it as a task), the login account that you are doing the backup with needs access as well. Depending on how you have SharePoint installed, you will need to add the SQL server's service account (or for a Standalone installation, the computer account of the server) to the location as well so it can copy database information.

Backing up is a two-step process. First you select the things you want to back up, and then you specify the configuration settings, type of backup, and backup location. On the first backup page is where you can see that there is a convenient Readiness check list at the top of the page, letting you know whether the Timer and Administration services are running and that there are no other backup or restore jobs in progress (there can be only one running at a time). This is also where you specify the components to back up (including the entire farm).

The second page, Step 2 Of 2, is where you decide whether you are doing a full or incremental backup (if you are backing up for the first time, it must be full; then after that can be differentials), as well as if you want to back up just the configuration data or configuration and all contents. Choosing to back up the configuration means that you can restore all configuration settings for the farm to a new installation without all that pesky (and important) content. Usually you back up everything. Finally, on that page (Figure 11.52), you have to specify the location where the backup will go (with a convenient display of the estimated amount of space the backup will take).

FIGURE 11.52
Performing a
backup: Step 2
Of 2 page

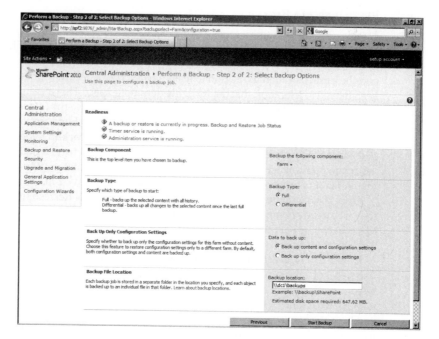

Backup files are stored in a folder automatically given the name spbr and four numbers (usually numbered incrementally in a backup location), along with a table of contents file (usually named spbrtoc). If you want to archive the backup elsewhere, you must keep the table of contents file and the backup folders together. And do not alter the files within the backup folders themselves in any way.

Backups are very resource intensive, so be sure to run them outside of peak production hours, especially since backing up uses the VSS Writer service; it is a good idea to keep activity on the databases at a minimum while they are being backed up. Also keep in mind that the timer job to run a backup is considered a one-time timer job. If the backup fails for some reason, you may have to go to the Timer Jobs page and delete the failed backup timer job in order to run another backup.

When a backup is started, you're taken to a Backup And Restore status page, where you can see what is happening during the backup. This also occurs during restores (of course), so you can see, in real time, the backup progress, success, or failures.

For more details on backing up SharePoint, see Chapter 13.

EVERYTHING BUT THE KITCHEN SINK

Also keep in mind that it is a good idea to back up other SharePoint components, such as the virtual directories and metadata used by SharePoint in IIS, SSL certificates (if you have any), as well as the SharePoint hive 14 folders to back up any customizations you might have made (like adding features and solutions).

RESTORE FROM A BACKUP

This process comes in three steps and has a few caveats. Each backup you do is contained in its own folder, with its own XML file to record what files are in the folder. The Restore process uses that XML file (usually called spbackup.xml) to identify all those backup files in the correct order and their exact location in relation to itself. Therefore, the restore won't work if any of the files have been moved to a location that the XML file does not expect. This means that if you need to move the backups, instead of moving the individual backup files, move the folder they are contained in. Or better yet, make a copy of the entire directory where the backups are so you preserve the backup history of the location with spbrtoc.xml, and retain each backup folder in its pristine state.

Because the restore is so dependent on that folder structure, it makes sense that the first step would be pointing to the backup location to find backup history file. In Figure 11.53, you can see that it defaults to the last successful place a backup was saved to.

Once you've pointed to the backup location and clicked Refresh (if the last place you backed up isn't already being displayed), it will read the backup history file and display the list of backups that can be restored from that location.

From there you select the backup you want to restore and click Next to go the next page.

In step 2, you select the components of the backup you want to restore (this looks very much like step 1 of a backup). It is in step 3 of the restore process that you specify whether you want to restore configuration and contents or just configuration settings (Figure 11.54). It is there that you identify what kind of restoration this will be. One of the nice things about full farm backups is you have the entire farm's components to choose from when restoring. In addition, if you have an incremental backup to restore, you need to restore the most recent full farm backup first and then the incremental one. Notice that although it was a full content backup, you can restore just the configuration settings. You didn't need to do a configuration backup to do a configuration restore.

FIGURE 11.53
Restoring from
backup: Step 1
Of 3 page

FIGURE 11.53
Restoring from
backup: Step 1
Of 3 page

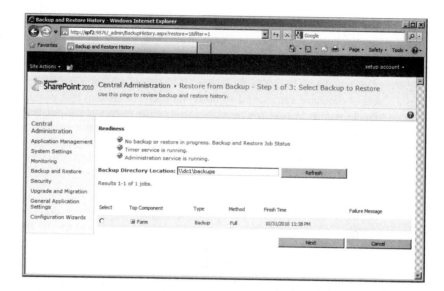

FIGURE 11.54
Restoring from
backup: Step 3 Of 3

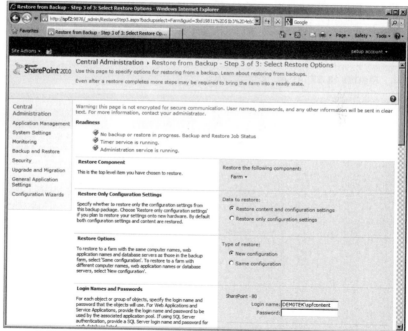

You can restore SharePoint locally (on the existing SharePoint server) if a web application or service has been corrupted or otherwise ruined, or you can restore the whole farm (or separate components) to a new SharePoint installation. This is generally considered a catastrophic restore, meaning that the first server or server farm has completely died and you're restoring that farm on a new server, where SharePoint has been installed to the point where you can open Central Administration and run a restore.

This is why the Step 3 Of 3 restore page has a section to choose Same Configuration or New Configuration. If you choose Same Configuration, it will restore your selected components (or whole farm) using the same URLs, database server, and database names, as well as the same application pool identity accounts. It's assuming you're restoring to the same server.

If you choose New Configuration, the page will prompt you to change the URL, database server, database names, and accounts for each component that you are restoring. It will suggest the old names, in case you need them. Once the restore is started, you'll be taken to the Backup And Restore Status page to watch the restore happen. Long after the restore, you can also check the Backup And Restore History page to see the details of past backups and restores.

For more details (and a step-by-step look at backups and restores), see Chapter 13.

CONFIGURE BACKUP SETTINGS

The Default Backup And Restore Settings page has only two sections and three settings (Figure 11.55). The Number Of Threads section allows you to specify the number of process threads that can be used for backup or restore (each has its own threads setting). The more threads allowed for a task (the maximum is 10), the faster it'll be done. However, that takes threads from other jobs SharePoint is doing. Sometimes, speed isn't everything. The default and suggested value is 3. I don't suggest you go lower.

The other section for this settings page is the default Backup File Location. This is really convenient if you have a location where you always put your backups. It's also useful if you change that location. Just change it here, and it will propagate to all the backups and restores you do after that point. Just make sure your permissions on the location are correct.

FIGURE 11.55
The Default
Backup
And Restore
Settings page

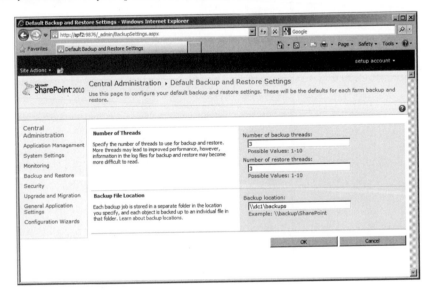

VIEW THE BACKUP AND RESTORE HISTORY

The Backup And Restore History page (Figure 11.56) looks suspiciously like the first Restore From Backup page. It has the Readiness list of services at the top of the page and a field for you to specify the backup location (along with a Refresh button in case you change it). Below that is the list of the backups at the location (based on the backup history file located there). If you select a backup from the list (in my case I have only one) and click the plus sign next to the heading, it will show you details for the selected item, such as when it was done, how long it took, the warning and error count, the directory where the files are actually located, the method used for the backup, and a list of error messages (if there were any). There is even a convenient Begin Restore Process link so you can start a restore right from the page.

FIGURE 11.56
The Backup
And Restore
History page

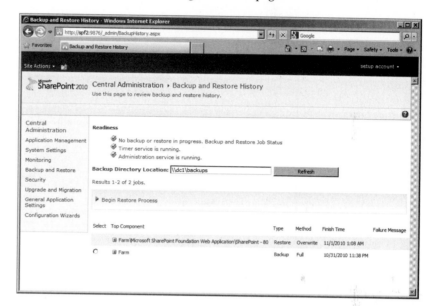

CHECK BACKUP AND RESTORE JOB STATUS

This settings link takes you to the page that is used by both the Backup And Restore processes to report the status of jobs (Figure 11.57). If you were to leave or close the Job Status page during a backup or restore, you could get back to that page by going to this link to see what has happened with the most recent backup or restore task. If you are not backing up or restoring a SharePoint component, this link will still take you to a page populated by the most recent status information of the last backup or restore job.

Granular Backup

New with this version of SharePoint, granular backup is a catchall subcategory for less comprehensive backups than the entire farm or its component web applications and services. In previous versions, site collection backups and exports were done at the command line. Keep in mind, however, that there is no restore option in this interface—only backup for some reason. You have to do your site collection restoration via the command line. In addition, there is a new and convenient means to access a content database that otherwise isn't used by SharePoint to recover individual objects.

FIGURE 11.57
The Backup
And Restore Job
Status page

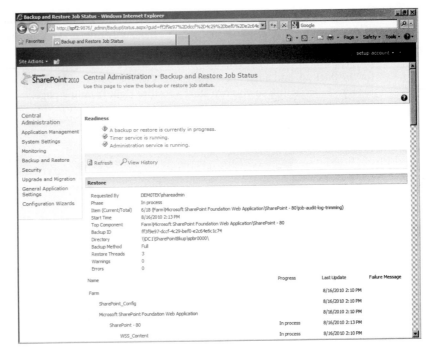

PERFORM A SITE COLLECTION BACKUP

In the previous version of SharePoint, this kind of backup was done only with the command-line tool, STSADM. Now it is available in the GUI for your convenience but still does about the same thing.

You have far fewer options on the Site Collection backup page than you do at the command line (with either STSADM or its new and favored cousin, PowerShell). However, it still works if you want to try a site collection backup in the GUI first, before trying it at the command line.

On the Site Collection Backup page there is just one setting, a field to specify the location and filename for the backup (Figure 11.58). Make sure the SharePoint farm account has read and write access to the location; otherwise, the backup can't be made.

Once you've entered a path and filename for the site collection backup and chosen whether to overwrite any file at that location with the same name (useful if you are doing regular backups), click Start Backup to begin.

The Granular Backup Job Status page will immediately open, displaying the current status of the backup job running, whether there is a backup or export running, if the timer job is running. There is also a convenient link to delete the backup timer job if it fails rather than having to go to the Timer Jobs page and do it.

EXPORT A SITE OR LIST

This page is very like the Site Backup page, only it exports sites, libraries, or lists. Exporting is very much like a backup, and I've often done exports to back up a particular site. Export will back up a path, meaning you can export site collections, subsites with sites below them, or a single site. Export creates .cmp files, which are a kind of .cab file and are imported into existing site collections or subsites. Like the STSADM Export command, this setting allows you to choose to export with full security (meaning that data such as who made what is retained) and the type of versioning for each file or list item. Like backups of site collections, these export files can be imported only using STSADM or PowerShell. As you can see in Figure 11.59, you first select the site collection, then the site, and even the list or library to export. Then you specify the location and name of the export file. Like the site collection backup, the farm account does need access to the location for the export to work.

FIGURE 11.58

The Site Collection Backup page

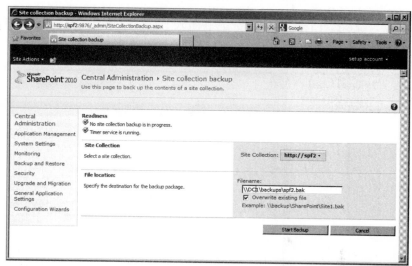

FIGURE 11.59

The Site Or List Export page

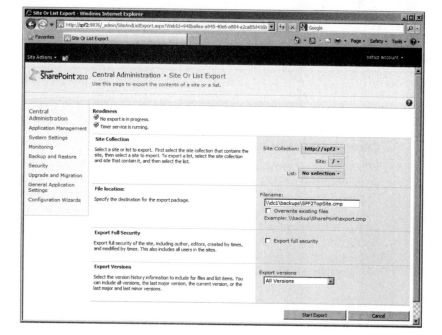

For more on how to back up and particularly restore site collections and import sites or lists, see Chapter 13.

RECOVER DATA FROM AN UNATTACHED CONTENT DATABASE

A particularly useful setting (and another that will be covered in more detail in Chapter 13), Recover Data From An Unattached Content Database does just that—it lets you specify a content database that isn't being used by a web application, possibly because the web application was removed, it came from a different farm, or it was a SQL database backup. Regardless, when all else fails, you can use this setting to browse the database's contents, run a site collection backup, or export a site, list, or library (Figure 11.60) and then restore them (wherever you'd like) to gain access to their contents.

FIGURE 11.60

The Unattached Content Database Data Recovery page

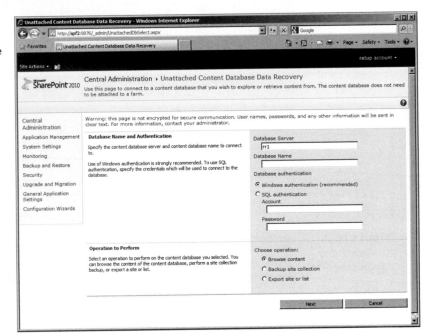

CHECK GRANULAR BACKUP JOB STATUS

When you do a granular backup or export, the Granular Backup Job Status page is where you go to watch the action's progress and check the status of recent backup and export activity (Figure 11.61). This page has a Readiness status area to let you know what is in process (either site collection or site/list export, which share this status page), as well as whether the timer service is running (and if it isn't, not only will no backups work, but you have bigger problems). Below that, while the backup job is in progress, there will be links to refresh the page and to delete the job (if it gets stuck). Beneath that is the area that will display the current or latest jobs, organized by whether they are backups or exports.

The current or most recent jobs will display details such as status (usually either initializing, success, or failure), duration of the job, when it was completed (if it's done), and recovery steps (usually referring to PowerShell, but you can also restore using STSADM).

If, for some reason, you accidentally close or move away from this page before you intended to, this is how you get back to it.

FIGURE 11.61
The Granular
Backup Job
Status page

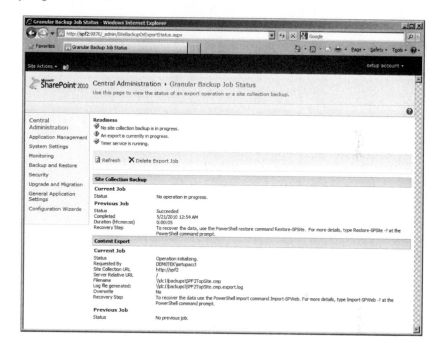

Security

This category includes all things related to SharePoint security, organized between user security, general SharePoint farm security, and, for those configured for it, information policy for information rights management.

Users

This subcategory seems to be a bit of a jumble, containing settings that relate to managing farm administrator accounts, web application policy for users (already accessible from the Manage Web Applications page), and approving or rejecting distribution groups. Only the web application policy settings seem to relate to users, and they are accessible elsewhere.

MANAGE THE FARM ADMINISTRATORS GROUP

This setting takes you to the People And Groups page for Central Administration. This group, Farm Administrators, gives members the full access to all settings on the farm, giving them the power to add, remove, or configure all web applications, services, or content databases and more. To add an account to the Farm Administrators group, simply click the New button (Figure 11.62).

FIGURE 11.62

People And
Groups – Farm
Administrators
page

Whatever you do, do not remove the farm account from the Farm Administrators group. It must be a member of the Central Administration site in order for Central Administration to work. For more information about managing farm administrators and permissions in general, see Chapter 12.

APPROVE OR REJECT DISTRIBUTION GROUPS

This settings page is useful if you have enabled Directory Management Services as part of the incoming email settings. (This service is not required for enabling incoming email, and it requires Exchange 2003 or higher somewhere on your network in order to function properly.) If you enable DMS, it will create an email contact item in an OU you specify for your incoming email-enabled lists and libraries, as well as make it possible to have distribution lists for groups. To keep groups from getting out of control, those distribution lists can be set for approval, requiring a farm administrator to approve the new distribution list before the object is added to Active Directory.

SPECIFY WEB APPLICATION USER POLICY

In the Manage Web Applications page, there is a User Policy button, which (if the site is configured for it) will pop up a form box for you to see what user policies are applied to a selected web application, as well as add, delete, or edit a user policy (there are buttons for the permission and anonymous policy on the page as well).

This setting does about the same thing, except it takes you to the page shown in Figure 11.63, reminiscent of the Policy For Web Application page from the previous version of SharePoint. Also in the Manage Web Applications page are buttons for Permission Policy and Anonymous Policy; here they are listed in addition to the Quick Launch bar on the left.

FIGURE 11.63

The Policy For Web Application page

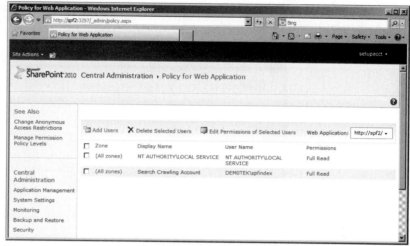

The page lists the user policies applied to the selected web application. The links on the page include Add Users, Delete Selected Users (more than one can be selected), and Edit Permissions Of Selected Users. On the left site of the page, above the Quick Launch bar, is a See Also section that has Manage Permission Policy Levels and Change Anonymous Access Restrictions links.

User policies are applied to a web application to give (or explicitly deny) an account or security group access to all the site collections in that web application. User policies are basically the combination of user or security groups and the permission levels applied to them. User policies are particularly useful for the search index account, so it can read all content in all site collections. They are also useful for accounts that need to be given permissions to site collections in a web application, even if the individual site collections don't add the user or security group to its membership.

Permission-level policies (also simply called *permission policies*) are the combinations of permissions that can be applied to the user or security accounts in the user policies. There are a few default permission levels: Full Control, Full Read, Deny Write, and Deny All (and two named permission levels: Site Administrators, which is the same as Full Control, and Auditors, which is the same as Full Read). New permission level policies can be created, and policies can be deleted as well (although the defaults should not, especially Full Read, which is used by the index account).

Anonymous access must be enabled at the web application first. Once enabled, anonymous access restrictions can be applied (otherwise the Anonymous Access Restrictions page settings are grayed out, as you can see in Figure 11.64). Those restrictions will apply to all site collections being accessed through the URL of the web application (or you can choose to specify one of the zones instead). The restrictions are Deny Write, Deny All, and None. Deny Write blocks anonymous users from contributing content to the site collections, no matter what is set at that level. Deny All simply blocks all anonymous users from accessing content, even if allowed at the site collection level. This makes None the least restrictive of the options and the one you choose if you want anonymous users for the URL or selected zone to be able to contribute in any of the site collections.

User policies and permission policy levels are covered in detail in Chapter 12, and anonymous access is covered in Chapter 10.

FIGURE 11.64

Anonymous Access
Restrictions page

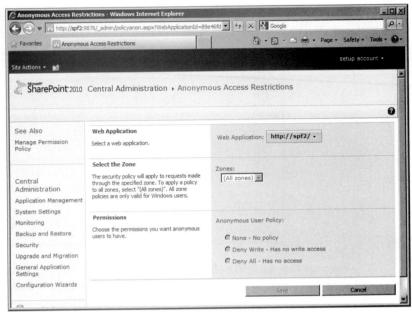

General Security

This subcategory has a number of useful and unique settings, such as configuring managed accounts and password change settings. But it also has some settings that appear elsewhere already. So, for those of you who have seen some of these setting elsewhere, you're right—you have. I will point out those settings as we get to them and direct you to where they are covered in detail.

CONFIGURE MANAGED ACCOUNTS

This version of SharePoint overcomes a service account problem that plagued it for years—the fact that much of what runs SharePoint requires an account identity to function, and if that account's password expires or is changed, SharePoint had no way of knowing it or doing anything about it.

Now it can. In fact, many of the services that SharePoint requires, that also require a user account, now must have SharePoint manage that account. Thus, at least SharePoint knows that its password is about to expire and can send you dire warnings, but it would prefer to be allowed to change the account's password regularly on its own. Yes, that means you won't know what that password is yourself, but at least SharePoint will know it. Configure Managed Accounts actually depends on what you set in the Configure Password Change settings to do its job. So, keep in mind that, once you've configured managed accounts, you need to configure password change settings as well.

When you click the Configure Managed Accounts link, it will take you to a page (Figure 11.65) that lists all the managed accounts for the farm, with information for each, such as the username, password change schedule, last password change (useful to see if it was successful), and next password change. You can also edit or delete each item listed. Being able to edit an existing managed account will be useful if, for some reason, you need to change the password for the account manually, rather than wait for it to be changed by SharePoint or have SharePoint realize there was a change.

To add a new managed account, click the Register Managed Account link.

On the Register Managed Account page, there are two sections, one for the user account and password and the other for managing the automatic password changes (Figure 11.66).

FIGURE 11.65
The Managed Accounts page

FIGURE 11.65
The Managed Accounts page

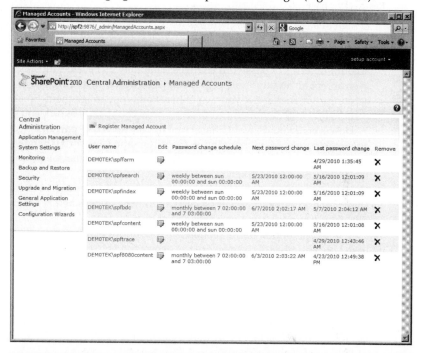

FIGURE 11.66
The Register Managed Account page

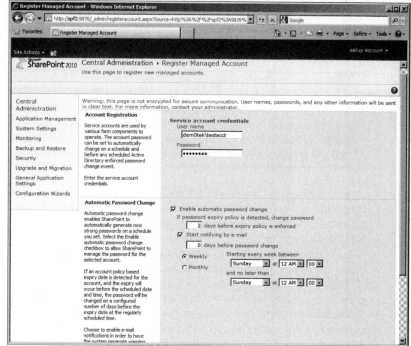

In the Account Registration section are the service account credentials fields, one for the username and one for the password.

The username field requires a *domain\username* (or if it's a local computer account *computername\username*) syntax.

You might notice that automatic password management is optional. In other words, you can add a registered account name and password and then not let SharePoint do anything with the account in terms of password changes. That may be because most SharePoint services won't even accept an account unless it's a managed account, forcing you to register most service accounts, whether or not you want SharePoint to manage them. So, it's only fair that if you don't want to buy into SharePoint controlling an account's password, you shouldn't have to do so.

However, if you do want SharePoint to play an active part in detecting the state of the account's password or changing it, the Automatic Password Change section is for you.

First check the Enable Automatic Password Change check box, and then the other settings in the section become available.

If a password expiration policy is detected, the first option in the section lets SharePoint change the account's password a certain number of days before the password actually expires. The default is two days, but you can change it.

The second option in the section is to start notifying by email that the password is expiring, based on a number of days before the expiration is to occur. The default is five days (supposedly giving you a three-day lead before the password is changed by SharePoint). The odd thing about this setting is that the notification email is apparently supposed to be sent out summary style; in other words, it can only be sent either weekly or monthly.

I can see where this could cause a problem, because the default notification schedule is five days before a password is changed, but even a weekly notification can be seven days away, making the email a little late to do anything about. And I can only imagine sending out the five-day warning email once a month is even less helpful.

For this reason, I tend to set the warning to be at least eight days, rather than five. Then I set the notification email for weekly—at least for the first few months, until I am sure that everything is working fine. Then I might edit the managed account and change the password settings.

HOW DOES IT KNOW WHO TO NOTIFY?

You may have noticed that this page seems to take for granted that it knows where to send these notification emails you're scheduling. This is why if you are configuring managed accounts, you also need to go to Configure Password Change Settings in the General Security subcategory. It is there that you specify the email address used by SharePoint for password expiration notification.

In this example (as you can see in Figure 11.66), I'm just going to register a test account I created in AD for this example (dem0tek\testacct), enable a password, and enable automatic password change. For this example, let's keep the two-day schedule for changing the password before expiration. And for the notification, choose eight days and a weekly notification schedule. Once your settings are complete, click OK. You'll return to the Managed Accounts page, where your new account will be listed.

To edit a managed account after it's been registered, go to the Managed Accounts page (where you should be if you've been following along). Just click the Edit button for the account (in the Edit column). That will open the Manage Account page; only this time, instead of a section for you to specify the username and password, there will be a section to change the password right now (Figure 11.67). There are radio button settings to let SharePoint generate a new password, or you can change the password yourself (giving you a chance to have some control over the account's password and making that notification email more useful).

FIGURE 11.67
The Manage
Account page,
editing an account

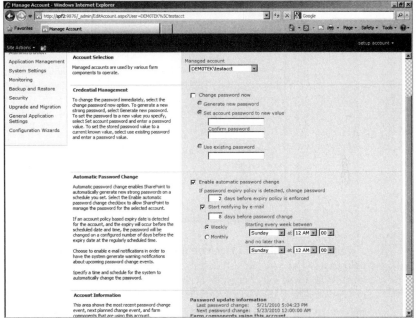

FIGURE 11.67
The Manage
Account page,
editing an account

Below the Credential Management settings are the Automatic Password Change settings, where you can change the password change policy and notification email settings. And at the bottom of the page is a convenient section that not only lists the most recent and next password changes scheduled but also shows what SharePoint components (web applications, services, or service applications) are using that account. Nice to know.

SHARING SHOULD BE CARING, BUT SOMETIMES IT ISN'T

If you enable password changes on an account that is also used by non-SharePoint services, those services may stop working once SharePoint changes the account's password, because SharePoint doesn't actually tell anybody else what the new password is. The other service is left unaware of what happened and unable to log in with that account anymore. This is just a friendly reminder.

CONFIGURE SERVICE ACCOUNTS

Service accounts are used by SharePoint's web applications and services. In this version of SharePoint, all significant services (except the search content access account and SharePoint tracing) require their service accounts to be managed. To see what service account each SharePoint component has and what services are available in the farm, go to the Service Accounts page (Figure 11.68).

FIGURE 11.68
The Service
Accounts page

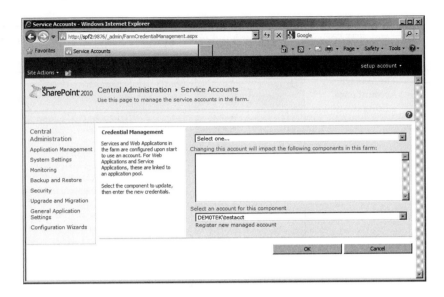

In the Credentials Management section of this page are three fields. The first is a drop-down field that (when you click it) displays all the services with service accounts available on the farm. When you select one, the second field conveniently displays the components impacted by changes made to that service (such as messing with the service account). The last field shows the service account that is currently being used by the selected service. You can click in that field and select a different managed account (which you had to set up before you got here). If you forgot to set up the account you want to use for the component, you can click the Register New Managed Account link. On its page you can set up the account. When you are done, clicking OK to finish will take you back to the page you were originally on (in this case Service Accounts), but your settings will usually have been cleared. So, expect to have to select the component you need to change again.

CONFIGURE PASSWORD CHANGE SETTINGS

This setting must be configured for the notification component of Managed Accounts to work. It also has additional settings that complement the password change settings used by Managed Accounts.

On the Password Management Settings page, there are three sections: Notification E-Mail Address, Account Monitoring Process Settings, and Automatic Password Change Settings (Figure 11.69).

The Notification E-Mail Address section allows only one address to be entered in its field. This means the email will go to only one address, although it can be a distribution or group address.

The Account Monitoring Process Settings section is interesting in that it, too, lets you schedule how long before the password of a managed account (no particular one, but all in general) expires to send out a notification email. Yes, this page also sets up a notification email concerning password expiration—but this one is completely independent of the one configured per password. This notification setting is so you will receive a notification email even if you do not enable automatic password change for a managed account. Just trying to be helpful, SharePoint is willing to let you configure an email here that warns you a certain number of days (the default is 10) before the account expires, regardless of its password change settings. This can trigger redundant emails, so keep this setting, as well as the notification setting for each managed account, in mind.

FIGURE 11.69
The Password
Management
Settings page

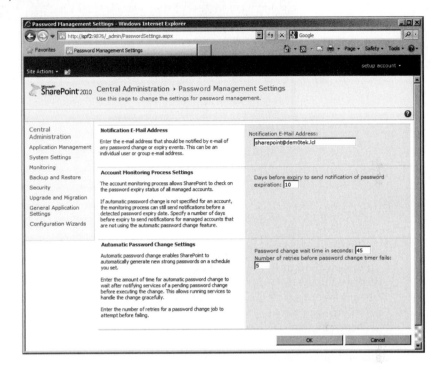

The Automatic Password Change Settings section lets you specify how long SharePoint waits after a password is changed to notify the affected components. This apparently lets those components change over gracefully. The default is 45 seconds (which I see no reason to change, but if your services seem to not be changing their passwords properly, try increasing it).

Also in the Automatic Password Change Settings section is the setting for the number of retries SharePoint will make when trying to change a password. Sometimes, because of network issues, or maybe a reboot, the domain controller might not be available for password changes. This setting will let you specify how many times SharePoint will try to make the change before giving up (you can always check the timer job for password changes for failure from time to time, just to be sure all is well).

SPECIFY AUTHENTICATION PROVIDERS

This setting is also located in Manage Web Applications, as it relates directly to web applications, and is available here for your convenience. It opens to a page as opposed to a form box, which can also be convenient. Authentication providers are covered in detail in Chapter 10.

If you click the Specify Authentication Providers link, it will open an Authentication Providers page (Figure 11.70), with a Web Application drop-down list on the right and the list of zones (and their authentication providers, referred to as Membership Providers here) in the center.

FIGURE 11.70
The Authentica-
tion Providers page

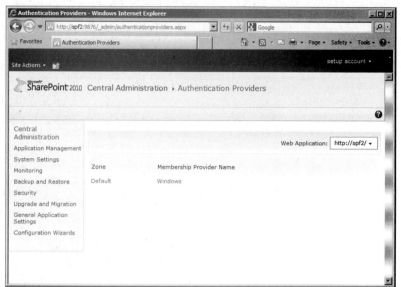

To view the authentication provider details for a particular web application, make sure it is displayed in the drop-down (to change the web application listed, click the drop-down, select Change Web Application, and in the pop-up select the preferred web application). Then click the zone name you want to view.

Depending on whether the zone is using classic or claims-based authentication, you will have a number of options to change authentication settings (Figure 11.71), such as anonymous access, require remote interfaces permissions, authentication types and sign-on URL (if you are using claims-based authentication, it can be customized), authentication settings in IIS (if you are using classic authentication), and client integration (enabled to launch client applications, but forms-based authentication might need it disabled).

MANAGE TRUSTS

Service applications, and Business Data Connectivity in particular, are new to this version of SharePoint (SharePoint services didn't have them). In addition, service applications can be shared across server farms, as a convenience. For two farms to be able to share resources, each must set up a trust relationship in SharePoint with the other. This involves exchanging root authority certificates and, if you want to provide trust to the other farm, a security token certificate (that can be optional).

Certificate management is rather outside the scope of this book, but in brief, using PowerShell, you can export, copy, or import root certificates. Then you can use Manage Trusts page to create a new trust (or see existing ones).

To create a new trust, in the Manage Trusts page, click the New button in the Trust Relationships ribbon (Figure 11.72).

FIGURE 11.71
The Edit Authentication page

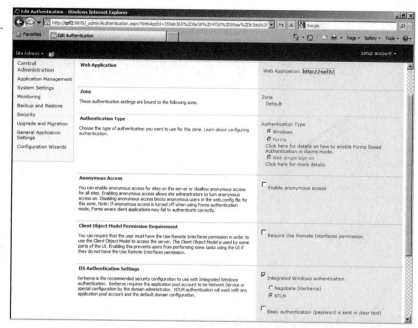

FIGURE 11.72
The Trust Relationships page

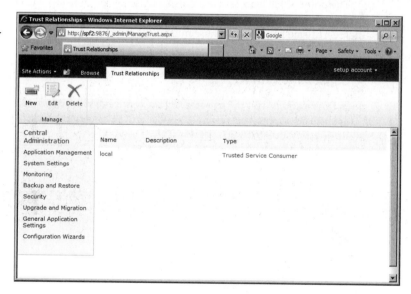

In the Establish Trust Relationship form box that pops up (Figure 11.73), there are sections for naming the relationship (so you will recognize it in the list of trusts in the Manage Trusts page), the root certificate for the trust relationship, and the Security Token Service (STS) certificate for providing trust.

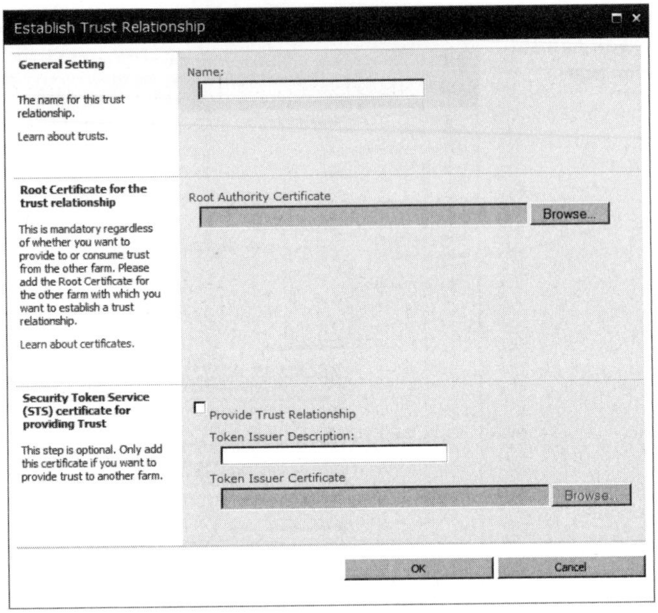

FIGURE 11.73
The Establish Trust
Relationship form

The point of the trust is to establish a trusting relationship with the other farm, so the Root Authority Certificate field is used to select the other farm's root certificate. If you have a copy of their certificate handy, then there must be a lot of trusting going on.

CONSUMING TRUST

In this relationship—the one offering the service to trust is providing trust, and the one who is going to be trusting that provided service will be consuming trust. The terminology may seem a little creepy, but that's just the way it is.

If you are also going to be trusted by the other farm (otherwise known as providing trust), then you also can offer a security token service certificate for the other farm to use in the trust relationship.

To edit an existing trust that you've created, you can select it in the Manage Trusts list and then click the Edit button. It should show you the certificates used by that trust, with a browse field to add more.

MANAGE ANTIVIRUS SETTINGS

This setting requires that you have a SharePoint-aware antivirus program installed on *all* front-end web servers on the farm. Once that software is installed, you must use this setting in Central Administration to allow SharePoint to scan uploaded or downloaded documents, attempt to clean infected documents, or even allow infected documents to be downloaded (I am not sure why anyone would want to do that, but it's there). Using the antivirus software takes up resources on the SharePoint servers and can cause lagging and delays, so you can set the default timeout period (the default is 300 seconds, which is five minutes) to wait before the antivirus scan times out (Figure 11.74). You can also decide how many processor threads a virus scanner can use on the server to curtail the amount of processor resources a single scan can consume. The default is five, but you can experiment with that to see what's right for you.

FIGURE 11.74

The Antivirus page

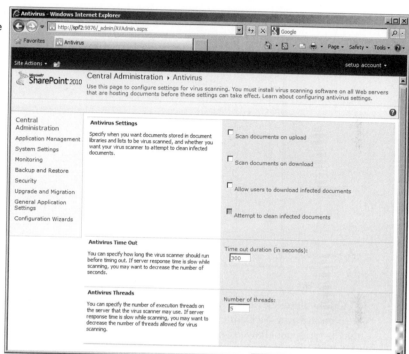

DEFINE BLOCKED FILE TYPES

This setting is also available on the Manage Web Applications page, but in a form box; from here, its settings are available in page format.

Obviously, you will want to block some file types, such as malicious executable files, from being uploaded. However, there may be times when your users will need to upload files that are on the blocked file types list. You'll need to familiarize yourself with what file types are blocked by default and how to add or remove file types from the list.

As you can see in Figure 11.75, this page is really simple. On the right, above the blocked file type list, you can see that blocked file types are applied by web application. This means that this setting can be applied to one web application and not affect the other web applications. The list of file types being blocked is just a multiple-line text box. To add a file extension to the list, simply scroll down to the last entry in the text box, put the cursor at the end of the entry, and press Enter. That will create a new line where you can type the extension you want to block—or you can go to whatever point in the list you'd like and add the extension there (alphanumerics only, no periods). To remove an extension, select the correct web application to apply the change to, then select the file extension in the list, and delete it.

FIGURE 11.75
The Blocked File
Types page

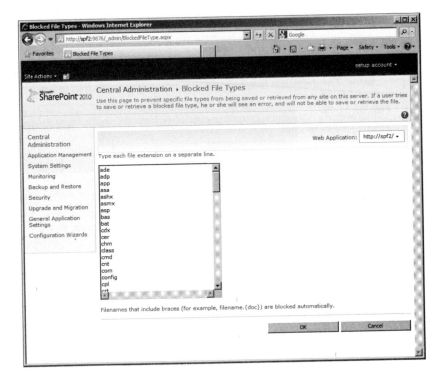

Oddly, although there are no global blocked file types, the tooltip that pops up if you move your mouse over the Define Blocked File Types link does mention that the setting is used to define the file types not allowed to be added to a web application or globally to the farm. There is no global blocked file type setting (it is applied only per web application), so disregard the tooltip.

EVADING BLOCKED FILES

As you can see, this is a pretty rudimentary way to block file uploads. It obviously only checks the file extension and not the file contents. This means that a clever user only needs to change a file's extension before they upload it to avoid the file being blocked.

MANAGE WEB PART SECURITY

This setting is actually applied per web application (despite the link's tooltip saying it's per site collection) and is available from the Manage Web Applications page. Web parts can take extra processing power to pass data between connected web parts, and they can be a security risk if you allow users to add or edit web parts that can run scripts. Because of that, you can set some restrictions on web parts used within a web application.

The Security For Web Part Pages page contains four sections. The first section lets you select the web application to which you want the web part security settings to apply.

The second section, Web Part Connections, lets you specify whether web part connections are allowed to be used on any page in any site collection in the web application. Now, the section says that the settings prevent or allow "users" to create connections between web parts. That might lead you to think the average members of the site will be prevented, but surely site collection administrators or owners will still be able to, right? Wrong. If you prevent creating connections between web parts, all users, including you, will be prevented from creating connections.

"BUT WHAT ABOUT THAT INSERT RELATED LISTS BUTTON?"

Interestingly, Microsoft was pretty effective at removing the capability to connect web parts from the web parts' drop-down list while in edit mode, but it did leave a few things that relate to connecting web parts, causing some interesting results.

Related lists can still be inserted on any page that contains list view web parts, even though the whole point of related list web parts is that they will be connected.

What happens when you use that button to insert a related list on a page? The related list will be inserted below the selected list view web part, and it will have Related Items appended to its title. But, the two lists simply will not be connected. They'll just both be on the page.

Also, the Miscellaneous section of list view web part tool panes will still have the setting for sending first-row data to connected web parts when the page loads—but it won't actually do anything, either. Just to let you know.

The third section, Online Web Part Gallery, is a throwback to an earlier age when Microsoft hosted an Online Web Part Gallery that offered, for free, useful and dynamic web parts, such as weather, stock tickers, and so on. Alas, those days are over, and there is no online web part gallery anymore. Yet the setting remains. Maybe Microsoft intends to resurrect the site someday? And if they do, you can use the settings in this section to allow or prevent anyone using sites in the web application from being able to access the gallery.

As of now, the usefulness of this setting might be that it is backward-compatible with online galleries that might have been created using the SharePoint developers kit.

The fourth section, Scriptable Web Parts, is useful to know. The default setting for this, unlike the previous two sections, is Prevent Contributors From Adding Or Editing Scriptable Web Parts (the other two sections are set to Allow by default). Notice in Figure 11.76 that it doesn't say "users." It says "contributors," meaning that those members of the site with contributor permissions (as opposed to owners or site collection administrators, for example) will be affected by this setting. What this truly means is that average users cannot add a Content Editor or XML Viewer web part to a page they are editing or personalizing. They can manipulate, but not edit, one that you've already added to the page, but they can't add one themselves. If that has been an issue, this is where you allow contributors to add scriptable web parts to pages.

FIGURE 11.76
The Security
For Web Part
Pages page

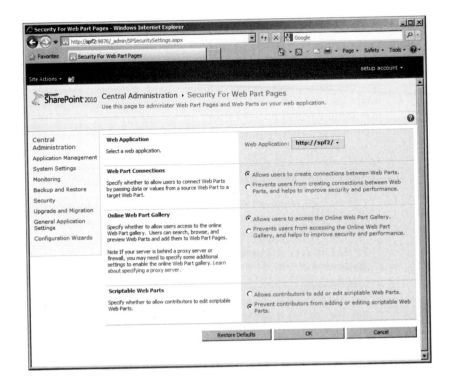

CONFIGURE SELF-SERVICE SITE CREATION

This setting is also listed under Application Management on the Manage Web Applications page and under Site Collections here in Central Administration, where it was covered in some detail. Because of that (and because it was demonstrated in Chapter 10), I'm not going to go over it in detail here.

Self-service site creation is set per web application. It requires that a site collection already be created at the root of the web application and requires that the top-level site for that site collection have an Announcements list.

Self-service site creation actually just gives the users who are members of the first site collection the right to create site collections of their very own. Site collections in a web application can be set with a size quota. If you had one site collection and each subsite was uniquely set with permissions for individual users, then they'd all contribute to the size of the site collection overall and could negatively affect one another. If each had its own site collection, they would each be limited by the quota and not have to worry about what others did on their sites.

Interestingly, you can configure self-service site creation under this subcategory but not quotas or automatic deletion. Also, I am not sure what enabling this capability actually has to do with security. For more about site collection settings, go to the Site Collection subcategory under Application Management, or see Chapter 10.

Information Policy

This section has only one setting, Configure Information Rights Management. This version of SharePoint doesn't really have much in the way of built-in IRM capabilities.

CONFIGURE INFORMATION RIGHTS MANAGEMENT

You can enable SharePoint for information rights management (IRM) using this setting. However, as you can see in Figure 11.77, you must have the Windows Rights Management (WRM) client (Service Pack 2 or higher) installed on the server, and you should have a Rights Management Server on your network for SharePoint to confer with concerning information rights. In addition, each file type that is going to be protected with IRM must have a protector (a file that encrypts and decrypts a particular file format in a list or library that is IRM-enabled) installed on the server that will be IRM-enabled. A number of those protectors are built into SharePoint Server 2010, but SharePoint Foundation has none. Rights management is configured at a list or library level and then applied to each individual file. Files are encrypted and restricted based on the SharePoint user's rights to access and use the file in the list or library where it is stored. When a user downloads a file from an IRM-enabled list or library, it is restricted by their SharePoint user access rights for that library or list. Common restrictions include making the file read-only and preventing the text from being copied, printed, or saved as a local copy. IRM is not really a SharePoint thing; it's a different server function altogether. SharePoint can just integrate with it. See the online document about Information Rights Management for more information.

FIGURE 11.77
The Information Rights Management page

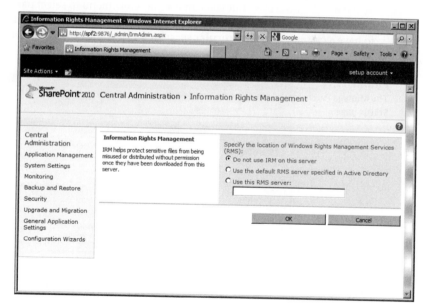

Upgrade and Migration

Ever want to check the version number of your farm quickly? Then this category is for you. It has only one subcategory, Upgrade And Patch Management. Despite that, these settings pages are some of my favorites. The settings are related to what version SharePoint thinks it is up to (regardless of what you might think) and the versions of the databases (well, mostly the content databases), and if you are in the middle of an upgrade to SharePoint Foundation, the upgrade status can be tracked here as well.

Upgrade and Patch Management

This subcategory has only a few settings: Check Product And Patch Installation Status, Review Database Status, and Check Upgrade Status. As anyone who's ever had an update go awry knows, these offerings still make this subcategory a useful one.

CHECK PRODUCT AND PATCH INSTALLATION STATUS

The page for Check Product And Patch Installation Status will just show you the products installed on the farm, on what server they are installed, their patch install status, and their version. This can be very useful in trying to figure out what updates and service packs have been installed, as well as what language packs and other additional products. All in all, it's very convenient.

The Manage Patch Status page opens viewing the farm products and their version numbers by default (Figure 11.78), but you can use the View menu to select particular servers to review as well. This becomes useful if they end up with a great many patches and updates and you need to have a closer look at a particular server. Often servers can get out of sync with their updates, since they often have to be installed on each one manually.

FIGURE 11.78
The Manage Patch Status page

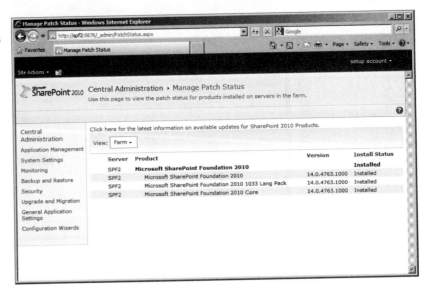

As if that weren't informative enough, there is also a link at the top of the page that takes you to the update center page for SharePoint and related servers. I find this link is particularly useful for keeping up with updates (particularly cumulative updates) and hotfixes. I suggest checking it monthly.

REVIEW DATABASE STATUS

This settings page is useful just to see, in one convenient place, all of the databases used for the SharePoint server farm, regardless of whether they are used by services, web applications, or the farm configuration database. If any of them were mid-upgrade or hadn't upgraded properly, you could come here and see their status.

If all is good, the Status column will list that no action is required (Figure 11.79).

FIGURE 11.79
The Manage Database Upgrade Status page

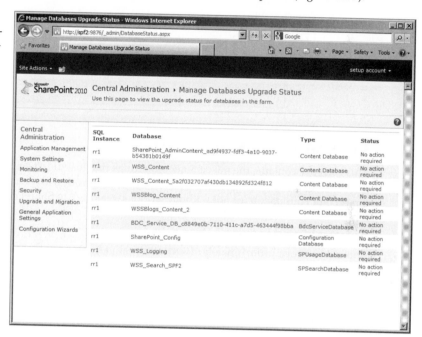

You might also notice that the content database names are links. These will take you to the Manage Content Database page for the database itself, so you can conveniently see the database version, schema, and upgrade information as well as other database settings.

CHECK UPGRADE STATUS

This setting is for checking the status of an existing or past upgrade process. It's useful if an in-place upgrade was done on this server (Figure 11.80). It will, quite reasonably, be empty of data if you did not upgrade to get to the current state of the SharePoint implementation (in my case, I did a fresh install).

FIGURE 11.80
The Upgrade Status page

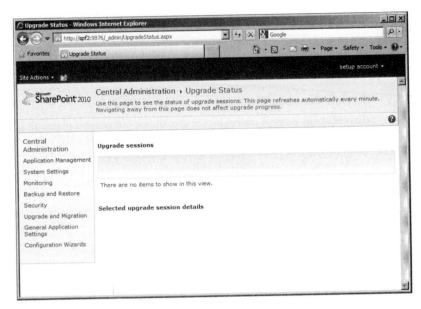

General Application Settings

This category contains the miscellaneous settings that just didn't seem to fit anywhere else, from external service connections that were meant to work with SharePoint Server 2010, not SharePoint Foundation (or not without serious tweaking), to SharePoint Designer restrictions.

External Service Connections

This subcategory, unfortunately, does not contain any settings that can be used by SharePoint Foundation out of the box. Both settings pages are simply part of the infrastructure used by the paid-for SharePoint Server 2010 version.

CONFIGURE SEND TO CONNECTIONS

Send-to connections, at this level, are used for records management and require an officiafile.asmx file in order to work—a file that is not available for SharePoint Foundation. There may be ways to build the file from scratch. But you cannot simply configure this and expect it to work.

Send To Connections lets you specify, for each web application, a send-to connection to a record center site (Figure 11.81). So when a document is complete, there will be the option, in the Send To menu, to send the document to the record center. You could even have more than one (each with a different description), per web application, which is new, and you can specify what action is taken per connection. If you have site subscriptions working, you can allow sites to send to sites outside their subscription.

The problem is that this capability first requires you to use the Record Center template, which SharePoint Foundation doesn't have. It also requires the officialfile.asmx file to be available under _vti _bin, which SharePoint Foundation doesn't have either. Because of this, this settings page is really of no use in SharePoint Foundation (without a lot of work and hacking on the back end) and is only here to prepare for SharePoint Server 2010.

FIGURE 11.81
The Configure
Send To Connec-
tions page

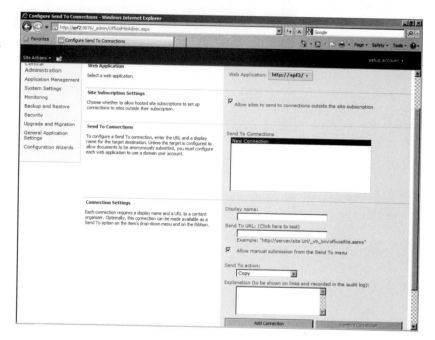

CONFIGURE DOCUMENT CONVERSIONS

This is another setting that is not really applicable for SharePoint Foundation; it is here to connect with SharePoint Server 2010, should you upgrade your farm to it at some point. Document conversions are set on individual web applications and make it possible to do document-type conversions within SharePoint. A document converter allows you to take a document of one type (such as a Word document) and convert it into another type (such as a PowerPoint document or PDF) using SharePoint rather than some other product. Primarily for SharePoint Server, this capability requires converter files and two services to be running and configured for this process to be successful. The files and two services already exist for SharePoint Server, but you have to make them for SharePoint Foundation. See the Microsoft Developers Network (MSDN) website for more information.

The Document Conversion Load Balancer service is in charge of accepting and balancing conversion requests for the server farm. The Document Conversion Launcher service is actually in charge of converting the document. The document conversion process requires the Document Conversion Launcher service to have access to the appropriate converter files so that it knows what it is converting from and what it's converting to.

If you examine Figure 11.82, you'll understand why a load-balancer server is required. This is not network load balancing, but instead SharePoint wants to know what SharePoint server on the farm is running the document conversion load-balancing service. Otherwise, you simply enable document conversion and set the schedule for when conversions should be processed.

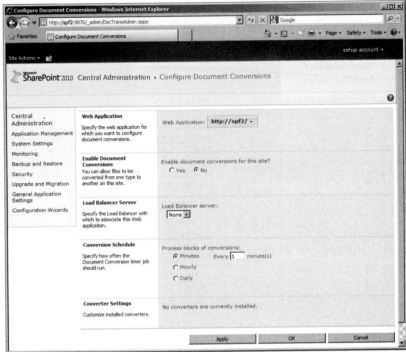

FIGURE 11.82
The Configure
Document Conver-
sions page

SharePoint Designer

SharePoint Designer's role with this version of SharePoint is an interesting one. It is marketed as a must-have tool to use with SharePoint 2010 (both Foundation and Server), with buttons and menu items to access it all over the place, but it is also understood to be a potential danger to SharePoint sites, lists, and security. For this reason, you can grant or deny the right for users (meaning everyone, even those with Designer permissions) to use SharePoint Designer on a web application basis. On the SharePoint Designer Settings page, there are five sections (all settings are enabled by default):

Web Application Used to select the web application the settings on this page will apply to (Figure 11.83).

Allow SharePoint To Be Used In This Web Application Select the box in this section to enable SharePoint Designer for the selected web application. If you disable it, no one will be able to access any of the sites in the web application from SharePoint Designer.

Unfortunately, that will not change all the tantalizing buttons and menu items begging users to click them to edit things with SharePoint Designer. Those menu items and buttons will actually trigger the locally installed SharePoint Designer or open an inviting splash screen to help you download SharePoint Designer. Then, while SharePoint Designer is opening, it will fail to access the website and will display a message that the site has been configured to disallow editing with SharePoint Designer. Would it have been better to not have the buttons or menu items work instead or have the buttons and items go away because the capability and been disabled? Probably. But this is what you get with this setting. The other settings are trumped by this one. If you can't access the site from SharePoint Designer, you can't detach or customize pages or see a URL structure there.

FIGURE 11.83
The SharePoint
Designer
Settings page

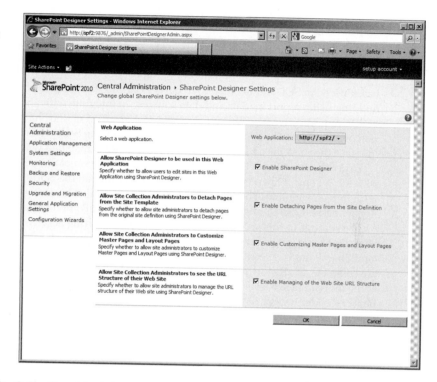

Allow Site Collection Administrators To Detach Pages From The Site Template Most users aren't allowed to detach pages from the site template to begin with, but if disabled, this basically denies anyone the right to detach pages. You can still try, because you'll only be told it won't work after you've opened SharePoint Designer and everything. But in the end, you will be denied.

Allow Site Collection Administrators To Customize Master Pages And Layout Pages
This setting, if disabled, will trigger a dialog box in SharePoint Designer saying that capability (such as master page editing) has been disabled for this site.

Allow Site Collection Administrators To See The URL Structure Of Their Web Site This setting, when disabled, doesn't necessarily block you from seeing the lists, subsites, or workflows, but it does remove the All Files folder from the Navigation bar.

A SLIGHT CONTRADICTION

You might've noticed that the titles for the sections and the actual setting name for the section are not exactly the same. For example, with the Allow Site Collection Administrators To See The URL Structure Of Their Web Site section, the actual setting is Enable Managing Of The Web Site URL Structure. That is different. But, as is the usual case in a GUI environment, if you can not see the thing you're trying to manage, you can't manage it (so that title is more correct). Keep that in mind when you're using SharePoint. For some reason, particularly with this version, setting links and their tooltips, the setting pages, and the settings themselves might not all seem to be referring to the same thing. When in doubt, pay attention to the setting title itself; it's often the right one.

Reporting Services

SQL Server 2000 introduced Reporting Services, and SQL 2005 and 2008 integrated it with SharePoint. This version of SharePoint uses SQL Server 2008 R2's Reporting Services to make it possible to create a SharePoint library of Report Builder documents that pull data from databases stored in SQL and to create web parts to surface that data as well. It allows ad hoc report building using report models and data sources. To integrate with SharePoint, previous versions of SQL required an add-on be downloaded and installed on the SharePoint servers. For this version of SharePoint, the settings for using SQL's Reporting Services are available by default in the interface (because the add-on for SQL Server 2008 R2 is installed with the prerequisites).

To get the most out of Reporting Services in this version of SharePoint, you need SQL Server 2008 R2. A copy of SharePoint must be installed locally on the SQL server (preferably in a server farm implementation). Then the report server service must be configured in SQL (using the Reporting Services Configuration Manager) to do SharePoint integration.

The settings in this section are for configuring Reporting Services for this version of SharePoint using SQL Server 2008 R2 after Reporting Services has been set up on the SQL server (and SharePoint has been installed there, and added to the farm as well). Once these settings are complete, the Reporting Services feature at the site collection level should be activated; and at the individual site level, you should be able to create Report Builder libraries (because the Report Builder Report, Data Source, and Model content types are added to the site collections), report services web parts, and configure site settings.

REPORTING SERVICES DETAILS?

Reporting Services requires pretty extensive knowledge of SQL and Report Builder, and although it integrates with SharePoint, much of the set up has nothing to do with SharePoint and is rather outside the scope of the book. However, there are numerous documents and articles online that will walk you, step-by-step, through setting up Reporting Services and using Report Builder.

There are three links to settings pages under the Reporting Services subcategory. They are Reporting Services Integration, Add A Report Server To The Integration, and Set Server Defaults.

REPORTING SERVICES INTEGRATION

For Reporting Services to be available for SharePoint to use it, these settings must be configured. If you click the Reporting Services Integration link, it will take you to a page that requires Reporting Services to already be configured in SQL in order for you to fill in the fields. These settings are critical for SharePoint to be able to find and use the Reporting Services instance on the SQL server.

The first section requires the URL for the report server instance. The Reporting Services Configuration Manager in SQL 2008 R2 usually defaults to the SQL server name, a port number (in my example I chose 81), and the word *ReportServer* if you allow SQL to use the default name for the Report Server database.

In the second section, you need to indicate the authentication mode to access Reporting Services in SQL. There are two options: Trusted Account and Windows Authentication. Windows Authentication requires Kerberos to be configured, and is the suggested option. If you do that, the users will need to be given permission to the databases being used to generate the reports. Trusted Account is an option if you are not using Kerberos, but is not suggested (unless you are using SQL Authentication).

In the third section, you need to enter the credentials of an account that has administrative privileges on the Reporting Services server. This should be the account specified for the reporting service on the SQL server. The syntax is *domain\username*.

In the final section, you need to specify the site collections to which you want to make Reporting Services (and particularly Report Builder libraries and web parts) available. You can choose all site collections, which means all site collections in all web applications on the farm will have Reporting Services features activated, or you can choose to specify the site collections instead. Interestingly, if you want to specify the site collections, it will drop down a list of all the *web applications* on the farm, with the option to select or deselect them (Figure 11.84). Once you've finished configuring, click OK.

FIGURE 11.84
Reporting Services Integration page

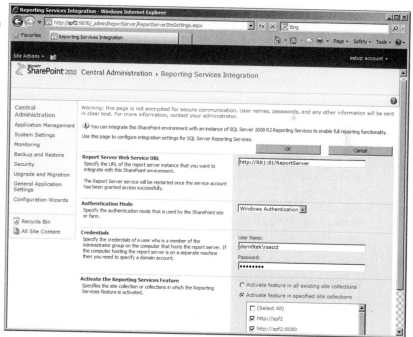

If your settings were correct (that is, if the URL and accounts were acceptable), it will generate a Reporting Services Summary page (Figure 11.85). No matter what account you use for the authentication mode, it will return the value of the service account specified by the Reporting Services Configuration Manager on the SQL server. Don't be alarmed by that.

FIGURE 11.85
Reporting Services
Integration Sum-
mary page

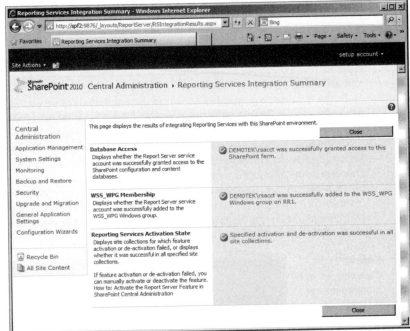

ADD A REPORT SERVER TO THE INTEGRATION

The Integrate A Report Server page that opens for this link is required to indicate to SharePoint which server on the network is the Reporting Services server (although it should have figured it out from the Reporting Services Integration page) and, if necessary, what instance is running reporting services. On this page is one section and two fields; the first is to specify the SQL server name (in my case, that would be RR1; for those of you keeping track, I did upgrade the SQL server to 2008 R2 for this exercise). The second field is to specify, if necessary, the instance name for Reporting Services if you aren't using the default (Figure 11.86). In my case, I am using the default instance on the SQL server.

Once you click OK, you may be prompted to enter a username and password for the Reporting Services service account on the SQL server. (You might even get a script error before the prompt. If so, just click Yes on the script error, and the prompt will appear.)

Integrating the report server is critical in order for several features to work at the site level, so do not skip this seemingly redundant and simple page.

There will be no summary page to indicate whether the integration was a success; you'll just be taken back to the General Application Settings page in Central Administration.

SET SERVER DEFAULTS

This Reporting Services Server Defaults page (Figure 11.87) contains settings that control the default behavior of Reporting Services across all selected web applications.

Reporting Services Reporting Services takes snapshots for report histories. You can limit the number of snapshots taken per report. The default is to not limit. Different limits can be set in the properties of individual reports.

Report Processing Time-Out Sometimes reports can take forever to process (if they have a lot of data to filter through), and sometimes they can take forever because something is wrong. You can set how long (in seconds) a report can process before timing out or let it run forever. The default is to time out at 1800 seconds.

FIGURE 11.86
Integrate A Report
Server page

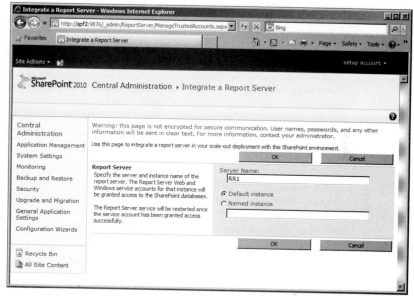

FIGURE 11.87
Reporting
Services Server
Defaults page

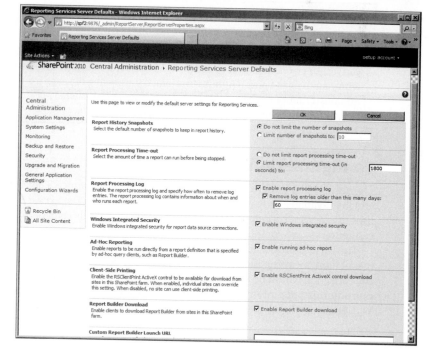

Report Processing Log Located on the SQL server, Reporting Services can generate report processing logs (basically trace logs for reporting services). A new log is created every time the service is started. You can specify in this section if logging is enabled and how old entries need to be before they are deleted.

Windows Integrated Security This section allows you to enable (or disable) Windows integrated security for report data source connections.

Ad-Hoc Reporting This setting allows reports to be run directly from a report from an ad hoc query client like Report Builder (this is an important setting to keep enabled if your users use Report Builder).

Client-Side Printing This setting enables the ActiveX control for printing reports. In the report window or in the Reporting Services web part, there is the option to print. To print, the users need to be able to download and install the ActiveX control into their browser. Without this setting enabled, they can't. This setting can be overridden at the site level.

Report Builder Download Report Builder 3.0 is a ClickOnce component of SQL Server 2008 R2. This means that because Reporting Services is integrated with SharePoint, the client's system will be checked for a local installation of Report Builder when the New Document button is clicked in a Report Builder document library. If Report Builder isn't installed, it will be downloaded, installed, and launched for the user automatically. With this setting disabled, that behavior won't occur.

Custom Report Builder Launch URL This setting is used to specify a custom URL if, for some reason, you are not using the default Report Builder URL.

CAN'T OPEN THE PAGE?

An interesting thing about the Report Services Server Defaults page is that it may not open if you have the wrong authentication mode configured in the Reporting Services Integration page. So if you get 401 errors whenever you click the Set Server Defaults link (when everything else works fine with your login in Central Administration), try accessing the page from the server hosting Central Administration or you can enable (even just temporarily) Trusted Account for the reporting services authentication mode and then try accessing the page again.

Configuration Wizards

The only setting under this category, out of the box, is Launch The Farm Configuration Wizard, which is available only if SharePoint was installed using the Server Farm option. Standalone uses this wizard by default, so it's not available under this category once the installation and configuration are complete.

The Farm Configuration Wizard sets up the farm almost exactly as if it were a Standalone installation, meaning the web application would be the default, classic SharePoint-80. The root site collection would be set up as a team site, with the installation account as the site collection administrator. Many, many of the farm settings would be configured without your input. You deserve to know exactly how to set up your farm yourself. There should be no part of an installation and initial configuration that you don't have control of (and with that control comes a fundamental understanding of SharePoint's underpinnings), and a wizard is all about doing things outside of your control.

I am against using wizards for doing something as important as setting up a SharePoint farm, and for that reason, I will not be demonstrating it.

The Bottom Line

Understand Central Administration's organization.   SharePoint's Central Administration is organized in categories and settings pages with a home page that has several useful web parts.

Master It   Is it a good idea to use Central Administration to hold shared library content, lists, and calendars? Why?

Configure managed accounts.   SharePoint can now manage its own service account passwords, avoiding the problem of services being unable to function after their passwords expire.

Master It   Are there any services in SharePoint Foundation that don't require or can't have a managed account? List an example.

Set the server farm's default database server.   In SharePoint, an administrator is often going to be doing work that involves databases. For this reason, having a default database server specified for the server farm is a great convenience.

Master It   If you are creating a new web application, can you specify a different database server other than the default set for the server farm?

Determine where to stop and start farm services.   The server farm services cannot be truly managed from the server's Services Management console. They can be started and stopped from the Services On Server Settings page under Topology And Services on the Operations page.

Master It   Name a server farm service that can be stopped or started from the Services On Server Settings page.

Manage a farm's solutions and features.   The settings for managing solutions and features are available on the System Settings page under Farm Management.. The Managing Farm Features page allows you to see what features are active (or inactive but available) at the farm level. Solution Management allows you to see what solutions have been added to SharePoint, as well as deploy or retract them.

Master It   Can you install a feature or add a solution to SharePoint from the Manage Features or Solution Management pages?

Chapter 12

Users and Permissions

Controlling user access is a fundamental concern to SharePoint administrators, and it is where we earn a lot of our bread and butter. I mean, really, what good is SharePoint if no one can use it? But the only thing worse than having users unable to access the information they need is having users able to access information they should not have. Access management is a prime area of focus in the administrator's life, and if you plan and implement user access correctly, life goes much more smoothly. In this chapter, you'll learn to

- ◆ Define users and groups in SharePoint
- ◆ Add users and groups in SharePoint
- ◆ Define permissions and permission levels in SharePoint
- ◆ Set permissions on a site/list/list item for a user or a group

What Are Users, Groups, and Permissions?

When you start looking at security, chances are good that you start with the basics: who is allowed to access SharePoint resources, what resources are they allowed to see, what resources are they allowed to use, and how are they allowed to use them.

The people who are allowed access to SharePoint are commonly referred to as *users*. To add user accounts, SharePoint utilizes the services of an authentication provider, such as Windows integrated authentication (which on a domain uses Active Directory; on a non-domain server, it is that server's security account manager database). Active Directory (AD) stores its own user accounts, and people use it to log into their workstations to access network resources all the time. SharePoint uses that authentication source for user accounts when setting up users in its own environment, which allows administrators to use accounts already available in AD to populate its users and group. And when a user logs into SharePoint, SharePoint passes the authentication information to the authentication provider. From that point, SharePoint authorizes user access to its resources based on its membership on the site. Once the user is there, SharePoint uses groups, permission levels, permissions, and other security to authorize their access to the resources that were meant for them and block their access to other resources.

This is why the term *user account* is used in two ways with Windows authentication:

Domain user accounts refers directly to the accounts in AD. If the server is a standalone server and not on a domain, then the user accounts would be local server accounts. They would, however, work the same way, because SharePoint would use the local servers users and groups for authentication by default instead of a domain's users and groups.

SharePoint user accounts refers to the user accounts added to SharePoint from AD (or other authentication source).

SharePoint manages what a user account can do with *permissions*. There is a large list of set permissions that are available at the web application level. These permissions, when applied to a user account, govern what it can do. Permissions are generally grouped together in what are called *permission levels*, to be applied to users based on the type of role they will play or tasks they will perform in SharePoint. There are a few default permission levels, such as Full Control (which usually is applied to administrators who require all permissions to be enabled) or Contribute (which is usually applied to users who will be viewing content, adding content, editing content, and so on). Individual permissions can't be applied to users directly, but permission levels can. For the convenience of administrators, in addition to permission levels putting together useful permissions into role-based combinations, SharePoint uses another convention: the SharePoint group (sometimes known as a site group). SharePoint groups are useful because they are associated with particular permission levels (or even combinations of permission levels if necessary), so when the users are added to the group, they are all given the same permissions. Changing a group's permissions changes them for all users contained therein. Groups are an excellent organizational device (which is why Microsoft keeps using them), allowing users to be grouped together by applied permissions so they can all be added to a resource's access list in one go (and removed that way as well). In addition, SharePoint has a People And Groups page that displays the users in a particular group. Members of the group can go to that page and see the other members and access their user information (if they have permission). If Directory Management Service is enabled, the group can have a distribution list associated with it in AD, allowing someone to email all members of the group at once.

You can add users individually to SharePoint groups, or you can take advantage of Active Directory by adding entire security groups (such as adding the Managers security group as members of the human resources site collection). This is a good thing from a SharePoint administrative point of view, because SharePoint can handle only so many security objects (otherwise known as *security principals*). As far as SharePoint is concerned, both a single user account and a security group are security objects, even though the security group can contain many user accounts. Using security groups to add users to SharePoint groups adds an extra layer of administration, because any change to that security group in AD (such as removing a user) could have an obvious effect on whether that user can access SharePoint. However, if you focus on managing users in groups at the AD level, then it's a snap to simply add their security groups to SharePoint and not really worry about the individual users and whether they've been demoted, promoted, or fired at that level. The changes occur in AD and then are reflected in SharePoint. All this talk of groups leaves you with two kinds of groups to consider:

Domain security groups are created and controlled by the AD administrators. A domain security group contains users and is a method for applying security uniformly to all domain users it contains. For a standalone server not on a domain, the local server's security groups would be used instead.

SharePoint groups are created and controlled by administrators in SharePoint. They are intended to apply permissions more easily to groups of users at once and manage their access to resources in SharePoint. Secondarily, they can be used to identify contained users by the role they play in SharePoint.

AD Is Not Strictly Required

If you have installed SharePoint on a single server, it doesn't need to be in a domain. In that case, instead of using Active Directory, SharePoint will use the local users and security groups for its Windows Authentication.

SharePoint groups are created at the site collection level and are available to any subsite in the site collection. However, you can choose to create a SharePoint group that has permissions only to a particular subsite, if you don't want it to inherit permissions from the parent site. Even groups specifically made for a subsite are listed at the site collection level, because they are a group in the collection of sites.

Although sites that are built on SharePoint can, of course, have additional SharePoint groups, SharePoint Foundation provides three default SharePoint groups for site collections:

♦ *Site name* Owners, such as Company Site Owners (default permission level: Full Control)

♦ *Site name* Members (default permission level: Contribute)

♦ *Site name* Visitors (default permission level: Read)

Each of these SharePoint groups is associated with a default permission level, but you can change the permission level for any SharePoint group as needed. Anyone who is assigned a permission level that includes the Create Groups permission can create custom SharePoint groups.

Users and groups are used at every level of SharePoint, from managing the entire farm to managing web applications, site collections, subsites, lists and libraries, and even individual items.

Before you start working with permissions or creating, editing, and changing groups, it helps to understand the difference between authentication and authorization. Both concepts are critical to a good fundamental understanding of how to secure SharePoint content. *Authentication* is the process of establishing identity, and in a security context this is assessing the credentials of a user seeking access to resources under the control of the authentication provider. You can compare this to matching up someone's face with the picture on their passport to make sure they are the same. Authentication verifies that they are who they claim to be so you can proceed to the next stage, which is authorization. People frequently talk about authentication and authorization as if they were the same thing, but they most definitely are not. *Authorization* allows a user to do something with or to the resources their authentication gave them access to. It is the permission to do a particular task in a system, such as opening a page, reading a document, or managing permissions. All permissions make up the level of authorization for a user. That level of authorization can be considered a permission level inside SharePoint. Simply put, SharePoint requires an authentication provider to do authentication and then gives authorization to users for resources after they have been authenticated.

AUTHENTICATION VARIES

Keep in mind that although my example uses Windows Authentication with Active Directory, SharePoint is easily meant to support other forms of authentication. As a matter of fact, SharePoint was built to be authentication-independent so it can take advantage of multiple kinds of authentication providers. One of the most useful is forms-based authentication, which takes advantage of a SQL database for its authentication source. It's a convenient, alternate form of authentication if Windows authentication is not a viable option for you. It takes a little work to configure, but once done, it works like any other authentication provider.

Permissions are the authorization to perform specific actions, such as viewing pages, opening items, and creating subsites. SharePoint Foundation provides 33 predefined permissions that you can use to allow users to perform specific actions. For example, users assigned the View Items permission can view items in a list. Each permission belongs to one of the following categories: List, Site, or Personal. Permissions are not assigned directly to users or SharePoint groups. Instead, permissions are enabled in one or more permission levels, which are in turn assigned to users and SharePoint groups. Permissions can be included in multiple permission levels, and it is possible to apply multiple permission levels to a single SharePoint group, user, or security group. Permission levels are covered in the "Permission Levels" section.

Individual Permissions

Permissions are rights to do something—to view, create, delete, or edit something. Permissions are allowed or disallowed at the web application level using the User Permissions For Web Applications setting on the Application Management page in Central Administration. SharePoint breaks these permissions down into categories for assignment to users and groups. There are 33 separate permissions divided across three categories (Site, List, and Personal). The following sections will describe them all (based on the standard tables for permissions available in the SharePoint help files and on www.technet.com).

Individual permissions are listed at the web application level to be made available to the site collections that web application contains. To see those permissions (so you can allow or disallow them), go to Central Administration and click Manage Web Applications on the home page. On the Web Applications Management page, select a web application and click the User Permissions button. It will display the permissions in three sections: List, Site, and Personal. Permissions that are unchecked will not be available to be used by the site collections within the web application.

The tables that follow are divided into four columns. The permission name is what appears on the pages where you select the permissions. The description explains what the permission allows you to do. The required permissions are additional permissions that the permission needs to have also enabled to function. The last column lists the default permission levels that contain this permission. This is also a useful guide to selecting or creating permission levels.

The list permissions are shown in Figure 12.1 and described in Table 12.1.

FIGURE 12.1
User permissions,
List permissions

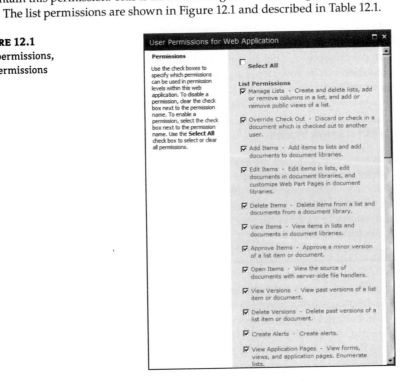

TABLE 12.1:   User Permissions, List Permissions

PERMISSION NAME	DESCRIPTION	REQUIRED PERMISSIONS	PERMISSION LEVELS BY DEFAULT
Manage Lists	Create and delete lists, add or remove columns in a list, and add or remove public views of a list. This is the main control permission to allow control of the lists on the site.	View Items, View Pages, Open, Manage Personal Views	Design, Full Control
Override Check Out	Discard or check in a document that is checked out to another user without saving the current changes. This is a key administration feature, because it allows those who have the permission to discard a checkout and return the document to available status.	View Items, View Pages, Open	Design, Full Control
Add Items	Add items to lists, add documents to document libraries, and add web discussion comments. This is a basic member-level right, allowing the user to interact with the contents of the site.	View Items, View Pages, Open	Contribute, Design, Full Control
Edit Items	Edit items in lists, edit documents in document libraries, edit web discussion comments in documents, and customize web part pages in document libraries. This is a basic member-level right, allowing the user to interact with the contents of the site.	View Items, View Pages, Open	Contribute, Design, Full Control
Delete Items	Delete items from a list, documents from a document library, and web discussion comments in documents. A Basic Member Level right, allowing the user to interact with the contents of the site.	View Items, View Pages, Open	Contribute, Design, Full Control
View Items	View items in lists, view documents in document libraries, and view web discussion comments. To use any of the items on the site, you must be able to view them first.	View Pages, Open	Read, Contribute, Design, Full Control

TABLE 12.1:   User Permissions, List Permissions   *(CONTINUED)*

PERMISSION NAME	DESCRIPTION	REQUIRED PERMISSIONS	PERMISSION LEVELS BY DEFAULT
Approve Items	Approve minor versions of list items or documents. Versioning would need to be enabled for this to be in effect.	Edit Items, View Items, View Pages, Open	Design, Full Control
Open Items	View the source of documents with server-side file handlers. This allows the user to open the document in the source application, such as Word or Excel.	View Items, View Pages, Open	Read, Contribute, Design, Full Control
View Versions	View past versions of list items or documents. Versioning would need to be enabled for this to be in effect.	View Items, Open Items, View Pages, Open	Read, Contribute, Design, Full Control
Delete Versions	Delete past versions of list items or documents. Versioning would need to be enabled for this to be in effect.	View Items, View Versions, View Pages, Open	Contribute, Design, Full Control
Create Alerts	Create email alerts so that the user can be notified via Outlook (or other email program) that something has changed in the item.	View Items, View Pages, Open	Read, Contribute, Design, Full Control
View Application Pages	View forms, views, and application pages. Enumerate lists. This allows you to open and use any pages, which is basic to all other functions.	Open	All

The list permissions govern the actions available to users in lists and on list items. You can combine them to reach your particular goals, but be careful about being overly gracious with what they are allowed to do, such as assuming that someone who needs to manage versioning and approve items should also manage lists. Also, keep in mind that when you look at list permissions, they will be dependent on the choices made for the lists. For instance, View Versions will work only if you have versioning turned on for the list; you could have permission to view versions but no ability to view them if versioning is turned off. Another interesting thing about the list permissions is that what you can do to a list item is broken out explicitly, but there are no explicit create list, delete list, or change list permissions; they are all lumped under the Manage List permission. Therefore, if you want someone to just be able to edit an existing list's settings or add columns, they also have to be allowed to create more lists. Currently permissions are not quite as granular as they could be, and that alone is useful to know.

The second category of permissions is site permissions. These permissions govern the user's access at the site and subsite level and what they can do concerning sites there. Most of the permissions for the SharePoint site are shown in Figure 12.2 and all of them are described in Table 12.2.

FIGURE 12.2

User permissions, Site permissions

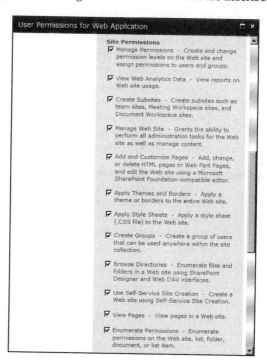

TABLE 12.2: User Permissions, Site Permissions

PERMISSION NAME	DESCRIPTION	REQUIRED PERMISSIONS	PERMISSION LEVELS BY DEFAULT
Manage Permissions	Create and change permission levels and groups on the website and assign permissions to users and groups. This permission enables control of other permissions. It is typically reserved for administration-level people.	View Items, Open Items, View Versions, Browse Directories, View Pages, Enumerate Permissions, Browse User Information, Open	Full Control
View Web Analytic Data	View reports on website usage. This is a key method of gathering metric data on the site. This permission is typically reserved for administration-level people.	View Pages, Open	Full Control

TABLE 12.2: User Permissions, Site Permissions *(CONTINUED)*

PERMISSION NAME	DESCRIPTION	REQUIRED PERMISSIONS	PERMISSION LEVELS BY DEFAULT
Create Subsites	Create subsites such as team sites, meeting workspaces, group work sites, and document workspaces. This permission deals with the structure of the site and should be reserved for administration-level people to allow for the tightest control of the environment.	View Pages, Browse User Information, Open	Full Control
Manage Web Site	Perform all administration tasks for the website and manage content. This permission is the high-level control permission that gives full administration control to the holder.	View Items, Add and Customize Pages, Browse Directories, View Pages, Enumerate Permissions, Browse User Information, Open	Full Control
Add and Customize Pages	Add, change, or delete HTML pages or web part pages, and edit the website by using a Windows SharePoint Services–compatible editor, such as SharePoint Designer. This permission enables more site changes.	View Items, Browse Directories, View Pages, Open	Design, Full Control
Apply Themes And Borders	Apply a theme or borders to the entire website. Because this permission deals with presentation and design, it is not restricted to administration-level people but should also include the designers and developers.	View Pages, Open	Design, Full Control
Apply Style Sheets	Apply a style sheet (CSS file) to the website. Because this permission deals with presentation and design, it is not restricted to administration-level people but should also include the designers and developers.	View Pages, Open	Design, Full Control
Create Groups	Create a group of users that can be used anywhere within the site collection. This is a security-based permission that will allow control of access to the site. This is an administration-level permission.	View Pages, Browse User Information, Open	Full Control

TABLE 12.2:   User Permissions, Site Permissions   *(CONTINUED)*

PERMISSION NAME	DESCRIPTION	REQUIRED PERMISSIONS	PERMISSION LEVELS BY DEFAULT
Browse Directories	Enumerate files and folders in a website by using Microsoft Office SharePoint Designer and Web DAV interfaces.	View Pages, Open	Contribute, Design, Full Control
Use Self-Service Site Creation	Create a website by using Self-Service Site Creation. This permission allows users to create site collections and is active only if Self-Service Site Creation is enabled on the web application; otherwise, it is ignored.	View Pages, Browse User Information, Open	Read, Contribute, Design, Full Control
View Pages	View pages in a website. This permission is for everyone.	Open	Read, Contribute, Design, Full Control
Enumerate Permissions	Enumerate permissions on the website, list, folder, document, or list item. This is a security-based permission that will allow control of access to the site. This is an administration-level permission.	Browse Directories, View Pages, Browse User Information, Open	Full Control
Browse User Information	View information about users of the website. This permission allows users to discover public information about other users and engage in social networking.	Open	All
Manage Alerts	Manage alerts for all users of the website. This permission allows the administrator to delete or change alerts for all users.	View Items, View Pages, Open	Full Control
Use Remote Interfaces	Use SOAP, Web DAV, or Office SharePoint Designer interfaces to access the website. This permission just allows external access to the site from other SharePoint component pieces.	Open	All

TABLE 12.2:   User Permissions, Site Permissions   *(CONTINUED)*

PERMISSION NAME	DESCRIPTION	REQUIRED PERMISSIONS	PERMISSION LEVELS BY DEFAULT
Use Client Integration Features	Use features that launch client applications. Without this permission, users must work on documents locally and then upload their changes. This permission enables the web-enabled collaboration that is the heart of SharePoint.	Use Remote Interfaces, Open	All
Open	Open a website, list, or folder to access items inside that container. This permission is needed for almost all other permissions to function.	None	All
Edit Personal User Information	Users can change their own user information, such as adding a picture. This permission is the one that allows users to make public the information others might browse if they have the Browse Information permission.	Browse User Information, Open	Contribute, Design, Full Control

Site permissions are the basis of control at the site level. Combinations of these permissions are what define a user's effective control of their environment. This category of permissions contains powerful administrative capabilities, such as managing permissions and seeing site usage information, as well as the ability to simply open documents using the correct client or see document libraries using WebDAV (Open With Explorer) for users. As a matter of fact, if a user is having a problem using Open With Explorer, make certain they have the Use Remote Interfaces permission. Despite the fact that the permission also makes it possible for them to open the page in SharePoint Designer, it's needed for all browsing of libraries with Explorer.

SELF-SERVICE SITE CREATION BLOCKING

If you want to block the possibility of Self-Service Site Creation ever being used in a particular web application, deny its permission here. Then, even if it is enabled in Central Administration, no user will be able to use it. It will make people angry when they try, but it is a fail-safe way of avoiding an "accidental" onslaught of new site collections. Another thing you can do is disable the permission in particular permission levels, allowing Self-Service Site Creation only to the permission levels you choose, not all of them.

The third category of permissions is Personal. The Personal permissions from the SharePoint site are shown in Figure 12.3 and described in Table 12.3.

FIGURE 12.3
User Permissions,
Personal
Permissions

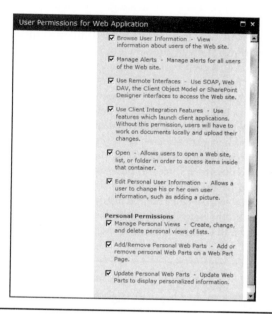

TABLE 12.3:   User Permissions, Personal Permissions

PERMISSION NAME	DESCRIPTION	REQUIRED PERMISSIONS	PERMISSION LEVELS BY DEFAULT
Manage Personal Views	Create, change, and delete personal views of lists.	View Items, View Pages, Open	Contribute, Design, Full Control
Add/Remove Personal Web Parts	Add or remove personal web parts on a web part page.	View Items, View Pages, Open, Update Personal Web Parts	Contribute, Design, Full Control
Update Personal Web Parts	Update web parts to display personalized changes.	View Items, View Pages, Open	Contribute, Design, Full Control

Personal permissions deal with an individual user's view of certain aspects of the website, including being able to manage their own personal view of lists, libraries, and web part pages (it does not affect wiki pages). Unfortunately, if you grant users the permission to change web parts, maybe intending to let them add related lists to a list view, they can also modify web parts on any other list and library pages as well. So, consider carefully the ramifications of what personalizations you allow. Permissions, individually, are never applied to users or groups. Instead, permission levels are created by making combinations of these permissions, and those permission levels are applied to users and groups in site collections. Therefore, it is only fitting that we take a look at permission levels next.

Permission Levels

Permission levels enable you to assign a set of permissions to users and SharePoint groups so that they can perform specific actions or *tasks* on your site. Most permission levels (and SharePoint groups for that matter) are role-related, aligning the set of permissions with a task that must be performed. With permission levels, you can control which permissions are granted to users and SharePoint groups on your site. For example, by default, the Read permission level includes the View Items, Open Items, View Pages, and View Versions permissions (among others), all of which are needed to read documents, items, and pages on a SharePoint site. The following permission levels are provided by default: Full Control, Design, Contribute, Read, and Limited Access. Anyone assigned a permission level that includes the Manage Permissions permission can customize permission levels (except for the Full Control and Limited Access) or create new ones. Site owners are assigned the Manage Permissions permission, by default. The defaults each have their own uses and purposes, which are described in Table 12.4. As you look at the levels and try to decide what to do with them, remember you always want to give the minimum permission to do a task that the user will need. You can see in the table that each succeeding level has all the permissions of the level before it and then adds more. You cannot directly edit either the Full Control or Limited Access permission levels, the two far ends of the spectrum.

TABLE 12.4: SharePoint Foundation Default Permission Levels for Site Collections

PERMISSION LEVEL	DESCRIPTION	INCLUDED PERMISSIONS
Limited Access	This level is designed to be combined with fine-grained permissions to give users access to a specific list, document library, item, or document, as well as shared site data such as the theme and navigation, without giving users access to the entire site. This level allows very focused control of access. *Cannot be customized or deleted.*	View Application Pages, Browse User Information, Use Remote Interfaces, Use Client Integration Features, Open
Read	Read-only access to the website. This is a default for the *<Site Name>* Visitors group. It's not intended to add, edit, or delete items, or be able to personalize their views.	Limited Access permissions plus: View Items, Open Items, View Versions, Create Alerts, Use Self-Service Site Creation (when enabled at web application), Browse User Information, View Application Pages, Use Remote Interfaces, Use Client Integration Features, View Pages, and all Personal Permissions

TABLE 12.4:   SharePoint Foundation Default Permission Levels for Site Collections   *(CONTINUED)*

PERMISSION LEVEL	DESCRIPTION	INCLUDED PERMISSIONS
Contribute	Can add and edit items in existing lists and libraries, and personalize page views. This is a default for the *<Site Name>* Members group. It's not intended to manage lists, create subsites, or manage permissions.	Read permissions plus: Add Items, Edit Items, Delete Items, Delete Versions, Browse Directories, Edit Personal User Information, Manage Personal Views, Add/Remove Personal Web Parts, Update Personal Web Parts
Design	Can create (and if necessary, manage) lists and document libraries, and edit pages in the website. This would generally be used for modifying the look and feel of your pages in the site. It cannot create or manage groups, alerts, sites, or permissions.	Contribute permissions plus: Manage Lists, Override Check Out, Approve Items, Add and Customize Pages, Apply Themes and Borders, Apply Style Sheets, Use Remote Interfaces, Use Client Integration Features, Manage Lists
Full Control	Has all permissions enabled. Specifically, this can manage and create sites, permission levels, alerts, groups, and view usage data. This is the default for the *<Site Name>* Owners group. *Cannot be customized or deleted.* It is required for full site management.	All permissions without restriction

Managing Permission Levels

Now that you've seen the out-of-the-box permission levels for site collections, you might need to do some customization. The Read, Design, and Contribute permission levels can be copied or modified, and otherwise, new permission levels can be created for a site. In other words, you can use the premade permission levels as they are, you can use those levels but modify them, you can copy those levels and then modify the copy (which is considered a better idea than modifying the originals), or you can apply your own and ignore the default levels (with the exception of Limited Access). For example, if you have a SharePoint server with a large number of users and groups assigned the Read permission level and you decide you want to restrict these users further (or give them more control), you can edit the Read permission level to provide the precise combination of permissions desired, without having to give all these users a new permission level. On the other hand, if you create a new site or want to add a lot of new users with unique permission needs to an existing site, you can create a new permission level with the correct permissions—either by using an existing level as a template or by creating one from scratch. Permission levels were meant to be easy to manage; as long as you know what the individual permissions actually do (particularly in combination), you can have a lot of control over your SharePoint resources and therefore over your users.

Permission levels are most often added, modified, or copied at the site collection's top-level site and then inherited by the subsites below it. So, most of the exercises concerning permissions and groups will be done at the top-level site of a site collection (which in my case is Company Site). Be aware that you can break inheritance at any subsite, where they then can do as they wish with their SharePoint groups at that point, but all permission levels are actually managed at the site collection level.

VIEWING SITE PERMISSIONS

To work with permission levels, you need to get to the Permissions page for the site collection. The quickest way to do so is to click Site Actions in the top ribbon bar and select Site Permissions in the drop-down menu. The Permissions page (Figure 12.4) will allow you to see all the groups and security principals on your site to which permission levels have been assigned directly, what those permissions are, and the type of object they are (user, SharePoint group, and so on). In most cases, permission levels will not be applied directly to a user or security group, so this list will generally contain only site groups (although there are exceptions).

FIGURE 12.4
The Permissions
page

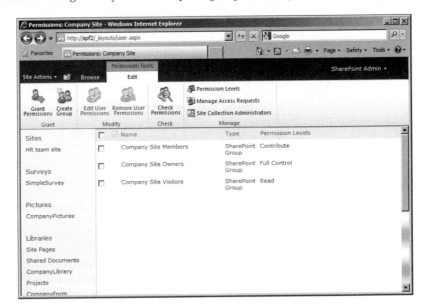

The Permissions page uses a Permissions tools ➤ Edit ribbon for its settings:

Grant Permissions   Basically an Add Users button, this opens a Grant Permissions box, where you can add users or security groups to SharePoint. You can add a user to a group (and inherit that group's permission level) or add a user or security group and then apply a permission level directly (this is good for permission levels not currently used by an existing group, such as Design). A user added with a permission directly applied will appear individually on the permissions page with the groups.

Create Group   This button opens a Create Group page, so you can add a new group to the site collection.

Edit User Permissions   If a user or group is selected, this button can be used to check the permission level (or levels) being applied.

Remove User Permissions   This button removes the permission level applied to the selected group or user, which makes them disappear from the page because it removes their access to the site collection. If they have no permission applied to them, they can't show up on the page (or in People And Groups)—but they still exist in the site collection as a security object. If you aren't just messing with the permissions applied to a group or user you plan to keep on the site, delete the user or group from the site collection instead.

DELETE FROM SITE COLLECTION

If you do want to delete a user or group from a site collection (rather than just remove permissions from them), click the name of the user or group in the Permissions page. In the User Information page that comes up, click Delete From Site Collection. That will not only remove permissions but will also remove the security object from the site collection. This is good housekeeping.

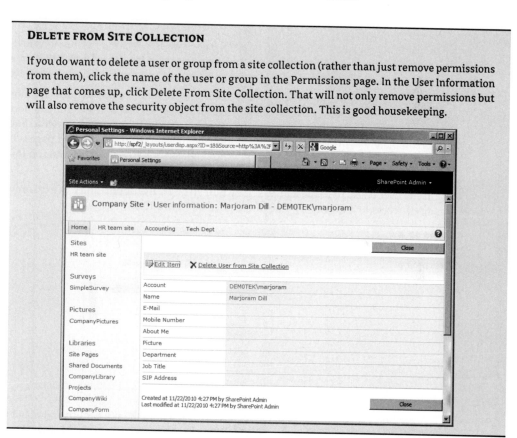

Check Permissions   This button doesn't need a user or group to be selected to work. It opens a box that lets you check the existing permission levels applied to a user or group. If you enter a username (as shown in Figure 12.5, I used the user Saffron I added in the installation chapters) and click Check Now, it will return information about the SharePoint group the user belongs to or permission level applied (if it was applied directly to the user).

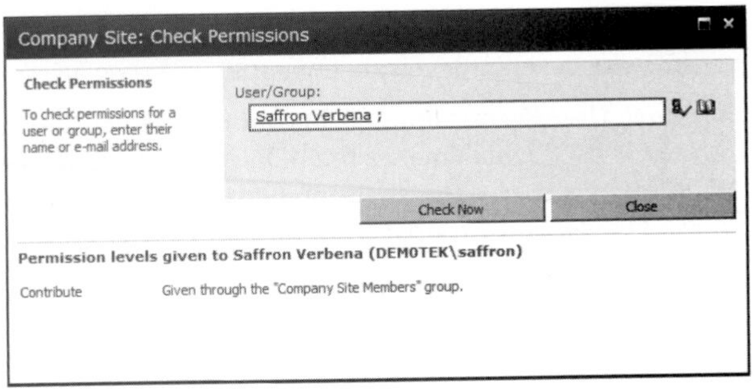

FIGURE 12.5

The Check Permissions box

Permission Levels This button opens a page that lists existing permissions levels, so you can select one to see the individual permissions it contains (in order to edit it) or select one (or several) to delete. Also on this page is the option to create new permission levels.

Manage Access Requests Generally enabled by default, Access Request is a site-level option. When users are faced with a denial of access, such as a missing menu item or a blocked list item, it allows them to click Request Access in the Account menu. But if a user is completely denied access to a list, library, or subsite, an Access Denied page will display a link to request access. If this option is not allowed, it will not be available on the Account menu or Access Denied page.

If the user clicks to request access, they will be given the opportunity to explain what they need access to and why they need that access (Figure 12.6).

FIGURE 12.6

The Request Access prompt

According to the menu option, the request will be sent to the site administrator, but it will actually be sent to the address in the Access Request Settings section of the Manage Access Requests box. (Figure 12.7). This address is by default the original site collection administrator's email address, but it can be changed.

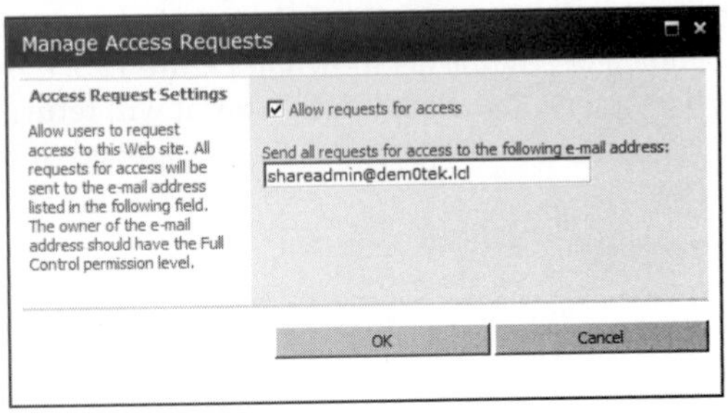

FIGURE 12.7

The Manage Access Requests box

This feature is a double-edged sword. It lets you know what lists, libraries, or subsites users would like to use, but it is also frustrating if they are denied access for a good reason that will not change. Obviously those requests for access can be disabled at the site level by going to the Permissions page and, on the ribbon, clicking Manage Access Requests.

Site Collection Administrators This button opens the Site Collection Administrators box (which is also available from the Site Settings page), where you can see the current site collection administrators, add more, or remove some. Site collection administrators have to be added individually. This is the only place adding security groups instead of individual user accounts is discouraged.

Copying an Existing Permission Level

As I mentioned, the preferred method of modifying a permission level is to copy and modify an existing one. This leaves the original permission level intact but gives you its settings to work with. However, if the custom permission level that you want is similar to an existing default permission level, you could just select to edit the existing permission level, make your changes, and be done. All groups or users that have that permission level applied to them will be affected by the change immediately. But if you need to keep the default permission level, you can copy the default permission level, modify the copy, and save it as a new permission level. The second option is a real time-saver and is standard practice.

To copy an existing permission level, make sure you are on the Permissions page and follow these steps:

1. Click Permission Levels on the ribbon.

   This will open a Permission Levels page (Figure 12.8). This page lists the permission levels for the site collection. Here, when you click on the name of a permission level, it opens a page to edit the permission level (or copy it). Also available on the Permission Levels page is a link to add a new permission level or delete selected permission levels.

FIGURE 12.8
The Permission Levels page

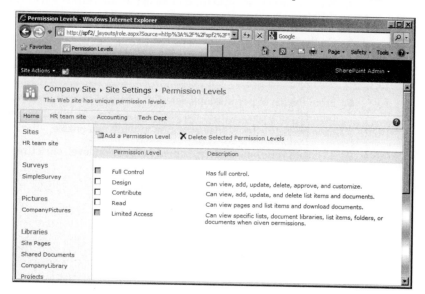

2. In the list of permission levels, click the name of the permission level you want to copy. For my example, I need to copy the Read permission level.

   This will open a page to edit the permission level. You could edit the permission level's settings, from name and description, to the permissions included (Figure 12.9).

FIGURE 12.9
The Read
permission level,
Edit Permission
Level page

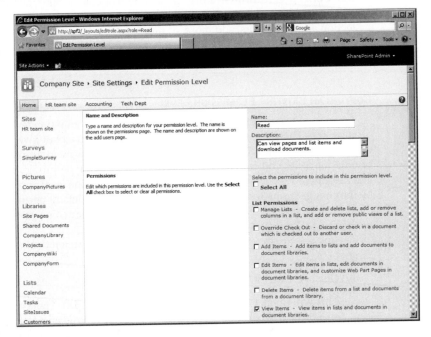

3. You will need to scroll to the bottom of the Edit Permission Level page to click the Copy Permission Level button (see Figure 12.10). This will open the Copy Permission Level page.

4. On the Copy Permission Level page (Figure 12.11), enter a name in the Name box for the new permission level. My example uses *New Read*.

5. In the Description box, enter a description for the new permission level.

6. From the list of permissions, select or clear the check boxes to add permissions to or remove permissions from the permission level. As you may remember, some permissions have prerequisites, so pay attention to what you enable.

7. To create your new custom, copied permission level, click Create at the bottom of the page.

FIGURE 12.10
The Edit Permission Level page, Copy Permission level button

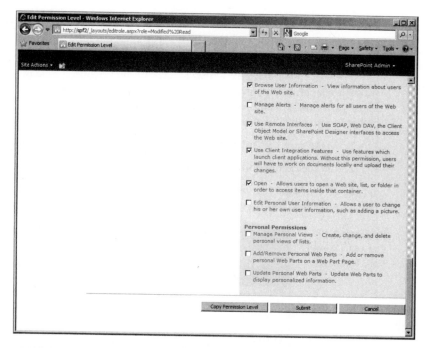

FIGURE 12.11
The Copy Permission Level page

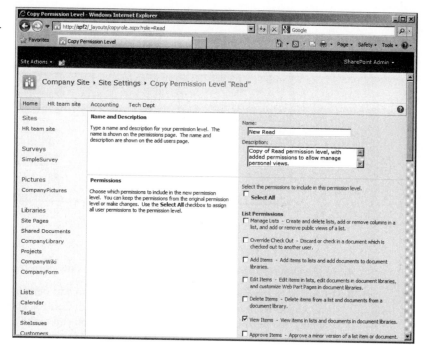

By using this method, you have created a new permission level while keeping the existing one in place, allowing you to use both permission levels in the site collection.

CREATING A NEW PERMISSION LEVEL

Creating a permission level from scratch is a good idea when none of the existing permission levels are close to what you need. You can create a permission level that will include exactly what you require. To create a new level, follow these steps:

1. Make sure you are on the Permissions page. In the ribbon, click Permission Levels.

2. On the Permission Levels page, click Add A Permission Level.

3. In the Name box on the Add A Permission Level page, enter a name for the new permission level (see Figure 12.12). My example will be a new permission level for *List Managers*.

FIGURE 12.12
The Add A Permission Level page

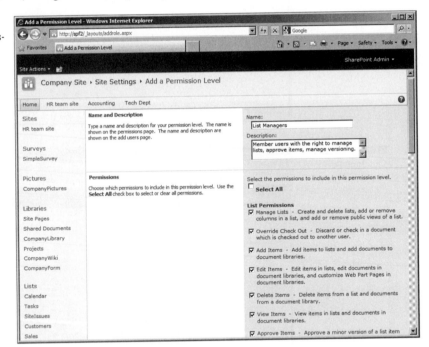

4. In the Description box, type a description for the new permission level.

5. In the list of permissions, select the check boxes to add permissions to the permission level. If you want to create a level with almost Full Control, click Select All and then uncheck the permissions you want to remove. You can make a permission level complete,

so it can be applied to a group of users as is and they can do everything they need to do, or you can create a limited permission level with only the exact permissions you want them to have and then add it as well as a standard permission level to a group, giving the users standard permissions (such as Contribute) plus the custom ones. In my case, I am enabling all of the list permissions to allow the list managers to work freely on lists in whatever capacity they require (especially to manage list settings, approvals, and versioning) as well as the standard Contribute permissions. This allows the level to be complete by itself.

6. Click the Create button at the bottom of the page to create your custom level.

In Figure 12.13, you can see the new permission level listed (as well as the one we modified and copied).

FIGURE 12.13

Permission Levels page with new and copied permission levels listed

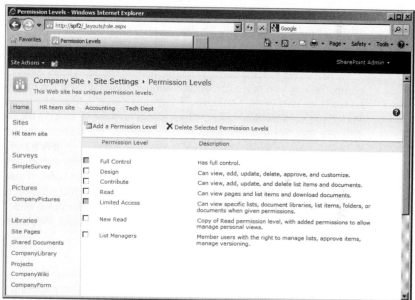

At this point, you know how to check the current permission levels of your sites to see what permissions they actually have, how to modify existing permission levels (and which you can't), how to create copies of existing permission levels for customization; and finally, you know how to create your own permission levels to combine exactly the permissions you want into a permission level.

Users and Groups

Now that you understand the foundation of permissions in SharePoint, it's time to start looking at applying them inside a SharePoint site collection.

When adding users to SharePoint, Microsoft recommends you add Active Directory security groups (usually just referred to as *security groups*) to SharePoint groups rather than individual users as much as possible. SharePoint has a limit of 5,000 security principals (users and security groups) for a site collection. According to Microsoft, going beyond this limit has been tested and could cause performance issues. However, adding Active Directory security groups, each of which can contain many users, allows the number of supported users (assuming they are all in no more than 5,000 AD security groups) to scale to 2 million.

Adding security groups rather than individual users provides another distinct advantage: ease of administration. Rather than having to manage users in two places, you only need to manage Active Directory group membership.

For example, you can add all the managers in your organization to a Managers security group in Active Directory and then add that security group to a Managers SharePoint group that you created. You want these managers to have read and write access on the Sales Events subsite, read-only access on the Accounting subsite, and full control access on the Management subsite. You can accomplish this by adding the Managers AD security group to a Managers group on the top-level site and then assigning the permissions you want for the Managers SharePoint group separately on each subsite.

As managers join the team, you add them to the Managers Active Directory security group, the way you normally would without SharePoint on the network. This automatically makes them part of the Managers SharePoint group, without having to add them manually to SharePoint as individual users. There is also no need to specify the permissions they have on different sites, because you have already assigned the permissions you want to the Managers SharePoint group for all three sites. If a manager leaves or gets transferred, you just remove the user account from the Managers Active Directory security group. And they will no longer be a member of the Managers SharePoint group. On the other hand, if you choose to add each manager directly to a site instead of using a security group and a SharePoint group, you must assign each manager the appropriate permissions on each of the three sites. If they then change job roles in the company, you need to change their permissions for each site manually.

Viewing People and Groups

Now that you are familiar with permissions and permission levels, let's take a look at how to manage user accounts and groups and how permissions are applied to them.

You can add groups and users using the Permission page. But when you want to look at the contents and settings of a group itself, you usually need to go to the People And Groups page. This page is where you end up if you click a SharePoint site group name. For this reason and because you already know about the Permission page, we'll work from within the People And Groups page to give you some experience with it.

Either make certain you are on the Site Settings page and click the People And Groups link, or click the Site Actions menu, select Site Permissions, and click the site group you want to view; they will both open the group's members list in the People And Groups page. Either way, find your way to the People And Groups page (see Figure 12.14).

FIGURE 12.14

The People And Groups – Company Site Members page

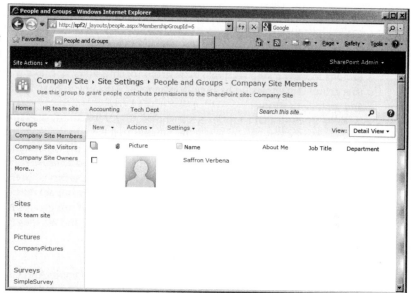

This page is essentially a list of the people and groups for the current site and generally defaults to displaying the users in the Members group (in my example Saffron is there because she was added in the installation chapters, Chapters 2 and 3). It allows you to manage the users in the groups as well as manage the groups themselves. On the Group Quick Launch bar, you can see the three default groups that SharePoint added to the site: Company Site Members, Company Site Visitors, and Company Site Owners. The Company Site Owners site group has the Full Control permission level assigned, the Company Site Members site group has been assigned the Contribute permission level, and the Company Site Visitors site group has the Read permission level assigned.

LOCATION, LOCATION, LOCATION

Note that members of the Company Site Owners group for a top-level website can control more options than site owners of a subsite. For example, they can perform actions such as specifying settings for web document discussions or alerts and viewing usage and quota data for the top-level site and all subsites.

In Chapters 2 and 3, as one of the post-configuration tasks, we added a user to the Company Site Members group, as an example. It's easy to add users to existing SharePoint groups. So, what we're going to do is create a new group to add users to.

When you create new permission levels, you can apply more than one to a group (you're not limited to one permission level per group); however, it's considered good practice to have one permission level associated with a group. The People And Groups page uses the old-style Action bar, with drop-down buttons for New, Actions, and Settings. New lets you create a new user. Actions requires that something be selected to act on; the options are to email, call or message, or remove (from the group) the selected user. Settings manages the group or the list itself, with options to view group settings, view group permissions, or make the group the default group (the group that shows up by default whenever someone goes to the People And Groups page), and go to list settings.

Keep in mind that a top-level site shows all groups for all sites in the collection. This includes unique groups specifically made for subsites that have broken inheritance. Even though those groups can't necessarily access or use any other site in the collection, they will still be listed at the top-level site. They are, after all, still groups applied *somewhere* in the site collection, and the top-level site is the one that contains the site collection settings. In the Groups page for the top-level site, the groups listed will indicate what sites they impact (although the groups for the top-level site, Company Site in my example, are also the default groups for the entire site collection). So, those top-level site groups impact the top-level site and all sites that inherit permissions.

Creating a New SharePoint Group

To manage and add groups to the site collection from People And Groups, you need to be on the All Groups page (from the Permissions page, just click Create Group).

To get to the All Groups page from the People And Groups page, you can click the Groups heading in the Groups Quick Launch , or you can click More… also in the Groups Quick Launch. On the All Groups page, there are New and Settings buttons. New only creates new groups, and Settings has one option, Edit Group Quick Launch.

1. While you are on the Groups page, click the New button (see Figure 12.15). You may notice, in my example, that there are groups for the Tech Dept subsite created in Chapter 10. The groups listed for your site collection may also vary, but you should at least have the site groups for the top-level site.

FIGURE 12.15
All Groups page

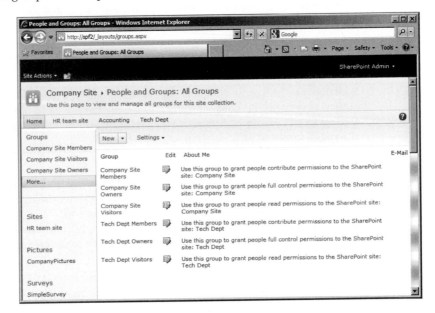

That will open the Create Group page (Figure 12.16), allowing you to add a new group to the site. If you clicked the down arrow next to the New button, click New Group from the menu to get to the page.

FIGURE 12.16

The top of the Create Group page

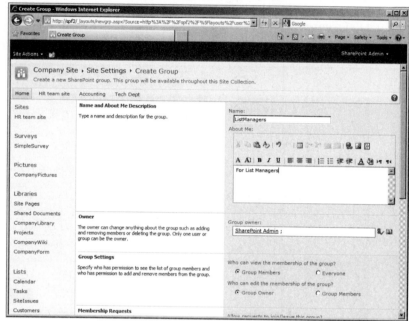

The top half of the page has several options that you can fill out:

◆ The first option is Group Name. Always enter a unique name for the group. My example uses *ListManagers*.

◆ Directly under Group Name is About Me, which is the description. My example uses *For List Managers*.

◆ The next section for the group is Owner. The owner can be any user, SharePoint group, or security group. But keep in mind that "owner" is not plural; there can be only one item in that field, even if it is actually a group of users. The owner will have full control of the group by default. My example uses my SharePoint Admin account (*shareadmin*). The field will default to the username of the person creating the group. Also keep in mind that the Owner of the group is the only one who is allowed to manage the group (other than the site collection administrator of course), so even if an account has full control permissions to a site, they won't be allowed to add users to a group they don't own.

◆ The following section is about the group members' settings, specifically who can view the group members (only that group or everyone) and who can edit the group members (only the owners or all members). The defaults are as shown, with the group members being able to view group membership and the group owner being able to edit the group members. Those defaults are fine for this example.

The bottom half of the page deals with the final options for the group, as shown in Figure 12.17.

FIGURE 12.17
The bottom of the
Create Group page

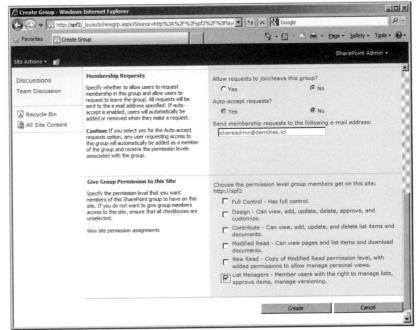

◆ The Membership Requests section is where you indicate whether to allow requests to join or leave the group and whether to automatically accept requests if they are allowed. The email address box is typically filled with the group owner or site administrator's email address, although the request can be sent to anyone who has authorization to edit the group. The defaults are fine for our example also.

◆ The Give Group Permission to this Site section is where you specify the permission levels for the group being added. My example assigns the new *List Managers* permission level I created earlier for this group.

MORE THAN ONE PERMISSION LEVEL CAN BE APPLIED

Notice that the option to select a permission level is a check box, which means you can select more than one. You certainly can apply more than one permission level to a group if necessary. This is useful if you create a permission level that is limited to some precise permissions but don't also cover those used for accessing, navigating, or contributing to the site. You can then combine that limited permission level with one that is more broad, such as the existing Contribute level, so the group members can use both.

2. Once you have made all your entries, click Create, and the group will be created and displayed (see Figure 12.18). By default, because a group cannot be empty of users, the owner/creator of the group is always the first member.

FIGURE 12.18
The ListManagers members page

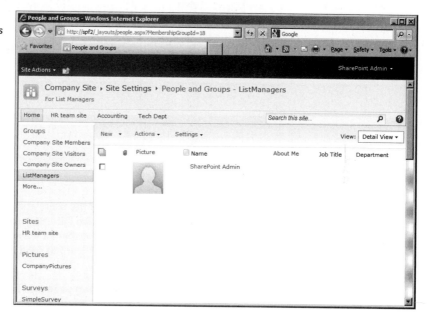

Adding a Security Group or User to a SharePoint Group

The People And Groups – ListManagers page indicates, in my case, that the group has one member, my SharePoint admin. To add new users, follow these steps:

1. You can add new members by clicking the New button on the People And Groups page for the group (if you were on the Permissions page, you would click the Grant Permissions button).

2. The Grant Permissions box shown in Figure 12.19 allows you to add a new user or security group to the SharePoint group. The first entry box is the People Picker into which you can add usernames. The username can be any existing SharePoint user, domain (or server) user, or security group in the system. In this box, you can enter multiple users and security groups separated by semicolons. You can enter the names in the format of Domain\UserName or Domain\GroupName, or you can just use the friendly name for the user or group and have the People Picker resolve it to the username in AD (you can do the same with accounts on a single server, using the server's name instead of the domain, it will also resolve to using the Check Name button). You could even use the email address listed for the user or group in Active Directory. My example adds my Active Directory security group *dem0tek\managers* and the individual user *Opal*.

FIGURE 12.19
Adding new users

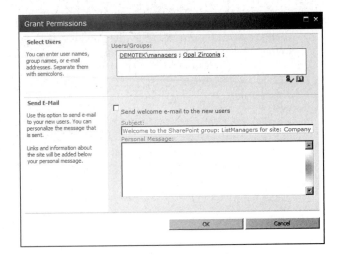

FIGURE 12.19
Adding new users

3. Below the Select Users section is Send E-mail. If the users and security groups have email addresses associated with their accounts in Active Directory (or if you used the email address for the accounts), you can choose to send them a welcome email letting them know that they've been added to the site. I don't want to send out the welcome email, so I am going to clear that check mark.

4. Once you click OK, you will be taken to the Group page (see Figure 12.20). My example has three members in the group: sharepoint admin (the owner of the group), *Opal*, and the *dem0tek\managers* security group.

FIGURE 12.20
The new
ListManagers
group has three
members.

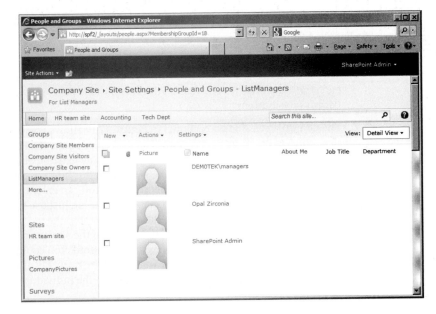

REMOVING A USER FROM A GROUP DOESN'T DELETE THEM FROM THE SITE

On the Permissions page there was a button to remove the permissions from a user account, and removing a user from a group is basically the same thing. You simply select the user or group you want to remove, click the Action button, and select Remove Users From Group (we'll do this later in the chapter). Keep in mind that if that was the only site group the user was a member of, this action just strips the account from being able to access the site; it does not actually remove the security principal from the site. So if the account is never going to be used in that site collection, delete it from the site collection (click the account in People And Groups, and choose Delete From Site Collection).

Now that we have covered a good bit of ground, it is time to look at how permissions work on the stuff inside SharePoint. Most objects can be secured in SharePoint. A securable object is an object upon which permissions can be configured (for example, a site, list, library, folder within a list or library, list item, or document). Permissions for users and SharePoint groups can be assigned to any securable object. The SharePoint system defaults to assigning permissions at the site collection level, and those permissions filter down through permission inheritance to the contained objects such as sites, lists, list items, and the like. A user with the Manage Permissions permission can edit the permissions for any of the contained objects, breaking the hierarchy of inheritance if they wish. This permission is assigned to the Site Owners group by default.

YOU CAN ADD A USER WITHOUT A GROUP

You might have noticed that there are only three default site collection groups (Members, Owners, Visitors) but four useful permission levels (Full Control, Contribute, Read, and Design). Thus, there is a fourth set of permissions that a user can't use if they are added to the existing groups. This is a good example of why you might want to add a user individually and apply permission level(s) to them directly.

1. To do that, in the Grant Permission box from the Permission page, enter a username (or users, if you'd like), and click the Grant Permission Directly radio button.

   This will propagate a list of the available permission levels for the site collection. You can then select the level (or levels) you want to apply to the user account.

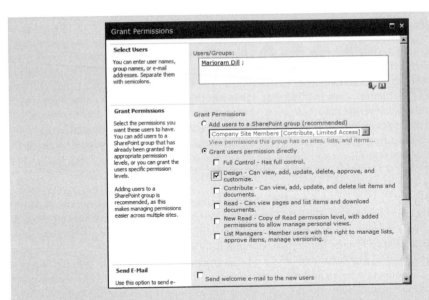

2. After clicking OK, you can go back to the Permissions page and see that the user is now listed, outside of the existing groups.

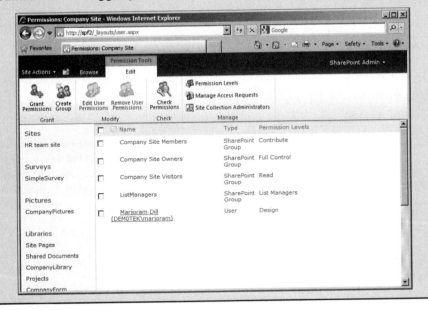

Inheritance

Now that you have a basic understanding of permissions, permission levels, groups, and users, it's time to explore inheritance.

Inheritance fundamentally means that a site and its contents inherit their permissions from their parent object. So, subsites get their groups, users, and permission levels from their parent site; the subsite's lists and libraries get their permissions from the subsite, and list and library items get their permissions from the list or library in which they reside. This chain of inheritance makes it possible to administer permissions for an entire site collection from one place and have those changes trickle down to all other objects contained therein.

The complicated part of this concept is when inheritance is broken.

Why would you want to break inheritance? Well, if inheritance (in this context) means that all users, groups, and permission levels are inherited by all subsites (and therefore their pages, lists, and libraries), then breaking inheritance should mean you select to break the object (be it a subsite, list/library, or item) from inheriting those users, groups, and permission levels with the intention of having its own, unique permission levels and groups.

But it doesn't quite mean that, especially not in this version of SharePoint.

To break inheritance on a subsite, you go to the Permissions page, and click the Stop Inheriting Permissions button. This button name is something of a misnomer, as you'll see in a moment.

When you click that button, nothing actually changes. The site collection groups that were there before are still there and function in the same way. But what really happens at this level, if you break inheritance, is that now the subsite owners (or a site collection administrator) can change the permissions allowed for those site collection groups within *that* site. If necessary, you can remove the site collection groups from the subsite, giving the site collection's users no access to the subsite at all (of course you'll make more groups at that level to add users to). Or you can change the permission level(s) on the site collection groups at that subsite, giving them different access to the subsite specifically (but not removing the groups entirely).

When you break inheritance of permissions and groups from the site collection, that subsite is saying, "I need to allow users other than those allowed throughout the rest of the site collection access to this subsite. Further, I need to give users different permission levels than those allowed throughout the site collection." But unfortunately, for this version of SharePoint, you cannot go so far as to create *new* permission levels for the subsite. However, you can apply existing permission levels in different ways to the users and groups in the subsite than the way the site collection does.

The fact that you can't break completely from the site collection and make your own permission levels for your unique subsite is a disappointment. All permission levels are held at the site collection level (much like site collection solutions are). However, you can create a permission level at the top of the site collection and *apply it only* at the subsite of your choosing. But you can't make a permission level specifically and only at the unique subsite that broke inheritance.

Further, because lists and libraries, even individual items, might need special security access configured on them, any one can be configured to break inheritance from its parent object, and then new permissions can be applied. Keep in mind that, if you break inheritance on a list and apply different permissions to that list, all items in that list will inherit those permissions. An individual item can even have unique permissions, if necessary (although going that granular with permissions can confuse the Search service, so use sparingly), by breaking its inheritance and applying new permissions to it.

If you break inheritance on a subsite and change the groups it uses, then everything on that subsite—its lists, libraries, and pages—inherits the new permissions from the subsite that contains them.

If you create a subsite *beneath* that unique subsite, then that sub-subsite inherits the permissions (meaning the groups and users and the permission levels applied to them) of that unique subsite above it, which is considered its parent (unless, of course, you set it not to inherit permissions).

To help you visualize how permissions are inherited, Figure 12.21 shows a top-level site with a set of permissions called Permission Set A. I'm considering a permission set to be a combination of groups, users, and the permission levels applied to them. The two subsites underneath that top-level site also have Permission Set A, as do the lists (I consider libraries to be included) and list items within the sites. All of the objects in my example are shown inheriting permissions from the top-level site.

FIGURE 12.21
Inherited
permissions

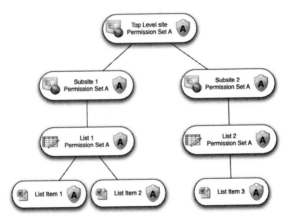

If you break inheritance on Subsite 2 and change permissions, such as the groups available for that subsite, as well as the permission levels applied to them (let's call those changes Permission Set B), the permissions for the list (and its list items) contained there will also change so that they both will have Permission Set B. See Figure 12.22.

FIGURE 12.22
Subsite 2 permissions changed

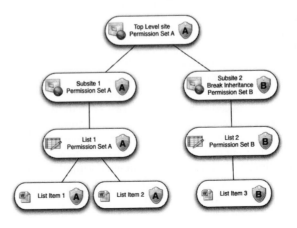

The same thing happens in lists or libraries. If you give them unique permissions by breaking inheritance, the new permissions will flow to every item in the list or library.

You could also break inheritance on an individual list item, like List Item 2, and give it a different set of permissions, Permission Set C in this example (see Figure 12.23).

FIGURE 12.23
List Item 2 permissions changed

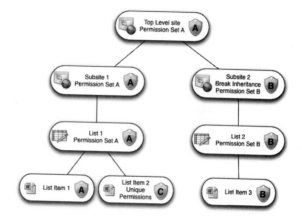

And on a larger scale, because inheritance goes from a parent object to its child objects, you can break inheritance on a site, and all subsites you create below it can inherit its unique settings (and by definition, all those sub-subsites' lists, libraries, items, and pages).

Figure 12.24 shows a top-level site with the same sort of permissions as our first example, which we'll call Permission Set A. Subsite 2 and all subsites beneath it are configured to inherit permissions and therefore also use Permission Set A throughout their pages, lists, and libraries.

However, in this diagram, one of the subsites two levels below the top-level site, Subsite 1-A, has broken inheritance to use its own groups and permissions. For the sake of discussion, we'll call its permissions Permission Set B. That means all lists and libraries on that site will be affected by Permission Set B (unless set to do otherwise). If any subsites are created beneath subsite 1-A and are set to inherit permissions, they will inherit Permission Set B. This gives subsite 1-A permission capabilities akin to a top-level site. Changes to the permissions at that level trickle to the other two subsites beneath it (Subsite 1-A-1 and Subsite 1-A-2).

FIGURE 12.24
Subsites with different inherited permissions

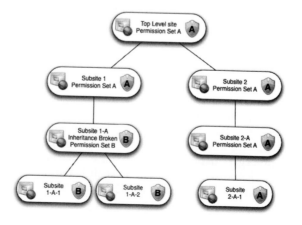

Breaking Inheritance on a Subsite

Occasionally a subsite in a site collection requires unique permissions, such as an event subsite that the site collection's Members group should only have Read access to. In that case, inheritance must be broken so those changes can be made.

To change a subsite's permissions if it is already inheriting permissions, go to the subsite's permissions page (in my example I created a meeting workspace for a Company Site picnic), and in the ribbon click Stop Inheriting Permissions (Figure 12.25). Notice that the page, until inheritance is broken, shows which site it is inheriting permissions from.

FIGURE 12.25
Choosing Stop
Inheriting Permissions on the subsite's Permissions
page

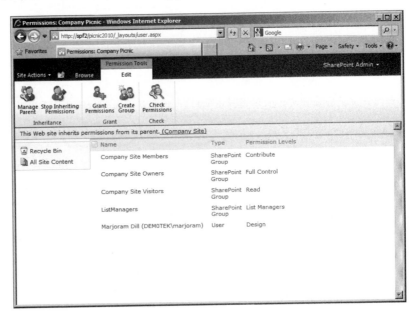

Choosing to stop inheriting permissions will trigger a warning dialog box reminding you that you will be breaking inherited permissions with the parent site (Figure 12.26).

FIGURE 12.26
The Breaking
Inheritance
warning

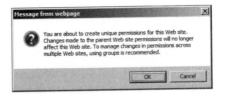

This warning is a little misleading. What it means is the groups that this site had originally inherited from the site collection, or *parent* site, will still be there, but the permissions applied to the groups are now broken from the parent, and if they are changed outside the site, the change won't propagate to this site. This also means that permissions applied to the groups at this site (now that it's broken inheritance) won't affect the parent sites permission on the same groups. Click OK. As you can see in Figure 12.27, inheritance has been broken with the parent on this site.

FIGURE 12.27
This website
has unique
permissions.

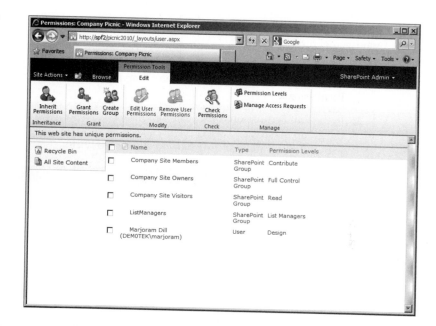

IF YOU CHANGE YOUR MIND

One of the nice things about SharePoint Foundation is that it allows you to reestablish the inheritance relationship. Anywhere inheritance can be applied, from the site level to the item level, inheritance can always be restored. This means these decisions are not unchangeable. On the Permissions page, after breaking permissions, the Manage Parent button (as in manage permissions from the parent site if you are inheriting them) turns into the Inherit Permissions button (you can see the change between Figures 12.27 and 12.29).

Once you choose to inherit permissions again, you will lose any and all customizations you have made to the current object (be it a site, list, or item), and you will revert to inheriting permissions from the parent object. Should you decide to return to custom permissions from inherited permissions, you would need to break inheritance again and redo the unique permissions for the object.

Once you've broken inheritance, you will see that the site collection groups are still there (as well as the group we created earlier and, in my case, the user I added to the parent site directly). They are still connected to the site collection, and if you add users to those groups, they will be added wherever those groups are applied. They still are the site collection groups. However, what makes it different at this level is that you can change not the users of the group uniquely but what *permissions* are applied to the group at this level. Or you can just remove those groups from having access to the site altogether.

APPLYING UNIQUE PERMISSIONS TO A GROUP AFTER INHERITANCE IS BROKEN

In this example, the site collection's members should only have the right to read content on this site but not the right to contribute. For that reason, you need to change the permission level on this group from Contribute to New Read (the permission level we copied and modified earlier).

1. On the Permissions page, select the group in which you want to change permissions (in my example I am going to select the Company Site Members group). Then click Edit User Permissions.

2. In the Edit Permissions box, clear the check box for the permission levels you don't want the group to have, and select the permission levels you do want. In my case, I am removing Contribute and selecting New Read (Figure 12.28).

FIGURE 12.28
Editing the permission level applied to the Company Site Members group for the unique subsite

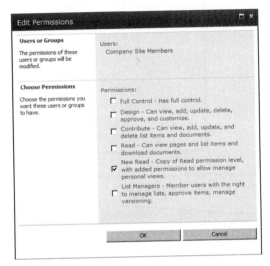

3. When your selection is complete, click OK to make the change and return to the Permissions page.

On the Permissions page, the group will now be listed with the New Read permission.

NOT AS INDEPENDENT AS YOU THINK

You might think that, if you broke inheritance from a parent site, even if their groups still show in the Permissions page, if you make changes, it won't propagate back up to the parent. If so, you are wrong.

If you were to add a user to one of the site collection groups while in the unique site, it would show up as a member of the site collection group at the top-level site.

The site collection groups didn't change their name when inheritance was broken, and that's because those are still the site collection groups. This way, if you still plan to let those users access your unique site but you want them to have different permissions, you can easily just keep the site collection groups where they are. But if you don't, remove the groups and just create ones specifically for your unique site (and any subsites beneath it, if you wish).

CREATING A UNIQUE GROUP FOR A SUBSITE

So, the site collection's Members group has had its permission level changed. It's now time to add a unique group to the site, so you can add users who can contribute to the site (now that the Members group cannot).

You know how to create a group using the Groups page in People And Groups, so this time we're going to use the Create Groups button, conveniently located on the ribbon bar in the Permissions page.

1. To create a unique group for this subsite, make sure you are on the Permissions page, and click the Create Group button.

   The Create Group page that opens is the same one you used to create a group earlier in the chapter.

2. Fill in the fields to create this group for the site. The name for the group should indicate what site it belongs to (since it will show up in the groups list for all groups in the site collection, it's good form to show where the group is applied). My example will use *Company Picnic Members* (Figure 12.29). Feel free to enter a description for the group.

3. Keep the account you are logged in as the owner of the group, and keep the defaults for group member settings and request.

4. For the Permissions section, let's choose to give the group the Contribute permission level so the users you add to it can contribute to the site (Figure 12.29). These will be people who will be organizing the picnic.

5. To finish creating the group, click Create.

FIGURE 12.29
Creating a new group for the unique subsite

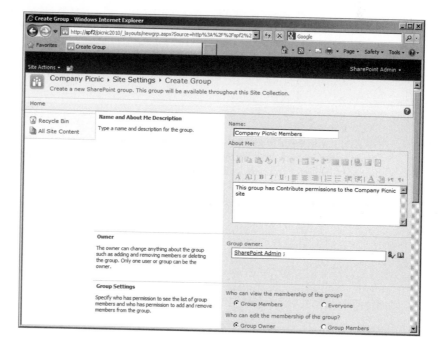

You will be taken to the People And Groups page for the new group, where you can add users. To follow my example, add one user. However, feel free to add other users or security groups to the new group for the site if you wish.

Once you've added a user (in my case, a user named Rosemary Leek, who is organizing the picnic this year), feel free to go to the home page of the site and log in with that user. You'll see that you can log in to the unique site with that user.

However, if you try to log in with that same user to the top-level site of the collection or any other subsite, you will get an Access Denied page because that group is used only by the site where it was created.

If you were to go back to the Permissions page for the site, you'd see the new group listed, with the correct permission level (Figure 12.30). Again, this group can be applied only to this site.

FIGURE 12.30
The new group listed in the Permissions page

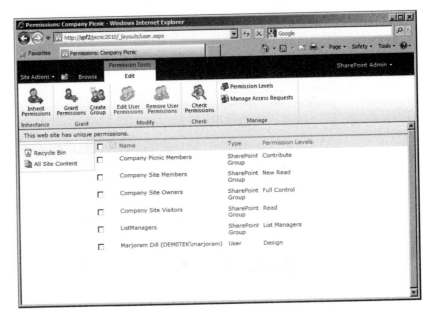

And if you were to go to the top-level site of the site collection, you would see that the group is not listed in that site's Permissions page (Figure 12.31). This means the group for the subsite is not applicable for that site (and therefore the whole site collection). The Permissions page at the top of the site collection shows you the groups that will be applied throughout the collection, if the subsites are inheriting permissions.

FIGURE 12.31
The site collection's Permissions page does not show the subsite group.

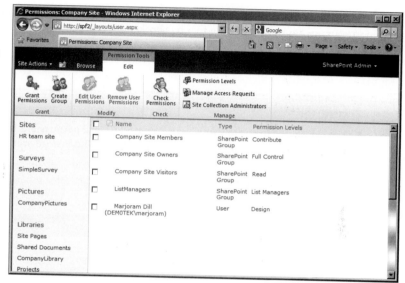

However, if you were to go to the All Groups page (using the Groups heading or More link in the Quick Launch of the People And Groups page) at the top-level site, you would see the group for the subsite that broke inheritance listed there (Figure 12.32). The group isn't being used by the top-level site (or the rest of the site collection), but it is listed on this page as a central location for all the site collection administrators to see what groups are used where throughout the collection.

FIGURE 12.32
The subsite group is listed for all groups in the site collection.

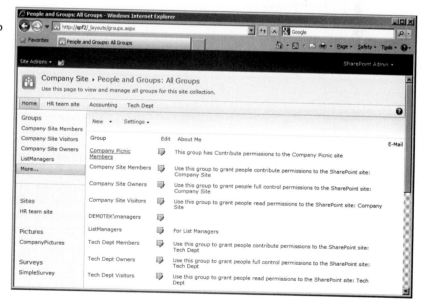

This should give you some insight into how to use the existing groups from a site collection to your advantage in a subsite that has broken inheritance (changing the permission levels). You've also seen how to create a group for the unique subsite, what that actually does, and why it is still listed (but not applied) at the top-level site.

CREATED WITHOUT INHERITANCE

You can choose to create a subsite that doesn't inherit permissions from the start. When you do that, the site doesn't end up with the parent's groups but instead prompts you to set up groups for the site right during site creation.

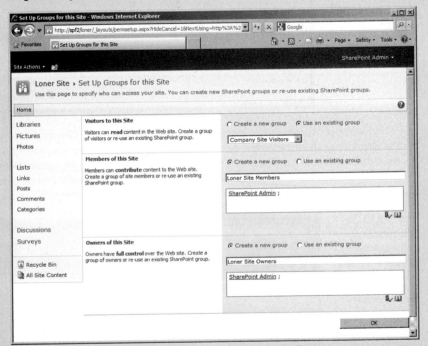

You can choose to use existing groups (like the site collection's visitors group), or you can create new ones. It will suggest group names based on its standards and suggest you use the naming convention of starting the group names with the site's name. You can add users to the groups here, although the account being used to create the site is automatically added. It only gives you the chance to set up three groups by default; you'll have to go to the site itself to add more.

REMOVING INHERITED GROUPS

At this point, you've been working with what you've got; you've changed the permission level on the site collection groups that can access the unique site, and you've created a new group to give specific people, specific access to the site. However, you may need to break completely with the site collection in terms of user access, meaning you need to completely remove at least some of site collection groups (and users) and simply use your own.

In my case, I only want the Company Site Members to be able to read content on the site and the Company Picnic Members to be able to contribute. This means I need to remove the other groups (and the user) the subsite originally inherited from the site collection.

A convenient way to stop groups (or users) from the parent site from accessing the site is to go to the Permissions page, check the box next to the groups (and/or users) to select them, and click Remove User Permissions. This will remove permission to the site from the groups (and users), *not* delete them from the site collection altogether (that is very important). A dialog box will pop up to warn you that you are removing groups from the site (which can reassure you that you are not deleting them from the site collection).

After you have clicked OK in the warning dialog box, it may take a few moments, but all the objects you removed from the Permissions page will go away and leave you with only the groups you want (Figure 12.33).

FIGURE 12.33
Permissions on the site after removing groups

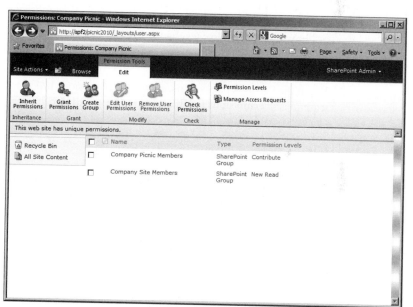

REMOVED GROUPS STILL SHOW UP ON THE SUBSITE'S GROUPS QUICK LAUNCH BAR

Now, the groups from the parent site, even though they've been removed from the site itself, will still show up in the subsite's Groups Quick Launch bar (and the All Groups page). To get rid of them from the Quick Launch bar, simply edit the Groups Quick Launch bar from the Settings menu on any Group page. However, even if those groups do show up on the Groups Quick Launch bar, they are truly no longer able to access the site.

I hope this discussion has given you an idea of how to break inheritance at the subsite level. You've seen what really happens; why the site collection groups remain there; and how to add new groups, change permission levels applied to groups, and remove the inherited site collection groups.

Changing List or Library Permissions

Sometimes the need to customize occurs not at the subsite level but at the list or library level (there was an example of that in Chapter 10 concerning blog comments). Often a document library needs to be created to hold secure documents that the users who otherwise populate the site should not see. Because of this, it needs to have custom permissions.

To change permissions on a list or library, you need to break inheritance from the parent site before you can set custom permissions. It's basically the same process to break inheritance for a subsite, list, library, document, or list item because each one of them has its own Permissions page.

1. To break inheritance on a list or library so you can change permissions, go to that list or library. My example uses the Picture Library for the unique subsite. Go to the list or library's settings page (in my case, I would click Settings in the Action bar since this library doesn't use a ribbon and then click Picture Library Settings).

2. When the Settings page opens, click the Permissions link for that list or library (my example is Permissions for this picture library) under the Permissions And Management category (see Figure 12.34).

FIGURE 12.34
The Picture Library
Settings page

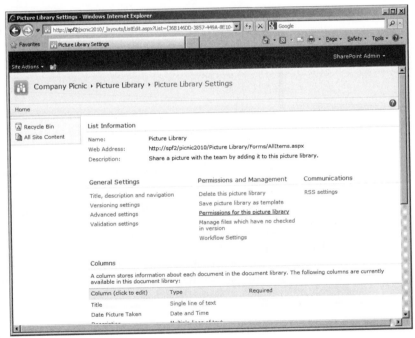

3. The Permissions: Picture Library page will open. This page contains the permissions currently inherited from the parent site and looks like your standard permissions page. Click the Stop Inheriting Permissions button. A dialog box will then warn you that you are about to create unique permissions for this library.

4. After you click OK on the dialog box, you'll be taken back to the Permissions page. You can then select any of the entries and modify their permissions, remove the groups, or add users (or security groups) directly to the list or library permissions. For example, in Figure 12.35, you can see that I've added a user and given them list manager permissions to the library.

FIGURE 12.35

The Permissions page for the library, with a unique user added after breaking inheritance

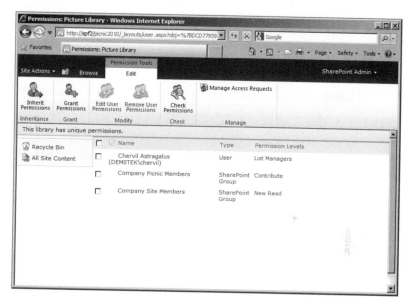

INTERESTING PERMISSIONS ISSUE WITH PICTURE LIBRARIES

If you use unique permissions for a picture library, there is something to consider. Users with permission to access the library must have permissions to the subsite containing the picture library in order to be able to use a picture editor to edit, download, or share pictures. For some reason, having unique, limited-access permissions to the Picture library only, and not to the subsite itself, will limit some of the things you can do with the library. The other library types don't have this issue.

Once you have broken inheritance, you'll have the following capabilities and restrictions:

♦ You can add new users or security groups to the library. To do this, simply click Grant Permissions on the permissions page of the library, and add the user or security group via the new user page.

♦ You can remove a SharePoint group allowed to access the library (or user if they were added with permission levels instead of a group), by selecting the group or user, going to ribbon bar, and selecting Remove User Permissions. The person or the people in the group will summarily be unable to access that library from that point (but can still easily access the rest of the site, unharmed).

◆ You can edit the permission levels applied to the SharePoint groups for the list. When you do this on a list or library that has broken inheritance, it does not change the true permission levels applied anywhere else on the site.

◆ You *cannot* simply create a new SharePoint group for the library.

◆ You *cannot* create anew or modify the permission levels applicable for the library.

The same thing applies to list or library items, in terms of breaking inheritance, and what you can do with permissions in terms of groups and permission levels. Keep in mind that you can always change your mind and restore inheritance by choosing Inherit Permissions at any time from the ribbon bar on the list or library's Permissions page. All changes you made during the noninheriting time will be undone.

Changing Individual List or Library Item Permissions

There are times when a single item in a list or library needs to have unique permissions, such as an announcement that should never be edited or deleted or the Home page in the Site Pages library. The rest of the library needs to have normal site permissions applied so users can contribute, edit, and so on. So , it stands to reason that if a single item needs to be locked down, its permissions should be changed. Keep in mind that this is considered "granular security," and too many items set with their own permissions can make it hard for the search service to security filter results properly. Therefore, securing individual items should be done only if absolutely necessary.

The procedure to give an individual item unique permissions is exactly like giving a list or library unique permissions. First you need to get to the item's permissions page and break inheritance, and then you need to apply the new permissions.

In this example, we are going to block the Home page wiki document (Home.aspx) from being able to be edited or deleted by users who are in the Members group. This will finally keep the users from being able to change, delete, or otherwise ruin the home page of the Company Site (since it is using the Home.aspx wiki page).

To do that, go to the Site Pages library. Select the Home document. Then, in either its drop-down menu, select Manage Permissions, or on the ribbon bar, click the Item Permissions button (in a library it would be Document Permissions). In Figure 12.36, I used the drop-down menu.

Once on the item's permissions page, click Stop Inheriting Permissions. Then, as you did with the list or library, you can add a user or security group to the item's permissions, edit the permissions of a selected group, and/or remove permissions from a selected group (effectively removing the group from accessing the item).

In this case, I want to change the access the Company Site Members get to the item from Contribute to Read. To do so, select the Company Site Members group, click Edit User Permissions in the ribbon bar, and change its permission level from Contribute to Read (and then click OK to commit the change).

FIGURE 12.36
Selecting to manage permissions on a library item

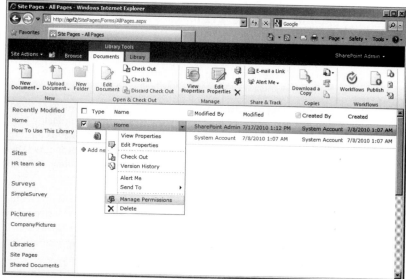

As you can see in Figure 12.37, the group is now listed with Read permissions for the item. This allows the users to see the home page (and open it in Site Pages) but not delete or edit it. Of course, be sure to test the home page as a user with only Read permissions to make sure all web parts work properly. Keep in mind that wiki pages are more like web part pages than the old text pages with special links of the past. And because of that, the permission of the *library* dictates if you can view and edit files that have been *added* to the wiki page itself. Those added files may well be editable.

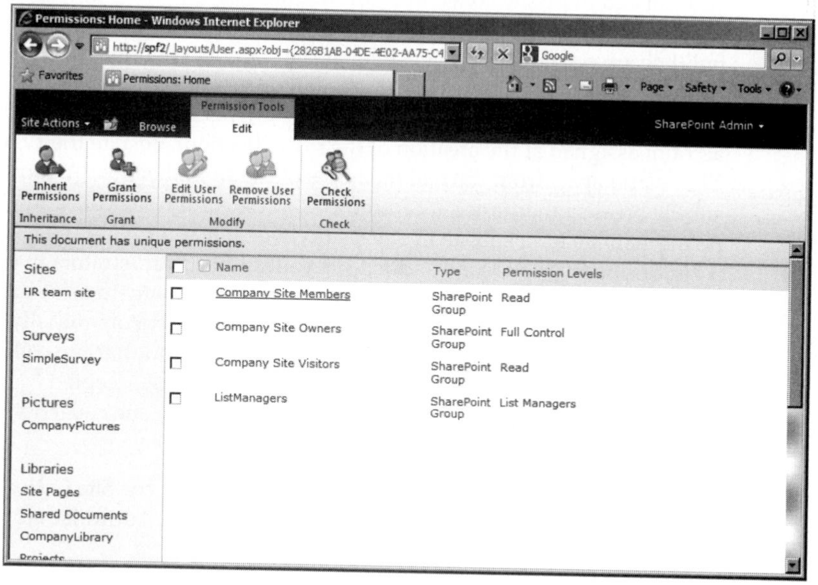

FIGURE 12.37
The document has a changed permission level for Members.

THROUGH THE USERS' EYES

Generally, as administrators, we will rarely log into a SharePoint site with less than administrative privileges. But because of security filtering, when a user with deprecated privileges such as Visitors (with the Read permission level) or Members (with the Contribute permission level) logs in, features that we take for granted are missing.

When a user logs on with only the permissions available with the Read permission level, they cannot personalize any pages or change any site settings, so most of the settings in the Site Actions menu are missing, except to view all the site content. The Account menu does not offer the user the chance to personalize the page. On lists and libraries, most of the buttons on ribbon bars are inactive, except those that allow the visitor to change the view, set an alert, open with Explorer (for libraries), export to a spreadsheet, or set an RSS feed.

When a user logs in with the Contribute permission level (Members have this by default), they can personalize their view of the home page but not change the site settings or create new pages, so there is an option on the Site Actions menu to edit the page. On a list or library, they are not allowed to change the settings, so that menu is completely missing for them, but both the New and Actions menus are available.

Just keep in mind when using and applying permission levels that the user experience will vary considerably, depending on the permissions they have.

Editing Site Collection Administrator Members

When a site collection is created, you are given the option to enter primary and secondary user accounts for site collection administration. However, once the site collection is up and running, you can add more site collection administrators.

Site collection administrators not only have Full Control permissions to the site collection, but they are considered responsible for the site collection in Central Administration and are the primary contacts for notification about the site collection. Ironically, however, site collection administrators are not members of the Owners SharePoint group by default (except for the account assigned at the creation of the site collection), despite their having full control of the site. They stand apart from the real members of the site collection. A good reason for this is that if a subsite breaks inheritance, it can remove access for the site collection Owners group. But there is no mechanism for a subsite to block site collection administrators from accessing their site.

In this book, I've casually added site collection administrators in Chapters 2 and 3, as well as in Chapter 10, but I didn't really go into the details of why to create a site collection administrator. It's also true that you can create only two administrators initially, but once the site collection is operational, you can add more. Further, keep in mind that site collection administrators have to be added as individual users, security groups are not accepted.

Take the following steps to get a look at the existing site collection administrators and make changes to the list, if necessary, at the site collection level:

1. Make sure you're on the Permission page. Click the Site Collection Administrators button in the ribbon. This will open the Site Collection Administrators box (Figure 12.38).

The box will show you the account (or accounts if you have a secondary) that are the current administrators. My example shows my default user, SharePoint admin (*shareadmin*), and an additional user added during the postinstallation tasks during the installation chapters (Chapters 2 and 3).

2. If you wanted to add another administrator or more, you could type in their AD user account names (separated by semicolons) in the People Picker field. Once the account is added to the People Picker field on the Site Collection Administrator's page, click OK to add the new site collection administrator.

Keep in mind that you can see and change the primary and secondary site collection administrators (only) from the SharePoint Central Administration site. The Applications Management page has a link to the Site Collection Administrators page, where you can change or remove those administrators if necessary.

User Policies and Permission Policies at the Web Application Level

Web applications have users and permission levels applied to them at the web application level, which then apply to all site collections contained in that web application. Now that you really understand about permission levels and users at the site collection level, web application user policies and permission policies can make more sense.

Site collections are managed at the site collection level. Site collection administrators can manage any site within the collection, even if they break inheritance. So, even if a subsite owner removes all the site collection groups and just makes their own, they cannot override the site collection administrator if those administrators want to browse to the subsite and make changes.

This can also be true at the web application level. Web applications are managed at the farm level, either at the command line (or shell) or in Central Administration. Farm administrators create and manage the web applications that contain the site collections. This allows them to override the site collection administrators by assigning permission levels to users (or security groups) in the form of permission policies and user policies.

Using these policies, farm administrators can explicitly allow or deny permissions to user accounts that apply to all site collections within a web application. This means they can explicitly allow someone to log into and work in a site collection without that person actually being added as a member (they can even be set to show up as a system account, obscuring their user-name). It also means they can be explicitly denied the right to permissions in the site collection, even if the site collection administrator adds the user specifically.

User and permission policies are also discussed in Chapter 10 in the context of managing web applications and again in Chapter 11. User and permission policies (as well as anonymous access, covered in Chapter 10) are managed either from the Web Applications page under Application Management in Central Administration or by going to the Security page and clicking Specify Web Application User Policy.

On the Manage Web Applications page, there is a User Policy button, which (if the site is configured for it) will pop up a form box for you to see what user policies are applied to a selected web application, as well as add, delete, or edit a user policy.

The User Policy setting under the Security heading in Central Administration does about the same thing, except it takes you to a page reminiscent of the Policy For Web Applications page from the previous version of SharePoint (Figure 12.39). Also in the Manage Web Applications page are Permission and Anonymous Policy buttons; here they are listed in an addition to the Quick Launch bar on the left.

FIGURE 12.39
The Policy For Web Application page

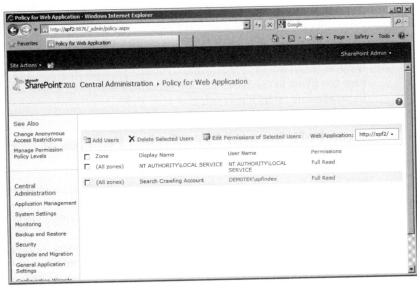

The page lists the user policies contained in the web application displayed in the drop-down list on the right. Add Users, Delete Selected Users (since you can select more than one), and Edit Permissions of Selected Users are links available above the list of user policies. In the list of user policies are columns for the web application zone that the user policy is applied to, the display and username of the accounts, and the applicable permissions for the policies.

On the left side of the page, above the Quick Launch bar, are Change Anonymous Access Restrictions and Manage Permission Policy Levels links. Although these were separate buttons on the Manage Web Applications page, they were all in the Policies section of the ribbon, so it makes sense that they are available on the same page.

Adding a User Policy

Unlike adding users to a group, at the web application level you simply add a user account or security group and apply permissions to them directly. However, as you'll see, it is very much like what you would do if you were adding a user directly to a site.

1. To add a user or security group (and therefore a user policy), just click the Add User link.

   As you can see in Figure 12.40, adding a user is a two-step process. On the first Add Users page, confirm the web application and the zone the user policy is going to apply to (or choose to have it apply to all zones of a web application, so the policy will apply no matter what URL the user uses to access the content).

FIGURE 12.40

Selecting a web application and zone in the first Add Users page

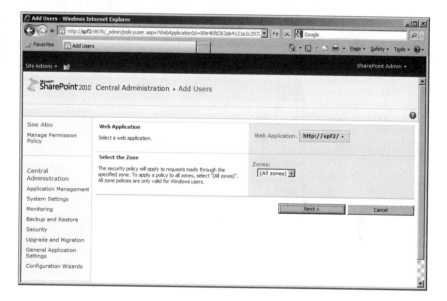

2. Once you've selected your web application and zone, click Next. The next step in the process (Figure 12.41) confirms the web application and zone you selected on the previous page. It also has sections for specifying the user account (accounts, or security groups), the permissions (you use Permission policy to remove, customize, or add Permission levels to be applied here), and whether the user(s) will operate as a system account (so when they access the site collections, their contributions will be listed as "system account" and not as their account name).

   The really interesting part of this page is the default permission levels that can be given to the accounts:

   Full Control   This is exactly like giving ownership or administrator permission. It is basically a site collection administrator setting, enabling all permissions.

   Full Read   When this setting says Full Read, it means it. This permission level allows users to read *everything*—every setting, list, library, and document—but they cannot change a darn thing anywhere. It's basically an auditor setting.

Deny Write   This is not what you probably think it is. You might think that the Deny Write permission-level policy gives someone the equivalent of a visitor's status on a site collection, but it doesn't. This setting is an "explicit deny," and it does not grant access to anything. Instead, it waits for a site or site collection to add the user (users, or group, whatever is added to the People Picker) as a contributor, full control, or some other permission level that allows viewing, editing, deleting, or adding of items, and then it forcibly and invisibly blocks those permissions and allows that user(s) to read-only. It is an absolute deny from the web-application level, regardless of the settings on the enclosed site collections.

Deny All   This permission level, if chosen, trumps anything done at the site collection. In other words, it blacklists whomever it is applied to; even if a site collection owner or administrator adds them explicitly to their site, they will not be able to log in.

FIGURE 12.41

Selecting an account and applying permission levels on the second Add Users page

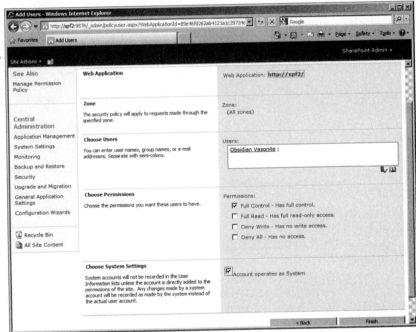

3.   Once you have configured the username or security group, permission level, and whether it will be a system account, you can click Finish to add it to the list of user policies.

If you were to log in with that account (or account from the security group, if that's what you added) to a site collection within the web application to which the user policy applies, the user would not need to show up in the list of all accounts allowed to access the site collection. They don't need to be given permission at the site collection level; they already have it at the web application level.

NO EASY WAY ANYMORE

The previous version of SharePoint offered an All People page in People And Groups, quickly showing all accounts that had access to the site collection (or wherever permission inheritance starts). But with this version of SharePoint, that page is no longer available. Now to quickly see all user accounts that have access to the site collection in one way or another (barring user policy), you need to use the PowerShell Get-SPuser cmdlet.

Adding a Permission Policy

You can change the permissions allowed (or denied) of a permission policy (sometimes considered permission policy levels) for a web application just as you can for a permission level in a site collection.

1. To see what permissions are available to allow or deny, and to create a custom permission policy level to apply to users, simply click Manage Permission Policy Levels in the See Also bar on the left side of the Policy for Web Application page (see Figure 12.40 for a look at the page) in the Quick Launch bar. Or if you are on the Manage Web Applications page, select a web application, and click the Permission Policy button.

   On the Manage Permission Policy Levels page is, as you'd expect, a list of what permission policy levels already exist (the page looks almost identical to the permission level page for managing site collection permission levels). There are links for Add Permission Policy Level and Delete Selected Permission Policy Levels (levels is plural because you can check more than one at a time). If you click a particular existing level in the list, it will open a page displaying what permissions it is explicitly allowing or denying.

2. To continue creating a new policy level, simply click the Add Permission Policy Level link on the Manage Permission Policy Levels page.

The page that opens looks a lot like the User Permission page used to specify the permissions to be admissible for a web application (a setting that would have been well located in this subcategory), except for two things:

- Each permission has two columns to check: an explicit Grant (or allow) and an explicit Deny.

- There is a section called Site Collection Permissions, which conveniently lets you just choose an existing Administrator (Full Control) or Auditor (Full Read) permission with which to begin.

You could create something like a List Manager permission policy level so you can force site collections to allow the users to whom you assign this permission policy level to manage lists (and read content on the site), even if they are not explicitly added as site members. On the flip side, if you wanted, you could explicitly deny an account or security group ever having certain permissions.

3. In this case, as you can guess from Figure 12.42, it's easy to grant the auditor settings and all the list permissions to the level and then click OK, creating the new permission policy.

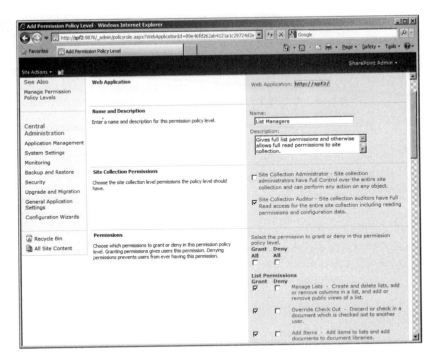

FIGURE 12.42
The Add Permission Policy Level page

PERMISSIONS CAN OVERLAP

You can have a permission policy level that gives a user rights to a site collection. However, if that person is also added to the site as a user with a different permission level, those two levels can merge, giving them more permissions than you might have expected.

Use Deny if you need to ensure that certain permissions are never attainable by the users to whom the permission policy levels are assigned.

Back on the Manage Permission Policy Levels page, there would be a new permission policy level. And if you add a user policy to the web application, you can apply the new permission policy level (Figure 12.43). This grants the user access to the web application (and the site collections it contains) in the selected zone, so if the user logs in to a contained site collection that does not have them as an explicit member, they can still manage lists using their account.

The Policy for Web Application page also manages (and overrides) the default anonymous access behavior for site collections in a selected web application or its individual zones. For this setting to be applied, the web application must have anonymous access enabled (otherwise, it's not applicable). For more information on anonymous access, see Chapter 10.

FIGURE 12.43
A new user policy with the new permission policy level

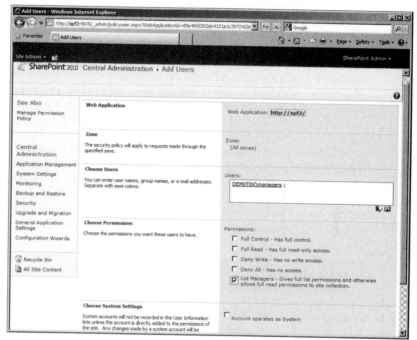

Farm-Level Users and Groups

Central Administration has its own web application, on its own custom port. In that web application is one site collection, for which the Central Administration site is the top-level site. It uses its own, special site definition, which is why it looks a lot different than your standard SharePoint site. This site was meant to be used only to manage the SharePoint server (or farm, depending on how you installed it). It is focused on the organization and display of settings and settings pages. The changes you make to the settings in Central Administration are saved to the configuration database for the server (or farm).

ADMINISTRATIVE CONTENT

The Central Administration site itself also has its own content database in case you want to populate it with lists and other data. If you do that, however, be aware that the site cannot normally be restored from backup should there be a catastrophe. It might be a better idea to create a different site collection for that kind of data and back it up separately.

Central Administration has two groups meant specifically for managing SharePoint itself: Farm Administrators and Delegated Administrators. They fall outside the standard site collection groups or permissions. A farm administrator, added in Central Administration (or with an STSADM or PowerShell command), essentially has full control of the farm settings and can take control of any site collection in the farm. There are some quirks to farm administrator accounts, though. The first is that the farm account *must* be farm administrator, even though you shouldn't log in as that account to manage the farm. (The farm account is used by SharePoint as the identity running SharePoint timer jobs and is the application pool identity used to access the configuration database for SharePoint.) Do not remove that account from the group. Second, farm administrators should be able to add, remove configure all web applications and databases, start and stop services, and more. This requires that the account have administrative rights on the local server itself (either by being a local admin or by being a domain admin). If you add a user account to the Farm Administrators group that *does not* have administrative rights to the server, it will therefore not be allowed to stop or start services on the server or add or remove things in IIS, for example. That account will be able to log into Central Administration, and it will be able to administer existing web applications, content databases, services, and settings, but it will be limited to only doing things that do not require local administrative access. This is a quirk in Central Administration and can be used to create junior farm administrators, who can work on existing web applications, site collections, farm settings, and service applications.

FARM ADMINISTRATORS ARE NOT MEMBERS OF THE SITE COLLECTION ADMINISTRATORS GROUP

Interestingly, Central Administration is also just the top-level site of the site collection in the Central Administration web application. Site collections must have site collection administrators, and because of that, the account you used to install SharePoint is the default site collection administrator (and is also automatically a farm administrator). This fact is not particularly useful in the administration of the farm, but it is useful if you are going to be doing anything on the site itself that only a site collection administrator could do.

Delegated administrators are new with this version of SharePoint and are intended to let you assign administrators to specific service applications or application connections. They essentially have very, very limited access to Central Administration and can only see and manage the service application they are assigned to.

To be able to do anything in SharePoint, there need to be farm administrators. At the beginning of the book, in Chapters 2 and 3, adding an additional user account to the Farm Administrators group was covered as a post-installation task. But as a reminder, you can do so by going to Central Administration. On the home page is a link, under the Security heading, for managing the Farm Administrators group.

Clicking it opens the People And Groups page for Central Administration, displaying the members of the Farm Administrators group.

As you can see in Figure 12.44, the members I have currently are the SharePoint farm account (in my case, *dem0tek\spffarm*), the setup account, and the account I added after installation—my SharePoint utility account, *shareadmin*. Since being a farm administrator generally requires that the account also have administrative rights to the SharePoint servers (or server in a standalone implementation), during installation (despite the potential security risk), all members of the server's BUILTIN\Administrators group for the initial server are added as farm administrators by default. This ensures that accounts with administrative rights to the server will be able to log in, in case of emergency.

FIGURE 12.44

The Farm Administrators group

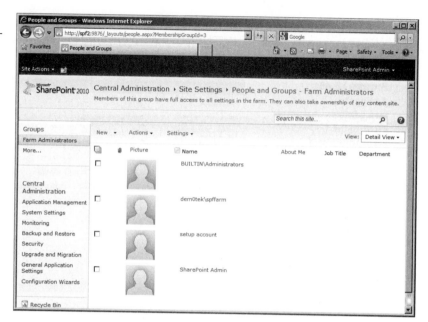

For this example, I have created a security group in Active Directory called *farmadmins* and have added some users (in particular, the user account *Beryl Malachite*, who I will be logging in as later). As I said earlier, you can add AD (or local) security groups to groups in SharePoint (except for site collection administrators; for some reason, they must be added individually). This is particularly useful for two reasons. First, SharePoint can handle only so many security objects, and security groups and users are considered objects. So, why not add a bunch of users to a group and then add the group to SharePoint (considered one object instead of many)? Second, because it's easy. Because most user accounts in a domain are being managed in Active Directory, it's more efficient to manage the users in those AD groups used by SharePoint than to manage the users in AD and also have to go into SharePoint and add or remove people there as well.

My *farmadmins* group has been added to the domain admins group for my domain, so all members of the *farmadmins* group will have administrative rights to the SharePoint server (if it is in the domain).

Adding Farm Administrators

To add an AD security group to the Farm Administrators group in Central Administration, take the following steps:

1. On the Farm Administrators People And Groups page, click the New button in the Action bar (what I call the old SharePoint interface that has links that act like drop-down buttons for actions in the content area of a page).

2. In the Grant Permissions box, enter the account or security group you want to add to the Farm Administrators group. For the added account(s) to be able to do full farm administration, make sure that they are members of the Domain Admins or local Administrators group.

3. In my example, I am adding the AD security group *farmadmins* that I created in Active Directory for this task (Figure 12.45). The security group doesn't have an email address, so I am going to deselect sending a welcome email. To Finish, click OK.

FIGURE 12.45
Adding the farmadmins group to the Farm Administrators group

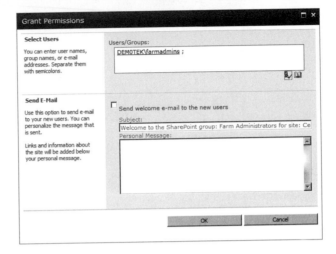

Once you've added the group, it will show up in the People And Groups list just like the BUILTIN\Administrators group does (Figure 12.46).

FIGURE 12.46
New AD group added to farm administrators

When you add users by security group to SharePoint, it doesn't create user information for the individual accounts the group contains until the users log in for the first time. In addition, the user will not show up in People And Groups as an individual user like individually added accounts will (see Figure 12.47, where I am logged in as one of the users in the added security group). This is one of the shortcomings of adding users via AD security group; it makes it harder to find the individual account to check their email address or see what group they are a member of.

FIGURE 12.47

Logged in with a new farm administrator, despite their account not being listed individually in Farm Administrators group

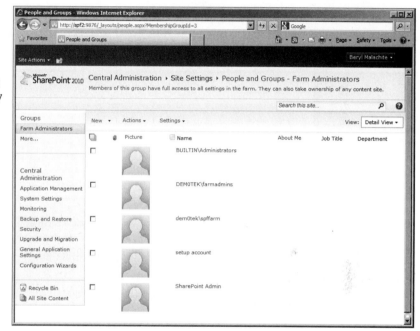

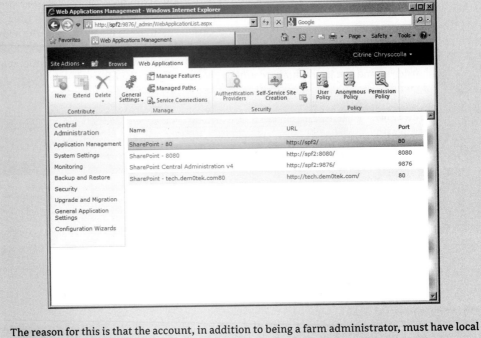

The reason for this is that the account, in addition to being a farm administrator, must have local administrative rights, which the account I am logged in with doesn't have.

The following settings pages are missing for a junior administrator:

◆ Manage Services On Server

◆ Configure Incoming Email Settings

◆ Configure Usage and Health Data Collection

◆ Perform A Backup Or Restore, Or Configure Backup Settings

◆ Launch The Configuration Wizard

Removing a User or Group from Farm Administrators

Now that we've added users to the Farm Administrators group, we have plenty of people who can log into Central Administration.

In most environments, after making sure you've added accounts to the Farm Administrators group, you quickly remove the builtin\administrators from the group. Generally those administrators are not necessarily SharePoint administrators and therefore shouldn't have farm administrator rights to the farm. To remove a user or security group from the Farm Administrators group, make sure you are in People And Groups, Farm Administrators group.

1. Put a check mark next to the security group or user you want to remove (in my case that would be BUILTIN\Administrators, the first member in the list). Keep in mind that, because there are check boxes, more than one user or security group can be removed at a time.

2. Then click Actions in the Action bar. It will drop down a menu. Select Remove Users From Group (Figure 12.48).

FIGURE 12.48
Removing selected group from farm administrators

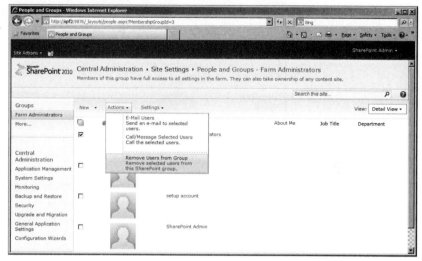

3. You will get a warning dialog box asking whether you are sure you want to delete the selected members. Check to make sure you are removing the correct member, and then click OK. That will take you back to the Farm Administrators group page, with one less item listed.

And that's it. The BUILTIN\Administrators security group is removed from Farm Administrators group. And that means that only the accounts listed on the page (and those in the group we added earlier) will be able to log into Central Administration.

So, that introduces you to the Farm Administrators group, the only group available from the Central Administration's home page. However, there is another group available for Central Administration, and that is Delegated Administrators.

Adding Delegated Administrators

Because SharePoint Foundation now supports several service applications, particularly Business Data Connectivity, it is possible that there could be a user account needed to access that specific service application to set up external connections without needing to have real administrative power over SharePoint.

So, you can add a user to the permissions of a service application, and the account will be added to the Delegated Administrators group.

1. To see this in action, while in Central Administration, go to the home page, and under the Application Management heading, click Manage Service Applications.

2. On the Manage Service Applications page, select the service you want to add an administrator to; in my case I am selecting Business Data Connectivity. Once it is highlighted, you can click the Administrators button on the ribbon (Figure 12.49).

FIGURE 12.49
Business Data Con-
nectivity selected,
Administrators
button, Manage
Service Applica-
tions page

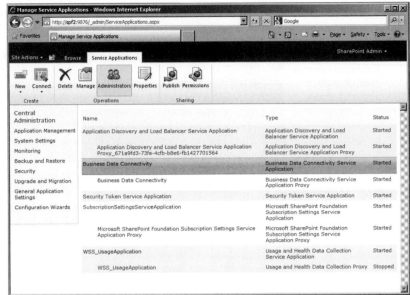

In the Administrators For Business Data Connectivity form box, you can see that there are two fields and a box—one for entering accounts or security groups with an Add button, one to display the accounts added, and the box containing the permission levels that can be applied to the account.

3. Enter the account or security group you want to give administrator rights to this service application, and click Add. In my case, I am going to add a user account (see Figure 12.50 for my example).

FIGURE 12.50
Adding user to
manage BDC
service

4. In the Permissions box is only one permission that can be given to administrators for this service application, Full Control. Click the check box to select it. To finish, click OK.

Now that you have an administrator delegated to managing a single service application but not part of the Farm Administrators group, if you log in as that account, you will see a very different Central Administration home page. This is because all settings have been stripped but the one that the administrator to the service application is allowed to manage (Figure 12.51).

FIGURE 12.51
Logged in as a delegated administrator

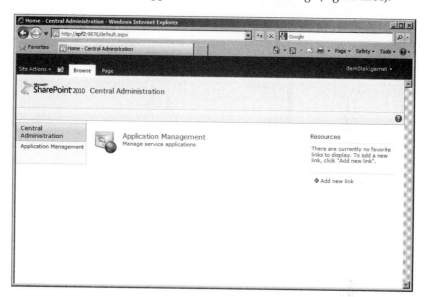

If you click the Manage Service Applications link, it will take you to the only service application the account is allowed to access. To see the account in the Delegated Administrator's group, do the following:

1. Go back to the People And Groups page (the easiest way is to make sure you are logged in as a farm administrator, and on the home page, click Manage The Farm Administrators group, under Security).

2. On the People And Groups page, in the top area of the Quick Launch bar, click either the Groups heading or More... It will take you to a page listing all groups that were ever added to Central Administration (even if they were removed from their site group, such as the BUILTIN\Administrators), and existing site groups, such as Farm Administrators or Delegated Administrators. This is just like the All Groups page for a site collection.

3. If you click Delegated Administrators in the All Groups page, it will open a page displaying the accounts the group contains (Figure 12.52). In this case, that would be the account that has administrative rights to the service application (and the account that you used to install SharePoint).

FIGURE 12.52
The Delegated
Administrators
group page

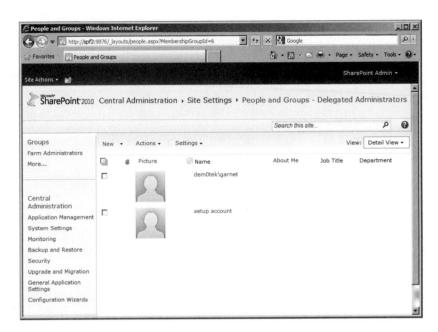

FIGURE 12.52
The Delegated
Administrators
group page

You now have some idea what groups are available to manage SharePoint at the farm level, what they can do, and how to add users to them.

Overall, you have learned about users and groups from the farm level to the individual items. You know what individual permissions are, where they can be allowed (and disallowed) at the web application level, and applied as permission levels for site collections and subsites. You now know how to create, remove, modify, and copy permission levels, as well as how to break inheritance.

The Bottom Line

Define users and groups in SharePoint. SharePoint users are individuals with user accounts that can be authorized to use SharePoint resources. Users can be stored in one or more groups. SharePoint understands two types of groups: SharePoint groups and security groups.

> **Master It** Differentiate between a SharePoint group and a security group. Determine the preferred method for adding users to SharePoint.

Add users and groups in SharePoint. New SharePoint groups can be created to organize user access to websites. User accounts and security groups from Active Directory (or whatever authentication provider you are using) can be added to the SharePoint site directly or by being placed into a SharePoint group.

> **Master It** If you add a security group to a SharePoint group and then later delete that SharePoint group, how do you apply a permission level to the security group directly?

Define permissions and permission levels in SharePoint.   Authorization in SharePoint is handled by 33 distinct permissions. These permissions provide user access to lists, sites, and personal settings. They also determine whether the user's access is restricted to simply reading or browsing, can allow editing of objects, or can even permit creation of new objects.

Permission levels are simply groups of permissions. A permission level can contain any or all of the 33 permissions and can depend on prerequisite permissions. The permission level is then applied to SharePoint groups to provide authorization to members of that group. They can also be applied directly to users and security groups.

Master It   Describe what the Manage Permissions permission does and what dependent permissions it requires. What permission level contains manage permissions by default?

Set permissions on a site/list/list item for a user or a group.   Permission levels are assigned to SharePoint groups, security groups, or individual users starting at the top-level site of the site collection. By default, these users and groups (along with their assigned permission levels) propagate throughout the site collection using permission inheritance. You can go to any object (site, list, library, or item) in the site collection and break inheritance, adding users and groups to the object manually, and then give them different permission levels.

Master It   If you break inheritance on a subsite of the main Company Site and start using custom permissions for that subsite, do the lists on the subsite retain their original permission settings from Company Site, or do they also gain the custom permissions set on the subsite?

Chapter 13

Maintenance and Monitoring

As a SharePoint administrator, your job is never done, particularly once the server is set up and functioning. You have servers to nurture and protect, databases to manage, and websites to control. Lists are being built, data is being processed, and web pages are being accessed. SharePoint was meant to grow, and grow it will. Now is the time to create a baseline of how your SharePoint services work optimally and prepare for possible emergencies. It's beneficial to recognize what your server looks like on a good day, when all is working well, so you can anticipate when things are going to start lagging before the users start to complain.

Tools to monitor your SharePoint server's health are built into both Windows Server 2008 R2 and SharePoint Foundation 2010. There are, of course, many third-party products you could use for monitoring as well, but let's start with what we all should have.

To monitor your server, you first need to create a baseline. To do so, you should be familiar with the Performance Monitor. This server tool has been around for a long time, and you should already be using it to monitor your existing Windows Server systems. In this chapter, you'll learn how to

◆ Monitor server performance

◆ Use SharePoint Backup and Restore

◆ Back up separate SharePoint components

◆ Recover from disaster

Why Monitor?

SharePoint can be resource-intensive, putting a strain on the server's hardware from the beginning. Because it depends heavily on processor and RAM, SharePoint will begin to show signs of stress if your server's hardware struggles to support it. In addition, SharePoint is very dependent on network access. If you can't reach the server because its network card (NIC) is overwhelmed or the network itself is too busy, SharePoint is broken as far as users are concerned. The hard drive can be pelted by paging requests if the system's RAM is not up to SharePoint's activity requirements (not to mention the extra RAM requirements each web application adds). SharePoint's databases can fill quickly with mission-critical data that requires user access practically 24/7. It's a closed circle—Processor ➤ RAM ➤ hard disk ➤ network card—so you must watch for all of these things.

Performance Monitor

To open the Performance Monitor, either you can go to Start, enter **perf** in the search field, and select Performance Monitor from the results list or you can click Start ➤ Administrative Tools ➤ Performance Monitor. The Performance Monitor window appears as in Figure 13.1. In the center of the console is a short system summary of performance counters that give you a quick idea of how your server is doing.

FIGURE 13.1

The Performance Monitor

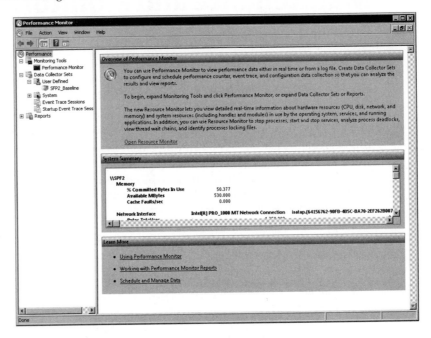

On the left under Monitoring Tools you can see the default Performance Monitor graph. When you click on Performance Monitor, it shows in real time what is happening on your server with the performance counters listed beneath the graph (see Figure 13.2). By default the graph contains one counter: *% Processor Time*. The long, vertical red line running the height of the graph always indicates the current activity.

> **MY PERFORMANCE MONITOR DOESN'T QUITE LOOK LIKE YOUR PERFORMANCE MONITOR**
>
> The Performance Monitor that we are using for this chapter is the Performance Monitor that comes with Windows Server 2008 R2. If you are running Windows Server 2008, your Performance Monitor may look a little different. The differences are pretty small, so don't worry; you will find everything in relatively the same place.

FIGURE 13.2

A Performance
Monitor graph

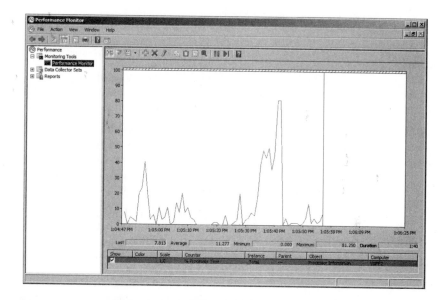

Adding Counters to Performance Monitor

Four critical parts of the server are CPU, RAM, disk drives, and network interface. You can add
other counters to measure the size of the queue for things the disk must do, how much paging
the RAM is doing to the hard drive per second, and the health of the network card.

1. To add a counter to the Performance Monitor, just click the button with the plus sign over
   the graph. The Add Counters dialog box (Figure 13.3) contains many counters based on
   all the objects available on your server.

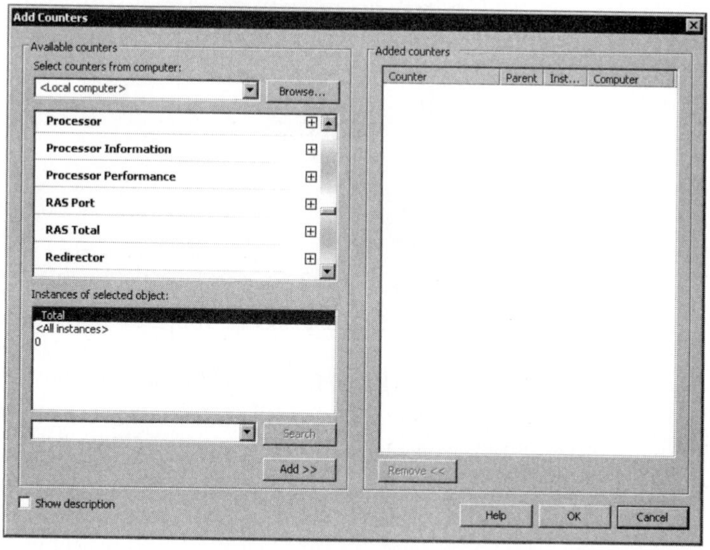

FIGURE 13.3

Adding a counter

This dialog box allows you to pull the performance objects and their counters from the local computer, or you can specify a different computer (if you have the permissions). By default, it specifies the local computer for the counters.

The Available Counters list is huge. By default, it shows you a list of objects, but each one contains multiple counters that can be monitored with Windows Server 2008 R2 (or Server 2008, if that's what you have).

2. To add the network interface counter to monitor its performance, just find Network Interface in the Available Counters section, and click the plus sign to expand that section. Notice how many things you can monitor. The number will vary from server to server depending on their roles. Many Microsoft products add their own counters to the monitor, and SharePoint is no exception.

There are so many counters in the Network Interface section alone that you may not be sure what to choose. If that is the case, simply pick a counter such as Bytes Total/Sec (as shown in Figure 13.4), and check the Show Description box at the bottom. A small window will display a brief explanation of the counter; this window stays attached at the bottom of the dialog box for easy reference.

FIGURE 13.4

Displaying a description for a selected network interface counter

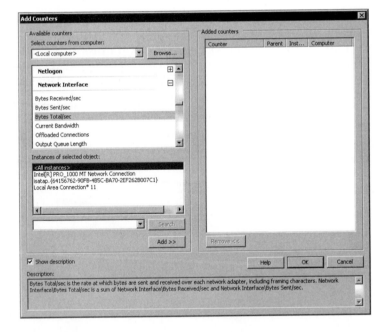

3. In the counters list, choose Bytes Total/Sec to track the network activity. In the instances list, if you have more than one NIC, choose the one you want to monitor (or you can select all instances). Once you have made your selection, click the Add button to add it to the Performance Monitor.

4. Now browse to Memory, select the % Committed Bytes In Use counter, and add that to the list. Then browse to Logical Disk and add the counter for Current Disk Queue Length. When you're done, click OK to add these counters to the graph.

As you can see, the Performance Monitor in Figure 13.5 shows a lot of activity. You can quickly see that the RAM usage is hovering around 50 percent, and the disk queue and network are pretty idle.

FIGURE 13.5

Multiple counters added to the Performance Monitor

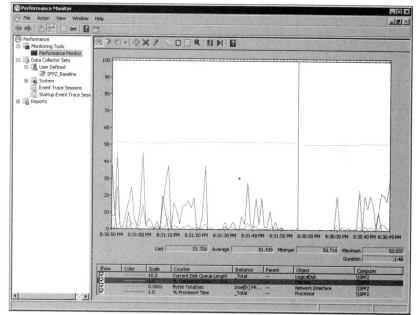

This book's sample server is running in a virtual machine with as little RAM as possible to keep it going. Figure 13.5 gives you a chance to see what a stressed-out SharePoint server looks like when people access it.

Being able to see what's going on with the Performance Monitor is great. After you've surfed through all the performance objects and read all the explanations of the counters, you may be tempted to try to monitor all of them. Don't. Performance Monitor will become too crowded and hard to read. Keep it simple—maybe no more than six or so counters as a maximum.

Creating a Data Collector Set

What if you want to keep track of more than a few significant counters, or you want a longer sample time? In that case, you'll need a baseline report that collects data over time to give you the big picture of what your server is doing. It will give you the chance to spot trends using multiple counters and anticipate the need for upgrades and repairs before the users complain. To build a baseline report, you'll first need to create a performance log (or a *data collection set* as it is called in Performance Monitor).

To create a data collection set, follow these steps:

1. Double-click Data Collector Sets in the Performance console.

2. Right-click User Defined, and select New Data Collector Set.

3. You'll be prompted to name the set. My example is going to be used to track the baseline performance of the SharePoint server. Name the log **SFP2_Baseline**. You can also build a set from an existing template or create it manually with the counters. My example will create it manually, so select Create Manually. See Figure 13.6.

FIGURE 13.6

Creating a new
data collector set

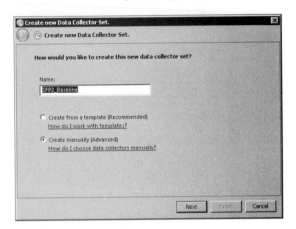

4. Click Next.

   Next you are asked what type of data to include in the data collection set (either data logs or performance counter alert); there are three types of information under Create data logs: performance counter (the same collection of counters you can apply to the graph shown earlier), event trace data, and system configuration information (settings and configuration information, such as memory installed, network adapter settings, and registry settings).

5. Check the Performance Counter box (since you need to generate a performance baseline), and click Next.

You are now asked to populate the performance counter data collector with whatever counters you want to log.

Because you are going to use this log to create a performance baseline for your server, it would help to know what kind of counters are available. There is no list of official counters to use when creating a baseline for monitoring a Windows server, and the optimum collection of counters will vary from server to server based on hardware, environment, and server use. There are several Microsoft white papers that can assist you in picking the right counters for your situation. Keep in mind that SharePoint has added custom counters to the server, most of them relating to Search, which can be added as well.

SharePoint counter performance problems are often corroborated by events in the application log. If you see levels that don't look good in your logs, remember that you should see what events SharePoint has generated to better troubleshoot the problem. Table 13.1 lists some counters you can use for your baseline.

TABLE 13.1: Common Baseline Counters

PERFORMANCE OBJECT	COUNTER	LOOK FOR THESE MAXIMUMS
Memory	%Committed Bytes in Use	Greater than 80 percent can mean you don't have enough RAM.
Memory	Available MB	Less than 50 MB is bad because the default file maximum for uploads is 50 MB; at least 128 to 256 MB is better.
Memory	Pages/Sec	If your server is paging memory at 220 pages per second or more, you need to increase the RAM.
Logical Disk	%Idle Time	Less than 20 percent means that the disk is being overworked. Each partition can be measured as an instance.
Network Interface	Bytes Total/Sec	If you are using more than 50 percent of your NIC's total bandwidth, you could have real problems during peak times. If you are monitoring a 100 MB NIC, that would be 50 MB, or 536,870,912 bytes, give or take.
Physical Disk	%Disk Time	Indicates the percentage of time a disk is busy. If it is busy 80 percent of the time, you have a bottleneck (you can also do this for logical disks). Can count all disks total or individual disks as instances.
Physical Disk	Avg Disk Queue Length	A standard counter for the physical disk. If it's above 2 or 3 per hard disk (depending on your environment), you need either more RAM or faster disks. Also can measure each disk individually as an instance.
Processor	%processor time_total	Total of all processors on the server. Greater than 80 percent means it's overutilized. You can also measure the performance of individual processors if you think one is failing.
System	Processor Queue Length	More than 10 threads may mean that your processor is too slow or overworked.
Web Service	Connection Attempts/Sec	500 or more a second could mean that you need to think about adding another server to your farm. There is an instance for each web application.

TABLE 13.1: Common Baseline Counters *(CONTINUED)*

PERFORMANCE OBJECT	COUNTER	LOOK FOR THESE MAXIMUMS
SharePoint Foundation*	Incoming Page Requests Rate	The number of page requests received in the last second. A quick snapshot of how many page views the server is handling. There is an instance for each web application.
SharePoint Foundation*	Sql Query Executing time	The average time it takes for SharePoint to execute a query to the SQL server. If this is high when the rest of the counters (network, processors, and so on) are slow, you may want to run Performance Monitor on the SQL server. There is an instance for each web application.
SharePoint Foundation Search Gatherer*	System IO traffic rate	The amount of traffic (in KB/s) the search gatherer (also known as the search crawler or index) is applying to the physical disks. A quick way to see how Search is impacting the disk.
SharePoint Foundation Search Gatherer*	Heartbeats/ Heartbeats Rate	Gatherer heartbeats occur every 10 seconds. If the number of ticks does not increment for this counter, the Gatherer's heart isn't beating, and therefore it is not running. Check the event logs for errors, and make sure the Search service is running somewhere on your farm. This counter is good for alerts.
SharePoint Foundation Search Gatherer Project*	Retries	How many times the Search Gatherer had to retry when accessing a document. A high number may indicate communication problems between the crawler and the database.

*SharePoint counters require the log to run as an administrator on the domain. The other counters can run as the local system (the default) without a problem.

To add these counters to the log, follow these steps:

1. Click the Add button. The Add Counters dialog box will open.

2. Select one of the performance objects from Table 13.1, select the correct counter in the counters list (and instance where applicable), and click Add. The dialog box will stay open until you close it manually. For example, select Memory from the Available Counters list, and then select %Committed Bytes In Use.

3. There are no additional instances for this counter, so click Add to add it to the log.

4. Repeat steps 1 through 3 for each counter (you can see Figure 13.6 for an idea of the counters I chose).

5. When you are done, click OK to leave the Add Counters dialog box. This will return you to the data collector set up for SPF2_Baseline (see Figure 13.7). A lot of counters now appear in the list.

FIGURE 13.7

SPF2_Baseline log counters

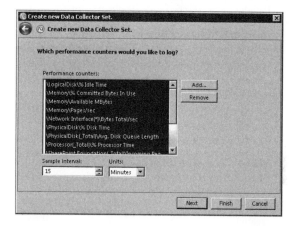

The Create New Data Collector Set window also has another setting: Sample Interval. This indicates the interval of time for which the log will *sample* counter data (that is, collect counter data). In this case, you should consider sampling at least every 5 minutes or so. You don't want to add extra processing strain on a server you might already be worried about, which is why you should consider avoiding a sampling interval that is too short, especially in the long run. For this example, since we are going to be making a baseline of performance over a longer period of time, we will set it for 15-minute sample intervals.

6. Set the Interval to 15, and set the Units to Minutes. Click Next.

SPEAKING OF COUNTERS

You may think some of the counters from Table 13.1 are redundant, and that's fine. A lean data collector set makes the log easier to read and uses fewer machine resources. However, you do need to know the various counter options that can assist you in assessing your server's performance. Once you get the hang of using counters, feel free to experiment with your own baseline monitoring until you use only the counters that are right for you. Remember, monitoring takes resources, so keep your sampling intervals as long as you can, and try to save the logs to a drive other than the one being sampled. Remember that the real-time Performance Monitor does take resources, so just using logs and not running the monitor helps conserve resources.

Also note that if there are maximum values listed in Table 13.1, they can be used as alert triggers to warn you when an unacceptable performance threshold has been met. Those values are not only so you can interpret the baseline logs you will create but also so you can be alerted. Alerts will be covered in the section "Setting a Performance Counter Alert."

You are now prompted to choose a location to store all the log files. If possible, keep these on a separate disk from the ones you're monitoring, so they don't impact the performance of the disks (and skew your reports).

7. For the example, leave the default in place, and click Next.

Using the Run As field, you can monitor counters from other computers on the network or monitor counters that are managed by services with domain accounts that access network resources. To do that successfully, you may need to run the log under a domain account with the permission to access the services and resources necessary to measure performance. To use the SharePoint counters in my example, you need this log to run in a context that is allowed to access other resources on the network and local services. My example uses an account I created for this exercise, the monitor@dem0tek.lcl account. This account was created as a member of the Domain Admins group.

8. When you're done make sure Save and Close is selected, and then click Finish. You'll see the new data collection set in Performance Monitor (Figure 13.8).

FIGURE 13.8

The newly created data collection set

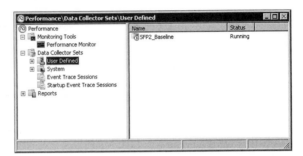

If you now right-click the data collection set and go to Properties, you can configure other options, most notably scheduling the set to run at specific times and setting stop conditions. As you can see in Figure 13.9, on the Schedule tab you can add a schedule; my example has a simple schedule to start the data collection set every day at 5 a.m.

FIGURE 13.9

Scheduling the data collection set

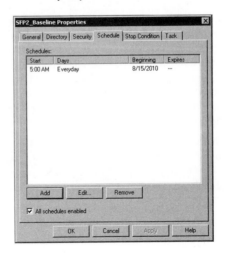

On the Stop Condition tab (shown in Figure 13.10), you can provide certain settings that will trigger the data collection to stop. My example stops the jobs after 15 hours (around 8 p.m., assuming it started at 5 a.m.). You may want the log to stop when each log reaches 10 MB and then start again with a new log file. To do that, check the box to restart the data collector when the maximum size limit is reached. Keep an eye on the logs, because they do take up space on the drive where they are stored.

FIGURE 13.10
The Stop
Condition tab

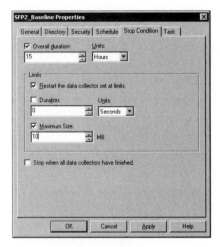

Once it's all configured, you can also manually run the data collector set by selecting it from the window and clicking Run on the toolbar. The data collectors will create new log files storing the information gathered. To make certain that your logs have been created, open Windows Explorer, and navigate to your log file location (in my example, it's `c:\perflogs\Admin\SPF2_Baseline`, as you can see in Figure 13.11).

FIGURE 13.11
Log files that have
been created

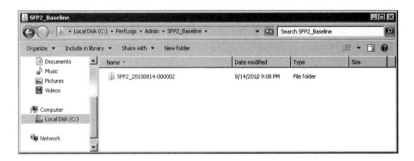

By default the log files are stored as binary `*.blg` files. It is possible to have the data collector save the file in other formats by editing the properties of the data collector (inside the data collector set). It's recommended you leave the log file format as binary so Performance Monitor can easily open these files later. Other format options include comma-delimited, tab-delimited, and SQL.

ANALYZING YOUR LOG FILES

If you've got some quiet time on a Friday night, why not spend it analyzing your log files? For example, you could convert the logs to CSV (comma separate value) files and open them in Excel to format the results conditionally so you can tell at a glance whether any totals are outside your acceptable range. It's easy and takes only a second in Excel 2007 or Excel 2010.

To convert the log files (which are binary by default) to CSV, open a command prompt and type this:

```
Relog logfilename.blg -f CSV -o Newfile.csv
```

Just keep in mind that you don't have to open your comma-delimited log file and read it as a text file. The point is to have it parsed elsewhere. You can open it in Excel of course, but you can also open it in Access to make a database out of it, or you can choose an SQL database file type (using -f SQL in place of -f CSV) for your logs so you can query them with SQL. Logs aren't just simple text files anymore. Logs are only as useful as you make them. If you don't analyze them, they are just taking up space.

When your data collection set has completed (either because it hit a stop condition or because you clicked the Stop button), you can view the resulting report. In Performance Monitor, on the left browse under Reports ➤ User Defined to see your newly created reports (Figure 13.12).

FIGURE 13.12
The latest report for the SPF2_Baseline data collection

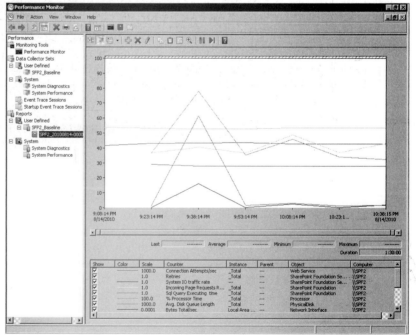

Setting a Performance Counter Alert

Now that you've created your baseline, you must wait for it to build up some data. After a while, when data has been collected, you'll have to look at it. That's good, but what if one of those counters passed a threshold you think is dangerous and you didn't have time to check the log at that particular moment? Wouldn't you like to know whether something catastrophic may be brewing? That's why you can set alerts for performance counters. To do so, follow these steps:

1. To set an alert, browse to your existing data collection set (My example is called SFP2_ Baseline), right-click on it, and choose New ➤ Data Collector.

2. A Create New Data Collector wizard will come up so you can name the alert. My example calls the alert **free disk space**. Choose the option to create a Performance Counter Alert (rather than Performance Counter Data Collector), and click Next.

3. To add the counter for this alert, click Add to open the Add Counters dialog box.

4. Because you are adding a counter for the logical disk, browse to that section, and select % Free Space in the counters list.

5. In the instance field, choose a drive as the logical partition that you want to monitor (see Figure 13.13); my example selects the C: drive.

6. Click Add to add this counter to the alert. You could add more, but all of their values would have to be triggered for the alert to go off. Therefore, it's a good idea to create alerts based on as few counters as possible. Click OK after you've chosen your counters.

FIGURE 13.13
Configuring the %
Free Space counter

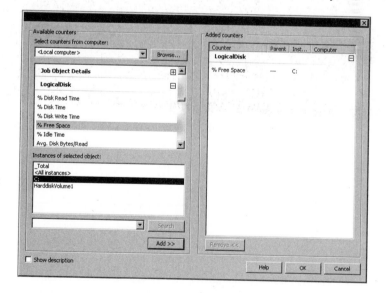

7. The *alert value*, or the value that the counter needs to reach in order to trigger the alert, is set in the Alert dialog box. The alert can be triggered when a value is either over or under the specified value. For this example, set the alert value to Below 30. The alert will trigger when the percentage of free space on the C: partition is less than 30 percent (see Figure 13.14).

FIGURE 13.14
Setting an alert value

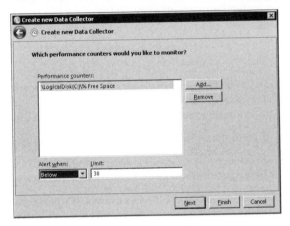

8. Click Next, and then check the box to open the Alert item's properties for this data collector, and click Finish (you may be prompted to enter the username for the set).

9. Performance Monitor will create the alert under your data collection set and open the properties for the alert (if the data collection set is running, it warns you that changes will take effect at next start; just click OK). The Alert tab contains the settings you just entered (along with a Sample Interval setting you can change). The Alert Action tab is where you specify what happens when the trigger value is reached. The alert can log an entry in the application event log or start a particular data collection set. Go ahead and have it log an entry in the Application event log.

10. On the Alert Task tab, you can have the alert run a WMI task when the alert conditions are met. You can use an existing task or create your own in Task Scheduler (we are not going to set a WMI task in this example). When you are done, click OK to finish setting up the alert.

ALERT TASK?

So, how do you use the new Alert Task tab's WMI Task options to do something useful when you're not really sure what WMI tasks are?

The easiest way to create a new task is to use Scheduled Tasks. As you probably know, this is the place you can schedule simple batch files, programs, and other events under Windows Server 2008 R2. Well, every scheduled task is actually a WMI Task and can be used with the Performance Monitor alert.

For example, say you want the server to email the account *shareadmin* when the disk space goes below 30 percent. Go to Start ➤ Administrative Tools ➤ Task Scheduler (under Administrative Tools) and then create a new task. On the General tab, enter the name, description, and other settings for the task (for example, I edited the task to run as demotek\monitor and set it to run with highest privileges).

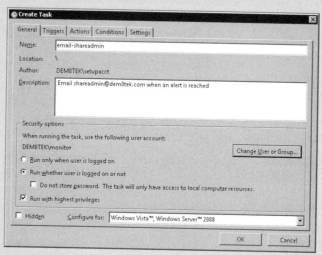

Don't worry about adding triggers; the task will be triggered by the alert in Performance Monitor. Under Actions, click New and choose Send An Email. Enter the desired email contents (I keep the email body vague in case I want to use this task for multiple alerts in the future). For the SMTP server, add your email server. By default Task Scheduler will attempt to authenticate using NTLM and the credentials of the account running the task (in my example, dem0tek\monitor). If NTLM authentication fails, it will attempt anonymous access. In my example, I'm using the local server's SMTP service (configured in Chapter 3), which I've adjusted to allow open relay from its own IP address.

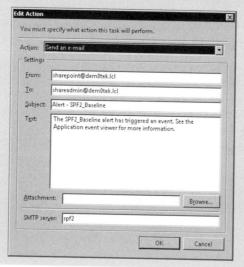

You can examine the conditions and settings to make any changes you might want. I'm happy with the defaults. Go ahead and click OK to create the new task (it will prompt for the run-as user's password); you now have a WMI task that emails *shareadmin*.

Go back to your alert in Performance Monitor, and open its properties. Go to the Alert Task tab, and enter the name of the task you created (my example was **email-shareadmin**). Now, when the alert is triggered, it will run this task, sending an email to *shareadmin*.

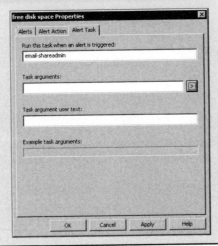

Alerts do not run automatically—they run as part of a data collection set. So if you want the server to alert you independently of the data collection in our SPF2_Baseline collection set, you'll need to create a new data collection set for the alert and schedule it to run constantly.

Resource Monitor

Sometimes you need to see what's going on in real time—the server is misbehaving *right now*, and it's critical that you fix it. When this happens, the first go-to tool for an IT professional is the Task Manager (right-click the task bar, and select Start Task Manager). This familiar tool will quickly show you what processes are running, the CPU load, memory in use, and users.

With Windows Server 2008 R2 there's a new tool called Resource Monitor that's accessible from Task Manager (as a button on the Performance tab) or launched directly via the Start menu (Located in Accessories ➤ System Tools). Launching this program takes you to the Overview screen for Resource Monitor (Figure 13.15).

Here at a glance you can see the current processes using CPU time, disk access, network access, and memory. There are tabs along the top to give you more information about each section—and allow you to quickly view what resources are being used (or abused) by what process. For example, clicking the Disk tab brings up a list of the processes currently writing or reading from the physical disk, as shown in Figure 13.16.

FIGURE 13.15
The Resource Monitor Overview display

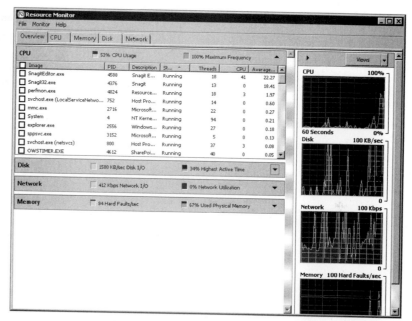

FIGURE 13.16
The Resource Monitor Disk tab

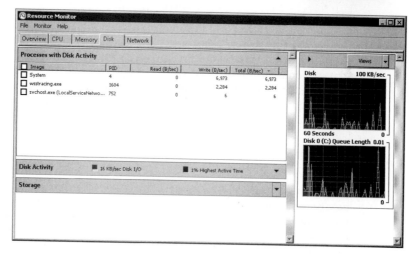

If you click one of the running processes, the display below it will filter the Disk Activity section by that process, showing you exactly which files on the disk are being accessed right now. For example, if you click the wsstracing.exe process, you'll see that it's accessing three files on the local disk (Figure 13.17).

FIGURE 13.17
Filtered disk access
by process

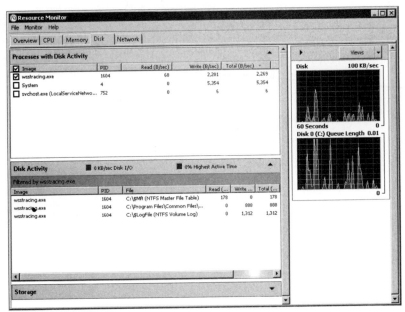

Then, on the CPU tab, you can filter by the wsstracing.exe process and view the currently used Services, Associated Handles, and Associated Modules for that process. Under Network, you can view what current TCP connections each process is using (including what remote IP address and port they are connecting to). It's a great way to see if an unfamiliar process is sending data out onto the Internet.

All of this information is much more useful than the basics found in Task Manager, and it gives you a quick way to see what each running process is doing, so you can find and resolve your issue quickly.

SPDIAG

In addition to the server's resources, the SharePoint Administrators Toolkit for WSS 3.0 and MOSS 2007 had a great tool called SharePoint Diagnostics (SPDiag). This tool is not currently bundled with the updated SharePoint Administrators Toolkit 2010. But the good news is that the old 2007 version of the tool still works perfectly with SharePoint Foundation 2010. And it's an extremely handy tool to have. If you search Microsoft's download site for SPDiag, you can download the SPDiag user's guide and find the link to download the SharePoint Administrators Toolkit. Note that the system requirements say it's for WSS 3.0 and MOSS 2007, but the SPDiag tool does work fine with SPF 2010.

Once it's installed, you can create a new "project" and have it examine your current SharePoint environment. SPDiag doesn't let you make any changes; it simply pulls all the configuration settings, IIS logs, PerfMon logs, and other statistics together to provide you with a comprehensive look at your SharePoint systems. (It's also a really handy way to become familiar with a SharePoint environment you may not have built yourself but are now expected to maintain.)

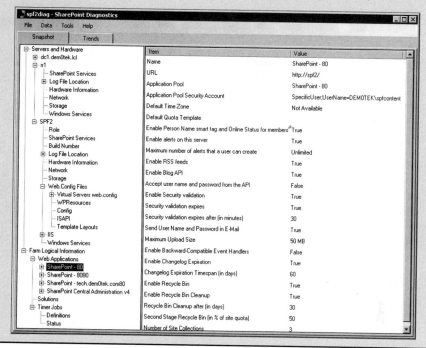

IIS Logs

By default, IIS keeps logs for all IIS Web Sites, which means it keeps logs for each web application. These logs keep approximately the same information as the SharePoint Usage Data Collection does (another means to monitor your sites and site collections, by the way). However, it's possible to control what the IIS log tracks and how you look at it. To see what the IIS logs are for each web application, just follow these steps:

1. Open the IIS console on the SharePoint server by choosing Start ➢ Administrative Tools ➢ Internet Information Services (IIS) Manager.

2. Inside the console, expand the server icon, and then expand Sites in the connections pane so you can see your website icons.

3. Click one of the SharePoint web applications (my example uses SharePoint-80), and double click on Logging from the IIS section of the workspace in the middle of the console. This opens the logging settings for the website. See Figure 13.18.

FIGURE 13.18
Logging for
SharePoint-80

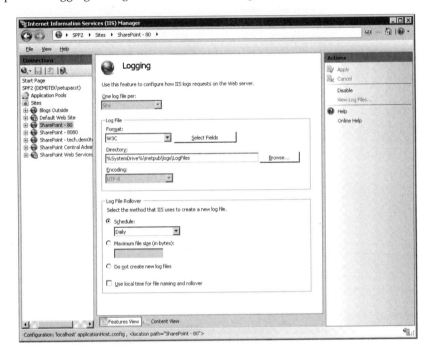

4. In the Log File section you'll see that the format for the log is W3C. This is the default format for IIS log files, and its use is highly recommended (see the IIS help files for lots of information about logging and log file formats) we will keep the default W3C format.

5. The Directory section shows you the location of the log files. For this example we will use the default directory that is already present in the Directory box.

6. The Log File Rollover section lets you change the schedule of the log rollover. The default is Daily, which is fine for this example.

7. Because the log file type is W3C extended, the log can contain extended information. To see what data this log file is collecting, click the Select Fields button. You will see the extended options that are available to collect. Not all of the fields are selected by default,

but many of the most important ones are. You can select more, which can be useful later when you are trying to parse the log for critical information. Close the W3C Logging Fields dialog box when you are done to go back to the console.

8. Back on the IIS Manager console, copy the path in the Directory field. Open an Explorer window, and copy the path from the Log File Directory field into the address bar of the Explorer window and press Enter.

That will take you to the folder where your IIS log files are located, organized by folders. (My example is the default path of c:\inetpub\logs\LogFiles\.) The first thing you'll notice is that the log folders are unhelpfully named. Each Web Site stores its logs in a folder called W3SVC<website id>, where <website id> is a long numerical string.

9. To determine your site's ID you need to go back into IIS Manager, right-click the Web Site in question, and go to Manage Web Site ➢ Advanced Settings (or select the Web Site in the connections pane and then click Advanced Settings in the Actions pane). The Advanced Settings dialog box that opens (Figure 13.19) is where you can see the ID for the site.

FIGURE 13.19
The ID for
SharePoint-80

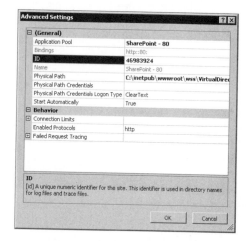

Because SharePoint-80 has the ID 46983924 in my example, the logs are found in the W3SVC46983924 folder. In this folder are the log files for the Web Site.

10. A log file is actually a text document. To see its contents, you can just open the file. Open your most recent log file (as shown in Figure 13.20). The very top of the text file lists the headings for data that the log will be collecting, in the order it will be reported for each entry. The activities that IIS recorded for that particular web application are listed below that. As you scroll, you'll see a lot of GET and POST commands. You'll see the browsers that people used to access the web application, what pages they went to, and what account they used. You can even see the pages that the Index service accessed (yet another good reason to give each service its own account).

FIGURE 13.20

The IIS log file for SharePoint-80

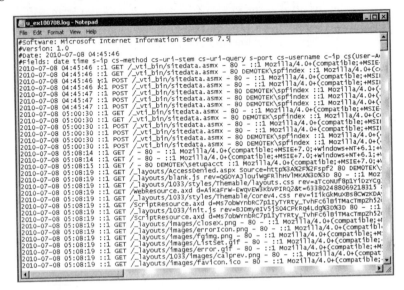

These log files can be long, tedious, and full of stuff. This is why using a log-parsing tool can be useful. It's also why SharePoint collects the same sort of data to display in its usage analysis; the IIS logs are kind of ponderous. Nonetheless, they are priceless during times of trouble.

OTHER HELPFUL TOOLS

If you are familiar with SQL queries, you can use the Log Parser 2.2 utility from Microsoft to actually run queries against the logs to make them more useful.

You may also want to try Indihiang, a free IIS log viewer for both IIS6 and IIS7. This tool is available on CodePlex: http://indihiang.codeplex.com/. It provides graphs and nice visuals for your log files, and it can be run on an individual log file or a group of files. Make sure you download the x64 version.

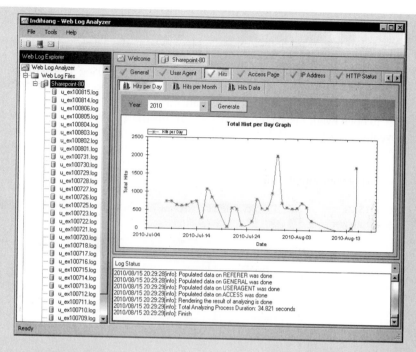

Another useful tool is Webalizer GUI. I use the one from www.tobias-schwarz.net (the direct link to the download page is: http://www.tobias-schwarz.net/programmierung/webalizer_guie.html). The executable I use is the Webalyzer GUI+ Executable. This tool generates an HTML report full of statistics, including a list of which users logged in and when.

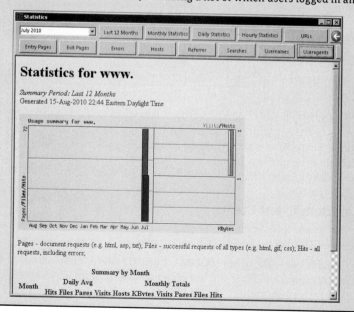

Event Viewer

The Event Viewer is another important tool in your arsenal. This console can be used in conjunction with the Performance Monitor to see what events SharePoint is reporting in the system's event logs. If you get any extreme readings in the log files or alerts for unacceptable thresholds, the next place you should go is Event Viewer to see if there are any error events that may shed light on how these log anomalies are affecting SharePoint.

To open Event Viewer, go to Start ➤ Administrative Tools ➤ Event Viewer. The Application event log (see Figure 13.21) is where SharePoint will record most of its significant application events. The System event log is also important—occasionally SharePoint will cause a more general system error to be recorded in the System log. You should check the Event Viewer regularly as part of your monitoring rituals.

FIGURE 13.21

The Event Viewer

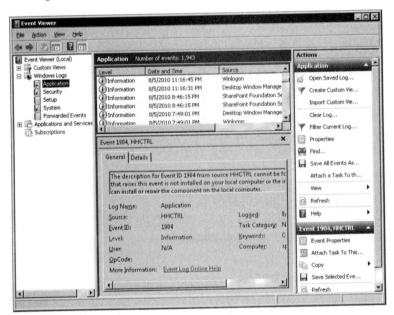

SharePoint tends to be a bit verbose, so expect to see a fair number of informational event entries in the Application log. They will at least let you know when things are going well. Of course, SharePoint is not shy about announcing when something is not going well, even if the problem is temporary. Keep in mind that the event throttling you might have configured in Central Administration will affect the events listed.

Common Event Errors

In the System and Application logs, you should look for events referring to the SharePoint Services, DCOM, and ASP. NET, such as these:

System Log – DistributedCOM – EventID 10016 This standard DCOM event usually means that SharePoint did not give the farm account, or a content database account, the local activation right to the IIS WAMREG Admin Service DCOM. For some reason it most often does this when creating web applications. Often it forgets to give the web application's application pool account local activation rights to that DCOM component. So when creating a new web application using a unique user account for the application pool, check the System logs for DCOM errors. The WAMREG errors will reference a CLSID that starts with 61738644. There is another DCOM error you may encounter that references a CLSID starting with 000C101C (the CLSID for MsiInstaller). The fix for this error is the same as the one for WAMREG, but for the DCOM object of MsiInstaller.

 Real World Scenario

A Practical Romp through Component Services

For those of you suffering from the DCOM error 10016 (for example, if the CLSID starts with 61738644), it's easy to fix.

Follow these steps:

1. Grant yourself permission to access the DCOM object. Launch Regedit.exe (from Start ➢ Run), and navigate to the hive:

```
Computer\HKEY_CLASSES_ROOT\AppID\{61738644-F196-11D0-9953-00C04D919C1}
```

2. Right-click this key, and select Permissions. Click on Advanced and then the Owner tab. Make your account (my example is the *setupacct* user) the owner of the key. Do not make any other changes to the security settings. Do *not* check the Replace Owner On Subcontainers And Objects box.

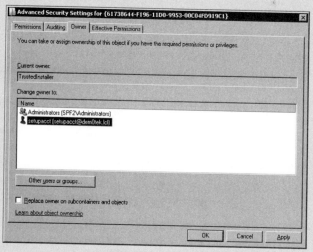

3. Click OK to close the Advanced window and go back to the Security tab. Now that you're the owner of the key, you are able to add your account to the permissions list so that you explicitly have Full Control. To do this, click the Add button, and add the account. Once added, select Full Control for the account in the list of users on the Security tab.

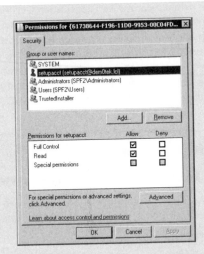

4. Go back into Advanced, and change the Owner of the key back to NT Service\TrustedInstaller (when adding this user, you may have to change the location for searched objects from the domain to the local server. You have now granted yourself rights to edit the DCOM object. Apply changes, and close Regedit.

5. Open the Component Services console (Start ➤ Administrative Tools ➤ Component Services), and click Component Services.

6. In the Component Services console, double-click the Computers folder in the details pane. Then double-click the My Computer icon that was inside the folder, and double-click the DCOM Config folder. Scroll down the list of DCOM objects until you reach the IIS WAMREG admin Service icon.

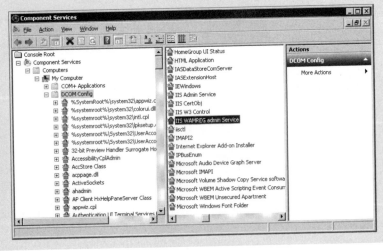

7. Right-click the IIS WAMREG admin Service, and select Properties from the pop-up menu. Go to the Security tab. Thanks to our registry change, you can now edit these settings.

8. In the Launch And Activation Permissions section, make sure Customize is selected, and click the Edit button.

9. In the Launch Permission dialog box, add the local group WSS_WPG to the list. This local group contains all the SharePoint content database accounts, the same accounts you will see listed in the DCOM errors (assuming you used separate accounts for each web application). Make sure you explicitly give them the Local Launch and Local Activation rights.

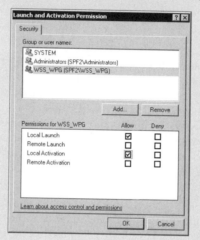

10. Save and close Component Services. This will stop the DCOM error and may also help you troubleshoot search errors.

If you get a DCOM error with a CLSID that does not start with 61738644 (like 000C101C for the MSIServer DCOM service), chances are good that you'll have to search the registry to resolve the CLSID to the correct DCOM application ID (which is what the DCOM applications are listed by in the Component Services console, except, ironically, MSIServer, which remains listed by its CLSID.) Open the Registry Editor, and search for the CLSID that the DCOM error displays. You may have to click Next a few times, but it will eventually display the friendly name and AppID mapped to the CLSID. Then use that AppID to find the correct DCOM application to modify in the console.

Application Log – SharePoint 2010 Products Configuration Wizard – EventID 107 You might have noticed, just moments after installation, that there is a SharePoint warning in the application log of Event Viewer about a service connection point. This appears thanks to a new (and, in my opinion, not quite ready for prime time) feature of SharePoint that is a nod toward server governance and allows Active Directory to keep track of SharePoint installations. It requires that you configure Active Directory, using ADSI Edit (available under Administrative Tools on the Domain Controller), to create a container called "Microsoft SharePoint Products," then give the group Authenticated Users the Create serviceConnectionPoint Object permission, and finally ensure, generally using Group Policy, that the servers have a registry key for

`HKEY_LOCAL_MACHINE\SOFTWARE\Policies\Microsoft\SharePoint`, with a string value for `ContainerDistinguishedName` that exactly matches the distinguished name of the Microsoft SharePoint Products container.

When this registry key has been applied to all servers on the domain, installing SharePoint (2010 or higher) on one of those servers generates a connection point object in the container in Active Directory. It also helps if you do not configure SharePoint using PowerShell but, instead, using the standard GUI interface or `psconfig` command.

For more details on setting it up, see the TechNet article "Track or Block SharePoint Foundation 2010 Installations."

If you don't need to use Active Directory to track your SharePoint installations (that is, you find all of this work just to see your SPF servers show up in AD a bit much), you can safely ignore the warning in the Application log.

Application Log – User Profile Service – EventID 1511   This error will start to occur as soon as you create a web application that uses its own application pool identity (instead of using the farm account, which is a bad idea). This is because there is something in SharePoint 2010 that needs the application pool for the content database to have a user profile. And, for some reason, Server 2008 R2 finds it difficult to give content database accounts local profiles. There are a few ways to fix this issue; I'll point out the one that's worked for me. Your mileage may vary.

Local accounts on a server create a profile when they log in, and the application pool identities for content databases are added to the WSS_WPG group on the server. So, first run an IISRESET (because IIS might have the profile locked). Then log in with the content database account (sometimes I log in twice if the first time it warns me that it is using a temporary account). Then log back in as the SharePoint administrator for the server and see whether the user profile is local (type **user profile** in the Start menu search field, and click Configure Advanced User Profile Properties). It may take a few tries, but the profile should eventually be listed as local.

There are suggestions online for other things you can do, such as deleting the temporary profile from the TEMP folder for the account (you may have to first stop IIS to unlock the profile folder), adding the account to the local administrators, executing a `runas` command (`runas /u:domain\accountname /profile cmd`) to create a profile for the account, and then removing the account from the local administrators group.

For more information about those other options, do a search (I used *SharePoint 2010 user profile error 1511*, for example) for the error. As of this writing, there are numerous blog posts concerning this issue and how to fix it. Just keep in mind that this may have to be done every time you use a new content database account.

Application Log – SharePoint Foundation – EventID 2137   Whenever you set up a web application that uses claims-based authentication, the SharePoint Health Analyzer will log this error. In brief, there's a security issue with claims-based authentication and a corresponding patch to correct it. It will also trigger an alert in Central Administration, in the form of a scary red bar across the top, indicating the Health Analyzer has discovered a problem. Clicking this bar will take you to the Review Problems And Solutions page, where you can view the details of the alert (see Figure 13.22).

FIGURE 13.22
Claims-based
authentication
security update
required

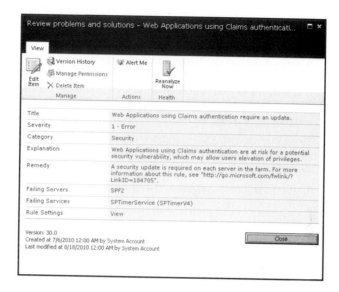

At the time of this writing, the patch was still classified as a hotfix and required a reboot to apply. Once the hotfix is applied, the error will clear from Central Administration the next time the Health Analyzer runs (you can also manually trigger a reanalyze command in the window shown in Figure 13.21, after you've applied the update) See KB article 979917 for details on the problem and to obtain the hotfix.

SEARCH NOT WORKING? CAN'T BROWSE A SITE LOCALLY ON THE SHAREPOINT SERVER?

If both of the issues are occurring, you may be suffering from a loopback check issue. This occurs most often when you are using a fully qualified domain name or host header for a web application address.

Windows Server (2003 SP1 and higher) has a security feature that prevents access to a web application if the request takes place on the local server. You, and the search service that does indexing, will see 401 errors when trying to access data in your SharePoint sites. Or worse, you simply can't log in to the page to get a 401 error. But you can access the site from any other computer on the network.

Although most access to SharePoint resources occurs off the server, Search (particularly the index service) runs on the SharePoint server and therefore can be blocked by this loopback check security feature.

To fix this issue, you need to disable loopback check for the SharePoint server hosting the Search service in particular and any server on which you locally browse your SharePoint sites.

The definitive KB article from Microsoft on this issue and its workaround is 896861. It says it applies to Server 2000 and 2003, but in fact it applies to all Windows servers to date.

There are two steps to this fix. First, you disable strict name checking. Then, you can use either of the two disabling loopback check options. The first is to create the registry value BackConnectionHostNames and enter exactly the host names of the local websites. This bypasses loopback checking for the listed hosts and only requires an IISRESET whenever a new host name is added. The second option, which is much more insecure and not recommended in a production environment, is to create the registry value DisableLookbackCheck. That option is one-time-only and requires a server reboot.

To get started with disabling strict name checking, you need to open the registry (from the Start menu, type **regedit** in the search field, and double-click regedit.exe to open the program). This setting will require a reboot.

1. In the registry, navigate to the following location:

   HKEY_LOCAL_MACHINE\System\CurrentControlSet\Services\LanmanServer\Parameters

2. Right-click Parameters, select New, and add the DWORD value: **DisableStrictNameChecking**. Enter the decimal value of 1 for the value. Close out of regedit, and reboot the server.

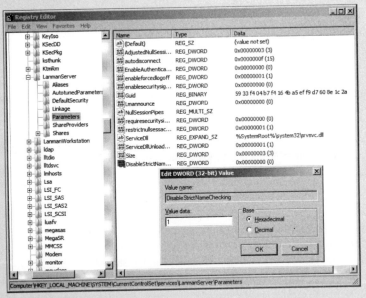

3. After the server reboots, to do the first, and more secure, option BackConnectionHostNames, reopen the Registry Editor (regedit).

4. Navigate to HKEY_LOCAL_MACHINE\SYSTEM\CurrentControlSet\Control\Lsa\MSV1_0.

5. Add the multistring value BackConnectionHostNames (right-click MSV1_0 and click New ➢ Multi-String Value). Then double-click the new item after it's created, and enter the host names of the web applications you (and Search) will be accessing locally. Use the host name and not the URL. My examples include spf2.dem0tek.lcl, spf.dem0tek.com, tech.dem0tek.com, and so on. Any fully qualified domain name that a web application address will resolve to needs to be in the list

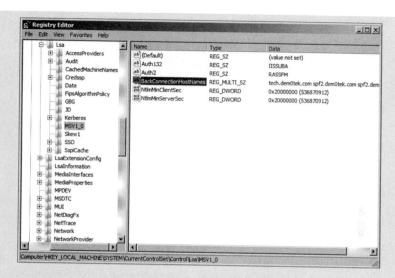

To simply disable loopback checking for the whole server instead, open the Registry Editor (regedit.exe).

1. Navigate to the following location:

   HKEY_LOCAL_MACHINE\SYSTEM\CurrentControlSet\Control\Lsa

2. Create a new DWORD value named DisableLoopbackCheck. Give it the decimal value of 1. Close out of the Registry Editor, and reboot the server.

These fixes should help if you, and Search, suddenly become locked out of a web application.

SharePoint error events are usually pretty self-explanatory (which is good because Microsoft doesn't have much online help for SharePoint events) and often inform you whether an action failed because a service isn't running (just as restores will fail without the administrative service) or if the problem is database access. Often the event log entry will suggest ways to fix the problem right in the description.

Event IDs will vary, but the root cause of many SharePoint problems is with the databases or access to SQL. If you reboot the SQL server (say, because you innocently installed a security update), SharePoint will panic because its access to SQL was broken, even momentarily, and you will see error events. Search, Gatherer, and Timer will all throw errors if their access to their SQL is broken for any length of time. If you see these errors, make certain that SharePoint was able to reestablish its connection with SQL after the reboot and that all is well. Another cause can be changing service account passwords. Most accounts for services must be registered as managed accounts in SharePoint. This means that not only is SharePoint aware of the passwords of the managed accounts, but it can manage their passwords itself. However, sometimes the automatic password change can fail, causing significant errors. Also, the Search index account does not use a managed account, so if its account password is changed, that will cause an issue. Additionally, when you restore a web application and its database, make certain that the access accounts have the correct permissions to the correct databases.

Reporting and Monitoring in SharePoint

SharePoint is not just an application onto itself; it is a combination of services that work together to give SharePoint the functionality that more and more businesses are coming to rely on. The ability to monitor SharePoint, and those services, effectively has become increasingly important. So, it doesn't come as a surprise that SharePoint Foundation has some added monitoring tools to the SharePoint Administrator's toolbox.

The Health Analyzer, health reports, diagnostic logging, health and usage data collection, and web analytic reports all offer SharePoint administrators a glimpse at how their SharePoint farm is running. In this section, we will be covering the tools that are built in to Central Administration, Site Collection Administration, and Site Administration.

The monitoring tools in Central Administration are found on the Monitoring page. To get there, open the Central Administration site, and click the Monitoring link. When the Monitoring page opens, you will see three main categories: Health Analyzer, Timer Jobs, and Reporting. Let's see what each has to offer.

The Health Analyzer

SharePoint has a number of moving parts and requires a certain baseline of component settings to function properly. In previous versions, there was an art to keeping in mind all the little things that help keep a SharePoint farm healthy.

New in SharePoint Foundation 2010 is the Health Analyzer, comprising a set of rules concerning known issues that might compromise SharePoint's health. These rules can be updated from time to time by Microsoft, and developers can add their own rules programmatically. The Health Analyzer runs these rules against the farm regularly to check its health status. You can also run the rules yourself at will if you want. If a rule should find a problem, it will trigger an alert bar on the Central Administration home page, offering you the chance to see what the issue is, with suggestions for its remedy.

The Health Analyzer subcategory has two review options, one to review a list of outstanding problems (with suggestions as to their solutions) and one to review all the health rules available for the SharePoint farm.

REVIEWING OUTSTANDING PROBLEMS AND THEIR SOLUTIONS

The first item in the Health Analyzer section is Review Problems And Solutions. Click it to open the Review Problems And Solutions page, where you will see the problems that were found, grouped into categories that might include Security, Performance, Configuration, and so on. (I triggered some of the problems in Figure 13.23 so you could see an example of multiple error categories.) If there are no categories listed, it's because no problems were found.

FIGURE 13.23
The Review
Problems And
Solutions page

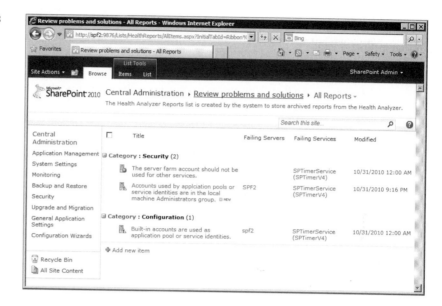

Click a problem to see detailed information about it, along with information about how to remedy it (see Figure 13.24).

FIGURE 13.24
Viewing the details
of a problem

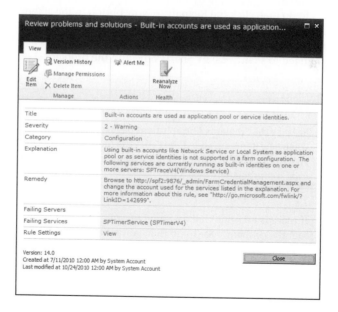

This page gives you quite a bit of information about the issue that triggered the alert, including its severity, the type or category it is listed under, an explanation of the problem (those vary in usefulness), and a suggested remedy, as well as which server and/or service triggered the issue.

The severity of the problem can help you understand not only whether something really *is* a problem but also how to disable notification of the problem, if you want. Severity levels run from 1 to 4; should the rule not run cleanly or fail to provide a severity level, it registers a zero (for an execution error).

1 – Error An item with this severity causes the red bar on the Central Administration home page to be triggered; the list item icon will have a red circle with an X in it. Typically this means something has gone wrong or needs to be corrected to ensure smooth operation.

2 – Warning The icon will have a yellow triangle with an exclamation point in it. Less severe than an error, a warning means something happened but may not happen again.

3 – Information The list icon has a blue circle with the letter *I* in it. A benign result.

4– Success At this level the alert leaves the list; there is no icon for this level.

0 – Rule Execution Failure Caused by the rule itself not running properly, not necessarily the servers or services failing; the list item icon will have a yellow diamond with an exclamation point, subtly different from the warning.

You can view the actual rule that triggered the item by clicking the View link in the Rule Settings section when viewing the item.

The Remedy section often comes with suggestions about how to fix the issue and often has a link to use, which may or may not be current. Nonetheless, any suggestions are better than nothing. Often the remedy to fix an issue is simple, such as changing a service account. And if you do manage to remedy the problem, you would probably like to clear it from the problem list.

To do that, click the Reanalyze Now button in the ribbon bar while you are viewing the item. That will cause the Health Analyzer to check the status of the problem again. If you did fix it properly (or at least in a way that SharePoint expects), the severity of the issue should be changed to 4 (success) by SharePoint, and the problem should stop appearing in the list.

PROBLEM ALERTS

Because the Problems And Solutions page is a list, you can create an alert on the list to let you know when new items are added. Just click the Alert Me button on the List ribbon, or click Alert Me while viewing a problem item and configure an alert. This lets you know right away if there is a new Health Analyzer problem to deal with.

If there is an issue that for some reason you don't want to fix or can't, you may want to clear it from the problem list. To do that, just edit the item and change its severity setting to 4 – success, as shown in Figure 13.25, and that should get rid of the list item until the rule runs again (you could also select the item and delete it from the ribbon bar). To keep the rule from running again and generating the same issue, you need to disable that rule. Think carefully before disabling any rules, though, because they are there for a reason.

FIGURE 13.25
Editing the severity of a problem

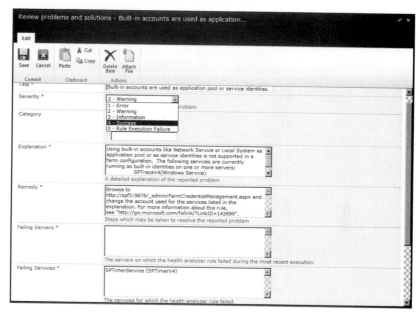

To see what rules are available, when they are scheduled to run, and how to disable them (in case you don't want to regularly have to clear the problem list of items you aren't going to fix), you can simply use the other link under Health Analyzer, Review Rule Definitions.

ADD ITEMS...

Because both Review Problems And Solutions and the Rule Definitions pages are lists, there is an Add Item link at the bottom of the content area. You can add items to either list at will. This is useful if you want to indicate a problem manually that doesn't have a rule to generate it. However, in the case of the Rule Definitions page, the form used to create the rule from the Add Item link doesn't actually do anything because it requires programmatic coding on the backend.

REVIEWING THE RULE DEFINITIONS

The second item in the Health Analyzer section of the Monitoring page is Review Rule Definitions. Click this link to open the Health Analyzer Rule Definitions page (see Figure 13.26). From this page you can see all the rules for each category. You can see how often they are scheduled to run a check, whether the rule is enabled or not, and whether there is an automatic repair option.

To change the settings of a rule, just edit the list item (click the title of a rule and then click Edit Item in the View item's form, or select an item and then click the Edit Item button in the Items ribbon).

FIGURE 13.26
The Health Analyzer Rule Definitions page

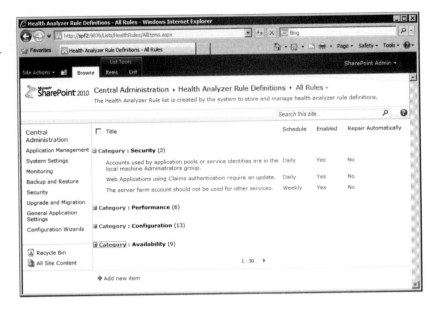

In the Edit Item form box shown in Figure 13.27, you can see that a number of the settings can be changed.

Title You can change the title, although I generally don't.

Scope You can choose whether the rule will trigger if the issue occurs on any server in the farm or all servers in the farm. All Servers works for me, as I'd rather not have any of them have issues.

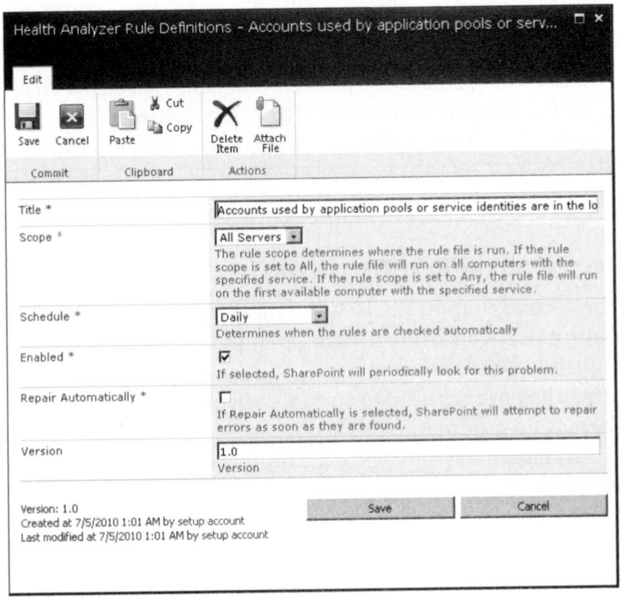

FIGURE 13.27
Editing rule definitions

Schedule   The rule can be scheduled to run Hourly (which takes up a lot of resources), Daily, Weekly, Monthly, or OnDemandOnly, meaning it doesn't run until you click the Run Now button when you view the item.

Enabled   The rule can be disabled here, if necessary. And, of course, when you disable it, it remains in the list in case you change your mind but otherwise doesn't run. It differs from OnDemandOnly in that clicking the Run Now button won't work on a disabled rule, no matter how hard you click it. This is how you disable a rule that you don't want triggering problems in the Problems And Solutions list.

Repair Automatically   If SharePoint can fix an item automatically, generally this setting is already enabled. Trying to set it to fix automatically, when SharePoint can't do so won't help. However, there may be cases when you *don't* want SharePoint to try to fix something itself. In that case, disable it here. You might also notice that this setting has an asterisk, as if it were required. It obviously is not.

Version   Although it appears to be one that can be edited, this field actually indicates the version of the list item and increments whenever you change its settings.

According to Microsoft, these rules may be updated from time to time to keep SharePoint aligned with current best practices and aware of updates.

Timer Jobs

The Timer service is a utility in SharePoint that runs scheduled tasks, or jobs, for SharePoint. Some jobs will run immediately; others run daily, weekly, or monthly. Some jobs can be set to run hourly, or every X number of minutes. When SharePoint starts a job, that job is added to the list of job titles as the server prepares to begin. This list is where you can see if a job has initialized, what progress it has had, and whether (when done) it has succeeded or failed. With this version of SharePoint, the number of Timer jobs available in this list is far greater than in the last version.

The links beneath the Timer Jobs subcategory both take you to the same set of list pages, only one opens with a view of timer job definitions and the other displays the status of jobs currently running or scheduled to run, as well as a useful history of previously run timer jobs (which lets you see which have succeeded, which have failed, and when).

REVIEWING TIMER JOB DEFINITIONS

The Jobs Definitions page displays all the timer jobs available for the farm (Figure 13.28). As you can see, a number of timed tasks are listed there, including the Customer Experience Improvement Program (CEIP) data collection. That job is not supposed to send data if you do not allow it; however, it has succeeded in collecting the data anyway. Do not be surprised if you see some timer jobs that you have not enabled, such as gradual site deletion or usage analysis. They are built into SharePoint and are ready to complete their tasks as soon as you enable them.

FIGURE 13.28
The Job
Definitions page

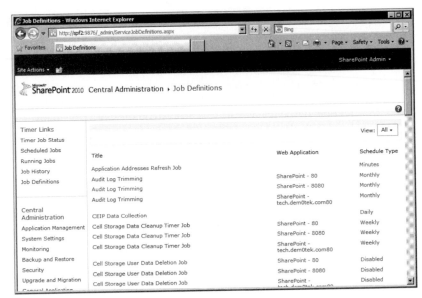

GRADUAL SITE DELETION AND OTHER GOODIES

There are a few interesting new timer jobs for this version of SharePoint, such as the Gradual Site Deletion timer job (which helps manage deleting a large site by first removing its URL from the configuration database, effectively removing it from user access, and then, over time, deleting all the tables and other objects) or the Cell Storage Cleanup timer jobs, which help keep the SQL databases for SharePoint tidy.

Most of these timer jobs are configured for you. In addition, there can be a number of instances of the same job definition, as they pertain to each individual web application or service.

The Timer Job pages have extra links in the Quick Launch area:

Timer Job Status   This shows the status of all timer jobs, those scheduled to run, those currently running, and a history of past timer jobs (when they ran and whether they succeeded). Each part of the page is a list view web part (sort of like a timer jobs dashboard), set to display 30 items at a time, so each can be advanced individually. The next three links are subset views of this page.

Scheduled Jobs   This displays only the timer jobs currently scheduled to run.

Running Jobs   This displays only the currently running jobs. This page can be empty if no jobs are running at the moment.

Job History   Shown in Figure 13.29, this page displays all the past timer jobs, when they completed, how long they took, and whether they succeeded. Because over time the job history for a farm may get long, a drop-down list at the top of the content area lets you choose how many items to show per page (from 100 to 2,000). For this page, the View drop-down's filtering options also include Failed Jobs, which can be very useful while troubleshooting.

FIGURE 13.29
The Job
History page

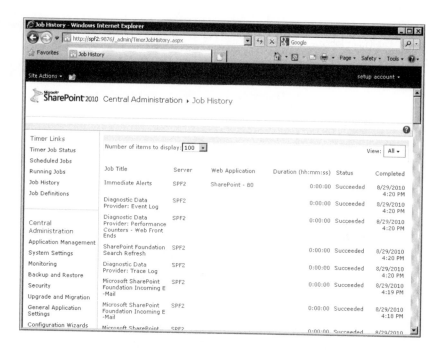

A TIMER JOB FOR DELETING TIMER JOBS

Obviously the Job History list could get ridiculously long, so there is a timer job to schedule the regular deletion of older list items—Delete Job History. By default it is set to delete older history entries every week. You can change that schedule, but the longest you can go without deleting is a month. Beyond that you would have to just disable the job. The Delete Job History job cannot be deleted.

Job Definitions   This is the page you should be on if you selected Review under the Monitoring subcategory. It simply lists all the timer jobs available for the SharePoint farm, what web application they are associated with (if they are associated with one), and their schedules. Keep in mind that timer jobs can be created as part of a solution or feature that you might have added to the farm, so this list can change over time.

In addition, these pages have a View drop-down list that lets you filter the timer jobs displayed by All (the default), Services, or Web Application. This lets you quickly see all the timer jobs associated with a particular web application or service. It can also show the page as something like a dashboard, as it displays not just scheduled timer jobs but also the running jobs and job history of the selected web application. This can help you pinpoint an issue if you have a number of timer jobs failing or taking too long to complete. In Figure 13.30, I've limited the timer job definition list to those associated with one web application. You can use this filtering technique on any of the different timer job pages. It is particularly handy for troubleshooting purposes, while checking the timer job history of a particular web application or service.

FIGURE 13.30
The Timer Job Status page filtered by web application

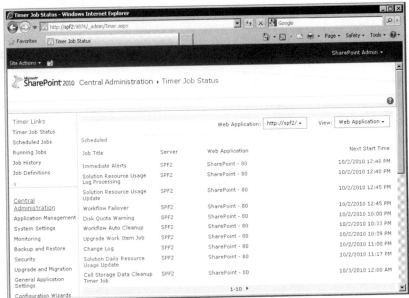

Most timer jobs can be run immediately, have their schedule changed, or even be disabled (which can save server resources, so it is something to consider for timer jobs that are never used). To edit a timer job's settings, just click its title in any of the timer job pages.

In the Edit Timer Job page, you can see the title of the timer job, a job description (which can be very useful in explaining what the job is for), and the job's properties (primarily if it is associated with a web application and when it last ran). The last section, Recurring Schedule, is the only one that can really be changed, and it lets you manage how often, and exactly when, a job will run (Figure 13.31).

At the bottom of the Edit Timer Job page can be buttons to Run Now (to run the job once at that moment), Disable, OK, and Cancel. In most, cases, there will be no Delete button.

EXECADMSVCJOBS

You can make some changes to the properties of several of the timer jobs using STSADM or PowerShell, as well as force all administrative service jobs to execute (should one be lagging). For more information about doing that, you might also want to check out the STSADM operation execadmsvcjobs.

In addition, there are a number of new commands for getting, setting, starting, disabling, and enabling timer jobs using the SPTimerjob cmdlet. For more about PowerShell, see Chapter 14.

FIGURE 13.31

The Edit Timer Job page

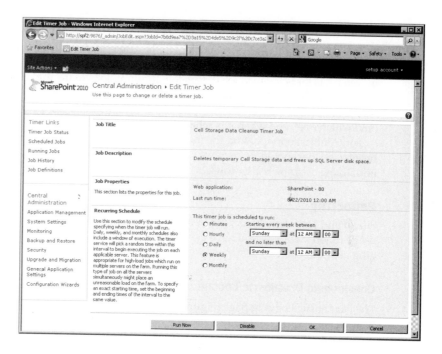

Most timer jobs are required at one point or another, so they can only be disabled and not deleted. Because they are scheduled tasks, there is always the chance that although you don't want one now, you might want it later. Other timer jobs might be one-time jobs that you can delete if you need to (for example, a backup job that failed but needs to be deleted before you can try again). Unfortunately, you can't add a new job to the list from any of the timer job pages. Those changes are strictly in the domain of the developer.

IF A TIMER JOB GOES BAD

What should you do if you start a timer job, such as a backup, and it fails?

If you simply try to do the task again, you will get an error because the job failed, and you won't be able to do it again until it has been removed. When a timer job fails, it remains in the queue, so you will know what has happened. However, this procedure can be inconvenient.

If a timer job fails, go to the Timer Job Definitions page, and select the title of the job that failed. This will give you the chance to delete the offending job and clear the failure from the definitions list so you can try again.

If you do have a job that doesn't seem to behave properly, you can see whether that job has succeeded or failed here. Then you can check the trace logs to find any errors related to the job or go to the Job Definitions page.

CHECKING THE STATUS OF TIMER JOBS

The Check Job Status link will take you to the Timer Jobs Status page (the same one as the Timer Links list above the Quick Launch). This page displays the status of all the timer jobs, laid out in web parts for Scheduled jobs at the top, Running Jobs in the middle, and Job History at the bottom. Each list can be scrolled through individually (they show only 30 items a piece in this view). The title of the job, the server it runs on, whether it is associated with a web application (and which one), and when it is scheduled to run (or was completed) are also listed.

For troubleshooting, I find the Running section to be the most useful; it lets me know the status of a job that should be currently running. This is where I can often find a job that is stuck on initializing or going really slowly.

Reporting

SharePoint Foundation has built-in capabilities to run diagnostic reports, as well as health and usage reports. But first you have to configure diagnostic logging and usage and health data logging in SharePoint.

CONFIGURING DIAGNOSTIC LOGGING

The Diagnostic Logging page (Figure 13.32) lets you configure event throttling for diagnostic logging, as well as configure some Trace Log (otherwise known as ULS logs) settings. The first section is Event Throttling. Here you decide what categories you will be running logging for, what the least critical event will be that you want reported to the event log, and the least critical event that you want reported to the trace log.

FIGURE 13.32
The Diagnostic
Logging page

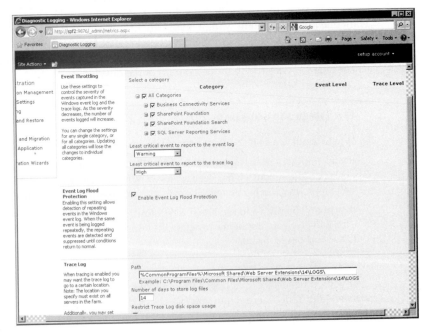

Before you say, "What the heck, let's see it all," keep in mind that as the severity of the event you will report on decreases, the size of your log will increase. You can minimize this somewhat by enabling Event Log Flood Protection in the second section; this will suppress repeating events from being logged over and over, but the log can still grow very large, very quickly.

Events are throttled by severity, going from the highest to the lowest level of severity you care to see. So if you wanted to only see warnings or worse but didn't want to be bothered with the many informational events that SharePoint can generate, you can set it to avoid recording events below the warning level. Further, you can even select what categories of SharePoint events are throttled at a particular severity or choose to apply the severity level to all events (if you choose to do that, your specific settings will be lost).

The categories that are available to throttle are as follows:

Business Data Connectivity Services   This category has only one type of event, Business Data.

SharePoint Foundation   This category has many, many types of events lists. However, there are events that have nothing to do with SharePoint Foundation; they are there to support the infrastructure of SharePoint Server, such as the Document Conversion events.

SharePoint Foundation Search   This category covers all events related to search and indexing. There are a few events that relate more to features available in the SharePoint Server and SharePoint Search Server roles than SharePoint Foundation.

SQL Server Reporting Services   This category covers all events related to reporting services.

WHEN IN DOUBT

So, you have dozens and dozens of events you can throttle for diagnostic logging, many of which may not be familiar to you. One option is to run with no diagnostic events throttled for a short time to see what events are logged during an average business day or week. Then, when you see what events are too chatty or what events don't show up at all, you can decide what to throttle and what not to throttle.

In addition to event throttling, this page also allows you to configure Event Log Protection, which keeps repeated events from flooding the logs, bloating them immensely, and some Trace Log settings. The trace log settings that can be configured are where the trace logs will be located, how many days worth of logs will be kept, and the maximum amount of space those files can take up. Trace logs can take up a considerable amount of space, and you may need to allow that in order for all the event information necessary for troubleshooting as complicated a product as SharePoint to be available. It's a good idea to store those trace logs outside the SharePoint root.

OUTSIDE THE HIVE

Keep in mind that if you do move the trace logs to a different location, it must be the same on all web front-end servers. Also note that if you move the trace logs, the PSCDiagnostics logs that are created whenever Central Administration is opened will also go along. This is part of what adds to the weight of the trace logs' folder. Make certain that the location for the logs has the same permissions as the previous location so the necessary SharePoint services can still access it. (WSS_ADMIN_WPG is the local group needed to generate those reports.)

The maximum storage limit alone is worth visiting this settings page. Trace logs can get huge if they are not managed, and that restriction does help. However, keep in mind that if the limit is reached, the oldest logs will be deleted to avoid going over. If keeping an archive of old trace logs is important to you, consider backing them up to a different location on a regular basis.

Example: Configuring Event Throttling

Diagnostic logging has not been configured for SharePoint up to this point, so let's set some limits.

You may want to be more specific in the future concerning the individual events and their severity levels, but at this point, to cut down on the idle chatter that can fill the Application logs in the Event Viewer of the server, you will select all categories and set the minimum severity to Warning for event logs and High for the trace logs. That will cut down on how large the logs will get without (ideally) compromising too much important information; this limits the information to bad news, rather than any news.

To do that, take the following steps:

1. Select All Categories in the Event Throttling section (shown earlier, in Figure 13.32). That will put a check mark in all categories and their events.

2. Select Warning as the least critical event to report to the event log, and select High as the least critical event to report to the trace log.

3. Make sure Event Flood Protection is enabled (it should be by default).

4. In the Trace Log section, leave the default address as it is. At least you know where it is and that all SharePoint servers on the farm will have this folder structure available. Keep in mind that your environment might be different and require you to put the logs on a different drive or partition. Make sure the location matches for all SharePoint servers and that the WSS_ADMIN_WPG group for each server has the correct permissions to the location.

5. For the number of days to store the log files, the default is two weeks. That seems more than enough time to discover any issue that requires delving into the trace logs, so for this exercise, leave that default. In your own environment, your mileage may vary.

   The Restrict Trace Log Disk Space Usage setting is not enabled by default. In addition, it appears that the default size is 1000 GB. You might be tempted to bring that size down to less than a gigabyte and keep the logs for fewer days (and I have nothing against that), but the setting will not let you go below 1 GB as the minimum size for trace log storage.

6. At this point I am going to go for a 1 GB restriction; your log may need more space. If it does, you'll get an error in the event logs stating that you have reached your storage limit for the trace logs and that you should increase the storage size or older logs will be deleted.

7. Once the settings are complete, click OK.

The changes will be saved, and then you'll be returned to the Monitoring subcategories page. If you go back to the Diagnostic Logging page, you'll see that any category of events that you changed will now be listed in bold and its current level of warning listed (Figure 13.33). If you check to see how they are listed now, you'll see the change (the check boxes are empty so you can select one to change).

FIGURE 13.33
The Diagnostic
Logging page after
changes

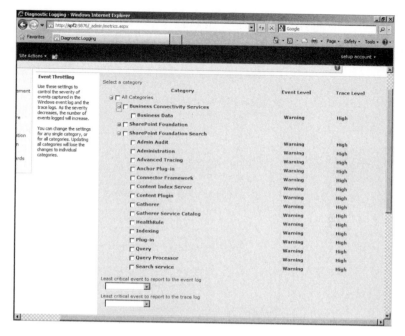

THE TRICK TO INDIVIDUAL EVENT SETTINGS

If you do want to change the severity of the events that an individual category uses, click OK after you set each one; and do that after each change, or it won't take.

That's inconvenient, but you can use the Set-SpLogLevel PowerShell command to change event throttling for categories and avoid dealing with the GUI's limitations. See Chapter 14 for more information about the syntax of PowerShell commands.

THE VIEW HEALTH REPORTS PAGE

Unfortunately, the View Health Reports settings page doesn't really give you a health report per se. It simply shows you the slowest pages on a server in a given range of time and the most active users. In addition, it has no Quick Launch bar, so navigation depends on either the Navigate Up button or the title breadcrumb.

To use this page, you first choose between two reports, one for Slowest Pages and one for Top Active Users. Then you can specify a particular server and web application you want to focus on, or you can choose to see the results from all servers and web applications on the farm, within a given range of time (last day, week, month), and limit the number displayed on the page.

Once you have selected your display criteria, clicking Go will populate the list with results matching your criteria.

Now the Slowest Pages report appears to list all the pages that have had any activity (Figure 13.34), not just the slowest, and it reports the Average/Minimum/Maximum duration it took to the load the page, Average/Minimum/Maximum Database Queries, and the Number of times the page was requested.

FIGURE 13.34

The Slowest Pages health report

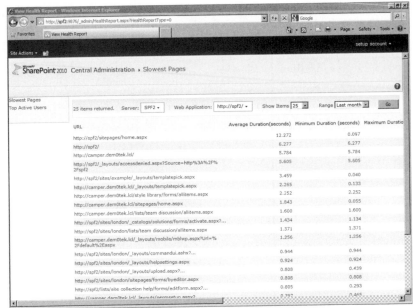

The Top Active Users report (Figure 13.35) also seems to list the majority of the active users based on the selected criteria (accessing a particular server or web application), not just the top ones. It displays the number of requests a given account has made, the last time they made it (and thus were active), and the percentage of successful requests (which lets you see if there have been significant failures). Notice that the search content access account (spfindex in my case) is regularly accessing the web application content that is search-enabled.

FIGURE 13.35

The Top Active Users health report

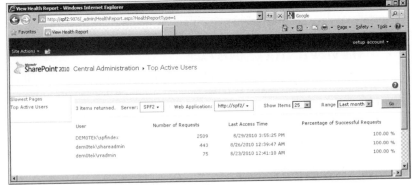

CONFIGURING USAGE AND HEALTH DATA COLLECTION

Configure Usage And Health Data Collection is the third item in the Reporting section. Click the link to open the Configure Web Analytics And Health Data Collection page. Here you can see settings for enabling usage data collection, complete with what events should be collected, as well as where the log file for the data should go (make sure that location is the same for every front end server on the farm), and how large those logs can get (in gigabytes). You can also enable health data collection here as well.

The first thing you need to do is enable usage data collection by checking the box in the Usage Data Collection section. Next choose the events you want to log. Your options are as follows:

◆ Content Import Usage

◆ Content Export Usage

◆ Page Requests

◆ Feature Use

◆ Search Query Usage

◆ Site Inventory Usage

◆ Timer Jobs

◆ Rating Usage

Logging uses system resources and can have an adverse effect on system performance, so you may not want to report on all events all the time. Instead, you may want to consider which events you want to run regular reports for and only log other events for occasional reports and troubleshooting (see Figure 13.36).

In the Usage Data Collection Settings section, you can choose where to save the log files or just stick with the default location, and you can set a maximum file size to keep your log from growing out of control.

FIGURE 13.36

The Usage Data
Collection settings

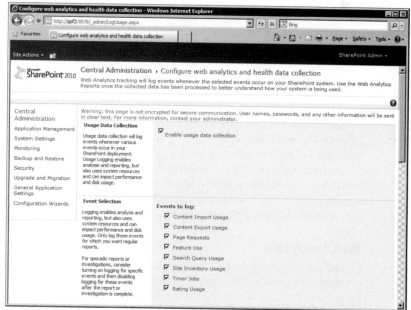

> **USELESS RATING?**
>
> If you enable the usage data collection service, notice the events that can be collected. SharePoint Foundation does not have a rating service built in; that is for the Server version. Therefore, collecting data for rating usage might be a waste of effort. You may not want to enable that event for collection.

In the Health Data Collection section, you can enable health data collection by checking the box. Click the Health Logging Schedule link to modify the timer job definition (see Figure 13.37).

FIGURE 13.37
Setting the health logging schedule

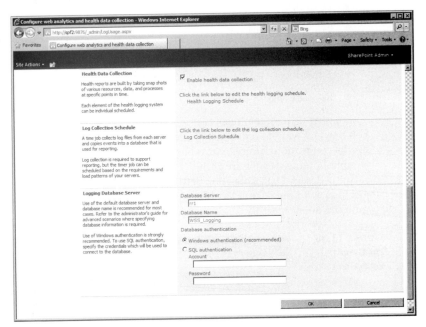

The next section is Log Collection Schedule. Now that you have logged the data, you need to collect it for use by the reports. If you click the Log Collection Schedule link, you can modify the timer job for collecting the log data.

The last section is Logging Database Server. In most cases, using the default database is the preferred way to go if your database server uses Windows authentication; just click the radio button. If you are using SQL Authentication, click the SQL Authentication radio button, and then enter a SQL user account and password that will be used to connect to the SQL Server database.

Web Analytics

The Slowest Pages report and the Top Active Users report both give you good information about problem pages and active users; sometimes, however, you want to see some web analytics—you know, page hits, storage used, number of visitors, and so forth. We can do that!

SharePoint Foundation has built-in web analytic reports that come in two flavors: Site Collection Web Analytic Reports (introduced in Chapter 10) and Site Web Analytic Reports (introduced in Chapter 9). Both let you quickly see the overall usage of individual site collections and sites, so if your server is showing high demand, you can narrow down exactly which site is so popular.

THE SITE COLLECTION WEB ANALYTICS REPORTS

Let's start at the top with the Site Collection Web Analytics reports and work our way down.

1. To view the Site Collection Web Analytics report, open your browser, and browse to the top-level site of one of your site collections. For this demonstration, I will use my root-level site, `http://spf2`.

2. Once the site is opened, click Site Actions, and select Site Settings.

3. When the Site Settings page opens, under Site Actions click the Site Collection Web Analytic Reports link. The Web Analytics Reports – Summary page will open, revealing three sections to the report (see Figure 13.38).

Storage: Here you can see how much disk space the Site Collection is currently using, how much of that disk space is taken up by web discussions, and, if a quota has been applied, how much storage space the site collection can use.

Users: This section shows how many users have been added to the site collection and whether there are any restrictions on how many users can be invited, or added, to the site collection.

Activity: This will tell you how many hits the site collection has received and how much bandwidth has been used.

FIGURE 13.38
A Site Collection Web Analytics report

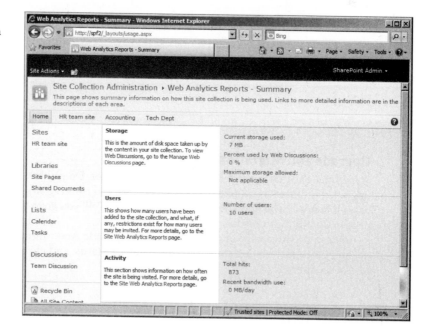

THE SITE WEB ANALYTICS REPORTS

It is in the Site Web Analytics reports that you really start to get to the nitty-gritty of your web analytics. Figure 13.39 shows one of seven Site Web Analytic reports that are available and can be run for individual sites and subsites within the site collection. The reports that are available are as follows:

◆ Number of Page Views (by day)

◆ Number of Unique Visitors (by day)

◆ Number of Referrers (by day)

◆ Top Pages (page with the most hits on top)

◆ Top Visitors (by user account)

◆ Top Referrers (the page the visitor came from)

◆ Top Browsers (as reported by the visitor's browser user agent). Chapter 9 describes these reports in more detail.

FIGURE 13.39

The Top Visitors report

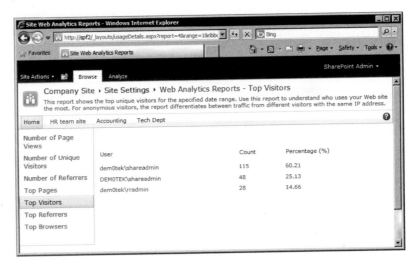

Upgrade and Migration

Something else that needs to be monitored is upgrades. Do you have the latest and greatest upgrades and patches installed? What version are you running anyway? Do you have any databases that need to be upgraded? How can you tell? Well, you go to the Upgrade And Migration page in Central Administration.

You can do three very important things in Upgrade And Migration. You can check product and patch installation status, review database status, and check on the status and progress of an upgrade.

CHECKING THE PRODUCT AND PATCH INSTALLATION STATUS

There is so much to see, do, build, and monitor in SharePoint that it is easy to miss an upgrade or a patch. That is where the Check Product And Patch Installation Status page comes in handy.

Open the Central Administration site, and click Upgrade And Migration. When the Upgrade And Migration page opens, you will see that there is only one section, Upgrade And Patch Management.

The first item is Check Product And Patch Installation Status. Click the link to open the Manage Patch Status page. On this page, you will see what products have been installed and on what servers. You will also see the version number and the install status, such as Installed (Figure 13.40). You can view patch information about all servers in the farm, or you can select which server you want to see patch information for by clicking the View down arrow at the top of the page.

FIGURE 13.40
Manage Patch
Status page

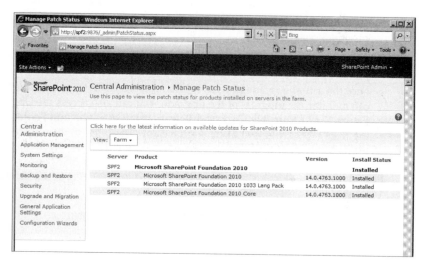

At the very top of the page, in blue, is a Click Here For The Latest Information On Available Updates For SharePoint 2010 Products link. If you click this link, it will open the Updates For SharePoint 2010 Products page in your web browser. About halfway down the page you will see a listing of the latest available updates. See an update you don't have? Click its link, and you will be taken to the download page. How simple is that?

REVIEWING THE STATUS OF SHAREPOINT DATABASES

The second item on the Upgrade And Migration Page is Review Database Status. Click on the link to open the Manage Databases Upgrade Status page (shown in Figure 13.41). On this page you will see a listing of the SharePoint databases, along with the SQL Server instance each one is in, its database type, and its status.

FIGURE 13.41
The Manage Databases Upgrade Status page

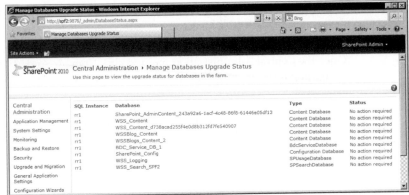

CHECKING UPGRADE STATUS

The third item on the Upgrade And Migration page is Check Upgrade Status. When you are performing an upgrade from WSS 3 SP2 to SharePoint Foundation, as described in Chapter 15, once the actual upgrade process begins, you are taken to an Upgrade Status page where you can monitor the progress of the upgrade. You can also access the Upgrade Status page here (see Figure 13.42.) Note that if you did a clean install of SharePoint Foundation, instead of upgrading from WSS 3, you will likely not have any "sessions" to view since you haven't done any upgrades.

FIGURE 13.42
The Upgrade Status page

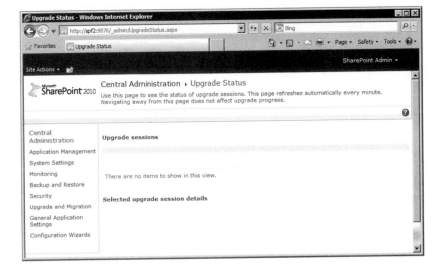

Backing Up and Restoring a SharePoint Farm

At this point you have tools to help you recognize when your SharePoint farm is having a problem or load issue and why it might be happening. But then what? If you use those tools now to prepare for catastrophes before they happen, then when they do, you will be able to recover your data and get SharePoint back up and running when it fails.

SharePoint has a couple of points of failure: IIS and SQL.

To give users access to SharePoint sites, IIS depends on configuration data about SharePoint sites (and their virtual directories). There are no SharePoint websites. Therefore, backing up IIS and the virtual directory information for the web applications is critical for continued web access to SharePoint.

In addition to IIS, SharePoint also depends on its databases, so it is a good idea to back up your databases independently in SQL, in case they become corrupted, damaged, or lost. Fortunately, Microsoft has also given SharePoint a way to defend itself against catastrophe with built-in backup and restore capabilities. SharePoint's Backup tool backs up the IIS configuration and virtual directories for each web application, as well as all the content databases for those web applications. Restoring a web application is just a matter of getting to Central Administration, selecting what to restore and where to restore it to (you can overwrite an existing web application or create an all new web application), and then running the restore.

There are several ways to perform backups with SharePoint, and each has its merits. But SharePoint's own backup tool can perform a full backup of SharePoint's IIS configuration data and virtual directory information, as well as the SQL content databases for each web application, which makes it a great place to start. SharePoint will allow you choose to back up everything all at once in a full backup or just the web applications you choose. When SharePoint performs a backup, a folder is created containing a series of backup files and an XML file that catalogs all of the folder's contents. If you ever need to move the backup files, move the entire folder structure.

You should be aware that even though the SharePoint backup tool can back up the whole farm, it can't actually restore the configuration database or the administrative site. Why? The configuration database contains all the settings and configuration information for the entire farm in absolute terms, and this makes it very complex. To restore the configuration database, all servers on the farm, and their configurations, must be identical to the state of the backed-up configuration database so the configuration data will match. So, Microsoft felt it would be easier for you to, "real quick," reinstall SharePoint and create a new, almost blank configuration database. Then you can simply restore all the web applications on the farm, and you will be up and running.

The first type of backup you should perform is a *full* backup. In a full backup all the web applications in the farm are backed up in one shot. Once you have made a full backup, you can do *differential* backups, in which only the changes made since the last full backup are backed up. To restore a server, you would apply the most recent full backup and then the most recent differential backup. Keep in mind that if you make a big change, such as adding a new content database, you won't be able to make another differential backup until another full one is made.

Because differential backups take less time, you can perform them more frequently. However, all backups and restores take considerable RAM and processor power to perform, so you will want to wait until off-hours (like 3 a.m.) to perform your backups. Be careful not to perform your backups at the same time as you are performing usage process analysis. SharePoint backups are a little fragile, and this is just one way your backups can get corrupted.

Backing Up and Restoring a SharePoint Farm

In this section, you'll learn how to back up and restore the example SharePoint farm. There are a few gotchas with SharePoint backups to watch out for. To help avoid them, remember these tips:

♦ Make sure the SharePoint 2010 Administrative Service is running on all front-end servers for the duration of the backup (WSSADMIN in Task Manager). Be aware that this service is often stopped on single-server installs. It should go without saying, but the Timer service must also be running.

♦ The Volume Snapshot Service (also called Volume Shadow Copy Service or simply VSS) services on both SharePoint and SQL are used during the backup process. (Theoretically, the backup or restore process should trigger it to start.)

♦ Make certain that the SQL service account is a domain account. If the service account is a local account on the server, you'll need to give the SQL server's machine account permissions to the file share where the backups are stored. There is no guarantee that this will always work. It is easier just to give the SQL Server service account a domain account and then give it permission to the file share.

♦ Make certain that the location where you are going to save the backup (and probably restore from there as well) has enough disk space as well as read and write permissions assigned to the Timer service account and the SQL Server service account. It also must be accessible to the SharePoint server from the network.

♦ Make certain that the account you are logged in with while doing the backup also has read and write permissions to the backup location.

CONFIGURING SHAREPOINT BACKUP

Before we jump into SharePoint backups, it's a good idea to examine the Central Administration Backup And Restore page. Open the Central Administration site by going to Start ➢ All Programs ➢ SharePoint 2010 Product ➢ SharePoint 2010 Central Administration, and click the Backup And Restore link. On the Backup And Restore page, you can see that there are two main types of backup you can perform in Central Administration: farm backup and restore and granular backup (see Figure 13.43).

FIGURE 13.43
Farm and granular backup options

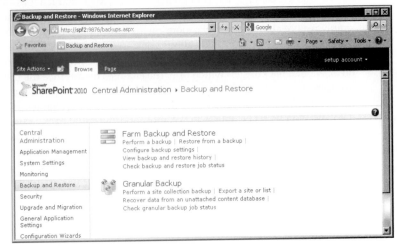

Farm Backup And Restore is the backup setting you are probably already familiar with; it allows you to back up the whole farm or specific web applications. In this section, you can choose to perform a backup or a restore, or you can view your backup and restore history. You can check the status of a backup or restore job, and you can configure your backup settings.

You will take a much closer look at how to perform a backup and restore in the next two sections, and after that, we will walk you through how to view your backup and restore history and how to check on the status of your backup or restore job. But for now let's configure the backup settings:

1. Click on Configure Backup Settings.

2. The first section is Number Of Threads. You can choose to have anywhere from 1 to 10 threads running when performing a SharePoint backup. Using more threads may speed up the backup performance, but it also means that it will be more difficult to sift through the logs should something go wrong. For SharePoint Foundation, three is the commonly recommended number of threads; this will give you increased performance without creating chaos with your logs (see Figure 13.44).

3. The last section is Backup File Location. This is the location where you want SharePoint to save your backup to. It is always good practice to save your backup files to a file share outside the SharePoint farm, so for the examples in this chapter, I am going to save my backups to a file share located on a computer named DC1, in a file share called SharePointBkup that I created for this example. So, for this example, I will enter it in the text box as **\\DC1\SharePointBackup**.

4. Click OK to save.

FIGURE 13.44
Setting the number of backup threads

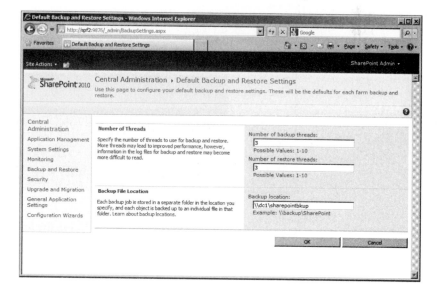

PERFORMING A SHAREPOINT BACKUP

Now that you have configured the backup settings, you are ready to jump feet first into your first backup:

1. On the Central Administration home page, click Perform A Backup.

2. On the Perform A Backup Step 1 Of 2 page (see Figure 13.45), you will see three Readiness indicators. SharePoint will check to be sure that there are no other backup or restore jobs running, that the Timer service is running, and that the Administration service is running. A check mark indicates that each component is ready. Under Readiness is the Select A Component To Back Up section. The layout of the components to back up basically conforms to the databases that are used by SharePoint, either as content databases for the web applications or as the databases used by Search. To back up everything SharePoint will let you, select Farm. Click the Farm check box to select everything, and then click Next.

FIGURE 13.45

Perform A Backup Step 1 Of 2 page: Select Component To Back Up

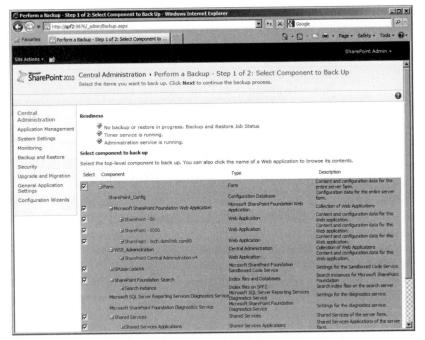

3. On the Perform Backup Step 2 Of 2 page (Figure 13.46), the first section confirms that you have selected to back up the entire farm. You can change your mind here by clicking Farm and selecting Change Backup Component from the drop-down menu, which would be the equivalent of clicking the Back button. Leave it set to Farm.

4. In the second section, you will choose between a full and differential backup. For this example, choose a full backup; however, you could choose to do a differential backup if

a full backup has already been done. Remember that a differential backup only backs up changes made since the last full backup. Leave the type set to Full. For the first backup, it's always a good idea to do a full backup, and then you can plan for doing differential backups regularly after that.

5. Something that is new with SharePoint Foundation is the Backup Only Configuration Settings section. You can now specify whether you want to back up both the content databases and the configuration settings or just the configuration settings. In this exercise, you will back up both the content databases and the configuration settings.

Copying only the configuration setting is useful in situations where you would want to copy the configuration settings from one farm to another, such as when creating a development or testing environment, creating a standard set of configuration settings to be used in more than one farm, or preparing for disaster recovery.

6. The last section is Backup File Location, where you will tell SharePoint where to save the backup files. SharePoint even lets you know how large it estimates the file will be, so you can be sure you have enough free space in the file share. Make sure to choose a location where the Timer service has Read, Write, and Modify rights to the file share; also, it is good practice to save the file on a server outside of the SharePoint farm (or at least not on the SharePoint server itself).

7. Once you have entered the file location for your backup, click the Start Backup button to begin.

FIGURE 13.46
Perform A
Backup Step 2 Of 2
page: Backup File
Location

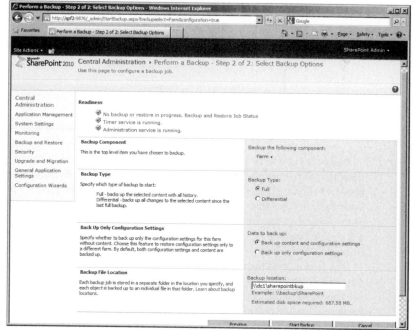

The Backup And Restore Job Status page will appear (see Figure 13.47). It will take a moment before information will begin to display on the page, because you will need to wait for the Timer job to get the backup task and begin processing. The page will refresh every 30 seconds, but if you are like me and can't seem to wait 30 seconds to see whether the job is running, you can always click the manual Refresh link. Each time the page refreshes, you can see what is happening with your backup. The Phase tells you if your backup is In Progress, Completing Backup, or Completed. Below that you will see the number of errors and warnings.

Farther down the page, you will see each component listed along with information progress, the date of the last backup, and any failure messages for each component.

FIGURE 13.47

The Backup And Restore Job Status page

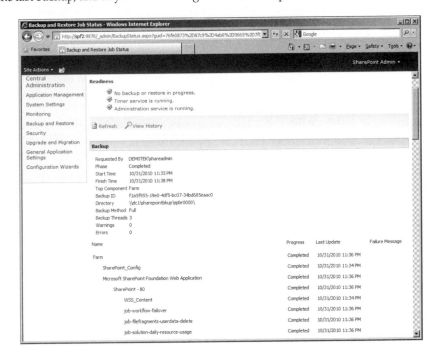

Now that you have performed a backup, it will be listed in the backup history. For most backup and restore pages, the link to the backup history is usually in the Action bar. From here just click the View History link in the Action bar. The History page will show a listing for your backup. This data is pulled from the last location where you stored backups. To display SharePoint backups from a different location, you'll need to click the Change Directory link in the Action bar (see Figure 13.48). It is also from here that you can easily start the restore process on a selected backup.

The folders and files that were created when you did a backup were named automatically; you had no choice in the matter. If you go to the location where the backup was made, you will see there is a folder containing the separate backup files for this particular backup. The backup folder names are prefaced with spbr followed by a four-digit number. This number is incremented by 1 for each new backup. In addition, in the backup location there is always a backup history document or spbr toc, which is the backup XML file. If you have to move the backup files, always move all the folders and the TOC file together. The TOC file lists exactly where all the files are in the folders. If you move the backups away from their TOC file, the SharePoint Restore tool may not know how to restore them because they can't be listed in the location history. In each backup folder is also a critical XML file indicating all the individual backup files and their order.

FIGURE 13.48
The Backup
And Restore
History page

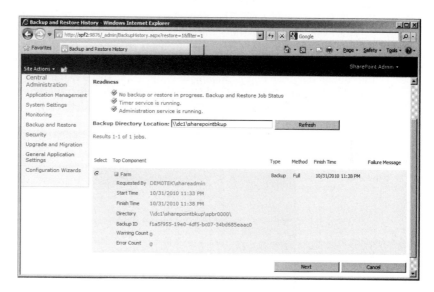

Now that you've backed up your SharePoint server farm, you can use the backup file to recover if something should go wrong with your web applications. Although you did a full farm backup, that backup is structured so you can perform restores of any individual web application or the Search service and database. To restore to a new server, SharePoint must already be installed, so the restore command can run. This means that Central Administration is already there and already has its own configuration and admin content databases. This is part of the reason why they are not restored.

Now should any of the content on a web application become corrupted, a site collection get accidentally deleted, the IIS Web Site become corrupted, a database become inaccessible, or any other type of catastrophe, you will be prepared. Remember that you can't restore a single-server installation to a farm installation, or vice versa, or restore an earlier version of SharePoint to a more current one.

The beauty of SharePoint backups is that they are complete. They cover all the areas that are critical for access to SharePoint sites. They are *full fidelity*, which means they keep all the content and settings they can and all user security settings that are possible if you stay in the same domain (alternate access mapping will have to be reset; solutions, custom web parts, and features will have to be returned). The backups can be used to recover all the web applications in a farm, or just one. Web applications can be restored to the same server, to a different server, or even to another farm. They are your first stop in restoring SharePoint functionality.

RESTORING FROM A SHAREPOINT BACKUP

When there are errors in the event logs, when the content databases seem to have gone sour, when IIS doesn't seem to remember your SharePoint website (it's there, but not quite working), or when the application pool seems to have forgotten its identity, often the best thing to do is restore from a SharePoint backup. Sometimes it is just faster and easier to restore from backup than it is to spend fruitless hours trying to fix a bizarre problem.

This example demonstrates the simplicity and power of restoring from an existing backup. For this example, I will make some noticeable changes to the theme and layout of the home page for the http://spf2 site (see Figure 13.49). The changes will emulate a possible corruption of the content database that is causing unexpected changes to the sites. Fortunately, this happened just after the most recent full backup was made to the site (otherwise, you would need to restore the most recent full backup and then the most recent differential).

FIGURE 13.49
An example of a corrupted Share-Point site

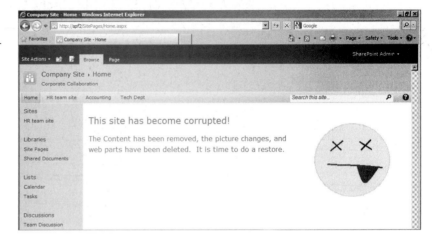

The option to recover the same configuration of the site from a backup will restore the content database of the web application and return it to its precorruption condition.

1. On the Central Administration home page, click Restore From A Back Up, under Backup And Restore.

2. On the Restore From Backup-Step 1 Of 3 page, look in the Readiness section to be sure that you have check marks indicating that there are no other backup or restores in progress, that the Timer service is running, and that the Administration service is running. If you have all three check marks, you are ready to begin (see Figure 13.50).

3. Next enter the backup directory location. The directory location that you used when performing your last backup will be displayed by default, but you can change the directory by typing an alternate location in the box and then clicking Refresh to display the backup files located in the new location.

4. Select the backup file you want to restore from. To see more information for each backup file, click the plus sign (+) next to the top component for each file, and click the Next button to continue.

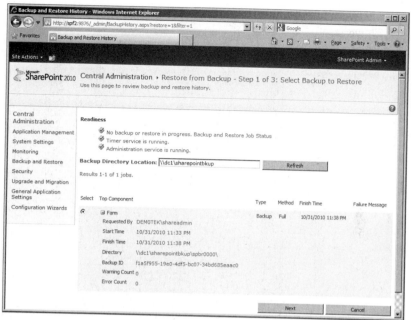

5. On the Restore From Backup Step 2 Of 3 page (Figure 13.51), you will select the components you want to restore. The backup file contains everything you would need to restore the whole farm, but you can choose to restore only selected parts of the farm. For this example, you need to restore the SharePoint-80 web application only, so let's select the box next to the web application. If you expand the web application, you will see that you can restore just the content database, or you can restore the database and the web application information (just in case). Let's restore both.

On the Restore From Backup Step 3 Of 3 page, the first section simply confirms the component you are going to restore (see Figure 13.52).

In the Restore Options section, you can choose to restore the good data right over top of the bad data using all the same web application names, database servers, and URL by choosing Same Configuration. Or you can recover the web application without disturbing the existing web application by restoring to a new configuration using new URLs, web application names, and database server names.

6. For this example, we need to replace a corrupted version of SharePoint-80 web application, so select Same Configuration. This will trigger a dialog box warning that selected components will be overwritten. Click OK.

FIGURE 13.51
Restore From
Backup Step 2 Of 3
page: Select Component To Restore

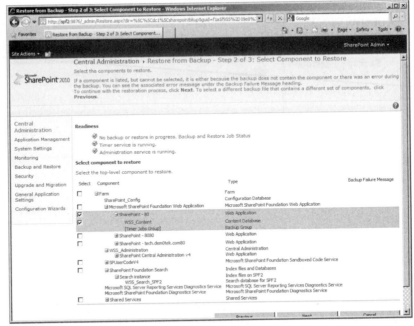

FIGURE 13.52
Restore From
Backup Step 3
Of 3 page: Select
Restore Options

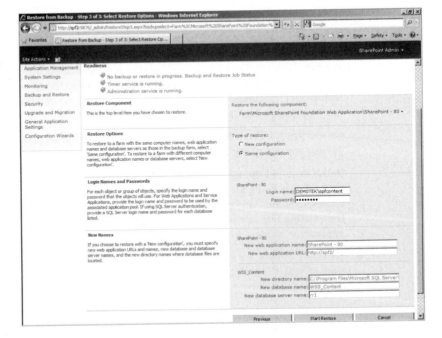

TWO WAYS TO RESTORE

Keep in mind that there are two distinct ways to perform a SharePoint restore: to the same configuration or to a new configuration. SharePoint remembers the exact configuration of the web applications and the exact web address, port, service account, virtual directory, database server, and database name.

If you are simply overwriting a web application, use the Same Configuration setting. If you are restoring the backup to a different server, you must use the New Configuration setting and specify the new server name in the web address (or addresses if you are restoring more than one web application at a time). When you perform a New Configuration restore, you can use the same web address as before, but you usually must use a different database name. When you restore to a different server (and/or domain), you will need to use the new configuration and all new addresses if necessary to reflect the new environment. If that new environment doesn't already have databases with the same names as those being restored, you can keep the names if you'd like.

When a farm is restored (particularly as a New Configuration), service applications may not automatically be started, and they may not be in the correct proxy group to be associated with web applications. BDC service settings are backed up and restored, but the external resources are not (of course).

Here are some things to keep in mind when using the Same Configuration restore option:

◆ Restores to the same configuration are primarily for the restoration of existing content.

◆ Same-configuration restores will not fix a deleted or corrupted IIS Web Site or application pool.

◆ Same-configuration restores apply only to existing settings and content database information to existing IIS websites and content databases.

◆ The application pool identity is not reset in a same-configuration restore. (This is where restoring the IIS metabase or IIS Web Site configuration comes in handy.)

If you need to rebuild the IIS Web Site, IIS application pool, and database of a web application using SharePoint, you must use the new configuration option. Here are some things to keep in mind when using the New Configuration restore option:

◆ A new configuration is meant to fully restore a farm or farm components (such as web applications, search, or services) in case of catastrophe. This is why it assumes it may need to use a different URL for the IIS Web Sites (because it may be on a different server), SQL server, service accounts, and database names. A new configuration tells SharePoint to create a new IIS Web Site and application pool for the new web applications and services.

◆ A new configuration creates a new content database in SQL based on the backup information. This means you can restore a web application side by side with the existing one, if you use a different address and database name, so you can recover something from the backup without overwriting the original.

◆ Because a new configuration requires that the database be unique, you must use a different database name (unless the old database is missing).

7. For the Login Names And Passwords section, enter the username and password for the application pool associated with the web application, or if you are using SQL Server authentication, use a SQL Server login and password. If it is a managed account, you may have to reset the password in order to use it. The last section on this page is New Names. If you have chosen to restore to the same configuration, the New Names section will be grayed out. If you have chosen to restore to a new configuration, you will need to specify the new web application name and URL, as well as the name of the database directory, database name, and database server for the new web application. For more details about doing a new configuration restore, see Chapter 15.

THE WEB APPLICATION AND URL

If you choose to restore to a new web application and use the same default URL as that of the original SharePoint site (for example, http://spf2), SharePoint has no choice but to give the new web application a different port number. This page will have a condensed version of the information used when creating a new web application.

So, it is here you specify either the host header for the new web application or the URL based on a managed path. If you want to use a port number and use the default web address, specify the port in the New Web Application field (although I have seen SharePoint assign its own port number despite that).

---

8. Once you have everything filled in, click the Start Restore button to begin the recovery process.

The Backup And Restore Job Status page will appear (see Figure 13.53). At the top of the page under Readiness, you can now see a red exclamation point, indicating that a backup or restore is currently in progress. This tells you that the Timer service is receiving the restore job and beginning the restore process. It will take a moment before any additional information will begin to appear on the page. The page will refresh every 30 seconds, but again, you can you can click the manual Refresh link to refresh the page at any time. Each time the page refreshes, you can see what is happening with your restore. The Phase tells you if your backup is In Progress or Completed. Below that you will see the number of errors and warnings.

Farther down the page, you will see each component listed along with its progress, the date of the last update, and any failure messages. You can also get to the Restore Job Status page from the Backup And Restore page in Central Administration; just click Check Backup And Restore Status.

Once the Backup And Restore Job Status page shows that the restore has been completed, let's open up the http://spf2 site and see what it looks like now (Figure 13.54).

And *voilá*, the home page has successfully restored!

FIGURE 13.53
The Backup
And Restore Job
Status page

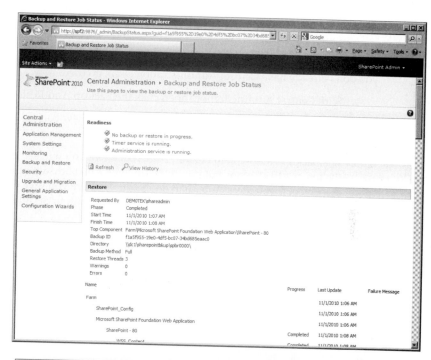

FIGURE 13.54
The restored
home page

Keep in mind that restores are not a game. They can really push a server's resources. If you just want to restore a single site collection, site, or list, there are better, less invasive ways to do it. Think of Restore as sledgehammer. If you really need to hit something large really hard, it's perfect, but if you need to just tap something small, it's too much.

VIEWING YOUR BACKUP AND RESTORE HISTORY

Now that you have successfully created a backup and successfully restored a web application, those jobs will be listed on the View Backup And Restore History page, so let's take a look. If you don't already have Central Administration open, go there now.

1. With Central Administration, open click the Backup And Restore link.

2. When the Backup And Restore page opens, click View Backup And Restore History, under Farm Backup And Restore.

3. The Backup And Restore History page will open. You will see the Readiness section at the top just like before, but it will also include a text box with the backup file location displayed. If you have more than one location where you save your backup files and want to see the history for the other location, type the path to the alternate directory in the text box and click the Refresh button (see Figure 13.55).

FIGURE 13.55
The Backup
And Restore
History page

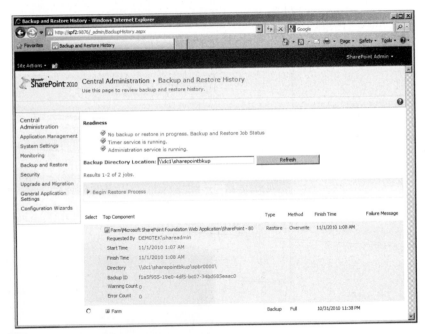

4. Below the Readiness section, all of the backup jobs you performed that were saved to this location will be listed, along with a record of each time you performed a restore job. They will be listed in order with the newest entries on top.

If you expand the job, the details for each job will be listed on this page: the username of the account that was used to run the backup or restore job, when it started, when it finished, and the directory either where the files were saved if it was a backup job or where the files that were used to perform the restore were stored. It will also list the number of warnings and errors that were generated while the job was being performed.

Want to know whether there were any problems with last night's backup? This is where you can go to look and see whether there were any errors generated or warnings issued. Luckily for us, both our backup and restore were performed without errors or warnings.

BACKING UP AND RESTORING USING STSADM AND POWERSHELL

Remember that STSADM, and now PowerShell, can do anything at the command line that SharePoint does in the GUI—and more. The GUI is simply executing STSADM/PowerShell commands for you. One of the problems with using the GUI is that it has no scheduling capabilities. That is where STSADM or PowerShell comes in handy. You can write a script to run your SharePoint site collection or web application backup and then schedule it to run as a task. Sweet!

Chapter 14 is dedicated to using STSADM and PowerShell, so this is just a brief overview of the relevant commands. Although using STSADM is as simple as always, configuring your accounts to use PowerShell is a bit more involved, so you will want to read Chapter 14 before trying to run any of these commands. Something to keep in mind, in order for an account to run a backup using PowerShell, it must be a shell admin for all databases used by the farm (which means it has owner rights to all databases). Needing to own all databases can also be true for STSADM backups run at the command line for more complex implementations (simple, single server farms often don't require the account own everything- test it and see). This is not the case for backups done in the GUI because all the heavy lifting is done by the farm account.

STSADM COMMANDS

The STSADM command to back up a SharePoint farm is:

```
Stsadm.exe -o backup -directory <location of backup> -backupmethod <full or
differential>
```

You must use the -directory parameter to tell SharePoint where to save the backup files. It is recommended that you use a UNC path when backing up a farm. Make certain that the correct services are running and that all necessary accounts have read and write access to the backup location (of course). If you want to do a configuration-only backup, you can specify it with a -configurationonly parameter. There are additional parameters, but directory and backupmethod are required. For backupmethod, indicate whether you want to run a full or differential backup. The first time you run a backup, it must be a full backup. You can't back up all the changes made since the last full backup if there has never been a full backup, can you?

The STSADM command to restore a farm is:

```
Stsadm.exe -o restore -directory <location of backup> -restoremethod <Overwrite
or New>
```

You must again specify the directory where the backup files are stored using the -directory parameter. You must also specify the restoremethod: to overwrite the existing web application (overwrite) or restore the files to a new web application (new). This is the equivalent of choosing a new or same configuration restore. You can also use the -configurationonly parameter to restore a configuration only backup. There are a number of additional parameters, but the only required ones are -directory and -restoremethod. Keep in mind, in more complex implementations, that the account you use to run the STSADM command, may need ownership of all databases on the farm to back up. This is not the case in simple, single server scenarios.

You can run SharePoint STSADM commands in the SharePoint 2010 Management Shell console. This PowerShell console conveniently already has all the SharePoint commands added to it. No muss, no fuss for you! Just make sure the account has permissions set up in PowerShell to access the farm and its databases. Otherwise, open a command prompt, and navigate to the SharePoint root's BIN folder to run the command.

PowerShell Commands

The PowerShell command to back up a farm is (if the backup location is a folder called sharepoint on a server named dc1):

```
Backup-SPFarm -directory \\dc1\sharepoint\ -backupmethod <Full or Differentia>}
```

where *backupmethod* may be Full or Differential. Look familiar? It should if you have been following along. It should look an awful lot like the STSADM command we ran earlier.

The PowerShell command to restore a farm is:

```
Restore-SPFarm -Directory \\dc1\sharepoint\ -restoremethod <Overwrite or New>
```

where *restoremethod* may be Overwrite or New.

Again, it is almost exactly like the command we used with STSADM.

Now that you know how to write the command for backing up, you can create a script (for PowerShell) or a batch file, for STSADM, and use Task Scheduler to run the script or batch file at regular intervals.

To use a STSADM batch file, simply open Task Scheduler, create a task, specify the interval (such as daily or weekly), specify the start time and the account that will be used to run the task (be sure it owns all farm databases and that it doesn't need to be logged in to run), and for the action specify the text file containing the STSADM command saved with a .bat or .cmd extension as the program to start for the task. Be sure to include the path to the stsadm command executable in the file, so the task scheduler knows where it is.

An example of the text that should be in the batch file is: cd C:\Program Files\Common Files\ Microsoft Shared\Web Server Extensions\14\BIN stsadm -o backup -directory <backuplocation> -backupmethod <full or differential>. To use a PowerShell script to do a scheduled backup, it is slightly more complicated. Open Task Scheduler, create a task, specify the schedule, the account that will run the task (without being logged in). For the Action, specify the script file to be used, and for the argument, be sure to specify the path to the powershell executable and the -noexit parameter. In the script, be sure to add the SharePoint snapin in the first line so SharePoint commands can be run. For more specifics about scheduling a PowerShell Script, see Chapter 14.

When scheduling backups, consider creating a scheduled task for differential backups on a frequent basis, daily for example, and a separate scheduled task for full backups that is not as frequent, say, weekly. Also keep in mind that backups are resource-intensive, so always schedule them at off-peak times.

Granular Backup and Restore

There will probably be times when you need to back up and restore smaller things than an entire web application. The smallest component of SharePoint that you can actually back up and restore is an entire site collection. Smaller components such as individual sites, lists, and libraries are technically exported/imported, or made into a template, but are not technically backed up and restored.

Granular backups are new to SharePoint and really have some cool new features. In the previous version of SharePoint, there was no GUI in Central Administration to back up a site collection, nor was there a GUI for exporting/importing a site, library, or list. Now in SharePoint Foundation, the ability to back up a site collection or export a site or list is built into the Backup And Restore page.

There is just one small downside to using granular backups in Central Administration. There is no GUI in Central Administration that you can use to restore the granular backups, so you will need to use a command-line utility such as STSADM or PowerShell to perform the restore. Don't ask me why you can back up in Central Administration but you can't restore; maybe they ran out of time to finish it, who knows?

You can run four basic granular backup operations from Central Administration's Backup And Restore page (as you saw in Figure 13.43):

- Perform a site collection backup

- Export a site or list

- Recover data from an unattached content database

- Check the granular backup job status

Granular backup and exports are even more resource-intensive than farm backups, so you will not want to try to run a granular backup during times when site usage is high. So, why use granular backup?

Remember earlier when we talked about using a sledgehammer when you only needed to tap something? Granular backups allow you to set aside the sledgehammer and pick up a regular nail hammer. With a farm backup in Central Administration, you can't back up anything smaller than the whole web application, but with granular backup you can choose to back up a site collection, single site, or even just a list.

Remember, you can't restore from a granular backup in Central Administration, so you will need to use STSADM or PowerShell, as shown later in this chapter, when it comes time to restore your site collection, site, or list.

BACKING UP A SITE COLLECTION

Site collection backups are full-fidelity, meaning that they keep as many custom and security settings as possible. Let's say you wanted to back up a single site collection, but you didn't want to back up all the site collections in the web application just to back up this one site collection. Here's what you would need to do:

1. Open the Central Administration site, and choose Backup And Restore.

2. On the Backup And Restore page, click Perform A Site Collection Backup in the Granular Backup section.

3. The Site Collection Backup page will open. At the top you will see the now familiar Readiness section, showing you that there are no other site collection backups in

progress, and that the Timer service is running. Everything you need to perform this backup is ready to go (see Figure 13.56).

FIGURE 13.56

The Site Collection Backup page

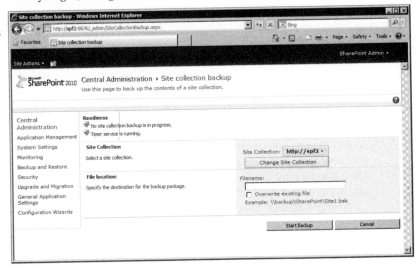

   4. In the Site Collection section, select the site collection you want to back up.

If the site collection that is displayed by default is not the site collection you want to back up, you can change it by clicking the Site Collection down arrow and choosing Change Site Collection.

The Select Site Collection dialog page will open, showing a list of all the site collections. Click the name of the site collection you want to back up, and it will be highlighted in yellow. Once you have made your selection, click OK (see Figure 13.57). For this example, I am going to back up the London site collection to demonstrate how you can use this to back up any site collection just by changing the site collection selected.

FIGURE 13.57

The Select Site Collection page

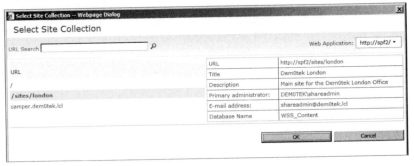

   5. After selecting your site collection, specify the location where you want your backup files to be saved, and specify the name of the backup file, in the File Location section. I am going to use the \\dc1\backups\londoncollection.bak directory and filename. Remember to add the .bak at the end of your filename.

6. If you have used this directory and filename before and want to overwrite the existing file, check the Overwrite Existing File box (Figure 13.58).

7. Click the Start Backup button to begin the backup process.

FIGURE 13.58
Specifying the site collection backup file

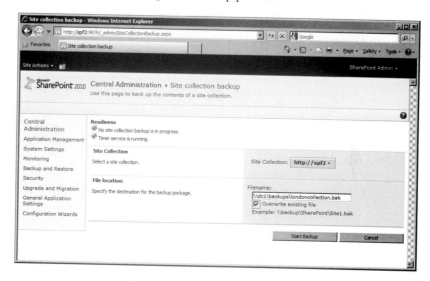

After you click the Start Backup button, the Granular Backup And Job Status page will open, allowing you to track the progress of your backup job. This page is almost like the Farm Backup Job Status page, but note that there are two sections on this page. The first section gives you the details and status of site collection backup jobs, and the second gives you the details and status of export jobs (see Figure 13.59).

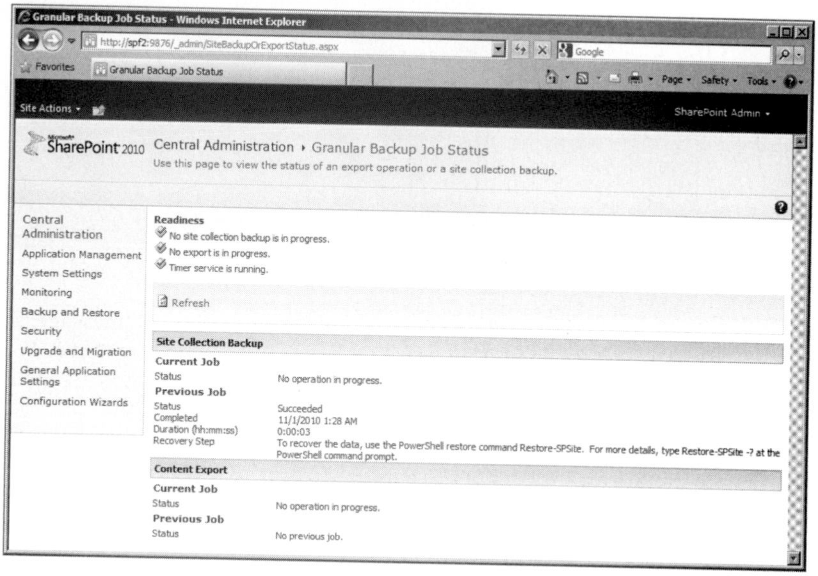

FIGURE 13.59
The Granular Backup Job Status page

Now you have a successful backup of your site collection, but remember that there is no GUI option for restoring the site collection from Central Administration. In the next sections, you'll see how to restore a site collection using STSADM and PowerShell.

RESTORING A SITE COLLECTION USING STSADM

Restoring a site collection is just as simple, and just like the backup file, it is very similar to the restore command for a farm.

An example of a restore command looks like this:

```
Stsadm.exe -o restore -url http://spf2/sites/london -filename \\dc1\backups\
londoncollection.bak -overwrite
```

Remember when I had the home page become corrupted? Well, it has happened again (for this example). However, this time instead of restoring the whole farm, I am going to restore only the site collection.

To restore the site collection using STSADM, just follow these steps:

1. Open the SharePoint Management Shell (remember, this PowerShell also supports traditional STSADM commands). Make sure you launch the management shell as a user with permission to perform the commands you plan to execute. In my case, this is shareadmin (because this affects the site collections in the WSS_Content database, the account has to have shell admin rights to the database; see Chapter 14 for more about it).

2. Type in the following command for this example, and press Enter (see Figure 13.60):
   ```
   Stsadm.exe -o restore -url http://spf2/sites/london -filename \\dc1\backups\
   londoncollection.bak -overwrite
   ```

FIGURE 13.60

Executing a restore command

When you see the "Operation completed successfully" message, the restore process has finished. Now let's open the home page to see if it has been restored. You should see your site collection back to normal.

BACKUP AND RESTORE A SITE COLLECTION USING POWERSHELL

You can also back up a site collection using PowerShell. The commands for backing up the site collection are very similar to the ones we used to back up the whole farm.

The PowerShell command to back up a site collection is (for example):

```
Backup-spsite -identity http://spf2 -path \\dc1\backups\pssitecollect.bak
```

When using PowerShell instead of a URL parameter, you use the -identity parameter, but it is still just looking for the web address of the site collection. Also, instead of the -filename parameter, you use a -path parameter; both are used to indicate the UNC file path to the location where the backup files are to be stored.

The PowerShell command to restore a site collection is (using the same example as the backup):

```
Restore-SPSite -identity http://spf2 -path \\spf2\backup\pssitecollect.bak -force
```

Again, the restore command is practically identical to the backup command except that this time you will use the -force parameter to force SharePoint to overwrite any existing site collection with the recovered site collection.

EXPORTING A SITE

Being able to export a site collection is nice, but sometimes even a nail hammer is too big for the job you need to do. Sometimes what you need is a ball-peen hammer, something just big enough to give it a little tap. That is where Export A Site Or List comes into play.

Exporting and importing are operations that cross the boundary between backing up and restoring site collections and backing up and restoring sites and lists. They aren't officially considered backup and restore, but they do very similar things.

Export saves a site collection, site, or list so it can be exported from its current location and imported into a new web application or server. Export is full-fidelity, saving as many settings and as much security as possible. When you export a subsite, alone at the end of a path, that site is all that is saved in the export file to be imported later. However, since export really specifies only the address of a site, if it does have subsites, it exports everything in that path, including subsites as one unit. This is useful to know if you want to break off a site and its subsites and make them their own site collection.

For this example, you are going to back up the *HRTeam* site so you can move it to a new site collection and import it as a top-level site. To export a site in Central Administration, follow these steps (see Figure 13.61):

1. Open Central Administration.

2. Click the Backup And Restore link.

3. Click the Export A Site Or List link in the Granular Backup section.

4. Click the down arrow on the Site Collection box, and select Change Site Collection.

5. When the Select Site Collection window opens, click the name of the site collection that has the site you want to export, and then click OK.

6. Click the down arrow on the Site box, and choose Change Site.

7. When the Select Site window opens, click on the name of the site you want to export (*HRTeam* in my example), and then click OK.

8. Leave the list box set at No Selection, since you are exporting the whole site.

9. Enter the path to the location where you want the file to be saved, include the filename (the expected extension for exports is .cmp).

10. If you have exported this site before, you will want to select the Overwrite Existing Files check box (otherwise be sure to use a different filename). In this example, you are overwriting.

11. To include user security settings, check the Export Full Security box.

12. Choose what version information you would like to export. Your choices are All Versions, Last Major Version, Current Version, and Last Major Version and Last Minor Version. My example uses All Versions.

13. Click Start Export.

FIGURE 13.61
Exporting a site

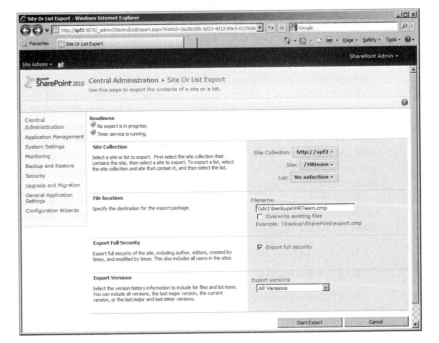

The now familiar Granular Backup Job Status page will open displaying information about the progress of the export job. Once the export job shows as Succeeded, you are ready to import your site into a new site collection.

IMPORTING A SITE USING STSADM

Importing a site or a site collection can take two steps. The first step is to ensure that there is a site to import to. This can be an existing site (which will be written over) or a new site you created. For this demonstration, you will quickly create a new site collection and then import the HRTeam site to it as the top level site.

To do this, you must first create a new site collection. You can do this in Central Administration, but since you will be working with STSADM for this example, you will create the site collection using STSADM as well.

In this example, I will be creating a new site collection named Newsite. To create a new site collection using STSADM, you use the `createsite` command (to create just a subsite, it's `createweb`).

The `createsite` command requires you to specify who the site administrator is by their email address (for notifications) and the URL for the new site collection. Make sure that the account you want to use for the site collection administrator has that email address associated with its account in AD. I also like to specify the owner login as well, to be sure. There are a number of additional, optional parameters, but only the URL and owner's email address are required.

The `createsite` command to create the site collection looks like this (remember that the -ownerlogin parameter is optional):

```
stsadm -o createsite -url <URLofSiteCollection> -owneremail
<EmailAddressofSiteCollectionAdmin> -ownerlogin <domain\username>
```

To create a new site collection using STSADM, follow these steps:

1. Open the command prompt and navigate to the SharePoint root's BIN folder, or open the SharePoint Management Shell (remember, this PowerShell also supports traditional STSADM commands). Make sure you launch the management shell as a user with permission to perform the commands you plan on executing. In our case, this is shareadmin.

2. For this example, we will use the shareadmin account and email address, so type the following command and press Enter:

```
stsadm -o createsite -url http://spf2/sites/newsite -owneremail Shareadmin@
dem0tek.com -ownerlogin dem0tek\shareadmin
```

Running this command will create a new site collection (minus the site template, which we don't need since we will be importing one into the new site collection when we import our site).

The second step of importing a subsite as a new top-level site is to perform the site import. For this example, I will be importing my HRTeam site, which I exported earlier. You would of course substitute your site collection address and account information when you run this command. The `import` command looks like this:

```
Stsadm.exe -o import -url http://spf2/sites/newsite -filename \\dc1\backups\
hrteam.cmp -includeusersecurity -haltonwarning -updateversions 3
```

You have seen the `import` command and the `-url`, `-filename`, and `-includeusersecurity` parameters before, but the `-haltonwarning` and `-update` versions are some parameters you haven't come across yet.

`-haltonwarning` will cause the import process to stop at the first warning it receives of a problem. Instead of waiting for the import to attempt to finish, this allows you to fix the problem and try again. There is also a `-haltonfatalerror` parameter you can use as well.

The `-updateversions` parameter allows you to specify how to handle file or item versions. Because imports are often used to recover a site or site collections, there are likely to be version conflicts. Using this parameter allows you to decide the default behavior when it comes to versions. Your options are as follows:

Add New Versions The default option, this leaves the old versions and adds the imported versions as new versions.

Overwrite The File And All Its Versions This will delete the items and files that it finds and inserts the imported versions as the only versions.

Ignore The File If It Already Exists This is the option I will be using in my example.

There are other parameters, but these are the only ones we need for this example. To import a site to a new site collection using STADM, follow these steps:

1. Open the command prompt, and navigate to the SharePoint root's BIN folder, or open the SharePoint Management Shell.

2. Type in the following command (using the files and paths of my example), and press Enter: `Stsadm.exe -o import -url http://spf2/sites/newsite -filename \\spf2\backup\Hrteam.cmp -includeusersecurity -haltonwarning -updateversions 3.`

After the `import` command has completed successfully, open Internet Explorer, and open the new site collection to confirm that the site imported successfully. Figure 13.62 shows what our new site should look like.

FIGURE 13.62
Newly imported HR team site

Don't forget to check the security settings and file versions to make sure that they were imported correctly. You will also need to reset your alerts.

EXPORT AND IMPORT A SITE USING POWERSHELL

You may want to use PowerShell to do your exporting and importing (since you're already in the management console). It is very much like using the STSADM command.

The command to export a site using PowerShell is:

```
Export-spweb -identity <URLfortheSite> -path <LocationandFilenameofExport.cmp>
```

This command is very straightforward, and you should be pretty familiar by now with the parameters. It simply tells SharePoint which site to export, where to export it to, and what to call the exported file.

The command to import a site using PowerShell is:

```
Import-spweb -identity <URLfortheSite> -path <LocationandFileNameofExportFile.
cmp> -force
```

Again, it's a very straightforward command; the only difference between the import and export commands is the -force parameter (instead of -overwrite) at the end to force SharePoint to overwrite the existing site with the imported site.

There are additional optional parameters, such as -whatif, which will display a message about what happens after running the command, rather than executing it. Useful for testing.

EXPORT A LIST

For this example, you'll back up the Links list that is located in the SPF2 site collection. Take the following steps to do this:

1. Open Central Administration.

2. Click the Backup And Restore link.

3. Click the Export A Site Or List link in the Granular Backup section.

4. On the Site Or List Export page (shown in Figure 13.63), in the Site Collection section, choose the site collection that contains the site or list you want to export.

5. Next, choose either the site you want to export or the site that contains the list you want to export.

6. If you are exporting a site, leave the List field blank; if you want to export a list, choose the list you want to export.

   Selecting or changing the site collection, site, or list that you want to export works just like changing the site collection did when you backed up the site collection. Click the down arrow, and then choose the menu option to change the object (for example, to change a list, it would say Change List). The Select page will open, showing you a list of all the site collections, sites, and lists (depending on what you're changing) that are available. Click the name you want, and then click OK.

7. In the File Location section, enter the directory where you want to save the backup file to and the filename you want to use for the export. Remember to add the .cmp to the end of the filename. For this example, I will use \\dc1\backups\LinkList.cmp.

8. If you have backed up this list before, you may want to overwrite the old file with the new one; if that is the case, be sure to check the Overwrite Existing Files check box.

9. If you want to include all of the author, editor, created, and modified by time information, as well as all security and users, for the site in your export, check the Export Full Security check box.

10. One of my favorite features of the site/list export is the ability to export the version history for the list items. You can export all versions, just the current version, the last major version, or the last major and the last minor version. For this example, I am going to bring over all the versions.

FIGURE 13.63
The Site Or List
Export page

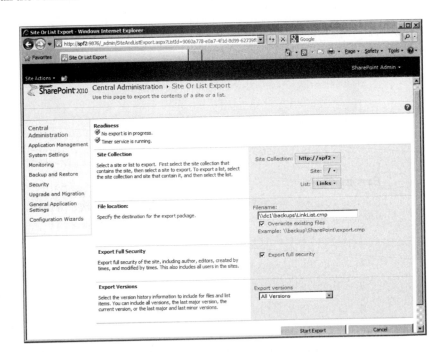

After you click the Start Export button, the Granular Backup Job Status page will open. This time, the detailed information will appear under the Content Export section. On this page, you can follow the progress of your export job. When the job has completed, the status will say Succeeded.

IMPORTING A LIST USING POWERSHELL

Being able to export and import a list is new to this version of SharePoint, and because of that, import is done only in PowerShell. There is no equivalent STSADM command. So, before you go any further, make sure you read through how to set up proper account access and permissions to run PowerShell commands in Chapter 14. Once you have everything configured so that you can run PowerShell commands, return here and follow these steps to import a list using PowerShell:

Import basically takes whatever is in an export file and restores it to an address; you use the same command to import an exported site, site collection, list, or library. The difference is what's in the export file.

The command to import a list or library using PowerShell is:

```
import-spweb -identity <URLforList> -path <PathtoExportfile>
```

So, our example would use the command below:

```
import-spweb -identity http://spf2/hrteam/ -path \\spf2\backup\hrteamtasks.cmp
```

Running this command will create the list at the relative address and then import all items that are in the export file into the list. You can also import over the top of an existing list (say a disgruntled employee ruined all list items in a large list), replacing items. If you are importing the list items into a new or empty list, this is fine. But what if you only want to restore some missing items and don't want to make any changes to, or new versions of, the existing items? Remember that the import command (be it STSADM or PowerShell) has a grasp of versioning. This means you can tell SharePoint to ignore any existing items in the list you are overwriting; to do that, you will need to add the -updateversions parameter with ignore.

EXPORT A LIST

Now that you know how to import a list or library using PowerShell, you can also use PowerShell to export the list. Although the GUI is useful for doing an export, you can create a PowerShell script (see Chapter 14) and then make a basic scheduled task (using Task Scheduler) to schedule the export. This gives you some additional control concerning doing backups.

Now you're going to want to pay close attention to the URL paths you use for this command because the -itemurl parameter is a root relative path. That means that when you add the -itemurl parameter, you must enter the part of the URL path that comes after the site URL address, like /lists/tasks (the leading slash helps).

This is important because examples of the command on the Internet do not use a root-relative path, and when you run the command, you will get an error that the URL is not valid. You must use a root-relative path, or it will not work.

The following is the command to export a list or library using PowerShell:

```
export-spweb -identity <siteURL> -path <exportfilelocation> -itemurl < root
relative path in the site to the list, such as /hrteam/lists/tasks>
```

BACKING UP AND RESTORING A SITE TEMPLATE, LIST, OR LIBRARY

Chapter 9 covered site, list, and library templates and how to create, export, and restore them in great detail, so here I'll just provide a few reminders.

To create a site template, you simply go to the Site Settings page of that site and click on the Save this site as a template link. Be sure, when specifying the name, filename, and description of the template, to also select Include Content. The default size limit is 50 MB for templates, but it can be raised to 200 MB. This is true of any site, list, or library template. Importing and exporting do not have that limit.

Once the site template is saved, you can go to the site collection's Solution Gallery and download the template for safekeeping. To restore the site template, simply add it to the Solution Gallery of the site collection of your choice, and then use it to create a new site.

To create a list (or library, as the steps are the same) template, go to that list's Settings page. Click Save List As Template. Specify a name, filename, and description, and select Include Content. In the site collection settings, open the List Template Gallery, and download the template. To restore, simply add the template to the correct site collection's List Template Gallery, and then create a new list using the list template.

RECOVERING DATA FROM AN UNATTACHED CONTENT DATABASE

At some point, in every SharePoint administrator's life, you will be faced with the task of recovering lost or deleted data. In the past, it has been difficult to recover, and it often required using third-party tools or building a recovery farm. You now know that if you have a backup or export file, you can recover everything from the entire farm down to list items. However, if all you have is a database, maybe from a SQL backup or maybe a database that was formerly attached to a web application, there is a new tool to use to recover lists, libraries, sites, or site collections: Unattached Content Database Data Recovery (yes, it is a mouthful).

All that is required is a SharePoint Foundation content database (preferably equally up-to-date on its updates as the farm itself) in SQL. You simply specify the server name, the database name, and what you want to recover.

This example demonstrates how to use the Recover Data From An Unattached Content Database to export a site, even a site that isn't in the root site collection. The site collection http://spf2/sites/London contains a site called techdept. I have created a restored version of the WSS_Content database on the SQL Server, which is named RR1, and I named the new database UnattachContent. This new content database is not attached or associated with any SharePoint web application. I will export a copy of the techdept site from the UnattachContent database. To export a copy of the techdept site, follow these steps (see Figure 13.64):

1. Open Central Administration.

2. Click the Backup And Restore link.

3. Click the Recover Data From An Unattached Content Database link under Granular Backup.

4. In Database Name And Authentication, enter the name of you database server. For my example, I am using a SQL Server named RR1.

5. Next enter the name of the unattached database you want to export data from. The name of the unattached database that I created for this example is UnattachContent.

6. Select the type of database authentication your database server uses. The SQL server in my example uses Windows authentication.

7. In the Operation To Perform section, you have three choices: you can browse the content in the database, back up a site collection, or export a site or list.

FIGURE 13.64
Unattached Content Database Data Recovery

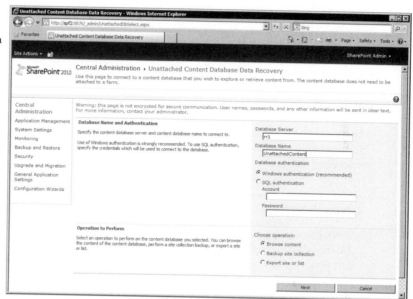

Here is where things start to get interesting. The three choices available on this page let you either back up a site collection, export a site or list, or simply look at the site collections, sites, and lists or libraries available in the database (so you can either back them up or export them):

Browse Content This option takes you to a page with the Site Collection section of the Site Or List Export page, offering the option to select a site collection, site, and even list contained in the database. The only other section in this page is Operation to Perform, and it offers you the option to either back up the selected site collection or export the selected list or site.

Export Site Or List This option simply takes you directly to the Site Or List Export page, so you can select the site or list from the database to export. The site collection will display as the Central Administration address, but if you select to change the site collection, it will display the correct database. When in doubt, check the site collection's database name.

Backup Site Collection This option will simply take you to the Site Collection Backup page so you can back up a site collection from the database. Again, the site collection might look like it's in Central Administration, but it's really showing the site collections from the unattached database.

So, what good is this unattached database recovery feature? If you have content in a database that you don't want to add to a web application on your server (or farm), you can simply access its contents, in the form of site collection, subsite, list, or library, and recover the data you want, without having to do the extra work. Using the Unattached Content Database Data Recovery, you can back up and export data from outside your farm, even from a whole other farm entirely. It opens whole new avenues for data recovery that you never had before.

Backup and Restore Using Other Tools

Although this chapter has focused on how to back up and restore using SharePoint's tools, you can restore data in other ways. Let's look at IIS to start. All IIS Web Sites have configuration data, application pools, and file data. The configurations are stored in the IIS metabase (although you can separately back up individual website and application pool configuration files). This is the data that you see in the IIS console or the Properties dialog box for an IIS Web Site. This means if someone accidentally deletes a website from the IIS console, you can recover it easily and SharePoint need never know it was missing.

BEST PRACTICES

SharePoint seems to resent it when you restore IIS or an SQL database without using its backup (Microsoft cryptically hints at the fact in its TechNet documents). Because SharePoint does not like to work with a mix of backups (databases, the IIS metabase, and so on), when you are forced to do a backup of that type, it might be a good idea to do a new SharePoint backup to incorporate the changes into a new SharePoint backup folder.

Always test your restores. I cannot emphasize this enough. Use a test environment that echoes the real one, even if only on a small scale simply to periodically test your backup and restore scheme. Try restoring the IIS metabase to see whether you can restore SharePoint properly. Then try to restore a SharePoint backup to ensure that it will work. Test your database backup and restores, and watch your event logs and Performance Monitor to see whether any issues were introduced after the restore. Check to make sure everything is running smoothly as part of your regular maintenance program, and you will always know if you are ready for an emergency.

Backing Up and Restoring the IIS Metabase

The IIS metabase backup is a complete backup of all the configuration information for all website and application pools for the server. Although powerful, complete, and easy to use, this kind of backup does have the drawback of being server-specific; if you back up the IIS metabase of one server, it can only be restored for that one server and cannot be restored anywhere else. For a server farm, this means that metabase backups would have to be made for each individual server.

BACKING UP THE IIS METABASE

To back up an IIS metabase, you need to use the appcmd tool:

1. Open a command prompt as the administrator (right-click Command Prompt on the Start menu, and choose Run As Administrator).

2. Browse to %windir%\system32\inetsrv.

3. Run the following command: **appcmd add backup <backupname>**. See Figure 13.65.

   You can find your backup located in %windir%\system32\inetsrv\ backup\<backupname>.

FIGURE 13.65
Backing up the IIS metabase

ENCRYPTING YOUR BACKUPS

Encrypting your backups is always a good idea, but that is just the tip of the iceberg. Remember to secure your backups as if they contained your personal information, because in a way they do. They generally always contain data you don't want strangers, clients, or competitors to access—so protect them. In my environment, it is unlikely that anyone else is going to access my machines or network. A business environment, however, is more dangerous. Pay attention to where you put your backups. Don't make them available to just anyone. From cleaning staff to disgruntled employees, you just never know who might be considering the value of your data.

What exactly was backed up? The configuration settings for all application pools, websites (even FTP sites), and references to virtual directories in IIS were backed up. The metabase data can be restored in case of an emergency. Each backup has five files. If you are going to copy those backups to another location for safekeeping, don't split up these files; they are all required to restore IIS. Remember that metabases are unique per server, so keep one for each server in the farm if necessary, and label them accordingly.

RESTORING THE IIS METABASE

Be aware that when you restore the IIS metabase, it overwrites everything in the console. To help avoid damaging the rest of what may be in IIS (and make it possible to restore to different servers), the backup options in SharePoint only back up configuration data for each individual web application, without touching the rest of IIS. The metabase is nothing to mess with, but it is a good last defense when all else fails, because it can return everything in the console to a functional state.

How do you restore an IIS metabase? Let's say that the application pool for the `http://spf2` web application was accidentally deleted by an overzealous junior administrator (see Figure 13.66). Even worse, he doesn't really know *what else* he did, but it's obvious that nothing is working. Everyone needs to learn, but you don't have the time it will take to find out all the IIS settings he changed or time to try to re-create the application pool.

FIGURE 13.66

IIS missing an application pool for SharePoint-80

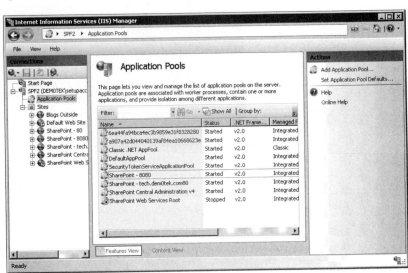

That sort of situation really could use a metabase restore (mind you, currently my farm has one SharePoint server). That's right; if no changes have been made to web applications since the last metabase backup, restore the application pool (and undo all the administrative mistakes) by restoring an IIS metabase backup. To do so, follow these steps:

1. Open a command prompt as the administrator (right-click Command Prompt on the Start menu, and choose Run as Administrator).

2. Browse to `%windir%\system32\inetsrv`.

3. Run the following command: **appcmd restore backup <backupname>**.

4. IIS can take several minutes and cause a significant slowdown on the server as it rebuilds all the site and application pool data. Eventually, you should receive a response indicating the configuration has been restored from backup. Checking IIS confirms that everything is back to normal (see Figure 13.67).

FIGURE 13.67
IIS repaired

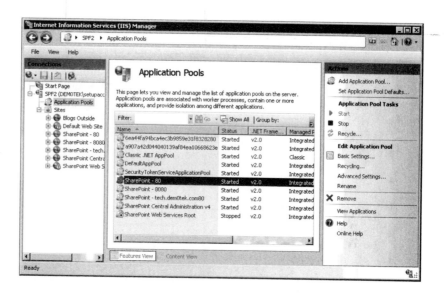

NO GUI FOR IIS BACKUPS?

Most of you will have noticed that IIS7 doesn't have a nice GUI tool for backups, while IIS6 did. Since it's well past Y2K, this lack of a GUI is somewhat disturbing. Fortunately, it's easily fixed thanks to an IIS module written by Rakki Muthukumar and found on his MSDN blog site (search for IIS7 – Improved Backup Restore Tool and a UI Module). Both a DLL file to integrate into the IIS Manager and a stand-alone Windows Forms application are available.

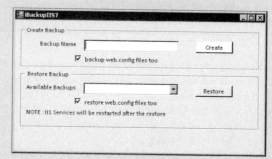

The DLL file you can install into the IIS Manager is a bit more tricky; it requires installing the DLL into the global cache and editing the `administration.config` file for IIS7. It's much easier to use the stand-alone executable

Virtual Directories and SharePoint Folders

To back up SharePoint web applications, you also need to include the virtual directories and the SharePoint-specific folders in the file system. Backing up the IIS metabase will store configuration information about virtual directories but not the *contents* of those directories. Virtual directories contain the actual ASPX pages, images, layout information, and more. You can't have an IIS Web Site for SharePoint without virtual directories any more than a SharePoint web application is of any use without a site collection.

The virtual directories are located in a folder called, intuitively enough, `virtualdirectories` under a folder used for all things IIS called `Inetpub` (I'll show you that in a moment). The full path to the virtual directories is `C:\inetpub\wwwroot\wss\VirtualDirectories\`. See Figure 13.68.

FIGURE 13.68
Viewing the Virtual Directories folder

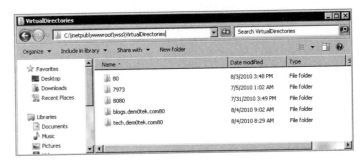

HEY! I DON'T RECOGNIZE THAT NUMBER

In Figure 13.68, the folder name for the SharePoint web application's folder is 80 (meaning the port number), and the blogging web application is 8080, but the Central Administration site's folder is 7973. You may have noticed that, throughout the book, the port for Central Administration is 9876, so why 7973? When I was installing SharePoint, I was given the choice to either take the default random port that SharePoint wanted to assign for the Central Administration site or create my own. I chose to specify 9876, but SharePoint remembered its random number anyway, and chose to name the virtual directory after it.

When backing up your files for IIS (and therefore, by extension, SharePoint), it is always good to actually back up not just the virtual directories but the whole `Inetpub` folder. Why? The `Inetpub` folder also contains the files used by SMTP. So, in one step, you back up both your virtual directories and the drop mail folder (in case anything goes awry with incoming email). I will be demonstrating backing up using `Inetpub`, but if you don't want to, feel free to back up only the virtual directories instead.

In addition to the virtual directory files, SharePoint uses other files to define its website. These files are located in the SharePoint folders, starting with a folder named 14, at the path: `%ProgramFiles%\Common Files\Microsoft Shared\web server extensions\14\`. This path contains so much critical SharePoint stuff that it is actually referred to as the *SharePoint root* (or sometimes the *14 hive*). The folders most critical for SharePoint IIS Web Sites to function are under the TEMPLATE and ISAPI folders in the SharePoint root.

One folder that SharePoint uses is outside the SharePoint root—the wpresources folder. This folder contains, at minimum, a `web.config` file that is used for web part resources and the global assembly cache (GAC). This folder is particularly useful if you have custom web parts. If you do, consider backing up this folder; it is located in the same directory as the SharePoint root.

CUSTOM SOLUTIONS AND TEMPLATES

Pay attention to the web parts, features, solutions, and templates you may add to SharePoint over time. You should keep a backup copy of the source files (usually they are .wsp files) in case you need to redeploy them in the future.

So at a minimum, you need to make sure you back up the following folders for each Web Front End server:

◆ `C:\inetpub`

◆ `%ProgramFiles%\Common Files\Microsoft Shared\web server extensions\14`

◆ `%ProgramFiles%\Common Files\Microsoft Shared\web server extensions\ wpresources`

To back up those essential folders and the files they contain, you could go directly to the folders that I suggest and directly copy them to a network share or backup disk, or you can use backup software or a scheduled task to automate the backup.

In Figure 13.69, I've copied the folders to a share on the DC1 server, located at `\\dc1\ backups\spf2\`.

FIGURE 13.69
Manual file
copy backup

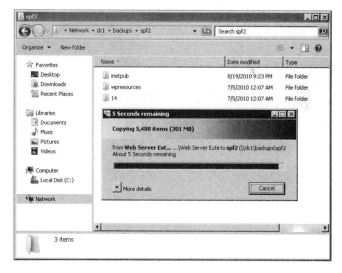

Should something happen to these files on your server—for example, the files in the SharePoint-80 virtual directory becomes corrupt—you can easily restore these files by copying them from your backup location to the server. Note that you will usually need to perform an `iisreset` to allow IIS to access the recovered files.

Backing Up and Restoring Databases in SQL Server

At this point, the farm, web applications, site collections, sites, and even the list and libraries have been backed up in preparation for a catastrophe. You have also backed up IIS and the virtual directories. But what about the databases? How the databases are backed up depends on whether you are running SharePoint as a stand-alone server, which uses SQL Server Express, or as a farm using SQL Server.

BACKING UP A DATABASE USING SQL SERVER MANAGEMENT STUDIO

You are going to first look at how to back up the server farm using SQL Server Management Studio. In a server farm, by definition, SharePoint will use SQL Server. This well-documented Microsoft product can be used to back up and restore any databases you might have stored there. SQL has its own built-in options, the details of which have filled their own books. But we will look at the basic database-by-database backup procedure.

You will want to back up SharePoint_AdminContent, SharePoint_Config, any content databases (such as WSS_Content), and any search databases. To manually back up individual databases using SQL Server, follow these steps:

1. Log onto SQL Server.

2. Open Management Studio by going to Start ➤ All Programs ➤ Microsoft SQL Server 2008 ➤ SQL Server Management Studio.

3. The Connect To Server dialog box opens (Figure 13.70). Enter the name of your SQL Server into the Server name text box. My SQL Server is named RR1.

FIGURE 13.70
The Connect To Server page in SQL Server Management Studio

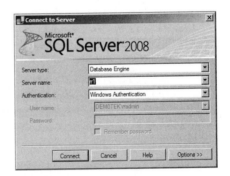

4. When you are connected, expand the Databases folder.

5. Right-click the database you want to back up (like WSS_Content Database), select Tasks, and then Backup (see Figure 13.71).

6. When the Backup Database page opens, you can choose the source of the backup, what you will name the backup (the backup set), and the destination of the backup file. For this example, we are going to go with the default information. Make sure the backup type is set to Full, the backup component is Database, the backup set is a name you can remember, and that it is set not to expire (expire after zero days).

7. To change the default location of the backup file, click the Add button.

8. When the Select Backup Destination dialog box opens, the file is set to the local default file location. Just type the location where you want to save the backup file. You must also give the backup file a name. Remember to use a meaningful name for the backup file, such as WSS_Content_Bkup.bak, so you can easily identify it later, and then click OK.

FIGURE 13.71
Selecting a database to back up

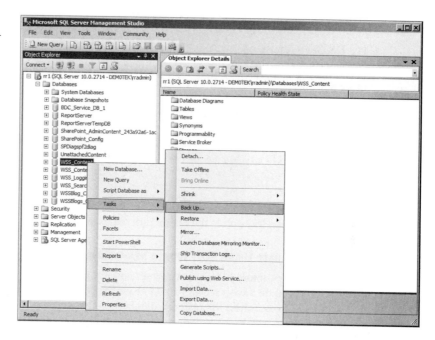

9. You will now be returned to the Select Backup Destination dialog box, shown in Figure 13.72; click OK.

FIGURE 13.72
Selecting a backup destination

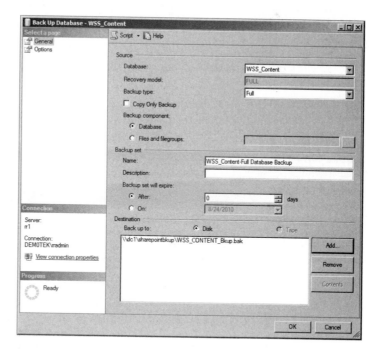

10. In the Select A Page area, choose Options.

11. Under Overwrite Media, select the Overwrite All Existing Media Sets radio button. This lets you overwrite backups in the destination location that might have expired.

12. Click OK.

13. You will know the backup job is finished when you see the message box (Figure 13.73) that reads "The Backup of the Database completed successfully."

FIGURE 13.73
A successful database backup

Repeat these steps for each of the SharePoint databases.

RESTORING A DATABASE USING SQL SERVER MANAGEMENT STUDIO

What if one of your content databases becomes corrupt and you don't have a recent SharePoint backup of it but you do have a recent full database backup? You can restore it in SQL. You will most likely need to reconnect the restored database to the web application in SharePoint, but this is just one more way to cover your bases in case of catastrophic failure.

Before you attempt to restore the database (if it hasn't been deleted), you first need to make sure it is offline. To take a database offline, follow these steps:

1. Open the Central Administration site, and click the Application Management link.

2. When the Application Management page opens, click the Manage Content Databases link in the Databases section.

3. Click the name of the database you want to restore; for this example, I will be restoring WSS_Content.

4. The Manage Content Database Setting page will open. In the first section, there is a drop-down menu called Database Status. The menu as two options, Ready (meaning online) and Offline; choose Offline. See Figure 13.74.

FIGURE 13.74
Database offline

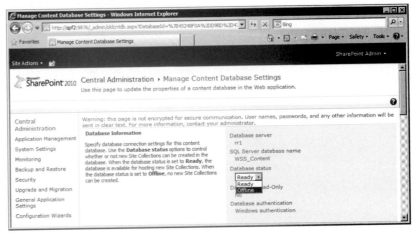

5. Click OK at the bottom of the page.

6. When you return to the Manage Content Databases page, the database you selected should now show a database status of Offline.

Now your database is offline, and you are ready to restore it in SQL Server Management Studio. To restore the database, follow these steps:

1. Right-click the database you want to replace (for this example WSS_Content), select Tasks, and select Detach (see Figure 13.75). You can, of course, restore over the existing database, but it can be safer to just replace it.

FIGURE 13.75
Detaching a
database

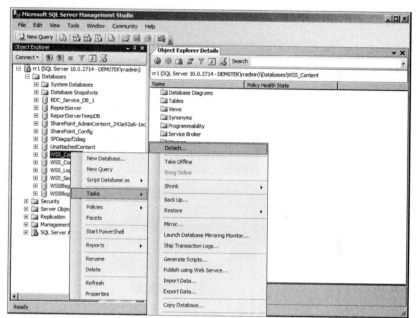

2. In the Database Detach window, you can see that there is one active connection to the database. Since this would cause our restore to fail, you need to put a check mark in the Drop Connections column and click OK (see Figure 13.76).

3. The database will disappear from the database window.

4. To restore the database, right-click the Database folder, and select Restore Database from the menu (see Figure 13.77).

FIGURE 13.76
Drop Connections
column

FIGURE 13.77
Selecting Restore
Database in SQL
Server Manage-
ment Studio

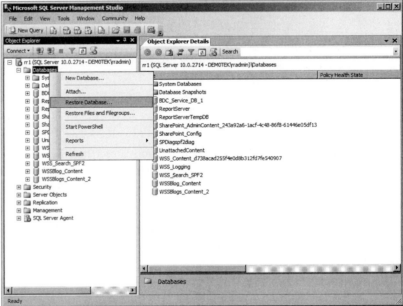

5. When the Restore Database page opens, type the name of the database you want to
restore in the To Database field (for this example, use the database's original name, WSS
Content). See Figure 13.78.

FIGURE 13.78
Restoring a
media set

6. In the Specify The Source And Location Of Backup Sets To Restore section, click the drop-down arrow, and select the database you want to restore (WSS_Content for this example). When you select the database that you want to restore, the most recent backup for that database will appear in the Backup Sets To Restore box.

7. Make sure there is a check mark in the Restore column. If there is more than one backup, check the most recent.

   The database you detached and want to restore is technically still on the server; it's just not listed in the console. So in order for the restore to succeed, you need to give it permission to overwrite the current copy of the database, even if it is detached.

8. In the Select A Page pane, go to the Options page, check the Overwrite The Existing Database (WITH REPLACE) check box, and then click OK.

In a few minutes, depending on the size of the database, you will see a dialog box either giving you an error or telling you the database was restored successfully. Click OK to finish.

Now that the database has been restored and reattached in SQL, you need to bring the database back online in SharePoint. To do that, follow these steps:

1. Open the Central Administration site.

2. Click the Application Management link.

3. Click the Manage Content Databases link in the Databases section.

4. When the Manage Content Databases page opens, click the name of the database you just restored.

5. When the Manage Content Database Settings page opens, set Database Status to Ready and click OK.

6. The database status should now show as Started on the Manage Content Databases page.

That's all it takes to restore your SharePoint web application to functionality.

BACKING UP AND RESTORING DATABASES FOR A STAND-ALONE SERVER

When running a stand-alone server install of SharePoint, there are two ways to back up the SQL Server Express databases:

◆ Turn off the services that might be using the database (and consider taking the databases offline in SharePoint), and then copy those databases and their log files to a different location. Then turn the services back on (and bring the databases back to a Ready status).

◆ Use a third-party backup solution that leverages Volume Shadow Copy (also known as Volume Snapshot Service or VSS) to create a backup without causing any locking issues with the active database.

WINDOWS SERVER BACKUP

Windows Server does have a built-in backup solution that supports VSS/Windows Server Backup. I'll show how to use it shortly for a full server backup, but it can also be used to back up individual files and folders. It has some limits regarding scheduling but is a viable option if you need a VSS-enabled backup solution.

Manual Database Backup

To be cautious with SharePoint, you can turn all the services off when you are copying a database on a stand-alone server. But remember that stopping SharePoint stops it for everyone, so you won't want to do this while users are trying to access SharePoint.

To turn off services and copy databases manually, follow these steps:

1. Open the Services console by going to Start ➤ Administrative Tools ➤ Services.

2. Scroll through the services until you get to the SharePoint services. You will know them because the names all start with SharePoint 2010. Stop all the services.

3. Next scroll to the SQL Server (SharePoint) service, and stop it as well.

4. Now that you have all the services stopped, navigate to the folder that contains the databases (see Figure 13.79):

   ```
   %Program Files%\Common Files\Microsoft Shared\Web Server extensions\14\Data\
   MSSQL10.SHAREPOINT\MSSQL\DATA
   ```

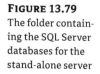

FIGURE 13.79

The folder containing the SQL Server databases for the stand-alone server

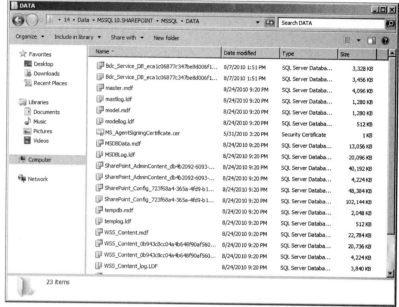

---

5. Now that the databases are not being used, you will be allowed to copy them. Don't forget that the databases must also have their corresponding log files with them.

6. The databases you want to back up or copy have names such as WSS_Content and WSS_Search , or they use the word SharePoint in their name (a dead give away). You may have created other web applications, and they may have different names than the ones listed here. These are just a sampling of what to look for. Select the databases (these will have the .mdf file extension) and their log files (these will have the .ldf file extension) that you want to back up. Then copy them to the backup location (see Figure 13.80).

FIGURE 13.80
Backup file
location

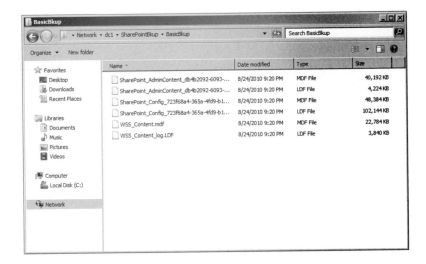

7. Restart all the services you stopped, including SQL Server (SharePoint). If you took the databases offline, set them back to a Ready Status.

Well, that's it for the old-school "Stop all services and copy the database" method for back-ups. The process runs in reverse to recover the databases. Remember that the `.mdf` files and the `.ldf` files go together, so if you copy over the database file, you must also copy over the log file. This is true for both backing up and restoring the databases.

Restoring a Stand-Alone Server Database

Restoring a stand-alone server database is pretty easy. Just repeat the steps for a manual backup, but reverse the direction of the file copy:

1. Stop all the running SharePoint 2010 and SQL Server services.

2. Copy back your saved database and log files from your backup. Place them in `C:\ Program Files\Common Files\Microsoft Shared\Web Server extensions\14\Data\ MSSQL10.SHAREPOINT\MSSQL\DATA`.

   Remember to get them all, including the `.ldf` log files.

3. Once all the database files are restored to the correct folder in the SharePointRoot, restart all the services.

Backing Up and Restoring a Complete Server

Now that you've spent some time backing up individual parts of SharePoint—from individual lists to SQL databases, IIS metadata, and the critical files—let's look at backing up the entire server. Although it's handy for any server, this is perhaps most useful in a single-server configuration where everything is on one machine (such as both SQL Express and SharePoint). Having a "bare-metal" backup solution in place can save you time and headaches should the unthinkable occur and the entire server go down.

BACKING UP THE FULL SERVER

There are many third-party solutions for backup and restore of the entire server, but there's also a free feature that comes with Windows Server 2008 R2, called Windows Server Backup. Previous versions also have a Windows backup product that does full-server restores, but my example is using Windows Server 2008 R2. So, that's what you'll be using in this example to completely back up and restore SPF2.

For this example, I've attached a second physical hard drive to the server to use for dedicated backups. This is the recommended setup for Windows Server Backup. You can also back up to nondedicated disks or even network shares. But for best results, having a dedicated physical disk is recommended.

When you attach the new disk, make sure you initialize it and create a partition. Windows Server Backup is going to promptly reformat that partition, but it doesn't know how to use an unpartitioned disk.

1. Go to Start ➢ Administrative Tools ➢ Windows Server Backup (Figure 13.81).

WINDOWS SERVER BACKUP IS NOT INSTALLED

It's possible your server doesn't have the backup software installed. In that case, open Server Manager, and go to Add Features in the Features section. Here you'll find Windows Server Backup Features listed as a feature—go ahead and install it. Once that's done, you can open Windows Server Backup normally.

FIGURE 13.81
Windows
Server Backup

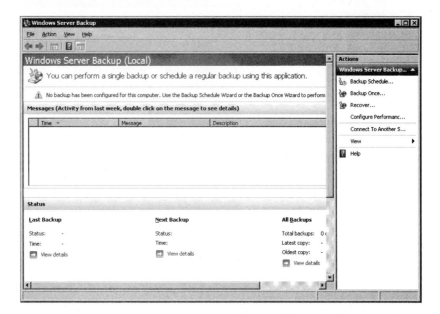

2. On the right in the Actions pane, click on Backup Schedule to schedule a nightly backup job.

3. For the Backup Configuration (Figure 13.82), you can select Full Server (the default) or Custom to back up individual files. I'll show how to back up the full server. Click Next.

FIGURE 13.82
Backup
configuration

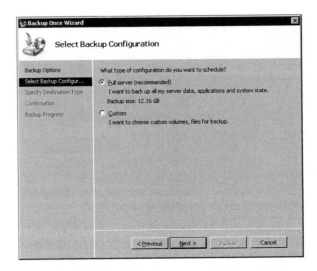

4. For the backup time (Figure 13.83), the default is a nightly backup at 9 p.m. You can adjust this time or back up more frequently. Note you cannot backup less frequently; once a day is the minimum. Keep this in mind if this is an issue. Leave the default in place for this example, and click Next.

FIGURE 13.83
Specify Backup
Time page

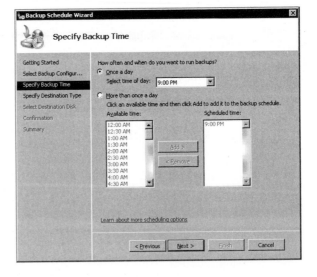

5. Under Specify Destination Type, you have three options. The first is to use the dedicated disk. This reformats the disk and uses it exclusively for Windows Server Backup. The second choice is to back up to a different volume (one that is not dedicated and can be used for other things). The final choice is to use a network share. We're going to be using the recommended first option (see Figure 13.84).

FIGURE 13.84
Specify Destination Type page

6. Go ahead and select your dedicated disk. If you don't see it in the list, click the Show All Available Disks button to scan for nonformatted physical disks detected by Windows. Once you have the disk selected (I'm using a disk called VMware virtual1 in my example, Figure 13.85), click Next.

FIGURE 13.85
Select Destination Disk page

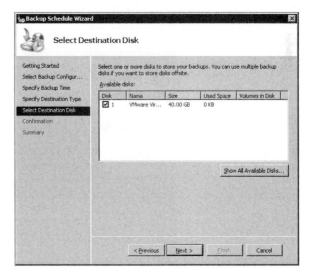

7. A dialog box will pop up reminding you that this will completely erase the chosen disk, and it will become unavailable to Windows Explorer; click Yes.

8. Finally, the confirmation window (see Figure 13.86) will appear, showing the options chosen, including the destination disk with a preassigned label. Choose Finish.

FIGURE 13.86
The final confirmation screen

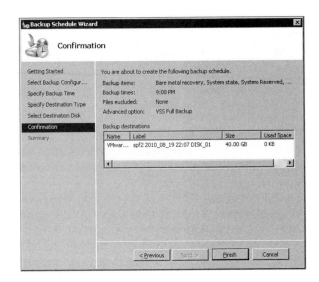

The backup is now scheduled to run at 9 p.m. If you want to run it right away, you can do so by going back to the main Windows Server Backup window and, in the Actions pane, choosing Backup Once. Choosing Backup Once will prompt you to either run your existing scheduled backup or create a new one-time-only backup job. Select the existing, scheduled backup, and click Next and then Finish.

The backup will start running and provide you with a progress window (see Figure 13.87). Let it run until completed. It may take a while.

FIGURE 13.87
The Backup Progress window

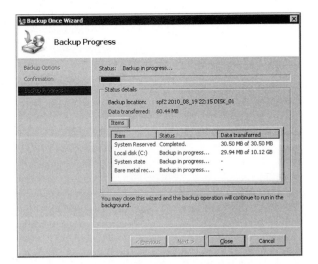

RESTORING THE FULL SERVER

Now you have a full backup of the server—and it's scheduled to run every night at 9 p.m. Should a disaster occur and the server's entire disk become unusable, you can restore the complete OS as of 9 p.m. the night before. The process requires you to have your Windows Server 2008 R2 disk handy and the backup drive to be attached to the server.

In my example, I've removed the primary hard drive from SPF2 (to simulate a spectacular failure) and replaced it with an empty disk. So, now the boot drive is completely blank—no OS, no SharePoint, nothing. All it has is an empty disk, the backup disk (containing our Windows Server Backup system image) and the Windows Server 2008 R2 DVD in the drive.

1. Boot the server from the DVD—it will launch into the standard installation options and ask you for your preferred language and keyboard layout.

2. At the installation screen, instead of choosing Install Now, click the Repair Your Computer option (Figure 13.88).

FIGURE 13.88
The Install Windows screen

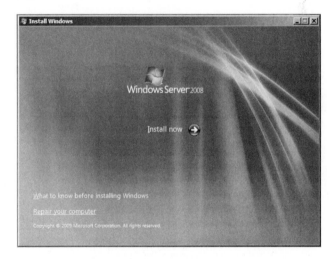

3. In the System Recovery Options window shown in Figure 13.89, select the option to Restore Your Computer Using A System Image That You Created Earlier, and hit Next.

FIGURE 13.89
The System Recovery Options window

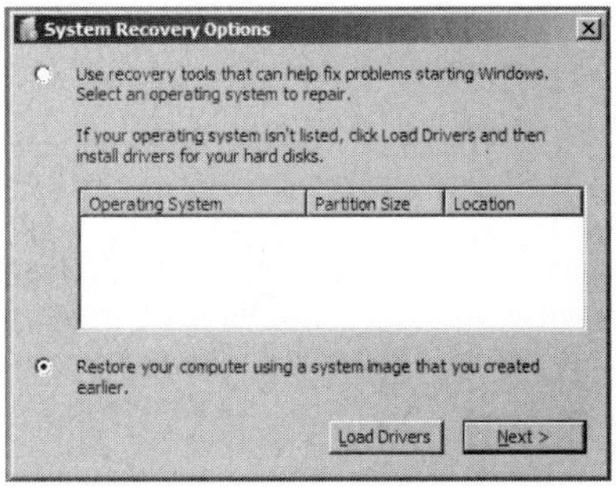

4. The recovery service will scan the local disks looking for a recent system image to use. It will prompt you to restore the most recent backup it can find, but you can also choose to back up from a specific system image. I'm going to restore the image I created earlier (see Figure 13.90).

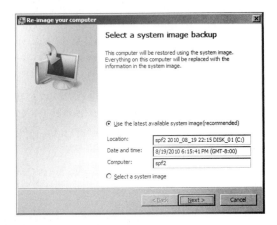

SYSTEM IMAGE? AS IN HYPER-V?

Windows Server Backup tries very hard to keep things tucked neatly away behind the GUI, but the underlying technology is pretty straightforward and can be quite useful in other ways.

The backup we created of the complete system is actually a set of VHD files (one for each partition on your server). These *virtual hard disk* files are the same ones used by Virtual Server, Virtual PC, and Hyper-V. This means that could take your system image and restore it to a virtual machine (rather than a physical one) should you need it up and running again while the physical server is being repaired.

5. Before you reimage, you can choose additional options (see Figure 13.91). Here you can specify any custom formatting or partitioning you may want to do, install drivers to access disks not discovered by the boot DVD (maybe you have a custom RAID card that needs drivers), or restore only some disks and exclude others. We're going to leave the defaults in place and click Next.

DATE STAMPS AND REDMOND

You'll notice the date stamp for your system images might be a bit off. It could be off by a couple of hours, or even almost a full day. This is because you've booted from the Windows Server 2008 R2 DVD. When you boot from this DVD, the machine is always in the GMT-8:00 time zone. Until you install an OS and say otherwise, it assumes you're in Redmond. So, be sure to mentally adjust the date stamps you see accordingly.

FIGURE 13.91
Additional recovery options

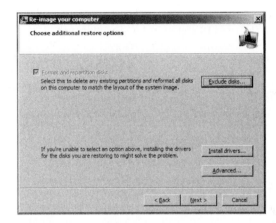

6. You'll have one final confirmation window (Figure 13.92) showing you what system image is going to be restored onto what disk. Click Finish.

FIGURE 13.92
Final restore confirmation

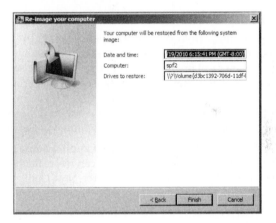

7. The computer will now restore the image to the bare disk, recovering the entire server from our backup. Be patient and let it run. Depending on the size of the disk, it could take a while.

8. When the restore is done, it will automatically reboot the server. It should come up fine, running on our new physical disk with no indication anything ever went wrong.

Being able to restore *everything* on one server is handy—but not a substitute for more modular backups. Having to rebuild an entire server because someone destroyed a list is a bit extreme (besides, in my example it wouldn't work since the content databases reside on the SQL server and not SPF2). So, although this is a great tool to avert major disaster, it should not be your only backup system.

PARTIAL RESTORE FROM A SYSTEM IMAGE

Another handy feature of Windows Server Backup is the ability to restore select files and folder from your system image. In Windows Server Backup, choose the Recover option from the Action pane. You choose the local machine for the backup location, select the latest backup, and then choose the Files And Folders option. WSB will connect to the backup disk, mount the VHD file, and allow you to browse the file structure, select the needed files, and restore them.

Suggested Recovery Scenarios

You know how to prepare for the loss or corruption of a site collection, subsite, list, and even a web application or two. You can even recover the server farm data by using the SharePoint backup and restore capability. But what if something big goes wrong? Here are some suggestions for handling common disasters based on the knowledge you already have (or should have).

For a Full Recovery of a Standalone-Server Installation

Restore an image from Windows Server Backup. This means you simply restore the entire server's OS and all applications. This scenario assumes that a regular Windows Server Backup image or other full image consists of the SharePoint server (especially useful for a standalone implementation). It makes sense in this situation because all the SharePoint services are running on one computer.

If you have an image of the server, it can restore the server fully to the point in time the backup was made. But if you have added web applications and databases since then, these are your options:

Do a SharePoint restore of the web applications, New Configuration settings. If you have more recent full backups, you can re-create the web applications that are missing from the backup by restoring them with the New Configuration settings. This will re-create the databases and all other information necessary to get the web applications back up and running. Doing a SharePoint restore is always a good starting point, if you have one.

Do an IIS metabase restore of the most recent backup you have for the server. If you don't have a full SharePoint restore available, you can restore the missing bits from scratch, starting with restoring the IIS metabase. This means you will need to copy your IIS metabase backup files for that particular server (there are two, as you know) to the %windir%\ system32\inetsrv\backup folder. Then run **appcmd restore backup <backupname>**. That should restore the settings in IIS to exactly the state of the last IIS backup. Complete with application pools and correct settings for all.

Restore the virtual directories (and customizations) from a recent backup. After you restore your IIS metabase, if there are new web applications that weren't there when you did the Windows Server Backup image, you will need to restore their virtual directories. In the IIS console, right-click each new IIS Web Site, go to Properties, and check the Home Directory tab for the path to the web application's virtual directory. Once you know which ones you need, restore them using your virtual directories backup. If there were any customizations, you should return them to the SharePoint Root folders as well.

Do a restore of the most recent backups of the embedded databases.   Simply restore the backups of the databases. It's that easy. You could also stop all SQL and SharePoint services, replace the existing databases, and then restart the services again.

Make sure that each web application in SharePoint indicates that it is connected to the correct database and that those databases have the status of Ready.

DO A FULL REINSTALLATION

If you don't have a full image backup of the server, you are not entirely out of luck. You can do a complete recovery anyway. If you can reinstall the server and get it back up and running, simply reinstall SharePoint using the Standalone Install. Then do a full farm recovery, New Configuration. This will restore SharePoint to the point when the backup was made.

If you don't have a full farm backup, you can, since SharePoint is running, create new web applications, remove their new databases (since they're empty), and add the existing databases that you backed up instead.

To do that, use STSADM and add the databases manually to each web application at the command line (remember that this is for the Standalone, single-server install):

```
STSADM -o addcontentdb -url <web address of web application> -databasename
<name of the database you want to restore> -databaseserver <servername>
Microsoft##SSEE
```

You can also optionally specify the site warning and maximum levels, as well as the search server in the command as well.

To do the same thing with PowerShell, you can use:

```
Mount-SPContentDatabase -Name <yourdatabasename> -WebApplication <http://
webapplicationURL>
```

If you had any customizations; new solutions, features, or web parts, you should restore the `wpresources` folder and SharePoint root as well. You might have to reconfigure the features, solutions, and other customizations manually (yes, that's a pain, but it's better than losing them altogether).

For a Web Front-End Server

In this scenario, we are assuming a single front end server in the farm has failed. So using Windows Server Backup or some other full-system image is a good idea. The front end server does not contain a lot of data per se because all the data is on an SQL server elsewhere, but it can contain the web parts, customizations, images, solutions, and features saved locally. If the SQL databases are perfectly intact, all you'll need to do is bring the server back online and the services on the server itself; otherwise, they'll use the databases as if nothing happened.

Restore IIS.   If SharePoint is installed, but Web Sites have been lost in IIS, or somehow have been corrupted. You can restore the IIS metabase for that server (metabases are server-specific). Remember to make the corresponding application pools if necessary.

Restore virtual directories and customizations.   If you've lost customizations or virtual directory content. Use your manual backup (or third party file backup) to restore whatever virtual directories or custom web parts, templates, and so on, that might be required by the new web applications. Usually the databases on SQL were never compromised and are likely not going to need restoration.

Install SharePoint and connect to the farm.   This is if you need to restore the entire server. Install the OS and add it to the domain, install the prerequisites (and SMTP if that server was the one supporting incoming email), and then run a Complete install of SharePoint. In the configuration wizard, choose to connect to an existing farm, then specify the correct SQL server and configuration database for the farm. You will also need to provide the farm passphrase for the farm as well, so keep it handy. SharePoint will add the necessary files where they need to go, and it will configure IIS for you (you may need to do an `IISRESET/noforce`), bringing the server into alignment again. Be sure to reconfigure those items that are outside the scope of a SharePoint installation such as network load balancing, SSL certificates, and other customizations, if necessary.

Keep in mind that, if the server that hosted Central Administration is the one that failed, you should start the Central Administration service on one of the other servers in the farm so administration of SharePoint as a whole can continue. (For more about adding front end servers to a farm, see Chapter 16.)

For a Full Recovery of a Server Farm

If your SharePoint server and the SQL server—even if your entire network—suffers a disaster, you can still rebuild it if you have your backups.

First, make certain you have a domain available with DNS. Then make sure you also have the necessary service accounts (with the setup account correctly configured in SQL), with a SQL server up, running on the domain, and accessible from the new SharePoint server.

Install SharePoint on the first, primary server.   Do a server farm, complete installation of SharePoint on that qualified server (running server 2008 or 2008 R2 on a domain, with IIS and SMTP installed, and all the prerequisites), and choose to create a new server farm in the configuration wizard. This will create a new configuration database, as well as the Central Administration site and its content database. That gives you the foundation to re-create your whole SharePoint farm by just resetting your configurations, restoring the web applications, and maybe restoring the customizations, alternate access mappings, and so on.

Use the most recent SharePoint restores.   When that server farm installation is complete, do a full restore from your most recent backup of all of the web applications. Make sure you do New Configuration restores, because there will be a new database server and possibly a new server name for the SharePoint server. If you've done a differential restore since the full backup, apply it if necessary. Check your configuration settings to ensure they are all there, and reset your alternate access mapping (don't forget your DNS settings to access any host header sites). Then copy over whatever files were used for your customizations.

Install SharePoint and customizations on the rest of the farm servers.   Once the first server is up, running, and completely recovered, install the prerequisites, install SharePoint, complete installation on the other web front end servers, choosing to add it to the existing farm (remember the passphrase for the restored farm). That should be all that is needed, however, customizations, including images, may need to be copied over. You might also need to reconfigure the settings if the additional servers were used to support search or other services on the farm instead of the first server.

TIPS AND TRICKS FOR RESTORING WEB APPLICATIONS TO A NEW FARM

Sometimes when SharePoint does a restore on a new server, it does not correctly add all the security accounts to their respective databases. This may well occur if restored databases are attached to the SQL instance with the old security intact and without the new accounts added. If this occurs, you will have a successful restore except for the databases. If you check the logs, as well as the event log for both the SharePoint server and the SQL server, they will all indicate that the farm account cannot access the restored content database and that possibly the new content database access account cannot log in either.

To fix this, simply add the necessary accounts as database owners of the correct databases. Then, in Central Administration, be sure to add the now functional databases to the restored web applications to which they belong.

The problem is caused by the fact that the web applications did not get to finish the process of connecting to their databases because the SharePoint service accounts could not take ownership properly. If the procedure just described does not give the web applications access to the databases within about five minutes, you may need to take the databases offline and then set them to Ready again to force the connection. Resetting IIS and even restarting the SharePoint or SQL services might be necessary to make certain all the services involved are clearly aware of the change. You should now have plenty of ideas about how to monitor and maintain your SharePoint servers and help you prepare for any disaster. Being unprepared is not an option. No one will think it's acceptable that you simply didn't think a catastrophe could happen.

Make sure you have plenty of storage space for your backups, make sure they are always readily accessible, and test them as often as you can. Monitor your servers to prepare for any problems that might arise. *Do* your backups; scheduled tasks are your friends.

If you can, back up your backups. Have a strategy in place that is appropriate for the value of your data, how long it would take to recover, and how much money and productivity would be lost during that time. If possible, have extra, regularly scheduled backups of the backups stored offsite (in case of fire, flood, or earthquake). Have a hot-swappable virtual twin of your network to go online in case of emergency. Mirror your SQL databases, and more. You cannot be too protected. From saving a list to saving a farm, it's all worth it when disaster strikes.

The Bottom Line

Monitor server performance. Use the Performance Monitor to view real-time server performance or create a data collection set to measure performance over time. You can create custom alerts that read the logs and warn you if something passes a counter limit.

Master It You have an existing server that has been tasked as your new SharePoint server. The installation is done, and it's about to go live. Because it's an existing server, you're worried that the addition of SharePoint will require more RAM than the server has installed. Build a performance alert that will register an event in the Application event log if the available RAM ever gets below 50 MB.

Use SharePoint Backup and Restore.   SharePoint has its own backup and restore features—both in the GUI and using the STSADM or PowerShell commands. These tools allow you to back up the whole farm, a site collection, web applications, or even a list or library. The GUI has some easy-to-use steps found in Central Administration, while the STSADM and PowerShell commands can be scripted, allowing for automation and scheduling.

>   **Master It**   You are getting ready to decommission a site collection and want to make a final backup of it in case it needs to be referenced or resurrected in the future. This archive needs to be done in such a fashion that you are able to restore it to a different SharePoint server (in case this server is gone by the time the archive is needed). How do you go about creating this final backup?

Back up separate SharePoint components.   In addition to SharePoint's built-in backup and recovery options, you can back up individual components of SharePoint using a variety of different tools. At a more granular level than a site collection, it is possible to use import/export to back up individual lists, libraries, and subsites. You can also use the backup features of IIS and SQL to back up SharePoint's IIS Web Sites and SQL databases.

>   **Master It**   After a large amount of work was done to a list on the SharePoint server, one of the users has accidentally deleted it. It's been too soon for the list to be backed up using the nightly STSADM script, but there's a possibility the list was exported to a backup file after it was created. What's the first step you should take to recover this deleted list?

Recover from disaster.   You can recover SharePoint from catastrophe in several ways. The SharePoint built-in back up has an option to perform a catastrophic backup (and back up the entire farm). IIS Web Sites can be moved to a new web front-end server, and SQL databases can be transferred to a new database server. Finally, Windows Server Backup is available to completely rebuild the Windows Server (and SharePoint), even to disparate hardware.

>   **Master It**   It's been raining, the ceiling has burst, and your server room has just been given an impromptu shower. Now the SharePoint server is a smoking, dripping ruin, and SharePoint is "down for routine maintenance." You had a full system image backup and a recent SharePoint catastrophic backup on an external hard drive (stored offsite at your house) and access to a freshly installed Windows server at your co-location site. What's the fastest way to get SharePoint back up and running?

Part 4

Special Topics in SharePoint Foundation 2010

Chapter 14

STSADM and PowerShell

Why should you learn about managing SharePoint Foundation with STSADM and PowerShell? Some tasks are unique to the command line; others, such as bulk management, require scripting to perform efficiently. (And you can impress your friends at parties.)

Using the command line is still a very useful and powerful approach for many SharePoint activities, so much so that Microsoft continues to provide the traditional, DOS-like STSADM. With SharePoint Foundation, however, Microsoft officially recommends that you use PowerShell, because it intends to deprecate STSADM in the future. To that end, Microsoft has developed a full set of PowerShell cmdlets (pronounced "commandlets").

This chapter will explain what PowerShell is and then teach you how to use it. Throughout the chapter, you'll review the tasks that have to be done via the command line (whether PowerShell or STSADM). Much of the early content will be focused on how to use PowerShell in general (using SharePoint-specific commands as examples).

In this chapter, you'll learn to

- ◆ Start and use the SharePoint 2010 Management Shell

- ◆ Understand the basic syntax for PowerShell cmdlets

- ◆ Use pipelining to make cmdlets work well together

- ◆ Use basic PowerShell scripting techniques

- ◆ Perform common SharePoint Foundation management tasks using PowerShell

PowerShell or STSADM?

So, which should you use, PowerShell or STSADM? That's a tough question and is one with no definite answer. For some management tasks, the flexibility of PowerShell makes it a clear winner. Scripting is easier using PowerShell, and using it you can access every property and method of every object. That is something STSADM has never been able to do. However, for some tasks, the STSADM command is actually simpler and easier than achieving the same result using a PowerShell cmdlet. STSADM also requires less permission configuration.

The reality is that for many administrators, PowerShell is still a bit of a mystery. It's been around for a few years, but many of us haven't had the time, the need, or (perhaps) the inclination to learn what on the surface can appear pretty daunting. Many of the admins I've encountered who do use PowerShell have come to it for one of two reasons:

◆ They were experienced scripters/developers who are familiar with complex command environments—DOS, VBScript, JScript, or others—and were keen to learn a new one and probably able to get the hang of it pretty quickly.

◆ They were forced to use it by a particular product. Microsoft Exchange is a good example of this. Starting with Microsoft Exchange 2007, the only command-line interface to manage Exchange is PowerShell. And there are many things that can be done only via PowerShell. (SharePoint could have gone that route, but the SharePoint team obviously decided a phased approach would work better for them.)

If you don't happen to match either profile, there is a good chance you have not had any significant need to use PowerShell. This chapter is for you. It assumes that you have very little/no experience, so it starts from the beginning. If you are already familiar with PowerShell, you may want to focus on the later sections, covering specific SharePoint activities.

It's important to remember that even though Microsoft intends to deprecate STSADM in the future, it hasn't done so just yet. So, although the focus of this chapter is on the PowerShell cmdlets, I will discuss both approaches (PowerShell and STSADM) and—where appropriate—make a specific recommendation as to which tool is better suited to a given task.

Starting the SharePoint 2010 Management Shell

For those familiar with Microsoft's increasing use of dedicated PowerShells for specific products, it will come as no surprise that with SharePoint Foundation 2010, it is important to start the correct shell in the correct manner. If the correct shell isn't loaded, the SharePoint cmdlets are not available to you.

The correct console to start is the SharePoint 2010 Management Shell, found in the Microsoft SharePoint Products 2010 folder in your Start menu (Figure 14.1). If you have run this console recently, you may also find it pinned to the root of your Start menu.

FIGURE 14.1
Starting the Share-Point 2010 Management Shell

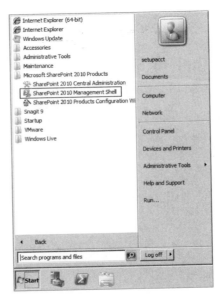

> **PIN IT UP!**
>
> Opening the console by choosing All Programs from the Start menu and then opening a folder in the list is tedious. That's why most people right-click the items they use often and choose Pin To Start Menu or Pin To Taskbar. If the SharePoint 2010 Management Shell is pinned to the Start menu, it shows up right at the top of the menu. You may also notice that some extra options pop out from the pinned shortcut when you select SharePoint 2010 Management Shell, most notably Run As Administrator. Assuming you have the right to run the shell, you may need to choose this option if permissions error messages appear within the shell when you try to start it and you have UAC enabled. If UAC is not turned on, this won't be necessary. As a matter of fact, it helps if UAC is turned off on the server on which you are administering SharePoint, especially if you are using PowerShell, because UAC can cause permission issues on its own.
>
> Another option that appears in the pinned shortcut callout is Windows PowerShell Help. This is a useful help file, but it provides general PowerShell assistance and makes no specific mention of SharePoint.

How do you know you have the right console open? That's easy. The SharePoint 2010 Management Shell uses white text on a black background, and the title bar of the shell window normally reads "Administrator: SharePoint 2010 Management Shell."

If you chose the basic PowerShell shortcut instead (which is easy enough to do), your management shell will probably consist of white text on a *blue* background, and the title bar will read "Administrator: Windows PowerShell." If that has happened, simply close the incorrect shell and open the correct shell. Failing that, it is possible to load the SharePoint 2010 PowerShell cmdlets manually by using the following command:

```
Add-PSSnapin Microsoft.SharePoint.PowerShell
```

Now you know you have the right shell, but before you can dive in and start managing, you will need to make sure you have the rights to manage SharePoint via PowerShell.

Security Requirements to Use PowerShell

To run the SharePoint cmdlets, the account being used to run the shell needs to be granted the appropriate permissions. For shell management, those permissions are configured at two levels. The account needs to have appropriate permissions to access the various databases that the cmdlets will be accessing, and it also needs to have the correct permissions within the SharePoint environment itself.

Permissions for Shell Management

Any account you want to use to run the SharePoint PowerShell cmdlets needs three settings to use PowerShell:

♦ It has to be added to the WSS_Admin_WPG local groups on all the Web Front End (WFE) servers. This occurs automatically if the account is a farm administrator. Basically, the account should be a member of the Farm Administrators group for SharePoint.

◆ It must be an owner of the databases that the account will need to administer. It also helps to be added to the SharePoint_Shell_Access role on those databases.

◆ To do many administrative tasks, the account also needs to be a local administrator for the SharePoint server (or a domain admin for the domain).

PowerShell has a command that enables accounts or security groups to be shell admins, configuring the settings listed above:

```
Add-SpShellAdmin
```

This command does two things. First, if you simply run the command without specifying any particular database, it will give that account or security group shell admin rights to the configuration database for the farm alone and add the account to the WSS_Admin_WPG local group on the SharePoint server, if necessary (but not add it explicitly to the Farm Administrators group). Second, if you also specify content databases in the command, it will also give the account or security group shell admin rights to those databases as well as the configuration database.

This lets you specify which accounts will be able to administer which content databases (and therefore web applications) in PowerShell. All shell admins must have rights to the configuration database.

Keep in mind that this means PowerShell shell admins will have incredibly dangerous power over the SQL databases used by SharePoint, because they will truly own the databases in SQL. Therefore, they can rename, delete, detach, and so on, any of those databases. This is not a right to give an untrusted co-worker.

To make matters a little more confusing, you must be a shell admin to be able to run the shell admin command to make more shell admins. So, how does that work? You can't have a shell admin without a shell admin, but first you need to make a shell admin.

Well, the account that will create more shell admins has to have ownership of all the databases used by SharePoint and be a farm administrator. In addition, that account needs to be allowed to add other user accounts to database roles in SQL, meaning that it has to also have the securityadmin role in SQL. (Other than running the Add-SpShellAdmin command itself, other shell admins don't need to have that role.) And there is only one account that owns everything and has the securityadmin role in SQL—the farm account. You should never, ever log in with the farm account under normal circumstances, but in this case, it is the only account that is automatically the shell admin for the farm by default.

The farm account would need to be added to the local administrators group for the SharePoint server temporarily (it must be temporary); then you'd log in with it. At that point, you can open the SharePoint 2010 Management Shell (usually just called the management shell or management console), and then you can run the Add-SpShellAdmins cmdlet.

Your other option is to take an account that is a farm administrator and a local admin of the SharePoint server, make it the owner of all SharePoint databases, give it the securityadmin role in SQL, log in with it, and use it to run the Add-SpShellAdmin cmdlet instead.

This is a more complicated way of creating a super shell admin (an account that is allowed to create other shell admins and give them rights to any and all existing SharePoint databases), but it avoids logging in as the farm account.

STANDALONE VS. COMPLETE, AND A WORD ABOUT SITE COLLECTION ADMINISTRATORS

You may be running PowerShell on a standalone server. If that is the case, the installation or setup account will have enough power to be the super shell admin for the server. This makes it much easier to create other shell admins and practice using PowerShell.

If you are using PowerShell in a farm implementation, then the details mentioned earlier, concerning who owns what database, become important. PowerShell for SharePoint is rather new, and ideally, in later versions, this requirement that admins need full ownership of databases, and its security issue, will go away.

Something else to consider is that if you have a site collection administrator whom you want to give command-line access to work on their site collection, it is not good security to let them work in PowerShell, because they'll have to own the entire content database where their site collection is held. This gives them the right to administer the web application or delete the database in SQL, as well as simply to administer everyone else's site collections in that database.

So, that is why you should not give up on STSADM. With STSADM, the site collection administrator can navigate to the BIN folder in the SharePoint root, open a command prompt (they do have to be an admin on the SharePoint server and work locally there), and run STSADM commands. It will work because, as long as they only use commands that affect their site collection, they will have the permission to do so. They don't need extensive, additional permissions.

Once you are logged in as the account that can run the shell admin cmdlet, it's time to try using the cmdlet.

FARM ADMINISTRATION ONLY

To add a shell admin that can do simple farm administrator commands, such as starting or stopping a service, they only need the right to work in the configuration database itself. So if you want to just give shell admin rights to the configuration database, you simply would run the following on an account or security group that is a farm administrator:

```
Add-SpShellAdmin -UserName <domain\accountorsecuritygroup>
```

The cmdlet is `Add-SpShellAdmin`, with the parameter (or switch as it's commonly called) of `-username`. This will add an account or security group as a shell admin to the farm (it is good form to specify the domain name with the account or security group name, but it's not required).

ALL DATABASES IN THE FARM

It gets a little more complicated if you want to add an account as a shell admin with permission to additional databases (which is kind of the point of administering SharePoint).

One of the reasons is that you are running PowerShell commands without really learning PowerShell yet (which isn't that uncommon with PowerShell, unfortunately). So, this section includes a brief overview of how the commands work and their syntax, but "PowerShell Primer" later in the chapter will go more completely into the details.

So, to make a shell admin that can administer other databases in the farm, you need to first find out the name (and the GUID) of the databases and then specify in the Add-SPShellAdmin command that you want to use those databases (as well as the configuration database, added by default when you run the command). However, if you want to cut to the chase and just add all the databases for the shell admin, you need to first have PowerShell get that list of databases (and their GUIDs) and then pass it to the Add_SpShellAdmin command. This is called *pipelining* and is covered in more detail in the "About Pipelines" sidebar.

To first get the list of SharePoint databases, you run the following (remember that you should be logged in and running PowerShell with an account that is already a shell account):

```
Get-SpDatabase
```

That will generate a list of the SharePoint databases for the farm this server is part of (and if it's a standalone, then its local databases).

To run that command and pass it to the shell admin command, you put a pipeline (|) between the two commands, passing the results of the first command to the second one. It really saves time.

That command would look like this:

```
Get-SpDatabase | Add-SpShellAdmin -UserName <domain\accountorsecuritygroup>
```

This will add the account or group you specified as a shell admin of all the SharePoint databases.

In a quick example of adding shell admins, I am going to make the farm account a local administrator on my SharePoint server, log in with that account, and then add a security group as a shell admin. In my example, that will be a group called *spadmins* that I set up in AD for this exercise, and my account, *shareadmin*, is a member so I can log in as that account to use PowerShell from that point on. Using the security group rather than adding a single account will allow me to simply add users (or remove them) from the group in Active Directory, rather than having to run this cmdlet every time I want to add a shell admin.

To do that, I would use the following cmdlet:

```
Get-SpDatabase | Add-SpShellAdmin -UserName dem0tek\spadmins
```

If you want to check to see if an account has been added correctly as a shell admin account, you can run the following command:

```
Get-SpShellAdmin
```

It will generate a list, as most "get" commands do, of the current shell admins available for the SharePoint implementation. You can see in Figure 14.2 that the farm account and the security group you've added are listed (as well as the Get-SpDatabase cmdlet's list of databases for the farm).

Being able to check to see if an account is a shell admin is important. Often if you get an error because a command cannot be run, check to make sure the account you are logged in with is a shell admin, and make sure that it has the correct permissions to the correct databases.

To remove shell admins, use Remove-SpShellAdmin (specifying the username parameter of course). Something to note about Remove-SpShellAdmin is that it removes the designated user from the SharePoint_Shell_Admin role on the SQL databases (thus removing the permissions), but it does not "clean up" the Windows groups. The user account remains in the WSS_Admin_WPG group on the SharePoint server, as well as listed in the security node of the database properties in SQL. If you want to fully clear out the changes the SpShellAdmin command left, you will need to remember to clean up the group memberships and SQL security.

FIGURE 14.2

Getting a list of SharePoint databases and adding and viewing shell admins in the Management Shell console

ABOUT PIPELINES

Pipelining (or *Piping*) is a key feature of PowerShell, one of the things that make it very useful. Pipelining is the ability to take the output of one cmdlet and feed it directly into a second cmdlet. The "command" used to add shell admins to all databases was actually two cmdlets being pipelined.

There is no limit to the number of cmdlets you can put in a single pipeline. In the previous case, the Get-SpDatabase cmdlet returns all the SharePoint databases in the farm. Those database GUIDs were then fed as input into the Add-SpShelladmin cmdlet. Since the input was coming from the pipeline, we did not have to type in the -database switch for Add-SpShelladmin. PowerShell was given all the information about the databases, found what it needed (the GUIDs of each database), and used it as needed without requiring you to type in a -database switch and specify each database GUID individually.

Here's the great thing, though—if there are multiple results being fed into a cmdlet, then the next one in the pipeline will run multiple times. Get-SpDatabase with no other switches will return a list of all the databases. If you pipe that into Add-SpShellAdmin, then Add-SpShellAdmin will run once for each database coming down the pipeline.

MEASURE TWICE, CUT ONCE

One tip for the PowerShell newcomer: until you get confident in what you're doing, you may put yourself at ease by testing your command in stages. To test the example from Figure 14.2, you would run the commands in the following order:

```
Get-Spdatabase
Get-SpDatabase |Add-SpShellAdmin -UserName dem0tek\spadmins
Get-SPShellAdmin
```

After each command, you can check to make sure you are getting the result you expect or need. The first command would return a list of all SharePoint databases, displayed as a table. The second command, as you know, passes the databases to the Add-SPShellAdmin command and adds the user as a shell admin to those databases. The third confirms that the user was added as a shell admin. If you had any issues with either of the first two commands, you can confirm it with the last command.

As you gain experience with PowerShell cmdlets, you may find that you don't need to do this kind of checking as often. Having said that, I still do this when I'm dealing with specific cmdlets that I'm not familiar with.

Some of the Databases in the Farm

There might be circumstances in which you don't want to simply give an account or security group shell admin rights to all the databases in the farm but to specific databases. This means you would have to run the `Add-SpShellAdmin` command with the `-username` and `-database` parameters. The `-database` parameter requires that you specify the *identity* of the database, which in this case is, unfortunately, the GUID of the database.

So if you ran a `Get_SpDatabase` command to list the databases, you could mark the GUID listed for a particular database and copy it. Then type out the `Add-SpShellAdmin` command, pasting the GUID as the identity for the database. Here's an example of the command:

```
Add-SpShellAdmin -UserName <domain\accountorsecuritygroup> -Database <GUID>
```

This would let you specify just that database (and of course, whenever you run the command, the user account is added as an owner with SharePoint_Shell_Access role to the configuration database as well).

But as you learned in the "About Pipelines" sidebar, there is a much easier way to get the GUID of all databases and simply pass it to the `Add-SpShellAdmin` command. In the following example, first look at the list of available databases. This gives you a chance to see the exact spelling of all the database names.

Next, you need to pass the database information to the `Add-SpShellAdmin` command for just one database. Instead of doing the GUID mark and paste trick we did a moment ago, we can use a filter to narrow down what is used by the cmdlet to add shell admin rights to one database. We do this by using a cmdlet (and its syntax) we'll go into detail about later, called `Where-Object`. This cmdlet let's you get object information on something you specify with a variable and an operator. A variable, in this case is indicated by a `$_.Name`, and the operator meaning equals or equal to, is `-eq`. Again, keep in mind that filtering and variables will be covered in much more detail later in the chapter.

So if we wanted to add a user as a shell admin for one database, we could first confirm what the database names are with the syntax:

```
Get-SpDatabase
```

Then we could use the following syntax to first get a list of all the databases, then filter it down to one database, returning information about that object that can be passed to other cmdlets in the pipeline (be sure to use the braces, or squiggly brackets for this):

```
Get-SpDatabase | Where-Object {$_.Name -eq "WSS_Content"}
```

And finally, we could use this information to specify only that database be used by the `Add-SpShellAdmin` cmdlet with the following syntax:

```
Get-SpDatabase | Where-Object {$_.Name -eq "WSS_Content"} | Add-SpShellAdmin
    -UserName "dem0tek\spadmins"
```

This pipeline will add the spadmins group to only that database as a shell admin. (Keep in mind that we will be covering both the `where-object` cmdlet and variables in detail later in the chapter.)

SharePoint Permission for Administration

Configuring the database permissions for your administration account will allow you to open the shell and run the cmdlets. But it *does not* provide anyone else with a security back door. You basically have configured the account with the right to try. When a specific cmdlet is executed, it is still subject to the SharePoint permissions within the service, web application, site collection, site, or whatever you are attempting to manage. If the administrator does not have the rights within SharePoint to do something, the cmdlet (or STSADM for that matter) will return some kind of Access Denied error. If the account is not a farm administrator, they still can't do farm administrative commands.

PowerShell Primer

Although this single chapter isn't meant to be a comprehensive PowerShell tutorial, it's useful to take a quick look at the basics. Once you feel comfortable with how PowerShell works in general, you'll be better able to focus on the outcome you need, rather than how you got there. If you already have a good grounding in PowerShell, feel free to skip this and move on to "STSADM.EXE Basics." However, if you're new to PowerShell, this should give you a start.

Cmdlet Structure

PowerShell uses a basic "verb-noun" structure for most of its cmdlets so that they look like this:

```
Get-SPweb
new-spsite
Set-SpList
```

PowerShell is not case-sensitive, and it is reasonably common to see cmdlets with various capitalization formats. If you were to type any of these three cmdlets, they would work. When reading documentation about PowerShell, you are likely to see the cmdlets capitalized in one of the three formats shown here. In the first example, the first letter of both the verb and the noun are capitalized. In the second, nothing is capitalized. The final example capitalizes the verb and key letters of the noun component. Many times the noun part of a cmdlet is two or three words run together with no spaces, so each word is capitalized, making it easier to read. In this book, we'll use the third convention, because it's easiest to read in this format, but when you're actually typing these commands, it doesn't really matter.

You will find that there is a reasonably small set of commonly used verbs, such as Get, New, and Set. Cmdlets that start with Get are mostly used to retrieve (or get) information. For example, Get-SPWeb is used to retrieve all the SharePoint sites in a specified site collection. You can see an example of this first command in Figure 14.3 in which the identity of the site collection is specified as http://spf2.

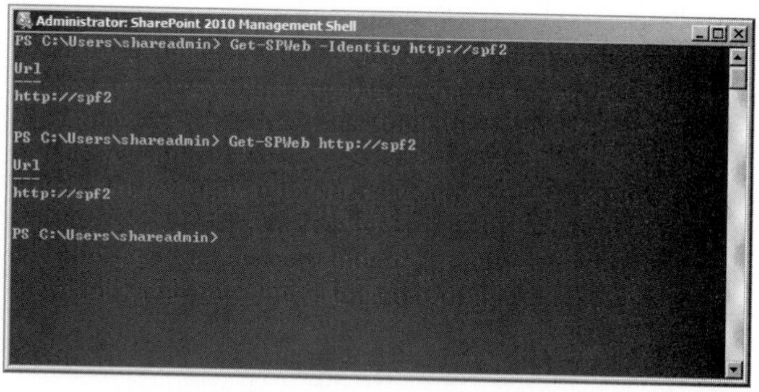

FIGURE 14.3
Getting the sites in a site collection

Depending on the number of results (and the whims of the SharePoint development team at Microsoft), the presentation of the results is likely to be in either a list or a table. In Figure 14.3, the results are displayed in a table format. I will discuss ways to manipulate output later in the chapter.

The `Set` verb is usually paired with `Get`. By that I mean that if there is a `Get`-something cmdlet, there is likely to be a `Set`-something cmdlet as well. `Get` cmdlets retrieve objects and their settings, and `Set` cmdlets allow you to modify the objects and their settings.

DUDE, WHERE'S MY SWITCH?

Take a close look at Figure 14.3. You will notice that `Get-SpWeb` was actually executed twice—once with the `-identity` switch and once without. In both cases, the required identity (in this case the URL of a top level site) was provided.

Most Get and Set cmdlets (as well as other cmdlets) have this switch. It allows you to specify items you want to retrieve or configure or work against without having to write complex queries. Feed an acceptable ID into the cmdlet, and it will execute against whatever has been identified.

In an effort to be user-friendly, most PowerShell cmdlets that have an `-identity` switch allow you to specify the identity in two other ways. Instead of `-identity`, you can use `-id` (but note that tab completion pulls up `-identity`); the final option is not to include a switch at all but to make sure the required data is listed after the cmdlet and before any other switches. In that instance, the data is assumed to be the identity data and is treated as such. This is one of the reasons we can pipeline commands: if the correct data is fed into a cmdlet—either manually or via the previous command in the pipeline—PowerShell takes and uses that data correctly, with or without the switch being present.

That is what you are seeing in the second cmdlet in Figure 14.3. In this book, you should always see the `-identity` switch listed in any examples, but it's very common for it not to be directly shown, especially in cmdlet examples on the Internet.

It's important to remember that most switches *don't* work this way; they need to be properly typed in and fed the appropriate data. But there are some switches that do.

You will also find that it's common for a given noun to have a set of commands, each with a different verb. `Get-SPWeb` and `Set-SPWeb` are just two of a set of cmdlets that all have the SPWeb noun. You can see in Figure 14.4 the entire set of cmdlets that have the SPWeb noun (I used the `Get-Command` cmdlet to list anything that ends with SPWeb; I'll be mentioning it in more detail in the next section).

FIGURE 14.4

The SPWeb cmdlets

You don't have be a SharePoint 2010 guru to make a pretty good guess what each of these cmdlets does. What you'll learn is that knowing what cmdlet to use, while important, is really only half the battle. Just like any command interface, the devil is in the details. In this case, the details are the many switches that a cmdlet may have.

Most SharePoint cmdlets have additional parameters (or switches) that are required for them to complete their task and a number of optional switches as well. These switches all start with a minus sign (-) and do not require a colon after them, just a space and the required data. The presence of the next switch's - is enough of a separator. You can see an example of a full cmdlet and its switches in all their glory in Figure 14.5.

FIGURE 14.5

Creating a new subsite with PowerShell

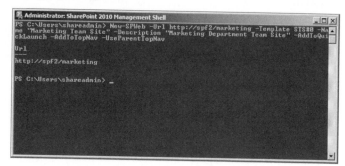

When you look at Figure 14.5, you can see that several switches were used to provide all the information needed to create a new subsite under `http://spf2`. The `-url` switch provides the URL that you want to assign to the new site, followed by switches for the site template to use, the name, the description, and three navigation options. It's interesting to note that some of these switches (`-url`, `-template`, and others) require data, and some of them (`-AddToTopNav` for example) just have to be listed. This is all very much like the syntax used by STSADM.

TAB COMPLETION IS YOUR FRIEND

Most cmdlets have lots of switches, just as most STSADM operations do. But one of the things that makes PowerShell more user friendly is *tab completion*. Simply put, this feature reduces the amount of time you spend searching for cmdlets and their arguments and also reduces typos in your cmdlets by helping you complete the cmdlet. If you have a PowerShell shell open, type `get-` and then press Tab.

This will bring up the first Get cmdlet, and for each time you Tab, it cycles through the set alphabetically. When you get to the one you want, press the spacebar to select it, and then finish typing in what you need to get it to run.

The more of the command you know, the better, because PowerShell cycles through all the cmdlets that match what you've typed. Try typing **get-sp** and then hitting Tab. You'll start cycling through all the SharePoint `get-` cmdlets starting from those that begin with `get-sp`.

Once you have the cmdlet you want, type - after it and then press Tab again. Now it cycles through all the switches for the cmdlet you chose.

If you know the first few letters of the switch you want to use, type the first two or three letters of the switch and hit Tab. If there happen to be a few different switches that start the same, you might have to cycle through them, but this is pretty unlikely.

Although this doesn't fix every problem, it does make using PowerShell-based management shells considerably easier.

Getting Help

Even for experienced administrators, the new PowerShell-based management shells can be somewhat intimidating. You often forget that all the management tools (command-based or otherwise) you now use without a second thought were new to you at some point, and there was probably a steep initial learning curve. And as the tools evolved, what you needed to learn was incremental. When an entirely new tool is introduced into the mix, one that at first glance doesn't look or behave like anything you're familiar with, it's somewhat daunting. That's why it's important to understand where and how to get assistance.

Many external sources of guidance are available. Books have been written, blogs composed, and videos recorded. Microsoft provides a comprehensive reference on its TechNet site. You can find detailed SharePoint cmdlet help as well as overall PowerShell help. For SharePoint Foundation 2010 cmdlet help, go to the TechNet article "Windows PowerShell for SharePoint Foundation 2010." For a general PowerShell reference, look in the Scripting, Windows PowerShell area of the TechNet Library. In addition to those two references, I'm particularly fond of www.PowerShell.com. I've found it to be a great reference, especially when I want to do more complex tasks, such as writing scripts.

In addition to all of these resources, there is built-in help available when you are in the throes of PowerShell. Use the following cmdlets to get help:

To see a complete alphabetical list of cmdlets available when you are in any PowerShell window, use this:

```
Get-command
```

If you want to know the commands for a specific verb, you can use the same command but tell it which verb you want using a basic search string. For example, to see the list of Get cmdlets, use this:

```
Get-command get-*
```

If you want to see a list of all the SharePoint-specific cmdlets, you need to be aware that the noun part of each cmdlet starts with the letters SP. Once you know that, you can retrieve the list of these cmdlets by using the following cmdlet:

```
Get-command *-SP*
```

If the results go by too quickly, you can redirect the output using a traditional redirection of the output to a text file instead of the screen.

```
Get-command *-SP* > c:\spcommands.txt
```

Once that completes, you can use whatever text editor you like to see the results. You can redirect the screen output of any PowerShell cmdlet in this manner.

Assuming you have figured out what cmdlet you want to run, you may still want help on all the details for that command and its switches. All the PowerShell cmdlets have help built into them. The quick and easy way to access it is to run the cmdlet with the -? switch. This will give you all the switches for the cmdlet and a basic description.

Figure 14.6 illustrates this type of help for the set-spweb cmdlet.

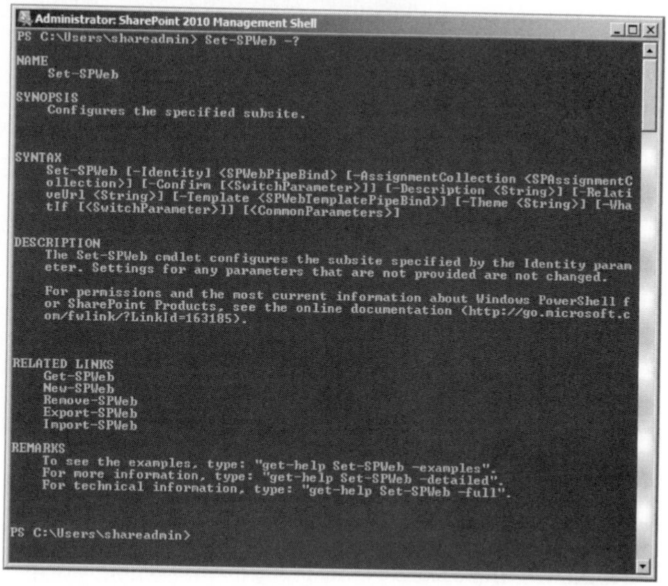

FIGURE 14.6

Inline help using the -? switch

If you look closely at Figure 14.6, you can see that this command is used to configure a subsite, and you'll also notice all the switches, which each starts with -. Square brackets around a switch indicate that it is optional. In angle brackets after each switch is a description of the type of data needed for that switch.

This is great help if you are somewhat familiar with what the cmdlet does and how it does it but need a quick refresher on the switch names and details.

You may have also noticed that at the very bottom of the help are a couple of suggestions for getting more help. Each of these suggestions uses get-help. This cmdlet exposes more detailed and complete help. Figure 14.7 illustrates the detailed help available for Set-SPWeb using this expanded help option. There's too much detail to show on one screen's worth of space, but you can clearly see how it details what information is required for each switch, and if you scroll down, there are examples of common usage of the cmdlet.

When working in PowerShell, the help you need really is right at your fingertips; you just have to remember to use it!

FIGURE 14.7
Retrieving
detailed help

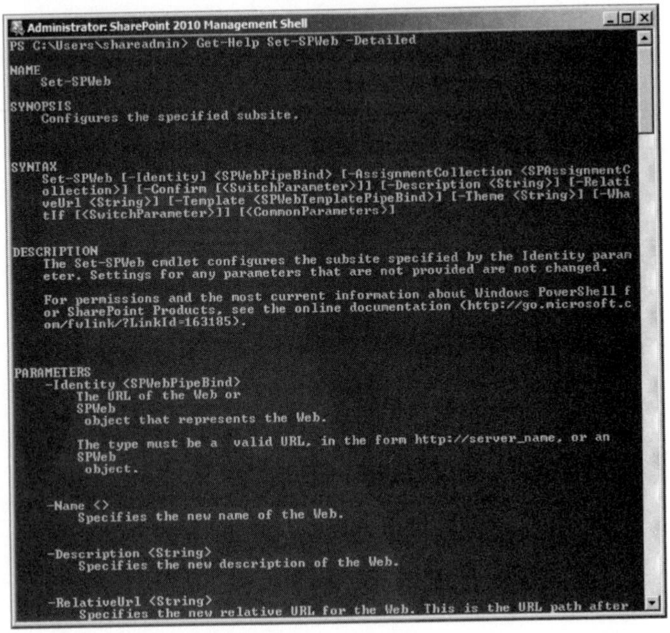

Output

For many of the commands that you run, there isn't much data returned to you (see the sidebar "No News Can Be Good News"). The main exceptions to this are the cmdlets that use Get. The purpose of these commands is to query and retrieve objects and data, so they actually generate some data to output. Obviously, we want to see the data on-screen or perhaps rerouted to a text file for documentation purposes. But we can actually do much more with it. So let's take a moment to look at what you can do to and with your output.

Data vs. Objects

One of the most important but least noticeable features of PowerShell is that when you run Get cmdlets, they return an object. STSADM just returns data, usually text. If you're among a large part of the population not familiar with programming or scripting, you might be wondering what the difference is. Here's a simple analogy.

Imagine that you said to two people, "Hey, I need to learn about a soccer ball. Would you help me out?" The people you asked bolt off and return a short while later.

The first person did some research and has come back to you with a nicely written report on soccer balls. It tells you size and weight statistics, gives a list of manufacturers, describes what it's used for, and so on. Now, this is useful to you. You can learn about soccer balls from this.

The second person ran off and bought a soccer ball and brought it back to you. They also picked up a little bit of information about the ball and made sure it was in the box too, as well as a pamphlet on how to kick a soccer ball. You have data, but more importantly you have a ball that you can feel, inflate, deflate, kick, and anything else you want to do. You have an object.

The first person provided you with data about soccer balls. And that data seems to be useful. Great. You now know more about soccer balls than you would have expected. But to have something you can kick around, manipulate, and experiment with—that gives you so much more opportunity.

STSADM outputs data in the form of text strings. This is great for reporting or for documenting. But it does have one key drawback: you only get the data that is presented to you. There's no easy way to get more or different data. Someone else has decided, on your behalf, what was important for you to know.

PowerShell retrieves objects and returns them, and their properties, to you. Just as with STSADM, someone has made a decision about what properties to display and how to display them. But here's the kicker—you can change what gets displayed, and you can use the objects as inputs to the next cmdlet (remember pipelines?).

CHANGING THE DISPLAY FORMAT

The most basic way to manipulate the output of a cmdlet is to change which properties are displayed and how they are displayed. Each cmdlet has a default format that was decided by its developer, and that decision revolves around two things: which properties to display and how to display them. This usually results in a table format with somebody's idea of the most useful or common properties being displayed. Much of the time, this will be enough, but not all of the time.

To change these settings, you use the four Format cmdlets: Format-List, Format-Table, Format-Wide, and Format-Custom. At this time, you probably only need to worry about using Format-List and Format-Table.

Format cmdlets need at least one other cmdlet to feed them data. In other words, they need to be the last cmdlet in the pipeline. Figure 14.8 demonstrates the use of Format-Wide, in this case being fed the objects returned by Get-SPWebApplication.

FIGURE 14.8

A basic use of Format cmdlets

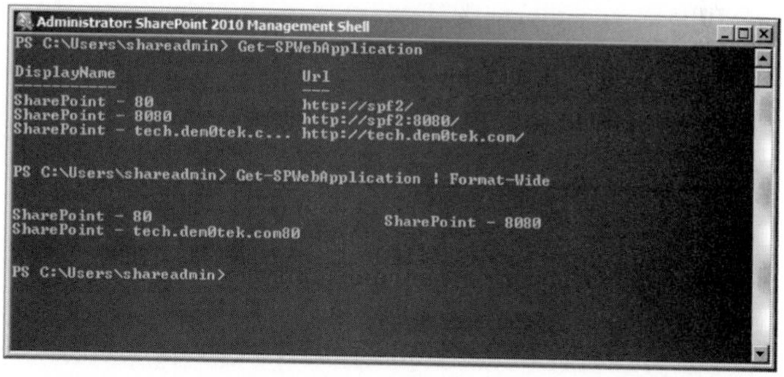

Format-List presents every property of the object—too much to include in a single screenshot (but my favorite of the Format cmdlets). To see it in action, pipeline Get-SPWebApplication into it.

Format-Custom allows you to call custom display formatting that has already been defined and registered.

If you want to see a list of just the properties and methods (things you can do to the object) for the SPWebApplication, without any data run this:

```
Get-SPWebApplication | Get-Member
```

The Get-Member cmdlet lets you see the properties and methods of an object (since you can't right click an object in PowerShell). This will give you a very long and detailed list (too long to effectively capture in a single screenshot) of all the properties and methods for the object in your variable or piped command.

You've probably noticed in Figure 14.8 that the default formatting was basically a table format, so formatting didn't really manipulate the output much. If you use the Format cmdlets without any additional parameters, they will show the default properties. If you know the names of the properties you want to display, you can tell PowerShell that, and it will display those instead. You have access to every property of the result set. If you want to display a property, you most likely can.

Figure 14.9 demonstrates how this is done, displaying the owners and all subsites of all the site collections in http://spf2. Note that the properties listed by Format-List are comma-separated (in this case, URL, Owner, and AllWebs).

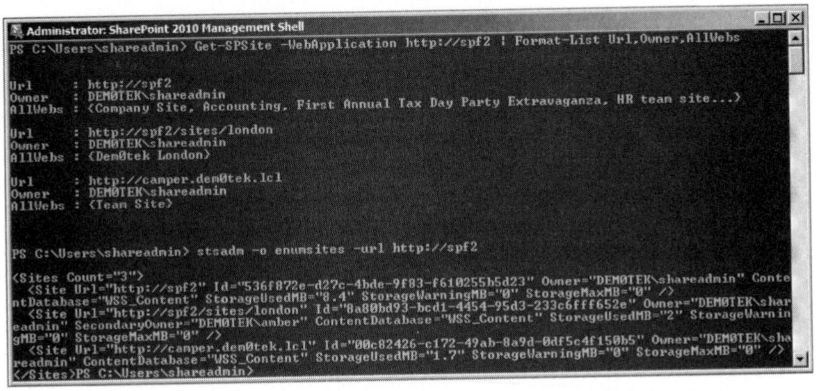

FIGURE 14.9
Controlling the output of Format-List vs. using STSADM to enumerate sites

When you compare the formatted output from Get-SPSite to the STSADM equivalent, which is the second command shown in Figure 14.9, you start to see the benefits of being passed objects and the use of the Format cmdlets.

There is one caveat to using the Format cmdlets: *they must be the last position in the pipeline*. If they are not, any cmdlets that occur later in the pipeline may not get the full result set.

ALIASES

In this book, we're using the full cmdlet names and full switch names, but you should be aware that you don't always have to. Earlier I mentioned that the -identity switch can be shortened to -id. This is because PowerShell supports *aliases*, which allow you to use a shorter cmdlet or switch, making it a little easier to work in PowerShell.

In the case of the switches, the alias was written into the code for the cmdlet. But the cmdlets themselves have aliases. There are several built-in aliases, and if you want to get a full list, run alias (which, interestingly enough, is an alias for get-alias).

The aliases we are concerned with at the moment have to do with manipulating our output. See the following table for a listing of common output aliases and their corresponding cmdlets.

We will continue to use the full cmdlets, but don't be surprised to see these aliases when you are looking at other documentation.

OUTPUT ALIASES

ALIAS	CMDLET
Fl	Format-List
Ft	Format-Table
Fw	Format-Wide
Where	Where-Object
Sort	Sort-Object

SORTING THE OUTPUT

The default output for most Get cmdlets sorts alphabetically by the name property (or equivalent, depending on what you're retrieving). Using Sort-Object, you can modify that behavior:

```
Sort-Object <OptionalProperty> [-descending]
```

Figure 14.10 demonstrates the most common uses of Sort-Object. The first command returns the list of web applications with default sorting. The second line uses Sort-Object to change it from ascending to descending. Note the use of the -descending switch. If you don't put that switch in, it will sort ascending by whatever properties you listed or the default property. The third sorts by the web application ID property (and you've pipelined to format-table so you can see what the ID is). The fourth demonstrates that you can sort on any property that is returned, even if you choose not to display it on the screen. This is something you need to be a little bit careful with. In Figure 14.10, it doesn't make any significant difference, but depending on the data that is being returned, it could. It's likely to cause confusion for whoever is looking at the output. Results could be ordered according to logic that is not readily apparent.

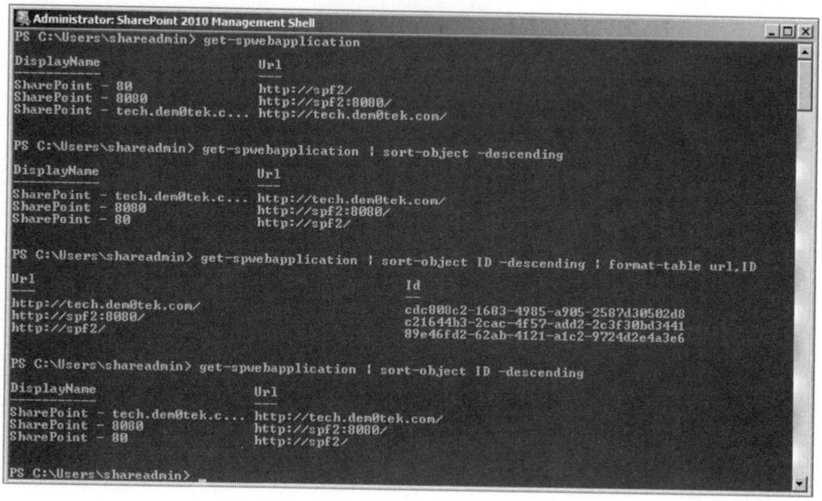

FIGURE 14.10
Using
Sort-Object
in a pipeline

FILTERING THE OUTPUT

Choosing properties to display and how to sort the results is all very useful. But there are also times when you need to reduce the result to display or pipeline. For example, what if you wanted to know which sites were based on the Team Site template (STS#0)?

There are two possible ways to do achieve this—one you can be sure will work, and one is somewhat hit-or-miss.

```
Where-Object {FilterString}
Get-<Noun> -Filter{FilterString}
```

Some Get cmdlets have a `-filter` switch you can use to control which objects are returned. This is a great idea. Unfortunately, not every Get cmdlet has a `-Filter` switch, and there doesn't appear to be any rhyme or reason why. You just have to check using `-?` to see whether the cmdlet you want to use has this switch.

Just to make that method even more unreliable, among the commands that do have `-filter` available, there is no consistency to the properties you can filter on. And it can be somewhat difficult to figure it out. If you miss it in the built-in help, then you're looking at some trial-and-error time.

Figure 14.11 shows three things. At the top, you can see the section of the online help for Get-SPWeb that addresses what can and can't be filtered. It's clear enough but pretty easy to miss because all the help flies by on-screen.

FIGURE 14.11
Reviewing filter switch errors

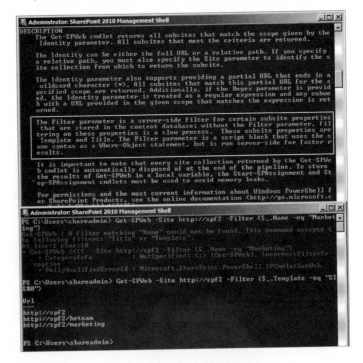

In the bottom area, you can see what the error looks like when you try to filter on a property that is not supported by the cmdlet. Fortunately, it does inform you what properties are available, so you won't waste any more time. Finally, you see the results when you use it correctly.

So, what's the other option? Use `Where-Object`.

`Where-Object` lets you filter on any property. If there is a property, you can likely filter on it. The only downside is that it is a separate cmdlet that needs to be part of a command pipeline. This cmdlet should always immediately follow the `Get` cmdlet that will provide the objects to be filtered. You can feed this further down the pipeline to sort and format the output as needed.

It's important to note that just because the property or its value isn't displayed on-screen doesn't mean you can't filter on it, and just because you filtered based on that property doesn't mean you have to show it on-screen.

How do you know what you can filter on? Remember the `get-member` cmdlet I mentioned earlier? That list of properties can be used to filter objects using Where-Object. For example, you can use this to return a list of sites in a particular site collection that are based on the Team Site template (one of the properties listed is the template used). This is done using the following command (see Figure 14.12 in the next section for an example of the results):

```
Get-SPWeb -Site http://spf2 | Where-Object {$_.WebTemplate -eq "STS"}
```

In other management shells it is not as easy to query for a property and filter results as easily as this. Knowing about the properties available for an object, and being able to filter by them is convenient and a real time saver. Although we're focusing on Where-Object and Sort-Object here, once you've mastered them, consider exploring the other two object oriented commands, Select-Object and Group-Object to additionally filter output.

BUILDING THE FILTER STRING

The `-Filter` switch and `Where-Object` both need a filter string (called a *scriptblock* in the help documentation). The syntax for the filter string is the same, regardless of which cmdlet uses it.

◆ The filter string itself is always put inside braces (aka curly brackets). This is non-negotiable. PowerShell uses the different brackets for different things, so having the correct brackets is very important:

```
{}
```

◆ The first part of the filter is the property to be evaluated (or filtered on). This takes the form `$_.<PropertyName>`, where `$_` is a placeholder (also known as a variable) that represents each object being filtered. If you wanted to filter on the Name property of an object, the filter string would look like this:

```
{$_.Name}
```

◆ The final component of a filter string is to identify what it is you're looking for, the value of the property. The structure of this part is `-comparisonoperator "Value"`. If you are looking for all the objects with a name of Saffron, your string would look like this:

```
{$_.Name -eq "Saffron"}
```

You now have a filter string that will return all objects with a name equal to Saffron. The value part of this must be in quotation marks for the filter string to execute properly. There are 12 comparison operators available, outlined in the following table.

POWERSHELL COMPARISON OPERATORS

OPERATOR	DEFINITION/USAGE
-lt	Less than
-le	Less than or equal to
-gt	Greater than
-ge	Greater than or equal to
-eq	Equal to
-ne	Not equal to
-contains	Checks whether items in a multivalue property are present
-notcontains	Checks whether items in a multivalue property are not present
-like	Uses wildcards for pattern matching
-notlike	Uses wildcards for pattern matching
-match	Uses regular expressions for pattern matching
-notmatch	Uses regular expressions for pattern matching

Using SharePoint cmdlets as a starting point, let's look at how to build and use these filter strings with some practical examples. You can test these in your own environments.

COMMON SHAREPOINT COMMANDS THAT USE FILTERS

COMMAND	EXPECTED OUTCOME
Get-SPDatabase | Where-Object {$_.Name -like "WSS_Content*"}	Returns all SharePoint databases whose name starts with *WSS_Content*
Get-SPWeb -Identity -site http://spf2 | Where-Object {$_.WebTemplate -eq "STS"}	Returns all SharePoint sites within http://spf2 that are based on the Team Site template
Get-SPWebApplication | Where-Object {$_.MaximumFileSize -gt 50}	Returns all web applications that have a maximum upload size greater than 50 MB

FILTERING ON TWO OR MORE CRITERIA

So far, you've been filtering on a single criterion. What if you need multiple criteria? One option is to pipeline the results of one Where-Object into another. This works well if your filters have a logical AND relationship. For example, if you require a list of all web applications that have a maximum upload size between 30 and 50 MB, then you have a logical AND; your target is greater than or equal to 30 MB AND less than or equal to 50 MB. If you used two `Where-Object` cmdlets, it would look like this:

```
Get-SPWebApplication | Where-Object {$_.MaximumFileSize -ge 30} | Where-Object
{$_.MaximumFileSize -le 50}
```

You can do as many of these as you need to get the appropriate result set, as long as each new criterion is a logical AND.

Especially when you are new to PowerShell, sometimes this is the most effective way to make sure you get the filter right. It's easy to test each filter as you go along. As you gain experience and confidence, you might look for a more efficient approach to achieve the same thing.

PowerShell has two other operators that can be useful in this scenario, `-and` and `-or`. You can use these operators to build a single filter string.

Combining multiple criteria into a single filter string changes the structure of the filter string slightly (as you can see in Figure 14.12). The entire filter string still needs to be encapsulated in braces, but each criterion is now enclosed inside standard parentheses, with the operator separating the criteria. To achieve the same outcome as the preceding example, you would create a pipeline that looks like this:

```
Get-SPWebApplication | Where-Object {($_.MaximumFileSize -ge 30) -and ($_.
MaximumFileSize -le 50)}
```

You'll notice that inside the parentheses, the structure of the filter string has not changed.

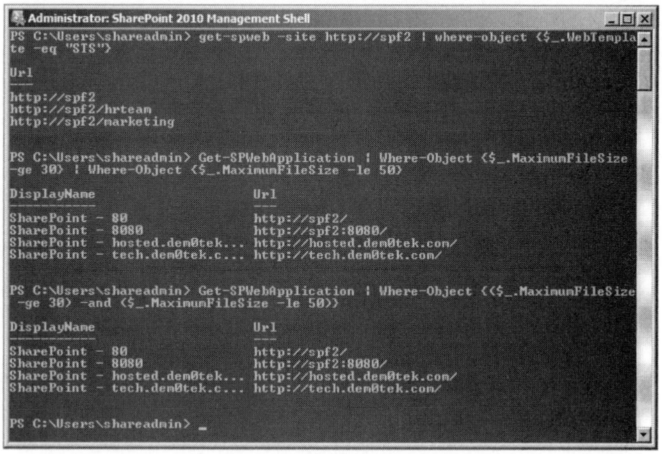

FIGURE 14.12
Filtering with
Where-Object
cmdlets

SharePoint Configuration with PowerShell

So far, all you've done is retrieve objects and data, and that is very useful. But there is more to PowerShell than that. At some point, you will probably need to configure SharePoint. Fortunately for us, for every `Get` cmdlet there is usually a `Set` cmdlet, which allows you configure objects.

The syntax for most of these cmdlets is straightforward:

```
Set-<Noun> -Identity <objectid> -<settingname> <value>
```

Clear as mud, right? Take a look at this command to set the size limit to 200 MB for a site collection:

```
Set-SPSite -Identity http://spf2 -MaxSize 200MB
```

If you compare the two, you can see the structure a little more clearly. In that cmdlet, you adjusted only one setting. Unless specifically prohibited from doing so (and it's rare but not completely unheard of), you can configure multiple settings in a single cmdlet, as shown next. This cmdlet sets the storage limit and the warning limit for the site collection:

```
Set-SPSite -Identity http://spf2 -MaxSize 200MB -WarningSize 175MB
```

This may be the first time you've run across it, but PowerShell is good with disk size calculations. In these set commands, you can put the size limits in whatever scale you want (KB/MB/GB) as long as you tell PowerShell. This would work with any switch that requires storage/memory data.

The real questions are, what can you configure with a specific cmdlet, and how do you know which cmdlet to use?

The answer to the first question is simple: use the inline help. In other words, remember the `-?` switch and `get-help`. Between those two, you can get the level of detail you need to understand exactly what you can and cannot do with a particular `Set` cmdlet.

The second question is a little trickier to answer. Just like any command shell, PowerShell has no one absolute place to find cmdlets. In time, you will remember the ones you use frequently and have to look up the ones you don't. In the meantime, you have all the options found in the "Getting Help" section of this chapter to figure that out, and all the SharePoint cmdlets and STSADM operations are listed in the accompanying download Bonus Chapter 2, "PowerShell Cmdlets and STSADM Operations at a Glance," available at www.sybex.com/go/masteringsharepointfoundation2010.

No News Can Be Good News

You may have already noticed that there is no output for most of the cmdlets (such as the `Set-SPSite` command) and STSADM operations. This is a case of "No news is good news." If there is an error, your PowerShell window will fill with red text. As you can probably guess, that's not a good sign.

If you are a trusting soul, you will take the lack of an error as a positive thing. If, however, you are like me, you may want a little more proof that all is well. In PowerShell this will be up to you. There is no "one way" to check your results. Ultimately, you will need to be aware of what your expected outcome is and then run the appropriate STSADM operation or PowerShell cmdlet to verify that it occurred.

For example, when the `export-spweb` is run, it doesn't actually generate any feedback when it succeeds. So, often commands are run back-to-back without delay, as is the case here, to export a site and then a single list.

To prove the exports worked, you can use another cmdlet, `get-childitem` (which shows the objects in a container of some sort) against the directory where the exported files should be, displaying the exported files that were just created.

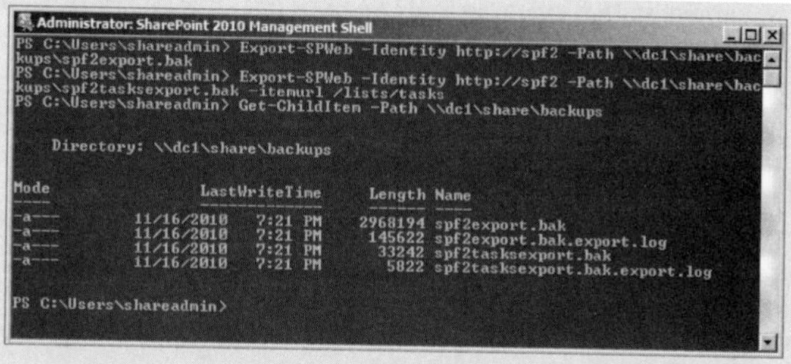

In this instance, you can see that the backup files are created, along with a log file, and you can also see that the task list backup file is significantly smaller than the site backup file, so it would confirm that not only did it run, but it seems to have done what we expected.

For more detail, you would need to read the log files to see exactly what did or did not occur.

Bulk Configuration

The cmdlets you've just seen were great for the configuration of a single object (a site collection in this case), but how do you adjust the settings for multiple objects? If you've been reading this straight through, then you should already know—pipelines!

Up to now you've used pipelines to retrieve data and then sort and filter it before displaying it on-screen. You can just as easily use pipelines to simplify the management of multiple objects of the same type. For example, Figure 14.13 demonstrates how to pipeline `Get-SPSite` into `Set-SPSite` so that all the site collections in the default web application have the same maximum and warning sizes. In this case, I specified the web application `where-object` is any web application name that ends with an "-80" using the comparison operator `-Like`.

In this case we could use the following commands to first get site collections that match the criteria of having a web application name that ends with *-80:*

```
Get-SpSite | Where-Object {$_.WebApplication -like "* - 80"}
```

To use the same criteria but to set properties on the site collections that are returned, you can use a command like this:

```
Get-SpSite | Where-Object {$_.WebApplication -like "* - 80"} | Set-SPSite -MaxSize
200MB -WarningSize 175MB
```

FIGURE 14.13
Configuring size limits on multiple site collections

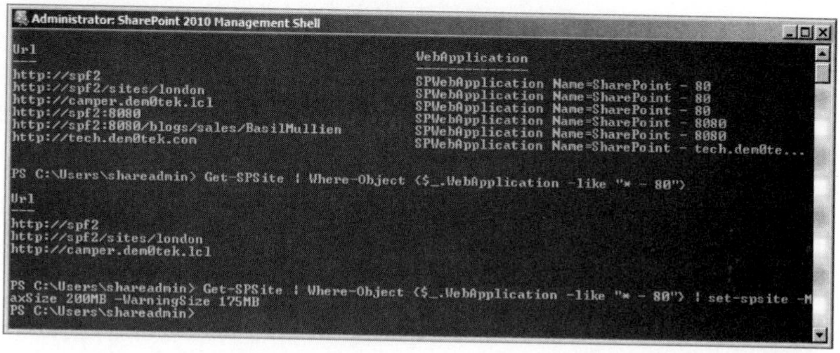

You can see in that example that I've used my "measure twice, cut once" approach. The first pipeline returns the site collection URLs and their parent web application. The second one is used to select only those that are part of the default web application. Lastly, you take that set and feed it into Set-SPSite to configure the quota settings.

Variables, Properties, and Scripts, Oh My!

One of the main benefits of using any command shell, PowerShell or otherwise, is that you can group together a series of tasks, save the instructions to a file (called a *script*), and then execute the script later or execute it repeatedly. Additionally, your command shell may also give you access to advanced tools and properties that aren't exposed anywhere else. PowerShell delivers on both counts.

VARIABLES

You've seen how PowerShell can make use of a placeholder ($_) when you use a Where Object command. Technically, that placeholder is called a *variable*. Variables are just placeholders that you can use to make your PowerShell life easier, usually by simplifying the syntax of your cmdlets. Think back to high-school algebra—you learned that if a − b = c, then c + b = a. Those are all variables, in other words, placeholders for numbers you can put in later. You can work on the logic of the equations without having to worry about the details.

Variables fulfill the same purpose when working with PowerShell, as you've already seen with the $_ variable used earlier in the chapter. That is very useful when working in those pipelines. But you can also create your own variables to use.

Variable names in PowerShell must start with $. What follows is up to you, with two exceptions: $True and $False. Those two names are reserved, and you cannot use them to create variables. You don't need to know any fancy syntax to create a variable in PowerShell; you just need to type in the variable name and then populate it with data or objects, usually by setting it to equal one of the Get cmdlets. Figure 14.14 demonstrates two different variables being created and displayed.

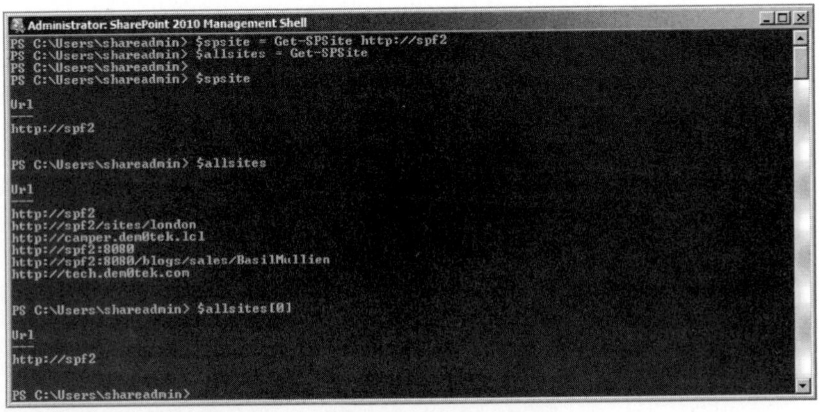

FIGURE 14.14

Basic use of variables: $spsite to contain just one site collection, $allsites to contain all sites collections for farm

In Figure 14.14, you see two variables being created. The first, $spsite, was filled with the data about a particular site.

```
$spsite = Get-SPSite http://spf2
```

The second variable, $allsites, was populated with the results of Get-SPSite without any switches.

```
$allsites = Get-SpSite
```

So now these variables contain the objects from the Get commands. To see the contents of a variable once it has been populated, you just need to type in the name of the variable and press Enter. This has been done for both variables, and you can see the differing results in Figure 14.14.

Pay particular attention to the order of the list of site collections that make up the $allsites variable. The first result in the list is considered to be at position 0 (or [0] as it were). So if you entered the syntax of $allsites[0], the result is a single site, the first one in the list. There are two things at play when a variable is populated with multiple objects. The first is that PowerShell treats it as an array. An array is really just a specific name for a variable that has multiple objects. When only the variable name is used, it returned all the default properties of all the objects in the array. If you want to use a particular entry in that list, you have to tell it which one to use, which you do by putting the number in brackets (make sure they're brackets and not parentheses or braces). That seems pretty straightforward; the only thing you need to remember is that arrays number their objects starting with zero, not one. So, if you want to use the first object in the array, you reference it with [0].

Once you have your variables populated, you will likely want to use them. You use them in the same way you would use the cmdlet that you used to populate them. You can use them in a pipeline to configure something about them, dump them out to the screen, or do anything else you can do with the results of a Get cmdlet.

Figure 14.15 demonstrates how to use the variables we just created. There are five examples.

The first example just retrieves and displays some of the properties of the site you mapped to $SPSite, laid out in a table.

```
$spsite | Format-Table url,owner,resourcequotaexceeded
```

The second feeds all the site collections into Set-SPSite to adjust their quota settings (remember, no news is good news). As you can see, besides the advantage that you don't need to type the entire Get cmdlet every time, you can also do a lot of work with a variable.

```
$allsites | Set-SpSite -WarningSize 100MB -MaxSize 120MB
```

FIGURE 14.15
Using variables to format a table, set size limits, list usage properties, and lock and unlock a site collection

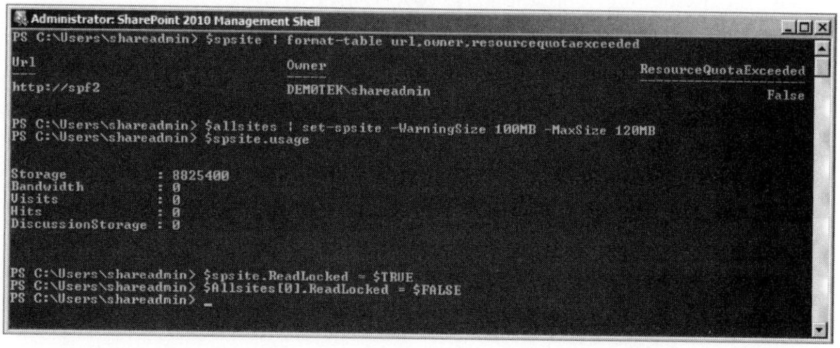

The third, fourth, and fifth examples are where you start to see some of the power of PowerShell. There is no specific cmdlet or STSADM operation to return the size of the site collection. With PowerShell, once you've populated a variable with an object or objects, you have access to *every* property for that object.

For example, with the third cmdlet in Figure 14.15, we use:

```
$spsite.usage
```

This shows you how big (in bytes) the site collection is. The syntax of this cmdlet indicates the property of a specific object by using the object name (or in this case, a variable containing the object), then a period, then the property. So in this example, it would be `$spsite.usage` to display the usage information for `http://spf2`.

The fourth and fifth examples demonstrate how to adjust the properties, first for a variable containing a single object and then for a single object in an array.

```
$spsite.ReadLocked = $True
$allsites[0].ReadLocked = $False
```

In this example, the two lines are referring to the same site collection, so you locked the site collection for read-only access and then turned the lock back off. This is because `$spsite` contains `http://spf2`, and for `$allsites`, the object in the array at position [0] is `http://spf2`.

PROPERTIES

In Figure 14.15, you saw how to set a property on an object that has been put into a variable. It's not likely that you will remember every property of an object, so remember that pipelining the object (via either cmdlet or variable) into `get-member` will show all the properties and methods. You could also pipeline into `format-list`, so you can see the *values* for the properties.

When you look at the values for all the properties, you will notice some of the properties will have a value, some will be blank, but a few seem to have a value that doesn't make sense. To see an example of this, enter the following (use the first line in case you need to populate your $spsite variable):

```
$spsite = Get-SPSite -identity http://spf2
$spsite | format-list
```

Remember that using `format-list` will give you an extensive list of properties. Scroll through the results until you find the property called Usage. Its value reads `Microsoft.SharePoint.SPSite+UsageInfo`. The Usage and Quota properties are two examples that you might find yourself using frequently. Unfortunately, properties like these don't display nicely when you try to feed them into the normal Format cmdlets directly from the Get cmdlet. If you want to see or configure them, you'll need to use a variable (luckily, we have one). Continuing on from the code you just typed, try these four commands:

```
$spsite.Usage
$spsite.Usage | Format-Table
$spsite.Usage.Storage
$spsite.Usage.Storage /1MB
```

The first two commands show you the usage statistics for `http:/spf2`, in the default list format and then in a table format. You can see in Figure 14.16 that there are five types of usage. The next two commands show how to reference the next level of properties in the hierarchy, showing the size of the site collection, first in bytes (which isn't that intuitive to read) and then converted to megabytes (which is more intuitive to read).

FIGURE 14.16

Using a variable to view and change properties

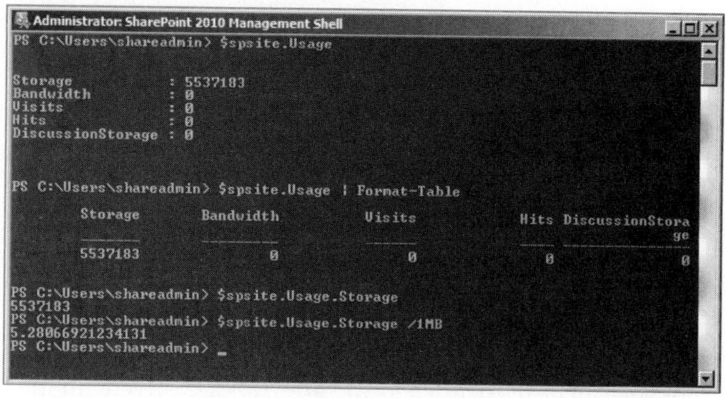

You can do the same thing for individual members of an array using the same syntax you used earlier (specifying the individual site collection by number in brackets). You can try these (assuming you still have `$allsites` populated with all site collections):

```
$allsites[0].Usage
$allsites[0].Usage.Storage
```

They will return the same results as when you used the variable that was populated with a single object (since the site collection at position zero in the array is the same as the single object variable for this example).

That's great for a single item in the array, but what if you want to see that information for all the site collections? Try these commands, and after the third one, press Enter *twice* (pressing Enter twice is important):

```
ForEach($i in $allsites)
{$i.url
$i.usage}
```

When you enter the `ForEach` cmdlet and press Enter, it goes into a sort of interactive mode (this cmdlet uses a variable in an array, or in our case `$i in $allsites`). `$i` stands for `$item` in this case. This mode will encourage you with double greater-than symbols (>>) to enter the actions you want to run. In this case, you're pulling and displaying the URL and usage properties of items in `$allsites`, letting you enter the sequence of actions you want, considered *script blocks,* as you can see in Figure 14.17. The script block has to be formatted, even in interactive mode, so it starts and ends with braces. That is why the two properties for this exercise are formatted the way they are. Using this command in an interactive way lets you see how `ForEach` steps through each item and script block. This is covered in a little more detail in "Scripting Flows."

FIGURE 14.17

Using ForEach in interactive mode

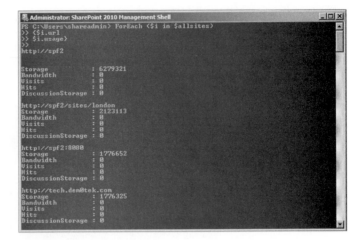

This sequence is most commonly used when creating scripts and complex command flows. But you can also use it when you are working directly in the shell. I mention it here because it is something that you will likely see the more you use PowerShell. The point is that you have some reasonably straightforward ways to use the properties that PowerShell makes available to you, especially the ones that aren't available to you in any other way.

SCRIPTING

At some point, you are likely to want to save the commands you've run so that you can run them again (without as much typing) or schedule them. When you do this, you are scripting. The most basic scripts would be nothing more than taking one or more of the cmdlets we've done and saving them in a script file. A script file can written in Notepad and saved with the .ps1 extension.

To run those scripts, you need to have your management shell open and type in the full path to the script you want to run. Trying to run a PowerShell script by double-clicking it will likely open the script in Notepad or whatever scripting tool you may have installed.

If you want your script to run at a specific time, you may want to use the Windows Task Scheduler to schedule it to run.

To do this, you will need to configure the scheduler to run PowerShell.exe, register the SharePoint snapin, and then have the script text you want to run.

The easiest way to do this is to create a new task in Task Scheduler (covered in more detail in Chapter 13).

On the Actions tab, specify the path to the PowerShell executable (%Windows%\System32\ WindowsPowerShell\v1.0\powershell.exe). In the script itself, add the command to add the SharePoint snapin (Add-SPSnapin Microsoft.SharePoint.PowerShell) at the top of the file, as the first line in the script. Then specify the file name of the script file itself as the argument of the task in task scheduler. In Figure 14.18, you can see the simple script with the Add-Snapin cmdlet at the top in a notepad window in the background, with the new task being configured in the foreground, with the path to powershell.exe in the Program field, the parameter -noexit (so the PowerShell window doesn't close if there is an error), and the path and filename for the script in the arguments field. Be sure to run the task using a login that is a shell admin permitted to run the cmdlets.

FIGURE 14.18
Configuring
a scheduled
task to run a
PowerShell script

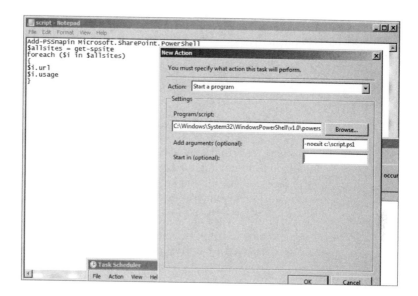

Scripting Flows

Some scripts may be very simple, with a very small number of cmdlets, each doing their one task. However, at some point you are going to need to do more than that. This requires understanding some basic scripting structures. The two that are used most frequently are ForEach and If.

If you have a bit of a developer or scripter background, you might be thinking "Shouldn't that be For-Next loops and If-Then statements?" Not in PowerShell. To try to make it easier, you don't have to put Next at the end of script blocks or Then after the initial If command.

ForEach blocks are very useful when you need to process each item individually in an array. You saw an example of a ForEach block in the code you looked at in the "Properties" section of this chapter. In this case, you are going to write the script blocks sequentially, rather than running them in interactive mode.

When using ForEach, there are two things to remember:

◆ A ForEach block starts with the following syntax:

```
ForEach ($variable in array)
```

Here's an example:

```
ForEach ($item in $spsite)
```

The most common variable to use in a ForEach line is $i or $item, but you can use whatever variable name you like. The variable is a placeholder for each object in the array. It is then used in the script block. If you have already populated an array, then put the variable name for the array in there. In previous examples, the variable $allsites would be considered an array because it contains multiple objects.

◆ Immediately following the ForEach command is the script block:

```
ForEach ($item in $spsite)
{powershell cmdlets to execute}
```

An example of this would be (based on our interactive exercise earlier, assuming the $spsite variable is populated):

```
ForEach ($i in $spsite)
{
$i.url
$i.usage
}
```

This is where the actual work gets done. The script block *must start and end with braces*. The cmdlets and code you put in there is completely up to you. In simple scripts, there may be three or four cmdlets. In complex scripts, you may have more ForEach or If blocks nested, so you can have more analysis and logic. You can manipulate data, save it, and write it to file. Basically, whatever you can do directly in the shell should also execute here.

The other commonly used type of block is the If block, used to evaluate properties or conditions and then determine what to do next. You can do multiple evaluations by using ElseIf statements and an Else statement if required. There are a few keys to making If blocks work.

◆ The basic structure is as follows:

```
If(evaluation)
{script block to execute if True}
ElseIf(optional second evaluation)
{script block to execute if the ElseIf is True}
Else
{script block to execute if none of the evaluations are True}
```

If you've ever done work in spreadsheets or conditional formatting, this basic idea should be somewhat familiar. It's important to remember that the evaluations are in parentheses and the script blocks are in braces.

◆ The evaluations have to be Boolean; in other words, they must have an answer of either True or False. The syntax you looked at earlier in this chapter in "Building the Filter String" works here.

◆ You don't have to have ElseIf or Else. You do have to use If but if there is no second thing to check, then you don't need ElseIf. If there are no cmdlets to run if the test returns False, then you don't need Else.

Here is an example of a simple If block that compares the site collection size to the warning and maximum quotas and displays messages on-screen (write-host is like using echo in DOS).

```
$SPSite = http://spf2

If ($SPSite.usage.storage -ge $SPSite.quota.storagemaximumlevel)
    {write-host "This site collection is over the maximum size."}
ElseIf ($SPSite.usage.storage -ge $SPSite.quota.storagewarninglevel)
```

```
{write-host "This site collection is over the warning size."}
Else
    {write-host "This site collection is of acceptable size."}
```

Obviously, you will likely want to do more complex things in your script blocks, but that is a start. Always check that you have the logic part of the If block correct; from there you can go and start developing the script blocks for each evaluation.

 Real World Scenario

USING SCRIPTS TO DOCUMENT AND DIAGNOSE

The pipeline capability of PowerShell reduces (but does not entirely eliminate) the need to write complex scripts. One of the more common uses of PowerShell scripting is for ongoing documentation and diagnostic work, especially in environments where external monitoring tools are not an option.

For example, you fairly often need to report on what your storage quotas are set to for a site collection. In Central Administration, you can see this one site collection at a time. For day-to-day management and monitoring, it is much more useful to be able to collect this data together. The following script collects and writes the URLs and quota information of site collections for the farm to a file, which can be viewed later. It also formats to view immediately in the shell each site collection's URL, storage, bandwidth, visits, hits, discussion storage. You could then schedule this script to run at whatever interval you require.

```
##PowerShell Script to collect quota settings for all Site Collections

##BLOCK ONE:Check to make sure that the SharePoint modules are loaded. Load them
##if not
$snapin=Get-PSsnapin
Foreach ($i in $snapin)
{
  If ($i.Name -ne "Microsoft.SharePoint.PowerShell")
  {
        $counter = $counter + 0
  }
  ElseIf ($i.Name -eq "Microsoft.SharePoint.PowerShell")
  {
        $counter = $counter + 1
  }
}
If($counter -ne 0)
{
        Write-Host "SharePoint PowerShell Module Loaded`n"
}
```

```
ElseIf ($counter -eq 0)
{
        Write-Host "Loading SharePoint PowerShell Module"
        Add-PSsnapin Microsoft.SharePoint.PowerShell
        Write-Host "SharePoint PowerShell Module Loaded`n"
}
## BLOCK TWO: Get the URL and usage information for the site collections and
##write them to a file named output.txt, and display usage information in the
##shell window in table format. Out-File tells the script to output data to a
##file specified in the -filepath
$SPSite = Get-SPSite
Foreach ($tls in $SPSite)
{
  $tls.url | write-host
  $tls.url | out-file -filepath c:\output.txt -append
  $tls.quota | out-file -filepath c:\output.txt -append
  $tls.usage | format-table
}
```

This script has two main blocks of code. The first (and ironically the harder to write) checks to see whether the SharePoint PowerShell modules are loaded. To do this, you pull the list of snapins into a variable ($snapin) and then use ForEach to look at each snapin and see whether it is the SharePoint snapin. If not, do nothing, and check the next one in the set. If it does run across the SharePoint snapin, then increase a counter to one.

Once all the snapins have been evaluated, check the value of the counter. If it is still zero, then the SharePoint snapins are not loaded, so trigger add-pssnapin. If it is anything other than zero, then the SharePoint module has been loaded.

Now comes the easy part—retrieving the list of site collections and outputting the information you want. In this particular script, you again use a ForEach loop to go through each site collection in the set. For each item, you are capturing the URL and the set of quota properties and then outputting them to screen and adding them to a text file. If you were going to run this on a schedule, then you might decide to leave the lines out that display on-screen. What you'd be after is the text file.

This is a good example of a simple documentation/diagnostic script. The next logical step would be to somehow use the results to effect the changes you want. You might want to try to display the current size of the site collection in the results or go through and set quotas on the site collections that don't have any set. That's particularly handy if you are using Self-Service Site Creation. But those are changes for you to make to this script, for you to learn from.

This is really just the tip of the iceberg when it comes to what you can do with PowerShell, but it should give you enough of a grounding to make sense of the cmdlets and code snippets you'll see as you start to work with PowerShell. There are many resources available to gain further knowledge, both in books and on the Internet.

SCRIPTING TIPS AND TRICKS

Here are some tips and tricks:

- *Address your main need first.* When I wrote the script, the first part I got sorted out was the second block. I focused on getting the data I wanted and building the resulting text string and outputting it where I needed it. Once that was working, I started addressing the "extras" such as trying to make sure it works even if it is started from the wrong shell. If I want to schedule this script to run automatically, this part was important to get right.

- *Use a good PowerShell scripting tool.* You can use Notepad if you want, but there are a lot of good tools out there to help you write PowerShell scripts. Most of them help with syntax, have tab completion built in to them, check for mismatched brackets, and provide some kind of line-by-line code-checking tool. Windows Server 2008 has an optional feature called the Windows PowerShell ISE that provides very basic support for these things. Although not as fancy as the third-party tools, it's free and is better than Notepad. Whatever you choose, a good scripting tool will save you a lot of time and headaches.

- *There's a fine line between self-documenting and script bloat.* Although it is a good idea to put comments into your script to help you remember what you did and why you did it when you have to edit the script six months after you wrote it, you can go overboard. I overdid it in the sample script, but that was for demonstration purposes. For a final script that I was going to use in production, I'd reduce the amount of comments.

- *Scripts are never finished; they're just at the current version.* The script as written works and is useful. But there's nothing wrong with trying to make it work better or make it more useful. When I finished this script initially, my first thought was "Good. Done. It works. Now, what property displays the size of the site collection? And how would I color-code the results to highlight ones that exceed their limit? And how hard would it be to make it email me the results instead of a file? Or perhaps build it as an HTML string instead of plain text so I could save it to a website directory or page library?" This script is version 1.0. By the time you're reading this, I'll probably be on version 3.something. And that's a good thing; it's how you learn and gain experience.

- *The Internet is your friend.* If someone puts a script sample that is useful to you in their blog, it's not stealing; they want you to use it. It would almost be rude not to. But, if someone asks, remember to correctly attribute the original material to the correct person, especially if it is particularly clever. Someone may do the same for you someday.

- *Reduce, reuse, recycle.* Build your own script repository, including a text file with snippets of code you want to reuse and entire scripts that you can call from other scripts. Make your life as easy as possible. I'd take that Block One code and save it somewhere so with the next script I write I just need to copy and paste it in.

STSADM.EXE Basics

Even though Microsoft would like you to stop using STSADM and switch to PowerShell, there is still a lot going for STSADM. In a few cases, it's easier to use STSADM than it is PowerShell, and there are still some tasks that can be done in STSADM that have no PowerShell equivalent. Given that, let's make sure we have covered the basics of how to use STSADM. If you have experience with STSADM from your work with previous versions of SharePoint, then you probably don't need to worry about this. However, if SharePoint Foundation 2010 is your first tilt at the windmill, you might find this handy. Keep in mind that many commands used in PowerShell are very similar to their counterparts in STSADM. So if you know one pretty well, it gives you a head start with the other environment.

You must have local administrator rights on the SharePoint computer that you are running STSADM on. And remember, there is no remote execution (that is, no ability within the commands to tell it to "run against that server over there") for STSADM. Unlike PowerShell, which can be used remotely, STSADM has usually been run from a traditional command prompt, and the directory within that shell needs to be set to the directory containing STSADM (`%program files%\common files\microsoft shared\web server extensions\14\bin`), or that directory needs to be added to the PATH system variable. And you can still do this if you want. Or you can take the easy approach and just open the SharePoint 2010 Management Shell. Yes, that is where you run the PowerShell cmdlets, but it also runs STSADM (and other DOS commands), and you don't have to do all that fiddling with environment variables.

The syntax of STSADM is pretty straightforward:

```
STSADM.exe -o <operation> [parameters required for the operation]
```

Although it is straightforward, there are more than 100 different operations, and most of those operations have several parameters. Once you've committed all those to memory, you'll be on your way. Actually, STSADM has good inline help, so you don't need to do that.

To get a list of all the STSADM operations at your disposal, simply run `stsadm.exe -help` (or you can just use the command name, `stsadm`, without the file extension) . That command will output a list of all the operations. You may want to redirect that output to a text file for later reference, with a command like the following:

```
STSADM.exe -help > c:\stsadm.txt
```

Once you have identified the operation you want to execute, you can get detailed instructions/options for that operation by running this command:

```
STSADM.exe -help <operation>
```

You can see an example of this in Figure 14.19.

FIGURE 14.19
STSADM help for the `createsite` operation

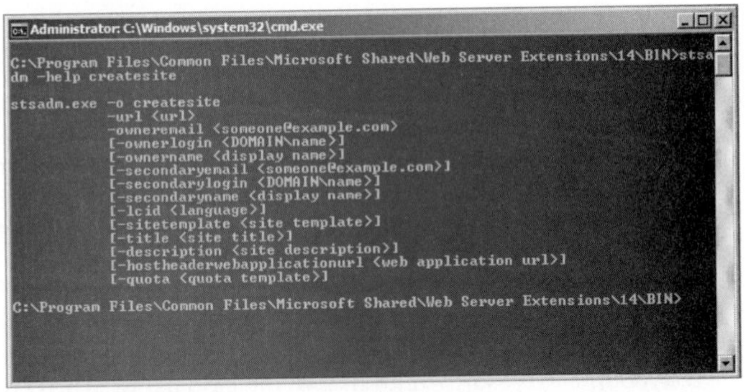

Once you know the possible parameters, you should be able to construct the command you require to achieve the outcome you want. See the next section for several examples of how to use STSADM commands.

Command-Line Only Tasks and Options

Now that you have the basics of using the command-line tools at your disposal, you are ready to figure out what cmdlet or STSADM operation does what you need. As stated earlier, the inline help is useful for seeing the list of all your options, as well as the syntax required. TechNet has many articles and lists to help you find commands. However, to supplement this chapter, I have created tables, broadly organized by task, of the more than 200 PowerShell and 100 STSADM commands in Bonus Chapter 2, "PowerShell Cmdlets and STSADM Operations at a Glance" available online at www.sybex.com/go/masteringsharepointfoundation2010.

As mentioned briefly earlier in this chapter, there are some activities that can be done only using command-line tools. In some cases, these tasks make up part of a bigger picture (that is, they are single steps in a process). In others, they are the whole task/activity in themselves. In still other cases, command-line tools present you with additional options that aren't available with equivalent GUI tools.

Several areas require a command line (usually PowerShell), many having to do with security, such as claims providers and trust relationships. Other individual tasks that require using the command line include enabling/disabling the Developer Dashboard, adjusting the New Item display length, and changing a web application's authentication provider. Other commands available only at the command line, such as adding solutions, testing content databases, and importing exported sites or lists, were covered in previous chapters.

Regardless, one of the frustrating things about SharePoint management is that these command line–only tasks and options aren't consistently referenced in the GUIs. For example, when dealing with the management of farm solutions, the page specifically states that you must use STSADM to add a solution to be managed. That is fine, but what it doesn't mention is that there is a PowerShell cmdlet to do the same thing.

You can find a complete PowerShell-to-STSADM mapping at the TechNet website, or you can simply download the bonus material for the book.

JUST BECAUSE WE WROTE IT DOESN'T MEAN WE'RE GOING TO TELL YOU ABOUT IT

One thing you will find somewhat frustrating about both of the command-line tools is that although Microsoft does provide decent inline help, it's not always right. STSADM's help generally is pretty solid, because it has been around for nearly a decade. Unfortunately, the cmdlet inline help isn't as mature yet, and you will probably find more discrepancies.

The discrepancies at this time seem to fall into two broad categories:

- Microsoft doesn't mention it at all. The STSADM property to turn the Developer Dashboard on and off doesn't show up in the inline help. If you don't know what it is, you won't find it there. See Chapter 4 for more about the Developer Dashboard.

◆ The information is wrong or incomplete. This is probably more frustrating than the things that aren't there. For example, the inline help for Export-SPWeb doesn't mention that to export a single list, the URL has to be root-relative (meaning the path has to be relative to the root of the site specified, such as /lists/tasks if you're exporting the Tasks list). The help file's example actually displays the wrong syntax, indicating a "valid URL" of http://*server_name*, and it won't work. That's an important little piece of information to leave out. Likewise, the inline help for adjusting the quota levels of a site collection explicitly states that the number you put is megabytes. That's wrong. The number you enter is in bytes unless you specify megabytes explicitly. As another example, the inline help for adding shell admins indicates that you can use the common name for specifying databases, when it requires a GUID. These are just a few examples of the kinds of things that can drive you nuts.

There's not much you can do about this, except to document problems when you find them so you can save time and effort in the future. This chapter identifies some of these discrepancies, but you shouldn't assume that they have all been found. Often your best bet is to scour the Internet for blogs and forums that indicate what others have gotten to successfully work. You also might want to consider posting your successes so others can avoid frustration.

To round out the chapter, here are some of the more common tasks that can't be done in Central Administration.

Working with Developer Dashboard

Discussed in Chapter 4, this tool appends a Developer Dashboard page to the bottom of each page on a SharePoint site so you can see details about how long each component took to load, what data it accessed, and more.

This tool cannot be enabled in the GUI and has to be enabled at the command line. It is one of the few commands that is better suited to be run using STSADM than PowerShell, because the PowerShell command takes several lines to complete. It is much easier to enable (or disable) via STSADM. Keep in mind that it is an all-or-nothing setting; once enabled, it is enabled for the farm, not for specific web applications or site collections.

The Developer Dashboard has three simple modes: on, off, and on-demand. The first two are self-explanatory. When you enable the developer dashboard to run on-demand, it will put a small icon to the right of the Account menu on all pages. This icon lets you enable or disable the Developer Dashboard at will.

To simply enable the Developer Dashboard and have it on for every page, use this command:

```
stsadm -o setproperty -pn developer-dashboard -pv on
```

The syntax of the command uses the setproperty operation, with the property name of developer-dashboard and the property value of on. You can use setproperty to set many, many properties of objects in SharePoint.

To turn off the Developer Dashboard, use this command:

```
stsadm -o setproperty -pn developer-dashboard -pv off
```

To enable Developer Dashboard to run on-demand, use this command:

```
stsadm -o setproperty -pn developer-dashboard -pv ondemand
```

Managing the User Account Directory

Using Active Directory for user authentication is convenient, but by default, it gives site collections access to add users from all of Active Directory. If you want your site collections to be more isolated in terms of what users it can and cannot add from Active Directory, there are some options available. The simplest of which is organizing the user accounts you want to access specific site collections by organizational unit. Then you specify, per site collection, what organizational unit you want each site collection to access when looking for or adding users. This would allow you to isolate the users for each site collection by OU, so no one from one site collection could possibly be added to another.

If you want to specify that a site collection only pull user accounts from a particular OU in Active Directory, you can use this STSADM command (the path for the OU can vary, depending on how your domain is set up; here it's a simple domainname.suffix, like dem0tek.lcl):

```
stsadm -o setsiteuseraccountdirectorypath -path "<OU=YourOU ,
DC=DomainName,DC=suffix>" -url <URLofSiteCollection>
```

For PowerShell, the command is as follows:

```
Set-SPSite -Identity "<URLofSiteCollection>" -UserAccountDirectoryPath "<ou=OUname,
dc=domainname,dc=suffix>"
```

So if I wanted to use PowerShell to isolate the accounts the london site collection uses for this book to an OU I created called London, I could use this:

```
Set-SPSite -Identity "http://spf2/sites/london" -UserAccountDirectoryPath
"OU=London,DC=dem0tek,DC=lcl"
```

If the site collection already has users from elsewhere in Active Directory, they won't be removed, but from now on, only users in the OU will be available to be added to the site collection.

Managing HTTP Request Monitoring and Throttling Thresholds

SharePoint Foundation supports throttling of resource-intensive tasks, such as viewing large lists. That sort of throttling can be enabled, and values set, in Central Administration. While HTTP Request Monitoring and Throttling can only be turned on or off in the GUI, the values can only be changed in PowerShell. This setting keeps track of acceptable values of performance on a web front-end server in terms of memory and ASP.NET requests using health score bucket values. The two values that are most important in that set are the upper limit and lower limit, especially because the upper limit will trigger low-priority requests (such as those of the Search service) to be ignored. Actually seeing what the minimum and maximum levels are (and to set them) requires PowerShell.

To enable or disable the setting in PowerShell (if you don't want to do it in Central Administration), use the following:

```
Enable-SPWebApplicationHttpThrottling <URL>
Disable-SPWebApplicationHttpThrottling <URL>
```

If you don't specify a URL, it will prompt to you enter one.

To see what settings are configured for HTTP Request Monitoring and Throttling, use this:

```
Get-SPWebApplicationHttpThrottlingMonitor
```

This will display the categories (usually Memory and ASP.NET) that are being monitored and their health score calculator, with highest and lowest values at the start and end of the list. To change the value of those settings, you can use the `Set-SPWebApplicationHttpThrottling` cmdlet. Again, as is standard with PowerShell, if you don't specify a URL, you'll be prompted to enter one.

The next command has a number of parameters, so you should check its detailed help for more, but as an example, to change the upper limit of the available memory in megabytes to 3000 before throttling begins, you use the following:

```
Set-SPWebApplicationHttpThrottlingMonitor <URL> -Category Memory -Counter
"Available Mbytes" -IsDesc -UpperLimit 3000
```

Then you can use the `Get` command to list that cmdlet's settings and make sure it is correct.

Setting the New Item Display Length

Every time you add a new item to a list or library, a little green "new" icon displays next to it. By default this icon tends to display for about two days before disappearing. If you'd like to change the length of time that little new item icon displays (such as setting it to zero so it never displays), you need to use an STSADM command. This setting is per web application. I have not been able to find this setting's equivalent for PowerShell.

```
stsadm -o setproperty -pn days-to-show-new-icon -pv 0 -url <webapplicationURL>
```

This command uses the `setproperty` operation, specifying the property name as "days-to-show-new-icon" and the property value of zero, on the web application URL (an example could be `http://spf2:8080`). This will disable the new item icon from appearing next to any new item on any site in the web application.

Working with Multi-Tenancy

Multi-tenancy is a service that must be configured entirely using PowerShell. Using the Site Subscription Settings service, it allows a SharePoint administrator to set up site collections organized by subscription IDs. Although it is demonstrated extensively in Chapter 16, here is a quick look at the basics.

An example for the basic pattern for setting up tenancy is as follows:

```
##Create application pool for service application
$appPool = New-SPServiceApplicationPool -Name SettingsServiceApppool -Account
dem0tek\spsubset

##Create Site Subscription Service application and its database
$sapp = New-SpSubscriptionSettingsServiceApplication –Name
SubscriptionSettingsServiceApplication –Databasename
SubscriptionSettingsServiceDB -applicationpool $appPool

##Create Service Proxy
new-SPSubscriptionSettingsServiceApplicationProxy –ServiceApplication $sapp

##Create a Site Subscription
```

```
$subscription=New-SPSiteSubscription

##Create the Tenant Administration Site The Tenant Administration Site is actually
##the top level site of a site collection, and you must make sure the URL works
##and you specify the Tenant Adminsite template.

$site = New-SPSite -url http://<computername>/sites/tenant -Template
TenantAdmin#0 -OwnerAlias <domain\username> -SiteSubscription $subscription

##If you had created the tenant site earlier, skip the previous step
##and do the following instead (without the two hashes)
##$site = Get-SPSite -Identity <url of already created tenant administration site>
##Then align the subscription to the Tenant Administration SiteSet-SPSite
-Identity $site -SiteSubscription $subscription

##Assign the Tenant Administration Site so it takes over site collection management
##Set-SPSiteAdministration -Identity "http://<computername>/sites/tenant"
-AdministrationSiteType TenantAdministration -SiteSubscription $subscription
```

In the online bonus chapter, cmdlets that reference the subscriptions are found in the reference table for their core task.

Ideally this chapter has given you insights into using the command-line and shell tools for SharePoint. You've seen throughout the book where these commands (and cmdlets) are used to do tasks in SharePoint, and now you have the foundational knowledge to use those tools yourself. Don't forget to download the bonus material that is an addendum to this chapter, Bonus Chapter 2.

The Bottom Line

Start and use the SharePoint 2010 Management Shell.   The SharePoint 2010 Management Shell is found in the menu, but you must have the appropriate permissions to run the shell and the commands in it.

Master It   What cmdlet do you need to run to grant someone the ability to run the SharePoint 2010 Management Shell?

Understand the basic syntax for PowerShell cmdlets.   PowerShell cmdlets take a verb-noun structure, along with multiple switches that can also govern how the cmdlet functions. Often a single noun will have multiple verbs for it.

Master It   How do you retrieve a list of all available PowerShell cmdlets?

Use pipelining to make cmdlets work well together.   PowerShell cmdlets typically output objects, not text. Those objects can be fed as input to other cmdlets. This is called pipelining. You can pipeline to adjust the result set, and you can pipeline to configure multiple objects with a single-line command.

Master It   How would you retrieve all the subsites based on the Team Site template of the site collection found at `http://spf2`?

Use basic PowerShell scripting techniques. The real power of any command shell is the ability to write a script that can be reused as needed. Variables help with this, as does the direct access to properties of objects. PowerShell supports IF and FOREACH structures, as well as others.

> **Master It** Which code block should you use to analyze a property of an object and then make a decision as to what you should do next?

Perform common SharePoint Foundation management tasks using PowerShell. There are 244 SharePoint cmdlets, which address many of the management activities that you want to do. However, PowerShell also exposes every property of every object.

> **Master It** How would you set the quota settings for all of your site collection to a maximum 150 MB and 100 MB warning?

Chapter 15

Migrating from Windows SharePoint Services 3.0 to Microsoft SharePoint Foundation 2010

Upgrades can be exciting for users—a new look, new features, and new capabilities—but for SharePoint administrators, they can become an inevitable chore. SharePoint Foundation was designed for improved scalability and performance and to take advantage of 64-bit architecture. To do this, it has some new hardware and software requirements that for 32-bit environments entail extra steps in the upgrade process. However, with a little planning and preparation, upgrades don't have to become a nightmare.

In this chapter, you'll learn to

◆ Determine which upgrade method to use

◆ Prepare for migration

◆ Move WSS 3.0 from 32-bit hardware to 64-bit hardware

◆ Upgrade Windows SharePoint Services 3.0 to SharePoint Foundation 2010

◆ Use Visual Upgrade

Determine Which Upgrade Method Is Right for You

If you are reading this chapter, there is a good chance you already have a Windows SharePoint Services 3.0 (WSS 3.0) Standalone or Server Farm installation up and running, and you want to upgrade to SharePoint Foundation so you can get your hands on some of the cool new features. You may have opened this book, checked the table of contents for the migration chapter, and come straight here past all the other chapters. That's OK, but you may have missed some important information along the way. Not to worry, I will touch on these things as we go along and refer you to the chapters where they were discussed in depth.

What's more, although each migration or upgrade is unique, they all have some steps in common (the two terms can be synonymous). Rather than repeat the steps in detail for each method, I will explain the steps in depth the first time and then just summarize or refer you to the detailed section each time after that. Now let's get started so you can get your hands on all those new SharePoint Foundation features.

One size simply doesn't fit all. SharePoint comes in all different shapes and sizes too, from standalone servers to farms that span multiple servers. Some companies use lots of customizations, while others do everything out of the box. So, there isn't a one-size-fits-all path to upgrade for SharePoint either. This chapter will explore the different paths to upgrade, discuss which paths work best in what situations, and then walk you through each of them step-by-step. Upgrading is easy once you know the way to go about it.

For previous upgrades, you had three options: in-place upgrade, gradual upgrade, and database-attach upgrade. However, with SharePoint Foundation, support for gradual migration has been discontinued because of problems with compatibility and poor performance. That leaves us with the in-place and database-attach methods of migration. Each method has its pros and cons.

DOMAIN NAME CONSIDERATIONS BEFORE YOU MIGRATE

SharePoint Foundation and SharePoint Server 2010 no longer support internationalized domain names or single-label domain names (domain names that don't have a suffix, such as `server .companyname`, instead of `server.companyname.com`). If you require either type of domain name in your implementation, you might want to reconsider upgrading.

The In-Place Migration Method

In-place migration (or in-place upgrade as it is commonly called) involves upgrading from Windows SharePoint Services 3.0 to SharePoint Foundation on the same machine as your current installation. Everything in your current installation is upgraded in a fixed sequence. During the in-place upgrade, all farm settings are upgraded, and customizations are preserved and available after upgrade, but they may still need to be modified in order to work in the new SharePoint Foundation environment.

However, you need to be aware that all servers in the farm will be unavailable during the upgrade process, which takes the server offline. Also, once the upgrade process has begun, it will run through to the end, and you will not be able to cancel it once it has started. So if you choose this method, allow enough time for all your content to be upgraded. (See the sidebar "SharePoint Will Be Unavailable for How Long?!" for tips on estimating how long the upgrade is likely to take.)

An in-place upgrade works well if you have a Standalone installation or plan to install SharePoint Foundation on the same hardware as your current installation, but to do this, your current hardware and software must meet minimum requirements. Most notably, it must be 64-bit, and your WSS 3.0 server must be at Service Pack 2 or higher. With an in-place upgrade, the actual upgrade process takes more time to complete, but you won't have to spend as much time manually moving settings and customizations.

The in-place method is particularly useful if you have sites based on STP files. The 2010 version of SharePoint no longer supports `.stp` files. You can't add any more STP sites to SharePoint Foundation once you upgrade, but you can keep the ones you have already.

HOW DO I KNOW WHICH VERSION OF SHAREPOINT I AM RUNNING?

You must be running at least WSS 3.0 with Service Pack 2 in order to upgrade to SharePoint Foundation, but how can you tell? Just go to any SharePoint site, and then select Site Settings. The version number is listed under Site Information. Then use the following table to determine which version you are running.

SharePoint Versions

Version Number	Version Name
12.0.0.6529	SP2+ February 10 Cumulative Update
12.0.0.6524	SP2+ December 09 Cumulative Update
12.0.0.6520	SP2+ October 09 Cumulative Update
12.0.0.6514	SP2+ August 09 Cumulative Update
12.0.0.6510	SP2+ June 09 Cumulative Update
12.0.0.6504	SP2+ April 9 Cumulative Update
12.0.0.6421	Service Pack 2
12.0.0.6341	SP1 + February 09 Cumulative Update
12.0.0.6335	SP1 + December 08 Cumulative Update
12.0.0.6331	SP1 + October 08 Cumulative Update
12.0.0.6327	SP1 + August 08 Cumulative Update
12.0.0.6318	SP1 + Infrastructure Update
12.0.0.6303	SP1 + Post SP1 Hotfix
12.0.0.6301	SP1 + Post SP1 Hotfix
12.0.0.6300	SP1 + Post SP1 Hotfix
12.0.0.6219	Service Pack 1
12.0.0.6039	October Public Update
12.0.0.6036	August 24, 2007 Hotfix Package
12.0.0.4518	WSS 3.0 RTM

The Database-Attach Migration Method

A *database-attach* upgrade allows you to upgrade and move the content from your WSS 3.0 implementation to a separate SharePoint Foundation implementation. During a database-attach upgrade, you will move your content databases from your current WSS 3.0 farm and then attach them to a new SharePoint Foundation farm or standalone server. Your content databases will be upgraded automatically when you attach the databases to your new SharePoint Foundation implementation.

One of the nice features of this method is the ability to upgrade your databases in any order and even upgrade several databases at the same time. This method is also good if you have more than one farm you want to combine into a single farm.

If you are considering restructuring your environment by changing, adding, combining, or deleting your web applications and their URLs, the database-attach method has the advantage of being able to attach your content databases to whatever web application you want.

One of the biggest advantages of this method is the ability to upgrade directly from WSS 32-bit to SharePoint Foundation 64-bit without migrating WSS 3.0 to a 64-bit environment before upgrading to SharePoint Foundation. You can just move the databases over to the new SharePoint Foundation implementation straight from the WSS 3.0 32-bit implementation.

However, if you choose this method, you need to be aware that no settings, services, or customizations are upgraded or moved, so you will need to manually enter your settings (such as those in Central Administration) and transfer your customizations to the new SharePoint Foundation server or farm. As with the in-place upgrade, your SharePoint installation will be unavailable while you're moving your databases around, so you will need to allow enough time to complete the process. If you are running a SharePoint Foundation farm, you will also require direct access to the database server.

This method of upgrade defaults to showing the old interface until you choose to use Visual Upgrade to upgrade to the new SharePoint Foundation interface (an approach that can be convenient when testing list views, pages, and customizations). Visual Upgrade is also available as an option with in-place server farm upgrades.

If you plan to move to new hardware or from a Standalone installation to a Server Farm installation, then you may want to consider using the database-attach method. A database-attach upgrade takes less time to complete but requires more time to be spent on manually moving and adding settings, permissions, and customizations.

SHAREPOINT WILL BE UNAVAILABLE FOR HOW LONG?!

Many factors can affect how long it takes to complete your upgrade; the number of site collections, subsites, lists, and libraries, as well as the performance of your servers, can all affect how long it takes to complete the upgrade process.

You can plan to perform the upgrade during a time when users won't be accessing your SharePoint sites or when shutting down SharePoint will have the least impact on users, but sometimes there just isn't a good time. What then?

You can reduce the amount of "downtime" by using one of two hybrid approaches to upgrading. A hybrid upgrade is a combination of an in-place upgrade and a database-attach upgrade.

The first hybrid approach is to set the databases on your current farm to read-only so that your users can see their data even if they can't make any changes to it. This allows the users to access the original server(s) using their original URL until the new server(s) are ready to be used.

To use this method, take the following steps:

1. First set up your new SharePoint Foundation server or farm, and then set the databases, on the server you're upgrading, to read-only.

2. Back up your content databases, and restore them to the new SharePoint Foundation server. (If you are simply copying the databases, as in the case of a Standalone installation, you may need to stop services temporarily but turn them back on as soon as copying is complete so users can continue to access content during the upgrade process.)

3. Finally, you switch users to the new farm (either have them use the new server's URL or add the original address as an Alternate Access Mapping for the new server and then configure the correct records in DNS to set the old server address as an alias to the new server).

4. Shut the old farm down.

The second hybrid approach does interrupt service, but it is intended to do so very briefly and uses the database-attach method to speed up the process by detaching the content databases from the WSS 3.0 implementation you are upgrading, upgrading WSS 3.0 on that server without the databases (which is quicker), and then attaching the databases to the upgraded server—upgrading the attached databases in the process. You don't get all the benefits of a true in-place upgrade on the content, but it does go pretty fast.

To use this method, do the following:

1. Take the current WSS 3.0 server or farm down.

2. Detach the content database(s) from the original server or farm.

3. Run the in-place upgrade on the WSS 3.0 server or farm.

4. Finally, attach the content database to the newly upgraded server or farm and upgrade the content. It is important to note that the content will not be available to users during this process, but it can reduce the amount of time it is unavailable. This is convenient because you don't have move customizations or re-enter settings.

For more information about the hybrid upgrade method, see the TechNet article "Upgrade process overview (SharePoint Foundation 2010)."

Preparing for Migration: Best-Laid Plans

Now that you know which method you are going to use, you can start to put your plan in place. There are some simple things you can do to get ready for your upgrade, such as identify potential "gotchas" and prepare your environment for migration.

Reviewing System Requirements

SharePoint Foundation system requirements were discussed in detail in Chapter 1, "SharePoint Foundation 2010 under the Hood." Briefly, a installation requires the following technologies.

SOFTWARE REQUIREMENTS

♦ Windows Server 2008 (Service Pack 1 or higher. If you are running Service Pack 1, the installer will upgrade you to Service Pack 2, so be warned if anything else on the server needs SP1 only). The OS architecture must be 64-bit, and it must be Windows Server 2008 or higher; Windows Server 2003 is not compatible with SharePoint Foundation. **Therefore, the hardware, obviously, must support 64-bit.** There are no 32-bit options here, not even for evaluation. SharePoint installation is supported on Standard, Enterprise, and Web editions. It cannot be installed on Server Core for Windows and is not supported if you try to install it on a domain controller. (Although there are hacks to get it to work, it's not suggested.)

◆ A number of prerequisites are required before SharePoint Foundation will install properly. Luckily, all those fiddly-bits, like Filter Pack 2.0, Chart Controls, or Sync Framework are installed for you by the Prerequisite installation process available from the SharePoint Foundation installation screen. So, be sure, before upgrading to SharePoint Foundation, to run the prerequisite installation on the new server first (it does require Internet access). For more details on exactly what the SharePoint Foundation installation prerequisites are, see Chapter 1. If you need help running the prerequisites installer, see Chapter 2, "Standalone Installation."

◆ Along with installing SharePoint, you must always consider the fact that SharePoint depends on SQL databases of some sort on the backend. Therefore, it goes without saying that either you will need to have a 64-bit version of SQL Server (2005 SP3 or higher) somewhere or you'll be installing SQL Server 2008 Express during the Standalone installation.

PLAN FOR DATABASE GROWTH DURING UPGRADE

While you're checking your hardware and software requirements, you might want to take a look at the available disk space on the server that will be housing your database. During the upgrade process, your databases will undergo some changes that will cause them to grow. The changes will be logged in the transaction log, which will cause the log to grow as well. So, you will want to make sure that there is enough space to accommodate this immediate growth (plus more, of course, for continued growth in standard day-to-day use).

Since the database can grow as much as 50 percent, you will want to make sure you have 1.5 times the size of your databases available on your destination server. For example, if all your WSS 3.0 databases together total 100 GB of space, be sure that you will have 150 GB of free space on the SharePoint Foundation database server just for the upgrade alone.

Your databases may not grow that much, but the upgrade will cause a size increase to some degree, so it's better to be safe than sorry. The good news is that most of this extra space can be recovered after the upgrade is finished, leaving you with room for future growth.

◆ The server OS, either 2008 or 2008 R2, requires a hotfix before SharePoint is configured (the prerequisite installer should install the hotfix, but check for it). For Windows Server 2008 SP2, you can download `Windows6.0-KB979919-x64.msu`, and for Windows Server 2008 R2, download `Windows6.1-KB979917-x64.msu`.

◆ Finally, your current WSS 3.0 farm will need to be 64-bit and at Service Pack 2 or higher before you can do an in-place upgrade to SharePoint Foundation. If you're going to use the database attach method, make sure WSS 3.0 is up to Service pack 2 before migrating.

HARDWARE REQUIREMENTS

To run a 64-bit operating system, you will need at least one processor that supports 64-bit (Microsoft suggests at least one quad-core processor, 2.5 GHz or better). The suggested minimum amount of RAM is 4 GB for a development environment and 8 GB for a production environment. And finally, you'll need an 80 GB disk drive for your system drive (for the operating system and SharePoint Foundation files alone).

HOW MUCH FREE SPACE DO I NEED?

An 80 GB system drive can seem big, but in reality it can fill up fast, and if you are low on free space, it can adversely affect the performance of SharePoint Foundation.

So, how much free space do you need? A good rule of thumb is to maintain a minimum of twice the amount of RAM you are running in free space for the paging file alone. So, for example, if you are running the suggested 8 GB of RAM on your production server, you will want to maintain 16 GB of free space on your system drive at all times.

In other words, if you don't have your database files on your system drive (as would be the case in a standalone server), you still need to plan for storing the operating system files, SharePoint binaries, log files, update/hotfix/service packs, custom web parts, features, and solutions, as well as index files (if you have them in the default location) on that system drive. Growth in these files is practically inevitable, but it can be controlled with careful management. So in addition to the need for the free 16 GB of storage in this scenario, keep in mind those files that can silently fill up your drive.

What about Customizations?

One of the wonderful things about SharePoint is how customizable it is. And one of the downsides of SharePoint, in terms of upgrades, is how customizable it is. Developers are able to customize the way SharePoint looks and functions, allowing them to create solutions that meet specific needs, and this is good. However, when upgrade time comes around, all those customizations can give administrators headaches trying to identify all of them and decide which need to be kept and which can be discarded. And if they are kept, will they work in the new environment, or will they need to be reworked? This process can be challenging; just how challenging may depend on the extent of the customizations.

Good or bad, customizations are part of SharePoint and therefore will need to be planned for when upgrading. The first step is to identify your customizations. This doesn't have to be fancy or elaborate; a simple list of what is available in Central Administration, site collections, and even sites will do. Look for any custom solutions, site templates, features, or web parts and add them to the list, keeping in mind anything that might have an absolute URL, such as alerts or links. Don't forget to list any event handlers, customized master pages, or page layouts.

A QUICK WORD ABOUT SITE TEMPLATES

In previous versions of SharePoint, site template files were stored as `.stp` files. SharePoint 2010 (Foundation and Server) now stores site template files as `.wsp` files, making `.stp` files incompatible.

If you are currently using sites based on `.stp` site template files, not to worry; when you upgrade to SharePoint Foundation, the sites will be upgraded as well. However, you will not be able to create new sites from those site templates.

One alternative is to, after you upgrade, open a site you have that was based on an `.stp` template, open site settings for that site, and save the site as a template. This will save the modified site as a `.wsp` file so you will be able to use it again. Although this trick will work for most `.stp` site templates, sometimes the process of making a `.stp` site into a `.wsp` solution file may damage some web parts and custom code. So, be sure to test the template after you've made the new template, just in case.

Something to keep in mind concerning the Fantastic 40 site templates used for WSS 3.0, particularly the `.stp` files, is that not all the site templates (particularly the `.stp` files) will upgrade properly. They won't stop the migration, but test them thoroughly, and make sure that those you need work properly after the upgrade process.

Custom components such as features, third-party web parts, or solutions require files to be stored in the server's file system. For this reason, you will probably have to add them manually to the new server in order to have them work properly (SharePoint will be pointing to them, but the required files might not have copied over). This is specifically the case if you are using the database-attach method of migrating.

PREPARATION TOOLS

There are two tools to remember in your migration arsenal when upgrading to SharePoint Foundation: the pre-upgrade checker, which we will discuss in detail later in the chapter, and the PowerShell cmdlet `Test-SPContentDatabase`.

The `Test-SPContentDatabase` PowerShell cmdlet is run on the SharePoint Foundation server to which you will be attaching databases. Once you've restored the databases from the WSS 3.0 implementation to the 64-bit SQL server the SharePoint Foundation server will be using, you can use the `Test-SPContentDatabase` cmdlet to check those databases before attaching them to the SharePoint Foundation server (or server farm). This is obviously specifically used in a database-attach migration scenario, once you've created the web applications the databases will attach to. However, it can also be useful to just check the state of any content database in the farm to be sure it's healthy.

You can also use this command to verify your custom components. If your new farm is missing any customizations on the front-end servers, it could cause the upgrade to fail. You can verify you have all your customizations installed using the PowerShell cmdlet `Test-SPContentDatabase`.

1. To use the PowerShell cmdlet, on your SharePoint server, open the management shell (**Start** ➢ **All Programs** ➢ **Microsoft SharePoint 2010 Products** ➢ **SharePoint 2010 Management Shell**).

2. In the management shell console, type the following command and press Enter:

```
Test-SpContentDatabase -name <name of the database>
```

3. You will then be prompted to provide the name of the web application the database can be compared to. Here you will see if there are any customizations missing. Enter it, using the syntax `http://<yoursiteURL>`, and press **Enter**.

What follows is a list of any features, web parts, site definitions, or files that you may be missing.

You can find more information about PowerShell cmdlets and using PowerShell with SharePoint in Chapter 14, "STSADM and PowerShell," and for more information about these tools, see the TechNet article "What's new in upgrade (SharePoint Foundation 2010)," an excellent source of information about preparing for migration.

So, after you run the pre-upgrade checker before even starting the upgrade process on your WSS 3.0 server (or the `Test-SPContentDatabase` cmdlet on the SharePoint Foundation server before or even after attaching the databases), make note of the customizations it has found. Record what customizations you've made to the `web.config` file (if you made any), in Central Administration's farm features and solutions galleries, and at the site and site-collection level, and indicate what has been activated and what hasn't. (This is also a good time to do some housecleaning and maybe not migrate over anything you aren't really using or that never really worked.) Make sure you have copies of all the solution, web part, or feature files you need to apply to the upgraded server (or farm). Then, to help ensure success, after you install SharePoint Foundation but before you attach the content databases, apply the customizations. So, when the databases attach, they will be referring to files that now exist, because you put them there. You might as well not invite problems.

Plan for Visual Upgrade

Visual Upgrade is a new SharePoint 2010 feature that allows you to retain the look and feel of your WSS 3.0 sites after you upgrade. You may not want to use the new SharePoint Foundation ribbons and wiki-like user interface. Maybe your current WSS 3.0 sites are so easy to use and so well-designed that your users don't want them to change, or maybe they just prefer some simple menus over numerous, complicated ribbons for their sites. Whatever the reason, you don't have to change anything in the interface if you don't want to.

You can choose to keep the appearance of your WSS 3.0 sites and never move your site to the new SharePoint Foundation interface. You will still get most of the infrastructure improvements that come with upgrading; you just won't be able to take advantage of some of the new features of the SharePoint Foundation interface (mostly the visual ones, but it will still support .stp files, not .wsp, for templates, for example) unless you permanently upgrade your site to the new user interface.

To help you evaluate whether to retain the look of your WSS 3.0 sites or make the change to the new SharePoint Foundation interface, Visual Upgrade allows site collection owners and site owners to switch between the WSS 3.0 user interface and the new SharePoint Foundation user interface and preview how the site will look and function under the new interface. In this way, they will be able to see how their site would appear and test how their site will function in the new SharePoint Foundation interface before deciding whether to keep their sites as they are in WSS 3 or upgrade to the new SharePoint Foundation look.

You can also use Visual Upgrade to identify any issues that will need to be addressed before permanently moving their site to the new user interface. Your customized pages can be reworked, or if there are issues, you can decide to retain the WSS 3.0 look and feel permanently. The choice is yours.

Visual Upgrade is enabled by default for in-place standalone as well as database-attach upgrades, both standalone and farm, and is an option with in-place farm upgrades (which we'll choose in the example). So, most readers should plan to take advantage of this testing opportunity and then upgrade to the new interface when ready. Later in this chapter, we'll go through the steps of enabling Visual Upgrade.

Plan for Remote BLOB Storage (RBS)

BLOB stands for Binary Large Object and refers to a large file, or a collection of binary data, that gets stored as a single file in a database. A BLOB is typically an image, sound, or multimedia file. Because BLOB files are so large, they tend to take up a lot of file space in the database they are stored in.

Remote BLOB Storage (RBS) is an API add-on to SQL Server 2008 that takes those BLOB files and stores them outside the database, freeing up file space inside the database but appearing to users as if the files are right where they have always been. RBS requires the use of a provider program to act as a middleman for the RBS API and the SQL Server. Conveniently, both SQL Server 2008 Express, and SQL Server 2008 R2 Express come with the FILESTREAM provider included. SharePoint Foundation uses the version of RBS that is included with the Feature Pack for SQL Server2008 R2.

SQL Server 2008 Express has a database size limit of 4 GB per database. So if you are using the built-in database version that is included as part of the Standalone installation and *any* of your content databases from WSS 3.0 are over 4 GB, then you basically have two choices: use RBS, or purchase a copy of SQL Server (2005, 2008, 2008 R2, or higher), because they're too big to be upgraded to SharePoint Foundation's built-in SQL Express 2008. You could also upgrade the built-in SQL Express 2008 to 2008 R2 before migrating, but that only increases the database limit from 4 GB to 10 GB, which (depending on your circumstances) may not be enough.

If you are using SQL Server 2005 with Service Pack 3, you will not be able to use RBS, because it does not support this feature.

RBS can only be used for the content databases in SharePoint Foundation, not the databases used for the services or configuration. If your database is located on the local server, you can use RBS with Microsoft SQL Server 2008 R2, SQL Server 2008, and SQL Server 2008 Express (which is what a Standalone installation uses). However, if your database is on a remote server, you are limited to using SQL Server 2008 R2 Enterprise edition if you want to use RBS.

If you are running SQL Server 2008 or SQL Server 2008 R2, you may benefit from using RBS if your content databases are larger than 500 GB, if your BLOB data files are larger than 256 KB, or if your BLOB data files are causing a performance bottleneck.

The section "Upgrade a Standalone Server with Remote BLOB Storage" presents the procedure for installing RBS as part of your upgrade.

PLAYING THE NAME GAME

As we go through the chapter, you can follow along as I walk through the steps for each of the various types of upgrades. To do this, I have set up a test environment with nine servers that are listed in the following table. As I go from one example to the next and from one machine to another, it can be easy to get confused. So, to make it easier to follow along, I have named the machines as follows.

TEST ENVIRONMENT

SERVER NAME	DESCRIPTION	PURPOSE
SP1	32-bit, WSS 3.0, Standalone	Will be backed up in migrating a WSS 3.0 32-bit server to WSS 3.0 64-bit. Its contents are the original WSS 3.0 standalone server contents.
SP2	32-bit, WSS 3.0, Server Farm	The WSS 3.0 server farm server. Its contents will be backed up and restored to a WSS 3.0 64-bit on MIGC, and the content databases from this server are used in the database-attach upgrade for server farms on MIGD.
DC1	Domain controller	This server is where the file share is for saving backups and files.
RR1	32-bit SQL Server for WSS 3.0 farm	The database server for the 32-bit WSS 3.0 server farm. Its databases will be used in the upgrade of WSS 3.0 server farm scenarios. It is where the databases for the farm will be coming from.
SQL64	64-bit SQL Server for SharePoint Foundation server farm	This is the 64-bit database server, which will be used in the server farm migration scenarios. This 64-bit server is where the databases for the server farm upgrade scenarios will be going.
MIGA	64-bit 2008 R2 server, first used for WSS 3.0 and then SharePoint Foundation Standalone in-place upgrade	This server will be used first as a WSS 3.0 server for the migration of WSS 3.0 from a 32-bit server to a 64-bit server and then later for the in-place upgrade to SharePoint Foundation, and then reused for the in-place upgrade with Remote BLOB Storage.
MIGB	64-bit 2008 R2, SharePoint Foundation, standalone	This server is used in the database-attach upgrade for a standalone server.
MIGC	64-bit 2008 R2, SharePoint Foundation, server farm	This server will be used for the in-place upgrade for a server farm.
MIGD	64-bit, 2008 R2, SharePoint Foundation, server farm	This server will be used in the database-attach upgrade for a server farm.

So when you see references to these machines in the examples, you will know that I am referring to the names of the machines in my test environment.

When Planning to Succeed, Plan to Fail

Sometimes bad things happen to good plans. No matter how carefully you plan your upgrade, things can still go awry, and if they do, you need to be prepared. Part of every good migration plan is what to do in case of a failure.

When starting your upgrade, the very first thing you should do is a full farm backup. Then, if something should go wrong with your upgrade, you can restore your WSS 3.0 environment to its current state (remember, there is no rollback capability for an in-place upgrade). Although backing up and restoring SharePoint Foundation was covered earlier in the book, some settings are a little different with WSS 3.0; so we'll step through the process here.

FULL FARM BACKUP OF WSS 3.0

To back up WSS 3.0 through Central Administration, you must be logged in as a member of the Farm Administrator group.

1. First you will need to open the **Central Administration** website.

2. Click the **Operations** tab.

3. In the **Backup and Restore** section, click Perform a Backup.

4. To back up the entire farm, click the **Farm** check box. Once you do, all the check boxes below Farm will be checked automatically, and the entire region will be highlighted in blue (Figure 15.1).

FIGURE 15.1
Selecting components to back up

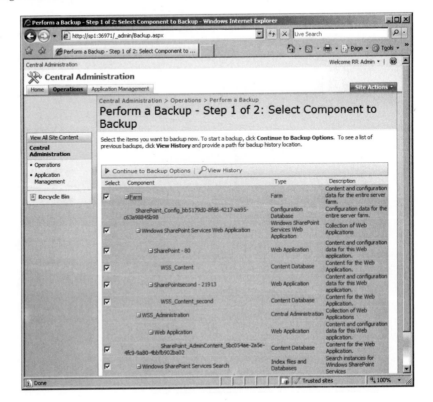

5. Click the **Continue To Backup Options** button.

6. In the **Backup Content** section, leave the default setting of **Farm**, and for the **Type Of Backup** setting, leave the **Full** radio button selected.

7. In the **Backup File Location** section, enter a file path where you can save your backup file. Whenever possible, it is a good idea to save these files on a server share outside the farm but where they're accessible to the WSS 3.0 server. In this example, we will save the files in a file share on the domain controller named dc1, so our path is \\dc1\sp1backup. Figure 15.2 shows all the backup options.

FIGURE 15.2
Selecting backup options

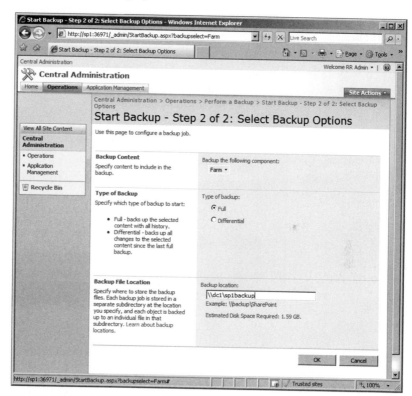

Make certain that the account you are logged in with, the SQL service account (if you are backing up a standalone server, the server computer account instead), and the farm account all have at least read and write access to the backup location. Also make sure the account is a member of the db_owner database role on all the databases that need an upgrade, as this can cause your upgrade to fail. The SharePoint Administration service should be running for this process (and especially for the restore), so be certain it is started before you start the backup or restore process.

Just below the **Backup Location** file path you will see **Estimated Disk Space Required**. If you have any concerns about whether you have enough disk space on your file share to save the backup files, you can compare the amount of free space you have to the Estimated Disk Space Required.

8. Click the **OK** button. The backup timer job will begin.

Next you'll see the Backup And Restore Status page, shown in Figure 15.3. It shows you the progress of your backup job and any errors that might occur (ideally there won't be any; if there are, fix the issues listed, and run the backup again).

FIGURE 15.3

The Backup
And Restore
Status page

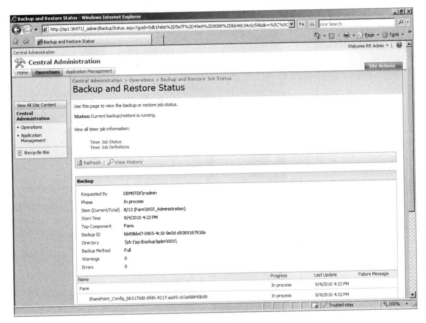

At the top of the page is a summary displaying information such as the phase, top component, number of warnings, and errors that have occurred. Below the summary you will find a listing of all the components being backed up and the progress of each. The information on the page is refreshed automatically every 30 seconds, but you can refresh it manually at any time with the Refresh button.

You will know when the backup job has completed when the summary at the top of the page shows the Phase as Completed and shows the Progress as Completed for each of the components in the list.

Any errors during the backup job will be listed by component under Failure Message in the component listing. You will need to review the messages and correct any issues listed. If there are no errors, then you have successfully completed your backup.

By the end of this chapter, you will be tired of me reminding you to back up your farm over and over again, but trust me, if something goes wrong, you will be thanking me later.

Moving from a 32-Bit to a 64-Bit Environment

Many companies today are running their WSS 3.0 standalone server or server farm in a 32-bit environment, but to run SharePoint Foundation, you will have to move SharePoint to a 64-bit environment. This can seem like it's going to be a real chore, but trust me, it really won't be difficult.

As you can see with a quick Internet search, there is more than one way to move SharePoint from a 32-bit server to a 64-bit server.

If you have a WSS 3.0 Standalone server, you can use the Backup And Restore feature in Central Administration to back up your farm on your current server and restore it to your new server.

Another solution would be to use the database-attach method to upgrade directly from WSS 32-bit to SharePoint Foundation on 64-bit. Do not pass Go; do not collect $200.

Generally, if you are running a WSS 3.0 32-bit environment, you will want to use the database-attach method to upgrade directly to a SharePoint Foundation 64-bit environment. However, there are some good reasons to move your WSS 3.0 32-bit implementation to a 64-bit server first before upgrade (other than performance improvements).

If you plan to use the database-attach method, then you can skip ahead to the section "The Database-Attach Upgrade Method for Standalone Servers" of the chapter. Remember that you can take the databases directly from the 32-bit WSS 3.0 environment to the SharePoint Foundation environment. The databases don't care about 32-bit vs. 64-bit. Whatever method you choose, we will walk you through each of these processes one step at a time. So, let's get started!

Moving a Standalone Server from 32-Bit to 64-Bit

You might be wondering why anyone would go to all the trouble of moving a WSS 3.0 Standalone installation to a 64-bit server and then do an in-place upgrade, when you can use database-attach to upgrade directly to SharePoint Foundation without all the extra steps.

One answer would be that you'll need to move WSS 3.0 to 64-bit if you have a database that exceeds 4 GB and therefore need to install Remote BLOB Storage. RBS was discussed earlier in this chapter. SharePoint is configured to use RBS when the configuration wizard is run. In the database-attach method, the configuration wizard is run before the databases are attached, so the wizard wouldn't know to configure SharePoint Foundation to use RBS. Therefore, you would need to move WSS 3.0 over to a 64-bit server and then perform an in-place upgrade with RBS.

Another good reason to move WSS 3.0 to a 64-bit server is to be able to do an in-place installation of SharePoint Foundation. This way, URL addressing (it simply doesn't change, which is nice), and all features, custom web parts, solutions, alerts, absolute links (such as those that might be added to the Quick Launch bar and Top Link bar) will all be right where you left them. When you do a database-attach to a different server, you have to be aware of configuration settings, security, addressing issues, such as absolute links and AAM (Alternate Address Mapping) settings, and you have to copy over all the necessary files for features, solutions, and web parts as well as redeploy them to the new server before upgrade.

PREPARE TO MOVE A STANDALONE SERVER

Before you can move your 32-bit WSS 3.0 standalone server to a 64-bit WSS 3.0 standalone server, you must first be sure that your 32-bit WSS 3.0 standalone server is on SP2 or higher. Next, on the 64-bit server, install the 64-bit version of WSS 3.0. Finally, install any service packs and hotfixes required to bring your 64-bit WSS 3.0 server up to the same service pack as your 32-bit WSS 3.0 server. Then just back up your 32-bit WSS 3.0 server, and restore that backup on the 64-bit WSS 3.0 server. Easy peasy.

BACK UP AND RESTORE YOUR STANDALONE FARM USING CENTRAL ADMINISTRATION

Moving your WSS 3.0 installation using the **Backup And Restore** process in Central Administration is, for the most part, like doing any other backup and restore. For this example, I will be backing up my WSS 3.0 standalone server (which is named SP1) and restoring it to a new 64-bit WSS 3.0 server (which is named MIGA). Figure 15.4 shows an overview. Later we will upgrade the MIGA server from WSS 3 to SharePoint Foundation.

FIGURE 15.4

Overview of the standalone backup and restore

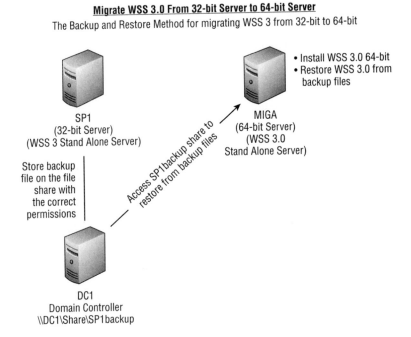

Migrate WSS 3.0 From 32-bit Server to 64-bit Server

The Backup and Restore Method for migrating WSS 3 from 32-bit to 64-bit

SP1
(32-bit Server)
(WSS 3 Stand Alone Server)

Store backup file on the file share with the correct permissions

Access SP1backup share to restore from backup files

- Install WSS 3.0 64-bit
- Restore WSS 3.0 from backup files

MIGA
(64-bit Server)
(WSS 3.0 Stand Alone Server)

DC1
Domain Controller
\\DC1\Share\SP1backup

First, log onto your 32-bit WSS 3.0 server, and create a full farm backup, as described in "When Planning to Succeed, Plan to Fail." Since I want to be sure that I back up my files to a file share that is accessible to my 64-bit server (MIGA), I have used the file share at \\dc1\share\sp1backup.

Once you have a complete farm backup, log onto your 64-bit WSS 3.0 server (MIGA in my example), and install WSS 3.0 for 64-bit. To install WSS 3.0 as a standalone server, you will need to click "Basic" when choosing which kind of installation you want to perform. When you run the **SharePoint Products And Technologies Configuration Wizard** on your new WSS 3.0 server, a new web application and site collection will be created by the configuration wizard by default. However, we will not be using this web application or site, so you will need to delete the web application (it contains the site collection) in Central Administration.

1. To do this, open your Central Administration site, and click the **Application Management** tab. Then click **Delete Web Application** in the **SharePoint Web Application Management** section.

When the **Delete Web Application** page opens, you'll see the newly created web application (it should be SharePoint-80) in the Web Application section. Since there is only one web application (besides Central Administration, which we need to keep), it should be selected by default. If it isn't, click the drop-down arrow, and select Change Web Application. This will take you to a page where all the web applications are listed, and you can select your web application by clicking the name. Make certain the correct web application is selected before choosing to delete the web application. It is always a good idea to check in the **Delete Database** window to make certain the correct web application is being deleted.

Under **Delete Options**, you have two selections to make. The first is whether to delete the content database for the web application, and the second is whether to delete the IIS Web Sites.

If you choose No, not to delete the content database, then the content database would not be deleted and would be available to be used or added to other web applications. If you choose Yes to delete it, the database would be deleted, and the only way you could recover it would be from a backup.

If you choose No, not to delete the IIS Web Sites, the Web Site will no longer be associated with this web application, but it will still be available to other, non-SharePoint applications. If you choose Yes, to delete, the IIS Web Site and all the metabase entries will be removed, and the web application will not be available to any application.

2. Select **Yes** to delete the databases and **Yes** to delete the IIS Web Sites as well. Figure 15.5 shows our settings.

3. Click the **Delete** button.

FIGURE 15.5
Setting the Delete Web Application options

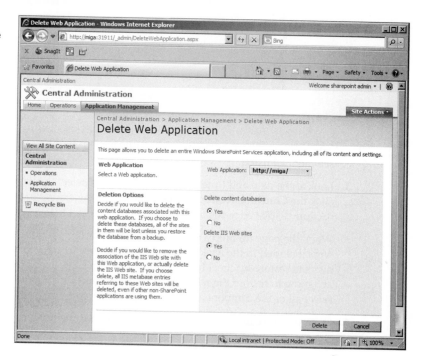

You now have a clean implementation to restore our farm to, so let's get started.

1. On the Central Administration site, click the **Operations** tab, and then click **Restore From Backup** in the **Backup And Restore** section.

2. The page for Step 1 of 4 will open asking you for the location of your backup file (Figure 15.6). I saved my backup files to a server share outside the server farm, on my DC1 server. So, I will enter the backup location as **\\DC1\share\sp1backup**. You will need to enter the location you used when you performed your own backup (and make sure it's accessible from this server with the account you are using to run the restore; for more details about restores, see Chapter 13, "Maintenance and Monitoring").

FIGURE 15.6
Selecting the backup location

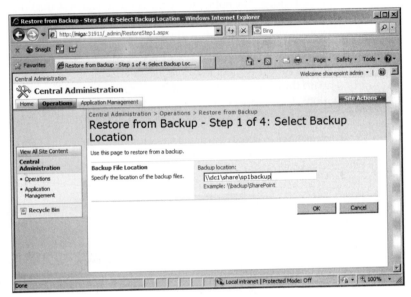

On the page for Step 2 of 4 (Figure 15.7), you will select which backup you want to restore from. You may have saved more than one backup in the same location, and if so, you will see them all listed.

3. Look at the date and time of each one carefully, select the backup you want, and then click the **Continue Restore Process** button. In my example, I am restoring my most recent backup, displayed at the top of the list.

When the page for Step 3 of 4 (Figure 15.8) opens, you will see a list of components that were included in the backup you chose to restore from. You can select individual components to restore by checking their boxes, or you can select to restore all of them. Since we are going to restore the whole farm, we will check the **Farm** box, which will automatically select all of the components.

4. Once you have made your selections, click **Continue Restore Process**.

The fourth and final step is to select the restore options (Figure 15.9); and this is where things are a little different, and you need take some extra care. The first section of the page is **Restore Component**, which we will leave at **Farm**, since we aren't restoring particular web applications but the entire farm.

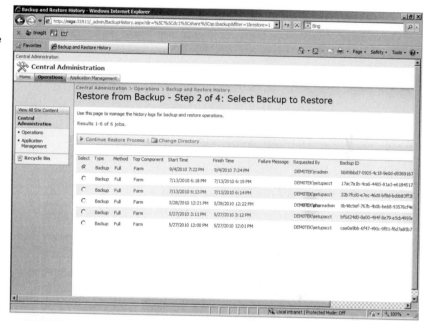

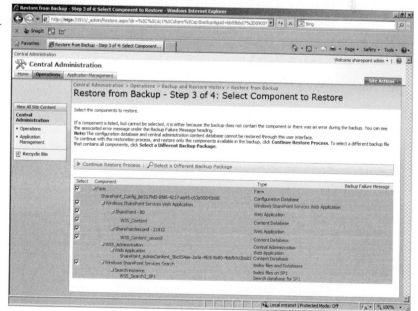

FIGURE 15.9

Selecting restore options—the Restore Component and Restore Options sections

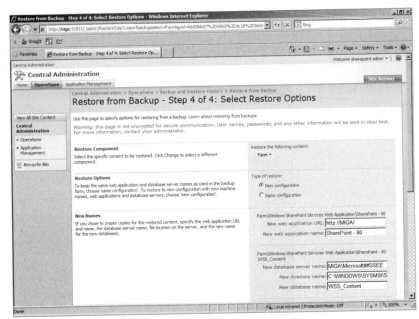

The next section is **Restore Options**, and this is also the first "gotcha." If you were restoring to the same server the backup was created from (SP1 in my example) and you just wanted to overwrite everything and return to a previous state, you would choose Same Configuration.

However, you are restoring to a new server, so you need to use new server names. Also, this machine doesn't have the web applications created yet, so you will have to create new web applications to hold your site collections.

5. Select the **New Configuration** option.

Once you've selected **New Configuration**, the next section, which would be grayed out if you had chosen Same Configuration, is now active and can be edited.

In the **New Names** section (Figure 15.10), the server name of the farm where the backup was taken (SP1 in my example) may be still listed in all the relevant fields. So, you will need to go through and everywhere you see the old server name, replace it with the new name (which for me is MIGA). While you're there, you might consider also adding the server name to the name of the databases as well. It makes it easier to tell which databases go with which servers for backup and restores later, if there are any questions. There may also be fields for entering SQL authentication for the databases, if you require it. I use Windows authentication, so I'm leaving it blank.

6. Make sure that all URLs for web applications include the new server name (you can have them accept the address of the old server in AAM later), that the database server name is correct (for a standalone WSS 3.0 server, the server name is always the local server name itself, then ##SSEE for the instance name), and the database name itself is one you want. Don't forget to change the server names for the Search service and search database names as well. If the search database name doesn't include the server name, I usually append it to the name, just for clarity's sake.

IF AT FIRST SEARCH DOES NOT SUCCEED...

Sometimes, when I restore Search for WSS 3.0, it doesn't quite work. In that case, I just stop the service, change the name of the search database, and start it again. I don't know why, but sometimes it just doesn't like to reuse the restored database. Don't worry. This particularly happens if you have a custom location for your index files. This will cause some lag while the restored web applications are reindexed, but at least you'll be prepared for it if it happens.

---

7. Once you have selected all your options, click the **OK** button to begin the restore process.

FIGURE 15.10
Selecting restore options—the New Names section

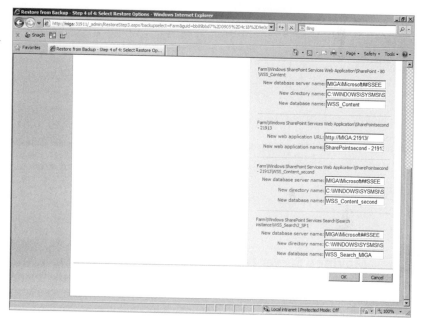

You can follow the restore progress on the Backup And Restore Status page. This page works just like the Backup Progress page we discussed earlier in the chapter. The page will refresh itself automatically every 30 seconds, or you can refresh the page manually by clicking the Refresh button.

Once the restore process is completed, you should see a status page much like Figure 15.11. You can see the status of the job overall, as well as each component and whether there were any errors or warnings. The details of any error or warning is listed with its component in the Failure Message column.

Next you will want to transfer over and install any customizations. This means adding and deploying solutions (see "Adding and Deploying Solutions" later in the chapter), activating features, or adding web parts.

After you have transferred your customizations, you are ready to test your new SharePoint environment. Open your web browser, and type in the URL for your root site. This would be `http://yourservername/`, which for my example would be `http://miga`.

You should see your SharePoint home page displayed just like it was on your 32-bit server. Take a few minutes and check out all your sites. Make sure everything is working and that you haven't forgotten to bring over any of your customizations. Also be sure that all security is in place, make certain your alternate access mappings are set up, and that alerts and workflows are working.

FIGURE 15.11

The Backup
And Restore
Status page

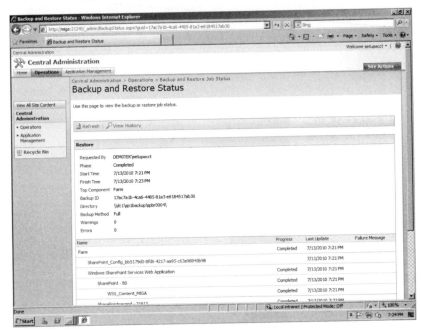

Moving a Server Farm from 32-Bit to 64-Bit

As I mentioned at the beginning of this section, if you have a 32-bit WSS 3.0 server farm, then you don't have to move WWS 3.0 to a 64-bit server before upgrading to SharePoint Foundation. Rather, you can use the database-attach method to move your content databases directly to your new SharePoint Foundation farm servers.

If you have a specific need to move your WSS 3.0 32-bit server farm to a 64-bit WSS 3.0 server before performing an in-place upgrade to SharePoint Foundation, you can follow the basic instructions in the section "The Database-Attach Upgrade Method for Standalone Servers." Just install WSS 3.0 64-bit on the server you want to move to instead of SharePoint Foundation. Keep in mind that you can use the backup and restore method to move, just as you did with the standalone server, but the database-attach method can be fast and give you more control. So, feel free to jump directly to that section now before proceeding with the upgrade.

Upgrading a Standalone Server

This section will walk through upgrading a WSS 3.0 standalone server to a SharePoint Foundation standalone server. You will see how to perform both in-place and database-attach upgrades.

For the in-place upgrade method, I am assuming that you are already running your WSS 3.0 environment on a 64-bit server and that your WSS 3.0 is up to SP2, with the latest cumulative updates (to use the most recent pre-upgrade checker).

For the database-attach method, the WSS 3.0 server can be running at either 64-bit or 32-bit, as long as the SharePoint Foundation server you will be upgrading to is on a 64-bit server.

The Prep Work

In the spirit of "measure twice, cut once," it is important to be sure you are well prepared before performing an upgrade. The time it takes to perform these simple steps can save you hours of work down the road. Before attempting to upgrade to SharePoint Foundation, you need to do a few preparatory steps. In particular, you should do the following:

- Run the pre-upgrade checker (make note of any issues and customizations).

- Back up your farm, of course.

- Install your prerequisites on your SharePoint Foundation Server.

THE PRE-UPGRADE CHECKER

I don't know about you, but when it comes to upgrading, I hate surprises, especially surprises that can cause my upgrade to fail. To help you avoid those nasty surprises, Microsoft came up with this neat little tool called the *pre-upgrade checker.*

The pre-upgrade checker is a handy command-line tool that checks your current WSS 3.0 environment, assesses its readiness to be upgraded, and then generates a printable report. In addition to identifying issues that could cause your upgrade to fail so that you can fix them *before* trying the upgrade, this report also lists all the components, features, web parts, databases, web applications, and so on, in your environment. The pre-upgrade checker was added to WSS 3.0 with Service Pack 2, so if it is not available, check to see what service packs are installed. There has also been at least one update since then that also improved the pre-upgrade checker; so be sure to be fully updated before running the checker.

DOCUMENT YOUR ENVIRONMENT

I see this stated all the time: you should document your environment. What I rarely see, however, is anything that tells you exactly how to do that. Yes, there are worksheets out there, but because each implementation is so different, only you can know what you have configured and what you need to remember. Regardless of the size of your implementation, you should keep a regular list of all Central Administration settings, security settings at every level, changes made at the command line, and all features, solutions, alternate access mappings, custom site templates, and third-party web parts. Pay particular attention to any absolute links, alerts, self-service, or host header site collections, because their URL addressing may need extra attention.

If you don't already have your WSS 3.0 environment documented and you want to document your environment before you upgrade so you can use it to verify that your sites, components, and customizations are all present and accounted for after upgrade, printing out the pre-upgrade check report is a fast and easy way to document your WSS 3.0 environment without having to spend a lot of time and effort to do it.

---

1. To run the pre-upgrade checker on the WSS 3.0 server, open the command prompt window, and navigate to the bin folder in the 12 hive:

   `%program files%\common files\microsoft shared\web server extensions\12\bin`

2. Once you are in the correct directory, you can start the pre-upgrade checker by entering the following STSADM command:

   `Stsadm.exe -o preupgradecheck`

   You will see the message "Processing configuration file: WssPreUpgradeCheck.xml," followed by a list of components that are being analyzed, as shown in Figure 15.12. As each one is checked, it will be marked as Passed in green, Failed in red, or Information Only in yellow.

FIGURE 15.12
Running the pre-upgrade check

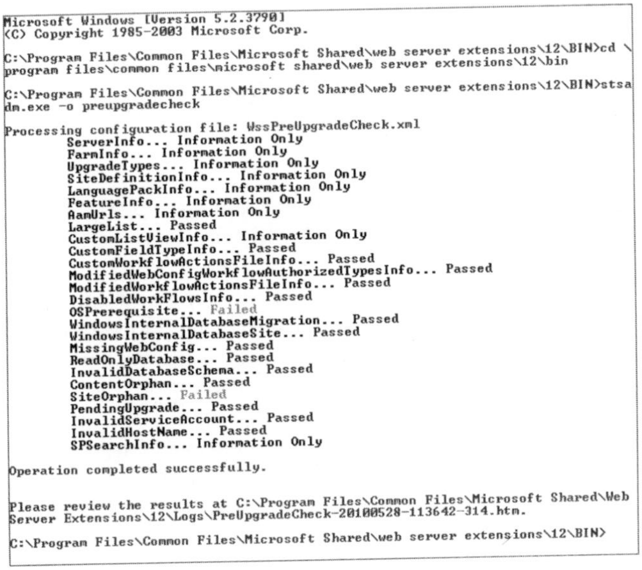

```
Microsoft Windows [Version 5.2.3790]
(C) Copyright 1985-2003 Microsoft Corp.

C:\Program Files\Common Files\Microsoft Shared\web server extensions\12\BIN>cd \
program files\common files\microsoft shared\web server extensions\12\bin

C:\Program Files\Common Files\Microsoft Shared\web server extensions\12\BIN>stsa
dm.exe -o preupgradecheck

Processing configuration file: WssPreUpgradeCheck.xml
        ServerInfo... Information Only
        FarmInfo... Information Only
        UpgradeTypes... Information Only
        SiteDefinitionInfo... Information Only
        LanguagePackInfo... Information Only
        FeatureInfo... Information Only
        AamUrls... Information Only
        LargeList... Passed
        CustomListViewInfo... Information Only
        CustomFieldTypeInfo... Passed
        CustomWorkflowActionsFileInfo... Passed
        ModifiedWebConfigWorkflowAuthorizedTypesInfo... Passed
        ModifiedWorkflowActionsFileInfo... Passed
        DisabledWorkFlowsInfo... Passed
        OSPrerequisite... Failed
        WindowsInternalDatabaseMigration... Passed
        WindowsInternalDatabaseSite... Passed
        MissingWebConfig... Passed
        ReadOnlyDatabase... Passed
        InvalidDatabaseSchema... Passed
        ContentOrphan... Passed
        SiteOrphan... Failed
        PendingUpgrade... Passed
        InvalidServiceAccount... Passed
        InvalidHostName... Passed
        SPSearchInfo... Information Only

Operation completed successfully.

Please review the results at C:\Program Files\Common Files\Microsoft Shared\Web
Server Extensions\12\Logs\PreUpgradeCheck-20100528-113642-314.htm.

C:\Program Files\Common Files\Microsoft Shared\web server extensions\12\BIN>
```

WAIT, THE PRE-UPGRADE PASS WASN'T PERFECT

In my case, everything passed except the OS (because I ran it on the 32-bit server before backing it up), and there is an orphaned site. I was messing with the site that indicates it's orphaned, and I could delete it before the upgrade. However, sometimes, depending on why it's orphaned (especially if its information is a little corrupt in the content database), simply attaching the content database containing it to a different server fixes the problem (which is what will happen here). In other words, sometimes Fails are more informative than critical errors.

When the analysis is complete, you will get your printable HTML report (it will open in the browser). Print that report, and you can add it to your documentation for future reference. The report is pretty detailed (Figure 15.13 shows the first screenful) and contains information pertaining to everything about the SharePoint implementation from components to site definitions, features, language packs, AAM settings, search topology, and more. In the Failed section (if you had any failures), it will specify exactly what failed. In every section, there are links to a massive Knowledge Base article concerning the rules that generated a given section and additional KB articles to help you fix failures or issues, or at least explain what is listed.

FIGURE 15.13
A pre-upgrade
check report

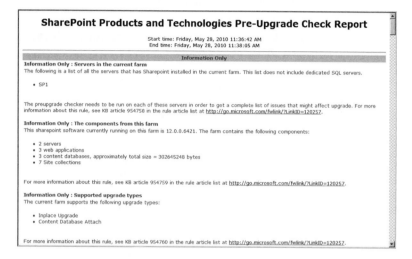

Keep whatever customizations you might have documented in mind. In the case of a database-attach upgrade, after installing SharePoint Foundation but before you attach databases, you will likely need to add your customizations back to the farm (or server in a standalone situation).

BACK UP YOUR FARM

Once your environment is cleaned up and ready to upgrade, don't forget to take a moment and get a current full farm backup so if something unexpected happens, you can restore your farm to its current, ready-to-upgrade state. This way, in the event you need to restore your farm, you won't have to go back and clean up any issues in your environment all over again. Backups are your friend!

INSTALL THE PREREQUISITES

Installing the prerequisites was covered in the installation chapters; for detailed instructions, please refer to Chapters 2 and 3. Briefly, to get to the prerequisite installer, you double-click the `SharePointFoundation.exe` installation file. It will unpack some files necessary to check for and install prerequisites, among other things. After the installation screen comes up, click the Install Software Prerequisites link to run the preparation wizard. Remember that to install and configure prerequisites using this wizard, you must have Internet access. Otherwise, note the items listed in the wizard interface, download the ones you don't have, and install them manually. Once they are installed, run the prerequisites wizard again to be sure that SharePoint sees that everything is OK (if it doesn't reboot and rerun on its own). You may also want to add the SMTP service at this point as well, if you need it for incoming email.

Now that the prep work is done, you are ready to upgrade your WSS 3.0 standalone server to a SharePoint Foundation standalone server.

The In-Place Upgrade Method for Standalone Servers

Now you are ready for the moment you have been planning and working for—upgrading to SharePoint Foundation.

In this example, we will perform an in-place upgrade of WSS 3.0 to SharePoint Foundation on a 64-bit server named MIGA. Earlier in the chapter we moved a 32-bit WSS 3.0 standalone implementation to this 64-bit server, so we could do this in-place upgrade. Figure 15.14 shows a conceptual overview of this upgrade method.

FIGURE 15.14

Overview of a standalone in-place upgrade

In-Place Upgrade of a Stand Alone Server

Upgrading WSS 3.0 to SharePoint Foundation on the same server.

MIGA
(64-bit Server)
Server is running WSS 3.0 and
will be upgraded to SharePoint Foundation.

1. Browse to the location where you saved the SharePoint Foundation installation file (`SharePointFoundation.exe`), and double-click it. As it starts to run, a splash screen (Figure 15.15) will be displayed.

2. Click Install SharePoint Foundation in the Install section on the splash screen. This will start the installer to install SharePoint Foundation.

3. The first screen displays the license agreement for you to accept. Click the **I Accept The Terms Of This Agreement** check box, and then click the **Continue** button.

   Next you will see the **Upgrade Earlier Versions** page (Figure 15.16), which will explain that the installer has detected an earlier version installed on the computer. It also goes on to explain about the order in which the databases will be upgraded and that you can monitor the upgrade process from the upgraded Central Administration website.

   It also warns that during the upgrade process the SharePoint environment will be unavailable. Finally, it reminds you one last time to run the pre-upgrade check tool before starting your upgrade just in case you haven't already.

FIGURE 15.15

The SharePoint
Foundation
splash screen

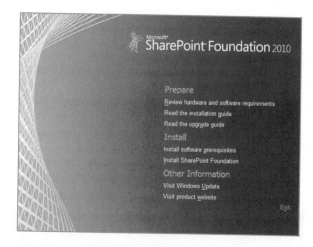

FIGURE 15.16

The Upgrade Earlier Versions page

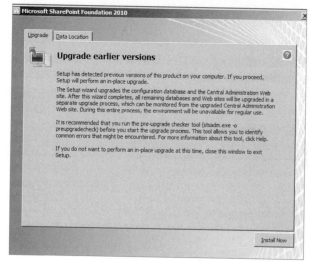

4. When you are ready to start the installation, click the **Install Now** button to start the process. You can follow the overall progress on the **Installation Progress** screen.

5. After the upgrade has finished, you will see the **Run Configuration Wizard** page, with a **Run The SharePoint Products Configuration Wizard Now** check box that is selected by default. If you leave it selected and click **Close**, the wizard will launch automatically.

However, if you need to install any language packs, you will want to deselect that box before clicking the Close button. Then, after you have installed your language packs, you can go back and run the wizard manually from the Start Menu, Microsoft SharePoint 2010 Products, and SharePoint 2010 Products Configuration Wizard.

Do You Speak My Language?

Site owners and site collection administrators can use language packs to create sites using language-specific templates. This doesn't mean that you can change the language in which a site template is viewed but rather that a site owner or site collection administrator can choose a language for a new site collection or subsite when they create it. Different sites or site collections can be based on different languages all in the same SharePoint Foundation installation.

Language packs are not available in multilingual packs, so you will need to download a pack for each language you want to deploy to your SharePoint environment. Each pack uses the same name for its installer (SharePointLanguagePack.exe), so you will need to save each downloaded pack in a separate folder to avoid overwriting this file with the file from another language.

You can download SharePoint Foundation language packs from Microsoft; take the following steps:

1. Do an Internet search for SharePoint Foundation 2010 language packs you require. On the download page, select the language you want to deploy from the Change Language listing.

2. Click Change and then Download. Clicking Change is critical; otherwise, you will just download the default language (usually English), even if the correct language is in the field.

3. When the download dialog box appears, choose to save the file to your computer.

4. To install the language pack, browse to the location where you saved the file, and double-click the installer file.

5. Click the **I Accept The Terms Of This Agreement** check box, and then click Continue.

The wizard will run and install the language pack. You then need to run the configuration wizard so the SharePoint implementation can be updated. Language packs can be added after configuration, but adding them before configuration is recommended.

When the SharePoint Products Configuration Wizard starts, you will see a screen welcoming you to SharePoint Products, just in case you didn't realize that you have spent all this time installing a SharePoint product.

6. Click the **Next** button.

A message box will open warning you that the IIS, SharePoint Administration, and SharePoint Timer services may be started or reset during the configuration process. This is fine, so you can click the **Yes** button and continue.

The configuration process will go through 10 steps, or tasks, as it configures your new SharePoint 2010 environment. You will be able to follow the overall progress on the **Configuring SharePoint Products** page (Figure 15.17).

If all goes well, then the next screen you see, after all 10 steps have been completed, will proclaim your success (Figure 15.18). You should see the message that reads "Configuration Successful, Upgrade In Progress." It will include an explanation that the upgrade has not completed yet. A timer job will be created to finish the upgrade process, but during this time, some of your content may not be available until the upgrade completes. You can monitor the upgrade progress by viewing the log files or the **Upgrade Status** page in Central Administration. When you click the **Finish** button to close the wizard, you'll return to the Upgrade Status page.

Check out all your sites, confirm your settings, make sure all your customizations are installed and working, and check that nothing is missing. There should be nothing missing since you simply upgraded the server as is, but it's always good to check.

Congratulations, you have upgraded your WSS 3.0 server to SharePoint Foundation!

FIGURE 15.17
The Configuring SharePoint Products page

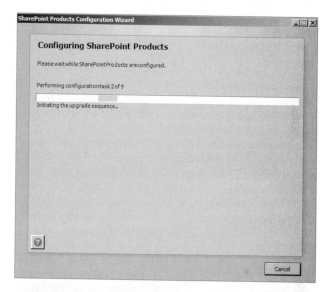

FIGURE 15.18
Configuration successful

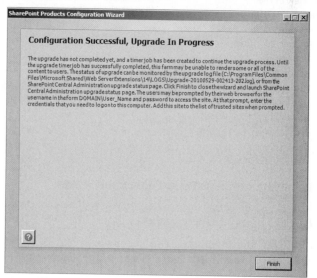

The Database-Attach Upgrade Method for Standalone Servers

As discussed earlier in the chapter, the database-attach upgrade method is best if you need or want to do any of the following while upgrading:

◆ Move your content to new hardware.

◆ Go directly from a 32-bit implementation of WSS 3.0 to SharePoint Foundation.

◆ Do some housecleaning as you upgrade and get rid of some web applications.

◆ Change web application URL naming schemes.

With this method, you will first install SharePoint Foundation on a new 64-bit server and then configure your farm settings, web applications, and customizations on the new SharePoint Foundation server. After that, you just need to get your databases from your WSS 3.0 server, add or restore them (depending) to the SharePoint Foundation server, and attach them to your new SharePoint Foundation implementation.

For this example, I am going to use a content database (WSS_Content) from my 32-bit WSS 3.0 server (named SP1) and use the database-attach method to upgrade to SharePoint Foundation on the 64-bit server I have named MIGB. Although it might have been a good idea to have the server name mirror the original server, for clarity's sake in this scenario I am keeping the server name as MIGB. When migrating using the database-attach method, it is standard that the first database to be migrated to the new SharePoint server be the one for the web application at the root of the farm. In my case, that would be the content in WSS_Content, and it will be added to the web application at SharePoint-80 on the new server. Figure 15.19 shows a conceptual overview.

FIGURE 15.19
Overview of the database-attach standalone upgrade

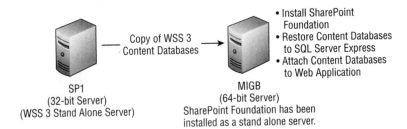

Database Attach Upgrade of a Stand Alone Server
The databases from the WSS 3 server (SP1) will be copied and then attached to the SharePoint Foundation server (MIGB).

Copy of WSS 3 Content Databases

• Install SharePoint Foundation
• Restore Content Databases to SQL Server Express
• Attach Content Databases to Web Application

SP1
(32-bit Server)
(WSS 3 Stand Alone Server)

MIGB
(64-bit Server)
SharePoint Foundation has been installed as a stand alone server.

PREPARING THE SHAREPOINT FOUNDATION SERVER

Just as you did earlier in the chapter, you will need to prepare your new 64-bit SharePoint Foundation server to receive the databases from WSS 3.0 by completing the following tasks:

◆ Run the pre-upgrade checker on your WSS 3.0 server if you haven't done so already. Make certain nothing failed, and if anything did, resolve the issues before doing the upgrade.

◆ Back up your WSS 3.0 installation (as a precaution) if you haven't done so already.

◆ Install the SharePoint prerequisites on the machine that will be your SharePoint Foundation server.

- ◆ Install SharePoint Foundation, and then install language packs if necessary.
- ◆ Run the configuration wizard on the new installation.
- ◆ Transfer customizations and settings to the new installation (before attaching databases).

PREPARING TO MOVE THE DATABASE

Keep in mind that, while you are preparing the server, you need to plan to move the databases from the WSS 3.0 server to the SharePoint Foundation server. Once there, you will be attaching the databases to SQL Express on the SharePoint Foundation server so SharePoint can then use them. So, this process has two parts, one in SharePoint itself and one in SQL Express.

After you install and configure SharePoint Foundation on your new 64-bit server, the configuration wizard will create a new web application and top-level site as part of the configuration process. You will need to re-create any additional web applications that you had on your WSS server and then re-create all the permissions and security settings for those web applications. (Note that forms-based authentication now requires its web application to support claims-based authentication.) The process of creating new web applications is covered in depth in Chapter 10, "Site Collections and Web Applications."

When you create web applications, SharePoint automatically creates a content database for each new web application. However, since you will be replacing the new web application databases (in our case we're just doing one, but you may have more) with the databases from your WSS 3.0 server, you won't need the databases that were created when you created that new web application, so your first task will be to remove them.

1. To do this, log onto your SharePoint Foundation server, and open the **Central Administration** website.

2. Click **Manage Content Databases** under **Web Application Management**.

3. Click the name of the database you want to remove.

   Once the **Manage Content Database Settings** page is open, the only setting we are interested in right now is the **Remove Content Database** check box. Selecting this box does not delete the database; it only removes the association of the database with the web application. Any sites contained in the database will no longer be available to SharePoint, but the site data remains in the database and can be used again later.

4. **Check** the **Remove Content Database** box, and click **OK**.

5. A confirmation dialog box will open asking you to confirm that you want to delete the database; click **OK**.

   When you return to the Manage **Content Database Settings** page, the database will no longer be listed.

6. Repeat these steps until all the new content databases have been removed from the web applications you have created.

Finally, you need to transfer your customizations to your SharePoint Foundation server. This usually involves copying over the solution, feature, or web part files to the server and then going through the steps you went through originally to add, deploy, or activate your customizations as needed.

Downloading SQL Server Management Studio Express

At this point, I would like to introduce you to Microsoft SQL Server Management Studio Express. If you have ever used SQL Server, you will already be familiar with Management Studio. Well, this is its little brother. It is a free graphical tool that you can download and install, which will enable you to manage, configure, and administer your SQL Server Express databases using a GUI interface that is essentially the SQL Server Management Studio minus the advanced capabilities to manage the SQL Analysis, Integration, Notification, or Reporting Services, nor can you manage SQL Server mobile edition with this tool. SQL Server Management Studio Express is meant to give you a graphic user interface to do the basic tasks of adding, removing, attaching, detaching, backing up, restoring, and managing databases on the local server.

For this upgrade scenario, we will simply copy the database we will attach from the WSS 3.0 server. But for the SharePoint Foundation server, we will be using Microsoft SQL Server Management Studio Express to attach the database during the database-attach process. So, take the following steps to install it:

1. First download the 64-bit installation file for **SQL Server Management Studio Express** to the server to which you will be attaching the databases.

2. Run the **setup** file on your SharePoint Foundation server, and when the **SQL Server Installation Center** opens, click **New Installation Or Add New Feature To An Existing Installation**.

   The installer will run through some setup rules and open the **License Agreement** page. As you go through the installation process, you may occasionally see a message that the installation can't be completed until the computer is restarted. You don't need to restart the computer right then; just click **OK** and continue with the installation. Once the installation process has finished, you will restart your computer to complete the installation.

3. On the **License Agreement page**, select the **I Accept The Terms Of This License Agreement** radio button before clicking **Next**.

4. When the **Feature Selection** page (Figure 15.20) opens, make sure that the **Management Tools – Basic** feature is checked; then click **Next** to begin the installation.

   Complete the rest of the steps (they're pretty self-explanatory) until the wizard has completed the installation. After the installation process is completed, you will see the **Completing The Microsoft SQL Server Management Studio Express Setup** screen, and it will display the message that Setup has installed Microsoft SQL Server Management Studio Express successfully.

5. **Restart** your computer, and you're done.

FIGURE 15.20
The Feature
Selection page

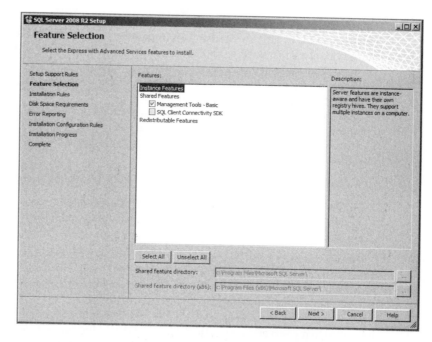

I CAN'T GET SQL SERVER EXPRESS TO INSTALL ON MY WINDOWS SERVER 2008 R2 SERVER!

If you are running Windows Server 2008 R2 and having trouble installing SQL Server Management Studio, you can download and install the Management Tools for SQL Server 2008 R2 Express. They will work just fine with previous versions of SQL Express.

At the time of the writing of this book, you could download these tools by going to `http://Microsoft.com/express/database/installoptions.aspx`. On the page you will see four Installation Options and each has a 32-bit download and a 64-bit download. The options are Database Only, Management Tools, Database With Management Tools, and Database With Advanced Services. Just click the purple 64-bit button under **Management Tools** to download the file.

Now we are almost ready to start moving databases from the WSS 3.0 server to the new SharePoint Foundation server. For this example, we will move a content database from the WSS 3.0 server named SP1 to a SharePoint Foundation server named MIGB. Before moving the files, we need to copy them, and that means locking them from any changes during the move.

Taking the Sites Offline and Copying the Files

One of the things you want to do is avoid having your users try to add or change data on your WSS 3.0 SharePoint sites while you're busy moving the databases. The best way I know to avoid this problem is simply to take your SharePoint sites offline. You can go into Central Administration, Application Management page, Manage Content Databases and set the content databases to Read

Only (and you should), but to be more thorough, log onto your WSS 3.0 server and open the Services console by going to **Start ▶ Administrative Tools ▶ Services**. When it opens, look for any service name that starts with *Windows SharePoint Services*, and stop the service (just to be sure).

And while you're at it, you need to make sure that there are no open connections to the databases by stopping the SQL service, too. Look for the service called SQL Server Embedded Edition (SSEE), and stop it as well.

Now that WSS is offline, you can safely make copies of your content databases and move those copies to your SharePoint Foundation server.

To make copies of your content databases log onto your WSS 3.0 standalone server, and take the following steps:

1. Go to `C:\WINDOWS\SYSMSI\SSEE\MSSQL.2005\MSSQL\Data`.

2. Find all your content databases; the `.mdf` files; and their corresponding log files, the `.ldf` files. Right-click them, select Copy, browse to a shared folder on your network, and paste the files into the shared folder.

For my example, I will be making copies of the `WSS_Content.mdf` file and the `WSS_Content_Log.ldf` files (the database files for my SharePoint-80 web application) and then moving them to a shared folder on my network. The log files are easy to spot because they are named the same as the database files but with _LOG appended to the name.

To make it easy to remember which files are the original files and which ones are going to be moved to my server named MIGB, I have renamed the copies to `MIGB_Content.mdf`. You don't have to rename the file, and as you'll see in a moment, changing the filename in the file share doesn't really make a difference in SQL. It's for convenience only. Once you have copied all your content databases to the shared folder, log off of your WSS 3.0 server, and log onto your SharePoint Foundation server.

PREFER A GUI?

Although you can see how easy it is to manage (and manhandle) database files on a standalone WSS 3.0 server, you can install SQL Server Management Studio Express (SSMSE) on the WSS 3.0 server too (there is a 32-bit version available).

To access the WID databases of a WSS 3.0 implementation using SSMSE, in the Connect To Server dialog box, you need to enter `\\.\pipe\mssql$microsoft##ssee\sql\query` in the Server Name field. This is the trick to using SSMSE with a WID database—it requires the named pipe query string because otherwise it does not allow remote connections. This is handy when simply managing databases on a standalone WSS 3.0 implementation, even if you are not migrating.

Once in the SSMSE console, open the **Databases** node, and **right-click the database(s)** you want to migrate. You can detach the database or just make a backup of it (which I prefer, so that in case something goes wrong, the original is fine). Be sure the destination for the backup is a shared location that is accessible from the SharePoint Foundation server.

MOVING THE STANDALONE SERVER DATABASES

Start the database-attach process by browsing to the shared folder where you saved your database file copies, and copy them to the hard drive of your SharePoint Foundation server, in my case MIGB.

Once you have the database files copied to your server, **open SQL Server Management Studio Express**. When the Connect To Server window (Figure 15.21) opens, type YOUR_SERVER_NAME\ sharepoint into the Server Name field, and click the **Connect** button. In my example, my SharePoint Foundation server is named MIGB, so I would type MIGB\sharepoint (SharePoint is the default instance name) in the database server field, and then click the **Connect** button.

FIGURE 15.21

The Connect To Server window

After the **SQL Server Management Studio Express** connects to your database server, you will see a list of folders appear in the left side navigation pane. The folder that we are interested in is the database folder. If you click the **(+)** sign to expand the database folder, you will see a list of all your databases.

When we removed all the content databases from our web applications, I said that it would remove the database from the web application association but wouldn't delete the database. Now, as you look at your lists of databases, you will see each of those databases listed. Since we will not be using those databases and they are now just cluttering up the joint, we can delete them entirely. This is particularly important if a database you need to delete (like WSS_Content) has the same database name as one you need to attach. Be aware that if you delete the databases from **SQL Management Studio Express**, you are indeed deleting them entirely, and they will no longer be available unless you have a backup copy you can use to restore them.

1. As shown in Figure 15.22, **right-click the name of the database** you want to delete, and select **Delete**.

FIGURE 15.22

Deleting a database

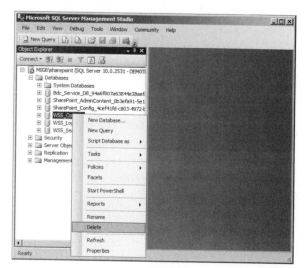

2. The Delete Object window (Figure 15.23) will open. At the bottom of the screen, check the **Delete Backup And Restore History Information For Databases** and **Close Existing Connections** boxes, and then click **OK**.

FIGURE 15.23

The Delete Object window

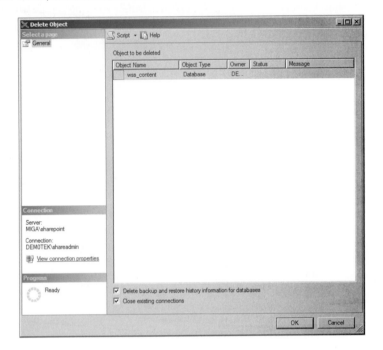

Now that you have cleaned up some of the clutter, you can start to attach the databases that you copied over from your WSS 3.0 server.

1. Right-click the **Databases** folder, and select **Attach**, as shown in Figure 15.24.

2. At this point, you need to select the database file to attach (that's the database file with the .mdf extension). In the **Attach Databases** window, click the **Add** button.

3. The **Locate Database Files** window will open, allowing you to browse to the location on your hard drive where you saved your database copies earlier. It has to be a local directory; the window doesn't let you browse to remote shares unless you type in the exact path (now you know why I suggested we save it locally). I saved my database copies in a folder on the C: drive named imageshare. For my example, the database copy file is named MIGB_Content.mdf. Select the **MDF** file for your database copy, and click **OK**.

The database file is now added to the **Databases To Attach** box, and in the **Database Details** box below it, I can now see two entries, one for WSS_Content.mdf and one for WSS_Content_LOG.ldf (Figure 15.25).

FIGURE 15.24
Choosing to attach
a database

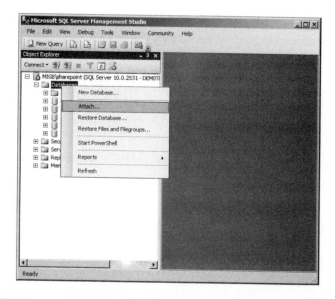

FIGURE 15.25
The Attach Data-
bases window with
databases selected
for attaching

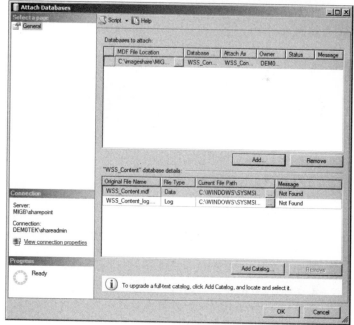

Although we renamed the database files after we copied them, so they'd be easy for us to identify, the database the MDF files contain is still the WSS_Content database from the WSS 3.0 server.
Further, SQL Server Management Studio Express has read the MDF file and may be looking for

the database and log file based on the location where the files were originally stored (often the Management Studio does not have this problem, but it can happen). Given that, you may need to tell the Management Studio where to find the files it needs to attach the database:

1. To get the **Attach Databases** window to point to the correct location for the MDF file, click the ellipsis (**...**) button next to the first entry in the Database details section, which is for the database .mdf file. It will open the **Locate Database Files** window. Navigate to the location where the MDF file that you are attaching is located (in my case that would be the local folder imageshare).

2. Select the **MDF** file, in my case MIGB_Content.mdf, and click **OK**.

    You can see in Figure 15.26 that the entry previously for WSS_Content.mdf now shows MIGB_Content.mdf.

FIGURE 15.26

Database details

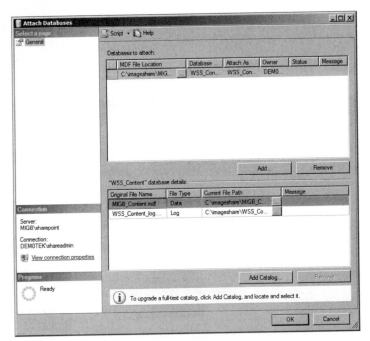

3. For the log file, the second entry, do the same.

4. Once you have selected all the correct files, click the **OK** button to attach the database. You will get a pop-up window asking you whether you need to add any additional full-text catalogs. You don't, so just click **OK** to continue.

After the database is attached successfully, you will be able to see it listed in the Databases folder; if you don't, click the **Refresh** button to refresh your screen.

Notice in Figure 15.27 that the database that was attached is named WSS_Content, not MIGB_Content. Although we renamed the file to MIGB_Content when we copied the original database, when the database is attached, it is attached using the same name as original database. That shows that renaming the copied files for the databases was purely a convenience so I'd recognize the files in the share to use for the migration.

FIGURE 15.27
The original
database name
is retained.

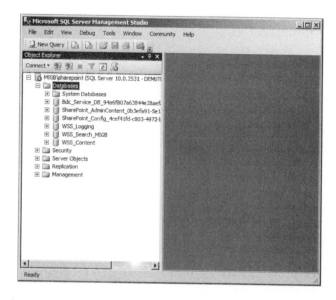

If you have any additional content databases, you will need to move each one to your SharePoint Foundation server and attach them following the steps just listed. Once you have moved all your content databases to your SharePoint Foundation server and attached them using SQL Server Management Studio Express, the next step is to add the content databases to their new web applications and upgrade them.

ADD CONTENT DATABASE TO THE WEB APPLICATION

Because the content databases have not been upgraded yet, you can't add them to their web applications through Central Administration. This means you need to use a command-line tool, such as STSADM or PowerShell. In our case, we'll be using the STSADM command-line tool. When you use STSADM to add your WSS 3.0 content database to a SharePoint Foundation web application, the databases will automatically be upgraded. This is also true if you want to use the PowerShell cmdlets instead.

One of the convenient new features in SharePoint Foundation is that you can run STSADM commands from the **SharePoint 2010 Management Shell** (otherwise known as the management shell or management console). You no longer have to open a command prompt and change the directory before you can run your commands (although you can if you want to). Now you can just open the Management Shell by going to **Start ➤ All Programs ➤ SharePoint Foundation 2010 Products ➤ SharePoint 2010 Management Shell**. The permissions to run the commands are the same, and the commands are all the same, so you can just open it and start entering STSADM commands (actually, it supports any standard DOS commands as well).

1. Open the SharePoint 2010 Management Shell.

   Next you will add the content database to the web application using the URL of the web application. Always start with your first, root URL. In my example, my root web application is http://MIGB, and the database I want to use for that web application is WSS_Content.

2. Type in the following command:

```
Stsadm.exe -o addcontentdb -url http://[YOUR_SERVER_NAME] -databasename
[DATABASE_NAME]
```

Using my example, I would enter the command like this:

```
Stsadm.exe -o addcontentdb -url http://MIGB -databasename WSS_Content
```

By default with this kind of upgrade, the old user experience is preserved so you can use Visual Upgrade (covered later in the chapter). To force the content in the database to be upgraded to the new interface without delay, you can use the `-preserveolduserexperience` parameter, but specify the value to be `False`.

It will take a few moments, but then the percentage of the upgrade that has been completed will begin to show on the screen. Once you reach 100 percent, you will get a message telling you the operation has been completed successfully, which means your database has been added and the upgrade completed.

The PowerShell cmdlet for this process requires more data to be specified (namely, the database server name; STSADM assumes the farm database is being used). The syntax would be as follows:

```
Mount-SPDatabase -Name <databasename> -DatabaseServer <databaseservername>
-WebApplication <url>
```

It will also accept the parameter `-UpdateUserExperience <true or false>`, in case you want to force an interface upgrade and not use Visual Upgrade.

"UPGRADE COMPLETED WITH ERRORS"! DID IT WORK OR NOT?

Did you forget to transfer a customization? Missing customizations are a very common cause for this message. If you log onto your SharePoint Foundation site, you will most likely find that it is working, except for anything that depends on that missing customization. Go back and install that customization, and generally your site will function as expected.

Once all your databases have been added successfully, log onto your sites, and make sure everything is as it should be and works correctly.

Congratulations! You are now the proud owner of a brand new SharePoint Foundation web server! Don't be surprised if it still looks like WSS 3.0 (Figure 15.28)—that's because Visual Upgrade is enabled by default, so the content was upgraded, but the visual interface will not be upgraded until you choose to do so.

ADDING AND DEPLOYING SOLUTIONS

The site I migrated in this example has a lot of subsites (some of which are from the Fantastic 40 templates that were available from Microsoft for WSS 3.0 but will not be available for SharePoint Foundation). Many of these subsites are simply created from standard site template files, but there is one subsite that is based on two solutions that were deployed to the WSS 3.0 farm. For that subsite's features to all work, we need to redeploy those solutions.

FIGURE 15.28

The upgraded site on MIGB

To do that, we need to use STSADM or PowerShell to add the solution to the farm's file store. Then we can deploy or retract the solutions in Central Administration (you could also deploy the solutions at the command line as well).

Solutions are really files packaged together in a CAB file with the .wsp extension. A solution can be as big as a site definition with site templates and their features and web parts or as small as a single feature and its supporting files.

Solutions are often made of features that can be scoped to be activated at different levels of SharePoint. When a solution is deployed to a web application, only the site collections or sites in that particular web application can have access to the new features, depending on how they're written.

In my example, I am going to add `ApplicationTemplateCore.wsp` (which must be added and deployed before other Fantastic 40 solutions can be added) and `Helpdesk.wsp` solutions using STSADM, and then I will deploy them from Central Administration.

Although STSADM will be covered in detail in Chapter 14, it is easy to add a solution to SharePoint by following these steps:

1. Open the **SharePoint Management Shell** by going to **Start ➢ All Programs ➢ Microsoft SharePoint 2010 Products ➢ SharePoint Management Shell** (you could also just use a command prompt, but you don't have to navigate to the SharePoint root, bin folder in the PowerShell console).

2. Once the management shell is open and the prompt is displayed, type the following command:

```
stsadm -o addsolution -filename "pathtofile\filename.wsp"
```

In my case, that would be (for the first of the two solutions I need to add):

```
stsadm -o addsolution -filename c:\imageshare\applicationcoretemplate.wsp
```

Use that command to add as many solutions as you need. In my example, I will be adding the two solutions listed earlier.

Once added to SharePoint, the solution is available to be viewed and managed on the **Solution Management** page in Central Administration. (You can also deploy a solution at the command line, using the command `Stsadm -o deploysolution -name "pathtofile\filename.wsp"`, but the GUI is often considered more user friendly.)

To manage a particular solution in Central Administration, on the site, click **System Settings** and then **Manage Farm Solutions** under **Farm Management**. When the **Solution Management Page** opens, you will see the solutions you added. In our example, there are two solutions (`applicationtemplatecore.wsp` and `helpdesk.wsp`) listed on the page. See Figure 15.29.

FIGURE 15.29
Solutions installed but not deployed

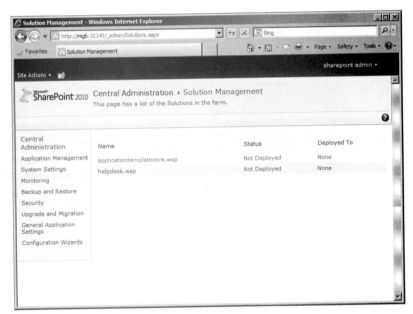

First we will deploy the **ApplicationTemplateCore** solution file, so select it on the page. You will be taken to that solution's **Solution Properties** page (Figure 15.30). You can check the solution properties, such as whether it was deployed and the scope of the deployment.

From there, you can deploy the solution by clicking the **Deploy Solution** link. This will give you the option to deploy the solution to a specific web application (Figure 15.31).

You can deploy the solution now or at a time that might put less strain on the server. You can deploy it to the global assembly cache (this is particularly useful if your solution needs to use secure controls) or to a particular web application's bin folder (if the solution is scoped with that flexibility). You will be warned that everything in there is trusted. The global assembly cache is useful because it's globally accessible and it's a high-level security location, so all solutions there run in a highly trusted context. That also means you shouldn't just download any old solution from the Internet and install it to the global assembly cache (in my case, the solutions are known to be good).

FIGURE 15.30
Solution Proper-
ties page

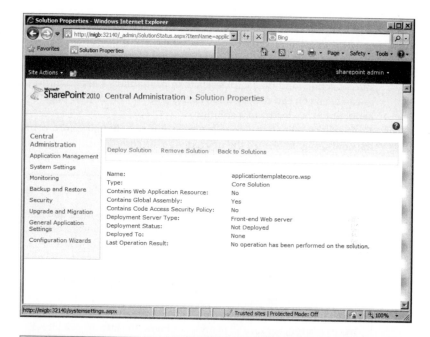

FIGURE 15.31
The Deploy
Solution page

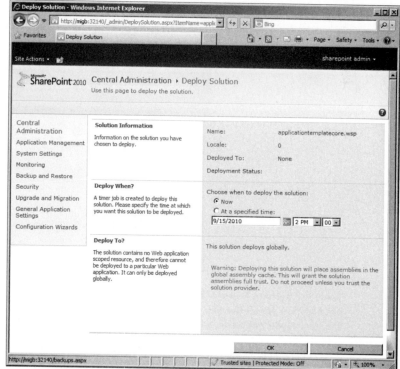

In my case, I am deploying the solution to the global assembly cache, immediately.

Once you deploy a solution, the **Manage Solutions** page will show its deployment state and the scope it's deployed to. Repeat this same process for the other solution files you might have (HelpDesk solution file in my example) in order to complete moving the customizations for the site collection (and the HelpDesk site in particular). Keep in mind that you can retract solutions as easily as you can deploy them in the Solution Properties page, should you change your mind about how you deployed a solution.

As you've seen in this brief example, it is easy to make sure your solutions are deployed on the new server to ensure the upgrade is a success.

Concerning Addressing

One of the more important aspects of upgrading is to limit downtime, loss of productivity, and inconvenience. Often, you don't even want users to know the server has changed (except in terms of improvements). In that way, you often don't want the users to have to learn a new URL for the new SharePoint Foundation server; you want them to use the old one.

Redirecting servers is an art as much as a science, and there are a number of ways to do it.

In my simple example, I want to change the address on the MIGB server (which is nonintuitive now that we've finished the migration) and have it respond to the address http://spf, as well as http://migb, because all of my users know the http://spf address.

All I have to do to make that address change happen is create a CNAME alias for SharePoint Foundation in DNS that points to the MIGB server's Fully Qualified Domain Name (FQDN).

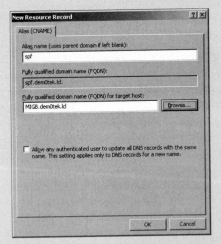

Then, in Alternate Access Mappings for the MIGB server, add a new public URL that responds to http://SPF for all the web applications (or, for slow database-attach migrations, as each web application gets upgraded, add a public URL to respond to the alternate address).

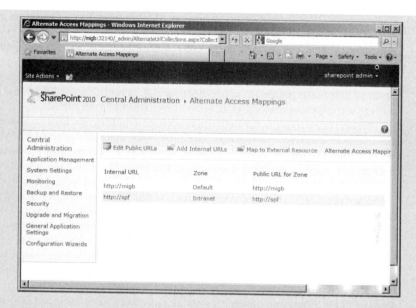

Now, within the office, the SPF address will resolve to the correct server, and searches will also display the correct server address.

If you want to replace an old server and have users use its old URL to access the upgraded content on a new server, do the following:

1. After the old server is decommissioned, delete its A record in DNS.

2. Create a CNAME alias that uses the same name (like my old WSS 3.0 *sp1*), but point the alias at the new server's FQDN.

3. In AAM for the new server's web applications, create a new public URL that contains the old server's URL, such as http://sp1.

If you are working with a server farm in a load-balanced situation, then you need to take the CNAME alias into consideration for the web applications' load-balanced URL as well.

This is one of the few times when it makes sense to use a web application zone for a manually entered URL, rather than adding the URL via extending a web application.

Upgrade a Standalone Server with Remote BLOB Storage

As we discussed earlier in the chapter, BLOB stands for Binary Large Object and refers to a large file, or a collection of binary data that gets stored as a single file in a database. A BLOB is typically an image, sound, or multimedia file. Because BLOB files are so large, they tend to take up a lot of file space in the database they are stored in.

Remote BLOB Storage (RBS) is an add-on API that takes those BLOB files and stores them outside the database, freeing up file space in the database but making it appear to users that the data is just where it has always been. RBS requires the use of a provider program that acts as a middleman between the database and the Remote BLOB Storage.

When you install SharePoint Foundation using the standalone option, it uses SQL Server Express 2008 for its database engine. Because SQL Server Express 2008 has a 4 GB size limit, if any of your databases exceed 4 GB, you will be required to install RBS.

This section walks you through the process of installing the RBS for SharePoint Foundation. For this example, I assume that you have previously upgraded your 64-bit WSS 3.0 server to Service Pack 2 or higher, everything is configured and running, and you have performed a farm backup just in case something goes wrong. You know that you have at least one database that exceeds 4 GB, so you know you will need to install RBS when you upgrade.

Before performing the upgrade, be sure you will have enough free disk space for your BLOB database(s). You will need at least twice as much free disk space as your largest content database(s) and twice the free disk space of all your other content databases combined.

Much of the in-place upgrade with Remote BLOB Storage is identical to a regular in-place standalone server upgrade, which the section "In-Place Upgrade for Standalone Server" covered in detail. Refer to that coverage if at any point you have a question or need more details.

For my example (if you are following along), I am going to do an in-place upgrade with Remote BLOB Storage on a WSS 3.0 standalone server I have named MIGA (Figure 15.32).

FIGURE 15.32

Overview of an in-place upgrade with RBS

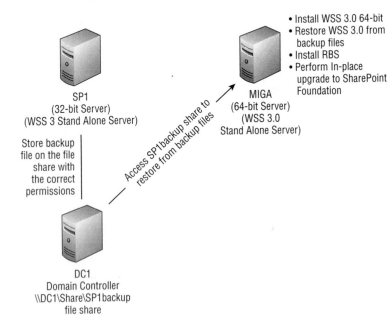

In-Place Upgrade with RBS for Standalone Server
Backup and Restore Method for migrating WSS 3 from 32-bit to 64-bit
Install RBS on the Server, then Perform an in-place upgrade

- Install WSS 3.0 64-bit
- Restore WSS 3.0 from backup files
- Install RBS
- Perform In-place upgrade to SharePoint Foundation

SP1
(32-bit Server)
(WSS 3 Stand Alone Server)

MIGA
(64-bit Server)
(WSS 3.0
Stand Alone Server)

Store backup file on the file share with the correct permissions

Access SP1backup share to restore from backup files

DC1
Domain Controller
\\DC1\Share\SP1backup
file share

REUSING MIGA

Now you're probably saying "Wait a minute, didn't we just upgrade that server?" and yes we did. This time I am going to go back and demonstrate how to do the same upgrade, only this time adding Remote BLOB Storage. So, for this demonstration, I have removed SharePoint Foundation, reinstalled WSS 3.0 for 64-bit, and migrated WSS 3.0 from my 32-bit WSS 3.0 server to the MIGA 64-bit server again, making it a WSS 3.0 server again, ready for upgrade. I am simply doing this to demonstrate how to add Remote BLOB Storage on a server we know is being used to demonstrate different standalone-server, in-place upgrades.

The process is very simple and painless—simply download and install the RBS API, and then perform an in-place upgrade just like you would normally. SharePoint Foundation will take care of the setting up RBS to work with SharePoint Foundation as part of the upgrade processes. Let's go download the RBS provider setup file so we can install it:

1. Open your web browser, and do an Internet search for the download page for **Microsoft SQL Server 2008 R2 Feature Pack**.

2. When the page opens, ignore the Download button because it will only download a text file that says "Microsoft SQL Server 2008 R2 Feature Pack." Instead, scroll down the page until you get to the **Microsoft SQL Server 2008 R2 Remote Blob Storage** section. There you will find the **X64** Package (RBS.msi); click the link to download the file.

3. When prompted, **save** the setup file to a location on the server's hard drive. After the file has been downloaded and saved, you will be prompted to run the setup or close the download program. Click the **Run** button, and launch the installer.

4. As usual, the first screen in the setup wizard will be the Welcome screen. You don't need to do anything here except click the **Next** button.

5. The License Agreement screen is next; select the **I Accept The Terms Of This License Agreement** radio button, and click **Next**.

6. The next step is to fill out the registration information. Enter a username in the **Name** field, or leave **Windows User** in the box. Then enter the name of your company in the Company box. Click the **Next** button.

7. Now you are at the **Feature Selection** screen, where you can select how each feature will be installed. By default, all features are set to install to the local hard drive. Expand the **Server** section, click the down arrow next to **Execute Scripts**, and choose **Entire Feature Will Be Unavailable**. The execute scripts need a database to act on, and there aren't any yet. The scripts will be made automatically when SharePoint Foundation installs.

8. Then expand the **FILESTREAM Provider** section, expand the **Server** section under it, and click the down arrow next to **Execute Scripts**, as shown in Figure 15.33; again, choose **Entire Feature Will Be Unavailable**, and click **Next**.

FIGURE 15.33
Feature
Selection page

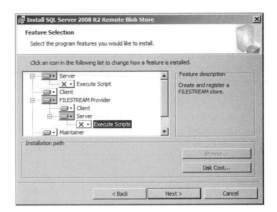

9. On the next screen (Figure 15.34), you configure the connection to the Remote Blob Storage database. For my example, the Server\Instance is MIGA because that is the name of the server I am upgrading. I will just go with the default database name and file group of internal tables. I have my SharePoint databases set up to use Windows authentication, so that is what I will use for the BLOB database as well.

FIGURE 15.34
Database
connection

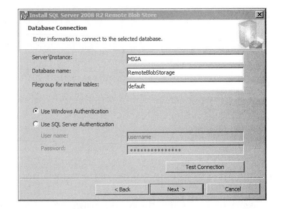

10. The next page is **Maintainer Task** (Figure 15.35). On this screen you have the option of setting a maintainer task. This is selected by default, and for this example you can leave it set to defaults. If you don't want to run maintenance on the BLOB storage, just uncheck the **Schedule To Run The Maintainer** check box. It is a good idea to leave it checked though.

11. Now you come to the **Client Configuration** page (Figure 15.36), where you set the logging detail level. You can set the level of detail each of the logs will track. Remember, the more detail you track, the bigger the logs will grow. After setting the detail level for each log, click **Next**.

12. Now you are ready to install the program. When the **Ready To Install The Program** screen appears, just click the **Install** button.

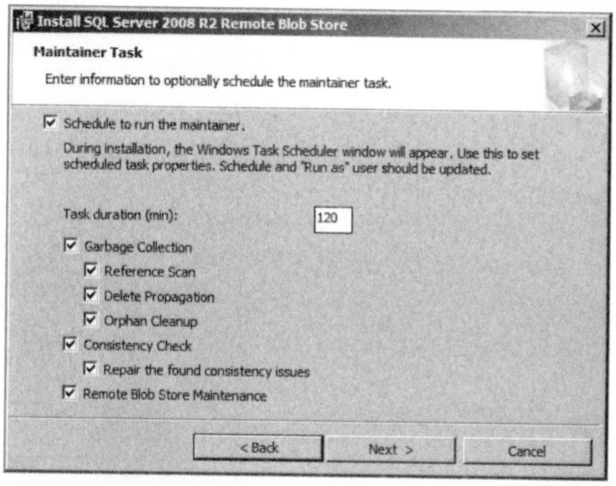

FIGURE 15.35
The Maintainer
Task window

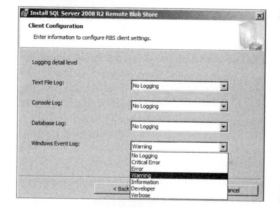

FIGURE 15.36
Setting the
logging level

If you decided to set up the maintainer task, you will need to configure some settings so it can run properly. After the install process starts, the setting screens for the maintainer box will open. Note that the RBSMaintainerTask_1050 dialog box will often open behind the Installing Remote Blob Store windows. You may need to move your window around to find it.

1. On the **Task** tab, you will need to configure the **Run As** user and password. To set the username, simply type the name of the user you would like to run the tasks as in the **Run As** field. To set the username and password, click the **Set Password** button, which will open a window where you will enter the password, and then retype it to confirm the password (Figure 15.37).

2. On the **Schedule** tab, you set the maintainer task to run at a scheduled time by clicking the **New** button to add a new schedule. This is the kind of task that doesn't need to run every day, so for this example, set the task to run once a month. It is a good idea to run these sorts of tasks either when users will not be using the system or when usage is low. For this reason, we will set the task to run at 3 a.m. on the first day of every month.

3. Once you have configured the task to run exactly the way you want, click the **Apply** or **OK** button to continue with the install.

FIGURE 15.37
Setting the Run
As account and
password

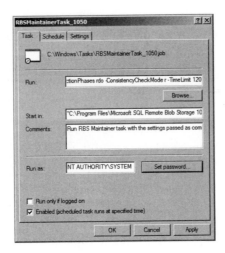

Once the installation is completed successfully, you can perform an in-place upgrade of your standalone server, as described in detail earlier in the chapter.

The only difference will be that when you run the configuration wizard, you will see a warning about the databases being over the size limit. Just click **OK**, and the configuration wizard will continue. Since you have already installed RBS, the wizard will be able to configure your databases to work with it. Now your upgrade is complete, with Remote BLOB Storage in place, and you're ready to go!

 Real World Scenario

HOW TO AVOID THE 4 GB DATABASE SIZE LIMIT AND THE DREADED BLOB

If you are running a standalone WSS 3.0 server, and you already know you have at least one database that is over the 4 GB database size limit imposed by SQL Express 2008, then when you go to upgrade to SharePoint Foundation 2010, you will get a message telling you that you must install Remote BLOB Storage.

Although this is true, there is a way you can get around the puny 4 GB size limit. You can upgrade to SQL Server Express 2008 R2, which has an increased database size limit of 10 GB. If any of your databases exceed 10 GB, you still need to install RBS, but it does give you a little more breathing room.

The process is fairly simple: install SharePoint Foundation prerequisites, install SharePoint Foundation as a standalone server, upgrade SQL Server Express 2008 to SQL Server Express 2008 R2, and then do a database-attach upgrade.

To do this, you will need to download the SharePoint Foundation installation file and the SQL Server Express 2008 R2 database with Management Tools x64 installation file. It is important to get the SQL Server Express 2008 R2 download that includes the management tools, so you can also install SQL Server Management Studio Express, which we will use to perform the database-attach upgrade.

For this example, I will be upgrading from a WSS 3.0 standalone server to a SharePoint Foundation standalone server. My WSS 3.0 server has a content database that is 4.65 GB in size, just over the 4 GB limit, and if I tried to migrate it to a SharePoint Foundation server that uses SQL Server Express 2008 (which the standalone installation installs), it would fail saying that it exceeds the 4GB limit. So if I want to migrate that database to a new SharePoint Foundation standalone installation, and not use RBS, then I need to take advantage of SQL Express 2008 R2's increased database limit.

You can upgrade SQL Express either after installing SharePoint Foundation but before running the configuration wizard (since SQL Server Express is installed before configuration, you can do that) or any time after configuration. In this example, we are going to do the complete installation and configuration, minus the database-attach, then upgrade SQL Server Express, and then do the database-attach migration. Either way is good.

So, in this case, there are a few things we need to do before we upgrade SQL Server Express:Back up the WSS 3.0 standalone server.Install SharePoint Foundation prerequisites on the 64-bit server (that is running a supported OS, of course).

◆ Install SharePoint Foundation as a standalone server on the 64-bit server.

◆ Run the SharePoint Foundation Configuration Wizard. Configure farm settings as appropriate.

All of these steps have been covered earlier in this chapter and in the installation chapters.

Once the those steps have been completed, to continue to prepare for the database-attach migration, you will need to re-create the web applications from your WSS 3.0 server on your new SharePoint Foundation server. You will need to transfer or re-create all the security and permissions for each of the web applications as well.

Since we will be using the database-attach method, we will replace the databases that get created with the new web applications with the databases from your WSS 3.0 standalone server. So, you can delete these new databases from the web application. See the "Preparing to Move the Database" section for details on how to remove content databases.

Once you are prepared, you can upgrade SQL Server Express 2008 to SQL Server Express 2008 R2 and finish doing the database-attach migration. To this, follow these steps:

1. Double-click the setup file for SQL Server Express 2008 R2 **(SQLEXPRWT_X64_ENU.exe)** to start the installation.

2. Choose the second option on the right of the splash screen, **Upgrade From SQL Server 2000, SQL Server 2005 Or SQL Server 2008**.

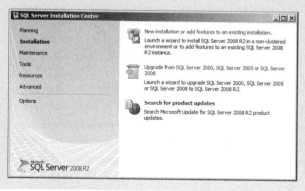

3. You'll see a License Terms page. Accept the license terms, and click **Next**. Setup Support Files will be installed.

   During the upgrade process, a message box may pop open telling you that "One or more affected files have operations pending. You must restart your computer to complete this process." You might see this message several times during the upgrade, and it can be misleading. You *do not* need to restart your computer right that second, just click **OK**, and the installation will continue. *After* the installation has been completed, you can restart your computer, and the upgrade will finish all pending operations.

4. **Setup Support** rules will run. On the next page, you will be asked to choose the instance you want to upgrade. The instance we want to upgrade is called **SHAREPOINT** and will likely already be selected by default; if not, select it from the drop-down list, and then click **Next**.

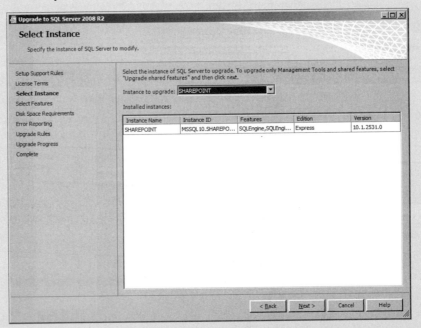

The installation will continue through the next few screens automatically. The next screen where you will be required to take action will be the Error Reporting page, where you will need to decide whether you want to send error reports to Microsoft.

5. If you want to share error reports with Microsoft, check the box; if not, leave it unchecked, and then click the **Next** button.

   The installation will continue through the Upgrade Rules screen without any user interaction, and then you will be able to follow the installation progress on the Upgrade Progress screen.

6. When the upgrade is completed, you will see the Computer Restart Required message again. Simply click **OK** and then **Close** to close the installation wizard.

7. Now you can restart your computer if necessary.

At this point, you have upgraded your SQL Server Express 2008 to SQL Server Express 2008 R2, but you still need to install the Management Studio Express.

1. After your computer has restarted (if it needed to reboot), log back on, and double-click the **SQL Server Express 2008 R2** installation file again.

2. When the splash screen opens again, this time click **New Installation Or Add Features To An Existing Installation**.

   The first screen where you be asked to make a decision is **Installation Type**. Here you will indicate whether you want to create a new installation of SQL Server Express or add a shared feature such as Management Studio. You can also choose to add a feature to an existing instance of SQL Server. If you're not careful, this can be confusing. Management Studio Express is a shared feature, which means it can be used by all instances of SQL Server installed on the computer, so you do not install it to a specific instance. For this reason, you need to choose New Installation Or Add Shared Feature.

3. Select the first radio button, **New Installation Or Add Shared Feature**.

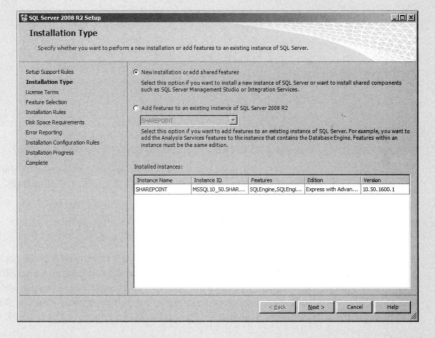

4. Check the **I Accept The License Terms** box in the next screen, and then click the **Next** button.

   On the next screen, **Feature Selection**, you select the features you want to be installed. By default Database Engine, SQL Server Replication, and Management Tools-Basic are all selected.

5. Be sure **Management Tools-Basic** is the only thing checked (the others do not need to be checked; you are only adding the management tools here), and then click **Next**.

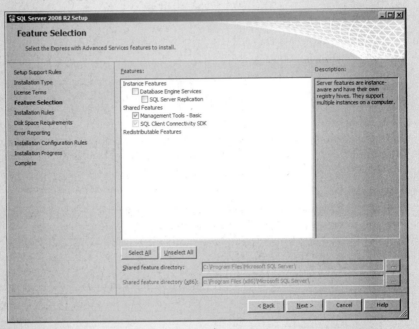

6. A License Terms screen will open. Accept the license terms, and click **Next**.

7. On the **Error Reporting** screen, if you want to share error reports with Microsoft, check the box at the bottom of the page; otherwise, leave it blank, and then click **Next**.

   Just as with the upgrade, you will be able to follow the progress of the installation on the **Installation Progress** screen.

8. When the installation is complete, click the **Close** button.

You now have upgraded your SQL Server Express 2008 database to SQL Server Express 2008 R2 so you can take advantage of the larger 10 GB database size limits and have installed SQL Server Management Studio Express. To be sure SQL Server Express upgraded properly, you can check the server name in the Management Studio console. In parenthesis after the server name it will indicate 10.50.1600 (for SQL Server Express 2008 R2) and not 10.0.2531, which is for SQL Server Express 2008.

From here you would run the configuration wizard and use the database-attach method for a stand-alone server, described earlier in the chapter, to upgrade to SharePoint Foundation just as you would normally. Congratulations, you now can have content databases larger than 4GB on this server

Upgrading a Server Farm

Up until now we have been working with standalone installations. Now we will look at what is involved in upgrading a server farm. The most direct route for upgrading a 32-bit WSS 3.0 server farm to a 64-bit SharePoint Foundation server farm is to use the database-attach method. The process is similar to a database-attach upgrade for a standalone farm, but since there is usually more than one machine in a server farm, there will be a few extra steps involved.

The Prep Work

The steps that need to be done to prepare for upgrading a server farm to SharePoint Foundation are the same as discussed earlier for upgrading a standalone installation. Essentially, before attempting to upgrade to SharePoint Foundation, you should do the following:

- Run the pre-upgrade checker (make note of any issues and customizations).

- Back up your farm, of course.

- Install your prerequisites on your SharePoint Foundation server.

Once you have completed all your preparations, you can begin your upgrade.

The In-Place Upgrade Method for Server Farms

If your company is already running WSS 3.0 on 64-bit servers, including a 64-bit SQL Server, then you are already ahead of the game. No need to worry about moving to new servers. All you need to do is perform an in-place upgrade on your servers.

If you are running WSS 3.0 on 32-bit, you will need to move to a 64-bit server before you can perform an in-place upgrade, because SharePoint Foundation will not run on a 32-bit server. Moving WSS 3.0 from 32-bit to 64-bit was discussed in more detail earlier in the chapter.

Let's say your company has decided they want to upgrade to SharePoint Foundation 2010, and they are already running WSS 3.0 on a 64-bit server. An in-place upgrade is the right method for this situation. So, let's get started.

For this example (for simplicity's sake), I will be using a SharePoint farm consisting of one 64-bit WSS 3.0 server named MIGC and one SQL Server 2008 server named SQL64. Figure 15.38 shows an overview.

1. Log on to the SharePoint server with the setup account (of course). Run the SharePoint Foundation installation file, and click **Install SharePoint Foundation** on the splash screen to launch the install wizard (assuming you have installed the prerequisites).

More Than One Server

In a server farm environment, it is likely that you will have more than one server to upgrade. Keep in mind that the server that hosts the Central Administration site must be upgraded and configured before any other server in the farm. There needs to be at least one server hosting Central Administration, but in most implementations, there's only one. If there are more, they should be upgraded before other SharePoint servers.

FIGURE 15.38

Overview of an in-place upgrade for a server farm

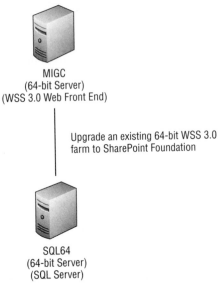

In-Place Upgrade of a 64-bit WSS 3.0 Server Farm

MIGC
(64-bit Server)
(WSS 3.0 Web Front End)

Upgrade an existing 64-bit WSS 3.0 farm to SharePoint Foundation

SQL64
(64-bit Server)
(SQL Server)

2. First you will see the **Welcome** screen; click the **Next** button, and you will be taken to the **License Agreement** screen. Select the **I Accept The Terms Of This License Agreement** box, and then click the **Continue** button to continue.

3. **Upgrade Earlier Versions** is the next screen you will see. Click the **Install Now** button.

   The wizard will now start to install the files. It will take it a few minutes to complete the installation, but once it does, you will come to the **Run SharePoint Products Configuration Wizard Now** screen. Unless you clear the check box on this screen, it will automatically launch the Configuration Wizard after the installer closes. If you have more than one server in the farm, stop here.

   If you have more than one server to upgrade, be sure to run the SharePoint Foundation installation on each of them before running the configuration wizard (then come back and run the configuration wizard on the server hosting Central Administration first). Also, remember to install any language packs before you run the wizard.

4. Launch the **Configuration Wizard** (after making sure all SharePoint servers in the farm have SharePoint Foundation installed but not configured and you've installed your language packs on all servers in the farm, if necessary).

5. When the Configuration Wizard launches, it opens to the usual **Welcome** screen. Just click **Next** here.

6. You will again see the warning dialog about restarting services; just click **OK**.

   The next screen, **Specify Farm Security Settings** (Figure 15.39), is something new with SharePoint Foundation. You are asked to create a farm passphrase, which is kind of like a password for the SharePoint Farm configuration database. You will need this passphrase each time you add a server to the farm. So, you will want to put this somewhere safe and add it to your farm documentation.

FIGURE 15.39
Specifying a
farm passphrase

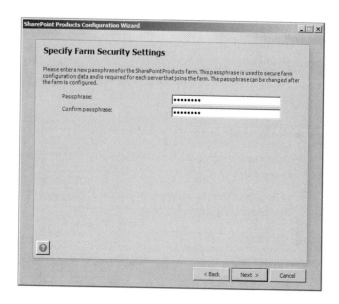

7. Enter an effective passphrase. Make note of what it is before clicking **Next** to move on.

   Visual Upgrade is the next screen (Figure 15.40). You will be asked to decide whether
   to change the user interface to the new SharePoint Foundation user experience or preserve the current look and feel of your sites. As discussed when this tool (the default in
   database-attach upgrades) was introduced earlier in the chapter, it allows site administrators and site collection administrators to test their sites and then upgrade them to the new
   look and feel once everything looks OK or to never upgrade if they choose. If you choose
   to change to the new user experience, you have the option to keep page customizations or
   reset them to the pages' new templates, which cannot be undone.

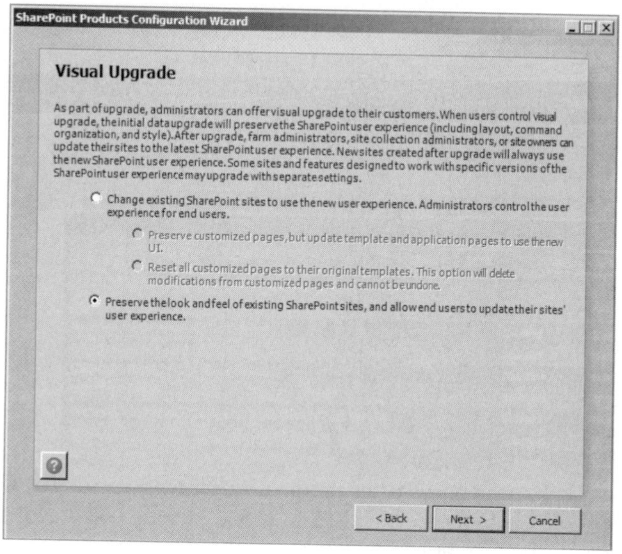

FIGURE 15.40
Choosing whether
to use Visual
Upgrade

8. For this example, I am going to preserve the current look and feel. This will let our administrators upgrade when they are ready (and allow me to demonstrate using the Visual Upgrade option).

   The final screen, **Completing The SharePoint Products Configuration Wizard**, is a summary of the settings that will be applied. This is your last chance to make any changes.

9. When you are ready, click the **Next** button.

10. When the configuration starts to run, a message window opens reminding you that you must run the upgrade on all other farm servers. Click the **Next** button, and the configuration continues.

    When the configuration wizard is finished, you will be presented with the **Configuration Successful, Upgrade In Progress** screen. It's done, but it's not.

    This message means that the configuration portion of the upgrade is done; now a timer job that will complete the upgrade has been set to run. When you click **Finish**, the wizard will close, and the timer job will start.

11. Click **Finish** to close the wizard.

After the wizard closes, your web browser will open to the **Upgrade Status page**, where you can monitor the progress of your upgrade. Much like the status pages for Backup And Restore, this screen tells you the status of your upgrade, whether it is in progress, has succeeded, or has failed. It will list the number of errors, and warnings, if you have any. It will show you what step out of how many you are on, even the percentage of the upgrade that has completed. It will refresh itself every 30 seconds so you can follow the progress. When the timer job has completed, you should see the status (Figure 15.41).

FIGURE 15.41
Upgrade completed successfully

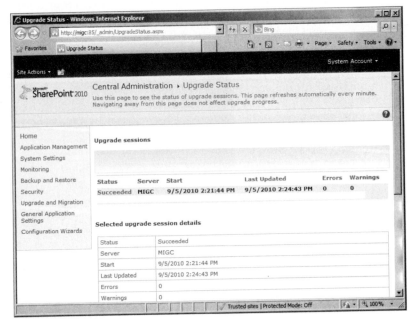

If you have other servers in the farm, now that the first server has finished configuration and upgraded successfully, you can move on to configure them as well. Make note of the upgrade status of each before moving on to the next, just in case.

Log onto your new SharePoint Foundation sites, look around, and make sure everything is working. That is all there is to it! Your WSS 3.0 server farm has now been upgraded to SharePoint Foundation 2010. You can skip ahead to the "Using Visual Upgrade" section or continue reading to explore the alternative database-attach upgrade method.

The Database-Attach Upgrade Method for Server Farms

If you are running a WSS 3.0 server farm on 32-bit server(s) with a 32-bit SQL Server and you want to upgrade to SharePoint Foundation, you will probably want to use the database-attach method so that you can upgrade directly to 64-bit SharePoint Foundation server(s) with a 64-bit version of SQL Server.

Let's say your company is currently running its 32-bit WSS farm, which we will call farm A, with a 32-bit SQL 2005 server named RR1, and a single WSS 3.0 application server named SP2. Business has been booming, and the company has really grown, so the company wants to upgrade to SharePoint Foundation to take advantage of the new features.

So, the new 64-bit SharePoint server farm, which we will call farm B, will start off with one SharePoint Foundation server named MIGD and one 64-bit SQL Server named SQL64. Figure 15.42 shows an overview.

FIGURE 15.42

Overview of a database-attach upgrade for a server farm

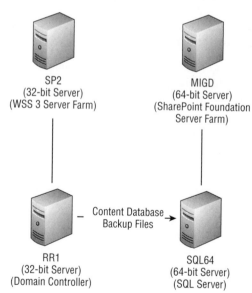

Database Attach Upgrade for a Server Farm

For the Database Attach upgrade, SharePoint Foundation is installed on (MIGD), then the content databases on the WSS 3.0 SQL Server (RR1) are backed up and restored to SharePoint Foundation SQL Server (SQL64)

SP2
(32-bit Server)
(WSS 3 Server Farm)

MIGD
(64-bit Server)
(SharePoint Foundation
Server Farm)

• Install SharePoint
  Foundation on 64-bit Server
• Backup content databases
  on 32-bit SQL server
• Move backup files to 64-bit
  SQL server
• Restore content databases
  on 64-SQL server
• Add content databases to
  web applications

Content Database
Backup Files

RR1
(32-bit Server)
(Domain Controller)

SQL64
(64-bit Server)
(SQL Server)

PREP WORK

As usual, you will need to do a little prep work before you can start moving your WSS 3.0 databases to your new SharePoint Foundation farm. You will need to complete the following tasks:

◆ Run the pre-upgrade checker on the WSS 3.0 server. Make sure there are no issues that would cause your migration to fail.

◆ Back up your WSS 3.0 farm (just in case).

◆ Install SharePoint Foundation prerequisites on the farm B server that will host the Central Administration site; for my example, that would be the server named MIGD. Remember to use the setup account, which is an account configured to hold the necessary roles in SQL, and be able to configure prerequisites and install software on the SharePoint servers.

◆ Do a SharePoint Foundation Server Farm Complete installation on the SharePoint server. If you want to select a different location for the search index files, be sure to specify a data location.

◆ Run the Configuration Wizard first on the server that will contain Central Administration.

◆ Then install and configure the other web front-end servers (if you have any more). The additional servers need to at least run the configuration wizard *after* the first server because the first server on the farm needs to establish the passphrase and configuration database the rest of the servers will use.

The Complete installation of SharePoint Foundation was covered in detail in Chapter 3, "Complete Installation." For more information about installing additional servers on a farm, see Chapter 16, "Advanced Installation and Configuration."

IF YOU HAVE ADDITIONAL SERVERS

You can now log onto the other farm servers with the same setup account and install SharePoint Foundation; only this time, when you run the configuration wizard, you will choose to join the existing server farm. Also, you'll be asked for the passphrase you set up when creating the farm, so keep it in mind.

Otherwise, specify the same configuration database and farm account information, as well as the farm passphrase you created when installing the first server in the SharePoint Foundation farm.

Farm B now consists of a SQL Server database named SQL64 and a SharePoint Foundation server named MIGD. On your new SharePoint Foundation farm, you will need to re-create the web applications that you had on your WSS 3.0 farm. You can either use the Farm Configuration Wizard or enter the information manually (I prefer not to use the wizard, because the manual method offers greater control over the services and their service accounts). You can find more information on how to do this in Chapters 3 and 10. After you have created your web applications, go into Manage Content Databases in Central Administration, and remove the databases that are created when you create a new web applications. You will also need to re-create the security settings and permissions, as well as transfer your customizations to your new SharePoint Foundation farm.

After preparations are complete, all you need to do is move the 32-bit SharePoint farm databases into their new home.

BACKING UP THE SERVER FARM DATABASES

Now that you have prepared a new home for your WSS 3.0 databases, it is time to move them in.

1. You need to log onto the SQL Server being used by WSS 3.0. Once logged on, open your **SQL Server Management Studio** by going to **Start ➢ All Programs ➢ Microsoft SQL Server 2005** (or whatever version you are running) ➢ **SQL Server Management Studio**.

2. The Management Studio will open with the familiar **Connect To Server** dialog box. In this dialog box, you will need to enter the name of the server you want to connect to (for my example that would be RR1 for the server name). You might also need to specify an instance; mine uses the default.

TO BE THOROUGH, OFFLINE THE DATABASES

If you want to be extra picky, you can set the database(s) that you are going to be backing up and moving to be offline in SharePoint, to avoid errors and ensure that users don't try to enter new data into the database while we are trying to back it up. To do so, go to **Central Administration ➢ Application Management ➢ Content Databases**, select the correct database, and on its settings page set the database status to **Offline**. This will make sure that at least no new sites are made during all this and no errors are generated in SharePoint.

Once the Management Studio is connected, the **Object Explorer** will populate on the left side of the screen. In it you will see your database server and a bunch of folders beneath it. The folder we are interested in right now is the **Database** folder. Expand the **Database** folder to reveal all your SharePoint databases.

We will be backing up the content databases from Farm A. In my example, there is only one web application on SP2, so I have only one content database, WSS_Content. If your SharePoint farm has multiple web applications, you will have multiple content databases, and you need to back them all up.

To ensure that we don't cause any conflicts, it is a good thing to first set the database (or databases, if you have more than one) to read-only.

1. To do this, right-click the name of the database, and then click **Properties**.

2. The **Database Properties** page (Figure 15.43) will open. Click **Options** under the **Select A Page** navigation pane on the left side of the screen. Then slide the scroll bar all the way down until you get to the **State** options. The first State option will be **Database Read-only**. Set it to True, and click **OK**.

   You will see a warning message that to change the settings, all connections will have to be closed; this is **OK**. Repeat this process with all your content databases. Now you are ready to back up the database.

3. To back up each database, right-click the name of the database, click **Tasks**, and then click **Back Up**, as shown in Figure 15.44.

FIGURE 15.43
Database Properties page

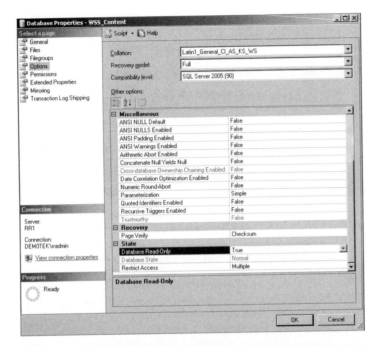

FIGURE 15.44
Selecting the database to back up

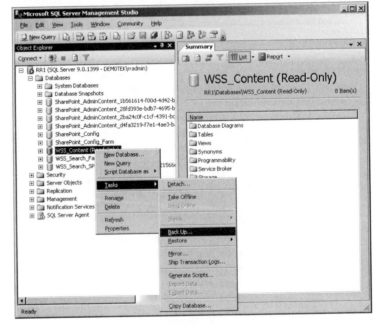

The **Back Up Database** screen (Figure 15.45) will open. On the **General** page, under the **Source** section, the database name should already be in the **Database** box. If it is not, select it from the drop-down menu. The backup type should be set to Full.

FIGURE 15.45
Database backup
settings

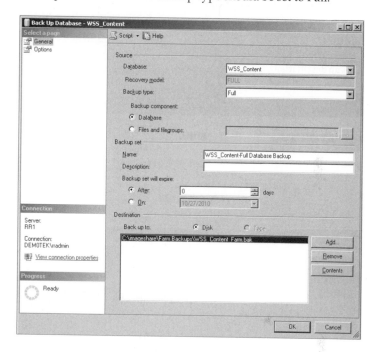

4. Select **Database** for **Backup Component**. Leave everything under the **Backup Set** section at the defaults.

5. In the **Destination** section, select **Disk**, and either accept the default location for backup files or click the **Remove** button to clear the default and add your own destination (which is what I have to do because the server doesn't have my backup location listed).

6. To add your own location to save the backup files to, click the **Add** button in the **Destination** section. The **Select Backup Destination** screen will open, with the default file location. To choose an alternate location, click the (...) button to browse to a new location.

7. The **Locate Database Files** window (Figure 15.46) will open. Browse to your alternate location, and then type the name of your backup file in the **File Name** box. You will also need to append the file extension to the filename. For this example, we will be using the filename WSS_Content_Farm.bak. Click **OK** to continue.

   You will now return to the **Select Database Destination** screen, this time with your alternate file location in the **File Name** box.

8. Click the **OK** button.

This brings us all the way back to the **Back Up Database** screen. The alternate file location you selected will now appear in the Destination file box.

9. Click **OK** to start the backup.

FIGURE 15.46

Selecting the backup destination

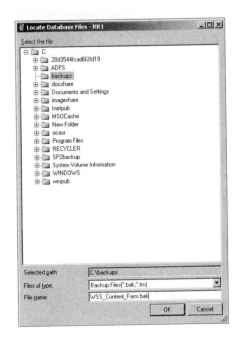

You can follow the progress in the **Progress** section, which is in the lower-left corner of the screen. When the backup is completed, a message box will state that the database backup was completed successfully. Click **OK**.

Repeat this process with each of the content databases files for your farm. Keep in mind that if you have web applications that have more than one content database, then you need to back up, restore, and attach them to their respective web applications as well.

RESTORING THE SERVER FARM DATABASES TO THE NEW SQL SERVER

After you have created your backups, copy them to the 64-bit SQL server, either 2008 or 2008 (R2) in farm B (for me that's the server named SQL64).

1. Open the **SQL Server Management Studio**. However, this time when you enter the SQL Server name, you will need to enter the name of your 64-bit SQL server; for this example, I will be using SQL64.

2. Once you are connected, expand the **Databases** folder by clicking its plus sign. You will now be able to see a list of all the databases installed on the server. This is helpful to let you know the names of any of the databases already on the server (in case there might be any name conflicts).

3. The next step will be to use the backup files we copied from the source server and restore them using SQL Server Management Studio. Right-click the Databases folder, and select **Restore Database**.

When the **Restore Database** page opens, you will need to specify a name for your database in the **To Database** box.

When you re-created your web applications, there was a content database created for each web application. Instead of deleting those databases, as you did in the standalone upgrade, you can restore the backup copies of your WSS 3.0 databases to these new SharePoint Foundation databases.

This lets you choose which database you will restore to, by clicking it in the drop-down menu.

You should always start with the first, root web application, so we will be restoring that database first. Now once you do this, it's still a good idea to run the STSADM command `addcontentdb` (or the PowerShell equivalent) to attach the databases to their respective web applications, even though you just wrote over their databases, even if all names remain the same.

Also, if you are restoring over an existing database, make sure that database is in the same **Read-Only** state as the backup. In this case, you may need to set the database you are going to restore over to **Read-Only** in the database's properties. If that is necessary, you will be prompted during the restore, or you can prepare for it to start.

RATHER NOT OVERWRITE?

You can always delete the databases in SQL that were used by the web applications that you made and then create new ones with names you specify during the restore. We're just giving you a chance to see that you can restore over existing databases, rather than just create new ones.

---

4. For my example, my first, root web application content database is WSS_Content_Farm, so I will select it from the drop-down menu in the To Database field (Figure 15.47).

5. In the **Source For Restore** section, select **From Device** as our source, and then click the Browse button (...) to select the location of the backup file to restore from.

6. After clicking the button, the **Specify Backup** window will open. The **Backup Media** setting should already be set to **File**, so all you have to do is click the **Add** button to add the file location.

7. After you click **Add**, the **Locate Backup File** window (Figure 15.48) will open, and you can browse to the file location where the database backup files were stored. Click the file you want to restore from, and then click **OK**.

This will take you back to the **Specify Backup** window; only this time the file is showing in the **Backup Location** box, so just click **OK** to continue. You will return to the **Restore Database** page, only now the database backup file location is listed in the **Select The Backup Sets To Restore** box.

FIGURE 15.47
Database to restore

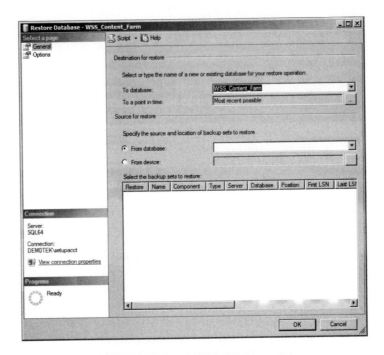

FIGURE 15.48
Selecting the
backup file for the
restore

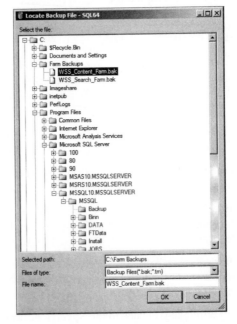

8. As shown in Figure 15.49, click the check box next to the filename to select it as the backup set you want to restore from (notice that the original database was called WSS_Content, but the database will restore on this server with the name specified, in my case WSS_Content_Farm). This is a good reason to do the `addcontentdb` command to be sure SharePoint is aware that the newly restored database belongs with the root web application.

FIGURE 15.49
Selecting the backup set to restore from

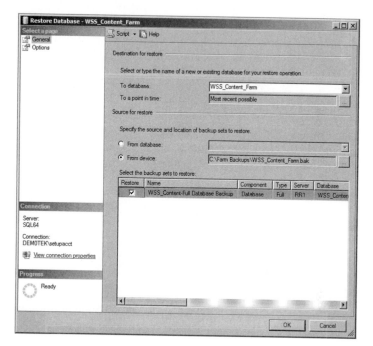

Finally, since you are using the content database that was created when we first configured SharePoint Foundation, be sure to overwrite the empty database with our restored database.

9. So, click **Option** in the **Select A Page** navigation pane, and then check **the Overwrite Existing Database (WITH REPLACE)** box (Figure 15.50). Now you can click **OK** to start the restore.

10. Once the restore process is complete, you will see a message box open saying the database restore was completed successfully. Click **OK** to close.

You'll end up back on the **Object Explorer**, where your new database is now listed, but it is listed as (Read Only). In order to be able to use it, you will need to set the **Database Read-Only** property to False. Click the database, go to **Properties** in the drop-down menu, and in the **Database Properties** window, select **Options** from the list on the left, and scroll down to change the **Database Read-Only** state from True to **False**.

You will need to repeat the previous steps for every content database that you backed up from farm A that you want to migrate to farm B.

FIGURE 15.50
Overwriting
database

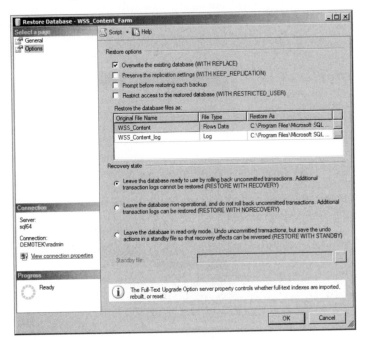

ATTACHING THE SERVER FARM DATABASES TO SHAREPOINT FOUNDATION

Once you've restored all the databases you want to migrate, you are ready for the next step, adding the restored content databases to the web applications. (Well, in our example, we'll add only one, but you'll get the idea.) You can use a PowerShell or STSADM command to add the content databases to their web applications. In our case, we'll use STSADM.

1. Open the **SharePoint 2010 Management Shell** (since it's so convenient).

2. Type in the following STSADM command to add the content database to the root web application, SharePoint-80 (of course filling in the variables for *yourrootsite* and *your_db_name* with the correct information for your environment).

   ```
   Stsadm.exe -o addcontentdb -url http://YOURROOTSITE -databasename <YOUR_DB_NAME>
   ```

   For our example, I will be adding the WSS_Content_Farm database that we restored to the root web application http://migd, so my command will look like this:

   ```
   Stsadm.exe -o addcontentdb -url http://MIGD -databasename WSS_Content_Farm
   ```

3. Press **Enter** to start the attach and upgrade process.

It will take a few minutes for the process to run, so you only see the status of the process by the percentage complete message displayed in the command prompt window. When the process is complete, you will see the message Operation Completed Successfully.

You will most likely have more than one content database to restore and attach, so you will need to repeat the process for each content database and attach them to their new web application.

YOU CAN ALSO USE POWERSHELL TO ATTACH THE DATABASE

If you prefer to use one of the new PowerShell cmdlets to attach your database, open the PowerShell application by going to **Start ➤ All Programs ➤ Microsoft SharePoint 2010 Products** folder ➤ **SharePoint 2010 Management Shell**.

This is the cmdlet you will want to use:

```
Mount-SPContentDatabase -Name YOUR_DATABASE_NAME -WebApplication http://YOUR_
ROOT_SITE
```

So, for my example, I would use this:

```
Mount -SPContentDatabase -Name WSS_Content_Farm -WebApplication http://MIGD
```

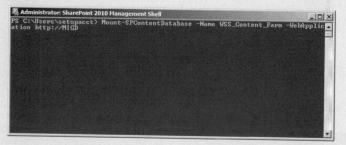

There is another cmdlet, `Upgrade -SPContentDatabase`, that is often confused with `Mount -SPContentDatabase`. The Upgrade cmdlet is used only if your database upgrade fails and you need to retry.

We're almost there. If you created any additional front-end servers, you will want to log on to them and do an IISRESET so that the changes you just made will be updated on those servers.

Finally, open up your new SharePoint site to see how it looks! Take some time, and click around; make sure everything is working correctly and that nothing was forgotten. Congratulations! You are now the proud owner of a new SharePoint Foundation server farm!

Using Visual Upgrade

Your new SharePoint Foundation farm is up and running! Take a deep breath, and congratulate yourself on a job well done! All your time, effort, and planning paid off.

But now it is time for the post-game wrap-up.

As discussed earlier in the chapter, Visual Upgrade is a tool enabled by default in all database-attach upgrades, and in the in-place server farm upgrade, we decided to allow for transitioning users to the new interface with Visual Upgrade as well.

There really isn't much to using Visual Upgrade. Start by logging onto your SharePoint Foundation top-level site at the root of the web application you just upgraded. Figure 15.51 shows what the site in my example looks like using the older user experience (look and feel).

To preview what the site will look like with the new SharePoint Foundation user experience, click **Site Actions**, and then click **Visual Upgrade** in the menu that drops down (Figure 15.52).

The **Site Setting** ➢ **Title, Description, And Icon** page will open. On this page you can give the page a title, add a description, and add a logo for your home page. More important for our purpose is that you can also choose what you want to do with Visual Upgrade.

FIGURE 15.51
A site using the previous user interface

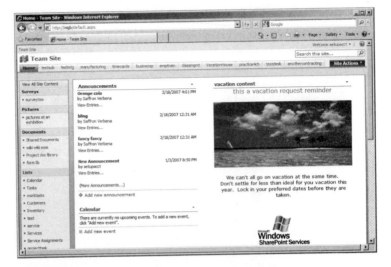

FIGURE 15.52
Visual Upgrade

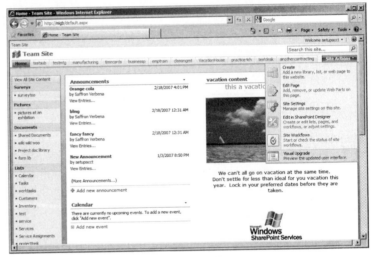

If you choose **Use The Previous User Interface**, the site will display as they did in WSS 3.0. If you choose **Preview The Updated User Interface**, the site will display as it will when the user interface is permanently upgraded to use the new SharePoint Foundation user interface and will include the new features and options. This option will allow you to see how the sites will look, feel, and function under the SharePoint Foundation interface. If you make any changes to the pages under the new interface and then notice that your pages display incorrectly when you return to the previous interface because of the changes you made, you can reset the pages.

The last option is **Update The User Interface**, and it will permanently upgrade the page to the new SharePoint Foundation interface.

For this example, we will select **Preview The Updated User Interface** (Figure 15.53) just so we can see what the site will look like under the new user experience.

FIGURE 15.53

Choosing to preview the new user interface

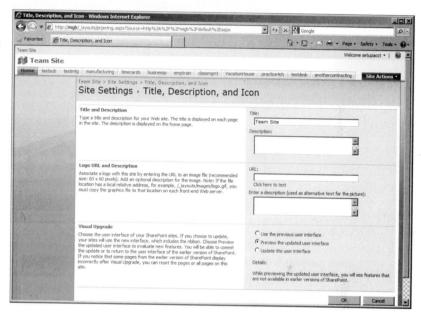

Figure 15.54 shows what the site will look like under the new user interface.

FIGURE 15.54

The new user interface

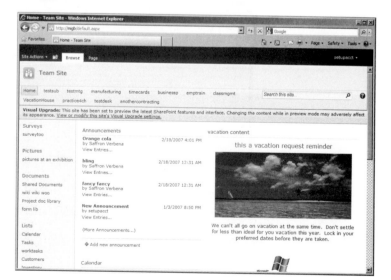

Now if you want to either go back to the previous user experience or permanently upgrade to the new look and feel, you can do this by clicking **Site Actions** again (this time it is on the left of the new top ribbon bar) and then choosing **Visual Upgrade** (Figure 15.55).

FIGURE 15.55

Selecting Visual Upgrade from the Site Actions list

This time we will select **Use The Previous User Interface** (Figure 15.56), and the site will return to the way it looked in WSS 3.0.

FIGURE 15.56

Returning to previous user interface

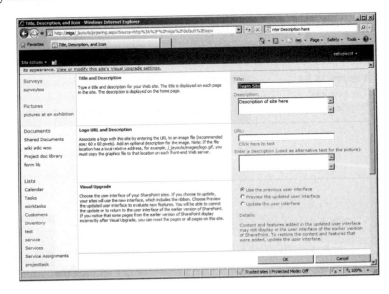

When you are ready to upgrade your site permanently to the new user experience, choose **Update The User Interface**, and the site will always display in the new user interface.

Each site must be updated individually, so you can task your site collection administrators and/or site administrators with testing their sites under the new user experience and ultimately with deciding when to permanently update them to the new look and feel. You now have a handle on how to migrate your WSS 3.0 environment to SharePoint Foundation so you, and your users, can take advantage of the new capabilities and features. Congratulations.

The Bottom Line

Determine which upgrade method to use.   The decision about which upgrade method to use is influenced by many factors. Do you need to move to new hardware? Do you need to restructure your environment? And finally, what type of server farm are you currently running?

> **Master It**   Which upgrade method will allow you to upgrade databases from a 32-bit WSS 3.0 farm directly to 64-bit SharePoint Foundation farm?

Prepare for Upgrade.   When you are preparing for an upgrade there are many things you can do to identify potential problems that could cause your upgrade to fail. You can ensure you are on the correct hardware and running the correct software. You can ensure you have enough memory and free disk space. There are also preparation tools that you can run to identify potential "gotchas."

> **Master It**   Which preparation tool generates a printable HTML report that lists all of the SharePoint components and identifies any issues that could cause your upgrade to fail?

Move from 32-bit hardware to 64-bit hardware.   Many companies today are running WSS 3.0 on 32-bit hardware and operating system; however, SharePoint Foundation requires 64-bit hardware.

> **Master It**   Name an upgrade method that would requires a WSS 3.0 farm be moved to 64-bit hardware and operating system before upgrading to SharePoint Foundation.

Upgrade Windows SharePoint Services 3.0 to SharePoint Foundation 2010.   There are two main methods available to upgrade or migrate from Windows SharePoint Services 3.0 to SharePoint Foundation: database-attach and in-place. Database-attach method is used to migrate WSS 3.0 content database to a SharePoint Foundation installation and attach them to existing web applications. In-place method simply upgrades an existing WSS 3.0 installation to SharePoint Foundation.

> **Master It**   Under what circumstances might it be easier to do a database-attach upgrade than an in-place upgrade? When might an in-place upgrade be a better option?

Use Visual Upgrade.   Visual Upgrade is a new feature of SharePoint 2010 that allows you to retain the current look and feel of your SharePoint sites. After WSS has been upgraded to SharePoint Foundation, site owners and site collection administrators will be able to preview their sites in the new user interface, allowing them to test the functionality of their sites before upgrading permanently to the new user interface.

> **Master It**   Where would a site owner or site collection administrator do to preview their site with the new user interface?

Chapter 16

Advanced Installation and Configuration

Generally you install SharePoint on your network for a reason. Maybe you intend to use it for document storage, collaboration, data gathering, or calendar and contact management. But behind the scenes you might need more than the default settings allow. You may need to host isolated site collections for clients or separate departments of your business. You might be considering offering access, from within SharePoint, to external data for your users to view or modify. Your data might need the security of SSL, or you might need Kerberos authentication. You might be planning on having tens of thousands of users and require multiple front-end servers managed centrally from one Central Administration site. These requirements involve a more complicated SharePoint installation and configuration. They will also have limitations that must be considered before implementation.

This chapter covers the more advanced features, configurations, and settings that were not appropriate earlier in the book. These include the practical concepts behind installing additional servers to the SharePoint farm and network load balancing SharePoint; securing SharePoint web applications with SSL; and enabling Kerberos authentication. Other useful concepts include multi-tenancy, configuring Business Data Connectivity to create an external list and explore a lookup field, Office Web Apps.

In this chapter, you'll learn to

- Use the Business Data Connectivity service to create external data connections

- Set a service principal name

- Configure Network Load Balancing

- Configure Multi-tenancy

Configuring New SharePoint Capabilities

Business Data Connectivity is new to SharePoint Foundation. Until this point, the free version of SharePoint could not make use of this external data access tool. However, because the Foundation version of SharePoint is intended to contain more of the true SharePoint infrastructure features, things such as Business Data Connectivity are now built right in. There may be added features and conveniences in the paid for version, SharePoint Server 2010, but there are quite a number of things you can do in SharePoint Foundation, as long you know how to configure them.

Using Business Data Connectivity

To start, Business Data Connectivity (BDC, but also known as Business Connectivity Services or BCS) is a service application used by SharePoint to access data external to SharePoint's content databases. Up until this version, Windows SharePoint Services could not access external data and use it natively in lists or libraries without considerable customization. Now, with SharePoint Foundation, access to external business data is possible. Using BDC models and external content types (which basically define the external connection parameters, data source being accessed, and so on), you can create external lists at the site level that users can read or even edit and add data to the external source. External data lookup fields can be added to SharePoint lists as well, giving them access to data from the external source that otherwise would not have been available.

The BDC service needs to be configured on the SharePoint server first, and then external content types need to be set up using SharePoint Designer 2010 or Visual Studio 2010. SharePoint Designer 2010 (SPD) is free and is meant to be used to customize SharePoint without writing code, so we will be using it in this chapter to set up external content types for BDC.

We configured and enabled the service in Central Administration in Chapter 3, and now it's time to set up an external connection.

To do that, you need to have SharePoint Designer 2010 (earlier versions are not compatible) installed on your network, and an external data source, such as a non-SharePoint related SQL database. You need to be logged in as a farm administrator because SPD will be using your credentials for this endeavor. I have installed SPD 2010 32-bit on a Windows 7 client on the network. (I installed the 32-bit version because I already had the 32-bit version of Office 2010 on that workstation, and the two products must match in architecture.) This book has not really explored SharePoint Designer 2010, because there are numerous good books dedicated to learning SPD 2010, so teaching it again here would be redundant. Therefore I am going to cover just enough about SPD to accomplish our task. But it should give you some idea of the usefulness of the tool, and why it is well worth downloading and installing.

 Real World Scenario

PERMISSIONS CHECK

Something to keep in mind when preparing to use the Business Data Connectivity service to access external content is the permissions required. The account you will use to configure the external connection for BDC, the BDC service account itself, and the content database account for the web application containing the site that will use the external list or lookup fields must have at least read and write access to the external data source (in my case, that will be a SQL database called *sampleDB*).

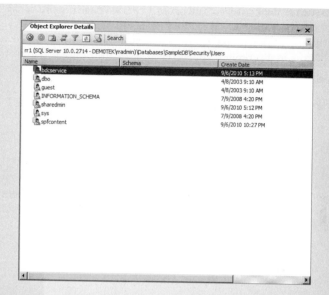

To enable the BDC service to access the SQL database, I had to add its account, in my case dem0tek\ spfbdc, to the database's users and give it db_datareader and db_datawriter permissions (it does not need to be an owner of the database; least privilege is good). The account I am using to set up the external content type for the database (for me that's dem0tek\shareadmin) and the content database account for the web application to contain the external list (for me, dem0tek\spfcontent) will also need to be added as users with the same permissions (db_datareader and db_datawriter) to the data source.

All farm administrators have the right to administer service applications, regardless of whether they are explicitly added to the service application's permissions. The only caveat to this is, in order to apply permissions directly to accounts for the service application, you do need the right specifically to do so (we'll set that up later in the chapter).Therefore, when I configure permissions on the external content type for the BDC service in Central Administration, I am going to give my *shareadmin* account full rights to manage permissions. Although it's not strictly required, I am also going to be logged in as that *shareadmin* account when creating the external list that points to the external content type.

CREATING AN EXTERNAL CONTENT TYPE

Take the following steps to begin creating an external content type in SharePoint Designer 2010, once you've installed it:

1. Make certain you are logged in with a farm account (in my case, that's my *shareadmin* account). Open SharePoint Designer. If you have never opened the product before, it will be located under the SharePoint folder in All Programs.

SharePoint Designer 2010 opens to a Sites page (as you can see in Figure 16.1). In my case, I have `http://spf2` and `http://spf1` listed under Recent Sites because I've been doing work with my SharePoint servers using this product. Your Recent Sites might be blank at this point if you've never used any Office product on the workstation to access a SharePoint site.

FIGURE 16.1
The SharePoint Designer 2010 Sites page

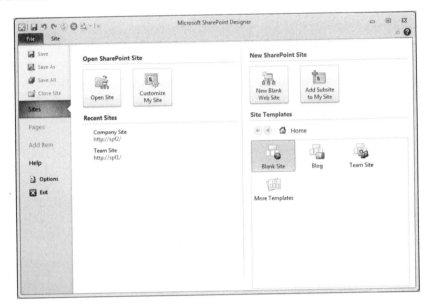

SharePoint Designer focuses on a particular site and its resources, such as lists, pages, libraries, workflows, or web parts. So if you are planning on using BDC external content on a particular site on a server, it's convenient to have its address here under Recent Sites. In my case, I am going to use `http://spf2`. This is the address of the Company Site created early in the book and will be the site that eventually will use the external data we are connecting to in a list. It is a site collection in a web application that has the BDC service application connection enabled.

REMEMBER SERVICE APPLICATION CONNECTIONS?

Back when you were creating web applications, there was a setting for service application connections. The default was to simply allow all service applications, of which we have two out of the box (if configured): BDC and Usage and Health. Because a web application contains the site you might be working on, it defines whether the site can use a service. If one of yours can't, check to see whether that service application connection (elsewhere in the interface it is called a *service application association*) was disabled for that web application.

---

2. To open a site to work on, click Open Site, type in its address in the Open Site dialog box, and click Open.

It may take a moment as SPD establishes communication with the site. Then it will display the workspace for the site. Here you have a plethora of objects to work on, everything from web parts and site groups to master pages and external content types. Notice in Figure 16.2 that site objects are listed in the pane on the left, and the workspace currently displays a page to view and manage settings for the site. When you select something in the Site Objects pane, its properties and relevant information display in the workspace on its own page. The workspace can be tabbed, so there can be more than one page to look at in that area (it basically remembers everything you've worked on while you've had the program open). And it can get crowded, so remember that tabs can be closed. Pay attention to which one you are working on if objects are similar.

FIGURE 16.2
The workspace for a selected site

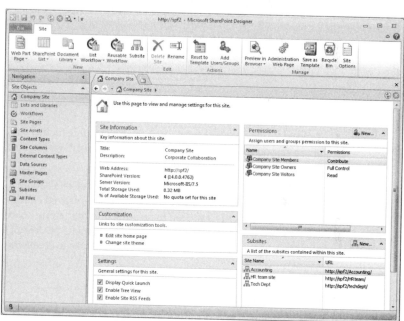

For this exercise, we are going to focus on creating an external content type to use with our Business Data Connectivity service. It should be noted that this is a great place to get to know for customizing and extending the use of SharePoint. For busy administrators in particular, it is simply the best and easiest way to set up BDC external data access.

You will be working on the external content type as a farm administrator who also has access to the data source. Remember that the BDC service, the account you're using, and the content database for the web application that will contain the external list must have read and write permissions to the data source.

3. Click the External Content Types object in the Site Objects pane.

There may be a delay while data is gathered from the server concerning the BDC service and its external content types (or ECTs). In my case, I have no external content types yet, so this page should be blank until I create one (Figure 16.3).

FIGURE 16.3
The External Content Types page before a type is created

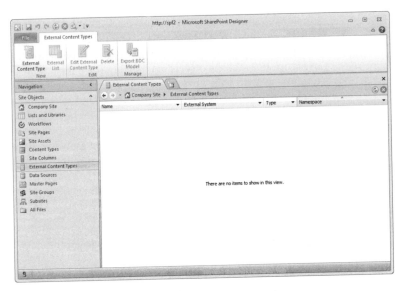

4. To create a new content type, click the External Content Type button in the New section of the ribbon (you may need to click in the empty workspace to activate the External Content Type button if it is grayed out).

The tab in the workspace will change to New External Content Type * (the asterisk means it's new and hasn't been saved yet, or there are unsaved changes), as shown in Figure 16.4. It will fill with sections related to creating and managing an external content type. There are two views for this tab—Summary, which opens by default and contains the sections, and Operations Design, which is the view you use to create the connection to external data sources.

FIGURE 16.4
The new ECT workspace

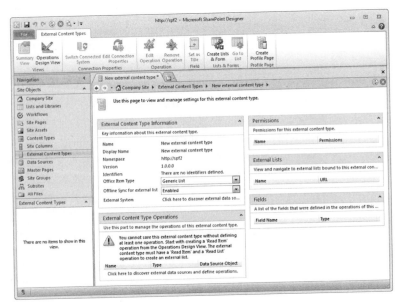

In the Summary view, External Content Type information lists the Name, Display Name (essentially the friendly name is optional), Namespace (URL of site), and Version. (You can specify the version of the external content type if you want to track changes you make. Use the four digits separated by period format to avoid issues.) If there is an identifier specified for the external content type, it will be here. There are also fields for specifying the type of list to use for the external content type (I'm just keeping the generic list option) and whether to allow offline sync for the external list. Offline sync is enabled by default (used by SharePoint Workspace), but if the data pulled by the external content type is really large, you might want to disable it. Finally, the external system information (the source for the data) will be displayed at the bottom of the section.

THE OFFICE ITEM TYPE

Although we are just going to use a generic list type for this example, you could select a type of list that would map to something Outlook could use, such as a Task, Contact, or Calendar. So if you have data in the external content that would map to the fields of an existing list type, you can select it and map the fields in the field parameters when setting up operations for the external content type.

The other sections, External Content Type Operations, Permissions, External Lists, and Fields, will propagate with data after the external content type is configured, as you will see in a moment.

5. To get started with configuration, give the external content type a name by clicking New External Content type in the Name field. For my example, I am going to enter *ExampleData*. If you tab out of the field, it will propagate the display name with the same data.

   You can also specify a display name if you'd like; I'm going to use the same name (often the name of a connection isn't as friendly as the display name).

   Now that you've named the external content type, it's time to create a connection to an external data source and define the operations that can be done with that connection.

6. To create a new connection, either click the Operations Design View button in the ribbon or click the Click Here To Discover The External Data Source Link In The External System field at the bottom of the External Connection Type Information section in the summary view.

   Once on the Operations Design View page, you'll see that this is where you click the big Add Connection button to specify your data source (Figure 16.5).

   The data source I am using for my example is a little database I made in SQL with one small sample table in it. With this version of SharePoint, external data sources can be accessed via SharePoint to do more than just passively read the data. Now (depending on your source database) you can also *CRUD* (do create, read, update, and delete operations) on the database. When setting up these operations, remember that fields can be required, read-only, and identifiers (or primary keys). Keep in mind that tables can be designed with autogenerating data that is read-only (identifier fields often are) and might make it hard for SharePoint to create a new item if there are fields that can't be empty but can't be filled with anything from SharePoint either. Test your database as a data source for an external list to be sure what will work and what won't.

FIGURE 16.5
Adding a new
connection on the
Operations Design
View page

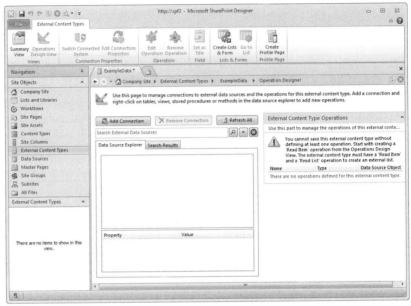

FIGURE 16.5
Adding a new
connection on the
Operations Design
View page

7. To add a data source connection to the external content type, click Add Connection in the workspace.

   This will trigger a dialog box in which to select the data source type for the external connection. In my case, the type of data I will be accessing is SQL Server (see Figure 16.6 for my example selection). The other types of data connection require some coding and are .NET type and WCF service (WCF stands for Windows Communications Foundation). If you have data stored in a form not available through SQL Server, you may need to opt for using .NET or WCF connectors for the BDC to be able to figure out how to access the data.

8. In my case, my external, non-SharePoint data is stored in a SQL database. So, I will select SQL Server as my data source. Select the correct data source for you.

FIGURE 16.6
Selecting the
external data
source type

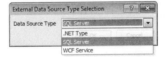

Once you've selected the type of data source access you'll be using, a Connection dialog box will come up (in my case, it's a SQL Server Connection box). This dialog box requires a server name, a database name, a name for the connection (that one's optional), and the type of identity that will be used to access the database.

The User Identity option simply passes through the user's identity they are using to access the external list to the back-end data source to access the data. That user account (and all user accounts that will use the data on the site) needs to have permissions to the database. This option also requires Kerberos to be configured.

Connect with Impersonated Windows Identity and Connect with Impersonated Custom Identity both have to do with the Secure Store service, which is not available for SharePoint Foundation.

So at this point, the only option available to give users access to the data source is to choose User Identity. And that would work if the users all had permissions set on the source database and if you had Kerberos set up (we'll look at Kerberos later in the chapter).

However, there is another option. And because it isn't obvious, it's the one I am going to demonstrate—using the BDC identity for this external content type to access the data source on behalf of the users so they don't all have to be added to the database's permissions nor Kerberos-configured (this is particularly good if you are looking at doing this for external or anonymous users, although anonymous users take extra configuration).

Now you may have noticed that using the BDC identity is not an option in the dialog box. It becomes available *after* you create the connection. So, we'll create the connection, configure a few things, and then come back and change User Identity to BDC Identity.

9. In the dialog box, enter the data source (mine would be the SQL server name), the database you are going to use as the source (mine is *sampledb*), enter a shorter friendly name if you want, and select Connect With User's Identity, because that's the only option of the three that SharePoint Foundation can use. You can see Figure 16.7 for my example.

FIGURE 16.7
Configuring connection properties in the SQL Server Connection dialog box

10. Once the connection properties are configured as you wish, click OK to continue.

Back in the workspace, the database you chose as the data source is displayed in the data source explorer list. You can select a table to use or a view. In my case, I am going to use a simple table I made for this example.

At this point, you need to navigate in the Data Source Explorer to the item you are going to use for this connection. Once you can see the table or view you want to use for your data source, you need to decide what operations the users can do in the external list on the site connected to this data source. With this version of SharePoint Designer and SharePoint Foundation, you can allow (depending on the data source) the user to read (item and/or list), as well as write, update, and delete items in the list and therefore the underlying external database. Once you can see your data source listed, you right-click it to select the operations you want your users to be able to do on the data source.

11. Right-click your data source to access the operations available to give to your users. In the drop-down menu, select the operation you want to offer (this has to be done one at a time if you want more than one); or, if you want to give users all the options (which I do), select Create All Operations (Figure 16.8). In my case, this will give my users the right to read, create, edit, and delete items from the data source.

FIGURE 16.8
Selecting Operations to apply to data source

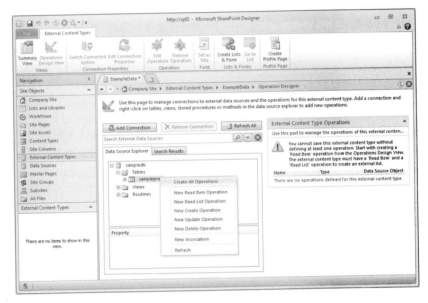

12. An Operations configuration window will open. It starts with an Operation Properties page to confirm the operations you selected. Click Next to set up field parameters for your operations.

13. Once on the Parameters page, you select the fields and set up their properties. Properties for fields are listed on the right, such as Map To Identifier, Required, Read-Only, Show In Picker, and TimeStamp Field. If a field is a unique key or ID field, set it to Map To Identifier, so it will be identified with a key (see Figure 16.9). The fields should be configured here to match their configuration in the underlying table, except that you also choose which field will be the main field for searching (the Show In Picker field). Keep in mind that SPD can only handle identifier fields that are read-only and required. In this context, when you add a new item, you can enter data into that field (if it's not read-only in the underlying database) but you cannot edit the identifier field otherwise. See the sidebar below for more. If you selected a type of list (instead of generic) for the external content type, you can map the field from the external data source to the type of list's field, in the Office Property field.

You will notice that there are some warnings and suggestions at the bottom of the page. You will find that some warnings can be ignored (it doesn't like that my Price field has a decimal limit, for example). In addition, at least one field needs to be set to Show In Picker. This field controls how the external content type will show up in the picker box when you need to select an external content type to create a new external list. For this example, the Name field should have Show In Picker selected. At a minimum, you need to set a Map To Identifier field and one to Show In Picker.

FIGURE 16.9
Configuring field
parameters in All
Operations

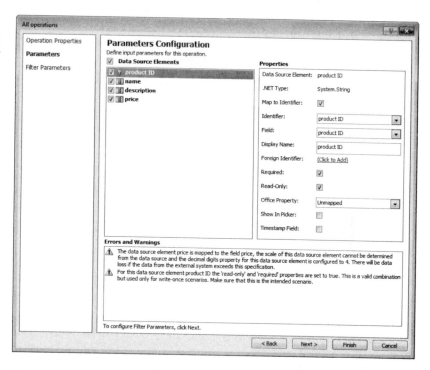

PRE-UPDATER FIELD WARNING

Even if you set the identifier field of your data source *not* to be read-only in SPD, you will still not be able to edit data in the external list using that data source. You will easily be able to create, delete, or read data, but in order for identifier fields to be editable, the UpdaterField = True attribute in the underlying BDC model XML file must be changed to PreUpdaterField = True for the identifier field in the Update method instance. By design, SPD cannot make that change, so you must either edit the BDC model manually or purchase, install, and use Visual Studio to do it (both of which are a bit outside the scope of this book). SharePoint Designer cannot edit an external connection if its BDC model has been edited.

---

14. Once you've configured your field parameters, click Next to continue.

On the Filter Parameters page, in the Errors And Warnings area, you'll see that it suggests you set up at least a filter to limit the number of items returned to avoid large result sets. Remember that if the data source has thousands of records and the users need to see all of them, limiting the results they get in SharePoint may not be a good idea. For this example, however, let's create a filter that limits the items to 1,000 (the maximum for a limit filter is 2,000 items).

15. To do this, click the Add Filter Parameters button. It will add some unconfigured filter parameters to the page (Figure 16.10).

FIGURE 16.10

The Filter Param-
eters page

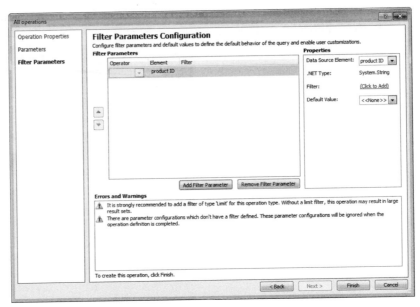

FIGURE 16.10

The Filter Param-
eters page

16. To create a limits filter, click (Click To Add) in the Properties area on the right of the page, in the Filter field.

This will open a Filter Configuration dialog box. In the box, you can name the new filter (I'm not going to bother). In the Filter Properties area, click the Filter Type down arrow, and select Limit (Figure 16.11).

FIGURE 16.11

Setting Filter
Properties in the
Filter Configura-
tion dialog box

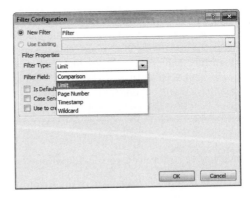

17. There are other options in the dialog box that aren't really applicable to the limit filter, so simply click OK to finish configuration.

18. Back on the Filter Parameters page, you now need to configure the default value—the amount you want the filter to limit data that will display from this data source in the

external list in SharePoint. For this example, enter **1000** as the limit (Figure 16.12), but keep in mind how many items your data source actually contains.

FIGURE 16.12
Entering a default value in Filter Parameters

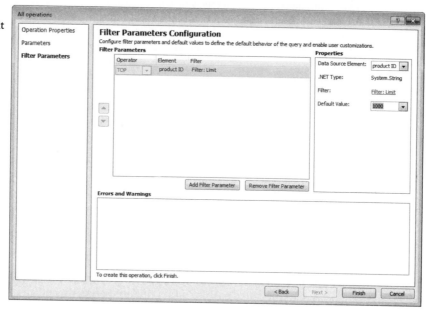

FIGURE 16.12
Entering a default value in Filter Parameters

19. To finish configuring parameters for your operations, click Finish. This will bring you back to the workspace. Notice that your connection is listed, with the data source you selected on the left, and the operations you configured are now listed under External Content Type Operations on the right (Figure 16.13).

FIGURE 16.13
External Content Type Operations in Design view with operations listed

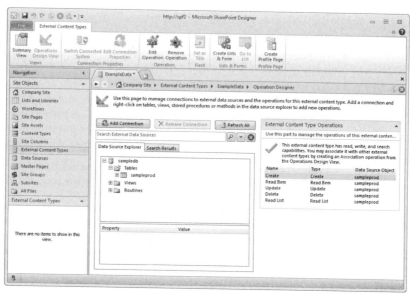

WHY USING A VIEW AS A DATA SOURCE CAN BE HANDY

I've mentioned that you can select either a table or a view in a database as the data source. If you have a table of data that has far more than 1,000 to 2,000 records (the maximum the Limit filter can allow), you can simply choose not to limit the data that returns from this source. However, that can really slow down the experience of the user trying to open the external list. So if you are going to limit the result set of a connection, you should consider filtering the data at the database by creating views. That way, the users will get all the relevant records they need but fewer of the ones they don't need. Then create multiple connections, one to each view, and multiple external lists. Then the users can go to the correct list to get the data they need and, if you're good, never exceed 2,000 records.

Now that we've set up the external content type's connection and operations, you need to consider what kind of identity you are going to use so that the users can access the external data source. Initially we selected Connect With User Identity as the authentication mode for the external content type, but that was essentially just a placeholder until we could go back in and select BDC Identity.

CONFIGURING A SERVICE APPLICATION FOR BDC IDENTITY

To use the User identity, SharePoint just passes the credentials through to the data source. This works if you have Kerberos enabled and configured properly, and all users who will need to use the external list in SharePoint personally have permissions set up on the data source (the SQL database in my case). When you use BDC identity, only a few accounts need read and write access to the data source (the BDC service, the content database account that will house the external lists, and the account that is configuring the external content type). In addition, when you choose to use the BDC identity, the service needs to be able to *revert to self* for its credentials. This allows SharePoint to act as the BDC identity when accessing the data source on behalf of the users.

The Revert To Self capability is not enabled by default for the BDC service, so you need to enable it in order for the BDC identity to work. This is a sneaky extra thing you have to do, and it requires PowerShell.

1. Go back to your SharePoint server's desktop, and make sure you are logged in with an account with the correct PowerShell permissions. That can be a super shell admin account (one with PowerShell admin permissions to all databases in the farm, and the right to create new shell admins), or at least one that is a farm administrator, that has access (actually owner permissions) to the BDC service's database, the content database that will be using the external lists, and the configuration database. If you are logged in with the correct account, open the SharePoint management shell console.

   When the management shell console opens, you will need to know the BDC service application's GUID, because you will have to change the property RevertToSelfAllowed from False to True.

   Now there are ways to pipe a PowerShell command so that it passes the correct GUID to the variable, but I am going to simply mark and paste the GUID for simplicity's sake. It's a straightforward way to make sure you are using the correct data.

2. To get that information (which you can see in Figure 16.14), first list the service applications:

```
Get-SPServiceApplication
```

3. Then you can mark the GUID for the service and copy it. (To mark, right-click in the console and select Mark in the menu; then click and drag to select the GUID. When it is highlighted, press Enter to copy it to the Clipboard.)

4. You will need to fill a variable with the BDC service information, so use the following command, pasting (by right-clicking) the GUID marked earlier as the identity value:

```
$bapp= get-spserviceapplication -identity <BDCserviceGUID>
```

(I just made up my own variable, $bapp; you don't have to use mine exactly.) For confirmation, just type the variable name and hit Enter to see what it returns. It should display the correct service application information.

5. It is a good idea to check what the current state of RevertToSelfAllowed is for the service application. RevertToSelf is a property of the BDC service application, so it's easy to check what its value is. To do so, use this command:

```
$bapp.RevertToSelfAllowed
```

It should return the value of False, which is the default and means it hasn't been changed. And it means you need to change it to True. (If it's already True, then you got lucky and can skip having to change or update it.)

6. To change the BDC service's RevertToSelfAllowed property value to True, enter the following:

```
$bapp.RevertToSelfAllowed = $true
```

7. Finally, to make sure the value updates immediately, enter this:

```
$bapp.Update()
```

You can again check the state of RevertToSelf by using the variable to make sure it is $True. And that's it; the BDC service will now be able to use its identity.

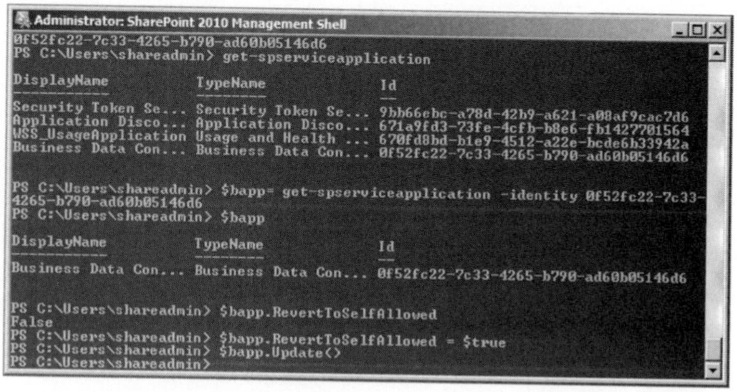

FIGURE 16.14
PowerShell commands to enable BDC Identity

ABOUT POWERSHELL

Keep in mind that there are a few things that really can't be done outside PowerShell. And this appears to be one of them. Later, when we enable subscription services to do multi-tenant site hosting, you'll see that almost all of the process is done in the SharePoint management shell console. So, it would help for you to become comfortable with PowerShell. If you aren't, you may want to check out Chapter 14, "STSADM and PowerShell." Also keep in mind that since the console can run both PowerShell commands *and* STSADM, it's no problem to do a PowerShell command, then an STSADM one, and then go back to some more PowerShell. Do whatever is easiest. Experiment and find what works for you, but don't avoid the console just because it's new. You'll be shortchanging yourself.

And now we can go back to SharePoint Designer 2010 and reset the authentication mode for the external content type.

RESETING AUTHENTICATION MODE TO BDC IDENTITY

To do that, back in the workspace (we were in Operation Design view adding a connection type), we need to be in the summary view for the External Content Type.

1. Click the Summary View button on the ribbon.

   On the Summary View page (Figure 16.15), you'll see that many of the sections are now full of information.

FIGURE 16.15
Summary View with external content type data

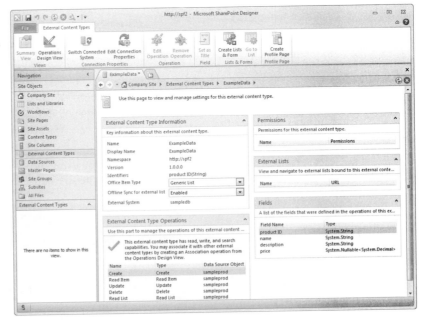

You might have noticed that the option to change the identity for authentication is not openly displayed anywhere. SPD thinks of this process in terms of the external content type, which defines the settings in terms of name, version, and URL for the site, and contains the connection and external system information. An external connection simply defines what type of data source connection will be made (be it .NET, SQL Server, or WCF), what operations will be done on the data source, and their parameters. And an external system is the data source itself and the connection properties to access the source.

2. Given that the way to change the identity to do authentication, or *authentication mode*, is to go to External System in the External Content Type section and click its data source name (in my case *sampledb*).

That will open a Connection Properties dialog box (Figure 16.16). There are two tabs for Connection Properties, but stay on the Default tab. Notice that most settings concerning the data source are here, such as server name, database name, and data source type (now called Database Access Provider).

3. For the Authentication Mode field, change the value from User Identity to BDC Identity (it will be in the drop-down list now).

FIGURE 16.16
Connection Properties for the external system, changing to BDC Identity

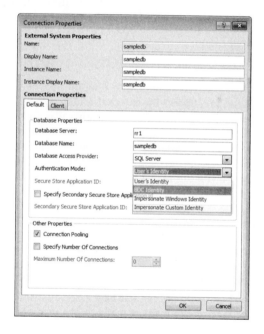

4. Once you've changed the authentication mode to BDC Identity, click OK.

Back on the workspace, it's time to save this external content type and go back to SharePoint and see what happened.

5. If all settings are complete for your external content type, click the Save button in the Quick Access Toolbar (that little group of icons in the title bar of the window).

   There may be a delay while the external content type is saved to the business data connectivity metadata store. Once the save is complete, you could create an external list right in SharePoint Designer, but I'd rather show you how it's done in SharePoint, since that's where everyone else will be working.

6. Feel free to close out of SharePoint Designer.

To continue to configure the external content type (because we're not done yet), you need to open Central Administration.

CONFIGURING PERMISSIONS FOR THE BDC SERVICE IN CENTRAL ADMINISTRATION

In Central Administration, you need to add the permissions necessary to give the BDC service some idea as to what users it can allow to use the external data. To do that, go to the Application Management page. Adding permissions, in this case, comes in two part; the first sets up the account that will be doing administration of all objects in the metadata store for the service application, and the second is to configure user access to the external content type.

1. On the Application Management page, under Service Applications, click Manage Service Applications.

2. On the Manage Service Applications page, click the Business Data Connectivity service.

   This will open a page containing the objects the BDC service uses. Currently the view of the page shows the external content type (Figure 16.17). However, what was really uploaded from SharePoint Designer was an XML file containing all the information the BDC service needs to use the external content type, its external connection, and external system. The XML file is called the *BDC model* and can be exported for safekeeping. That said, the external content type and external system information are surfaced in this interface so you can manage their settings, such as changing the authentication mode.

EXTERNAL ACTIONS AND ASSOCIATIONS

An interesting capability of external content types is that you can set up actions for the fields it will pull from the data source. What this means is you can have that action listed in a drop-down menu for a specified field or all fields when used as lookup fields *only*.

External content types can also have associations. This means the underlying table data sources might have a one-to-many or many-to-one relationship with each other, allowing them to have connected data as well.

As you can see, the external content type we created in SharePoint Designer is listed here, showing the display name, namespace, version, and external system. Right now the external content type has no permissions set on it. So if you were to just skip to the site and create a new external list based on it, it would fail, because no one is set to access it yet. It is here that you tell BDC who is allowed to access the external data and how.

FIGURE 16.17

The View External
Content Types
page for a Business
Data Connectivity
service application

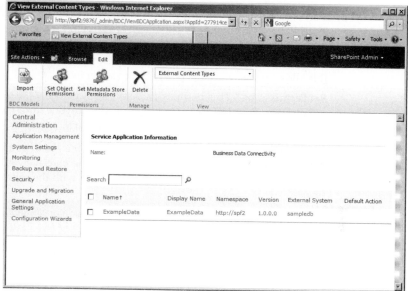

There are essentially three levels of permissions. One is for the BDC service itself. That's set to allow farm administrators full control by default (and that setting works, so we're not going to change it in this exercise). That's farm-wide. Then there is the metadata store, which stores all the external content types (and other information) for the BDC service. Finally, there is the object permissions for the object, such as an individual external content type. If all your external content types require granting the same permissions to the same people, then configure permissions on the metadata store.

Before you can set permissions for the external content type, you need to set a permission to allow someone to set permissions; that is a requirement. In my case, I want to give my SharePoint admin account the right to simply administer all external content types in one effort.

3. To do this, click the Metadata Store button.

In the Metadata Store Permissions box, you will need to add an account and give it permissions, especially Set Permissions. In my case, I am going to give my *shareadmin* account all the permissions to all items in the metadata store. This will let me test any part of the BDC service with this account. That said, always test your external lists and lookup fields while logged in as a user to see what their more limited permissions do. It would be a shame if it worked only for you.

The following is a quick rundown of the permissions listed. Keep in mind that although these permissions are being applied to the metadata store, they are basically the same set for all BDC permission levels:

Edit This permission should be for administrators only and has to do with editing settings on the objects at the administrative level. It has nothing to do with editing fields in an external list.

Execute This permission gives access the external systems. It's a permission often given, at the object level, to users so they can access data sources.

Selectable in Clients This oddly named permission lets you select the external content type to create lists and lookup fields. Another permission that is useful for user access, this allows users to use the picker box to select items.

Set Permissions This permission is specifically to give the assignee the right to apply permissions. Permissions cannot be applied to anyone until there is at least one account with this permission to do so. Administrative only.

Notice in Figure 16.18 that beneath the permissions list is a check box to propagate these settings to all BDC models, external systems, and external content types. Checking it allows this account to have access to everything with the selected permissions.

FIGURE 16.18
Metadata store permissions

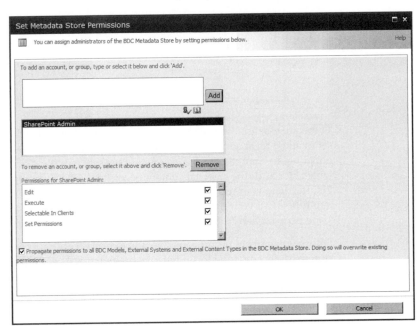

4. Enter the name of the account or security group you want to apply these permissions to, and click Add. Once they are in the center box, select the permissions you want to apply (in my case that is all of them). You can also select to have these permissions propagate to everything else in the metadata store, which is what I am going to do. Once your settings are complete, click OK. That will take you back to the View External Content Types page.

Now you can set permissions on all other objects related to the BDC service. So, let's give our authenticated users permission to access and use the external content type.

5. Click the selection box for the external content type, and then click Set Object Permissions in the ribbon (or you can select Permissions from the item's drop-down menu; this is a list after all).

Once in the Set Object Permissions box, you'll see that the administrator you added at the metadata store level is already here. You could add the individual users you want to be able to access this external content type, their AD security group, or all authenticated users.

6. To follow my example, add All Authenticated Users, and give them Execute And Selectable in Clients permissions (Figure 16.19); then click OK (propagating to all methods for this external content type is fine). You could also specify a certain group of users to have access. In my case, I want all users who are authorized to access SharePoint to be able to use the external content.

FIGURE 16.19

Set Object Permissions for the ExampleData external content type

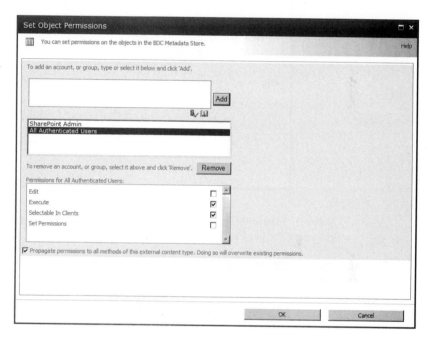

That's it for setting up permissions for the users. Now it's time to create an external list.

CREATING AN EXTERNAL LIST

Now that we have the external connection to the data source set up, with access and permissions configured, it's time to use the external data from within SharePoint. Two ways are supported: create External Lists, which simply display the table or view for the external content type for users to work with, or use lookup fields from the external content type in lists and libraries.

1. Go to the site you intended to add the external list. In my case, that is `http://spf2`. Log in as the administrator with full permissions to the external content type, in my case that would be *shareadmin*.

2. On the home page, click Site Actions, and select More Options in the menu.

3. On the Create page, select External List (Figure 16.20).

FIGURE 16.20
Selecting
External List on
the Create page

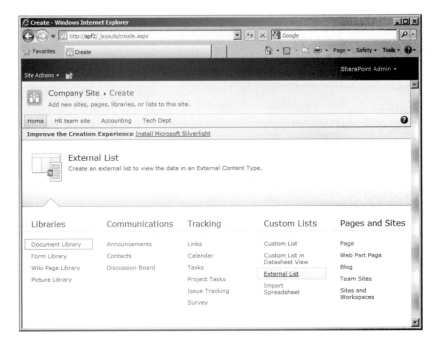

Notice, in Figure 16.21, that the options to set for this list are pretty sparse. For this example, let's name the list ExampleList.

FIGURE 16.21
Creating the new
external list

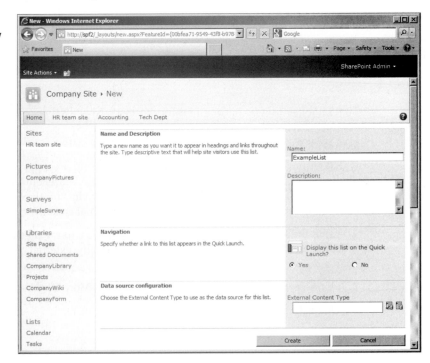

To enter an external content type for the data source, you can simply type it in the External Content Type field, but if you click the Select Internal Content Type button (the second icon after the field), you can see the external content types available for the site.

4. As you can see in Figure 16.22, the ExampleData external content type will be listed in this case. Simply select it (or whatever you named your external content type), and click OK.

FIGURE 16.22

The external content type picker

5. Back on the New List page, the external content type you selected will display in the field. Click Create to create the list.

It might take a moment, but the list will be created, with all of its contents displayed (as you can see, by my sample data in Figure 16.23). The identifier field (in my case, that's product ID) is the linked field for this list, meaning it will have the drop-down menu for the list items.

You should be currently logged in as the account with full permissions on the list. To truly be sure that it works, you need to log in as a user. This list was supposed to support all operations, meaning that items can be viewed, added, deleted, and edited for all authenticated users. For this example, we are just going to add an item.

6. To test the list, log in as a user with contribute permissions (in my case, that's the user Saffron, a member of the site with no special permissions). Logging in with the user account while on the list will verify that she can see the external list's contents (Figure 16.24). If you can't, check your permissions; first on the data source itself (remember, the BDC service and the content database account for the web application containing the list have dbreader and dbwriter roles), make sure the BDC identity is selected in SPD for the external connection, RevertToSelfAllowed on the server is set to true, and that the permissions for the external content type in Central Administration is correct.

FIGURE 16.23
The new external list, filled with sample data from data source

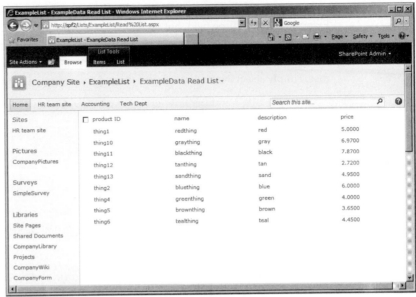

FIGURE 16.24
The external list works for a site member.

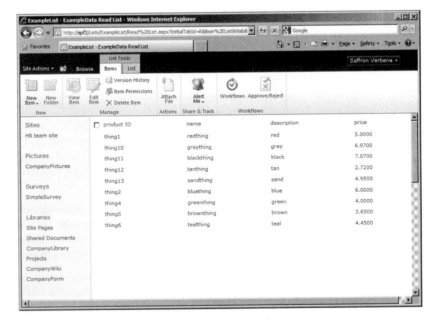

7. Now that we're sure the user can see the list, you can try adding an item using her account. There is no convenient Add Item link in the list itself, so use the New Item button in the Items ribbon.

8. Create a list item using the user's name in one of the fields; in my case, that would be Saffron in the Name field for the item. As you can see in Figure 16.25, her item is added (I selected it for better visibility).

FIGURE 16.25

The site member added as a list item

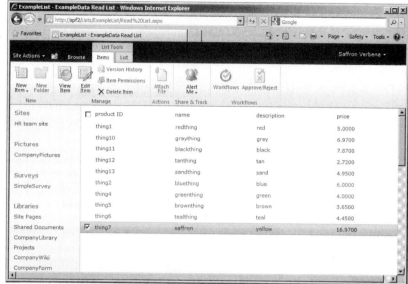

You can also delete and edit items here, although the product ID cannot be modified after an item is saved.

9. To prove that the data you've added here with the user account was added to the underlying table, you can go to the database on the database server and check. The table now contains the new item (Figure 16.26).

FIGURE 16.26

The underlying table in the data source with the new list item added

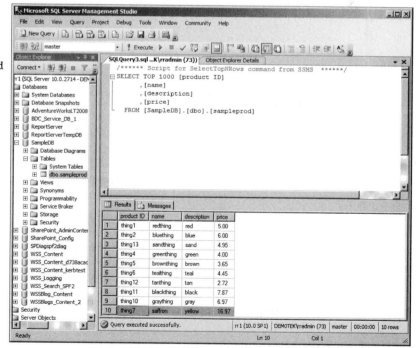

CREATING AN EXTERNAL LOOKUP FIELD

You can also use the external content type to pull lookup field information for lists. I used an existing list (make sure you're logged in with an account able to create lists or modify them) and simply added a new column. In the settings for a new column, External Data is available (Figure 16.27). If the option is selected, you can specify the external content type and then the field. As with any lookup field, you can also show additional fields. Notice that there is an option to display an Actions menu if you configured it for the external content type in Central Administration. If it's on and no actions are set, the menu will show up but be empty, leaving it available for use should you configure actions later.

1. In the list to which you want to add the external data lookup field, go to List Settings, and add a column. Name it what you'd like (in my case, mine is named *External*), and select External Data for the type of information for the column. This example uses the Name field for the Lookup and Price as an additional field.

FIGURE 16.27
Creating an External Data lookup field

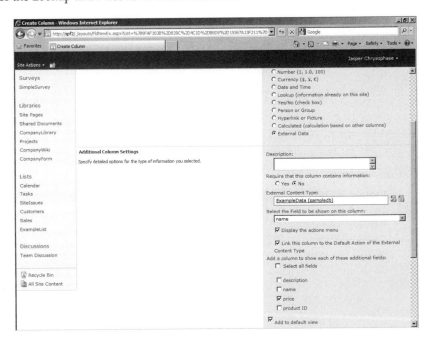

2. Once you've created the new column, you can add a new item to the list. You can see in Figure 16.28 that there is a field for the new external data lookup.

3. If you click the Select External Item(s) button (second on to the right of the field), a Choose ExampleData (the name of my external content type, if you remember; yours might be different) box comes up. Notice in Figure 16.29 that items are listed by the field I chose to show in the picker back when setting up operation parameters. Choose a name, and click OK.

FIGURE 16.28
New External Data
field in New Item
form for list

FIGURE 16.29
Choosing external
data list item

4. For the new item itself, click Save to create the new list item.

Once on the list, you'll see that the external field and its additional field are visible (this list was cleared of other items so this would be easier to see). Note that there is an icon next to the first external lookup field. It's for the Actions menu. If you were to click it, it would be empty at this point (Figure 16.30).

FIGURE 16.30
External data
lookup fields in
list, with Actions
drop-down menu

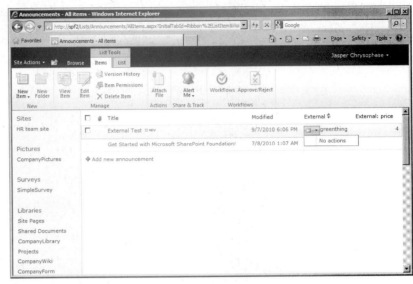

You've now seen how to use that Business Data Connectivity service we enabled at the beginning of the book. It took several steps, but because you know how to use it, you have your permissions set up in the metadata store, you know how to set the BDC identity (and how to be sure the service is set to allow that authentication mode to work), and you know how to use SharePoint Designer, you can now create many more external content types more easily. You know what permissions it takes for users to be able to access the external content and how to create the external lists and lookup fields.

Now let's take a look at something else built into this version of SharePoint—multi-tenancy. This capability, based on the Subscription Settings Service, lets you host isolated site collections for your clients, departments, or whatever entity in your environment might need isolated site collections, users, and features.

Using this capability is *very* PowerShell-intensive. If you do not have much understanding of PowerShell, I suggest you check out Chapter 14 first and then come back to try this capability.

Enabling Multi-Tenancy

In many SharePoint environments, it would be handy to offer departments or clients the ability to control their own site collections. You know how to create a web application and give users the right to create their own site collections, but that has limited management control. With multi-tenancy (also called *hosting*), you can offer a "tenant" administrator the right to create, control, and manage site collections grouped together under a subscription ID. This adds a level of self-administration for a subscription of site collections that otherwise is missing from the self-service scenario. This allows you, with some configuration, to isolate management of the site collections to a qualified administrator. Giving them the administrative rights to manage the site collections (including adding other accounts and create groups as site collection administrators to the individual site collections), apply quotas, see the status of the site collections, and access site collection settings. You can configure separate subscriptions of site collections to have (or be blocked from having) certain features and isolate what users are available to add to the site collections for that subscription.

Multi-tenancy for SharePoint Foundation overall is a great way to allow you to offer hosting of site collections for departments, division, clients, and whoever might need to be able to manage a group of site collections in a set. This lets you isolate, delegate control, and identify what resources those site collections are using. However, it is still early days for multi-tenancy, and it can be clunky. There are some caveats to consider:

♦ Tenants (as the site collection subscription administrators and their users are called) can have their own administration website to administer the site collections in their subscription. They can add new site collections (if you enable it for the web application containing the subscription) and manage those they have. Although that may be a good thing, some might find it limited.

♦ You have to manage the source of user accounts. That's not a big deal if the tenant is allowed to pull users from the entire authentication provider's pool of accounts. But if you need to isolate those users to just a particular group, it will take extra configuration. Even if you are simply isolating users by OU in AD, for example, there will need to be ongoing management of those accounts in terms of adding and removing users from the OU, since you won't want the tenants to have administrative rights to Active Directory.

♦ If you want your tenants to be able to create site collections for their subscription, you will need to enable self-service site creation on the web application containing the tenants. Keep in mind that there is still no limit on how many they can create. There will also need to be a root site collection, even if no one uses it. Something else to consider, if you have tenants that you do not want to be able to create their own site collections, they will need to be in a different web application with self-service site creation disabled.

♦ Site collections can have host headers for their address, rather than being in a managed path, of course. But, you have to set the site collections up manually (using STSADM or PowerShell so you can specify the host header). If a tenant wants to use their administrative site to create more site collections, their only option will be to use a managed path, because that's what the GUI offers for self-service site creation. If they truly want a custom header for their site collections, they may need to be in their own web application (which defeats the purpose of multi-tenancy) or at least access their sites through an extended web application just for them (and you have very few zones per web application for that sort of thing).

♦ Features available to site collections in a subscription can be managed in *feature packs*, which group together the features allowed for a subscription. Features can be scoped at either the farm, web application, site collection, even subsite level, and explicitly selected to be applied to subscriptions. However, you will need to manage deploying or adding features to the farm, and what features are available to subscriptions manually. However, if a tenant pays for a solution that is deployed to the whole web application, you can isolate that solution's features to only that tenant. This makes sure tenants that don't pay for them, don't get them. Feature packs are managed in PowerShell, so tenants can't manage that themselves; you will have to. As an alternative, sandboxed solutions can be uploaded, activated, and managed at the site collection level (and have the added bonus of being limited in the resources they use on the server overall).

So, planning for your multi-tenant or hosted environment does take some effort. But if this is something you need, it's good to know.

There are a few steps required to prepare to set up multi-tenancy for SharePoint. We'll actually do them later in the chapter, but this shows the overall tasks in a reasonable order:

1. Create a managed account for the Subscription service. SharePoint will want that service to have a different account than the farm account, which it will use by default.

2. Enable the Subscription service in Central Administration.

3. Create a web application for the tenants. Subscriptions are per site collection. This is optional; you can use an existing web application, but it's best to plan for a good, general URL for the web application such as my example, `hosted.dem0tek.com`. Also plan its available zones as alternate addresses as well. Create the site collection at the root of the web application if you are going to enable self-service site creation.

4. Make sure you have an account with the spshelladmin capability for that web applications database as well as the configuration database. The account must also have the dbcreator and securityadmin login roles on the SQL server (it will be creating the database for the Subscription Settings service, which means it will own it as well).

5. If you want your tenants to be able to make more site collections within a subscription, you need to enable self-service site creation on the web application.

6. You also may want to consider creating custom managed paths for your tenants, if the `/Sites/` path isn't enough. For this example, we are going to add a wildcard managed path, `/admin/`, for the tenant administrative sites. This will put the administrative sites on a different path than the hosted site collections.

7. Consider how to manage the tenant user accounts and set up that infrastructure. There will need to be accounts for the tenant administrators and tenant users. If OU s will be used to isolate user accounts for example, create and populate them in Active Directory.

8. Finally, using PowerShell, configure the service application, database, and proxy.

At that point you will be ready and able to generate new subscription IDs and apply them to new or existing site collections, as well as generate tenant administration sites. Multi-tenancy will be up and running. You can create and apply feature packs as necessary. These plans may seem extensive, but once you know what you plan to do, it makes creating and maintaining the subscriptions much easier.

Now that you've prepared yourself, let's configure multi-tenancy.

REGISTERING A MANAGED ACCOUNT AND STARTING THE SUBSCRIPTION SETTINGS SERVICE

In Central Administration, to add a managed account for the Subscription Settings service, go to Configure Managed Accounts on the Security page.

1. In the Configure Managed Accounts page, click the Register Managed Account link to do your account registration. I will be using an account I created in AD, dem0tek\spsubset, for my example (Figure 16.31). You can have it manage the password if you'd like, but I am not going to bother for this example.

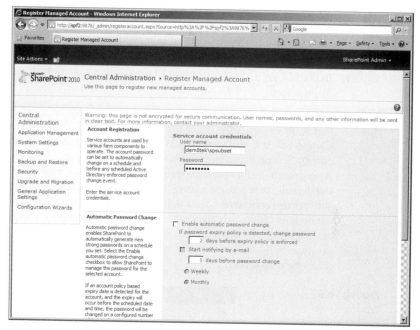

2. Once you've added the account, start the Subscription Settings service. To do that, go to the Services On The Farm page, click the Manage Services On Server link, and then choose the System Settings page.

3. The SharePoint Foundation Subscription Settings service is stopped by default. To start it, click Start for the service (Figure 16.32).

FIGURE 16.32
Starting the Subscription Settings service

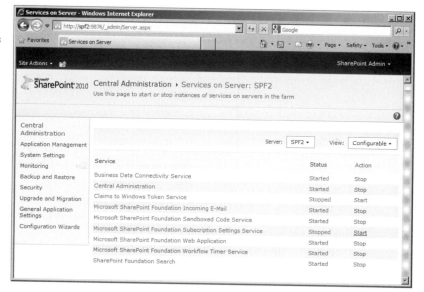

CREATING A WEB APPLICATION FOR MULTI-TENANT SITE COLLECTIONS

Now that the service is started, we need to create the web application to contain the tenant site collections.

1. To do that, go to the Application Management page and choose Manage Web Applications.

2. On the Manage Web Application page, create a web application (click the New button). Figure 16.33 shows the settings I've chosen: Classic Authentication (you could choose Claims-Based if you wanted to; Classic works fine for me here), the host header `hosted .dem0tek.com` (be sure that if you use a host header, it resolves in DNS), using port 80. Also give the content database an identifiable name, name the application pool (or keep the default name), use a managed account for the database account, and so on. Once the settings are complete, click OK to create the web application. After the web application is created, feel free to create a root site collection. You don't need to create a site collection at the root of the web application's URL unless you are going to enable self-service site creation. Self-service site creation requires a site collection to put its announcement, even if no one ever sees it.

FIGURE 16.33
Creating a web application to use for multi-tenant site collections

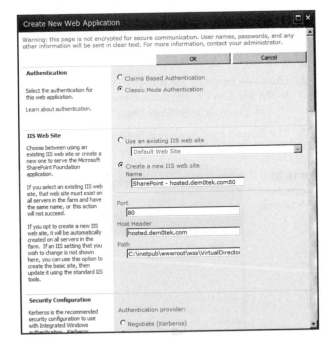

At this point be sure to enable self-service site creation (in the Web Applications management page, select the web application and click the Self-service site creation button) and turn it on. Requiring a secondary administrator is not necessary.

Also, to have an *admin* path for the tenant administration sites, be sure to click the Manage Paths button for the web application, and configure it there. For more step-by-step details about creating and configuring web applications and site collections, see Chapter 10, "Site Collections and Web Applications."

PERMISSION TO CONFIGURE SUBSCRIPTION SETTINGS SERVICES

Once you've created your web application (and root site collection if necessary), be sure you are logged into the SharePoint server with an account that has shell admin permissions to at least the configuration database and the content database for the web application you are using for subscription services in PowerShell (for more about that, see Chapter 14). Then open the SharePoint management shell.

After you are certain that the account you will be using to do this task has the correct permissions in PowerShell, open the SQL Management Studio on the SQL server, and make sure that account has a SQL login and actually has the permission to create databases and assign users to them. Just like the setup account, that means the account requires at least dbcreator and securityadmin roles on the SQL server, as you can see in Figure 16.34.

FIGURE 16.34
Confirm permission in SQL for the account configuring the Subscription Settings service.

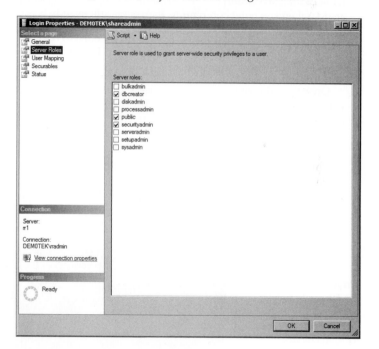

Once you are sure your SQL permissions are in order, you can start using the commands necessary to set up the Subscription Settings service and the multi-tenant site collections.

CONFIGURING THE SUBSCRIPTION SETTINGS SERVICE APPLICATION POOL ACCOUNT, SERVICE APPLICATION, AND PROXY

Make sure you are logged into the SharePoint server with the account with the correct permissions, and that the SharePoint management shell is open. Once in the console, you need to start by first setting up the application pool account to access the service's database. This will be the account you registered earlier as a managed account.

It will be helpful to create a variable, $appPool (you can actually name it anything you like), to use for creating the new application pool for the Subscription Settings service and then configuring the Subscription Settings service's database. The application pool account in my case will be *dem0tek\spsubset*. The variable will contain the application pool account information so it can be reused in more than one command.

The command to enter in this case is this:

```
$appPool = New-SPServiceApplicationPool -Name SettingsServiceApppool -Account
dem0tek\spsubset
```

After you hit Enter, you will not see any indication that anything happened. That means it worked.

Then to create the service application and its database, I am going to use a new variable name, $sapp, to contain the Subscription Settings service, as well as use the $appPool variable again (when you enter commands, they generally need to be one line):

```
$sapp = new-spsubscriptionsettingsserviceapplication
  -Name SubscriptionSettingsServiceApplication -Databasename
SubscriptionSettingsServiceDB -applicationpool $appPool
```

Once the subscription setting service and its database is created (this may take a moment), you need to create the service proxy. This is what the web application actually connects to instead of the service application directly:

```
new-SPSubscriptionSettingsServiceApplicationProxy -ServiceApplication $sapp
```

This will generate a display name, type name, and GUID for the proxy (Figure 16.35). And that's it. After all that prep of setting up a web application, setting up a managed path, enabling self-service site creation, and getting the permissions configured, all it took was three PowerShell commands to configure the service application. Now it's on to creating the new site subscriptions and site collections and then exploring them.

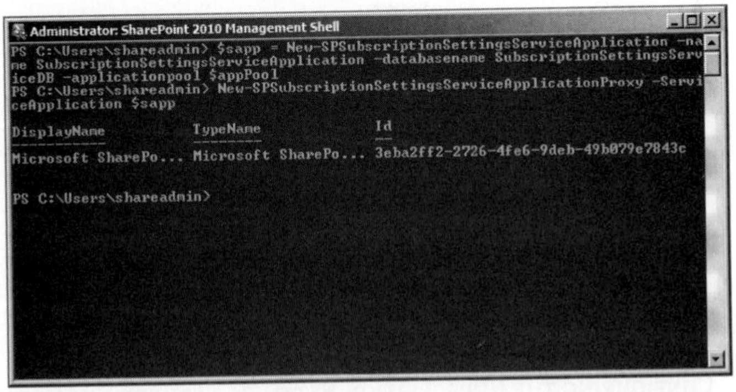

FIGURE 16.35

Creating new Subscription Settings service application pool, service application and database, and service application proxy

CREATE NEW SITE SUBSCRIPTIONS AND THEIR SITE COLLECTIONS

Now that the Subscription Settings service is up and running, it's time to create some site subscriptions. In this example, there are going to be two subscriptions—one for the red tenant and one for the blue tenant. I have added accounts in AD for the tenant administrators, redtenantadmin and bluetenantadmin, as well as OUs (Red Tenant and Blue Tenant) and user accounts in Active Directory for each tenant in this scenario. I am assuming you know how to create user accounts and OUs, so I am not going to walk you through it.

We will create each site subscription, and then the site collections that belong with them, including the tenant administration site collections.

This will require a variable to use for the subscription ID when creating the site collections. You can create a variable for each subscription, or you can reuse the same one. It's up to you.

1. So, to create the new site subscription, you invoke a new site subscription that will generate a new subscription ID, which the variable will contain. To do this, you can enter the following:

```
$sub = New-SPSiteSubscription
```

The site subscription will be created with no real feedback. You can check to see whether the command worked by just typing the variable and pressing Enter. It should return the value it is holding. If it's blank, run get-spsitesubscription, and see whether the new site subscription GUID is listed. You should be able to use that instead of the variable if necessary.

Now that we have the site subscription ID generated, we can apply it to site collections. In this example, we are creating new site collections to use the subscription now. We are also not using host headers (otherwise known as *host-named*) site collections for this, but you can easily do so if you'd like. It's just a site collection. Keep in mind that if you want your clients to have host-named site collections, you will have to create them manually. Tenants can't use the self-service site creation capability of the administration page to create host named site collections; they can only use managed paths off the web application URL (or extended web application address).

The command to create a new site collection has a parameter, OwnerAlias, to specify the site collection administrator; for this, use the tenant admin account you created (remember that I have my tenant admins ready, redtenantadmin and bluetenantadmin). It also specifies the Team Site template for the site collection's top-level site with STS#0. If you didn't specify a site template, you'd be prompted to select one when you log into the site for the first time. In addition, I used the OwnerEmail parameter, so notifications for the site collection will have an address to be sent to. It is good practice, but not required.

2. Here is an example of how to create a new site collection with the subscription ID (see Figure 16.36 for an example of the command completed successfully) for the first of my two tenants:

```
New-SPSite -Url http://hosted.dem0tek.com/sites/redtenant"-OwnerAlias dem0tek\
redtenantadmin -OwnerEmail redtenantadmin@dem0tek.lcl -Template STS#0
-SiteSubscription $sub
```

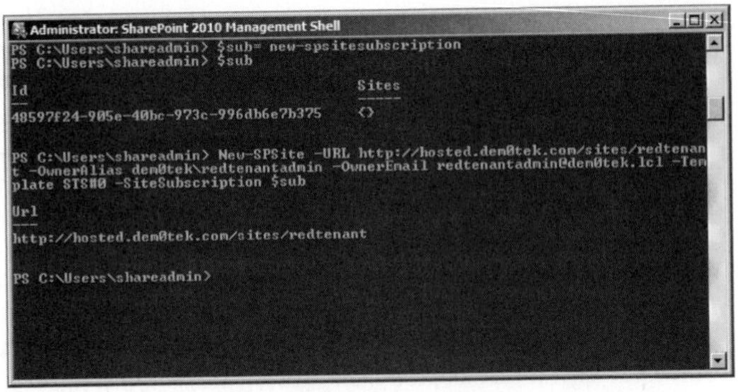

FIGURE 16.36

New site collection with subscription ID

SITE TEMPLATES

I specified a site template for the site by using its template ID. To find out what the different template IDs are, use the command get-SPWebTemplate. It will list all templates available.

Now that you've created the site collection to be used by the tenant (in my case the red tenant), let's create the administrative site collection for the subscription. You can create them in either order.

1. To create the tenant administration site for the subscription, enter the following (note that this example is using the admin managed path created earlier):

   ```
   New-SPSite -Url http://hosted.dem0tek.com/admin/redtenant" -OwnerAlias
   dem0tek\redtenantadmin "-OwnerEmail redtenantadmin@dem0tek.lcl"
   -Template tenantadmin#0" -SiteSubscription $sub -AdministrationSiteType
   tenantadministration
   ```

2. Now that the subscription and sites for the red tenant are complete, simply do the same for the blue tenant (or whatever you want to name your second tenant). To review, you need to create a new site subscription, create a new site and use the subscription ID, and create a new tenant administration site using the subscription ID. There should always be only one administration site, but you can have as many sites collections in the subscription as you'd like.

   If you forget which ID to use, enter Get-SPSiteSubscription, and see what IDs show up. And to see what site collections belong to those site subscriptions, you can use Get-SPSiteSubscription | Format-List. That command will display not only the subscription GUIDs but the site collections using them.

Now that we have some site collections to play with, let's take a look at them.

WHAT IF YOU HAVE A SITE COLLECTION YOU WANT TO ADD TO A SUBSCRIPTION?

As long as the site collection is in the web application that is using the Subscription Settings service, you can apply the subscription ID to it. To do so, simply use the -identity switch with the Set-SPSite command:

```
SPSite -identity <URLofSiteCollection> -SiteSubscription <GUIDofsubscription>
```

EXPLORING THE TENANT ADMINISTRATION SITE

First, let's look at the tenant administration site for the first subscription tenant (in this example, that is the red tenant).

1. Open a browser, and browse to the address of the tenant administration site (for this example, that would be http://hosted.dem0tek.com/admin/redtenant).

2. Log in with the account you specified as the OwnerAlias; in my case that would be *dem0tek\redtenantadmin*. Once logged in, you will come to a very abbreviated Central Administration site (Figure 16.37).

FIGURE 16.37

Tenant Administration site

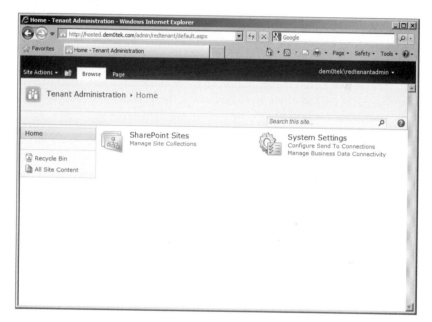

You can see that the site has the top ribbon bar, the Quick Launch bar, and a central content area containing only two categories, SharePoint Sites and System Settings. Beneath SharePoint Sites is a link to manage site collections.

3. Managing the site collections is the focus now, so click the Manage Site Collections link beneath the SharePoint Sites heading.

4. On the page that comes up (see Figure 16.41 for an idea of the page), you'll see the other site collection in this subscription. Select it, and you'll see some options in the ribbon bar to explore. The buttons available to manage site collections are Properties, Owners, and Disk Quota.

    ◆ If you click the Properties button, there is a limited report concerning the site collection (Figure 16.38). There you can see some fundamentals about the site collection, such as the Owner (the primary site collection administrator), any other site collection administrators who might have been added, the template the top-level site is using, how big the site collection is in megabytes, and if a quota is applied.

FIGURE 16.38

Site Collection Properties page

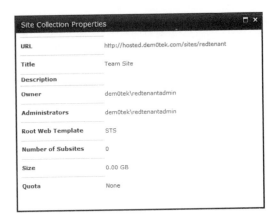

◆ The Owners button on the Manage Site Collections page is something of a misnomer, and offers you a box listing the primary site collection administrator for the site, and a field to add and display additional administrators.

◆ The Disk Quota button allows you to set a quota on the selected site collection (Figure 16.39).

FIGURE 16.39

Disk Quota settings for a selected site collection

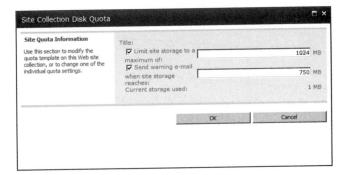

◆ The New button available on the ribbon makes it possible for the tenant administrator to create new site collections in the subscription. This works only if self-service site creation is enabled for the web application.

In this example, we enabled self-service site creation, so you could try creating another site collection from here that will also be in the same subscription.

1. To test it, click the New button.

It opens a New Site Collection box, which lets you configure the title, description, URL (from the web application's managed paths), template, and site collection administrator. You can also add your account as an administrator, as a convenience.

2. In this case, we're going to create a site collection for the red marketing division. We are also going to make the red tenant administrator the primary site collection administrator, so we don't need to add the account as well (Figure 16.40). Click OK when the settings are complete to create the site collection.

FIGURE 16.40
Creating a
new tenant site
collection

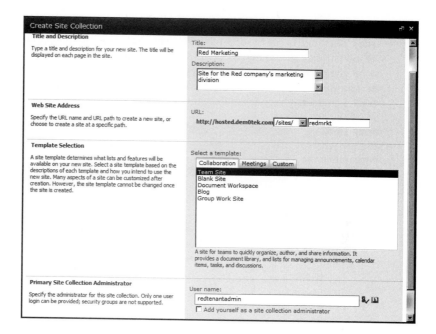

Back on the Tenant Administration page, you'll see that there are now two site collections to be managed for this tenant. For each site collection listed, there is a Manage icon (Figure 16.41).

FIGURE 16.41
The new site col-
lection listed

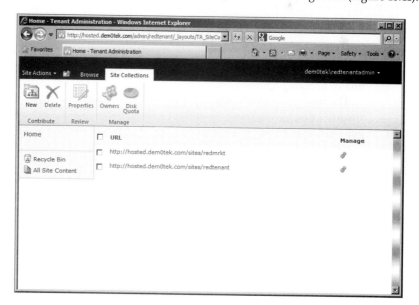

To manage one of the site collections, click its Manage icon, and it will take you to the Site Collection Settings page for that site collection. If your account doesn't have permissions to the site, you will be prompted to log in.

You may remember that there were two subscriptions created for this scenario, with additional site collections. To see the difference between the two subscriptions, browse to the other tenant's administration site (in my case that would be `http://hosted.dem0tek.com/admin/bluetenant`).

If you click to Manage Site Collections, once you've logged into the site, you'll see that it contains a single site collection, the one meant to be in this subscription (Figure 16.42). This demonstrates that what happens in one subscription really does not affect the other.

FIGURE 16.42

The second tenant administration site

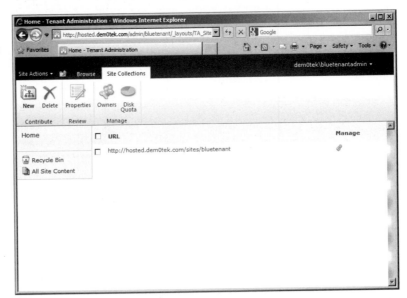

So far, we've proven that the subscription works, seen what the tenant administration pages look like, and added a new site collection. Now let's take a look at isolating users and then, finally, applying feature packs.

The two subscriptions have their own administrators, but when it comes to users, because you are using classic Windows authentication, they will use the same Active Directory users to populate their site collections.

ISOLATING THE TENANT ACCOUNTS

There are a number of ways to fix this, and one of the simplest is that you can create some OUs in Active Directory and then run a quick STSADM command to point the site collections to look only in their OU to find users. In this example, two OUs have been created in AD, one called Red Tenant and one called Blue Tenant. These OUs have one user apiece (red user and blue user, one for each tenant).

1. To get the site collections to look only for users in the correct OU, go back to the SharePoint management shell console, and use the following command. You can see Figure 16.43 for an example of the command completing successfully. The syntax for the OU is the common name (CN) path.

```
stsadm -o setsiteuseraccountdirectorypath -path "OU=Red
Tenant,DC=dem0tek,DC=1c1" -url http://hosted.dem0tek.com/sites/redtenant
```

Figure 16.43

A successful
STSADM
command

2. To prove the command was successful, log into the site you just applied the STSADM setting to (for this example, the redtenant site collection), and open the site's permissions page.

3. Click the Grant Permission button, and in the Grant Permission box, click the People Picker button.

4. In the People Picker box, try typing in a user that you know is in Active Directory but not in the OU you specified. It will fail. This shows that it will not let you search outside the OU for users, nor will it display anyone from outside the OU (unless they are already in the site permissions).

5. If you try part of a name you know is in the OU, it will appear in the list (Figure 16.44). You can add the user to the site if you'd like. Feel free to also set up the user account directory path for the other tenant site as well, now that you know how.

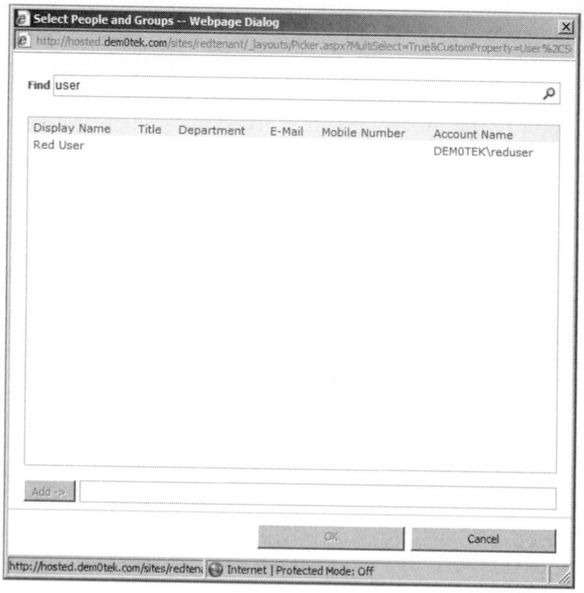

Figure 16.44

A user from the
specified OU in the
People Picker

Now that we've gotten the hang of creating site collections from the tenant administration site and have learned to isolate tenant site users from the rest of Active Directory so the tenants can only add users they are allowed to, we need to take a look at specifying what features the site collections can have. When a solution is deployed at the farm level, it often adds features scoped to the site collection or subsite level.

Managing Features

You can control what features a tenant site may have, so if a tenant asks for a solution to be deployed, you can let that tenant have the features the solution offers but block it from being used by other tenants.

Doing this requires *feature packs* (as I mentioned earlier). These are combinations of features that make up the functionality of a site collection. What is not widely known is that most things available on a site created by a site template (such as the team site) are features. If you specify that a feature pack be applied to a site collection, then any feature that was part of the site collection but isn't listed in the feature pack is gone for that site collection, until you add it to the feature pack and apply it again. In other words, if you apply no feature pack, then the site collections in a subscription will get all the features available. If you want to use a feature pack to block some features, then you need to explicitly specify what features are allowed in order for the site collections to get any features.

There are a few useful PowerShell commands concerning features. First, to find out just what features are available to the site collections in this web application, you need to run this command:

```
Get-SPFeature
```

You can see in Figure 16.45 that there are a lot of features applied to a new site collection. Some of them are scoped to the web application or farm level. Those features cannot be managed with feature packs, only those applied to the site collection or subsite.

After scrolling through the list, to see all the features, you probably realize you want most of them. If you just create a new feature pack, it's empty. If you apply it to a site collection, it will empty the site collection of all features, such as collaborative lists, many web parts, search, and so on.

So, what you need to do is create a feature pack and then add back in all the features you might need, such as those that are scoped at the site collection and subsite (called Web in PowerShell) levels. Then you can take out the ones you want. There is also a command to add features one by one, in case there are features you want to add in the future.

Creating a New Feature Pack

To start, let's create a new feature pack with a variable that will hold its identity to use later:

```
$fp = new-SPsiteSubscriptionFeaturePack
```

FIGURE 16.45

Listing all features available for a site collection

Adding Features to the Feature Pack

Then let's fill the feature pack with all the features scoped for the subsite level first.

The command for this is a little complex. It gets the features list and filters it to just items scoped to "Web" and then adds those items (considered Site Subscription feature pack members) to the feature pack we created. The command is as follows:

```
Get-SPFeature -limit all | Where{ $_.Scope -eq "WEB" } | Add-SPSiteSubscriptionFe
aturePackMember -id $fp
```

Then enter this command to get all the features scoped at the site collection level ("Sites") and add them to the feature pack:

```
Get-SPFeature -limit all | Where{ $_.Scope -eq "SITE" } | Add-SPSiteSubscriptionF
eaturePackMember -id $fp
```

(Tip: To do this quickly, you can just hit the up arrow at the command prompt in the console and then change WEB to SITE and hit Enter.) That gives you a feature pack that contains, basically, all the features already available to the site collections.

ONE BY ONE

To add a single feature to a feature pack, get the GUID for the feature, and then type the following:

```
Add-SPSiteSubscriptionFeaturePackMember –identity $fp –FeatureDefinition
<feature id>
```

Removing Features from a Feature Pack

Now that you've added a lot of the features back to the pack, you might want to remove a few. To remove features, you first need to select them, and to do that, you need to know their GUIDs. Then, when you apply the feature pack, the site collections in the subscription will lose the removed features.

The features in question for my example are the team collaboration lists and the wiki home page feature. You can get their GUIDs in the feature list you retrieved earlier:

TeamCollab   00bfea71-4ea5-48d4-a4ad-7ea5c011abe5

WikiPageHomePage   00bfea71-d8fe-4fec-8dad-01c19a6e4053

So to remove the Team Collaboration feature for example, you can use the following command, pasting the GUID you marked from the `get-feature` list:

```
Remove-SPSiteSubscriptionFeaturePackMember –identity $fp –FeatureDefinition
00bfea71-4ea5-48d4-a4ad-7ea5c011abe5
```

The console will want confirmation before continuing, as shown in Figure 16.46. To continue, press Y and press Enter.

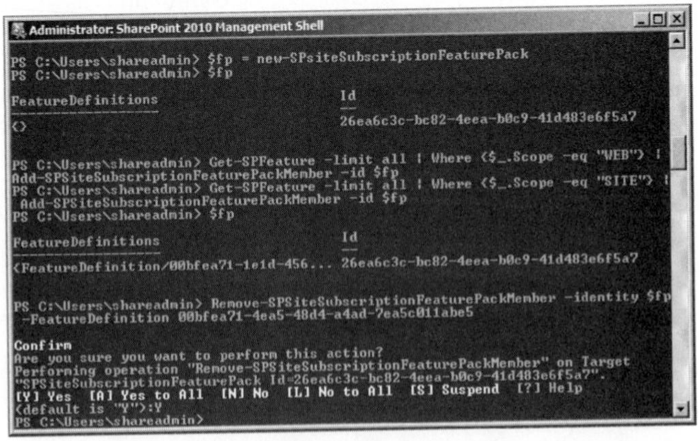

FIGURE 16.46
Last command confirming the removal of a feature from a feature pack

To remove the wiki page home page feature, just replace the GUID for the TeamCollab feature with the wiki page home page GUID, and run the command again (expect the confirmation prompt as well).

Once the two features are removed from the pack, you need to apply them to the site subscription of your choice so all new site collections will be missing the features.

Apply the Feature Pack to a Site Subscription

You may need to reset the $sub variable to match the correct site subscription. In this example, you are going to apply this feature pack to the red tenant's site subscription, so the command is this:

```
$sub = Get-SPSiteSubscription –Identity http://hosted.dem0tek.com/sites/redtenant
```

Then, once the variable, in this case, $sub, contains the correct subscription information, you can use it apply the feature pack to the site subscription with this command:

```
Set-SPSiteSubscriptionConfig –Identity $sub –FeaturePack $fp
```

That will apply the feature pack to the red tenant's site collection.

If you browse to the site collection and look at its site features, you'll see that the two features you removed are now missing (Figure 16.47).

FIGURE 16.47
Missing features for site collection with feature pack applied

But if you were to browse to the other tenant's site collection, which has a different site subscription, you'd see that it has been unaffected (Figure 16.48).

FIGURE 16.48
No missing
features for site
collection using
a different site
subscription

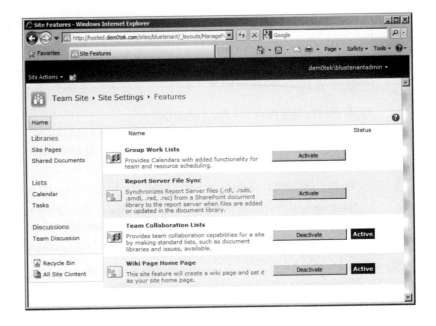

You should now have a solid understanding of multi-tenancy fundamentals. You configured the Subscription Settings service, its application pool and database, and the service proxy. You then created some site subscriptions and applied them to new site collections and administration sites for those tenants. User accounts were isolated by site collection, and features were managed per site subscription. There are a few more things that can be done with multi-tenancy, but this gives you a solid foundation to work with when considering SharePoint multi-tenant hosting.

Now that you've configured some new capabilities for this version of SharePoint Foundation, it's time to step back and cover some of the fundamentals concerning installing more SharePoint servers, load balancing them, applying SSL to their web applications, and more.

Advanced Installation

The advanced installation topics covered next include installing additional web front-end servers for the SharePoint farm, load-balancing them, and spreading some services between the two servers. Depending on your requirements, how you install SharePoint is integral to its function. A single mouse click or a single missed button will change a web front-end server's function, even the whole farm's function, if you are not careful.

An example of this is installing a second SharePoint server in a farm. That installation of the second web front-end server is a bit different from the installation for the first server in the farm, as is its configuration.

Installing an Additional SharePoint Server on a Server Farm

Because SharePoint was meant to be able to support tens of thousands of users, it can be deployed in a server farm fashion. Up to this point, we have been using a server farm/web front-end installation of SharePoint for the single SharePoint server to make use of SQL 2008 for the SharePoint databases (instead of using SQL Express databases locally). But the real point of having a SharePoint server farm is to have multiple, identical, front-end web servers offering the same content for uninterrupted user access and to spread out the services that might consume extra processor time, such as Search, among those servers.

To make this possible, you must install at least a second web front-end server (probably more). This server will simply access the same configuration and content databases as the first SharePoint server, with the intention of being used to continue to offer SharePoint to clients without a hitch or break in service, should the first server become busy or unresponsive. The additional server will literally be a mirror of the first SharePoint server and is not really intended to host web applications and sites independently.

SOMETIMES YOU FEEL LIKE MIRRORING, SOMETIMES YOU DON'T

If you want to manage your resources by splitting web applications between the first server and additional servers, then you may not want to add the extra servers to the existing server farm. Instead, if you want them to be accessible individually, install them each as independent server farms (or if it works for you, as standalone servers).

The problem then becomes trying to remember what site is on what server and teaching users which server to access for what resource.

When you offer load balancing by having all the servers mirror the first, all the web applications are identical among the servers. With load balancing, this allows the users to learn one server address to access their SharePoint resources. Then, if the first server becomes overloaded or nonresponsive, the users are transparently sent to one of the other servers that can host the same data.

Each option has its strengths and weaknesses, so choose carefully before you install SharePoint on any additional servers.

Installing SharePoint on a server intended to be part of a farm is easy. It's just like installing SharePoint on a server intended to be the first in a server farm, except that in the configuration wizard, you choose to connect to an existing configuration database rather than creating a new one. Once you choose to add the server to an existing farm, you will be prompted to enter a passphrase, ensuring that you are qualified to be adding servers to the farm (a new security feature for this version of SharePoint).

When you install SharePoint on the first server of the farm, you need to enable all the services on that server if you want to use them. However, when other SharePoint servers are added to the farm, some of those services can be assigned to the new servers instead, easing the strain on the resources of the first server.

When installing SharePoint on a server intended to be an addition to the SharePoint server farm, you need to be sure that the server meets the minimum hardware requirements or better and is running Windows 2008 SP2 (or higher). The Prerequisites tool will install the various bits required behind the scenes (for more about the prerequisites, see Chapter 2 or 3) for SharePoint to function. Be sure to have Internet access for the installer to acquire those prerequisites. SharePoint will require IIS 7.0 (or higher), and it is a good idea to also enable SMTP in IIS for incoming email (in case the service needs to be supported on the new server at any point), if it isn't already installed.

ADDING A SHAREPOINT SERVER TO AN EXISTING SERVER FARM

To have the installation go smoothly, you should be logged in with the farm's setup account, or at least an account that is a farm administrator, which has the right to install software and modify services on the local server and has dbcreator and securityadmin rights on the SQL server.

1. When installing the SharePoint software itself, make certain you are logged in to the server locally (mine is SPF3) with the correct account. When you double-click the SharePointFoundation.exe installer, you will go through the wizard screens just as you would any other server farm install: install the software prerequisites (you may have to reboot), and then install the SMTP service (make sure it's on). Then, on the installer screen, select to Install SharePoint Foundation, accept the license terms, choose Server Farm, select Complete as the Server Type, and click Install Now. It is only when you get to the Configuration Wizard that you specify that this will be an additional server and not a new server farm installation.

INSTALLATION LOCATION MATTERS

Something to keep in mind about installing SharePoint on additional servers in a server farm is the need to install it on the same drive for each server. SharePoint has some file location information written to the configuration database that requires that the same SharePoint files be in the same location on each web front-end server.

---

2. After you choose to Run Configuration Wizard, you'll need to click Next past the welcome screen and click Yes in the warning dialog box to reach the screen where you make the choice that decides whether the server will be part of an existing farm or beginning a new farm.

3. On that Connect To A Server Farm screen (Figure 16.49), you have two choices: to make this installation part of an existing server farm or to create a new farm. To make this installation part of an existing server farm, make certain Connect To An Existing Server Farm is chosen. It is the default, conveniently enough. To continue the installation, click Next.

4. On the Specify Configuration Database Settings screen, enter the SQL server name (my example is *RR1*). To confirm that the server can be found from here, click Retrieve Database Names. This will also, once the database server is found, populate the Database Name field with the most likely configuration databases that are available on that server (if there is more than one, they'll all be listed). In my case, it was correct, choosing SharePoint_Config from the databases on my SQL 2008 server (Figure 16.50). Click Next to continue the installation. You might notice that there is no field to specify the farm account to access the configuration database. That because it assumes you'll be using the existing account already set up for the farm.

FIGURE 16.49

Connect To A
Server Farm screen

FIGURE 16.50

Specify Configuration Database Settings screen

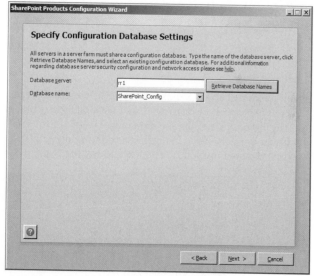

The Specify Farm Security Settings screen will appear (Figure 16.51). This is new to this version of SharePoint and is used to confirm that you are qualified to add servers to the farm by offering the correct passphrase. This passphrase was created when the first server in the farm was installed.

5. In my case, that passphrase was *MasteringSPF2010*. Enter your passphrase, and click Next.

FIGURE 16.51
The passphrase
screen

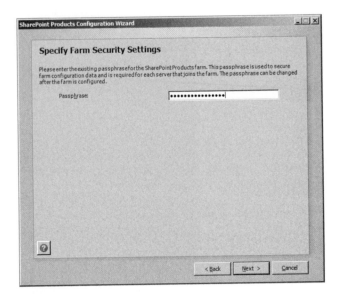

FORGET YOUR PASSPHRASE?

It can happen. And if it does, you can reset your passphrase by using PowerShell. Although there doesn't seem to be any way to retrieve an existing one, it is easy to change your farm passphrase in PowerShell.

The command is Set-SPPassphrase. The command needs to be run in the SharePoint management shell console on a SharePoint server already in the farm. When you use Set-SPPassphrase at the prompt in the SharePoint management shell console (with a farm administrator's account with the permissions to perform shell admin commands), it will prompt you to enter a new farm passphrase, prompt you to retype again, and then ask you for confirmation.

Once you've confirmed that you want to change the passphrase, there is no indication that it worked, but it did. Keep in mind that the new passphrase may not propagate to all servers on the farm immediately, so you can set it manually on each one (just in case) using the -localserveronly parameter. For more information about PowerShell, see Chapter 14.

This is so easy to do that you must be careful who you give shell admin rights for the farm.

6. A Completing SharePoint Products and Technologies Configuration Wizard Summary screen will be next. Make certain that the database server and database name are correct (Figure 16.52).

FIGURE 16.52
Completing Con-
figuration Wizard
Summary screen

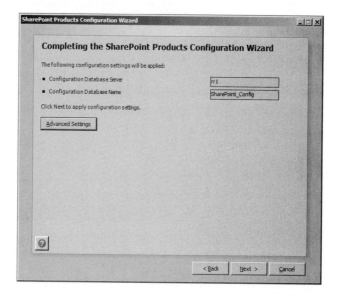

The Advanced Settings button on this screen allows you to configure whether this server will be used to also host the Central Administration website.

The option to not use this machine to host the Central Administration website is selected by default (Figure 16.53). This means that the Central Administration web application will not be created in IIS on this server. If load-balancing Central Administration was required for the server farm, then using the server to host the website on this machine would be necessary. Often the site is isolated to one server for security's sake.

Although SharePoint is being installed on a second server to mirror the content of the SharePoint sites on the original server, we are not going to load-balance the Central Administration site at this time, so you don't need this server to host the site (we'll do it later).

7. After you make your choice, you can either click OK to save the change, or click Cancel if you made no change, to just go back to the summary screen. Once on the summary screen, click Next to continue the installation.

At that point, the Configuration Wizard will connect to the configuration database and do the necessary things to get SharePoint up and running.

8. Once the Configuration Wizard is done, you should get a Configuration Successful screen. Click Finish to open the default browser on the server (ideally Internet Explorer) to go to the Central Administration site.

FIGURE 16.53
Advanced Settings, host Central Administration screen

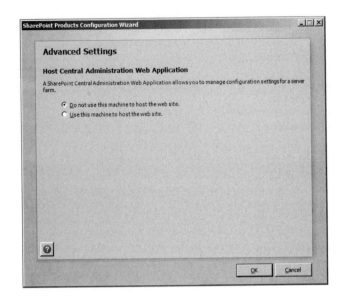

Strangely, you will be taken to a Configure Your SharePoint Farm page on the Central Administration site, despite that the farm has long since been configured (Figure 16.54). If the account you're using to install SharePoint isn't a farm administrator, you will need to log in as one to proceed.

FIGURE 16.54
Initial Farm Configuration Wizard page

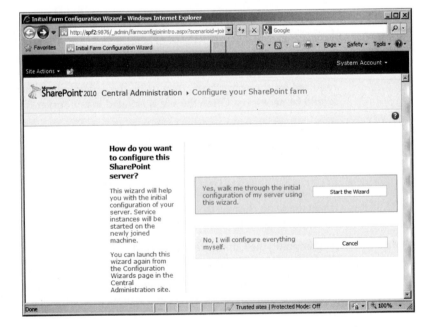

9. You could simply hit Cancel, but I suggest you click the Start The Wizard button, because it does some processing and then takes you to a This Completes The Farm Configuration Wizard page (Figure 16.55).

FIGURE 16.55
This Completes
The Farm Configu-
ration Wizard page

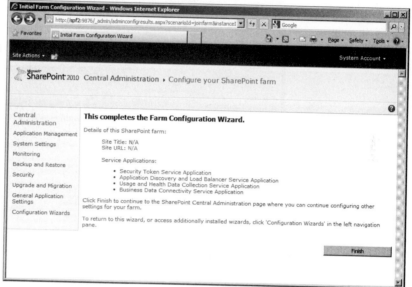

10. Clicking Finish should take you out to the Central Administration home page. Notice that the address bar indicates it is actually accessing Central Administration on the original SharePoint server (in my case, `http://spf2:9876`).

CONFIRMING THE NEW SERVER IN CENTRAL ADMINISTRATION

On the Central Administration home page, let's see whether the new server is displayed as part of the topology of the farm.

1. To do that, click Manage Servers In This Farm, under System Settings. That will take you to a Servers In Farm page. In Figure 16.56, notice that I've logged in using my SharePoint admin account to avoid working with the setup account.

In the Servers In Farm page, notice that the Incoming E-mail, Business Data Connectivity, Workflow Timer, and Web Application services are running on the new server. That means this server, when used with network load balancing, will be able to support all the web application services that the first server does, as well as accept email if necessary. (You may have notice that the outgoing email server is indicated as not configured. This is a bug; it's configured.)

FIGURE 16.56
The new server
listed in the farm

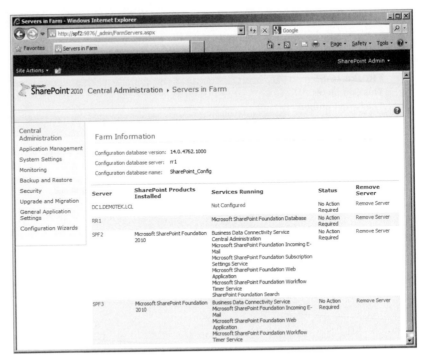

SOME SERVICES WERE MEANT FOR FAILOVER

Incoming email wasn't necessarily intended to be load-balanced, but if the first server's incoming email goes down, the service can be stopped there and shifted to the second server. It's more of a failover feature than a load-balancing one. In this case, Central Administration is really just reporting that SMTP is running on the second server, not that incoming email is configured there.

The additional server was meant either to host services that may need to be shared with or removed from the first server, to work with that first server in a load-balanced environment, or possibly do a bit of both. It does have the same web applications in IIS locally that the first server has, but they were meant to be used to keep service to the SharePoint clients seamlessly effective, offering its web application pages when the first server's load might slow it down.

2. To see what services are available to be configured on a server, you need to go that server's Services On Server page. The easiest way to do that is to click the server's name (mine is SPF3) on the Servers In Farm page (since we're here).

That will open the Services On Server page for that server (Figure 16.57).

FIGURE 16.57
Services On
Server page

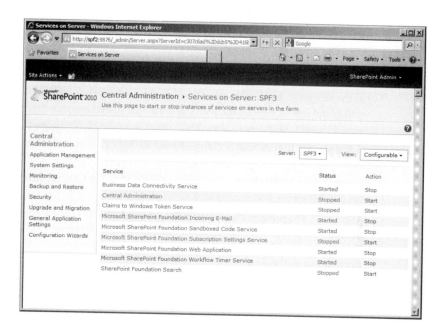

On the Services On Server page is a Server field in which you can choose the server you want to manage (if the one displayed isn't the one you want). There is also a View menu so you can see only the configurable services for a server (the default view) or all services (even the ones you can do nothing about). Beneath that are the services displayed in the chosen view for that particular server, with columns for the current status of the service on the server, and a Status column, containing the actions available concerning the service. Services that are not configured or running on the server are considered Stopped; those that are configured or running locally are considered Started.

In my example, there are only two truly configurable services for the new server (SPF3) on this page:

Microsoft SharePoint Foundation Workflow Timer Service   This service processes workflow events for the server each time interval. The default is 100 per batch but can go as high as 50,000, or if you want the server not to process workflows, you can set it to 0. This service is started and running automatically on the server. You can specify, in the content database settings for a web application, which server you'd like to handle timer jobs, particularly workflow timer jobs, for that content database. This helps you keep one server from being overloaded with jobs during the course of the day.

SharePoint Foundation Search   Search can be assigned to more than one server in the farm. This service is not enabled on this server. When enabled, it runs the search and index services in order for data to be indexed from the content databases and accessed via search query. Currently this service is being hosted by the first server in the farm.

Other services can be started or stopped on the Services On Server page but are configured elsewhere:

Business Data Connectivity Service   This service is configured elsewhere on the site. It allows SharePoint to access external data and use that data in external lists and lookup fields at the site level. It is automatically started on new web front-end servers on the farm, so there will be no loss of service for users in a load-balanced environment.

Claims to Windows Token Service   This service is managed by one server in the farm and is the service that supports claims-based authentication and token service for the SharePoint farm.

Central Administration   This service both adds the Central Administration web application to the server and manages it.

Microsoft SharePoint Foundation Incoming E-mail   This service is available on this server because the SMTP service is locally enabled in IIS. However, in the Incoming E-mail settings, this server is not indicated as the incoming email server for the farm. It can be, should something occur to the first server. This is primarily for failover events.

Microsoft SharePoint Foundation Web Application   This service will be running by default on any web front-end server. It is what adds the SharePoint web applications to this server in IIS and keeps this server's IIS synchronized with changes that might occur on the server farm.

Microsoft SharePoint Foundation Subscription Settings Service   This service supports multi-tenancy and subscription IDs. Multi-tenancy is discussed earlier in the chapter. This service is not enabled by default. In a load-balanced situation, this service should run on all servers. This is not enabled by default on additional servers on the farm if the first one has it running. It needs to be enabled manually per server.

Microsoft SharePoint Foundation Sandboxed Code Service   This service supports isolating solutions to a single site collection, limiting the resources the solutions can use and the damage they can do to the rest of the farm. On standalone servers, this service is started by default, but for Complete installations, this service needs to be enabled manually. If the additional servers will be load-balanced, you should enable the service on those servers as well (it should be enabled by default if the other servers have it running). If you don't have this service enabled and you add a sandboxed solution to a site collection Solutions gallery, you will be unable to activate it. A good rule of thumb is that if the Activate button is grayed out for a solution in the Solutions gallery, something is wrong with this service.

A FRONTLESS FRONT-END SERVER

Theoretically, if you want this server to host only services such as search or incoming email, you can disable the web application service to conserve server resources. The server will then be on the farm to run those services and nothing else.

Right now, this server is not supporting the Central Administration service. This means it isn't hosting Central Administration locally but using the site on the first server. But what if, in case something happens to the first server, you want to add that service to this server as well? Adding (or *provisioning*) the Central Administration service to a server is one of those configuration settings you can do at any time. As a matter of fact, you can start or stop this service whenever you need to do so.

First, to confirm that the Central Administration web application is, in fact, not supported on this server, let's check the IIS management console.

CONFIRMING SHAREPOINT WEB SITES IN IIS

To check what SharePoint did or did not add to IIS for the additional server, open the IIS management console (Start ➤ Administrative Tools ➤ Internet Information Services (IIS) Manager). In the console, open the Web Sites node to view the IIS Web Sites available (Figure 16.58). You'll see that the default IIS Web Site is stopped and that there is only SharePoint-80.

FIGURE 16.58
IIS Web Sites on the additional SharePoint server

This confirms that Central Administration is not being supported on this server.

ENABLING SERVICES ON THE NEW SERVER

To enable most services on this server, you simply click their associated Start link in the Action column. They'll use the service account already applied to them for the farm. A good example of this is enabling Central Administration. It makes some big changes on the server, but it takes only a single click.

On the other hand, starting the Search service requires that specific settings be enabled. So, just clicking Start won't work in that case. It requires that you confirm service accounts, a search database, and so on.

To give you an idea, let's run through enabling both services.

Central Administration

In this example, Central Administration is not listed on the second server because we chose not to support it during the installation (it is running on the other server, however). Central Administration is not a service that must be run on only one server on the farm; it is up to you how many servers on your farm end up running Central Administration. It is suggested that it be enabled on at least two servers on the farm or more, for redundancy's sake. However, this point can be hotly contested by those who think Central Administration should be secured on one server only. But it's always good to know how to enable it on more than one server, even if you don't end up implementing it.

To enable the Central Administration service on the additional server, simply return to the Services On Server page for that server in your browser, find Central Administration in the services list for the additional server, and click its Start link in the Action column.

The status of the service will initially change to Starting while the web application is added to IIS and then change to Started (Figure 16.59). Also notice that, once the service is started on this server, the indicator that the service is available on a different server disappears. This does not mean the service was disabled; apparently it just isn't necessary to mention it, now that the service is running locally.

FIGURE 16.59
Central Administration started on new server in server farm

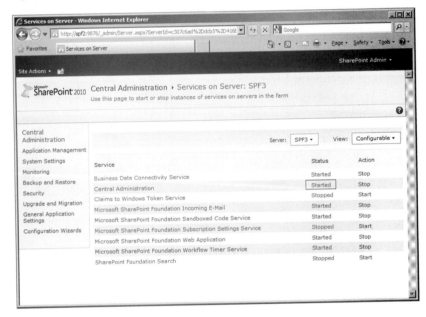

And if you go to the IIS management console on the new server (Figure 16.60), it will now contain the Central Administration Web Site (no need for an iisreset).

FIGURE 16.60
Central Administration Web Site on new server in server farm

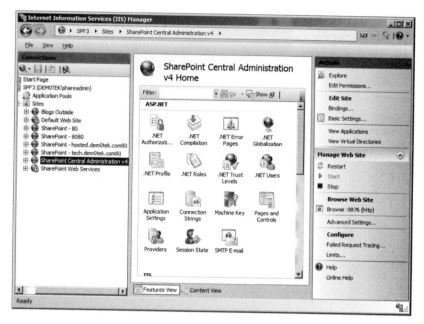

Now the new server is also hosting Central Administration. If necessary, the Central Administration site can be assigned a load-balanced URL and accessed even when the first server is unresponsive. This is an example of enabling a service on an additional server.

Search

There are many reasons why a SharePoint server might be slow in its response to clients, not the least of which is while SharePoint is indexing the content databases for the Search service.

Search can be resource intensive, both when running search queries and when indexing new data. And because of that, you might want to offload all the search services to one server and free up others to support user requests. Or you can split the search queries so more than one server can be running Search and then specify what web applications (or more specifically, their content databases) will utilize which search server. This gives you more control over which server will handle the search load of particular web application.

If you are considering enabling Search for a second server, you should use the same farm search accounts that the first server uses for the Search service and the indexing service (also called crawler, gatherer, or content access account). First you enable the service on the new server, and then you set the web application content databases to use the new server for searches.

1. To start the service on the second server, click Start for the SharePoint Foundation Search service on the Services on Server page (make sure you are looking at the services for the new server).

2. On the search configuration page, the search account (which has to be managed) will already be listed. The content access account will have the account listed, but you will need to enter the password, because this account isn't managed for some reason (Figure 16.61). Then specify the search database account for that server (the default is WSS_Search_*Servername*; in my case that would be WSS_Search_SPF3). Finally, specify the index schedule for the index account to use for indexing.

FIGURE 16.61
Configuring the Search service to run on the second SharePoint server

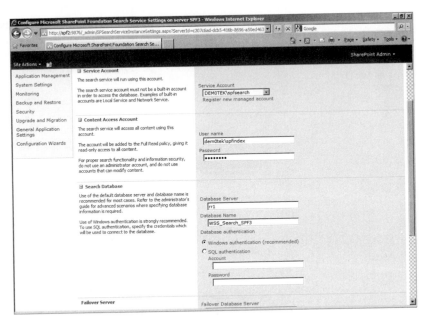

3. Once you click OK, the service will begin. You can then go to the content databases of the web applications that will use the new server to do their searching and select that server in the Search Server drop-down (Figure 16.62). The new server will also be available to be selected as the search server for any additional web applications made.

FIGURE 16.62
The new server is available as a search server for the content database.

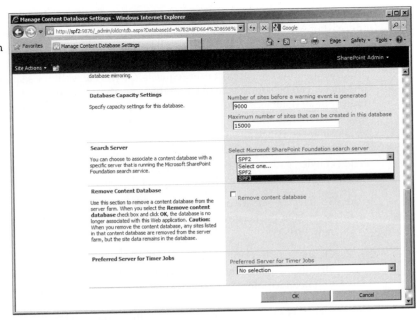

To modify a search's settings or index schedule, click the name of the service *only* to access the fields and make changes. Do not click Start and change settings there, because that can stop and restart the service. Search cannot reuse its database, so if you restart the service, you have to specify a new database for Search to use. So, don't play with the Start or Stop link for the Search service unless you need to do so.

INDEX JUGGLING

There is a catch to adding Search to another server. The second server you start the Search service on will automatically become the index server. This is often a good thing, because newer servers are often more powerful than old servers. But if this is not good, you can juggle the service:

1. Start Search on the new server.

2. Run an IISRESET, and stop the Search service on the original server.

3. Do another IISRESET, this time start the Search service again on the original server. You will need to specify a new database name for the service, search cannot reuse databases.

4. Do an IISRESET (preferably on both servers). So the original server gets the index service again.

You don't absolutely have to do an IISRESET on each pass, but it quickly tells SharePoint that changes have been made.

CONFIRMING ALTERNATE ACCESS MAPPING

A second server has been added to the farm. The Search service for the server farm has been added to the new server. You've seen that the new server mirrors the web applications of the original server, and you've learned how easy it is to make a SharePoint server host the Central Administration site.

But what you may not realize is that aside from supporting the Search service or a spare copy of the Central Administration site, this server is not very useful until Network Load Balancing of some sort is enabled on the web front-end servers of the farm. That's because the web applications hosted on the new server are not actually accessible on that server unless you explicitly configure the server's address in Alternate Access Mapping (AAM). Of course, you would think that if the SharePoint-80 Web Site is hosted on this server, you should be able to open a browser and access it on this server's address. But that is not the case. The new server's websites are not meant to be accessed directly but only as load-balanced content.

In SharePoint, Alternate Access Mapping controls what URLs are accepted by web applications. Up to this point, our internal URL for the main SharePoint-80 web application has been the first server's address. In this example, that is http://spf2. This address is the correct address for that site, if it were on only one server. But now it is echoed identically on a second server as well. It's the same web application, in two places. This is essentially step 1 of load balancing, to have two web servers with identical content. Step 2 is to have a shared URL that both servers recognize and accept to access that identical data. When you create a new web application, you can specify its load-balanced URL (the field is called Public URL). By default, SharePoint fills in that field for you with the URL you configured for that web application (including port, host header, whatever). But you can, and should, change it to the real shared address that you specify when implementing network load balancing. However, in this case, with SharePoint-80, the server's URL was left as the default (the original server's address) for the load-balanced, public URL because load balancing hasn't been enabled and it was the only server on the network.

This is why, in AAM, the internal URL for the SharePoint-80 web application is still `http://spf2`. It is assumed by SharePoint to be the load-balanced URL, even though it's not and points only to one server.

You can see this by going to the Alternate Access Mappings page. It is important enough to be listed in several places in Central Administration. The easiest is to click the Configure Alternate Access Mappings link on the Central Administration home page.

On the Alternate Access Mappings page, you can see the internal URL for the SharePoint-80 web application and Central Administration (Figure 16.63) as well as all of the other web applications created throughout this book.

Most of these addresses are the default zones for the farm's web applications, and under normal circumstances the default zone for a web application is also its load-balanced URL (although the newly enabled Central Administration site does show up for SPF3, because we specifically started that service for the server). And since there is already a load-balanced URL for these web applications (it is listed as the public URL when creating a web application, but it is the load-balanced address as well), SharePoint didn't need to enter the new server's address into AAM for any of them. That server should be responding to the public/load-balanced URL anyway.

FIGURE 16.63
URLs listed in the
Alternate Access
Mappings page

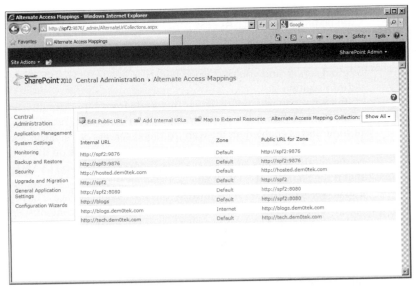

Nowhere in Alternate Access Mapping is a listing for the new server (Figure 16.64), except for Central Administration. And that makes sense now that you know the default addresses for the server farm's Internal URLs are supposed to be shared, load-balanced URLs. And when load balancing is enabled and the correct load-balancing URL is used, that default zone URL will work for both servers. If you try to access the SharePoint web applications (except Central Administration, of course) on the new server directly by using its address in the address bar of the browser (my example is `http://spf3`), SharePoint will try to accommodate your address request. But if you try to do a search, which you should be able to do, it will fail because there is no alternate address mapping for that server (Figure 16.64). This means it's not really resolving the new server's address correctly.

FIGURE 16.64
The address cannot be found.

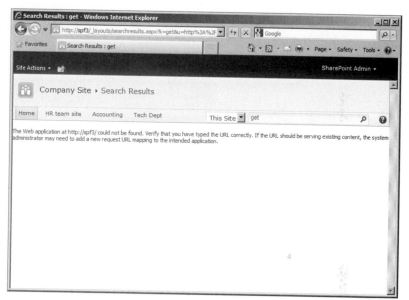

To really demonstrate how both servers using the same load-balanced URL works, I need to enable network load balancing. There are numerous network load-balancing products, both hardware and software, on the market today. However, for our purposes, the network load balancing functionality built into Windows Server 2008 R2 will do just fine.

Network Load Balancing the Server Farm

Now that we have two servers in the SharePoint server farm, it's time to see what SharePoint does when network load balanced. To install SharePoint, the operating system must be Windows Server 2008 Service Pack 2 or higher. That server has the Windows Network Load Balancing (NLB) technology built in. In this section, I'll demonstrate how to enable load balancing using Windows Network Load Balancing in order to show how it applies to SharePoint. However, once you have the concept down, it is applicable to any load-balancing product your organization may use instead. NLB is not the most complex or feature rich load balancer out there, so you may want to shop around to find the most appropriate product for your needs.

The point of network load balancing is to balance the network load between web front-end servers (considered, together, a cluster) by distributing network traffic among the servers to increase availability, scalability, and performance. The servers are set up to all respond to a shared virtual IP address and full Internet name. Among the servers, each has a unique identifier called a *priority number,* but they also keep their dedicated addresses to respond to any packets directly addressed to them as well as address any outbound connections. In addition, the full Internet name that will be shared among the load-balanced servers must be configured in DNS to resolve to the virtual IP.

RESOLVE IN DNS?

The full Internet name requires a host name, such as SharePoint, to resolve to the virtual IP you are going to use for the NLB cluster. To do that, you can create an A record in DNS that uses the host name and resolves to the virtual IP address.

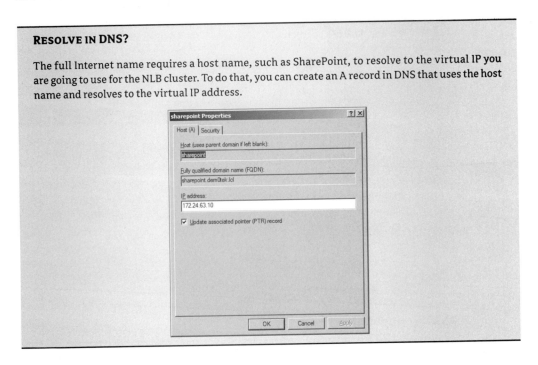

The servers in the cluster, when network load balancing, share a virtual IP (VIP) and a virtual Media Access Control (MAC) address. Essentially it looks like they all have the same network card and IP address to the clients outside the cluster. Because of this, the NLB settings among the servers in the cluster must be identical. NLB will work for servers with a single network card (the servers in this example are single-card machines). However, each server should be multihomed (have multiple network cards), with one dedicated to, and configured for, NLB.

If the servers are multihomed, with a dedicated NLB network card, they should run in Unicast mode. The shortcoming of Unicast mode is that a network card configured to use it cannot communicate directly with other hosts in the cluster, because Unicast basically means that card will be dedicated to solely support incoming NLB traffic and not be able to speak to the other members of the cluster (because as far as Unicast is concerned, they are all the same computer). This is not a problem if the servers have other network cards installed; the other network cards can be used to communicate within the cluster. However, if the servers have only one network card each (or at least one server in the cluster has only one card, because all of their clustering parameters must match), they should use Multicast mode, because that mode allows the servers within the cluster to communicate with one another directly. The shortcoming of Multicast mode is that it can cause some switch flooding issues under certain circumstances (see Windows Server's Network Load Balancing help for more information).

TESTING, TESTING...IS THIS THING ON?

Single network card hosts for NLB cluster hosts are fine for testing and demonstration. To prove it works and get practice before installing a second network card to be used in production, it is often a good idea to use multicast mode on the single network card the servers have. Then, if it works, invest in the time, effort, and money to add additional network cards to the load-balanced servers to dedicate to NLB.

Generally NLB is a Network Connection property (that is, a feature added to the function of a network card). And the network card's TCP/IP properties do need to be configured in that connection's properties, but NLB will do it for you while adding the host (server) to the cluster. Although the settings for enabling NLB are available in the properties of the network connection, it is strongly recommended you use only the NLB console to create and manage NLB clusters.

The servers that will be in the cluster must be on the same subnet. Also keep in mind that Windows NLB can support only up to 32 different hosts. If you need to load balance more, then it is time to look elsewhere for a more sophisticated load-balancing product.

When configuring NLB, keep in mind that there will be cluster parameters, host parameters, and port rules:

◆ Cluster parameters are the shared virtual IP, its subnet mask, cluster mode (Unicast or Multicast), and whether remote access (to manage the cluster from a machine outside of the cluster—not a good idea security-wise) will be enabled.

◆ Host parameters are the dedicated IP address and subnet mask of the host, as well as the initial state the server will be in when it reenters the cluster.

◆ Port rules, which can be configured per host or per cluster, are similar to the rules or policies used to filter packets on a router, Internet authentication service, or firewall. The port rules are used to set the cluster IP addresses (if there is more than one), the port range and protocols that the cluster will listen for and respond to, as well as the filter mode. Filter mode indicates whether the cluster contains a single server or multiple servers. Port rules also include Affinity and Load Weight. Affinity means allowing a connection to be "sticky" or continue to try to keep a connection with the server that answered their request throughout a session. It can be set to None, Single, or Class C. Setting Affinity to None means the client can be shifted from one server to another during a session to load balance, setting it to Single (the default when UDP protocol is being supported) means that Affinity will stick a connection to the single server that responded for the entire session, and setting it to Class C means it will try to keep a client session, from within a specific class C subnet, stuck to the correct server (useful if the client accesses the server through proxy servers). Load Weight can also be set as a port rule, which specifies the relative load weight this host would hold in a cluster. A Load Weight setting of zero means the server will handle no client traffic.

CONFIGURING NETWORK LOAD BALANCING

Network Load Balancing should be configured almost exactly the same way on every server intended to be in the NLB cluster. Each server needs to enable and configure Network Load Balancing. You may want to be sure that, after a server is added to an NLB cluster, it doesn't register its connection with DNS, because two or more servers will be registering the same IP address in DNS to their name. Sharing is bad in DNS. When a host is added to an NLB cluster, then that shared virtual IP will be added to the network card's IP addresses.

Network Load Balancing is a feature of Server 2008 and 2008 R2 and needs to be added and configured on all servers that will be load-balancing content through the operating system. Take the following steps to add Network Load Balancing to a server (if necessary):

1. Make sure you are logged into the SharePoint server as a domain admin or a local administrator for all servers in the cluster.

2. Go to the Server Manager console, click Features in the navigation pane on the left, and select Add A Feature in the content area.

3. In the Add Features Wizard, select Network Load Balancing, and click Next.

4. When asked to confirm that you want to add the feature, click Install to add the feature. It may take a moment. Once the feature is installed, it will add a Network Load Balancing Manager to the Administrative Tools on the Start menu.

Once the feature is added, you can immediately start creating the cluster. If there are any changes to be made to the other servers, such as binding new IP addresses to their network cards, it will be done by the NLB Manager—which is why you need to be logged in as someone who is allowed to change network card settings on the other servers (such as a domain admin).

Be sure to install the Network Load Balancing feature on the other servers. Once you've done that, you're ready to create the cluster in Network Load Balancing Manager. To open it, go to Start ➤ Administrative Tools ➤ Network Load Balancing Manager. When the NLB Manager console opens, in the tree pane on the left you'll see an Network Load Balancing Clusters icon. On the right is the details pane, and across the bottom is a pane containing log information concerning NLB activities.

1. To create the NLB cluster, right-click the Network Load Balancing Clusters icon in the tree pane. In the pop-up menu, select New Cluster (Figure 16.65). This will walk you through the three steps of preparing a new cluster: Cluster Parameters, Host Parameters, and Port Rules.

FIGURE 16.65
Creating a new cluster in the NLB Manager console

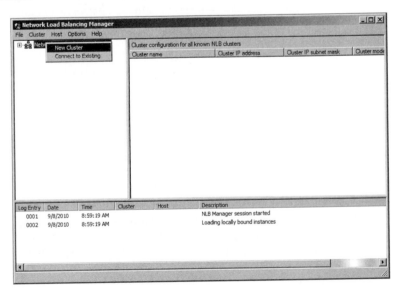

2. On the Connect screen of this process, enter the IP address or server name (in my example it's *spf2*) of one of the servers that will be added to this cluster, and click the Connect button. This will display the server's network connections and their IP addresses. If the server had more than one network card installed, you could choose the one you wanted to apply Network Load Balancing to. However, as you can see in Figure 16.66, this server has only a single network card. Select its dedicated IP, and click Next.

FIGURE 16.66
Connecting the
host to the cluster

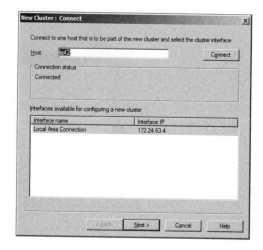

3. The next screen contains the Host Parameters for the host chosen in the previous screen. Each host must have a unique identifier. Keep the default of 1 in this case (Figure 16.67).

FIGURE 16.67
The Host Param-
eters settings

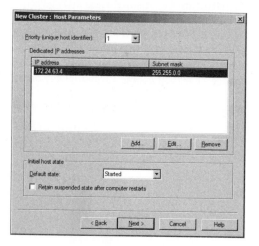

4. Confirm that the server's dedicated IP address and subnet mask are correct. The server's original IP should be the only IP address listed. A dedicated IP address is the address used by the server for *non*clustered traffic. This should be, in our case, the original server IP address. Initial host state refers to the default state that the host should start in when being added to the cluster in the future. Leave Started as the default. Click Next.

5. In the Cluster IP Address page, click the Add button, and enter the Virtual IP that you are going to use for the cluster (it's possible to have more than one, but we're keeping this example simple). My IP is going to be 172.24.63.10. Be sure your IP address and subnet mask are correct (Figure 16.68). Click Next.

FIGURE 16.68

Entering the cluster IP address

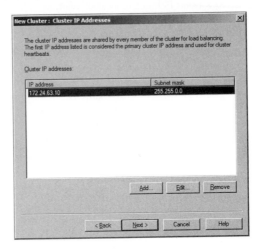

6. In the Cluster Parameters screen, you need to specify (if it's not already selected) the Network Load Balancing Virtual IP, its subnet mask, and the full Internet name for the virtual IP. This name will be used as the basis for the load-balanced (Public) URL for web applications in SharePoint and must be compatible with, and configured in, your organization's DNS structure. So, be sure to add an A record for the load-balanced URL to the correct zone in DNS for your network. In my case, I have an A record in DNS for sharePoint.dem0tek.lcl on 172.24.63.10. So, the full Internet name for my example is sharePoint.dem0tek.lcl. Notice in Figure 16.69 that below this section is the automatically generated virtual MAC address. (Tip: If you have other sites, particularly host-headered ones, that you want to load-balance, have their cname aliases in DNS point to the load-balanced A record.)

FIGURE 16.69

The Cluster Parameter settings

7. In the Cluster Operating mode section, select Multicast. *Do not* keep the default of Unicast, unless you want the SharePoint servers with only one network card to be unable to communicate directly with each other for this cluster. Click Next if all information is correct.

This will bring you to the Port Rules screen. Notice that at the top is the Port Rules list for this cluster (each host should have identical port rules settings). The settings for port rules are similar to the rules or policies used to filter packets on a router, Internet authentication service, or firewall.

To add or edit a port rule, click the Add or Edit button below the Port Rules list. The Add/Edit Port Rules dialog box contains settings for the Cluster IP address (or all if there are more than one Virtual IP for the network card), port range, protocols, and filtering mode. The default Port Rule settings, shown in Figure 16.70, will load-balance all virtual IPs for the server (which in our case is only one) and all ports from 0 to 65535 as well as both UDP and TCP protocols. The default of multiple host filtering mode means there will be more than one server in this cluster, and supporting UDP means that Affinity is set to Single by default.

FIGURE 16.70

The default NLB
Port Rules settings

8. There are no settings that require editing in the Port Rules settings at this time, so click Finish to create the new cluster.

This will create the parameters of the first cluster and add the first host. The other hosts will need to be added manually. Each time you open the console to manage the cluster, it will recognize the host it is running on, and the other host will need to be added.

HOST LIST CONVENIENCE

If you expect to use the console frequently, you can create a host list to populate the console easily the next time. Once the hosts are displayed in the console, click File in the menu bar, and select Save Host List. At that point, you simply save the file to a convenient location to be opened using the File menu the next time you need to manage that cluster. If you save the host list to a file share, it can be used if you open the console on a different server in the cluster.

In the NLB Manager console, there will now be a cluster identified by the full Internet name entered during the creation process. The details pane will contain general information about the cluster, the hosts in the cluster, or a particular host, depending on what is selected in the tree pane. The tree pane should now also display the host you added, but it is obvious that the next host needs to be included to make load balancing work. The log pane at the bottom of the window will display the outcome of creating the new cluster. You can double-click the Update Succeeded log entry for more details.

To add the second server (and any others) to the cluster, right-click the cluster icon, and select Add Host To Cluster from the menu (Figure 16.71).

FIGURE 16.71

Add Host To Cluster in NLB Manager console

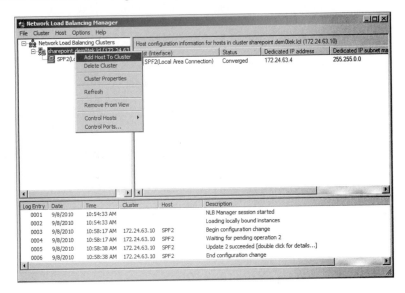

This will open a Connect dialog box. Enter the server name or IP address, click the Connect button, select the network connection that will be using NLB, and click Next. On the next screen, which contains the Host Parameters for the new host, the priority number (unique identifier) should be 2 or at least any number but 1. Confirm the dedicated host IP address and subnet mask, and leave the initial state for this host at the default Started state. Click Finish to add the host to the cluster (the virtual IP and other parameters for the cluster were already established, so no need to enter them again).

In the console, there will now be two hosts listed, although the second host may take a few moments to update. In the log area at the bottom of the console, the status of the host being added to the console will be reported as successful. You can also right-click a host and select Host Status for more information. Hosts added to the cluster are considered *converged*.

Check the Event logs for both servers to ensure that there are no WLBS (Windows Load Balancing Service) errors. Make certain there are no typing errors, skipped steps, or possible DNS registration issues before continuing.

NETWORK LOAD BALANCING MANAGEMENT

Once Network Load Balancing is enabled on both servers, it is time to manage the cluster. The Network Load Balancing Manager console is where clusters are stopped, started, and administered. And in this particular example, we are going to use the Network Load Balancing Manager to make sure that NLB is running on the server cluster and what servers are reporting that they are in the cluster.

It is also here that you can test if clustering is working per host. To see whether load-balancing failover is functioning, you can simply turn off one of the servers and see whether the cluster IP still services clients by using the other server. However, that is a little extreme (and it can be time-consuming to wait for the server to shut down gracefully and then boot back up). Instead, you can check to see whether NLB is working by using the NLB Manager and see whether there is an interruption of service. In this case, we will ping the full Internet name for the cluster. If service is interrupted, then you know that NLB is not working.

During this time, the cluster has been displayed (if all is working correctly) with the server icons outlined in green. This means they are functioning properly as members of the NLB cluster (Figure 16.72 shows the effect in black and white). If the icons are not both green, check the log entries at the bottom of the console for an idea as to what is malfunctioning.

FIGURE 16.72
Servers connected to the cluster as displayed in NLB Manager

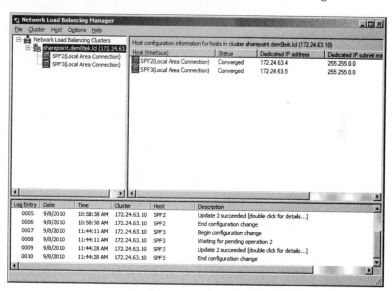

If the cluster icon is selected, you can see the host information in the details pane, which shows the status of the two servers. They both indicate that they have been converged, meaning they have been added to the cluster. Convergence occurs when a member is added or returned to a cluster. All members must be informed that there is a new member so they can figure out each other's relative weight in the port rules and compare priority numbers.

Knowing that network load balancing is working by viewing it in the NLB manager console is one thing. But let's test it. For SharePoint to make use of network load balancing from a web server point of view, the full Internet name for the cluster must work and resolve correctly to the virtual IP. To test this, ping the full Internet name for the cluster:

1. Open a command prompt window or the SharePoint management shell console.

2. At the prompt, type **ping**, a space, and the cluster's name, such as **ping sharepoint** (the domain part of the name is not necessary for this); then press Enter.

   This will cause the server to resolve that DNS name to the virtual IP address, send four sets of packets, and then report the results. As you can see in Figure 16.73, my cluster Internet name SharePoint resolved to the cluster's virtual IP of 172.24.63.10.

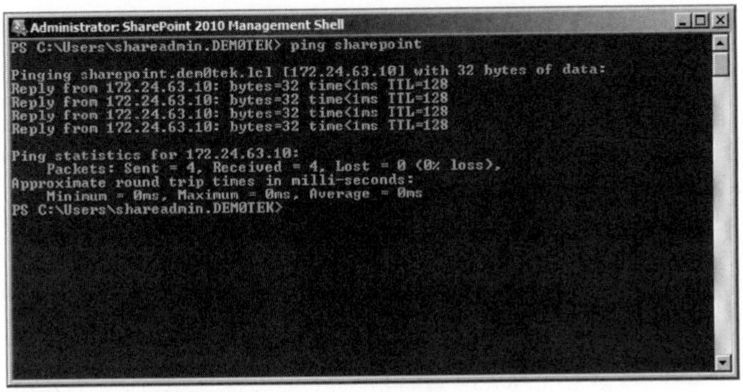

FIGURE 16.73

Testing the Share-
Point NLB cluster
virtual IP address

NLB looks happy in the Manager console. So if the ping test did not work, the problem is likely that DNS does not have a Host (A record) for the full Internet name of the cluster that resolves to the cluster's virtual IP address. Check the event logs on the server to make certain there are no issues concerning communicating with the DNS server and then check DNS for the cluster's host record. Repeat the ping test when the issue is resolved.

Now that you know that the cluster is working, let's see what happens if we break it—or at least, *simulate* breaking it. This is a standard load-balancing test of the cluster intended to demonstrate the failover capabilities of NLB. First we will try a ping test that continuously pings the cluster address. Then we will apply a test called *drainstopping* to one of the servers in the cluster. This cuts it off temporarily from the cluster, simulating a server failure. If NLB is working correctly, the ping test will not falter during the drainstop, because NLB will transparently, in milliseconds, transfer activity to the second server.

1. To do this, first start the ping test at the command prompt (or in my case, the SharePoint management shell). Enter the ping command you used earlier but at the -t switch. Here's an example:

   ```
   ping sharepoint -t
   ```

   where *sharepoint* is the name of the cluster that resolves to the load-balancing virtual IP.

2. When the test is returning results, return to the NLB Manager console. Right-click the first server (the one with the lowest number and therefore highest priority), and from the pop-up menu, choose Control Host ➤ Drainstop (Figure 16.74).

FIGURE 16.74

Drainstop a host in the NLB Manager console to test cluster functionality.

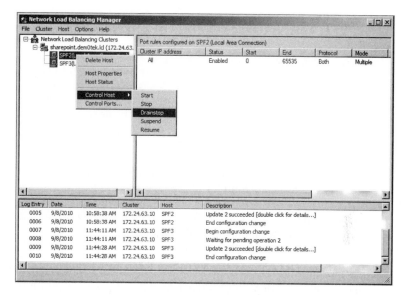

The server icon's outline will turn yellow as it stops and then red when it has stopped entirely. Return to the command prompt, and you will see that the ping test is still going (Figure 16.75), uninterrupted, at no loss in speed. This helps prove that NLB is working correctly.

FIGURE 16.75

Testing cluster connectivity with `ping`

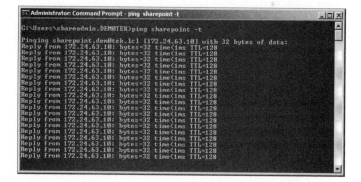

3. Of course, because we drainstopped one of the cluster's servers, it is not responding to client requests on that IP. This is not a state we want to leave that server in. To return that server to the cluster, go back to the NLB Manager console, right-click the drainstopped server, and select Start.

4. The server's icon outline will turn yellow while its status is converging. Then, after its status returns to converged, the outline will return to green (if you are impatient, you can hit Refresh to speed up the color change). All the while, the cluster is still (because we haven't stopped pinging) responding to ping requests as if nothing had ever happened. To stop the ping test, you can close the command prompt window or select the window and type Ctrl+C to cancel the command.

REAL ADMINS UNPLUG THE SERVER'S NETWORK CARD

Instead of drainstopping, which is convenient, you can also simply disable the network connection of the server you want to use to emulate a failure (be careful, of course, that your users aren't using that server for anything that isn't load-balanced) or, if you can access it, just pull out the network cable from the server's physical network card. Then try pinging it directly—it should fail. Then try pinging the load-balanced host name, and it should respond correctly, because the other server in the cluster is responding to the request. As long as one of them is available, all is well.

So, now we know that NLB works between the servers for uninterrupted service. But in order for requests for SharePoint resources to be captured and filtered by the NLB, the load-balanced URL must be used as the default zone for any web application you'd like to balance. For any web application that you do not want load-balanced (such as Central Administration), do not use the load-balanced URL for its default zone address.

CONFIGURE SHAREPOINT FOR NETWORK LOAD BALANCING

Currently the example SharePoint installation has a Central Administration web application and several other web applications. The SharePoint-80 web application has the default internal URL of *http://spf2*. This is the server's address, and it works fine to access the sites in that web application. To keep things simple, I am going to use that web application to demonstrate using the load-balanced URL. Now that we are using NLB, we should change that default address to the Internet name for the cluster. Then, clients will always be able to access the web application, even if one of the servers is off.

1. To set up a load-balanced URL for a web application after it has been created, you need to access Alternate Access Mappings. So, go to Central Administration ➤ System Settings, and click the Configure Alternate Access Mappings link under Farm Management (or you can just click the link to configure Alternate Access Mappings from the home page).

2. On the Alternate Access Mapping page, click the internal URL of the web application you'd like to change (my example is *http://spf2*). This will open a page that displays the current internal URL and its zone. Make certain the zone is set to Default (Figure 16.76).

3. Change the URL to the Internet name for the cluster (my example will be *http://sharepoint* because that will resolve to the full Internet name and the virtual IP for the cluster), and click OK. That will take you to the Alternate Access Mappings page for the web application, displaying the new default URL (Figure 16.77). If you wanted the web application to also be accessible by the server address (in case NLB has a problem), enter that address in one of the other public zones for the site. (You might think that you should just change the default Public URL for the web application, but it will do the same thing: change both the internal and public addresses for the default zone.)

FIGURE 16.76
Displaying the internal, default URL for a web application

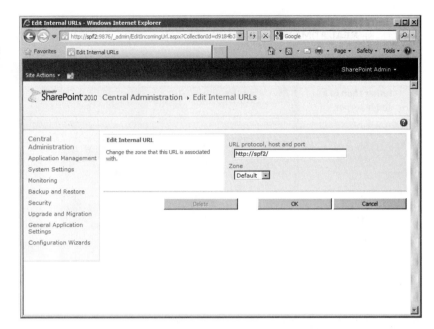

FIGURE 16.77
The new load-balancing URL for the web application

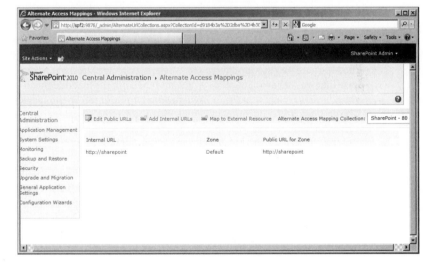

4. To test the new URL, go to a different server or workstation on the network than the SharePoint server (just to prove that the network load balancing service is working), open Internet Explorer, and browse to `http://sharepoint` (or whatever your load balanced address is). You may be prompted for your username and password from SharePoint (not to the server itself, which is good), and then the home page of the top-level site will load without a problem (Figure 16.78).

FIGURE 16.78
The SharePoint
site address now
resolves to the
NLB cluster name
rather than to a
single server.

WANT TO KEEP ANSWERING REQUESTS ON THE ORIGINAL ADDRESS?

If you don't want to simply replace the default zone's internal URL address with the load-balanced one, you can just add a new internal URL. To add a new internal URL, click Add Internal URLs in the Alternate Access Mappings page. Select the correct Alternate Access Mapping collection (in my case that would be for SharePoint -80), and then use the load-balanced URL there. Keep the default zone, because that is what search will need to be able to return the correct address for search results. The problem with not completely replacing the original, single server's URL is that if users are still using that address to access SharePoint, their traffic will not be load-balanced.

From this point on, when you create new web applications (or extended web applications) for the SharePoint server farm, you can always use the cluster's Internet name as the load-balanced URL, if you are using ports. And for host-headered web applications, make sure their CNAME Alias in DNS points to the A record for the load-balanced URL.

To see an example of a web application using the load balanced URL, create a new web application:

1. Go to the Application Management page of Central Administration, and click the **Create Or Extend Web Application** link in the SharePoint Web Application Management category.

2. On the Create Or Extend Web Application page, select Create A New Web Application.

3. On the Create New Web Application page, configure the web application's address and other settings. My example uses the server name and unique port to address the web application, as you can see in Figure 16.79. In the Public URL section (named Load Balanced URL in previous versions), you may notice that the default URL is the server name and the port number. That is, it will not be load-balanced because it is pointing

specifically to the server's address. To configure it properly (now that you have load balancing in place), enter the cluster Internet name rather than the server name.

FIGURE 16.79
Configuring a new, load-balanced web application

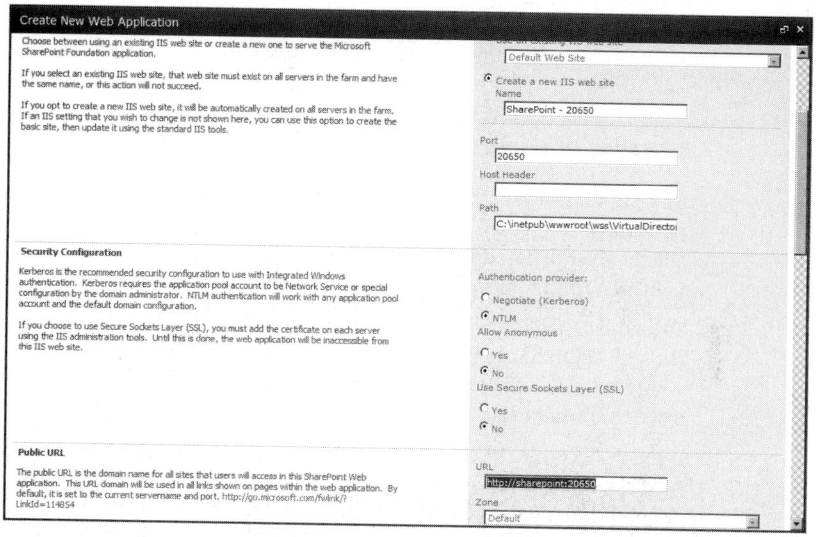

4. When you have completed the rest of the web application's configuration (including defining a content database account and database name and specifying a search server), click Create to finish. Create the site collection, and then run `iisreset /noforce` at the command prompt of the SharePoint server.

In the Alternate Access Mappings page, you'll see that the default internal URL for that web application is, in fact, the load-balanced URL (Figure 16.80).

FIGURE 16.80
Internal URL reflects load-balanced URL for new web application

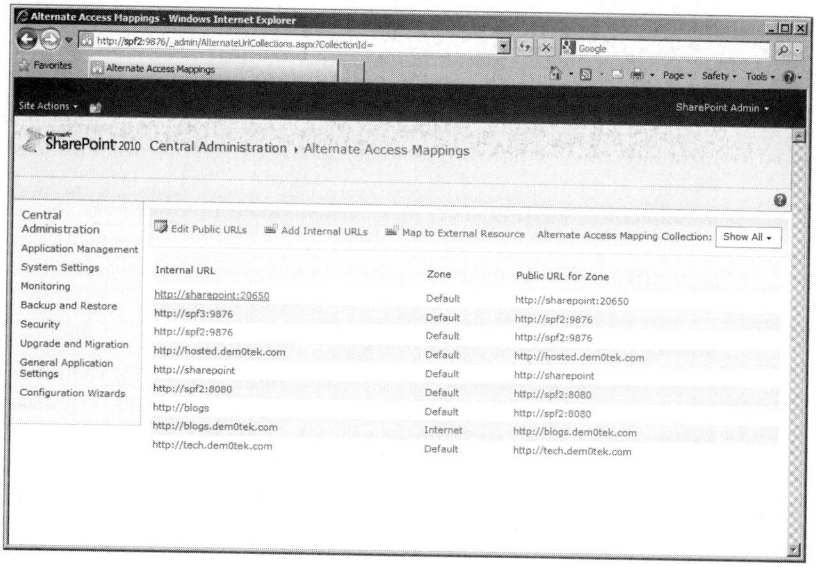

To access the site from any machine on the network, simply use the load-balanced URL. As a matter of fact, that URL is the only web address that SharePoint will accept for the web application. If you want to access the new web application by any other addresses, be sure to add them as alternate access mappings. (For more about creating web applications, site collections, and alternate access mappings, check out Chapter 10.)

CENTRAL ADMINISTRATION AND LOAD BALANCING

Since Central Administration is running on both servers, you could load-balance it, too. That is a possibility if high availability is a priority. However, it is considered a more secure practice to instead add the URLs of the additional servers that will be hosting Central Administration. This obscures the Central Administration website's address further if it is not the common load-balanced address.

To load-balance Central Administration, make certain that all servers in the NLB cluster are hosting the site. Then change the default internal URL for the site to resolve to the cluster Internet name (or whatever alias will resolve to the cluster virtual IP). In my case, that would be changing `http://spf2:9876` to `http://SharePoint:9876`.

If you decide to go the other way and simply make it possible for the Central Administration website on the additional server to be accessible by its own address if the original server were to go offline, simply add that server's address for the site as an internal URL. In my case, that would mean adding `http://spf3:9876` to AAM.

Although we have tested NLB by completely stopping access to one of the servers, remember that, in addition to failover capabilities, NLB also continuously monitors the activity of the cluster servers and distributes client requests to the server with the least load at any given time. Keep in mind that Windows NLB is not application-aware. If the web applications become unavailable in IIS on one of the servers, NLB will be unaware of it and will continue to send that server client requests if it is next in line or the least busy of the cluster.

Advanced Configuration

At this point, you know how to administer your SharePoint implementation including planning, installing, and configuring services; creating web applications and site collections; managing security at the farm, web application, and site collection levels; and monitoring, performing maintenance, and preparing for disaster. However, there were two additional, more advanced configuration settings—configuring Kerberos as an authentication method and securing a web application's data transfer with SSL—that we haven't done, until now.

Using SSL with SharePoint

Often external access to company data through SharePoint requires the additional protection of SSL. Secure Socket Layer (SSL) encrypts data sent over HTTP (making it HTTPS, the *S* meaning *secure*) to help avoid any tampering while in transit. SSL uses certificates, as well as public and private keys to encrypt and decrypt data. When a client requests access to a site that uses SSL, the server sends back the certificate and its public key. The client checks the certificate information to make certain it can be trusted (that the site is authentic and can be trusted to be who they say they are), and then it creates a premaster key of its own and encrypts that with the server's public key. The server gets the premaster key, decrypts it with its private key, and uses that to create a master key (with the agreement of the client) to create a session key to encrypt all data to that client during that session. Both the client and the server know what the session key is that encrypts and decrypts the data that is traveling between them, but no one else does. This secures the traffic from snooping or any other exploitation while it is between destinations.

To use SSL to encrypt traffic to and from your SharePoint websites, the server (servers if you are using a load-balanced server farm) must have a certificate. The URL covered by the certificate must match the URL that the user is using to access a website. There are two kinds of SSL certificates that are really relevant under these circumstances: the wildcard certificate and the standard website certificate. A wildcard certificate is more expensive and covers any site that uses the same domain name in the URL. A wildcard certificate for `*.dem0tek.com` would cover `SharePoint.dem0tek.com`, `sales.dem0tek.com`, `marketing.dem0tek.com`, and so on. A standard SSL certificate must match the full address exactly. So if there were a certificate for `marketing.dem0tek.com`, that URL is the only one that could use it.

In this example, just to demonstrate how to enable SSL with SharePoint, we are going to use a standard certificate and secure a public-facing web application. As a matter of fact, we are going to create a new web application and use a host header to address it. This site will be accessed from outside the office, and it must have the data encrypted between the server and the client.

GETTING FANCY WITH HOST HEADERS AND NLB

This exercise can also demonstrate a more advanced use of load balancing. Instead of using the Internet name for the web application, we are going to use a host header that resolves to the load-balanced IP address using DNS.

Create a new forward lookup zone for the external domain in DNS. Then create an alias for the new host header and map it to `SharePoint.dem0tek.lcl` (or whatever your cluster's Internet name is).

When you access the site using the host header, it will resolve (as this example will demonstrate) to the cluster's VIP and therefore be load balanced; that is why its default address can also be the load-balancing address.

Setting up for SSL requires three stages. First, decide on the URL. Then, enable the web application to do SSL in SharePoint. Finally, configure SSL in IIS, generate the certificate request, and then add the certificate to the IIS Web Site. There is even an optional fourth stage, which is to export the certificate to import it to the web application on the other servers in the farm for load-balancing purposes.

CHOOSE AN APPROPRIATE URL

It is important to decide what URL will be secured. In this example, we'll use `collaborate .dem0tek.com`. The domain `dem0tek.com` has been registered by the company with the correct DNS record to allow traffic to reach your internal SharePoint server. Internally, in this example, the router is configured to pass HTTP and HTTPS traffic to the SharePoint servers, and DNS has a record for `collaborate.dem0tek.com` that resolves to the internal server's VIP address.

CREATE A WEB APPLICATION TO USE SSL

Stage 2 of the process involves creating a web application and preparing it to use SSL.

1. To do that, go to the Central Administration website, go to the Application Management page, and click Manage Web Applications. On the Manage Web Applications page, click New in the ribbon bar.

2. Once you're in the Create New Web Application box, configure the new web application to use a host header that matches the URL to be used on the SSL certificate. As you can see in Figure 16.81, my example is `collaborate.dem0tek.com`. Make certain that the port for this web application is 80 at this point (you'll change it in IIS later).

FIGURE 16.81

Configuring the new web application to use SSL

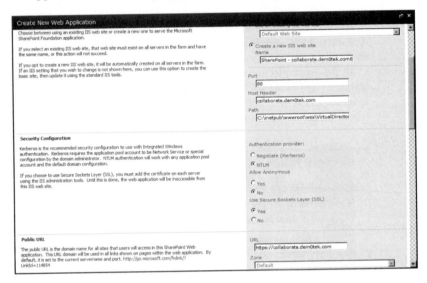

3. In the Security Configuration section, leave NTLM as the authentication method, do not enable anonymous (for this example), and select Yes to enable SSL for this web application.

    In the Public URL field, the protocol at the beginning of the address changes from HTTP to HTTPS and otherwise matches the host header address. That default is good for this example, because this is the address that will be used for the SSL certificate. For SSL to work, the users must type in an address for the web application that exactly matches the one used by the certificate. The host header is what you will be using and is an exact match (although you should remove the port number from the end, because it's not necessary). The Public URL will be the default zone for the web application in AAM and therefore the only address (at least initially) that SharePoint will accept for that web application. The default (minus the port number) is good.

4. Configure the Content Database account and the database name, and select a search server. When configuration is complete, click OK.

5. Once the web application has been created, you will be prompted to create a site collection. Create a new site collection, and then, on each SharePoint server in the farm, open a command prompt or the SharePoint management shell and run `iisreset / noforce` just to be sure all settings have propagated to IIS correctly.

The new web application will be created with the new host header address as the default zone (in my example that's the `SharePoint-collaborate.dem0tek.com80` web application), as you can see in Figure 16.82.

FIGURE 16.82

The new web application's default, internal URL

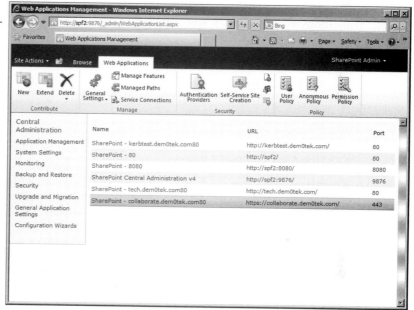

This configuration of the new web application is not entirely complete. Because the web application is supposed to be using SSL, SharePoint configures the IIS Web Site for the new web application to be stopped until SSL is configured.

To prepare to move to stage 3 of this process, the web application's IIS Web Site must be configured properly before you start it.

CONFIGURING AN EXISTING WEB APPLICATION TO USE SSL

You may wonder where the setting is to enable SSL for *existing* web applications. There really isn't one. You just change the URL in Alternate Access Mappings from HTTP to HTTPS. That's essentially all that the Enable SSL setting does when you create/extend a web application.

Keep in mind that enabling SSL on a SharePoint site requires that you enable SharePoint to accept requests for the web application using an HTTPS address and *then* you configure it in IIS.

CONFIGURE SSL FOR A SHAREPOINT WEB APPLICATION IN IIS

In the third stage of the process, with the web application created, you must get an SSL certificate and configure the IIS Web Site of the web application. You can use the Windows Certificate Authority console to create a certificate on your network. It may not be from one of the publicly trusted Certificate Authorities, but it can be trusted by your clients since you made it for them. Or you can use a trusted authority online, such as VeriSign or GeoTrust. These vendors do nothing but vouch for the authenticity of other people's websites and generate certificates for them. These authorities can put you through a rigorous application process; they'll make certain you own the domain and that your contact and company information is correct; then they'll move on to questions more appropriate when applying for security clearance.

Purchasing an SSL certificate from a third-party vendor is convenient but potentially expensive (depending on the kind of certificate you choose). It is convenient because many of them are already trusted publishers of certificates, so Internet Explorer will accept their certificates readily and because they offer additional support if the certificate expires (they generally are designed to expire), is lost, or becomes corrupt. Because companies often use third-party certificates, that's the process this example will use.

CERTIFICATES GENERATE IN-HOUSE WORK

A certificate that is generated by the certificate authority on your network may cause users outside the network to get a warning that it may have expired or is not known. Keep in mind that SSL does two things: it sends a certificate to verify the site's authenticity, and then it negotiates the master key to encrypt the session traffic. Both steps are needed: authentication and then encryption. So if a user is warned by their browser that the certificate from your company's Certificate Authority is not trusted (because the browser knows nothing about your company) and then clicks to accept the certificate manually, the key passing will proceed, and all data between the two computers, server and client, will be exchanged. If the user rejects the certificate, then they don't access the site.

Just because the browser doesn't like the look of a certificate does not mean it is automatically a problem if you know where it came from. Authenticity may not be established, but the encryption will still work if it is accepted.

Generating a Certificate Request

To get an SSL certificate, you first have to apply for one. IIS has a convenient wizard that helps you set up a certificate request that you can use to acquire a certificate from a trusted Certificate Authority. It is often a good idea to try the certificate before you buy it, so most vendors offer trial certificates that expire in a few weeks.

1. To generate a certificate request for a particular IIS Web Site, open the IIS Manager console (Start ➤ Administrative Tools ➤ Internet Information Server (IIS) Manager).

   You may notice that new web application is stopped. That is to be expected; SharePoint does that to keep anyone from accessing an SSL-enabled web application until SSL is in place. After you finish configuring it to require SSL, you can start it.

2. In the IIS Manager console, select the server name in the navigation pane, and scroll down in the workspace to Server Certificates. Even though the certificates will be

primarily for individual IIS Web Sites, they are applied to the server, and the icon to add certificates is for the server (Figure 16.83).

3. Double-click the Server Certificates icon. The workspace will display existing certificates (there might be a machine certificate for server identification in there). In the Actions pane, you can create self-signed or domain certificates, as well as create and complete certificate requests (Figure 16.84).

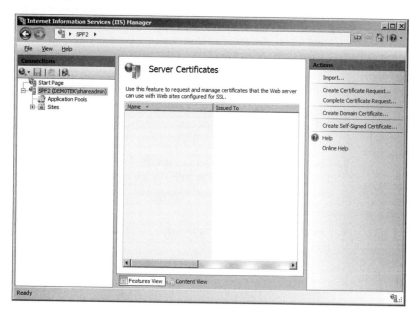

4. We need to create a certificate request, so click Create Certificate Request in the Actions pane.

    On the first page of the Request Certificate Wizard, you need to specify required information. City/Locality must be official names and can't be abbreviated.

5. This Distinguished Name screen needs quite a bit of information. The first field, Common Name, is the most important one. It must match the URL of the web application you are requesting the certificate for. In my example, that would be *collaborate.dem0tek.com* (Figure 16.85). If the certificate were being used by internal clients only, then the server's NetBIOS name would be acceptable. However, that is not the case in this instance.

FIGURE 16.85

The Distinguished Name screen of the Certificate Request Wizard

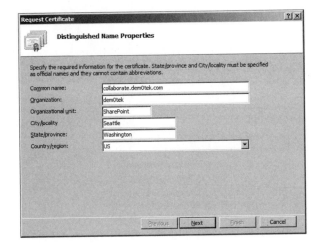

6. Once you've entered your web application's URL into the Common Name field, enter information for the organization or company name for the certificate. You also need to enter an Organizational Unit. Even if you don't really have one, make something up (but remember that all data in a certificate can be viewed by the user, so keep it professional— my example uses *SharePoint*). Also enter country, state/province, city/locality information in this screen (avoid abbreviations), and click Next.

7. On the Cryptographic Service Properties screen, the default of RSA SChannel Provider, 1024-bit length is good for me. You can choose a different bit length and use the DH SChannel provider if you'd like. Then click Next.

8. On the next screen is a field to specify the filename and location for the certificate request. Save it to a handy location, and use an intuitive filename. For my example, I am going to use `certreq.txt` for the filename. The certificate request is just some hashed text, nothing fancy.

9. Once you've specified the location and filename for the request, click Finish to generate the certificate request file.

The certificate request will have been generated, and you will find yourself back in the IIS console.

Request an SSL Certificate from an Online Certificate Authority

Actually using the request information to get a certificate varies depending on which Certificate Authority you use. In many cases, you fill out a form with the name, phone number, and email address of the authoritative contact used to register the domain you are using for the common name in the certificate.

In my case, I used a trial certificate from an online Certificate Authority.

1. To request a certificate, open the certificate request file that you just generated. Select the data (be sure not to miss anything) in the text file (see Figure 16.86).

FIGURE 16.86

Selecting text in the certificate request text file

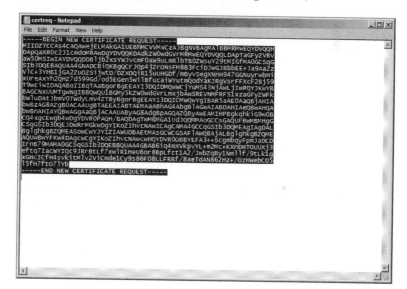

2. Paste that data into the certificate request field of the Certificate Authority you've chosen. Figure 16.87 illustrates a standard request form might look like, and you can see where to paste the request data.

FIGURE 16.87

A sample request form at an online certificate authority

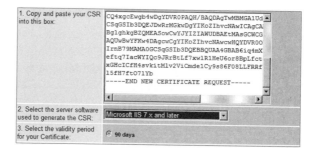

The rest of the authentication process depends on the Authority. In my case, for the trial certificate, it did a whois query on my domain. It then returned the email address of the person authoritative for that domain. The Authority then sends an email to that authoritative email address for confirmation. When you get the email, click the link to confirm that the certificate is legitimate (and one you requested). The new certificate will then be generated and sent to you in the form of a text string just like the request.

Apply the SSL Certificate from an Online Certificate Authority to a Web Site

Now you may be wondering, "What can I do with this text? Where is the attached file that is the certificate?" That text *is* the SSL certificate. Simply copy (from five dashes of the Begin Certificate header of the data to the last five dashes of the End Certificate footer) and paste it into a text file.

Name the text file something you can remember, with the file extension of .cer (I used the name *collaborate.cer*). That indicates to Windows that the file contains certificate information and the public and private key combination associated with that certificate (remember, SSL both proves authenticity and encrypts data).

Once the text file is saved somewhere accessible, it's time to add it to the web application that requested it:

1. To apply a certificate to an IIS Web Site (and therefore a SharePoint web application), go back to the Internet Information Services (IIS) Manager console, and with the server name selected, scroll to and double-click the Server Certificate icon.

2. In the Actions pane, click Complete Certificate Request.

3. In the wizard, on the Specify Certificate Authority Response screen, browse to or enter the location of the file and the filename. Beneath that field, enter a friendly name for the certificate (I used certreq in Figure 16.88).

FIGURE 16.88
The Specify Certificate Authority Response page

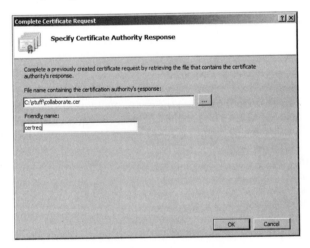

4. Click OK to complete the certificate request and apply the certificate to the server.

That will take you back to the IIS console. Now the certificate is listed in the Server Certificate's workspace (Figure 16.89).

FIGURE 16.89

The certificate listed in its workspace in IIS

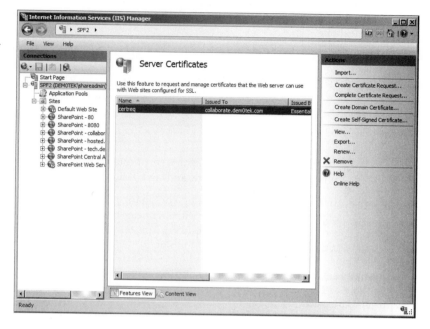

Congratulations, your server now has its a new SSL certificate, ready to be applied to the Web Site that bears the Issued To name.

There are a few steps left to complete this process. First the binding for the IIS Web Site has to be changed from 80 to 443, and the certificate needs to be specified. Then the IIS Web Site has to be started and then tested by accessing it with Internet Explorer. If it doesn't work, chances are good there is something wrong with the certificate.

If it works, then the certificate has to be exported. Why? Well, the certificate has to be imported to the other SharePoint servers in the farm for the same web application. Remember, they all have to match, and that includes having the same certificate on all servers in the cluster. Then, after the certificate is imported to the other servers, the IIS Web Site has to be started there as well.

Change the Web Site Binding and Apply the Certificate to the Web Site

Although SharePoint knows that the IIS Web Site should be listening on port 443, SSL requires a little more configuration.

1. To make sure the web application is listening on the correct port (we originally set the web application for port 80 in SharePoint before we enabled SSL), open the Server And Sites nodes in the Connections pane. Then right-click the IIS Web Site that you are configuring to use SSL (in my case that would be SharePoint - collaborate.dem0tek.com80), and select Edit Bindings from the pop-up menu.

In the Site Bindings dialog box, you can see that the site is listening on the default HTTP port of 80 (Figure 16.90). It needs to be changed to port 443, which is what SSL uses.

FIGURE 16.90
The default site binding

2. To change the port and select the certificate to apply to this specific IIS Web Site, select the binding you want to change, and click Edit.

3. In the Edit Site Binding dialog box, change the port to 443 (leaving the IP as all unassigned is fine). And, in the SSL Certificate drop-down, select the correct certificate (my example is `certreq`, Figure 16.91). You can even view the certificate to be sure it's the right one by using the View button.

FIGURE 16.91
Editing the site binding to include the SSL port and certificate

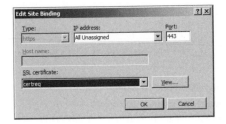

4. When you are certain your settings are correct, click OK.

Now the IIS Web Site is bound to the correct port and uses the correct SSL certificate.

Start the Web Site

Next we need to start the IIS Web Site that we just configured to use SSL.

1. Click Close to close the Site Bindings dialog box. Now that the correct port is selected and the certificate is set for the IIS Web Site, it's time to start it. In the IIS Manager console, right-click the IIS Web Site and click Start in the pop-up menu, or with the Web Site selected, click Start in the Actions pane.

2. Open Internet Explorer, type the web application's URL in the address bar, and hit Enter. Be sure to use HTTPS instead of HTTP in the address.

3. It may prompt you to log in. Use the username you chose for the site collection administrator when you were configuring it. It may also prompt you to add the site to the Trusted Site zone on that computer. That is a very good sign and indicates that the browser found the site.

Once you have added the site to the Trusted sites zone, the home page for the SSL secured web application's first site collection should load (see Figure 16.92 for my example).

FIGURE 16.92

Website secured with SSL certificate

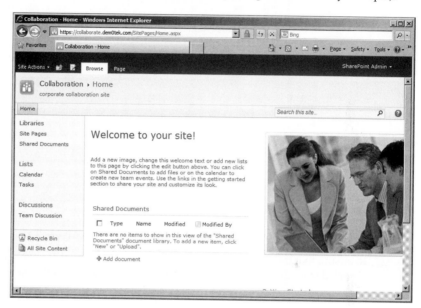

This indicates that SSL is working for the web application. To require SSL security to be used exclusively to access the site, go back to the IIS Manager console, and open the Properties dialog box (right-click the Web Site and select Properties) for the SSL-enabled Web Site we were just working on.

4. Make sure the site we've applied SSL to is selected in the Connections pane and that the workspace is in Features view. Select SSL Settings.

5. In the SSL Settings in the workspace, check the Require SSL check box (Figure 16.93).

6. In the Actions pane, click Apply to apply the change.

Open Internet Explorer, and browse to the secure site again. Confirm that you can access the site. Once you've established that SSL is working with that site, it must be configured on all other servers on the farm. That means they all need exactly the same certificate running on their copy of the IIS Web Site to be secured.

FIGURE 16.93
Requiring SSL

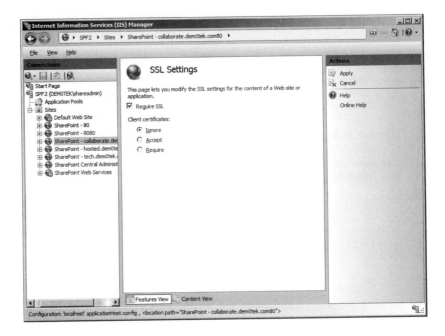

EXPORTING AND IMPORTING THE SSL CERTIFICATE TO THE OTHER FARM SERVERS

To ensure that the certificate is exactly the same for each server, the certificate needs to be exported from the working IIS Web Site and installed on all other servers.

1. To do this, select the server in the connections pane, and scroll to the Server Certificates icon and double-click.

2. In the workspace, select the certificate, and click Export in the Actions pane.

3. As you can see in Figure 16.94, a dialog box opens to export the current certificate to a .pfx file. A password will be applied to it, so it will require a password to import. Specify a filename and location, and then enter a password. Click OK.

FIGURE 16.94
Exporting the cur-
rent certificate

Now that the certificate has been exported, it is time to add it to the second server on the farm. The IIS Web Site will be stopped on that server because it doesn't have an SSL certificate yet.

4. To import the certificate so the IIS Web Site can become functional, go to the Service Certificate workspace, and click Import in the Actions pane.

5. It will open a dialog box where you can browse to the exported certificate file, and enter the password (Figure 16.95). When you've got the correct file and password entered, click OK.

FIGURE 16.95

Importing the certificate to the second server

The certificate will then appear in the Server Certificate workspace. Now it can be selected when setting up the site binding for the IIS Web Site on that server.

Just as a reminder, now that you have imported the certificate, you need to bind it. Right-click the Web Site associated with the web application you enabled SSL on. In the drop-down menu, select Edit Bindings. In the Site Bindings dialog box, select the binding that is there (it will be for port 80), and click Edit. In the Edit Bindings dialog box, enter the correct port for SSL, **443**, and select the imported certificate. Click OK. Then start the Web Site, while it is still selected, by clicking Start in the Actions pane.

Repeat the import certificate, and prepare the Web Site process with each server in the farm that hosts the Web Site that requires the certificate.

Keep in mind that Search may not work on the web application until the server running Search that was selected for that web application has a working, SSL-enabled IIS Web Site. Consider configuring that server's IIS Web Site first.

Here are some things to keep in mind when using SSL:

◆ The IIS Web Site for each server on the farm will be stopped and require manual configuration before they are all functional.

◆ If there is a web application already using the default SSL port, you will need to assign a different one. Each corresponding Web Site can have a different host header on port 80, but each Web Site must have a unique SSL port (or they need to either use a unique IP address or use a wildcard certificate). This is because traffic is *encrypted* when it gets to IIS, and therefore the host header information cannot be read to give IIS any change to figure out what IIS Web Site to send the data to. Thus, having a unique port for each site is critical. If you have any load-balancing port rules governing the unique port, they will, obviously, have to change.

◆ If the IIS Web Site needs a custom SSL port, then the SSL certificate must have the port as part of the common name (such as collaborate.dem0tek.com:444).

◆ Search may be delayed and errors may occur as each server is configured to start the new web application.

◆ The IIS certificate for each server's copy of the web application must be an exact duplicate of the others. Do not request a new certificate for each server. Even if they contain the same data, their keys will not be the same.

◆ Keep in mind that SSL session IDs linger in Internet Explorer. If you move away from an SSL site on a load-balanced server farm and then try to go back, you may be redirected to a different server. However, IE will have a session ID for the other server it accessed earlier. Features of the page, such as Search or changing views, may not work properly. Try closing out of Internet Explorer altogether and then trying again. That will give IE a chance to clear the old session ID from its cache.

Using Kerberos for Authentication

When you are using Windows authentication, there are two primary authentication methods: NTLM and Kerberos (Negotiate). NTLM is the default Windows authentication method, and it requires no additional configuration to work in an Active Directory—or even a workgroup environment. Kerberos requires that both the client and server support that authentication method. Kerberos uses port 88 by default, so make certain, if you are using Kerberos authentication with external clients, that both the network firewall and the client's firewall allow Kerberos traffic on port 88. Also keep in mind that keeping the same time is critical for Kerberos to work with external clients, so make certain they are pulling time from the same source and are updating their time adequately. Often issues of time are the biggest reason not to use Kerberos for authentication.

Kerberos is a ticket-based system, allowing an authenticated user to access resources based on their session ticket given by the key distribution center—usually the domain controller. However, sometimes a front-end product needs to be allowed to delegate authentication in order to give a user access to a back-end resource like the SQL server. This means that when someone logs into SharePoint, it needs to grant that user the right to access SharePoint resources in the SQL databases through a delegated service. For each web application that will be using Kerberos, the content database account (otherwise known as the application pool account for that web application) must be given the right to access this data on behalf of the user. Only service principal accounts are allowed to delegate authentication with Kerberos. So if you want to use Kerberos authentication, the content database account must be registered as a service principal name (SPN) for the server (or servers) hosting its web application. Kerberos authentication has several bonuses. It is more secure, and in distributed environments, it works faster because of the session tickets, and it supports delegation of authentication, allowing service applications to pass through authentication to network resources, which NTLM cannot do.

Because there can be only one service principal name, per service class and per server registered, if you are going to enable Kerberos on more than one web application (especially if they are going to use custom ports and otherwise the same server address), it is recommended that you register one account that will be used as a content database account for all of those web applications. This will make it more convenient to manage Kerberos and avoid duplicate principal name errors. Keep in mind that the same account can be registered as a service principal name on several different servers. If there is more than one name used by the service being configured (such as a FQDN and NetBIOS), then each name needs to be set manually, so Kerberos knows how to do authentication for the name being used.

In addition to registering a service principal name, in more complex environments you might need to also give the account *trusted for delegation rights* in Active Directory. Also keep in mind that the Search service (particularly the index service) often has problems authenticating using Kerberos (particularly on web applications that are using non-standard ports). This is why it is common practice to have a main web application using NTLM authentication for the sake of search and have everyone else access the content by using an extended web application, which will be using Kerberos for authentication.

Setting up for Kerberos is pretty easy to do. The main worry is that it does give a user account (or user accounts) that otherwise ran in a least-privilege context access to the network as a service principal. However, that said, some service applications need to use Kerberos to allow pass-through authentication where the user authenticates to use SharePoint, then SharePoint needs to pass their credentials to the external resource. NTLM cannot do that, but Kerberos can. It depends on the service application, and there are often work arounds.

In a single-server installation of SharePoint, local services such as the Network Service already work with Kerberos. However, if they need to access network resources, you will need to register the computer object to be trusted for delegation and set as a service principal name on behalf of the local service. It is strongly suggested that you use a domain account for web application pools (content database accounts).

USING SETSPN TO REGISTER SERVICE PRINCIPAL NAMES

Before you enable Kerberos authentication on a web application, you need to register the content database account as a service principal name in Active Directory. The tool to use to set service principal names is SetSPN. This command is built into the Windows Server 2008/2008 R2 operating system (you used to have to download it). It will run on any server in the domain, but it needs to query the domain controller for principal names.

To register an account as a service principal name in Active Directory for a standard SharePoint web application, open a command prompt or SharePoint management shell, and run the `setspn` command with the following syntax:

```
setspn -s http/servernamefqdn domain\contentdbaccount
setspn -s http/NetBIOSname domain\contentdbaccount
```

where the *servernamefqdn* is the FQDN of the SharePoint server, *NetBIOSname* is the NetBIOS name of the server, *domain* is your domain name, and *contentdbaccount* is the domain account that will be used as the application pool for accessing the content database of the web applications requiring Kerberos authentication.

TO TRULY MASTER SETSPN, ONE MUST ASK FOR HELP...

There are more parameters to the `setspn` command than are commonly used. Most people just use the -A parameter to register arbitrary service principal names, but Server 2008 R2 also has the -S parameter, which will do the same things as -A but also check for duplicates.

For more information about `setspn`, use the -? parameter. It will generate informative help information about the various modes and switches available with the command. You can use it from any command prompt or SharePoint management shell on the servers in the domain.

This means you are going to register an arbitrary service principal, using the HTTP service class (because IIS needs to use it), for the server and the content database account. You are specifying HTTP as a class, and that's why there are not two slashes, only one. An example is as follows:

```
setspn -s http/spf2.dem0tek.lcl dem0tek\spfcontent
setspn -s http/spf2 dem0tek\spfcontent
```

This will allow SharePoint to access resources on behalf of a SharePoint user who is using the http://spf2 website via the content database account.

If you have one server, you can register the SPN for that server and be done. In Figure 16.96, you can see the example of setting the service principal name for my SPF2 server for the content database account of dem0tek\spfcontent.

FIGURE 16.96
Registering an SPN
for a server

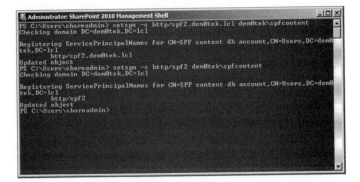

To confirm the service principal names registrations for an account, use the list parameter for setspn:

```
Setspn -l accountname
```

such as setspn -l spfcontent. That will, in my example, display all registrations for the dem0tek\ spfcontent account (Figure 16.97).

FIGURE 16.97
Listing SPN reg-
istrations for a
domain account

If you are doing network load balancing, there is a little more labor involved. You will need to register the content database account as a service principal name for each NLB server in the cluster, and the cluster server Internet name.

Here's an example:

```
Setspn -s http/spf2.dem0tek.1cl dem0tek\spfcontent
Setspn -s http/spf3.dem0tek.1cl dem0tek\spfcontent
Setspn -s http/SharePoint.dem0tek.1cl dem0tek\spfcontent
```

QUIRKY KERBEROS

Kerberos can be a bit moody. I have worked with NLB networks that don't require the cluster Internet name to be registered, and in others all clients but the SharePoint servers themselves can access the web application without the cluster name registered. The vast majority of SharePoint deployments don't need the content database account to be trusted to delegate, but a few (usually those with custom or complex web parts) do.

Kerberos does not report errors very well. Generally, if there are Kerberos (or key distribution center, sometimes called KDC, errors), they will be on the domain controller. Otherwise (without installing a network monitoring tool), the best way to know if there is a problem is to see whether the web application can be accessed by all users and servers in the browser and if search works.

If a web application is having any problems with authentication, Search is often the first to know. Check all Application logs on the servers hosting search for the Kerberos-authenticated web applications. If search is having no problems, chances are good there are no problems.

So, I think you are seeing a pattern; you need to set the principal name for the content database account for a web application, both for its NetBIOS name and its FQDN (essentially any name it will be accessed with). But what about web applications with a host header, or host-named, address? In that case, because the users are not going to be accessing the web application using any other address, then you need to use just that address for setting up the service principal name.

For example, I created a web application at the address http://kerberos.dem0tek.com. I also created a domain account specifically for this exercise, dem0tek\kerbcontent, and used it as the content database account for the web application. Use your own information if it's different.

To make sure that this content database account is set as a service principal name for its web application, its fully qualified name need to be specified (Figure 16.98). Open the SharePoint management shell (if you have the correct permissions) or a command prompt, and run the following setspn command:

```
setspn -s http:/kerberos.dem0tek.com dem0tek\kerbcontent
```

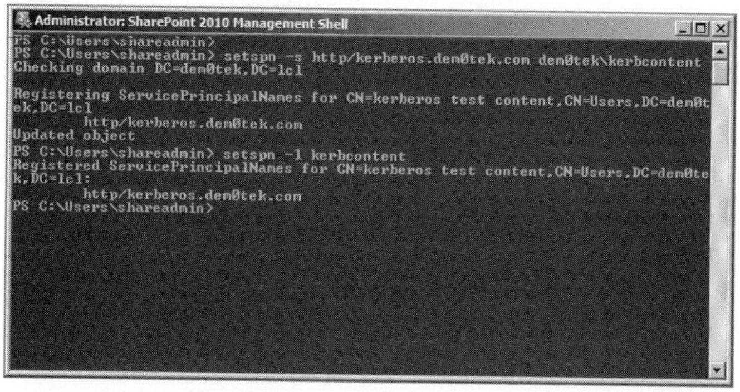

FIGURE 16.98
Configuring service principal names for the content database account

Once the registrations are complete, it is time to enable Kerberos on the web application.

JUST IN CASE

If there is a chance the users will just use the alias for an address, such as kerberos in this example, consider setting the spn for the content database account for that address too.

ENABLING KERBEROS ON A WEB APPLICATION

You can enable Kerberos on any web application or extended web application. It's easy to do while creating new ones, because there is a setting right there. It's a little less intuitive to change authentication for an existing web application (or extended web application), which is why I am going to demonstrate enabling Kerberos on an existing web application.

1. To do so, you first need to open the Manage Web Applications page, select the web application in question, and click the Authentication Providers button. For my example, I created a web application that uses the host name *http://kerberos.dem0tek.com*.

WHERE'S THE BEEF?

To modify the authentication for an existing extended web application, first choose the web application it extends. Then click Authentication Providers, and select the zone for that extended web application uses. It is easy to forget that extended web applications are considered only zones of the web applications they extend.

2. In the Authentication Providers box, select the zone you want to have Kerberos for its authentication. In my case, I only have the default zone.

3. In the IIS Authentication Settings section of the Edit Authentication box is the setting to enable Kerberos. If you select it, you will get a warning (Figure 16.99) that Kerberos requires additional configuration if the application pool's account isn't the server's network service account. We already manually prepared for Kerberos, so click OK on the warning, and then save the changes.

4. This will put you back on the Authentication Provider box; just close out of it to get back to the Manage Web Applications page.

5. To be on the safe side, open a command prompt or SharePoint management shell, and run an `iisreset /noforce` on all the servers in the farm to be sure they know about the authentication change.

FIGURE 16.99
Enabling Kerberos authentication on an existing web application

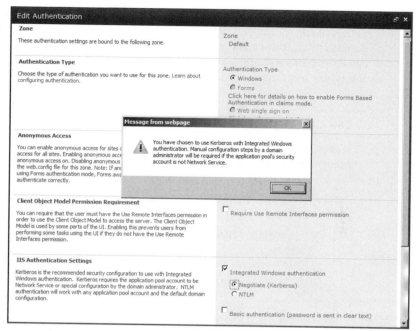

Once you have run iisreset on the servers, it's time to see whether Kerberos is working. Log into the site as a user with at least contribute permissions. To truly test it, do some common tasks. As you can see in Figure 16.100, I managed to access the top-level site at the root of the web application just fine.

FIGURE 16.100
Logged into the Kerberos-enabled site

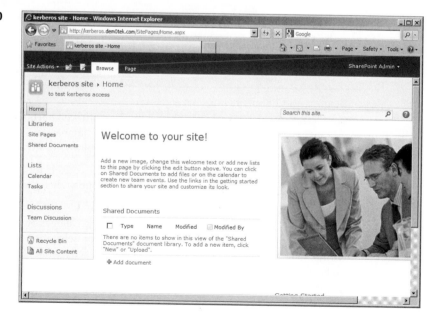

Just to be thorough, check the Event Viewer logs for errors on all servers in the cluster, as well as the domain controller. There should be no errors, but it never hurts to check. Sometimes it does take SharePoint a few minutes to realize that Kerberos is being used to access the content databases of the web application (if you don't do an `iisreset`). So, if Search is not working, wait at least one indexing cycle and try again before beginning troubleshooting procedures.

CAN'T LEAVE WELL ENOUGH ALONE

Because Kerberos for SharePoint negotiates, I am never completely confident that SharePoint isn't falling back to authenticating via NTLM. So, I installed Network Monitor 3.4 (it used to come free with Windows Server). I ran it while I was trying to access the Kerberos-enabled site for the first time.

According to Network Monitor, Kerberos was being used for authentication successfully. Now you know.

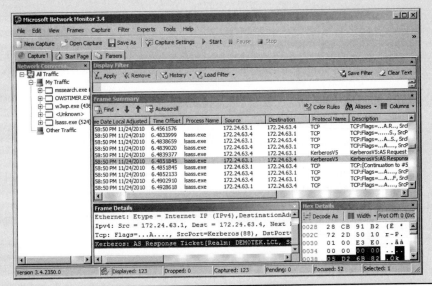

If your SharePoint environment is more complex, with web parts that access external resources, for example, you may need to set the content database account to be trusted for delegation in Active Directory. If this is the case, take the following steps:

1. Open the Active Directory Users And Computers console for the domain. Click the Users node in the tree pane of the console, and then double-click the Content Database user account.

2. This will open its Properties dialog box. Select the Delegation tab (Figure 16.101). You have a few options here. You can trust the user for delegation to any service (Kerberos Only), which works for me, or you can specify exactly what SPNs you want the account to be able to delegate for. This approach is more controlled and specific, and many white papers suggest it for complicated environments, when the account will be handling

Kerberos for multiple services. Select (and possibly configure) the correct delegation type for you, and click OK. In my example, I am simply letting the account delegate to all services (Kerberos only).

You may have to do an `iisreset/noforce` on the SharePoint servers for them to realize the change.

FIGURE 16.101

Configuring the domain account for trusted delegation

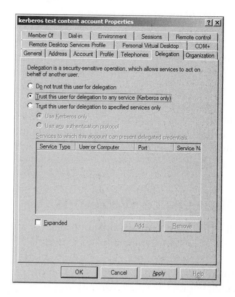

You should now be able to access the extended web application with no problems using Kerberos authentication. I have noticed that some of my servers do seem to perform a little better when Kerberos is enabled, not to mention that it can be very useful to use if you are doing authentication passthrough when using BDC. Give it a try.

TESTING THE CLUSTER

Remember that this example is built on the network that was load-balanced earlier in the chapter. This means that this Kerberos authentication is working across the cluster. To test it, feel free to drainstop a server or two (or disable its network connection) to confirm that load balancing is working.

Authenticating is an important part of accessing shared resources on a network. Being able to conveniently access sites, lists, and libraries is what SharePoint is all about.

So far in this chapter we've explored external content types and Business Data Connectivity, multi-tenancy, load balancing, SSL, and Kerberos. We installed a second server on the farm and moved the index service to it. We also enabled the Search service on the second server and enabled Central Administration for fault tolerance. These advanced capabilities come with SharePoint Foundation. However, there are some additions that can be added to SharePoint at a cost. One of those additions is Office Web Apps.

Office Web Apps adds rudimentary Office viewer and editor capabilities to SharePoint so you can open Excel, Word, PowerPoint, and OneNote files from libraries right in the browser. It is likely Office Web Apps will be a popular add-on, allowing users to do work in libraries without opening a local copy of the product.

This seems to mean that the user doesn't need to have those Office products on their computer to open and edit those files. It looks like a chance to save on licensing fees and use Word, Excel, PowerPoint, or OneNote for free.

But, just to get the installer for Office Web Apps requires a volume license of Office 2010 (you can download an installer from TechNet, but that's not for production). Each user who uses SharePoint with the Office Web Apps capability added to it must have an Office 2010 Pro Plus or Office 2010 Standard client license. Essentially, the Office 2010 license on their computer gives the user the right to use Office Web Apps from any computer. In other words, Office Web Apps was meant to be a convenience, not a free way to use Office products. (For that you have to go online and use the ad-supported Windows Live offerings).

Despite that shortcoming, it is likely to be helpful to have some idea of what makes Office Web Apps tick from an administrative standpoint before you're asked to install and maintain it on your network.

Installing Office Web Apps

To install Office Web Applications (popularly known as Office Web Apps), you must have a volume license of Office 2010 Pro Plus or Standard for your organization. This product requires a license key, that you will not get for free, to use in a production environment. The installer itself can be downloaded from the Microsoft Volume License Servicing Center (of course, you have to have a valid, volume license customer login).

It can be installed on a single Standalone server (and when it is, the Office Web App services will run as service instances) or in a server farm (where the services run per server).

When it is installing, the Office Web Apps installer runs a setup program and then the configuration wizard (otherwise referred to by its command-line equivalent, `psconfig`), which registers services, starts service instances (in the Standalone configuration), creates service applications and proxies, and activates features. For a farm, you can configure the service applications and proxies yourself. It's like deploying an immense solution to the farm. The Word Viewing service, PowerPoint service, and Excel Calculation services are added to the farm when Office Web Apps is installed. This essentially upgrades the SharePoint Foundation implementation to a quasi-SharePoint Server installation, meaning that when you do updates, service packs, and hotfixes, check to be sure whether you need the SharePoint Foundation ones or the SharePoint Server version. This also applies to language packs. If you install a language pack on a SharePoint Foundation server after Office Web Apps has been installed, you will need to use the SharePoint Server version.

How you install Office Web Apps, and how the services are handled, depends a bit on the type of installation you do. Just as an introduction, I am going to install it on a Standalone server. There are other installation types, such as installing Office Web Apps on an existing server farm or installing Office Web Apps on a new server farm (essentially during the installation process for the new farm after you run the SharePoint installer but before you run the configuration wizard to set up the farm for the first time).

LIGHT READING

To learn more about the different options you have for installing Office Web Apps, do an Internet search for *Deploy Office Web Apps* (Installed on SharePoint 2010).

Installing Office Web Apps comes in three parts. First you run the installation (after planning for it). Then you start services, and then you activate features. Of course, in a standalone environment, the services, service applications, and proxies will be started and configured, and all you really need to do is check out the settings of the service applications (to change them if you want to) and activate the Office Web App features at the site collection level.

Something to keep in mind is that Office Web Apps takes over the way Office files open from libraries. The default behavior is to open files with the desktop client software. Office Web Apps understandably changes that so just about everything opens in the browser. You can change that at the site collection level by activating the Open Documents In Client Application By Default feature. Or you can change the open file behavior for each library.

Services can be load-balanced in farm environments, and because several of the services do caching on the server (so files open faster), caching can be managed to a certain extent as well.

For farms, there can be a lag between the farm-wide default for opening files because it is changed during installation from open in client to open in browser only and during the activation of services. During this time, users might have problems opening library files. So, plan carefully—you might want to consider installing Office Web Apps when production is slow.

Office Web Apps needs basically the same hardware, software, and browser requirements as SharePoint (although it apparently runs well in the Chrome browser). It is strongly recommended that you don't install Office Web Apps on a domain controller. It is also suggested that, when you install Office Web Apps, you are logged in as a farm administrator, you are a PowerShell shell admin, and you are in the Local Administrators group on the local server. In the case of a Standalone installation of SharePoint, you need to be a local administrator, and it helps if you use the account that you installed SharePoint with to begin with.

LOOKING FOR TROUBLE

Some troubleshooting tips if a user cannot open a file: Check to see what version of Internet Explorer the user is using. Office Web App features are not entirely compatible with the 64-bit version of Internet Explorer. Nor does it play well with browsers of an older version than IE 7. It requires Active X controls, so it won't work in browsers that don't support Active X. It will work with Firefox, but you need to install the add-on so it can Open Office documents. If the user has a version of Office installed on their computer that is older than Office 2003, Office Web Apps won't work when opened on that machine. In addition, if security settings in the browser are blocking Active X, it will also cause issues.

This exercise assumes you have a volume license for Office 2010 and that you've downloaded the installer from the Microsoft licensing site. It will require a product key, so be sure to have it handy.

To start the installation, make sure you are logged in with the correct account, and then double-click the installation file for Office web apps, or you can right-click and run it as an administrator if you'd like.

During the installation, you will be prompted for a product key, to accept the EULA, and to specify where the installation files for the product (as well as the search index files, as if this were a new SharePoint installation) will be located.

After the installation files finish, the configuration wizard will start (if you didn't clear the Run The Wizard Now box, and you shouldn't because it does need configuration). It will stop the SharePoint services temporarily (although on a standalone installation, you will need to restart the Administration service manually) and then configure 11 tasks, including installing and registering services.

DELUSIONS OF GRANDEUR

The Configuration Wizard considers this an upgrade installation, although the version number in the upgrade and status page for SharePoint itself does not increase. However, a lot of new components were added.

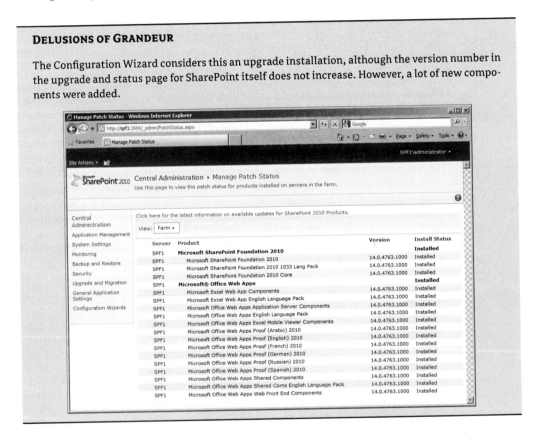

Once the installation and configuration of Office Web Apps is complete, let's go to Central Administration and see what has happened.

To see what services were installed and if they have been started, open Services On Server under System Settings on the Central Administration home page.

In Figure 16.102, you can see that the expected services, Excel Calculation, PowerPoint, and Word Viewing, were created and started by the Configuration Wizard.

FIGURE 16.102
Services now available in Services On Server page

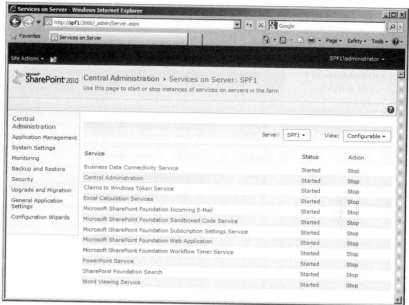

To take a closer look, because obviously the services can't be managed here, open Manage Service Applications under Service Applications on the Application Management page (Figure 16.103).

FIGURE 16.103
New Office Web Apps–related service applications

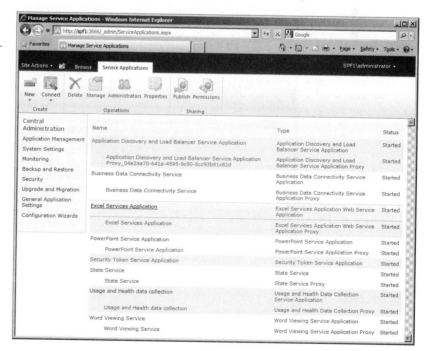

The new services are listed, along with a service that cannot be managed, State Service. It helps services that handle high quantities of data flow, such as PowerPoint broadcasts, by storing temporary data. The state service does have its own database (Figure 16.104).

FIGURE 16.104

State Service database

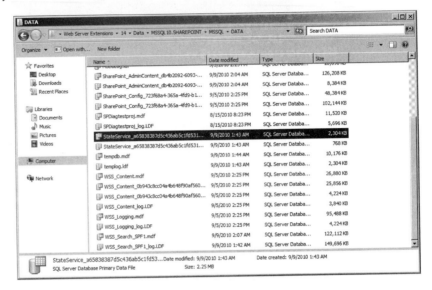

Each one of these service applications has additional management settings.

If you click the Excel Services application, it has a page of links to settings pages (Figure 16.105).

FIGURE 16.105

Manage Excel Services application page

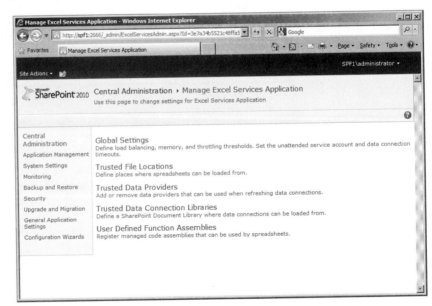

Global Settings   This link goes to a page where you can manage security in terms of file access methods, connection encryption, and allowing cross-domain access, load-balancing schemes, session management with maximum sessions per users, memory utilization, workbook caching, and settings concerning external data.

Trusted File Locations   The SharePoint implementation is trusted by default, but you can add more trusted file locations here. Excel will not open workbooks from untrusted locations.

Trusted Data Providers   Excel Services application has a long list of trusted types of data sources for spreadsheets, from SQL server to Oracle providers to IBM. You can add providers here if what you need isn't listed.

Trusted Database Connection Library   It's possible to store data connection files (such as ODC or UDC files) to use in order to make the same database connections again. To use this setting, you have to make a dedicated library for it (there isn't one by default) and then specify that library's location and description.

User Defined Function Assemblies   This is used to manage and register DLL files that provide Excel functions.

The Excel Services Application also created some farm features (Figure 16.106). It is the only one to do so.

FIGURE 16.106
Excel farm features

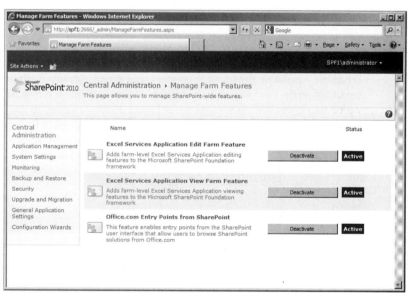

The PowerPoint Service application settings are less broad. As you can see in Figure 16.107, they primarily relate to file format support, extra checking for older format files, and presentation broadcasting. The service will scan older PowerPoint files before opening them, because those files can have issues running as a presentation. However, scanning those files is resource intensive, so this can be skipped if all files are trusted. The Broadcast site section displays the default site that gets created during installation and configuration of Office Web Apps. There is also a link to create a broadcast site at a different location using the broadcast site template.

FIGURE 16.107
PowerPoint
service application
settings

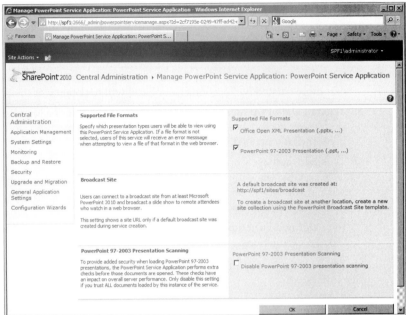

FIGURE 16.107
PowerPoint
service application
settings

The PowerPoint broadcast site is an added capability of the PowerPoint service. The service creates a site collection specifically for broadcasting presentations. It has three member groups—Broadcast Attendees, Broadcast Presenters, and Broadcast Administrators. To be able to see a broadcast on the site, users need to be added to the Attendees group. The site is tightly integrated with PowerPoint 2010. As you can see in Figure 16.108, you need to use PowerPoint 2010 to basically publish a presentation to the site. After setting up a broadcast in PowerPoint, you'll get a temporary link to the broadcast of the presentation to give out to everyone. If they have permission to access the site, they can see a synchronized view of the slides as you present.

FIGURE 16.108
PowerPoint
Broadcast Site

The Word Viewing service's application settings (Figure 16.109) include managing total active processes, recycle threshold for processes, older format document scanning, embedded font support, and supported file formats for viewing.

FIGURE 16.109

Word Viewing service's application settings

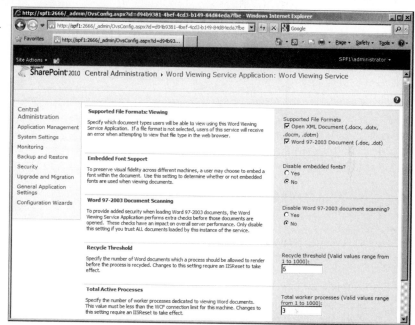

In IIS, several applications were created under the SharePoint Web Services Web Site; they coincide, not surprisingly, with the Office Web App service applications. Also, if you check in Central Administration (or at the command line), every web application (except Central Administration) will have a new site collection dedicated to caching views of Office files, Office_Viewing_Service_Cache. The Broadcast site collection will be created in only one web application, usually the root. You can create more, so it can be located in a different web application if you'd like. Remember that PowerPoint broadcasting is very resource intensive. Enable and use with caution.

On the site collection level, there are two new site collection features to enable (Figure 16.110). Open Documents In Client Applications By Default allows you to override the default Office Web Apps behavior of opening all files in the browser. The other feature, simply called Office Web Apps, is what actually enables Office Web Apps in the site collection libraries.

FIGURE 16.110
Office Web Apps–
related site collec-
tion features

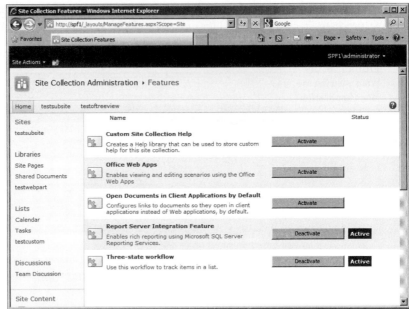

FIGURE 16.110
Office Web Apps–
related site collection features

If you activate the Office Web Apps service, you can use its viewer/editor capabilities in libraries on the site. I am not going to go into the details of using the individual Office Web Apps that much because Microsoft uses Office Web Apps online at `http://office.live.com`. All you need is a live ID and you can explore the product to your heart's content. In general, if you know how to use the Office products, you know how to use the web apps, although there will obviously be some features missing.

Briefly, if you were to click a Word document in a library, it would trigger the View capability of the Word Viewing service, opening the file in the browser in an interface with the options to open the document in Word 2010 if you have it installed, edit in browser, and even use find to search in the text. There is even a tiny button on the top right of the page that lets you "pop out" the document so it is not constrained by the boundaries of the browser window. Notice also in Figure 16.111 that there are extra features in a drop-down menu, including the option to print from SharePoint. That is a useful option.

You can also click Edit In Browser to trigger the ribbon. It is very much like the ribbon available for the rich-text area of wiki pages (Figure 16.112). There are tabs for formatting text (although it's called Home), Insert and View. To return to just viewing the document, you can use the View tab and click Reading View.

FIGURE 16.111
View document
using Office
Web Apps

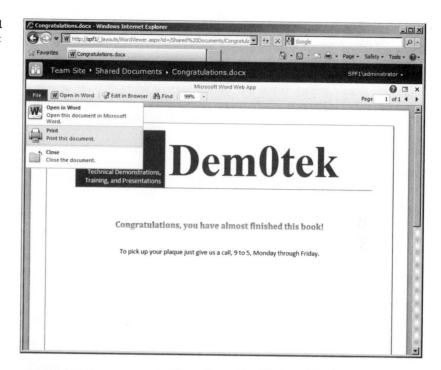

FIGURE 16.112
Editing a
document in
the browser

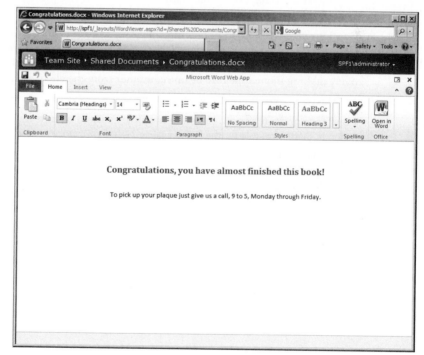

And that's my whirlwind tour of Office Web Apps from an administrator's perspective. You have a fundamental understanding of what it takes to install Office Web Apps; what service applications are created; and what databases, site collections, and farm and site collection features need to be activated.

I hope this gives you the courage to try it yourself. It can be convenient for commuting users, for those who roam and aren't always at the same workstation, or for those who just want to quickly share a document, spreadsheet, PowerPoint presentation, or OneNote file, without opening the client application locally.

As a matter of fact, I hope this chapter has given you insights into the more advanced capabilities and configurations of SharePoint and has rounded out your mastery of the product. Good luck with SharePoint and happy collaboration.

The Bottom Line

Use Business Data Connectivity and create external data connections. Business Data Connectivity is a service application that makes it possible to surface external data sources in SharePoint to create lists and lookup fields.

Master It What free product can I use to configure external content types?

Set a service principal name. For Kerberos authentication to work with SharePoint, additional configuration is required. The content database account for the web application using Kerberos must be registered as a service principal name for the SharePoint server (or servers).

Master It What executable is used to register service principal names? How do you access it?

Configure Network Load Balancing. Network Load Balancing is a network connection feature built into Windows Server 2008 and 2008 R2 (although there are other hardware and software solutions). It balances client requests and activity between servers in a cluster, effectively making them appear to be one computer from the client's perspective.

Master It What is a drainstop, and what is it for?

Configure multi-tenancy. Hosting multiple, isolated tenants on one SharePoint implementation is made possible by the Subscription Settings service application.

Master It What is a site subscription?

Appendix

The Bottom Line

Each of The Bottom Line sections in the chapters suggest exercises to deepen skills and understanding. Sometimes there is only one possible solution, but often you are encouraged to use your skills and creativity to create something that builds on what you know and lets you explore one of many possible solutions.

Chapter 1: SharePoint Foundation 2010 Under the Hood

Determine the software and hardware requirements you need for installing SharePoint Foundation. SharePoint has some stringent software and hardware requirements. Be sure you know what you need before you become the proud owner of your own SharePoint server or servers. SharePoint depends on Windows Server components and services in order to function.

Master It What software architecture is required for both the server OS and SQL to successfully install and run SharePoint?

Solution Both the SharePoint server and the SQL server must be 64-bit. 32-bit is not supported.

Identify the three ways of installing SharePoint Foundation. Choose the best three ways of installing SharePoint Foundation for you. With SharePoint, how you choose to install it defines how it works. Making the wrong choice can come back to haunt you. Know what you're in for, and choose the correct installation type for your business.

Master It If you were going to install SharePoint on one server (no existing SQL server) for a small business of about 50 people, what installation type would you choose?

Solution You could simply choose the Standalone installation. Or, if you expect to have a lot of content to search and need to specify a location for the index files (instead of the system partition of the SharePoint server), you can use the Server Farm Standalone installation. It is exactly the same as a standard Standalone installation, except that you can specify where the index files will go.

Set up the necessary accounts that SharePoint needs to run. When SharePoint is installed on a domain, it needs user accounts to assign to its services. Knowing what permissions and roles those accounts require will help you avoid problems when installing and running SharePoint.

Master It What is a Database Access Account? Is it known by any other names?

Solution The Database Access Account is also known as the Index account, crawler, or gatherer. It is used as part of the Search service to index data.

Recognize the new features and requirements of SharePoint. SharePoint has features that require additional planning and setup to function properly. Make sure you know what they are and what they require.

Master It What new feature of SharePoint Foundation allows SharePoint to access data from external data sources?

Solution The Business Data Connectivity service. It used to be available only with the paid-for SharePoint Server product.

Plan for hardware requirements. Don't let SharePoint outgrow its hardware before it really gets started. Prepare for growth. Establish your company's baseline operations per second and storage needs before installing SharePoint.

Master It What is the formula to calculate the storage requirements that a SharePoint server would need in a given environment?

Solution Database size = $((D \times V) \times S) + (10 \text{ KB} \times (L + (V \times D)))$

Chapter 2: Standalone Installation

Prepare for the installation of SharePoint. SharePoint has certain software and hardware requirements before it can be installed. In addition, some of those requirements vary depending on the type of installation you choose. It is good to know what to install, how to install them, and in what order to be prepared for installing SharePoint.

Master It SharePoint has a number of prerequisites that must be installed before it is installed. Do they each need to be downloaded and installed separately?

Solution No. You can if you so wish, but the SharePoint installer now includes a preparation tool that will install and configure the prerequisites that allow SharePoint to install and function.

Install SharePoint using the Standalone installation option. Several types of SharePoint installations are available: Standalone, which is a single-server installation that installs without intervention with all default settings and uses a SQL Server Express database; Server Farm Standalone, which is essentially the Standalone installation but with an additional configuration option before installation begins; and Server Farm Complete installation, which allows you to manage all configuration options and specify the SQL server that will manage the databases. Each installation type has its strengths and weaknesses, and it's good to know about them before you begin.

Master It   Can you install and use SharePoint if you don't have a SQL server on your network?

Solution   Yes. By using the Standalone installation option, you can have SharePoint install and use SQL Server 2008 Express if you don't have a SQL server on your network.

Determine what gets created when SharePoint installs.   From Standalone to Complete, it is good to know every step of the way the repercussions of each installation, configuration, and service that SharePoint adds and/or enables.

Master It   What is one way to confirm that the SharePoint services are running properly on the server?

Solution   There are actually several right answers to this question. Generally, you go to Service On Server and see whether the services are running. You can also check event logs or trace logs on the server to see whether there are any errors. You can check the Services console (or the Task Manager's Services tab), and make certain the correct services, with the correct accounts, are running. You can even check the Health Analyzer to see whether any of the services have broken any of the preset rules concerning best practices.

Perform the initial configuration tasks after a SharePoint install (and understand why you perform them).   After installation, SharePoint can require additional configuration before you can call it your own. It is good to know what the necessary settings are to quickly get SharePoint up and running to the point where an administrator can start working on it.

Master It   Does incoming email require Directory Management Service to function?

Solution   No. Many resources might imply otherwise, but DMS is not required to configure incoming email.

Chapter 3: Complete Installation

Prepare for a Complete installation.   SharePoint has certain software and hardware requirements before it can be installed. In addition, some of those requirements vary depending on the type of installation you choose. To be prepared for installing SharePoint, it is good to know what to install, how to install it, and in what order.

Master It   During the installation process, in what way does the Complete installation vary from the Standalone installation?

Solution   The Standalone installation configures most services for you, using local, network service, or system accounts, as well as installing an instance of SQL Express to use for its databases. The Complete installation gives you the opportunity to specify the SQL server instance to use for the SharePoint databases, as well as the service accounts and database names. In addition, it does not configure the services or the first web application and site collection for you. The Complete installation requires user accounts (either domain or local) for its services; it cannot use the built-in local, network service, or system accounts like Standalone can.

Install SharePoint using the Complete installation option. Several types of SharePoint installation are available: Standalone, which is a single-server installation that installs without intervention with all default settings and uses a SQL Server Express database; Server Farm, Stand-alone, which is essentially the Standalone Installation but with an additional configuration option before installation begins; and Server Farm, Complete installation, which allows you to manage all configuration options and specify the SQL server that will manage the databases. Each installation type has its strengths and weaknesses, and it's good to know about them before you begin.

Master It Does SQL have to be on a different server when you install SharePoint using the Complete installation option?

Solution No. SQL can be installed on the same server as SharePoint. Just use the server's address (and instance if necessary) during the configuration wizard to let SharePoint know where you want the databases to go. It doesn't mind running on the same server as SQL, as long as you have the resources to handle the extra load.

Determine what service accounts SharePoint requires and how to set them up. The SharePoint Complete installation requires you to have accounts available to be used by its services. It is best if the accounts are created ahead of time. They should use the least possible privileges on the domain. In addition, most services require you to register and manage their service accounts.

Master It List three service accounts that SharePoint uses and what they are used for.

Solution *The SharePoint farm account* is the most important; this account is the application pool identity to access SharePoint's configuration database and run the SharePoint timer jobs. *Search service* and *content access or index accounts* are used by SharePoint to support the Search service. The index account is used to index content databases, and the search account is the one that does search queries. The *Business Data Connectivity service account* is used to access external content from within SharePoint (to make external lists and lookup fields); it requires an application pool identity and that its account be permitted access to those external sources. The *Sandboxed Code service account* is the user account used to run the service, which manages and allows sandboxed or user solutions to be uploaded and activated at the site collection level. The *content database or web application account*, each web application has at least one database in which to store its content. It requires an application pool identity to access its databases. The Subscription Settings Service is used to support multi-tenant hosting, and uses a service account to access its database.

Manually configure necessary SharePoint services. Because the Complete installation does not make assumptions about if and how you want to configure services, it leaves you to configure them yourself. This lets you specify details, such as indexing schedules, service accounts, database names, and more.

Master It Is there a service account that you have to configure in a Complete installation that does not require a managed account?

Solution Yes. The content access or *index* service, which is part of Search, does not require a managed account for some reason. Because of that, you should seriously consider setting that account to never expire. You might also consider setting it so the user cannot change the password in case the account is ever compromised.

Chapter 4: Introduction to the SharePoint Interface

Identify SharePoint's navigation tools and understand how to use them. SharePoint makes a point of ensuring that a user always has a way to get where they need to go without using the Back button in the browser. Recognizing these features makes navigation easier and increases productivity.

Master It List three ways to get back to the home page should you be in a list or library.

Solution You can use the Navigate Up button, the title area, and the Home tab in the top link bar (if they are showing; if not, use the Browse tab to display them).

Find a list or library. SharePoint uses the Quick Launch bar as a quick, convenient, and consistent way for users to find the SharePoint lists and libraries they need to access.

Master It How do you find a list or library if it is not on the Quick Launch bar?

Solution Either you open All Site Content or you can click a Quick Launch bar heading that relates to the thing you are looking for, which will open All Site Content filtered to show only that kind of object in the site.

Use the Quick Launch bar. The Quick Launch bar is more than a list of lists. It also contains an easy way to navigate through all contents of a site, check the Recycle Bin, and create new site contents.

Master It By default, when SharePoint is initially installed, the Quick Launch bar does not have Surveys as a heading. Why?

Solution SharePoint doesn't generate headings in the Quick Launch bar for types of site objects that don't exist, such as surveys or picture libraries.

Use the Top Ribbon bar. The interfaces containing the settings and actions to apply to objects in this version of SharePoint are ribbon bars. These ribbons contain buttons and drop-down lists to apply changes, access settings, or to configure whatever is selected in the environment.

Master It Is there a limit to how many ribbon bars there can be for a selected item or page?

Solution No. SharePoint will generate as many relevant ribbons to work on an object as necessary.

Master It There is a button that appears on both the top ribbon bar and in the Documents ribbon for a library. It seems to be the same button; does it do the same thing when used from the top ribbon bar as it does from the Documents ribbon?

Solution The button is called the Navigate Up button, and no, it does not do the same thing in both places. In the top ribbon bar, the Navigate Up button is used to navigate back up the path taken to get to the current location through the site. In the Documents ribbon, the button that looks the same and has the same name actually navigates only through the folder structure of a library.

Understand a content page. All lists and libraries contain content. To display that content in a consistent and easy to use manner, SharePoint uses content pages. This simply refers to list or library pages that contain content. Otherwise known as view pages, they can be configured to display the list or library data in different ways, depending on your needs.

Master It Every page on the site has at least one feature that is consistent throughout the site. What is that new consistent feature? What unique attribute does it have that allows it to remain always in view?

Solution The new feature is the top ribbon bar. Always at the top of the page, it displays the Account menu, Site Actions, and Navigate Up button (other tabs and buttons can vary). It remains always in view (in case you need to access its contents) because it is locked to the top of the page, and if you scroll, you can lose the title area, top link bar, even parts of the Quick Launch bar (depending on how far you scroll), but never the top ribbon bar. It is always at the top of the page.

Chapter 5: Introduction to Web Parts

Identify web parts. Web parts are small, independent applications intended to quickly and conveniently display the contents of lists, libraries, folders, or pages.

Master It What are List View web parts?

Solution List View web parts are generated whenever a list or library is created. The List View web parts are used to view a list or library's contents. They are automatically added to the list or library's content pages, but they can also be added to any page that can hold a web part.

Use edit mode. To work on web parts in SharePoint, the page containing the web parts should be in edit mode. Edit mode is a page state in which web parts can be moved, removed, added, imported, and edited. No data entry occurs in edit mode.

Master It How do you enter edit mode to edit a shared version of a page? How do you know for certain that you are editing the shared version?

Solution To edit the shared version of a page, go to Site Actions, and select Edit Page. The only way you know you are editing a shared version of a page, and not the personal version, is that the personal version will have a golden yellow banner saying that you are editing the personal version of the page.

Master It How do you edit a wiki page home page?

Solution Click Site Actions, select Edit Page, or click Edit Page in the top ribbon bar. Or click the Page tab, and then click the Edit button in the ribbon.

Distinguish between personal and shared versions. SharePoint offers the luxury of allowing users to have their own personal version of any web part page in which they can rearrange, remove, or add web parts to their pages for their convenience.

Master It How can a user tell whether they are viewing the personal or shared version of a page?

Solution There is no indication that you're looking at a personal version of a page, except that you can go to the Account menu and see whether the option listed indicates that you are in the personal version (Show Shared View is available) or in the shared version (Show Personal View).

Work with web parts.   Adding, moving, removing, and customizing web parts while in the browser are all possible with SharePoint. There are built-in List View web parts to quickly populate the home page with web parts relevant to users. There are also built-in web part templates to easily customize web parts with no coding necessary.

Master It   How do you change the title of a web part?

Solution   Edit the web part; then, in the tool pane's Appearance section, change the text in the Title field.

Export and import web parts.   Web parts aren't just static little applications. You can customize them, export them to a web part definition file, and import them to a different page or site collection.

Master It   How do you export a web part?

Solution   To export a web part, if the web part can be exported, just click the down arrow in the title bar of the web part, and click Export.

Chapter 6: Introduction to Lists

Use and modify a list.   Lists are the collaboration core of SharePoint. With the content stored in a database, lists can be used to track data, hold discussions, manage issues, and more.

Master It   How do you get to a list if it isn't displayed on the home page?

Solution   Go to the All Site Content page by clicking its link at the bottom of the Quick Launch, by clicking its All Site Content link in the Site Actions menu, or by clicking the List heading in the Quick Launch bar.

Modify a view and create a view.   SharePoint uses views to display the content of lists. Much like reports, views can be modified to display any field in a list in any order. Custom views can be created, with four different view formats to choose from.

Master It   What are the view formats, and which would you choose to display data grouped by a particular field?

Solution   View formats are basically view-type templates that define the look, feel, and capabilities of a view, such as Gantt, Standard, Calendar, and Datasheet. The best view to display data grouped by a particular field is Standard view.

Customize a list.   The settings of any SharePoint list can be customized in a number of ways to more conveniently store, secure, and track data.

Master It   Is it possible for users to add items to lists or libraries without having to use their browser? Are there any configuration considerations, or is it simply built in?

Solution   Yes, some lists and libraries (such as a document library, announcement, or calendar) allow users to email their item or document to the list or library, rather than having to log in and use the browser. Incoming email must be enabled and configured in Central Administration first and then enabled and set up for each list or library that requires it (not all can). An incoming email–enabled list or library must have a unique alias for users to email to, such as *announcements@dem0tek.com*. In addition, you can choose to allow a list or library to accept email from anyone who sends it, or you can limit acceptance to just those who have the permission to contribute.

Chapter 7: Creating Lists

Create a list from a template. SharePoint sites offer, in addition to a few convenient prebuilt lists, ready-to-go templates of common lists. This makes it very easy to simply create a new list based on an existing template and then customize it, rather than having to create one like it from scratch.

> **Master It** What list template creates a list that is meant to work with the Three-State workflow? How would you go about creating that list?

> **Solution** The list intended to use the Three-State workflow is the Issue Tracking list. To create an Issue Tracking list, go to the Create page, and in the Tracking category, select Issue Tracking. On the New List page, configure the list name, description, and whether a link to it should be listed in the Quick Launch bar.

Create a custom list. In addition to the prebuilt lists and the templates, SharePoint has the option to create custom lists from scratch. Lists can be custom made in two ways: by importing from an Excel spreadsheet or by manually building one. All lists require at least one field (by default the Title field) and include system-generated columns for ID, Created By, and Modified By.

> **Master It** You're creating a custom list to track inventory. You need to make sure that, during the data entry process, the item number field is never left blank and is unique for each item and that purchase levels never exceed storage levels.

> **Solution** To ensure that the item number field contains a value, set its Require column to contain information by setting it to Yes, set Enforce Unique Value to Yes, and set the List Validation with a calculation, such as =[Purchase Level]<[Storage Level], if those are the names of the fields in question. Column validation cannot be used because the formula has to compare two different fields in the list.

Display related lists. This version of SharePoint has expanded its capabilities regarding related lists, from enforcing relationships and allowing additional related fields to more easily displaying related data in list view web parts.

> **Master It** How would you go about filtering the contents of one list based upon the value in another, related list? What is the essential element that allows you to do this?

> **Solution** On the content page of the source list or on a new page, you can use the new Insert Related List feature to easily insert the target list's list view web part below the source list's list view web part. Alternatively, you can use the Connections options of a list view web part to connect the two lists with more control over the connection. The essential thing is that the two lists must have (and be displaying) a field in common, related via a lookup field.

Chapter 8: Introduction to Libraries

Create a library. A library is a kind of list that focuses primarily on the files that are attached to the list items. There are several different types of libraries, depending on the type of file they are intended to store. Creating a library is as easy as opening the Create page, selecting the type of library, and configuring it. There are several different types of libraries.

> **Master It** If you do not have any Microsoft Office products installed on your machine, what two main features of document libraries are not available?

Solution   Upload multiple files, and the New Document button will not be able to open the required Office product to use the library's template. Files will have to be downloaded/uploaded to edit them.

Use the different kinds of libraries.   Document libraries can be used to store practically any type of file, but SharePoint has four main kinds of libraries with different features and views. These four libraries are the document library, form library, wiki page library, and picture library.

Master It   You're restructuring the content of some of your libraries and are planning on moving content from one library to another. What key facts do you need to keep in mind regarding wiki libraries when it comes to moving or uploading files?

Solution   Wiki libraries do not support any form of uploading, so there is no way to place existing wiki pages into a library. Rather than moving the content to a new library, you should move the entire library as a whole.

Set checkout, content approval, and versioning.   Require Check Out forces users of a document library to check out a document if they intend to edit it. This helps enforce version management by allowing only one person to edit a document at a time. When a document is checked out, it can only be read by other users, but they cannot edit the document until the person with it checked out checks it back in.

Content approval can allow items to remain invisible to most list or library viewers until someone with approval rights approves the item. In a library with content approval and major and minor versions enabled, only major versions of a document can be approved.

Versioning means that whenever a list or library item (or its attached document) is changed, that change is saved as a different version. That means that if an edit was a mistake, you can restore a previous version of the item.

Master It   Brian has left the company, but some of the documents in your Shared Documents library are still checked out by him. Several of the documents have multiple versions stored, but one was a new document that Brian uploaded to the server recently. What three methods are available to check these documents back in?

Solution   It is possible to check in all the documents by simply logging into the SharePoint server using Brian's account. Once logged in as Brian, you can check in all the documents.

Without using his account, a site administrator can revert most of the documents to a previous (precheckout) version, making this available to other users. Anything Brian has done to the document since the checkout would be lost.

For the new document that has no previous versions, the site administrator must first *take ownership* of the file and then can check it in.

Manage content types.   By default each library (like most lists) has one content type. The content type of a library item is one that can have a single template associated with it such as Word documents, PowerPoint presentations, or Excel spreadsheets. However, it is possible to have a document library with multiple content types, allowing the library to create a mix of documents and use multiple templates.

Master It   You have a general document library for the public relations department. They want to use the library to manage a large number of different file types—from Word to pictures to movie clips to more obscure things. Many of them were created in products other than Office. More importantly, the type of files they're going to use is likely to change over time. How should you configure the content types for this library?

Solution   Any library can have any file type uploaded to it (that has not been blocked); it does not depend on the content type. You can reasonably leave the default content type or add some new document-based content types that use different Office templates so they'll show up under the New button, but the majority of their unique files will need to be uploaded rather than created using a template.

Chapter 9: Sites, Subsites, and Workspaces

Create and customize a new site.   Using the New SharePoint Site page, you can create a new subsite or workspace from one of several templates, or you can create a new workspace from an existing document or calendar event. The site can be customized using themes, custom logos, lists, and libraries.

Master It   After you create a new site, you discover you left a space in the URL, making it hard for users to type (since it contains that darn %20 ASCII code). What steps do you need to take to safely change the URL without breaking links to the site and its subsequent subsites? Will anything fail the moment you change the URL?

Solution   Change the URL in the Site Settings ➤ Look And Feel ➤ Title, Description, And Icon section. When the URL is changed, all the paths and links (unless they were manually created and therefore *unmanaged*) are automatically updated. All of the site's subsites will also automatically show this change. The only thing that may fail is search, since it could take a while for the indexing service to notice the change. This is corrected by simply waiting until the indexer next runs.

Adjust a site's settings for administrative purposes.   You can configure sites to inherit or set unique permissions on a site. You can also configure subsites to use tree view, manage user alerts, place the site on the top link bar, adjust regional settings, enable features such as RSS, and view usage reports.

Master It   If you create a new subsite and choose to not place a link to this subsite on the parent site's top link bar and then set the subsite to inherit the top link bar from the parent, what happens when you click the Home link on the subsite?

Solution   The link takes you back to the parent site. The top link bar is inherited, so Home is the parent site. There is no link on the top link bar that directly takes you to the subsite.

Understand the different types of SharePoint site templates available.   By default, SharePoint can create team sites, document workspaces, blogs, group sites, and meeting workspaces (from the Basic, Decision, Social, and Multipage templates).

Master It   You create a new event on a calendar and select the option to create a new meeting workspace. Once it's created and you've entered attendees and objectives, someone accidently deletes the event from the calendar. What happens to the linked workspace?

Solution   The workspace doesn't get deleted but does alert you that the linked event no longer exists. If multiple events were linked, it will allow you to merge your items into another instance. Otherwise, it will simply be an unlinked workspace.

Chapter 10: Site Collections and Web Applications

Create and customize a new site collection. A new site collection has separate permissions, its own Recycle Bins, its own storage quota, and its own site collection galleries. You can change the regional settings and grant someone site administrator rights on a new site collection without compromising your existing sites.

Master It You created a new site collection with a storage quota of 100 MB. Since then, it has hit capacity, and no one can add new documents or list items. You asked quite a few users to delete data to free up space, but it didn't appear to help. Short of increasing the quota, what can you do?

Solution When the users deleted data, it was moved to their Recycle Bins, which still counts against the quota. Have the users empty their Recycle Bins to actually free up the space (to be more thorough, you can also empty the site collection recycle bin).

Create a new web application. A new web application is fundamentally a new IIS Web Site with a new content database on the back end. Using a new IIS Web Site allows you to change the port for accessing the web application, use a host header, and adjust the IIS-level authentication such as anonymous access. Web applications, in addition to being a security boundary, are also a boundary for settings such as RSS, sending alerts, upload size limits, and blocked file types that affect all contained site collections. All SharePoint site collections must reside in a web application. At this level, serious changes can affect the way the site collections are accessed and controlled.

Master It You want to create a new web application but don't want to use a custom port, so you set up a host header instead. But although it appears to have been created correctly and you created a site collection, you cannot seem to access the site. What is the most likely problem?

Solution You forgot to make sure DNS has a record for the new host header—if DNS cannot resolve the host header's URL to the server's IP address, the browser can't get there.

Use managed paths. SharePoint uses managed paths to tell IIS which paths in a URL are handled by SharePoint and are, therefore, *managed*. All other paths are considered *excluded*, and IIS is free to use them with traditional websites. You can add your own managed paths, adjusting the URL of site collections.

By default, SharePoint site collections have two managed paths: the path (root), which is explicit, and the path /sites/, which is a wildcard path.

Master It You create a new wildcard managed path at `http://myserver/sales` but cannot seem to place a site collection in this URL without adding another piece to the path. What is wrong?

Solution You set up the managed path as a *wildcard*, which means the path cannot be used for a site—instead, it's intended to hold multiple site collections (like `http://myserver/sales/bob`). You should have created the managed path to be *explicit*.

Configure anonymous access. One of the features of web applications is the ability to allow anonymous access to the site collections they contain. Anonymous access can allow the site to be viewed without requiring a login while retaining all the needed permissions for authenticated users to add, edit, modify, or delete site content. Anonymous access is enabled in two core steps: first by permitting anonymous access at the web-application level and then by enabling anonymous access at the site collection level.

Master It Someone else has allowed anonymous access on the web application, and you're configuring your site collection. You want anonymous users to view only the Status list and nothing else. How do you configure the site?

Solution First, at the site collection level, you enable anonymous access for Lists And Libraries and not Entire Site under Site Permissions. Then you need to edit the permission for the Status list, break inheritance (if needed), and configure anonymous access to the list.

Set different zones for different access methods. Each web application can support up to five public URLs that it displays in the address bar and on the page in links and paths. Four of the public URLs can be used for manually entered alternate web addresses or used by extending the web application to a new IIS Web Site, providing a new URL (including a new port if desired), and applying different authentication policies to the same site. For example, one web application within the local network can permit anonymous access, but authentication can be required for anyone accessing the site through the Internet public URL. The five public URLs are identified by their *zone*, and additional internal URLs can be mapped to each zone.

Master It Your web application has three zones configured with extended web applications, each with their own public URL. Because of a company policy change, you need to remove the Internet zone from the web application. What is the recommended method for doing this?

Solution Go to Manage Web Applications, and select the web application in question. Click the drop-down menu for the Delete button, and select Remove SharePoint From IIS Web Site. Choose the Internet zone, and choose the radio button to delete the IIS website. Then click OK.

Chapter 11: Central Administration

Understand Central Administration's organization. SharePoint's Central Administration is organized by category page, with a home page that displays each category heading and an abbreviated list of tasks for each.

Master It Is it a good idea to use Central Administration to hold shared library content, lists, and calendars? Why?

Solution No. Central Administration's site, although it can be backed up, can't be restored, so that content will not be recoverable if there should be a disaster. Instead, consider creating a different site collection in the same web application to contain that information—and then back it up regularly. That way, you can restore it to the Central Administration web application should something go awry.

Configure managed accounts. SharePoint can now manage its own service account passwords, avoiding the problem of services being unable to function after their passwords expire.

Master It Are there any services in SharePoint Foundation that don't require or can't have a managed account? List an example.

Solution Yes. The Tracing service and Search's content access account (otherwise known as the index account or crawler) both can have accounts that are not managed.

This is important to know in case they fail; it could be because their passwords have expired or been changed.

Set the server farm's default database server.   In SharePoint, an administrator is often going to be doing work that involves databases. For this reason, having a default database server specified for the server farm is a great convenience.

Master It   If you are creating a new web application, can you specify a different database server other than the default set for the server farm?

Solution   Yes. On the settings page, when a new web application is created, the database server field will already contain the default server's name, but it can be changed.

Determine where to stop and start farm services.   The server farm services cannot be managed from the server's Services Management console. They can be started and stopped from the Services On Server Settings page from the link "Manage services on server" under System Settings on the home page.

Master It   Name a server farm service that can be stopped or started from the Services On Server Settings page.

Solution   Most services available on the farm, regardless of whether they can actually be modified from the Services On Server page, can be stopped or started from there. These include services such as Search, the Claims to Windows Token service, the Workflow Timer service, Incoming E-mail, and even Central Administration.

Manage a farm's solutions and features.   The settings for managing solutions and features are available on the System Settings page, under Servers. The Managing Farm Features page allows you to see what features are active (or inactive but available) at the farm level. Solutions management allows you to see what solutions have been added to SharePoint, as well as deploy or retract them.

Master It   Can you install a feature or add a solution to SharePoint from the Manage Features or Solution Management pages?

Solution   No. Those functions must be done at the command line (using STSADM or PowerShell) first before you can use those management pages to deploy, retract, activate, or otherwise manage those solutions or features.

Chapter 12: Users and Permissions

Define users and groups in SharePoint.   SharePoint users are individuals with user accounts that can be authenticated by SharePoint server. Users can be stored in one or more groups. SharePoint understands two types of groups: SharePoint groups and security groups.

Master It   Differentiate between a SharePoint group and a security group. Determine the preferred method for adding users to SharePoint.

Solution   A security group is used in Active Directory (or in the SAM of a Windows server) to contain users with the intention to give those users permissions to shared resources. A SharePoint group is a group in SharePoint that can contain users. The group uses permission levels to give the users it contains permission to SharePoint resources.

Add users and groups in SharePoint. New SharePoint groups can be created to organize user access to SharePoint resources. User accounts and security groups from Active Directory can be added to the SharePoint site directly or by being placed into a SharePoint group.

Master It If you add a security group to a SharePoint group and then later delete that SharePoint group, how do you apply a permission level to the security group directly?

Solution By adding the group to the site directly and, in the Grant Permissions box, selecting to apply permissions directly to the security group, rather than choosing a group to put it in.

Define permissions and permission levels in SharePoint. Authorization in SharePoint is handled by 33 distinct permissions. These permissions provide user access to lists, sites, and personal settings. They also determine whether the user's access is restricted to simply reading or browsing, can allow editing of objects, or can even permit creation of new objects.

Permission levels are simply groups of permissions. A permission level can contain any or all of the 33 permissions. The permission level is then applied to SharePoint groups to provide authorization to members of that group. They can also be applied directly to users and security groups.

Master It Describe what the Manage Permissions permission does and what dependent permissions it requires. What permission level contains manage permissions by default?

Solution Manage Permissions allows for the creation and management of permission levels and groups. The permission requires the View Items, Open Items, View Versions, Browse Directories, View Pages, Enumerate Permissions, Browse User Information, and Open permissions. Full Control permission level contains Manage Permissions by default (as does the site collection administrators group, of course).

Set permissions on a site/list/list item for a user or a group. Permission levels are assigned to SharePoint groups, security groups, or individual users starting at the top-level site of the site collection. By default, these users and groups (along with their assigned permission levels) propagate throughout the site collection using permission inheritance. You can go to any object (site, list, library, or item) in the site collection and break inheritance, adding users to and modifying the group permissions of the object manually, and then give them different permission levels.

Master It If you break inheritance on a subsite of the main Company Site and start using custom permissions for that subsite, do the lists on the subsite retain their original permission settings from Company Site, or do they also gain the custom permissions set on the subsite?

Solution Those lists, libraries, pages, and items on that subsite are subject to the permissions of the subsite that contains them.

Chapter 13: Maintenance and Monitoring

Monitor server performance. Use the Performance Monitor to view real-time server performance or create a data collection set to measure performance over time. You can create custom alerts that read the logs and warn you if something passes a counter limit.

Master It   You have an existing server that has been tasked as your new SharePoint server. The installation is done, and it's about to go live. Because it's an existing server, you're worried that the addition of SharePoint will require more RAM than the server has installed. Build a performance alert that will register an event in the Application event log if the available RAM ever gets below 50 MB.

Solution   Create a new data collection set and add a new Data Collector ➢ Performance Counter Alert. Add the Memory counter Available *Mbytes*, and set it to alert if it goes below 50. Create the data collector, open its properties, and go to the Alert Action tab and check the box to log an entry in the application event log.

Use SharePoint Backup and Restore.   SharePoint has its own backup and restore features— both in the GUI and using the STSADM or PowerShell commands. These tools allow you to back up the whole farm, a site collection, web applications, or even a list or library. The GUI has some easy-to-use steps found in Central Administration, while the STSADM and PowerShell commands can be scripted, allowing for automation and scheduling.

Master It   You are getting ready to decommission a site collection and want to make a final backup of it in case it needs to be referenced or resurrected in the future. This archive needs to be done in such a fashion that you are able to restore it to a different SharePoint server (in case this server is gone by the time the archive is needed). How do you go about creating this final backup?

Solution   You open the Central Administration site, click the Backup A Site Collection link under the Backup And Restore section. Following the wizard, you select the site collection you wanted to back up and specify the location where the backup is to be saved and the name of the backup file.

You could also use the STSADM or PowerShell commands to back up the site collection. The STSADM command is as follows:

```
Stsadm.exe -o backup -url http://servername/sitecollection -filename \\server\
folder\backupfilename.bak -overwrite
```

The PowerShell command is as follows:

```
Backup-spsite -identity http://servername/sitecollection -path \\server\
folder\backupfilename.bak
```

Back up separate SharePoint components.   In addition to SharePoint's built-in backup and recovery options, you can back up individual components of SharePoint using a variety of different tools. At a more granular level than a site collection, it is possible to use import/ export to back up individual lists, libraries, and subsites. You can also use the backup features of IIS and SQL to back up SharePoint's IIS Web Sites and SQL databases.

Master It   After a large amount of work was done to a list on the SharePoint server, one of the users has accidentally deleted it. It's been too soon for the list to be backed up using the nightly STSADM script, but there's a possibility the list was exported to a backup file after it was created. What's the first step you should take to recover this deleted list?

Solution   You would locate where the exported file was saved, and run the PowerShell command to import it back into its site collection:

```
Import-spweb -identity http://servername/sites/sitecollection -path \\server\
folder\backupfilename.cmp -force.
```

Recover from disaster.   You can recover SharePoint from catastrophe in several ways. The SharePoint built-in back up has an option to perform a catastrophic backup (and back up the entire farm). IIS Web Sites can be moved to a new web front-end server, and SQL databases can be transferred to a new database server. Finally, Windows Server Backup is available to completely rebuild the Windows Server (and SharePoint), even to disparate hardware.

Master It   It's been raining, the ceiling has burst, and your server room has just been given an impromptu shower. Now the SharePoint server is a smoking, dripping ruin, and SharePoint is "down for routine maintenance." You had a full system image backup and a recent SharePoint catastrophic backup on an external hard drive (stored offsite at your house) and access to a freshly installed Windows server at your co-location site. What's the fastest way to get SharePoint back up and running?

Solution   At the co-location site, image the server with the system image using a Windows 2008 R2 DVD and the full system image backup. Make sure the IP subnet, DNS, and domain structure at your co-location matches the main location (so the server will function cleanly). Then launch Central Administration, and restore the SharePoint catastrophic backup to the newly created server.

Chapter 14: STSADM and PowerShell

Start and use the SharePoint 2010 Management Shell.   The SharePoint 2010 Management Shell is found in the menu, but you must have the appropriate permissions to run the shell and the commands in it.

Master It   What cmdlet do you need to run to grant someone the ability to run the SharePoint 2010 Management Shell?

Solution   Add-SPShellAdmin allows you to grant other accounts the right to run the cmdlets.

Understand the basic syntax for PowerShell cmdlets.   PowerShell cmdlets take a verb-noun structure, along with multiple switches that can also govern how the cmdlet functions. Often a single noun will have multiple verbs for it.

Master It   How do you retrieve a list of all available PowerShell cmdlets?

Solution   Get-Command lists all PowerShell cmdlets.

Use pipelining to make cmdlets work well together.   PowerShell cmdlets typically output objects, not text. Those objects can be fed as input to other cmdlets. This is called pipelining. You can pipeline to adjust the result set, and you can pipeline to configure multiple objects with a single-line command.

Master It   How would you retrieve all the subsites based on the Team Site template of the site collection found at http://spf2?

Solution   Use the following cmdlet:

```
Get-SPWeb -site http://spf2 | Where-Object {$_.WebTemplate -eq "STS"}"
```

Use basic PowerShell scripting techniques.   The real power of any command shell is the ability to write a script that can be reused as needed. Variables help with this, as does the direct access to properties of objects. PowerShell supports IF and FOREACH structures, as well as others.

> **Master It**   Which code block should you use to analyze a property of an object and then make a decision as to what you should do next?

> **Solution**

> IF/ELSEIF/ELSE

Perform common SharePoint Foundation management tasks using PowerShell.   There are 244 SharePoint cmdlets, which address many of the management activities that you want to do. However, PowerShell also exposes every property of every object.

> **Master It**   How would you set the quota settings for all of your site collection to a maximum 150 MB and 100 MB warning?

> **Solution**

> Get-SPSITE | Set-SPSite -MaxSize 150MB -WarningSize 100MB

Chapter 15: Migrating from Windows SharePoint Services 3.0 to Microsoft SharePoint Foundation 2010

Determine which upgrade method to use.   The decision about which upgrade method to use is influenced by many factors. Do you need to move to new hardware? Do you need to restructure your environment? And finally, what type of server farm are you currently running?

> **Master It**   Which upgrade method will allow you to upgrade databases from a 32-bit WSS 3.0 farm directly to 64-bit SharePoint Foundation farm?

> **Solution**   The database-attach method.

Prepare for Upgrade.   When you are preparing for an upgrade there are many things you can do to identify potential problems that could cause your upgrade to fail. You can ensure you are on the correct hardware and running the correct software. You can ensure you have enough memory and free disk space. There are also preparation tools that you can run to identify potential "gotchas"

> **Master It**   Which preparation tool generates a printable HTML report that lists all the SharePoint components , and identifies any issues that could cause your upgrade to fail.

> **Solution**   The Pre-Upgrade Checker.

Move from 32-bit hardware to 64-bit hardware.   Many companies today are running WSS 3.0 on 32-bit hardware and operating system; however, SharePoint Foundation requires 64-bit hardware.

> **Master It**   Name an upgrade method that would requires a WSS 3.0 farm be moved to 64-bit hardware and operating system before upgrading to SharePoint Foundation.

> **Solution**   In-place upgrade.

Upgrade Windows SharePoint Services 3.0 to SharePoint Foundation 2010. There are two main methods available to upgrade or migrate from Windows SharePoint Services 3.0 to SharePoint Foundation; database-attach and in-place. Database-attach method is used to migrate WSS 3.0 content database to a SharePoint Foundation installation and attach them to existing web applications. In-place method simply upgrades an existing WSS 3.0 installation to SharePoint Foundation.

> **Master It** Under what circumstances might it be easier to do a database-attach upgrade than an in-place upgrade? When might an in-place upgrade be a better option?

> **Solution** Database-attach: when the WSS 3.0 server is 32-bit. In-place: when the stand-alone WSS 3.0 server is 64-bit or the databases are larger than 4 GB so that you will need to use Remote BLOB storage which can only be installed using the In-place upgrade method.

Use Visual Upgrade. Visual Upgrade is a new feature of SharePoint 2010 that allows you to retain the current look and feel of your SharePoint sites. After WSS has been upgraded to SharePoint Foundation, site owners and site collection administrators will be able to preview their sites in the new user interface, allowing them to test the functionality of their sites before upgrading permanently to the new user interface.

> **Master It** Where would a site owner or site collection administrator go to preview their site with the new user interface?

> **Solution** They would open the site and then go to Site Actions ➤ Visual Upgrade.

Chapter 16: Advanced Installation and Configuration

Use Business Data Connectivity and create external data connections. Business Data Connectivity is a service application that makes it possible to surface external data sources in SharePoint to create lists and lookup fields.

> **Master It** What free product can I use to configure external content types?

> **Solution** SharePoint Designer 2010. It is a free download from Microsoft and was meant to be the go-to tool for customizing SharePoint.

Set a service principal name. For Kerberos authentication to work with SharePoint, additional configuration is required. The content database account for the web application using Kerberos must be registered as a service principal name for the SharePoint server (or servers).

> **Master It** What executable is used to register service principal names? How do you access it?

> **Solution** The `setspn.exe` program is now built into Server 2008 and 2008 R2, so you no longer have to download it; just open a prompt and type in the command.

Configure Network Load Balancing. Network Load Balancing is a network connection feature built into Windows Server 2008 and 2008 R2 (although there are other hardware and software solutions). It balances client requests and activity between servers in a cluster, effectively making them appear to be one computer from the client's perspective.

> **Master It** What is a drainstop, and what is it for?

> **Solution** It will emulate a server failure so you can see whether load balancing sends clients to other servers in the cluster.

Configure multi-tenancy.   Hosting multiple, isolated tenants on one SharePoint implementation is made possible by the Subscription Settings service application.

Master It   What is a site subscription?

Solution   A site subscription is an ID that can be used to group together site collections and their resources. No site collection can be in more than one site subscription, but there can be more than one site collection using the same site subscription.

Index

Note to the reader: Throughout this index **boldfaced** page numbers indicate primary discussions of a topic. *Italicized* page numbers indicate illustrations.